Microsoft®
VISUAL BASIC® 2012

for Windows®, Web, Office, and Database Applications: Comprehensive

Corinne Hoisington
Central Virginia Community College

CENGAGE
Learning®

SHELLY
CASHMAN
SERIES®

Australia • Brazil • Japan • Korea • Mexico • Singapore • Spain • United Kingdom • United States

Microsoft® Visual Basic® 2012 for Windows®, Web, Office, and Database Applications: Comprehensive
Corinne Hoisington

Vice President, General Manager:
  Dawn Germain

Product Director:
  Kathleen McMahon

Senior Product Manager: Jim Gish

Senior Content Developer: Alyssa Pratt

Product Assistant: Sarah Timm

Rights Acquisition Specialist: Christine
  Myaskovsky

Manufacturing Planner: Julio Esperas

Content Project Manager:
  Jennifer Feltri-George

Development Editor: Lisa Ruffolo

Copyeditor: Michael Beckett

Proofreader: Kim Kosmatka

Indexer: Sharon Hilgenberg

QA Manuscript Reviewer: Serge Palladino

Art Director: Cheryl Pearl, GEX

Cover Designer: Lisa Kuhn, Curio Press, LLC

Cover Photo: Tom Kates Photography

Text Designer: Joel Sadagursky

Compositor: PreMediaGlobal

Microsoft and the Office logo are either registered trademarks or trademarks of Microsoft Corporation in the United States and/or other countries. Cengage Learning is an independent entity from the Microsoft Corporation, and not affiliated with Microsoft in any manner.

For product information and technology assistance, contact us at
Cengage Learning Customer & Sales Support, www.cengage.com/support

For permission to use material from this text or product,
submit all requests online at **cengage.com/permissions**
Further permissions questions can be emailed to
permissionrequest@cengage.com

Library of Congress Control Number: 2013945908

ISBN-13: 978-1-285-19797-5
ISBN-10: 1-285-19797-6

Cengage Learning
200 First Stamford Place, 4th Floor
Stamford, CT 06902
USA

Cengage Learning is a leading provider of customized learning solutions with office locations around the globe, including Singapore, the United Kingdom, Australia, Mexico, Brazil, and Japan. Locate your local office at: **international.cengage.com/region**

Cengage Learning products are represented in Canada by Nelson Education, Ltd.

To learn more about Cengage Learning, visit **www.cengage.com**

Purchase any of our products at your local college bookstore or at our preferred online store at **www.cengagebrain.com**

Printed in the United States of America
1 2 3 4 5 6 7 19 18 17 16 15 14 13

CONTENTS

The Shelly Cashman Series® offers the finest textbooks in computer education. This *Microsoft Visual Basic 2012* book utilizes an innovative step-by-step pedagogy, which integrates demonstrations of professional-quality programs with in-depth discussions of programming concepts and techniques and opportunities for hands-on practice and reinforcement. The popular Guided Program Development section supports students as they work independently to create useful, realistic, and appealing applications, building their confidence and skills while guiding them to select appropriate Visual Basic 2012 programming methods. Online Reinforcement boxes direct students to online videos that show how to perform a series of steps. Other marginal elements, such as In the Real World boxes, provide expert tips to add interest and depth to topics. A robust and varied collection of exercises, including a series of practical case-based programming projects, ensures students gain the knowledge and expertise they need to succeed when developing professional programs.

Visual Basic 2012 builds on the features of Visual Basic 2010, which emphasized coding once and deploying on multiple devices. Some of the major enhancements to Visual Basic 2012 include enhanced code editing, a robust collection of online samples, an improved interface that makes it easier to access frequently used files, and more efficient build management. Using Visual Basic 2012, you can design, create, and deploy Windows, Mobile, Web, Database, Office, and Windows Store applications. Visual Studio 2012 includes several productivity enhancements including debugging tools, more powerful searching tools, Windows Store sample applications, and more.

Objectives of this Textbook

Microsoft Visual Basic 2012 for Windows, Web, Office, and Database Applications: Comprehensive is intended for a year-long course that introduces students to the correct ways to design and write programs using Visual Basic 2012. The goal of this text is to provide a rigorous and comprehensive course in computer programming for students with little or no previous programming experience. The objectives of this book are:

- To teach the fundamentals of the Microsoft Visual Basic 2012 programming language
- To understand and apply graphical user interface design principles
- To emphasize the development cycle when creating applications, which mirrors the same approach that professional developers use
- To illustrate well-written and readable programs using a disciplined coding style, including documentation and indentation standards

- To create Visual Basic applications that deploy on multiple platforms such as mobile computers, Web pages, and Windows Store environments
- To demonstrate how to implement logic involving sequence, selection, and repetition using Visual Basic 2012
- To write useful, well-designed programs for personal computers and mobile computers that solve practical business problems
- To write useful, well-designed programs that solve practical business problems
- To create appealing, interactive Web applications that can be delivered and executed on the Internet
- To organize complex programs by using procedures and to anticipate and prevent errors by managing exceptions
- To produce sophisticated, professional programs by using arrays and files that handle data and to make programs more robust by defining classes and using the power of inheritance
- To encourage independent study and help those who are working on their own in a distance education environment

The Shelly Cashman Approach

Features of this *Microsoft Visual Basic 2012* book include:

- **Realistic, Up-to-Date Applications** Each programming chapter focuses on building a sample project, a complete, useful application that showcases Visual Basic 2012 features and the latest technology.
- **Guided Steps to Encourage Independence** After observing how a professional developer would build the chapter project and exploring related programming concepts and Visual Basic 2012 techniques, students create the sample application on their own in the Guided Program Development section. This step-by-step section provides enough guidance for students to work independently, with Hint Screens that verify students are performing the tasks correctly.
- **More Than Step-By-Step** Each chapter offers clear, thorough discussions of the programming concepts students need to understand to build the sample application. Important Visual Basic 2012 design and programming features are also highlighted, including time-saving techniques such as using IntelliSense, code snippets, and the Toolbox. As appropriate, students design and prepare for applications the way professional developers do — by creating or analyzing requirements documents, use case definitions, and event planning documents.
- **Online Reinforcement Boxes** The Online Reinforcement boxes send students to the Student Companion site at CengageBrain.com to watch videos illustrating each step in the chapter project. Students can refer to the Online Reinforcement boxes when they work through or review the chapter, watching videos as they prepare to create the chapter application on their own.

- **Heads Up Boxes** Heads Up boxes appear in the margin to give advice for following best programming practices and tips about alternative ways of completing the same task.
- **In the Real World Boxes** This marginal feature provides insight into how developers use Visual Basic tools or programming techniques to save time or enhance professional development projects.
- **Watch Out For Boxes** These boxes explain how to avoid common pitfalls when using a particular command, programming structure, or technique.
- **Consider This Boxes** This element encourages critical thinking and independent problem solving by posing thought-provoking questions and providing answers related to programming and Visual Basic.

Organization of this Textbook

Microsoft Visual Basic 2012 for Windows, Web, Office, and Database Applications: Comprehensive provides detailed instructions on how to use Visual Basic 2012 to build authentic, effective, and appealing applications for Microsoft Windows personal computers and mobile devices. The material is divided into 12 chapters and 3 appendices as follows:

Chapter 1 — Introduction to Visual Basic 2012 Programming
Chapter 1 provides an overview of programming with Visual Basic 2012. The chapter defines a computer program, describes the role of a developer in creating computer programs, and discusses event-driven programs that have a graphical user interface (GUI). The chapter also explains the roles of input, processing, output, and data when running a program on a computer; examines the basic arithmetic and logical operations a program can perform; and explores the use of databases and computer programming languages in general. Finally, the chapter introduces Visual Studio 2012 and the .NET 4.5 Framework, including the .NET class libraries and related features, and surveys the types of Visual Basic 2012 applications.

Chapter 2 — Program and Graphical User Interface Design
Chapter 2 introduces students to the major elements of the Visual Studio 2012 integrated development environment (IDE) while designing a graphical user interface mock-up. Topics include opening Visual Studio 2012, creating a Windows Forms Application project, adding objects to a Windows form, assigning properties to objects, aligning objects on the Windows form, and saving Visual Basic projects. The chapter also discusses how to apply GUI design principles and examines the first two phases of the program development life cycle (PDLC).

Chapter 3 — Program Design and Coding
Chapter 3 provides students with the skills and knowledge necessary to complete phases 2, 3, and 4 of the PDLC by enhancing a GUI mock-up, designing program processing objects, and coding a program. Topics include using IntelliSense when writing code and enhancing

a Visual Basic 2012 form by changing the BackColor property of an object and displaying images. This chapter also explains how to enter Visual Basic 2012 code, correct errors, and run a completed program. Finally, the chapter discusses the value of creating an event planning document.

Chapter 4 — Variables and Arithmetic Operations Chapter 4 introduces variables and arithmetic operations used in the coding of a Visual Basic application. The chapter provides in-depth coverage of declaring variables, gathering input for an application, differentiating data types, performing mathematical calculations, and understanding the proper scope of variables. The chapter also shows how to use various types of TextBox objects.

Chapter 5 — Decision Structures Chapter 5 explains how to create a Visual Basic 2012 Windows application that uses decision structures to take different actions depending on the user's input. Topics include using If...Then statements, If...Then...Else statements, nested If statements, logical operators, and Case statements. The chapter also explores how to use the GroupBox object, place RadioButton objects, display a message box, insert code snippets, and test input to ensure it is valid.

Chapter 6 — Loop Structures Chapter 6 presents another type of fundamental programming structure — the repetition structure, including Do While, Do Until, For...Next, For Each...Next, and While...End While loops. Topics include repeating a process using the For...Next and Do loops; priming a loop; creating a nested loop; selecting the best type of loop; avoiding infinite loops; validating data; and understanding compound operators, counters, and accumulators. The chapter also shows how to insert a MenuStrip object, use the InputBox function, display data using the ListBox object, debug programs using DataTips at breakpoints, and publish a finished application using ClickOnce technology.

Chapter 7 — Using Procedures and Exception Handling Chapter 7 focuses on using procedures to organize complex programs and handling exceptions to prevent errors. The chapter begins by demonstrating how to create a splash screen that is displayed as a program loads. It then explores how to organize long, complex programs into procedures, including Sub and Function procedures, and shows how to pass an argument to a procedure by value and by reference, how to code a Function procedure to return a value, and how to create a class-level variable. The chapter concludes by discussing exception handling and using Try-Catch blocks to detect errors and take corrective actions.

Chapter 8 — Using Arrays and File Handling Chapter 8 explains how to develop applications that maintain data for later processing, including sorting, calculating, and displaying the data. The chapter project demonstrates an application that reads data from a file, displays the data in a ComboBox object, and then uses the data in calculations. This chapter also shows how to create a Windows application that uses more than one form.

Chapter 9 — Creating Web Applications

Chapter 9 explains how to create a Web application by building an interactive Web form, a page displayed in a browser that requests data from users. The chapter examines ASP.NET 4.5 technology and explores tools that help to create appealing, useful Web applications, including Web form properties, CheckBox, DropDownList, and Calendar objects, and custom tables. The chapter also explains how to validate data on Web forms and format text using the HTML <br> tag and the string manipulation properties and procedures in the Visual Basic String class.

Chapter 10 — Incorporating Databases with ADO.NET

Chapter 10 examines databases and explores the ADO.NET 4.5 technology. The chapter discusses how to take advantage of the data access technology of ADO.NET 4.5 to connect to databases and update, add, and delete data and retrieve database information for viewing and decision making. The chapter project demonstrates how to create a professional application that connects to a Microsoft Access database, temporarily stores data from the database, and lets users add, select, and delete records.

Chapter 11 — Multiple Classes and Inheritance

Chapter 11 explores the advanced topics of defining classes, using inheritance, and designing a three-tier structure for a program. The chapter begins by introducing the three-tier program structure and thoroughly defining classes and the object-oriented programming concepts related to classes. The chapter project shows how to create a class, instantiate an object, write a class constructor, call a procedure in a separate class, and use inheritance to code a base class and a subclass. Other topics include calling procedures in a base and subclass, writing overridable and overrides procedures, and creating and writing a comma-delimited text file.

Chapter 12 (Enrichment Chapter) — Windows Store Apps

Chapter 12 explains how to design a touch-first app as required for the Windows Store, the online marketplace for programs created for Windows 8. The chapter outlines the Windows Store application life cycle and explains how to obtain a free Windows developer license. After demonstrating how to create a Windows Store app that includes a customized splash screen (required for the Windows Store), appealing images, and TextBlock, TextBox, and ComboBox objects, the chapter guides readers through running the app in a simulator, and then packaging, certifying, and publishing the app.

Appendices

This book concludes with three appendices. Appendix A explains the purpose of Unicode and provides a table listing Unicode characters and their equivalents. Appendix B examines the My namespace element of Visual Basic 2012 in detail. Appendix C lists the common data types used in Visual Basic 2012, including the recommended naming convention for the three-character prefix preceding variable names.

End-of-Chapter Activities

A notable strength of this *Microsoft Visual Basic 2012* book is the extensive student activities at the end of each chapter. Well-structured student activities can make the difference between students merely participating in a class and retaining the information they learn. These end-of-chapter activities include the following:

- **Learn Online** The Learn Online section directs students to Web-based exercises, which are fun, interactive activities that include chapter reinforcement (true/false, multiple choice, and short answer questions), practice tests, and a crossword puzzle challenge to augment concepts, key terms, techniques, and other material in the chapter.

- **Knowledge Check** The Knowledge Check section includes short exercises and review questions that reinforce concepts and provide opportunities to practice skills.

- **Debugging Exercises** In these exercises, students examine short code samples to identify errors and solve programming problems.

- **Program Analysis** The Program Analysis exercises let students apply their knowledge of Visual Basic 2012 and programming techniques. In some exercises, students write programming statements that meet a practical goal or solve a problem. In other exercises, students analyze code samples and identify the output.

- **Case Programming Assignments** Nine programming assignments for each chapter challenge students to create applications using the skills learned in the chapter. Each assignment presents a realistic business scenario and requires students to create programs of varying difficulty.

  - Easiest: The first three assignments provide most of the program design information, such as a requirements document and use case definition, for a business application. Students design an application, create an event planning document, and write the code for the application.

  - Intermediate: The next three assignments provide some of the program design information, such as a requirements document. Students create other design documents, such as a use case definition and event planning document, and then build the user interface and code the application.

  - Challenging: The final three assignments provide only a description of a business problem, and students create all the design documents, design the user interface, and code the application.

To the Instructor

Each chapter in this book focuses on a realistic, appealing Visual Basic 2012 application. A chapter begins with a completed application, which you can run to demonstrate how it works, the tasks it performs, and the problems it solves. The chapter introduction also identifies the application's users and their requirements, such as running the program on a mobile computer or validating input data.

The steps in the next section of a chapter show how to create the user interface for the application. You can perform these steps in class — each step clearly explains an action, describes the results, and includes a figure showing the results, with callouts directing your attention to key elements on the screen. Some marginal features, such as the Heads Up boxes, provide additional tips for completing the steps. The Online Reinforcement boxes direct students to videos that replay the steps, which is especially helpful for review and for distance learning students.

This section also explains the Visual Basic 2012 tools and properties needed to understand and create the user interface. For example, while placing a text box in an application, the chapter describes the purpose of a text box and why you should set its maximum and minimum size. You can discuss these ideas and strategies, and then continue your demonstration to show students how to apply them to the chapter application.

After completing the user interface, the chapter explores the programming concepts students should understand to create the application, such as proper syntax, variables, data types, conditional statements, and loops. This section uses the same types of steps, figures, and marginal features to demonstrate how to enter code to complete and test the application.

To prepare students for building the application on their own, the chapter next considers the program design and logic by examining planning documents:

- *Requirements document* — The requirements document identifies the purpose, procedures, and calculations of the program, and specifies details such as the application title, restrictions, and comments that help to explain the program.
- *Use case definition* — The use case definition describes what the user does and how the program responds to each action.
- *Event planning document* — The event planning document lists each object in the user interface that causes an event, the action the user takes to trigger the event, and the event processing that must occur.

You can discuss these documents in class and encourage students to review them as they create a program, reinforcing how professional developers create applications in the modern workplace.

In the innovative Guided Program Development section, students work on their own to create the chapter application. They complete the tasks within each numbered step, referring to Hint Screens when they need a reminder about how to perform a step or which method to use. Many tasks reference figures shown earlier in the chapter. Students can refer to these figures for further help — they show exactly how to use a particular technique for completing a task. Steps end with a results figure, which illustrates how the application should look if students performed the tasks correctly. To reinforce how students learned the chapter material, the Guided Program Development section also focuses first on designing the user interface and then on coding the application. A complete program listing appears at the end of this section, which students can use to check their work.

At the end of each chapter, you'll find plenty of activities that provide review, practice, and challenge for your students, including a summary table that lists skills and corresponding figures and videos, descriptions of online learning opportunities, and exercises ranging from short, focused review questions to assignments requiring complete programs and related planning documents. You can assign the Learn Online, Knowledge Check, Debugging Exercises, and Program Analysis activities as necessary to reinforce and assess learning. Depending on the expertise of your class, you can assign the Case Programming Assignments as independent projects, selecting one from each level of difficulty (easiest, intermediate, and challenging) or concentrating on the level that is most appropriate for your class.

INSTRUCTOR RESOURCES

The following resources are available through www.cengage.com to instructors who have adopted this book. Search for this title by ISBN, title, author, or keyword. From the Product Overview page, select the Instructor's Companion Site to access your complementary resources.

- **Instructor's Manual** The Instructor's Manual consists of Microsoft Word files, which include chapter objectives, lecture notes, teaching tips, classroom activities, lab activities, quick quizzes, figures and boxed elements summarized in the chapters, and a glossary page.

- **Syllabus** Sample syllabi, which can be customized easily to a course, cover policies, assignments, exams, and procedural information.

- **Figure Files** Illustrations for every figure in the textbook are available in electronic form. Figures are provided both with and without callouts.

- **PowerPoint Presentation** PowerPoint is a multimedia lecture presentation system that provides slides for each chapter. Presentations are based on chapter objectives. Use this presentation system to present well-organized lectures that are both interesting and knowledge based. PowerPoint Presentations provide consistent coverage at schools that use multiple lecturers.

- **Solutions to Exercises** Solutions are included for all end-of-chapter and chapter reinforcement exercises.

- **Test Bank & Test Engine** Test Banks include a wide range of questions for every chapter, featuring objective-based and critical-thinking question types, and include page number references and figure references, when appropriate. Also included is the test engine, ExamView, the ultimate tool for your objective-based testing needs.

- **Printed Test Bank** A printable Rich Text File (.rtf) version of the test bank is included.

- **Data Files for Students** Includes all the files that are required by students to complete the exercises.

- **Additional Activities for Students** These additional activities consist of Chapter Reinforcement Exercises, which are true/false, multiple-choice, and short answer questions that help students gain confidence in the material learned.

About Our Covers

The Shelly Cashman Series® is continually updating our approach and content to reflect the way today's students learn and experience new technology. This focus on student success is reflected on our covers, which feature real students from University of Rhode Island using the Shelly Cashman Series in their courses, and reflect the varied ages and backgrounds of the students learning with our books. When you use the Shelly Cashman Series®, you can be assured that you are learning computer skills using the most effective courseware available.

To the Student

Getting the Most Out of Your Book

Welcome to *Microsoft Visual Basic 2012 for Windows, Web, Office, and Database Applications: Comprehensive*. To save yourself time and gain a better understanding of the elements in this text, spend a few minutes reviewing the descriptions and figures in this section.

Introduction and Initial Chapter Figures Each chapter presents a programming project and shows the solution in the first figure of the chapter. The introduction and initial chapter figure let you see first-hand how your finished product will look and illustrate your programming goals.

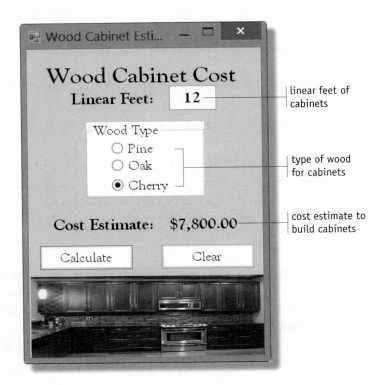

Guided Program Development After reading through the chapter and observing how to create the chapter application, the Guided Program Development section takes you through building the chapter project step by step. As you perform each task, you can refer to Hint Screens that remind you how to complete a step or use a particular technique. If you need further help, some steps include references to figures shown earlier in the chapter — you can revisit these figures to review exactly how to perform a task. Each step ends with a results figure, so you can make sure your application is on the right track. A complete program listing also appears at the end of the Guided Program Development section, which you can use to check your work.

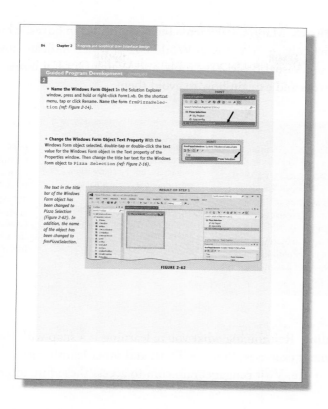

Visual Basic 2012 Online Reinforcement Videos The first of their kind, the Shelly Cashman Online Companion provides video reenactments of every new Visual Basic process that is introduced in each chapter. These animated tutorials provide a Web-based visual instruction on how to complete a Visual Basic task. You can watch these videos to learn how to perform the steps shown in the book or to review the steps and techniques.

To access the Online Reinforcement videos, you need only a computer with an Internet connection. Use your Web browser to visit cengagebrain.com, navigate to the resources for this title, tap or click the link to the appropriate chapter, and then tap or click the link to a video to play a video.

Marginal Boxes Marginal elements include Heads Up boxes, which offer tips and programming advice, In the Real World boxes, which indicate how professional developers use Visual Basic 2012 tools, and Watch Out For boxes, which identify common errors and explain how to avoid them.

HEADS UP	IN THE REAL WORLD	WATCH OUT FOR
Visual Basic 2012 can run on Windows 7 or Windows 8. In this book, the default operating system is Windows 8 with a screen resolution of 1366×768, but Windows applications such as the program in this chapter work in both operating systems. Windows Store apps can only be written and executed using Windows 8.	Program names can contain spaces and some special characters, but by convention most developers use a name with capital letters at the beginning of each word. This naming convention is called camel case.	In Figure 2-9, the Common Controls category of tools is open and all its tools are visible. If the Common Category tab is not expanded, a right triangle appears to the left of the Common Controls tab. To open the tab, tap or click the right triangle.

Learn Online Reinforcing what you're learning is a snap with the Chapter Reinforcement exercises, Practice Tests, and other learning games on the Student Companion site. Visit cengagebrain.com to access these fun, interactive exercises.

Knowledge Check To verify you've learned the essential information in the chapter, you can work through the Knowledge Check exercises. Use these short exercises to test your knowledge of concepts and tools and to prepare for longer programming assignments.

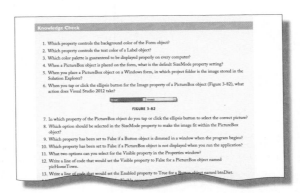

Debugging Exercises and Program Analysis Analyzing programs and finding the errors in code lines are common tasks for programmers. The debugging exercises and program analysis activities help you develop and fine-tune these vital skills.

Case Programming Assignments To pull together everything you've learned, you can complete the Case Programming assignments. These describe realistic business problems, and then ask you to design and code applications that solve the problems. Every chapter provides nine case programming assignments. The first three are the easiest, the next three are of intermediate difficulty, and the last three are the most challenging. By the end of the course, you should have a full portfolio of programs to demonstrate your competence.

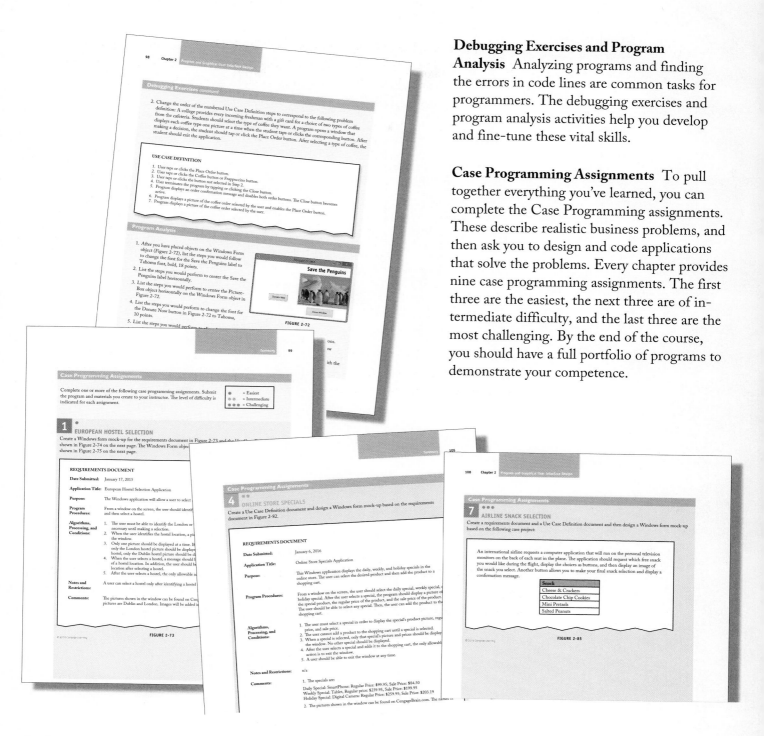

Acknowledgements

To Tim, my husband, for sharing this wonderful world that is full of beauty, adventure, and frequent flyer miles. To Liam, my grandson, without whose loving attention this book would have been finished in half the time. To Gary Shelly, for teaching me to write with passion and clarity. To Lisa Ruffolo, my editor, for her analytical flair and creative panache. To Melinda White (Seminole State College) and John Hoye (Kellogg Community College), my reviewers, for their brilliant insight.

— Corinne Hoisington

CHAPTER 1

Introduction to Visual Basic 2012 Programming

OBJECTIVES

You will have mastered the material in this chapter when you can:

- Understand software and computer programs

- State the role of a developer in creating computer programs

- Specify the use of a graphical user interface and describe an event-driven program

- Specify the roles of input, processing, output, and data when running a program on a computer

- Describe the arithmetic operations a computer program can perform

- Explain the logical operations a computer program can perform

- Define and describe the use of a database

- Identify the use of a computer programming language in general, and Visual Basic 2012 in particular

- Explain the use of Visual Studio 2012 when developing Visual Basic 2012 programs

- Specify the programming languages available for use with Visual Studio 2012

- Explain .NET Framework 4.5

- Explain RAD

- Describe classes, objects, and the .NET Framework 4.5 class libraries

- Explain ADO.NET 4.5, ASP.NET 4.5, MSIL, and CLR

- Specify the types of Visual Basic 2012 applications

Introduction

A computer is an electronic device that completes tasks under the direction of a sequence of instructions to produce useful results for people. Computers include desktop models, laptops, tablets, and smartphones. The set of instructions that directs a computer to perform tasks is called **computer software**, or a **computer program**. A computer program on a mobile device or Windows 8 computer is also called an **app**.

When controlled by programs, computers and mobile devices can accomplish a wide variety of activities. For example, computers can interpret and display a page from the web, compute and write payroll checks for millions of employees, display video and play audio from the web, post to a social network on a smartphone, and be used to write a book (Figure 1-1).

FIGURE 1-1

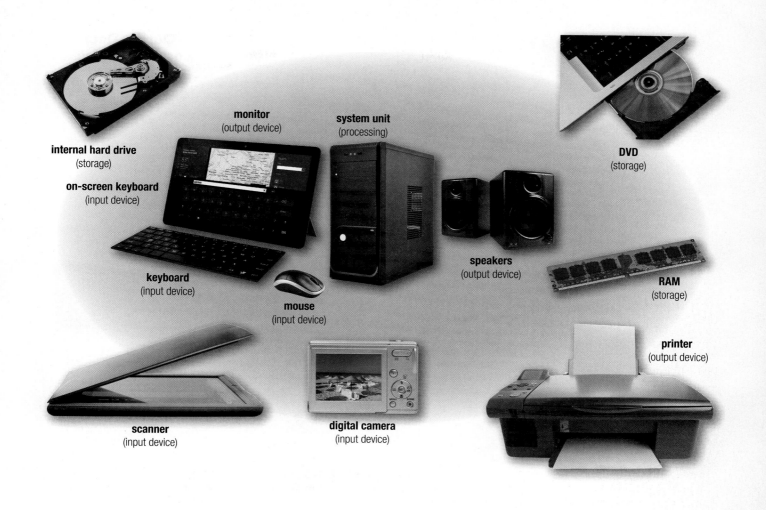

FIGURE 1-2

Two vital components of a computer must interact with one another for any activity to be performed. These components are computer hardware and computer software. **Computer hardware** is the physical equipment associated with a computer. This includes the keyboard (traditional or on-screen), mouse, touch screen or monitor, central processing unit (CPU), smartphone, random access memory (RAM), hard disk, and other devices (Figure 1-2).

A computer program or app is a set of electronic instructions that directs the hardware to perform tasks such as displaying a character on the screen when a key is pressed on the keyboard, adding an employee's regular pay and overtime pay to calculate the employee's total pay, or displaying a picture from an attached digital camera on the monitor. Computer hardware cannot perform any activity unless an instruction directs that hardware to act. In most cases, the instruction is part of a computer program a developer has created to carry out the desired activity. A third component required is data. **Data** includes words, numbers, videos, graphics, and sound that programs manipulate, display, and otherwise process. The basic function

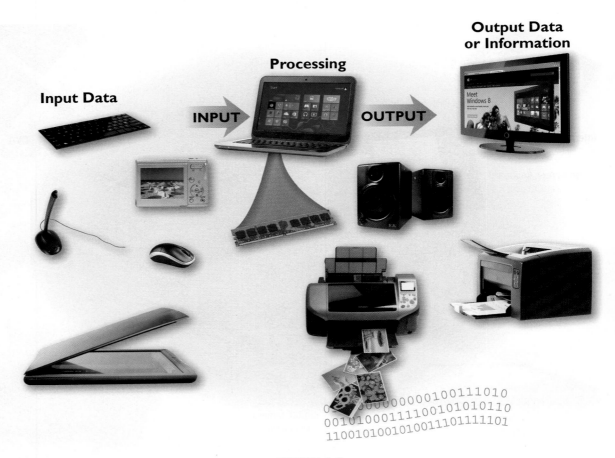

FIGURE 1-3

of many programs is to accept some form of data (sometimes called **input data**), manipulate the data in some manner (sometimes called **processing**), and create some form of data that is usable by people or other computers (sometimes called **output data,** or **information**) (Figure 1-3). In short, many computer programs perform the following general steps: accept input data, process the data, and create output data. The data that acts as input to a program, the processing that occurs, and the output that is created vary with the requirements of the program.

In order for the computer to execute a program, both the program and the data must be placed in the computer's **random access memory (RAM)** (Figure 1-4). Once the program is stored in RAM, the computer's **central processing unit (CPU)** can access the program instructions and the data in RAM to perform activities as directed by the program.

One other activity that hardware and software typically carry out is saving both the data and other software. **Saving,** or **storing,** data refers to placing the data or software electronically on a storage medium such as a hard disk or Universal Serial Bus (USB) drive or saving to a cloud storage server. The software and data are stored so they can be accessed and retrieved at a later time. Stored local data is said to be **persistent** because it remains available even after the computer power is turned off.

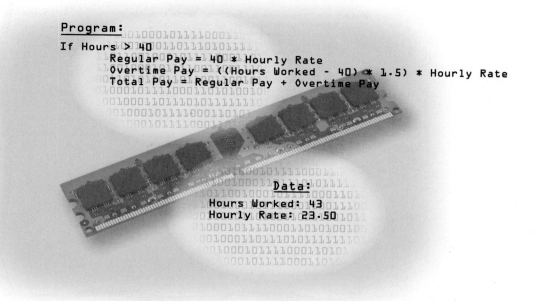

```
Program:
If Hours > 40
        Regular Pay = 40 * Hourly Rate
        Overtime Pay = ((Hours Worked - 40) * 1.5) * Hourly Rate
        Total Pay = Regular Pay + Overtime Pay

                              Data:
                       Hours Worked: 43
                       Hourly Rate: 23.50
```

FIGURE 1-4

© Tatiana Popova / Photos.com; © 2014 Cengage Learning

Computer Programmers and Developers

A computer program is designed and developed by people known as **computer programmers,** or developers. **Developers** are people skilled in designing computer programs and creating them using programming languages. Some computer programs are small and relatively simple, but often a problem to be solved on a computer requires more than one program. Developers speak of developing an **application**, which can mean several computer programs working together to solve a problem.

When designing a program, developers analyze the problem and determine how to solve it. Once a computer program or an application is designed, the developer must create it so it can be executed on a computer. In most cases, the developer creates the program by writing code using a **programming language**, which is a set of words and symbols that can be interpreted by special computer software and eventually executed as instructions by a computer. In this book, you will learn the skills required both to design and create computer programs and apps using the Visual Basic 2012 programming language (Figure 1-5 on the next page).

Will I be able to find a job in computer programming?

According to the National Association of Colleges and Employers (NACE), the top employable degrees for 2013 include the following majors, which all require programming skills:

- Computer & Information Science — #2
- Management Information Systems — #6
- Computer Engineering — #8

(www.thebestschools.org/blog/2012/10/15/20-best-it-jobs-2013/)

CONSIDER THIS

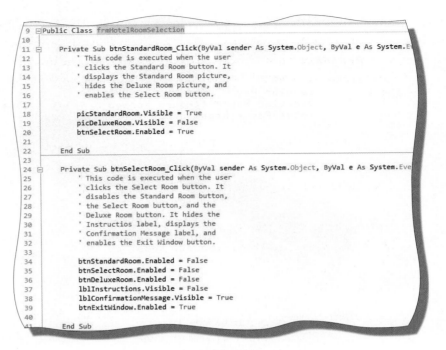

```
 9  □Public Class frmHotelRoomSelection
10
11  □    Private Sub btnStandardRoom_Click(ByVal sender As System.Object, ByVal e As System.E
12           ' This code is executed when the user
13           ' clicks the Standard Room button. It
14           ' displays the Standard Room picture,
15           ' hides the Deluxe Room picture, and
16           ' enables the Select Room button.
17
18           picStandardRoom.Visible = True
19           picDeluxeRoom.Visible = False
20           btnSelectRoom.Enabled = True
21
22       End Sub
23
24  □    Private Sub btnSelectRoom_Click(ByVal sender As System.Object, ByVal e As System.Eve
25           ' This code is executed when the user
26           ' clicks the Select Room button. It
27           ' disables the Standard Room button,
28           ' the Select Room button, and the
29           ' Deluxe Room button. It hides the
30           ' Instructios label, displays the
31           ' Confirmation Message label, and
32           ' enables the Exit Window button.
33
34           btnStandardRoom.Enabled = False
35           btnSelectRoom.Enabled = False
36           btnDeluxeRoom.Enabled = False
37           lblInstructions.Visible = False
38           lblConfirmationMessage.Visible = True
39           btnExitWindow.Enabled = True
40
41       End Sub
```

FIGURE 1-5

Event-Driven Computer Programs with a Graphical User Interface

Most Visual Basic 2012 programs are **event-driven programs** that communicate with the user through a **graphical user interface (GUI)**. The GUI usually consists of a window that contains a variety of objects and that can be displayed on various devices such as a computer monitor or a smartphone screen. Users employ the GUI objects to select options, enter data, and cause events to occur. An **event** is an action the user initiates and causes the program to perform a type of processing in response. For example, a user might enter data into the program, and then tap or click a button. The button action triggers an event, resulting in the program performing the appropriate processing in response.

To illustrate the process of entering data when using a graphical user interface and then triggering an event, consider the window shown in Figure 1-6.

FIGURE 1-6

This window is part of a banking application. When it is displayed, the teller at the bank or a user on the web can enter an account number. Then the user can click the Display Account Balance button (that is, trigger an event) and the program displays the account balance. The following steps illustrate the dynamics of the interaction with the program:

STEP 1 The user enters the account number in the Account Number box.

The account number the user entered is displayed in the Account Number text box (Figure 1-7). The Account Balance label displays no information.

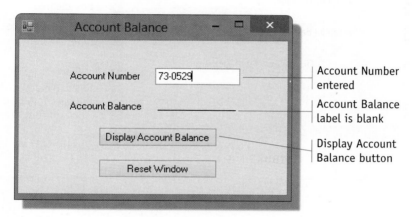

FIGURE 1-7

STEP 2 The user clicks the Display Account Balance button.

The account balance is displayed in the Account Balance label (Figure 1-8). Clicking the Display Account Balance button triggered the event that caused the program to determine and display the account balance based on data that the program accessed.

FIGURE 1-8

STEP 3   The user clicks the Reset Window button to clear the text box and the label and prepare the user interface for the next account number.

Clicking the Reset Window button triggers another event. The text box and the label are cleared and the insertion point is placed in the Account Number text box (Figure 1-9). The user now can enter a new account number to determine the account balance.

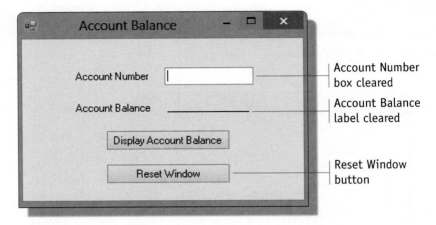

FIGURE 1-9

The events in the previous example consist of clicking the Display Account Balance button and clicking the Reset Window button. The program reacts to the events by performing specific actions (showing the account balance and resetting the text box and label). This is an example of an event-driven program. The Visual Basic developer designs the user interface and writes the program code that performs these event-triggered actions.

Basic Program Operations

All programs, regardless of their size and complexity, execute only a few fundamental operations: input, output, basic arithmetic operations, and logical operations. These operations can be combined in countless different ways to accomplish the tasks required of the program. The following pages describe these basic program operations.

Input Operation

As noted previously, a fundamental operation in most computer programs involves a user who enters data. For instance, in Figure 1-7 on the previous page, the user entered the account number. The steps that occurred when the user typed the account number are shown in Figure 1-10.

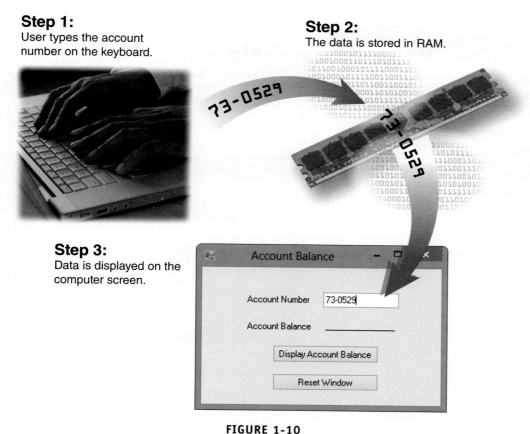

Step 1:
User types the account
number on the keyboard.

Step 2:
The data is stored in RAM.

73-0529

Step 3:
Data is displayed on the
computer screen.

Account Balance — ☐ ✕

Account Number   73-0529|

Account Balance   _____

Display Account Balance

Reset Window

FIGURE 1-10

© Wesley Thornberry / Thinkstock; © Tatiana Popova / Photos.com; © 2014 Cengage Learning

In Figure 1-10, the banking computer program that processes the user's request
is stored in RAM. The data entered by the user also is stored in RAM. Depending
on the input device, entered data might also be displayed on the computer screen.
The input device used to enter data depends on the application. In Figure 1-10, the
user typed the account number on a keyboard. Other applications might allow data
to be entered with a scanner, digital camera, video camera, mouse, or other device. In
each instance, the data is stored in the computer's RAM. When the data is in RAM,
instructions in the program can operate on the data.

Output Operation

The second basic program operation is creating output, or information. As you
learned previously, a major goal of most computer programs is to create output data,
or information, that is useful to people. In Figure 1-8 on page 7, the information
requested of the program is the account balance. The process of creating output is
shown in Figure 1-11 on the next page.

As always, the program must be stored in RAM to control the operations of the
computer. In the example, the program sets the text of the Account Balance label
equal to the account balance, and then displays it on the screen.

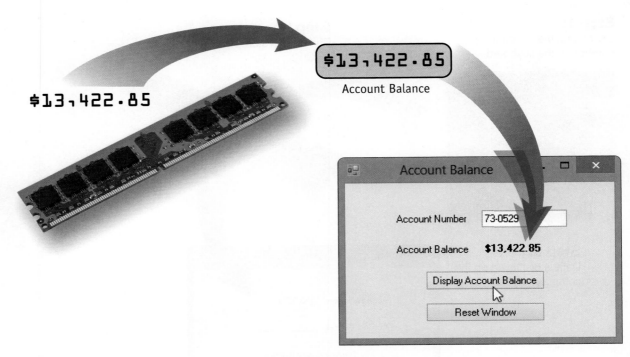

FIGURE 1-11

As with input operations, a variety of devices can present output. In addition to computer monitors, common output devices include printers, gaming console screens, and smartphone screens (Figure 1-12).

Input and output operations are basic to all computers and most computer programs. The ability to enter data, process it in some manner, and create output in the form of useful information is what makes a computer valuable. Understanding input/output operations is essential because they provide the foundation for many of the programs you will write in this text.

Basic Arithmetic Operations

Once data is stored in main computer memory as a result of an input operation, the program can process it in some manner. In many programs, arithmetic operations (addition, subtraction, multiplication, and division) are performed on numeric data to produce useful output.

Prior to performing arithmetic operations, the numeric data used in calculations must be stored in RAM. Then, program instructions that also are stored in RAM can direct the computer to add, subtract, multiply, or divide the numbers. The answers from arithmetic operations can be used in additional calculations and processing, stored for future use, and used as output from the program.

The example in Figure 1-13 on page 12 illustrates the steps an application performs to calculate an average test score. The average score is calculated from the three test scores a user enters.

smartphones

printer

73-0529
$13,422.85

FIGURE 1-12
© iStockphoto / Torian Dixon / MrIncredible; © iStockphoto / Gergana Valcheva / gerisima; © Murat Baysan / Photos.com

In the example in Figure 1-13 on the next page, the program adds the three test scores the user enters, and then divides the total by 3 to obtain the average score. As always, both the program and the data required to calculate the average test score must be stored in the computer's RAM. As you can see, when the user enters data in a text box, the data is stored in RAM and is available for arithmetic and other operations.

This example demonstrates the three fundamental operations of input (entering the three test scores), processing (calculating the average test score), and output (displaying the average test score). Although most applications are more complex than the one illustrated, the input, process, and output operations are used; arithmetic operations are commonly part of the processing step.

Logical Operations

The ability of a computer to perform logical operations separates it from other types of calculating devices. Computers, through the use of programs, can compare numbers, letters of the alphabet, and special characters. Based on the result of these comparisons, the program can perform one processing task if the tested condition

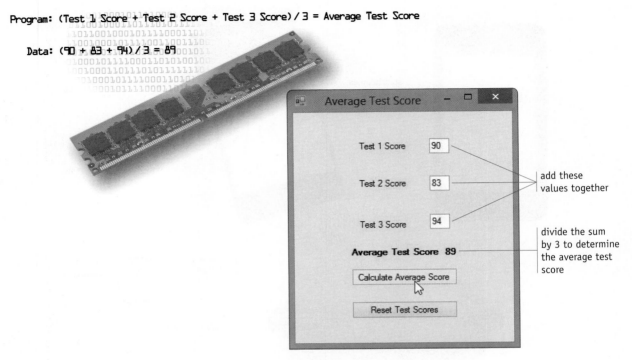

Program: (Test 1 Score + Test 2 Score + Test 3 Score) / 3 = Average Test Score

Data: (90 + 83 + 94) / 3 = 89

FIGURE 1-13

© Tatiana Popova / Photos.com; © 2014 Cengage Learning

is true and another processing task if the condition is not true. Using a program to compare data and perform alternative operations allows the computer to complete sophisticated tasks such as predicting weather, formatting and altering digital photographs, editing digital video, and running high-speed games.

A program can perform the following types of logical operations:

* Comparing to determine if two values are equal
* Comparing to determine if one value is greater than another value
* Comparing to determine if one value is less than another value

Based on the results of these comparisons, the program can direct the computer to take alternative actions.

Comparing — Equal Condition

A program can compare two values stored in RAM to determine whether they are equal. If the values are equal, one set of instructions will be executed; if they are not equal, another set of instructions will be executed.

Comparing to determine if two values are equal requires comparing one value to another. In an application for calculating student tuition, different rates might apply based on the student's residence. If the school is located in Texas and the student resides in Texas, the tuition per unit is one value; if the student does not reside in Texas, the tuition per unit is another value (Figure 1-14).

BEFORE:

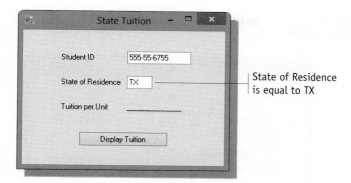

State of Residence is equal to TX

AFTER:

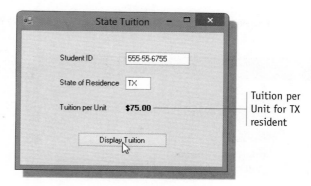

Tuition per Unit for TX resident

BEFORE:

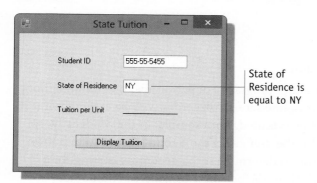

State of Residence is equal to NY

AFTER:

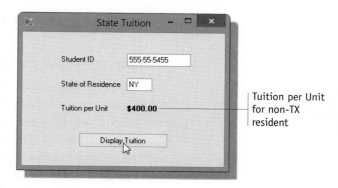

Tuition per Unit for non-TX resident

FIGURE 1-14

When the Display Tuition button is clicked and the state is equal to TX, the program displays the in-state tuition per unit. If the state is not equal to TX, the program displays the out-of-state tuition per unit.

Comparing can be used to determine if a condition is selected. For example, in Figure 1-15 on the next page, the Campus Parking Fees window contains a Student Name text box that provides space for the student's name and On-Campus Housing and Off-Campus Housing option buttons, or radio buttons, that allow the user to select either on-campus housing or off-campus housing. When the user clicks the Calculate Parking Fees button, the program displays the appropriate parking fee.

In Example 1, the user name is Athir Gomez and the On-Campus Housing option button is selected. When the user clicks the Calculate Parking Fees button, the program performs a comparison and determines that the On-Campus Housing button is selected. Because it is selected, the result of the comparison is true and the program displays the parking fee for on-campus housing. In Example 2, the Off-Campus Housing button is selected, so the program displays the parking fee for off-campus housing.

EXAMPLE 1:

On-Campus
Housing selected

Parking fee for
On-Campus Housing

EXAMPLE 2:

Off-Campus
Housing selected

Parking fee for
Off-Campus Housing

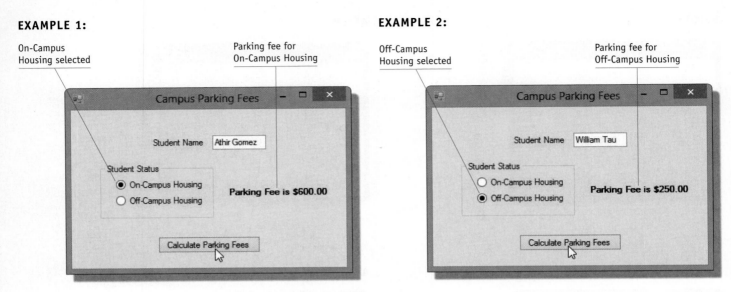

FIGURE 1-15

Comparing — Less than Condition

A second type of comparison a computer program can perform is to determine if one value is less than another value. If it is, one set of instructions will be executed; if it is not, another set of instructions will be executed. For example, in the Student Dorm Assignment program in Figure 1-16, the user clicks the Submit Application button and the program makes a comparison to determine if the person registering for a dorm room is less than 18 years old. If so, the person is considered a minor and a parent's signature is required. If not, no signature is required. An instruction is performed in the program to place a check in the Parent Signature Required check box if the age is less than 18, and the instruction is not executed if the age is 18 or more.

BEFORE:

Student Age
is less than 18

AFTER:

parent
signature is
required
because
Student Age
is less than 18

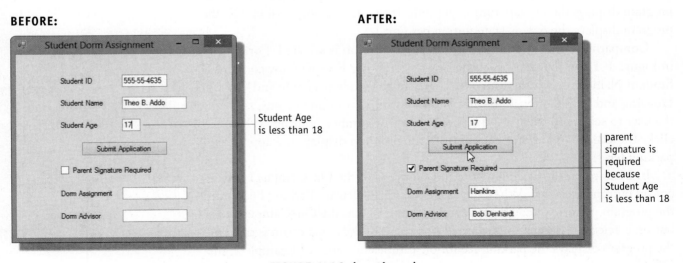

FIGURE 1-16 *(continues)*

BEFORE:

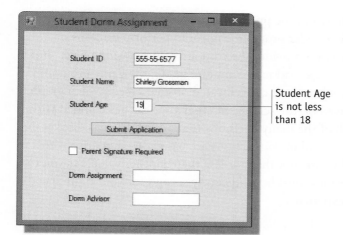

Student Age is not less than 18

AFTER:

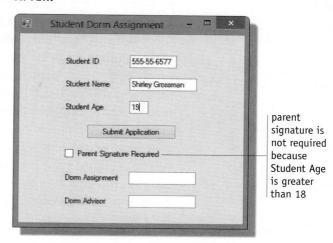

parent signature is not required because Student Age is greater than 18

FIGURE 1-16 *(continued)*

Comparing — Greater than Condition

The other condition a computer program can determine is whether one value is greater than another value. For example, in a payroll application, the hours worked by an employee can be compared to the value 40. If the hours worked are greater than 40, then overtime pay (1.5 times the hourly rate) is calculated for the hours over 40. If the employee worked 40 hours or less, no overtime pay is calculated. This comparing operation is shown in Figure 1-17.

In Figure 1-17a, the Hours Worked box contains 42, so the program calculates overtime pay for employee Lisa Hueve. In Figure 1-17b, Mia Ortega worked 30 hours, so no overtime pay is calculated. When the Hours Worked value is greater than 40, the program executes one set of instructions; if the Hours Worked value is not greater than 40, the program executes another set of instructions.

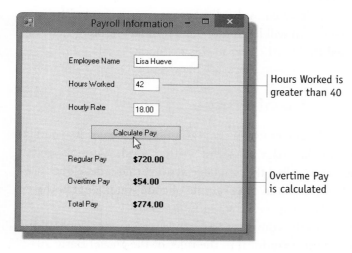

Hours Worked is greater than 40

Overtime Pay is calculated

FIGURE 1-17a

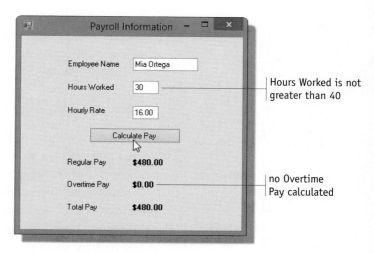

Hours Worked is not greater than 40

no Overtime Pay calculated

FIGURE 1-17b

Logical Operations Summary

While the logical operations shown in the previous examples might seem simple, the ability of a computer running under program control to perform millions of these comparisons in a single second provides the computer's processing power. For example, if you are participating in a road race computer game, the game program uses comparisons to determine where your car is located on the screen, which graphic road elements should be displayed on the screen, whether your car has collided with your competitor, and so on. All of the many decisions that are required to display your game on the screen and respond to your actions are based on comparisons to determine if one value is equal to, greater than, or less than another value. As you can imagine, millions of these decisions must be made every second for your high-speed game to provide an enjoyable experience.

Saving Software and Data

When you develop and write a program, the code you write and other features, such as the graphical user interface, must be saved on disk. Then, when you want the program to run, you can make the program load into RAM and execute. By saving the program on disk, you can execute the same program many times without rewriting it each time you want to run it.

The program you write, however, also can save data. This data, which can be generated from the processing in the program, can be saved on disk for future use. For example, in a banking application, a customer might open an account. The computer program that is used to open the account saves the customer's information, such as name, address, account number, and account balance, to a local file on the device or in the cloud on a remote server. Later, when the customer makes a deposit or withdrawal, the customer information will be retrieved and modified to reflect the deposit or withdrawal.

In most cases, data such as a customer's name and address is saved in a database. A **database** is a collection of data organized in a manner that allows access, retrieval, and use of that data. Once the data is saved in the database, any programs with permission can reference the data. You will learn more about databases and their use when programming using Visual Basic 2012 later in this textbook.

Visual Basic 2012 and Visual Studio 2012

To write a computer program, a developer uses a programming language. As you learned previously, a programming language is a set of written words, symbols, and codes, with a strict set of usage rules called the language **syntax**, that a developer uses to communicate instructions to a computer. An example of code statements in the Visual Basic 2012 programming language is shown in Figure 1-18.

Each program statement causes the computer to perform one or more operations. When written, these instructions must conform to the rules of the Visual Basic 2012 language. Coding a program is a precise skill. The developer must follow the syntax,

```
41    Do Until intNumberOfEntries > intMaxNumberOfEntries Or strVehicleSpeed = strCancelC
42
43        If IsNumeric(strVehicleSpeed) Then
44            decVehicleSpeed = Convert.ToDecimal(strVehicleSpeed)
45            If decVehicleSpeed > 0 Then
46                lstRadarSpeed.Items.Add(decVehicleSpeed)
47                decTotalOfAllSpeeds += decVehicleSpeed
48                intNumberOfEntries += 1
49                strInputMessage = strNormalMessage
50            Else
51                strInputMessage = strNegativeError
52            End If
53        Else
54            strInputMessage = strNonNumericError
55        End If
56
57        If intNumberOfEntries <= intMaxNumberOfEntries Then
58            strVehicleSpeed = InputBox(strInputMessage & intNumberOfEntries, strInputHe
59        End If
60
61    Loop
62
63    ' Makes label visible
64    lblAverageSpeed.Visible = True
65
66    'Calculates and displays average speed
67    If intNumberOfEntries > 1 Then
68        decAverageSpeed = decTotalOfAllSpeeds / (intNumberOfEntries - 1)
69        lblAverageSpeed.Text = "Average speed at checkpoint is " & _
70            decAverageSpeed.ToString("F1") & " mph"
71    Else
72        lblAverageSpeed.Text = "No speed entered"
73    End If
```

FIGURE 1-18

or **programming rules**, of the programming language precisely. Even a single coding error can cause a program to execute improperly. Therefore, the developer must pay strict attention to coding an error-free program.

When writing Visual Basic 2012 programs, most developers use a tool called Visual Studio 2012. **Visual Studio 2012** is a software application that allows you to develop Visual Basic 2012 programs using code you write, code prewritten by others that can be incorporated into your program, and sophisticated tools that speed up the programming process significantly while building better executing and more reliable programs. In this book, you will use Visual Studio 2012 to write Visual Basic 2012 programs.

Visual Studio 2012 is a type of **integrated development environment (IDE)**, which provides services and tools that enable a developer to code, test, and implement a single program, or sometimes the series of programs that comprise an application. Visual Studio 2012, which was developed by Microsoft Corporation, works specifically with Visual Basic 2012 as well as other programming languages to develop program code.

Visual Basic, part of Visual Studio 2012, can be installed on a Windows 7 computer with Service Pack 1, a Windows 8 computer, Windows Server 2008, or Windows Server 2012. Visual Studio 2012 can be installed on a 32-bit or 64-bit computer. Students, educators, and academic institutions can access a free copy of Visual Studio 2012 at *www.dreamspark.com*. DreamSpark (Figure 1-19 on the next page) is a Microsoft program that supports technical education by providing access to Microsoft software for learning, teaching, and research purposes. This text uses the Microsoft Visual Studio 2012 Professional version to present the programming topics.

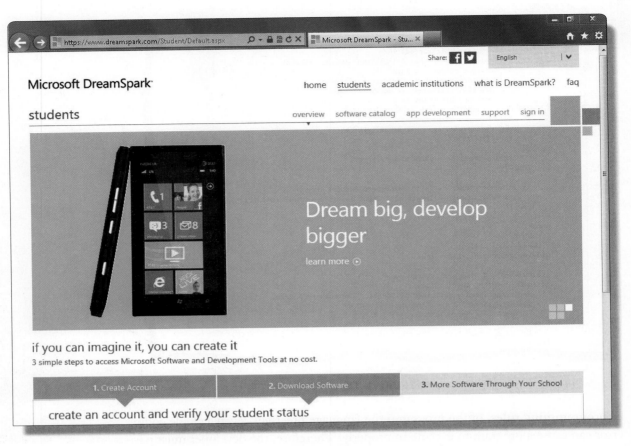

FIGURE 1-19

After you start the Visual Studio 2012 application, the Visual Studio 2012 window is displayed. In this window, you can develop and write your Visual Basic 2012 program, as shown in Figure 1-20.

The following elements help you use the Visual Studio 2012 window. In subsequent chapters, you will learn to use each of the elements found in this window.

Title bar: The title bar identifies the window and the application open in the window. In Figure 1-20, the open application is Payroll.

Menu bar: The menu bar displays the Visual Studio 2012 menu names. The menus contain lists of commands that allow you to create, edit, save, print, test, and run a Visual Basic program, and to perform other functions that are critical to developing Visual Basic programs.

Standard toolbar: The Standard toolbar contains buttons that execute frequently used commands such as Open Project, New Project, Save, Cut, Copy, Paste, and Undo.

Toolbox: The Toolbox contains **.NET components** that help you develop the graphical user interface for your program. For example, you can use the Toolbox to place buttons, picture boxes, labels, radio buttons, and other Windows GUI objects in the windows of your program.

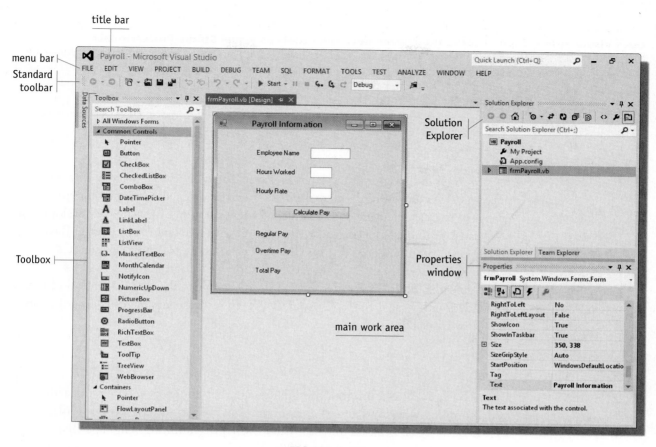

FIGURE 1-20

Main work area: The main work area contains the item you are currently developing. In Figure 1-20, this area contains the Payroll Information window of the Payroll program.

Solution Explorer: The Solution Explorer window displays the elements of the Visual Basic **solution**, which is the name for the Visual Basic program and other items generated by Visual Studio to help the program execute properly. You will learn about these items and how to use the Solution Explorer window throughout this book.

Properties window: An item that is a visible part of a graphical user interface, such as the Calculate Pay button in Figure 1-20, is called an **object** or **control**. Each object in a Visual Basic program has a set of characteristics called the **properties** of the object. These properties, such as the size of the button and the text displayed within the button, can be set in the Properties window within Visual Studio. You will learn about the properties of many objects throughout this book.

To code a Visual Basic program, the developer starts the Visual Studio program, identifies the kind of program to be developed, and then uses the tools and features of Visual Studio to create the program.

Does Visual Studio Express contain the same developer tools as Visual Studio Professional?
Microsoft Visual Studio Express is a free software IDE developed by Microsoft with multiple products that include lightweight versions of the Microsoft Visual Studio product line. The Visual Studio Express product line includes a subset of the full Visual Studio Professional product. Express 2012 products include Express for Web, Express for Windows 8, Express for Windows Desktop, Express for Windows Phone, and Team Foundation Server Express.

Programming Languages

Several thousand programming languages exist today. Each language has its own rules and syntax for writing instructions. Languages often are designed for specific purposes, such as scientific applications, business solutions, or webpage development.

Visual Studio can be used to write programs in five languages: Visual Basic, Visual C++ (pronounced Cee Plus Plus and called C++ for short), Visual C# (pronounced Cee Sharp and called C# for short), JavaScript, and Visual F# (pronounced F Sharp and called F# for short). You can develop a Windows Store app coded with Visual Basic, C++, or C#. Each of these languages is described in the following sections.

Visual Basic

Visual Basic 2012 is a programming language that allows developers to easily build complex Windows and Web programs, as well as other software tools. Visual Basic 2012 is based on the Visual Basic programming language that Microsoft developed in the early 1990s. Visual Basic, in turn, was based on the BASIC (Beginner's All-purpose Symbolic Instruction Code) language, which was developed in the 1960s.

Visual Basic's popularity evolved from the wide range of productivity features that enabled developers to quickly generate high-quality software applications for Windows. Today, Visual Basic is one of the most widely used programming languages in the world because it is English-like and is considered one of the easier enterprise-level programming languages to learn. Visual Basic is the only language in Visual Studio that is not case sensitive, which makes it easy for entry-level programmers. It is as powerful as the other programming languages in the Visual Studio suite, such as C++ or C#. An example of Visual Basic 2012 code is shown in Figure 1-18 on page 17.

In this book, you will learn to become a proficient Visual Basic developer.

C++

C++ is a derivative of the programming language C, which originally was developed at Bell Labs in the 1970s. It gives developers exacting control of their applications through optimized code and access to system-provided services. It contains powerful language constructs, though at the price of added complexity. C++ provides unrivaled performance and precision for applications that require a high degree of control.

Visual C#

Introduced in 2001 by Microsoft, Visual C# offers a synthesis of the elegance and syntax of C++ with many of the productivity benefits enjoyed in Visual Basic. Visual C# can be used to create both Windows and Web applications, as well as other types of software tools. Microsoft designed Visual C# to overcome some of the limitations of C++ while still providing the depth of control that C++ developers demand. Visual C# includes aspects of several other programming languages, such as C++, Java, and Delphi, with a strong emphasis on code simplification.

JavaScript

JavaScript (JS) is fully included in the Visual Studio 2012 version. JS is an open source client-side scripting language that enhances web browser user interfaces and dynamic websites. Visual Studio 2012 provides complete IntelliSense and debugging support for all JavaScript objects and methods.

Visual F#

A Microsoft .NET object-oriented language that debuted with Visual Studio 2010 is called F#. A multipurpose language similar to Visual Basic and C#, the F# language is known for its math-intensive focus, making it perfect for heavy-duty scientific programming applications. The language is relatively new and is just beginning to gain popularity in the business and science environments.

.NET Framework 4.5

In 2000, Microsoft announced a set of software technologies and products under the umbrella name of .NET. The .NET technologies and products were designed to work together to allow businesses to connect information, people, systems, and devices through software. Much of this connection occurs over the Internet.

The software environment in which programs and applications can be developed for .NET is called the **.NET Framework**, which provides tools and processes developers can use to produce and run programs. The .NET Framework is a development platform for building apps for Windows, Windows Phone, Windows Server, and Windows Azure (Microsoft's professional cloud computing platform). The most recent version is called **.NET Framework 4.5**. Visual Studio 2012 provides the development environment for the developer to have access to the .NET Framework 4.5 tools and processes.

Major features of .NET Framework 4.5 include the .NET class library, ADO.NET 4.5 (provides the ability to read and write data in databases), ASP. NET 4.5 (provides the ability to develop Web applications), Windows Presentation Foundation (WPF), Windows services, and the Common Language Runtime (allows programs to run on different computers under different operating systems). Each of these features is explained in the following sections.

.NET Class Library

As you have learned, most programs written using Visual Basic 2012 are event-driven programs in which a user performs an action, such as clicking a button, and the program executes the appropriate instructions. The instructions a program executes when a user clicks a button are normally written by the Visual Basic developer and are unique to the processing required by the program. For example, when a user clicks a button in one program, the overtime pay is calculated for an employee, whereas in another program parking fees are calculated. Each program responds to the events triggered by users with unique processing based on the requirements of the program.

In many programs, however, much of the programming code that must be developed is common for all the programs. For example, in all the programs you have seen in this chapter, a button was used to trigger an event in the program. The button appears in a window on a screen and senses when it has been clicked through the use of program instructions.

When certain code is common to multiple programs, the best approach is to write the code one time and then reuse it when appropriate. For example, when a button is required in the graphical user interface of a program, it is more efficient to use common programming code to insert the button than to require a developer to write all the code for a button each time one is required. When a common task must be performed or a new object such as a button is required, a developer can write the code one time and save it as a class. That class then can be referenced by all other programs when the task or object is required.

In short, the coding required for a button can be placed in a class. A **class** is a named group of program code. Once the class is coded, it can be stored in a **class library**, which makes the class available to all developers who need to use it. For example, when you as a developer need to place a button in the user interface, you can use the Button class stored in a class library to create the button without writing all the programming code associated with the button (Figure 1-21).

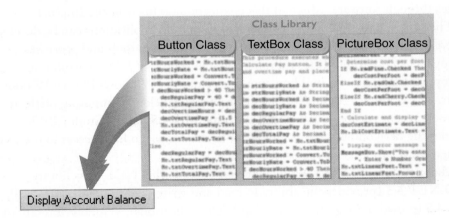

FIGURE 1-21

A button created from a class is called an **object**, or sometimes an **instance** of a class. In programming terminology, the process of creating a Button object from the Button class is called **instantiation**. In other words, a class acts as a general template, while an object is a specific item that is generated based on the class template. All buttons can be generated, or instantiated, from the Button class. The Display Account Balance button in Figure 1-21 is a specific Button object instantiated from the Button class.

To create a Button object from the Button class in Visual Studio 2012, you only need to drag the Button .NET component from the Toolbox to a Windows Form object, as you will learn in Chapter 2.

A button in a graphical user interface is only a single example of using classes and class libraries. The .NET Framework 4.5 class library contains thousands of classes and many class libraries for Visual Basic developers who use Visual Studio to create programs.

With so many classes available in .NET Framework 4.5, developers use a method of program development called rapid application development. **Rapid application development (RAD)** refers to the process of using prebuilt classes to make application development faster, easier, and more reliable. Throughout this book, you will gain a further understanding of classes and their use in modern computer programming, and will see how the classes in the .NET Framework 4.5 class libraries can be used for RAD.

ADO.NET 4.5

Often, programs you write must access data stored in a database. A set of prewritten classes called ADO.NET 4.5 (ADO stands for ActiveX Data Objects) provides the functionality for a program to perform the four primary tasks required when working with a database: getting the data, examining the data, editing the data, and updating the data.

Getting the data refers to retrieving it from the database and making it available to the program. Once the data is retrieved from the database, ADO.NET 4.5 provides the tools for the program to examine the data and determine how to use it. For example, a program might retrieve data from a database to create a printed report. The program can examine the data to determine its use for the report.

In other applications, the program might examine the data to determine if it is appropriate to display for a user. Thus, in a banking application such as in Figure 1-22 on the next page, the program might require the user to enter a special value, such as her mother's maiden name, to verify her identity before displaying the requested information. The program, using ADO.NET 4.5 classes, can compare the special value to the data retrieved from the database to determine if the user is permitted to access the data.

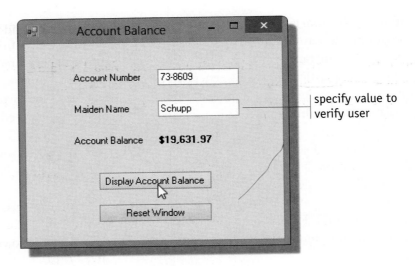

specify value to verify user

FIGURE 1-22

A third facility provided by ADO.NET 4.5 is the ability to edit the data, which means to make changes to it. For example, if you change your address or telephone number, those values should be changed in your account database information. ADO.NET 4.5 supports the ability to make those changes.

Finally, once changes have been made to data, ADO.NET 4.5 enables a program to update the database with the new information by writing the data into the database.

ADO.NET 4.5 is a powerful and necessary part of .NET Framework 4.5. The developer uses Visual Studio 2012 to access the ADO.NET 4.5 classes.

ASP.NET 4.5

The Internet and the web are integral technological resources. Modern websites provide services from selling products to sharing the latest medical research on any known disease. The development and maintenance of these websites is a constant requirement and consumes many developer hours.

Recognizing the importance of the web, Microsoft developed .NET Framework 4.5 to include a programming framework called ASP.NET 4.5. Developers can use this framework through Visual Studio 2012 to build powerful and sophisticated Web applications on a web server. Using ASP.NET 4.5 classes, Visual Basic 2012 programmers can create websites that perform any function available on the web today. In addition to traditional websites, you can automatically adapt Web applications to target mobile devices with enhanced ASP.NET support for mobile browsers.

ASP.NET 4.5 offers several advantages for developers. First, almost all the objects available in the .NET framework, such as buttons, text boxes, and picture boxes, are available in ASP.NET 4.5. Developers can use the same techniques to create a Web application that they use to create Windows applications, such as those shown in this chapter. In addition, deploying the Web application on a web server almost is automatic. Visual Studio 2012 incorporates a new Web designer interface into ASP.NET 4.5 that uses the design engine of a popular webpage designing program named Microsoft Expression Web. This design engine greatly improves moving between HTML5 (Hypertext Markup Language) source code, cascading style sheets (CSS3) that assist in layout, and Visual Basic code. The new ASP.NET 4.5 editor within Visual Studio provides tools to develop interactive HTML5 Web applications easily and efficiently with JavaScript and jQuery.

Important web requirements such as performance and security are enhanced and maximized through use of the tools offered with ASP.NET 4.5. In short, ASP.NET 4.5 offers a complete solution for developing modern Web applications for computers, tablets, and smartphones.

Microsoft Intermediate Language (MSIL) and Common Language Runtime (CLR)

After a developer writes a program in a programming language such as Visual Basic 2012 using Visual Studio 2012, the programming statements must be translated into a collection of instructions that eventually can be understood by the electronics of the computer. These electronic instructions then are executed by the computer to carry out the tasks of the program. This process of translation is called **program compilation**.

Program compilation for a Visual Basic 2012 program creates a set of electronic code expressed in an intermediate language called the **Microsoft Intermediate Language (MSIL)**. When the program is executed, a portion of .NET 4.5 called the **Common Language Runtime (CLR)** reads the MSIL and causes the instructions within the program to be executed (Figure 1-23 on the next page).

In Figure 1-23, the Visual Basic program written by a developer is compiled, which translates the human-readable statements in Visual Basic into MSIL, the set of electronic code that forms the input to CLR. Then, when the program is ready for execution, the CLR reads the MSIL in RAM in a form that allows the computer's CPU to execute the instructions in the program.

The use of MSIL and CLR offers multiple benefits that provide speed and flexibility for both the development and execution environments of a program. Utmost among these benefits is that a program written using Visual Studio 2012 and compiled into MSIL can be executed on any computer using any operating system, as long as .NET Framework 4.5 is available on the computer. For example, with no changes to a program you write, the program could be executed on a Dell computer running Windows 8 or an older operating system or on an IBM computer using the Linux operating system. This ability to execute programs on different computers running different operating systems is a primary benefit of using .NET Framework 4.5.

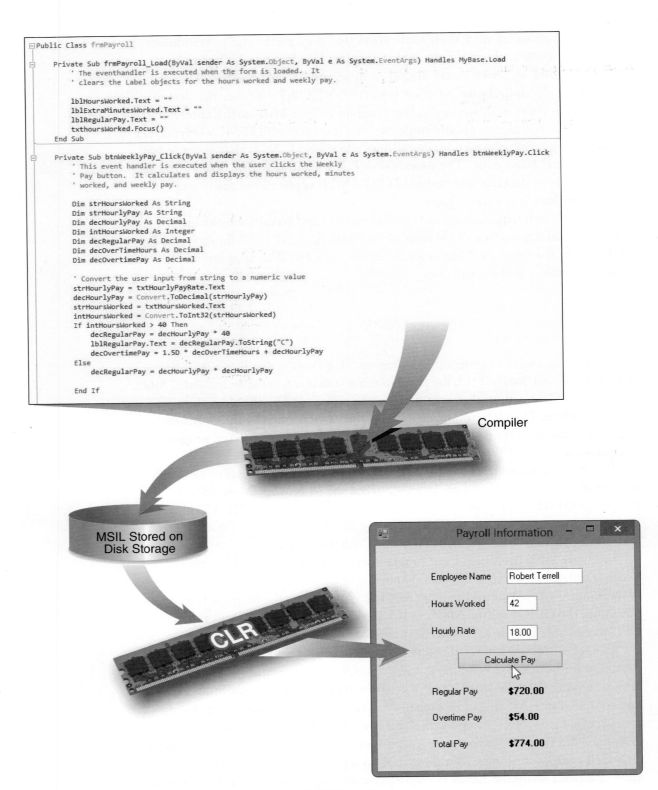

```
Public Class frmPayroll

    Private Sub frmPayroll_Load(ByVal sender As System.Object, ByVal e As System.EventArgs) Handles MyBase.Load
        ' The eventhandler is executed when the form is loaded.  It
        ' clears the Label objects for the hours worked and weekly pay.

        lblHoursWorked.Text = ""
        lblExtraMinutesWorked.Text = ""
        lblRegularPay.Text = ""
        txthoursWorked.Focus()
    End Sub

    Private Sub btnWeeklyPay_Click(ByVal sender As System.Object, ByVal e As System.EventArgs) Handles btnWeeklyPay.Click
        ' This event handler is executed when the user clicks the Weekly
        ' Pay button.  It calculates and displays the hours worked, minutes
        ' worked, and weekly pay.

        Dim strHoursWorked As String
        Dim strHourlyPay As String
        Dim decHourlyPay As Decimal
        Dim intHoursWorked As Integer
        Dim decRegularPay As Decimal
        Dim decOverTimeHours As Decimal
        Dim decOvertimePay As Decimal

        ' Convert the user input from string to a numeric value
        strHourlyPay = txtHourlyPayRate.Text
        decHourlyPay = Convert.ToDecimal(strHourlyPay)
        strHoursWorked = txtHoursWorked.Text
        intHoursWorked = Convert.ToInt32(strHoursWorked)
        If intHoursWorked > 40 Then
            decRegularPay = decHourlyPay * 40
            lblRegularPay.Text = decRegularPay.ToString("C")
            decOvertimePay = 1.5D * decOverTimeHours + decHourlyPay
        Else
            decRegularPay = decHourlyPay * decHourlyPay

        End If
```

Compiler

MSIL Stored on
Disk Storage

CLR

Payroll Information

Employee Name   Robert Terrell

Hours Worked   42

Hourly Rate   18.00

Calculate Pay

Regular Pay $720.00

Overtime Pay $54.00

Total Pay $774.00

FIGURE 1-23

Types of Visual Basic 2012 Applications

When you begin creating a new Visual Basic 2012 program in Visual Studio 2012, you must choose the type of application you will be developing. Based on your choice, Visual Studio 2012 provides the classes, tools, and features required for that type of application.

Five major types of applications are Windows applications, Windows Store apps, website applications, Office applications, and database applications. A **Windows application** means the program will run on a computer or other device that supports the Windows GUI. You can run Windows applications on a variety of computers.

You can create **Windows Store apps** that are designed to run on Windows 8 computers and mobile devices such as smartphones and tablets. Windows Store apps have a new look and feel, run on a variety of devices, and can be sold in the Windows Store. Unlike traditional desktop apps, a Windows Store app has a single, chromeless window that fills the entire screen by default. (Chrome consists of the borders, controls, and other features of a window that frame the content.) To develop a Windows Store app, you must have Visual Studio 2012 installed on a Windows 8 computer. You cannot develop Windows Store apps on Windows 7 or Windows Server products. You must obtain a free developer license to develop and test Windows Store apps before the Windows Store can certify them. The free developer license is provided on a per-machine basis and for a fixed amount of time.

You create a **Web application** using ASP.NET 4.5. The application runs on a web server. It produces HTML5 code that is downloaded to the client computer, where the browser interprets the HTML and displays the contents of a webpage. In a Web application created with ASP.NET 4.5, the developer can include items such as security and forms processing to provide all the services required of a modern website on a computer or mobile device.

An **Office application** includes writing Visual Basic 2012 code to automate and manipulate documents created using Microsoft Office 2010 and Office 2013.

A **database application** is written using ADO.NET 4.5 to reference, access, display, and update data stored in a database. The Visual Basic 2012 developer writes the code to process the data.

Other types of applications Visual Basic 2012 developers can create include console applications, classes for class libraries, certain controls to use in Windows applications, Web services, and device-specific applications.

Summary

In this chapter, you have learned the fundamentals of computer programming and have been introduced to the Visual Studio 2012 and Visual Basic 2012 program development environments. In subsequent chapters, you will learn to use Visual Studio 2012 and Visual Basic 2012 to create Windows applications, Windows Store apps, database applications, and Web applications.

Knowledge Check

1. Explain the differences between computer hardware and computer software.   *a Physical*   *a collection of instruction*

2. The basic functions of many programs are: a. ___Input___ ; b. ___processing___ *Logical* ;
   c. ___output___ .

3. Match the following terms and their definitions:

√2 a. Developer   1. A collection of classes that are available for use in programs

√4 b. Persistent data   2. Someone skilled in designing computer programs and implementing them in programming languages

√7 c. Programming language   3. A window with a variety of objects that can be displayed on a variety of devices

√3 d. Graphical user interface   4. Data that is stored on a storage medium

√6 e. Database   5. The process of using prebuilt classes to make application development faster, easier, and more reliable

√1 f. Class library   6. A collection of data organized in a manner that allows access, retrieval, and use of that data

√5 g. Rapid application development (RAD) 7. A set of words and symbols that can be interpreted by special computer software and eventually can be executed as instructions by a computer

4. Explain what an event is in the context of event-driven programs. Give two examples.

5. Give examples of the differences between an input operation and an output operation.

6. What are the four primary arithmetic operations a computer program can perform? Give an example of each.

7. In the following examples, identify the condition a program would detect (the first exercise is solved for you):

   a. 4 is _____ 3   a. greater than

   b. 9 is _____ 9   b. __equal to__

   c. 17 is _____ 17.8   c. __less than__

   d. 75 is _____ 85   d. __less than__

   e. "Microsoft" is _____ "Microsoft" e. __equal to__

8. Describe three different databases where you think information about yourself might be stored.

9. What is programming language syntax? Why is it important?

10. What is a Toolbox in Visual Studio 2012? Why is it valuable?

11. Name two properties that a Button object can possess.

12. What are the five programming languages you can use with Visual Studio 2012?

13. Where can you sell the Windows Store apps that you develop?

Knowledge Check *continued*

14. State three reasons that Visual Basic is one of the most widely used programming languages in the world.

15. What are four major features of .NET Framework 4.5?

16. Why is a class developed? How are classes organized and stored?

17. Differentiate between a class and an object. Give three examples each of classes and objects.

18. What is the primary use of ADO.NET 4.5?

19. What do you call the process of translating statements written by a developer? What is the result of this process?

20. What are five types of applications you can create in Visual Basic 2012?

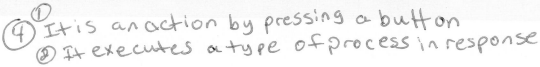

④ ① It is an action by pressing a button
② It executes a type of process in response

⑤

CHAPTER 2

Program and Graphical User Interface Design

OBJECTIVES

You will have mastered the material in this chapter when you can:

- Open and close Visual Studio 2012

- Create a Visual Basic 2012 Windows Application project

- Name and set the title bar text in a Windows Form object; resize a Windows Form object

- Add a Label object to a Windows Form object; name the Label object; set the text in the Label object; change the

- Font properties of the text in the Label object

- Add a PictureBox object to the Windows Form object; name the PictureBox object; resize the PictureBox object

- Add a Button object to the Windows Form object; name the Button object; set the text in the Button object; change the Button object's size

- Align objects on the Windows Form object

- Save and open Visual Basic projects

- Understand and implement design principles of the graphical user interface

- Understand and implement the first two phases of the program development life cycle

Introduction

Before a program can be coded using Visual Basic 2012, it must be designed. Designing a program can be compared to constructing a building. Before cement slabs are poured, steel beams are put in place and walls are built. Architects and engineers must design a building to ensure it will perform as required and be safe and reliable. The same holds true for a computer program. Once the program is designed, it can be implemented through the Visual Basic 2012 programming language to perform its intended functions.

To illustrate the process of creating a computer program in Visual Basic 2012 using **Visual Studio 2012** as the integrated development environment, you will design and implement the application shown in Figure 2-1 throughout this chapter and Chapter 3.

The application in Figure 2-1 could be part of a larger menu application used to select your pizza order. The program that creates the window in Figure 2-1 will run on a personal computer using the Windows operating system. The program will allow customers to select their favorite pizza type between the two options of Chicago deep-dish pizza and New York thin-crust pizza.

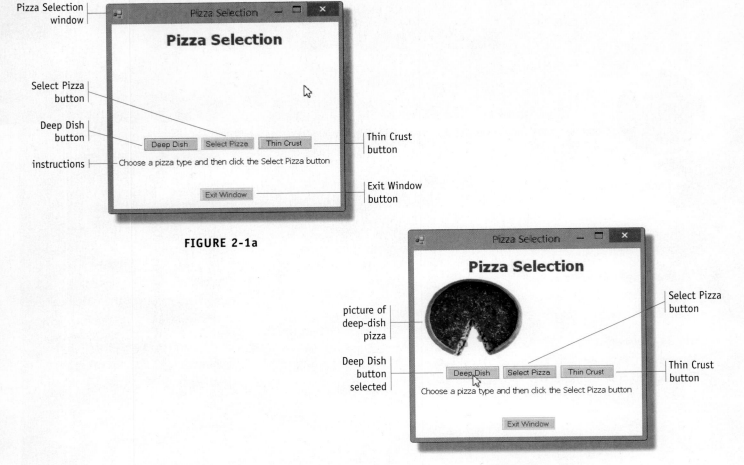

FIGURE 2-1a

FIGURE 2-1b

Brand X Pictures/Getty Images

In Figure 2-1a, the program begins by displaying the Pizza Selection window on a PC monitor. The program provides instructions for the user to choose the pizza type by tapping or clicking the Deep Dish or Thin Crust button, and then to complete the selection by tapping or clicking the Select Pizza button. If the user taps or clicks the Deep Dish button, a picture of a deep-dish pizza is displayed (Figure 2-1b). If the user taps or clicks the Thin Crust button, a picture of a thin-crust pizza is displayed (Figure 2-1c). After choosing a pizza type, the user can tap or click the Select Pizza button and the program informs the user that pizza selection has been completed (Figure 2-1d). To close the window and exit the program, the user can tap or click the Exit Window button after making a pizza selection.

By the end of Chapter 3, you will have completed the design and implementation of this program.

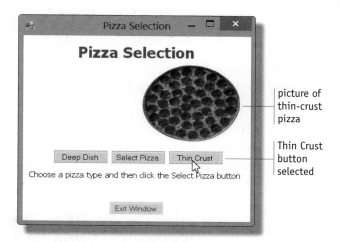

FIGURE 2-1c

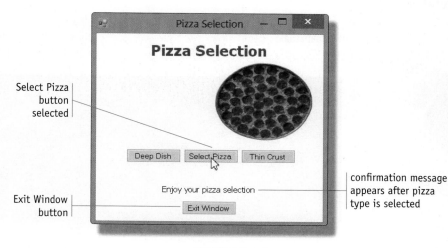

FIGURE 2-1d

© Brand X Pictures / Getty Images

Use Visual Studio 2012

When designing an event-driven program that uses a graphical user interface (GUI), such as the program in this chapter, one of the first steps after defining the purpose for the program is to design the user interface itself. Recall that the user interface is the window that appears on the screen when the program is running. The user interface includes a variety of objects such as buttons that are displayed in the window. Before beginning to design the user interface, however, the developer should know how to use Visual Studio and Visual Basic **rapid application development** (**RAD**) tools in the design process. For example, you use the Visual Studio tools to place a button on the window. Before starting the design of the program shown in Figure 2-1, you should know how to accomplish the Visual Studio tasks described on the following pages. In this text, you can complete steps by tapping if you are using a touch screen or by clicking if you are using a mouse.

Open Visual Studio 2012

To design a user interface using Visual Studio, the developer opens Visual Studio 2012 and then uses the tools the program provides. To open Visual Studio 2012, you can complete the following steps:

STEP 1   In Windows 8, open the Search charm and type `Visual Studio 2012`. In Windows 7, tap or click the Start button on the Windows taskbar, point to All Programs on the Start menu, and then tap or click Microsoft Visual Studio 2012 on the All Programs submenu.

The program name, Microsoft Visual Studio 2012, is displayed on the left side of the Windows 8 Apps screen (Figure 2-2).

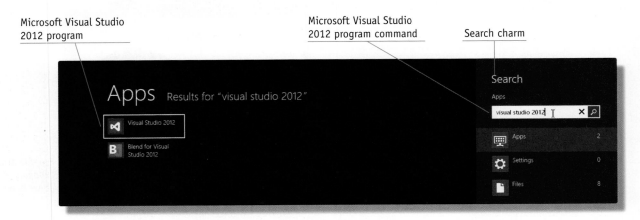

Microsoft Visual Studio 2012 program

Microsoft Visual Studio 2012 program command

Search charm

FIGURE 2-2

STEP 2 Tap or click Visual Studio 2012.

*A Visual Studio splash screen appears briefly, and then Microsoft Visual Studio 2012 opens
(Figure 2-3). The title of the window is Microsoft Visual Studio. The menu bar and the
Standard toolbar are displayed at the top of the window. The Start Page contains informa-
tion about Visual Basic. To close the Start Page, tap or click the Close button on the Start
Page title bar. You will learn the other elements of this window as you progress through this
book.*

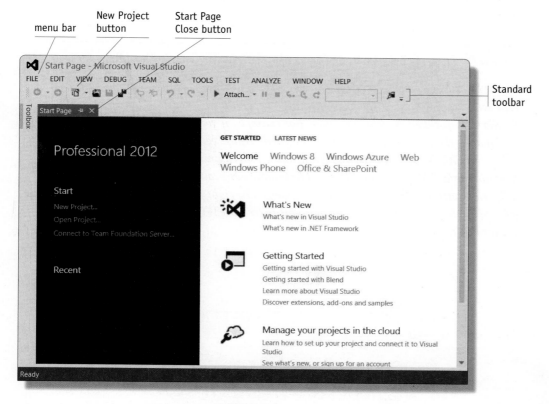

FIGURE 2-3

ONLINE REINFORCEMENT

To view a video of the process
in the previous steps, visit
CengageBrain.com and navigate
to the resources for this title.
Tap or click the link for Chapter 2
and then navigate to Video 2-2.

Create a New Visual Basic 2012 Windows Application Project

A **project** is equivalent to a single program created using Visual Studio. A **Windows Application project** is a program that includes a user interface whose windows are created using the Windows operating system. When the program is executed, the user interacts with the program by using its windows and components (the user interface).

To create a new project using Visual Studio, you must specify the programming language you want to use and the type of program or application you will create. To create a new Visual Basic Windows Application project, you can take the following steps:

STEP 1   Tap or click the New Project button on the Standard toolbar.

Visual Studio opens the New Project window (Figure 2-4). The New Project window on your computer might be displayed differently, depending on selections made when Visual Studio was installed on your computer. For example, if you are using Windows 7, you will not see the Windows Store templates listed because you need Windows 8 to develop a Windows Store app. The left pane contains the programming languages and other types of templates available in Visual Studio. The middle pane contains the types of applications you can create within each programming language. The right pane displays a description of the selected application. At this point, you want to create a Windows Forms Application using Visual Basic.

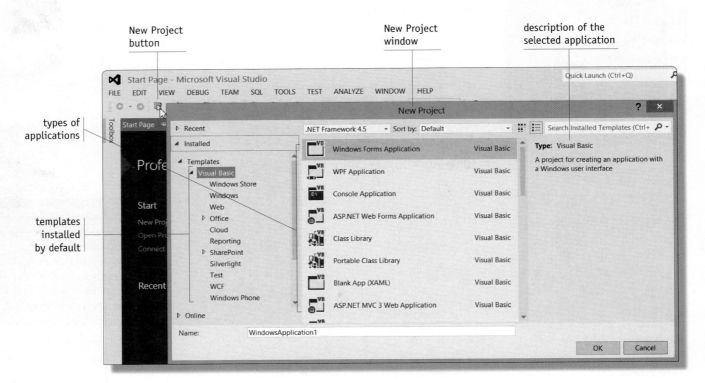

New Project button

New Project window

description of the selected application

types of applications

templates installed by default

FIGURE 2-4

STEP 2   If necessary, tap or click Windows in the left pane so it is selected.

Windows is highlighted in the left pane and the types of Windows projects you can create using Visual Basic are listed in the middle pane (Figure 2-5).

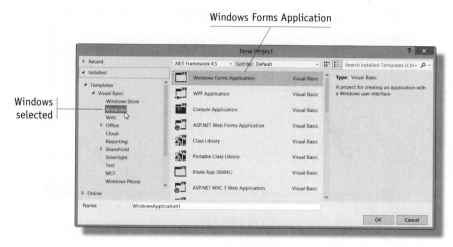

FIGURE 2-5

STEP 3   If necessary, tap or click Windows Forms Application in the middle pane.

Windows Forms Application is selected in the middle pane (Figure 2-6). By making this selection, you have specified you want to create a program that will run under the Windows operating system using the Windows graphical user interface.

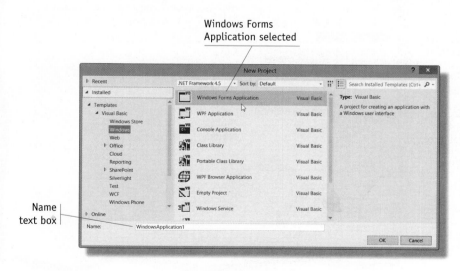

FIGURE 2-6

STEP 4 Type the project name. For this example, you could type `Pizza Selection` as the name.

The project name appears in the Name text box (Figure 2-7).

FIGURE 2-7

STEP 5 Tap or click the OK button in the New Project window.

Visual Studio creates a new project (Figure 2-8). The project name is displayed in the title bar of the window.

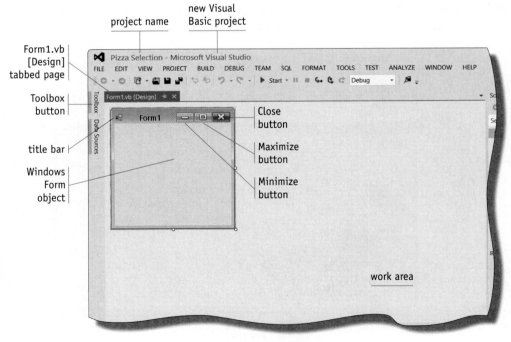

FIGURE 2-8

The Visual Studio window contains several important features you should know. First, in the portion of the window known as the **work area**, a tabbed page named Form1.vb [Design] contains a Windows Form object called Form1. A **Windows Form object** is the window you will use to build the program and then display it on your screen when you execute the program. The Windows Form object is the fundamental object in the graphical user interface you will create using Visual Studio tools. Notice in Figure 2-8 that the Windows Form object contains a blue title bar, a window title (Form1), a Minimize button, a Maximize button, and a Close button.

A second important element is displayed on the left side of the window. Depending on the settings in Visual Studio, the left portion of the window will appear as shown in Figure 2-8 or Figure 2-9. In Figure 2-8, the left margin contains the Toolbox button. The Toolbox button also appears on the Standard toolbar.

Display the Toolbox

You can use the **Toolbox button** to display the Toolbox. The **Toolbox** is the primary tool you use to place objects such as buttons on the Windows Form object. Items in the Toolbox are grouped into sections called **tabs**. To display the Toolbox, you can take the following steps:

STEP 1   If the window does not already display the Toolbox, tap or click the Toolbox button in the left margin of the window. If necessary, tap or click Common Controls to display the Common Controls tab.

When you point to the Toolbox button, the Toolbox is displayed on the window (Figure 2-9). Notice that the Toolbox hides the Form1 Windows Form object.

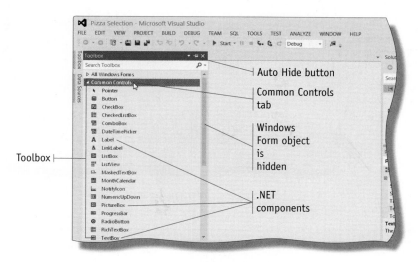

FIGURE 2-9

WATCH OUT FOR

In Figure 2-9, the Common Controls category of tools is open and all its tools are visible. If the Common Category tab is not expanded, a right triangle appears to the left of the Common Controls tab. To open the tab, tap or click the right triangle.

ONLINE REINFORCEMENT

To view a video of the process in the previous steps, visit CengageBrain.com and navigate to the resources for this title. Tap or click the link for Chapter 2 and then navigate to Video 2-4.

Among other things, the Toolbox contains many graphical elements called **controls** that you can place on the Windows Form object as graphical user interface objects. For example, the Toolbox contains buttons that can be placed on the Windows Form object. You will learn how to perform this activity in the next section of this chapter.

Permanently Display the Toolbox

When you tap or click outside the Toolbox, it no longer is displayed. When you are designing the graphical user interface, normally it helps to display the Toolbox at all times. To always display the Toolbox, you can complete the following step:

STEP 1   If necessary, tap or click the Toolbox button in the left margin of the window to display the Toolbox. Then, tap or click the **Auto Hide button** (Pushpin icon) on the Toolbox title bar.

When you tap or click the Auto Hide button, the Pushpin icon on the button changes from being horizontal, which indicates Auto Hide, to vertical, which indicates the Toolbox has been "pinned" to the window and will remain there (Figure 2-10). Form1 is moved to the right so you can see both the Toolbox and all of Form1.

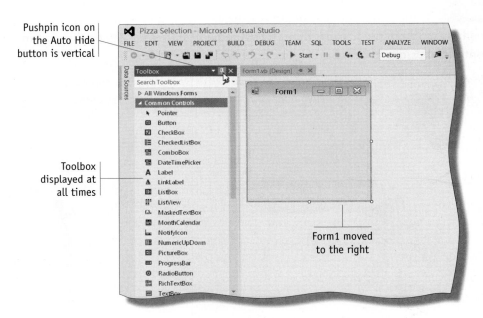

Pushpin icon on the Auto Hide button is vertical

Toolbox displayed at all times

Form1 moved to the right

FIGURE 2-10

When the Pushpin icon is vertical, the Toolbox is said to be in Dockable mode, which means it can be dragged around and placed anywhere within the Visual Studio window. In most applications, it should remain on the left side of the window, as shown in Figure 2-10. Later, you can change the Toolbox back to Auto Hide mode by tapping or clicking the Auto Hide button again.

View Object Properties

Every object you create in the user interface, including the Windows Form object, has properties. **Properties** can describe a multitude of characteristics about the object, including its color, size, name, and position on the screen. You will learn about the properties of all the objects you create using the Toolbox.

To view the properties for an object in Visual Studio, you use the Properties window. By default, the Properties window is displayed in the lower-right section of the Visual Studio window (Figure 2-11).

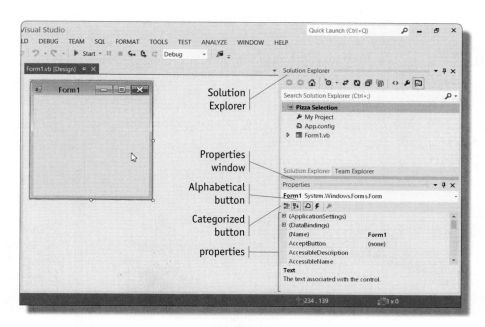

FIGURE 2-11

In the **Properties window** shown in Figure 2-11, the property names in the left list appear in Alphabetical view. Many developers find the Alphabetical view the easiest to use when searching for properties. Some developers, however, prefer the Categorized view, in which properties are organized according to type. You can change the order of the properties to Categorized if you tap or click the Categorized button on the Properties window toolbar (see Figure 2-11). In this book, the properties are shown in Alphabetical view, which you select by tapping or clicking the Alphabetical button on the Properties window toolbar.

Name the Windows Form Object

Visual Studio assigns a default name to every object in a Visual Basic graphical user interface. For example, the first Windows Form object in a project is named Form1. In virtually every instance, a developer should assign a meaningful name to an object so the program can reference it if required. The name of an object should reflect the object's use. For example, a good name for the Pizza Selection window might be frmPizzaSelection. Notice in the name that each word is capitalized and the remaining letters are lowercase. You should always follow this naming method when naming objects.

No spaces or other special characters are allowed in the object name. Also, by convention, each object name should begin with a prefix that identifies the type of object. For Windows Form objects, the prefix is frm. Therefore, the complete name for the Windows Form object would be frmPizzaSelection. The form name should be changed from Form1 to a more descriptive name in the Solution Explorer.

To give the name frmPizzaSelection to the form in Figure 2-11 on the previous page, you can complete the following steps:

STEP 1   Tap or click anywhere in the Windows Form object to select it.

When you tap or click within any object, including a Windows Form object, it is selected (Figure 2-12). Sizing handles and a heavier border surround the selected object. In addition, the Properties window displays the properties of the selected object.

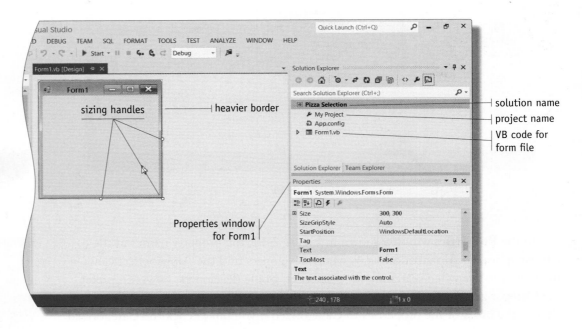

FIGURE 2-12

STEP 2   In the Solution Explorer window, press and hold or right-click the Form1. vb filename. On the shortcut menu, point to Rename.

The shortcut menu for the Form1.vb file appears in the Solution Explorer. Rename is highlighted (Figure 2-13).

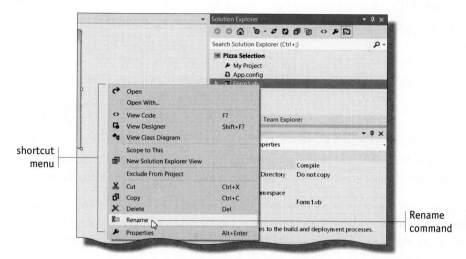

shortcut
menu

Rename
command

FIGURE 2-13

STEP 3 Tap or click Rename. Type `frmPizzaSelection.vb` and press the ENTER key.

The Form1.vb form file is given the new name frmPizzaSelection.vb in the Solution Explorer window (Figure 2-14).

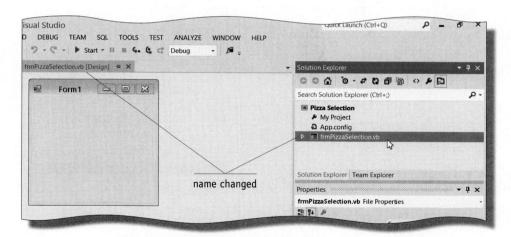

name changed

FIGURE 2-14

CONSIDER THIS

Set the Title Bar Text in a Windows Form Object

After you name the Windows Form object, often the next step in graphical user interface design is to change the title bar text to reflect the function of the program. In this example, the name used is Pizza Selection. The **Text property** in the Properties window for the Windows Form object contains the value displayed in the title bar of the window. You can set the Text property using the following steps:

STEP 1   With the Windows Form object selected, scroll in the Properties window as necessary until you find the Text property. (Remember that the properties are in alphabetical order.) Then, double-tap or double-click the Text property in the right column.

The text, Form1, is selected in the Properties window (Figure 2–15). Form1 is the default text value for the first Windows Form object created in a project. Whenever a property is selected, you can change the property.

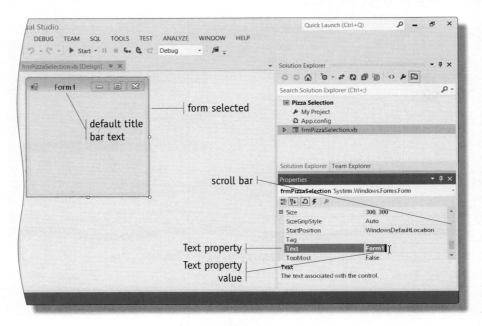

FIGURE 2-15

STEP 2 Type `Pizza Selection` and then press the ENTER key.

The value, Pizza Selection, is displayed for the Text property in the Properties window and is partially displayed in the title bar of the Windows Form object (Figure 2-16). You can enter any value you like for the Text property of the Windows Form object.

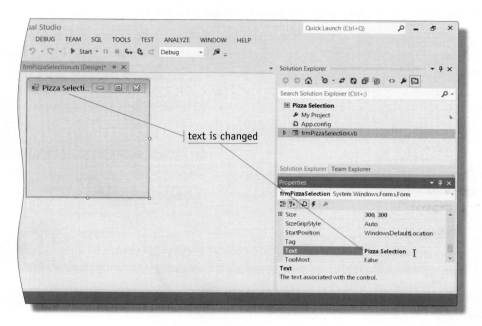

FIGURE 2-16

You can change many of the properties for any object in the graphical user interface using the techniques just illustrated.

Resize a Form

To resize a Windows Form object, you can change the **Size property** in the Properties window to the exact number of horizontal and vertical pixels you desire. You can change the Size property in the Properties window, or you can drag the vertical border to change the width of the window and the horizontal border to change the height. Another way to change the size is to drag a corner sizing handle, which allows you to change the width and height at the same time.

The following steps illustrate how to change the Size property of the Windows Form object shown in Figure 2-17:

STEP 1 With the Windows Form object selected, double-click the Size property in the right column.

The Size property is selected in the Properties window (Figure 2-17).

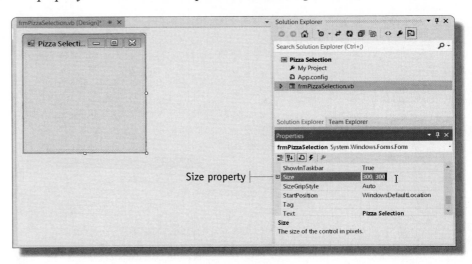

Size property

FIGURE 2-17

STEP 2 Type 430, 395 and then press the ENTER key.

The Windows Form object has been resized (Figure 2-18). The exact size of the Windows Form object is shown on the status bar as (number of horizontal pixels, number of vertical pixels). In Figure 2-18, the size of the Windows Form object is 430 pixels horizontally by 395 pixels vertically.

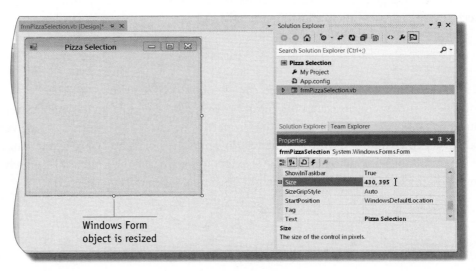

Windows Form object is resized

FIGURE 2-18

Add a Label Object

After sizing the Windows Form object, you can use the Toolbox to add other GUI objects as required. For example, a graphical user interface often displays a message or labels an item in the window. To accomplish this, you can use the **Label .NET component** in the Toolbox to place a **Label object** on the Windows Form object. To add a Label object to a Windows Form object, you can complete the following steps.

STEP 1 Drag the Label .NET component from the Common Controls tab in the Toolbox over the Windows Form object to the approximate location where you want to place the Label object.

The pointer changes to a crosshair and small rectangle when you place it over the Windows Form object (Figure 2-19). The Label object will be placed on the form at the location of the small rectangle in the pointer.

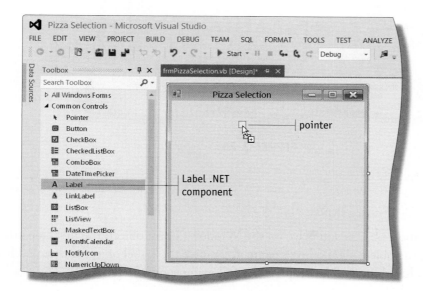

FIGURE 2-19

STEP 2 When the Label object is in the correct location, release the left mouse button.

The Label object is placed on the Windows Form object at the location you selected (Figure 2-20). The label is selected, as identified by the dotted border surrounding it. The default text within the label is Label1. In virtually all cases, you must change the label text to reflect the needs of the interface.

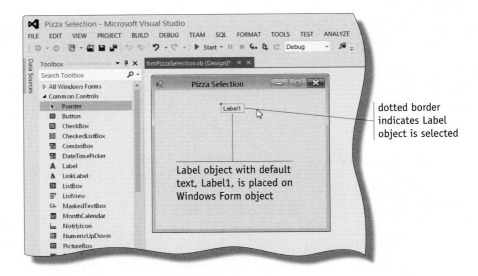

FIGURE 2-20

Name the Label Object

As with most objects you place on the Windows Form object, the first step after creating the object should be to name it. To give the Label object the name Heading with the Label prefix lbl, complete the following steps:

STEP 1 With the Label object selected, scroll in the Properties window until you find the (Name) property. Then, double-click the (Name) property in the right column.

The default name, Label1, is selected (Figure 2-21). When a property is selected, you can change the property.

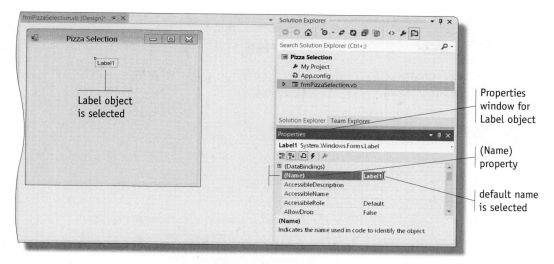

FIGURE 2-21

STEP 2 Type the new name as `lblHeading` and then press the ENTER key.

The name you entered is displayed in the Name property in the Properties window (Figure 2–22). You now can reference the Label object by its name in other parts of the program.

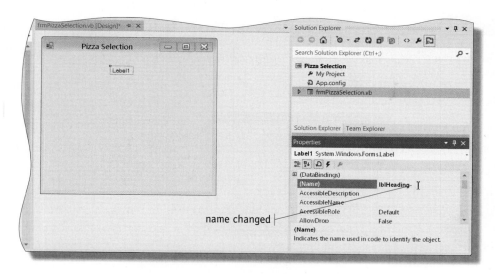

FIGURE 2-22

WATCH OUT FOR

If you make an error while typing a property, such as the name, you can press the backspace key to erase your mistake and then type the correct data. You also can double-tap or double-click the property you want to change and start over.

ONLINE REINFORCEMENT

To view a video of the process in the previous steps, visit CengageBrain.com and navigate to the resources for this title. Tap or click the link for Chapter 2 and then navigate to Video 2-10.

Change the Text in a Label Object

The default text in a Label object, Label1, normally is not the text you want to display in the label. Therefore, you should change the Text property for the Label object to the value you want. To change the text on the label in Figure 2-21 to Pizza Selection, you can complete the following steps:

STEP 1   With the Label object selected, scroll in the Properties window until you find the Text property. Then, double-tap or double-click the Text value in the right column.

The text value is selected in the right column of the Text property. The same text is displayed on the label (Figure 2-23). When the Text value is selected, you can change it.

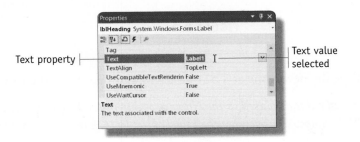

FIGURE 2-23

STEP 2   Type `Pizza Selection` for the Text property.

The text you typed, Pizza Selection, is displayed in the Text property for the Label object (Figure 2-24).

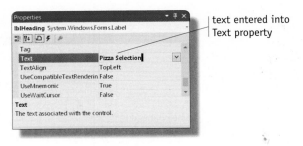

FIGURE 2-24

STEP 3   To enter the Text property, press the ENTER key.

The text you entered, Pizza Selection, is displayed in the Text property and in the label itself (Figure 2-25). By default, the text is 8 points in size. The Label object automatically expanded horizontally to accommodate the text you typed. By default, Label objects change to be the right size for the text in the Text property.

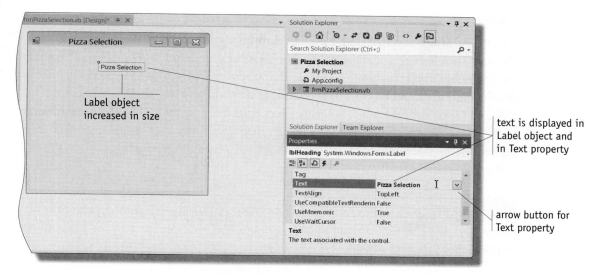

FIGURE 2-25

The text in a Label object can span multiple lines. To enter multiple lines for a Label object, you can complete the following steps:

STEP 1 With the Label object selected, tap or click the Text property name in the left column of the Properties window. Then, tap or click the arrow button in the right column of the Text property.

A box opens in which you can enter multiple lines (Figure 2–26). As you type, you can move the insertion point to the next line by pressing the ENTER key. To accept the text for the label, press CTRL + ENTER. (In other words, hold down the CTRL key, press the ENTER key, and then release both keys.)

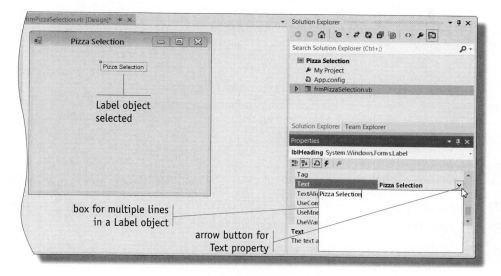

FIGURE 2-26

ONLINE REINFORCEMENT

To view a video of the process in the previous steps, visit CengageBrain.com and navigate to the resources for this title. Tap or click the link for Chapter 2 and then navigate to Video 2-11.

ONLINE REINFORCEMENT

To view a video of the process in the previous step, visit CengageBrain.com and navigate to the resources for this title. Tap or click the link for Chapter 2 and then navigate to Video 2-12.

Change the Label Font, Font Style, and Font Size

The default font, font style, and font size of the text in a Label object often must be changed to reflect the purpose of the label. For example, in a label used as a heading for a window, the text should be larger than the default 8-point font used for Label objects, and it should be bold to stand out as a heading. To change the font, font style, and font size of a label, you can select the label and then use the **Font property** to make the change. To change the text in the lblHeading label to Tahoma font, make the font bold, and increase the font size to 16 points, you can complete the following steps:

STEP 1   Tap or click the Label object to select it. Scroll until you find the Font property in the Properties window. Tap or click the Font property in the left column of the Label Properties window.

The Label object is selected, as shown by the dotted border surrounding it (Figure 2-27). When you tap or click the Font property in the Properties window, a button with an ellipsis (three dots) is displayed in the right column. In the Properties window, an ellipsis button indicates that multiple choices for the property will be made available when you tap or click the button.

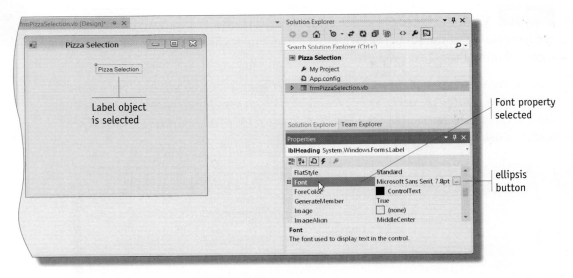

Label object is selected

Font property selected

ellipsis button

FIGURE 2-27

STEP 2   Tap or click the ellipsis button for the Font property.

The Font dialog box is displayed (Figure 2-28). Using the Font dialog box, you can change the font, font style, and size of the text in the Label object.

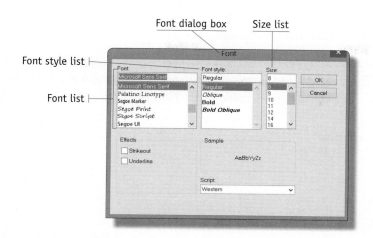

FIGURE 2-28

STEP 3 In the Font dialog box, scroll in the Font list until you find Tahoma and then tap or click it. Tap or click Bold in the Font style list. Tap or click 16 in the Size list.

The selections are highlighted in the Font dialog box (Figure 2-29).

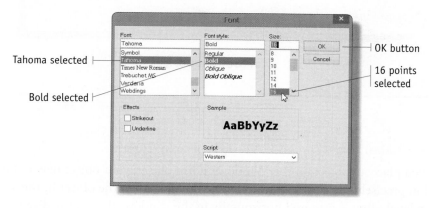

FIGURE 2-29

STEP 4   Tap or click the OK button.

The font, font style, and font size in the Label object are changed as specified in the Font dialog box (Figure 2-30). The Label object automatically expands to accommodate the changed font. The changes also are made for the Font property in the Properties window.

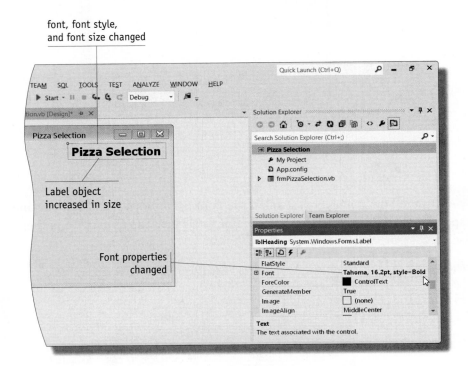

FIGURE 2-30

Center a Label Object in the Windows Form Object

When you place an object on the Windows Form object, your object may not be located in precisely the correct position. So, you must align the object in the window. A single label often is centered horizontally in the window; that is, the distance from the left frame of the window to the beginning of the text should be the same as the distance from the end of the text to the right frame of the window. To horizontally center the label that contains the heading, you can complete the following steps:

STEP 1   With the Label object selected, tap or click FORMAT on the menu bar and then point to Center in Form on the FORMAT menu.

The FORMAT menu is displayed and the pointer is located on the Center in Form command (Figure 2-31). The Center in Form submenu also is displayed. The two choices on the Center in Form submenu are Horizontally and Vertically. Horizontally means the label will be centered between the left and right edges of the window. Vertically means the label will be centered between the top edge and the bottom edge of the window.

FORMAT on menu bar

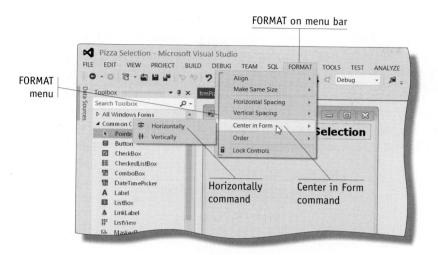

FORMAT
menu

Horizontally
command

Center in Form
command

FIGURE 2-31

STEP 2 Tap or click Horizontally on the Center in Form submenu.

The label is centered horizontally in the window (Figure 2–32).

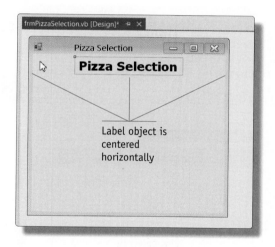

Label object is
centered
horizontally

FIGURE 2-32

Aligning objects is an important aspect of user interface design because it makes objects and the interface easy to use. Centering within the Windows Form object is the first of several alignments you will make in this chapter.

Delete GUI Objects

In some instances, you might add an object to the Windows Form object and later discover you do not need the object in the user interface. When this occurs, you should delete the object from the Windows Form object. Visual Studio provides two primary ways to delete an object from the Windows Form object: the keyboard and a shortcut menu. To delete an object using the keyboard, perform the following steps:

STEP 1   Select the object to delete by tapping or clicking it.

When you tap or click an object, such as the label in Figure 2-33, the object is selected. When a label is selected, it is surrounded by a dotted border. As you saw with the Windows Form object (Figure 2-12), other objects are surrounded by a heavier border and sizing handles.

FIGURE 2-33

STEP 2   Press the DELETE key.

When you press the DELETE key, Visual Studio removes the object from the screen (Figure 2-34).

FIGURE 2-34

A second way to delete an object is to use a shortcut menu. To do so, press or right-click the object to be deleted and then select Delete on the shortcut menu.

Use the Undo Button on the Standard Toolbar

As you work in Visual Studio to create a graphical user interface, you might delete an object or perform another activity that you realize was an error. You can undo an action you just performed by tapping or clicking the Undo button on the Standard toolbar. To undo the action of deleting the heading label, you can perform the following step:

STEP 1 Tap or click the Undo button on the Standard toolbar.

When you tap or click the Undo button, the last action performed in Visual Studio is "undone." In Figure 2-35, the action that deleted the label (Figure 2-34) is undone and the Label object now appears on the Windows Form object again.

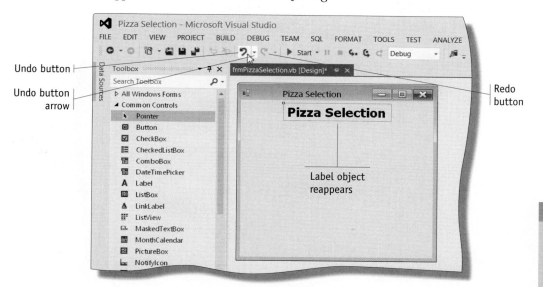

FIGURE 2-35

You can use the Undo button to undo more than just the last action performed. If you tap or click the Undo button arrow (Figure 2-35), many of the previous activities are shown in a list. You can undo any displayed activity by tapping or clicking it in the list.

When you use the Undo button, you might undo something you do not want to undo. You can tap or click the Redo button on the Standard toolbar to redo an action.

Learning to use the Undo and Redo buttons on the Standard toolbar means you can add or delete items in the graphical user interface with the assurance that any error you make can be corrected immediately.

Add a PictureBox Object

When you want to display a picture in a window, such as the pizza pictures shown in Figure 2-1b and Figure 2-1c on pages 32 and 33, you must place a PictureBox object on the Windows Form object. Then, you place the picture in the PictureBox object.

In this section, you will learn to add a PictureBox object to the Windows Form object. In Chapter 3, you will learn how to place a picture in the PictureBox object.

A **PictureBox** is an object much like a label. To add a PictureBox object to the window, you can use the Toolbox, as shown in the following steps:

STEP 1   With the Toolbox visible, drag the PictureBox .NET component on the Toolbox over the Windows Form object to the approximate location where you want the PictureBox object to be displayed.

The pointer changes when you place it over the Windows Form object (Figure 2-36). The upper-left corner of the PictureBox object will be placed on the form at the location of the small square in the pointer.

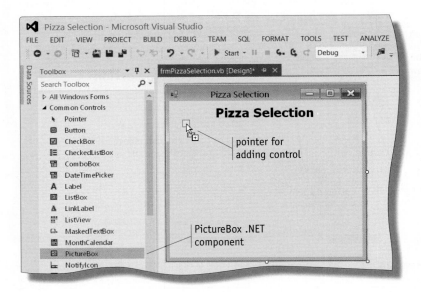

FIGURE 2-36

STEP 2   When the pointer is in the correct location, release the left mouse button.

A PictureBox object is placed on the Windows Form object in the default size (Figure 2-37). The PictureBox object is selected, as indicated by the sizing handles and the heavier border. Notice that when the pointer is inside the PictureBox object, it changes to a crosshair with four arrowheads. This indicates you can drag the PictureBox object anywhere on the Windows Form object.

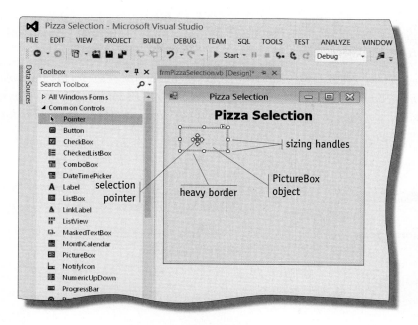

FIGURE 2-37

As you can see, placing a PictureBox object on the Windows Form object is similar to placing a Label object on the Windows Form object. You can use the same technique for most objects within the Toolbox.

Name a PictureBox Object

When you add an object to the Windows Form object, your next action should be to name the object. The technique for naming a PictureBox object is identical to that for a Label object, except that the prefix for a PictureBox object is pic. For example, to give the name picDeepDish to the PictureBox object just added to the form, you can complete the following steps:

1. Select the PictureBox object.
2. Locate the (Name) property in the Properties window for the PictureBox object.
3. Double-tap or double-click the value in the right column for the (Name) property, type picDeepDish as the name, and then press the ENTER key.

Resize a PictureBox Object

When you place a PictureBox object on the Windows Form object, it often is not the size required for the application. You can resize a PictureBox object using the same technique you used to resize the Windows Form object. The step on the next page will resize the PictureBox object:

STEP 1 Double-tap or double-click to the right of the Size property of the PictureBox object, type 185,150, and then press the ENTER key.

When you change the Size property, the width and height of the PictureBox object are changed. In Figure 2-38, the width and height of the PictureBox object are increased. The actual size of the PictureBox object in pixels (185 horizontal pixels, 150 vertical pixels) is shown on the status bar.

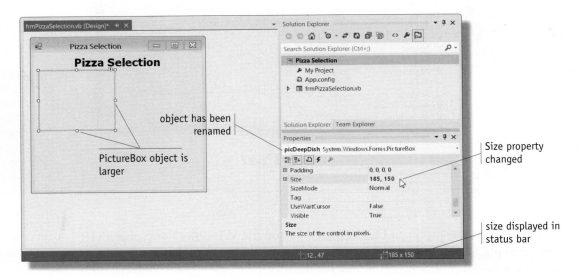

FIGURE 2-38

Add a Second PictureBox Object

You can add a second PictureBox object to the Windows Form object by performing the same technique you used previously, as in the following step:

STEP 1   Drag the PictureBox .NET component in the Toolbox to any location in the Windows Form object, and then release the left mouse button.

The PictureBox object is placed on the Windows Form object (Figure 2-39). Notice that the PictureBox objects in Figure 2-39 are different sizes. If you see a blue line as you drag the PictureBox object onto the Windows Form object, ignore it. You will learn about these lines later in this chapter.

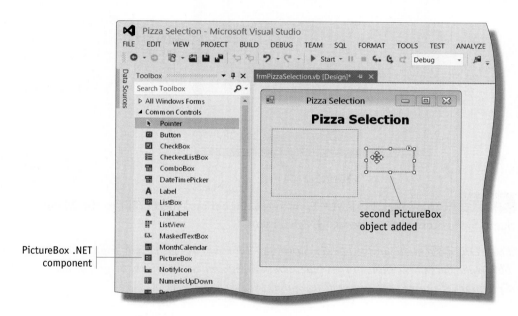

FIGURE 2-39

ONLINE REINFORCEMENT

To view a video of the process in the previous step, visit CengageBrain.com and navigate to the resources for this title. Tap or click the link for Chapter 2 and then navigate to Video 2-19.

As with all objects you add to the Windows Form object, you should name the PictureBox object immediately after adding it. A good name for the second PictureBox object is picThinCrust.

Make Objects the Same Size

Often you will want picture boxes and other GUI elements in your user interface to be the same size. You can use the FORMAT menu to make GUI objects the same size, as shown in the steps on the next page:

STEP 1 Select the object whose size you want to duplicate (in this example, the left PictureBox object in the window), and then hold down the CTRL key and tap or click the object you want to resize (the right PictureBox object in the window).

The left and right PictureBox objects are selected (Figure 2–40). The left PictureBox object is surrounded by white sizing handles and the right PictureBox object is surrounded by black siz-ing handles, which indicates the left PictureBox object is the "controlling" object when sizing or alignment commands are executed. The first object selected always is the controlling object.

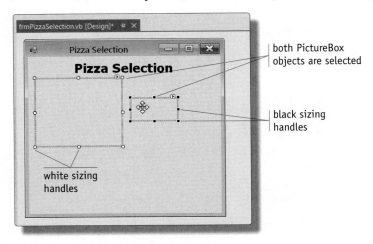

FIGURE 2-40

STEP 2 Tap or click FORMAT on the menu bar and then point to the Make Same Size command on the FORMAT menu.

The FORMAT menu and the Make Same Size submenu are displayed (Figure 2–41). The Make Same Size submenu provides commands to make the width, height, or both dimensions the same as the controlling object.

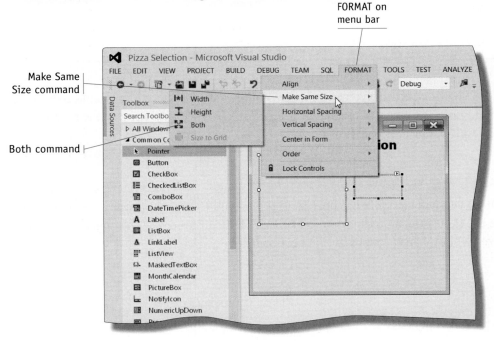

FIGURE 2-41

STEP 3   Tap or click Both on the Make Same Size submenu.

Visual Studio changes the size of the right PictureBox object to match the size of the left PictureBox object (Figure 2–42). Both the width and the height of the right PictureBox object are changed.

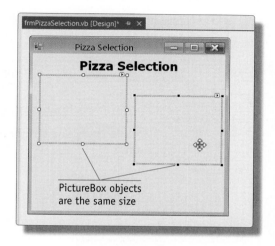

FIGURE 2-42

ONLINE REINFORCEMENT

To view a video of the process in the previous steps, visit CengageBrain.com and navigate to the resources for this title. Tap or click the link for Chapter 2 and then navigate to Video 2-20.

Align the PictureBox Objects

Notice in Figure 2-42 that the left PictureBox object is higher in the form than the right PictureBox object. When designing a graphical user interface, you should consider aligning the elements to create a clean, uncluttered look for the user. **Alignment** means one element in the GUI is lined up horizontally (left and right) or vertically (up and down) with another element in the window. For example, in Figure 2-42 the GUI would look better if the PictureBox objects were aligned horizontally so their tops and bottoms were even across the window.

When you want to align objects that are already on the Windows Form object, select the objects to align and then specify the alignment you want. As you saw when changing the object size, the first object selected is the controlling object; when aligning, this means the other selected objects will be aligned with the first object selected. To horizontally align the two PictureBox objects in Figure 2-42, you can perform the steps on the next page:

STEP 1 With the left and right PictureBox objects selected, as shown in Figure 2-42 on the previous page, tap or click FORMAT on the menu bar and then point to Align on the FORMAT menu.

The FORMAT menu and the Align submenu are displayed (Figure 2-43). The left PictureBox object is the "controlling" object, as indicated by the white sizing handles, so the right PictureBox object will be aligned horizontally with the left PictureBox object.

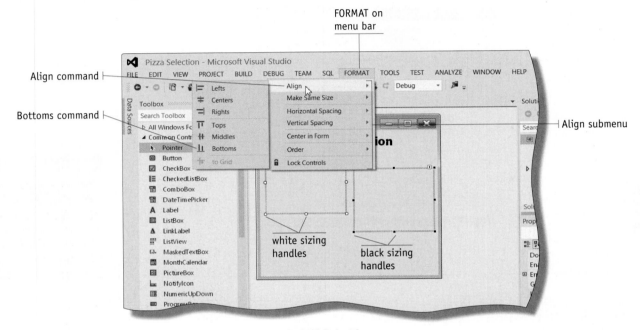

FORMAT on menu bar

Align command

Bottoms command

Align submenu

white sizing handles

black sizing handles

FIGURE 2-43

STEP 2 Tap or click Bottoms on the Align submenu.

The bottom of the right PictureBox object is aligned horizontally with the bottom of the left PictureBox object (Figure 2-44). Because the PictureBox objects are the same size, the tops also are aligned.

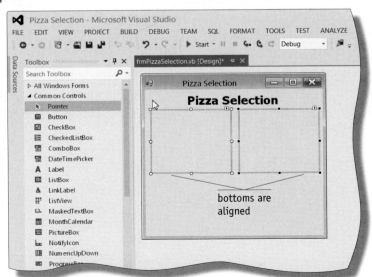

bottoms are aligned

ONLINE REINFORCEMENT

To view a video of the process in the previous steps, visit CengageBrain.com and navigate to the resources for this title. Tap or click the link for Chapter 2 and then navigate to Video 2-21.

FIGURE 2-44

Notice on the Align submenu in Figure 2-43 that Visual Studio offers seven choices for alignment. When you are aligning objects horizontally, you should choose from the Tops, Middles, and Bottoms group. When you are aligning objects vertically, you should choose from the Lefts, Centers, and Rights group. You will learn how to align to a grid later in this book.

Center Multiple Objects Horizontally in the Window

From Figure 2-44, you can see that the PictureBox objects are not centered horizontally in the Windows Form object. As you learned, you can center one or more objects horizontally within the Windows Form object by using a command from the FORMAT menu. To center the two PictureBox objects as a unit, you can complete the following steps:

STEP 1 With both PictureBox objects selected, tap or click FORMAT on the menu bar and then point to the Center in Form command.

The FORMAT menu is displayed (Figure 2-45). The Center in Form submenu also is displayed.

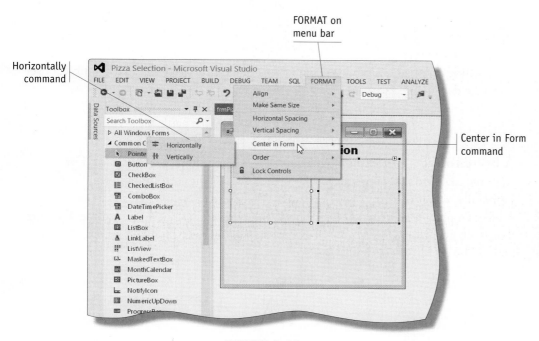

FORMAT on
menu bar

Horizontally
command

Center in Form
command

FIGURE 2-45

STEP 2   Tap or click Horizontally on the Center in Form submenu.

The two PictureBox objects are centered horizontally as a unit in the Windows Form object (Figure 2–46). The left border of the left PictureBox object is the same distance from the window frame as the right border of the right PictureBox object.

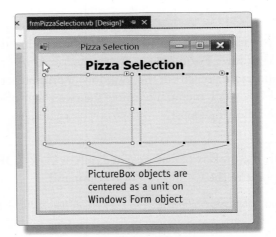

FIGURE 2-46

ONLINE REINFORCEMENT

To view a video of the process in the previous steps, visit CengageBrain.com and navigate to the resources for this title. Tap or click the link for Chapter 2 and then navigate to Video 2-22.

Adding an object, naming it, sizing it, and aligning it are basic to graphical user interface design.

Add a Button Object

A **Button object** is a commonly used object in a graphical user interface. For example, you probably are familiar with the OK button used in many applications. Generally, when the program is executing, buttons are used to cause an event to occur. To place a Button object on the Windows Form object, you use the Toolbox. To create a Button object, you can complete the following steps:

STEP 1   With the Toolbox displayed in the Visual Studio window, drag the Button control in the Toolbox over the Windows Form object to the position where you want to place the button below the first PictureBox object.

When you drag the button over the Windows Form object, the pointer changes (Figure 2–47). The upper-left corner of the Button object will be placed at the lower-left corner of the rectangle.

Button .NET component

control pointer

FIGURE 2-47

STEP 2   When the pointer is positioned properly, release the left mouse button.

A standard-sized Button object is added to the Windows Form object (Figure 2–48). The text on the button is the default, Button1. The button is selected, as indicated by the heavier border and sizing handles.

default text

Button object is selected

Button object added

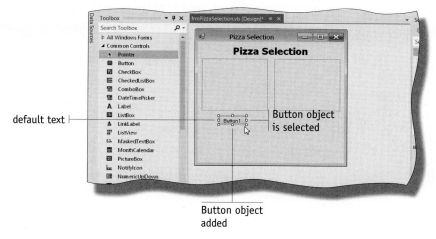

FIGURE 2-48

Name and Set Text for a Button Object

As with other objects you add to the Windows Form object, the first step after adding the Button object is to name it. A Button object name should contain the prefix btn. For example, the name for the button you just added could be btnDeepDish.

In most cases, you also will change the text that appears on the Button object. To change the text on the btnDeepDish button, you can do the following:

STEP 1 With the Button object selected, scroll in the Properties window until you find the Text property. Double-click the Text value in the right column, type Deep Dish, and then press the ENTER key.

The text for the Deep Dish button is changed on the button and in the Properties window (Figure 2–49). The button is not large enough to contain the words Deep Dish, so only Deep is displayed. In the next set of steps, you will learn how to increase the size of the Button object.

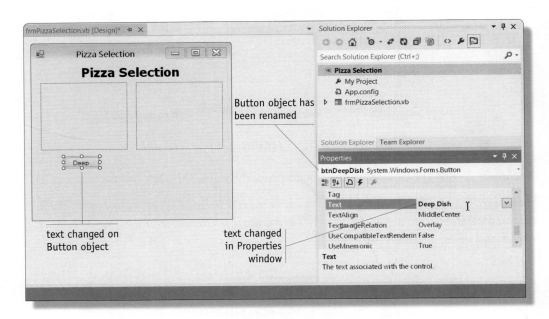

FIGURE 2-49

Change a Button Object's Size

Sometimes, a button may not be big enough to display the button text (see Figure 2-49). To change a Button object's size to accommodate the text, you can perform the following steps:

STEP 1   Place the pointer over the right edge of the Button object until the pointer changes to a double-headed arrow.

The pointer changes to a double-headed arrow, which indicates you can drag the border of the button to increase or decrease its size (Figure 2-50).

FIGURE 2-50

STEP 2   Drag the pointer to the right until the Button object is just big enough to display the text Deep Dish, and then release the left mouse button.

As you drag the pointer to the right, the button becomes bigger (Figure 2-51). When the button is big enough to display the text, it is the right size.

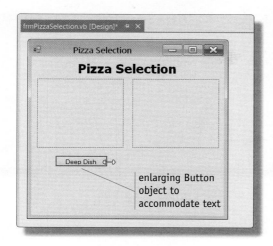

FIGURE 2-51

ONLINE REINFORCEMENT

To view a video of the process in the previous steps, visit CengageBrain.com and navigate to the resources for this title. Tap or click the link for Chapter 2 and then navigate to Video 2-25.

To move a Button object, first place the pointer on the button; when the pointer changes to a crosshair with four arrowheads, drag the button to any location on the Windows Form object. You can move other objects on the Windows Form object using the same technique.

Add and Align a Second Button

Often, a window requires more than one button. When a second button is added to the window, a normal requirement is to align the buttons. As with PictureBox objects, you can align Button objects horizontally or vertically.

With the PictureBox objects, you saw that you can align objects after placing them on the Windows Form object. You also can align objects when you place them on the Windows Form object. To add a second button to the Windows Form object in Figure 2-51 on the previous page and align it horizontally at the same time, you can complete the following steps:

STEP 1   Drag the Button .NET component from the Toolbox to the right of the Deep Dish button on the Windows Form object. Align the top of the rectangle in the pointer to the top of the Deep Dish button until a red line appears under the text of the buttons.

*The red line, called a **snap line**, indicates the text on the Deep Dish button is aligned with the text on the Button object being added to the Windows Form object (Figure 2-52). You can drag the Button object left or right to obtain the desired spacing between the buttons. If the red line disappears while you are dragging, move the pointer up or down until the red line reappears, signaling the objects are aligned horizontally.*

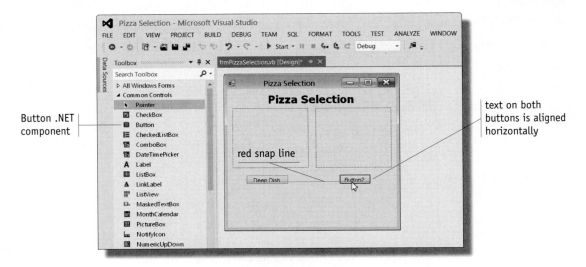

FIGURE 2-52

STEP 2 When the buttons are aligned and spaced as you like, release the left mouse button.

The Button2 object is aligned horizontally with the Deep Dish button (Figure 2-53). The text of each button is on the same line.

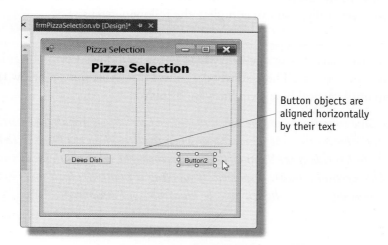

FIGURE 2-53

After adding the second Button object, you should name it, change the text as needed, and size the Button object if necessary. Assume you have named the second Button object btnThinCrust, changed the button text to Thin Crust, and made the two buttons the same size. Recall that you can make the Thin Crust button the same size as the Deep Dish button by completing the following steps:

Step 1:   Tap or click the Deep Dish button and then, while holding down the CTRL key, tap or click the Thin Crust button.

Step 2:   Tap or click FORMAT on the menu bar, point to Make Same Size on the FORMAT menu, and then tap or click Both on the Make Same Size submenu.

Step 3:   To deselect the Button objects, tap or click anywhere on the Windows Form object except on another object.

ONLINE REINFORCEMENT

To view a video of the process in the previous steps, visit CengageBrain.com and navigate to the resources for this title. Tap or click the link for Chapter 2 and then navigate to Video 2-26.

Align Objects Vertically

The buttons in Figure 2-53 on the previous page are aligned horizontally, but they also can be aligned vertically. To illustrate this point and to use snap lines to align objects that are already on the Windows Form object, assume that the Deep Dish and Thin Crust buttons should be aligned vertically on the left side of the Windows Form object, with the Deep Dish button above the Thin Crust button. To align the Button objects vertically, you can complete the following steps:

STEP 1 If necessary, tap or click anywhere in the Windows Form object to deselect any other objects. Then, slowly drag the Thin Crust button below the Deep Dish button until vertical blue snap lines are displayed.

*As you drag, **blue snap lines** indicate when the sides of the objects are aligned vertically. In Figure 2-54, the buttons are the same size, so when the left side of the Deep Dish button is aligned with the left side of the Thin Crust button, the right sides are aligned as well. As a result, two blue vertical lines are displayed. If you drag the button a little more to the left or right, the buttons will not be aligned and the blue lines will disappear.*

FIGURE 2-54

STEP 2 When the blue lines appear, indicating the buttons are aligned vertically, drag the Thin Crust button up or down to create the proper spacing between the buttons, and then release the left mouse button.

The proper vertical distance between the buttons is a judgment call based on the needs of the application, the size of the Windows Form object, and the number of other elements in the window (Figure 2-55). As with many aspects of GUI design, the eye of the developer is critical when placing objects in the window.

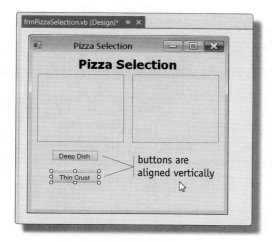

FIGURE 2-55

FIGURE 2-55

ONLINE REINFORCEMENT

To view a video of the process in the previous steps, visit CengageBrain.com and navigate to the resources for this title. Tap or click the link for Chapter 2 and then navigate to Video 2-27.

In the previous examples, you have seen the use of blue snap lines. As you drag objects, you also might see red snap lines flash on the screen. A red snap line indicates text is aligned within an object. For example, if you drag a button that contains text and the text aligns horizontally with the text in another button, a red snap line will be displayed. The use of red and blue snap lines allows you to align objects on the Windows Form object by dragging instead of selecting the objects and using the FORMAT menu.

Visual Studio offers a variety of tools to create and align elements in the graphical user interface, and to make the user interface as effective and useful as possible.

Save a Visual Basic Project

As you are working on a Visual Basic project, you must save your work on a regular basis. Some developers save every 10 to 15 minutes, while others might wait for a natural break to save their work. Regardless, it is important to develop the habit of regularly saving your work.

To save the work you have completed, you can tap or click the Save All button on the Standard toolbar. The first time you save a project, the Save Project dialog box is displayed (Figure 2-56).

location for
saving project

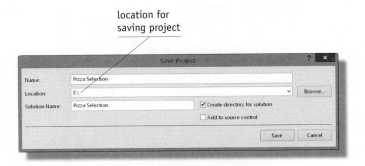

FIGURE 2-56

Select the location where you want to store your program. You might use a USB drive, the hard drive on your computer, or a network drive. If you have questions about where to store your program, check with your instructor or network administrator.

After you save the program the first time, tap or click the Save All button on the Standard toolbar to save your program in the same location with the same name.

Close Visual Studio 2012

To close Visual Studio, you can tap or click the Close button to the right of the title bar in the Visual Studio window. If you try to close Visual Studio but you have never saved your program, Visual Studio will display the Close Project dialog box (Figure 2-57).

FIGURE 2-57

You can choose to save your program or discard it. If you tap or click the Save button, the Save Project dialog box will be displayed (Figure 2-56) and you can save the program. If you tap or click the Discard button, your program will be discarded and not saved.

If you try to close Visual Studio but you have done more work since last saving your project, Visual Studio will ask if you want to save your recent work. In most cases, you should choose Yes.

Open a Visual Basic Project

After you save a project and close Visual Studio, you often will want to open the project and work on it again. To open a saved project, you can use one of several methods:

Method 1: Double-tap or double-click the solution file in the folder where it is stored. This method will open the solution and allow you to continue your work.

Method 2: With Visual Studio open, tap or click the Open File button on the Standard toolbar, locate the solution file, and open it in the same manner you use for most Windows programs.

Method 3: With Visual Studio open, tap or click FILE on the menu bar and then point to Recent Projects and Solutions on the FILE menu. A list of recent projects is displayed. Tap or click the name of the project you want to open. This method might not work well if you are not using your own computer because other projects might be listed.

After using one of these methods, you can continue working on your project.

WATCH OUT FOR

Sometimes when you open a Visual Basic project, the Form1.vb[Design] tabbed page is not displayed. (This page is renamed frmPizzaSelection.vb in your project.) To display the page, double-click Form1 or the new name of this project, frmPizzaSelection.vb, which appears in the Solution Explorer window in the upper-right section of the Visual Studio window.

Program Development Life Cycle

Now that you have learned the necessary skills to design a user interface in Visual Studio and Visual Basic, you are ready to learn about the program development life cycle. The **program development life cycle** is a set of phases and steps that developers follow to design, create, and maintain a computer program. The phases of the program development life cycle are:

1. **Gather and Analyze the Program Requirements** — The developer must obtain information that identifies the program requirements and then document these requirements.
2. **Design the User Interface** — After the developer understands the program requirements, the next step is to design the user interface. The user interface provides the framework for the processing that will occur within the program.
3. **Design the Program Processing Objects** — A computer program consists of one or more processing objects that perform the tasks required by the program. The developer must determine what processing objects are required and then determine the requirements of each object.
4. **Code the Program** — After a processing object has been designed, the object must be implemented in program code. **Program code** is the set of instructions, written using a programming language such as Visual Basic 2012, that a computer executes.
5. **Test the Program** — As the program is being coded, and after the coding is completed, the developer should test the program code to ensure it is executing properly. The testing process is ongoing and includes a variety of stages.

6. **Document the Program/System** — As a program is being designed and coded, and after the process is completed, the developer should document the program. **Documenting a program** means using a prescribed method to write down the instructions for using the program, the way the program performs its tasks, and other items that users, developers, and management might require.

7. **Maintain the Program/System** — After a program is put into use, it probably will have to be modified in the future. For example, if a third type of pizza is added to the pizza selection program, it must be changed to reflect the new pizza type. The process of changing and updating programs is called **program and system maintenance**.

The program development life cycle rarely is accomplished in a linear fashion, with one phase completed before the next phase starts. Rather, programs are developed iteratively, which means phases and steps within phases might have to be repeated several times before the program is completed. For example, the requirements for a program might change after the developer has begun coding the program. If so, the developer must return to Phase 1 and gather and document the new requirements. Then, changes might be needed to the user interface or other parts of the program to accommodate the updated requirements. This process of moving back and forth within the program development cycle is normal when developing a computer program.

The next sections in this chapter explain Phase 1 and Phase 2 of the program development life cycle in more detail. The remaining phases are explained in Chapter 3.

Phase 1: Gather and Analyze the Program Requirements

An old programming adage states, "If you don't understand the problem to be solved, you will never develop a solution." While this seems self-evident, too often a program does not perform as desired because the designer did not understand the problem to be solved. Before beginning the user interface design, it is mandatory that the developer understand the problem.

In many programming projects, the developer is responsible for gathering program requirements by interviewing users, reviewing current procedures, and completing other fact-gathering tasks. The emphasis in this book is on learning to program using the Visual Basic 2012 language, so the process of gathering program requirements is beyond the scope of the book. You will be given the program requirements for each program in this book.

When the requirements have been determined, they must be documented so the developers can proceed to design and implement the program. The exact form of the requirements documentation can vary significantly. The format and amount of documentation might be dictated by the application itself or by the documentation standards of the organization for which the program is being developed. For Windows applications in this book, two types of requirements documentation will be provided for you. The first is the requirements document.

A **requirements document** identifies the purpose of the program being developed, the application title, the procedures to be followed when using the program, any equations and calculations required by the program, any conditions within the program that must be tested, notes and restrictions that the program must follow, and any other comments that would be helpful to understanding the problem.

Recall that the program being developed in this chapter and Chapter 3 is the Pizza Selection program (see Figure 2-1 on pages 32 and 33). The requirements document for the Pizza Selection program is shown in Figure 2-58.

REQUIREMENTS DOCUMENT

Date Submitted:	January 23, 2015
Application Title:	Pizza Selection Application
Purpose:	This Windows application will allow a user to select a type of pizza.
Program Procedures:	From a window on the screen, the user should view two different pizza types and then make a pizza selection.
Algorithms, Processing, and Conditions:	1. The user must be able to view choices for a deep-dish and thin-crust pizza until the user selects a pizza type.
	2. When the user chooses a pizza type, a picture of the selected type should appear in the window.
	3. Only one picture should be displayed at a time, so if a user chooses deep-dish pizza, only its picture should be displayed. If a user then chooses thin-crust pizza, its picture should be displayed instead of deep-dish pizza.
	4. When the user makes a pizza selection, a confirming message should be displayed. In addition, the user should be prevented from identifying a pizza type after making the pizza selection.
	5. After the user makes a pizza selection, the only allowable action is to exit the window.
Notes and Restrictions:	The user should only be able to make a pizza selection after choosing a pizza type.
Comments:	The pictures shown in the window should be selected from pictures available on the web.

FIGURE 2-58

The requirements document contains all the information a developer needs to design the program. In an event-driven program such as the Pizza Selection program, however, one additional document often is needed to clarify for the developer what should occur in the program. This document is the Use Case Definition.

A **use case** is a sequence of actions a user will perform when using the program. The **Use Case Definition** specifies each of these sequences by describing what the user will do and how the program will respond. The Use Case Definition for the Pizza Selection program is shown in Figure 2-59.

USE CASE DEFINITION

1. User clicks Deep Dish or Thin Crust button.
2. Program displays a picture of the pizza chosen by the user and enables the pizza selection button.
3. User clicks pizza type buttons to view the types of pizza as desired. Program displays the picture of the chosen pizza type.
4. User clicks the Select Pizza button.
5. Program displays a pizza selection confirmation message, and disables both pizza type buttons and the Select Pizza button. The Exit Window button becomes active.
6. User terminates the program by clicking the Exit Window button.

FIGURE 2-59

© 2014 Cengage Learning

As you can see, the Use Case Definition specifies the actions that the user performs and the actions the program must take in response.

The Use Case Definition is an important part of the requirements documentation for two reasons: 1) It defines for the developer exactly what will occur as the user operates the program; 2) It allows users to review the requirements documentation and ensure that the specifications are correct before the developer begins designing the program.

When gathering and documenting the program requirements, it is critical that users be involved. After all, the program is being developed for their use. When the users concur that the requirements documentation is correct, the developer can move forward into the design phases of the program with confidence that it will fulfill users' needs.

For the programs you will design in this book, the program requirements, including the requirements document and the Use Case Definition, will be provided to you. However, be aware that in many cases in industry, an experienced developer must gather the requirements as well as implement them in a program.

Phase 2: Design the User Interface

Virtually all programs developed for a graphical user interface are driven by the user's actions within the interface. These actions dictate the processing that the program should execute. Therefore, by designing the user interface, the developer will obtain a foundation for designing the rest of the program. By designing the user interface early in the design process, the developer also can interact with users and ensure that the interface will fulfill their requirements.

Expert program developers recognize the importance of the graphical user interface. These developers spend 25 to 40 percent of program design on the user interface, which sometimes is called the **presentation layer** of the program because it is so critical to the program's success. Mobile devices use small screens, so an easy-to-follow user interface assists in clear navigation that relies on fingers instead of keyboard input.

In the past, developers would draw the user interface on paper and present the drawings to users for their approval. When using Visual Studio 2012, however, the developer should use the program's rapid application development tools to create the user interface. The interface is created with no functionality; that is, none of the buttons or other GUI elements will cause processing to occur. Often, these interface designs are called **mock-ups** because they are provided only for approval of the design. When the users or others approve the interface design, the developer can design the program elements required to implement the functions of the program.

An additional benefit of using Visual Studio to design the user interface is that you can use the completed design in the actual program; you do not have to re-create the design using other software.

My boss at my programming job asked me to design a prototype for the layout of the user interface. What is a prototype?

A prototype is a model of a software product or information system built for customer approval. It is similar to a mock-up of a user interface.

CONSIDER THIS

Principles of User Interface Design

Because the presentation layer of the program is so important, a number of principles and guidelines have been developed over the years for user interface design. While the intent of this book is not to create experts in user interface design, you should understand some of the principles so you can develop programs that are useful and usable. The following are some **design principles** you should incorporate into your user interface designs:

1. The most important principle to remember is that the user's ability to operate the program effectively depends on the design of the interface. If the GUI is easy to use and follow, the user will have a productive and enjoyable experience. On the other hand, if the user struggles to figure out how to enter data or which button to tap or click, the user interface design is defeating the purpose of the program.

2. If the user interface is not easy to use, the user will not be satisfied with the application regardless of how well it works.

3. The user interface includes the windows, graphics, and text shown on the screen, as well as the methods that interact with your program and cause operations to occur. Four primary means of interacting with a user interface are the keyboard, a pointing device such as a mouse, a touch interface, and voice input. The correct use of these tools significantly increases the probability of success for a traditional or touch-based user interface.

4. Using the interface should feel natural and normal. The developer must be aware of who the user is and how the user is accustomed to working. For example, the interface for a banking program in which a teller enters account information will be different from that of a graphic arts program that allows manipulation of graphics and photographs. Each must reflect the needs of the user.

5. Visual Studio contains a wide variety of objects, many of which can be used for similar purposes in the GUI. A good user interface provides the most appropriate object for each requirement. You will learn about all these objects and their correct use throughout this text.

6. Once an object is used for a particular purpose in the user interface, such as a button that causes a particular action, the object should be used for the same purpose throughout the program interface.

7. Objects must be arranged in the sequence in which they are used so the user can move from item to item on the screen in a logical, straightforward manner. Following this principle helps create an interface that is clean and easy to use. Again, the developer must understand the needs of the user. When this principle is not followed, a confusing interface can result.

8. The interface should be kept as simple as possible while containing all required functionality. Generally, the simpler the interface is, the more effective it will be. Consider using colors that are "easy on the eyes" to prevent eye fatigue.

9. When implemented, the user interface should be intuitive, which means the user should be able to use it with little or no instruction. In fact, the user should feel that no other interface could have been designed because the one they are using is the most "natural."

By following these principles, you will create user interfaces that assist the user. The success of your program can depend on the user interface you design.

Sample Program

As you learned earlier, the Pizza Selection program is the sample program for this chapter and Chapter 3 (see Figure 2-1 on pages 32 and 33). The requirements document for this program is shown in Figure 2-58 on page 77, and the Use Case Definition is shown in Figure 2-59 on page 78. With these documents in hand, the first phase of the program development cycle is complete.

Sample Program — Phase 2: User Interface Design

When beginning the design of the user interface, the primary sources of reference are the requirements document and the Use Case Definition for the program. Using these documents, the developer must analyze the program requirements and determine which elements are required in the user interface.

On a line-for-line basis, the analysis of the requirements document in Figure 2-58 on page 77 could proceed as follows:

1. The application will be presented in a window on the screen, so a Windows Forms Application using a Windows Form object is the appropriate means for creating the program.

2. The user will choose either a deep-dish or thin-crust pizza and then make a pizza selection. When the pizza is chosen, a picture of the pizza should be displayed. To choose each pizza, the program uses a Button object, a common tool that is familiar to users. When a user taps or clicks a button, the user has made a choice and the program responds appropriately. In this application, a good design decision is to use buttons so the user can decide between pizza types and then make a pizza selection. When the user taps or clicks the Deep Dish button, a picture of deep-dish pizza will be displayed. When the user taps or clicks the Thin Crust button, a picture of thin-crust pizza will be displayed. The user then taps or clicks the Select Pizza button to make the selection.

3. Two pictures must be displayed in the user interface — a deep-dish picture and a thin-crust picture. Although it is possible to display two different pictures in a single PictureBox object depending on the user's choice, you can develop a simpler and more easily understood user interface if a PictureBox object and a button work together. In other words, when the user taps or clicks the Deep Dish button, the deep-dish picture is displayed in the Deep Dish PictureBox object; when the user taps or clicks the Thin Crust button, the thin-crust picture is displayed in the Thin Crust PictureBox object. In this way, the user can associate a button with a picture box location and the user interface is intuitive and easy to use.

4. When the user makes a pizza selection by tapping or clicking the Select Pizza button, a message must be displayed to confirm the pizza selection. Therefore, a Label object must be included for the confirmation message.

5. After the user makes a pizza selection, the only action available to the user is to exit the window, so an Exit Window button is required.

6. In addition to the requirements in the program requirements document, standard procedure usually dictates that a heading should appear in the program window. Also, it is common practice to include simple instructions in the window so the user is not confused while using the interface. The heading and instructions can be included as Label objects.

7. As a result of this analysis, the user interface should include the following items: a Windows Form object that will contain all the other objects; two PictureBox objects to contain pictures of deep-dish and thin-crust pizzas; four Button objects (Deep Dish button, Thin Crust button, Select Pizza button, and Exit Window button); and three Label objects (Heading, Instructions, and Pizza Selection Confirmation).

After determining the elements required for the user interface, the developer can use Visual Studio 2012 to create a mock-up of the user interface. The exact placement of objects in the window is a creative process, and is guided by the principles of user interface design you have learned. Usually, no "right answer" exists because each developer will see a slightly different solution, but you must adhere to the principles of good user interface design. Figure 2-60 shows the mock-up created for the Pizza Selection program.

FIGURE 2-60

Guided Program Development

This section on guided program development takes you step by step through the process of creating the sample program in this chapter. To create the mock-up shown in Figure 2-60, complete the steps on the following pages.

Guided Program Development

1

- **Open Visual Studio 2012**
Open Visual Studio using the
Search charm (Windows 8) or
the Start button on the Windows
taskbar and the All Programs
submenu (Windows 7) *(ref: Figure
2-2)*. If necessary, maximize the
Visual Studio window. If necessary, close the Start page.

HINT

HEADS UP

While developing the program,
you should save it periodically
to keep from losing your work.

- **Create a New Visual Basic Windows Forms
Application** Create a new Visual Basic Windows
Forms Application project by tapping or clicking the
New Project button, selecting Windows in the left
pane, selecting Windows Forms Application in the
middle pane, naming the project `Pizza Selec-
tion`, and then tapping or clicking the OK button
in the New Project window *(ref: Figure 2-4)*.

HINT

- **Keep the Toolbox Visible** If necessary, tap or
click the Auto Hide button to keep the Toolbox
visible *(ref: Figure 2-10)*.

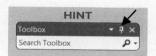

HINT

*The Visual Studio
application opens
and a new project
is displayed in the
window (Figure
2-61). The Toolbox
remains visible
regardless of the
location of the
pointer.*

RESULT OF STEP I

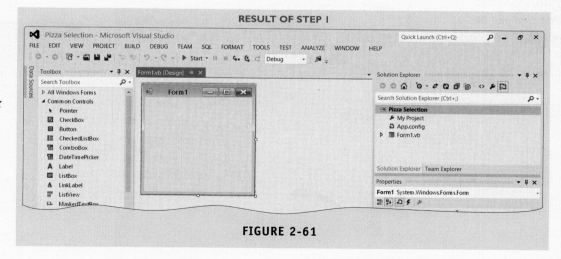

FIGURE 2-61

(continues)

Guided Program Development   *continued*

2

● **Name the Windows Form Object** In the Solution Explorer window, press and hold or right-click Form1.vb. On the shortcut menu, tap or click Rename. Name the form `frmPizzaSelection` *(ref: Figure 2-14)*.

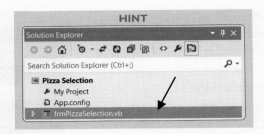

● **Change the Windows Form Object Text Property** With the Windows Form object selected, double-tap or double-click the text value for the Windows Form object in the Text property of the Properties window. Then change the title bar text for the Windows Form object to `Pizza Selection` *(ref: Figure 2-16)*.

The text in the title bar of the Windows Form object has been changed to Pizza Selection (Figure 2-62). In addition, the name of the object has been changed to frmPizzaSelection.

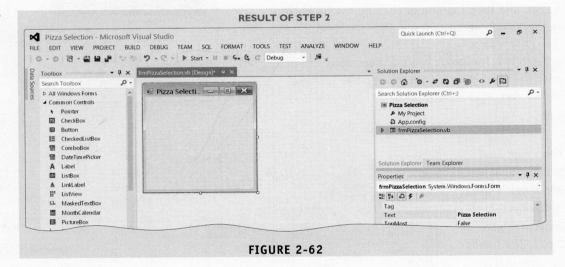

RESULT OF STEP 2

FIGURE 2-62

3

- **Resize the Windows Form Object** Resize the Windows Form object to the approximate size shown in Figure 2-60 (430 × 395) by changing the Size property in the Properties window to `430,395` *(ref: Figure 2-18)*.

4

- **Add a Label Object** Add a Label object by dragging the Label .NET component from the Toolbox to the Windows Form object. Place the label near the center and top of the Windows Form object *(ref: Figure 2-19)*.

- **Name the Label Object** Change the name of the Label object to `lblHeading` by using the (Name) property in the Properties window for the Label object *(ref: Figure 2-21)*.

- **Change the Label Object Text Property** Double-tap or double-click the text value for the Label object in the Text property of the Properties window, and then change the Text property of the lblHeading Label object to `Pizza Selection` *(ref: Figure 2-23)*.

- **Open the Font Dialog Box** Tap or click the Font property for the Label object in the Properties window, and then tap or click the ellipsis button (...) for the Font property *(ref: Figure 2-27)*.

- **Change the Font for the Label Object** In the Font list of the Font dialog box, change the font in the lblHeading Label object to Tahoma *(ref: Figure 2-29)*.

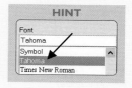

- **Change the Font Style for the Label Object** Using the Font style list in the Font dialog box, change the font style in the lblHeading Label object to Bold *(ref: Figure 2-29)*.

- **Change the Size for the Label Object** Using the Size list in the Font dialog box, change the font size in the lblHeading Label object to 16 points *(ref: Figure 2-29)*.

(continues)

Guided Program Development *continued*

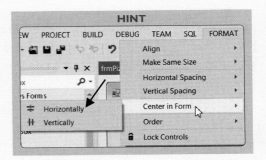

● **Center the Heading Horizontally** If necessary, select
the lblHeading Label object. Then, using the Center in Form
command on the FORMAT menu, tap or click the Horizontally command on the Center in Form submenu to center the
lblHeading Label object horizontally on the Windows Form
object *(ref: Figure 2-31)*.

*The lbl Heading Label object text has been changed and the label object is centered horizontally on the Windows
Form object (Figure 2-63). The vertical placement of the label (that is, the distance from the top of the window
frame) depends on the eye of the developer, the size of the Windows Form object, and the other objects in
the graphical user interface. Although your label might be a little higher or lower, your window should closely
resemble the one in Figure 2-63.*

RESULT OF STEPS 3 AND 4

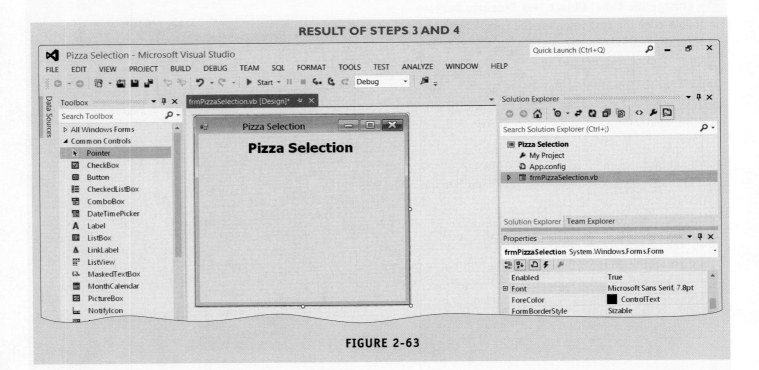

FIGURE 2-63

● **Add a PictureBox Object** Add a PictureBox object to the Windows Form object by dragging a PictureBox .NET component from the Toolbox to the Windows Form object. Place the Picture-Box object below and to the left of the heading label, as shown in Figure 2-64 *(ref: Figure 2-36)*.

● **Name the PictureBox Object** Using the (Name) property in the PictureBox Properties window, name the PictureBox object `picDeepDish`.

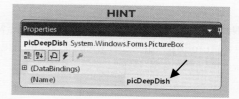

● **Resize the PictureBox Object** Resize the PictureBox object by changing its Size property to `139, 122` *(ref: Figure 2-38)*.

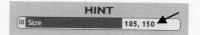

A properly sized PictureBox object is displayed in the Windows Form object (Figure 2-64). This PictureBox object will display a picture of a deep-dish pizza when the program is completed in Chapter 3.

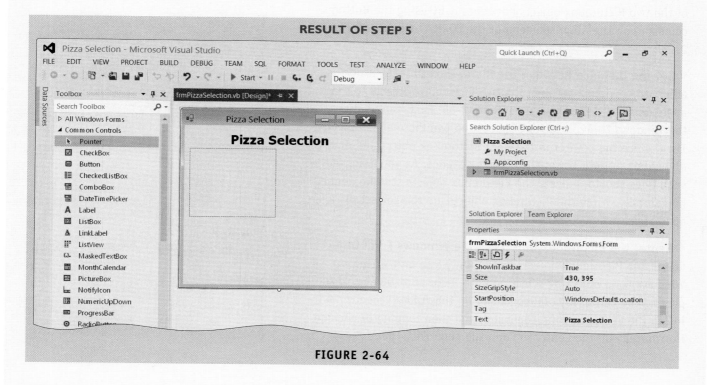

FIGURE 2-64

(continues)

- **Add a PictureBox Object** Add a second PictureBox object to the Windows Form object by dragging a PictureBox .NET component from the Toolbox to the Windows Form object. Place it to the right of the first PictureBox object in the Windows Form object *(ref: Figure 2-39)*.

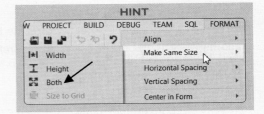

- **Name the PictureBox Object** Using the (Name) property in the PictureBox Properties window, name the PictureBox object `picThinCrust`.

- **Size the PictureBox Object** Make the second PictureBox object on the Windows Form object the same size as the first by using the Both command on the Make Same Size submenu of the FORMAT menu *(ref: Figure 2-41)*.

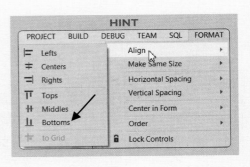

- **Align the PictureBox Objects Horizontally** Align the bottoms of the two PictureBox objects horizontally by using the Bottoms command on the Align submenu of the FORMAT menu *(ref: Figure 2-43)*.

- **Set the Distance Between the PictureBox Objects** If necessary, adjust the distance between the two PictureBox objects to the approximate distance shown in Figure 2-65. First, tap or click the Windows Form object to deselect the two PictureBox objects. Then, place the pointer in the right PictureBox object and drag the object left or right to set the correct distance. As you drag, red snap lines should indicate the PictureBox objects still are aligned horizontally. When the PictureBox objects are the correct distance apart, release the object.

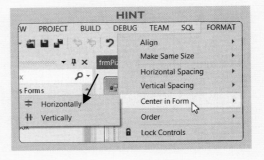

- **Center the PictureBox Objects in the Windows Form Object** Center the PictureBox objects horizontally as a unit within the Windows Form object by selecting both PictureBox objects, displaying the Center in Form command on the FORMAT menu, pointing to the Center in Form command, and then tapping or clicking Horizontally on the Center in Form submenu *(ref: Figure 2-45)*.

The PictureBox objects are sized and located properly within the Windows Form object (Figure 2-65).

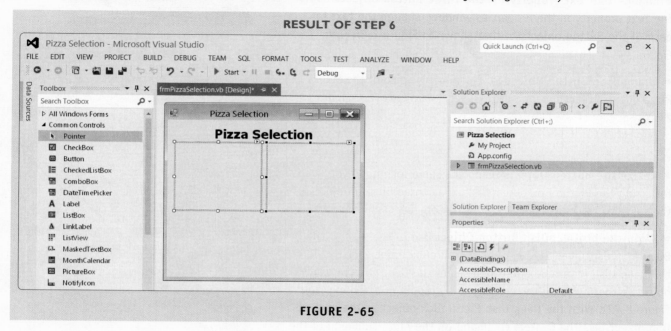

RESULT OF STEP 6

FIGURE 2-65

7

- **Add Three Button Objects to the Windows Form Object** Add three Button objects by dragging them onto the Windows Form object. Align them horizontally below the PictureBox objects at about the same locations shown in Figure 2-60 on page 82. Use blue snap lines to align horizontally the buttons on the Windows Form object as you drag them onto the form *(ref: Figure 2-47, Figure 2-52).*

- **Name the Three Button Objects** Using the (Name) property in the Properties window, name the left Button object btnDeep-Dish, the center Button object btnSelectPizza, and the right Button object btnThinCrust.

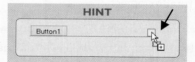

HINT

(continues)

● **Change the Text Property for the Three Button Objects** Using the Text property in the Properties window, change the text for each of the Button objects to that shown in Figure 2-66 *(ref: Figure 2-49)*.

● **Change the Button Object Size** Change the size of the Select Pizza button to accommodate the Select Pizza text *(ref: Figure 2-50)*.

● **Resize the Button Objects** Using the same technique you used for sizing the PictureBox objects, make all three Button objects the same size as the Select Pizza Button object.

● **Align the btnDeepDish Button Object** Center the Deep Dish Button object under the Deep Dish PictureBox object. First, select the Deep Dish PictureBox and then select the Deep Dish Button object, either by using the CTRL key or by tapping or clicking *(ref: Figure 2-40)*. With the Deep Dish PictureBox object as the controlling object, use the Centers command on the Align submenu of the FORMAT menu to align the PictureBox object and the Deep Dish Button object *(ref: Figure 2-43)*.

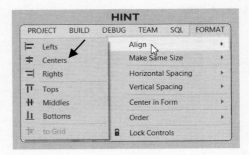

● **Align the btnThinCrust Button Object** Using the same technique, center the Thin Crust Button object below the Thin Crust PictureBox object.

● **Center the btnSelectPizza Button Object** Center the Select Pizza Button object horizontally within the Windows Form object by selecting the Select Pizza Button object and then using the Horizontally command on the Center in Form submenu of the FORMAT menu *(ref: Figure 2-31)*.

The Button objects are sized and placed properly within the Windows Form object (Figure 2-66). All three buttons are the same size. The Deep Dish and Thin Crust buttons are centered under their respective PictureBox objects, and the Select Pizza button is centered in the Windows Form object.

RESULT OF STEP 7

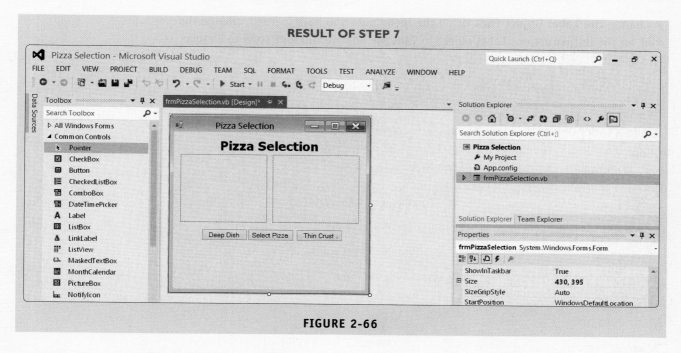

FIGURE 2-66

8

- **Add a Label Object** Add the instructions Label object to the Windows Form object by dragging a Label .NET object from the Toolbox to the Windows Form object. Place it below the Button objects at the approximate location shown in Figure 2-60 on page 82 *(ref: Figure 2-19)*.

- **Name a Label Object** Using the techniques you have learned, name the Label object lblInstructions.

HINT

(continues)

- **Change the Label Object Text Property** Using the techniques you have learned, change the text in the lblInstructions Label object to `Choose a pizza type and then click the Select Pizza button`.

- **Change the Label Object Font** Using the techniques you have learned, change the font for the lblInstructions Label object to Tahoma, change the font style to Regular, and change the size to 9 points.

- **Center the Label Object** Using the techniques you have learned, center the lblInstructions Label object horizontally within the Windows Form object.

- **Add a Label Object** Using the techniques you have learned, add the final message Label object to the Windows Form object. The text of the label should read `Enjoy your pizza selection`. Place the Label object in the location shown in Figure 2-67. Name it `lblConfirmation`. Change the font to Tahoma, the font style to Regular, and the size to 9 points. Center the Label object within the Windows Form object.

The two Label objects contain the correct text and are centered horizontally in the Windows Form object (Figure 2-67).

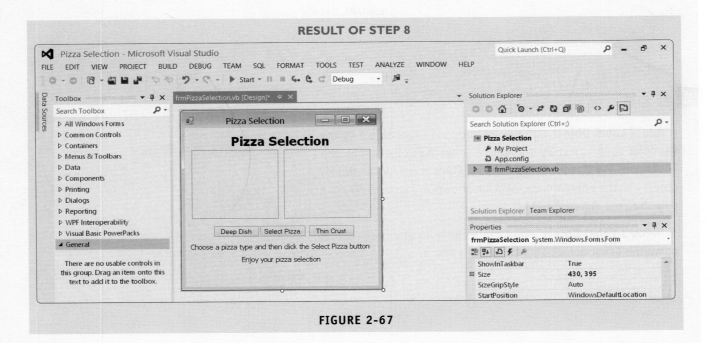

RESULT OF STEP 8

FIGURE 2-67

● **Add a Button Object** Add the Exit Window Button object by dragging a Button control onto the Windows Form object. Place it in the approximate location shown in Figure 2-68. Then, using the techniques you have learned, give the name `btnExit` to the Button object, change its text to `Exit Window`, make the Exit Window Button object the same size as the other Button objects in the window, and center the Exit Window Button object horizontally in the window.

The user interface mock-up is complete (Figure 2-68).

RESULT OF STEP 9

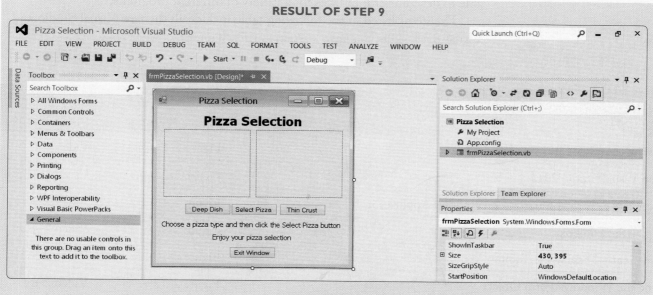

FIGURE 2-68

After completing the user interface mock-up, the designers will distribute the design to the users and others for approval. In many cases, the developers must implement changes the users request. Then they will resubmit the design for approval.

Summary

You have completed the steps to create the graphical user interface mock-up for the Pizza Selection program. As you can see, many of the required steps are somewhat repetitive; the same technique is used repeatedly to accomplish similar tasks. When you master these techniques and other principles of user interface design, you will be able to design user interfaces for a variety of different programs.

The items listed in the following table include all the new Visual Studio and Visual Basic skills you have learned in this chapter.

Visual Basic Skills		
Skill	**Figure Number**	**Video Number**
Run the completed program	Figure 2-1	Video 2-1
Open Visual Studio 2012	Figure 2-2	Video 2-2
Create a New Visual Basic 2012 Windows Application	Figure 2-4	Video 2-3
Display the Toolbox	Figure 2-9	Video 2-4
Permanently Display the Toolbox	Figure 2-10	Video 2-5
Name the Windows Form Object	Figure 2-12	Video 2-6
Set the Title Bar Text in a Windows Form Object	Figure 2-15	Video 2-7
Resize a Form	Figure 2-17	Video 2-8
Add a Label Object	Figure 2-19	Video 2-9
Name a Label Object	Figure 2-21	Video 2-10
Change the Text in a Label Object	Figure 2-23	Video 2-11
Enter Multiple Lines for a Label Object	Figure 2-26	Video 2-12
Change the Label Font, Font Style, and Font Size	Figure 2-27	Video 2-13
Center a Label Object in the Windows Form Object	Figure 2-31	Video 2-14
Delete GUI Objects	Figure 2-33	Video 2-15
Use the Undo Button on the Standard Toolbar	Figure 2-35	Video 2-16
Add a PictureBox Object	Figure 2-36	Video 2-17

Visual Basic Skills (continued)

Skill	Figure Number	Video Number
Resize a PictureBox Object	Figure 2-38	Video 2-18
Add a Second PictureBox Object	Figure 2-39	Video 2-19
Make Objects the Same Size	Figure 2-40	Video 2-20
Align PictureBox Objects	Figure 2-43	Video 2-21
Center Multiple Objects Horizontally	Figure 2-45	Video 2-22
Add a Button Object	Figure 2-47	Video 2-23
Name a Button Object	Figure 2-49	Video 2-24
Set Text for a Button Object	Figure 2-49	Video 2-24
Change the Button Object's Size	Figure 2-50	Video 2-25
Add a Button with Alignment (Use Snap Lines)	Figure 2-52	Video 2-26
Align Objects Vertically	Figure 2-54	Video 2-27
Save and Close a Visual Basic Project	Figure 2-56, 2-57	
Open a Visual Basic project	Page 75	

FIGURE 2-69

Knowledge Check

1–5. Label the following parts of the window:

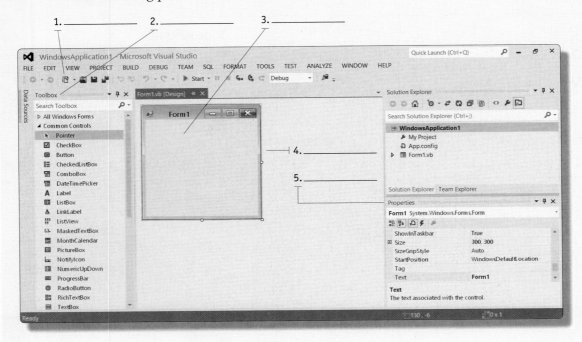

FIGURE 2-70

(continues)

Knowledge Check *continued*

6. What does RAD stand for?

7. What is the purpose of the Auto Hide button on the Toolbox title bar?

8. What is the difference between red and blue snap lines?

9. What is the prefix of the Form object?

10. A Button, a Label, and a PictureBox are all _____.

11. How do you select four Button objects on the Windows Form object at the same time for alignment purposes?

12. What is the purpose of a mock-up?

13. What are the first two phases of the program development life cycle?

14. Write the Label object name "Video" with the correct prefix.

15. Write the Button object name "Submit" with the correct prefix.

16. Write the PictureBox object name "Tablet" with the correct prefix.

17. Which property of the Label object do you use to change the name of the label from Label1?

18. Which button can you tap or click to sort the property names in the Properties window from A to Z?

19. How do you save the project you have created for the user interface mock-up?

20. Name the four objects you learned in Chapter 2 and briefly describe the purpose of each object.

Debugging Exercises

1. List the steps required to change the poorly aligned buttons on the left to the properly aligned buttons on the right.

BEFORE

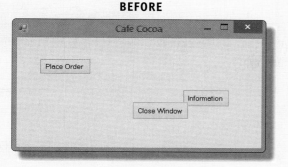

FIGURE 2-71a

AFTER

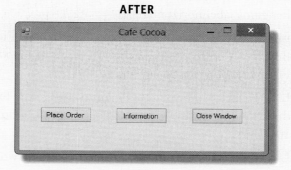

FIGURE 2-71b

(continues)

Debugging Exercises *continued*

2. Change the order of the numbered Use Case Definition steps to correspond to the following problem definition: A college provides every incoming freshman with a gift card for a choice of two types of coffee from the cafeteria. Students should select the type of coffee they want. A program opens a window that displays each coffee type one picture at a time when the student taps or clicks the corresponding button. After making a decision, the student should tap or click the Place Order button. After selecting a type of coffee, the student should exit the application.

USE CASE DEFINITION

1. User taps or clicks the Place Order button.
2. User taps or clicks the Coffee button or Frappuccino button.
3. User taps or clicks the button not selected in Step 2.
4. User terminates the program by tapping or clicking the Close button.
5. Program displays an order confirmation message and disables both order buttons. The Close button becomes active.
6. Program displays a picture of the coffee order selected by the user and enables the Place Order button.
7. Program displays a picture of the coffee order selected by the user.

Program Analysis

1. After you have placed objects on the Windows Form object (Figure 2-72), list the steps you would follow to change the font for the Save the Penguins label to Tahoma font, bold, 18 points.

2. List the steps you would perform to center the Save the Penguins label horizontally.

3. List the steps you would perform to center the Picture-Box object horizontally on the Windows Form object in Figure 2-72.

4. List the steps you would perform to change the font for the Donate Now button in Figure 2-72 to Tahoma, 10 points.

FIGURE 2-72

5. List the steps you would perform to align the two Button objects horizontally by the tops of the buttons.

6. List the steps you would perform to make the Donate Now button the same size as the Close Window button.

7. In the real world, why is it important to have a user interface mock-up approved before proceeding with the rest of the project?

Case Programming Assignments

Complete one or more of the following case programming assignments. Submit the program and materials you create to your instructor. The level of difficulty is indicated for each assignment.

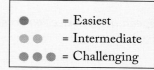

● = Easiest
●● = Intermediate
●●● = Challenging

1 ●
EUROPEAN HOSTEL SELECTION

Create a Windows form mock-up for the requirements document in Figure 2-73 and the Use Case Definition shown in Figure 2-74 on the next page. The Windows Form object and the other objects in the user interface are shown in Figure 2-75 on the next page.

REQUIREMENTS DOCUMENT

Date Submitted: January 17, 2015

Application Title: European Hostel Selection Application

Purpose: The Windows application will allow a user to select a location in London or Dublin.

Program Procedures: From a window on the screen, the user should identify a hostel location (London or Dublin) and then select a hostel.

Algorithms, Processing, and Conditions:
1. The user must be able to identify the London or Dublin hostel as many times as necessary until making a selection.
2. When the user identifies the hostel location, a picture of that hostel should appear in the window.
3. Only one picture should be displayed at a time. If a user identifies the London hostel, only the London hostel picture should be displayed; if a user identifies the Dublin hostel, only the Dublin hostel picture should be displayed.
4. When the user selects a hostel, a message should be displayed to confirm the selection of a hostel location. In addition, the user should be prevented from identifying another location after selecting a hostel.
5. After the user selects a hostel, the only allowable action is to exit the window.

Notes and Restrictions: A user can select a hostel only after identifying a hostel location.

Comments: The pictures shown in the window can be found on CengageBrain.com. The names of the pictures are Dublin and London. Images will be added in Chapter 3.

FIGURE 2-73

(continues)

Case Programming Assignments

European Hostel Selection (continued)

USE CASE DEFINITION

1. User taps or clicks London Hostel button or Dublin Hostel button.
2. Program displays a picture of the hostel identified by the user and enables the location selection button.
3. User taps or clicks hostel buttons to view hostel locations as desired. Program displays the picture of the identified hostel.
4. User taps or clicks the Select Location button.
5. Program displays a hostel selection confirmation message and disables both hostel buttons and the Select Location button. The Exit Window button becomes active.
6. User terminates the program by tapping or clicking the Exit Window button.

FIGURE 2-74

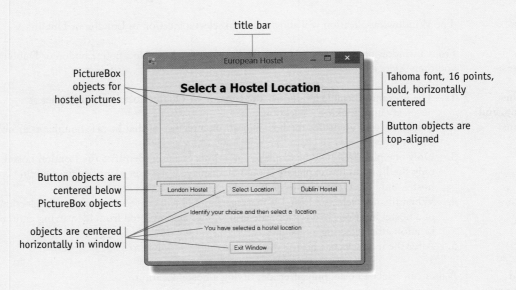

FIGURE 2-75

2
STUDENT PICNIC

Create a Windows form mock-up for the requirements document shown in Figure 2-76 and the Use Case Definition shown in Figure 2-77 on the next page. The Windows Form object and the other objects in the user interface are shown in Figure 2-78 on the next page.

REQUIREMENTS DOCUMENT

Date Submitted:	January 14, 2015
Application Title:	Student Picnic Application
Purpose:	This Windows application displays a welcome screen for the Annual Spring Fling Picnic. The user can choose an option to view the date and location.
Program Procedures:	From a window on the screen, the user makes a request to see the picnic's date and location.
Algorithms, Processing, and Conditions:	1. The user first views a Student Picnic window that displays the picnic name (Annual Spring Fling Picnic), a picnic picture, and a phrase that states all students are welcome. 2. When the user chooses to view the picnic date and location, the following information is displayed: April 17, 2015 Located in the Quad in front of the Barnard Building 3. After the user views the picnic information, the only allowable action is to exit the window.
Notes and Restrictions:	n/a
Comments:	The picture shown in the window can be found on CengageBrain.com. The name of the picture is Picnic. Images will be added in Chapter 3.

FIGURE 2-76

(continues)

Case Programming Assignments

Student Picnic (continued)

USE CASE DEFINITION

1. The window opens, displaying the name of the picnic, a picnic picture, and a message stating all students are welcome. All buttons are enabled.
2. User taps or clicks the View Picnic Information button.
3. Program displays the picnic time and location between the buttons. The View Picnic Information button is disabled.
4. User taps or clicks the Exit Window button to terminate the application.

FIGURE 2-77

© 2014 Cengage Learning

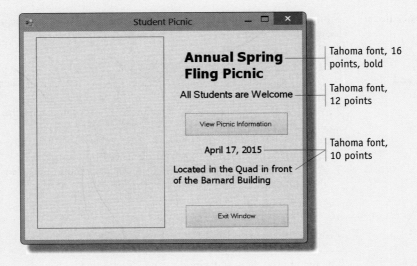

FIGURE 2-78

© 2014 Cengage Learning

3 •

VISUAL BASIC 2012 TERMS

Create a Windows form mock-up for the requirements document shown in Figure 2-79 and the Use Case Definition shown in Figure 2-80 on the next page. The Windows Form object and the other objects in the user interface are shown in Figure 2-81 on the next page.

REQUIREMENTS DOCUMENT

Date Submitted:	August 16, 2015
Application Title:	Visual Basic 2012 Terms Application
Purpose:	This Windows application displays the definitions of common Visual Basic terms. When the user chooses to view a definition, the term's definition is displayed.
Program Procedures:	From a window on the screen, the user makes a request to see one of three VB definitions.
Algorithms, Processing, and Conditions:	1. The user first views a screen that displays three VB terms. 2. A logo is displayed at the top of the window throughout the running of the application. 3. The user can select any of the three terms displayed on the buttons to view the definition. 4. When the user taps or clicks a term button to display the definition, any previous definitions will disappear. 5. An exit button is available at all times, allowing the user to end the application.
Notes and Restrictions:	Only one definition should be displayed at a time, so if a user selects a second term, only the second definition should be displayed.
Comments:	n/a

FIGURE 2-79

(continues)

Case Programming Assignments

Visual Basic 2012 Terms (continued)

USE CASE DEFINITION

1. The window opens and displays a logo (Professional 2012), a title (Visual Basic 2012 Terms), three buttons labeled with VB terms, and an Exit Window button. All buttons are enabled.
2. User taps or clicks each of the term buttons to review the definitions.
3. Program displays the definitions to the right of the buttons.
4. Only one definition is displayed at a time.
5. User taps or clicks the Exit Window button to terminate the application.

FIGURE 2-80

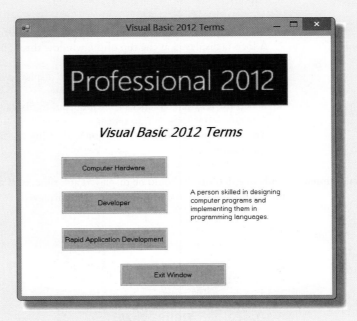

FIGURE 2-81

4 ●●
ONLINE STORE SPECIALS

Create a Use Case Definition document and design a Windows form mock-up based on the requirements document in Figure 2-82.

REQUIREMENTS DOCUMENT

Date Submitted:	January 6, 2016
Application Title:	Online Store Specials Application
Purpose:	This Windows application displays the daily, weekly, and holiday specials in the online store. The user can select the desired product and then add the product to a shopping cart.
Program Procedures:	From a window on the screen, the user should select the daily special, weekly special, or holiday special. After the user selects a special, the program should display a picture of the special product, the regular price of the product, and the sale price of the product. The user should be able to select any special. Then, the user can add the product to the shopping cart.
Algorithms, Processing, and Conditions:	1. The user must select a special in order to display the special's product picture, regular price, and sale price.
	2. The user cannot add a product to the shopping cart until a special is selected.
	3. When a special is selected, only that special's picture and prices should be displayed in the window. No other special should be displayed.
	4. After the user selects a special and adds it to the shopping cart, the only allowable user action is to exit the window.
	5. A user should be able to exit the window at any time.
Notes and Restrictions:	n/a
Comments:	1. The specials are:

Daily Special: SmartPhone: Regular Price: $99.95; Sale Price: $84.50
Weekly Special: Tablet, Regular Price: $239.95, Sale Price: $199.95
Holiday Special: Digital Camera: Regular Price: $259.95; Sale Price: $203.19

2. The pictures shown in the window can be found on CengageBrain.com. The names of the pictures are SmartPhone, Tablet, and DigitalCamera.

FIGURE 2-82

5 ●●
GUITAR STORE

Create a Use Case Definition document and design a Windows form mock-up based on the requirements document in Figure 2-83.

REQUIREMENTS DOCUMENT

Date Submitted: March 21, 2015

Application Title: Guitar Store Application

Purpose: A local guitar store has three guitars on special this week. A customer can choose one of three guitar types. The program must display each of the guitars upon request. The customer can then select a guitar for purchase.

Program Procedures: From a window on the screen, the user selects one of three guitars. A picture of the selected guitar is displayed in the window. The user then can choose a guitar for purchase.

Algorithms, Processing, and Conditions:
1. The user selects a guitar. Then, a picture of the guitar is displayed in the window.
2. The user can select any of the three guitars. Only the picture of the selected guitar should be displayed.
3. The user can select guitars as many times as necessary and display the pictures of the guitars.
4. The user finds a guitar, chooses it for purchase, and taps or clicks the Purchase button.
5. After the user chooses a guitar, a message stating "Enjoy your guitar!" should be displayed.
6. After the user chooses a guitar, the only allowable action is to exit the window.

Notes and Restrictions: The user should not be able to choose a guitar until viewing at least one guitar image.

Comments:
1. The available guitars are classical acoustic, steel-string acoustic, and electric.
2. The pictures shown in the window can be found on CengageBrain.com. The names of the pictures are Classical, Electric, and Steel.

FIGURE 2-83

6 ●● SONG VOTING

Create a Use Case Definition document and design a Windows form mock-up based on the requirements document in Figure 2-84.

REQUIREMENTS DOCUMENT

Date Submitted: February 22, 2015

Application Title: Song Voting Application

Purpose: In your mall, a music store named Millennium Music wants an application that shows the #1 song in each of three music genres and allows users to vote for their overall favorite. The user should be able to select one of three music genres and then vote for one.

Program Procedures: From a window on the screen, the user selects one of three music genres. The name of the #1 song in the selected genre is displayed with a picture of the performing artist or band. Then, the user can vote for that song or genre as his or her overall favorite.

Algorithms, Processing, and Conditions:
1. The user selects a music genre. The title of the #1 song in that genre and a picture of the artist or band are displayed in the window.
2. The user can select any of the three music genres. Only the name of the song and the picture for the selected genre should be displayed.
3. The user can select music genres as many times as necessary to see the #1 song for each genre and the associated artist or band.
4. After selecting a genre, the user should be able to vote for that genre and song as the favorite. The user can vote only after selecting a genre.
5. After the user votes, a message confirming the vote should be displayed.

Notes and Restrictions: The user should only be able to vote after selecting a musical genre.

Comments:
1. You (the developer) should select the three music genres and the #1 song for each of the genres.
2. The pictures of the artist or band will depend on your selection of music genres and the #1 song in those genres. You should download pictures of artists or bands from the web. You can search anywhere on the web for the pictures. You will find that *www.google.com/images* is a good source.

FIGURE 2-84

Case Programming Assignments

7 ●●● AIRLINE SNACK SELECTION

Create a requirements document and a Use Case Definition document and then design a Windows form mock-up based on the following case project:

An international airline requests a computer application that will run on the personal television monitors on the back of each seat in the plane. The application should request which free snack you would like during the flight, display the choices as buttons, and then display an image of the snack you select. Another button allows you to make your final snack selection and display a confirmation message.

Snack
Cheese & Crackers
Chocolate Chip Cookies
Mini Pretzels
Salted Peanuts

FIGURE 2-85

Case Programming Assignments

8 ●●● TRAVEL SPECIALS

Create a requirements document and a Use Case Definition document and then design a Windows form mock-up based on the following case project:

Your local travel agent requests a computer application that advertises the travel specials of the week from your city. This week's flight specials are:

Destination	Price
New York City	$399 round trip
Las Vegas	$419 round trip
Miami	$520 round trip
St. Thomas	$619 round trip
Hawaii	$828 round trip

Write an application that allows the user to select any of the five vacation destinations. When the user selects a vacation destination, the corresponding flight price and a picture of the destination should be displayed. Clear each prior price and picture when the user selects a different vacation destination. In addition to a picture of the destination, include a web page address that features the selected location. After selecting a destination, the user should be able to book the flight and then exit the window.

FIGURE 2-86

Case Programming Assignments

9 ●●● LACROSSE TICKETS

Create a requirements document and a Use Case Definition document and then design a Windows form mock-up based on the following case project:

Your favorite university lacrosse team has asked you to develop a Windows application that allows the user to see the four types of game tickets offered, one at a time. Then, the user should be able to reserve a single game ticket for the selected seat type. The four types of stadium seating and their base prices are as follows:

Name of Ticket	Minimum Price
Upper Endline Seating	$15.00
Lower Endline Seating	$25.00
Sideline Seating	$30.00
Club Seats	$50.00

For each type of seating, your program should display the base price and a picture depicting an example of the seating type. Clear each price and picture when the user selects a different seating type. After selecting a ticket, the user should be able to purchase the ticket and then exit the window.

FIGURE 2-87

CHAPTER 3

Program Design and Coding

OBJECTIVES

You will have mastered the material in this chapter when you can:

- Change the color properties of an object

- Add images to a PictureBox object

- Locate and save an image from the World Wide Web

- Import an image into the Program Resources folder

- Size an image

- Set the Visible property in the Properties window

- Set the Enabled property in the Properties window

- Run a Visual Basic 2012 program

- Enter Visual Basic 2012 code

- Understand Visual Basic 2012 code statement formats

- Use IntelliSense to enter Visual Basic 2012 code statements

- Use code to set the Visible property of an object

- Use code to set the Enabled property of an object

- Enter comments in Visual Basic 2012 code

- Correct errors in Visual Basic 2012 code

- Write code to use the Close() procedure

- Print code

- Prepare an event planning document

Introduction

In Chapter 2 you completed the design of the graphical user interface (GUI) mock-up. While users and others can approve the mock-up as being functional, the developer normally must make a variety of changes to the GUI to prepare it for the actual production version of the program. Among these changes are:

- Adding color to the interface to make it more visually appealing
- Acquiring and including images that are required for the program
- Setting interface object properties in accordance with the needs of the program

Once these tasks have been completed, Phase 2 of the program development life cycle (PDLC) is complete.

The next two phases of the PDLC are:

- Phase 3: Design the program processing objects
- Phase 4: Code the program

This chapter will provide the skills and knowledge necessary to complete Phase 2 of the PDLC and then complete Phases 3 and 4.

Sample Program

You will recall that the sample program for Chapter 2 and this chapter is the Pizza Selection program. Windows for the program are shown in Figure 3-1.

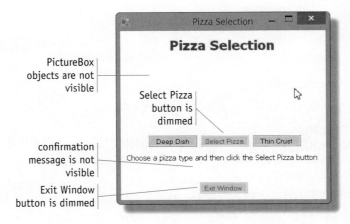

FIGURE 3-1a

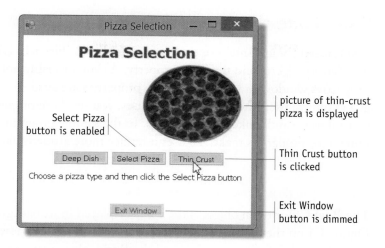

FIGURE 3-1b

© Brand X Pictures/Getty Images

FIGURE 3-1c

© Brand X Pictures/Getty Images

In the opening window (Figure 3-1a), no images appear in the PictureBox objects, and the Select Pizza button and Exit Window button are dimmed, which means they are disabled (visible, but not available for selection) when the program begins. In Figure 3-1b, the user tapped or clicked the Thin Crust button, so the picture is displayed. In addition, the Select Pizza button is enabled. The Exit Window button still is dimmed. In Figure 3-1c, the user has selected a type of pizza, so the pizza selection confirmation message is displayed. The Deep Dish, Select Pizza, and Thin Crust buttons are dimmed and the Exit Window button is enabled. When the program runs, each of these changes occurs through the use of code you enter into the program, as you will discover later in this chapter.

Fine-Tune the User Interface

You learned about some properties of Visual Basic objects in Chapter 2, including the Name property and the Text property. As you probably noted while viewing the Properties window in Chapter 2, more properties are available for each of the objects in a graphical user interface. In many cases, you set these properties to fine-tune the user interface and make it more usable. In the sample program, the BackColor and ForeColor properties make the user interface more attractive and effective.

BackColor and ForeColor Properties

The **BackColor** of an object is the color displayed in its background. For example, in Figure 3-1 on the previous page the BackColor of the Windows Form object is white instead of the default gray color, and the BackColor of the Button objects is a wheat shade. You can select the BackColor of an object by using the **BackColor property** in the Properties window. The **ForeColor** of an object is the color displayed in the text of the object. The heading Label object that displays the Pizza Selection text uses a text color called Firebrick. To change the BackColor of a Windows Form object from its default color of Control (gray) to White, you can complete the following steps:

STEP 1 Tap or click the Windows Form object to select it. (Do not tap or click any of the objects on the Windows Form object.)

The Windows Form object is selected, as indicated by the thick border and the sizing handles (Figure 3-2).

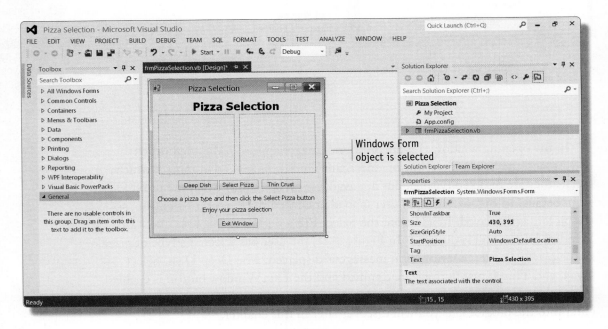

FIGURE 3-2

STEP 2 If necessary, scroll in the Properties window until the BackColor property is displayed, and then tap or click the right column of the BackColor property.

The BackColor property is selected, and the BackColor arrow is displayed (Figure 3-3).

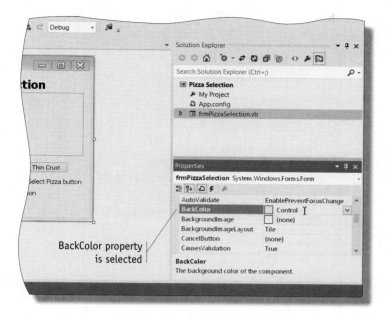

FIGURE 3-3

STEP 3 Tap or click the BackColor arrow. Then, tap or click the Web tab to display the Web tabbed page.

The color window opens within the Properties window (Figure 3-4). The Web tabbed page contains more than 100 named colors you can display as the BackColor for the selected object, which in this case is the Windows Form object.

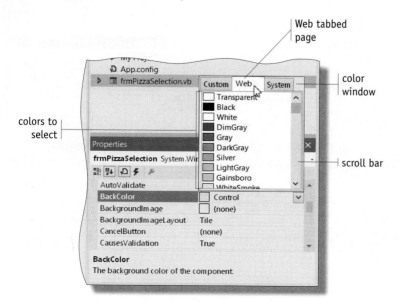

FIGURE 3-4

HEADS UP

Carefully consider your choice
for the BackColor of a window.
Generally, use light colors so
objects in the window are easily
visible. In some instances, you
might choose a darker color for
the BackColor, but then you
should use lighter colors for the
objects within the window. If
you choose a darker BackColor
and the object contains text,
such as a Button or Label
object, then the text color
should be light. You specify
text colors with the **ForeColor
property**. The choice of a
BackColor can be critical to the
usability of the window.

STEP 4   If necessary, scroll until the color White is displayed in the list of colors.

The name and a sample of the White color are displayed (Figure 3–5).

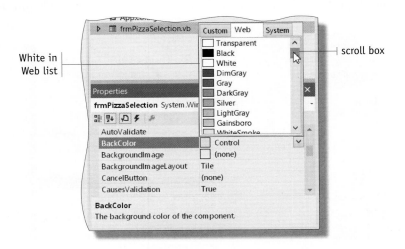

FIGURE 3-5

STEP 5   Tap or click White on the color list.

The background color in the Windows Form object is changed to White (Figure 3–6).

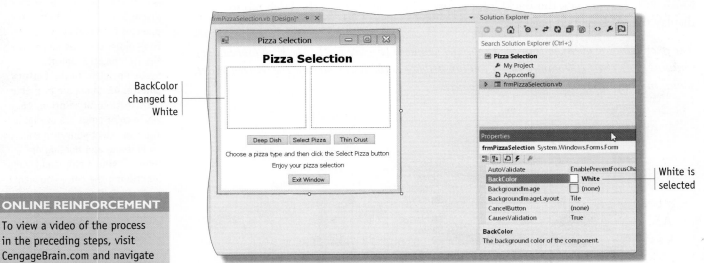

FIGURE 3-6

ONLINE REINFORCEMENT

To view a video of the process
in the preceding steps, visit
CengageBrain.com and navigate
to the resources for this title.
Tap or click the link for Chapter 3
and then navigate to Video 3-2.

You can use the same technique to change the BackColor or ForeColor on any object that contains the BackColor or ForeColor properties, including Button and Label objects.

Add Images to a PictureBox Object

PictureBox objects are used to display a graphic image. The sample program can display a picture of a deep-dish pizza and a thin-crust pizza. You must specify the image that will be displayed in a particular PictureBox object. Before specifying the image, however, you must locate the image and then place it in the Resources folder that is linked to the application. The general steps for displaying an image in a PictureBox object are:

1. Locate the image to be displayed in the PictureBox object. You might locate this image on the Web, in which case you must store the image in a folder on your computer, or the image might already be stored on your computer or a local network.
2. Import the image into the **Resources folder**. This step makes the image available for display within the PictureBox object. Multiple images can be placed in the Resources folder.
3. Specify the image to be displayed within the PictureBox object.

Each of these steps will be explained on the following pages.

Locate and Save an Image from the World Wide Web

Images are available from a multitude of sources, from your own digital camera to millions of publicly available images on the Web. If you work for a company, it might have photos and graphic images that can be used in company applications.

In this book, you can use the Student Companion Site to retrieve an image. For example, to retrieve the DeepDish image from this site, you could complete the following steps:

STEP 1   Open your Web browser. (This example uses Internet Explorer; steps for other browsers might vary slightly.) Enter www.cengagebrain.com in the Address box, and then press the ENTER key. Enter 9781285197975 (the book's ISBN) in the Search text box, and then click the Search button. Select the Free Materials tab, and then click the Access Now button to display your student resources.

The browser window opens and the Student Companion Site for this book is displayed (Figure 3–7).

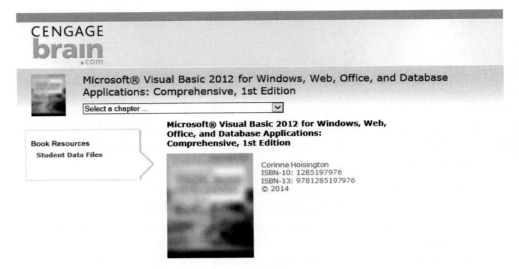

FIGURE 3-7

© 2014 Cengage Learning

STEP 2   In the left pane, click Student Data Files, and then click the Download Now link for Chapters 1-6.

The Information bar is displayed at the bottom of the browser window (Figure 3–8).

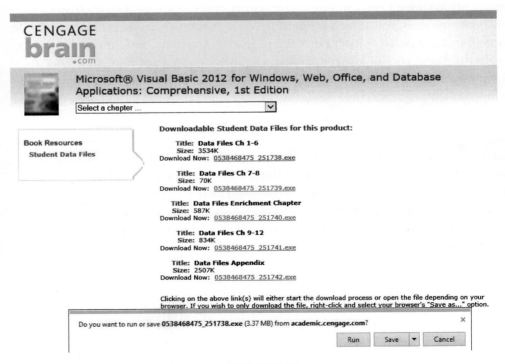

FIGURE 3-8

© 2014 Cengage Learning

STEP 3   Click Save as, and then navigate to the location on your computer where
you store downloaded files.

*In the Save As dialog box (Figure 3-9), you must identify the drive and folder in which you
want to store the image files. The location depends on your computer and drives. In all sample
programs in this book, images are stored on a USB drive that is designated as drive E.*

Save As
dialog box

FIGURE 3-9

STEP 4   Click the Save button to save the zipped file. Navigate to the location
of the downloaded file, and then double-click the file. Click the Browse button,
navigate to the folder where you want to store files for this book, and then click the
OK button. Click the Extract all button on the Extract tab to extract the files to the
selected folder. Click the Extract button. Open the extracted folder for Chapter 3 to
display its contents.

*The image files for Chapter 3 are displayed in a folder window (Figure 3-10). Remember
where you save the images because later you must locate and import them into the Resources
folder for use in the program. Image file names should not contain spaces.*

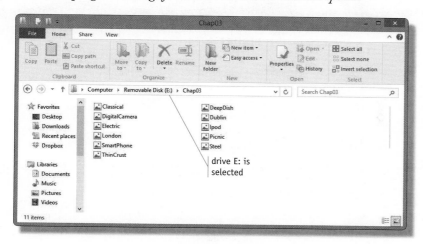

drive E: is
selected

FIGURE 3-10

ONLINE REINFORCEMENT

To view a video of the process
in the preceding steps, visit
CengageBrain.com and navigate
to the resources for this title.
Tap or click the link for Chapter 3
and then navigate to Video 3-3.

Import the Image into the Program Resources Folder

After you have saved an image on a storage device that is available to your computer, you should import the image into the program's Resources folder so the image is available for use. To import the DeepDish image into the Resources folder, you can complete the following steps:

STEP 1   If necessary, open Visual Studio 2012 and the Pizza Selection Visual Basic program. Select the picDeepDish PictureBox object by tapping or clicking it. Scroll in the PictureBox Properties window until the Image property is visible. Tap or click the Image property name in the left list of the Properties window.

*With the PictureBox object selected, the Properties window displays all the properties of the object (Figure 3-11). The **Image property** specifies the image that should be displayed in the selected PictureBox object. The Image property is selected in the Properties window. The Image property's ellipsis button is displayed in the right column of the Image property.*

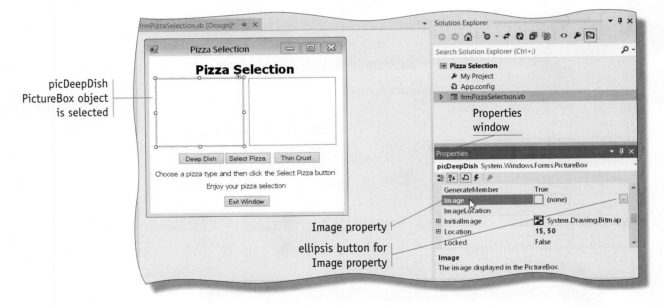

FIGURE 3-11

STEP 2   Tap or click the ellipsis button in the right column of the Image property.

*The **Select Resource dialog box** opens (Figure 3-12) and displays the resources that have been imported for the program. In Figure 3-12, no resources have been imported.*

Select Resource
dialog box

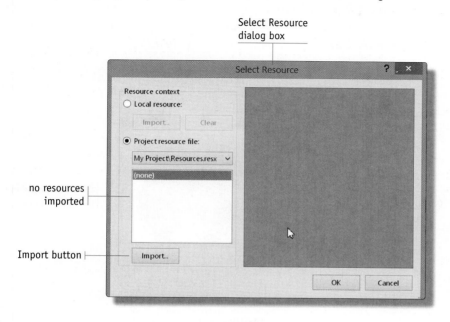

no resources
imported

Import button

FIGURE 3-12

STEP 3   Tap or click the Import button in the Select Resource dialog box. Use the features of the Open dialog box to locate the file you want to import into the program. In this case, you want to import the DeepDish.jpg file stored on drive E, which is a USB drive.

The Open dialog box opens when you tap or click the Import button (Figure 3-13). The DeepDish.jpg file is stored on drive E.

Open dialog
box

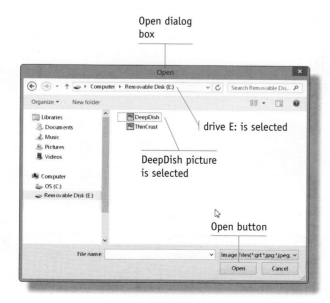

drive E: is selected

DeepDish picture
is selected

Open button

FIGURE 3-13

STEP 4 Select DeepDish.jpg. Tap or click the Open button in the Open dialog box.

The Select Resource dialog box is displayed again, but now the DeepDish image is identified in the Project resource file list (Figure 3-14). The image appears in the preview window. This means the image is now part of the resources for the program. You no longer need to locate the image on the USB drive to include the image in a PictureBox object.

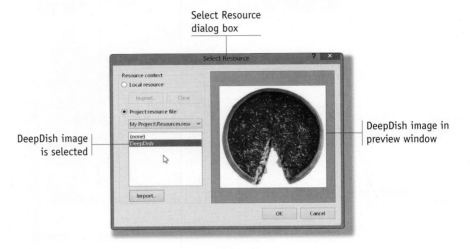

FIGURE 3-14

© Brand X Pictures/Getty Images

STEP 5 With the DeepDish file name selected in the Project resource file list, tap or click the OK button in the Select Resource dialog box.

The DeepDish image is displayed in the picDeepDish PictureBox object (Figure 3-15). In addition, the Resources folder is added to the Solution Explorer window, indicating the Resources folder now is part of the program.

ONLINE REINFORCEMENT

To view a video of the process in the previous steps, visit CengageBrain.com and navigate to the resources for this title. Tap or click the link for Chapter 3 and then navigate to Video 3-4.

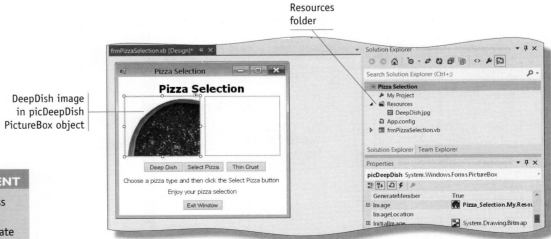

FIGURE 3-15

© Brand X Pictures/Getty Images

Size an Image

In most cases, when you import an image into a program, the image will not fit in the PictureBox object perfectly because the two items have different sizes or dimensions. The developer must adjust the size of the image to fit in the PictureBox object or adjust the size of the PictureBox object to accommodate the image.

By comparing the images in Figures 3-14 and 3-15, you can see that the image is larger than the PictureBox object. Because the PictureBox object must remain its current size, the image must be adjusted using the **SizeMode property**. To adjust an image's size to fit in a PictureBox object, you can complete the following steps:

STEP 1   Select the PictureBox object that contains the DeepDish image, and then scroll in the picDeepDish Properties window until you see the SizeMode property. Tap or click the SizeMode property name in the left column, and then tap or click the SizeMode arrow in the right column of the SizeMode property.

The SizeMode property list is displayed (Figure 3-16). The list contains five choices you can use to change either the size of the image or the size of the PictureBox object. Normal is selected because it is the default value.

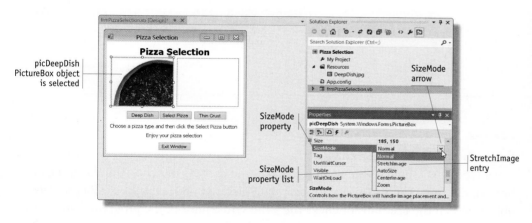

FIGURE 3-16

In the example, StretchImage is selected from the SizeMode list in the Properties window for PictureBox objects (see Figure 3-16). The other choices and their actions are:

- **Normal** — No changes are made to the image size or the size of the PictureBox object. Visual Studio places the image in the PictureBox object and aligns the upper-left corner of the image with the upper-left corner of the PictureBox object.

- **AutoSize** — Visual Studio increases or decreases the size of the PictureBox object to accommodate the size of the image. The entire image is visible and fits precisely in the PictureBox object.

- **CenterImage** — No changes are made to the image size or the size of the PictureBox object. Visual Studio places the image in the PictureBox object and aligns the center of the image with the center of the PictureBox object.

- **Zoom** — The image size is either reduced or enlarged to fit in the PictureBox object. The fit can be left and right or up and down, depending on the dimensions of the image and the PictureBox object. If the image and PictureBox object are not exactly proportional to one another, the image will not fill out the entire PictureBox object.

STEP 2   Tap or click StretchImage in the SizeMode list.

*The SizeMode list is closed and the image is resized to fit within the picDeepDish PictureBox object (Figure 3-17). When you use the **StretchImage option**, some image distortion might occur to make it fit within the PictureBox object. Therefore, you should select an image that has the same approximate dimensions (or at least the same aspect ratio) as the selected PictureBox object.*

image is
resized

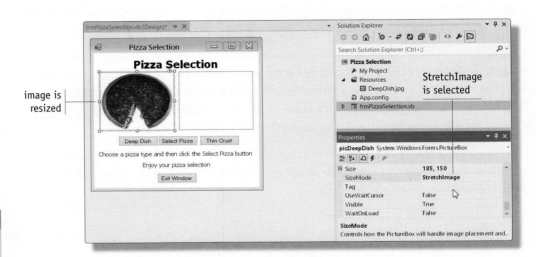

© Brand X Pictures/Getty Images

FIGURE 3-17

Set the Visible Property

As you have learned, when the Pizza Selection program begins, neither of the two pizza types is pictured in the window. When the user taps or clicks the Deep Dish button, the program displays the appropriate picture in the Deep Dish PictureBox object. When the user taps or clicks the Thin Crust button, the program displays the appropriate picture in the other PictureBox object.

The **Visible property** controls whether an object is displayed on the Windows Form object. By default, the Visible property is set to True so that any object you place on the Windows Form object is displayed when the program runs. If you do not want an object to be displayed, you must set the Visible property to False. To set the Visible property to False for the picDeepDish PictureBox object, you can complete the following steps:

STEP 1 If necessary, select the picDeepDish PictureBox object. Scroll in the Properties window until the Visible property is displayed. Tap or click the Visible property name in the left column, and then tap or click the Visible arrow in the right column of the Visible property.

When you tap or click the Visible arrow, the list displays the words True and False (Figure 3-18). To make the object visible when the program starts, select True. If you do not want the object to be visible when the program starts, select False.

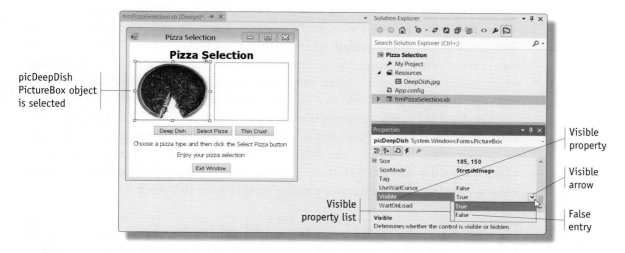

picDeepDish PictureBox object is selected

Visible property list

Visible property

Visible arrow

False entry

FIGURE 3-18

© Brand X Pictures/Getty Images

STEP 2 Tap or click False on the Visible property list.

The Visible property is set to False (Figure 3-19). When the program begins, the DeepDish picture will not be displayed on the Windows Form object. Note that the image and object are displayed on the frmPizzaSelection.vb [Design] tabbed page regardless of the Visible property setting.

image is visible in Design mode

Visible property is set to False

FIGURE 3-19

© Brand X Pictures/Getty Images

ONLINE REINFORCEMENT

To view a video of the process in the previous steps, visit CengageBrain.com and navigate to the resources for this title. Tap or click the link for Chapter 3 and then navigate to Video 3-6.

Once you have set an object's Visible property to False, the only way to display the object on the Windows Form object while the program is running is to set the Visible property to True. You can do this by writing code, as you will see later in this chapter.

Set the Enabled Property

In an event-driven program, objects such as Button objects can be used to make events occur. For example, when you tap or click the Deep Dish button, a picture of a deep-dish pizza is displayed in the PictureBox object. In addition, the Select Pizza Button object becomes **enabled**, which means it can be tapped or clicked to make an event occur. When the program begins, however, the Select Pizza button is **disabled**, which means nothing will happen when you tap or click the button. A disabled button is displayed as dimmed (see Figure 3-1a on page 112).

The **Enabled property** controls when a Button object is enabled. The property also controls when a Button object is not enabled, which means tapping or clicking the button causes no action. The default selection for the Enabled property is True, which means the associated Button object is enabled. To set the Enabled property to False for the Select Pizza button, you can complete the following steps:

STEP 1   Select the btnSelectPizza object. Scroll in the Properties window until the Enabled property is displayed. Tap or click the Enabled property name in the left column, and then tap or click the Enabled arrow in the right column of the Enabled property.

When you tap or click the Enabled arrow, the list contains the words True and False (Figure 3-20). To make the object enabled when the program starts, select True. If you do not want the object to be enabled when the program starts, select False.

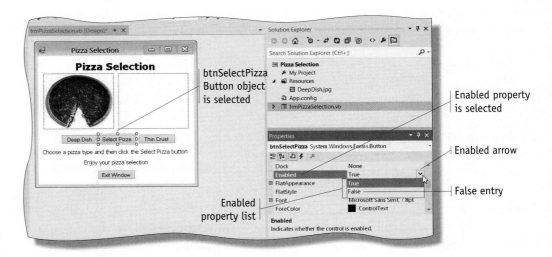

FIGURE 3-20

STEP 2   Tap or click False on the Enabled property list.

The Enabled property is set to False (Figure 3-21). When the program begins, the btnSelectPizza Button object will not be enabled on the Windows Form object.

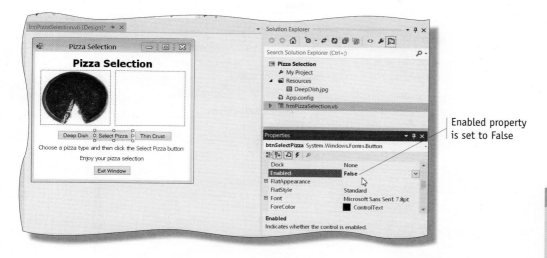

Enabled property is set to False

FIGURE 3-21

© Brand X Pictures/Getty Images

Once you have set the Enabled property to False, the only way to enable a Button object on the Windows Form object while the program is running is to set the Enabled property to True. You can do this by writing code, as you will see later in this chapter.

Run a Program

When you set some object properties, the effect of their changes might not be evident until you run the program. For example, you have set the Visible property to False for the picDeepDish PictureBox object, and you have set the Enabled property to False for the btnSelectPizza Button object. Neither change is evident, however, when you view the Pizza Selection Windows Form object on the frmPizzaSelection.vb [Design] tabbed page in Visual Studio. These settings are applied only when you actually run the program.

To ensure the settings are correct for the user interface, you must run the program. **Running the program** means it is compiled, or translated, from the instructions you have written or generated in Visual Basic into a form of instructions that the computer can execute. These instructions are saved and then executed as a program.

To run the program you have created, you can tap or click the Start Debugging button on the Standard toolbar, as shown in the steps on the next page:

STEP 1   Point to the Start Debugging button on the Standard toolbar.

The pointer appears over the Start Debugging button (Figure 3-22).

Start Debugging
button

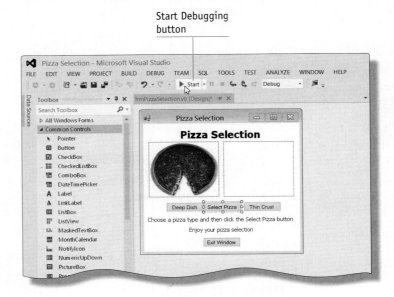

FIGURE 3-22

© Brand X Pictures/Getty Images

STEP 2   Tap or click the Start Debugging button on the Standard toolbar.

The program is compiled and saved, and then it runs on the computer. When the program runs, the Pizza Selection window is displayed on the screen (Figure 3-23). Notice that the DeepDish image is not displayed in the window because the Visible property was set to False for the picDeepDish PictureBox object (see Figure 3-19 on page 125). Notice also that the Select Pizza button is dimmed, which indicates its Enabled property is set to False.

Pizza Selection
window

Close button

DeepDish image
is not displayed

Select Pizza
button is dimmed

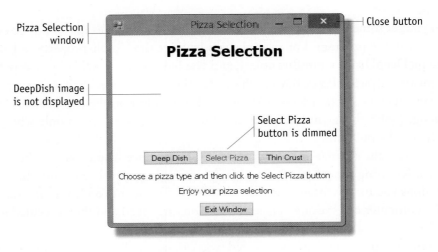

FIGURE 3-23

Once you start running the program, it continues to run until you close it. To close a program, tap or click the Close button on the right side of the window title bar (see Figure 3-23).

After you set all the properties for the objects in the user interface, the design of the user interface is complete. You now are ready to move to the next phase of the program development life cycle — designing the program processing objects.

Visual Basic Program Coding

Before beginning to design the program processing objects, the developer must understand certain program coding principles and techniques. **Program code** is the set of instructions written by the developer that direct the program to carry out its required processing. The following sections explain the Visual Basic 2012 code required for the Pizza Selection program.

Enter Visual Basic Code for Event Handling

As you have learned, most processing in an event-driven program occurs when the user triggers an event. For example, when a user taps or clicks a button on the graphical user interface, the activity can trigger an event and the program performs the required processing. The developer writes program code to carry out the processing. This code is placed in a section of the program called an **event handler** — it "handles" the event that the user action triggers by executing code that performs the required processing.

To write the code for an event handler, the developer first must identify the GUI object that will be used to trigger the event. For example, when the Deep Dish button is tapped or clicked in the sample program, the DeepDish picture should appear in the picDeepDish PictureBox object. To write the code that will display the DeepDish picture, the developer must inform Visual Studio that the Deep Dish button is the object for which the code is being written, and that an event handler must be created for the tap or click event. You can create the event handler using the steps on the next page:

STEP 1   If necessary, open Visual Studio 2012 and the Pizza Selection program and make the frmPizzaSelection.vb [Design] tabbed window visible. Point to the Deep Dish Button object in the Windows Form object.

The pointer appears over the Deep Dish Button object (Figure 3-24). The four-headed arrow pointer indicates you can drag the Button object to another location in the window.

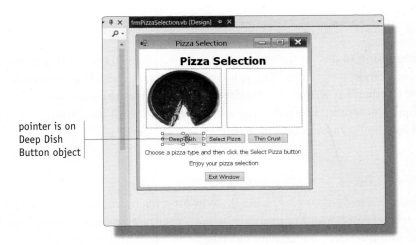

pointer is on
Deep Dish
Button object

FIGURE 3-24

© Brand X Pictures/Getty Images

STEP 2   Double-click the Deep Dish Button object.

The code window is displayed on the frmPizzaSelection.vb* tabbed page (Figure 3-25). The code in the window is generated by Visual Studio. This code identifies an event handler, which is the code that executes when an event is triggered. When the Deep Dish button is tapped or clicked, the program will execute the code in this event handler. The list box in the upper-left corner of the tabbed page identifies the object for which the event handler will execute — in this case, the btnDeepDish object. The list box in the upper-right corner of the tabbed page identifies the event that must occur to execute the code in the event handler. The event identified in Figure 3-25 is "Click." When the user taps or clicks the Deep Dish button, the program executes the code between the Private Sub statement and the End Sub statement. In Figure 3-25, no code has been entered other than the event handler identification code generated by Visual Studio. The insertion point is located where the developer should begin entering the code that executes when the user taps or clicks the btnDeepDish Button object.

Toolbox
Close button

frmPizzaSelection.vb*
tabbed page

object for which event
handler will execute

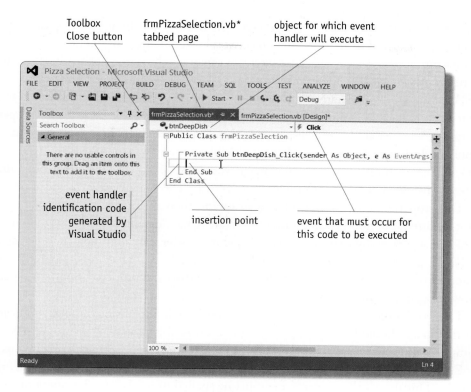

event handler
identification code
generated by
Visual Studio

insertion point

event that must occur for
this code to be executed

FIGURE 3-25

Visual Basic 2012 Coding Statements

A Visual Basic 2012 coding statement contains instructions that the computer eventually executes. Visual Basic has a set of rules, or **syntax**, that specifies how each statement must be written.

When the user taps or clicks the Deep Dish button while the Pizza Selection program is running, the DeepDish image should be displayed in the picDeepDish PictureBox object. Figure 3-26 shows a Visual Basic coding statement that sets the Visible property to True for the picDeepDish PictureBox object so the image is displayed in the picture box after the statement executes.

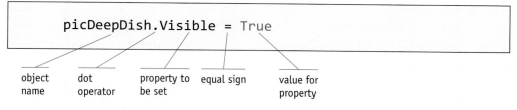

```
picDeepDish.Visible = True
```

object
name

dot
operator

property to
be set

equal sign

value for
property

FIGURE 3-26

The first part of the statement, picDeepDish, identifies the object that contains the property to set. The name of the object is followed by the dot operator (period) with no intervening spaces. The dot operator separates the name of the object from the next entry in the statement and is required.

Following the dot operator is the name of the property to set. In Figure 3-26 on the previous page, the name of the property is Visible. You will recall that the Visible property determines whether an image is displayed in the PictureBox object when the program is running. In Figure 3-19 on page 125, the Visible property was set to False for the picDeepDish PictureBox object so the image would not be displayed when the program started. This statement sets the Visible property to True so the image will be displayed.

The property name is followed by a space and then an equal sign. The space is not required, but good coding practice dictates that elements within a statement should be separated by a space so the statement is easier to read. One or more spaces can be used, but most developers use only one space. The equal sign is required because it indicates that the value to be used for setting the property follows. A space follows the equal sign for readability.

The word True follows the space. The value True in the Visible property indicates that the image should be displayed in the PictureBox object. When the program is running and the Visible property is set to True, the image appears in the picture box.

Each entry within the program statement must be correct or the program will not compile. This means the object name must be spelled properly, the dot operator must be placed in the correct location, the name of the property must be spelled properly, the equal sign must be present, and a valid entry for the property must follow the equal sign. For the Visible property, the only valid entries are True and False.

General Format of a Visual Basic Statement

The general format of the Visual Basic statement shown in Figure 3-26 appears in Figure 3-27.

General Format: Property Value Assignment Statement

```
objectname.property = propertyvalue
```

EXAMPLE	RESULT
picDeepDish.Visible = True	Picture is visible
btnSelectPizza.Enabled = False	Button is dimmed

FIGURE 3-27

© 2014 Cengage Learning

In the general format, the object name always is the first item in the Visual Basic statement. The object name is the name you specified in the (Name) property of the Properties window. In Figure 3-26 on page 131, the object name is picDeepDish because that name was given to the Deep Dish PictureBox object.

The dot operator (period) is required. It follows the object name with no space between them. Immediately following the dot operator is the name of the property that will be set by the statement. The property name must be spelled correctly and must be a valid property for the object named in the statement. Valid properties that can be specified in the statement are identified in the Properties window associated with the object.

The equal sign must follow the property name in the statement. Visual Basic statements do not require spaces, nor is there a limit to how many spaces you can place between elements in the statement. The equal sign identifies the statement as an **assignment statement**, which means the value on the right side of the equal sign is assigned to the element on the left side of the equal sign. When setting properties, the element on the left side of the equal sign is the property.

The property value specified in the assignment statement must be a valid value for the property identified on the left side of the equal sign. You can see the valid values for a given property by looking in the Properties window for the object whose property you are setting.

After you have entered the property value, the Visual Basic statement is complete. Because correct programming protocol dictates that only one statement should appear on a line, the next step is to press the ENTER key to move the insertion point to the next line in the code window.

The general statement format shown in Figure 3-27 is used for all statements in which the code sets the value of an object property.

HEADS UP

Unlike some programming languages, the capitalization of object names, properties, property values, and other values is not important in Visual Basic. Therefore, the object name picDeepDish is equivalent to the object name picdeepdish. Capitalization is used within the object name to make the name easier to read.

IntelliSense

In Figure 3-25 on page 131, the insertion point is located in the code window. To enter the statement in Figure 3-26 into the program using the code window, you can type the entire statement. Visual Studio, however, provides help so that you will be less prone to make a typing error when entering the statement. This help feature is called IntelliSense.

IntelliSense displays all allowable entries you can make in a Visual Basic statement each time a dot (period), equal sign, or other special character is required for the statement. When you type the prefix pic as shown in Figure 3-28, an IntelliSense window opens with all the objects that begin with the prefix. Instead of possibly misspelling the object name, you can select it from the IntelliSense list. The complete Visual Basic statement is shown in Figure 3-28.

IN THE REAL WORLD

Microsoft created IntelliSense in response to the demands of rapid application development so statements can be entered accurately and easily. Most developers use IntelliSense; it is the standard within the software industry.

```
picDeepDish.Visible = True
```


FIGURE 3-28

When you type the first few letters of the object name, IntelliSense displays a list of all the objects and other entries that can be specified in the statement.

Enter a Visual Basic Statement

To enter the Visual Basic statement in Figure 3-28 on the previous page using IntelliSense, you can complete the following steps:

STEP 1   Tap or click the Close button to close the Toolbox. With the code window open and the insertion point positioned as shown in Figure 3-25 on page 131, type pic.

The characters "pic" are displayed in the code window (Figure 3-29). IntelliSense displays a list of all the entries that can follow the prefix in the statement. Sometimes the selected entry is correct for the statement you are entering, but often it is not. Therefore, you must identify the correct statement in the list before entering it.

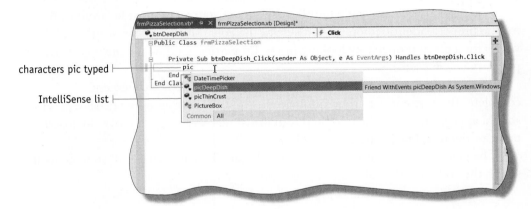

FIGURE 3-29

STEP 2   To identify the correct entry, type its next letter until the entry is selected. In this case, type d.

As you type, IntelliSense highlights an entry in the list that begins with the letters you enter (Figure 3-30). When you enter picd, IntelliSense highlights the only term in the list that begins with picd, which is picDeepDish. This is the object name you want to enter into the Visual Basic statement.

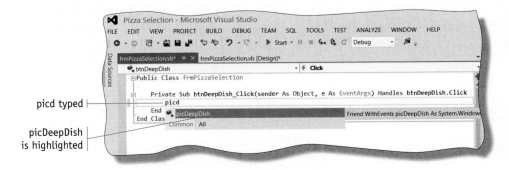

FIGURE 3-30

STEP 3 When IntelliSense highlights the correct object name, press the key corresponding to the entry that follows the object name. In this case, press the PERIOD key.

IntelliSense automatically enters the entire object name into the Visual Basic statement and the period you typed following the object name (Figure 3-31). In addition, IntelliSense realizes that the dot you entered means more information is required in the statement, so it displays a list of the allowable entries following the dot.

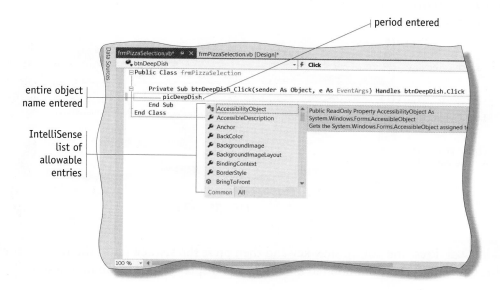

FIGURE 3-31

STEP 4 As with the object name in Step 2, the next step is to enter one or more characters until IntelliSense highlights the desired property in the list. Type the letter v for the Visible property.

IntelliSense highlights the properties in the list that begin with the letter v (Visible) or that contain the letter v, such as ProductVersion (Figure 3-32). Because the Visible property is highlighted, no further action is required to select it.

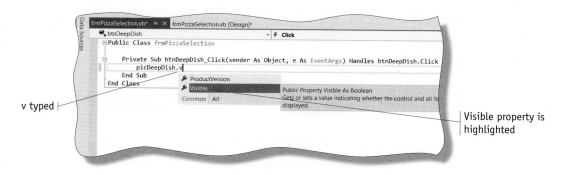

FIGURE 3-32

STEP 5 Press the key for the character that follows the property name. In this case, press the SPACEBAR.

IntelliSense enters the highlighted property name (Visible) followed by the space you typed (Figure 3-33). The space indicates to Visual Basic that the object name and property name entry is complete. Notice also that the IntelliSense tip specifies what the statement will do. In Figure 3-33, the statement gets or sets a value indicating whether the control is displayed. This means the Visible property indicates whether the picDeepDish PictureBox object is displayed.

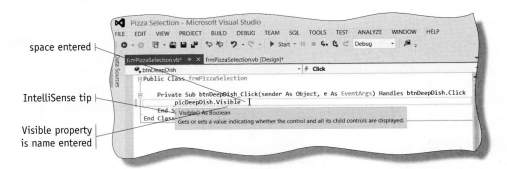

FIGURE 3-33

STEP 6 Press the EQUAL SIGN key and then press the SPACEBAR. In the IntelliSense list, tap or click the Common tab if necessary to display the most common results.

The equal sign and a space are displayed and then IntelliSense displays a list of the entries you can make (Figure 3-34). For the Visible property, the only possible entries following the equal sign are False and True. An entry of False indicates the PictureBox object should not be visible; True indicates the opposite.

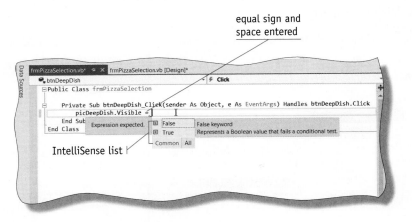

FIGURE 3-34

STEP 7 Type t for True.

IntelliSense highlights the True entry (Figure 3-35).

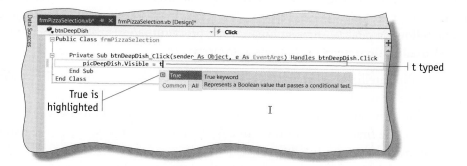

t typed

True is highlighted

FIGURE 3-35

STEP 8 Press the key for the character that follows the True entry. In this case, press the ENTER key.

Because you pressed the ENTER key, IntelliSense enters True into the statement and then Visual Studio moves the indented insertion point to the next line (Figure 3-36). The Visual Basic statement now is entered completely.

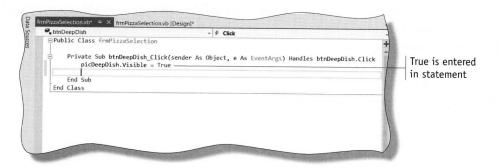

True is entered in statement

FIGURE 3-36

IN THE REAL WORLD

You can highlight entries in the lists that IntelliSense displays in a variety of ways. In the previous example, you typed the first character of the entry. Other ways to highlight an entry include pressing the UP ARROW key and DOWN ARROW key, and using the mouse to scroll in the list until the entry is visible and then tapping or clicking the entry.

To enter the item selected in the list, the example illustrated how to press the key for the character that follows the entry from the list. Other methods include pressing the Tab key and double-tapping or double-clicking the entry in the list. In both these cases, you still must enter the next character in the statement, but in the example, that character is entered when you press the corresponding key to select the IntelliSense entry from the list.

ONLINE REINFORCEMENT

To view a video of the process in the previous steps, visit CengageBrain.com and navigate to the resources for this title. Tap or click the link for Chapter 3 and then navigate to Video 3-10.

Can I turn on line numbers to receive assistance while creating my program?

Line numbers help identify each line of code in the code window. They do not appear by default, however, so you must instruct Visual Studio to display the line numbers. If line numbers do not appear in the code window on your computer, you can display them by completing the following steps:

1. Tap or click TOOLS on the menu bar.
2. Tap or click Options on the TOOLS menu.
3. If necessary, tap or click the triangle next to Text Editor in the Options dialog box.
4. If necessary, tap or click the triangle next to Basic in the list below Text Editor.
5. Tap or click General in the list below Basic.
6. Place a check mark in the Line numbers check box.
7. Tap or click the OK button in the Options dialog box.

CONSIDER THIS

Visual Studio and IntelliSense automatically create the indentations in the program statements in Figure 3-36 on the previous page because indentations make the statements easier to read and understand. As programs become more complex, proper indentation of program statements can be an important factor in developing error-free programs.

The following general steps summarize the procedure for using IntelliSense to enter a Visual Basic statement that sets a property:

1. In the IntelliSense list, type the first letter(s) of the name of the object whose property will be set.
2. When the object name is selected in the list, press the PERIOD key.
3. Type the first letter(s) of the name of the property to be set until the name is highlighted in the IntelliSense list.
4. Press the SPACEBAR to complete the first portion of the statement.
5. Press the EQUAL SIGN key.
6. Press the SPACEBAR.
7. Press the first letter(s) of the entry you want to select in the list until the entry is highlighted. If IntelliSense does not display a list, type the value for the property.
8. Press the ENTER key.

Using IntelliSense to enter a Visual Basic statement provides two significant advantages. First, it is faster to enter a statement using IntelliSense than it is to type the statement. Second, using IntelliSense drastically reduces the number of errors when entering statements. By using only the entries in the IntelliSense lists, the developer seldom will make an invalid entry. In addition, because the entry is chosen from a list, it cannot possibly be misspelled or mistyped.

Entering a programming statement is a fundamental skill for a Visual Basic programmer. You should thoroughly understand how to enter a programming statement using IntelliSense.

Set the Visible Property to False

In Figure 3-36 on the previous page, the programming statement set the Visible property to True for the picDeepDish PictureBox object, which will display the image in the picture box when the statement is executed. The statement will execute when the user taps or clicks the Deep Dish button because the statement is part of the btnDeepDish_Click event handler.

When the user taps or clicks the Deep Dish button, the Visible property also must be set to False for the picThinCrust PictureBox so the ThinCrust picture is not displayed alongside the DeepDish picture. To set the Visible property to False for the picThinCrust PictureBox object, you could complete the following steps:

STEP 1 With the insertion point on the next line of the code window for the Deep Dish button click event, type `pic`.

The letters you typed are displayed in the code window and the IntelliSense list shows the valid entries you can choose (Figure 3-37). The entry picDeepDish is highlighted because it is the last entry that was selected from this list.

pic typed

IntelliSense list

picDeepDish is highlighted

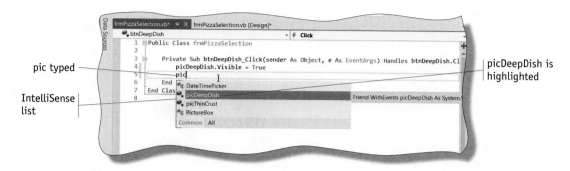

FIGURE 3-37

STEP 2 Type `t` to highlight the picThinCrust entry in the IntelliSense list.

IntelliSense highlights picThinCrust in the list because it is the only entry that starts with the characters "pict" (Figure 3-38).

pict typed

picThinCrust is highlighted

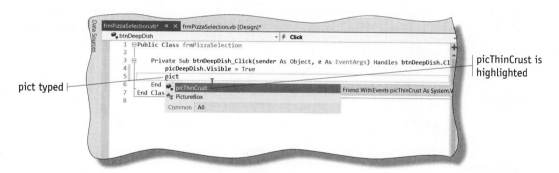

FIGURE 3-38

STEP 3 Press the key for the character that follows the object name. In this case, press the PERIOD key.

The picThinCrust entry is placed in the statement followed by the dot operator (period) you typed (Figure 3-39 on the next page). In addition, IntelliSense displays the list of allowable entries.

The Visible entry is highlighted in the list because it was selected the last time the list was used. If Visible was not highlighted, you could type the letter v to highlight Visible in the list.

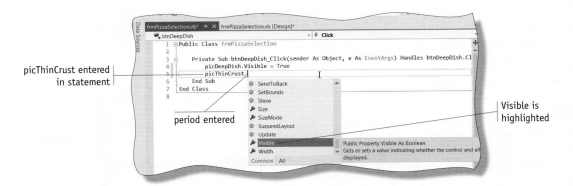

picThinCrust entered in statement

period entered

Visible is highlighted

FIGURE 3-39

STEP 4 Press the SPACEBAR, press the EQUAL SIGN key, and then press the SPACEBAR.

IntelliSense places the Visible entry in the statement (Figure 3-40). Next, the space you typed appears, followed by the equal sign and the second space you typed. When you typed the equal sign, IntelliSense displayed the list of allowable entries following the equal sign.

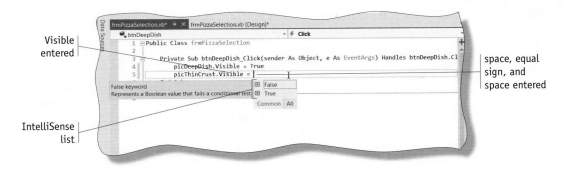

Visible entered

IntelliSense list

space, equal sign, and space entered

FIGURE 3-40

STEP 5 Type f and then press the ENTER key.

When you type the letter f, IntelliSense highlights False in the list. When you press the ENTER key, IntelliSense inserts False (Figure 3-41).

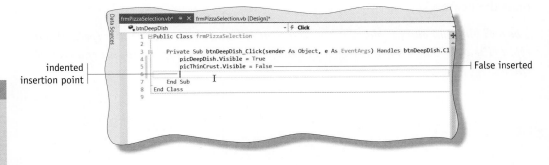

indented insertion point

False inserted

FIGURE 3-41

ONLINE REINFORCEMENT

To view a video of the process in the previous steps, visit CengageBrain.com and navigate to the resources for this title. Tap or click the link for Chapter 3 and then navigate to Video 3-11.

Again, using IntelliSense to enter a Visual Basic programming statement results in a correct statement entered in minimal time with a reduced chance of errors.

Set the Enabled Property

You learned earlier that if the Enabled property is True for a Button object, the tap or click event code will be executed for the button when the user taps or clicks it. If the Enabled property is False for a Button object, the event code for the button will not be executed. In Figure 3-21 on page 127, the Enabled property was set to False for the Select Pizza button so that the button is not active when the program begins. When the user taps or clicks a picture button such as the Deep Dish button, however, the Enabled property must be set to True so the Select Pizza button is active. To set the Enabled property to True, the developer must enter a coding statement for the btnSelectPizza Button object. To enter the coding statement into the btnDeepDish_ Click event handler, you can complete the following steps:

STEP 1   Type `btn` to display the IntelliSense list (Figure 3-42).

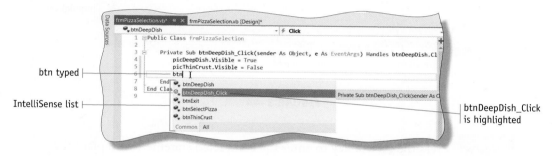

FIGURE 3-42

STEP 2   Type `s` (or more characters if necessary) until IntelliSense highlights the btnSelectPizza entry in the list.

IntelliSense highlights btnSelectPizza, the only entry that starts with the characters "btns" (Figure 3-43). Sometimes, the correct entry will be highlighted before you type all the distinguishing characters. If so, you need not type more characters.

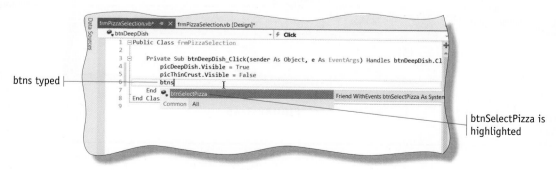

FIGURE 3-43

STEP 3   Type a period, type e, press the SPACEBAR, press the EQUAL SIGN key, press the SPACEBAR again, and then type t to select True in the IntelliSense list.

IntelliSense places the highlighted entry (btnSelectPizza) in the statement and displays a list of the next allowable entries. When you typed e, Enabled was selected in the list. Pressing the SPACEBAR caused IntelliSense to place Enabled and then the space in the statement. When you typed the equal sign and second space, IntelliSense inserted both and displayed the list of entries that can follow the equal sign (Figure 3–44). When you typed the letter t, IntelliSense highlighted True in the list.

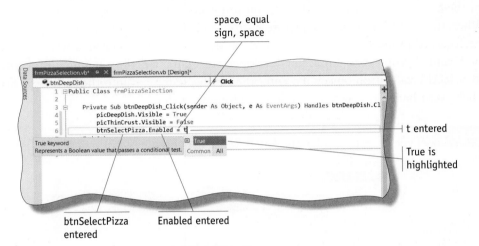

space, equal sign, space

t entered

True is highlighted

btnSelectPizza entered

Enabled entered

FIGURE 3-44

STEP 4   Press the ENTER key to enter the completed statement and place the insertion point on the next line.

IntelliSense enters True in the statement (Figure 3–45). Pressing the ENTER key completes the statement and moves the indented insertion point to the next line.

indented insertion point

True entered

FIGURE 3-45

ONLINE REINFORCEMENT

To view a video of the process in the previous steps, visit CengageBrain.com and navigate to the resources for this title. Tap or click the link for Chapter 3 and then navigate to Video 3-12.

Learning how to enter program statements using IntelliSense is fundamental to writing programs using the Visual Basic 2012 language.

Comments in Program Statements

A well-written Visual Basic 2012 program normally contains **comment statements** within the code itself to document what the code is doing. The general purpose of comments is to help code readers understand the code and how it accomplishes its tasks. An example of comment statements used in code is shown in Figure 3-46.

apostrophes
indicate
comment lines

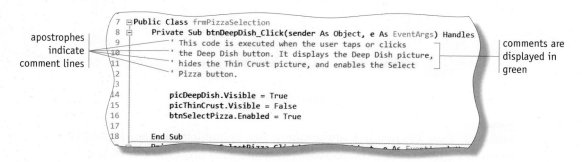

comments are
displayed in
green

FIGURE 3-46

A comment is preceded by an apostrophe. Whenever the Visual Basic compiler encounters an apostrophe in the code, it ignores the remaining characters on the line. To the compiler, it's as if the comments do not exist.

The comments in the code are displayed in green text and describe the processing that will occur in the code that follows. Because comments are ignored by the Visual Basic compiler, developers must not include programming language syntax in the comments. Any letters or characters are allowed within comments.

To enter comments, first type an apostrophe in the code. All characters following the apostrophe on a line of code are considered a comment. To enter the comment code shown in Figure 3-46, you could complete the following steps:

STEP 1 To insert a blank line following the event code generated by Visual Studio that begins with the word Private, tap or click anywhere in that line and then press the END key.

Visual Studio positions the insertion point at the end of the line that you tapped or clicked (Figure 3-47).

code generated by
Visual Studio

insertion point
at end of line

FIGURE 3-47

STEP 2 Press the ENTER key.

Visual Studio inserts a blank line in the code and then moves the insertion point to the blank line (Figure 3–48). The comments can be inserted on the blank line.

insertion point moved to next line

Visual Studio inserts blank line

FIGURE 3-48

STEP 3 Type the first line of the comments, beginning with an apostrophe as shown in Figure 3-46 on the previous page, and then press the ENTER key.

The apostrophe identifies the rest of the line as a comment (Figure 3–49). The comment line is displayed in green text. When you press the ENTER key, Visual Studio creates a new blank line and places the indented insertion point on that line.

apostrophe indicates comment line

comment line is displayed in green

blank line

indented insertion point

FIGURE 3-49

You can continue to enter lines of comments by typing an apostrophe and the comment and then pressing the ENTER key until all comments are completed.

Same-line Comments

Because the Visual Basic compiler treats all characters following an apostrophe as comments, it is possible to place a comment on the same line as executable code. In Figure 3-50, a comment is shown on the same line as the statement that sets the btnSelectPizza Enabled property to True.

```
 3   Private Sub btnDeepDish_Click(sender As Object, e As EventArgs) Handles btnDeepDish.Cl
 4       ' This code is executed when the user taps or clicks
 5       ' the Deep Dish button. It displays the Deep Dish picture,
 6       ' hides the Thin Crust picture, and enables the Select
 7       ' Pizza button.
 8
 9       picDeepDish.Visible = True
10       picThinCrust.Visible = False
11       btnSelectPizza.Enabled = True ' Enable button
12
13   End Sub
14 End Class
15
```

apostrophe identifies comment

FIGURE 3-50

In Figure 3-50, the apostrophe specifies that subsequent characters on the line are to be treated as comments. Therefore, the Enable button text is displayed in green and is treated as a comment. To enter a comment on any line, enter an apostrophe and then type the comment. Remember that all characters after an apostrophe are treated as comments on a line of code.

Introductory Comments

Every program should begin with comments that state the name of the program, the developer's name, the date, and the purpose of the program. These introductory comments should precede all code in the program — even the code generated by Visual Studio (Figure 3-51).

introductory comments

```
frmPizzaSelection.vb*  ⊟ ✕  frmPizzaSelection.vb [Design]*
 (General)                                    ▼  (Declarations)
 1   ' Program Name:  Pizza Selection
 2   ' Developer:     Corinne Hoisington
 3   ' Date:          January 28, 2015
 4   ' Purpose:       This application displays two pizza types
 5   '                (deep dish and thin crust). The user can select a pizza type.
 6
 7 Public Class frmPizzaSelection
```

FIGURE 3-51

To enter introductory comments, you can complete the steps on the next page:

STEP 1   Tap or click to the left of the word Public on line 1 of the program to place the insertion point on that line.

The insertion point is positioned at the beginning of line 1 in the code (Figure 3-52).

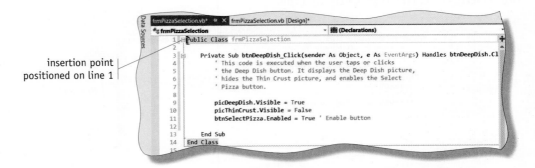

insertion point
positioned on line 1

FIGURE 3-52

STEP 2   Press the ENTER key and then press the UP ARROW key.

When you press the ENTER key, Visual Studio inserts a blank line on line 1 of the code and moves the line that begins with the words Public Class down to line 2 (Figure 3-53). Visual Studio also moves the insertion point to line 2 when you press the ENTER key. When you press the UP ARROW key, the insertion point moves to the first line, which is blank.

insertion point

blank line

Public Class line
now on line 2

FIGURE 3-53

STEP 3   Type an apostrophe, a space, the text `Program Name:`, and then press the TAB key.

The apostrophe identifies all characters and words that follow as comments, so those characters are displayed in green (Figure 3-54). The first line of introductory comments normally specifies the name of the program. Pressing the TAB key moves the insertion point to the right.

comment 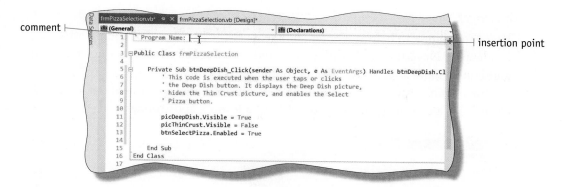 insertion point

FIGURE 3-54

STEP 4 Type Pizza Selection as the name of the program, and then press the ENTER key.

The program name appears in the first line of comments and the insertion point is moved to line 2 (Figure 3-55).

insertion
point  program name

FIGURE 3-55

You can enter the remaining comments using the same techniques. Press the TAB key one or more times to vertically align the paragraphs on the right so they appear as shown in Figure 3-51 on page 145.

What do the yellow and green lines represent to the left of the code?
The yellow lines indicate lines that have not been saved. The green lines indicate the changes in code that have been saved. The yellow and green lines are a method of tracking your most recent changes in code.

CONSIDER THIS

Correct Errors in Code

Using IntelliSense to help you enter code reduces the likelihood of coding errors considerably. Nevertheless, because you could create errors when entering code, you should understand what to do when a coding error occurs.

One possible error would be to forget an apostrophe in a comment statement. In Figure 3-56, a comment was entered without a leading apostrophe.

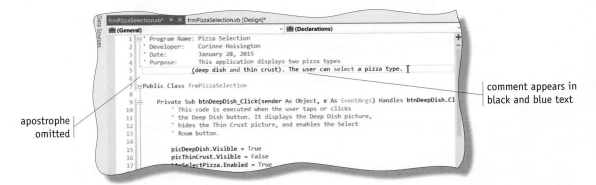

FIGURE 3-56

In Figure 3-56, the comment words are displayed in black and blue text, which indicates an error because comment characters normally are displayed in green text. Visual Studio gives no other indication that an error has occurred.

From this point where the error occurred, the developer might take any course of action. For example, she might immediately run the program. Or, she might tap or click anywhere in the window to move the insertion point, or press the ENTER key to insert a blank line. If the program in Figure 3-56 is executed immediately by tapping or clicking the Start Debugging button on the Standard toolbar, the window shown in Figure 3-57 will be displayed.

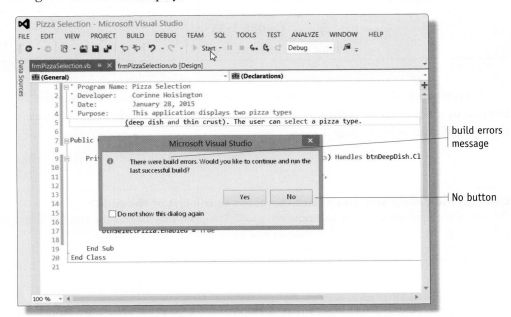

FIGURE 3-57

The **build errors message** means the Visual Basic compiler detected a coding error in the program. An absolute requirement when creating Visual Basic programs is that when you see the build errors message, you *always tap or click the No button.* Under no circumstances should you tap or click the Yes button in the dialog box. When you tap or click the No button, you can perform the following steps to make corrections in your program:

STEP 1   Tap or click the No button in the Microsoft Visual Studio dialog box that informs you of a build error (see Figure 3-57).

*When you tap or click the No button, Visual Studio displays the program code and the Error List window (Figure 3-58). The **Error List window** identifies the number of errors that occurred and displays descriptions of the errors. For example, the Syntax error in Figure 3-58 means Visual Studio expected to find a different type of statement. The window also contains the file name in which the error occurred (frmPizzaSelection.vb), the line number of the statement in error (5), and the vertical column within the statement where the error was detected (15). In the code window, the location of the error is noted by a blue squiggly line.*

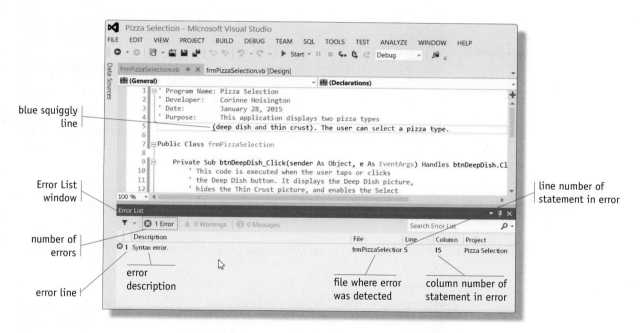

FIGURE 3-58

STEP 2 Double-click anywhere on the error line.

Visual Studio highlights the error with a blue squiggly line. The developer can type and replace the highlighted text with the correct code (Figure 3-59). With the error highlighted, the developer must examine the statement to determine the error. By looking at line 5, column 15, where the left parenthesis is highlighted, it is clear that the developer created a line that was intended to be a comment. Further examination reveals the required apostrophe is missing.

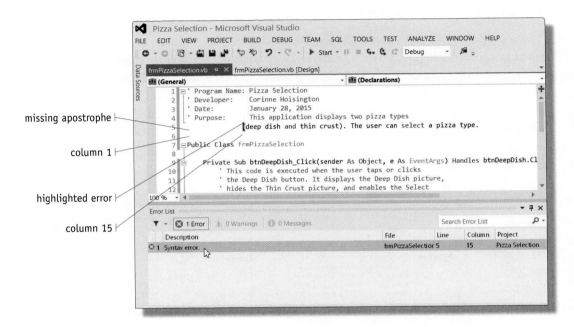

FIGURE 3-59

STEP 3 Tap or click in the far left column on line 5 to place the insertion point there.

The insertion point is placed in the far left column on line 5 of the program (Figure 3-60).

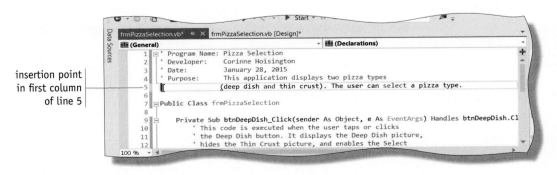

FIGURE 3-60

STEP 4   Type an apostrophe.

The apostrophe is placed in the first column on line 5 of the program (Figure 3-61).

apostrophe in
column 1, line 5

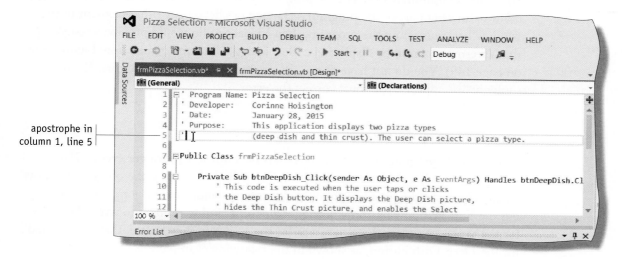

FIGURE 3-61

STEP 5   Tap or click anywhere in the code window.

When you tap or click anywhere in the window, the insertion point moves to that location (Figure 3-62). If the statement has been corrected, the error line is removed from the Error List window, and the number of errors is reduced by one. In Figure 3-62, the number of errors now is zero because the one error found in the program has been corrected. Multiple errors can be detected when the program is compiled.

comment in green
and no blue
squiggly line

insertion point

0 errors in
program

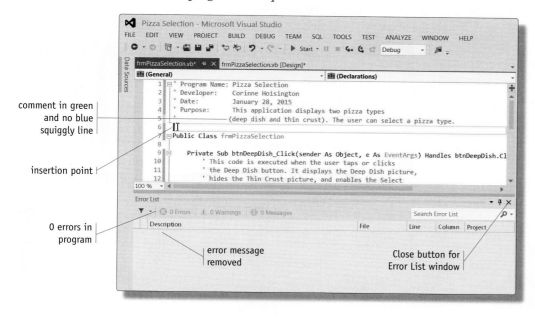

error message
removed

Close button for
Error List window

FIGURE 3-62

ONLINE REINFORCEMENT

To view a video of the process in the previous steps, visit CengageBrain.com and navigate to the resources for this title. Tap or click the link for Chapter 3 and then navigate to Video 3-15.

You can close the Error List window by tapping or clicking its Close button (see Figure 3-62 on the previous page).

In Figure 3-57 on page 148, the example assumed that the developer made an error and then immediately ran the program. If the developer moved the insertion point to another part of the program or tapped or clicked any other element in the window before running the program, then Visual Studio would provide a visual cue that an error occurred by displaying a blue squiggly line under the error (Figure 3-58 on page 149). You do not have to run the program to find coding errors. If a blue squiggly line appears, you must correct the error.

Additional Tap or Click Events

In the sample program in this chapter, multiple buttons can trigger events. For example, when the user taps or clicks the Exit Window button, the program window should close and the program should terminate. To indicate that tapping or clicking the Exit Window button will trigger an event, and to prepare to write the code for the event, complete the same steps for the Exit Window button that you learned for the Deep Dish button, as shown in the following example:

STEP 1   On the frmPizzaSelection.vb [Design] tabbed page, double-click the Exit Window Button object.

Visual Studio opens the code window and displays the frmPizzaSelection.vb tabbed page (Figure 3-63). Visual Studio also inserts the event handler code for the tap or click event on the btnExit object. Two horizontal lines separate the event handler code for the btnExit object from code for other event handlers that might be in the program. The developer must write the code that will be executed when the tap or click event occurs. The insertion point is located in the proper place to begin writing code.

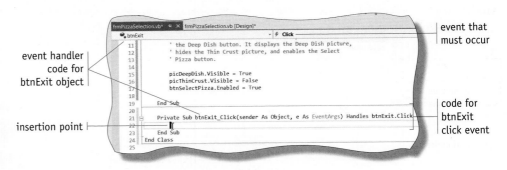

FIGURE 3-63

Enter Comments

As you have learned, you can enter code in the code window using the IntelliSense tools. The first code written for an event, however, should be comment code that identifies the event and the processing that will occur. The comment code for the Exit Window event handler is shown in Figure 3-64.

comments for
btnExit event
handler

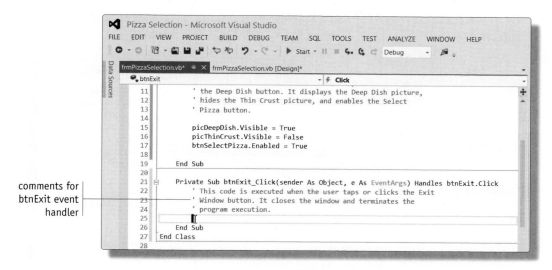

FIGURE 3-64

Close Procedure

The Visual Basic statement to close the window and terminate the program calls a procedure that performs the actual processing. A **procedure** is a set of prewritten code that can be called by a statement in the Visual Basic program. When the procedure is called, the program processes the code. The procedure used to close a window and terminate a program is the Close procedure.

You can use the statement in Figure 3-65 to call the Close procedure.

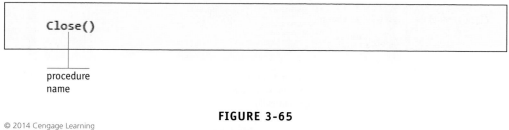

procedure
name

FIGURE 3-65

The word Close specifies the name of the procedure to be called. The left and right parentheses immediately following the procedure name identify the Visual Basic statement as a **procedure call statement**.

When the statement in Figure 3-65 is executed, the Close procedure will be called and control will be given to the prewritten programming statements in the Close procedure. These statements will close the window and terminate the application.

To enter the Close statement into the program, you can type "clo" and then select Close in the IntelliSense list, as shown in the following steps.

STEP 1 With the insertion point positioned as shown in Figure 3-64 on the previous page, type `clo` to highlight Close in the IntelliSense list.

When you type the letters "clo," IntelliSense highlights the word Close in the IntelliSense list (Figure 3-66).

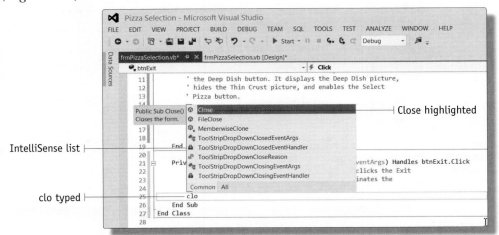

FIGURE 3-66

STEP 2 Press the ENTER key.

IntelliSense enters Close in the statement and, because it knows Close is a procedure call, automatically appends the open and closed parentheses to the statement (Figure 3-67). Then, Visual Studio returns the insertion point to the next line.

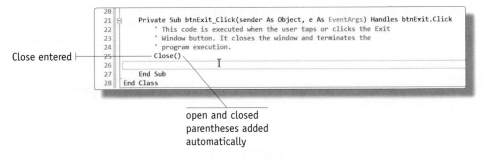

FIGURE 3-67

Prewritten procedures are an important element when using rapid application development in Visual Basic and Visual Studio because the developer is not required to write the procedure code. The developer merely writes a single statement to call the procedure. You will use many procedures in this book for a variety of reasons.

Print Code

In some instances, you will need to print the code in the program. While reviewing code, you might find it easier to read and understand the code on a printed page rather than on your computer screen. In other cases, you might want to share the code with another developer; the printed page often is a better tool for sharing than a monitor screen. To print the code in a program, you can complete the following steps:

1. Tap or click FILE on the menu bar to display the File menu.
2. Tap or click Print on the FILE menu to display the Print dialog box.
3. Ensure that a check mark appears in the Include line numbers check box if you want to include line numbers on your printout. Most developers prefer line numbers on printouts.
4. Make any other needed selections in the Print dialog box.
5. Tap or click the OK button in the Print dialog box to print the code.

If you have a color printer, the code will be printed with correct color. Otherwise, shades of gray will represent the colors shown in the code window. If a line of code extends beyond one printed line, an arrow will appear at the end of the first line to indicate it continues to the next printed line.

Coding Summary

Writing code is the essence of programming in Visual Basic 2012. Much of the emphasis in this book will be on writing the code required to implement applications of all kinds.

Once you understand coding and the statements shown in this chapter, you are ready to continue the process of designing and implementing the Pizza Selection program.

Phase 3 — Design the Program Processing Objects

The next phase in the program development life cycle requires determining the processing objects for the program and creating the event planning document. In the Pizza Selection program and programs of similar complexity, the designer need not be concerned about determining the processing objects. The only processing object required for the program is the Windows Form object. In more complex programs, determining processing objects will become important.

For the Pizza Selection program, the next task is to design the event planning document.

Event Planning Document

As you have learned, programs written using a graphical user interface normally are event-driven programs. An **event** means the user has initiated an action that causes the program to perform the appropriate type of processing in response. Once the mock-up has been created for the user interface, the developer must document the events that can occur based on the user interface.

The **event planning document** is a table that specifies objects in the user interface that will cause events, the actions taken by the user to trigger the events, and the event processing that must occur. The event planning document for the Pizza Selection program is shown in Figure 3-68.

EVENT PLANNING DOCUMENT

Program Name:	Developer:	Object:	Date:
Pizza Selection	Corinne Hoisington	frmPizzaSelection	January 28, 2015

Object	Event Trigger	Event Processing	
btnDeepDish	Tap or click	Display the DeepDish picture Hide the ThinCrust picture Enable the Select Pizza button	
btnSelectPizza	Tap or click	Disable the Deep Dish button Disable the Select Pizza button Disable the Thin Crust button Hide the Instructions label Display the Confirmation Message label Enable the Exit Window button	
btnThinCrust	Tap or click	Display the ThinCrust picture Hide the DeepDish picture Enable the Select Pizza button	
btnExitWindow	Tap or click	Close the window and terminate the program	

FIGURE 3-68

The left column in the event planning document identifies the object in the graphical user interface that can trigger an event. In the Pizza Selection program, each of the four Button objects can be used to trigger an event, so each must be included in the event planning document. Notice each Button object is identified by its name. Using this technique ensures that the documentation is precise, and provides little room for error when the developer creates the code to implement these events.

The middle column identifies the event trigger, which is the action a user takes to cause the event. In all four event cases in Figure 3-68, tapping or clicking a button triggers the event. As you will learn in this book, users can perform a variety of acts to trigger an event. For example, a user might point to an object, press or right-click the object, or double-tap or double-click the object. Each event trigger could trigger a different event.

The right column in the event planning document specifies the event processing that the program must perform when the event occurs. This list of tasks for each event is a critical element in the program design. It must be precise and accurate. No processing step that must occur should be left out of the event processing column. The tasks should be listed in the same sequence as they will be performed in the program.

For example, the first task for the btnDeepDish_Click event is to display the DeepDish picture. This is the primary task for the Deep Dish button. However, several other tasks must be completed. When the program begins, the ThinCrust picture is not visible, but if the user taps or clicks the Thin Crust button, then the picture will be visible. When the user taps or clicks the Deep Dish button, however, the ThinCrust picture should not be visible. Therefore, each time the user taps or clicks the Deep Dish button, the processing must hide the ThinCrust picture.

You also will recall that when the program begins, the Select Pizza button is dimmed (disabled). After the user taps or clicks a pizza type button, the Select Pizza button must be enabled. For example, each time the user taps or clicks the Deep Dish button, the Select Pizza button must be enabled.

As you review the event planning document in Figure 3-68, be sure you understand the processing that must occur for each event.

You should note that the event processing tasks in the right column identify *what* processing must be done when the event occurs. *How* these tasks will be accomplished is not identified specifically, although the information in the event planning document must be precise enough that the developer can easily write the code to implement the specified tasks.

Phase 4 — Code the Program

After the events and tasks within the events have been identified, the developer is ready to code the program. As you have learned in this chapter, coding the program means entering Visual Basic statements to accomplish the tasks specified in the event planning document. As the developer enters the code, she also will implement the logic to carry out the required processing.

Guided Program Development

To fine-tune the user interface in the Pizza Selection program and enter the code required to process each event in the program, complete the following steps to create the program shown in Figure 3-1 on pages 112 and 113.

NOTE TO THE LEARNER

In the following activity, you should complete the tasks within the specified steps. Each of the tasks is accompanied by a Hint Screen. The purpose of the Hint Screen is to indicate where you should perform the activity in the Visual Studio window and to remind you which method to use. If you need further help completing a step, refer to the figure identified by *ref:*.

Guided Program Development

1

- **Open the Mock-Up File** Open Visual Studio and then open the mock-up file for the user interface you created in Chapter 2. (If you did not create a mock-up file in Chapter 2, consult with your instructor to obtain the file.)

- **Show the Windows Form Object's BackColor Property** To finish the user interface, you must specify the BackColor of the Windows Form object. Select the frmPizzaSelection Windows Form object. In the Properties window, scroll until the BackColor property is visible, tap or click the BackColor property name in the left column, and then tap or click the BackColor arrow in the right column. If necessary, tap or click the Web tab (*ref: Figure 3-3*).

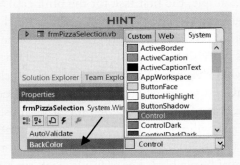

- **Choose the Windows Form Object's BackColor** Scroll the Web tabbed page until White is visible, and then tap or click White in the list (*ref: Figure 3-5*).

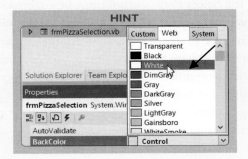

- **Select the BackColor for Buttons** Next, you must specify the BackColor for the Button objects. Select the four buttons in the window using techniques you have learned and change the color to Wheat.

- **Change the ForeColor of a Label Object** Select lblHeading and tap or click the ForeColor property name in the left column, and then tap or click the ForeColor arrow in the right column. If necessary, tap or click the Web tab and select Firebrick in the list.

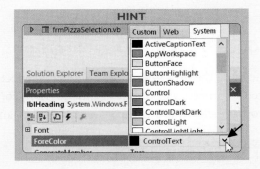

1

The BackColor for the Windows Form object is changed to White, the ForeColor of the heading is changed to Firebrick, and the BackColor for the buttons in the window is changed to Wheat (Figure 3-69).

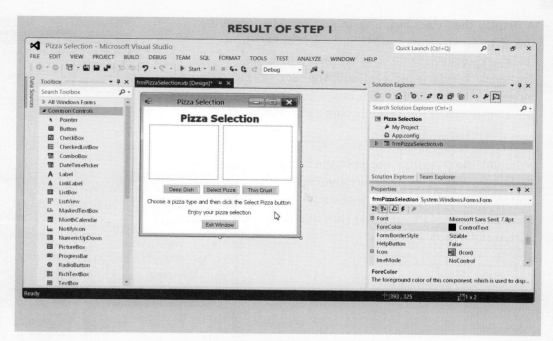

FIGURE 3-69

2

● **Download the DeepDish Image** To display the pictures in the PictureBox object, you might need to use your Web browser to download the pictures from the book's Web page at *CengageBrain.com* and store them on your computer. After downloading the files for Chapter 3, save the DeepDish image on a USB drive or other available storage media on your computer (*ref: Figure 3-7*).

● **Download the ThinCrust Image** Save the ThinCrust image on a USB drive or other storage media on your computer (*ref: Figure 3-7*).

(continues)

3

● **Display the Select Resource Dialog Box** After acquiring
the pictures, you must import them into the Resources
folder and specify the PictureBox object where they will be
displayed. Select the picDeepDish PictureBox object. In the
Properties window, tap or click Image and then tap or click
the ellipsis button in the right column (*ref: Figure 3-11*).

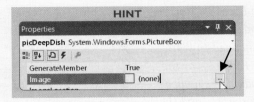

● **Import the DeepDish Image** In the Select
Resource dialog box, tap or click the Import
button, import the DeepDish image from its
saved location, and then tap or click the OK
button (*ref: Figure 3-14*).

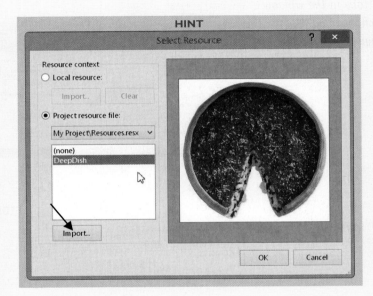

© Brand X Pictures/Getty Images

● **Import the ThinCrust Image** Using the same
technique, specify the ThinCrust image as the
image for the picThinCrust PictureBox object.

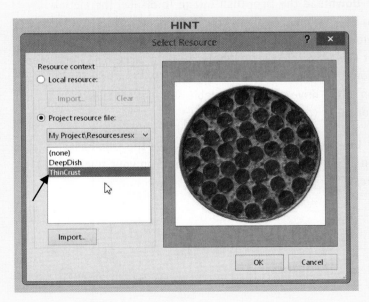

© Brand X Pictures/Getty Images

● **Set the SizeMode Property to StretchImage for the DeepDish Image** When you import a picture, normally you must resize it or the PictureBox object so the picture is displayed properly. To resize the DeepDish image, select the picDeepDish PictureBox object. In the Properties window for the picDeepDish PictureBox object, tap or click the SizeMode property name, tap or click the SizeMode arrow, and then set the property to StretchImage (*ref: Figure 3-16*).

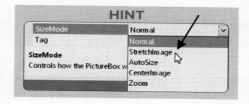

● **Set the SizeMode Property to StretchImage for the ThinCrust Image** Using the same technique, set the SizeMode property to StretchImage for the picThinCrust PictureBox object.

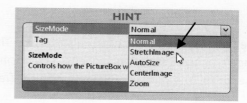

The images are displayed in the correct PictureBox objects (Figure 3-70).

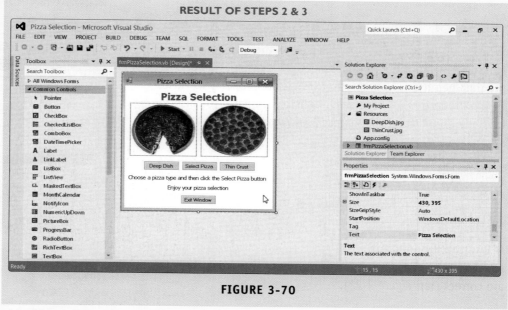

FIGURE 3-70

© Brand X Pictures/Getty Images

(continues)

Guided Program Development *continued*

4

- **Set the Visible Property to False for the DeepDish Image**
When the program begins, the pictures are not displayed in
the window, so you must set their Visible property to False.
In the Properties window for the picDeepDish PictureBox
object, tap or click the Visible property name in the left
column, tap or click the Visible arrow for the Visible property,
and then set the Visible property to False for the picDeepDish
PictureBox object (*ref: Figure 3-18*).

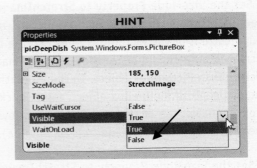

- **Set the Visible Property to False for the ThinCrust
Image** Using the same technique, set the Visible property to
False for the picThinCrust PictureBox object (*ref: Figure 3-18*).

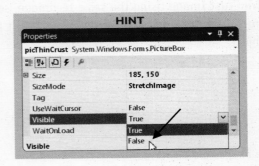

- **Set the Visible Property to False for the Confirmation
Message** The confirmation message is not displayed when the
program begins, so you must set its Visible property to False.
In the Properties window, set the Visible property to False for
the lblConfirmation Label object (*ref: Figure 3-18*).

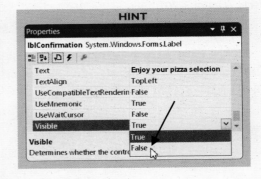

- **Run the Program** After you make changes to a program,
you should run it to ensure your changes work properly and
are correct (*ref: Figure 3-22*).

In Figure 3-71, the pizza type pictures are not displayed. In addition, the confirmation message is not displayed.

FIGURE 3-71

5

● **Set the Select Pizza Button's Enabled Property to False**
Initially, the Select Pizza button and the Exit Window button must be dimmed. In the Properties window for the btnSelect-Pizza object, tap or click the Enabled property name, tap or click the Enabled arrow, and then set the Enabled property to False for the btnSelectPizza Button object (*ref: Figure 3-20*).

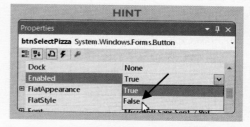

● **Set the Exit Window Button's Enabled Property to False**
Using the same technique, set the Enabled property to False for the btnExit Button object (*ref: Figure 3-20*).

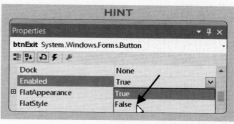

● **Run the Program** Again, after you make changes, always ensure the changes are correct. Run the program.

Both the Select Pizza button and the Exit Window button are dimmed, indicating the Enabled property for both buttons is False (Figure 3-72).

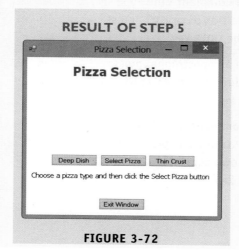

FIGURE 3-72

(continues)

Guided Program Development   *continued*

6

- **Open the Code Window for the btnDeepDish Event Handler** The user interface now is complete, so you should begin writing the code for the program. To write code, you must open the code window. Double-click the Deep Dish button to open the code window for the btnDeepDish_Click event (*ref: Figure 3-24*).

- **Position the Insertion Point** Close the Toolbox window. When you begin writing the code for a program, the first step is to write the introductory comments. Tap or click in the far left position of the first line of code (Public Class) (*ref: Figure 3-52*).

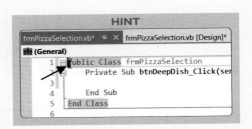

- **Create a Blank Line and Position the Insertion Point** Press the ENTER key and then press the UP ARROW key (*ref: Figure 3-53*).

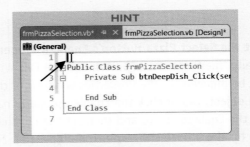

- **Enter the First Line of the Introductory Comments** The introductory comments provide the code reader with important information about the program. The first line normally specifies the name of the program. Type an apostrophe, press the SPACEBAR, type `Program Name:`, press TAB, type `Pizza Selection`, and then press the ENTER key (*ref: Figure 3-55*).

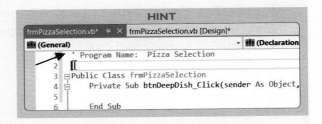

- **Enter the Developer Identification Comment Line** Type an apostrophe, press the SPACEBAR, type `Developer:`, press TAB, type your name, and then press the ENTER key.

- **Enter the Date Comment Line** Type an apostrophe, press the SPACEBAR, type `Date:`, press TAB three times, enter the current date, and then press the ENTER key.

- **Enter the First Program Purpose Comment Line** Type an apostrophe, press the SPACEBAR, type `Purpose:`, press TAB two times, enter the first line of your own comments about the program, and then press the ENTER key.

- **Enter the Remaining Program Purpose Comment Lines**
Insert additional lines of comments about the purpose of the
program as you see fit.

*The comments appear at
the top of the program
code (Figure 3-73).*

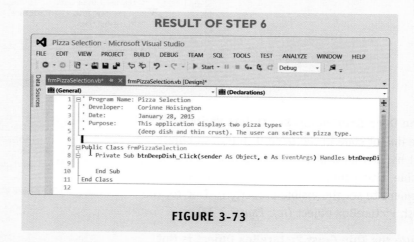

RESULT OF STEP 6

```
1 ' Program Name: Pizza Selection
2 ' Developer:    Corinne Hoisington
3 ' Date:         January 28, 2015
4 ' Purpose:      This application displays two pizza types
5 '               (deep dish and thin crust). The user can select a pizza type.
6 '
7 Public Class frmPizzaSelection
8     Private Sub btnDeepDish_Click(sender As Object, e As EventArgs) Handles btnDeepDi
9
10        End Sub
11 End Class
12
```

FIGURE 3-73

7

- **Position the Insertion Point Inside
the Click Event Handler** With the
insertion point located on the line
above the line of code that begins
with Public Class (see Figure 3-73),
press the DOWN ARROW key four times
and then press TAB two times to position
the insertion point (*ref: Figure 3-48*).

HINT

```
7 Public Class frmPizzaSelection
8     Private Sub btnDeepDish_Click(sender As Object, e As EventArgs) Handles btnDeepDi
9
10        End Sub
11 End Class
12
```

- **Enter the First Line of the Event
Handler Comments** Each event handler
should begin with comments describing
what the event handler accomplishes.
Type an apostrophe, press the SPACEBAR,
and then enter the first line of comments
for the btnDeepDish_Click event handler.
Press the ENTER key (*ref: Figure 3-49*).

HINT

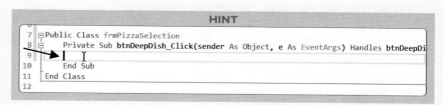

```
7 Public Class frmPizzaSelection
8     Private Sub btnDeepDish_Click(sender As Object, e As EventArgs) Han
9         ' This code is executed when the user taps or clicks
10
11        End Sub
12 End Class
13
```

(continues)

● **Enter the Remaining Event Handler Comments** Enter the remaining comments for the btnDeepDish_Click event handler.

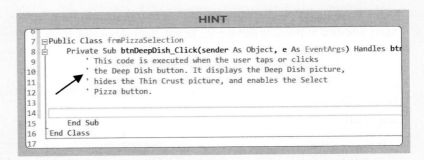

HINT
```
6
7  ⊟Public Class frmPizzaSelection
8  ⊟    Private Sub btnDeepDish_Click(sender As Object, e As EventArgs) Handles btn
9          ' This code is executed when the user taps or clicks
10         ' the Deep Dish button. It displays the Deep Dish picture,
11         ' hides the Thin Crust picture, and enables the Select
12         ' Pizza button.
13
14
15         End Sub
16 End Class
17
```

● **Make the Deep Dish PictureBox Object Visible** The first executable line of code in the Deep Dish Button object click event handler must make the Deep Dish PictureBox object visible. Using IntelliSense, enter the Visual Basic code statement to set the Visible property to True for the picDeepDish PictureBox object (*ref: Figure 3-32*).

HINT
```
13
14          picDeepDish.v
15      End Sub           🔧 ProductVersion
16  End Class             🔧 Visible
17
                          Common  All
```

● **Make Sure the Thin Crust PictureBox Object is Not Visible** As documented in the event planning document, the next task is to make sure the ThinCrust picture is not visible in the window. Using IntelliSense, enter the Visual Basic code statement to set the Visible property to False for the picThinCrust PictureBox object (*ref: Figure 3-40*).

HINT
```
3  ⊟    Private Sub btnDeepDish_Click(sender As
4          picDeepDish.Visible = True
5          picThinCrust.Visible =
False keyword                        ▣ False
```

● **Enable the Select Pizza Button Object** The last task for the Deep Dish button click event is to enable the Select Pizza button. Using IntelliSense, enter the Visual Basic code statement to set the Enabled property to True for the btnSelectPizza Button object (*ref: Figure 3-44*).

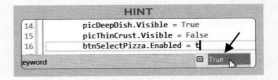

HINT
```
14          picDeepDish.Visible = True
15          picThinCrust.Visible = False
16          btnSelectPizza.Enabled = t
eyword                              ▣ True
```

The lines of code are entered in the Deep Dish Button object's click event handler (Figure 3-74). The code will set the Visible property to True for the picDeepDish PictureBox object, set the Visible property to False for the picThinCrust PictureBox object, and set the Enabled property to True for the btnSelectPizza Button object.

HEADS UP

As you enter executable code, you should refer to the event planning document to ensure the code implements the identified tasks. The event planning document is the guide to the code you write in each event handler.

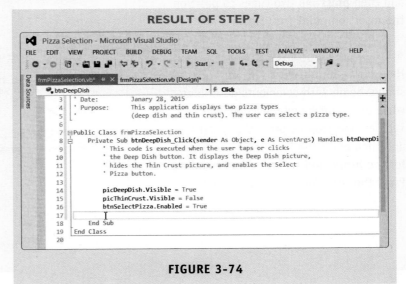

RESULT OF STEP 7
```
Pizza Selection - Microsoft Visual Studio
FILE  EDIT  VIEW  PROJECT  BUILD  DEBUG  TEAM  SQL  TOOLS  TEST  ANALYZE  WINDOW  HELP

frmPizzaSelection.vb*  frmPizzaSelection.vb [Design]*
● btnDeepDish                              ⚡ Click
3   ' Date:        Janary 28, 2015
4   ' Purpose:     This application displays two pizza types
5                  (deep dish and thin crust). The user can select a pizza type.
6
7  ⊟Public Class frmPizzaSelection
8  ⊟    Private Sub btnDeepDish_Click(sender As Object, e As EventArgs) Handles btnDeepDi
9          ' This code is executed when the user taps or clicks
10         ' the Deep Dish button. It displays the Deep Dish picture,
11         ' hides the Thin Crust picture, and enables the Select
12         ' Pizza button.
13
14         picDeepDish.Visible = True
15         picThinCrust.Visible = False
16         btnSelectPizza.Enabled = True
17
18         End Sub
19 End Class
20
```

FIGURE 3-74

8

● **Run the Program** When the code for an event handler is complete, good practice dictates that you should run the program to ensure the event handler code works properly. Run the program. Tap or click the Deep Dish button.

When you tap or click the Deep Dish button, the DeepDish picture is displayed, the ThinCrust picture is not displayed, and the Select Pizza button is enabled (Figure 3-75). These are the correct results. Note that if you tap or click any of the other buttons in the window, nothing happens because you have not yet written the event handler code for these objects.

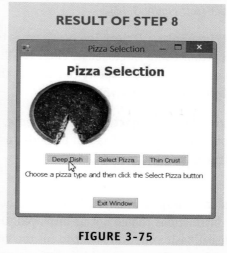

RESULT OF STEP 8

FIGURE 3-75

© Brand X Pictures/Getty Images

9

● **Display the Design Window** When the code for an event handler is completed, the next task is often to write the code for another event handler. To do so, you must go to the Design tabbed page and indicate the object for which the code will be written. Tap or click the frmPizzaSelection.vb [Design] tab to return to the Design tabbed page.

● **Open the Code Window for the btnSelectPizza Event Handler** You must open the code window for the btnSelectPizza Button object to enter code for the event handler. Double-tap or double-click the Select Pizza button to open the code window for the btnSelectPizza_Click event *(ref: Figure 3-24).*

```
19
20      Private Sub btnSelectPizza_Click(sender As Object, e As EventArgs) Handles btnSel
21
22      End Sub
```

● **Enter Event Handler Comments** When beginning the code for an event handler, the first step is to enter the event handler comments. Enter the comments that describe the processing in the btnSelectPizza_Click event handler.

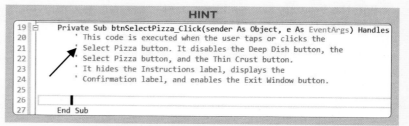

```
19      Private Sub btnSelectPizza_Click(sender As Object, e As EventArgs) Handles
20          ' This code is executed when the user taps or clicks the
21          ' Select Pizza button. It disables the Deep Dish button, the
22          ' Select Pizza button, and the Thin Crust button.
23          ' It hides the Instructions label, displays the
24          ' Confirmation label, and enables the Exit Window button.
25
26
27      End Sub
```

(continues)

- **Disable the btnDeepDish Button Object** According to the event planning document (Figure 3-68 on page 156), the next task is to disable the Deep Dish button. Using IntelliSense, enter the Visual Basic code statement to set the Enabled property to False for the btnDeepDish Button object (*ref: Figure 3-42*).

- **Disable the btnSelectPizza Button Object** The next task is to disable the Select Pizza button. Using IntelliSense, enter the Visual Basic code statement to set the Enabled property to False for the btnSelectPizza Button object (*ref: Figure 3-42*).

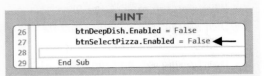

- **Disable the btnThinCrust Button Object** Using IntelliSense, enter the Visual Basic code statement to set the Enabled property to False for the btnThinCrust Button object (*ref: Figure 3-42*).

- **Hide the Instructions Label Object** When the Select Pizza button is tapped or clicked, the instructions should not be displayed. Using IntelliSense, enter the Visual Basic code statement to set the Visible property to False for the lblInstructions Label object (*ref: Figure 3-32*).

- **Display the Confirmation Message** The confirmation message must be displayed when the user taps or clicks the Select Pizza button. Using IntelliSense, enter the Visual Basic code statement to set the Visible property to True for the lblConfirmation Label object (*ref: Figure 3-32*).

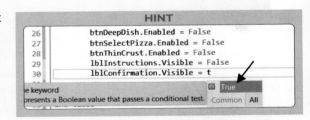

- **Enable the Exit Window Button** After the user taps or clicks the Select Pizza button, the only allowable action is to tap or click the Exit Window button and close the application. Therefore, the Exit Window button must be enabled. Using IntelliSense, enter the Visual Basic code statement to set the Enabled property to True for the btnExit Button object (*ref: Figure 3-42*).

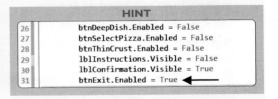

- **Run the Program** Save and then run the program to ensure that it works correctly. Tap or click the Deep Dish button and then tap or click the Select Pizza button.

After tapping or clicking the two buttons, the DeepDish picture is displayed; the Deep Dish, Select Pizza, and Thin Crust buttons are disabled; the Instructions label is not displayed; the Confirmation Message label is displayed; and the Exit Window button is enabled (Figure 3-76).

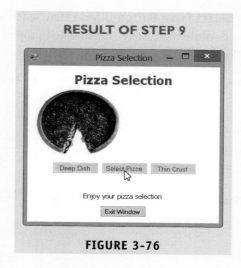

RESULT OF STEP 9

FIGURE 3-76

© Brand X Pictures/Getty Images

10

• **Display the Design Window** The next task is to write the code for the btnThinCrust event handler. To return to the Design tabbed page so you can select the Thin Crust button, tap or click the frmPizzaSelection.vb [Design] tab.

• **Open the Code Window for the btnThinCrust Event Handler** Double-tap or double-click the Thin Crust button to open the code window for the btnThinCrust_Click event (*ref: Figure 3-24*).

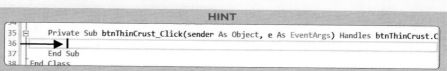

• **Enter the Event Handler Comments** Using the techniques you have learned, enter the comments that describe the processing in the btnThinCrust_Click event handler.

• **Make the ThinCrust PictureBox Object Visible** According to the event planning document, the next task is to make the ThinCrust picture visible. Using IntelliSense, enter the Visual Basic code statement to set the Visible property to True for the picThinCrust PictureBox object (*ref: Figure 3-32*).

• **Make Sure the DeepDish Picture is Not Visible** Using IntelliSense, enter the Visual Basic code statement to set the Visible property to False for the picDeepDish PictureBox object (*ref: Figure 3-32*).

(continues)

- **Enable the Select Pizza Button** Using IntelliSense, enter the Visual Basic code statement to set the Enabled property to True for the btnSelectPizza Button object (*ref: Figure 3-42*).

- **Run the Program** Run the program and then tap or click the Thin Crust button to ensure your code works correctly.

The completed code for the Select Pizza button event handler and the Thin Crust button event handler is shown in Figure 3-77.

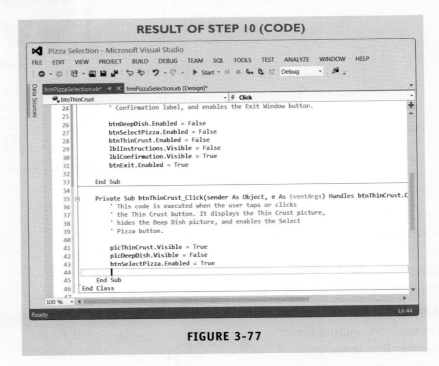

RESULT OF STEP 10 (CODE)

```
          ' Confirmation label, and enables the Exit Window button.
24
25
26              btnDeepDish.Enabled = False
27              btnSelectPizza.Enabled = False
28              btnThinCrust.Enabled = False
29              lblInstructions.Visible = False
30              lblConfirmation.Visible = True
31              btnExit.Enabled = True
32
33          End Sub
34
35   ⊟   Private Sub btnThinCrust_Click(sender As Object, e As EventArgs) Handles btnThinCrust.C
36              ' This code is executed when the user taps or clicks
37              ' the Thin Crust button. It displays the Thin Crust picture,
38              ' hides the Deep Dish picture, and enables the Select
39              ' Pizza button.
40
41              picThinCrust.Visible = True
42              picDeepDish.Visible = False
43              btnSelectPizza.Enabled = True
44
45          End Sub
46      End Class
```

FIGURE 3-77

When you tap or click the Thin Crust button, the ThinCrust picture is displayed, the DeepDish picture is not displayed, and the Select Pizza button is enabled (Figure 3-78). The program is working properly.

RESULT OF STEP 10 (PROGRAM EXECUTION)

FIGURE 3-78

© Brand X Pictures/Getty Images

11

- **Display the Design Window** Tap or click the frmPizzaSelection. vb [Design] tab to return to the Design tabbed page.

HINT

- **Open the Code Window for the btnExit Event Handler** Double-tap or double-click the Exit Window button to open the code window for the btnExit_Click event (*ref: Figure 3-24*).

- **Enter the Event Handler Comments** Using the techniques you have learned, enter the comments that describe the processing in the btnExit_Click event handler.

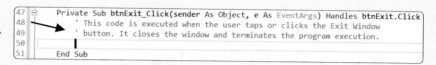

```
47    Private Sub btnExit_Click(sender As Object, e As EventArgs) Handles btnExit.Click
48        ' This code is executed when the user taps or clicks the Exit Window
49        ' button. It closes the window and terminates the program execution.
50
51    End Sub
```

- **Enter the Close() Procedure Call** Using IntelliSense, enter the Visual Basic code statement to close the window and terminate the program (*ref: Figure 3-66*).

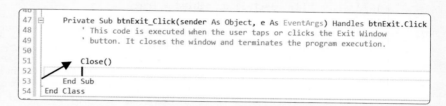

```
47    Private Sub btnExit_Click(sender As Object, e As EventArgs) Handles btnExit.Click
48        ' This code is executed when the user taps or clicks the Exit Window
49        ' button. It closes the window and terminates the program execution.
50
51        Close()
52
53    End Sub
54 End Class
```

The Close() procedure call statement is entered (Figure 3-79). When the procedure call is executed, the application will be closed.

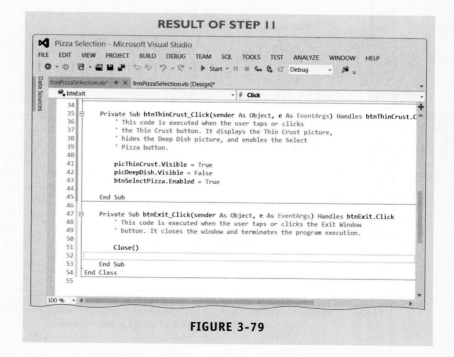

RESULT OF STEP 11

FIGURE 3-79

12

- **Run the Program** Run the program to ensure that it works correctly. Tap or click the Deep Dish button, the Thin Crust button, the Select Pizza button, and the Exit Window button.

Code Listing

The complete code for the sample program is shown in Figure 3-80.

```vbnet
1  ' Program Name: Pizza Selection
2  ' Developer:    Corinne Hoisington
3  ' Date:         January 28, 2015
4  ' Purpose:      This application displays two pizza types
5  '               (deep dish and thin crust). The user can select a pizza type.
6
7  Public Class frmPizzaSelection
8      Private Sub btnDeepDish_Click(sender As Object, e As EventArgs) Handles btnDeepDish.Click
9          ' This code is executed when the user taps or clicks
10         ' the Deep Dish button. It displays the Deep Dish picture,
11         ' hides the Thin Crust picture, and enables the Select
12         ' Pizza button.
13
14         picDeepDish.Visible = True
15         picThinCrust.Visible = False
16         btnSelectPizza.Enabled = True
17
18     End Sub
19     Private Sub btnSelectPizza_Click(sender As Object, e As EventArgs) Handles btnSelectPizza.Click
20         ' This code is executed when the user taps or clicks the
21         ' Select Pizza button. It disables the Deep Dish button,
22         ' the Select Pizza button, and the Thin Crust button.
23         ' It hides the Instructions label, displays the Confirmation
24         ' label, and enables the Exit Window button.
25
26         btnDeepDish.Enabled = False
27         btnSelectPizza.Enabled = False
28         btnThinCrust.Enabled = False
29         lblInstructions.Visible = False
30         lblConfirmation.Visible = True
31         btnExit.Enabled = True
32
33     End Sub
34
35     Private Sub btnThinCrust_Click(sender As Object, e As EventArgs) Handles btnThinCrust.Click
36         ' This code is executed when the user taps or clicks
37         ' the Thin Crust button. It displays the Thin Crust picture,
38         ' hides the Deep Dish picture, and enables the Select
39         ' Pizza button.
40
41         picThinCrust.Visible = True
42         picDeepDish.Visible = False
43         btnSelectPizza.Enabled = True
44
45     End Sub
46
47     Private Sub btnExit_Click(sender As Object, e As EventArgs) Handles btnExit.Click
48         ' This code is executed when the user taps or clicks the Exit Window
49         ' button. It closes the window and terminates the program execution.
50
51         Close()
52
53     End Sub
54  End Class
```

FIGURE 3-80

Summary

In this chapter you have learned to fine-tune a graphical user interface to maximize its usefulness and to enter code for object event handlers.

The items listed in the table in Figure 3-81 include all the new Visual Studio and Visual Basic skills you have learned in this chapter. Video 3-1 demonstrates the complete program execution.

Visual Basic Skills		
Skill	**Figure Number**	**Video Number**
Run the completed program	Figure 3-1	Video 3-1
Set the BackColor Property	Figure 3-2	Video 3-2
Locate and Save an Image from the World Wide Web	Figure 3-7	Video 3-3
Import an Image into the Program Resources Folder	Figure 3-11	Video 3-4
Size an Image	Figure 3-16	Video 3-5
Set the Visible Property in the Properties Window	Figure 3-18	Video 3-6
Set the Enabled Property in the Properties Window	Figure 3-20	Video 3-7
Run a Visual Basic 2012 Program	Figure 3-22	Video 3-8
Enter Visual Basic 2012 Code for Event Handling	Figure 3-24	Video 3-9
Enter a Visual Basic 2012 Statement Using IntelliSense	Figure 3-29	Video 3-10
Enter a Visual Basic 2012 Statement to Set the Visible Property to True	Figure 3-29	Video 3-10
Enter a Visual Basic 2012 Statement to Set the Visible Property to False	Figure 3-37	Video 3-11
Enter a Visual Basic 2012 Statement to Set the Enabled Property to True	Figure 3-42	Video 3-12
Enter Comments in Visual Basic 2012 Code	Figure 3-47	Video 3-13
Enter Introductory Comments in Visual Basic Code	Figure 3-52	Video 3-14
Correct Errors in a Visual Basic 2012 Program	Figure 3-58	Video 3-15
Enter Additional Tap or Click Events	Figure 3-63	Video 3-16
Enter a Close() Statement into Visual Basic 2012 Code	Figure 3-66	Video 3-17
Print Code	Pages 155	

FIGURE 3-81

Knowledge Check

1. Which property controls the background color of the Form object?

2. Which property controls the text color of a Label object?

3. Which color palette is guaranteed to be displayed properly on every computer?

4. When a PictureBox object is placed on the form, what is the default SizeMode property setting?

5. When you place a PictureBox object on a Windows form, in which project folder is the image stored in the Solution Explorer?

6. When you tap or click the ellipsis button for the Image property of a PictureBox object (Figure 3-82), what action does Visual Studio 2012 take?

FIGURE 3-82

7. In which property of the PictureBox object do you tap or click the ellipsis button to select the correct picture?

8. Which option should be selected in the SizeMode property to make the image fit within the PictureBox object?

9. Which property has been set to False if a Button object is dimmed in a window when the program begins?

10. Which property has been set to False if a PictureBox object is not displayed when you run the application?

11. What two options can you select for the Visible property in the Properties window?

12. Write a line of code that would set the Visible property to False for a PictureBox object named picHomeTown.

13. Write a line of code that would set the Enabled property to True for a Button object named btnDiet.

14. Write a line of code that would set the Visible property to True for a PictureBox object named picHeadphones.

15. Write a comment line of code that states, "This code displays the headphone image."

16. What color is used to display comments in the code window of Visual Basic 2012?

17. Write a line of code that will close an application window and terminate the application.

18. What does a blue squiggly line mean in the code window?

19. Which symbol is associated with the assignment statement?

20. Why is it best to use IntelliSense when you enter code in the code window? List two reasons.

Debugging Exercises

1. Fix the following line of code to set the Enabled property to False for the btnDisplayCartoon Button object.

   ```
   btnCartoon.Enable.False
   ```

2. Fix the following line of code to change the visibility of the btnExitProgram Button object so that you can view it when the program runs.

   ```
   btnExitProgram.Visibilty = Yes
   ```

3. Fix the following line of code to set the Visible property to False for the lblDirections Label object.

   ```
   lblDirections.Visible = ' False
   ```

4. Fix the following comment line of code.

   ```
   The ' following line of code makes the college logo visible
   ```

5. Fix the following line of code.

   ```
   Close
   ```

6. Examine the code window and the Error List window in Figure 3-83. Then, write a line of code to replace the erroneous line.

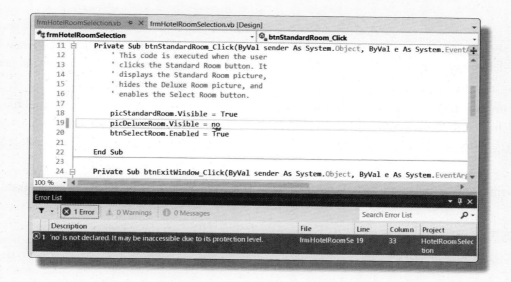

FIGURE 3-83

Program Analysis

1. For the hiking application shown in Figure 3-84, write the Visual Basic 2012 coding statement to view the picture when the user taps or clicks the btnView button, assuming the Visible property had been set to False for the picHike PictureBox object in the Properties window.

background is Bisque

btnView

picHike

Hike.jpg

FIGURE 3-84

Photo courtesy of Corinne Hoisington

2. Which property in the Properties window controls whether the picHike image is displayed when the program begins? Which option for the property would you select to make the button dimmed when the program begins?

3. When you import the picture into the Resources folder and select the image to use in the picHike PictureBox object, which SizeMode property option would you select to view the complete picture?

4. Write the Visual Basic 2012 coding statement for the btnView click event that would cause the image to be displayed.

5. To change the window background color to Bisque as shown in Figure 3-84, what property should you modify?

6. What property is used to display the text "Enjoy your Italian Hike" in the window title bar?

Case Programming Assignments

Complete one or more of the following case programming assignments. Submit the program and materials you create to your instructor. The level of difficulty is indicated for each assignment.

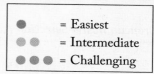

●	= Easiest
●●	= Intermediate
●●●	= Challenging

1 ●
EUROPEAN HOSTEL SELECTION

Based on the Windows form mock-up you created in Chapter 2, complete the European Hostel Selection program by changing the window background color, downloading and adding the images, and writing the code that will execute according to the program requirements shown in Figure 3-85 and the Use Case Definition shown in Figure 3-86 on the next page. Before writing the code, create an event planning document for each event in the program. The completed Windows Form object and the other objects in the user interface are shown in Figure 3-87a, Figure 3-87b, and Figure 3-87c on the next page.

REQUIREMENTS DOCUMENT

Date Submitted:	January 17, 2015
Application Title:	European Hostel Selection Application
Purpose:	The Windows application will allow a user to select a location in London or Dublin.
Program Procedures:	From a window on the screen, the user should identify a hostel location (London or Dublin) and then select a hostel.
Algorithms, Processing, and Conditions:	1. The user must be able to identify the London or Dublin hostel as many times as necessary until making a selection.
	2. When the user identifies the hostel location, a picture of that hostel should appear in the window.
	3. Only one picture should be displayed at a time. If a user identifies the London hostel, only the London hostel picture should be displayed; if a user identifies the Dublin hostel, only the Dublin hostel picture should be displayed.
	4. When the user selects a hostel, a message should be displayed to confirm the selection of a hostel location. In addition, the user should be prevented from identifying another location after selecting a hostel.
	5. After the user selects a hostel, the only allowable action is to exit the window.
Notes and Restrictions:	A user can select a hostel only after identifying a hostel location.
Comments:	The pictures shown in the window can be found on CengageBrain.com. The names of the pictures are Dublin and London.

FIGURE 3-85

(continues)

Case Programming Assignments

European Hostel Selection (continued)

USE CASE DEFINITION

1. User taps or clicks London Hostel button or Dublin Hostel button.
2. Program displays a picture of the hostel identified by the user and enables the location selection button.
3. User taps or clicks hostel buttons to view hostel locations as desired. Program displays the picture of the identified hostel.
4. User taps or clicks the Select Location button.
5. Program displays a hostel selection confirmation message and disables both hostel buttons and the Select Location button. The Exit Window button becomes active.
6. User terminates the program by tapping or clicking the Exit Window button.

FIGURE 3-86

© 2014 Cengage Learning

In Figure 3-87a, no button has been tapped or clicked. In Figure 3-87b, the user has tapped or clicked the Dublin Hostel button. In Figure 3-87c, the user has tapped or clicked the Select Location button.

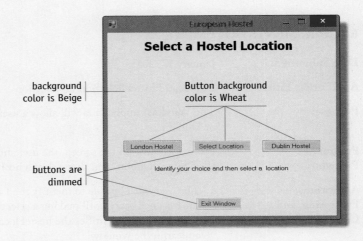

FIGURE 3-87a

FIGURE 3-87b
© DreamPictures/Photodisc/Getty Images

FIGURE 3-87c
© DreamPictures/Photodisc/Getty Images

2 STUDENT PICNIC

Based on the Windows form mock-up you created in Chapter 2, complete the Student Picnic program by changing the window background color, downloading and adding the image, and writing the code that will execute according to the program requirements shown in Figure 3-88. The Use Case Definition is shown in Figure 3-89 on the next page. Before writing the code, create an event planning document for each event in the program. The completed Windows Form object and the other objects in the user interface are shown in Figure 3-90a and Figure 3-90b on the next page.

REQUIREMENTS DOCUMENT

Date Submitted: January 14, 2015

Application Title: Student Picnic Application

Purpose: This Windows application displays a welcome screen for the Annual Spring Fling Picnic. The user can choose an option to view the date and location.

Program Procedures: From a window on the screen, the user makes a request to see the picnic's date and location.

Algorithms, Processing, and Conditions:
1. The user first views a Student Picnic window that displays the picnic name (Annual Spring Fling Picnic), a picnic picture, and a phrase that states all students are welcome.
2. When the user chooses to view the picnic date and location, the following information is displayed:

   April 17, 2015
   Located in the Quad in front of the Barnard Building
3. After the user views the picnic information, the only allowable action is to exit the window.

Notes and Restrictions: n/a

Comments: The picture shown in the window can be found on CengageBrain.com. The name of the picture is Picnic.

FIGURE 3-88

(continues)

Case Programming Assignments

Student Picnic (continued)

USE CASE DEFINITION

1. The window opens, displaying the name of the picnic, a picnic picture, and a message stating all students are welcome. All buttons are enabled.
2. User taps or clicks the View Picnic Information button.
3. Program displays the picnic time and location between the buttons. The View Picnic Information button is disabled.
4. User taps or clicks the Exit Window button to terminate the application.

FIGURE 3-89

© 2014 Cengage Learning

In Figure 3-90a, no button has been tapped or clicked. In Figure 3-90b, the user has tapped or clicked the View Picnic Information button.

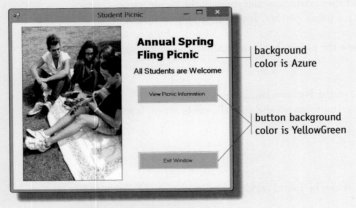

background color is Azure

button background color is YellowGreen

FIGURE 3-90a

© Angela Sorrentino/E+/Getty Images

FIGURE 3-90b

© Angela Sorrentino/E+/Getty Images

3
VISUAL BASIC 2012 TERMS

Based on the Windows form mock-up you created in Chapter 2, complete the Visual Basic 2012 Terms program by changing the window background color and writing the code that will execute according to the program requirements shown in Figure 3-91. The Use Case Definition is shown in Figure 3-92 on the next page. Before writing the code, create an event planning document for each event in the program. The completed Windows Form object and the other objects in the user interface are shown in Figure 3-93a and Figure 3-93b on the next page.

REQUIREMENTS DOCUMENT

Date Submitted:	August 16, 2015
Application Title:	Visual Basic 2012 Terms Application
Purpose:	This Windows application displays the definitions of common Visual Basic terms. When the user chooses to view a definition, the term's definition is displayed.
Program Procedures:	From a window on the screen, the user makes a request to see one of three VB definitions.
Algorithms, Processing, and Conditions:	1. The user first views a screen that displays three VB terms. 2. A logo is displayed at the top of the window throughout the running of the application. 3. The user can select any of the three terms displayed on the buttons to view the definition. 4. When the user taps or clicks a term button to display the definition, any previous definitions will disappear. 5. An exit button is available at all times, allowing the user to end the application.
Notes and Restrictions:	Only one definition should be displayed at a time, so if a user selects a second term, only the second definition should be displayed.
Comments:	n/a

FIGURE 3-91

(continues)

Case Programming Assignments

Visual Basic 2012 Terms (continued)

USE CASE DEFINITION

1. The window opens and displays a logo (Professional 2012), a title (Visual Basic 2012 Terms), three buttons labeled with VB terms, and an Exit Window button. All buttons are enabled.
2. User taps or clicks each of the term buttons to review the definitions.
3. Program displays the definitions to the right of the buttons.
4. Only one definition is displayed at a time.
5. User taps or clicks the Exit Window button to terminate the application.

FIGURE 3-92

In Figure 3-93a, no button has been tapped or clicked. In Figure 3-93b, the user has tapped or clicked the Developer button.

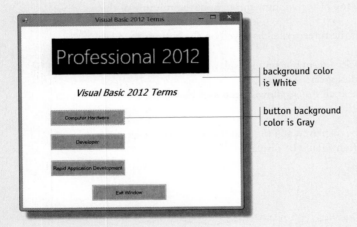

background color is White

button background color is Gray

FIGURE 3-93a

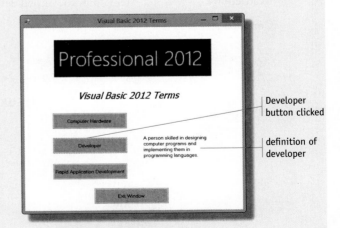

Developer button clicked

definition of developer

FIGURE 3-93b

Case Programming Assignments

4 •• ONLINE STORE SPECIALS

Based on the Windows form mock-up you created in Chapter 2, complete the Online Store Specials program by finishing the user interface, downloading and adding the images, and writing the code that will execute according to the program requirements shown in Figure 3-94. Before writing the code, create an event planning document for each event in the program.

REQUIREMENTS DOCUMENT

Date Submitted:	January 6, 2016
Application Title:	Online Store Specials Application
Purpose:	This Windows application displays the daily, weekly, and holiday specials in the online store. The user can select the desired product and then add the product to a shopping cart.
Program Procedures:	From a window on the screen, the user should select the daily special, weekly special, or holiday special. After the user selects a special, the program should display a picture of the special product, the regular price of the product, and the sale price of the product. The user should be able to select any special. Then, the user can add the product to the shopping cart.
Algorithms, Processing, and Conditions:	1. The user must select a special in order to display the special's product picture, regular price, and sale price.
	2. The user cannot add a product to the shopping cart until a special is selected.
	3. When a special is selected, only that special's picture and prices should be displayed in the window. No other special should be displayed.
	4. After the user selects a special and adds it to the shopping cart, the only allowable user action is to exit the window.
	5. A user should be able to exit the window at any time.
Notes and Restrictions:	n/a
Comments:	1. The specials are:
	Daily Special: SmartPhone: Regular Price: $99.95; Sale Price: $84.50
	Weekly Special: Tablet: Regular Price: $239.95; Sale Price: $199.95
	Holiday Special: Digital Camera: Regular Price: $259.95; Sale Price: $203.19
	2. The pictures shown in the window can be found on CengageBrain.com. The names of the pictures are SmartPhone, Tablet, and DigitalCamera.

FIGURE 3-94

5 ●●
GUITAR STORE

Based on the Windows form mock-up you created in Chapter 2, complete the Guitar Store program by finishing the user interface, downloading and adding the images, and writing the code that will execute according to the program requirements shown in Figure 3-95. Before writing the code, create an event planning document for each event in the program.

REQUIREMENTS DOCUMENT

Date Submitted: March 21, 2015

Application Title: Guitar Store Application

Purpose: A local guitar store has three guitars on special this week. A customer can choose one of three guitar types. The program must display each of the guitars upon request. The customer can then select a guitar for purchase.

Program Procedures: From a window on the screen, the user selects one of three guitars. A picture of the selected guitar is displayed in the window. The user then can choose a guitar for purchase.

Algorithms, Processing, and Conditions:
1. The user selects a guitar. Then, a picture of the guitar is displayed in the window.
2. The user can select any of the three guitars. Only the picture of the selected guitar should be displayed.
3. The user can select guitars as many times as necessary and display the pictures of the guitars.
4. The user finds a guitar, chooses it for purchase, and taps or clicks the Purchase button.
5. After the user chooses a guitar, a message stating "Enjoy your guitar!" should be displayed.
6. After the user chooses a guitar, the only allowable action is to exit the window.

Notes and Restrictions: The user should not be able to choose a guitar until viewing at least one guitar image.

Comments:
1. The available guitars are classical acoustic, steel-string acoustic, and electric.
2. The pictures shown in the window can be found on CengageBrain.com. The names of the pictures are Classical, Electric, and Steel.

FIGURE 3-95

6 ●●
SONG VOTING

Based on the Windows form mock-up you created in Chapter 2, complete the Song Voting program by finishing the user interface, downloading and adding the images, and writing the code that will execute according to the program requirements shown in Figure 3-96. Before writing the code, create an event planning document for each event in the program.

REQUIREMENTS DOCUMENT

Date Submitted:	February 22, 2015
Application Title:	Song Voting Application
Purpose:	In your mall, a music store named Millennium Music wants an application that shows the #1 song in each of three music genres and allows users to vote for their overall favorite. The user should be able to select one of three music genres and then vote for one.
Program Procedures:	From a window on the screen, the user selects one of three music genres. The name of the #1 song in the selected genre is displayed with a picture of the performing artist or band. Then, the user can vote for that song or genre as his or her overall favorite.
Algorithms, Processing, and Conditions:	1. The user selects a music genre. The title of the #1 song in that genre and a picture of the artist or band are displayed in the window. 2. The user can select any of the three music genres. Only the name of the song and the picture for the selected genre should be displayed. 3. The user can select music genres as many times as necessary to see the #1 song for each genre and the associated artist or band. 4. After selecting a genre, the user should be able to vote for that genre and song as the favorite. The user can vote only after selecting a genre. 5. After the user votes, a message confirming the vote should be displayed.
Notes and Restrictions:	The user should only be able to vote after selecting a musical genre.
Comments:	1. You (the developer) should select the three music genres and the #1 song for each of the genres. 2. The pictures of the artist or band will depend on your selection of music genres and the #1 song in those genres. You should download pictures of artists or bands from the web. You can search anywhere on the web for the pictures. You will find that *www.google.com/images* is a good source.

FIGURE 3-96

Case Programming Assignments

7 ●●● AIRLINE SNACK SELECTION

Based on the problem definition (Figure 3-97) and the Windows form mock-up you created in Chapter 2, complete the airline snack selection program by finishing the user interface, downloading and adding any required images, and writing the code that will execute according to the program requirements. Before writing the code, create an event planning document for each event in the program.

An international airline requests a computer application that will run on the personal television monitors on the back of each seat in the plane. The application should request which free snack you would like during the flight, display the choices as buttons, and then display an image of the snack you select. Another button allows you to make your final snack selection and display a confirmation message.

Snack
Cheese & Crackers
Chocolate Chip Cookies
Mini Pretzels
Salted Peanuts

FIGURE 3-97

Case Programming Assignments

8 ●●●
TRAVEL SPECIALS

Based on the problem definition (Figure 3-98) and the Windows form mock-up you created in Chapter 2, complete the Travel Specials program by finishing the user interface, downloading and adding any required images, and writing the code that will execute according to the program requirements. Before writing the code, create an event planning document for each event in the program.

Your local travel agent requests a computer application that advertises the travel specials of the week from your city. This week's flight specials are:

Destination	Price
New York City	$399 round trip
Las Vegas	$419 round trip
Miami	$520 round trip
St. Thomas	$619 round trip
Hawaii	$828 round trip

Write an application that allows the user to select any of the five vacation destinations. When the user selects a vacation destination, the corresponding flight price and a picture of the destination should be displayed. Clear each prior price and picture when the user selects a different vacation destination. In addition to a picture of the destination, include a Web page address that features the selected location. After selecting a destination, the user should be able to book the flight and then exit the window.

FIGURE 3-98

9
LACROSSE TICKETS

Based on the problem definition (Figure 3-99) and the Windows form mock-up you created in Chapter 2, complete the Lacrosse Tickets program by finishing the user interface, downloading and adding any required images, and writing the code that will execute according to the program requirements. Before writing the code, create an event planning document for each event in the program.

Your favorite university lacrosse team has asked you to develop a Windows application that allows the user to see the four types of game tickets offered, one at a time. Then, the user should be able to reserve a single game ticket for the selected seat type. The four types of stadium seating and their base prices are as follows:

Name of Ticket	Minimum Price
Upper Endline Seating	$15.00
Lower Endline Seating	$25.00
Sideline Seating	$30.00
Club Seats	$50.00

For each type of seating, your program should display the base price and a picture depicting an example of the seating type. Clear each price and picture when the user selects a different seating type. After selecting a ticket, the user should be able to purchase the ticket and then exit the window.

FIGURE 3-99

© 2014 Cengage Learning

CHAPTER 4
Variables and Arithmetic Operations

OBJECTIVES

You will have mastered the material in this chapter when you can:

- Create, modify, and program a TextBox object

- Use code to place data in the Text property of a Label object

- Use the AcceptButton and CancelButton properties

- Understand and declare String and Numeric variables

- Use assignment statements to place data in variables

- Use literals and constants in coding statements

- Understand scope rules for variables

- Convert string and numeric data

- Understand and use arithmetic operators and arithmetic operations

- Format and display numeric data as a string

- Create a form load event

- Create a concatenated string

- Debug a program

Introduction

In the Pizza Selection program you developed in Chapter 2 and Chapter 3, you tapped or clicked buttons in the user interface to trigger events, but you did not enter data. In many applications, users must enter data that the program then uses in its processing.

When processing data entered by a user, a common requirement is to perform arithmetic operations on the data to generate useful output. Arithmetic operations include adding, subtracting, multiplying, and dividing numeric data.

To illustrate user data input and arithmetic operations, the application in this chapter allows the user to specify a number of songs to download from the World Wide Web. The application then calculates the total cost of downloading the files. The user interface for the program is shown in Figure 4-1.

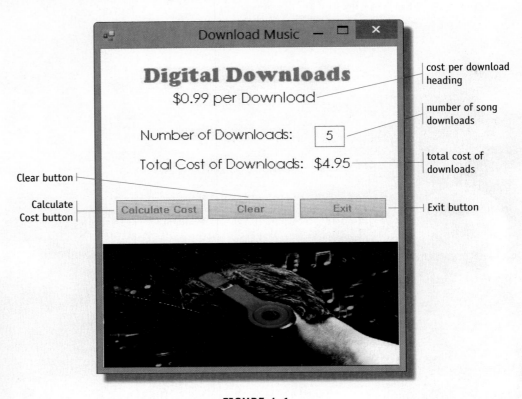

FIGURE 4-1
© Luca Pierro PHOTOGRAPHY/Flickr/Getty Images

In Figure 4-1, the user entered 5 as the number of songs to download. When the user tapped or clicked the Calculate Cost button, the program multiplied 5 by the cost per song (99 cents) and then displayed the result as the total cost of downloads. When the user taps or clicks the Clear button, the values for the number of song downloads and the total cost of downloads are cleared so the next user can enter a value. Tapping or clicking the Exit button closes the window and terminates the program.

To create this application, the developer must understand how to perform the following processes, among others:

1. Define a text box for data entry.
2. Define a label to hold the results of arithmetic operations.
3. Convert data in a text box to data that can be used for arithmetic operations.
4. Perform arithmetic operations on data entered by a user.

The following pages describe the tools and techniques required to create the program shown in Figure 4-1.

Design the User Interface

As you have learned in Chapter 2 and Chapter 3, the next step after completing the program requirements document for an application is to define the graphical user interface. In this chapter, three new elements are introduced:

- TextBox objects
- Labels intended for variable text property values
- Accept buttons

Each of these elements is described in the following sections.

TextBox Objects

A **TextBox object** allows users to enter data into a program. In Figure 4-2, the user can enter a value into the text box.

FIGURE 4-2

In Figure 4-2 on the previous page, the TextBox object is placed on the Windows Form object. A TextBox object automatically allows the user to enter data in the text box. To place a TextBox object on the Windows Form object, you can complete the following steps. (Note that the examples in this chapter illustrate new objects in the user interface. Portions of the user interface have already been completed for you. You should not expect to "tap or click along" with these examples unless you create all the elements or follow the steps using an unformatted user interface.)

STEP 1 With Visual Studio open, the Digital Downloads Windows application created, and the frmDownloads.vb [Design] tabbed page visible, point to the TextBox .NET component in the Toolbox.

The TextBox .NET component is highlighted in the Toolbox (Figure 4-3).

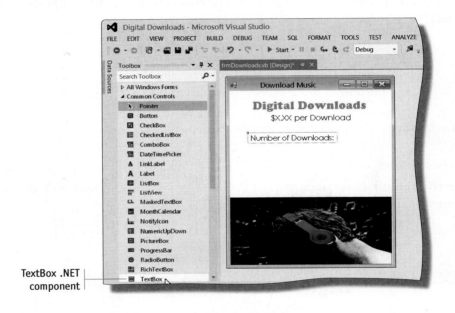

TextBox .NET component

FIGURE 4-3
© Luca Pierro PHOTOGRAPHY/Flickr/Getty Images

STEP 2 Drag the TextBox .NET component onto the Windows Form object at the desired location.

While you drag, the mouse pointer changes to indicate a TextBox object will be placed on the Windows Form object (Figure 4-4). Snap lines indicate where the TextBox object aligns with other objects on the Windows Form object. In Figure 4-4, the bottom of the TextBox object aligns with the bottom of the Label object. When adding a TextBox object to the Windows Form object, bottom alignment often provides a good beginning position.

upper-left corner
of pointer

snap line

pointer

FIGURE 4-4
© Luca Pierro PHOTOGRAPHY/Flickr/Getty Images

STEP 3 When the upper-left corner of the pointer is located where you want to place the TextBox object's upper-left corner, release the left mouse button.

Visual Studio places the TextBox object at the location identified by the mouse pointer (Figure 4-5). The default size of the TextBox object is 100 pixels wide by 22 pixels high. Notice that by default the TextBox object contains no text. You can change that by entering text in the Text property of the TextBox object.

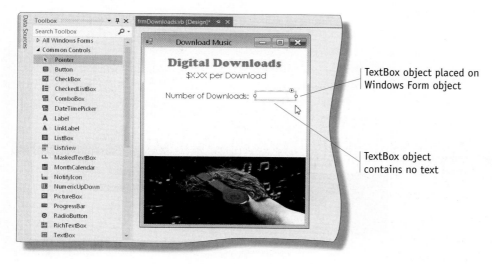

TextBox object placed on
Windows Form object

TextBox object
contains no text

FIGURE 4-5
© Luca Pierro PHOTOGRAPHY/Flickr/Getty Images

ONLINE REINFORCEMENT

To view a video of the process in the preceding steps, visit CengageBrain.com and navigate to the resources for this title. Tap or click the link for Chapter 4 and then navigate to Video 4-2.

As you have learned, whenever you place an object on the Windows Form object, you must name the object. When naming a TextBox object, the prefix should be txt. Therefore, the name of the TextBox object in Figure 4-5 on the previous page could be txtNumberOfDownloads.

Size and Position a TextBox Object

To properly place a TextBox object on the Windows Form object, you need to know the minimum and maximum size of the text box. The minimum size normally is determined by the maximum number of characters the user will enter into the text box. For example, if the user can enter 999 in the sample program as the maximum number of downloads, the minimum size of the text box must be large enough to display three numbers. Although it can be larger, it should not be smaller.

The maximum size of the text box often is determined by the design of the user interface; that is, the size should "look and feel good" in the user interface. To determine the minimum size of the text box, you can use the technique in the following steps:

STEP 1   Select the TextBox object. Select the (Name) property and name the TextBox object `txtNumberOfDownloads`. Scroll in the Properties window until the Text property is visible and then tap or click the right column for the Text property.

The TextBox object is selected, as shown by the thick border and sizing handles (Figure 4-6). The TextBox object is named txtNumberOfDownloads. The Text property for the TextBox object is highlighted and the insertion point indicates you can enter text for the Text property.

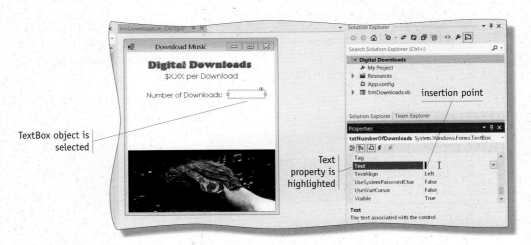

FIGURE 4-6

STEP 2   Type the maximum number of characters the user normally will enter into the text box and then press the ENTER key. Programmers often use the digit 8 in this situation because it is wider than other digits. This example uses the value 888 because three digits is the maximum number the user normally will enter.

When the value is entered in the Text property of the TextBox object, the value is displayed in the TextBox object (Figure 4-7).

FIGURE 4-7

STEP 3   Using the Properties window, change the Font property to the correct font and font size. For this application, change the font to Century Gothic and change the font size to 11. Then, drag the right edge of the TextBox object and resize it to be slightly wider than the 888 entry.

As you drag, the size of the TextBox object changes (Figure 4-8). When you release the left mouse button, the text box will be resized. When the font size is changed, the horizontal alignment of the text will change.

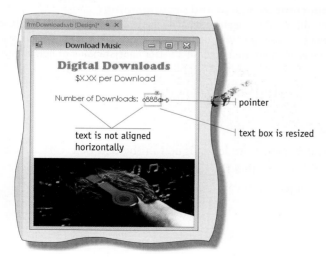

FIGURE 4-8

STEP 4   To horizontally align the text in the label and the text in the text box, drag the text box up until a red snap line indicates the bottoms of the text are aligned (Figure 4-9). Then, release the left mouse button.

As you drag the TextBox object, the red snap line indicates when the bottoms of the text are aligned (Figure 4-9). When you release the left mouse button, the TextBox object will be placed so the bottoms of the text are aligned.

FIGURE 4-9
© Luca Pierro PHOTOGRAPHY/Flickr/Getty Images

ONLINE REINFORCEMENT

To view a video of the process in the preceding steps, visit CengageBrain.com and navigate to the resources for this title. Tap or click the link for Chapter 4 and then navigate to Video 4-3.

Are smaller details like alignment important in design and programming?
The user interface is more important than ever with Windows application and mobile design. Many colleges teach entire courses on interface design. Remember, your users need consistency in your design layout. Language is another interface element that needs consistency. A consistent interface enables your users to have a better understanding of how things will work and increases their efficiency.

CONSIDER THIS

Align Text in a TextBox Object

In Figure 4-9, the numbers are left-aligned in the text box. Often, the user interface will be more useful if the value the user enters is centered in the text box. To align the text in a TextBox object, you can use the following method:

STEP 1   Select the TextBox object. In the Properties window, scroll until the TextAlign property is visible, tap or click the TextAlign property in the left column, and then tap or click the list arrow in the right column of the TextAlign property.

The TextAlign property list contains the values Left, Right, and Center (Figure 4-10).

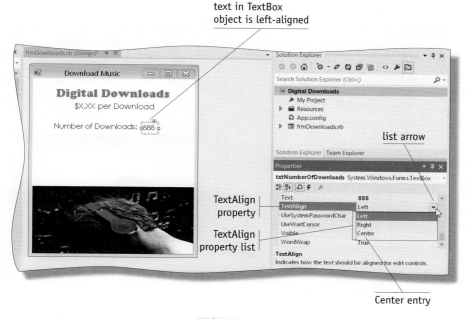

FIGURE 4-10

© Luca Pierro PHOTOGRAPHY/Flickr/Getty Images

STEP 2   Tap or click Center in the TextAlign property list.

The text in the TextBox object is centered (Figure 4-11). When a user enters data in the text box, the data also will be centered.

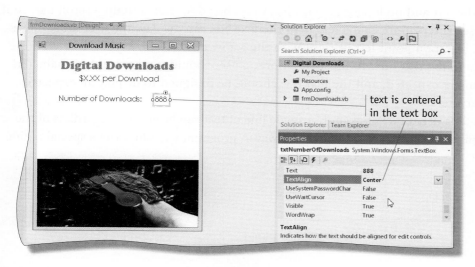

FIGURE 4-11

© Luca Pierro PHOTOGRAPHY/Flickr/Getty Images

STEP 3   Because the TextBox object is sized properly, remove the digits in the TextBox object. Select the characters 888 in the Text property, press the DELETE key on your keyboard, and then press the ENTER key.

The TextBox object contains no text and is ready for use in the user interface (Figure 4-12).

© Luca Pierro PHOTOGRAPHY/Flickr/Getty Images

FIGURE 4-12

Enter Data in a TextBox Object

When the program is executed, the user can enter data in the text box. Users can enter letters, numbers, and other characters. If the user enters more characters than the text box can display, the characters that have already been entered scroll to the left and no longer are visible. A text box does not contain a scroll bar, so if a user enters more characters than the text box can display, the user must move the insertion point left or right with the arrow keys on the keyboard to view the data in the text box. In most situations, a user should not enter more characters than are expected, and the text box should be designed to display all expected characters.

In a default text box, only a single line of text can be entered regardless of the number of characters in the line. However, programmers can select a special option for a text box to allow the user to enter multiple lines of text. Additionally, the MaskedTextBox object can be used to control the format of data that a user enters. These types of text boxes are explained in the following sections.

Create a MultiLine Text Box

A MultiLine text box allows the user to enter multiple lines in the text box. The TextBox object must be resized vertically to display the multiple lines. To create a TextBox object that can accept multiple lines, you can complete the following steps:

STEP 1   Select the TextBox object, tap or click the Action tag, and then point to the MultiLine check box.

The TextBox Tasks list is displayed with the MultiLine check box (Figure 4-13). When you tap or click the MultiLine check box, the TextBox object will be able to accept multiple lines.

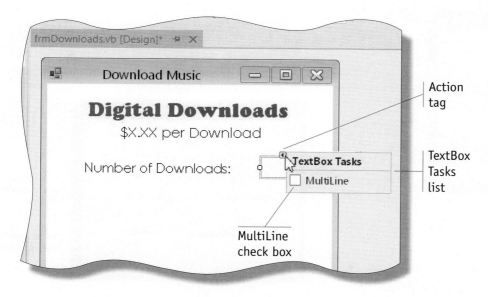

FIGURE 4-13

STEP 2   Tap or click the MultiLine check box.

The text box is enabled to accept multiple lines.

In addition to enabling multiple lines, you should increase the vertical size of the TextBox object so the multiple lines will be visible when the user enters them.

Create a MaskedTextBox Object

The MaskedTextBox object allows you to specify the data format of the value typed into the text box. Using the MaskedTextBox object removes confusion about which format should be used for data the user enters. The term *mask* refers to a predefined layout for the data. Figure 4-14 shows three examples of the MaskedTextBox used for the Short date input mask, the Phone number input mask, and the Social Security number input mask.

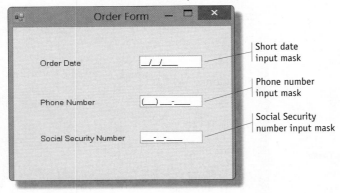

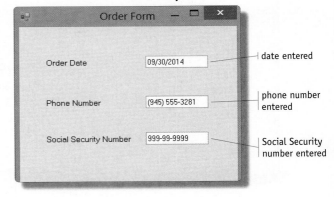

FIGURE 4-14

In Figure 4-14, before the user enters data, the mask demonstrates the format of the data to be entered. To enter data, the user selects the text box and then types data into it. The user need not enter punctuation or spacing. To enter the date in the Order Date text box, the user typed 09302014 with no spaces, punctuation, or other keystrokes. Similarly, for the phone number, the user typed 9455553281, again with no spaces or other keystrokes. For the Social Security number, the user typed 999999999.

To place a MaskedTextBox object on the Windows Form object, you can complete the following steps:

STEP 1 Drag a MaskedTextBox .NET component from the Toolbox to the Windows Form object. Then, tap or click the Action tag on the TextBox object and point to the Set Mask command.

The MaskedTextBox object is placed on the Windows Form object (Figure 4-15). When the Action tag is tapped or clicked, the MaskedTextBox Tasks list is displayed. The Set Mask command is the only command in the list.

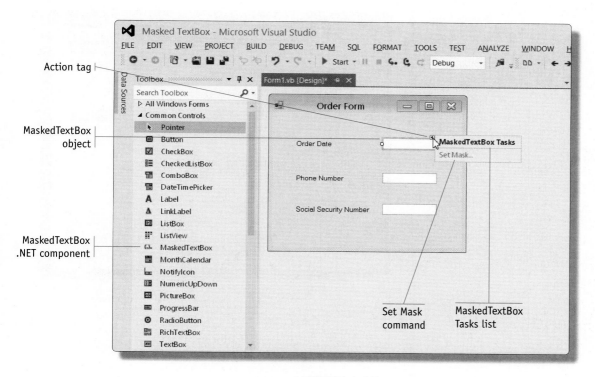

FIGURE 4-15

STEP 2 Tap or click Set Mask on the MaskedTextBox Tasks list and then tap or click the Short date mask description in the Input Mask dialog box.

Visual Studio displays the Input Mask dialog box (Figure 4-16). The Mask Description column contains all the masks that can be used for the MaskedTextBox object. The Short date mask description is highlighted. In the Preview box, you can type data to see how the mask will perform when it is used in the MaskedTextBox object. The Use Validating Type check box is selected to verify that the user entered valid numeric data.

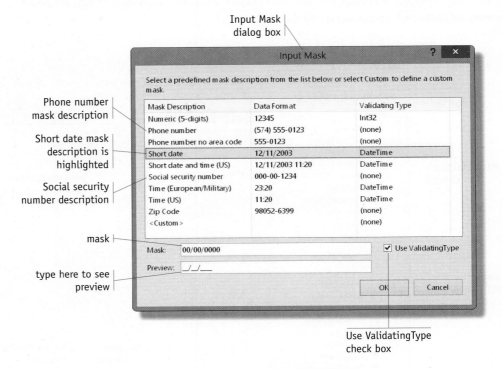

Input Mask dialog box

Phone number mask description

Short date mask description is highlighted

Social security number description

mask

type here to see preview

Use ValidatingType check box

FIGURE 4-16

STEP 3   Tap or click the OK button in the Input Mask dialog box and then tap or click anywhere in the Windows Form object.

The mask is placed in the MaskedTextBox object (Figure 4-17).

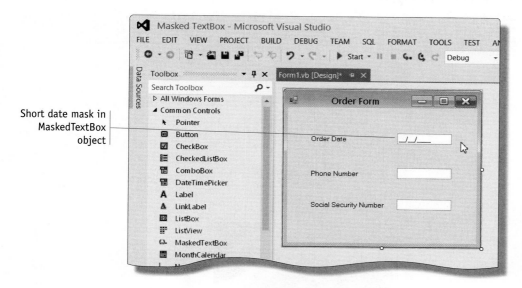

Short date mask in
MaskedTextBox
object

FIGURE 4-17

ONLINE REINFORCEMENT

To view a video of the process in the preceding steps, visit CengageBrain.com and navigate to the resources for this title. Tap or click the link for Chapter 4 and then navigate to Video 4-7.

You can use the same technique to place the phone number and Social Security number in the MaskedTextBox.

Label Objects

In the sample program, a Label object is used to display the total cost of downloads (see Figure 4-1 on page 190). The developer must accomplish two tasks to prepare the label for this purpose: Place the label on the Windows Form object in the correct location, and then ensure that when the Label object contains its maximum value, its location will work within the user interface design.

To accomplish these two tasks, you can complete the steps on the next page:

STEP 1   Drag a Label object onto the Windows Form object to the correct location. Name the label `lblTotalCost`. Change the label to the appropriate font and size (Century Gothic, 11 points). In the Text property for the Label object, enter the maximum number of characters ($888.88) that will appear in the label during execution of the program.

The properly sized characters appear in the label (Figure 4-18). The label is aligned vertically, but should be moved up to align horizontally with the Total Cost of Downloads label.

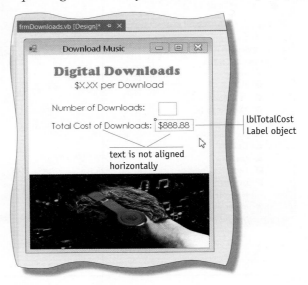

FIGURE 4-18
© Luca Pierro PHOTOGRAPHY/Flickr/Getty Images

STEP 2   Drag the Label object up until the red snap line appears (Figure 4-19). Then release the left mouse button.

The label is aligned (Figure 4-19).

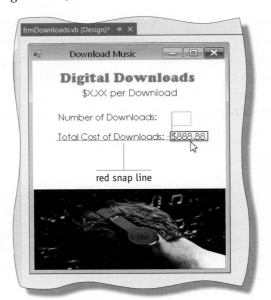

FIGURE 4-19
© Luca Pierro PHOTOGRAPHY/Flickr/Getty Images

ONLINE REINFORCEMENT

To view a video of the process in the preceding steps, visit CengageBrain.com and navigate to the resources for this title. Tap or click the link for Chapter 4 and then navigate to Video 4-8.

When program execution begins, the label that will contain the total cost of downloads should be blank. In Figure 4-19, however, it contains the value in the Text property of the Label object ($888.88). If the Text property in a Label object is set to hold no content, it will not be displayed in the Windows Form object during the design phase, which makes the Label object difficult to work with in Design mode. Therefore, most designers place a value in the Text property of the Label object and leave it there during user interface design. Then, when the program begins, the label Text property will be set to blank. You will learn to perform this task later in the chapter.

Accept Button in Form Properties

Computer users often press the ENTER key to enter data in a text box and cause processing to occur. For instance, in the sample program for this chapter, users might prefer to type the number of downloads and press the ENTER key instead of typing the number and tapping or clicking the Calculate Cost button.

You can assign a button to be an Accept button in the user interface, which means the program will carry out the event handler processing associated with the button if the user taps or clicks it or presses the ENTER key. To assign the Calculate Cost button as the Accept button, you can complete the following steps:

STEP 1   After the Button objects are added, tap or click a blank area in the Windows Form object to select it. Scroll in the Properties window until the Accept-Button property is visible. Tap or click the AcceptButton property name in the left column and then tap or click the AcceptButton property list arrow in the right column.

The AcceptButton property list displays the names of the Button objects on the selected Windows Form object (Figure 4-20). Any of these buttons can be specified as the Accept button.

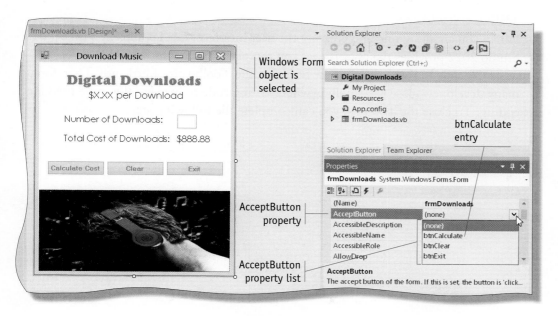

FIGURE 4-20

© Luca Pierro PHOTOGRAPHY/Flickr/Getty Images

STEP 2 Tap or click btnCalculate in the AcceptButton property list.

The btnCalculate Button object is designated as the Accept button. When the program is running, the user can press the ENTER key after entering data to execute the event handler processing for the Calculate Cost button.

Cancel Button in Form Properties

In the same manner as the Accept button, you can designate a Cancel button for the Windows Form object. When the user presses the esc key, the event handler processing will be executed for the button identified as the Cancel button. In the sample program, the Cancel button will be used to clear the text box and the total cost of downloads and place the insertion point in the text box. Thus, it performs the same activity that occurs when the user taps or clicks the Clear button. To specify the Cancel button for the sample program, you complete the following steps:

Step 1: Tap or click a blank area in the Windows Form object to select it.

Step 2: Tap or click the CancelButton property name in the left column of the Properties window for the Windows Form object, and then tap or click the CancelButton list arrow.

Step 3: Tap or click the button name (btnClear) in the CancelButton property list.

When the program is executed, the user can press the esc key to perform the same processing as when the Clear button is tapped or clicked.

Visual Studio Preparation for Code Entry

When you are designing and creating the user interface, the Toolbox in Visual Studio 2012 provides the objects that you can place in the interface. When you write the code in the code window, however, the Toolbox is of little use. Therefore, many developers close the Toolbox when writing code to increase the space used for coding. To close the Toolbox, you can complete the following step:

STEP 1   With the Toolbox visible (Figure 4-21), tap or click the Toolbox Close button. The Toolbox closes and the work area expands in size. To display the Toolbox after it has been closed, tap or click the VIEW menu and then tap or click Toolbox.

Figure 4-21 illustrates the screen before the Toolbox is closed. The Toolbox Close button is visible.

Toolbox Close button

FIGURE 4-21

© Luca Pierro PHOTOGRAPHY/Flickr/Getty Images

In the following sections, the Toolbox has been closed in the windows that show code.

Introduction to Data Entry and Data Types

As you have seen, the user can enter data into the program by using the TextBox object. When the user enters data, it becomes the value stored in the Text property of the object. For example, if the user enters 15 as the number of downloads, the Text property for the txtNumberOfDownloads TextBox object will contain the value 15.

String Data Type

When data is stored in RAM, it is stored as a particular data type. Each data type allows data to be used in a specific manner. For example, to add two values together, the values must be stored in one of the numeric data types. The **String** data type is used for values that the user enters in a TextBox object and that are stored in the Text property of the TextBox object. A String data type can store any character available on the computer.

When the user enters data into a TextBox object, it is good programming style to copy the entered value from the Text property of the TextBox object to a String variable. A **variable** is a named location in RAM where data is stored. A **String variable** is a named location in RAM that can store a string value. Thus, a person's name, a dollar amount, a telephone number, or the number of song downloads can be stored in a String variable.

The programmer defines a variable during the coding of the program. The statement in Figure 4-22 defines a string.

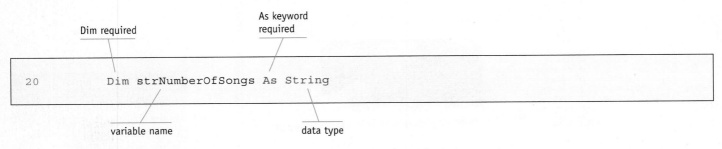

FIGURE 4-22

© 2014 Cengage Learning

To begin the statement, the keyword Dim is required. This keyword stands for *variable dimension*. It indicates to the Visual Basic compiler that the entries after Dim are defining a variable.

The next entry is the variable name. Every variable must have a name so it can be referenced in other statements within the program. By convention, every String variable name begins with the letters str followed by a descriptive name. The name in Figure 4-22 (strNumberOfSongs) indicates a String variable that will contain the number of songs entered by the user.

The keyword As must follow the name of the variable, as shown in Figure 4-22. If it is not included, a compilation error will occur. Following the word As is the declaration for the variable's data type. In Figure 4-22, the data type is specified as String.

As a result of the statement in Figure 4-22, when the program is compiled, the Visual Basic compiler will allocate an area in RAM that is reserved to contain the value in the string.

The general format to define a variable is shown in Figure 4-23.

General Format: Define a Variable

```
Dim VariableName As DataType
```

EXAMPLE	RESULT
Dim strNumberOfSongs As String	String variable
Dim intNumberOfSongs As Integer	Integer variable
Dim decFinalCosts As Decimal	Decimal variable

FIGURE 4-23

© 2014 Cengage Learning

HEADS UP

When defining variables, good programming practice dictates that the variable names should reflect the actual values to be placed in the variable. That way, anyone reading the program code can easily understand the use of the variable. For example, a good name for a String variable that contains an employee's last name would be strEmployeeLastName. You should not use names like strXXX, strLN, strEmp, or strName. Each of these names is imprecise and potentially misleading. You should consider the people who will read your code when you name the variables in your program. Your goal must be to make their task as clear and easy as possible.

The Integer and Decimal variables defined as examples in Figure 4-23 are numeric variables. You will learn about numeric variables shortly.

Assignment Statements

When a variable is defined as shown in Figure 4-22, the variable does not contain any data. One method used to place data in the variable is an **assignment statement**. The assignment statement shown in Figure 4-24 will copy the data from the Text property of the txtNumberOfDownloads TextBox object into the strNumberOfSongs String variable.

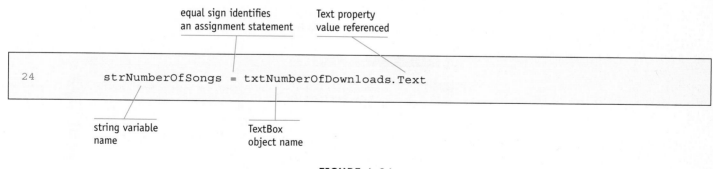

```
24        strNumberOfSongs = txtNumberOfDownloads.Text
```

equal sign identifies an assignment statement

Text property value referenced

string variable name

TextBox object name

FIGURE 4-24

© 2014 Cengage Learning

The variable name to the left of the assignment statement (strNumberOfSongs) identifies the variable to which a value will be copied. The equal sign indicates to the Visual Basic compiler that the statement is an assignment statement. The equal sign is required.

The value to the right of the equal sign will be copied to the variable to the left of the equal sign. In Figure 4-24, the value in the Text property of the txtNumberOfDownloads TextBox object will be copied to the strNumberOfSongs variable.

To enter the definition of the strNumberOfSongs variable and then enter the assignment statement in Figure 4-24 on the previous page using IntelliSense, you can complete the following steps:

STEP 1 With Visual Studio open to the code window and the insertion point located in the desired column, type `Dim` followed by a space. Then, type the name of the String variable you want to define, `strNumberOfSongs`.

The Dim keyword and the string name you typed are displayed in the code window (Figure 4-25). Notice that Dim is blue to indicate it is a keyword.

name of
String variable

Dim keyword

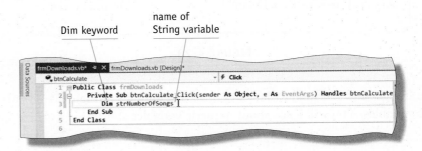

FIGURE 4-25

STEP 2 Press the SPACEBAR, type the word `As`, and then press the SPACEBAR again.

The letters you typed are entered. When you typed the space following the word As, IntelliSense displayed a list (Figure 4-26). The list contains all the allowable entries that can follow the As keyword. To define a String variable, the correct entry is String.

As keyword

IntelliSense list

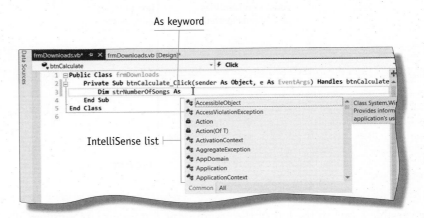

FIGURE 4-26

STEP 3 Because the correct entry is String, type `str`.

IntelliSense highlights String in the list (Figure 4-27).

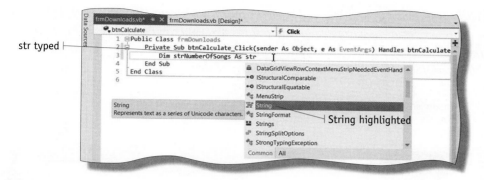

str typed ⊢

String highlighted

FIGURE 4-27

STEP 4 Press the ENTER key.

The Dim statement is entered (Figure 4-28). The green squiggly underline indicates the variable is not referenced within the program. Visual Studio will remove the underline when the variable is used in an assignment statement or other statement.

variable not referenced

Dim statement is complete

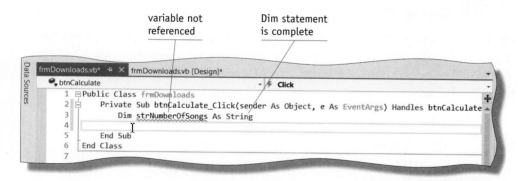

FIGURE 4-28

STEP 5   To begin the assignment statement, type strn. IntelliSense displays the only variable name that starts with the letters strn, which is the String variable strNumberOfSongs.

IntelliSense displays a list of allowable entries for the statement (Figure 4-29). Whenever you want to reference a variable name in a statement, you can type the first few letters of the name to have IntelliSense display a list of allowable entries. The variable name strNumberOfSongs is highlighted because you typed strn.

IntelliSense
list

strn typed

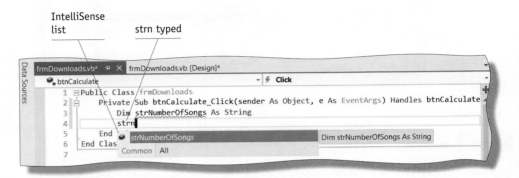

FIGURE 4-29

STEP 6   Press the SPACEBAR, press the EQUAL SIGN key, and then press the SPACEBAR.

IntelliSense enters the highlighted variable name, the spaces, and the equal sign you typed (Figure 4-30). The spaces are not required in Visual Basic but should be included in the statement for ease of reading. An IntelliSense list automatically appears and displays the possible valid entries.

IntelliSense entered
the variable name

equal sign and
spaces

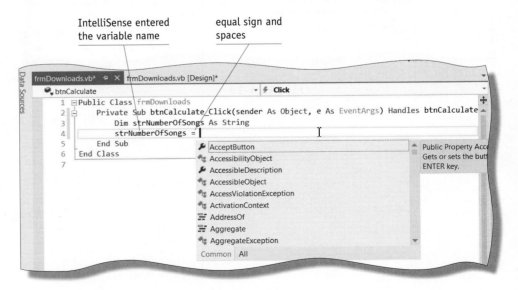

FIGURE 4-30

STEP 7   Type `txt` to display the IntelliSense list of Form objects, and then type `n` to identify the txtNumberOfDownloads TextBox object in the IntelliSense list.

The IntelliSense list contains the valid entries for the statement; in this case, only one object has the prefix of txt. The TextBox object txtNumberOfDownloads is highlighted in the list (Figure 4-31).

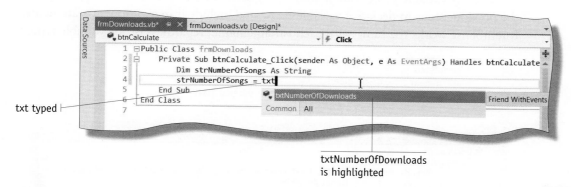

FIGURE 4-31

STEP 8   Press the PERIOD key. If necessary, next type `te` to highlight the Text entry in the IntelliSense list.

After the dot operator (period) and the txtNumberOfDownloads object name are entered, Visual Studio displays the IntelliSense list (Figure 4-32). When you typed te, the Text entry was highlighted in the IntelliSense list.

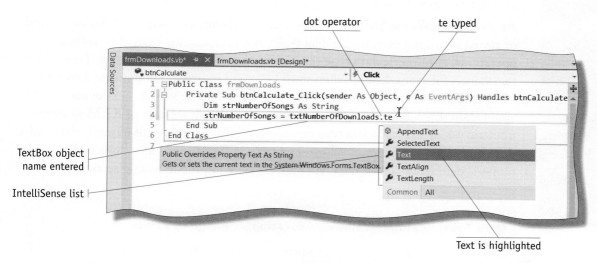

FIGURE 4-32

STEP 9 Press the ENTER key.

The assignment statement is entered (Figure 4–33). When the statement is executed, the value in the Text property of the txtNumberOfDownloads TextBox object will be copied to the location in memory identified by the strNumberOfSongs variable name. Notice also that the green squiggly lines in the Dim statement are removed because the variable now is referenced in a statement.

For any variable you define within a program, you can use the method shown in the previous steps to declare a variable name and include it in assignment statements. IntelliSense works the same with each variable name, regardless of the variable type.

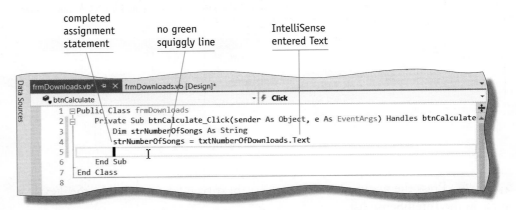

FIGURE 4-33

HEADS UP

IntelliSense has different rules for entering object names and variable names into a Visual Basic statement. To enter the name of an object that has been defined in the user interface, type the prefix. To enter a variable name you have declared in the program, type the first few letters of the variable name. In each case, IntelliSense will display a list of the allowable entries.

Numeric Data Types

As you will recall, the String data type can contain any character that can be entered or stored on a computer. String data types, however, cannot be used in arithmetic operations. A **numeric data type** must be used in arithmetic operations. To multiply two values, for example, the values must be stored in one of the numeric data types.

Visual Basic allows a variety of numeric data types depending on the need of the application. Each numeric data type requires a different amount of RAM to store the numeric value, and each data type can contain a different form of numeric data and a different maximum range of values. The table in Figure 4-34 lists three widely used numeric data types. These data types are explained in the following sections.

Data Type	Sample Value	Memory Allocation	Range of Values
Integer	48	4 bytes	−2,147,483,648 to +2,147,483,647
Decimal	3.14519	16 bytes	Decimal values that may have up to 28 significant digits
Double	5.3452307 or 673.6529	8 bytes	−1.79769313486232e308 to +1.79769313486232e308

FIGURE 4-34

Integer Data Type

An **Integer data type** holds a nondecimal whole number in Visual Basic. As you can see from Figure 4-34, an Integer data type can store a value that is greater or less than 2 billion. Examples of integers include the number of songs to download, the number of credit hours you are taking in a semester, and the number of points your favorite football team scored. Notice that each of these examples is a whole number.

Normally, an Integer data type is stored in an Integer variable. An **Integer variable** identifies a location in RAM where an integer value is stored. To define an Integer variable and place a value in the variable, you can use the Dim statement and the assignment statement, as shown in Figure 4-35.

```
6          Dim intNumberOfSongs As Integer
7          intNumberOfSongs = 34
```

FIGURE 4-35

The Dim statement in Figure 4-35 is similar to the Dim statement used to define the String variable (Figure 4-28 on page 211), except that the variable name begins with the prefix int and the word Integer follows the word As. Four bytes of RAM will be reserved for any value that is stored in the intNumberOfSongs Integer variable as a result of the Dim statement in Figure 4-35.

The definition in Figure 4-35 will not place a value in the intNumberOfSongs variable. To place a value in the variable, you can use an assignment statement. Enter the intNumberOfSongs variable that will hold the value on the left side of the equal sign, and enter the value to be placed in the variable (34) on the right side of the equal sign. When the statement is executed, the value 34 will be copied to the RAM location identified by the variable name intNumberOfSongs.

You also can place an initial value in the variable. For example, to define an Integer variable to hold the number of credit hours you are taking and to place the value 12 in that variable, you could write the Dim statement in Figure 4-36.

HEADS UP

Visual Basic 2012 now allows you to omit the data type without causing an error. For example, entering Dim intValue = 1 does not produce an error because the compiler infers that the value of intValue is an Integer data type. This feature is called type inference. While you are learning how to write programs, it is best to use the data types so you can understand the changes as you convert one data type to another.

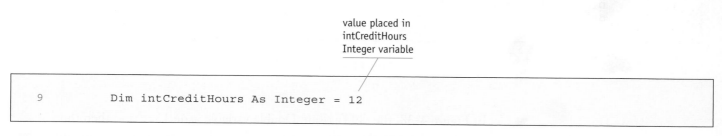

```
                              value placed in
                              intCreditHours
                              Integer variable

9          Dim intCreditHours As Integer = 12
```

FIGURE 4-36

The statement in Figure 4-36 defines the Integer variable named intCreditHours. The equal sign after the word Integer indicates to the Visual Basic compiler that the value to the right of the equal sign should be placed in the variable. The value 12 will be placed in the intCreditHours Integer variable when the program is compiled.

Decimal Data Type

A **Decimal data type** accurately represents large or very precise decimal numbers. It is ideal for use in the accounting and scientific fields to ensure that numbers keep their precision and are not subject to rounding errors. The Decimal data type can be accurate to 28 significant digits. (Significant digits are those that contribute to the precision of a number.) Often, Decimal data types are used to store dollar amounts. For example, to define the Decimal variable for the total cost of downloads in the sample program, you can use the statement in Figure 4-37.

```
22          Dim decTotalCostOfDownloads As Decimal
```

FIGURE 4-37

HEADS UP

A Double data type represents numbers in a way that might not be precisely correct. For example, the value 0.07875 might be represented as 0.078749999999 in the Double data type. Therefore, when exact precision is required, the Decimal data type is preferred over the Double data type. The Double data type does have advantages, however; it can store a much larger or much smaller number than the Decimal data type, and it requires only 8 bytes of memory for each variable as opposed to 16 bytes for each Decimal variable.

The Dim statement is used to define the Decimal variable. The dec prefix is used for all Decimal variable names. When the compiler processes the statement in Figure 4-37, 16 bytes of RAM will be reserved for a value to be placed in the decTotalCostOfDownloads variable. Initially, no value will be present in the variable unless you specify a value, as shown in Figure 4-36 on the previous page. You can use an assignment statement to place data into the decTotalCostOfDownloads variable.

Double Data Type

A **Double data type** can represent huge positive numbers and very small negative numbers that can include values to the right of the decimal point. Sometimes, a Double data type is said to represent floating-point numbers, which means the decimal point can be anywhere within the number. The Dim statement in Figure 4-38 declares a Double variable that could be used in a tax application.

```
13          Dim dblTaxRate As Double
14          dblTaxRate = 0.07875
```

FIGURE 4-38

In Figure 4-38, the dblTaxRate Double variable is declared and then the assignment statement places the value 0.07875 in the memory location identified by the variable name. Note that a Double variable begins with the dbl prefix.

Other Data Types

Visual Basic supports other data types that are used for more specialized situations. Two widely used data types are Char and Boolean (Figure 4-39).

Data Type	Sample Value	Memory Allocation	Range of Values
Char	A single character such as ? or M	2 bytes	Any single character
Boolean	True or False	2 bytes	True or False

FIGURE 4-39

© 2014 Cengage Learning

Char Data Type

The **Char data type** represents a single keystroke such as a letter of the alphabet, a punctuation mark, or a symbol. The prefix for a Char variable name is chr. When you assign a value to a Char variable, you must place quotation marks around the value. For example, in Figure 4-40, the value A is assigned to the chrTopGrade Char variable.

```
16        Dim chrTopGrade As Char
17        chrTopGrade = "A"
```

FIGURE 4-40

© 2014 Cengage Learning

The value A in the assignment statement has quotation marks around it. In addition, Visual Studio displays the letter and the quotation marks in red text, indicating they are not Visual Basic keywords, variable names, or object names. In fact, the value is called a literal. You will learn more about literals shortly.

Visual Studio allows 65,534 different characters in a program. These characters consist of numbers, letters, and punctuation symbols. In addition, a wide variety of technical characters, mathematical symbols, and worldwide textual characters are available, which allows developers to work in almost every known language, including Korean (Figure 4-41). These characters are represented by a coding system called Unicode. To learn more about Unicode, visit *www.unicode.org*.

유니코드에 대해 ?

어떤 플랫폼,
어떤 프로그램,
어떤 언어에도 상관없이
유니코드는 모든 문자에 대해 고유 번호를 제공합니다.

FIGURE 4-41

© 2014 Cengage Learning

Even though you can assign a number to a Char variable, it cannot be used in arithmetic operations. A number to be used in an arithmetic operation must be assigned a numeric variable.

Boolean Data Type

A Boolean data variable can contain a value that Visual Basic interprets as either true or false. A Boolean variable name begins with the bln prefix. If a variable in your program should represent whether a condition is true or not true, then the variable should be Boolean. In Figure 4-42, a Boolean variable called blnFullTimeStudent is declared and then the assignment statement sets the Boolean variable to True.

```
19        Dim blnFullTimeStudent As Boolean
20        blnFullTimeStudent = True
```

FIGURE 4-42

© 2014 Cengage Learning

In Figure 4-42, the Dim statement is used to declare the blnFullTimeStudent Boolean variable. The assignment statement sets the Boolean variable to True. This variable can be checked in the program to determine whether it is true or false, and appropriate processing can occur as a result.

Miscellaneous Data Types

Visual Basic has several other data types that are used less often than the ones you have seen so far. These data types are summarized in the table in Figure 4-43.

Data Type	Sample Value	Memory Allocation	Range of Values
Byte	A whole number such as 7	1 bytes	0 to 255
Date	April 22, 2014	8 bytes	Dates and times
Long	A whole number such as 342,534,538	8 bytes	−9,223,372,036,854,775,808 through +9,223,372,036,854,775,807
Object	Holds a reference	4 bytes	A memory address
Short	A whole number such as 16,546	2 bytes	−32,786 through 32,767
Single	A number such as 312,672.3274	4 bytes	$-3.4028235\text{E}+38$ through $1.401298\text{E}-45$ for negative values; and from $1.401298\text{E}-45$ through $3.4028235\text{E}+38$ for positive values

FIGURE 4-43

© 2014 Cengage Learning

As a review, the prefixes for each of the data type variable names are shown in Figure 4-44.

Data Type	Prefix
String	str
Integer	int
Decimal	dec
Double	dbl
Char	chr
Boolean	bln
Byte	byt
Date	dtm
Long	lng
Short	shr
Single	sng

FIGURE 4-44

© 2014 Cengage Learning

Literals

When an assignment statement includes a value like the one in Figure 4-38 on page 216 or Figure 4-40 on page 217, the value is called a **literal** because it literally is the value required by the assignment statement. It is not a variable. The Visual Basic compiler determines the data type of the value you use for a literal based on the value itself. For example, if you type "Chicago," the compiler treats the literal as a String data type, and if you type 49.327, the compiler treats the literal as a Double data type. The table in Figure 4-45 displays the default literal types as determined by the Visual Basic compiler.

Standard Literal Form	Default Data Type	Example
Numeric, no fractional part	Integer	104
Numeric, no fractional part, too large for Integer data type	Long	3987925494
Numeric, fractional part	Double	0.99 8.625
Enclosed within double quotes	String	"Brittany"
Enclosed within number signs	Date	#3/17/1990 3:30 PM#

FIGURE 4-45

© 2014 Cengage Learning

Forced Literal Types

Sometimes you might want a literal to be a different data type than the Visual Basic default type. For example, you may want to assign the number 0.99 to a Decimal data variable to take advantage of the precision of the Decimal data type. As you can see in Figure 4-45 on the previous page, Visual Basic will consider the value 0.99 a Double data type by default. To define the literal as a Decimal literal, you must use a special character to force Visual Basic to use a data type other than the default. Specifically, you place the literal-type character at the end of the literal value. The table in Figure 4-46 shows the available literal-type characters and examples of their use.

Literal-Type Character	Data Type	Example
S	Short	Dim shoAge As Short shoAge = 40S
I	Integer	Dim intHeight as Integer intHeight = 76I
D	Decimal	Dim decPricePerSong As Decimal decPricePerSong = 0.99D
R	Double	Dim dblWeight As Double dblWeight = 8491R
C	Char	Dim chrNumberOfDays As Char chrNumberOfDays = "7"C

FIGURE 4-46

© 2014 Cengage Learning

In the first example, the value 40 will be processed by Visual Basic as a Short data type literal, even though the value would be considered an Integer value by default. In the second example, the literal-type character confirms that the value should be treated as an Integer data type. In the third example, the value 0.99 will be processed as a Decimal data type, even though it would be considered a Double data type by default. In the next example, the value 8491 would be considered an Integer data value by default, but because the R literal-type character is used, Visual Basic will treat it as a Double data type. In the final example, the value 7 will be treated as a Char data type.

Constants

Recall that a variable identifies a location in memory where a value can be stored. By its nature, the value in a variable can be changed by statements within the program. For instance, in the sample program in this chapter, one user might request 5 downloads and another user might request 12 downloads; the value in the strNumberOfSongs variable can change based on the user's needs. In some instances, however, you might not want the value to be changed. For example, the price per download in the sample program is $0.99 per song. This value will not change, regardless of how many songs the user wants to download.

When a value will remain the same throughout the execution of the program, you should assign a meaningful name to a value. A **constant** contains one permanent value throughout the execution of the program. It cannot be changed by any statement within the program. To define a constant value, you can use the code in Figure 4-47.

```
12      Const cdecPricePerDownload As Decimal = 0.99D
```

FIGURE 4-47

© 2014 Cengage Learning

The following rules apply to a constant:

1. The declaration of a constant begins with the letters Const, not the letters Dim.
2. You must assign the value to be contained in the constant on the same line as its definition. In Figure 4-47, the value 0.99D is assigned to the constant on the same line as the Const definition.
3. You cannot attempt to change the value of the constant anywhere in the program. If you do, you will produce a compiler error.
4. The letter c often is placed before the constant name to identify it throughout the program as a variable that cannot be changed.
5. Other than the letter c, constant names are formed using the same rules and techniques as other variable names.

Using a named constant instead of a literal provides significant advantages:

1. The program becomes easier to read because the value is identified by the name. For example, instead of using the value 0.99D in a literal, you can use it in a constant called cdecPricePerDownload. This variable name describes the use of the value 0.99D and makes the program easier to read.
2. If you discover that a value must be changed in the code, it is much easier and more reliable to change the value one time in the constant as opposed to changing every occurrence of the value in a literal.

Reference a Variable

You learned earlier that when a variable is declared, it is underlined with a green squiggly line until it is referenced in a statement. This feature of Visual Basic is intended to ensure that you do not declare a variable and then forget to use it. It also helps ensure that you do not waste memory by declaring an unnecessary variable.

When using a variable in a program, it is mandatory that you define the variable before using the variable name in a statement. For example, the statements in Figure 4-48 *will cause an error* because the variable is used in an assignment statement before it is declared.

```
25        strNumberOfSongs = txtNumberOfDownloads.Text
26        Dim strNumberOfSongs As String
```

FIGURE 4-48

In the code in Figure 4-48, the variable strNumberOfSongs is referenced in an assignment statement (line 25) before it is defined (line 26). This creates a compile error, as indicated by the blue squiggly line beneath the variable name strNumberOfSongs on line 25. If you attempt to compile the statements on lines 25 and 26, you will receive a build error. Always define a variable before it is used in a statement.

Scope of Variables

When you declare a variable in Visual Basic, you not only declare the data type of the variable, you also implicitly define its scope. The **scope of a variable** specifies where the variable can be referenced in a Visual Basic statement within the program. In larger programs with multiple classes and forms, scope becomes critical, but it is important that you understand the concept at this point.

You declare a variable in a region within a program. For instance, in the sample program in this chapter, you can declare a variable in the tap or click event handler for the Calculate Cost button. You could declare another variable in the tap or click event handler for the Clear button. Scope determines where each of these variables can be referenced and used in the Visual Basic program. *The rule is: A variable can be referenced only within the region of the program where it is defined.* A region in the programs you have seen thus far in the book is the code between the Sub statement and the End Sub statement in the event handlers. The code between the Sub statement and the End Sub statement is a **procedure**.

Therefore, if you declare a variable within the tap or click event handler for the Calculate Cost button, that variable cannot be referenced in the tap or click event handler for the Clear button, and vice versa. A variable that can only be referenced within the region of the program where it is defined is called a **local variable**. This variable is defined in one region of the program and cannot be changed by a statement in another region of the program.

In addition, when a variable is defined in a procedure and the procedure ends, the values of the local variables within the procedure are destroyed. Thus, local variables have a certain **lifetime** in the program. They are only "alive" from the time the procedure begins until it ends. If the procedure is executed again, the value the variable once contained no longer is present. One execution of the procedure is a variable's lifetime. Therefore, if a user taps or clicks the Calculate Cost button, the values in the variables are valid until the tap or click event is completed. When the user taps or clicks the Calculate Cost button again, all values from the first tap or click are gone.

You can also define variables that can be used in multiple regions of a Visual Basic program. These variables are called **global variables**. In most programs, local variables should be used because they cause fewer errors than global variables.

Understanding the scope of a variable is important when developing a program. You will learn more about the scope of variables later in this chapter and throughout this book.

Convert Variable Data

Variables used in arithmetic statements in a Visual Basic program must be numeric. String variables cannot be used in an arithmetic statement. If you attempt to use them, you will create a compilation error.

A user often enters data in a text box. Data in the Text property of a TextBox object is treated as String data. Because String data cannot be used in an arithmetic statement, the String data entered by a user must be converted to numeric data before it can be used in an arithmetic statement.

For instance, in the sample program in this chapter, the user enters the number of songs to download. Before this number can be used in an arithmetic statement to determine the total cost of the downloads, the value must be converted to an Integer data type.

Visual Basic includes several procedures that allow you to convert one data type to another data type. You will recall that a procedure is a prewritten set of code that can be called by a statement in the Visual Basic program. When the procedure is called, it performs a particular task. In this case, the task is to convert the String value the user entered into an Integer data type that can be used in an arithmetic operation. One procedure that converts a String data type to an Integer data type is named ToInt32. The number 32 in the procedure name identifies that the representation of the integer will require 32 bits or 4 bytes, which is the amount of memory required for the Integer data type. The procedure is in the Convert class, which is available in a Visual Studio 2012 class library.

Use a Procedure

When you need to use a procedure to accomplish a task in your program, you must understand what the procedure does and how to code the procedure call in a program statement. A procedure can operate in one of two ways: It can perform its task and return a value, or it can perform its task without returning a value. You will recall in the Chapter 3 sample program that the Close() procedure closed the window and terminated the program. The procedure performed its task but did not return a value. A procedure of this type is called a **Sub procedure**.

In the Digital Downloads program in this chapter, the requirement is to convert the String value for the number of songs the user enters into an Integer data type. Then it can be used in an arithmetic operation. Therefore, the procedure must return a value (the Integer value for the number of songs). A procedure that returns a value is called a **Function procedure**, or a **function**.

In addition, a procedure might require data to be passed to it when called in order to carry out its processing. In the sample program in this chapter, the Function procedure to convert a String variable to an Integer variable first must be able to access the String variable. Therefore, in the statement that calls the Function procedure, the variable name for the String variable to be converted must be passed to the procedure. A value is passed to a procedure through the use of an argument.

An **argument** identifies a value required by a procedure. To pass the argument to the procedure, include its name within parentheses following the name of the procedure in the calling statement. For example, to pass the value stored in the strNumberOfSongs variable to the ToInt32 procedure, you could use the statement in Figure 4-49.

argument

```
...ToInt32(strNumberOfSongs)
```

name of
procedure

FIGURE 4-49

The name of the procedure is ToInt32. The argument is strNumberOfSongs, which is the String variable that contains the value to be converted to an Integer data type by the ToInt32 procedure. Notice that the argument is enclosed within parentheses.

Every procedure is part of a class in Visual Basic. You will recall from Chapter 1 that a **class** is a named grouping of program code. When the calling statement must call a procedure, it first must identify the class that contains the procedure. Thus, in Figure 4-49 the calling statement is incomplete because the class name is not included. The class that contains the ToInt32 procedure is the Convert class. To complete the procedure call statement, the class must be added, as shown in Figure 4-50.

procedure name   argument

```
Convert.ToInt32(strNumberOfSongs)
```

class name

FIGURE 4-50

In Figure 4-50, the class name Convert begins the procedure call. A dot operator separates the class name from the procedure name (ToInt32). The argument (strNumberOfSongs) within the parentheses completes the procedure call.

When a Function procedure returns a value, such as the ToInt32 procedure that returns an integer value, the returned value essentially replaces the Function procedure call in the assignment statement. So, in Figure 4-51, you can see that when the processing is completed within the Function procedure, the integer value is substituted for the procedure call in the assignment statement.

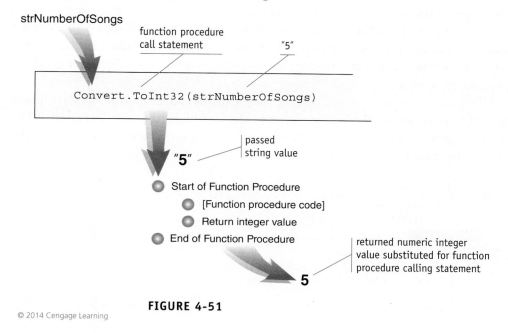

strNumberOfSongs

function procedure
call statement   "5"

Convert.ToInt32(strNumberOfSongs)

"5"   passed
string value

● Start of Function Procedure
    ● [Function procedure code]
    ● Return integer value
● End of Function Procedure

returned numeric integer
value substituted for function
procedure calling statement

5

FIGURE 4-51

Figure 4-52 shows the complete assignment statement to convert the String data type in the strNumberOfSongs variable to an Integer data type and place it in the intNumberOfSongs variable.

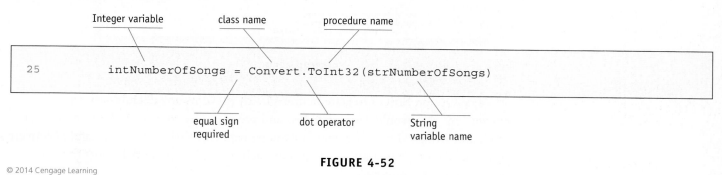

Integer variable   class name   procedure name

25   intNumberOfSongs = Convert.ToInt32(strNumberOfSongs)

equal sign   dot operator   String
required   variable name

FIGURE 4-52

The intNumberOfSongs variable name to the left of the equal sign identifies the Integer variable where the converted value will be copied. The equal sign in the assignment statement is required. As a result of the assignment statement in Figure 4-52, the ToInt32 Function procedure in the Convert class will convert the value in the strNumberOfSongs String variable to an integer value. The assignment statement will place that integer value in the intNumberOfSongs variable.

The use of Function procedures and arguments with procedure calls is common when programming in Visual Basic. You will encounter many examples of Function procedure calls throughout this book.

Option Strict On

In the previous section, you saw an example of how to explicitly change a value from one data type to another. By default, Visual Basic will automatically convert data types if the one on the right side of the equal sign in an assignment statement is different from the data type on the left side of the equal sign. Quite often, however, the automatic conversion can introduce errors and produce an incorrect converted value. Therefore, allowing automatic conversion typically is not good programming style.

To prevent automatic conversion of values, the developer must insert the Option Strict On statement in the program prior to any event handler code. In Figure 4-53, the Option Strict On statement is shown just after the introductory comments in the sample program for this chapter.

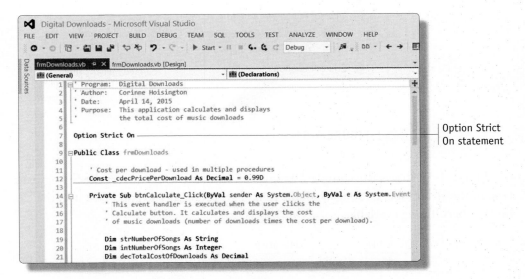

FIGURE 4-53

The Option Strict On statement explicitly prevents any default data type conversions that would cause data loss and prevents any conversion between numeric types and strings. Therefore, you must write explicit conversion statements to convert from one data type to another. This approach minimizes potential errors that can occur from data conversion.

Arithmetic Operations

The ability to perform arithmetic operations on numeric data is fundamental to computer programs. Many programs require arithmetic operations to add, subtract, multiply, and divide numeric data. For example, in the Digital Downloads program in this chapter, the price per song downloaded must be multiplied by the number of songs downloaded to calculate the total cost. The formula is shown in Figure 4-54.

Total Cost of Downloads = Number of Song Downloads times Price per Download

FIGURE 4-54

© 2014 Cengage Learning

An assignment statement is used in Visual Basic 2012 to perform the arithmetic operation shown in Figure 4-54. The statements used in the sample program and a depiction of the operation are shown in Figure 4-55.

```
20          Dim strNumberOfSongs As String
21          Dim intNumberOfSongs As Integer
22          Dim decTotalCostOfDownloads As Decimal
23          Const cdecPricePerDownload As Decimal = 0.99D
24
25          strNumberOfSongs = txtNumberOfDownloads.Text
26          intNumberOfSongs = Convert.ToInt32(strNumberOfSongs)
27          decTotalCostOfDownloads = intNumberOfSongs * cdecPricePerDownload
```

decTotalCostOfDownloads = intNumberOfSongs * cdecPricePerDownload

FIGURE 4-55

© 2014 Cengage Learning; © Tatiana Popova/Photos.com

In the code in Figure 4-55, the variable strNumberOfSongs is assigned the user's entered value by the assignment statement on line 25. (See Figure 4-24 on page 209 for a detailed explanation of this statement.) The statement on line 26 converts the value in the strNumberOfSongs variable to an integer and copies it to the intNumberOfSongs variable. (See Figure 4-52 on page 225 for an explanation of this statement.)

The statement on line 27 multiplies the integer value in the intNumberOfSongs variable by the constant value in the cdecPricePerDownload variable, and then copies the result to the decTotalCostOfDownloads variable. For example, if the user enters 5 as the number of downloads, the value 5 is multiplied by 0.99 (the value in the cdecPricePerDownload variable), and the result (4.95) is copied to the decTotalCostOfDownloads variable.

Arithmetic Operators

The asterisk (*) is an important element on the right side of the equal sign in the assignment statement on line 27. This asterisk is the multiplication **arithmetic operator**. Whenever the compiler encounters this operator, the value to the left of the operator is multiplied by the value to the right of the operator, and these values then are replaced in the assignment statement by the product of the two numbers. Thus, in Figure 4-55 on the previous page the arithmetic expression intNumberOfSongs * cdecPricePerDownload is replaced by the value 4.95. Then, the assignment statement places the value 4.95 in the decTotalCostOfDownloads variable.

The multiplication arithmetic operator is only one of the arithmetic operators available in Visual Basic 2012. The table in Figure 4-56 lists the arithmetic operators in Visual Basic 2012, describes their use, and provides an example of their use.

Arithmetic Operator	Use	Assignment Statement Showing Use
+	Addition	decTotal = decPrice + decTax
−	Subtraction	decCost = decRegularPrice − decDiscount
*	Multiplication	decTax = decItemPrice * decTaxRate
/	Division	decClassAverage = decTotalScores / intNumberOfStudents
^	Exponentiation	intSquareArea = intSquareSide ^ 2
\	Integer Division	intResult = 13 \ 5
Mod	Modulus Arithmetic (remainder)	intRemainder = 13 Mod 5

FIGURE 4-56

The arithmetic operators shown in Figure 4-56 are explained in the following paragraphs:

Addition

The **addition arithmetic operator** (+) adds the numeric values immediately to the left and right of the operator and replaces the arithmetic expression in the assignment statement. For example, in Figure 4-57, the value in the decPrice variable is added to the value in the decTax variable.

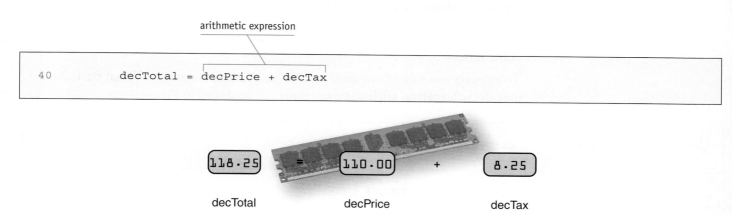

arithmetic expression

```
40        decTotal = decPrice + decTax
```

118.25   =   110.00   +   8.25

decTotal   decPrice   decTax

FIGURE 4-57

In Figure 4-57, the arithmetic expression (decPrice + decTax) is evaluated, and then the assignment statement copies the sum to the decTotal variable in RAM.

An arithmetic expression that uses the addition operator can contain more than two numeric values to be added. For example, in Figure 4-58, three variables are used in the arithmetic expression.

```
47        decTotalPay = decRegularPay + decOvertimePay + decBonusPay
```

FIGURE 4-58

In Figure 4-58, the value in decRegularPay is added to the value in decOvertimePay. The result then is added to decBonusPay, and that sum is copied to the decTotalPay variable. Visual Basic imposes no limit on the number of variables in an arithmetic expression.

In addition to variables, arithmetic expressions can contain literals. The assignment statement in Figure 4-59 uses a literal.

```
53        decTicketCost = decInternetTicketCost + 10.25
```

FIGURE 4-59

In Figure 4-59 on the previous page, the value 10.25 is added to the value in the decInternetTicketCost variable, and that sum is placed in the decTicketCost variable. Generally, literals should not be used in arithmetic expressions unless you know that the value will not change. For example, if the extra cost for the ticket could change in the future, good program design would dictate that the value be placed in a variable (perhaps even a constant).

Subtraction

To subtract one value from another in an assignment statement, Visual Basic 2012 uses the **subtraction arithmetic operator** (−), as shown in Figure 4-60.

```
59          decNetProfit = decRevenue - decCosts
```

FIGURE 4-60

© 2014 Cengage Learning

In Figure 4-60, the value in the decCosts variable is subtracted from the value in the decRevenue variable. The result then is copied into the decNetProfit variable. If the value in decCosts is greater than the value in decRevenue, the value placed in the decNetProfit variable will be negative.

Use Arithmetic Results

After an arithmetic operation has been performed using an assignment statement, the values used in the operation and the resulting answer can be used in subsequent arithmetic operations or for other purposes within the program. For example, the result of one operation can be used in a subsequent calculation (Figure 4-61).

```
67          decComputerCost = decMonitorCost + decSystemUnitCost
68          decNetComputerCost = decComputerCost - decSystemDiscount
```

FIGURE 4-61

© 2014 Cengage Learning

In Figure 4-61, the statement on line 67 determines the computer cost by adding the costs of the monitor and the system unit. The statement on line 68 calculates the net computer cost by subtracting the system discount from the computer cost calculated on line 67. Whenever a value is stored in a variable, it can be used in other statements within the program.

Multiplication

Multiplication is accomplished through the use of an assignment statement and the multiplication operator (*), as shown in Figure 4-62.

```
74          intLandPlotArea = intLandPlotLength * intLandPlotWidth
```

FIGURE 4-62

© 2014 Cengage Learning

In Figure 4-62, the value in the intLandPlotLength variable is multiplied by the value in the intLandPlotWidth variable. The product of the multiplication is placed in the intLandPlotArea variable.

If two positive numbers are multiplied, the answer is positive. If two negative numbers are multiplied, the answer is positive. If one positive number and one negative number are multiplied, the answer is negative.

When two numbers are multiplied, you must be aware of the size of the result. The largest number of digits that can appear as a result of multiplication is the sum of the number of digits in the values being multiplied. If the product is greater than the value that can be stored in the variable to the left of the assignment statement, an overflow error can occur and the program will be terminated.

How should I test my program to make sure it works properly?

When you allow user input, be sure to test every possible entry by the user. If a decimal value is input instead of an expected integer value, your program may stop functioning. As you learn more about coding in the next chapters, error validation will become an important part of developing your program.

CONSIDER THIS

Division

Visual Basic 2012 provides three arithmetic operators for division and related calculations: the slash (/), the backslash (\), and the MOD operator.

You use the slash for normal division. For example, in Figure 4-63, the value in the decTestScores variable is divided by 3 to obtain the average test score.

```
79          decAverageTestScore = decTestScores / 3
```

FIGURE 4-63

© 2014 Cengage Learning

You use the backslash (\) for integer division. With integer division, the quotient returned from the division operation is an integer. If the division operation produces a quotient with a remainder, the remainder is dropped, or truncated. The examples in Figure 4-64 on the next page illustrate the use of the integer division arithmetic operator.

WATCH OUT FOR

The divisor is the number to the right of the division operator. Make sure the divisor is not zero. If you attempt to divide by zero, your program will be terminated with an error.

Division Operation	Result
12\5	2
25\4	6
30\7	4

FIGURE 4-64

© 2014 Cengage Learning

Notice in each example in Figure 4-64 that the result is a whole number with the remainder truncated.

The MOD operator divides the number to the left of the operator by the number to the right of the operator and returns an integer value that is the remainder of the division operation. Integer division and the MOD operator often are used together, as shown in Figure 4-65.

```
86          intHours = intTotalNumberOfMinutes \ 60
87          intMinutes = intTotalNumberOfMinutes Mod 60
```

FIGURE 4-65

© 2014 Cengage Learning

In Figure 4-65, the operation on line 86 will return only the integer value of the division. For example, if the intTotalNumberOfMinutes variable contains 150, a result of 2 (2 = 150\60) will be placed in the intHours variable. The operation on line 87 will place the remainder in the intMinutes variable. The remainder in the example is 30; 150 divided by 60 is 2, with a remainder of 30.

Exponentiation

Exponentiation means raising a number to a power. It is accomplished in Visual Basic 2012 using the exponentiation arithmetic operator (^), as shown in Figure 4-66.

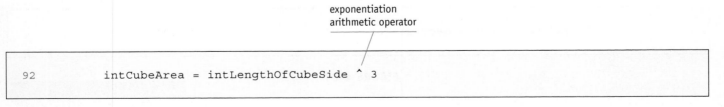

exponentiation
arithmetic operator

```
92          intCubeArea = intLengthOfCubeSide ^ 3
```

FIGURE 4-66

© 2014 Cengage Learning

In Figure 4-66, the arithmetic expression is the same as intLengthOfCubeSide *intLengthOfCubeSide* intLengthOfCubeSide. Therefore, the value is cubed and copied to the intCubeArea variable.

The exponent used in the operation can be a fraction. If so, the root is taken (Figure 4-67).

```
94          intLengthOfCubeSide = intCubeArea ^ (1 / 3)
```

FIGURE 4-67

In Figure 4-67, the cube root of the value in the intCubeArea variable is calculated and the result is copied to the intLengthOfCubeSide variable. Thus, if the area of the cube is 64, the value calculated for the length of the cube side would be 4 (4 * 4 * 4 = 64). The fractional exponent can never be negative, and it must be placed within parentheses.

Multiple Operations

A single assignment statement can contain multiple arithmetic operations. In Figure 4-68, the addition and subtraction operators are used to calculate the new balance in a savings account by adding the deposits to the old balance and subtracting withdrawals.

```
101         decNewBalance = decOldBalance + decDeposits - decWithdrawals
```

FIGURE 4-68

When the assignment statement is executed in Figure 4-68, the value in the decOldBalance variable is added to the value in the decDeposits variable. Then, the value in the decWithdrawals variable is subtracted from that sum and the result is copied to the decNewBalance variable.

Notice in Figure 4-68 that the calculations proceed from left to right in the arithmetic expression.

Hierarchy of Operations

When multiple operations are included in a single assignment statement, the sequence for performing the calculations is determined by the following rules:

1. Exponentiation (^) is performed first.
2. Multiplication (*) and division (/) are performed next.
3. Integer division (\) is next.
4. MOD then occurs.
5. Addition (+) and subtraction (−) are performed last.
6. Within each of the preceding five steps, calculations are performed from left to right.

As a result of this predetermined sequence, an arithmetic expression such as decBonus + decHours * decHourlyRate would result in the product of decHours * decHourlyRate being added to decBonus.

An arithmetic expression such as decGrade1 + decGrade2 / 2 would cause the value in the decGrade2 variable to be divided by 2 and then the quotient to be added to the value in decGrade1 because division is performed before addition. However, this calculation probably was not intended. Instead, the intent probably was to add the values in decGrade1 and decGrade2 and then divide the sum by 2. To force certain operations to be performed before others, you can use parentheses. Any arithmetic expression within parentheses is evaluated before expressions outside the parentheses, as shown in Figure 4-69.

```
108          decAverageGrade = (decGrade1 + decGrade2) / 2
```

FIGURE 4-69

© 2014 Cengage Learning

In Figure 4-69, the addition operation is inside the parentheses, so it will be completed before the division operation. Therefore, the result of the arithmetic expression is that the value in decGrade1 is added to the value in decGrade2. That sum then is divided by 2 and the quotient is copied to the decAverageGrade variable.

If you want to make the sequence of operations explicitly clear, you can use parentheses around multiple arithmetic operations in an arithmetic expression even if the predetermined sequence of operations will produce the correct answer.

IN THE REAL WORLD

You know that a procedure is a collection of code that a program can call to perform a particular function, such as converting data stored in a numeric data type to data stored as a String data type. In some programming languages, a procedure is called a method. Therefore, as you search the index or other areas in Visual Studio Help, you might find the word method *used*. Just remember that the terms *method* and *procedure* are virtually synonymous.

Display Numeric Output Data

As you have learned, the result of an arithmetic expression is a numeric value that typically is stored in a numeric variable. To display the numeric data as information in a graphical user interface, usually the data must be placed in the Text property of a Label object or a TextBox object. The Text property of these objects, however, requires that the data be a String data type. Therefore, to display a numeric value in a label or a text box, the numeric data must be converted to a String data type.

Each of the numeric data types provides a function called ToString that converts data from the numeric data type to the String data type. The general format of the function call for a Decimal numeric variable is shown in Figure 4-70.

General Format: ToString Function

```
decimalvariable.ToString()
```

FIGURE 4-70

© 2014 Cengage Learning

The statement shown in Figure 4-70 consists of the name of the Decimal variable that contains data to be converted, the dot operator (.), and the name of the function (ToString). Notice that the function name is followed immediately by closed parentheses, which indicates to the Visual Basic compiler that ToString is a procedure name. When the function call is executed, the value returned by the ToString function replaces the call.

The function call normally is contained within an assignment statement to assign the returned string value to the Text property of a Label or TextBox object. The example in Figure 4-71 shows the assignment statement to convert the numeric value in the decTemperature variable to a String value that then is placed in the Text property of the lblTemperature Label object.

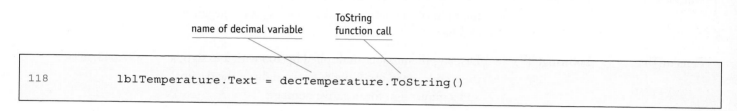

name of decimal variable   ToString function call

```
118        lblTemperature.Text = decTemperature.ToString()
```

FIGURE 4-71

© 2014 Cengage Learning

In Figure 4-71, the name of the Decimal variable (decTemperature) is followed by the dot operator and then the name of the function (ToString) with the required parentheses. When the statement on line 118 is executed, the ToString function is called. It converts the numeric value in the decTemperature variable to a String data type and returns the String data. The assignment statement then copies the returned String data to the Text property of the Temperature Label object.

Format Specifications for the ToString Function

In the example in Figure 4-71, the conversion from numeric value to String value is a straight conversion, which means the value is returned but not formatted in any manner. For example, if the numeric value in the Decimal variable was 47.235, then the same value was returned as a String value.

The ToString function, however, can convert numeric data to String data using a specified format. For example, the value 2317.49 could be returned as $2,317.49. The returned value is in the form of dollars and cents, or currency. To identify the format for the numeric data to be returned by the ToString function, the **format specifier** must be included as an argument in the parentheses following the ToString function name. The table in Figure 4-72 on the next page identifies the commonly used format specifiers; in the examples, the value in the numeric field is 8976.43561.

Format Specifier	Format	Description	Output from the Function
General(G)	ToString("G")	Displays the numbers as is	8976.43561
Currency(C)	ToString("C")	Displays the number with a dollar sign, a thousands separator (comma), 2 digits to the right of the decimal and negative numbers in parentheses	$8,976.44
Fixed(F)	ToString("F")	Displays the number with 2 digits to the right of the decimal and a minus sign for negative numbers	8976.44
Number(N)	ToString("N")	Displays a number with a thousands separator, 2 digits to the right of the decimal and a minus sign for negative numbers	8,976.44
Percent(P)	ToString("P")	Displays the number multiplied by 100 with a % sign, a thousands separator, 2 digits to the right of the decimal and a minus sign for negative numbers	897,643.56%
Scientific(E)	ToString("E")	Displays the number in E-notation and a minus sign for negative numbers	8.976436E+03

FIGURE 4-72

© 2014 Cengage Learning

In Figure 4-72, each format specifier is used as an argument within parentheses. The argument must be included in the quotation marks on each side of the format specifier, as shown. The letter for the format specifier can be uppercase or lowercase.

Precision Specifier

Each format specifier has a default number of digits that will be returned to the right of the decimal point. You can use a precision specifier, however, to override this default number. The **precision specifier** is a number included within the quotation marks in the function call that identifies the number of positions that should be returned to the right of the decimal point. The examples in Figure 4-73 illustrate the use of the precision specifier; assume that the value in the decNumericValue variable is 8976.43561.

Statement	Copied to Text Property of lblOutput Label Object
lblOutput = decNumericValue.ToString("C2")	$8,976.44
lblOutput = decNumericValue.ToString("C3")	$8,976.436
lblOutput = decNumericValue.ToString("F1")	8976.4
lblOutput = decNumericValue.ToString("N4")	8,976.4356
lblOutput = decNumericValue.ToString("P0")	897,644%

FIGURE 4-73

© 2014 Cengage Learning

As you can see, the precision specifier identifies the number of digits that should be displayed to the right of the decimal point in the string returned from the ToString function. Notice that if the precision specifier is 0, no digits are returned to the right of the decimal point.

As with all conversions, when the number of positions to the right of the decimal point in the returned string is less than the number of digits to the right of the decimal point in the numeric value being converted, the returned value is rounded to the specified number of decimal places.

Clear the Form — Clear Procedure and Focus Procedure

Earlier in this chapter, you learned that when the user taps or clicks the Clear button in the Digital Downloads program (see Figure 4-1 on page 190), the event handler for the Clear button must clear the results from the window and allow the user to enter the next number of downloads. To clear the results, the Clear button event handler must complete the following tasks:

1. Clear the Text property of the TextBox object.
2. Clear the Text property of the Label object that displays the total cost of the downloads.
3. Set the focus on the TextBox object, which means placing the insertion point in the text box.

You will learn to accomplish these tasks in the following sections.

Clear Procedure

The Clear procedure clears any data in the Text property of a TextBox object. The general format of the Clear procedure is shown in Figure 4-74.

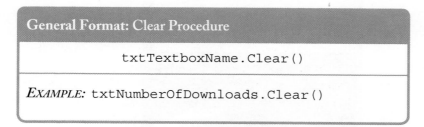

General Format: Clear Procedure

```
txtTextboxName.Clear()
```

EXAMPLE: txtNumberOfDownloads.Clear()

FIGURE 4-74

When the Clear procedure is executed, the Text property is cleared of data. As with every procedure call, the name of the procedure must be followed by parentheses.

Clear the Text Property of a Label

The Clear procedure cannot be used with a Label object. Instead, to clear the Text property of a Label object, you must write an assignment statement that assigns a null length string to the Text property. A null length string has no length, which means it is a string with no characters. A null length string is represented by two quotation marks with no character between them (""). To assign a null length string to the Text property, you can use the statement shown in Figure 4-75.

```
39          lblTotalCost.Text = ""
```

FIGURE 4-75

In Figure 4-75, the null length string represented by the two empty quotation marks is assigned to the Text property of the lblTotalCost Label object. As a result of the assignment statement, the Text property is cleared.

Set the Focus

When the focus is on a TextBox object, the insertion point is located in the text box (Figure 4-76).

insertion point
in text box

FIGURE 4-76
© Luca Pierro PHOTOGRAPHY/Flickr/Getty Images

When the user taps or clicks a button or other item in the graphical user interface, the focus shifts to that item. Therefore, to place the focus on a text box, the user can tap or click it. However, the programmer can use the Focus procedure to place the focus on a text box automatically without requiring the user to tap or click it first, thus making it easier for the user to enter data in the text box (Figure 4-77).

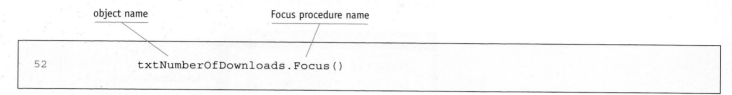

object name   Focus procedure name

52   txtNumberOfDownloads.Focus()

FIGURE 4-77

© 2014 Cengage Learning

   As with most procedure calls, the name of the object begins the statement, followed immediately by the dot operator (period). The name of the procedure (Focus) follows the dot operator. When the statement on line 52 is executed, the focus is placed on the txtNumberOfDownloads TextBox object, which means the insertion point is placed in the text box.

Form Load Event

In the sample programs in Chapter 3 and this chapter, you have seen that an event can occur when the user taps or clicks a button. The user's action triggers the code to execute in the event handler for the button tap or click. For example, in the Digital Downloads program in this chapter, the user taps or clicks the Calculate Cost button and the event handler code responds by multiplying the number of songs by the price per song and displaying the result (see Figure 4-1 on page 190).

   Tapping or clicking a button is not the only action that can trigger an event. For example, a form load event occurs each time a program is started and the Windows Form object is loaded into computer memory. For the program in this chapter, a form load event occurs when the program starts and the Digital Downloads form is loaded. In some programs, an event handler is not written for this particular event and no processing occurs. In the Digital Downloads program, however, a form loading event handler is required. This event handler completes the following tasks:

1. Display the cost per download heading.
2. Clear the placeholder from the lblTotalCost Text property.
3. Set the focus on the txtNumberOfDownloads text box.

Concatenation

In the Digital Downloads program, the lblCostHeading Label object displays the cost per download (see Figure 4-1 on page 190). In the user interface design, the lblCostHeading Label contains placeholder information for the label, but does not contain the actual cost per download (Figure 4-78).

lblCostHeading label does not contain actual cost per download

FIGURE 4-78

In Figure 4-78, the programmer had two reasons for not placing the actual download cost in the label during the design phase. First, in the original implementation of the program, the cost per download is 99 cents. In the future, however, the cost might change. Generally, data that might change should be placed in the Text property of a Label object during execution time, not at design time. Therefore, the cost per download should be placed in the label by the form load event handler when the form opens. Second, the cost per download is used in two places in the program — in the label and when the actual calculation is performed to determine the total cost (see Figure 4-55 on page 227). Instead of using the numeric value of 0.99 several times within the program, the value should be assigned to a variable. If the value must be changed in the future, only one change to the variable is necessary. For example, if the cost per download changes to 85 cents, the cost can be changed in the cost per download variable and then it will be correct for all uses of the variable. To illustrate, the variable for the cost per download is shown in Figure 4-79.

```
12    Const _cdecPricePerDownload As Decimal = 0.99D
```

FIGURE 4-79

As you can see, the price per download is declared as a constant that cannot be changed during program execution. If the price changes in the future, the developer can make one change to this declaration and all elements of the program that use the value will be correct.

To create the heading for the Digital Downloads program, the value in the variable declared in Figure 4-79 must be combined with the words Per Download and the result must be placed in the Text property of the lblCostHeading Label object. The process of joining two different values into a single string is called **concatenation**. When you use concatenation, the values being concatenated must be String data types. Note in Figure 4-79 that the _cdecPricePerDownload variable is a Decimal data type. Therefore, it must be changed to a String data type before being joined with the words in the heading.

The statement in Figure 4-80 converts the Decimal data type to a String data type, concatenates (or joins) the two strings together, and then places the result in the Text property of the lblCostHeading Label object.

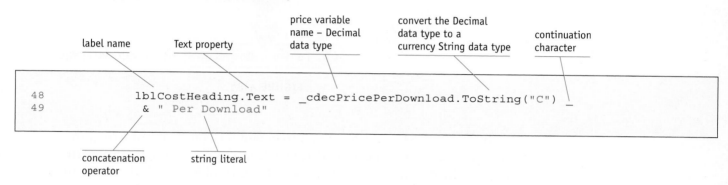

FIGURE 4-80

© 2014 Cengage Learning

In Figure 4-80, the string generated to the right of the equal sign will be placed in the Text property of the lblCostHeading Label object. The first entry to the right of the equal sign is the price variable name (see Figure 4-79). Following the dot operator is the ToString procedure name, followed by the currency argument within parentheses. Remember that the ToString procedure converts a numeric value to a String data type. When the currency argument ("C") is used, the String value returned is in a currency format. (See Figure 4-72 on page 236 for a detailed explanation.)

Following the conversion statement is the **concatenation operator (&)**. When the Visual Basic compiler encounters this operator, the string to the left of the operator is joined with the String data to the right of the operator to create a single concatenated string. The resulting string then is placed in the Text property of the lblCostHeading Label object.

The process that occurs to the right of the equal sign is illustrated in Figure 4-81.

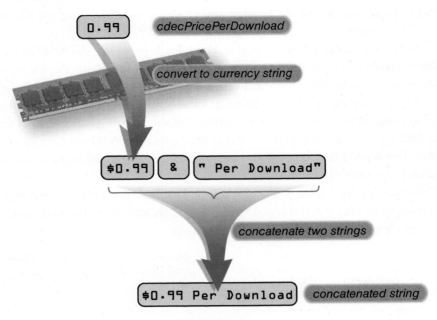

FIGURE 4-81

© 2014 Cengage Learning; © Tatiana Popova/Photos.com

In Figure 4-81 you can see that to obtain the concatenated string, the Decimal value in the cdecPricePerDownload Decimal variable is converted to a currency String data type. Then, that value is combined with the string literal to create the concatenated string. In the assignment statement in Figure 4-80 on the previous page, the concatenated string is assigned to the Text property of the lblCostHeading Label object.

Class Scope

Remember that when you declare a variable, you also define its scope. The scope of a variable identifies where within the program the variable can be referenced. For example, if a variable is declared within an event handler procedure, the variable can be referenced only within that procedure.

Sometimes, a variable must be referenced in multiple event handlers. In the Digital Downloads program, the value in the cdecPricePerDownload variable is referenced in the Calculate button event handler when the total cost is calculated (see Figure 4-55 on page 227). The value also is referenced in the form load event when the heading is displayed (see Figure 4-80 on the previous page). Because the variable is referenced in two different event handling procedures, it must be defined at the class level instead of the procedure (event handler) level. This means that the variable must be declared in the code before the first procedure in the program. As you can see in Figure 4-82, the declaration of the _cdecPricePerDownload variable follows the class definition statement but appears before the first event handler procedure.

beginning of program

class definition statement

```
 1  ' Program:   Digital Downloads
 2  ' Author:    Corinne Hoisington
 3  ' Date:      April 14, 2015
 4  ' Purpose:   This application calculates and displays
 5  '            the total cost of music downloads
 6
 7  Option Strict On
 8
 9  Public Class frmDownloads
10
11      ' Cost per download - used in multiple procedures
12      Const _cdecPricePerDownload As Decimal = 0.99D
13
14      Private Sub btnCalculate_Click(ByVal sender As System.Object, ByVal e As System
        .EventArgs) Handles btnCalculate.Click
15          ' This event handler is executed when the user clicks the
16          ' Calculate Cost button. It calculates and displays the cost
17          ' of music downloads (number of downloads times the cost per download).
```

first event handler

declaration of Price Per Download variable

FIGURE 4-82

© 2014 Cengage Learning

As a result of the code in Figure 4-82, the scope of the _cdecPricePerDownload variable will be all procedures within the class; that is, code in any event handler procedure within the class can reference the variable. Because the variable is declared as a constant, the value in the variable cannot be changed by code within the class; however, the value in the class can be referenced to calculate the total cost and to create the cost heading.

IN THE REAL WORLD

When a variable is declared for use throughout a class, the naming convention specifies that the name should begin with an underscore character (_). When you see a variable name that begins with the underscore character, you know the variable has class scope.

Debug Your Program

When your program processes numeric data entered by a user, you should be aware of several errors that can occur when the user enters data the program does not expect. The three errors that occur most often are Format Exceptions, Overflow Exceptions, and Divide By Zero Exceptions.

A **Format Exception** occurs when the user enters data that a statement within the program cannot process properly. In the Digital Downloads program, the user must enter a numeric value for the number of songs to download. When the user taps or clicks the Calculate Cost button, the program converts the entered value to an integer and then uses the numeric value in the calculation (see Figure 4-52 on page 225). If the user enters a nonnumeric value, such as abc (Figure 4-83a), the conversion process cannot take place because the argument passed to the Convert class is not a numeric value. In this situation, a Format Exception error is recognized and the error box in Figure 4-83b is displayed.

FIGURE 4-83a

© Luca Pierro PHOTOGRAPHY/Flickr/Getty Images

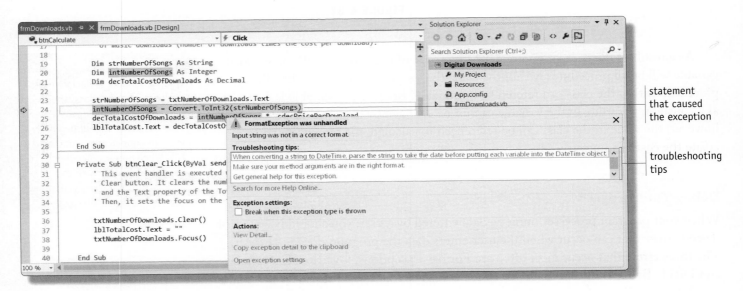

FIGURE 4-83b

In Figure 4-83a, the user entered the value abc and then tapped or clicked the Calculate Cost button. When control was passed to the ToInt32 procedure to convert the String value in the text box to an Integer, the Format Exception was triggered because the value in the strNumberOfSongs variable was not numeric. When an exception occurs, the execution of the program is terminated. With Visual Studio running, tap or click the Stop Debugging button on the Standard toolbar.

An **Overflow Exception** occurs when the user enters a value greater than the maximum value the statement can process. For example, in the Digital Downloads program, if the user enters a value in the text box that is too large for the ToInt32 procedure to convert, an Overflow Exception occurs.

An Overflow Exception also can occur when a calculation creates a value larger than a procedure can process. For example, if two large but valid numbers are multiplied, the product of the multiplication might be too large to process.

The third type of common error is the **Divide By Zero Exception**. It is not possible to divide by zero, so if your program contains a division operation and the divisor is zero, the Divide By Zero Exception will occur.

Whenever an exception occurs, a window similar to that in Figure 4-83b will be displayed.

To avoid exceptions, which should always be your goal, you can use certain techniques for editing the data and ensuring that the user has entered valid data. In Chapter 5 and Chapter 6, you will learn how to write code that checks user input to ensure that exceptions do not occur.

Program Design

As you have learned, the requirements document identifies the purpose of the program being developed, the application title, the procedures to be followed when using the program, any required equations and calculations, any conditions within the program that must be tested, notes and restrictions that must be followed by the program, and any other comments that would be helpful to understanding the problem. The requirements document for the Digital Downloads application is shown in Figure 4-84 on the following page.

REQUIREMENTS DOCUMENT

Date Submitted: April 14, 2015

Application Title: Digital Downloads

Purpose: The Digital Downloads program allows the user to enter the number of songs to be downloaded. The program calculates the total cost of the downloads based on a price of $0.99 per song.

Program Procedures: In a Windows application, the user enters the number of songs she wants to download. The program calculates the total cost of downloads. The user can clear the values on the screen and enter a new value for the number of downloads.

Algorithms, Processing, and Conditions:

1. The user must be able to enter the number of songs to be downloaded.
2. The user can initiate the calculation and display the total cost of the downloads.
3. The application computes the total cost by multiplying the number of downloads by the cost per download ($0.99).
4. The total cost of downloads is displayed as a currency value.
5. The user should be able to clear the value entered for the number of downloads and the total cost of downloads.
6. The user should be provided with a button to exit the program.

Notes and Restrictions: n/a

Comments: A graphic should depict a musical image. A graphic named Music is available on CengageBrain.com.

FIGURE 4-84

The Use Case Definition for the Digital Downloads program is shown in Figure 4-85.

USE CASE DEFINITION

1. The Windows application opens with a text box in which the user can enter a number of song downloads. The user interface includes the text box, an area to display the total cost of downloads, a Calculate Cost button, a Clear button, and an Exit button.
2. The user enters the number of song downloads.
3. The user taps or clicks the Calculate Cost button.
4. The program displays the total cost of the song downloads.
5. The user taps or clicks the Clear button to clear the Number of Downloads text box and erase the Total Cost of Downloads amount.
6. The user can repeat steps 2 through 5.
7. The user taps or clicks the Exit button to terminate the application.

FIGURE 4-85

Event Planning Document

You will recall that the event planning document is a table that specifies which objects in the user interface will cause events, the action taken by the user to trigger each event, and the event processing that must occur. The event planning document for the Digital Downloads program is shown in Figure 4-86.

EVENT PLANNING DOCUMENT

Program Name: Digital Downloads	Developer: Corinne Hoisington	Object: frmDownloads	Date: April 14, 2015

OBJECT	EVENT TRIGGER	EVENT PROCESSING
btnCalculate	Tap or click	Assign data entered in text box to a String variable Convert entered data to numeric integer Calculate total cost of downloads (number of downloads * price per download) Display total cost of downloads
btnClear	Tap or click	Clear Number of Downloads text box Clear Total Cost of Downloads label text Set focus on Number of Downloads text box
btnExit	Tap or click	Close the window and terminate the program
frmDownloads	Load	Display heading with price per download Clear the placement digits for Total Cost of Downloads Label object Set focus on Number of Downloads text box

FIGURE 4-86

© 2014 Cengage Learning

Code the Program

You are now ready to code the program by entering Visual Basic statements to accomplish the tasks specified in the event planning document. You also will implement the logic to carry out the required processing.

Guided Program Development

To design the user interface for the Digital Downloads program and enter the code required to process each event in the program, complete the following steps:

NOTE TO THE LEARNER

In the following activity, you should complete the tasks within the specified steps. Each of the tasks is accompanied by a Hint Screen. The purpose of the Hint Screen is to indicate where you should perform the activity in the Visual Studio window and to remind you which method to use. If you need further help completing a step, refer to the figure identified by *ref:*.

Guided Program Development

Phase 1: Create the User Interface Mockup

1

● **Create a Windows Application** Open Visual Studio using the Search charm (Windows 8) or the Start button on the Windows taskbar and the All Programs submenu (Windows 7). Close the Start page by tapping or clicking the Close button. To create a Windows application, tap or click the New Project button on the Standard toolbar. If necessary, tap or click Windows in the Installed Templates pane, tap or click Windows Forms Application in the center pane, and then type `Digital Downloads`. Tap or click the OK button in the New Project window.

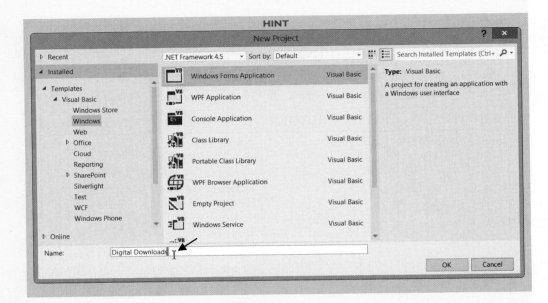

● **Display the Toolbox** Ensure that the Toolbox is displayed in the Visual Studio window. If it is not, tap or click VIEW and then Toolbox. If necessary, tap or click the triangle next to the Common Controls category name in the Toolbox and tap or click the Auto Hide button to display the tools.

● **Name the Windows Form Object** In the Solution Explorer window, press and hold or right-click the Form1.vb form file name and select Rename. Type `frmDownloads.vb` and then press the ENTER key.

• **Change the Title on the Title Bar** To change the title on the Windows Form object, tap or click the form, scroll in the Properties window until the Text property is displayed, double-tap or double-click in the right column of the Text property, type Download Music, and then press the ENTER key.

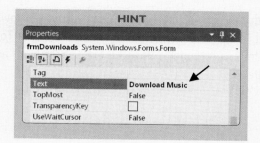

• **Resize the Windows Form Object** Change the Size property of the form to 425,500.

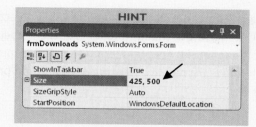

• **Add a PictureBox Object** Add a PictureBox object to the Windows Form object by dragging the PictureBox .NET component onto the Windows Form object. Place the object in the bottom of the Windows Form object.

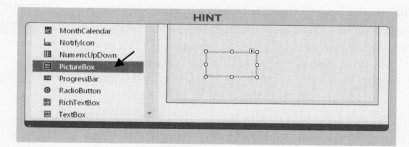

• **Name the PictureBox Object** With the PictureBox object selected, scroll in the Properties window until the (Name) property is visible. Double-tap or double-click in the right column of the (Name) property, type picMusic, and then press the ENTER key.

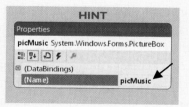

• **Resize the PictureBox Object** To resize the picMusic PictureBox object, first select it if necessary. Tap or click to the right of the Size property and change it to 405, 175.

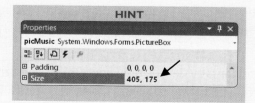

(continues)

● **Add a Heading Label** To insert the Digital Downloads heading label, drag the Label .NET component from the Toolbox to the Windows Form object. Position the Label object as shown in Figure 4-87.

● **Name the Label Object** Name the Label object `lblHeading` by scrolling to the (Name) property in the Properties window, double-tapping or double-clicking the (Name) property in the right column, typing `lblHeading`, and then pressing the ENTER key.

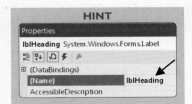

● **Change the Text of the Label Object** To change the text displayed in the Label object, scroll until the Text property is visible, double-tap or double-click in the right column of the Text property, type `Digital Downloads`, and then press the ENTER key.

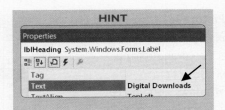

● **Change the Heading Font, Font Style, and Size** To make the heading stand out on the Windows form, its font should be larger and more prominent. To change the font to Cooper, its style to Black, and its size to 18, select the Label object and then scroll in the Properties window until the Font property is visible. Tap or click the Font property in the right column, and then tap or click the ellipsis button. In the Font dialog box, scroll if necessary, tap or click Cooper (or a similar font) in the Font list, tap or click Black in the Font style list, and then tap or click 18 in the Size list. Tap or click the OK button in the Font dialog box.

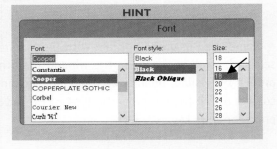

● **Horizontally Center the Label Object** The Label object should be centered horizontally in the form. Tap or click FORMAT on the menu bar, point to Center in Form on the FORMAT menu, and then tap or click Horizontally on the Center in Form submenu.

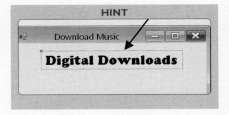

The PictureBox object and the Label object are placed on the resized Windows Form object (Figure 4-87). The font and font size for the Label object are appropriate for a heading in the window.

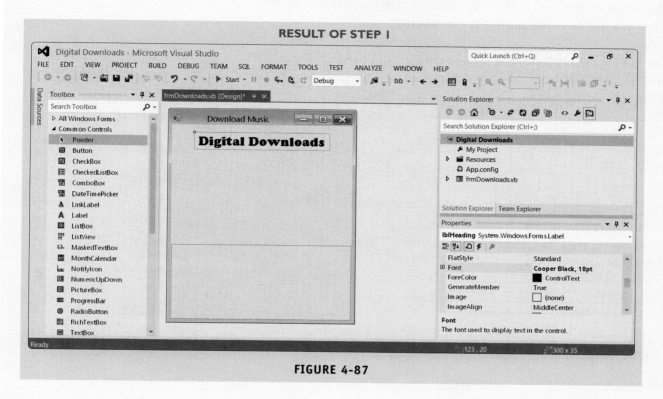

RESULT OF STEP 1

FIGURE 4-87

2

● **Add a Second Heading Label** To add the second heading label required for the window, drag a Label .NET component from the Toolbox to the Windows Form object. Place the second Label object below the lblHeading object.

HINT

● **Name the Label Object** Give the name `lblCostHeading` to the Label object you just placed on the Windows Form object.

(continues)

● **Change the Text in the Label Object** Change the text in the lblCostHeading object to `$X.XX per Download`. This text is a placeholder so that the Label object can be properly aligned and will be visible when it is not selected.

● **Set the Font, Font Style, and Size of the Font** Use the Font property and ellipsis button in the Properties window to display the Font dialog box, and then change the font to Century Gothic, the style to Regular, and the size to 12 points.

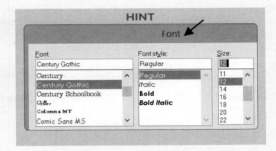

● **Center-Align the Label Object** Select the label, tap or click FORMAT on the menu bar, point to Center in Form, and then tap or click Horizontally.

The PictureBox object and the Label objects are properly aligned in the Windows Form object (Figure 4-88).

RESULT OF STEP 2

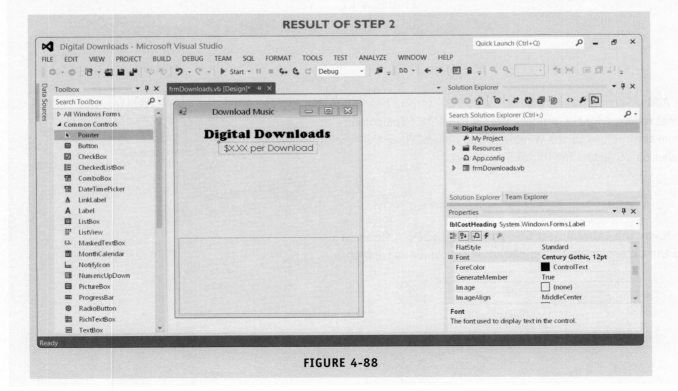

FIGURE 4-88

3

- **Add a Label for the Number of Song Downloads** Add the Label object for the number of song downloads by dragging it from the Toolbox. Place it below the two other Label objects, and then align the new Label object using the blue snap lines.

HINT

- **Change the Name, Enter Text, and Change the Font for the Number of Song Downloads Label** Using techniques you have learned previously, change the name of the Label object to `lblNumberOfDownloads`. In the Text property, enter `Number of Downloads:`. Using the Font property in the Properties window, change the font to Century Gothic, Regular style, and 11-point size.

HINT

- **Add a TextBox Object for the Number of Song Downloads** Drag a TextBox object to the Windows Form object. Name the TextBox object `txtNumberOfDownloads` *(ref: Figure 4-3)*.

HINT

- **Enter Data into the Text Property** As you learned in this chapter, even though the TextBox object will not contain text when the program begins, it still is necessary to enter text in the Text property of the TextBox object to size it properly. To enter text into the TextBox, select the TextBox object. In the Properties window, change the Text property to `888` *(ref: Figure 4-6)*.

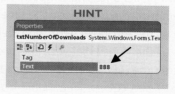

HINT

- **Change the Font and Size of the TextBox Object** Using the Properties window, change the font for the TextBox object to Century Gothic, Regular style, and 11-point size. Drag the right border of the TextBox object so the numbers fit properly in the text box *(ref: Figure 4-8)*.

HINT

(continues)

● **Align the Resized TextBox Object** To realign the resized TextBox object, drag it up until the red snap line indicates the text in the TextBox object is bottom-aligned with the label *(ref: Figure 4-9)*.

● **Center-Align Text in the TextBox Object** To center-align the text in the TextBox object, select the TextBox object, scroll in the Properties window until the TextAlign property is visible, tap or click the list arrow in the right column of the TextAlign property, and then tap or click Center in the TextAlign property list *(ref: Figure 4-10)*.

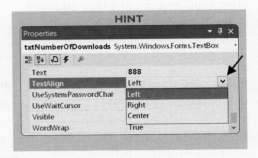

● **Remove Text from the TextBox Object** Because the TextBox object is sized properly, remove the digits from the TextBox object by selecting them in the Text property of the object and then pressing the DELETE key *(ref: Figure 4-12)*.

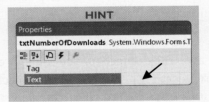

● **Add the Total Cost of Downloads Label Objects** A label that reports the total cost of the downloads must be displayed as the Text property of a Label object. A second label actually identifies the total cost. Drag two labels onto the Windows Form object and place them on the same horizontal line using the blue snap lines. Vertically align the left side of the left label with the label above it. Vertically align the left side of the right label with the text box above it. Name the Label object on the left `lblTotalCostLabel`. Name the label on the right `lblTotalCost` *(ref: Figure 4-18)*.

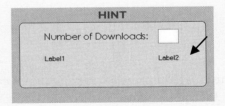

● **Enter Text for the Labels and Change the Font** Select the lblTotalCostLabel Label object and then double-tap or double-click the right column of the Text property for the label. Type the text `Total Cost of Downloads:` and then press the enter key. Select the lblTotalCost Label object and then double-tap or double-click the right column of the Text property for the label. Enter the value `$888.88` to represent the widest expected value for the label. With the right label selected, hold down the ctrl key and then tap or click the left label. With both labels selected, change the font to Century Gothic, Regular style, 11-point size.

- **Add Buttons** Three buttons are required for the user interface: the Calculate Cost button, the Clear button, and the Exit button. Drag three buttons onto the Windows Form object below the labels. Use blue snap lines to horizontally align the tops of the buttons. Using the (Name) property for each button, name the first button `btnCalculate`, the second button `btnClear`, and the third button `btnExit`.

- **Change the Button Text and the Font Style** Using the Text property for each button, change the text for the btnCalculate Button object to `Calculate Cost` and the text for the btnClear button to `Clear`. Change the text for the btnExit button to `Exit`. Select all three buttons by tapping or clicking the Calculate Cost button, holding down the CTRL key, and then tapping or clicking the other two buttons. Next, tap or click the Font property, tap or click the ellipsis button in the right column of the Font property, and then change the font style to Bold in the Font dialog box.

- **Change Button Size** The btnCalculate button does not display the entire Text property, so it must be enlarged. Drag the right border of the btnCalculate button until the entire Text property is visible.

- **Change the Size of the Other Buttons** Tap or click the btnCalculate button first, and then hold down the CTRL key and tap or click the other two buttons to select all three buttons. Make these buttons the same size by tapping or clicking FORMAT on the menu bar, pointing to Make Same Size on the FORMAT menu, and tapping or clicking Both on the Make Same Size submenu.

- **Space and Center the Buttons** With all three buttons selected, display the FORMAT menu, point to Horizontal Spacing on the FORMAT menu, and then tap or click Make Equal on the Horizontal Spacing submenu. Display the FORMAT menu, point to Center in Form on the FORMAT menu, and then tap or click Horizontally on the Center in Form submenu to center all three buttons horizontally in the Windows Form object.

(continues)

Guided Program Development   *continued*

The mockup for the user interface is complete (Figure 4-89).

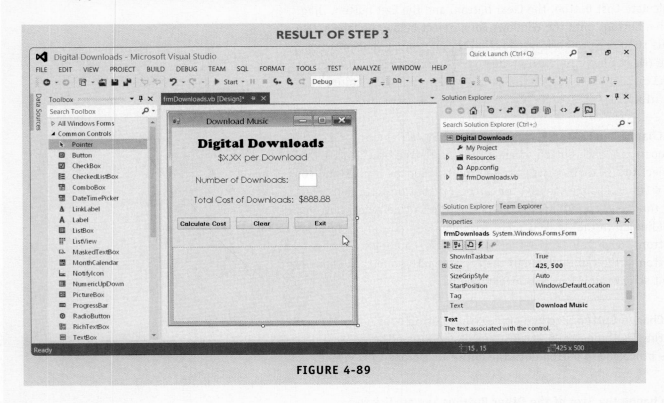

FIGURE 4-89

Phase 2: Fine-Tune the User Interface

4

● **Set the BackColor Property for the Windows Form Object** The user interface must be finished by setting the colors, adding images, and preparing for program execution. To set the BackColor property to White for the user interface, select the Windows Form object. In the Properties window, tap or click the BackColor property, and then tap or click the BackColor arrow in the right column of the BackColor property. If necessary, tap or click the Web tab. Scroll as required and then tap or click White in the BackColor list.

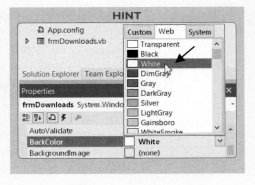

● **Set the ForeColor for the Button Objects and Label Object** To set the ForeColor to Red for the button objects and the first Label object, select all three buttons and the lblHeading object. Tap or click the ForeColor property in the Properties window, and then tap or click the ForeColor arrow in the right column of the ForeColor property. Tap or click the Web tab, if necessary. Scroll as required and then tap or click Red in the ForeColor list.

● **Set the Calculate Cost Button Object as the Accept Button** When the user enters the number of downloads, she should be able to calculate the total cost by tapping or clicking the Calculate Cost button or by pressing the ENTER key. To assign the Calculate Cost button as the Accept button, first select the Windows Form object by tapping or clicking anywhere in the window except on another object. Scroll in the Properties window until the AcceptButton property is visible, tap or click the AcceptButton property, tap or click the AcceptButton property arrow, and then tap or click btnCalculate *(ref: Figure 4-20)*.

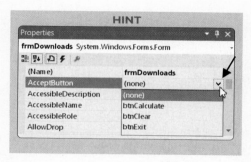

● **Set the Clear Button Object as the Cancel Button** By pressing the ESC key, the user should cause the same action as tapping or clicking the Clear button. To set the Clear button as the Cancel button, tap or click the Windows Form object, tap or click the CancelButton property in the Properties window, tap or click the CancelButton arrow, and then tap or click btnClear *(ref: Page 206)*.

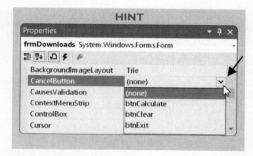

● **Insert the Music Image into the picMusic PictureBox Object** The last step to ready the user interface for execution is to insert the image into the PictureBox object. If necessary, download and save the Music image from the Student Companion Site. Then, with the picture box selected, tap or click the ellipsis button for the Image property in the Properties window, tap or click the Import button in the Select Resource dialog box, locate the Music image, and then import the image into the Resource folder. Tap or click the OK button in the Select Resource dialog box.

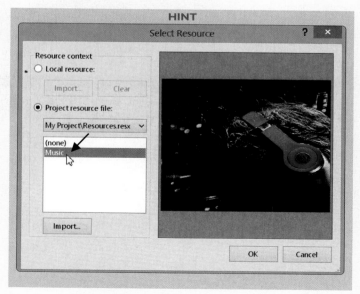

(continues)

● **Resize the Image** To resize the Music image, change the SizeMode property. With the picMusic PictureBox object selected, tap or click the SizeMode property in the Properties window, tap or click the SizeMode arrow in the right column, and then tap or click StretchImage.

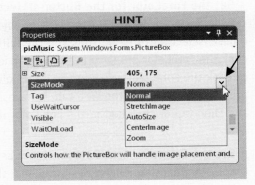

The user interface is complete (Figure 4-90).

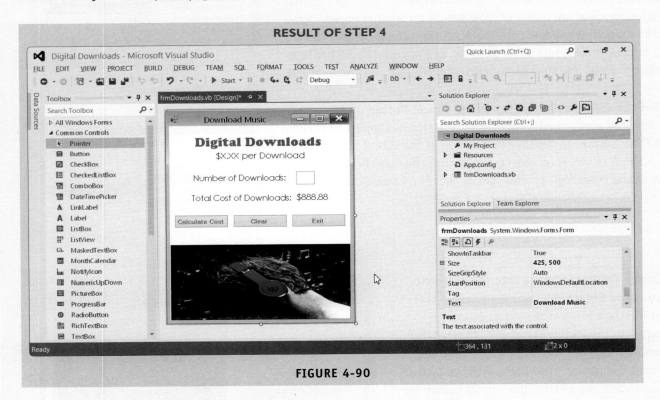

FIGURE 4-90

© Luca Pierro PHOTOGRAPHY/Flickr/Getty Images

Phase 3: Code the Application

5

● **Code the Comments** Double-click the btnCalculate Button object on the frmDownloads Windows Form object to open the code window and create the btnCalculate_Click event handler. Tap or click the Close button on the Toolbox title bar to close the Toolbox. Tap or click in front of the first words, Public Class frmDownloads, and press the ENTER key to create a blank line. Press the UP ARROW key and then insert the first four standard comments. Insert the Option Strict On command at the beginning of the code to turn on strict type checking *(ref: Figure 4-53)*.

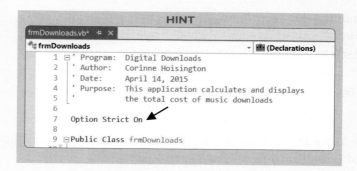

HINT

```
frmDownloads.vb*  ⊞ ✕
frmDownloads                              ▾  (Declarations)
  1 □ ' Program:   Digital Downloads
  2   ' Author:    Corinne Hoisington
  3   ' Date:      April 14, 2015
  4   ' Purpose:   This application calculates and displays
  5   '            the total cost of music downloads
  6
  7   Option Strict On  ←
  8
  9 □Public Class frmDownloads
```

● **Enter the _cdecPricePer Download Class Variable** The next step is to enter the class variable that is referenced in more than one event handler in this program. This variable contains the price per download and is referenced in the heading and to calculate the total cost. To enter this variable, press the DOWN ARROW key until the insertion point is on the blank line following the Public Class command (line 10). Press the ENTER key to add a blank line, and then type the comment that identifies the variable. Press the ENTER key and then write the declaration for the _cdecPrice-PerDownload variable. The constant Decimal variable should contain the value 0.99. The underline character (_) in the name indicates a class variable that is referenced in multiple procedures within the class *(ref: Figure 4-47)*.

HINT

```
  7   Option Strict On
  8
  9 □Public Class frmDownloads
 10
 11       ' Cost per download - used in multiple procedures  ←
 12       Const _cdecPricePerDownload As Decimal = 0.99D
 13
 14 □     Private Sub btnCalculate_Click(ByVal sender As System.Object, ByVal e As System.Event
```

● **Comment the btnCalculate Tap or Click Event Handler** Following the Private statement for the btnCalculate_Click event handler, enter a comment to describe the purpose of the btnCalculate_Click event.

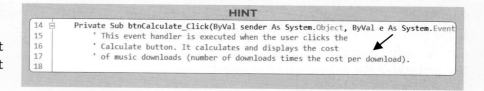

HINT

```
 14 □     Private Sub btnCalculate_Click(ByVal sender As System.Object, ByVal e As System.Event
 15         ' This event handler is executed when the user clicks the
 16         ' Calculate button. It calculates and displays the cost  ←
 17         ' of music downloads (number of downloads times the cost per download).
 18
```

(continues)

Guided Program Development   *continued*

- **Declare and Initialize the Variables** This event handler requires three variables: 1) strNumberOfSongs, which holds the number of song downloads entered by the user; 2) intNumberOfSongs, which holds the integer value for the number of song downloads entered by the user; and 3) decTotalCostOfDownloads, which holds the calculated total cost of downloads. Declare these three variables *(ref: Figure 4-22, Figure 4-35, Figure 4-37).*

```
HINT
19          Dim strNumberOfSongs As String
20          Dim intNumberOfSongs As Integer
21          Dim decTotalCostOfDownloads As Decimal
```

- **Write the Statements to Place the Number of Downloads in a Variable and Convert the Value to an Integer** The first steps in the event handler are to move the number of songs value from the Text property of the txtNumberOfDownloads TextBox object to a String variable and then convert that value to an Integer value. Using IntelliSense, write the code to complete these steps *(ref: Figure 4-29, Figure 4-52).*

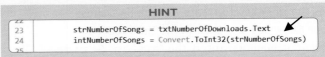

```
HINT
23          strNumberOfSongs = txtNumberOfDownloads.Text
24          intNumberOfSongs = Convert.ToInt32(strNumberOfSongs)
```

- **Calculate the Total Cost of Downloads** To calculate the total cost of downloads and place the result in the decTotalCostOfDownloads variable, the number of songs is multiplied by the price per download. Using IntelliSense, write the statement to perform this calculation *(ref: Figure 4-55).*

```
HINT
25       decTotalCostOfDownloads = intNumberOfSongs * _cdecPricePerDownload
```

- **Convert the Decimal Total Cost of Downloads to a String Currency Value and Place It in the Text Property of the lblTotalCost Label Object** After calculating the total cost of downloads, the result must be converted from a Decimal value to a currency String value so it can be displayed as the value in the Text property of a Label object. Write the statement to perform this conversion and place the converted value in the Text property of the lblTotalCost Label object

```
HINT
26       lblTotalCost.Text = decTotalCostOfDownloads.ToString("C")
```

The coding for the btnCalculate_Click event handler is complete (Figure 4-91).

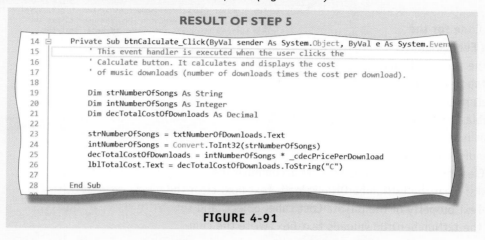

RESULT OF STEP 5

```
14  ⊟    Private Sub btnCalculate_Click(ByVal sender As System.Object, ByVal e As System.Even
15              ' This event handler is executed when the user clicks the
16              ' Calculate button. It calculates and displays the cost
17              ' of music downloads (number of downloads times the cost per download).
18
19              Dim strNumberOfSongs As String
20              Dim intNumberOfSongs As Integer
21              Dim decTotalCostOfDownloads As Decimal
22
23              strNumberOfSongs = txtNumberOfDownloads.Text
24              intNumberOfSongs = Convert.ToInt32(strNumberOfSongs)
25              decTotalCostOfDownloads = intNumberOfSongs * _cdecPricePerDownload
26              lblTotalCost.Text = decTotalCostOfDownloads.ToString("C")
27
28        End Sub
```

FIGURE 4-91

6

• **Run the Application** After you have entered code, you should run the application to ensure it is working properly. Run the Digital Downloads application by tapping or clicking the Start Debugging button on the Standard toolbar. Enter 10 for the number of song downloads and then tap or click the Calculate Cost button. The Total Cost of Downloads should be $9.90. Enter 15 for the number of song downloads and then press the ENTER key.

When the number of downloads is 10 songs, the total cost of the downloads is $9.90 (Figure 4-92).

RESULT OF STEP 6

FIGURE 4-92

(continues)

• **Write the Code for the Clear Button Event Handler**
Tap or click the frmDownloads.vb [Design] tab in the code window to return to the design window. Double-tap or double-click the Clear button to create the event handler for the Clear

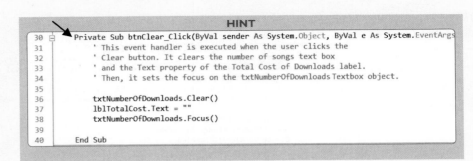

```
HINT
30    Private Sub btnClear_Click(ByVal sender As System.Object, ByVal e As System.EventArgs
31          ' This event handler is executed when the user clicks the
32          ' Clear button. It clears the number of songs text box
33          ' and the Text property of the Total Cost of Downloads label.
34          ' Then, it sets the focus on the txtNumberOfDownloads Textbox object.
35
36          txtNumberOfDownloads.Clear()
37          lblTotalCost.Text = ""
38          txtNumberOfDownloads.Focus()
39
40    End Sub
```

button. The Clear button event handler must accomplish the following tasks: Clear the txtNumberOfDownloads text box; clear the value in the Text property of the lblTotalCost Label object; and set the focus to the txtNumberOfDownloads text box. Write the comments for the event handler and then use IntelliSense to write the code for the event handler *(ref: Figure 4-74, Figure 4-75, Figure 4-77)*.

• **Write the Code for the Form Load Event Handler**
Tap or click the frmDownloads.vb [Design] tab in the code window to return to the design window. Double-tap or double-click the Windows Form object to create the event handler for the Form Load event. The Form Load event handler must

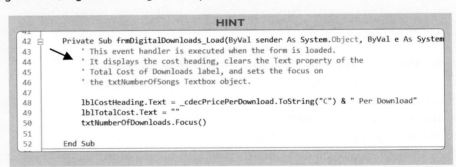

```
HINT
41
42    Private Sub frmDigitalDownloads_Load(ByVal sender As System.Object, ByVal e As System
43          ' This event handler is executed when the form is loaded.
44          ' It displays the cost heading, clears the Text property of the
45          ' Total Cost of Downloads label, and sets the focus on
46          ' the txtNumberOfSongs Textbox object.
47
48          lblCostHeading.Text = _cdecPricePerDownload.ToString("C") & " Per Download"
49          lblTotalCost.Text = ""
50          txtNumberOfDownloads.Focus()
51
52    End Sub
```

accomplish the following tasks: Using concatenation, create and display the Price per Download heading in the Text property of the lblCostHeading Label object; clear the Text property of the lblTotalCost Label object; and set the focus to the txtNumberOfDownloads TextBox object. Write the comments for the event handler and then use IntelliSense to write the code for the event handler *(ref: Figure 4-75, Figure 4-77, Figure 4-80)*.

• **Write the Code for the Exit Button Event Handler** Tap or click the frmDownloads.vb [Design] tab in the code window to return to the design window. Double-tap or double-click the Exit button to create its event handler. The Exit button event

```
HINT
54    Private Sub btnExit_Click(ByVal sender As System.Object, ByVal e As System.EventArgs)
55          ' Close the window and terminate the application
56
57          Close()
58
59    End Sub
60  End Class
```

handler must close the window and terminate the application. Write the comments and code for this event handler.

The coding is complete for the Clear button event handler, the Form load event handler, and the Exit button event handler (Figure 4-93).

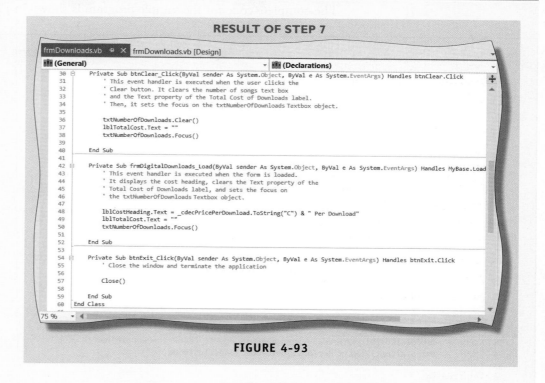

RESULT OF STEP 7

```
frmDownloads.vb    ⊕ ✕   frmDownloads.vb [Design]
▦ (General)                                                   ▾ ▦ (Declarations)
30 ⊟     Private Sub btnClear_Click(ByVal sender As System.Object, ByVal e As System.EventArgs) Handles btnClear.Click
31           ' This event handler is executed when the user clicks the
32           ' Clear button. It clears the number of songs text box
33           ' and the Text property of the Total Cost of Downloads label.
34           ' Then, it sets the focus on the txtNumberOfDownloads Textbox object.
35
36           txtNumberOfDownloads.Clear()
37           lblTotalCost.Text = ""
38           txtNumberOfDownloads.Focus()
39
40       End Sub
41
42 ⊟     Private Sub frmDigitalDownloads_Load(ByVal sender As System.Object, ByVal e As System.EventArgs) Handles MyBase.Load
43           ' This event handler is executed when the form is loaded.
44           ' It displays the cost heading, clears the Text property of the
45           ' Total Cost of Downloads label, and sets the focus on
46           ' the txtNumberOfDownloads Textbox object.
47
48           lblCostHeading.Text = _cdecPricePerDownload.ToString("C") & " Per Download"
49           lblTotalCost.Text = ""
50           txtNumberOfDownloads.Focus()
51
52       End Sub
53
54 ⊟     Private Sub btnExit_Click(ByVal sender As System.Object, ByVal e As System.EventArgs) Handles btnExit.Click
55           ' Close the window and terminate the application
56
57           Close()
58
59       End Sub
60   End Class
75 %   ▾ ◀
```

FIGURE 4-93

8

• **Test the Program** After finishing the coding, you should test the program to ensure it works properly. Run the Digital Downloads application by tapping or clicking the Start Debugging button on the Standard toolbar. Enter 20 for the number of song downloads and then tap or click the Calculate Cost button. The Total Cost of Downloads should be $19.80. Tap or click the Clear button to clear the text box and the label that contains the total cost of downloads. Enter 5 for the number of song downloads and then press the ENTER key on the keyboard. The Total Cost of Downloads should be $4.95. Press the ESC key to clear the text box and the label that contains the total cost of downloads. Enter other values to test the program completely.

The program runs properly (Figure 4-94).

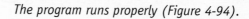

RESULT OF STEP 8

FIGURE 4-94

(continues)

Code Listing

The complete code for the sample program is shown in Figure 4-95.

```vb
1  ' Program:  Digital Downloads
2  ' Author:   Corinne Hoisington
3  ' Date:     April 14, 2015
4  ' Purpose:  This application calculates and displays
5  '           the total cost of music downloads
6
7  Option Strict On
8
9  Public Class frmDownloads
10
11     ' Cost per download - used in multiple procedures
12     Const _cdecPricePerDownload As Decimal = 0.99D
13
14     Private Sub btnCalculate_Click(ByVal sender As System.Object, ByVal e As System.EventArgs) Handles btnCalculate.Click
15         ' This event handler is executed when the user clicks the
16         ' Calculate button. It calculates and displays the cost
17         ' of music downloads (number of downloads times the cost per download).
18
19         Dim strNumberOfSongs As String
20         Dim intNumberOfSongs As Integer
21         Dim decTotalCostOfDownloads As Decimal
22
23         strNumberOfSongs = txtNumberOfDownloads.Text
24         intNumberOfSongs = Convert.ToInt32(strNumberOfSongs)
25         decTotalCostOfDownloads = intNumberOfSongs * _cdecPricePerDownload
26         lblTotalCost.Text = decTotalCostOfDownloads.ToString("C")
27
28     End Sub
29
30     Private Sub btnClear_Click(ByVal sender As System.Object, ByVal e As System.EventArgs) Handles btnClear.Click
31         ' This event handler is executed when the user clicks the
32         ' Clear button. It clears the number of songs text box
33         ' and the Text property of the Total Cost of Downloads label.
34         ' Then, it sets the focus on the txtNumberOfDownloads Textbox object.
35
36         txtNumberOfDownloads.Clear()
37         lblTotalCost.Text = ""
38         txtNumberOfDownloads.Focus()
39
40     End Sub
41
42     Private Sub frmDigitalDownloads_Load(ByVal sender As System.Object, ByVal e As System.EventArgs) Handles MyBase.Load
43         ' This event handler is executed when the form is loaded.
44         ' It displays the cost heading, clears the Text property of the
45         ' Total Cost of Downloads label, and sets the focus on
46         ' the txtNumberOfDownloads Textbox object.
47
48         lblCostHeading.Text = _cdecPricePerDownload.ToString("C") & " Per Download"
49         lblTotalCost.Text = ""
50         txtNumberOfDownloads.Focus()
51
52     End Sub
53
54     Private Sub btnExit_Click(ByVal sender As System.Object, ByVal e As System.EventArgs) Handles btnExit.Click
55         ' Close the window and terminate the application
56
57         Close()
58
59     End Sub
60  End Class
61
```

FIGURE 4-95

Summary

In this chapter you have learned to declare variables and write arithmetic operations. The items listed in the table in Figure 4-96 include all the new Visual Studio and Visual Basic skills you have learned in this chapter.

Visual Basic Skills

Skill	Figure Number	Video Number
Place a TextBox Object on the Windows Form Object	Figure 4-3	Video 4-2
Size and Position a TextBox Object	Figure 4-6	Video 4-3
Align Text in a TextBox Object	Figure 4-10	Video 4-4
Create a MultiLine TextBox Object	Figure 4-13	Video 4-5
Create a Masked TextBox Object	Figure 4-14	Video 4-6
Place a Masked TextBox Object on the Windows Form Object	Figure 4-15	Video 4-7
Place and Size a Label Object on the Windows Form Object	Figure 4-18	Video 4-8
Assign a Button Object as the Accept Button	Figure 4-20	Video 4-9
Assign a Button Object as the Cancel Button	Page 206	
Close the Toolbox	Figure 4-21	Video 4-10
Define a String Variable	Figure 4-22	
Write an Assignment Statement	Figure 4-24	
Use IntelliSense to Enter a Variable and an Assignment Statement	Figure 4-25	Video 4-11
Declare an Integer Data Type	Figure 4-35	
Declare a Decimal Data Type	Figure 4-37	
Declare a Char Data Type	Figure 4-40	
Declare a Boolean Data Type	Figure 4-42	
Declare a Constant	Figure 4-47	
Use an Argument in a Procedure Call Statement	Figure 4-49	
Write a Procedure Call Statement for the ToInt32 Procedure in the Convert Class	Figure 4-52	
Enter the Option Strict On Statement	Figure 4-53	
Perform Arithmetic Operations Using Arithmetic Operators	Figure 4-56	
Display Numeric Output Data	Figure 4-70	
Write a Procedure Call for the Clear Procedure	Figure 4-74	
Write a Procedure Call for the Focus Procedure	Figure 4-76	
Write a String Concatenation Statement	Figure 4-80	
Write a Variable with Class Scope	Figure 4-82	
Understand a Format Exception	Figure 4-83	

FIGURE 4-96

Learn Online

Reinforcement activities and resources are available at no additional cost on www.cengagebrain.com. Visit www.cengage.com/ct/studentdownload for detailed instructions about accessing the resources available at the Student Companion Site.

Knowledge Check

1. Name three numeric data types that can contain a decimal point.

2. Write a Dim statement for each of the following variables using the variable type and variable name that would be best for each value.

   a. The population of the state of Alaska

   b. Your weekly pay

   c. The smallest data type you can use for your age

   d. A constant for the first initial of your first name

   e. The minimum wage

   f. The name of the city where you live

   g. The answer to a true/false question

3. Determine whether each of the following variable names is valid or invalid. Explain the error in each invalid variable name.

   a. _intRadian

   b. PercentOfSales#

   c. first_Input_Value

   d. R743-L56

   e. 3CPO

   f. Close

   g. Name Of Client

4. List the steps that specify how you would perfectly align a group of TextBox objects along their left edges.

5. Which data type is best for currency amounts?

6. Explain the hierarchy in for the order of operations.

(continues)

7. What is the solution to each of the following arithmetic expressions?

   a. $3 + 4 * 2 + 6$

   b. $16 / 2 * 4 - 3$

   c. $40 - 6 \wedge 2 / 3$

   d. 68 Mod 9

   e. $9 \setminus 4 + 3$

   f. $2 \wedge 3 + (8 - 5)$

   g. $(15 \text{ Mod } 2) - 1 + 4 * (16 \setminus 5)$

8. What is the difference between a method and a procedure?

9. What is the difference between a variable and a literal?

10. Correct the following statements:

    a. `Dim itAge As Integr`

    b. `Dim dblDiscountRate As Dbl`

    c. `Constant cstrCollege As String = "CVCC"`

    d. `Dim strLastName As String`

    e. `strLastName = 'McNamara'`

    f. `1.5 * decHourlyPay = decOverTimePayRate`

11. Write a statement that sets the focus on the txtLastName TextBox object.

12. Write a statement that removes the contents of the txtAge TextBox object.

13. Write a statement that blanks the Text property of the lblEligibilityAge Label object.

14. Write a statement to convert the value in the String variable strWaistSize to an integer value and place the integer value in a variable named intWaistSize.

15. Write a statement to convert the value in the String variable strHourlyPay to a Decimal value and place the Decimal value in a variable named decWage.

16. Write a statement to close a form that currently is open.

17. Write a statement that declares a constant named decInsuranceDeductible as a Decimal data type and set its value to 379.25.

18. Which Windows Form property allows the user to press the enter key while the form is active and activate a button's event handler?

19. What is a local variable? How does its scope differ from that of a global variable?

20. When the following statements are executed, what would be displayed in the lblHourlyWage Label object?

```
decHourlyWage = 12.637
lblHourlyWage.Text = decHourlyWage.ToString("C")
```

Debugging Exercises

1. Fix the following code:

```
Option Strict On
Dim intDistance As Integer

intDistance = 17.5
```

2. Fix the following code:

```
Dim dblRegularPay As Double
Dim dblOvertimePay As Double

intRegularPay = 783.87
intOvertimePay = 105.92
lbl.TotalPay = (dblRegularPay + dblOvertimePay).ToString('C')
```

3. Analyze the code in Figure 4-97 and then correct it.

```
1  ⊟Public Class Form1
2
3  ⊟    Private Sub btnHeight_Click(sender As Object, e As EventArgs) Handles b
4          Dim intFeet As Integer
5          Dim strInches As String
6          Dim intInches As Integer
7
8          intInches = Convert.ToInt32(strInches)
9          intFeet = intInches / 12
10         lblFeet.Text = intFeet.ToString("P")
11
12     End Sub
13  End Class
14
```

FIGURE 4-97

Program Analysis

1. What will occur when the user taps or clicks the btnSlope Button in the following code?

```
Private Sub btnSlope_Click(ByVal sender As System.Object, ByVal e As System.
EventArgs) Handles btnSlope.Click
    Dim decRise As Decimal
    Dim decRun As Decimal
    Dim decSlope As Decimal
    decRise = 12.3D
    decRun = 2.1D
    decSlope = decRise / decRun
    lblSlope.Text = "The Line Slope is " & decSlope.ToString("F3")
End Sub
```

(continues)

2. How would the number .0256 be displayed if the format specifier ("P") is used in a Convert.ToString statement?

3. How would the number 3746.35555 be displayed if the format specifier ("F3") is used in a Convert.ToString statement?

4. If you want the user to enter her telephone number with the area code, which .NET component would be best to use on the Windows Form object?

5. Using the format specifier with the ToString procedure, write the statement that would display:

   a. The value in the decDvdCost variable with a dollar sign and two places to the right of the decimal point in a label named lblDvd

   b. The value in the decWithholdingTaxRate variable with a percent sign and one place to the right of the decimal point in a label named lblWithholdingTaxRate

   c. The value in the decOilRevenue variable with commas as needed, two places to the right of the decimal point, and no dollar sign in a label called lblOilRevenue

6. Write a single line of code to declare a variable decWindSpeed as a Decimal data type and assign it the value 25.47. Use a forced literal to ensure that the compiler views this number as a Decimal data type.

7. What would the values of these variables be at the end of the code that follows?

   a. intParts

   b. intBoxes

   c. intLeftovers

```
Dim intParts As Integer
Dim intBoxes As Integer
Dim intLeftovers As Integer

intParts = 77
intPartsPerBox = 9

intBoxes = intParts \ intPartsPerBox
intLeftovers = intParts Mod intBoxes
```

8. Are the following statements written correctly? If not, how should they be written?

```
Dim dblPay as Double
lblPay.Text = dblPay.ToString("C2")
```

Program Analysis *continued*

9. For a Button object named btnCalories, write the tap or click event handler to implement the following requirements and calculate the number of calories burned during a run:

   a. Declare variables named strMilesRan, decCaloriesConsumed, and decMilesRan.

   b. Declare a constant named cdecCaloriesBurnedPerHour and assign it the value 700. (Assume you burn 700 calories for every mile you run.)

   c. Allow the user to enter the number of miles she ran today.

   d. Convert the number of miles to a Decimal data type.

   e. Calculate the number of calories the user burned during her run.

   f. Display the result rounded to zero decimal places in a label named lblCaloriesBurned.

10. What would the output be when the user taps or clicks the btnDrivingAge Button?

```
Private Sub btnDrivingAge_Click(ByVal sender As System.Object, ByVal e As
System.EventArgs) Handles btnDrivingAge.Click
    Dim intPresentAge As Integer
    Const cintDrivingAge As Integer = 16
    Dim intYearsToDrive As Integer

    intPresentAge = 13
    intYearsToDrive = cintDrivingAge - intPresentAge
    lblYearsLeft.Text = intYearsToDrive.ToString() & " year(s) until you can
drive."
End Sub
```

Case Programming Assignments

Complete one or more of the following case programming assignments. Submit the program and materials you create to your instructor. The level of difficulty is indicated for each case programming assignment.

●   = Easiest
● ●   = Intermediate
● ● ● = Challenging

1 ●
STATE FAIR TICKETS

Design a Windows application and write the code that will execute according to the program requirements in Figure 4-98 and the Use Case Definition in Figure 4-99. Before writing the code, create an event planning document for each event in the program. The completed program is shown in Figure 4-100.

REQUIREMENTS DOCUMENT

Date Submitted:	January 31, 2015
Application Title:	State Fair Tickets Application
Purpose:	This Windows application allows a user to purchase tickets for a full day at your state or regional fair.
Program Procedures:	From a window on the screen, the user chooses the number of tickets needed for a group; the total cost of the tickets is displayed.
Algorithms, Processing, and Conditions:	1. The user must be able to enter the number of State Fair tickets. 2. A picture of women at the fair will be displayed throughout the entire process. 3. After entering the number of tickets needed, the user taps or clicks the Display Cost button. 4. Tickets cost $12.99 each; the total cost will be displayed in currency format.
Notes and Restrictions:	1. The user can use a Clear button to clear the number of tickets entered and the total cost and then enter another number of tickets. 2. An Exit button should close the application. 3. The cost per ticket can vary, so the program should allow a different price to be placed in any headings and be used in any calculations.
Comments:	The picture is named Fair and is available on CengageBrain.com.

FIGURE 4-98

(continues)

Case Programming Assignments

State fair tickets (continued)

USE CASE DEFINITION

1. The Windows application opens.
2. The user enters the number of State Fair tickets needed.
3. The user taps or clicks the Display Cost button.
4. The program displays the total cost of the State Fair tickets.
5. The user can tap or click the Clear button and repeat Steps 2 through 4.
6. The user terminates the program by tapping or clicking the Exit button.

FIGURE 4-99

FIGURE 4-100

2 TAXI FARE

Design a Windows application and write the code that will execute according to the program requirements in Figure 4-101 and the Use Case Definition in Figure 4-102. Before writing the code, create an event planning document for each event in the program. The completed program is shown in Figure 4-103.

REQUIREMENTS DOCUMENT

Date Submitted:	February 19, 2015
Application Title:	Taxi Fare Application
Purpose:	This Windows application computes the cost of a taxi fare.
Program Procedures:	From a window on the screen, the user enters the number of miles traveled in the taxi during one fare. The program calculates and displays the cost of the total fare.
Algorithms, Processing, and Conditions:	1. The user must be able to enter the number of miles traveled in a taxi cab for one fare. 2. The title of the program and a taxi logo will be displayed throughout the entire process. 3. After entering the number of miles traveled, the user taps or clicks the Display Fare button. 4. The formula for calculating the fare is: Flat fee ($2.25) + (number of miles * $2.75 per mile). 5. The program displays the fare in currency format.
Notes and Restrictions:	1. The user can clear the number of miles and make another entry. 2. An Exit button should close the application.
Comments:	The taxi logo is named Taxi and is available on CengageBrain.com.

FIGURE 4-101

(continues)

Case Programming Assignments

Taxi Fare (continued)

USE CASE DEFINITION

1. The Windows application opens.
2. The user enters the number of miles traveled.
3. The user taps or clicks the Display Fare button.
4. The program displays the total fare.
5. The user can tap or click the Clear button and repeat Steps 2 through 4.
6. The user terminates the program by tapping or clicking the Exit button.

FIGURE 4-102

© 2014 Cengage Learning

FIGURE 4-103

© Rouzes/E+/Getty Images

Case Programming Assignments

3

DOG YEARS

Design a Windows application and write the code that will execute according to the program requirements in Figure 4-104 and the Use Case Definition in Figure 4-105. Before writing the code, create an event planning document for each event in the program. The completed program is shown in Figure 4-106.

REQUIREMENTS DOCUMENT

Date Submitted: October 20, 2015

Application Title: Dog Years Application

Purpose: This Windows application calculates the age of a dog in human years.

Program Procedures: From a window on the screen, a dog owner enters a dog's age. The program displays the age of the dog and the comparison in human years.

Algorithms, Processing, and Conditions:
1. The dog owner must be able to enter the dog's age.
2. A picture of a dog will be displayed throughout the entire process.
3. After entering the dog's age, the dog owner taps or clicks the Compute button.
4. The dog's age in human years is displayed with the dog's age.

Notes and Restrictions:
1. The user can clear the dog's age by tapping or clicking a Clear button. The dog owner then can enter another dog's age.
2. An Exit button should close the application.

Comments: The dog picture is named Dog and is available on CengageBrain.com.

FIGURE 4-104

(continues)

Case Programming Assignments

Dog Years (continued)

USE CASE DEFINITION

1. The Windows application opens.
2. The dog owner enters the dog's age.
3. The dog owner taps or clicks the Compute button.
4. The program displays the dog's age and a computation of the age in human years.
5. The dog owner can tap or click the Clear button and then repeat Steps 2 through 4.
6. The user terminates the program by tapping or clicking the Exit button.

FIGURE 4-105

FIGURE 4-106

Photo courtesy of Corinne Hoisington

4 ●● SALES TAX CALCULATOR

Design a Windows application and write the code that will execute according to the program requirements in Figure 4-107. Before designing the user interface, create a Use Case Definition. Before writing the code, create an event planning document for each event in the program.

REQUIREMENTS DOCUMENT

Date Submitted: June 6, 2014

Application Title: Sales Tax Calculator Application

Purpose: This Windows application will compute the tax and final cost of a purchased item.

Program Procedures: From a window on the screen, the user enters the item name and cost of the item purchased. The program calculates the tax for the item and the final total, and then displays these values.

Algorithms, Processing, and Conditions:
1. The user must be able to enter the name of the item purchased and the cost of the item before tax.
2. A store name and store picture will be displayed throughout the entire process.
3. After the user enters the item name and the cost of the item, the user taps or clicks the Display Cost button.
4. The program displays the item name with the cost, tax, and final total.
5. The cost, tax, and final total should appear in currency format.
6. The tax rate for all items is 8.75%.
7. The final total is calculated by adding the cost and the tax.

Notes and Restrictions:
1. The user can clear the item name, cost, tax, and final total with a Clear button.
2. The user can tap or click an Exit button to close the application.

Comments: The store picture shown in the window should be selected from pictures available on the Web.

FIGURE 4-107

5   INCOME TAX CALCULATOR

Design a Windows application and write the code that will execute according to the program requirements in Figure 4-108. Before designing the user interface, create a Use Case Definition. Before writing the code, create an event planning document for each event in the program.

REQUIREMENTS DOCUMENT

Date Submitted:	January 4, 2015
Application Title:	Income Tax Calculator Application
Purpose:	This Windows application will compute and display the FICA tax, federal tax, and state tax for one year based on your income.
Program Procedures:	From a window on the screen, the user enters her yearly income. The program estimates the FICA tax, federal tax, and state tax for one year based on the user's income.
Algorithms, Processing, and Conditions:	1. Users must be able to enter their annual income. 2. The FICA tax (7.65%), federal tax (22%), and state income tax (3%) are computed. 3. The tax amounts should be displayed on separate lines and in currency format, two places past the decimal point. 4. The net pay should be displayed after the tax amounts have been deducted.
Notes and Restrictions:	1. The user can clear the income and taxes and then enter new data. 2. The user can use an Exit button to close the application.
Comments:	The designer should design the user interface, including all graphics and words displayed.

FIGURE 4-108

Case Programming Assignments

6 ●● CONVERT CURRENCY

Design a Windows application and write the code that will execute according to the program requirements in Figure 4-109. Before designing the user interface, create a Use Case Definition. Before writing the code, create an event planning document for each event in the program.

REQUIREMENTS DOCUMENT

Date Submitted:	November 4, 2014
Application Title:	Convert Currency Application
Purpose:	This Windows application will display the value of U.S. dollars in euros, Canadian dollars, and Mexican pesos.
Program Procedures:	From a window on the screen, the user should enter the number of U.S. dollars to be converted. The program will display the equivalent value in euros, Canadian dollars, and Mexican pesos.
Algorithms, Processing, and Conditions:	1. The user must be able to enter the number of U.S. dollars to be converted.
	2. After entering a number of U.S. dollars, the user taps or clicks the Convert Currency button.
	3. The program converts the number of U.S. dollars entered into the equivalent number of euros, Canadian dollars, and Mexican pesos. The program displays all three currency amounts with the amount in U.S. dollars.
	4. To find the conversion rates, the developer must consult appropriate Web sites. A possible site is *www.xe.com*.
	5. Because currency rates change dynamically, the user should enter the date and time that the conversion rates were applied. The date and time should be displayed in U.S. format.
	6. The user should be able to clear the date and time, the number of U.S. dollars entered, and the results of the calculations, and then enter new values.
Notes and Restrictions:	The user should be able to tap or click an Exit button to close the application.
Comments:	The designer must determine the design of the user interface and the words and graphics used in it.

FIGURE 4-109

Case Programming Assignments

7 MULCH CALCULATOR

Create a requirements document and a Use Case Definition document and then design a Windows application based on the case project shown in Figure 4-110. Before writing the code, create an event planning document for each event in the program.

A local landscaping design business requests a Windows application that allows you to compute how much rubber mulch you need to fill a playground. The rubber mulch is designed for safety and costs $9.87 per cubic foot. In addition, the mulch supplier charges a one-time delivery fee of $25. The Windows application should request the playground's length, width, and average depth (for example, 0.25 of a foot equals a mulch depth of 3 inches). The program then determines the volume of the playground in cubic feet (volume = length * width * depth) and displays the final cost of landscaping the playground, including the delivery fee. Allow the user to enter values with decimal places. The user should be able to clear all entries and then reenter data. To close the program, the user should be able to tap or click a button.

FIGURE 4-110

Case Programming Assignments

8 ●●● HOT TUB AREA AND CIRCUMFERENCE

Create a requirements document and a Use Case Definition document and then design a Windows application based on the case project shown in Figure 4-111. Before writing the code, create an event planning document for each event in the program.

You are interested in purchasing a hot tub. The listings on the Internet describe hot tubs that have a perfectly round shape. Each ad states the diameter of the hot tub. Create a Windows application that computes the area and circumference of a hot tub after the user enters the diameter in feet and inches (for example, 8 feet and 4 inches). The area and circumference results should display two decimal places. You should be able to clear the entry, enter a new diameter, and exit the form.

FIGURE 4-111

Case Programming Assignments

9 ●●● EXERCISE FOR A LIFETIME

Create a requirements document and a Use Case Definition document and then design a Windows application based on the case project shown in Figure 4-112. Before writing the code, create an event planning document for each event in the program.

The YMCA has asked you to write a Windows application that its members can use to determine the total number of hours they have exercised during their lifetimes, assuming they exercise an average of 3 hours per week. All users should enter their first name, their birth date, and the current date. For both dates, ask for the month, day, and year separately in numeric form. To calculate the number of hours exercised, assume 365 days per year and 30 days per month. The program must display the user's name and the number of hours the user has exercised in his or her lifetime. The user can tap or click a Clear button to clear all entries and results. An Exit button must be available to close the application.

FIGURE 4-112

CHAPTER 5
Decision Structures

OBJECTIVES

You will have mastered the material in this chapter when you can:

- Use the GroupBox object

- Place RadioButton objects in applications

- Display a message box

- Make decisions using If . . . Then statements

- Make decisions using If . . . Then . . . Else statements

- Make decisions using nested If statements

- Make decisions using logical operators

- Make decisions using Case statements

- Insert code snippets

- Test input to ensure a value is numeric

Introduction

Developers can code Visual Basic applications to make decisions based on the input of users or other conditions that occur. Decision making is one of the fundamental activities of a computer program. In this chapter, you will learn to write decision-making statements in Visual Basic 2012.

Visual Basic allows you to test conditions and perform different operations depending on the results. You can test whether a condition is true or false and change the flow of what happens in a program based on the user's input.

The sample program in this chapter is called the Wood Cabinet Estimate application. It is written for a carpenter or cabinetmaker who wants a program on the job site that can estimate the amount of wood needed for a job and the cost of building wood cabinets.

The application asks the user to enter the number of linear feet of cabinetry required and the desired wood type. The application then computes the cost of the cabinets based on a rate of $300.00 per linear foot for pine, $500.00 per linear foot for oak, and $650.00 per linear foot for cherry. Figure 5-1 shows the user interface for the application.

linear feet of cabinets

type of wood for cabinets

cost estimate to build cabinets

FIGURE 5-1
© Ivan Hunter/Digital Vision/Getty Images

ONLINE REINFORCEMENT

To view a video of the process described in the preceding paragraphs, visit CengageBrain. com and navigate to the resources for this title. Tap or click the link for Chapter 5 and then navigate to Video 5-1. Turn on your speakers to listen to the audio walkthrough of the steps.

In Figure 5-1, the Wood Cabinet Estimate Windows application displays the text "Wood Cabinet Estimate" in the title bar. The linear footage that the user enters in the TextBox object includes all cabinets for the job. The user chooses the wood type by selecting a RadioButton from the following list: Pine (the most common choice), Oak, or Cherry. After the user enters the number of linear feet of cabinetry and selects a type of wood, the user taps or clicks the Calculate button to obtain the cost estimate. The calculation is the linear feet multiplied by the cost of the selected wood. The cost estimate is displayed in currency format. In the example in Figure 5-1, the user entered 12 linear feet of cabinetry and selected cherry wood. After the user tapped or clicked the Calculate button, the application displayed a cost of $7,800.00 (12 × $650.00).

Tapping or clicking the Clear button clears the linear footage, resets the RadioButton selection to Pine, which is the most common wood type, and clears the calculation result.

Checking the validity of data the user entered is a requirement of the sample program in this chapter. In Chapter 4, you learned that if you enter nonnumeric data and attempt to use it in a calculation, the program will be terminated. To check for invalid data, the Wood Cabinet Estimate application ensures that the user enters a numeric value greater than zero in the Linear Feet TextBox object. A warning appears if the user leaves the TextBox blank or does not enter a valid number. Figure 5-2 displays the Input Error dialog box, called a Message Box, which directs the user to enter the linear feet for the cabinets.

FIGURE 5-2
© Ivan Hunter/Digital Vision/Getty Images

Checking input data for validity is an important task in Visual Basic programs. You will learn several data validation techniques in this chapter.

User Interface Design

The user interface for the Wood Cabinet Estimate application includes three new objects: a GroupBox, RadioButtons, and Message Boxes. The Message Boxes appear when the user enters a negative number or a nonnumeric value.

Use the GroupBox Object

The Wood Cabinet Estimate Form object requires a GroupBox object and RadioButton objects (Figure 5-3).

FIGURE 5-3
© Ivan Hunter/Digital Vision/Getty Images

A **GroupBox** object associates items as a group, allowing the user to select one item from the group. It also includes caption text. RadioButton objects allow the user to make choices. In Figure 5-3, the GroupBox object groups the radio buttons for selecting the wood type. When RadioButton objects are contained in a group box, the user can select only one radio button. For example, in Figure 5-3 the Pine radio button is selected. If the user taps or clicks the Oak radio button, it will be selected and the Pine radio button automatically will be deselected.

The GroupBox object shown in Figure 5-3 is displayed with the Text property of Wood Type as the caption text. The prefix for the GroupBox object (Name) property is grp. To place a GroupBox object on the Form object, you can complete the following steps:

STEP 1   Drag the GroupBox object from the Containers category of the Toolbox to the approximate location where you want to place the GroupBox object on the Form object.

The pointer changes when you place it over the Form object (Figure 5-4). The GroupBox object will be placed on the form at the location of the outline in the pointer.

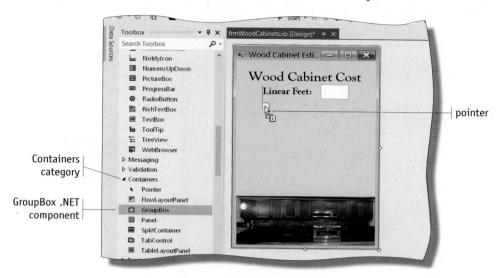

FIGURE 5-4

© Ivan Hunter/Digital Vision/Getty Images

STEP 2   When the pointer is in the correct location, release the object. With the GroupBox object selected, scroll in the Properties window to the (Name) property. Double-tap or double-click in the right column of the (Name) property, and then enter the name grpWoodType. Double-tap or double-click in the right column of the Text property to change the caption of the GroupBox object. Enter the text Wood Type. Click to the right of the Size property of the GroupBox object and enter 160, 100 as the size.

The name you entered is displayed in the (Name) property in the Properties window, the caption Wood Type is displayed, and the object is resized (Figure 5-5).

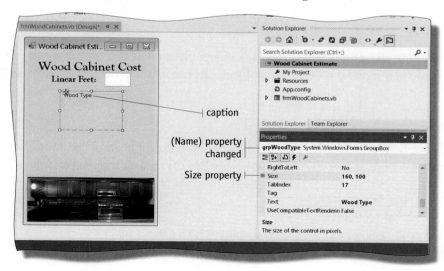

FIGURE 5-5

© Ivan Hunter/Digital Vision/Getty Images

STEP 3   Change the Font property to Goudy Old Style, Regular, 12 points. Change the BackColor property to White.

If you want to move the GroupBox to another location on the form, place the pointer over the drag box on the border of the GroupBox object and then drag it to the desired location. The Font property is set to Goudy Old Style, and the BackColor is white (Figure 5-6).

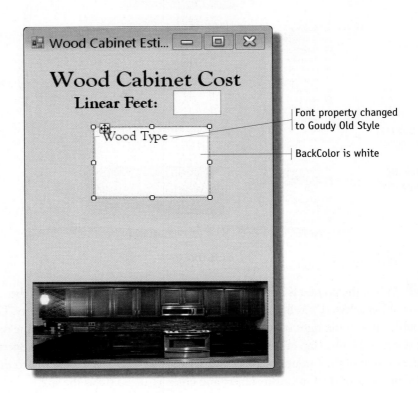

FIGURE 5-6
© Ivan Hunter/Digital Vision/Getty Images

Grouping all options in a GroupBox object gives the user a logical visual cue. Also, when you move the GroupBox object, all its contained objects move as well.

Add the RadioButton Objects

The GroupBox object in the Wood Cabinet Estimate application contains a set of RadioButton objects (see Figure 5-3 on page 286). The user may select only one type of wood: pine, oak, or cherry. To place RadioButton objects within the GroupBox object, you can complete the following steps:

STEP 1 Drag one RadioButton object from the Toolbox to the GroupBox object. Drag a second RadioButton object from the Toolbox into the GroupBox object, and use blue snap lines to align and separate the RadioButton objects vertically.

The second RadioButton object is aligned vertically with a blue snap line, which separates it vertically from the first RadioButton object (Figure 5-7).

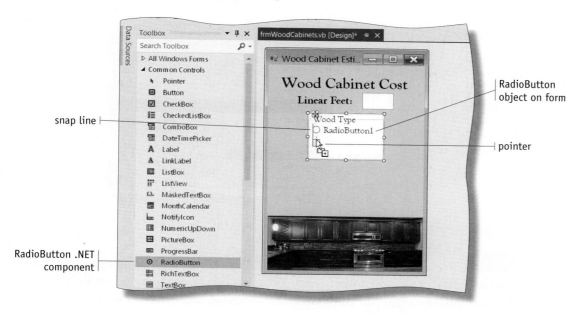

FIGURE 5-7

© Ivan Hunter/Digital Vision/Getty Images

STEP 2 Release the RadioButton object to place it within the GroupBox object. Using the same technique, add a third RadioButton object.

Three RadioButton objects are placed on the form and aligned within the GroupBox object (Figure 5-8).

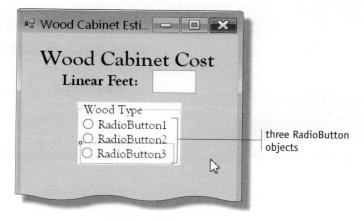

FIGURE 5-8

STEP 3   Name the RadioButton objects by selecting them one at a time, double-tapping or double-clicking in the right column of the (Name) property in the Properties window, and entering the name. The names for the radio buttons, from top to bottom, should be radPine, radOak, and radCherry.

The (Name) property is selected. The names radPine, radOak, and radCherry are entered (Figure 5-9).

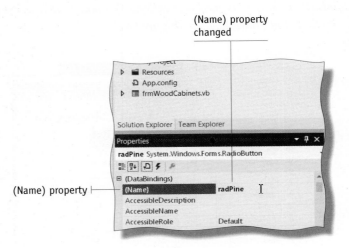

FIGURE 5-9

STEP 4   Change the Text property for each RadioButton by double-tapping or double-clicking the right column of the Text property and typing Pine for the first RadioButton, Oak for the second RadioButton, and Cherry for the third RadioButton.

The Text property is changed to the types of wood available: Pine, Oak, and Cherry (Figure 5-10).

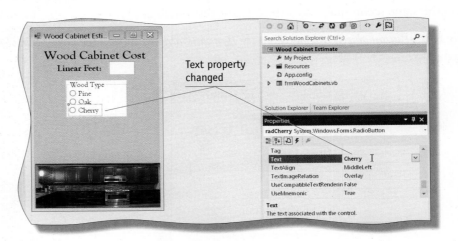

© Ivan Hunter/Digital Vision/Getty Images

FIGURE 5-10

A RadioButton object is best used when you have only one selection per group. What type of object would you use to select more than one option?

Checkbox objects are used with lists of options in which the user may select any number of choices. In other words, each Checkbox object is independent of all other check boxes in the list, so checking one box does not uncheck the others.

Use the Checked Property of RadioButton Objects

The RadioButton objects in the Wood Cabinet Estimate application allow the user to select one wood type. When the user selects Cherry, as shown in Figure 5-11, the RadioButton is selected, and the small circle in the radio button is shaded. When the Cherry RadioButton is selected, its Checked property changes from False (unselected) to True (selected).

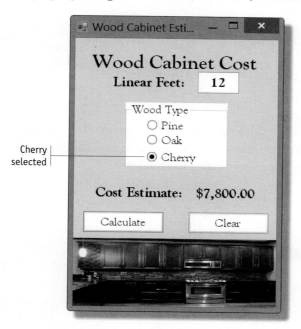

FIGURE 5-11
© Ivan Hunter/Digital Vision/Getty Images

During design time, you usually set the Checked property to True for the most commonly selected RadioButton to save the user from having to select it. In the Wood Cabinet Estimate application, the cabinetmaker uses Pine most often. To cause the Pine RadioButton object named radPine to appear selected (shaded) when the program begins, you change the Checked property for the radPine RadioButton from False to True (Figure 5-12).

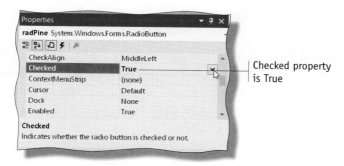

FIGURE 5-12

Windows Application Container Objects

The Panel object in a Windows application works like a GroupBox object. For Windows applications, Visual Basic provides four additional container objects: FlowLayoutPanel, SplitContainer, TabControl, and TableLayoutPanel. The GroupBox object is used most often; it provides several options that are not available with the Panel object. The table in Figure 5-13 shows the differences between the GroupBox and the Panel objects.

Option	GroupBox Object	Panel Object
Have a caption	Yes	No
Have scroll bars	Yes	No
Display a labeled border	Yes	No

FIGURE 5-13

© 2014 Cengage Learning

Figure 5-14 shows the Windows application Toolbox and a GroupBox object and Panel object in a Windows Form. Notice in the Toolbox that the GroupBox and Panel objects are in a category called Containers.

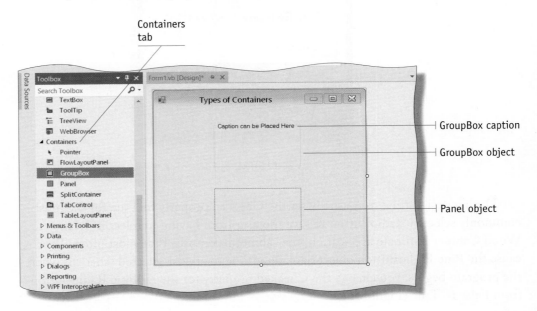

FIGURE 5-14

GroupBox and Panel objects have the same purpose of grouping RadioButtons and other objects, but they differ in their appearance. The GroupBox object in Figure 5-14 displays a border around its edges, with a text area in the upper-left portion for a caption. The Panel object has a black dashed border that does not appear when the application is executed.

Related sets of RadioButtons should be placed in separate container objects so that the user can select one radio button from each group. Always place the container object on the form first, and then drag the RadioButton objects into the container object.

The Course Sign-Up example in Figure 5-15 displays a Windows application that allows the user to sign up for a technology course. Notice the two separate groups of RadioButton objects. In the Choose Course Level GroupBox object, the user should select a course level. In the Choose Semester GroupBox object, the user should identify the semester for the course. As you can see, the user selects one radio button from the left group and one radio button from the right group.

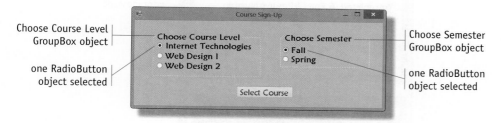

Choose Course Level GroupBox object

one RadioButton object selected

Choose Semester GroupBox object

one RadioButton object selected

FIGURE 5-15

Display a Message Box

In the Wood Cabinet Estimate application, a message box, also called a dialog box, opens if the user does not enter the length of the cabinets correctly. The dialog box displays an error message if the user omits the length or enters nonnumeric data (Figure 5-16).

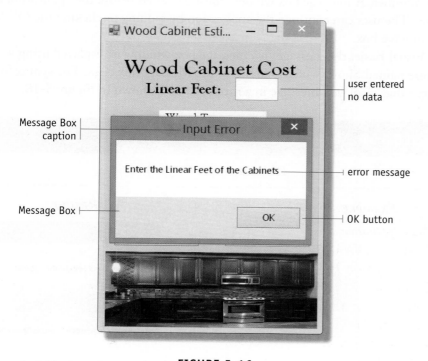

user entered no data

Message Box caption

error message

Message Box

OK button

FIGURE 5-16
© Ivan Hunter/Digital Vision/Getty Images

If the user enters a negative number for the length of the cabinets, a message box appears and indicates that a positive number is necessary (Figure 5-17).

FIGURE 5-17
© Ivan Hunter/Digital Vision/Getty Images

This message box reminds the user to enter the linear feet of the cabinets as a positive number. A message box window must be closed before the application can continue. The user can continue the application by tapping or clicking the OK button in the message box.

In Visual Basic, the message in a message box window is displayed using a procedure named Show, which is found in the MessageBox class. The syntax for the statement that displays a message in a message box is shown in Figure 5-18.

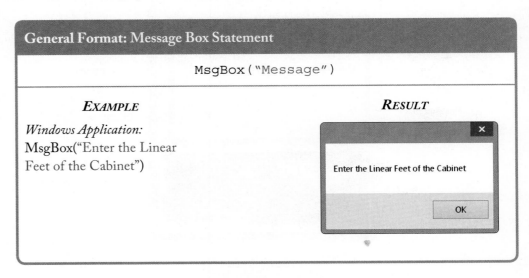

FIGURE 5-18

The string message shown in the parentheses will appear in the message box when the code is executed. The string message is considered an argument of the procedure. You will recall that an argument is a value passed to a procedure. The first argument for the MsgBox command contains the message to be printed in the message box window during execution.

The example in Figure 5-19 illustrates the code that could be used in the Calculate button click event handler. This code could be executed if the user taps or clicks the Calculate button without entering a numeric value in the Linear Feet text box (Figure 5-16 on page 293).

Display Message Box Captions

A message box can be displayed during execution with a variety of arguments. For example, by using the syntax shown in Figure 5-19, a message box can display a message and a caption in the title bar (two arguments with two commas between the two arguments).

notice the two commas between the two arguments

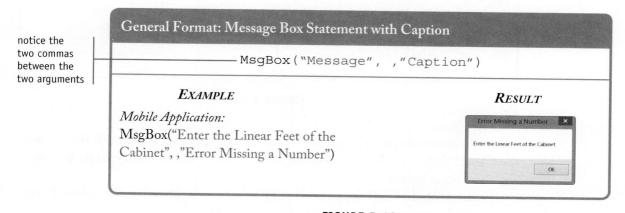

FIGURE 5-19

© 2014 Cengage Learning

The title bar in the example in Figure 5-19 displays a caption and the message box displays a message. In many applications, the caption is used to give further information to the user.

Message Box Buttons

The general format for changing the button command from OK to another button type is shown in Figure 5-20. The button entry can be a command or a value representing a command.

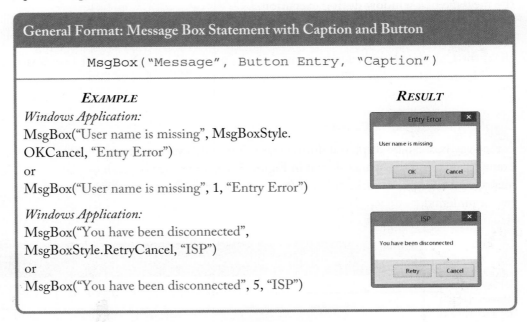

General Format: Message Box Statement with Caption and Button

```
MsgBox("Message", Button Entry, "Caption")
```

EXAMPLE

Windows Application:
MsgBox("User name is missing", MsgBoxStyle.
OKCancel, "Entry Error")
or
MsgBox("User name is missing", 1, "Entry Error")

Windows Application:
MsgBox("You have been disconnected",
MsgBoxStyle.RetryCancel, "ISP")
or
MsgBox("You have been disconnected", 5, "ISP")

RESULT

FIGURE 5-20

In the first example in Figure 5-20, the buttons specified are the OK button and the Cancel button. In the second example, the buttons shown are the Retry button and the Cancel button.

Figure 5-21 shows all the possible entries that can be placed in the Button Entry portion of the argument passed to the Show procedure.

MsgBoxStyle Arguments	Value	Use
MsgBoxStyle.OKOnly	0	Displays an OK button — default setting
MsgBoxStyle.OKCancel	1	Displays an OK and Cancel button
MsgBoxStyle.AbortRetryIgnore	2	After a failing situation, the user can choose to Abort, Retry, or Ignore
MsgBoxStyle.YesNoCancel	3	Displays Yes, No, and Cancel buttons
MsgBoxStyle.YesNo	4	Displays Yes and No buttons
MsgBoxStyle.RetryCancel	5	After an error occurs, the user can choose to Retry or Cancel

FIGURE 5-21

Message Box Icons

In the button entry portion of the argument (the second argument), you can add a message box icon (Figure 5-22). The word "or" connects the button entry to the icon entry.

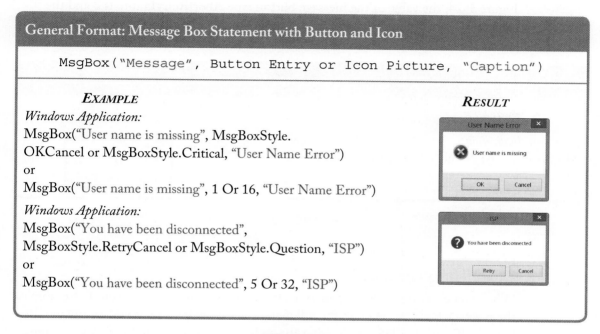

General Format: Message Box Statement with Button and Icon

```
MsgBox("Message", Button Entry or Icon Picture, "Caption")
```

EXAMPLE

Windows Application:
MsgBox("User name is missing", MsgBoxStyle.
OKCancel or MsgBoxStyle.Critical, "User Name Error")
or
MsgBox("User name is missing", 1 Or 16, "User Name Error")

Windows Application:
MsgBox("You have been disconnected",
MsgBoxStyle.RetryCancel or MsgBoxStyle.Question, "ISP")
or
MsgBox("You have been disconnected", 5 Or 32, "ISP")

RESULT

FIGURE 5-22

The picture icon represents the MsgBoxStyle that can be displayed as a graphic icon in the message box. Both examples in Figure 5-22 show a graphic icon added to the message box.

The picture icon in the second argument can contain any of the entries shown in Figure 5-23.

MsgBoxStyle Icons	Value	Icon	Use
MsgBoxStyle.Critical	16		Alerts the user to an error
MsgBoxStyle.Question	32		Displays a question mark
MsgBoxStyle.Exclamation	48		Alerts the user to a possible problem
MsgBoxStyle.Information	64		Displays an information icon

FIGURE 5-23

In the general formats shown for a message box, you must follow the syntax of the statements exactly, which means the commas, quotation marks, and parentheses must be placed in the statement as shown.

You can also add values to display both the buttons and a picture icon. In Figure 5-24, the value of the message button type AbortRetryIgnore is 2 and the value of the critical icon is 16. If you add 16 plus 2, the result is 18.

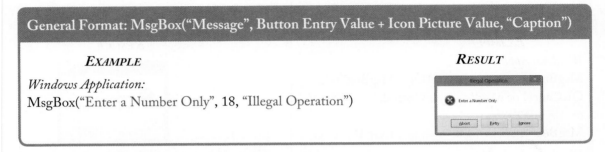

General Format: MsgBox("Message", Button Entry Value + Icon Picture Value, "Caption")

EXAMPLE	RESULT
Windows Application: MsgBox("Enter a Number Only", 18, "Illegal Operation")	

FIGURE 5-24

Message Box IntelliSense

When you enter the code for a message box, IntelliSense can assist you. For example, the message box you create in the following steps contains a message, caption, and buttons. To use IntelliSense to enter the code, you can complete the following steps:

STEP 1   In the code window, inside the event handler you are coding, type msg to display MsgBox in the IntelliSense list.

IntelliSense displays a list of the allowable entries (Figure 5-25). When you type msg, MsgBox is selected in the IntelliSense list.

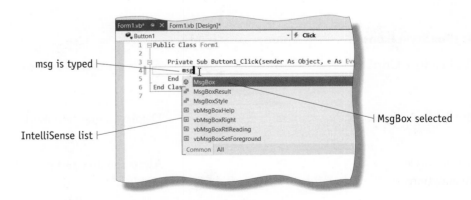

FIGURE 5-25

STEP 2   Press the tab key to select MsgBox in the IntelliSense list. Type the following text: ("You have been disconnected from the Internet", m)

The first argument for the message box is entered (Figure 5-26). IntelliSense displays a list of allowable entries for the second argument.

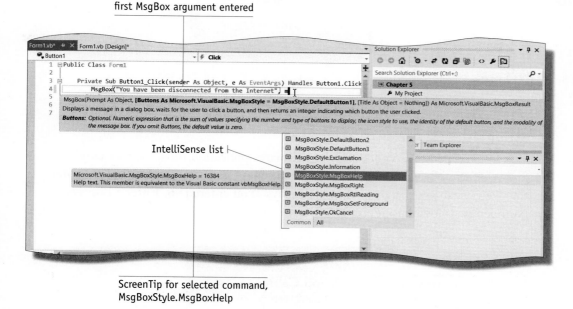

first MsgBox argument entered

IntelliSense list ⊢

ScreenTip for selected command,
MsgBoxStyle.MsgBoxHelp

FIGURE 5-26

STEP 3   Select the MsgBoxStyle.AbortRetryIgnore argument by pressing the up arrow until the correct argument is highlighted. Type a comma. Then type "ISP" and a right parenthesis.

The MsgBoxStyle.AbortRetryIgnore argument is selected. Next, the comma and the caption "ISP" are entered with a right parenthesis (Figure 5-27).

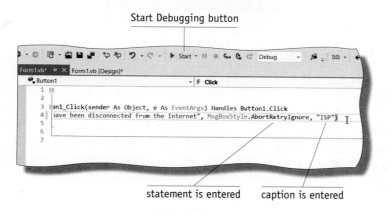

Start Debugging button

statement is entered   caption is entered

FIGURE 5-27

STEP 4   Tap or click the Start Debugging button on the Standard toolbar.

The application runs, displaying the message box that shows the message, buttons, and caption (Figure 5-28).

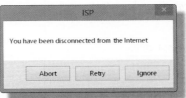

FIGURE 5-28

String Concatenation

Recall that when the Wood Cabinet Estimate application runs, the user enters the linear footage of the wood cabinets. If the user enters a number that is not greater than zero, such as –6, a message box displays "You entered –6. Enter a Positive Number", as shown in Figure 5-29.

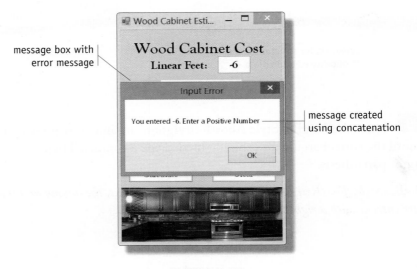

message box with error message

message created using concatenation

FIGURE 5-29
© Ivan Hunter/Digital Vision/Getty Images

To create the message in the message box, you can use concatenation, which you learned about in Chapter 4. In Figure 5-29, the string message is constructed by joining a string ("You entered"), a variable named decFeet that contains the entered linear footage (which must be converted to a string), and a string for the final part of the message (". Enter a Positive Number"). The code in Figure 5-30 creates the message box.

```
46    MsgBox("You entered " & decFeet.ToString() & ". Enter a Positive Number", , "Input Error")
```

FIGURE 5-30

You will recall that the operator to concatenate strings is the ampersand (&). When the statement is executed, the three string elements are joined together (concatenated) to form the one string that is displayed in the message box.

Make Decisions with Conditional Statements

HEADS UP

In older versions of Visual Basic, the plus (+) sign was used to concatenate strings instead of the ampersand (&) symbol. The + sign still functions for concatenation, but it can be confusing because it looks like the plus sign used in addition. You should always use the ampersand.

In the Wood Cabinet Estimate application, users can select one of three types of wood: pine, oak, or cherry. The price per linear foot is based on the user's choice of wood. To select the wood type, the user must tap or click one of three radio buttons titled Pine, Oak, and Cherry. Then, based on the choice, the application uses a different wood cost.

Visual Basic uses decision structures to deal with the different conditions that occur based on the values entered into an application. A **decision structure** is one of the three fundamental control structures used in computer programming. For example, if the user taps or clicks the Pine radio button, the wood cost is set to $300.00 per linear foot. The statement that tests the radio button is called a **conditional statement**. The condition to check is whether the Pine radio button is selected. If so, the wood cost is set to $300.00.

When a condition is tested in a Visual Basic program, the condition either is true or false. For example, when checking to determine if the Pine radio button is selected, the condition can either be true (the button is checked) or false (not checked). All conditional statements result in the tested condition either being true or false.

To implement a conditional statement and the statements that are executed when a condition is true or false, Visual Basic uses the If statement and its variety of formats. You will learn about the If statement in the following sections.

Use an If . . . Then Statement

In the sample program, an If . . . Then statement is used to determine the cost of the wood. The simplest form of the If . . . Then statement is shown in Figure 5-31.

```
5        If condition Then
6            Statement(s) executed when condition is true
7        End If
8
```

FIGURE 5-31

In Figure 5-31, when the condition tested in the If statement on line 5 is true, the statement(s) between the If and the End If keywords will be executed. If the condition is not true, no statements between the If and End If keywords will be executed, and program execution will continue with the statement(s) after the End If statement.

HEADS UP

If Visual Basic does not automatically indent the code in an If . . . Then statement, follow these steps: 1) Tap or click TOOLS on the menu bar, and then tap or click Options; 2) if necessary, expand Text Editor in the left panel; 3) if necessary, expand Basic in the left panel; 4) if necessary, tap or click VB specific in the left panel; 5) ensure the "Pretty listing (reformatting) of code" check box contains a check mark; 6) tap or click the ok button in the Options dialog box.

Visual Basic automatically indents statements to be executed when a condition is true or not true to indicate which lines of code are within the conditional If . . . Then structure. This is why the statement on line 6 in Figure 5-31 on the previous page is indented. The End If keywords terminate the If . . . Then block of code. After executing the If . . . Then block, execution continues with any statements that follow the closing End If statement.

Relational Operators

In Figure 5-31, the condition portion of the If . . . Then statement means a condition is tested to determine if it is true or false. The conditions that can be tested are:

1. Is one value equal to another value?
2. Is one value not equal to another value?
3. Is one value greater than another value?
4. Is one value less than another value?
5. Is one value greater than or equal to another value?
6. Is one value less than or equal to another value?

To test these conditions, Visual Basic provides relational operators that are used within the conditional statement to express the relationship being tested. Figure 5-32 shows these relational operators.

	Relational Operator	Meaning	Example	Resulting Condition
1	=	Equal to	8 = 8	True
2	<>	Not equal to	6 <> 6	False
3	>	Greater than	7 > 9	False
4	<	Less than	4 < 6	True
5	>=	Greater than or equal to	3 >= 3	True
6	<=	Less than or equal to	7 <= 5	False

FIGURE 5-32

A condition tested using a relational operator is evaluated as true or false. Example 1 tests whether 8 is equal to 8. Because it is, the resulting condition is true. Example 2 tests whether 6 is not equal to 6. Because they are equal, the resulting condition is false. Similarly, Example 5 tests whether 3 is greater than or equal to 3. Because they are equal, the resulting condition is true.

As an example of using a conditional operator, consider the following problem, in which an If statement is used to determine if someone is old enough to vote. If the value in the intAge variable is greater than or equal to 18, then the person is old enough to vote. If not, the person is not old enough to vote. The If . . . Then statement to test this condition is shown in Figure 5-33.

```
 8              If intAge >= 18 Then
 9                      lblVotingEligibility.Text = "You are old enough to vote"
10              End If
```

FIGURE 5-33

In Figure 5-33, if the value in the intAge variable is greater than or equal to 18, the string value "You are old enough to vote" is assigned to the Text property of the lblVotingEligibility Label object. If not, then no processing occurs based on the conditional statement and any statement(s) following the End If keywords will be executed.

You can see in Figure 5-33 that several keywords are required in an If . . . Then statement. The word If must be the first item. Next, the condition(s) to be tested are stated, followed by the word Then. This keyword is required in an If statement.

The End If keywords follow the statements to be executed when the condition is true. This entry also is required. It signals to the Visual Basic compiler that the statements following it must be executed regardless of the result of the conditional statement; that is, the End If keywords are the last element within the If block and no subsequent statements depend on the If block for execution.

To enter the If . . . Then statement shown in Figure 5-33, you can complete the following steps:

STEP 1   With the insertion point in the correct location in the code, type if and then press the SPACEBAR.

The statement begins with the word if (Figure 5-34). The If command is displayed in blue because it is a Visual Basic keyword. You can type uppercase or lowercase letters.

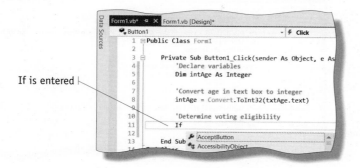

FIGURE 5-34

STEP 2 Type `inta` to select the variable named intAge in the IntelliSense list. Type `>=18` as the condition to be tested. Press the ENTER key.

The If... Then statement is entered in the code window (Figure 5–35). When the ENTER key is pressed, Visual Basic adds the keyword Then to the end of the If statement line of code and inserts spaces between the elements of the statement for ease of reading. In addition, Visual Basic inserts the End If keywords following a blank line. Notice the keywords Then and End If are capitalized and displayed in blue.

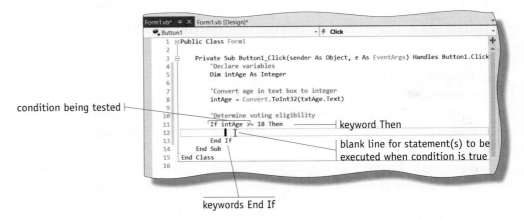

FIGURE 5-35

STEP 3 On the blank line (line 12 in Figure 5-35), enter the statement that should be executed when the condition is true. To place the message "You are old enough to vote" in the Text property of the lblVotingEligibility Label object, insert the code shown in Figure 5-33 on the previous page. Remember to use IntelliSense to reference the lblVotingEligibility Label object.

The resulting statement is entered between the If and End If keywords (Figure 5–36). Notice that Visual Basic automatically indents the line for ease of reading. The blank line allows you to enter more statements. If you have no further statements, you can press the DELETE key to delete the blank line in the If... Then statement.

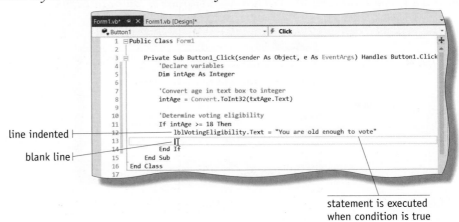

FIGURE 5-36

Compare Strings

You also can write an If . . . Then statement to compare string values using the relational operators shown in Figure 5-32 on page 302. A string value comparison compares each character in two strings, starting with the first character in each string. For example, in the two strings in Figure 5-37, the comparison begins with the first character (a) in each string. Because the characters are equal, the comparison continues with the second character in each string, which is b. Because these characters are equal, the comparison continues with the third character in each string, c. Because all three characters are equal, the strings are considered equal and the resulting condition from the If statement is true.

```
13          Dim String1 As String = "abc"
14          Dim String2 As String = "abc"
15
16          If String1 = String2 Then
17                  lblStringTest.Text = "Equal"
18          End If
```

© 2014 Cengage Learning

FIGURE 5-37

All characters found in strings, including letters, numbers, and special characters, are in a sequence based on how the characters are coded internally on the computer. In Visual Studio 2012, characters are stored and sequenced in Unicode, which is a coding methodology that can accommodate more than 60,000 characters. Appendix A in this book shows the Unicode sequence for the standard keyboard characters. You will find that numbers have lower Unicode values than uppercase letters, and uppercase letters have lower values than lowercase letters.

Using the If . . . Then statement, the following comparisons produce the following resulting conditions:

Example 1:

```
Dim String1 As String = "Powder"
Dim String2 As String = "Power"

If String1 < String2 Then
```

Resulting Condition: True because in the fourth character position, the letter d is less than the letter e.

Example 2:

```
Dim String1 As String = "6"
Dim String2 As String = "T"

If String1 < String2 Then
```

Resulting Condition: True because in a string comparison, a number is less than an uppercase letter.

Example 3:

```
Dim String1 As String = "12"
Dim String2 As String = "9"

If String1 < String2 Then
```

Resulting Condition: True because in a string comparison, the characters in the first position of the string are compared first. Because the value 1 in String1 is less than the value 9 in String2, the entire value in String1 is considered less than the value in String2.

Example 4:

```
Dim String1 As String = "anchor"
Dim String2 As String = "Anchorline"

If String1 > String2 Then
```

Resulting Condition: True because a lowercase letter (the a in the first position of String1) is considered greater than an uppercase letter (the A in the first position of String2).

Compare Different Data Types

Every type of data available in Visual Basic can be compared. Different numeric types can be compared to each other using an If statement. A single string character can be compared to a Char data type. The following examples illustrate some of the allowable comparisons.

Example 1: Decimal compared to Double

```
If decQuarterlySales > dblSalesQuota Then
```

If decQuarterlySales = 110,324.54 and dblSalesQuota = 112,435.54, the condition is false.

Example 2: Decimal compared to Integer

```
If decTirePressureReading > intTirePressureMaximum Then
```

If decTirePressureReading = 30.21 and intTirePressureMaximum = 30, the condition is true.

Example 3: Double compared to Integer

```
If dblCurrentTemperature >= intHeatDanger Then
```

If dblCurrentTemperature = 94.543 and intHeatDanger = 98, the condition is false.

Example 4: String compared to Char

```
If strChemistryGrade < chrPassingGrade Then
```

If strChemistryGrade = "B" and chrPassingGrade = "C", the condition is true.

Visual Basic allows comparisons between most data types. If you are unsure whether a comparison can be made, write an If statement to ensure the comparison is working properly.

Use the If . . . Then . . . Else Statement

An If . . . Then statement executes a set of instructions if a condition is true. If the condition is false, the instructions between the If statement and the End If statement are not executed and program execution continues with the statement(s) following the End If statement.

In many applications, the logic requires one set of instructions to be executed if a condition is true and another set of instructions to be executed if a condition is false. For example, a program requirement could specify that if a student's test score is 70 or greater, the message "You passed the examination" should be displayed, while if the test score is less than 70, the message "You failed the examination" should be displayed.

To execute one set of instructions if a condition is true and another set of instructions if the condition is false, you can use the If . . . Then . . . Else statement. Figure 5-38 illustrates the syntax of the If . . . Then . . . Else statement.

```
16        If condition Then
17            Statement(s) executed if condition is true
18        Else
19            Statement(s) executed if condition is false
20        End If
```

FIGURE 5-38

If the condition tested by the If statement is true, the statement(s) between the Then keyword and the Else keyword will be executed. If the condition tested is false, the statement(s) between the Else keyword and the End If keywords will be executed.

The example in Figure 5-39 shows the use of the If . . . Then . . . Else statement to calculate student fees by testing the student's status.

statement is executed if
student is a graduate

```
27          If strStudentStatus = "Graduate" Then
28              decStudentFees = decGraduateFee * intNumberOfUnits
29          Else
30              decStudentFees = decUndergraduateFee * intNumberOfUnits
31          End If
```

statement is executed if
student is not a graduate

FIGURE 5-39

HEADS UP

A condition cannot be true and false at the same time, so statements for a true condition and statements for a false condition cannot both be executed based on a single comparison.

If the student is in graduate school, the student fees are calculated by multiplying the graduate fee by the number of units. If the student is not a graduate student, fees are calculated by multiplying the undergraduate fee by the number of units. Notice that a student cannot be both an undergraduate and a graduate student, so either the statement following the Then keyword will be executed or the statement following the Else keyword will be executed.

Compare to an Arithmetic Expression

An If statement can compare an arithmetic expression to a constant or other data type. For example, in Figure 5-40, the withdrawals from a bank account are compared to the value obtained by adding the current balance to deposits and then subtracting account charges.

```
41          If decWithdrawals > decCurrentBalance + decDeposits - decAccountCharges Then
42              lblAccountStatus.Text = "Overdrawn"
43          Else
44              lblAccountStatus.Text = "Balance is Positive"
45          End If
```

FIGURE 5-40

In Figure 5-40, if the value in the decWithdrawals variable is greater than the current balance plus the deposits minus the account charges, the Text property of the lblAccountStatus Label object is set to Overdrawn. If the value in decWithdrawals is less than or equal to the value from the arithmetic expression, the message Balance is Positive is placed in the Text property of the lblAccountStatus Label object. Notice that the arithmetic expression is evaluated prior to the comparison. If the condition is true, the statement between the Then and Else keywords is executed. If the condition is false, the statement between the Else and End If keywords is executed.

Use the If . . . Then . . . ElseIf Statement

Complex logic problems might require a more complex structure than the If . . . Then . . . Else logic structure. For example, consider the following logical problem that must be solved in a computer program:

An online store charges a shipping fee based on the dollar amount of the order being shipped. The rules are:

1. If the order amount is above $500, the shipping cost is $30.
2. If the order amount is more than $400 and not greater than $500, the shipping cost is $25.
3. If the order amount is more than $200 and not greater than $400, the shipping cost is $20.
4. If the order amount is equal to or less than $200, the shipping cost is $15.

When one of the conditions is found to be true, the rest of the conditions are not tested because the correct condition has been found. To solve this problem, you should think this way:

1. If the order amount is greater than $500.00, then the shipping cost is $30.00 and no more processing is needed to determine the shipping cost.
2. If, however, the order amount is not greater than $500.00, I must check further to see if it is greater than $400.00 (400.01 through 500.00). If so, the shipping cost is $25.00.
3. If the order amount is not greater than $400.00, the next step is to check whether it is greater than $200.00. In other words, check within the range of $201.00 to $400.00. If this is true, the shipping cost is $20.00.
4. If none of the above is true, then the order amount must be less than or equal to $200. In this case, the shipping cost is $15.00.

As you can see, a simple If . . . Then . . . Else statement could not solve this logic problem because the structure tests only a single condition and specifies the processing based on whether the condition is true or false. For a problem in which multiple conditions must be tested, the If . . . Then . . . ElseIf statement might be appropriate. The general format of the If . . . Then . . . ElseIf statement is shown in Figure 5-41.

```
105        If decOrderAmount > 500D Then
106            Statement(s) executed if condition is true
107        ElseIf decOrderAmount > 400D Then
108            Statement(s) executed if condition is true
109        ElseIf decOrderAmount > 200D Then
110            Statement(s) executed if condition is true
111        ElseIf decOrderAmount > 0D Then
112            Statement(s) executed if condition is true
113        End If
```

FIGURE 5-41

HEADS UP

When testing conditions like those in the example in Figure 5-41, make sure you do not leave a number out of the range of numbers being tested. For example, if one ElseIf statement tests decOrderAmount > 400.00 and the next ElseIf statement tests < 400.00, the value 400.00 has not been tested and the program will not properly process the value 400.00.

Once a condition is true in the code in Figure 5-41 on the previous page, Visual Basic bypasses the rest of the ElseIf statements. For example, assume the order amount is $455. The first condition tests whether the order amount is greater than 500. The first condition would test false because 455 is not greater than 500.

Next, the ElseIf entry will test whether 455 is greater than 400. Because the value 455 is greater than 400, the condition is true and the statement(s) on line 108 will be executed. The remaining ElseIf statements will not be evaluated because the true condition has been found.

Separate If . . . Then statements are not used in the example in Figure 5-41 because each condition would have to be tested even though a condition had already been found to be true. When using an If . . . Then . . . ElseIf statement, any remaining conditions are not tested after a condition is found to be true, making the process faster and more efficient.

Trailing Else Statements

You may want to include a trailing Else statement at the end of an If . . . Then . . . ElseIf conditional statement to handle a condition that does not meet any of the previous conditions tested. In the example in Figure 5-42, the code is determining whether the user is eligible for Social Security benefits. If the user's age is greater than or equal to 65, the user receives full benefits. If the user's age is between 0 and 65, the user is not eligible for benefits.

```
115         If intAge >= 65 Then
116             lblSocialSecurity.Text = "Full Benefits"
117         ElseIf intAge > 0 Then
118             lblSocialSecurity.Text = "Not Eligible for Benefits"
119         Else
120             lblSocialSecurity.Text = "Invalid Age"
121         End If
```

FIGURE 5-42

In Figure 5-42, the statement on line 120 that follows the trailing Else statement on line 119 is executed if the number in the intAge variable does not meet the conditions stated in the previous If statements. For example, if the intAge variable contains a negative value such as −12, the Text property of the lblSocialSecurity Label object will be set to "Invalid Age".

Nested If Statements

At times, more than one decision has to be made to determine what processing must occur. For example, if one condition is true, a second condition may need to be tested before the correct code is executed. To test a second condition only after determining that a first condition is true (or false), you must place an If statement within another If statement. When you place one If statement within another one, the inner If statement is said to be nested within the outer If Statement. The syntax of a nested If statement is shown in Figure 5-43.

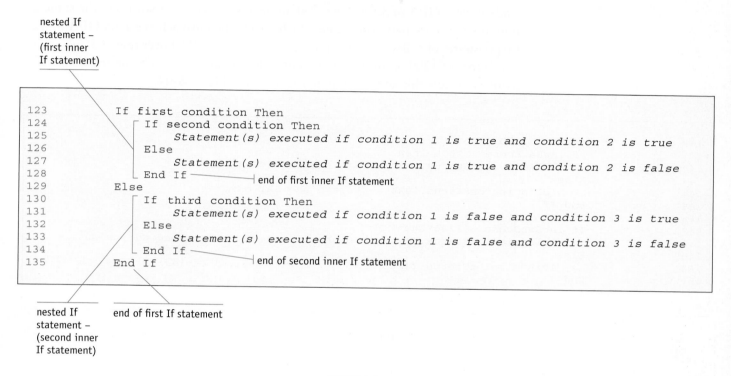

FIGURE 5-43

In Figure 5-43, if the first condition tested is true, the statements following the keyword Then are executed. The statement to be executed when the first condition is true is another If statement (line 124) that tests the second condition. This second If statement is said to be a nested If statement or an inner If statement. If the second condition is true, the program executes the statement(s) on line 125 following the keyword Then for the first inner If statement. If the second condition is not true, the program executes the statement(s) on line 127 following the keyword Else for the first inner If statement. The End If entry (line 128) follows the first inner If statement, indicating the end of the effect of the first inner If statement.

If the first condition is not true, then the program executes the statements following the keyword Else on line 129 for the first If statement. The statement to be executed when the first condition is not true is an If statement that tests the third condition (line 130). If the third condition is true, the program executes the statement(s) on line 131 following the Then keyword of the second inner If statement. Finally, if the second inner If statement that tests the third condition is false, the statement(s) on line 133 are executed.

To illustrate a nested If statement, assume a college has the following admissions policy: If an applying student has a GPA (grade point average) greater than 3.5 and a score greater than 1000 on the SAT college entrance exam, then that student is granted admission. If an applying student has a GPA greater than 3.5 but an SAT score of 1000 or lower, the student is advised to retake the SAT exam. If an applying student has a GPA of 3.5 or lower but an SAT score greater than 1200, the student is granted probationary admission, which means she must achieve a 2.5 GPA in the first semester of college. If an applying student has a GPA lower than 3.5 and an SAT score of 1200 or lower, the student is denied admission. The nested If statement to process this admission policy is shown in Figure 5-44.

```
140    If decGPA > 3.5D Then
141        If intSatScore > 1000 Then
142            lblAdmissionStatus.Text = "You have earned admission"
143        Else
144            lblAdmissionStatus.Text = "Retake the SAT exam"
145        End If
146    Else
147        If intSatScore > 1200 Then
148            lblAdmissionStatus.Text = "You have earned probationary admission"
149        Else
150            lblAdmissionStatus.Text = "You have been denied admission"
151        End If
152    End If
```

FIGURE 5-44

Notice in Figure 5-44 that the test for greater than 1000 on the SAT (line 141) must take place only after the test for a GPA greater than 3.5 (line 140), because the test for greater than 1000 is required only after the program determines that the GPA is greater than 3.5. Therefore, a nested If statement is required. In addition, the test for greater than 1200 (line 147) should occur only after the program determines that the GPA is less than 3.5. As you can see, you should use a nested If statement when a condition must be tested only after another condition has been tested.

Other Nested If Configurations

You can use nested If statements in a variety of forms. Assume, for example, that a school's admissions policy is as follows: If an applying student has a GPA greater than 3.5 and an SAT score greater than 1100, then that student is granted admission. If an applying student has a GPA greater than 3.5 but an SAT score of 1100 or lower, the student is advised to retake the SAT exam. If an applying student has a GPA of 3.5 or lower, the student is denied admission. The nested If statement in Figure 5-45 solves this logic problem.

```
154          If decGPA > 3.5D Then
155              If intSatScore > 1100 Then
156                  lblAdmissionStatus.Text = "You have earned admission"
157              Else
158                  lblAdmissionStatus.Text = "Retake the SAT exam"
159              End If
160          Else
161              lblAdmissionStatus.Text = "You have been denied admission"
162          End If
```

FIGURE 5-45

In Figure 5-45, if the GPA is greater than 3.5, then the first inner If statement on line 155 is executed to determine if the SAT score is greater than 1100. If so, the person has earned admission. If not, the person is advised to retake the SAT exam. If the GPA is not greater than 3.5, the student is denied admission. Notice that an If statement does not follow the Else keyword on line 160. An inner If statement need not follow both the If and the Else keywords.

Sometimes, after a condition is found to be true, a statement must be executed before the inner If statement is executed. For example, assume that if a student's GPA is greater than 3.5, then the student should be informed that her GPA is acceptable for admission. The code in Figure 5-46 implements this condition.

```
164          If decGPA > 3.5D Then
165              lblGPAStatus.Text = "Your GPA is acceptable"
166              If intSatScore > 1100 Then
167                  lblAdmissionStatus.Text = "You have earned admission"
168              Else
169                  lblAdmissionStatus.Text = "Retake the SAT exam"
170              End If
171          Else
172              lblGPAStatus.Text = "Your GPA is not acceptable"
173              lblAdmissionStatus.Text = "You have been denied admission"
174          End If
```

FIGURE 5-46

On line 165 in Figure 5-46, the message "Your GPA is acceptable" is assigned to the Text property of the lblGPAStatus Label object before checking the SAT score. As you can see, after the first condition has been tested, one or more statements can be executed prior to executing the inner If statement. This holds true for the Else portion of the If statement as well.

Match If, Else, and End If Entries

When you write a nested If statement, the inner If statement must be fully contained within the outer If statement. To accomplish this, you must ensure that each Else entry has a corresponding If entry, and an inner If statement must be terminated with an End If entry before either the Else entry or the End If entry for the outer If statement. If you code the nested If statement incorrectly, one or more of its entries will be shown with a blue squiggly line, indicating an error in the structure of the statement.

You also must place the correct executing statements with the If and Else statements within the nested If statement. For example, in Figure 5-47, the code is incorrect because the statements following the Else statements have been switched.

```
164        If decGPA > 3.5D Then
165            lblGPAStatus.Text = "Your GPA is acceptable"
166            If intSatScore > 1100 Then
167                lblAdmissionStatus.Text = "You have earned admission"
168            Else
169                lblAdmissionStatus.Text = "You have been denied admission"
170            End If
171        Else
172            lblGPAStatus Text = "Your GPA is not acceptable"
173            lblAdmissionStatus.Text = "Retake the SAT exam"
174        End If
```

incorrect
statements

FIGURE 5-47

You must be precise when placing the executing statements in the nested If statement. It is easy to miscode a nested If statement.

Nest Three or More Levels of If Statements

If statements are not limited to two levels of nesting. Three or more levels can be included in a nested If statement, although the statement can become difficult to understand and code. If more than two levels are required to solve a logic problem, great care must be taken to prevent errors such as the one shown in Figure 5-47.

Test the Status of a RadioButton Object in Code

In the Wood Cabinet Estimate application, the user selects one RadioButton in the GroupBox object to select the wood type. The code must check each RadioButton to determine if it has been selected by the user. When the user selects a radio button, its Checked property is changed from False to True. In addition, the Checked property for other RadioButton objects in the GroupBox object is set to False. This Checked property can be tested in an If statement to determine if the RadioButton object has been selected.

To test the status of the Checked property for the radPine RadioButton object, a programmer can write the general statement shown in Figure 5-48.

```
237        If radPine.Checked Then
238            Statement(s) to be executed if radio button is checked
239        End If
```

FIGURE 5-48

© 2014 Cengage Learning

Notice in Figure 5-48 that the RadioButton property is not compared using a relational operator. Instead, when a program tests a property that can contain only True or False, only the property must be specified in the If statement. When the property contains True, then the If statement is considered true, and when the property contains False, the If statement is considered false.

Test RadioButtons with the If . . . Then . . . ElseIf Statement

When a program contains multiple RadioButton objects in a Panel object or a GroupBox object, only one of the radio buttons can be selected. The If . . . Then . . . ElseIf statement is used to check multiple radio buttons because once the checked radio button is detected, checking the remaining radio buttons is unnecessary.

In the Wood Cabinet Estimate application, the user taps or clicks one of three radio buttons (Pine, Oak, or Cherry) to select the type of wood used for cabinets. When using an If . . . Then . . . ElseIf statement to check the status of the radio buttons, the most likely choice should be checked first. Thus, the fewest number of tests are performed. Therefore, the first If statement should test the status of the Pine radio button (radPine). If the radPine button is checked, the Cost Per Foot should be set to the value in the decPineCost variable, which is 300.00. No further testing should be done (Figure 5-49).

```
31        If radPine.Checked Then
32            decCostPerFoot = decPineCost
33        ElseIf radOak.Checked Then
34            decCostPerFoot = decOakCost
35        ElseIf radCherry.Checked Then
36            decCostPerFoot = decCherryCost
37        End If
```

FIGURE 5-49

© 2014 Cengage Learning

If the radPine button is not checked, then the radOak button should be tested. If it is checked, the Cost Per Foot should be set to the value in the decOakCost variable (500.00) and no further testing should be done. If the radOak button is not checked, then the radCherry button should be tested. If the other two buttons are not checked, then the radCherry button must be checked because one of the three must be checked. The Cost Per Foot will be set to the value in the decCherryCost variable (650.00).

As you learned earlier, during design time you can set the Checked property to True for the most frequently selected RadioButton to save the user from having to select it. In the Wood Cabinet Estimate application, after the Cost Per Foot has been determined and the Cost Estimate has been calculated, the user can tap or click the Clear button to clear the Linear Feet text box, clear the Cost Estimate, and reset the radio buttons so that the Pine button is selected. The code to reset the radio buttons is shown in Figure 5-50.

```
62          radPine.Checked = True
63          radOak.Checked = False
64          radCherry.Checked = False
```

FIGURE 5-50

In Figure 5-50, the Checked property for the radPine RadioButton object is set to True using the same method you have seen in previous chapters for setting an object property. Similarly, the Checked property for the other two RadioButton objects is set to False. As a result of these statements, the Pine radio button will be selected in the user interface, and the Oak and Cherry radio buttons will not be selected.

Block-Level Scope

In Chapter 4 you learned that the scope of a variable is defined by where it is declared within a program. For example, if a variable is declared within an event handler, then only code within that event handler can reference the variable. Code in one event handler within a program cannot reference a variable declared in another event handler.

Within an event handler, an If . . . Then . . . Else statement is considered a block of code. To review, this statement is the code beginning with the If keyword and ending with the corresponding Else keyword, or the code beginning with the Else keyword and ending with the End If keywords. Variables can be declared within the block of code, but they can be referenced only within the block of code where they are declared. For example, variables defined within an If . . . Then block of code fall out of scope (cannot be referenced) outside that block of code. To illustrate this concept, the code in Figure 5-51 shows a variable named intYears declared within an If . . . Then block of code.

```
11          If intAge < 18 Then
12              Dim intYears As Integer
13              intYears = 18 - intAge
14              lblMessage.Text = "You can vote in " & intYears & " years(s)."
15          Else
16              lblMessage.Text = "You can vote!"
17          End If
```

FIGURE 5-51

On line 12 in Figure 5-51, the variable intYears is declared as an Integer variable. On line 13, the variable is used in an arithmetic statement to receive the result of the calculation 18 – intAge, which determines the number of years less than 18 that is stored in intAge. The result in intYears is concatenated with literals in the statement on line 14. The intYears variable can be referenced in any statement between the If keyword and the Else keyword. It cannot be referenced anywhere else in the program, not even in the Else portion of the If statement. When a statement referencing the intYears variable is written outside the area between the If keyword and the Else keyword, a compilation error will occur and the program will not compile and execute.

Although the scope of the intYears variable in Figure 5-51 is between the If keyword on line 11 and the Else keyword on line 15, you should realize that the variable itself perseveres during the execution of the event handler procedure. Therefore, if the If statement in Figure 5-51 is executed a second time, the value in the intYears variable will be the same as when the If statement was completed the first time. To avoid unexpected results when the If statement is executed the second time, you should initialize block variables at the beginning of the block. In Figure 5-51, the statement on line 13 sets the value in the intYears variable immediately after it is declared, which is good programming technique.

Use Logical Operators

The If statements you have seen thus far test a single condition. In many cases, more than one condition must be true or one of several conditions must be true to execute the statements in the Then portion of the If . . . Then . . . Else statement. When more than one condition is included in an If . . . Then . . . Else statement, the conditions are called a **compound condition**. For example, consider the following business traveling rule: "If the flight costs less than $300.00 and the hotel is less than $120.00 per night, the business trip is approved." In this case, both conditions — flight less than $300.00 *and* hotel less than $120.00 per night — must be true for the trip to be approved. If either condition is not true, then the business trip is not approved.

To create an If statement that processes the business traveling rule, you must use a **logical operator**. The most common set of logical operators are listed in Figure 5-52.

Logical Operator	Meaning
And	All conditions tested in the If statement must be true
Or	One condition tested in the If statement must be true
Not	Negates a condition

FIGURE 5-52

© 2014 Cengage Learning

For the business traveling rule, you should use the And logical operator.

Use the And Logical Operator

The **And logical operator** allows you to combine two or more conditions into a compound condition that can be tested with an If statement. If any of the conditions stated in the compound condition is false, the compound condition is considered false and the statements following the Else portion of the If statement will be executed. The code in Figure 5-53 uses the And logical operator to implement the business traveling rule.

```
137        If decFlightCost < 300D And decHotelCost < 120D Then
138            lblTripMessage.Text = "Your business trip is approved"
139        Else
140            lblTripMessage.Text = "Your business trip is denied"
141        End If
```

FIGURE 5-53

© 2014 Cengage Learning

In Figure 5-53, both conditions in the compound condition (flight cost less than 300 and hotel cost less than 120) must be true for the business trip to be approved. If one of the conditions is false, then the compound condition is considered false and the If statement would return a false indication. For example, if the flight cost is 300 or more, the trip will not be approved regardless of the hotel cost. Similarly, if the hotel cost is 120 or more, the trip will not be approved regardless of the flight cost. This process is illustrated in Figure 5-54.

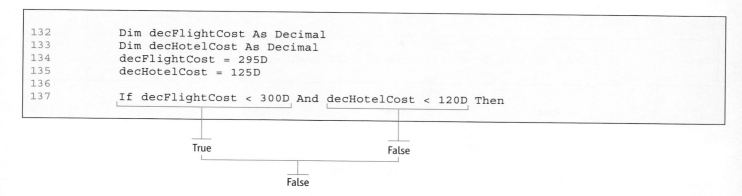

```
132          Dim decFlightCost As Decimal
133          Dim decHotelCost As Decimal
134          decFlightCost = 295D
135          decHotelCost = 125D
136
137          If decFlightCost < 300D And decHotelCost < 120D Then
```

                        True   False

                                      False

FIGURE 5-54

In Figure 5-54, the flight cost is 295, so it is less than 300 and the first part of the compound condition is true. Following the And logical operator, the hotel cost (125) is not less than 120. Therefore, the second part of the compound condition is false. When either condition is false with the And logical operator, the If statement considers the compound condition to be false. The result of the If statement in Figure 5-54 is that the compound condition is considered to be false.

Use the Or Logical Operator

When the **Or logical operator** is used to connect two or more conditions, the compound condition is true if any tested condition is true. Even if four conditional statements are included in the compound condition, only one conditional statement in the compound condition must be true for the entire statement to be considered true.

As an example, assume a college requires each student to have either at least a 3.5 GPA or at least a 1080 score on the SAT exam to be accepted for enrollment. If the student meets one or both conditions, the student is accepted. The If statement in Figure 5-55, which uses the Or logical operator, will solve this problem.

```
147          If decGPA >= 3.5D Or intSATScore >= 1080 Then
148             lblAcceptance.Text = "You have been accepted"
149          Else
150             lblAcceptance.Text = "You are not accepted"
151          End If
```

FIGURE 5-55

In Figure 5-55 on the previous page, if the decGPA is 3.2 but the intSATScore is 1130, the compound condition would be considered true because at least one of its conditions (intSATScore >= 1080) is true (Figure 5-56).

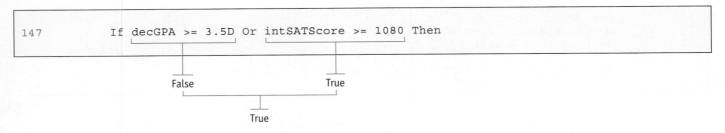

FIGURE 5-56

Use the Not Logical Operator

The **Not logical operator** allows you to state conditions that are best expressed in a negative way. In essence, the Not logical operator reverses the logical value of a condition on which it operates. For example, if a shoe store sells shoes under size 14 from its showroom but requires special orders for larger sizes, the code could use the Not logical operator shown in Figure 5-57 to negate the condition in the statement.

```
155        If Not decShoeSize >= 14 Then
156            lblOrderPolicy.Text = "Showroom shoe style available"
157        Else
158            lblOrderPolicy.Text = "Special order needed"
159        End If
```

FIGURE 5-57

The statement in Figure 5-57 works, but the use of the Not logical operator makes the If statement somewhat difficult to understand. Generally, a statement that avoids using the Not logical operator is more easily understood. For example, the code in Figure 5-58 accomplishes the same task as the code in Figure 5-57 and is easier to understand.

```
162        If decShoeSize < 14 Then
163            lblOrderPolicy.Text = "Showroom shoe style available"
164        Else
165            lblOrderPolicy.Text = "Special order needed"
166        End If
```

FIGURE 5-58

Other Logical Operators

The Visual Basic programming language provides three other logical operators, as shown in the table in Figure 5-59.

Logical Operator	Meaning
Xor	When one condition in the compound condition is true, but not both, the compound condition is true
AndAlso	As soon as a condition is found to be false, no further conditions are tested and the compound condition is false
OrElse	As soon as a condition is found to be true, no further conditions are tested and the compound condition is true

FIGURE 5-59

© 2014 Cengage Learning

Order of Operations for Logical Operators

You can combine more than one logical operator in the same If . . . Then statement. In an If statement, arithmetic operators are evaluated first, relational operators are evaluated next, and logical operators are evaluated last. The order of operations for logical operators is shown in Figure 5-60.

Logical Operator	Order
Not	Highest Precedence
And, AndAlso	Next Precedence
Or, OrElse, Xor	Last Precedence

FIGURE 5-60

© 2014 Cengage Learning

In most cases, if a developer uses multiple relational or logical operators in an If statement, the order of precedence should be established through the use of parentheses to clarify the sequence of evaluation. As in arithmetic expressions, conditional expressions within parentheses are evaluated before conditional expressions outside parentheses.

Select Case Statement

In some programming applications, different operations can occur based on the value in a single field. For example, in Figure 5-61, the user enters the number of the day in the week and the program displays the name of the day. The program must evaluate the number of the day value and display the name of the correct day.

FIGURE 5-61

In Figure 5-61, if the number of the day is 1, then the value Monday should be displayed. If the number of the day is 2, then Tuesday should be displayed, and so on. If the number of the day is 6 or 7, then the value Weekend should be displayed. If the user does not enter a value of 1 through 7, the user should be prompted to do so.

To solve this problem, a series of If . . . Then . . . ElseIf statements could be used, but an easier and clearer way to solve the problem is to use the Select Case statement.

When using a Select Case statement, the value in a single field, such as the day number, is evaluated. Based on the value in the field, a distinct action is taken. In this case, the name of the day is displayed.

A general example of the Select Case statement is shown in Figure 5-62.

```
168        Select Case Test Expression
169            Case First Expression
170                Statement(s) for First Case
171            Case Second Expression
172                Statement(s) for Second Case
173            Case Third Expression
174                Statement(s) for Third Case
175            Case Else
176                Statement(s) for when the Case Conditions do not match the
177                    test expressions above
178        End Select
```

FIGURE 5-62

The code for the Determine Day of Week application is shown in Figure 5-63.

```
13           Select Case intDayNumber
14               Case 1
15                   lblDayOfWeek.Text = "Monday"
16               Case 2
17                   lblDayOfWeek.Text = "Tuesday"
18               Case 3
19                   lblDayOfWeek.Text = "Wednesday"
20               Case 4
21                   lblDayOfWeek.Text = "Thursday"
22               Case 5
23                   lblDayOfWeek.Text = "Friday"
24               Case 6
25                   lblDayOfWeek.Text = "Weekend"
26               Case 7
27                   lblDayOfWeek.Text = "Weekend"
28               Case Else
29                   lblDayOfWeek.Text = "Enter 1 through 7"
30           End Select
```

FIGURE 5-63

The Select Case statement begins with the Select Case command. The test expression specifies the value or variable to be tested in the Select Case statement. In Figure 5-63, the variable is intDayNumber. So, when the Select Case statement is executed, each of the cases will be compared to the value in the intDayNumber variable.

Each Case statement specifies the value for which the test expression is checked. For example, the first Case statement on line 14 in Figure 5-63 specifies the value 1. If the value in the variable intDayNumber is equal to 1, the program executes the statement following the first Case statement up to the second Case statement (line 16). In Figure 5-63, the assignment statement on line 15 that sets the Text property of lblDayOfWeek to Monday is executed if the value in intDayNumber is equal to 1. More than one statement can follow a Case statement.

If the expression following the first Case statement is not true, then the next Case statement is evaluated. In Figure 5-63, the Case statement on line 16 checks if the value in intDayNumber is equal to 2. If so, the Text property of lblDayOf-Week is set to Tuesday. This process continues through the remainder of the Case statements.

The Case Else statement on line 28 is an optional entry that includes all conditions not specifically tested in the other Case statements. In Figure 5-63, if the value in the intDayNumber variable is not equal to 1 through 7, then the statement following the Case Else statement is executed. While not required, good program-ming practice dictates that the Case Else statement should be used so that all cases are accounted for and the program performs a specific action regardless of the value found in the test expression.

The End Select statement is required to end the Select Case statement. When you enter the Select Case statement in Visual Studio 2012, IntelliSense automatically includes the End Select statement.

Select Case Test Expressions

The example in Figure 5-63 on the previous page used an integer as the test expression value, but a value of any data type can be used in the test expression. For example, the test expression in Figure 5-64 uses the Text property of the txtStudentMajor TextBox object as a string value.

```
217        Select Case txtStudentMajor.Text
218            Case "Accounting"
219                lblDepartment.Text = "Business"
220            Case "Marketing"
221                lblDepartment.Text = "Business"
222            Case "Electrical Engineering"
223                lblDepartment.Text = "Engineering"
224            Case "Biochemistry"
225                lblDepartment.Text = "Chemistry"
226            Case "Shakespearean Literature"
227                lblDepartment.Text = "English"
228            Case "Web Design and E-Commerce"
229                lblDepartment.Text = "CIS"
230            Case Else
231                lblDepartment.Text = "Other"
232        End Select
```

FIGURE 5-64

HEADS UP

If you forget to type the Is keyword in the Case Is statement, Visual Studio will insert it for you.

In Figure 5-64, the Select Case statement is used to test the value in the Text property of the txtStudentMajor TextBox object and move the corresponding department name to the Text property of the lblDepartment object. The Case statements specify the values to be tested in the text box. The use of a string for the Select Case statement works in the same manner as other data types.

Use Relational Operators in a Select Case Statement

You can use relational operators in a Select Case statement, but you must use the keyword Is with the relational operator. For example, in Figure 5-41 on page 309, an If . . . Then . . . ElseIf statement was used to determine the shipping cost. That same processing could be accomplished using a Select Case statement, as shown in Figure 5-65.

```
191        Select Case decOrderAmount
192            Case Is > 500D
193                decShippingCost = 30D
194            Case Is > 400D
195                decShippingCost = 25D
196            Case Is > 200D
197                decShippingCost = 20D
198            Case Is > 0D
199                decShippingCost = 15D
200            Case Else
201                decShippingCost = 0D
202        End Select
203
```

FIGURE 5-65

Use Ranges in Select Case Statements

Another way to specify values in a Select Case statement is to use ranges. In Figure 5-66, the Case statements illustrate testing for six different conditions.

```
224        Select Case intGradeLevel
225            Case 1 To 3
226                lblGradeLevelExam.Text = "Early elementary"
227            Case 4 To 6
228                lblGradeLevelExam.Text = "Late elementary"
229            Case 7 To 8
230                lblGradeLevelExam.Text = "Middle school"
231            Case 9 To 10
232                lblGradeLevelExam.Text = "Early high school"
233            Case 11
234                lblGradeLevelExam.Text = "Late high school"
235            Case 12
236                lblGradeLevelExam.Text = "Final exam"
237            Case Else
238                lblGradeLevelExam.Text = "Invalid grade level"
239        End Select
```

FIGURE 5-66

© 2014 Cengage Learning

As you can see, a range of values is specified in a Case statement by stating the beginning value, the word To, and then the ending value in the range. The Case statements will test the value in the intGradeLevel variable and the appropriate statements will be executed.

You also can write Case statements so that more than one distinct value is tested. In Figure 5-67, the Case statement tests the individual values of 1, 3, 8, 11, and 17 against the value specified in the intDepartmentNumber variable.

```
230        Select Case intDepartmentNumber
231            Case 1, 3, 8, 11, 17
232
```

FIGURE 5-67

© 2014 Cengage Learning

Notice in Figure 5-67 that each value in the Case statement is separated by a comma. The code in Figure 5-68 shows a combination of the two techniques, using both commas and a To statement.

```
234        Select Case intDepartmentNumber
235            Case 2, 4, 7, 12 To 16, 22
```

FIGURE 5-68

© 2014 Cengage Learning

Select Which Decision Structure to Use

In some instances, you might need to determine if you should use the Select Case statement or the If . . . Then . . . ElseIf statement to solve a problem. Generally, the Select Case statement is most useful when more than two or three values must be tested for a given variable. For example, in Figure 5-64 on page 324, six different values are checked in the Text property of the txtStudentMajor TextBox object. This is a perfect example of when to use the Select Case statement.

The If . . . Then . . . ElseIf statement is more flexible because more than one variable can be used in the comparison. Programmers can also use compound conditions with the And, Or, and Not logical operators.

Use Code Snippets

Visual Basic includes a library of almost 500 pieces of code, called IntelliSense **code snippets**, that you can insert into an application. Each snippet consists of a complete programming task such as an If . . . Then . . . Else decision structure, sending an email message, or drawing a circle. Inserting these commonly used pieces of code is an effective way to enhance productivity. You also can create your own snippets and add them to the library.

In addition to inserting snippets in your program, you can display a code snippet to ensure you understand the syntax and requirements for a given type of statement. To insert and display a code snippet for the If . . . Then . . . Else statement, you can complete the following steps:

STEP 1   Press and hold or right-click the line in the code window where you want to insert the snippet.

Visual Studio displays a shortcut menu (Figure 5-69). It is important to press and hold or right-click the code window in the exact location where you want the code snippet to appear. If you press and hold or right-click outside this location, the shortcut menu might list customized choices for the wrong area of code. In addition, if you tap or click in the wrong place, the snippet will be positioned in the incorrect location in your program.

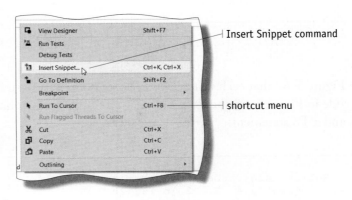

FIGURE 5-69

STEP 2   Tap or click Insert Snippet on the shortcut menu.

Visual Studio displays a menu of folders that contain snippets (Figure 5-70). The code snippets in each folder correspond to their folder titles.

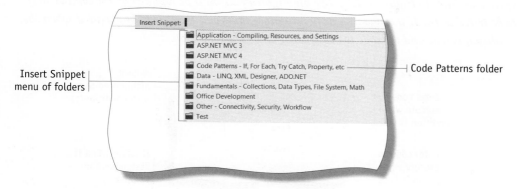

FIGURE 5-70

STEP 3   Double-tap or double-click the folder named Code Patterns - If, For Each, Try Catch, Property, etc, which contains commonly used code such as the If . . . Then . . . Else statement.

Visual Studio displays a menu of folders for code patterns (Figure 5-71).

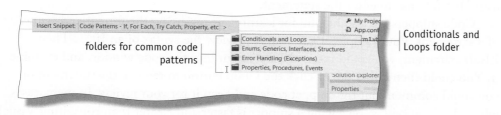

FIGURE 5-71

STEP 4   Double-tap or double-click the Conditionals and Loops folder because an If . . . Then . . . Else statement is a conditional statement.

Visual Studio displays the list of Conditionals and Loops code snippets (Figure 5-72). Some of these statements will be unfamiliar until you complete Chapter 6, but you can see that the list of code snippets includes several different types of If statements.

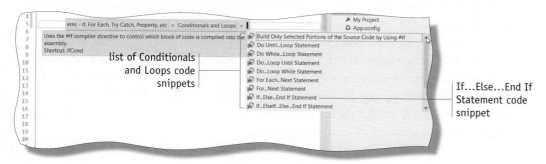

FIGURE 5-72

STEP 5   Double-tap or double-click the If . . . Else . . . End If Statement code snippet.

The If . . . Else . . . End If Statement code snippet is inserted into the code on the line selected in Step 1 (Figure 5-73). The highlighted text must be replaced by the condition(s) to be tested in the If statement. The programmer must add the code to be executed when the condition is true and the code to be executed when the condition is false.

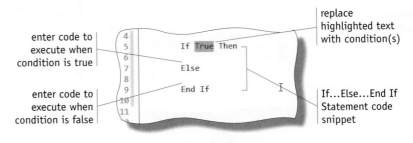

FIGURE 5-73

You must modify the code snippet shown in Figure 5-73 for the code to work properly. You may find that modifying a complicated code snippet is more work than using IntelliSense to enter the statement.

Code snippets are also helpful for learning or reviewing the format and syntax of a statement. For example, if you want to review the syntax of an If . . . Then . . . ElseIf statement, you could insert the statement into the code window and examine it. You could then either tap or click the Undo button to remove the statement or you could comment out the snippet code and keep it for your review. In many cases when checking syntax, reviewing a snippet is faster and clearer than consulting Visual Basic help.

Validate Data

Since the first days of computers, the phrase "garbage in, garbage out" has described the fact that allowing incorrect input data into a program produces incorrect output. Developers should anticipate that users will enter invalid data. Therefore, they must write code that prevents the invalid data from being used in the program to produce invalid output.

For example, in the Wood Cabinet Estimate application, the user is asked to enter the number of linear feet for the wood cabinets. If the user enters a negative number or a letter or even leaves the text box blank, the program should inform the user of the input error and allow the user to reenter a proper value. If the program attempts to process invalid data, unexpected errors can occur, which is not the way a program should respond to invalid input data.

To properly check the linear feet value entered by the user, two tests must be performed. First, the program must check the value to ensure it is numeric. Second, the numeric value entered by the user must be checked to ensure it is greater than zero. These tests are explained in the following sections.

Test Input to Determine If the Value Is Numeric

In the Wood Cabinet Estimate application, if no check is performed on the input data and the user accidentally enters a nonnumeric character such as an "a" or does not enter a value at all, the program will fail when Visual Basic attempts to convert that value to a number. An exception (error) screen will open and the program will be terminated. Therefore, the program must check the value entered by the user to ensure it is numeric. In addition, if the user enters a nonnumeric value, the program should inform the user of the error and request a valid numeric value.

The Visual Basic **IsNumeric function** can check the input value to determine if it can be converted into a numeric value such as an Integer or Decimal data type. If so, it returns a True Boolean value. If the value is not recognized as a numeric value, the IsNumeric function returns a False Boolean value.

For example, the IsNumeric function can check the value in the Text property of the Linear Feet text box. If the user enters a letter such as "a" in the text box, the IsNumeric function will return a False Boolean value because the letter "a" is not numeric.

Because the IsNumeric function returns a Boolean value (True or False), it can be placed within an If statement as the condition to be tested. If the returned value is True, the condition in the If statement is considered true. If the returned value is False, the condition in the If statement is considered false. The code in Figure 5-74 uses an If statement to determine if the Text property of the txtLinearFeet TextBox object is numeric.

```
                    IsNumeric      argument for
                    function       IsNumeric function

27          If IsNumeric(txtLinearFeet.Text) Then
 ⋮             Statement(s) executed when condition is true
50          Else
51             'Display MessageBox if user entered nonnumeric value
52             MsgBox("Enter the Linear Feet of the Cabinets.", , "Input Error")
53             txtLinearFeet.Text = ""
54             txtLinearFeet.Focus()
55          End If
```

FIGURE 5-74

In Figure 5-74, the If statement on line 27 calls the IsNumeric function. The Text property of the txtLinearFeet TextBox object is the argument for the IsNumeric function. As a result of this specification, the IsNumeric function will analyze the data in the Text property of the txtLinearFeet TextBox object. If the data can be converted to a numeric data type, then the function will return a Boolean value of True. If the data cannot be converted to a numeric data type, the function will return a Boolean value of False.

Once the function has returned a Boolean value, the If statement tests the Boolean value. If it is true, the value in the Text property of the txtLinearFeet Text-Box object is numeric, and the appropriate statements are executed. If the condition is false, meaning the value is not numeric, the statements on lines 51–55 are executed. The statement on line 52 displays a message box telling the user to enter the linear feet of the cabinet (see Figure 5-2 on page 285). The caption of the message box is "Input Error". The statement on line 53 clears the Text property. The statement on line 54 sets the focus on the text box so the user can reenter the value.

Check for a Positive Number

If the condition in Figure 5-74 on the previous page is true, the value in the Text property must be converted to a Decimal data type. Then, the program checks to ensure the entered value is greater than zero. These statements are shown in Figure 5-75.

```
27    If IsNumeric(txtLinearFeet.Text) Then
28        decLinearFeet = Convert.ToDecimal(txtLinearFeet.Text)
29
30        ' Is linear feet greater than zero
31        If decLinearFeet > 0 Then
          Statement(s) executed when condition is true
33        Else
34            ' Display error message if user entered a negative value
35            MsgBox("You entered " & decLinearFeet.ToString() &
36                ". Enter a Number Greater Than Zero.", , "Input Error")
37            txtLinearFeet.Text = ""
38            txtLinearFeet.Focus()
39        End If
40    Else
41        ' Display error message if user entered a nonnumeric value
42        MsgBox("Enter the Linear Feet of the Cabinets.", , "Input Error")
43        txtLinearFeet.Text = ""
44        txtLinearFeet.Focus()
45    End If
```

FIGURE 5-75

When the value in the Text property is numeric, it is converted to a Decimal value (line 28). On line 31, the Decimal value is compared to zero. If it is greater than zero, then the processing for a true statement is executed. If the value is not greater than zero, a message box is displayed to inform the user that an invalid entry was made (see Figure 5-29 on page 300). The user then can enter a valid value.

The process of validating input data is fundamental to programming when using a graphical user interface. A well-designed program must ensure the user enters valid data.

Program Design

As you have learned, the requirements document identifies the purpose of the program being developed, the application title, the procedures to be followed when using the program, any required equations and calculations, any conditions that must be tested, notes and restrictions that must be followed by the program, and any other comments that would be helpful to understanding the problem. The requirements document for the Wood Cabinet Estimate application is shown in Figure 5-76. The Use Case Definition document is shown in Figure 5-77 on the next page.

REQUIREMENTS DOCUMENT

Date Submitted:	January 29, 2015
Application Title:	Wood Cabinet Estimate
Purpose:	This application calculates the estimated cost of wood cabinetry for a job bid.
Program Procedures:	The user should enter the linear footage of cabinets needed and select the type of wood. The estimated cost for the cabinet job will be displayed.
Algorithms, Processing, and Conditions:	1. The user must be able to enter the number of linear feet of cabinetry.
	2. The user must be able to select one of three wood types — pine, oak, or cherry.
	3. The user can initiate the calculation and display the cost estimate for the wood cabinets.
	4. The application computes the cost estimate of the cabinets based on the number of linear feet and the cost of the wood. Pine costs $300 per linear foot of cabinets, oak costs $500 per linear foot, and cherry costs $650 per linear foot.
	5. The estimate calculation is linear feet x cost per linear foot.
	6. The cost estimate is displayed in currency format.
	7. The user should be able to clear the linear feet entered, reset the wood type to pine, and clear the cost estimate.
Notes and Restrictions:	1. If the user enters a nonnumeric value for the linear feet or leaves the TextBox object empty, the user should be advised and asked for a valid entry.
	2. If the user enters a negative number for the linear feet, the user should be advised and asked for a valid entry.
Comments:	The title of the Windows Form should be Wood Cabinet Estimate.

FIGURE 5-76

USE CASE DEFINITION

1. The window opens and displays the Wood Cabinet Estimate, a text box requesting the number of linear feet for the cabinets, radio buttons to select the wood type, and two buttons labeled Calculate and Clear.
2. The user enters the linear feet and selects one of the wood types.
3. The user clicks the Calculate button.
4. The user will be warned if a nonnumeric value is entered, the text box is left empty, or a negative number is entered.
5. The program displays the cost estimate for the cabinetry job.
6. The user clicks the Clear button to clear the Linear Feet text box, set the wood choice to Pine, and erase the cost estimate.
7. The user clicks the Close button to terminate the application.

FIGURE 5-77

© 2014 Cengage Learning

Event Planning Document

You will recall that the event planning document is a table that specifies which objects in the user interface will cause events, the action taken by the user to trigger each event, and the event processing that must occur. The event planning document for the Wood Cabinet Estimate application is shown in Figure 5-78.

EVENT PLANNING DOCUMENT

Program Name: Wood Cabinet Estimate	Developer: Corinne Hoisington	Object: frmWoodCabinets	Date: January 29, 2015
OBJECT	EVENT TRIGGER	EVENT PROCESSING	
btnCalculate	Click	Ensure data entered is numeric Display error message if data is not numeric or text box is empty Convert data entered to numeric Ensure data entered is greater than zero Display error message if data is not greater than zero Assign wood cost per foot based on type of wood selection Calculate cost (linear feet × cost per foot) Display cost	
btnClear	Click	Clear input text box Clear cost estimate Set the Pine radio button to checked Clear the Oak radio button Clear the Cherry radio button Set focus on input text box	
frmWoodCabinets	Load	Set focus on input text box Clear the placement zeros for cost	

FIGURE 5-78

© 2014 Cengage Learning

Design and Code the Program

After identifying the events and tasks within the events, the developer is ready to create the program. As you have learned, creating the program means designing the user interface and then entering Visual Basic statements to accomplish the tasks specified in the event planning document. As the developer enters the code, she also will implement the logic to carry out the required processing.

NOTE TO THE LEARNER

In the following activity, you should complete the tasks within the specified steps. Each of the tasks is accompanied by a Hint Screen. The purpose of the Hint Screen is to indicate where you should perform the activity in the Visual Studio window and to remind you which method to use. If you need further help completing a step, refer to the figure identified by *ref:*.

Guided Program Development

To design the user interface for the Wood Cabinet Estimate application and enter the code required to process each event in the program, complete the steps on the next page.

Guided Program Development

Phase 1: Design the Form

1

- **Create a Windows Application** Open Visual Studio using the Search charm (Windows 8) or the Start button on the Windows taskbar and the All Programs submenu (Windows 7). Create a new Visual Basic Windows Application project by completing the following: Tap or click the New Project button on the Standard toolbar; select and expand Windows in the left pane; select Windows Forms Application; name the project by entering Wood Cabinet Estimate in the Name text box; then tap or click the OK button in the New Project window.

- **Name the Form** In the Solution Explorer pane, press and hold or right-click Form1.vb and then tap or click Rename. Type frmWoodCabinets.vb, and then press the ENTER key. Tap or click the Yes button to automatically change the form (Name) in the Properties window.

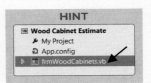

- **Change the Size Property** In the Properties window, change the Size property to 350, 500.

- **Change the BackColor Property** In the Properties window, change the BackColor property to Moccasin.

- **Change the Text on the Title Bar** To change the text on the title bar, tap or click the form, scroll down the Properties window until the Text property is displayed, double-tap or double-click the right column of the Text property, type Wood Cabinet Estimate, and then press the ENTER key.

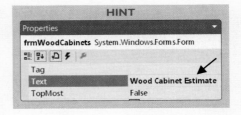

- **Add a Heading Title** Drag a label onto the form and name the label lblHeading. Set the Text property for the Label object to Wood Cabinet Cost. Set the font to Goudy Old Style, Bold, 20 points. Position the label horizontally in the center of the form.

- **Add a Label** Drag a second label onto the frmWoodCabinets Form object and name the label `lblLinearFeet`. Set the Text property of the Label object to `Linear Feet:`. Set the font to Goudy Old Style, Bold, 14 points. Position the label to resemble the one shown in Figure 5-79.

- **Add a TextBox Object** Drag a TextBox object onto the form. Using snap lines, align the top of the TextBox object with the top of the second Label object. Name the TextBox object `txtFeet`. Change the TextAlign property to Center. Change the font to Goudy Old Style, Bold, 14 points. Reduce the width of the TextBox object to closely resemble the one in Figure 5-79. Center the Label object and the TextBox object horizontally in the frmWoodCabinets Form object.

A title Label object is displayed on the first line of the form. A Label object and TextBox object occupy the second line of the frmWoodCabinets Form object (Figure 5-79). They are centered horizontally in the form.

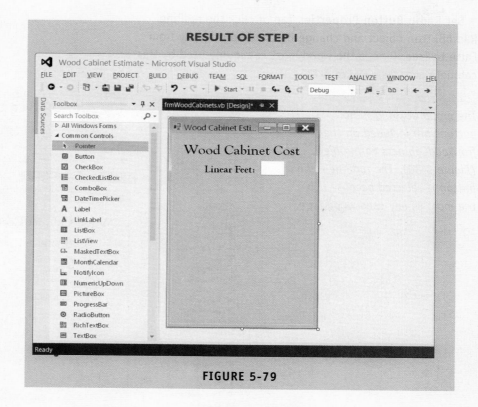

FIGURE 5-79

(continues)

Guided Program Development *continued*

2

● **Add a GroupBox** Drag a GroupBox object from the Container category of the Toolbox to the frmWoodCabinets Form object. Name the GroupBox `grpWoodType`. Change the Text property to `Wood Type`. Set the size of the GroupBox object to `160`, `100`. Change the BackColor of the GroupBox object to White. Center the GroupBox object horizontally in the frmWoodCabi-nets Form object, and change the font to Goudy Old Style, Regular, 12 points *(ref: Figure 5-4)*.

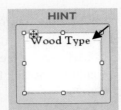

HINT

● **Add Radio Buttons** Place three RadioButton objects on the GroupBox object. Name the first RadioButton `radPine` and change its Text property to `Pine`. Name the second Radio-Button `radOak` and change its Text property to `Oak`. Name the third RadioButton `radCherry` and change its Text property to `Cherry`. If necessary, select the three Radio-Buttons and change the font to Goudy Old Style, Regular, 12 points *(ref: Figure 5-7)*.

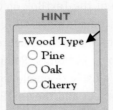

HINT

● **Set Radio Button Properties** Tap or click the radPine RadioButton object and change its Checked property from False to True. Pine is the wood most commonly used by this cabinetmaker *(ref: Figure 5-11)*.

The group box and radio buttons are included on the frmWoodCabinets Form object (Figure 5-80). The radPine radio button is selected because it is the most widely used wood type.

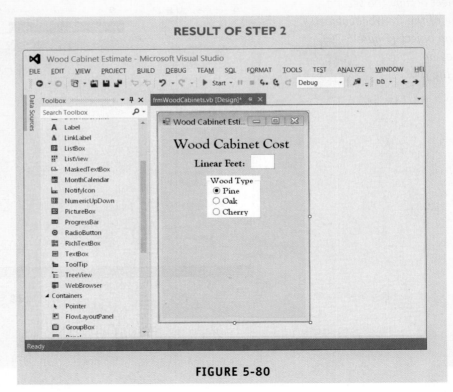

RESULT OF STEP 2

FIGURE 5-80

- **Add Estimate and Cost Labels** Drag two more Label objects onto the form below the GroupBox object. Align these labels by their tops using snap lines. Name the first label `lblCost`, change its Text property to `Cost Estimate:`, and resize the Label object to view the text. Name the second label `lblCostEstimate` and set its Text property to `$0000.00`. These placement zeros allow you to view the Label object when it is not selected. The placement zeros will be cleared using code when the form is loaded. Change the font for both Label objects to Goudy Old Style, Bold, 14 points. Horizontally center the labels as a unit on the frmWoodCabinets Form object.

- **Add Calculate and Clear Buttons** Drag two Button objects onto the form. Align the tops of the Button objects using snap lines. Name the left Button object `btnCalculate` and change its Text property to `Calculate`. Name the right Button object `btnClear` and change its Text property to `Clear`. Change the font for these two buttons to Goudy Old Style, Regular, 12 points. Change the size of each button to `100, 30`. Change the BackColor property for each button to White.

- **Add a Picture to the Windows Form** Download the Cabinets.jpg picture by visiting CengageBrain.com and accessing the resources for this chapter. Drag a PictureBox object to the bottom of the Windows Form. Name the picture `picCabinets`. Change the Size property of the PictureBox object to `330, 115`. Change the SizeMode property to StretchImage.

The user interface is complete (Figure 5-81).

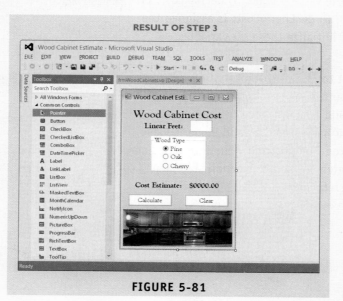

FIGURE 5-81

© Ivan Hunter/Digital Vision/Getty Images

(continues)

Phase 2: Code the Application

4

- **Code the Comments** Double-tap or double-click the btnCalculate Button object on the frmWoodCabinets Form object to open the code window and create the btnCalculate_Click event handler. Close the Toolbox. Tap or click in front of the first words, Public Class frmWoodCabinets, and then press the ENTER key to create a blank line. Insert the first four standard comments. Insert the Option Strict On command at the beginning of the code to turn on strict type checking.

HINT

```
frmWoodCabinets.vb*   ⊞ ×   frmWoodCabinets.vb [Design]*
⚞ frmWoodCabinets                              ▾  📖 (Declarations)
 1 ⊟ ' Program Name:  Wood Cabinet Estimate
 2   ' Author:        Corinne Hoisington
 3   ' Date:          January 29, 2015
 4   ' Purpose:       This Windows application computes the estimated cost
 5   '                of wood cabinets based on the number of linear feet of
 6   '                cabinets and the following cost per linear foot:
 7   '                Pine - $300.00 per linear foot; Oak - $500.00 per
 8   '                linear foot; Cherry - $650.00 per linear foot.
 9   '
10   Option Strict On
11
12 ⊟ Public Class frmWoodCabinets
```

- **Add Comments to the btnCalculate_ Click Event Handler** Enter a comment to describe the purpose of the btnCalculate_ Click event.

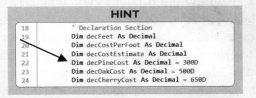

HINT

```
14 ⊟    Private Sub btnCalculate_Click(ByVal sender As System.Object, ByVal e As System.
15         ' The btnCalculate event handler calculates the estimated cost of
16         ' cabinets based on the linear feet and the wood type.
```

- **Declare and Initialize the Variables** This application requires six Decimal variables: 1) decFeet: Holds the estimated linear footage of the cabinets; 2) decCostPerFoot: Holds the cost per linear foot based on the wood type; 3) decCost Estimate: Is assigned the calculated final estimated cost; 4) decPineCost: Is assigned the value 300.00; 5) decOakCost: Is assigned the value 500.00; 6) decCherryCost: Is assigned the value 650.00. Declare and initialize these six variables.

HINT

```
18         ' Declaration Section
19         Dim decFeet As Decimal
20         Dim decCostPerFoot As Decimal
21         Dim decCostEstimate As Decimal
22         Dim decPineCost As Decimal = 300D
23         Dim decOakCost As Decimal = 500D
24         Dim decCherryCost As Decimal = 650D
```

- **Write the If Statement to Test for Numeric Data** When the user clicks the Calculate button, the program must first ensure that the user entered a valid numeric value in the txtFeet TextBox object. If the user has entered a valid numeric value, the value must be converted from a string value into a Decimal data type. Write the If statement and conversion statement required for this process *(ref: Figure 5-74)*.

HINT

```
26         ' Did user enter a numeric value?
27         If IsNumeric(txtFeet.Text) Then
28             decFeet = Convert.ToDecimal(txtFeet.Text)
```

- **Write the If Statement to Test for a Positive Number** If the value in the txtFeet TextBox object is numeric, then the converted numeric value must be checked to ensure it is a positive number. Write the If statement to check whether the converted numeric value is greater than zero *(ref: Figure 5-75)*.

```
29
30              ' Is Linear Feet greater than zero
31              If decFeet > 0 Then
```

- **Write the If Statements to Determine the Cost Per Linear Foot** When the value is greater than zero, the cost per linear foot is determined by checking the status of the RadioButton objects and placing the appropriate cost per linear foot in the decCostPerFoot variable. Using the If . . . Then . . . ElseIf structure, write the statements to identify the checked radio button and place the appropriate cost in the decCostPerFoot variable *(ref: Figure 5-49)*.

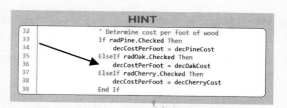

```
32                  ' Determine cost per foot of wood
33                  If radPine.Checked Then
34                      decCostPerFoot = decPineCost
35                  ElseIf radOak.Checked Then
36                      decCostPerFoot = decOakCost
37                  ElseIf radCherry.Checked Then
38                      decCostPerFoot = decCherryCost
39                  End If
```

- **Calculate and Display the Cost Estimate** The next step is to calculate the cost estimate by multiplying the value in the decCostPerFoot variable by the linear feet. Next, display the cost estimate in the cost estimate label. Write the statements to calculate and display the cost estimate in the currency format.

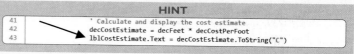

```
41                  ' Calculate and display the cost estimate
42                  decCostEstimate = decFeet * decCostPerFoot
43                  lblCostEstimate.Text = decCostEstimate.ToString("C")
```

- **Display a Message Box If the Value Entered Is Not Greater Than Zero** After the processing is finished for the true portion of the If statements, the Else portion of the If statements must be written. Write the code to display the message box that contains the error message when the user enters a value that is not greater than zero *(ref: Figure 5-24)*.

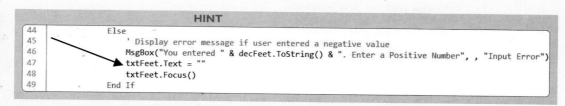

```
44              Else
45                  ' Display error message if user entered a negative value
46                  MsgBox("You entered " & decFeet.ToString() & ". Enter a Positive Number", , "Input Error")
47                  txtFeet.Text = ""
48                  txtFeet.Focus()
49              End If
```

- **Display an Error Message If the Value Entered Is Not Numeric** Write the Else portion of the If statement to display an error message if the value entered by the user is not numeric *(ref: Figure 5-24)*.

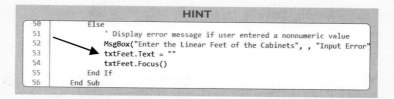

```
50          Else
51              ' Display error message if user entered a nonnumeric value
52              MsgBox("Enter the Linear Feet of the Cabinets", , "Input Error")
53              txtFeet.Text = ""
54              txtFeet.Focus()
55          End If
56      End Sub
```

(continues)

The code for the click event of the Calculate button is completed (Figure 5-82).

RESULT OF STEP 4

```vbnet
1  ' Program Name:  Wood Cabinet Estimate
2  ' Author:        Corinne Hoisington
3  ' Date:          January 29, 2015
4  ' Purpose:       This Windows application computes the estimated cost
5  '                of wood cabinets based on the number of linear feet of
6  '                cabinets and the following cost per linear foot:
7  '                Pine - $300.00 per linear foot; Oak - $500.00 per
8  '                linear foot; Cherry - $650.00 per linear foot.
9
10 Option Strict On
11
12 Public Class frmWoodCabinets
13
14     Private Sub btnCalculate_Click(ByVal sender As System.Object, ByVal e As System.EventArgs) Handles btnCalculate.Click
15         ' The btnCalculate event handler calculates the estimated cost of
16         ' cabinets based on the linear feet and the wood type.
17
18         ' Declaration Section
19         Dim decFeet As Decimal
20         Dim decCostPerFoot As Decimal
21         Dim decCostEstimate As Decimal
22         Dim decPineCost As Decimal = 300D
23         Dim decOakCost As Decimal = 500D
24         Dim decCherryCost As Decimal = 650D
25
26         ' Did user enter a numeric value?
27         If IsNumeric(txtFeet.Text) Then
28             decFeet = Convert.ToDecimal(txtFeet.Text)
29
30             ' Is Linear Feet greater than zero
31             If decFeet > 0 Then
32                 ' Determine cost per foot of wood
33                 If radPine.Checked Then
34                     decCostPerFoot = decPineCost
35                 ElseIf radOak.Checked Then
36                     decCostPerFoot = decOakCost
37                 ElseIf radCherry.Checked Then
38                     decCostPerFoot = decCherryCost
39                 End If
40
41                 ' Calculate and display the cost estimate
42                 decCostEstimate = decFeet * decCostPerFoot
43                 lblCostEstimate.Text = decCostEstimate.ToString("C")
44             Else
45                 ' Display error message if user entered a negative value
46                 MsgBox("You entered " & decFeet.ToString() & ". Enter a Positive Number", , "Input Error")
47                 txtFeet.Text = ""
48                 txtFeet.Focus()
49             End If
50         Else
51             ' Display error message if user entered a nonnumeric value
52             MsgBox("Enter the Linear Feet of the Cabinets", , "Input Error")
53             txtFeet.Text = ""
54             txtFeet.Focus()
55         End If
56     End Sub
```

FIGURE 5-82

5

• **Create the Clear Button Click Event Handler** The Clear Button click event includes the following processing: 1) Clear the txtFeet Text property; 2) Clear the lblCostEstimate Text property; 3) Set the radPine Checked property to True; 4) Set the radOak and radCherry Checked properties to False; 5) Set the focus in the txtFeet text box. To enter this code, tap or click the frmWood-Cabinets.vb [Design] tab and then double-tap or double-click the Clear button. Using IntelliSense, enter the required code.

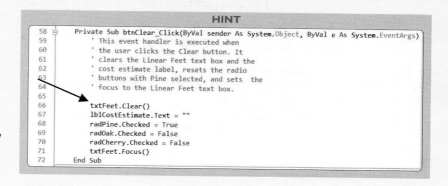

```
                                              HINT
58      Private Sub btnClear_Click(ByVal sender As System.Object, ByVal e As System.EventArgs)
59          ' This event handler is executed when
60          ' the user clicks the Clear button. It
61          ' clears the Linear Feet text box and the
62          ' cost estimate label, resets the radio
63          ' buttons with Pine selected, and sets  the
64          ' focus to the Linear Feet text box.
65
66          txtFeet.Clear()
67          lblCostEstimate.Text = ""
68          radPine.Checked = True
69          radOak.Checked = False
70          radCherry.Checked = False
71          txtFeet.Focus()
72      End Sub
```

• **Create the Form Load Event Handler** When the frmWoodCabinets Form object loads, the following processing should occur: 1) The focus is in the txtFeet text box; 2) The lblCostEstimate Text property is set to null. Tap or click the frmWoodCabinets.vb [Design] tab to return to Design view and then double-tap or double-click the form. Enter the code for the form load event handler.

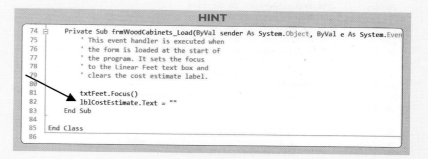

```
                                              HINT
74      Private Sub frmWoodCabinets_Load(ByVal sender As System.Object, ByVal e As System.Even
75          ' This event handler is executed when
76          ' the form is loaded at the start of
77          ' the program. It sets the focus
78          ' to the Linear Feet text box and
79          ' clears the cost estimate label.
80
81          txtFeet.Focus()
82          lblCostEstimate.Text = ""
83      End Sub
84
85  End Class
86
```

6

• **Run the Application** After you have completed the code, you should run the application to ensure it works properly.

• **Test the Application** Test the application with the following data: 1) Linear feet 25, wood type Oak; 2) Linear feet 9, wood type Cherry; 3) Linear feet 100, wood type Pine; 4) Linear feet Fifteen (use this word), wood type Cherry; 5) Linear feet −21, wood type Oak; 6) Use other values to thoroughly test the program. After each test, tap or click the Clear button before entering new data.

• **Close the Program** After testing the application, close the window by tapping or clicking the Close button in the title bar of the window.

Code Listing

The complete code for the sample program is shown in Figure 5-83.

```
1   ' Program Name: Wood Cabinet Estimate
2   ' Author:       Corinne Hoisington
3   ' Date:         January 29, 2015
4   ' Purpose:      This Windows application computes the estimated cost
5   '               of wood cabinets based on the number of linear feet of
6   '               cabinets and the following cost per linear foot:
7   '               Pine - $300.00 per linear foot; Oak - $500.00 per
8   '               linear foot; Cherry - $650.00 per linear foot.
9
10  Option Strict On
11
12  Public Class frmWoodCabinets
13
14      Private Sub btnCalculate_Click(ByVal sender As System.Object, ByVal e As System.EventArgs) Handles btnCalculate.Click
15          ' The btnCalculate event handler calculates the estimated cost of
16          ' cabinets based on the linear feet and the wood type.
17
18          ' Declaration Section
19          Dim decFeet As Decimal
20          Dim decCostPerFoot As Decimal
21          Dim decCostEstimate As Decimal
22          Dim decPineCost As Decimal = 300D
23          Dim decOakCost As Decimal = 500D
24          Dim decCherryCost As Decimal = 650D
25
26          ' Did user enter a numeric value?
27          If IsNumeric(txtFeet.Text) Then
28              decFeet = Convert.ToDecimal(txtFeet.Text)
29
30              ' Is Linear Feet greater than zero
31              If decFeet > 0 Then
32                  ' Determine cost per foot of wood
33                  If radPine.Checked Then
34                      decCostPerFoot = decPineCost
35                  ElseIf radOak.Checked Then
36                      decCostPerFoot = decOakCost
37                  ElseIf radCherry.Checked Then
38                      decCostPerFoot = decCherryCost
39                  End If
40
41                  ' Calculate and display the cost estimate
42                  decCostEstimate = decFeet * decCostPerFoot
43                  lblCostEstimate.Text = decCostEstimate.ToString("C")
44              Else
45                  ' Display error message if user entered a negative value
46                  MsgBox("You entered " & decFeet.ToString() & ". Enter a Positive Number", , "Input Error")
47                  txtFeet.Text = ""
48                  txtFeet.Focus()
49              End If
50          Else
51              ' Display error message if user entered a nonnumeric value
52              MsgBox("Enter the Linear Feet of the Cabinets", , "Input Error")
53              txtFeet.Text = ""
54              txtFeet.Focus()
55          End If
56      End Sub
```

FIGURE 5-83 (continues)

```
58 ⊟    Private Sub btnClear_Click(ByVal sender As System.Object, ByVal e As System.EventArgs) Handles btnClear.Click
59            ' This event handler is executed when
60            ' the user clicks the Clear button. It
61            ' clears the Linear Feet text box and the
62            ' cost estimate label, resets the radio
63            ' buttons with Pine selected, and sets  the
64            ' focus to the Linear Feet text box.
65
66            txtFeet.Clear()
67            lblCostEstimate.Text = ""
68            radPine.Checked = True
69            radOak.Checked = False
70            radCherry.Checked = False
71            txtFeet.Focus()
72        End Sub
73
74 ⊟    Private Sub frmCabinetCost_Load(ByVal sender As System.Object, ByVal e As System.EventArgs) Handles MyBase.Load
75            ' This event handler is executed when
76            ' the form is loaded at the start of
77            ' the program. It sets the focus
78            ' to the Linear Feet text box and
79            ' clears the cost estimate label.
80
81            txtFeet.Focus()
82            lblCostEstimate.Text = ""
83        End Sub
84
85  End Class
```

FIGURE 5-83 (continued)

Summary

In this chapter you have learned to make decisions based on the user's input.

The items listed in the table in Figure 5-84 on the next page include all the new Visual Studio and Visual Basic skills you have learned in this chapter.

Visual Basic Skills

Skill	Figure Number	Video Number
Explore the Wood Cabinet Estimate Application	Figure 5-1	Video 5-1
Use a GroupBox Object	Figure 5-4	Video 5-2
Add RadioButton Objects	Figure 5-7	Video 5-3
Use Windows Application Container Objects	Figure 5-14	
Display a Message Box	Figure 5-16	Video 5-4
Concatenate Strings	Figure 5-29	
Code an If...Then Statement	Figure 5-31	
Turn on Pretty Listing for Indentation	Page 302	
Use Relational Operators	Figure 5-32	
Enter an If...Then Statement	Figure 5-34	Video 5-5
Compare Strings	Figure 5-37	
Code If...Then...Else Statements	Figure 5-38	
Compare Values Using an Arithmetic Expression	Figure 5-40	
Code an If...Then...ElseIf Statement	Figure 5-41	
Code a Nested If Statement	Figure 5-43	
Test the Status of a RadioButton Object in Code	Figure 5-48	
Understand Block-Level Scope	Figure 5-51	
Code Logical Operators	Figure 5-52	
Code Select Case Statements	Figure 5-62	
Insert Code Snippets	Figure 5-69	Video 5-6
Validate Input Data	Figure 5-74	

FIGURE 5-84

Reinforcement activities and resources are available at no additional cost on www.cengagebrain.com. Visit www
.cengage.com/ct/studentdownload for detailed instructions about accessing the available resources at the Student
Companion Site.

Knowledge Check

1. If a form opens and the first of three RadioButtons is checked within a GroupBox object, what happens to the
   first RadioButton object when you tap or click the second RadioButton object?

2. Name the six relational operators and state the purpose of each operator.

3. Write an If . . . Then statement that tests whether the value in the variable decMaleShoeSize is between 9.0
   and 12.0. If the number is in that range, set the Text property for the lblResponse Label object to "Your size is
   in stock".

4. Write an If . . . Then . . . Else statement that assigns 65 to a variable named intSpeed if strHighway is equal
   to "I95". Otherwise, assign 45 to intSpeed.

5. List the three most common logical operators and explain their meaning.

6. Rewrite the following line of code without a Not logical operator, but keep the same logical processing:

   `If Not intHeight <= 75 Then`

7. The intent of the following statement is to check whether the radDormStudent RadioButton object is checked.
   What is the error in the statement? Rewrite the statement so it is correct.

   `If radDormStudent = Checked Then`

8. The intent of the following statement is to check whether the value in the intGrade variable is less than
   0 or greater than 100. What is the error in the statement? Rewrite the statement so it is correct.

   `If intGrade < 0 And intGrade > 100 Then`

9. What is the most commonly used container object?

10. Fix this statement.

    `If decMinWage > 7.25 and < 15.25 Then`

11. Why do most developers indent the code within a decision structure?

12. Write a statement that creates the dialog box shown in Figure 5-85 in a Windows
    application. Use a single numerical value to create the button and picture icon.

13. What is the difference between a Panel object and a GroupBox object?

14. What is the difference between the Or logical operator and the Xor logical
    operator?

15. Write a data validation statement that would check to ensure the value in the
    intAge variable is between 1 and 120. If the age is not valid, display an error
    message box that states the age is invalid.

FIGURE 5-85

(continues)

16. How many radio buttons in a group can be selected at one time?

17. Using the concatenation operator (&), write a statement that would create the compound word "smartphone" from the following two strings: strTerm1 = "smart" and strTerm2= "phone". Assign the compound word to the strCompound string variable.

18. Write a statement that would clear the radio button named radSurfboard.

19. Write a Select Case statement using the fewest Case statements possible to display the number of days in each month. The user enters the number of the month, such as 8, which is converted to an integer and assigned to the intMonth variable. The Select Case statement should display a message box that states the number of days in the month, such as "31 Days".

20. Which logical operator has the highest precedence in the order of operations?

Debugging Exercises

1. Explain how the two statements shown in Figure 5-86 are evaluated.

```
If strAirline = "Jet Green" AndAlso strHotel = "Homeland Suites" Then

    If strAirline = "Jet Green" And strHotel = "Homeland Suites" Then
```

FIGURE 5-86

2. Identify the error in the code shown in Figure 5-87 and explain how to correct the code.

```
If dblCommission >= 2500 Then
    Dim intBonus As Integer
    intBonus = 500
Else
    intBonus = 0
End If
```

FIGURE 5-87

Debugging Exercises

3. The Select Case statement shown in Figure 5-88 contains one or more errors. Identify the error(s) and rewrite the statements correctly.

```
Select Case intNumberOfSeats
    Case > 5000
        strVenueType = "Stadium"
    Case > 2000
        strVenueType = "Amphitheater"
    Case > 1000
        strVenueType = "Auditorium"
    Case > 200
        strVenueType = "Theater"
    Case > 0
        strVenueType = "Club"
    Else Case
        strVenueType = "Error"
Select End
```

FIGURE 5-88

4. The Select Case statement shown in Figure 5-89 contains one or more errors. Identify the error(s) and rewrite the statements correctly.

```
Select Case charFlightCode
    Case 'F', 'A'
        lblFare.Text = 'First Class'
    Case 'B', 'Q'
        lblFare.Text = 'Business Class'
    Case 'Y', 'S', 'M'
        lblFare.Text = 'Full Fare Economy'
    Case 'K', 'C'
        lblFare.Text = 'Preferred Economy'
    Case 'U', 'J', 'P', 'G'
        lblFare.Text = 'Economy'
    Else
        lblFare.Text = 'Unknown'
End Select
```

FIGURE 5-89

(continues)

Debugging Exercises *continued*

5. The If . . . Then . . . Else statement shown in Figure 5-90 contains one or more errors. Identify the error(s) and rewrite the statements correctly.

```
If strShippingMethod = "Overnite" Then
    If strDeliveryTime = "Morning"
        decDeliveryCost = 29.00D
    Else
        decDeliveryCost = 24.00D
Else
    If strShippingMethod = "Two Days" Then
        decDeliveryCost = 14.00D
    Else
        decDeliveryCost = 4.00D
End If
```

FIGURE 5-90

Program Analysis

1. Write an If . . . Then decision structure to compare the two numbers in the decDeveloperPay and decWebDesignerPay variables. Display a message box that states decDeveloperPay is greater than decWebDesignerPay.
2. Write an If statement that displays the message box “Sleet is possible” if the value in the variable decTemp is within the range from 30 to 35.
3. Write an If . . . Then . . . Else statement that checks the value in the variable chrGender for the value M (Male) or F (Female) and assigns the information shown in Figure 5-91 to lblCollegeExpectation.Text based on the gender. If the variable chrGender contains a value other than M or F, assign the message “Invalid Gender” to lblCollegeExpectation.Text.

Gender	College Expectation
Male	75% plan to graduate from college
Female	85% plan to graduate from college

FIGURE 5-91

4. Write a Select Case statement that tests the user's age in a variable named intAge and assigns the generation name of that age group to the variable strGeneration, according to the information shown in Figure 5-92.

Age Group	Generation Name
50 and above	Baby Boomers
39–49	Generation X
18–38	Generation Y
Below 18	Millennials

FIGURE 5-92

© 2014 Cengage Learning

5. Rewrite the Select Case statement shown in Figure 5-93 as an If . . . Then . . . Else statement.

```
Select Case chrDepartment
    Case "B", "b"
        strDept = "Baby / Infant Clothing"
    Case "T", "t"
        strDept = "Technology"
End Select
```

FIGURE 5-93

© 2014 Cengage Learning

6. Rewrite the If . . . Then . . . Else statement shown in Figure 5-94 as a Select Case statement.

```
If intGrade >= 9 And intGrade <= 12 Then
    lblSchool.Text = "High School"
ElseIf intGrade >= 7 Then
    lblSchool.Text = "Middle School"
ElseIf intGrade >= 1 Then
    lblSchool.Text = "Elementary School"
Else
    lblSchool.Text = "Invalid Grade"
End If
```

FIGURE 5-94

© 2014 Cengage Learning

(continues)

Program Analysis *continued*

7. What is the output of the code shown in Figure 5-95 if the word Black is entered in the txtSkiSlope text box?

```
Select Case Me.txtSkiSlope.Text
    Case "Green"
        MsgBox("Beginner Slope")
    Case "Blue"
        MsgBox("Intermediate Slope")
    Case "Black"
        MsgBox("Expert Slope")
    Case Else
        MsgBox("Invalid Entry")
End Select
```

FIGURE 5-95

8. After the execution of the Select Case structure in Figure 5-96, what value will be found in the Text property of lblFemaleHeight if the user enters the number 74 into the txtEnterHeight text box? If the number 81 is entered? If the number 59 is entered?

```
Dim intHeightInches As Integer
intHeightInches = Convert.ToInt32(txtEnterHeight.Text)
Select Case intHeightInches
    Case Is < 61
        lblFemaleHeight.Text = "Petite"
    Case 61 To 69
        lblFemaleHeight.Text = "Average"
    Case 70 To 80
        lblFemaleHeight.Text = "Tall"
    Case 80 To 120
        lblFemaleHeight.Text = "Towering"
    Case Else
        lblFemaleHeight.Text = "Not Possible"
End Select
```

FIGURE 5-96

9. In each of the following examples, is the condition True or False?

a. "CVCC" >= "GRCC"

b. "G" >= "g"

c. "Nerdy" < "Nerd"

d. "Cool" < > "cool"

e. "50" >= "Fifty"

f. ("Paris" < "Barcelona") And ("Amsterdam" <= "Prague")

g. ("Ford" > "Chevrolet") Or ("Toyota" < "Honda")

h. 3 ^ 2 <= 3 * 4

i. Not ("CNN" >= "ABC")

j. Not ("Tim" > "Tom") And Not ("Great" < > "great")

Complete one or more of the following case programming assignments. Submit the program and materials you create to your instructor. The level of difficulty is indicated for each case programming assignment.

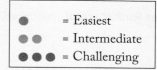

● = Easiest
●● = Intermediate
●●● = Challenging

1

● POWER WASHER RENTAL

Design a Windows application and write the code that will execute according to the program requirements in Figure 5-97. Before writing the code, create a Use Case Definition, as shown in Figure 5-98 on the next page. Before writing the code, create an event planning document for each event in the program. The completed Form object and other objects in the user interface are shown in Figure 5-99 on the next page.

REQUIREMENTS DOCUMENT

Date Submitted: May 6, 2015

Application Title: Power Washer Rental Application

Purpose: This Windows application calculates the cost of renting a power washer from a tool rental store.

Program Procedures: The user selects the duration of time for renting the power washer from the tool rental store. The user then requests that the program calculate and display the cost of renting the power washer.

Algorithms, Processing, and Conditions:
1. The user selects the duration of rental time.
2. The power washer can be rented for a half day ($24), full day ($35), or two full days ($50).
3. The user must be able to initiate the calculation of the rental fee.
4. The user should be able to clear the duration of the rental and the rental fee.

Notes and Restrictions: n/a

Comments: Obtain an image for this program from CengageBrain.com. The name of the image file is PowerWasher.

FIGURE 5-97

(continues)

Power Washer rental (continued)

USE CASE DEFINITION

1. The Windows application window opens.
2. The user selects the duration of time needed for the rental.
3. The user taps or clicks the Rental Fee button to display the cost of power washer rental.
4. The user clears the input and the result by tapping or clicking the Clear button.
5. If desired, the user repeats the process.

FIGURE 5-98

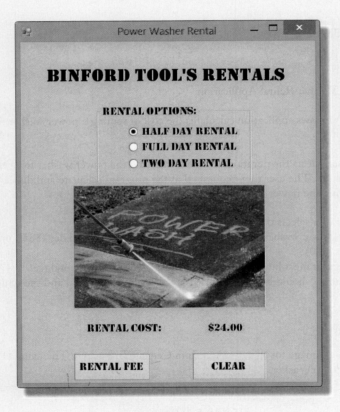

FIGURE 5-99

2 ● NEW YEAR'S EVE CELEBRATION TICKETS

Design a Windows application and write the code that will execute according to the program requirements in Figure 5-100 and the Use Case Definition in Figure 5-101 on the next page. Before writing the code, create an event planning document for each event in the program. The completed Form object and other objects in the user interface are shown in Figure 5-102 on the next page.

REQUIREMENTS DOCUMENT

Date Submitted: April 15, 2015

Application Title: New Year's Eve Celebration Tickets Application

Purpose: This Windows application calculates the cost of New Year's Eve celebration tickets.

Program Procedures: The user should enter the number of tickets for an exclusive New Year's Eve celebration. The event has three types of tickets. You cannot combine ticket types.

Algorithms, Processing, and Conditions:
1. The user enters the number of tickets to purchase.
2. The types of tickets include a full-evening dinner celebration for $125, an appetizers-only celebration for $75, and discounted entry with military ID (45% off the price of the full-evening dinner celebration). The user can only select one type of ticket for her entire party.
3. The user must be able to initiate the calculation and display the total cost of the tickets.
4. The user should be able to clear the number of tickets purchased, the type of ticket, and the total cost.

Notes and Restrictions:
1. If the user enters a negative number of tickets, the user should be advised and asked for a valid entry.
2. If the user enters a nonnumeric value for the number of tickets or does not enter a number, the user should be advised and asked for a valid entry.

Comments: Obtain an image for this program from CengageBrain.com. The name of the image file is NYE.

FIGURE 5-100

(continues)

New Year's Eve Celebration Tickets (continued)

USE CASE DEFINITION

1. The Windows application window opens.
2. The user enters the number of tickets and the ticket type needed for her party.
3. The user taps or clicks the Calculate button.
4. The program displays the total cost of the tickets, including any discount that applies.
5. A MsgBox appears and displays a warning if the user enters a negative number of tickets.
6. A MsgBox appears and displays a warning if the user enters a nonnumeric value for the number of tickets or does not enter a value.
7. The user can clear the input and the results by tapping or clicking the Clear button.

FIGURE 5-101

FIGURE 5-102

3
WINDOWS 8 ONLINE SHIPPING

Design a Windows application and write the code that will execute according to the program requirements in Figure 5-103 and the Use Case Definition in Figure 5-104 on the next page. Before writing the code, create an event planning document for each event in the program. The completed Form object and other objects in the user interface are shown in Figure 5-105 on the next page.

REQUIREMENTS DOCUMENT

Date Submitted:	May 11, 2015
Application Title:	Windows 8 Online Shipping Application
Purpose:	This Windows application computes the cost of shipping for an online Windows 8 accessories store.
Program Procedures:	The user enters the weight of the purchased item, the shipping destination, and the desired delivery time. The application computes the total shipping cost.

Algorithms, Processing, and Conditions:

1. A user must be able to enter the weight in pounds and select the destination and type of shipping. The user can select U.S. standard delivery or international delivery to Latin America or Canada.
2. The user must be able to enter the weight of the purchased item. If the item weighs less than 5 pounds, the standard and international rates apply. If the item weighs more than 5 pounds, add a 25% surcharge to the standard or international shipping rate. The shipping rates are $6.00 for U.S. standard delivery and $8.00 for Latin American or Canadian standard delivery.
3. If the customer requests overnight shipping, double the shipping cost.
4. The user must be able to initiate the shipping calculation and the display of the total cost of shipping.
5. The user must be able to clear the entries and results.

Notes and Restrictions:

1. If the user enters a nonnumeric value for the weight or does not enter a weight, the user should be advised and asked for a valid entry.
2. If the user enters a negative weight, the user should be advised and asked for a valid entry.
3. If the value entered is greater than 20 pounds, the user should be advised and asked for a valid entry.
4. The default delivery rate is for the United States.
5. The cost should be displayed in currency format.

Comments:

1. Use Case statements for the weight of the package.
2. Obtain an image for this program from CengageBrain.com. The name of the image file is Shipping.

FIGURE 5-103

(continues)

Case Programming Assignments

Windows 8 Online Shipping *(continued)*

USE CASE DEFINITION

1. The Windows application window opens.
2. The user enters the weight of the package in pounds.
3. The user selects the destination.
4. The user selects whether overnight shipping is required.
5. The user taps or clicks the Shipping Fee button to display the online shipping cost.
6. The user clears the input and the result by tapping or clicking the Clear button.
7. If desired, the user repeats the process.

FIGURE 5-104

FIGURE 5-105

4

PREMIUM GAMING SUBSCRIPTION

Design a Windows application and write the code that will execute according to the program requirements in Figure 5-106. Before designing the user interface, create a Use Case Definition. Before writing the code, create an event planning document for each event in the program.

REQUIREMENTS DOCUMENT

Date Submitted: April 22, 2015

Application Title: Premium Gaming Subscription Application

Purpose: This Windows application calculates the payment amount for a monthly membership to a cloud-based gaming subscription.

Program Procedures: The user should enter the name of the new member, the number of months the new member would like to prepay, and the type of membership. The gaming prepayment cost will be computed and displayed for the entered number of months. The monthly costs for the three types of membership are:
- Single Subscription: $12 per month
- Family Subscription (up to 5 members): $28 per month
- Game Developer Subscription: $7 per month

Algorithms, Processing, and Conditions:
1. The user must enter the name of the new member, the type of membership, and the number of months to prepay.
2. Based on the type of subscription, the prepayment cost is calculated using the following formula: number of prepaid months × cost per month.
3. The user must be able to initiate the calculation and display the prepaid amount for the gaming subscription, which covers the costs of unlimited gaming usage.
4. The user should be able to clear the name of the new member, the number of prepaid months, the type of membership, and the prepaid amount for the new member.

Notes and Restrictions:
1. If the user enters a nonnumeric value for the number of months, the user should be advised and asked for a valid entry.
2. If the user enters a negative number of months or does not enter a number, the user should be advised and asked for a valid entry.
3. If the user does not enter a member name, the user should be advised and asked for a valid entry.
4. The default subscription type is single membership.

Comments: n/a

FIGURE 5-106

5 ●●
WEIGHT ON THE MOON AND MARS

Design a Windows application and write the code that will execute according to the program requirements in Figure 5-107. Before designing the user interface, create a Use Case Definition. Before writing the code, create an event planning document for each event in the program.

REQUIREMENTS DOCUMENT

Date Submitted:	May 6, 2015
Application Title:	Weight on the Moon and Mars Application
Purpose:	This Windows application calculates a user's weight in pounds and kilograms on the Moon or on Mars.
Program Procedures:	The user enters her weight in pounds and selects either the Moon or Mars. The application will determine the user's weight on the Moon or Mars in pounds and kilograms.
Algorithms, Processing, and Conditions:	1. The user must be able to enter her weight in pounds and indicate that she wants to see her equivalent weight on the Moon or Mars. 2. One pound on the Moon is equivalent to 0.166 pounds. One pound on Mars is equivalent to 0.377 pounds. 3. One pound is equivalent to 0.454 kilograms. 4. The user must be able to initiate the calculation and the display of her weight on the Moon or Mars. 5. The user must be able to clear her input and the results.
Notes and Restrictions:	1. If the user's weight entry is blank or nonnumeric, the user should be advised and asked for a valid entry. 2. The results should be displayed one place past the decimal point.
Comments:	n/a

FIGURE 5-107

6 ●●

SECONDHAND STORE PAYROLL CALCULATOR

Design a Windows application and write the code that will execute according to the program requirements in Figure 5-108. Before designing the user interface, create a Use Case Definition. Before writing the code, create an event planning document for each event in the program.

REQUIREMENTS DOCUMENT

Date Submitted:	May 11, 2015
Application Title:	Secondhand Store Payroll Calculator Application
Purpose:	This application calculates the payroll for employees of a secondhand store.
Program Procedures:	In a Windows application, the user enters an employee's name, number of hours worked, and pay per hour. If the employee works more than 40 hours per week, the store pays time and a half for overtime. The tax rate can be a single rate (19%) or a family rate (16%). The application should compute and display the gross pay, the tax based on the single or family rate, and the net pay.
Algorithms, Processing, and Conditions:	1. The user must be able to enter the employee's name, hours worked, and pay per hour.
	2. The user must be able to indicate whether the tax rate is the single rate (19%) or the family rate (16%).
	3. The user must be able to initiate the calculation and display of the gross pay, the tax amount based on the single or family rate, and the net pay.
	4. A Clear button will clear the user's input and final results.
Notes and Restrictions:	1. If the employee name, hours worked, or pay per hour is left blank, the user should be advised and asked for a valid entry.
	2. If the hours worked or pay per hour is nonnumeric, the user should be advised and asked for a valid entry.
	3. The minimum value for hours worked is 5. The maximum for hours worked is 60. If the user enters a value that is not within the valid range, the user should be advised and asked for a valid entry.
	4. The minimum pay per hour is $8.00. The maximum pay per hour is $40.00. If the user enters a value that is not within the valid range, the user should be advised and asked for a valid entry.
	5. The user must be able to clear the employee's name, the hours worked, the pay per hour, and the other pay information.
Comments:	n/a

FIGURE 5-108

7 ●●●

TECHNOLOGY CONFERENCE REGISTRATION

Based on the case project shown in Figure 5-109, create a requirements document and a Use Case Definition document and then design a Windows application. Before writing the code, create an event planning document for each event in the program.

It is important that developers update their skills by attending developers' conferences. The Dynamic International Management Consortium (DIMC) runs and manages the DSE (Developers Skill Enhancement) Conference two times per year. To encourage companies to send multiple employees to the conference, the cost per attendee is determined based on the number of attending developers from a given company. The following table specifies the cost per attendee.

Number of Conference Registrations per Company	Cost per Attendee
1	$895
2–4	$645
5–8	$480
9–16	$395

DIMC has asked you to develop a Windows application that can determine and display the total cost per company for developers attending the conference. DIMC has a policy that if any company member has attended a previous DIMC conference, the company receives a 15% discount for the total cost of the conference. The policy also states that no more than 16 people from a single company can attend the conference. DIMC has asked you to design the program so that the user must enter valid data.

FIGURE 5-109

8 ●●●

OFFICE 365 SUBSCRIPTION PLANS

Based on the case project shown in Figure 5-110, create a requirements document and a Use Case Definition document and then design a Windows application. Before writing the code, create an event planning document for each event in the program.

Your school has asked that you create a Windows application to determine how much it would cost a university student, an entire family, or a small business to use Microsoft Office 365 subscription plans over several months. The user can enter the number of months and a price comparison can be made. The user also can select one of three plan options; you can research the cost of these plans at *office365.com*. After the user selects a plan, its total cost for the entered amount of months is displayed to compare the prices of the plans. Do not accept negative numbers of months or nonnumeric values.

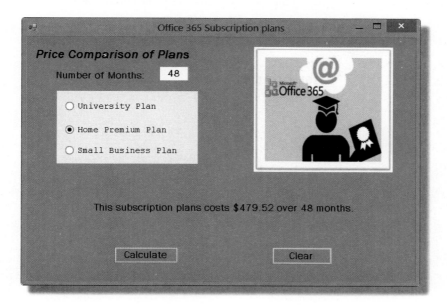

FIGURE 5-110

Case Programming Assignments

9 ●●● HUMMUS RESTAURANT

Based on the case project shown in Figure 5-111, create a requirements document and a Use Case Definition document and then design a Windows application. Before writing the code, create an event planning document for each event in the program.

A local restaurant offers hummus platters made to order. The hummus restaurant has asked you to create a Windows application that allows customers to enter their orders on a flat-screen computer. Create an application that allows the user to select one of five hummus platters. Create and display a list of platters, along with a display of prices for each platter, three types of pita bread choices at no additional cost, and two toppings at no additional cost. The hummus restaurant has a loyalty program that deducts 5% of the total order cost for every 10 points a customer has earned. Allow users to enter their total number of loyalty points and compute the cost of their order. Customers cannot receive money back if their loyalty points exceed the full cost of their order.

FIGURE 5-111

CHAPTER 6

Loop Structures

 **OBJECTIVES**

You will have mastered the material in this chapter when you can:

- Add a MenuStrip object
- Use the InputBox function
- Display data using the ListBox object
- Understand the use of counters and accumulators
- Understand the use of compound operators

- Repeat a process using a For… Next loop
- Repeat a process using a Do loop
- Avoid infinite loops
- Prime a loop
- Validate data
- Create a nested loop

- Select the best type of loop
- Debug using DataTips at breakpoints
- Publish a finished application using ClickOnce technology

Introduction

In Chapter 5, you learned about the decision structure, one of the major control structures used in computer programming. In this chapter you will learn another major structure called the **looping structure**, or the **iteration structure**.

A fundamental process in a computer program is to repeat a series of instructions either while a condition is true (or not true) or until a condition is true (or not true). For example, if a company is processing electronic paychecks for 5,000 employees, it can use the same set of instructions to post an electronic deposit for each employee, varying only the name of the employee and amount paid for each check. This process would continue until all checks are deposited. Unique check deposit instructions for each employee in the company are not required.

The process of repeating a set of instructions while a condition is true or until a condition is true is called **looping**. When the program is executing those instructions, it is said to be in a loop. Another term for looping is **iteration**.

The programming project in this chapter uses a loop to obtain input data and produce output information. A large company challenged groups of eight employees to form weight loss fitness teams. The Human Resource department requested a Windows application that determines the average weight loss for each team. This application, called the Fitness Challenge application, computes the average weight loss for up to eight team members that enter the total number of pounds they lost during their weight loss challenge. The application uses a loop to request and display the weight loss amounts of the team members. The application then displays the average weight loss by the fitness team (Figure 6-1).

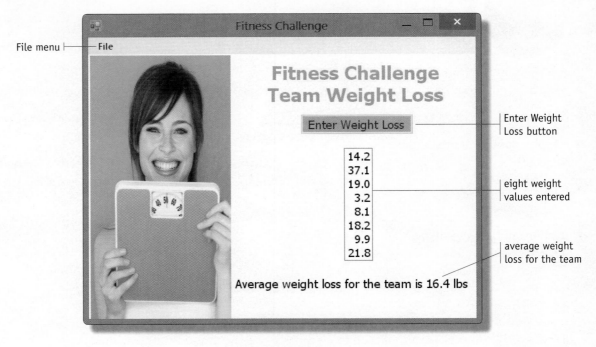

FIGURE 6-1

Figure 6-1 shows eight values the user entered in a list. After the user enters the weight loss values, the application calculates the average weight loss of the entire team.

When the Fitness Challenge application begins, the main window shows no weight loss values (Figure 6-2).

FIGURE 6-2

© Pando Hall/Photographer's Choice RF/Getty Images

When the user taps or clicks the Enter Weight Loss button, the Weight Loss dialog box opens (Figure 6-3), allowing the user to enter the weight loss of the first team member. This dialog box is called an **input box**.

FIGURE 6-3

ONLINE REINFORCEMENT

To view a video of the process described in the preceding paragraphs, visit CengageBrain. com and navigate to the resources for this title. Tap or click the link for Chapter 6 and then navigate to Video 6-1. Turn on your speakers to listen to the audio walkthrough of the steps.

After entering the first weight loss value, the user taps or clicks the OK button in the Weight Loss dialog box. The application lists the weight loss value in the main window, and then displays the input box again, requesting the next team member's weight loss. This process repeats for up to eight team members, and is implemented using a loop in the program. When the user is entering weight loss values, the program is said to be in a loop. The loop is terminated when the user enters the weight loss for the eighth team member or taps or clicks the Cancel button in the Weight Loss dialog box. After the loop is terminated, the Fitness Challenge application displays the average weight loss for the team, as shown in Figure 6-1 on page 364.

The Fitness Challenge application has several other features. Figure 6-1 shows a menu bar containing the File menu at the top of the window. The File menu contains the Clear command, which clears the list and the average weight loss, and the Exit command, which closes the window and terminates the application. In this chapter, you will learn to design and code a menu.

In addition, the application contains input validation. For example, if a user enters a nonnumeric or negative value for the weight loss, the application requests the weight loss amount again, until the user enters a reasonable value.

Finally, the application displays the average weight loss to one decimal place, such as 9.2 lbs.

User Interface Design

The user interface for the Fitness Challenge application includes three new elements: a menu, an input box, and a list for the weight loss values. The menu and the list of team member weight loss values are objects placed on the Windows Form object. The input box is created through the use of a function call in the program code. Each of these items is explained in the following sections.

Insert a MenuStrip Object

A **menu bar** is a strip across the top of a window that contains one or more menu names. A **menu** is a group of commands, or items, presented in a list. In the sample program, a File menu is created in the application window (Figure 6-4).

FIGURE 6-4
© Pando Hall/Photographer's Choice RF/Getty Images

When the user taps or clicks File on the menu bar during program execution, a menu appears with two commands: Clear and Exit. The user taps or clicks the Clear menu command to clear the entered weight values and the results. Tapping or clicking the Exit menu command closes the application. An advantage of a menu is that it conserves space instead of cluttering the form with objects such as buttons.

Using Visual Studio 2012, you can place menus at the top of a Windows Form using the MenuStrip object. To place a MenuStrip object on a Windows Form, you can complete the following steps:

STEP 1 With a Windows Form object open in the Visual Studio window, scroll in the Toolbox to display the Menus & Toolbars category. If the category is not open, tap or click the expand icon (the right-pointing triangle) next to the Menus & Toolbars category name. Drag the MenuStrip .NET component to the Windows Form object.

The pointer changes when you place it over the Windows Form object (Figure 6-5).

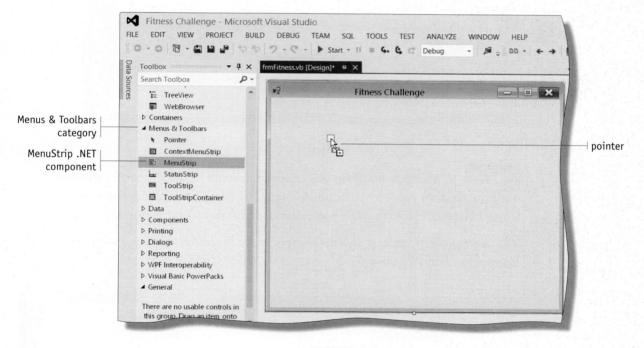

FIGURE 6-5

STEP 2   Release the object.

Visual Studio places the MenuStrip object at the top of the form regardless of where you released the object (Figure 6-6). The Component Tray, which is displayed below the form, organizes nongraphical Toolbox objects. It displays the MenuStrip1 object name.

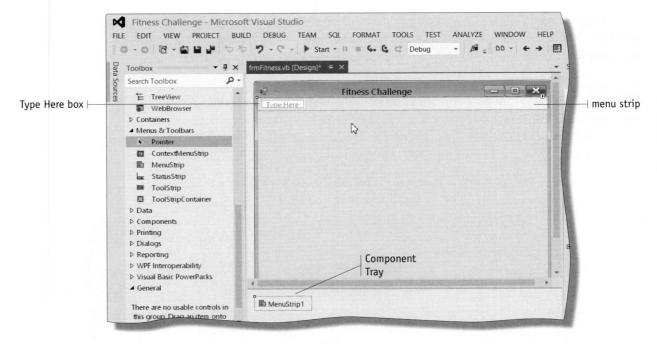

FIGURE 6-6

STEP 3   With the MenuStrip object selected, scroll in the Properties window until the (Name) property is visible. Change the MenuStrip object name to `mnuFitness`. (Note that the prefix for a MenuStrip object is mnu).

The name of the MenuStrip object is changed in the Properties window and in the Component Tray (Figure 6-7).

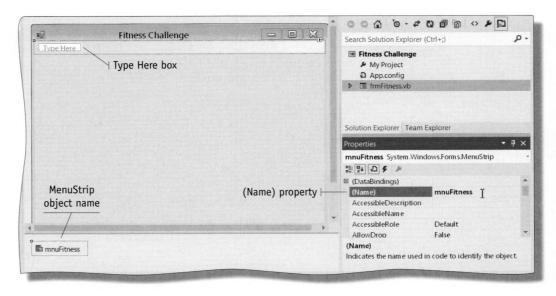

FIGURE 6-7

STEP 4 Tap or click the Type Here box on the menu bar. Type &File to identify the File menu, and then press the ENTER key.

The menu name File is displayed in the upper-left corner of the MenuStrip object and new Type Here boxes are available to create other menu items (Figure 6-8). The ampersand (&) you entered preceding the f indicates that F is a hot key. A hot key provides a keyboard shortcut for opening the menu. Instead of tapping or clicking File to open the menu, the user can press and hold the ALT key and then press the designated hot key, such as ALT+F. After you enter the menu name, the character following the ampersand is underlined to indicate it is the hot key.

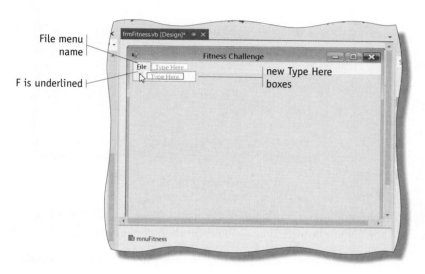

FIGURE 6-8

STEP 5 Tap or click File in the MenuStrip object to select it, scroll in the Properties window to the (Name) property, and then change the name to mnuFile.

The name of the File menu is displayed in the (Name) property in the Properties window (Figure 6-9).

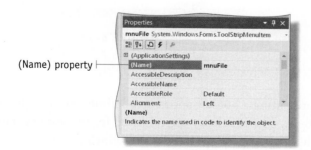

FIGURE 6-9

STEP 6   To add a menu item to the File menu, tap or click the Type Here box below the File menu name. Type &Clear and then press ENTER to create a new menu item named Clear with c as the hot key.

The Clear menu item is displayed below the File menu (Figure 6-10). After you press the ENTER key, the character following the ampersand is underlined to indicate it is the hot key.

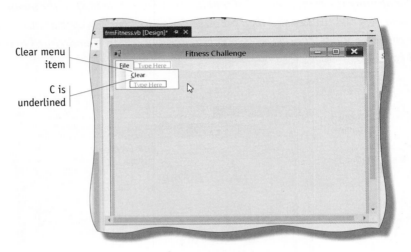

Clear menu item

C is underlined

FIGURE 6-10

STEP 7   On the File menu, tap or click Clear to select it, scroll in the Properties window until the (Name) property is visible, and then change the name to mnuClear.

The mnuClear name is displayed in the (Name) property in the Properties window (Figure 6-11).

(Name) property

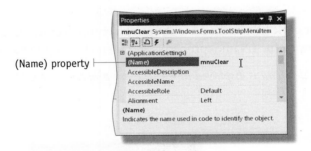

FIGURE 6-11

The letter representing a hot key appears underlined in the menu name, as shown in Figure 6-10. The first letter often is used for the hot key, but not always. For example, in the chapter project, the File menu includes the Exit item (see Figure 6-4 on page 366). The hot key typically used for the Exit item is the letter x. When entering the Exit menu item on the File menu, the developer can type E&xit, which assigns the letter following the & (x) as the hot key.

When assigning menu item hot keys, you should be aware that they are not case-sensitive. Therefore, you should not assign "T" to one menu item and "t" to another.

Event Handlers for Menu Items

Recall that the design of the user interface occurs before you write the code for event handlers. When you are ready to write code, however, you must write an event handler for each menu item because tapping or clicking it or using its hot key triggers an event. Writing a menu item event handler is the same as writing an event handler for a button tap or click.

To code the event handler for the Exit menu item, you can complete the following steps:

STEP 1   In Design view, double-tap or double-click the Exit menu item to open the code window.

The code window is displayed and the insertion point is located within the Exit item click event handler (Figure 6–12). When the user taps or clicks the Exit item on the File menu, the code in the event handler will be executed.

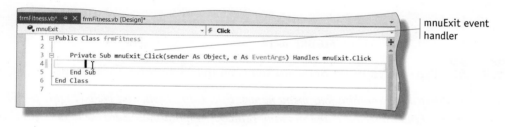

mnuExit event handler

FIGURE 6-12

STEP 2   Using IntelliSense, enter the Close procedure call to close the window and terminate the application.

When executed, the Close procedure will close the window and terminate the program (Figure 6–13).

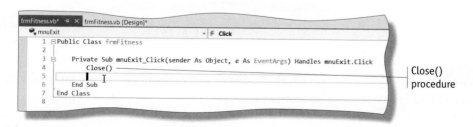

Close() procedure

FIGURE 6-13

Insert Standard Items for a Menu

Developers often customize the MenuStrip object for the specific needs of an application. In addition, Visual Basic 2012 contains an **Action Tag** that allows you to create a full standard menu bar commonly provided in Windows programs, with File, Edit, Tools, and Help menus. In Visual Basic 2012, an Action Tag (▶) appears in the upper-right corner of many objects, including a MenuStrip. Action Tags provide a way for you to specify a set of actions, called **smart actions**, for an object as you design a form. For example, to insert a full standard menu, you can complete the following steps:

STEP 1 With a new Windows Form object open, drag the MenuStrip .NET component onto the Windows Form object. Tap or click the Action Tag on the MenuStrip object.

The MenuStrip Tasks menu opens (Figure 6-14).

FIGURE 6-14

STEP 2 Tap or click Insert Standard Items on the MenuStrip Tasks menu.

The MenuStrip object contains four menu names: File, Edit, Tools, and Help (Figure 6-15). These are the standard menus found in many Windows applications. Each menu contains the items typically listed on the menus.

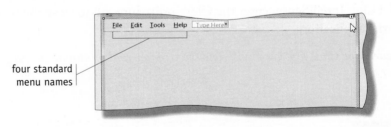

FIGURE 6-15

STEP 3 Tap or click File on the menu bar to view the individual menu items, their associated icons, and their shortcut keys.

The standard File menu items (New, Open, Save, Save As, Print, Print Preview, and Exit) are displayed with their associated icons and shortcut keys (Figure 6–16). The other menus also contain standard items. You can code an event handler for each menu item by double-tapping or double-clicking the item.

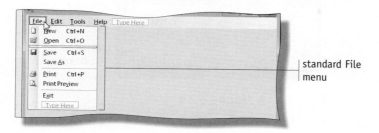

FIGURE 6-16

Use the InputBox Function

To calculate a team's weight loss, the Fitness Challenge application uses an InputBox object in which users enter the weight loss of each team member. The InputBox object is a dialog box that prompts the user to enter a value. You can use the InputBox function instead of a TextBox object to obtain input. Similar to coding a MessageBox object, you use the InputBox function to specify when the InputBox object appears. The InputBox function displays a dialog box that consists of a message asking for input, an input area, a title, an OK button, and a Cancel button (see Figure 6-3 on page 365). When the user enters the text and taps or clicks the OK button, the InputBox function returns the text as a string. If the user taps or clicks the Cancel button, the function returns a null string (""). Figure 6-17 shows the syntax of the InputBox function:

General Format: InputBox Function

```
strVariableName = InputBox("Question to Prompt User", "Title Bar")
```

FIGURE 6-17

© 2014 Cengage Learning

For example, the code in Figure 6-18 creates a dialog box that requests the user's age for a driver's license application. The string returned by the InputBox function is assigned to the strAge variable.

```
5        Dim strAge As String
6
7        strAge = InputBox("Please enter your age", "Driver's License Agency")
```

FIGURE 6-18

When the application is executed, the InputBox object in Figure 6-19 opens, requesting that the user enter her age.

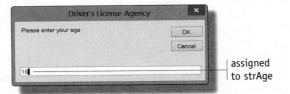

FIGURE 6-19

The InputBox object returns all data entered as a string, which then can be converted to the appropriate data type.

Display a Default Value in an InputBox Object

The InputBox object can be assigned a default value. For example, if a college application for admission requests the student's home state and the college or university is located in Virginia, the most likely state, Virginia, can be the default value in the InputBox, as shown in Figure 6-20.

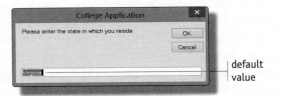

FIGURE 6-20

The code to produce this input box is shown in Figure 6-21.

```
 9        Dim strState As String
10
11        strState = InputBox("Please enter the state in which you reside:", _
12             "College Application", "Virginia")
```

FIGURE 6-21

As you can see, the third argument for the InputBox function call is the default value that is placed in the input box. It must be a String value and follow the syntax shown in Figure 6-21.

Create the InputBox Object for Fitness Challenge Application

The Fitness Challenge application uses an InputBox object that requests the weight loss amounts of team members numbered 1–8, as shown in Figure 6-22.

FIGURE 6-22

The code for the Weight Loss InputBox is shown in Figure 6-23. Notice that the prompt message for the user is assigned to the strInputMessage variable, and the title bar text (Weight Loss) is assigned to the strInputHeading variable.

```
15          Dim strWeightLoss As String
16          Dim strInputMessage As String = "Enter the weight loss for team member #"
17          Dim strInputHeading As String = "Weight Loss"
18          Dim intNumberOfEntries As Integer = 1
19
20          strWeightLoss = InputBox(strInputMessage & intNumberOfEntries, strInputHeading, " ")
21
```

FIGURE 6-23

The variable intNumberOfEntries identifies the team member's number. It is included in the prompt message through the use of concatenation. The variable intNumberOfEntries is incremented later in the code so that it refers to the correct team member each time the InputBox function call is executed.

In Figure 6-23, the default value is specified as a space (" "). When the input box is displayed, a space will be selected in the input area. This space is required so that if a user taps or clicks the OK button without entering any data, the InputBox will not return a null character (""), which indicates the user tapped or clicked the Cancel button. This normally is a good programming practice.

When the user taps or clicks the Cancel button in an input box and the InputBox function returns a null character, the program can test for the null character to determine further processing.

Display Data Using the ListBox Object

In the Fitness Challenge application, the user enters weight loss values into the InputBox object, and the application displays the weight loss values in a list box (see Figure 6-1 on page 364). To create such a list, you use the ListBox object provided in the Visual Basic Toolbox. A ListBox object displays a group of values, called items, with one item per line. To add a ListBox object to a Windows Form object, you can complete the following steps:

STEP 1 Drag the ListBox object from the Toolbox to where you want to place the ListBox object on the Windows Form object. When the pointer is in the correct location, release the object.

The ListBox object is placed on the form (Figure 6-24).

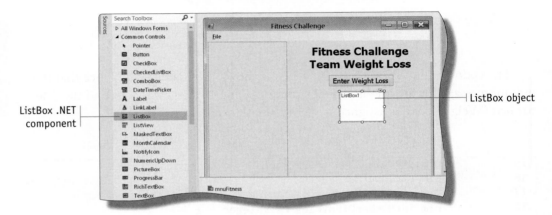

FIGURE 6-24

STEP 2 With the ListBox object selected, scroll in the Properties window to the (Name) property. Name the ListBox object `lstWeightLoss`.

The name you entered is displayed in the (Name) property in the Properties window (Figure 6-25). Notice a ListBox object name begins with lst (be sure to use a lowercase letter l, not a one).

ONLINE REINFORCEMENT

To view a video of the process in the previous steps, visit CengageBrain.com and navigate to the resources for this title. Tap or click the link for Chapter 6 and then navigate to Video 6-5.

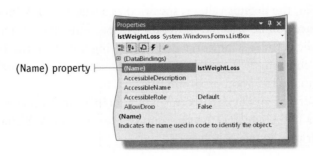

FIGURE 6-25

After placing a ListBox object on the Windows Form object, you can adjust the size by dragging the size handles (Figure 6-24). Be sure to resize the ListBox so that it is large enough to hold the application data. The ListBox object for the Fitness Challenge application is designed to be wide enough to hold three digits and a decimal point, and long enough to hold eight numbers (Figure 6-26).

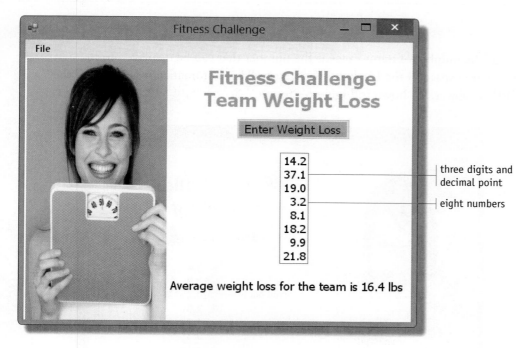

FIGURE 6-26

© Pando Hall/Photographer's Choice RF/Getty Images

To display the weight loss of each team member in the list box, you must write code to add each item to the ListBox object. After an item is added, it is displayed in the list box. The general format of the statement to add an item to a ListBox object is shown in Figure 6-27.

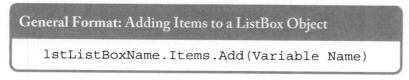

General Format: Adding Items to a ListBox Object

```
lstListBoxName.Items.Add(Variable Name)
```

FIGURE 6-27

© 2014 Cengage Learning

In Figure 6-27, the Add procedure will add the item contained in the variable identified by the Variable Name entry. The syntax for the statement must be followed precisely.

Figure 6-28 shows the code to add the team member weight loss values to the lstWeightLoss ListBox object and then display the weight loss of each team member (decWeightLoss) in the ListBox object.

| 45 | `lstWeightLoss.Items.Add(decWeightLoss)` |

FIGURE 6-28

If the number of items exceeds the number that can be displayed in the designated space of the ListBox object, a scroll bar automatically is added to the ListBox object, as shown in Figure 6-29.

FIGURE 6-29

© Pando Hall/Photographer's Choice RF/Getty Images

To clear the items in a ListBox object, the Clear method works as it does for the TextBox object. The syntax of the statement to clear the ListBox is shown in Figure 6-30.

General Format: Clear the ListBox Object

```
lstListBoxName.Items.Clear()
```

FIGURE 6-30

In the Fitness Challenge application, the user can select the Clear menu item to clear the form. The code in Figure 6-31 removes the items from the lstWeightLoss ListBox.

| 81 | `lstWeightLoss.Items.Clear()` |

FIGURE 6-31

CONSIDER THIS

Can I control where the InputBox appears on the screen?

To control the position of the InputBox, you can add an optional × position and Y position representing the upper-left edge of the dialog box. The syntax of the InputBox with sample × and Y positions is:

myValue = InputBox(message, title, defaultValue, 150, 100)

The 150 pixels represents the × position (horizontal) and the 100 pixels represents the Y position (vertical).

Add ListBox Items During Design

The Fitness Challenge application allows the user to add items to the ListBox object during program execution, but you also can add items to a ListBox object while designing the form. Adding items to the ListBox object during the design phase allows the user to select an item from the ListBox object during execution. For example, in an application to select a favorite clothing store, you can add items to a ListBox object named lstStores during the form design by completing the following steps:

STEP 1   Assume the lstStores ListBox object already has been placed and named on the Windows Form object. Select the ListBox object on the Windows Form object and then tap or click the Items property in the Properties window.

The Items property in the Properties window is selected. An ellipsis button appears to the right of the (Collection) entry (Figure 6-32).

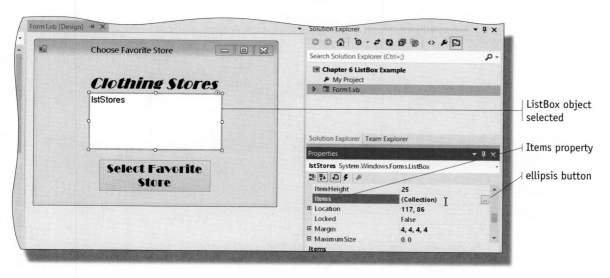

FIGURE 6-32

STEP 2   Tap or click the ellipsis button in the right column of the Items property.

The String Collection Editor window opens, allowing you to enter items that will be displayed in the lstStores ListBox object (Figure 6–33).

String Collection
Editor window

enter items to be
placed in the
ListBox object

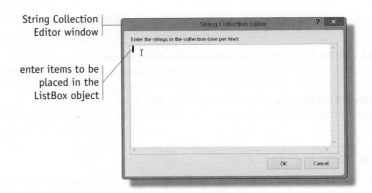

FIGURE 6-33

STEP 3   Tap or click the String Collection Editor window. Type the following items to represent popular retail stores, and then press ENTER at the end of each line:

```
Abercrombie & Fitch
Aeropostale
American Eagle
Express
Hollister
```

The items representing favorite retail stores appear in the String Collection Editor window on separate lines (Figure 6–34).

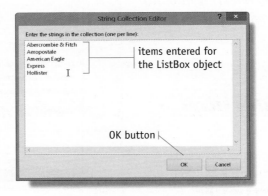

items entered for
the ListBox object

OK button

FIGURE 6-34

STEP 4 Tap or click the OK button.

The Windows Form object displays the stores in the lstStores ListBox object (Figure 6-35).
The user can select one of the items in the ListBox object during execution.

FIGURE 6-35

Use the SelectedItem Property

The SelectedItem property identifies which item in the ListBox is selected. An
assignment statement assigns that property to a variable, as shown in Figure 6-36.

General Format: Assign the Selected Item in a ListBox Object

```
strVariableName = lstListBoxName.SelectedItem
```

FIGURE 6-36

© 2014 Cengage Learning

Figure 6-37 shows the code to display the user's selection of her favorite store
from the lstStores ListBox object in a message box.

```
5       MsgBox("Your favorite store is "_
6       &lstStores.SelectedItem & ".")
```

FIGURE 6-37

Use Accumulators, Counters, and Compound Operators

After the user enters the weight loss values of up to eight team members, the Fitness Challenge application calculates the average weight loss (see Figure 6-1 on page 364). The formula to calculate the average weight loss is: (total of all weight loss values entered) / (number of team members). For example, if the total of all the weight loss values entered is 145.2 and weight loss values were entered for eight team members, the average weight loss is 18.2 pounds.

To calculate the average, the program must add the weight loss of each team member to a variable. The variable that contains an accumulated value such as the total of all the weight loss values is called an **accumulator**.

To compute the average weight loss, the program also must keep track of how many weight loss values have been entered. The variable that keeps track of this value is called a **counter**. A counter always is incremented with a constant value. This value can be positive or negative. In the Fitness Challenge application, the counter is incremented by 1 each time the user enters a weight loss number for a team member. Only positive values that indicate how many pounds were lost are accepted; for example, 8.3 represents 8.3 pounds lost.

You can use one of two techniques to add a value to a variable and then update the value in the variable, as with an accumulator or a counter. The first technique is shown in Figure 6-38.

```
26    decTotalWeightLoss = decTotalWeightLoss + decWeightLoss
27    intNumberOfEntries = intNumberOfEntries + 1
```

FIGURE 6-38

On line 26 in Figure 6-38, the value in the decTotalWeightLoss variable is added to the value in the decWeightLoss variable and the result is stored in the decTotalWeightLoss variable. This statement accumulates the weight loss values in the decTotalWeightLoss accumulator. The statement in line 27 increments the number of entries counter by 1. The effect is that the value in the number of entries counter is increased by 1 each time the statement is executed.

A second method for accomplishing this task is to use a shortcut mathematical operator called a **compound operator** that allows you to add, subtract, multiply, divide, use modulus or exponents, or concatenate strings, storing the result in the same variable. An assignment statement that includes a compound operator begins with the variable that will contain the accumulated value, such as an accumulator or a counter, followed by the compound operator. A compound operator consists of an arithmetic operator and an equal sign. The last element in the assignment statement is the variable or literal containing the value to be used in the calculation.

An assignment statement using a compound operator such as:

```
intNumberOfEntries += 1
```

is the same as:

```
intNumberOfEntries = intNumberOfEntries + 1
```

The += compound operator adds the value of the right operand to the value of the left operand and stores the result in the left operand's variable. Similarly, the statement:

```
decTotalWeightLoss += decWeightLoss
```

is the same as:

```
decTotalWeightLoss = decTotalWeightLoss + decWeightLoss
```

The table in Figure 6-39 shows an example of compound operators used in code. Assume that intResult = 24, decResult = 24, and strSample = "tree".

Operation	Example with Single Operators	Example with Compound Operator	Result
Addition	intResult = intResult + 1	intResult += 1	intResult = 25
Subtraction	intResult = intResult − 3	intResult −= 3	intResult = 21
Multiplication	intResult = intResult * 2	intResult *= 2	intResult = 48
Decimal Division	decResult = decResult / 5	decResult /= 5	decResult = 4.8
Integer Division	intResult = intResult \ 5	intResult \ =5	intResult = 4
Exponents	intResult = intResult ^ 2	intResult ^= 2	intResult = 576
Concatenate	strSample = strSample & "house"	strSample &= "house"	strSample = "treehouse"

FIGURE 6-39

© 2014 Cengage Learning

Developers often use compound operators in Visual Basic coding. The coding example in Figure 6-40 uses several compound operators and a MsgBox object. When the following code is executed, the result shown in the MsgBox object is "Final Result = 2".

```
30        Dim intTotal As Integer
31        intTotal = 7
32        intTotal += 6
33        intTotal *= 2
34        intTotal /= 13
35        MsgBox("Final Result = " & intTotal.ToString(), , "Compound Operators")
```

FIGURE 6-40

HEADS UP

The compound operators +=, −=, *=, /=, \=, ^=, and &= run faster than their regular longer equation counterparts because the statement is more compact.

Compound operators also can be used to connect two strings with the concatenation operator (&). The code in Figure 6-41 creates the phrase "To err is human!" in a MsgBox object by using compound operators to concatenate the strPhrase variable. Each compound operator joins another word to the end of the phrase assigned to the strPhrase variable.

```
30        Dim strPhrase As String
31        strPhrase = "To err"
32        strPhrase &= " is "
33        strPhrase &= "human!"
34        MsgBox(strPhrase, , "Compound Operators")
```

FIGURE 6-41

Use Loops to Perform Repetitive Tasks

In the Fitness Challenge application, the user enters weight loss values in an InputBox for up to eight team members. The repetitive process of entering eight weight loss values can be coded within a loop to simplify the task with fewer lines of code. Unlike If…Then statements that execute only once, loops repeat multiple times. Each repetition of the loop is called an **iteration**. An iteration is a single execution of a set of instructions that are to be repeated.

Loops are powerful structures that repeat a section of code a certain number of times or until a particular condition is met. Visual Basic has two main types of loops: For…Next loops and Do loops.

Repeat a Process Using the For…Next Loop

You can use a For…Next loop when a section of code should be executed an exact number of times. The syntax of a For…Next loop is shown in Figure 6-42.

General Format: For…Next loop

```
For Control Variable = Beginning Numeric Value To Ending Numeric Value

    ' Body of the Loop

Next
```

FIGURE 6-42

In Figure 6-42, the For...Next loop begins with the keyword For. Following this keyword is the control variable, which is the numeric variable that keeps track of the number of iterations the loop completes. To begin the loop, the For statement places the beginning numeric value in the control variable. The program then executes the code between the For and Next statements, which is called the body of the loop.

Upon reaching the Next statement, the program returns to the For statement and increments the value of the control variable. This process continues until the value in the control variable is greater than the ending numeric value. The program then executes the statement(s) that follows the Next command.

Figure 6-43 shows a For...Next loop designed to execute four times. The control value is a variable named intNumber.

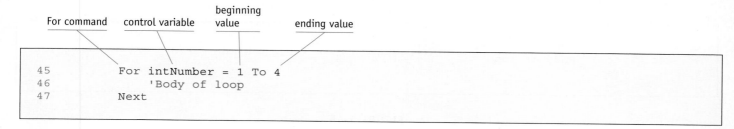

FIGURE 6-43

The first line in Figure 6-43 specifies that the control variable (intNumber) is assigned the value 1 because the literal 1 is the beginning value. Then the program executes the body of the loop. When the program encounters the Next statement, control returns to the For statement where, by default, the value 1 is added to the control variable. The code in the body of the loop is executed again. This process continues until the value in the control variable is greater than the ending value, which is 4 in this example. Then the program executes the statement(s) that follow the Next command. A loop never exits in the middle of the loop. The comparison is made to the upper limit of the For statement and when the value exceeds the upper limit, loop terminates. The table in Figure 6-44 illustrates the looping process.

Loop Iteration	Value of intNumber	Process
1	intNumber = 1	Executes the code inside the loop
2	intNumber = 2	Executes the code inside the loop
3	intNumber = 3	Executes the code inside the loop
4	intNumber = 4	Executes the code inside the loop
5 (exits the loop)	intNumber = 5	The control variable value exceeds the ending value, so the application exits the For...Next loop. This means the statement(s) following the Next command are executed.

FIGURE 6-44

Include a Step Value in a For...Next Loop

A Step value is the value in a For...Next loop that is added to or subtracted from the beginning value on each iteration of the loop. If you do not include a Step value in the For statement, as shown in Figure 6-45, by default the value in the control variable is incremented by 1 after each iteration of the loop.

In Figure 6-45, a Step value of 2 has been added to the For statement. The control variable intNumber is set to the initial value of 1, and the lines of code in the body of the loop are executed. After the first iteration of the loop, the Step value is added to the control variable, changing the value in the control variable to 3 (1 + 2 = 3). The For loop will continue until the value in intNumber is greater than 99.

Step value

```
49        For intNumber = 1 To 99 Step 2
50             ' Body of loop
51        Next
```

FIGURE 6-45

The Step value can be negative. If so, the value in the control variable is decreased on each iteration of the loop. To exit the loop, you must specify an ending value that is less than the beginning value, as shown in Figure 6-46.

negative
Step value

```
55        For intCount = 25 To -10 Step -5
56             ' Body of loop
57        Next
```

FIGURE 6-46

In the first iteration of the For...Next loop in Figure 6-46, the control variable value is 25. The value in the intCount control variable is decreased by 5 each time the loop repeats. This repetition continues until the value in intCount is less than −10. Then the loop ends.

You also can assign decimal values to the control variable in a For...Next loop. For example, the For loop in Figure 6-47 has a starting value of 3.1. The loop ends when the value in the control variable is greater than 4.5. The Step value is 0.1, which means the value in decNumber increments by 0.1 on each pass through the loop.

decimal
Step value

```
61          For decNumber = 3.1 To 4.5 Step 0.1
62              ' Body of loop
63          Next
```

FIGURE 6-47

A For...Next loop also can include variables and mathematical expressions, as shown in Figure 6-48.

```
69          For intNumber = intBegin To (intEnd * 2) Step intIncrement
70              'Body of loop
71          Next
```

FIGURE 6-48

In Figure 6-48, the intNumber control variable is initialized with the value in the intBegin variable. Each time the Next statement is encountered and control is returned to the For statement, the value in intNumber is incremented by the value in the intIncrement variable. The loop continues until the value in intNumber is greater than the product of the value in intEnd times 2.

Use IntelliSense to Enter the For...Next Loop Code

Suppose an application is designed to have a list box that displays the population growth for Alaska during the next six years. Assume that the current population of Alaska is 675,000 people and is expected to grow at 5 percent per year for the next six years. The code in Figure 6-49 accomplishes this processing.

```
4           Dim intAlaskaPopulation As Integer = 675000
5           Dim intYears As Integer
6
7           For intYears = 1 To 6
8               intAlaskaPopulation += (intAlaskaPopulation * 0.05)
9               lstGrowth.Items.Add("Year " & intYears & " Population " & intAlaskaPopulation)
10
11          Next
```

FIGURE 6-49

To use IntelliSense to enter the code shown in Figure 6-49 on the previous page, you can complete the following steps, which assume a lstGrowth ListBox object has been defined on a Windows Form object.

STEP 1　In the code window, type `Dim intAlaskaPopulation As Integer = 675000` and then press the ENTER key. Type `Dim intYears As Integer` and then press the ENTER key two times. Type `for` and a space to open an IntelliSense list.

When you press the SPACEBAR, For is capitalized because it is a reserved word. The IntelliSense list shows all available entries (Figure 6-50).

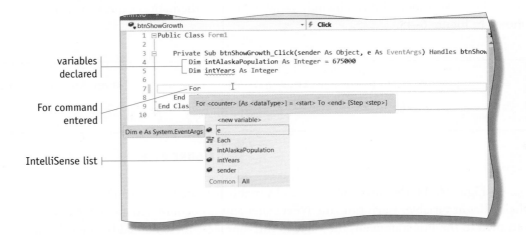

FIGURE 6-50

STEP 2　Type the first four letters of the intYears variable name (`intY`) to select intYears in the IntelliSense list. Type `= 1 to 6` and then press the ENTER key to specify the beginning value and ending value for the loop.

Visual Basic automatically inserts the Next statement in the code (Figure 6-51). For, To, and Next are blue to indicate they are keywords.

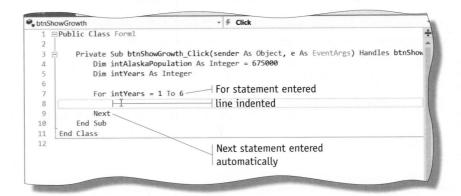

FIGURE 6-51

STEP 3 Use IntelliSense to select the appropriate variables. Enter the two new lines shown in Figure 6-52.

Each line of code automatically is indented between the For and Next statements (Figure 6-52).

statements in
body of loop

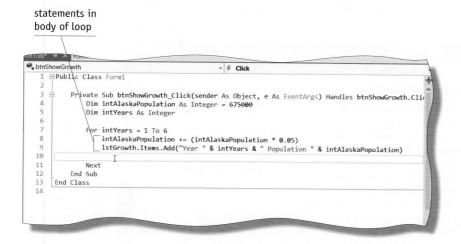

```
btnShowGrowth                                    ▾ ⚡ Click
  1 ⊟Public Class Form1
  2
  3 ⊟    Private Sub btnShowGrowth_Click(sender As Object, e As EventArgs) Handles btnShowGrowth.Cli
  4          Dim intAlaskaPopulation As Integer = 675000
  5          Dim intYears As Integer
  6
  7          For intYears = 1 To 6
  8              intAlaskaPopulation += (intAlaskaPopulation * 0.05)
  9              lstGrowth.Items.Add("Year " & intYears & " Population " & intAlaskaPopulation)
 10
 11          Next
 12      End Sub
 13 End Class
 14
```

FIGURE 6-52

STEP 4 Run the program to see the results of the loop.

The loop calculates and displays the Alaskan population growth for six years based on 5 percent growth per year (Figure 6-53).

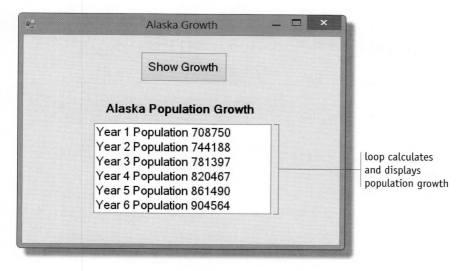

loop calculates
and displays
population growth

FIGURE 6-53

IN THE REAL WORLD

It is best to indent the body of the loop to clearly display what is being repeated. When you use IntelliSense to enter the loop, Visual Basic automatically indents the code properly. When other developers read the code, it is easy to identify the indented portion as the loop body.

ONLINE REINFORCEMENT

To view a video of the process in the previous steps, visit CengageBrain.com and navigate to the resources for this title. Tap or click the link for Chapter 6 and then navigate to Video 6-7.

Handle User Input in a For...Next Loop

The beginning, ending, and Step values used in a For...Next loop can vary based on user input. For example, the Squared Values application shown in Figure 6-54 displays the squared values of a range of numbers the user enters. The user enters the beginning (minimum) and ending (maximum) range of values, and then taps or clicks the Calculate Values button to view the squares of the numbers in the range.

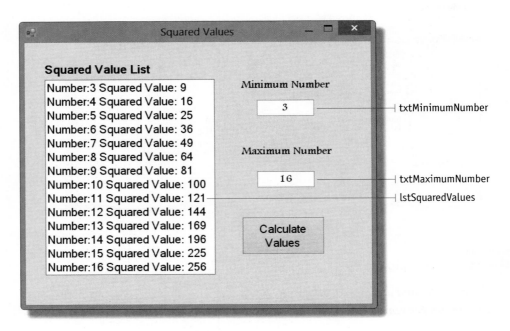

FIGURE 6-54

The code for the Squared Values application is shown in Figure 6-55.

```
5     Dim intCount As Integer
6     Dim intBegin As Integer
7     Dim intEnd As Integer
8
9     intBegin = Convert.ToInt32(txtMinimumNumber.Text)
10    intEnd = Convert.ToInt32(txtMaximumNumber.Text)
11
12    For intCount = intBegin To intEnd
13        lstSquaredValues.Items.Add("Number: " & intCount & " Squared Value: " & (intCount ^ 2))
14    Next
15
16    End Sub
```

FIGURE 6-55

On line 9 in Figure 6-55, the minimum value the user entered is converted to an integer and placed in the intBegin variable. Similarly, on line 10, the maximum value the user entered is converted to an integer and assigned to the intEnd variable.

On line 12, the value in intBegin is used as the beginning value in the For...Next loop, and the value in intEnd is used as the ending value. As you can see, the number of iterations for the loop is determined by values the user entered.

Within the loop, the value in intCount begins with the value in intBegin and is incremented by the default value of 1 each time through the loop. The application calculates the squared value from the number in intCount. As a result, the application calculates the squared values for all numbers beginning with the minimum number and ending with the maximum number.

Repeat a Process Using a Do Loop

You use a For...Next loop to repeat a process an exact number of times. In many applications, however, a loop should be repeated until a certain condition changes. For example, in the Fitness Challenge application, the user repeats the process of entering a weight loss value eight times, and then stops entering values by tapping or clicking the Cancel button. The loop in the Fitness Challenge application continues until one of two conditions becomes true: either the count of the weight loss values entered reaches 8 or the user taps or clicks the Cancel button on the InputBox object.

In a **Do loop**, the body of the loop is executed while or until a condition is true or false. The Do loop uses a condition similar to an If...Then decision structure to determine whether it should continue looping. In this way, you can use a Do loop to execute a body of statements an indefinite number of times. In the Fitness Challenge application, a Do loop can run an indefinite number of times because the user can end the loop at any time by tapping or clicking the Cancel button.

Visual Basic 2012 provides two types of Do loops: the Do While loop and the Do Until loop. Both Do loops execute statements repeatedly until a specified condition becomes true or false. Each loop examines a condition to determine whether the condition is true. The **Do While loop** executes as long as the condition is true. It is stated as, "Do the loop processing while the condition is true."

The **Do Until loop** executes until the condition becomes true. It is stated as, "Do the loop processing until a condition is true."

Do loops are either top-controlled or bottom-controlled, depending on whether the condition is tested before the loop begins or after the body of the loop has executed one time. A **top-controlled loop** is tested before the loop is entered. A top-controlled loop is also called a pre-test. The body of a top-controlled loop might not be executed at all because the condition being tested might be true before any processing in the loop occurs.

Bottom-controlled loops test the condition at the bottom of the loop, also called a post test, so the body of a bottom-controlled loop is executed at least once. Visual Basic provides top-controlled and bottom-controlled Do While and Do Until loops, meaning it can execute four types of Do loops.

Top-Controlled Do While Loops

You use a top-controlled Do While loop if you want the body of the loop to repeat as long as a condition remains true. Figure 6-56 shows the syntax of a top-controlled Do While loop.

> **General Format: Do While Loop (Top-Controlled)**
>
> ```
> Do While condition
>
>     ' Body of loop
>
> Loop
> ```

© 2014 Cengage Learning

FIGURE 6-56

A top-controlled Do While loop begins with the keywords Do While. Next, the condition is specified. The condition is expressed using the same relational operators that are available with the If statements that you learned in Chapter 5. Any condition that can be specified in an If statement can be specified in a Do While condition. The condition can compare numeric values or string values.

The body of the loop contains the instructions that are executed as long as the condition is true. The Loop keyword indicates the end of the loop. Visual Basic inserts it automatically when you enter the Do While keywords.

A statement within the body of the Do While loop must cause the condition to change at some point so the loop ends. For example, consider the following statement:

```
Do While strColor = "Red"
```

The loop continues to process as long as the value in the strColor variable remains Red. Based on the processing in the body of the loop, at some point the value in the strColor variable must be changed from Red. If not, the loop will not end. A loop that does not end is called an **infinite loop**.

The code in Figure 6-57 is an example of a top-controlled Do While loop. It continues to add 1 to the variable intScore while intScore is less than 5. It is considered a top-controlled loop because the condition is checked at the top of the loop.

```
17      Dim intScore As Integer = 0
18      Do While intScore < 5
19          intScore += 1
20      Loop
```

FIGURE 6-57

The loop in Figure 6-57 begins by testing whether intScore is less than 5. Because intScore starts with the value 0, the condition tested is true: 0 is less than 5. Next, the variable intScore is incremented by 1, and the loop repeats. The table in Figure 6-58 displays the values that are assigned to intScore each time the condition is checked in the code in Figure 6-57.

Loop Iteration	Value of intScore	Result of Condition Tested
1	intScore = 0	True
2	intScore = 1	True
3	intScore = 2	True
4	intScore = 3	True
5	intScore = 4	True
6	intScore = 5	False

FIGURE 6-58

© 2014 Cengage Learning

The loop in Figure 6-57 is executed five times because intScore is less than 5 during five iterations of the loop. As shown in Figure 6-57, if the value in the variable intScore is 5 or greater when the Do While statement is first executed, the body of the loop never will be executed because the condition is not true prior to the first iteration of the loop.

Enter a Do Loop Using IntelliSense

To use IntelliSense to enter the Do While loop shown in Figure 6-57, you can complete the following steps:

STEP 1 In the code window, enter the intScore variable declaration and then press the ENTER key. Type Do While and a space to display an IntelliSense list. Type ints to highlight intScore in the list.

The words Do While appear in blue because they are Visual Basic keywords (Figure 6-59). The IntelliSense list contains the valid entries and the intScore variable name is highlighted.

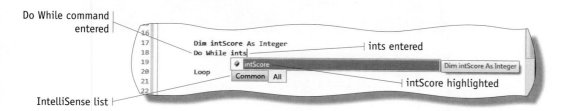

FIGURE 6-59

STEP 2   Type < 5 and then press the ENTER key.

Visual Basic automatically inserts the intScore variable name and the characters you typed (Figure 6-60). The keyword Loop also is inserted and the insertion point is located inside the loop, ready to enter the body of the loop.

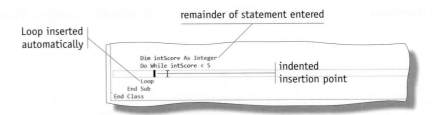

FIGURE 6-60

STEP 3   Type ints to highlight the intScore variable. Complete the statement by typing += 1 and then pressing the ENTER key. Press the DELETE key to delete the blank line.

The statement automatically is indented between the Do While and Loop statements (Figure 6-61). The intScore +=1 statement uses a compound operator to increment the intScore variable.

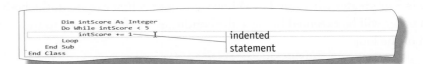

FIGURE 6-61

Bottom-Controlled Do While Loops

You can write a Do While loop in which the condition is tested at the bottom of the loop. A bottom-controlled loop works the same way as the top-controlled Do While loop except that the body of the loop is executed before the condition is checked the first time, guaranteeing that at least one iteration of a loop will be completed. The bottom-controlled Do While loop has the syntax shown in Figure 6-62.

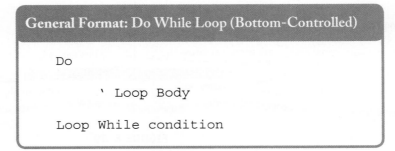

FIGURE 6-62

In Figure 6-62, the word Do appears on its own line at the beginning of the loop. The loop body follows, and the Loop While statement is the last statement in the loop. The Loop While statement contains the condition that is tested to determine if the loop should be terminated. Because the While condition is in the last statement of the loop, the body of the loop is executed one time regardless of the status of the condition.

The code in Figure 6-63 is an example of a bottom-controlled Do While loop.

```
22          Dim intScore As Integer = 0
23          Do
24              intScore = intScore + 1
25          Loop While intScore < 5
```

FIGURE 6-63

The body of the Do loop in Figure 6-63 is executed one time before the condition in the Loop While statement is checked. The variable intScore begins with the initial value of 0 and is incremented in the body of the loop, changing the value to 1. The condition is then tested and found to be true because 1 < 5. The loop repeats and the value of intScore increases, as shown in Figure 6-64.

The body of the loop in Figure 6-63 is executed four times because intScore is less than 5 during five iterations of the loop.

Loop Iteration	Value of intScore at Start of the Loop	Value of intScore When Checked	Result of Condition Tested
1	intScore = 0	intScore = 1	True
2	intScore = 1	intScore = 2	True
3	intScore = 2	intScore = 3	True
4	intScore = 3	intScore = 4	True
5	intScore = 4	intScore = 5	False

FIGURE 6-64

© 2014 Cengage Learning

Use Do Until Loops

A loop similar to a Do While loop is called a Do Until loop. The Do Until loop allows you to specify that an action repeats until a condition becomes true. When the condition in a Do Until loop becomes true, the loop ends.

Top-Controlled Do Until Loops

A Do Until loop can be both top-controlled and bottom-controlled. The syntax of the top-controlled Do Until loop is shown in Figure 6-65.

General Format: Do Until Loop (Top-Controlled)

```
Do Until condition

    ' Loop Body

Loop
```

FIGURE 6-65

A top-controlled Do Until loop begins with the keywords Do Until. Next, as with the Do While top-controlled loop, the condition is specified. The condition is expressed using the same relational operators that are available with If statements. Any condition that can be specified in an If statement can be specified in a Do Until condition. The condition can compare numeric values or string values.

The Do Until loop example shown in Figure 6-66 displays a parking meter application that computes the number of minutes a user can purchase based on the cost of 25 cents for each 15 minutes of parking. If the user only has 88 cents in pocket change, for example, the application computes how many minutes of parking time 88 cents will purchase.

```
4        Dim decAmount As Decimal = 0.88
5        Dim intQuarters As Integer = 0
6        Dim intTime As Integer = 15
7        Dim intParkingTime As Integer
8
9        Do Until decAmount < 0.25
10           intQuarters += 1
11           decAmount -= 0.25
12       Loop
13       intParkingTime = intQuarters * intTime
14       lblParkingTime.Text = "Parking Time: " &
15                       intParkingTime.ToString() & " minutes"
```

FIGURE 6-66

In the code example in Figure 6-66, the application checks the Do Until loop condition before executing the body of the loop. The first time the condition is tested, the expression decAmount < 0.25 is false because the decAmount variable contains 0.88. The body of the loop is executed because the Do Until statement specifies that the loop continues until the value in decAmount is less than 0.25. When the body of the loop is executed, it adds 1 to intQuarters to count the number of quarters the user has for the parking meter, and then subtracts 0.25 from decAmount because a quarter is worth 25 cents. Because decAmount is first assigned the value 0.88, the loop executes three times (decAmount = 0.88, decAmount = 0.63, and decAmount = 0.38) and stops when decAmount becomes less than 0.25. The lblParkingTime Label object displays the text "Parking Time: 45 minutes".

Bottom-Controlled Do Until Loops

The last of the four Do loops is the bottom-controlled Do Until loop. This Do Until loop checks the condition after the body of the loop is executed. The loop continues until the condition becomes true. The syntax of the bottom-controlled Do Until loop is shown in Figure 6-67.

General Format: Do Until Loop (Bottom-Controlled)

```
Do

        ' Loop Body

Loop Until condition
```

FIGURE 6-67

© 2014 Cengage Learning

In Figure 6-67, the bottom-controlled Do Until loop begins with the word Do. The body of the loop is executed one time regardless of the condition being tested. The Loop Until statement checks the condition. The loop will be repeated until the condition is true.

User Input Loops

Do loops often are written to end when the user enters a certain value or performs a certain action such as tapping or clicking the Cancel button in an input box. The developer determines the value or action. For example, the Do Until loop in Figure 6-68 accumulates the total of all the entered test scores until the user taps or clicks the Cancel button in the input box. If the user taps or clicks the Cancel button, the InputBox function returns a null string that is assigned to the strTestGrade variable. The Do Until statement tests the string. If it contains a null character, the loop is terminated.

```
40          Do Until strTestGrade = ""
41              strTestGrade = InputBox("Enter test grade", "Compute Average")
42              If IsNumeric(strTestGrade) Then
43                  decGrade = Convert.ToDecimal(strTestGrade)
44                  decTotal += decGrade
45              End If
46          Loop
```

FIGURE 6-68

Avoid Infinite Loops

Recall that an **infinite loop** is a loop that never ends. It happens when the condition specified to end the loop never occurs. If the loop does not end, it repeats until the program is interrupted. Figure 6-69 shows an example of an infinite loop.

```
22        Dim intProblem = 0
23        Do While intProblem <= 5
24            Box.Show("This loop will not end", "Infinite Loop")
25        Loop
```

FIGURE 6-69

The Do While loop in Figure 6-69 never ends because the value in the variable intProblem is never changed from its initial value of zero. Because the value in intProblem never exceeds 5, the condition in the Do While loop (intProblem <= 5) never becomes false. The processing in a loop eventually must change the condition being tested in the Do While loop so the loop will terminate. When working in Visual Basic 2012, you can interrupt an infinite loop by tapping or clicking the Stop Debugging button on the Standard toolbar.

CONSIDER THIS

How do I know which type of loop to use?
All loops have the same basic function of repeating certain lines of a program. Some loops are best suited under certain conditions. For example, if you want to check the condition before the loop is run, use a top-controlled loop. Often the type of loop you use is just programmer preference.

Prime the Loop

As you have learned, a top-controlled loop tests a condition prior to beginning the loop. In most cases, the value to test must be set before the condition is tested the first time in the Do While or Do Until statement. Starting a loop with a preset value in the variable(s) tested in the condition is called **priming the loop**. You have seen this in previous examples, such as in Figure 6-66 on page 396, where the value in decAmount is set before the condition is tested the first time.

In some applications, the loop is primed with a value the user enters or an action the user takes. For example, in the Fitness Challenge application, the user enters the weight loss value for each team member (up to eight values) or taps or clicks the Cancel button in the input box. Prior to executing the Do Until statement the first time in the Do Until loop that processes the data the user enters, the InputBox function must be executed to obtain an initial value. Then, the Do Until statement can test the action taken by the user (enter a value and tap or click the Cancel button). The coding to implement this processing is shown in Figure 6-70.

```
30          Dim strCancelClicked As String = ""
31          Dim intMaxNumberOfEntries As Integer = 8
32          Dim intNumberOfEntries As Integer = 1
   ⋮
38          strWeightLoss = InputBox(strInputMessage & intNumberOfEntries, strInputHeading, " ")
39
40          Do Until intNumberOfEntries > intMaxNumberOfEntries Or strWeightLoss = strCancelClicked
   ⋮
47                  intNumberOfEntries += 1
   ⋮
56              If intNumberOfEntries <= intMaxNumberOfEntries Then
57                  strWeightLoss = InputBox(strInputMessage & intNumberOfEntries, strInputHeading, " ")
58              End If
59
60          Loop
```

FIGURE 6-70

In the Do Until loop shown in Figure 6-70, the Do Until statement on line 40 tests two conditions: is the value in the intNumberOfEntries variable greater than the value in the intMaxNumberOfEntries variable, or is the value in the strWeight-Loss variable equal to the value in the strCancelClicked variable, which is a null character (see line 30)? If either condition is true, the body of the loop is not executed.

The Do Until loop must have two primed variables: the intNumberOfEntries variable and the strWeightLoss variable. The intNumberOfEntries variable is initialized to 1 on line 32. The strWeightLoss variable is initialized by the InputBox function call on line 38. In this function call, either the user entered a value or tapped or clicked the Cancel button. If the user tapped or clicked the Cancel button, the body of the loop should not be entered.

To continue the loop, the processing within the body of the loop eventually must change one of the conditions being tested in the Do Until statement or the loop never terminates. In the sample program, the conditions being tested are whether the user entered eight weight loss values or tapped or clicked the Cancel button. Therefore, within the loop, the variable containing intNumberOfEntries must be incremented when the user enters a valid weight loss value. The user then must be able to enter more weight loss values or tap or click the Cancel button. On line 47 in Figure 6-70, the value in intNumberOfEntries is incremented by 1 each time the user enters a valid weight loss value. In addition, the statement on line 57 displays an input box that allows the user to enter a new value or tap or click the Cancel button as long as the number of valid entries is not greater than the maximum number of entries.

Validate Data

As you learned in Chapter 5, you must test the data a user enters to ensure it is accurate and that its use in other programming statements, such as converting string data to numeric data, will not cause a program exception. When using an input box, the data should be checked using the IsNumeric function and If statements, as discussed in Chapter 5. If the data is not valid, the user must be notified of the error and an input box displayed to allow the user to enter valid data.

For example, if the user enters nonnumeric data, the input box in Figure 6-71 should be displayed.

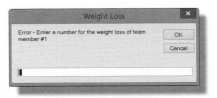

FIGURE 6-71

Similarly, if the user enters a negative number, the message in Figure 6-72 should be displayed in an input box.

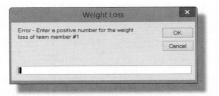

FIGURE 6-72

When error checking is performed within a loop and the user is asked to enter data in an input box, the body of the loop must be executed each time the user enters data, regardless of whether the data is valid or invalid. If the user enters valid data, then the data is processed according to the needs of the program.

If the user enters invalid data, an error message is displayed and the user is given the opportunity to enter valid data in the input box. The coding for the Fitness Challenge application that accomplishes these tasks is shown in Figure 6-73.

```
38          strWeightLoss = InputBox(strInputMessage & intNumberOfEntries, strInputHeading, " ")
39
40          Do Until intNumberOfEntries > intMaxNumberOfEntries Or strWeightLoss = strCancelClicked
41
42              If IsNumeric(strWeightLoss) Then
43                  decWeightLoss = Convert.ToDecimal(strWeightLoss)
44                  If decWeightLoss > 0 Then
45                      lstWeightLoss.Items.Add(decWeightLoss)
46                      decTotalWeightLoss += decWeightLoss
47                      intNumberOfEntries += 1
48                      strInputMessage = strNormalMessage
49                  Else
50                      strInputMessage = strNegativeError
51                  End If
52              Else
53                  strInputMessage = strNonNumericError
54              End If
55
56              If intNumberOfEntries <= intMaxNumberOfEntries Then
57                  strWeightLoss = InputBox(strInputMessage & intNumberOfEntries, strInputHeading, " ")
58              End If
59
60          Loop
```

FIGURE 6-73

In Figure 6-73, the loop is primed by the InputBox function call on line 38. The Do Until statement on line 40 checks the two conditions — if the value in the intNumberOfEntries counter is greater than the maximum number of entries, or if the user taps or clicks the Cancel button. In either case, the body of the loop is not executed.

When the body of the loop is executed, the application checks the data the user entered to verify it is numeric. If it is numeric, the value is converted to a Decimal data type and then is checked to ensure it is greater than zero (line 44). If it is greater than zero, it is added to the lstWeightLoss ListBox object, the decTotalWeightLoss accumulator is incremented by the weight loss value the user entered, the intNumberOfEntries counter is incremented by 1, and the normal message is moved to the strInputMessage variable. This variable contains the message that is displayed in the input box (see line 38).

If the value the user entered is not greater than zero, the statement following the Else statement on line 49 moves the value in the strNegativeError variable to the strInputMessage variable so that the next time the InputBox function is called, the message will indicate an error, as shown in Figure 6-72.

If the value the user entered was not numeric (as tested by the statement on line 42), the statement on line 53 moves the value in the strNonNumericError variable to the strInputMessage variable so that the next time the InputBox function is called, the message will indicate a nonnumeric error, as shown in Figure 6-71.

On lines 56 and 57, as long as the number of entries is not greater than the maximum number of entries, the InputBox function is called. The message that is displayed in the input box depends on whether an error occurred. The Do Until statement on line 40 is executed and the process begins again.

Create a Nested Loop

In the last chapter, you learned to nest If...Then...Else statements within each other. Loops also can be nested. You can place any type of loop within any other type of loop under the following conditions: interior loops must be completely contained inside the outer loop and must have a different control variable. The example in Figure 6-74 uses a nested For loop to display a list of the weeks in the first quarter of the year (13 weeks) along with the days in each week. The outer For...Next loop counts from 1 to 13 for the 13 weeks, and the inner For...Next loop counts from 1 to 7 for the days in each of the 13 weeks.

```
6        Dim intOuterCount As Integer ' Counts the first 13 weeks in a quarter
7        Dim intInnerCount As Integer ' Counts the 7 days in a week
8        For intOuterCount = 1 To 13 ' For weeks in the 1st quarter of the year
9            For intInnerCount = 1 To 7 ' For the 7 days in a week
10               lstDays.Items.Add("Week: " & intOuterCount.ToString() _
11                                 & " Day: " & intInnerCount.ToString())
12           Next
13       Next
```

FIGURE 6-74

The code in Figure 6-74 displays the output shown in Figure 6-75.

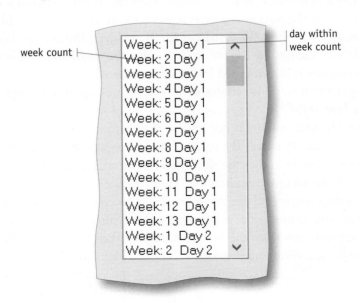

week count

day within week count

Week: 1 Day 1
Week: 2 Day 1
Week: 3 Day 1
Week: 4 Day 1
Week: 5 Day 1
Week: 6 Day 1
Week: 7 Day 1
Week: 8 Day 1
Week: 9 Day 1
Week: 10 Day 1
Week: 11 Day 1
Week: 12 Day 1
Week: 13 Day 1
Week: 1 Day 2
Week: 2 Day 2

FIGURE 6-75

Select the Best Loop

When writing a program, you might have to make a decision regarding which loop structure to use. For...Next loops are best when the number of repetitions is fixed. Do loops are best when the condition to enter or exit the loop needs to be re-evaluated continually. When deciding which loop to use, keep the following considerations in mind:

1. Use a Do loop if the number of repetitions is unknown and is based on a condition changing; a For...Next loop is best if the exact number of repetitions is fixed.
2. If a loop condition must be tested before the body of the loop is executed, use a top-controlled Do While or Do Until loop. If the instructions within a loop must be executed one time regardless of the status of a condition, use a bottom-controlled Do While or Do Until loop.
3. Use the keyword While if you want to continue execution of the loop while the condition is true. Use the keyword Until if you want to continue execution until the condition is true.

Use a DataTip with Breakpoints

As programs become longer and more complex, the likelihood of errors increases, and you need to carefully find and remove these errors. Resolving defects in code is called **debugging**. When you debug a program, you collect information and find out what is wrong with the code in the program. You then fix that code.

A good way to collect information is to pause the execution of the code where a possible error could occur. One way to pause execution is to use breakpoints. **Breakpoints** are stop points placed in the code to tell the Visual Studio 2012 debugger where and when to pause the execution of the application. During this pause, the program is in break mode. While in break mode, you can examine the values in all variables that are within the scope of execution through the use of **DataTips**. In the Fitness Challenge application, you can insert a breakpoint in the assignment statement that increments the decTotalWeightLoss accumulator to view its value after each iteration of the loop as the user enters each weight loss value. To set a breakpoint in your code and then check the data at the breakpoint using DataTips, you can complete the following steps:

STEP 1 With the Fitness Challenge application open in the code window, press and hold or right-click line 46, which contains the code where you want to set a breakpoint, and then point to Breakpoint on the shortcut menu.

A shortcut menu opens that contains the Breakpoint command (Figure 6-76). The Breakpoint submenu contains the Insert Breakpoint command. Setting a breakpoint on line 46 means that the program will pause at that line during execution so that the values in variables within the scope of execution can be examined.

set breakpoint on line 46

shortcut menu

Breakpoint submenu

Breakpoint command

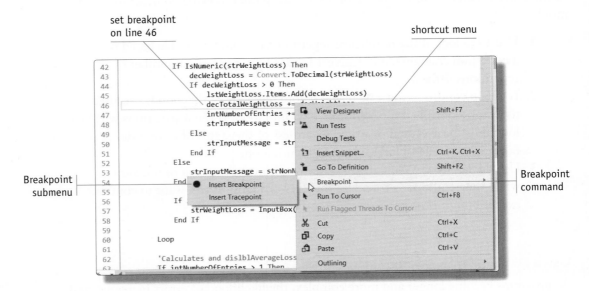

FIGURE 6-76

STEP 2 Tap or click Insert Breakpoint on the submenu.

A breakpoint is set on line 46, which is the line in the Do Until loop that adds the weight loss value the user entered to the weight loss accumulator — decTotalWeightLoss (Figure 6-77). The breakpoint is identified by the bullet to the left of the line numbers and the highlight effect on the code.

breakpoint set

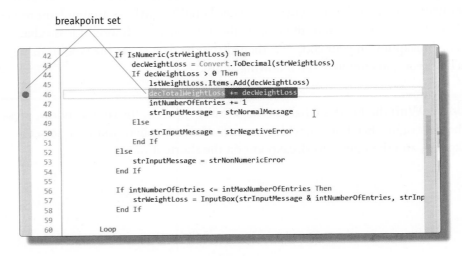

FIGURE 6-77

STEP 3 To run and test the program with the breakpoint, tap or click the Start Debugging button on the Standard toolbar.

The program starts and the Fitness Challenge window opens (Figure 6-78).

FIGURE 6-78

STEP 4 Tap or click the Enter Weight Loss button. Type 3 . 4 as the weight loss amount of the first team member.

The Weight Loss input box contains 3.4 as the weight loss amount of the first team member (Figure 6-79).

3.4 entered in Weight Loss input box

FIGURE 6-79

STEP 5   Tap or click the OK button in the input box.

The program executes the lines of code in the event handler until reaching the breakpoint, where it pauses execution on the accumulator line (Figure 6-80). The application is now in break mode. Notice the breakpoint line is highlighted in yellow.

program execution
paused at breakpoint

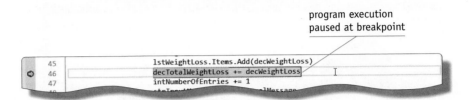

```
45              lstWeightLoss.Items.Add(decWeightLoss)
46              decTotalWeightLoss += decWeightLoss
47              intNumberOfEntries += 1
```

FIGURE 6-80

STEP 6   Point to the variable decWeightLoss on line 46.

A DataTip appears, displaying the value of the decWeightLoss variable when execution was paused (Figure 6-81). The value is 3.4 because the user entered this value in Step 4. It is a Decimal value (3.4D) because the statement in line 43 converted the value the user entered to a Decimal value.

pointer on
decWeightLoss variable

DataTip displays the value
in the decWeightLoss
variable

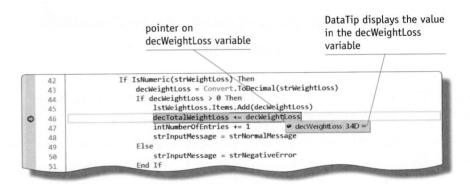

```
42          If IsNumeric(strWeightLoss) Then
43              decWeightLoss = Convert.ToDecimal(strWeightLoss)
44              If decWeightLoss > 0 Then
45                  lstWeightLoss.Items.Add(decWeightLoss)
46                  decTotalWeightLoss += decWeightLoss
47                  intNumberOfEntries += 1          ◉ decWeightLoss 3.4D ◎
48                  strInputMessage = strNormalMessage
49              Else
50                  strInputMessage = strNegativeError
51              End If
```

FIGURE 6-81

STEP 7   You can view the value in any other variable within execution scope by pointing to that variable. To illustrate, point to the variable decTotalWeightLoss on line 46.

The value in the decTotalWeightLoss variable is displayed (Figure 6–82). The value is zero, which means the assignment statement on line 46 has not yet been executed. When a breakpoint is set, the program pauses before executing the statement that contains the breakpoint.

pointer on
decTotalWeightLoss
variable

DataTip displays the value
in the decTotalWeightLoss
variable

```
44              If decWeightLoss > 0 Then
45                  lstWeightLoss.Items.Add(decWeightLoss)
46                  decTotalWeightLoss += decWeightLoss
47                  intl  decTotalWeightLoss 0D =
48                  strInputMessage = strNormalMessage
49              Else
50                  strInputMessage = strNegativeError
51              End If
```

FIGURE 6-82

STEP 8   Continue the program by tapping or clicking the Continue button on the Standard toolbar. Notice that the Continue button is the same as the Start Debugging button.

The program continues by opening the next InputBox function, where the user can enter the weight loss value for the next team member. The program runs until it again reaches the breakpoint, where it pauses so you can point to any variable to view its present value in a DataTip (Figure 6–83).

program execution
paused again

Continue button

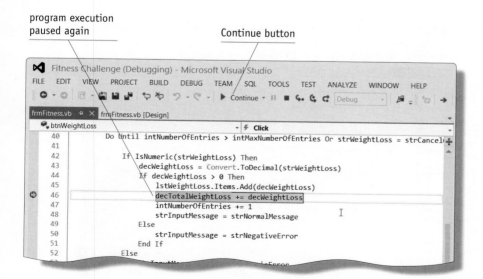

FIGURE 6-83

STEP 9   Point to the decTotalWeightLoss variable.

The updated value in the decTotalWeightLoss variable is displayed (Figure 6-84). The value 3.4D is in the variable as a result of the processing in the first iteration of the loop. You also can examine the values in other variables by pointing to the variable name.

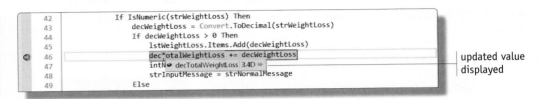

```
42          If IsNumeric(strWeightLoss) Then
43              decWeightLoss = Convert.ToDecimal(strWeightLoss)
44              If decWeightLoss > 0 Then
45                  lstWeightLoss.Items.Add(decWeightLoss)
46                  decTotalWeightLoss += decWeightLoss
47                  intN  decTotalWeightLoss  3.4D
48                  strInputMessage = strNormalMessage
49              Else
```

updated value displayed

FIGURE 6-84

The preceding example illustrated the use of one breakpoint, but you can include multiple breakpoints in a program if they will be useful. Sometimes, breakpoints before and after an instruction that you suspect is in error can pinpoint the problem.

To remove a breakpoint, you can complete the following steps:

STEP 1   Press and hold or right-click the statement containing the breakpoint, and then point to Breakpoint on the shortcut menu.

The shortcut menu is displayed, the pointer is located on the Breakpoint entry, and the Breakpoint submenu is displayed (Figure 6-85). You can press and hold or right-click the statement containing the breakpoint either when the program is running in Debugging mode or when the program is not running.

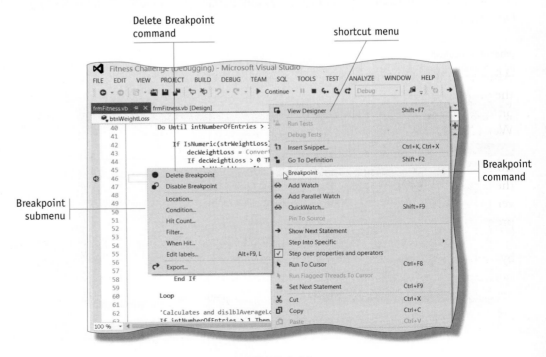

FIGURE 6-85

STEP 2   Tap or click Delete Breakpoint on the Breakpoint submenu.

If the program is running in Debugging mode, the breakpoint is removed when you tap or click the Continue button (Figure 6-86). If the program is not running, the breakpoint is removed immediately.

breakpoint is
removed, but variable
is highlighted

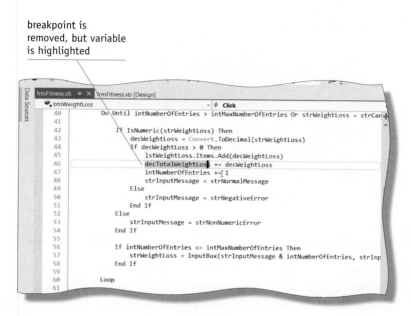

```
40        Do Until intNumberOfEntries > intMaxNumberOfEntries Or strWeightLoss = strCan
41
42             If IsNumeric(strWeightLoss) Then
43                 decWeightLoss = Convert.ToDecimal(strWeightLoss)
44                 If decWeightLoss > 0 Then
45                     lstWeightLoss.Items.Add(decWeightLoss)
46                     decTotalWeightLoss += decWeightLoss
47                     intNumberOfEntries += 1
48                     strInputMessage = strNormalMessage
49                 Else
50                     strInputMessage = strNegativeError
51                 End If
52             Else
53                 strInputMessage = strNonNumericError
54             End If
55
56             If intNumberOfEntries <= intMaxNumberOfEntries Then
57                 strWeightLoss = InputBox(strInputMessage & intNumberOfEntries, strInp
58             End If
59
60         Loop
61
```

FIGURE 6-86

Using breakpoints and DataTips allows you to examine any variables during the execution of the program. By moving step by step through the program, normally you can identify any errors that might occur in the program.

Publish an Application with ClickOnce Deployment

After an application is completely debugged and working properly, you can deploy the project. Deploying a project means placing an executable version of the program on your hard disk (which then can be placed on CD, DVD, or in the cloud), on a Web server, or on a network server.

You probably have purchased software on a CD or DVD or downloaded software from a cloud-based site. To install the application on your computer, you insert the CD or DVD into your computer and then follow the setup instructions. The version of the program you receive on the CD or DVD is the deployed version of the program.

When programming using Visual Basic 2012, you can create a deployed program by using **ClickOnce Deployment**. The deployed version of the program you create can be installed and executed on any computer that has the .NET framework installed. The computer does not need Visual Studio 2012 installed to run the program.

To publish the Fitness Challenge application using ClickOnce Deployment, you can complete the following steps:

STEP 1 With the Fitness Challenge application open, tap or click BUILD on the menu bar.

The BUILD menu is displayed (Figure 6-87).

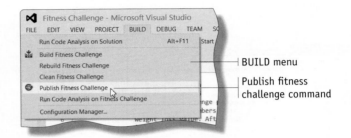

FIGURE 6-87

STEP 2 Tap or click Publish Fitness Challenge on the BUILD menu.

The Publish Wizard starts (Figure 6-88). The first Publish Wizard dialog box asks where you want to publish the application. The application can be published to a Web server, a network, or as a setup file on a hard disk or USB drive for burning on a CD or DVD. This dialog box includes publish\ as the default location, which you can change to a file location.

FIGURE 6-88

STEP 3   Change the default location from publish\ to a file location. To publish to a USB drive, type the drive letter. In this example, enter E: for a USB drive.

The Publish Wizard dialog box requests where you want to publish the application. The Fitness Challenge application will be saved to the USB drive, which is drive E: in this example (Figure 6-89).

location for publishing
application

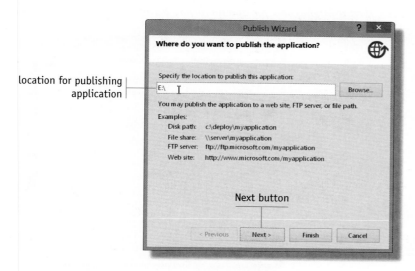

FIGURE 6-89

STEP 4   Tap or click the Next button. If necessary, tap or click the From a CD-ROM or DVD-ROM radio button.

Visual Basic displays a Publish Wizard dialog box that asks, "How will users install the application?" (Figure 6-90). When the user will install the application from a CD or DVD, such as when you purchase software, you should select the CD or DVD option.

From a CD-ROM or
DVD-ROM selected

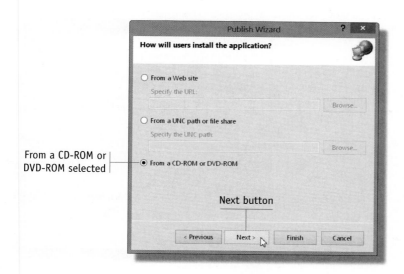

FIGURE 6-90

STEP 5 Tap or click the Next button. If necessary, tap or click the "The application will not check for updates" radio button.

The next Publish Wizard dialog box asks where the application will check for updates (Figure 6-91). You can select and enter a location or indicate that the application will not check for updates. Generally, when an application will be deployed to a CD or DVD, the application will not check for updates. If the application is deployed to a Web server or network server, then it might check for updates before being executed on the user's computer.

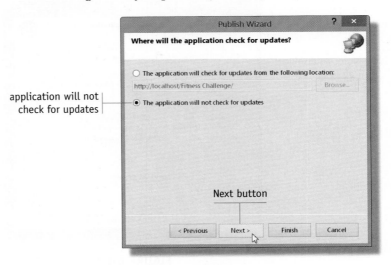

application will not
check for updates

Next button

FIGURE 6-91

STEP 6 Tap or click the Next button.

The Ready to Publish! window is displayed (Figure 6-92). Notice the message in this window — when the program is installed on the user's machine, a shortcut for the program will be added to the user's computer, and the program can be deleted using the Add/Remove Programs function in the Control Panel.

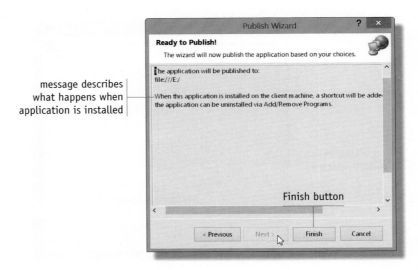

message describes
what happens when
application is installed

Finish button

FIGURE 6-92

STEP 7   Tap or click the Finish button.

The Visual Basic window displays several messages indicating that the application is being published. The last message is "Publish succeeded" (Figure 6-93).

Publish succeeded message

FIGURE 6-93

STEP 8   To view the finished result, minimize the Visual Studio window and then open the Search charm. Type Computer in the Search box. Double-tap or double-click the USB drive icon to view the published installation folder.

Installation files are placed on the USB drive (Figure 6-94). If all of these files are copied to a computer with the .NET framework, the user can double-tap or double-click the setup file to begin the installation.

installation files

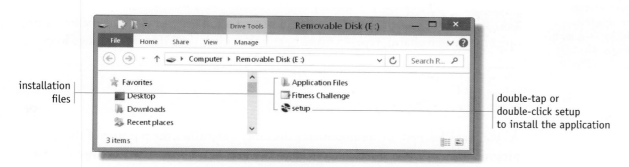

double-tap or double-click setup to install the application

FIGURE 6-94

STEP 9   To install the application, double-tap or double-click the setup file.

After the user double-taps or double-clicks the setup file, the application is installed on the local computer. During installation, Windows might display the dialog box shown in Figure 6-95. This dialog box is intended to protect you from installing programs that might harm your computer. Because you know the source of this program, you can tap or click the Install button to continue installing the program.

Application Install
– Security Warning
dialog box

FIGURE 6-95

STEP 10   After installation, the program runs. To run the installed application again, open the Search charm, type `Fitness`, and then click the Fitness Challenge icon.

Program Design

As you have learned, the requirements document identifies the purpose of the program being developed, the application title, the procedures to be followed when using the program, any required equations and calculations, any conditions that must be tested, notes and restrictions that must be followed by the program, and any other comments that would be helpful to understanding the problem. The requirements document for the Fitness Challenge application is shown in Figure 6-96.

REQUIREMENTS DOCUMENT

Date Submitted:	September 30, 2016
Application Title:	Fitness Challenge Application
Purpose:	This application finds the average weight loss of a team of eight employees.
Program Procedures:	In a Windows application, the user enters the weight loss amounts of eight employees as positive numbers to compute the average weight loss for the entire team.
Algorithms, Processing, and Conditions:	1. The user must be able to enter each of eight weight loss values in pounds after tapping or clicking the Enter Weight Loss button.
	2. Each weight loss value is validated to confirm it is numeric and greater than zero.
	3. Each weight loss value is displayed in a ListBox object.
	4. After the user enters eight weight loss values or taps or clicks the Cancel button in an input box, the program calculates and displays the average weight loss for the team.
	5. A menu bar includes the File menu, which contains Clear and Exit items. The Clear menu item clears the result and the weight loss values. The Exit menu item closes the application.
Notes and Restrictions:	1. If a nonnumeric or negative value is entered for the weight loss, the program should display an error message and ask the user to re-enter the value.
	2. If the user taps or clicks the Cancel button before entering any weight loss values, a message should indicate no weight loss values were entered. An average is not calculated when no weight loss values are entered.
Comments:	1. The picture shown in the window can be found on CengageBrain.com. The name of the picture is Weight.
	2. The average weight loss should be formatted as a Decimal value with one decimal place.

FIGURE 6-96

The Use Case Definition shown in Figure 6-97 specifies the procedures the user will follow to use this application.

USE CASE DEFINITION

1. The Windows application opens, displaying the Fitness Challenge title, a ListBox object to hold the numeric entries, and a Button object that allows the user to begin entering up to eight weight loss values.
2. A menu bar displays the File menu, which has two menu items: Clear and Exit.
3. In an InputBox object, the user enters up to eight values representing the number of pounds lost, such as 3.2 pounds.
4. The program asks the user for the weight loss value again if a value is nonnumeric or negative.
5. The user terminates data entry by entering eight values or by tapping or clicking the Cancel button in the InputBox object.
6. The program calculates the average weight loss for the values the user entered.
7. In a Label object, the program displays the average weight loss as a Decimal value with one decimal place.
8. The user can clear the input and the results by tapping or clicking the Clear menu item, and can then repeat Steps 3 through 7.
9. The user taps or clicks Exit on the File menu to close the application.

FIGURE 6-97

© 2014 Cengage Learning

Event Planning Document

You will recall that the event planning document is a table that specifies which objects in the user interface will cause events, the action taken by the user to trigger each event, and the event processing that must occur. The event planning document for the Fitness Challenge application is shown in Figure 6-98.

EVENT PLANNING DOCUMENT

Program Name: Fitness Challenge Application	Developer: Corinne Hoisington	Object: frmFitness Date: September 30, 2014
OBJECT	**EVENT TRIGGER**	**EVENT PROCESSING**
btnWeightLoss	Tap or click	Display an InputBox object to obtain each team member's weight loss up to eight times or until the user taps or clicks the Cancel button
		Check if strWeightLoss is numeric
		If the weight loss value is numeric, convert strWeightLoss to a Decimal value
		If strWeightLoss is numeric, check whether the value is positive
		If the weight loss value is positive: Display the value in lstWeightLoss Accumulate the total of the weight loss values in decTotalWeightLoss Update the number of entries Set the InputBox message to the normal message
		If the value entered is not numeric, display an error message in the input box
		If the value entered is not positive, display an error message in the input box
		After all weight loss values are entered, change the Visible property of lblAverageLoss to true
		If one or more weight loss values are entered: Calculate the average weight loss in decAverageLoss Display the average weight loss in lblAverageLoss
		If no values are entered: Display the text "No weight loss value entered"
		Disable the btnWeightLoss Button
mnuClear	Tap or click	Clear the lstWeightLoss ListBox
		Change the Visible property of lblAverageLoss to False
		Enable the btnWeightLoss Button
mnuExit	Tap or click	Exit the application

FIGURE 6-98

Design and Code the Program

After identifying the events and tasks within the events, the developer is ready to create the program. As you have learned, creating the program means designing the user interface and then entering Visual Basic statements to accomplish the tasks specified in the event planning document. As the developer enters the code, she also will implement the logic to carry out the required processing.

Guided Program Development

To design the user interface for the Fitness Challenge application and enter the code required to process each event in the program, complete the steps on the following pages:

NOTE TO THE LEARNER

In the following activity, you should complete the tasks within the specified steps. Each of the tasks is accompanied by a Hint Screen. The purpose of the Hint Screen is to indicate where you should perform the activity in the Visual Studio window and to remind you which method to use. If you need further help completing a step, refer to the figure identified by *ref:*.

Guided Program Development

Phase 1: Design the Form

1

• **Create a Windows Application** Open Visual Studio and then close the Start page. Create a new Visual Basic Windows Forms Application project by tapping or clicking the New Project button on the Standard toolbar, selecting Windows as the project type, selecting Windows Forms Application as the template, naming the project Fitness Challenge in the Name text box, and then tapping or clicking the OK button in the New Project window.

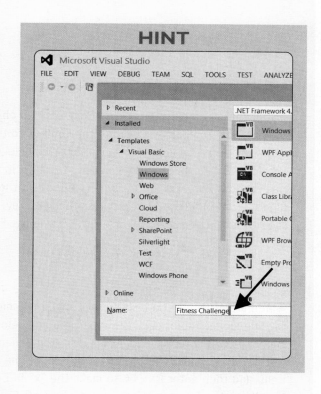

• **Display the Toolbox** Ensure that the Toolbox is displayed in the Visual Studio window and that the Common Controls are accessible.

• **Name the Windows Form Object** In the Solution Explorer window, press and hold or right-click Form1.vb, tap or click Rename, and then rename the form frmFitness.

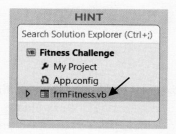

• **Change the Text on the Title Bar for the Windows Form Object** Change the title bar text of the Windows Form object to Fitness Challenge.

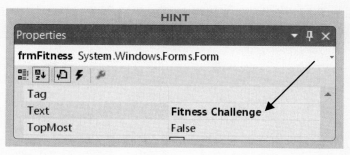

(continues)

Guided Program Development   *continued*

● **Change the Size of the Form Object** Resize the
Form object by changing the Size property to 625, 500.

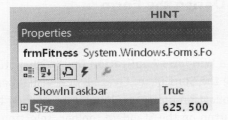

HINT

Properties

frmFitness System.Windows.Forms.Fo

ShowInTaskbar   True
⊞ Size   625. 500

● **Add the MenuStrip Object** Drag a MenuStrip object from
the Menus & Toolbars category of the Toolbox to the Windows
Form object. The MenuStrip snaps into place below the title
bar. Name the MenuStrip object mnuFitness in the Properties window. Tap or click the Type Here box on the MenuStrip
object, type &File, and then press the ENTER key. The ampersand creates a hot key for the letter F. Name the File menu
item mnuFile (*ref: Figure 6-5*).

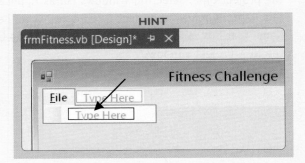

HINT

frmFitness.vb [Design]*   ⊕ ✕

Fitness Challenge

File   Type Here
       Type Here

● **Add Menu Items** The next step is to add two menu items to
the File menu. Tap or click the Type Here box below the word
File, and then enter &Clear. Name the Clear menu item mnu-
Clear. Tap or click the Type Here box below the Clear menu
item, and then enter E&xit to make the "x" in Exit the hot
key. Name the Exit menu item mnuExit (*ref: Figure 6-10*).

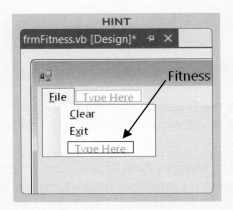

HINT

frmFitness.vb [Design]*   ⊕ ✕

Fitness

File   Type Here
    Clear
    Exit
    Type Here

● **Add a PictureBox Object** Drag a PictureBox .NET component
from the Toolbox to the left side of the Windows Form object.
Name the PictureBox object picFitness. Change the Size
property of the PictureBox object to 215, 450. Change the
Location property of the PictureBox object to 3, 30.

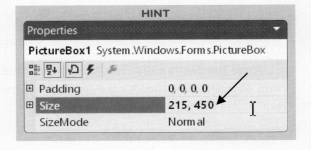

HINT

Properties

PictureBox1 System.Windows.Forms.PictureBox

⊞ Padding   0, 0, 0, 0
⊞ Size   215, 450
  SizeMode   Normal

● **Add the Title Label Object** Drag a Label
.NET component onto the Windows Form
object. Name the label `lblTitle`. Enter
the text for this label as `Fitness`
`Challenge Team Weight Loss` on
two lines. (*Hint*: Tap or click the Text
property list arrow in the Properties window
to enter a label with multiple lines. Press
the ENTER key to move to a new line.) Choose
Tahoma as the font, Bold as the font style,
and 18 points as the size. Change the
TextAlign property to MiddleCenter by tapping or
clicking the TextAlign list arrow and then tapping
or clicking the Center block. Change the Location
property of the lblTitle Label object to `275, 40`.

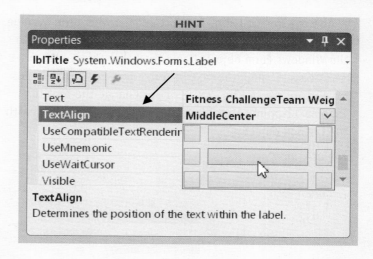

● **Add the Enter Weight Loss Button Object**
Drag a Button object onto the Windows Form
object below the title label. Name the Button
`btnWeightLoss`. Change the text of the
button to `Enter Weight Loss`. Change the font to
11-point Tahoma. Resize the Button object to view the
complete text. Align the centers of the Button object with the
title Label object.

● **Add the ListBox Object for the Team Members' Weight
Loss** To add the ListBox object that displays the team
members' weight loss, drag a ListBox object onto the Windows
Form object below the Button object. Name the ListBox
`lstWeightLoss`. Change the font of the text in the ListBox
object to 11-point Tahoma. Resize the ListBox to the width of
four characters because the top weight loss of a team member
could reach an amount such as 46.3 pounds. Lengthen the
ListBox object to display eight numbers. The Size property for
the ListBox object in the sample program is `45, 180`. Change
the RightToLeft property to No to right-align the numeric
values. Align the centers of the ListBox object with the Button
object (*ref: Figure 6-24*).

(continues)

- **Add the Result Label** To add the label where the average weight loss message is displayed, drag a Label object onto the Windows Form object. Name the Label object lblAverageLoss. Change the text to Average weight loss for the team is XX.X lbs. Change the font to Tahoma 11-point. Align the centers of the Label object with the ListBox object.

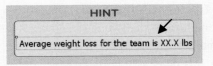

HINT

Average weight loss for the team is XX.X lbs

The user interface mockup is complete (Figure 6-99).

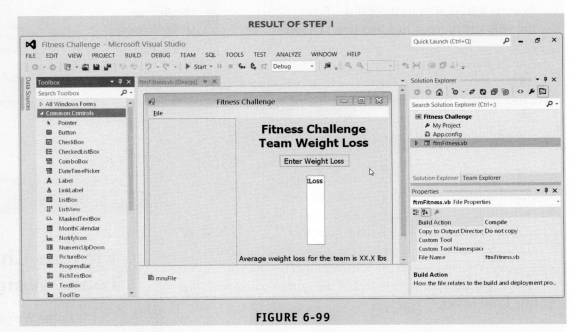

RESULT OF STEP 1

FIGURE 6-99

Phase 2: Fine-Tune the User Interface

2

- **Change the BackColor Property of the Windows Form Object** Select the Windows Form object and then change its BackColor property to White on the Web tab.

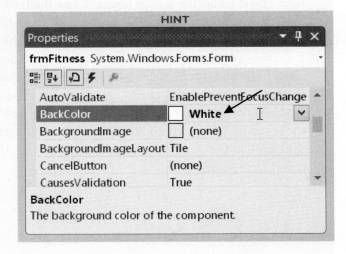

HINT

Properties

frmFitness System.Windows.Forms.Form

AutoValidate	EnablePreventFocusChange
BackColor	White
BackgroundImage	(none)
BackgroundImageLayout	Tile
CancelButton	(none)
CausesValidation	True

BackColor
The background color of the component.

● **Change the Color for the Title Label** Change
the ForeColor property for the lblTitle Label object
to DarkOrange on the Web tab.

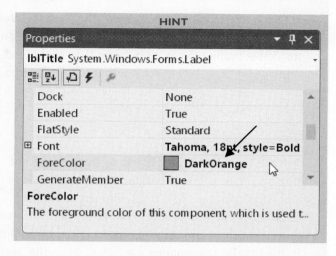

● **Change the Button Color** Change the BackColor property
of the btnWeightLoss Button object to Orange.

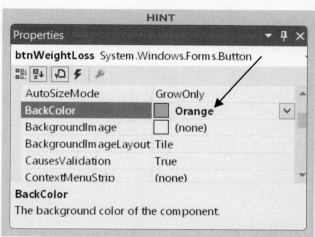

● **Insert the Fitness Image into the PictureBox Object
and Size the Image** Make sure you have the data files for
this chapter (available on CengageBrain.com). Select the
picFitness PictureBox object. In the Properties window,
select the Image property and then tap or click the ellipsis
button in the right column. Import the Fitness image from
the location where you saved it. Tap or click the OK button
in the Select Resource dialog box. Select the SizeMode
property, tap or click the SizeMode arrow, and then tap or
click StretchImage.

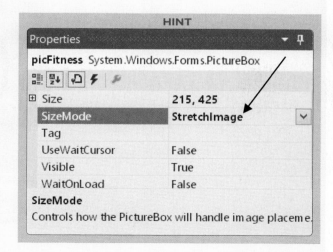

(continues)

Guided Program Development   *continued*

● **Change the Visible Property for the Average Weight Loss Label** Select the lblAverageLoss Label object and change its Visible property to False because the Label object is not displayed until the average weight loss is calculated.

HEADS UP

As you work on your program, do not forget to save it from time to time. You can save the work you have done by tapping or clicking the Save All button on the Standard toolbar.

● **Make the Enter Weight Loss Button the Accept Button** Tap or click the background of the Windows Form object to select it. In the Properties window, tap or click the AcceptButton list arrow to display the buttons in the user interface. Tap or click btnWeightLoss in the list. During program execution, when the user presses the ENTER key, the event handler for btnWeightLoss executes.

HINT

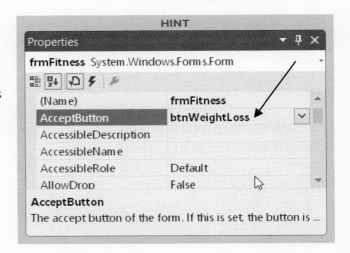

The user interface design is complete (Figure 6-100).

RESULT OF STEP 2

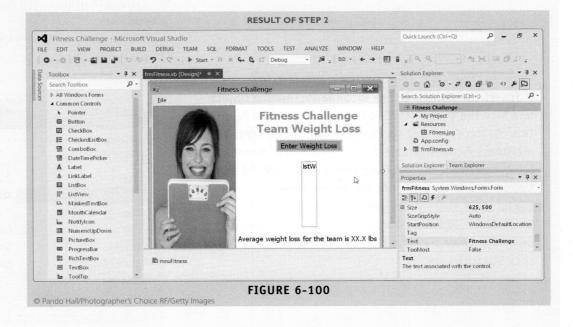

FIGURE 6-100

© Pando Hall/Photographer's Choice RF/Getty Images

Phase 3: Code the Program

3

● **Enter the Comments for the Enter Weight Loss Button Event Handler**
Double-tap or double-click the btnWeightLoss Button object on the Windows Form object to open the button event handler. Insert the first four standard comments at the top of the code window. Insert the command `Option Strict On` at the beginning of the code to turn on strict type checking.

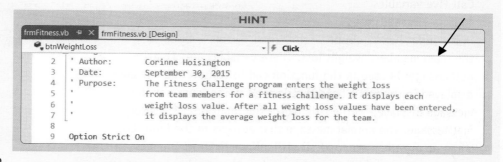

```
HINT
frmFitness.vb    ⇥ ✕  frmFitness.vb [Design]
🔧 btnWeightLoss                                    ▾ ⚡ Click
    2    ' Author:        Corinne Hoisington
    3    ' Date:          September 30, 2015
    4    ' Purpose:       The Fitness Challenge program enters the weight loss
    5    '                from team members for a fitness challenge. It displays each
    6    '                weight loss value. After all weight loss values have been entered,
    7    '                it displays the average weight loss for the team.
    8
    9    Option Strict On
```

● **Comment on the btnWeightLoss_Click Event Handler**
Enter a comment to describe the purpose of the btnWeightLoss_Click event handler.

```
HINT
   11  ⊟Public Class frmFitness
   12  ⊟    Private Sub btnWeightLoss_Click(sender As Object, e As EventArgs) Handles btnWeightL
   13            ' The btnWeightLoss_Click event accepts and displays up to 8 weight loss values
   14            ' and then calculates and displays the average weight loss for the team
   15
   16        End Sub
```

● **Declare and Initialize the Variables to Calculate the Average Weight Loss** Four variables are used to calculate the average weight loss (besides the team member count). These variables are: 1) strWeightLoss: Is assigned the value from the InputBox function call; 2) decWeightLoss: Is assigned the converted team member weight loss; 3) decAverageLoss: Contains the calculated average weight loss; 4) decTotalWeightLoss: The accumulator used to collect the total weight loss values entered by a user. Declare and initialize these four variables.

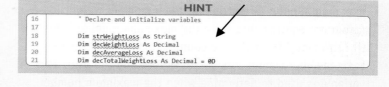

```
HINT
   16        ' Declare and initialize variables
   17
   18        Dim strWeightLoss As String
   19        Dim decWeightLoss As Decimal
   20        Dim decAverageLoss As Decimal
   21        Dim decTotalWeightLoss As Decimal = 0D
```

(continues)

Guided Program Development   *continued*

● **Declare and Initialize the Variables Used with the InputBox Function Call** Five variables contain messages used in the input box to obtain the team members' weight loss. These variables are: 1) strInputMessage: Is used in the function call to contain the message displayed in the input box; 2) strInputHeading: Contains the message displayed in the title bar of the input box; 3) strNormalMessage: The normal message that appears in the input box when no error has occurred; 4) strNonNumericError: The message that appears in the input box when the user has entered a nonnumeric value; 5) strNegativeError: The message that appears in the input box when the user has entered zero or a negative number. Declare and initialize these five variables.

```
HINT
22    Dim strInputMessage As String = "Enter the weight loss for team member #"
23    Dim strInputHeading As String = "Weight Loss"
24    Dim strNormalMessage As String = "Enter the weight loss for team member #"
25    Dim strNonNumericError As String = "Error - Enter a number for the weight loss of team member #"
26    Dim strNegativeError As String = "Error - Enter a positive number for the weight loss of team member #"
```

● **Declare and Initialize Variables Used in the Loop Processing** Three variables are used for processing the loop in the program. These variables are: 1) strCancelClicked: This variable contains a null string and is used to determine if the user tapped or clicked the Cancel button in the input box; 2) intMaxNumberOfEntries: Contains the maximum number of entries for team member weight losses (program requirements state the maximum number is eight); 3) intNumberOfEntries: The counter for the valid number of team member weight loss values entered by the user. This variable is used to determine when the maximum number of entries has been made and to act as the divisor when calculating the average weight loss per team member.

```
HINT
28          'Declare and initialize loop variables
29
30    Dim strCancelClicked As String = ""
31    Dim intMaxNumberOfEntries As Integer = 8
32    Dim intNumberOfEntries As Integer = 1
```

● **Write Comments for the Do Until Loop and Write the Priming InputBox Function Call** You often can use comments to document a loop or other set of major processing statements. The comments here alert the reader to the role of the Do Until loop. The priming InputBox function call obtains the first team members' weight loss, or allows the user to tap or click the Cancel button. The normal message is displayed. The space at the end of the argument list places a space in the input box so if the user taps or clicks the OK button without entering any data, the command will not be treated the same as tapping or clicking the Cancel button *(ref: Figure 6-70)*.

```
HINT
34        ' This loop allows the user to enter the weight loss of up to 8 team members.
35        ' The loop terminates when the user has entered 8 weight loss values or the user
36        ' taps or clicks the Cancel button or the Close button in the InputBox
37
38        strWeightLoss = InputBox(strInputMessage & intNumberOfEntries, strInputHeading, " ")
39
```

- **Code the Do Until Loop**
Because the application
requests the weight loss values
of up to eight team members,
the Do Until loop should continue until eight weight losses
are entered or until the user taps or clicks the Cancel or
Close button in the input box. Enter the Do Until loop using
IntelliSense *(ref: Figure 6-65, Figure 6-70)*.

```
40         Do Until intNumberOfEntries > intMaxNumberOfEntries Or strWeightLoss = strCancelClicked
41
42    Loop
```

- **Validate That the Entry Is a Number** The first
process in the Do Until loop is to validate that
the team member weight loss entered by the user
is a numeric value. Enter the If...Then statement to
test if the value in the strWeightLoss variable is numeric.

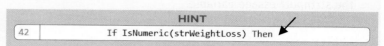

```
42              If IsNumeric(strWeightLoss) Then
```

- **Convert the Value Entered from a String
to the Decimal Data Type** If the user entered
a numeric value, the next step is to convert
the string value the user entered to a Decimal data type.
Using IntelliSense, enter the code to convert the value in the
strWeightLoss variable from the String to the Decimal data type
and place the result in the decWeightLoss variable.

```
43          decWeightLoss = Convert.ToDecimal(strWeightLoss)
```

- **Validate That the Entered Value Is a
Positive Number** After the value is converted,
the program must validate that the number is
positive. Write the If...Then statement to test whether the
value in the decWeightLoss variable is greater than zero.

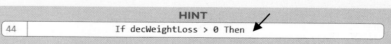

```
44          If decWeightLoss > 0 Then
```

- **Perform the Processing When the User
Enters a Valid Weight Loss** After ensuring
the weight loss entered by the user is valid,
the next steps are to perform the processing
for valid weight loss. Four steps are required:
1) Add the weight loss as an item to the lstWeightLoss ListBox
object *(ref: Figure 6-28)*; 2) Add the weight loss the user entered
to the decTotalWeightLoss accumulator *(ref: Figure 6-38)*. The
accumulated weight loss is used to calculate the average weight
loss; 3) Increment the intNumberOfEntries counter by 1 because
the user entered a valid weight loss *(ref: Figure 6-38)*. This value
is used as the divisor to determine the average weight loss, and
as one of the indicators that the loop should be terminated; 4)
Because the user entered a valid weight loss, the normal message
should appear the next time the input box is displayed. Therefore,
the normal message should be moved to the strInputMessage variable. Using IntelliSense, enter the code for these four activities.

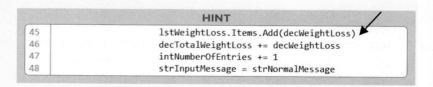

```
45              lstWeightLoss.Items.Add(decWeightLoss)
46              decTotalWeightLoss += decWeightLoss
47              intNumberOfEntries += 1
48              strInputMessage = strNormalMessage
```

(continues)

Guided Program Development *continued*

● **Assign an Error Message If the User Entered a Negative Weight Loss** If the user entered a negative weight loss, the next input box should display the negative number error message *(ref: Figure 6-73)*. Following the Else statement for the If statement that checks for a number greater than zero, enter the assignment statement that places the value in the strNegativeError variable in the strInputMessage variable.

```
        HINT
49              Else
50                      strInputMessage = strNegativeError
51              End If
```

● **Assign an Error Message If the User Enters a Nonnumeric Weight Loss** If the user enters a nonnumeric weight loss, the next input box should show the nonnumeric error message *(ref: Figure 6-73)*. Following the Else Statement for the If statement that checks for numeric data, enter the assignment statement that places the value in the strNonNumericError variable in the strInputMessage variable.

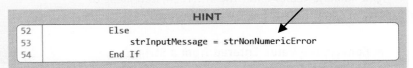

```
        HINT
52              Else
53                      strInputMessage = strNonNumericError
54              End If
```

● **Code the InputBox Function Call** The first InputBox function call was placed before the Do Until loop to prime the loop. To continue the process after the first value is entered, another InputBox function is needed as the last statement inside the loop to request subsequent values. This statement should be executed only if the maximum number of entries has not been exceeded. So, an If structure is required to determine if the maximum number of entries has been reached. If not, the InputBox function call is executed *(ref: Figure 6-73)*.

```
                                HINT
56      If intNumberOfEntries <= intMaxNumberOfEntries Then
57          strWeightLoss = InputBox(strInputMessage & intNumberOfEntries, strInputHeading, " ")
58      End If
```

The coding for the variables and Do Until loop that processes the data in the program is complete (Figure 6-101). It is important that you examine the code in Figure 6-101 and understand the loop processing. The priming of the loop, both by setting the value in the intNumberOfEntries variable (line 32) and calling the InputBox function (line 38), is critical for proper execution of the loop. Increasing the loop counter when a valid entry is made (line 46) also is fundamental in the loop processing because testing this counter is one way the Do Until loop can be terminated. Also, using variables for messages instead of literals in the actual code demonstrates how professional programs are coded. You should follow these examples in your programming.

RESULT OF STEP 3

```
28          'Declare and initialize loop variables
29
30          Dim strCancelClicked As String = ""
31          Dim intMaxNumberOfEntries As Integer = 8
32          Dim intNumberOfEntries As Integer = 1
33
34          ' This loop allows the user to enter the weight loss of up to 8 team members.
35          ' The loop terminates when the user has entered 8 weight loss vales or the user
36          ' taps or clicks the Cancel button or the Close button in the InputBox
37
38          strWeightLoss = InputBox(strInputMessage & intNumberOfEntries, strInputHeading, " ")
39
40          Do Until intNumberOfEntries > intMaxNumberOfEntries Or strWeightLoss = strCancelClicked
41              If IsNumeric(strWeightLoss) Then
42                  decWeightLoss = Convert.ToDecimal(strWeightLoss)
43                  If decWeightLoss > 0 Then
44                      lstWeightLoss.Items.Add(decWeightLoss)
45                      decTotalWeightLoss += decWeightLoss
46                      intNumberOfEntries += 1
47                      strInputMessage = strNormalMessage
48                  Else
49                      strInputMessage = strNegativeError
50                  End If
51              Else
52                  strInputMessage = strNonNumericError
53              End If
54              If intNumberOfEntries <= intMaxNumberOfEntries Then
55                  strWeightLoss = InputBox(strInputMessage & intNumberOfEntries, strInputHeading, " ")
56              End If
57
58          Loop
```

FIGURE 6-101

(continues)

Guided Program Development   *continued*

4

• **Set the Result Label's Visible Property** When you finish the Do Until loop, you

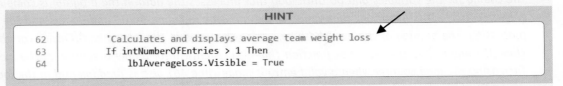

	HINT
62	'Calculates and displays average team weight loss
63	If intNumberOfEntries > 1 Then
64	lblAverageLoss.Visible = True

must complete three tasks to finish the Enter Weight Loss button click event handler: 1) Make the label that will contain the average weight loss visible; 2) Calculate and display the average weight loss; 3) Disable the Enter Weight Loss button. If at least one weight loss value has been entered using Intel-liSense, write the code to create the If statement and make the lblAverageLoss label visible.

• **Calculate the Average Weight Loss** To calculate the average of the weight loss values the user entered, the value in the decTotalWeightLoss variable (accumulator) must be divided by the number of team members entered (counter). At the end

	HINT
65	decAverageLoss = decTotalWeightLoss / (intNumberOfEntries - 1)
66	lblAverageLoss.Text = "Average weight loss for the team is " & _
67	decAverageLoss.ToString("F1") & " lbs"
68	Else
69	MsgBox("No weight loss value entered")
70	End If

of the loop shown in Figure 6-101 on the previous page, the value in the intNumberOfEntries variable always will be one greater than the actual number of team members entered, so the total weight loss must be divided by the value in intNumberOfEntries minus 1. This calculation should occur only if one or more team member weight loss values were entered, so an If statement must be used to check whether the value in the intNumberOfEntries variable is greater than 1. If so, the average weight loss is calculated; if not, the "No weight loss value entered" message should be displayed using a MsgBox. Using IntelliSense, write the code to perform this processing.

● **Change the Enter Weight Loss Button Enabled
Property to False** After the average weight loss is
calculated and displayed, the Enabled property of
the btnWeightLoss button is set to False to dim the
button. Using IntelliSense, write the code to accomplish
this processing.

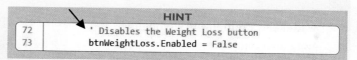

	HINT
72	' Disables the Weight Loss button
73	btnWeightLoss.Enabled = False

The code for the btnWeightLoss button click event handler is completed (Figure 6-102).

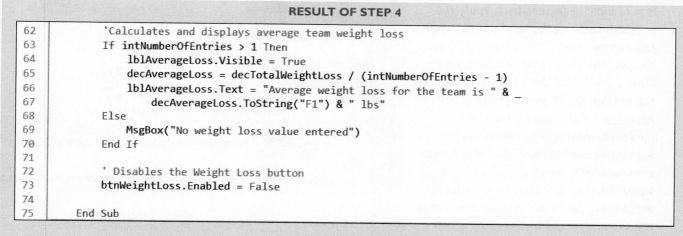

RESULT OF STEP 4

```
62        'Calculates and displays average team weight loss
63        If intNumberOfEntries > 1 Then
64            lblAverageLoss.Visible = True
65            decAverageLoss = decTotalWeightLoss / (intNumberOfEntries - 1)
66            lblAverageLoss.Text = "Average weight loss for the team is " & _
67                decAverageLoss.ToString("F1") & " lbs"
68        Else
69            MsgBox("No weight loss value entered")
70        End If
71
72        ' Disables the Weight Loss button
73        btnWeightLoss.Enabled = False
74
75    End Sub
```

FIGURE 6-102

(continues)

Guided Program Development   *continued*

5

- **Run the Program** After coding
a major section of the program, you
should run the program to ensure it
is working properly. Tap or click the
Start Debugging button on the Standard
toolbar to run the Fitness Challenge
application. Tap or click the Enter Weight
Loss button and then enter the weight
loss of eight team members. Verify the
weight losses are displayed properly and
the average weight loss is correct. Close
the program by tapping or clicking the
Close button. Run the program again,
tap or click the Enter Weight Loss button,
enter the weight loss for four team
members, enter a nonnumeric weight
loss, enter a weight loss that is less than
zero, and then tap or click the Cancel
button in the input box. Ensure that the
weight loss values are displayed properly,
the average weight loss is correct, and the error messages are
displayed properly in the input box. Close the program. Run the
program again, tap or click the Enter Weight Loss button, and
then tap or click the Cancel button in the input box. Ensure
that the "No weight loss value entered" message is displayed.
Close the program and then run it as many times as necessary
to ensure the program is working properly. If the program does
not run properly, consider setting a breakpoint and checking
the values in the variables *(ref: Figure 6-76)*.

HINT

Fitness Challenge

File

Fitness Challenge
Team Weight Loss

Enter Weight Loss

14.2
37.1
19.0
3.2
8.1
18.2
9.9
21.8

Average weight loss for the team is 16.4 lbs

6

- **Enter the Code for the Clear Menu
Item Click Event** Tap or click the
frmFitness.vb[Design]* tab in the code
window to display the design window.
Tap or click File on the MenuStrip object,
and then double-tap or double-click the
Clear menu item to open the Clear click
event handler in the code window. The
Clear click event handler must perform three tasks: 1) Clear the
lstWeightLoss list box; 2) Hide the average weight loss Label
object; 3) Enable the Enter Weight Loss Button object. Using
IntelliSense, write the code for these three tasks.

HINT

```
76
77   Private Sub mnuClear_Click(sender As Object, e As EventArgs) Handles mnuClear.Click
78       ' The mnuClear click event clears the ListBox object and hides
79       ' the average weight loss label. It also enables the Weight Loss button
80
81       lstWeightLoss.Items.Clear()
82       lblAverageLoss.Visible = False
83       btnWeightLoss.Enabled = True
84
85   End Sub
```

● **Enter the Code for the Exit Menu Item Click Event** Return to the design window. Double-tap or double-click the Exit menu item. In the code window, enter a Close procedure call that will close the window and terminate the program.

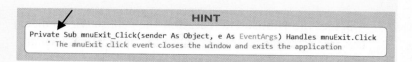

HINT

```
Private Sub mnuExit_Click(sender As Object, e As EventArgs) Handles mnuExit.Click
    ' The mnuExit click event closes the window and exits the application
```

The code for the Clear menu item click event and the Exit menu item click event is completed (Figure 6-103). The code for the program is also completed.

RESULT OF STEP 6

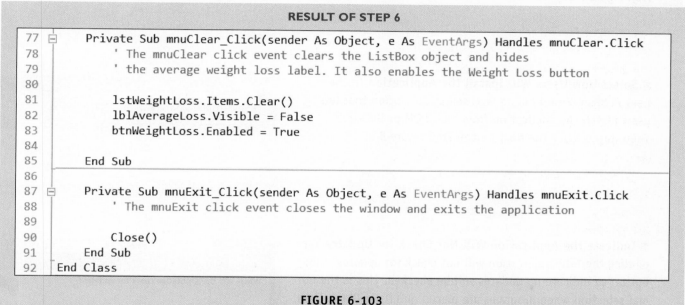

```
77      Private Sub mnuClear_Click(sender As Object, e As EventArgs) Handles mnuClear.Click
78          ' The mnuClear click event clears the ListBox object and hides
79          ' the average weight loss label. It also enables the Weight Loss button
80
81          lstWeightLoss.Items.Clear()
82          lblAverageLoss.Visible = False
83          btnWeightLoss.Enabled = True
84
85      End Sub
86
87      Private Sub mnuExit_Click(sender As Object, e As EventArgs) Handles mnuExit.Click
88          ' The mnuExit click event closes the window and exits the application
89
90          Close()
91      End Sub
92  End Class
```

FIGURE 6-103

7

● **Publish the Fitness Challenge Application** After completing the program, you can publish it using ClickOnce deployment so it can be installed on multiple computers. To open the Publish Wizard and begin the deployment process, tap or click BUILD on the menu bar and then tap or click Publish Fitness Challenge on the BUILD menu *(ref: Figure 6-87).*

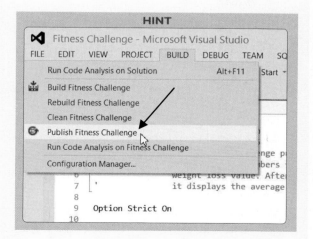

HINT

(continues)

● **Select the Publish File Location** The Publish Wizard dialog box asks where you want to publish the application. Change the default location to the same file location that you used to save your Windows application by tapping or clicking the Browse button and then selecting the drive. For example, select the E: drive, a USB drive. After selecting the drive, tap or click the Next button in the Publish Wizard dialog box *(ref: Figure 6-88)*.

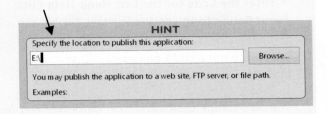

HINT

Specify the location to publish this application:

E:\   Browse...

You may publish the application to a web site, FTP server, or file path.

Examples:

● **Select How Users Will Install the Application** In the next Publish Wizard dialog box, select the option that lets users install the application from a CD-ROM or DVD-ROM. Then, tap or click the Next button *(ref: Figure 6-90)*.

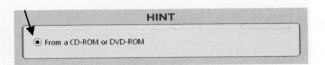

HINT

◉ From a CD-ROM or DVD-ROM

● **Indicate the Application Will Not Check for Updates** Tap or click the "The application will not check for updates" radio button to indicate no updates will be checked. This is the normal selection when programs are placed on CDs or DVDs. Then, tap or click the Next button in the Publish Wizard dialog box *(ref: Figure 6-91)*.

HINT

Publish Wizard   ?   ✕

Where will the application check for updates?

○ The application will check for updates from the following location:

http://localhost/Fitness Challenge/   Browse...

◉ The application will not check for updates

● **View the Summary Window** The Publish Wizard summary is displayed. Tap or click the Finish button to publish the application *(ref: Figure 6-92)*.

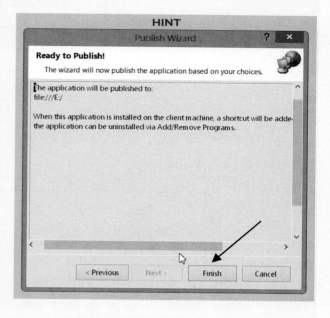

● **View the Installation Files** After the publishing succeeds, a folder is created with the installation files that could be placed on a CD, DVD, or other computer *(ref: Figure 6-94)*.

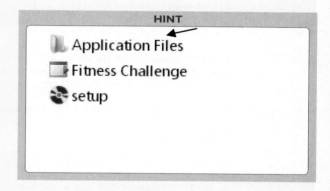

Code Listing

The complete code for the sample program is shown in Figure 6-104.

```vb
 1  ' Program Name: Fitness Challenge
 2  ' Author:       Corinne Hoisington
 3  ' Date:         September 30, 2015
 4  ' Purpose:      The Fitness Challenge program enters the weight loss
 5  '               from team members for a fitness challenge. It displays each
 6  '               weight loss value. After all weight loss values have been entered,
 7  '               it displays the average weight loss for the team.
 8
 9  Option Strict On
10
11  Public Class frmFitness
12      Private Sub btnWeightLoss_Click(sender As Object, e As EventArgs) Handles btnWeightLoss.Click
13          ' The btnWeightLoss_Click event accepts and displays up to 8 weight loss values
14          ' and then calculates and displays the average weight loss for the team
15
16          ' Declare and initialize variables
17
18          Dim strWeightLoss As String
19          Dim decWeightLoss As Decimal
20          Dim decAverageLoss As Decimal
21          Dim decTotalWeightLoss As Decimal = 0D
22          Dim strInputMessage As String = "Enter the weight loss for team member #"
23          Dim strInputHeading As String = "Weight Loss"
24          Dim strNormalMessage As String = "Enter the weight loss for team member #"
25          Dim strNonNumericError As String = "Error - Enter a number for the weight loss of team member #"
26          Dim strNegativeError As String = "Error - Enter a positive number for the weight loss of team member #"
27
28          'Declare and initialize loop variables
29
30          Dim strCancelClicked As String = ""
31          Dim intMaxNumberOfEntries As Integer = 8
32          Dim intNumberOfEntries As Integer = 1
33
34          ' This loop allows the user to enter the weight loss of up to 8 team members.
35          ' The loop terminates when the user has entered 8 weight loss values or the user
36          ' taps or clicks the Cancel button or the Close button in the InputBox
37
38          strWeightLoss = InputBox(strInputMessage & intNumberOfEntries, strInputHeading, " ")
39
40          Do Until intNumberOfEntries > intMaxNumberOfEntries Or strWeightLoss = strCancelClicked
41
42              If IsNumeric(strWeightLoss) Then
43                  decWeightLoss = Convert.ToDecimal(strWeightLoss)
44                  If decWeightLoss > 0 Then
45                      lstWeightLoss.Items.Add(decWeightLoss)
46                      decTotalWeightLoss += decWeightLoss
47                      intNumberOfEntries += 1
48                      strInputMessage = strNormalMessage
49                  Else
50                      strInputMessage = strNegativeError
51                  End If
52              Else
53                  strInputMessage = strNonNumericError
54              End If
55
56              If intNumberOfEntries <= intMaxNumberOfEntries Then
57                  strWeightLoss = InputBox(strInputMessage & intNumberOfEntries, strInputHeading, " ")
58              End If
59
```

FIGURE 6-104 (continues)

```
60          Loop
61
62          'Calculates and displays average team weight loss
63          If intNumberOfEntries > 1 Then
64              lblAverageLoss.Visible = True
65              decAverageLoss = decTotalWeightLoss / (intNumberOfEntries - 1)
66              lblAverageLoss.Text = "Average weight loss for the team is " & _
67                  decAverageLoss.ToString("F1") & " lbs"
68          Else
69              MsgBox("No weight loss value entered")
70          End If
71
72          ' Disables the Weight Loss button
73          btnWeightLoss.Enabled = False
74
75      End Sub
76
77      Private Sub mnuClear_Click(sender As Object, e As EventArgs) Handles mnuClear.Click
78          ' The mnuClear click event clears the ListBox object and hides
79          ' the average weight loss label. It also enables the Weight Loss button
80
81          lstWeightLoss.Items.Clear()
82          lblAverageLoss.Visible = False
83          btnWeightLoss.Enabled = True
84
85      End Sub
86
87      Private Sub mnuExit_Click(sender As Object, e As EventArgs) Handles mnuExit.Click
88          ' The mnuExit click event closes the window and exits the application
89
90          Close()
91      End Sub
92  End Class
93
```

FIGURE 6-104 (continued)

Summary

In this chapter you have learned to design and write code to implement loops and to create menus, list boxes, and an input box. The items listed in Figure 6-105 include all the new Visual Studio and Visual Basic skills you have learned in this chapter. Video 6-1 demonstrates the complete program execution.

Visual Basic Skills		
Skill	**Figure Number**	**Video Number**
Run the Completed Program	Figure 6-1	Video 6-1
Place a MenuStrip Object on the Windows Form Object	Figure 6-5	Video 6-2
Code the Exit Menu Item Event	Figure 6-12	Video 6-3
Insert a Full Standard Menu	Figure 6-14	Video 6-4
Code the InputBox Function	Figure 6-17	
Add a ListBox Object	Figure 6-24	Video 6-5
Add an Item to a ListBox Object	Figure 6-27	
Add Items to a ListBox Object During Design	Figure 6-32	Video 6-6
Assign a Selected Item from a ListBox Object	Figure 6-36	
Write Code using Compound Operators	Figure 6-39	
Write the Code for a For...Next Loop	Figure 6-42	
Use IntelliSense to Enter the Code for a For...Next Loop	Figure 6-50	Video 6-7
Write Code for a Top-controlled Do While Loop	Figure 6-56	
Use IntelliSense to Code a Do While Loop	Figure 6-59	Video 6-8
Write Code for a Bottom-Controlled Do While Loop	Figure 6-62	
Write Code for a Top-Controlled Do Until Loop	Figure 6-65	
Write Code for a Bottom-Controlled Do Until Loop	Figure 6-67	
Avoid Infinite Loops	Figure 6-69	
Prime a Loop	Figure 6-70	
Validate Data	Figure 6-73	
Create a Nested Loop	Figure 6-74	
Set a Breakpoint and Use a DataTip	Figure 6-76	Video 6-9
Publish an Application with ClickOnce Deployment	Figure 6-87	Video 6-10

FIGURE 6-105

Learn Online

Reinforcement activities and resources are available at no additional cost on *www.cengagebrain.com*. Visit *www.cengage.com/ct/studentdownload* for detailed instructions about accessing the resources available at the Student Companion Site.

Knowledge Check

1. Write a statement that displays the default value of 12 in the input box shown in Figure 6-106 and assigns the return value from the InputBox function to a variable named strMovieCount with the message Number of Instant Queue Movies with the title Hulu Plus.

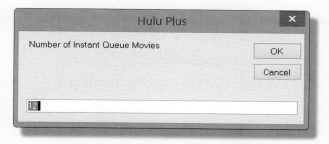

FIGURE 6-106

2. Write compound operators for the following equations:

   a. intTouchdown = intTouchdown + 6

   b. dblSquare = dblSquare ^ 2

   c. strFast = strFast & "Comet"

3. Write For...Next loops that calculate the sum of the following ranges and assign their sum to a variable named intSum:

   a. The first 100 numbers starting with 1

   b. The even numbers beginning at 10 and ending with 50

   c. The numbers 20, 30, 40, 50, and 60

4. Find the errors in the following For...Next header statements:

   a. For intCounter = "1" To "19"

   b. For intNumber = 98 To 71 Step 2

   c. For intValue = 12 To 52 Step –4

   d. For strCount = –15 To 5 Step 5

(continues)

5. Explain the purpose of placing an ampersand before or within a MenuStrip item.

6. Write the command to clear a ListBox object named lstBaseballPlayers.

7. Write a command to add your favorite sports team to a ListBox object named lstFavoriteTeam.

8. Using a compound operator, write an assignment statement to increment the value in intAmount by 7.

9. Using a compound operator, write an assignment statement to decrease the value in intCounter by 4.5.

10. Using a compound operator, write an assignment statement to increment the value in intQuantity by 10.

11. Write a top-controlled Do Until loop with an empty body that would continue until intValue is greater than 19.

12. Write a bottom-controlled Do While loop with an empty body that continues while the user enters "Yes" into the strContinue variable.

13. Write a Do While loop to validate that the user enters a nonzero integer into an input box for a variable named intDenominator.

14. Is the For...Next loop top-controlled or bottom-controlled?

15. Write the code for an infinite Do Until loop with the variable intInfinite.

16. Which loop should be used if you know the required number of times the loop will be executed?

17. What is the fewest number of times a top-controlled Do Until loop is executed?

18. Write a data validation Do loop to check that the variable intAge entered from an input box is between 1 and 115.

19. A loop inside another loop is called a _____ _____.

20. When you insert standard items in a MenuStrip object, what File menu items are automatically created by default?

Debugging Exercises

1. The loop shown in Figure 6-107 should repeat 10 times. If it will not repeat 10 times, change the code so it will.

```
7        For intRepeat = 20 To 10
8            MsgBox("The value is " & intRepeat.ToString("C0"))
9        Next
```

FIGURE 6-107

2. What output does the code shown in Figure 6-108 produce? How would you change the code to produce a list box containing the values 12–20?

```
15        intRate = 12
16        Do While intRate <= 10
17            lstDisplay.Items.Add(intRate)
18            intRate += 1
19        Loop
```

FIGURE 6-108

3. What is the output of the code shown in Figure 6-109?

```
5         Dim intAdd As Integer
6         Dim intOuterLoop As Integer
7         Dim intInnerLoop As Integer
8
9         intAdd = 0
10        For intOuterLoop = 1 To 8
11            For intInnerLoop = 3 To 7
12                intAdd += 1
13            Next
14        Next
          MsgBox.Show("The final value is " & intAdd.ToString())
```

FIGURE 6-109

4. What is the output of the code shown in Figure 6-110?

```
33        Dim intValue As Integer
34
35        intValue = 2
36        Do While intValue <= 9
37            lstDisplay.Items.Add(intValue & " " & intValue ^ 3)
38            intValue += 2
39        Loop
```

FIGURE 6-110

(continues)

5. Fix the errors in the loop shown in Figure 6-111.

```
41          Dim intStart As Integer = 8
42
43          Loop
44          intStart = +4
45          Do While intStart < 24
```

FIGURE 6-111

6. What is the output of the code shown in Figure 6-112?

```
53          intCount = 40
54          Do Until intCount < 26
55              intCount -= 2
56              lstCount.Items.Add(intCount)
57          Loop
```

FIGURE 6-112

7. Fix the errors in the code shown in Figure 6-113.

```
5           Dim decCost As Decimal = 3.5D
6
7           Do Until decCost > 10.5D
8               MsgBox("The cost is now " & decCost.ToString("F1"))
9               decCost -= 0.5
10          Loop
```

FIGURE 6-113

8. In the example shown in Figure 6-114, you want the code to count the odd numbers from 1 to 99. What is missing?

```
66          Dim intOddNumber As Integer = 1
67
68          Do While intOddNumber <= 99
69              lstDisplay.Items.Add("Odd Numbers: " & intOddNumber.ToString())
70          Loop
```

FIGURE 6-114

Program Analysis

1. What is the value of lblResult after the code shown in Figure 6-115 is executed?

```
73        Dim intCounter As Integer = -20
74
75        Do While intCount < 25
76            intCount += 5
77            lblResult.Text &= intCount.ToString() & " "
78        Loop
```

FIGURE 6-115

2. What is the value of lblResult after the code shown in Figure 6-116 is executed?

```
80        Dim intCountIt As Integer
81
82        intCountIt = 6
83        Do
84            intCountIt += 3
85            lblResult.Text &= intCountIt.ToString() & " "
86        Loop Until intCountIt = 21
```

FIGURE 6-116

3. Rewrite the top-controlled Do While loop shown in Figure 6-117 as a top-controlled Do Until loop.

```
88        Dim intQuantity As Integer
89
90        intQuantity = -5
91        Do While intQuantity < 30
92            intQuantity += 5
93        Loop
```

FIGURE 6-117

4. Convert the Do loop shown in Figure 6-118 to a For...Next loop.

```
95         Dim intIncrease As Integer
96
97         intIncrease = 10
98         Do While intIncrease < 40
99             lstDisplay.Items.Add(intIncrease)
100            intIncrease += 2
101        Loop
```

FIGURE 6-118

(continues)

5. How many times will the inner statement inside the nested loop in Figure 6-119 be executed?

```
103        For intOuterLoop = 3 To 5
104            For intInnerLoop = 6 To 10
105                lstDays.Items.Add("Value: " & intOuterLoop.ToString() & _
106                    " Count: " & intInnerLoop.ToString())
107            Next
108        Next
```

FIGURE 6-119

6. How many times will the loop in Figure 6-120 be executed?

```
110        Dim intQuantitySold As Integer
111        Dim decTax As Decimal
112
113        intQuantitySold = 1
114        Do Until intQuantitySold = 5
115            decTax = intQuantitySold * 0.07
116            lstDisplay.Items.Add("Tax Amount: " & decTax.ToString())
117            intQuantitySold += 1
118        Loop
```

FIGURE 6-120

7. Write a For...Next loop that adds the odd numbers 1 through 49 and assigns their sum to the variable intSum. The program should start with the lines shown in Figure 6-121 (use the variables shown in lines 120–123 in your code).

```
120        Dim intLoopValue As Integer
121        Dim intStartValue As Integer
122        Dim intEndValue As Integer
123        Dim intSum As Integer
124
125        intStartValue = 1
126        intEndValue = 49
127        intSum = 0
```

FIGURE 6-121

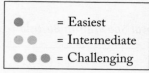

Complete one or more of the following case programming assignments. Submit the program and materials you create to your instructor. The level of difficulty is indicated for each case programming assignment.

●	= Easiest
● ●	= Intermediate
● ● ●	= Challenging

1 ●

TOTAL SNOWFALL IN BUFFALO

Design a Windows application and write the code that will execute according to the program requirements shown in Figure 6-122. Before writing the code, create an event planning document for each event in the program. The Use Case Definition document is shown in Figure 6-123 on the following page. The completed user interface is shown in Figure 6-124 on the following page.

REQUIREMENTS DOCUMENT

Date Submitted:	March 17, 2015
Application Title:	Total Snowfall in Buffalo
Purpose:	This Windows application is written for the city of Buffalo to compute the total snowfall for the months of October through April.
Program Procedures:	In a Windows application, the user enters up to seven monthly snowfall amounts to compute the total snowfall for Buffalo.
Algorithms, Processing, and Conditions:	1. The user enters up to seven monthly snowfall totals in inches in an InputBox object.
	2. Each month's total snowfall is displayed in a ListBox object.
	3. After seven months of snowfall totals are entered, the total snowfall is calculated and displayed.
	4. A File menu contains a Clear and an Exit option. The Clear menu item clears the total snowfall and the seven values representing the monthly snowfall totals. The Exit menu item closes the application.
	5. If the user taps or clicks the Cancel button in the input box before entering seven values, compute the total for the number of months entered.
	6. If the user taps or clicks the Cancel button before entering any snowfall values, display a message indicating the user did not enter a value.
Notes and Restrictions:	1. Nonnumeric values should not be accepted.
	2. Negative values should not be accepted.
	3. The average total snowfall should be rounded to the nearest tenth of an inch.
Comments:	1. The application allows decimal entries.
	2. Obtain an image for this program from CengageBrain.com. The name of the image file is Snowfall.

FIGURE 6-122

(continues)

Case Programming Assignments

Total Snowfall in Buffalo (continued)

USE CASE DEFINITION

1. The Windows application opens with the heading "Buffalo Total Snowfall," a ListBox object that displays the monthly snowfall amounts, an image, and a Button object that allows the user to begin entering the monthly snowfall.
2. A menu bar displays the File menu, which has two menu items: Clear and Exit.
3. The user enters up to seven values in an InputBox object, with each value representing one month of snowfall in inches.
4. The program asks the user for the monthly snowfall again if the value is a negative number or the entry is a nonnumeric value.
5. The program displays the total monthly snowfall rounded to one decimal place.
6. The user can clear the input and the result by tapping or clicking the Clear menu item, and then can repeat Steps 3–5. If the user taps or clicks the Cancel button in the input box, the average for the values entered is calculated. If the user did not enter any values, the program displays an appropriate message.
7. The user taps or clicks the Exit menu item to close the application.

FIGURE 6-123

FIGURE 6-124

Case Programming Assignments

2 WHERE OUR STUDENTS LIVE

Design a Windows application and write the code that will execute according to the program requirements shown in Figure 6-125. Before writing the code, create an event planning document for each event in the program. The Use Case Definition document is shown in Figure 6-126 on the following page. The completed user interface is shown in Figure 6-127 on the following page.

REQUIREMENTS DOCUMENT

Date Submitted:	July 31, 2015
Application Title:	Where Our Students Live
Purpose:	This Windows application finds the average distance from a school to the homes of students from all over the world.
Program Procedures:	In a Windows application, 10 students enter the distance from their home to their school and the average distance is displayed.
Algorithms, Processing, and Conditions:	1. The user taps or clicks the Enter Mileage button to enter the distance that the student lives from the campus.
	2. Each distance in miles is displayed in a ListBox object.
	3. After 10 distances have been entered, the average is displayed.
	4. A File menu contains a Clear and an Exit option. The Clear menu item clears the average and the 10 individual distance values. The Exit menu item closes the application.
	5. If the user taps or clicks the Cancel button in the input box after entering one distance but before entering 10 distance values, use the distances the user entered for the calculations.
	6. If the user taps or clicks the Cancel button before entering any distance values, display an appropriate message.
Notes and Restrictions:	1. The result should include two places after the decimal point.
	2. Nonnumeric values should not be accepted.
	3. Negative numbers should not be accepted.
Comments:	1. The application allows decimal entries.
	2. Obtain an image for this program from CengageBrain.com. The name of the image file is World.`

FIGURE 6-125

(continues)

Where Our Students Live *(continued)*

USE CASE DEFINITION

1. The Windows application opens, displaying Where Our Students Live as the heading, a ListBox object that will display the distance in miles from students' homes to their schools, and a Button object that allows the user to enter the distance.
2. A menu bar displays the File menu, which has two menu items: Clear and Exit.
3. In an InputBox object, the user enters up to 10 distances in miles from students' homes to their schools.
4. The program asks the user for the distance again if the value is a negative or nonnumeric number.
5. The program displays the average distance to 2 decimal places.
6. The user taps or clicks the Clear menu item to clear the input and the result.
7. If the user taps or clicks the Cancel button in the input box before entering 10 distance values, the program uses the mileage entered for calculations. If the user entered no distance values, an appropriate message is displayed.
8. The user taps or clicks the Exit menu item to close the application.

FIGURE 6-126

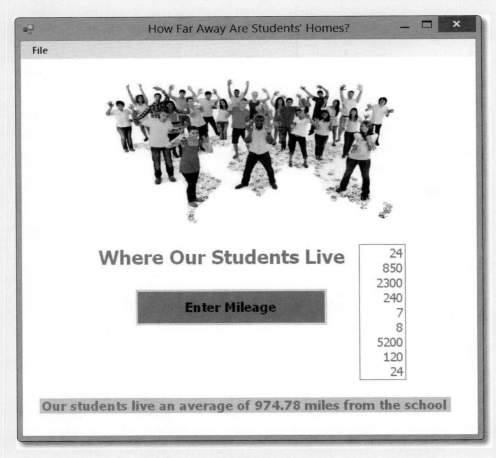

FIGURE 6-127

3 ● BOWLING SCOREBOARD

Design a Windows application and write the code that will execute according to the program requirements shown in Figure 6-128. Before writing the code, create an event planning document for each event in the program. The Use Case Definition document is shown in Figure 6-129 on the following page. The completed user interface is shown in Figure 6-130 on the following page.

REQUIREMENTS DOCUMENT

Date Submitted:	November 3, 2015
Application Title:	Bowling Scoreboard
Purpose:	This application calculates the score of each frame during a bowling game for one person.
Program Procedures:	In a Windows application, the user enters the score of each frame to display the total on the scoreboard after 10 frames of bowling.
Algorithms, Processing, and Conditions:	1. The user taps or clicks the Enter Score button in an InputBox object to enter a score after each frame in a game.
	2. The score for each frame and the running total is displayed in a ListBox.
	3. After the user taps or clicks the Cancel button in the InputBox object to end the game scoring, the total final score is displayed.
	4. A File menu contains a Clear and an Exit option. The Clear menu item clears the result and the frame scores. The Exit menu item closes the application.
Notes and Restrictions:	1. Nonnumeric values should not be accepted.
	2. A negative value should not be accepted.
Comments:	Obtain an image for this program from CengageBrain.com. The name of the image file is Bowling.

FIGURE 6-128

(continues)

Case Programming Assignments

Bowling Scoreboard (continued)

USE CASE DEFINITION

1. The Windows application opens with a heading, a Bowling Scoreboard subheading, a ListBox object that will display the frame scores throughout the game, and a Button object that allows the user to enter the scores.
2. A menu bar displays the File menu, which has two menu items: Clear and Exit.
3. In an InputBox object, the user enters points scored in each bowling frame.
4. The program asks the user for the score again if the value is a negative or nonnumeric number.
5. The program displays the running total score.
6. The program displays the final score when the user taps or clicks the Cancel button in the input box.
7. The user taps or clicks the Clear menu item to clear the input and the result.
8. The user taps or clicks the Exit menu item to close the application.

FIGURE 6-129

FIGURE 6-130

4 ●●
PENNY A DAY OR NICKEL A DAY

Design a Windows application and write the code that will execute according to the program requirements shown in Figure 6-131. Before writing the code, create an event planning document for each event in the program. Create a Use Case Definition document for the application.

REQUIREMENTS DOCUMENT

Date Submitted:	June 21, 2014
Application Title:	Penny a Day or Nickel a Day
Purpose:	This Windows application finds the amount of your monthly pay if you are paid a penny or nickel for the first workday and the pay is doubled each subsequent workday. New employees are paid a penny for the first workday and experienced employees are paid a nickel for the first day.
Program Procedures:	In a Windows application, the user enters the number of workdays in a monthly pay period and the pay for the first day. The program calculates and displays the amount of pay for the pay period.
Algorithms, Processing, and Conditions:	1. The user enters the number of days in the pay period. 2. The user selects a RadioButton object to indicate the pay amount for the first day: a penny or a nickel. 3. After the user enters the number of days and pay for the first day, the total amount earned is calculated and displayed. 4. A File menu contains a Clear and an Exit option. The Clear menu item clears the result and the RadioButton object. The Exit menu item closes the application.
Notes and Restrictions:	1. Nonnumeric values should not be accepted. 2. Negative values should not be accepted. 3. The minimum number of workdays in the pay period is 19 days for new employees and 16 days for experienced employees. The maximum number of workdays in a pay period is 22 days.
Comments:	n/a

FIGURE 6-131

5   VACATION DISTANCE CALCULATOR

Design a Windows application and write the code that will execute according to the program requirements shown in Figure 6-132. Before writing the code, create an event planning document for each event in the program. Create a Use Case Definition document for the application.

REQUIREMENTS DOCUMENT

Date Submitted:	December 5, 2014
Application Title:	Vacation Distance Calculator
Purpose:	This application computes the number of miles traveled given the speed limit and the number of days traveled while driving cross country.
Program Procedures:	In a Windows application, enter the speed limit and the number of days you plan to travel across the country. You will enter the number of hours you would like to drive for each of the days, based on places you plan to visit and other factors. For example, the first day you plan to drive only four hours because you are driving after work. The application displays the distance that you are able to travel for the entire trip based on the speed limit and the hours driven.
Algorithms, Processing, and Conditions:	1. The application opens and displays a title. Enter the speed limit and the number of days you plan to drive.
	2. Tap or click the Distance button to enter the number of hours you plan to drive each day. The resulting total number of miles you plan to drive over the entire trip will be displayed.
	3. A File menu contains a Clear and an Exit option. The Clear menu item clears the result, the entered number of miles, and the time traveled. The Exit menu item closes the application.
Notes and Restrictions:	1. Nonnumeric values should not be accepted.
	2. The number of hours for one day of travel should not exceed 20 hours.
Comments:	The application allows decimal entries.

FIGURE 6-132

6 •• NEXT DECADE PAY CALCULATOR

Design a Windows application and write the code that will execute according to the program requirements shown in Figure 6-133. Before writing the code, create an event planning document for each event in the program. Create a Use Case Definition document for the application.

REQUIREMENTS DOCUMENT

Date Submitted:	August 23, 2014
Application Title:	The Next Decade Pay Calculator
Purpose:	This Windows application computes the amount of money an employee will earn over the next decade based on a raise, which is a percentage amount.
Program Procedures:	In a Windows application, the user enters her present wage per hour and the raise percentage amount per year to compute her yearly pay over the next 10 years.
Algorithms, Processing, and Conditions:	1. The application opens, displaying a title and requesting the present amount of pay per hour and the expected raise percentage per year.
	2. When the Compute Future Pay button is tapped or clicked, the program calculates the yearly pay based on 40 hours per week and 52 weeks per year. The raise increases each amount after the first year.
	3. The yearly amount of pay earned is displayed for the next 10 years.
	4. A File menu contains a Clear and an Exit option. The Clear menu item clears the result. The Exit menu item closes the application.
Notes and Restrictions:	1. Nonnumeric values should not be accepted.
	2. Negative numbers should not be allowed.
Comments:	The application allows decimal entries.

FIGURE 6-133

Case Programming Assignments

7 •••
FACTORIAL MATH

Create a requirements document and a Use Case Definition document and design a Windows application based on the case project shown in Figure 6-134:

Most calculators have an operation called a "factorial," which is shown on a calculator key as an exclamation point. For example, 5! (5 factorial) multiplies 5 * 4 * 3 * 2 * 1 to calculate the result of 120. Using loops to compute the factorial, display the following factorials in a ListBox object:

1! 1
2! 2
3! 6
4! 24
5! 120
6! 720
7! 5040
8! 40320
9! 362880

FIGURE 6-134

© 2014 Cengage Learning

Case Programming Assignments

8 ●●● GALAXY HOTEL

Create a requirements document and a Use Case Definition document and design a Windows application based on the case project shown in Figure 6-135:

The Galaxy Hotel asks you to write a Windows application that computes the occupancy rate of the hotel. Occupancy rate is a percentage that is equal to the number of rooms sold divided by the total number of rooms available. The hotel has seven floors. The user should use an InputBox function to respond to two questions about each floor: How many rooms are occupied on that floor? How many rooms on the floor are vacant? Display which floor you are asking about in each question. Display how many rooms are occupied and vacant on each floor in a ListBox object. After the user has entered all the information, display the following results: the total number of rooms at the hotel, the number of occupied rooms, and the number of vacant rooms. Also display the occupancy rate as a percentage, such as 61%. Nonnumeric values should not be accepted. Do not accept negative numbers. Publish the application after testing it.

FIGURE 6-135

Case Programming Assignments

9 ●●● BUYING A GAMING COMPUTER

Create a requirements document and a Use Case Definition document and design a Windows application based on the case project shown in Figure 6-136:

The newest gaming computer costs $5000 for a 31-inch screen, two 1 TB hard drives, a metallic case, and a blazing fast processor. Ten years ago, your grandmother gave you $2500. The money has been in a savings CD that earns compound interest of 7.5 percent annually. Write a Windows application that allows you to enter the amount of money in your savings account, the interest rate, and a number of years. Display a ListBox object for each year and the amount of money in the account at the end of that year. Determine whether you have saved enough money for the gaming computer. Nonnumeric and negative values should not be accepted. Debug and then publish the application. *Hint*: The formula for compound interest for one year is: Amount = Principal * (1 + Rate). For 10 years of compound interest, this formula should be executed 10 times with the principal increasing to the new amount each year.

FIGURE 6-136

CHAPTER 7

Using Procedures
and Exception Handling

OBJECTIVES

You will have mastered the material in this chapter when you can:

- Create a splash screen

- Pause the splash screen

- Add a ComboBox object to a Windows Form

- Write code for a SelectedIndexChanged event

- Understand procedures

- Code a Sub procedure

- Pass an argument to a procedure by value

- Pass an argument to a procedure by reference

- Code a Function procedure to return a value

- Create a class-level variable

- Catch an exception using a Try-Catch block

- Determine the order of exceptions in a Try-Catch block

Introduction

The programs you have written thus far in this course were relatively small applications. Most real-world software, however, solves more expansive problems. As an application grows, it is important to divide each facet of a problem into separate sections of code called **procedures**. By using the principle of divide and conquer to create procedures, the code becomes more manageable.

In previous programs you have learned about data verification to ensure the user enters valid data before the data is processed. To expand your knowledge of data verification, you need to understand exception handling using Try-Catch blocks, which can check for any error a user might commit. By managing exceptions using Try-Catch blocks, you build high-quality, robust applications.

Finally, one way to make your programs more professional is to display a splash screen while the full program loads. In this chapter, you will learn to design and write procedures, include Try-Catch blocks in your program, and create a splash screen.

Chapter Project

The sample program in this chapter displays two Windows forms and is more complex than previous applications. A travel agent has requested a Windows application that provides pricing information for an island water-sports company named Ocean Tours. The purpose of the application is to display the pricing information for water sports at different island locations. Ocean Tours is located in Aruba, Jamaica, and Key West. Each island specializes in different water sports. The table in Figure 7-1 shows the available tours for each island, the length of the tour, and the tour cost.

Location	Tour Type	Tour Length	Tour Cost
Aruba	Deep Sea Fishing	8 hours	$199
	Kayaking	2 hours	$89
	Scuba	3 hours	$119
	Snorkeling	4 hours	$89
Jamaica	Glass Bottom Boat	2 hours	$39
	Parasailing	2 hours	$119
	Snorkeling	3 hours	$59
Key West	Deep Sea Fishing	4 hours	$89
	Glass Bottom Boat	2 hours	$29
	Scuba	3 hours	$119
	Snorkeling	3 hours	$59

FIGURE 7-1

The program begins with an opening screen called a splash screen. In Figure 7-2, the splash screen displays the company name and image logo for approximately five seconds.

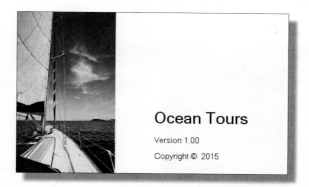

FIGURE 7-2

After the splash screen closes, the main form of the application opens and requests that the user select the island location. When the user taps or clicks the ComboBox arrow, the three island locations of Aruba, Jamaica, and Key West appear in the drop-down list, as shown in Figure 7-3.

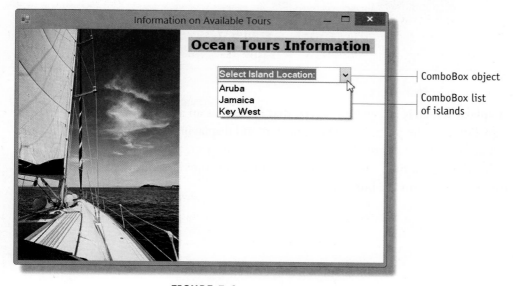

FIGURE 7-3

After the user selects the island location, the Windows form displays form controls that request the number of guests in the party and the type of tour. The user enters the number of guests, selects the type of tour she wants, and then taps or clicks the Find Cost of Tour button. As shown in Figure 7-4, the program displays the cost and length of the tour.

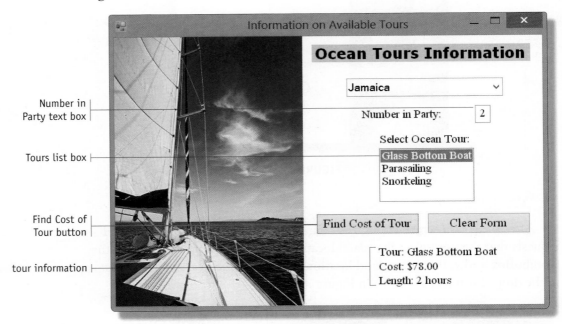

FIGURE 7-4

© Mbbirdy/E+/Getty Images

ONLINE REINFORCEMENT

To view a video of the process described in the preceding paragraphs, visit CengageBrain.com and navigate to the resources for this title. Tap or click the link for Chapter 7 and then navigate to Video 7-1. Turn on your speakers to listen to the audio walkthrough of the steps.

Create a Splash Screen

A **splash screen** is an opening screen that appears as an application is loading, signaling that the program is about to start and displaying an image and information to engage the user. In the Ocean Tours chapter project, the splash screen displays a sailboat image, a title, the application version, and copyright information (see Figure 7-2 on the previous page).

Visual Basic provides a generic splash screen template you can add to your project with or without modification. You can change the generic graphic on the splash screen by changing the BackgroundImage property on the Properties window. To use the generic splash screen, you can complete the following steps:

STEP 1   Create a Windows application named Ocean Tours. Name the form frmTours. Tap or click PROJECT on the menu bar and then tap or click Add New Item on the PROJECT menu. Scroll down to view Splash Screen.

The Add New Item dialog box is displayed (Figure 7-5).

Add New Item dialog box

FIGURE 7-5

STEP 2   In the Add New Item dialog box, select Splash Screen in the center pane.

The Splash Screen template is selected (Figure 7-6).

FIGURE 7-6

STEP 3   Tap or click the Add button in the Add New Item dialog box.

A form preconfigured by Visual Studio as a splash screen opens as a new tab named SplashScreen1.vb[Design] in the Design window (Figure 7-7). The splash screen can be customized with different graphics and text to suit an application.

tab for Splash
Screen form

click to select
Splash Screen form

preconfigured
Splash Screen

Solution
Explorer
window

Ocean Tours

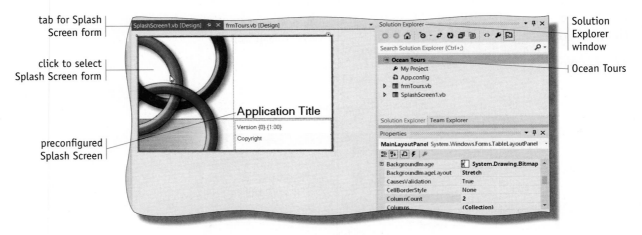

FIGURE 7-7

STEP 4   Tap or click the left side of the splash screen form to select it. To set the application to display the splash screen first, press and hold or right-click Ocean Tours in the Solution Explorer.

The splash screen form is selected (Figure 7-8). A shortcut menu opens.

Splash Screen
form selected

shortcut menu

Properties
command

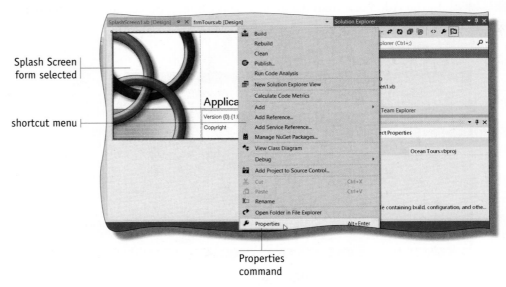

FIGURE 7-8

STEP 5   Tap or click Properties on the shortcut menu. Scroll down until the Splash screen option is displayed.

The Project Designer opens and displays the Application tab (Figure 7-9). The Project Designer provides a central location for managing project properties, settings, and resources. The Project Designer appears as a single window in the Visual Studio IDE. It contains a number of pages that are accessed through tabs on the left.

Project Designer | Application tab | tabs

Splash screen list arrow

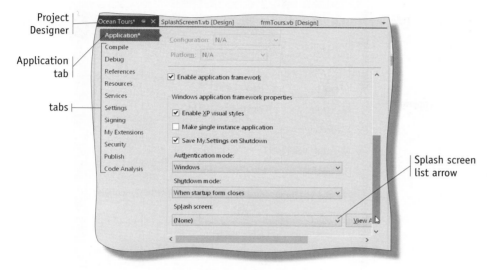

FIGURE 7-9

STEP 6   In the Windows application framework properties section, tap or click the Splash screen list arrow, and then tap or click SplashScreen1 to select it as the splash screen used for the project.

SplashScreen1 is selected in the Splash screen list (Figure 7-10).

SplashScreen1 selected as Splash screen

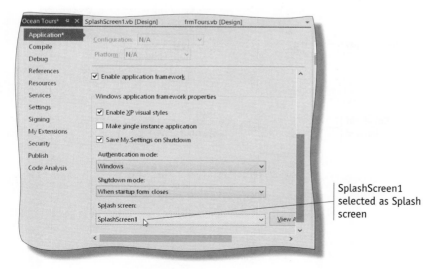

FIGURE 7-10

STEP 7 Scroll up and tap or click the Assembly Information button on the Project Designer to open the Assembly Information dialog box.

The Assembly Information dialog box opens (Figure 7–11).

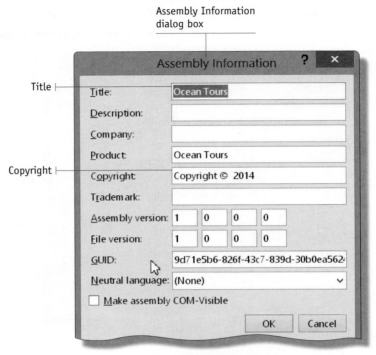

FIGURE 7-11

STEP 8 To customize the splash screen, if necessary, change the copyright to the present year. The numbers in the File version boxes can be changed as you update the application.

The copyright year is changed. The text on the splash screen form will not change until the application runs (Figure 7–12).

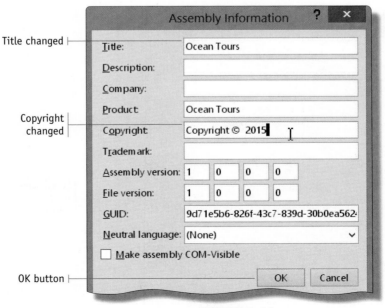

FIGURE 7-12

STEP 9   Tap or click the OK button on the Assembly Information dialog box. Close the Ocean Tours* Project Designer window. To change the predefined image, first make sure you have the Ocean.jpg picture (available on CengageBrain.com) and that you stored the image in a location you remember. Then, tap or click the SplashScreen1.vb [Design] tab. Tap or click the left side of the splash screen, making sure to select the entire splash screen form. The Properties window should identify MainLayoutPanel if you have selected the entire splash screen form. Tap or click to the right of the BackgroundImage property in the Properties window, and then tap or click the ellipsis button. In the Select Resource dialog box, tap or click the Project resource file radio button, if necessary. Import the Ocean.jpg picture by tapping or clicking the Import button in the Select Resource dialog box and selecting the Ocean.jpg image from the location where you stored it. Tap or click the OK button in the Select Resource dialog box.

The splash screen background image changes from the predefined image to the Ocean.jpg image (Figure 7-13).

SplashScreen1.vb [Design] tab

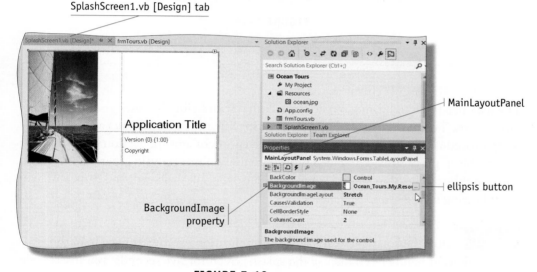

MainLayoutPanel

ellipsis button

BackgroundImage property

FIGURE 7-13

© Mbbirdy/E+/Getty Images

STEP 10 Run the application by tapping or clicking the Start Debugging button on the Standard toolbar.

The application begins to run. The splash screen appears for a moment and immediately closes (Figure 7-14). The amount of time the splash screen is displayed is based on the time needed to open the main form.

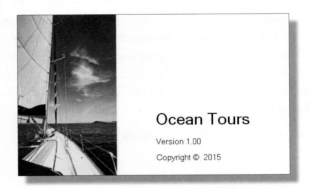

Ocean Tours

Version 1.00

Copyright © 2015

FIGURE 7-14

© Mbbirdy/E+/Getty Images

Pause the Splash Screen

The user needs enough time to read the splash screen before it closes and the main form opens. To pause the splash screen for a specific time period, you can call the Sleep procedure. In fact, you can pause the execution of any application by calling the Thread.Sleep procedure. The Sleep procedure uses an integer value that determines how long the application should pause. To pause the splash screen, you can complete the following steps:

STEP 1 After the splash screen loads, the application executes any code in the form load event handler. To display the splash screen for five seconds, you insert code that calls the Sleep procedure in the form load event handler. To open the code window and the form load event handler, double-tap or double-click the background of the frmTours Windows Form object in the Design window.

The frmTours_Load event handler opens in the code window (Figure 7-15).

frmTours_Load
event handler

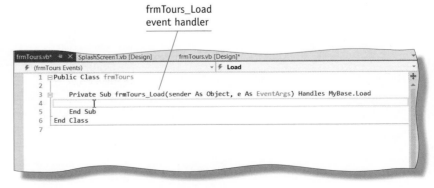

FIGURE 7-15

STEP 2 Tap or click inside the frmTours_Load event handler. Type `Threading.` (with an ending period) to have IntelliSense display a list of possible entries. If necessary, type `T` to select Thread from the IntelliSense list. Type `.S` to select Sleep from the IntelliSense list. Type `(5000)`.

The call for the Sleep procedure is entered (Figure 7-16). When the program runs and the frmTours_Load event is executed, the Sleep procedure suspends the execution of the application for 5000 milliseconds (5 seconds). This means that while the splash screen is displayed, the form will not be loaded for five seconds. You can increase the number of milliseconds if you want a longer pause.

Sleep procedure call   5000 milliseconds

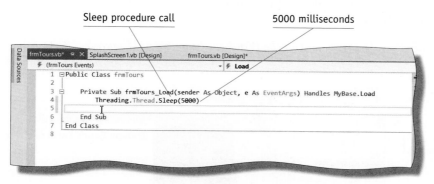

FIGURE 7-16

Add a ComboBox Object

The Ocean Tours sample program requires a new type of object, called a ComboBox object, to determine which island the user will select for touring (Figure 7-17).

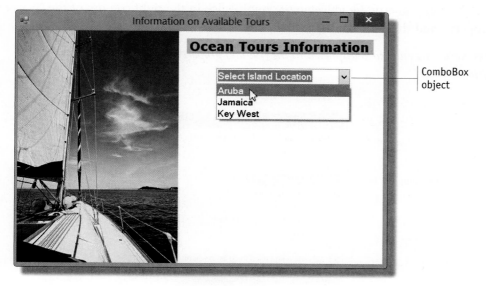

FIGURE 7-17

© Mbbirdy/E+/Getty Images

A ComboBox object consists of two parts. The top part is a text box that allows the user to enter text. The second part is a list box; when the user taps or clicks the arrow, the list box displays a list of items from which the user can select one item. To save space on a form, you can use a ComboBox object because the full list is not displayed until the user taps or clicks the list arrow. The prefix for the ComboBox object (Name) property is cbo. To place a ComboBox object on a Windows Form object, you can complete the following steps:

STEP 1   Drag the ComboBox .NET component from the Common Controls category of the Toolbox to the approximate location where you want to place the ComboBox object.

The ComboBox object is placed on the Windows Form object (Figure 7-18).

FIGURE 7-18

STEP 2   With the ComboBox object selected, scroll in the Properties window to the (Name) property. Double-tap or double-click in the right column of the (Name) property, and then enter the name `cboIsland`.

The name you entered is displayed in the (Name) property in the Properties window (Figure 7-19).

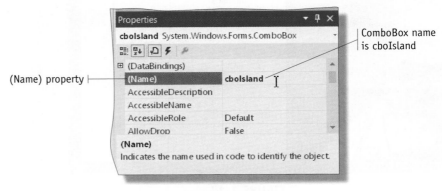

FIGURE 7-19

STEP 3   In the Properties window, scroll to the Text property. Tap or click to the right of the Text property and enter `Select Island Location:` to specify the text that appears in the combo box. Resize the ComboBox object as needed to display the data in the box.

The Text property is changed to the instructions to select an island location (Figure 7-20).

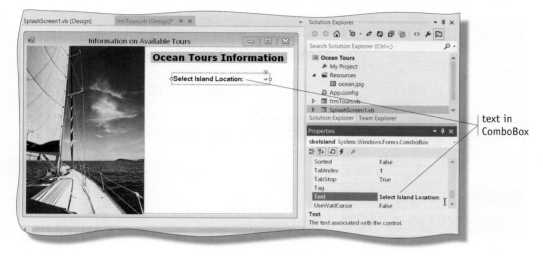

FIGURE 7-20

STEP 4   In the Properties window, scroll to the Items property, and then tap or click to the right of the Items property on the word (Collection). Tap or click the ellipsis button. The String Collection Editor dialog box opens. Enter the island locations `Aruba` (press ENTER), `Jamaica` (press ENTER), and `Key West`.

The three items for the ComboBox list are shown in the String Collection Editor dialog box (Figure 7-21).

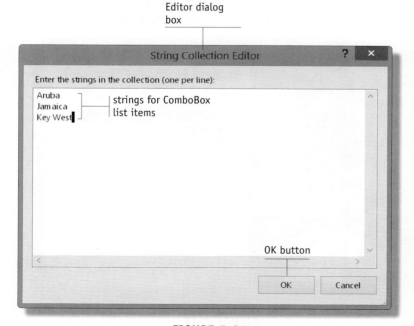

FIGURE 7-21

STEP 5   In the String Collection Editor dialog box, tap or click the OK button. Tap or click the Start Debugging button on the Standard toolbar to run the application. Tap or click the list arrow on the right side of the ComboBox object to view the contents. You can select a choice from the list.

The list in the ComboBox object contains the names previously entered in the String Collection Editor dialog box (Figure 7-22). The user can select one of the items in the list.

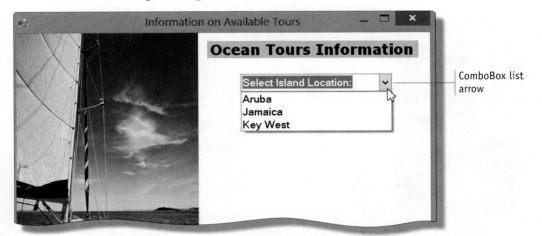

© Mbbirdy/E+/Getty Images

FIGURE 7-22

Determine the ComboBox Selected Index

To determine the cost of the tour selected in the Ocean Tours sample program, the user first selects the island location from the ComboBox object list. Code for the program must determine both that a value was selected and which one was selected. When the user selects an item in the ComboBox object list, the **SelectedIndex** property of the ComboBox object is assigned a number that represents the selected item. These numbers are a zero-based index, which means it begins with zero. For example, if the user selects Aruba, as shown in Figure 7-23, the index of 0 is the SelectedIndex for the ComboBox object. This index number can be assigned to an Integer data type variable.

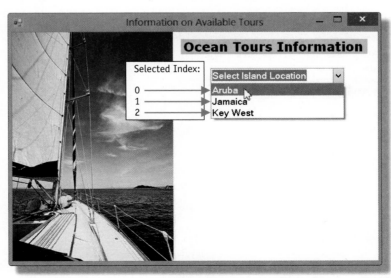

FIGURE 7-23

© Mbbirdy/E+/Getty Images

If the user has not made a selection, the SelectedIndex property is set to -1. To assign the item that the user selects using the SelectedIndex property, you can use a statement as shown in Figure 7-24.

```
32              intIslandChoice = cboIsland.SelectedIndex()
```

FIGURE 7-24

Handle SelectedIndexChanged Events

In the Ocean Tours application, the user's first action is to select the vacation island location. When the application opens, the user views the main title and a ComboBox object named cboIsland, as shown in Figure 7-25.

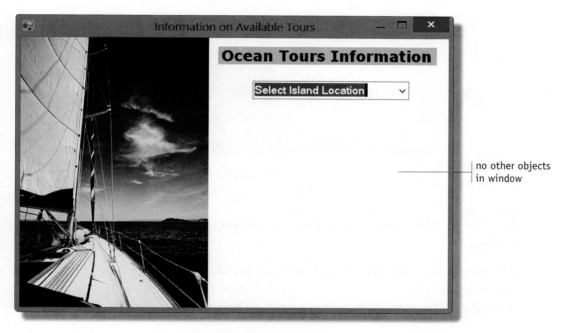

Ocean Tours Information

Select Island Location

no other objects in window

FIGURE 7-25

Notice that a Button object is not displayed in the window shown in Figure 7-25. When the user selects the island location, the application displays other objects on the form that request the number of people in the party and the list of possible tour choices for the selected island. Instead of using a button click event to begin this process, another type of event handler called the **SelectedIndexChanged** event handler is executed when the user selects the island location of the tour. The SelectedIndexChanged event is triggered by the user selecting an item in the ComboBox object because the selected index in the ComboBox object is changed when the user makes a selection. To create a SelectedIndexChanged event, you can complete the following steps:

STEP 1   Select the ComboBox object named cboIsland on the Windows Form object.

The cboIsland ComboBox object is selected on the form (Figure 7-26).

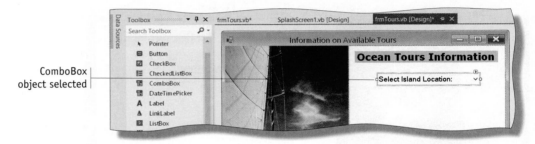

ComboBox object selected

FIGURE 7-26

© Mbbirdy/E+/Getty Images

STEP 2   Double-tap or double-click the ComboBox object, and then close the Toolbox.

The code window is opened and the code generated by Visual Studio for the SelectedIndex-Changed event handler is displayed (Figure 7-27). Within the event handler, you can write any code that should be executed when the user makes a selection in the cboIsland ComboBox object.

cboIsland _ SelectedIndexChanged event handler

FIGURE 7-27

By executing an event handler when the user selects a particular item in the cboIsland ComboBox object, the program works efficiently without multiple user taps or clicks. Many objects, such as the ListBox and DropDownList objects, can be used in the same manner as the ComboBox object with a SelectedIndexChanged event handler.

Procedures

The Ocean Tours application is a larger and more complex program than those in previous chapters. Because the code for each event handler will be long, you should divide the code into smaller parts, each of which completes a specific task for the event handler. It is easier to deal with a larger program if you can focus on code that accomplishes a single task.

When a program is broken into manageable parts, each part is called a **procedure**. A procedure is a named set of code that performs a given task. In previous programs you have called procedures, such as the Clear procedure and the ToString procedure that have been written by the developers of Visual Studio. In the Ocean Tours program in this chapter, you will both write and call procedures.

Visual Basic provides two types of procedures: Sub procedures and Function procedures. The following sections explain these two types of procedures and how to code them.

How is breaking your programs into procedures like taking a detour on a highway?
A Sub procedure call is like a detour on the highway. After the Sub procedure is completed, control returns to the calling procedure. It is much easier to debug a smaller set of statements in a procedure than in a large program.

CONSIDER THIS

Code a Sub Procedure

A **Sub procedure** is a procedure that completes its task but does not return any data to the calling procedure. A Sub procedure in Visual Basic 2012 is defined by using the Sub keyword. A **Sub** procedure is the series of Visual Basic statements enclosed by the Sub and End Sub statements. Each time the Sub procedure is called, its statements are executed, starting with the first executable statement after the Sub statement and ending with the first End Sub statement. A Sub procedure is called with a statement consisting of the procedure name and a set of parentheses in the form of a **procedure call**, as shown in Figure 7-28.

HEADS UP

The word *Private* before the Sub keyword specifies that the Sub procedure can be called only by code within the class where the Sub procedure is located. For Sub procedures that perform tasks required only within the class, you should use the Private keyword.

IN THE REAL WORLD

You can create your own Sub procedures to perform specific or repeated tasks. Sub procedures are not triggered by tapping or clicking a button or in reaction to an event. Sub procedures must be called within the code.

General Format: Procedure Call

The procedure call is made:

```
ProcedureName()
```

The **procedure declaration** that begins the Sub procedure has the form:

```
Private Sub ProcedureName()

    ' Line(s) of code

End Sub
```

FIGURE 7-28

In the Ocean Tours application, users can select ocean tours for each island. Based on the user's selection of an island location, the ListBox object in Figure 7-29 is filled with the various water tours that are available. For example, if the user selects Aruba, tours for Deep Sea Fishing, Kayaking, Scuba, and Snorkeling are displayed in the ListBox object.

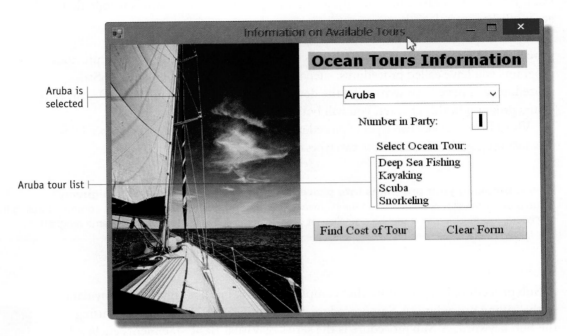

Aruba is selected

Aruba tour list

FIGURE 7-29

© Mbbirdy/E+/Getty Images

The items in the ListBox object are different based on the island selected. Figure 7-30 shows the code in the SelectedIndexChanged event handler that calls a Sub procedure to fill in the items in the ListBox object based on the island location selected by the user.

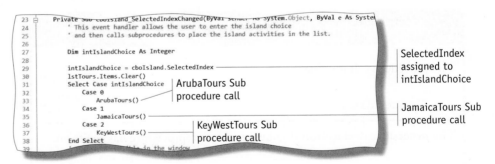

```
23   Private Sub cboIsland_SelectedIndexChanged(ByVal sender As System.Object, ByVal e As System
24       ' This event handler allows the user to enter the island choice
25       ' and then calls subprocedures to place the island activities in the list.
26
27       Dim intIslandChoice As Integer
28
29       intIslandChoice = cboIsland.SelectedIndex
30       lstTours.Items.Clear()
31       Select Case intIslandChoice
32           Case 0
33               ArubaTours()
34           Case 1
35               JamaicaTours()
36           Case 2
37               KeyWestTours()
38       End Select
39                              in the window
```

SelectedIndex assigned to intIslandChoice

ArubaTours Sub procedure call

JamaicaTours Sub procedure call

KeyWestTours Sub procedure call

FIGURE 7-30

In Figure 7-30 on the previous page, the selected index for the cboIsland ComboBox is assigned to the Integer variable named intIslandChoice. Then, in the Select Case statement, the appropriate Sub procedure is called based on the island the user selected. When the selected index is equal to zero, the user selected the first item in the ComboBox list, which is Aruba, so the ArubaTours Sub procedure is called. Notice that the name of the Sub procedure is specified with open and closed parentheses. As you learned previously, the Visual Basic compiler recognizes a procedure call by the parentheses.

The ArubaTours Sub procedure code is shown in Figure 7-31.

```
58     Private Sub ArubaTours()
59          ' This procedure fills in the possible ocean tours for Aruba
60          lstTours.Items.Add(_strDeepSeaFishing)
61          lstTours.Items.Add(_strKayaking)
62          lstTours.Items.Add(_strScuba)
63          lstTours.Items.Add(_strSnorkeling)
64
65     End Sub
```

FIGURE 7-31

In the code shown in Figure 7-31, the string values for the types of tours available on Aruba are added as items in the lstTours ListBox object. Notice that the String variables contain an underscore as the first character. You will recall that this designation identifies the variables as class variables that can be referenced in any procedure within the class.

In Figure 7-30, if the SelectedIndex value is 1, the Jamaica Sub procedure is called, and if the SelectedIndex value is 2, the Key West Sub procedure is called. Each Sub procedure adds items to the lstTours ListBox object, depending on what tours are available on each island.

A Sub procedure call may be used within a loop, If statements, or even Select Case statements, as shown in Figure 7-30. When a Sub procedure is called, the program gives control to the called Sub procedure and executes the lines of code within it. After the Sub procedure has completed its execution, program control returns to the calling procedure and program execution resumes in the calling procedure.

Pass Arguments

Earlier chapters defined and used the term *scope*, and explained that variables declared within a procedure are limited in scope to their procedure. Code outside a procedure cannot interact with the variables declared within another procedure.

When a procedure is called, however, the call statement can pass an argument to the called procedure. You have seen this in previous chapters when you passed a string value to the ToInt32 procedure to convert the string value to an integer value (Figure 7-32).

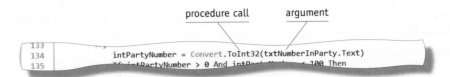

procedure call   argument

```
133
134       intPartyNumber = Convert.ToInt32(txtNumberInParty.Text)
135       If intPartyNumber > 0 And intP...    < 100 Then
```

FIGURE 7-32

In Figure 7-32, the argument is contained within parentheses. In this example, the argument is the Text property of the txtNumberInParty TextBox object.

In many applications, passing variables to another procedure is essential because the called procedure requires the value(s) in order to complete its processing. For example, in Figure 7-33, the btnDaysOfWeek_Click event determines whether a certain day of the week is part of the work week or the weekend. When the Weekday Sub procedure is called, a variable named intNumericDayOfWeek is passed to the Weekday Sub procedure because it must know the numeric day in order to perform its processing.

```
20      Private Sub btnDaysOfWeek_Click(ByVal sender As System.Object, ByVal e As System. ↙
        EventArgs) Handles btnDaysOfWeek.Click
21          Dim intNumericDayOfWeek As Integer
22
23          intNumericDayOfWeek = Convert.ToInt32(txtDay.Text)
24          Weekday(intNumericDayOfWeek)
25          MsgBox("Have a Great Week!", "Goodbye")  ◄
26      End Sub
27
28      Private Sub Weekday(ByVal intDay As Integer)
29        ► If intDay = 1 Or intDay = 7 Then
30              lblDisplayDay.Text = "Weekend"
31          End If
32          If intDay >= 2 And intDay <= 6 Then
33              lblDisplayDay.Text = "Weekday"
34          End If
35      End Sub
```

FIGURE 7-33

In Figure 7-33 on the previous page, the variable named intNumericDayOfWeek is passed to the Weekday Sub procedure by the calling statement on line 24. The value in the intNumericDayOfWeek variable should be 1 for Sunday, 2 for Monday, 3 for Tuesday, 4 for Wednesday, 5 for Thursday, 6 for Friday, and 7 for Saturday.

When a value is passed to a Sub procedure, its declaration, which identifies the name of the Sub procedure, also must contain an entry that defines the argument for use within the Sub procedure. In the Weekday Sub procedure in Figure 7-33, the parentheses following the Sub procedure name on line 28 contain the command ByVal intDay as Integer. This entry defines an Integer variable name (intDay) for use within the Sub procedure.

Visual Basic treats variables passed from a calling procedure to a called procedure in one of two ways: ByVal or ByRef. The following sections explain these two methods.

Pass Arguments by Value (ByVal)

When an argument is passed ByVal, it means the Sub procedure has access to the value of the passed argument, but does not actually reference the variable declared in the calling procedure. Instead, the value is copied into a variable whose name is specified in the Sub procedure declaration statement. For example, in Figure 7-33 the argument is passed ByVal, so the value in intNumericDayOfWeek is copied to the variable defined in the procedure declaration of the called Sub procedure (intDay).

The intDay variable contains the value passed from the calling procedure only as long as the called Sub procedure has processing control. When the Sub procedure has completed processing and passes control back to the calling procedure, the variable is lost. If the Sub procedure is called again, the variable is created again as a new variable with no preexisting value. So, you can consider the variable defined in the Sub procedure declaration as a temporary variable that exists only during processing within the Sub procedure when the argument is passed ByVal.

The temporary variable can be given any name, including the name of the variable in the calling procedure, but most developers use different names to avoid confusion. Notice that the name used in the calling procedure is intNumericDayOf-Week and the name used in the Sub procedure for the temporary variable is intDay.

When the argument is passed ByVal, the Sub procedure code can change the value in the temporary variable and use it in any manner required. The original value of the variable in the calling procedure is not affected because the value is copied into the temporary Sub procedure variable and the variable in the calling procedure is never referenced in the Sub procedure.

ByVal is the default option for all passed arguments. The keyword ByVal is added automatically if you do not enter it when you code the Sub procedure declaration.

The code in Figure 7-34 illustrates the fact that the Sub procedure can change the passed value, but that value is not changed in the calling procedure when the value is passed ByVal.

```
22    Private Sub btnShowMessages Click(ByVal sender As System.Object, ByVal e As System.↙
      EventArgs) Handles btnShowMessages.Click
23        Dim strMessage As String
24
25        strMessage = "The Original Welcome Message"
26        MsgBox(strMessage, ,"First Message")
27        DisplayMessage(strMessage)
28        MsgBox(strMessage, ,"Fourth Message")
29    End Sub
30
31    Private Sub DisplayMessage(ByVal strShowMessage As String)
32        MsgBox(strShowMessage, ,"Second Message")
33        strShowMessage = "The Changed Welcome Message"
34        MsgBox(strShowMessage, ,"Third Message")
35    End Sub
36 End Class
```

FIGURE 7-34

The output for the code in Figure 7-34 is shown in Figure 7-35.

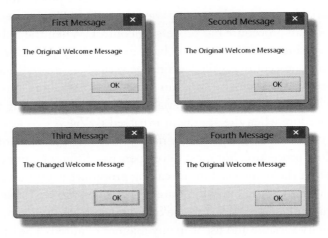

FIGURE 7-35

Figure 7-35 shows that the DisplayMessage Sub procedure in Figure 7-34 changed the message. The third message box displays this changed message: "The Changed Welcome Message". When the Sub procedure is finished and control is passed back to the calling procedure, however, the value in the strMessage variable is passed to the Sub procedure but is not changed, as shown in the Fourth Message window.

You can call the same Sub procedure repeatedly, as shown in Figure 7-36 on the next page. The Sub procedure DisplayMessage is called once and the Square Sub procedure is called three times. Notice that either literals or variables can be passed to a Sub procedure.

```
23        Private Sub btnSquare_Click(ByVal sender As System.Object, ByVal e As System.
          EventArgs) Handles btnSquare.Click
24
25            Dim decNum As Decimal
26
27            decNum = 3.3
28            DisplayMessage()
29            Square(7.9)
30            Square(4.0)
31            Square(decNum)
32
33        End Sub
34
35        Private Sub Square(ByVal decValue As Decimal)
36            lstResult.Items.Add("The square of " & decValue & " is " & _
37              (decValue * decValue))
38
39        End Sub
40
41        Private Sub DisplayMessage()
42            lstResult.Items.Add("Squares:")
43        End Sub
```

FIGURE 7-36

After executing the code in Figure 7-36, the ListBox object would contain the values shown in Figure 7-37.

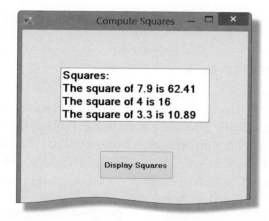

FIGURE 7-37

Pass Arguments by Reference (ByRef)

When an argument is passed ByVal, it means the Sub procedure has access to the value of the passed argument, but does not actually reference the variable declared in the calling procedure. Instead, the value is copied into a variable whose name is specified in the Sub procedure declaration statement. As Figure 7-33 on page 476 shows, because the argument is passed ByVal, the value in intNumericDayOfWeek is copied to the variable defined in the procedure declaration of the called Sub procedure (intDay).

Passing a value by reference allows code in the Sub procedure to modify the contents of the variable that is being passed because when you use ByRef, you are passing a reference to the variable that holds the value instead of the value itself, as when you use ByVal. Thus, if a Sub procedure changes the value of a variable passed ByRef, the original variable in the calling procedure is changed. You should select the option to pass a variable by reference if you intend to change the original value when it is passed to the Sub procedure.

In the code example in Figure 7-38, the calling procedure assigns the value Vincent Van Gogh to the strFavoriteArtist variable (line 49) and then passes the variable ByRef (line 55).

```
46      Private Sub btnDisplayMessage_Click(ByVal sender As System.Object, ByVal e As   ↙
        System.EventArgs) Handles btnDisplayMessage.Click
47          Dim strFavoriteArtist As String
48
49          strFavoriteArtist = "Vincent Van Gogh"
50          MsgBox("Favorite Artist is " & strFavoriteArtist, , "First Message")
51          DisplayMessage(strFavoriteArtist)
52          MsgBox("Favorite Artist is now " & strFavoriteArtist, , "Fourth Message")
53      End Sub
54
55      Private Sub DisplayMessage(ByRef strshowArtist As String)
56          MsgBox("Favorite Artist is " & strshowArtist, , "Second Message")
57          ' The artist name is changed
58          strshowArtist = "Paul Cezanne "
59          MsgBox("Favorite Artist is " & strshowArtist, , "Third Message")
60      End Sub
61 End Class
```

FIGURE 7-38

WATCH OUT FOR

Passing ByVal means the Sub procedure *cannot* change the original value. Passing ByRef means the Sub procedure *can* change the original value.

The Sub procedure changes the value of the passed variable to Paul Cezanne (line 58). Because the variable is passed by reference (ByRef), the value in the variable that is passed from the calling procedure is changed to Paul Cezanne. In the output shown in Figure 7-39, the changed value is displayed in the fourth message box when the btnDisplayMessage_Click event displays the last message box (line 52).

FIGURE 7-39

Pass Multiple Arguments

You can pass as many arguments as needed to a Sub procedure. If you have more than one argument, the variables are passed in the same order in which they appear in the procedure call statement.

Function Procedures

A **Function procedure** is similar to a Sub procedure except that a Function procedure returns a single value to the calling procedure. Just like a Sub procedure, you can pass variables to the Function procedure using ByVal and ByRef. A Function procedure uses the keyword Function (instead of the keyword Sub) in the procedure declaration. You also must specify a return data type in the procedure declaration to define the type of variable that is being returned to the calling procedure by the Function procedure. The Function procedure call has the syntax shown in Figure 7-40.

General Format: Function Procedure Call

The Function procedure call is made:

```
VariableName = FunctionProcedureName()
```

The **procedure declaration** that begins the Function procedure has the form:

```
Private Function FunctionProcedureName() as DataType

        ' Line(s) of code

        Return VariableName

End Function
```

FIGURE 7-40

The Private keyword is optional in the Function procedure declaration. If it is omitted, the default option is Public, which means any code in any class can reference the Function procedure. In many instances, Public access is not desirable, so the Private access modifier is used.

In the Function procedure call statement in Figure 7-40, the FunctionProcedureName on the right side of the assignment statement is replaced by the value that is returned from the Function procedure. That value then is assigned to the variable on the left side of the equal sign.

> **HEADS UP**
>
> You can exclude the receiving variable in the procedure call if you use the value immediately, as in lblResult.Text 5 "Price: " & FindPrice(intValue).ToString().

The Function procedure is different in appearance from a Sub procedure in the following ways:

- The Function procedure call has a receiving variable that is assigned the returned value from the Function procedure.
- The data type of the return value is listed in the procedure declaration.
- The keyword Return is used in the Function procedure to return a single value.

A Function procedure can pass only one value back to the calling procedure. The coding example in Figure 7-41 determines the gas mileage of a vehicle by dividing the number of miles driven by the number of gallons of gas used. The ComputeGasMileage Function procedure returns one value representing the gas mileage (Return statement on line 87). When the gas mileage value is returned, it is assigned to the receiving variable decMilesPerGallon (line 76 in the btnCompute_Click event).

```
69    Private Sub btnCompute_Click(ByVal sender As System.Object, ByVal e As System.   ↙
      EventArgs) Handles btnCompute.Click
70        Dim decMiles As Decimal
71        Dim decGallons As Decimal
72        Dim decMilesPerGallon As Decimal
73
74        decMiles = Convert.ToDecimal(txtMiles.Text)
75        decGallons = Convert.ToDecimal(txtGallons.Text)
76        decMilesPerGallon = ComputeGasMileage(decMiles, decGallons)
77        MsgBox("You are getting " & decMilesPerGallon.ToString("F1") & " miles per   ↙
      gallon", ,"MPG")
78
79    End Sub
80
81    Function ComputeGasMileage(ByVal decMiles As Decimal, ByVal decGallons As Decimal)
      As Decimal
82        Dim decMileage As Decimal
83
84        decMileage = decMiles / decGallons
85        ' The following statement returns control to the calling
86        ' procedure and returns the value in the decMileage variable.
87        Return decMileage
88
89    End Function
```

FIGURE 7-41

When writing a Function procedure, do not place any lines of its code after the Return statement because control returns to the calling procedure when the Return statement is executed.

It is best to use a Function procedure when you plan to return a value from a called procedure. In the Ocean Tours chapter project, a Function procedure returns the final cost of the selected tour, as shown in Figure 7-42 on the next page.

Calling Procedure

```
105                    Select Case intIslandChoice
106                        Case 0
107                            decTotalCost = ArubaFindCost(intTourChoice, _
108                                                  intGroupSize, intLengthOfTour)
```

Called Procedure

```
182        Private Function ArubaFindCost(ByVal intTourSelection As Integer, _
183         ByVal intGroupSize As Integer, ByRef intTourLength As Integer) As Decimal
184            ' This function calculates the cost of the tours to Aruba
185
186            Dim decTourCost As Decimal
187            Dim decFinalCost As Decimal
188            Dim decArubaDeepSeaCost As Decimal = 199D
189            Dim decArubaKayakCost As Decimal = 89D
190            Dim decArubaScubaCost As Decimal = 119D
191            Dim decArubaSnorkelCost As Decimal = 89D
192
193            Select Case intTourSelection
194                Case 0
195                    decTourCost = decArubaDeepSeaCost
196                    intTourLength = _intEightHours
197                Case 1
198                    decTourCost = decArubaKayakCost
199                    intTourLength = _intTwoHours
200                Case 2
201                    decTourCost = decArubaScubaCost
202                    intTourLength = _intThreeHours
203                Case 3
204                    decTourCost = decArubaSnorkelCost
205                    intTourLength = _intFourHours
206            End Select
207            decFinalCost = decTourCost * intGroupSize
208            Return decFinalCost
209
210        End Function
```

FIGURE 7-42

In Figure 7-42, the function call on line 107 calls the ArubaFindCost Function procedure. The arguments include the integer value of the user choice in the list box (intTourChoice), the integer value of the number in the party (intGroupSize), and a variable to contain the length of the chosen tour (intLengthOfTour).

WATCH OUT FOR

If you need to return more than one variable to the calling procedure, use ByRef. You can only return one value using the Return keyword.

In the called Function procedure, the tour choice and group size are passed ByVal. The length of the tour is passed ByRef. Therefore, when the Function procedure changes a value in the length of a tour, a change is made in the passed variable.

You can use Sub procedures and Function procedures in any Visual Basic application, including Windows applications, Web applications, and Visual Studio Tools for Office (VSTO) applications.

Create a Private Class-Level Variable

In previous programs within this book, you have defined class-level variables for use in multiple procedures or event handlers within the class. In those programs, the variable was declared using the Dim statement. You will recall that a class-level variable is defined within the class but outside any procedure. When a class-level variable is declared using the Dim statement, it can be referenced by any code within any procedure within the class.

It cannot, however, be referenced by any code outside the class. (In larger projects, multiple classes can be created.) When a class-level variable cannot be referenced outside the class in which it is declared, the variable is said to have Private access. Generally, it is a good programming practice to limit the scope of a class-level variable to the class in which it is declared.

By default, a class-level variable declared using the Dim statement has Private access. You also can declare class-level variables by using the Private keyword instead of the Dim keyword. The class-level variables used in the Ocean Tours program in this chapter are shown in Figure 7-43.

```
Public Class frmTours

    ' Class variables
    Private _intTwoHours As Integer = 2
    Private _intThreeHours As Integer = 3
    Private _intFourHours As Integer = 4
    Private _intEightHours As Integer = 8
    Private _strDeepSeaFishing As String = "Deep Sea Fishing"
    Private _strKayaking As String = "Kayaking"
    Private _strScuba As String = "Scuba"
    Private _strSnorkeling As String = "Snorkeling"
    Private _strGlassBottomBoat As String = "Glass Bottom Boat"
    Private _strParasailing As String = "Parasailing"
```

FIGURE 7-43

As you can see in Figure 7-43 on the previous page, each of the variables is declared using the Private keyword. All of the variables will have Private access, which means code in any procedure within the class can reference the variables but code in another class cannot.

Exception Handling

In previous programs in this book, you have learned how to ensure that users enter valid data, which is an essential task. You have used loops and If statements to check the values entered by users to ensure that the data does not cause an exception within the program.

Visual Basic provides another tool you can use to detect exceptions and take corrective action. This tool is called the **Try-Catch** set of statements. The Try keyword means "Try to execute this code." The Catch keyword means "Catch errors here." A Try-Catch block includes a statement or statements that are executed in the Try block and the statements that are executed in the Catch block(s) when an exception occurs. The format of the Try-Catch block is shown in Figure 7-44.

General Format: Try-Catch block

Try

     ' Try Block of Code – Executable statement(s) that may generate an exception.

Catch (filter for possible exceptions)

     ' Catch Block of Code for handling the exception

[Optional: Additional Catch blocks]

[Optional Finally]

     ' Optional statements that will always execute before finishing the Try block

End Try

FIGURE 7-44

To illustrate the use of a Try-Catch block, assume the value in one variable is being divided by the value in another variable. As you will recall, it is invalid to divide by zero. If a program tries to divide by zero, a DivideByZero exception will occur. Therefore, the division operation should be placed in a Try block and the Catch block should be set for a divide by zero exception. If the exception occurs, the code in Figure 7-45 will open a message box stating that an attempt was made to divide by zero.

```
91          Dim decNumerator As Decimal
92          Dim decDenominator As Decimal
93          Dim decDivision As Decimal
94
95          decNumerator = Convert.ToDecimal(txtNum.Text)
96          decDenominator = Convert.ToDecimal(txtDen.Text)
97          Try
98              decDivision = decNumerator / decDenominator
99          Catch Exception As DivideByZeroException
100             MsgBox("Attempt to divide by zero")
101         End Try
102
103     End Sub
104 End Class
```

FIGURE 7-45

In Figure 7-45, the division operation occurs in the statement on line 98. Note that the division operation is within the Try-Catch block, as defined by the Try keyword on line 97, the Catch keyword on line 99, and the End Try statement on line 101. You can define the particular class of exception in a Catch block by mentioning the name of the exception with the Catch keyword. In Figure 7-45, DivideByZero-Exception is included to catch the specific exception. If the value in decDenominator is zero when the division operation occurs, the code in the Catch block will display a message box with an error message. More importantly, the program will not be terminated. A Try-Catch block allows the program to handle exceptions elegantly so that the program does not abruptly terminate.

Different types of exceptions can occur. The table shown in Figure 7-46 identifies some of the possible exceptions.

Exception Type	Condition when Exception Occurs	Code Example
ArgumentNullException	A variable that has no value is passed to a procedure	`Dim strTerm As String` `lstDisplay.Items.Add(strTerm)`
DivideByZeroException	A value is divided by zero	`intResult = intNum / 0`
FormatException	A variable is converted to another type that is not possible	`strTerm = "Code"` `intValue = Convert.ToInt32(strTerm)`
NullReferenceException	A procedure is called when the result is not possible	`Dim strTerm As String` `intValue = strTerm.Length`
OverflowException	A value exceeds its assigned data type	`Dim intCost As Integer` `intCost = 58 ^ 4000000000`
SystemException	Generic	`Catches all other exceptions`

FIGURE 7-46

Figure 7-47 shows another example of a Try-Catch block, in which a very large number assigned to the variable intBaseValue is squared within a Try-Catch block. Notice that when the value intBaseValue is squared, the result will exceed the range for an Integer data type, causing an OverflowException. When the exception occurs within the Try block, the Catch block is called to deal with the OverflowException.

```
105          Dim intBaseValue As Integer
106          Dim intSquaredValue As Integer
107
108          intBaseValue = 50000000
109          Try
110              intSquaredValue = intBaseValue ^ 2
111          Catch Exception As OverflowException
112              'This catch block detects an overflow of the range of the data type
113              MsgBox("The value exceeds the range of the data type", , "Error")
114          End Try
```

FIGURE 7-47

Multiple Catch blocks can be defined for a single Try block, in which each Catch block will catch a particular class of exception. This approach is useful when you want to state which type of error occurred and tell users the mistake they made. It is best to order exceptions in Catch blocks from the most specific to the least specific. In other words, the Catch block that is most likely to be needed for the most common exception should appear first in a series of Catch statements. If an exception occurs during the execution of the Try block, Visual Basic examines each Catch statement within the Try-Catch block until it finds one whose condition matches that error. If a match is found, control transfers to the first line of code in the Catch block. If no matching Catch statement is found, the search proceeds to the next Catch statement in the Try-Catch block. This process continues through the entire code block until a matching Catch block is found in the current procedure. If no match is found, an exception occurs that stops the program.

In the Ocean Tours application, you need to validate the variable that is assigned the value of the number in the party. You want to make sure that the user enters a number, not a letter or other symbol, and that the number is from 1 to 99. The code in Figure 7-48 displays a Try-Catch block used within a Function procedure named ValidateNumberInParty. It uses three Catch blocks.

```
124   Private Function ValidateNumberInParty() As Boolean
125       ' This procedure validates the value entered for the number in party
126
127       Dim intPartyNumber As Integer
128       Dim blnValidityCheck As Boolean = False
129       Dim strNumberInPartyErrorMessage As String = _
130           "Please enter the number of people in your party (1-99)"
131       Dim strMessageBoxTitle As String = "Error"
132
133       Try
134           intPartyNumber = Convert.ToInt32(txtNumberInParty.Text)
135           If intPartyNumber > 0 And intPartyNumber < 100 Then
136               blnValidityCheck = True
137           Else
138               MsgBox(strNumberInPartyErrorMessage, , strMessageBoxTitle)
139               txtNumberInParty.Focus()
140               txtNumberInParty.Clear()
141           End If
142       Catch Exception As FormatException
143           MsgBox(strNumberInPartyErrorMessage, , strMessageBoxTitle)
144           txtNumberInParty.Focus()
145           txtNumberInParty.Clear()
146       Catch Exception As OverflowException
147           MsgBox(strNumberInPartyErrorMessage, , strMessageBoxTitle)
148           txtNumberInParty.Focus()
149           txtNumberInParty.Clear()
150       Catch Exception As SystemException
151           MsgBox(strNumberInPartyErrorMessage, , strMessageBoxTitle)
152           txtNumberInParty.Focus()
153           txtNumberInParty.Clear()
154       End Try
155
156       Return blnValidityCheck
157
158   End Function
```

FIGURE 7-48

The Boolean variable blnValidityCheck (line 128 in the code in Figure 7-48) is initially set to false, but it is set to true if an exception is not thrown (line 136); in other words, the Catch block is not executed if an exception is not thrown. This Boolean variable set to True then is returned to the calling procedure (line 156), which can continue its processing.

If an exception is thrown when the value in the Text property of the txtNumberInParty TextBox is converted to an integer (line 134), the statements below the Convert.ToInt32 statement will not be executed because control is passed to the appropriate Catch statement. The processing in each of the Catch blocks displays a message box with an error message, places the focus on the text box where the user enters the number in the party, and clears the text box.

When the processing in the Try-Catch block is complete, the Return statement on line 156 returns the value of the Boolean variable. If the data was valid, the Boolean variable contains the True value. If the data was not valid, the variable contains False because it initially was set to False (line 128) and its value was not changed by the Catch block processing.

An optional portion of the Try-Catch block is the Finally statement. The code in the Finally section always executes last, regardless of whether the code in the Catch blocks has been executed. Place cleanup code, such as code that closes files, in the Finally section. Code in the Finally section always is executed, no matter what happens in the Try-Catch blocks.

Program Design

As you have learned, the requirements document identifies the purpose of the program being developed, the application title, the procedures to be followed when using the program, any required equations and calculations, any conditions that must be tested, notes and restrictions that must be followed by the program, and any other comments that would be helpful to understanding the problem. The requirements document for the Ocean Tours application is shown in Figure 7-49.

REQUIREMENTS DOCUMENT

Date Submitted:	June 22, 2015
Application Title:	Ocean Tours Trip Selection
Purpose:	This Windows application allows a customer to view ocean tours available in the Caribbean islands.
Program Procedures:	From a Windows application, the user can select ocean tours and find out pricing information.
Algorithms, Processing, and Conditions:	1. The user first selects the island location. No other objects are displayed at this point.
	2. When the user selects an island, the following items are displayed in the window: the Number in Party text box, a custom list of the available tours on the chosen island, a button to find the cost of the tour, and a button to clear the form.
	3. The user enters the number of guests in her party.
	4. From the custom list of tours that are available for the chosen island, the user selects a tour.
	5. The total group price of the ocean tour is displayed.
Notes and Restrictions:	1. Validate numeric input with Try-Catch blocks.
	2. Use multiple procedures to break the application into manageable sections.
Comments:	1. The picture shown in the window is available on CengageBrain.com. The name of the picture is Ocean.
	2. A splash screen is shown for approximately five seconds before the main window is displayed.

FIGURE 7-49

The Use Case Definition for the application is shown in Figure 7-50.

USE CASE DEFINITION

1. A splash screen welcomes the user for approximately five seconds.
2. The user selects an island.
3. The program displays a text box for the number of people in the party and a list of available ocean tours for the selected island.
4. The user enters the number of people in the party, selects a tour, and taps or clicks the Find Cost of Tour button.
5. The program identifies the tour, calculates and displays the tour cost for the entire party, and specifies the length of the tour in hours.
6. The user can change any of the entries (island choice, number in party, and tour) and tap or click the Find Cost of Tour button to recalculate the tour cost.
7. The user can clear the form by tapping or clicking the Clear Form button.

FIGURE 7-50

© 2014 Cengage Learning

The table in Figure 7-51 contains information about available tour types for each island, the tour lengths, and the tour costs.

Location	Tour Type	Tour Length	Tour Cost
Aruba	Deep Sea Fishing	8 hours	$199
	Kayaking	2 hours	$89
	Scuba	3 hours	$119
	Snorkeling	4 hours	$89
Jamaica	Glass Bottom Boat	2 hours	$39
	Parasailing	2 hours	$119
	Snorkeling	3 hours	$59
Key West	Deep Sea Fishing	4 hours	$89
	Glass Bottom Boat	2 hours	$29
	Scuba	3 hours	$119
	Snorkeling	3 hours	$59

FIGURE 7-51

© 2014 Cengage Learning

Program Design When Using Sub and Function Procedures

As noted previously, larger programs often should be divided into procedures that perform specific tasks within the program. The goal of using procedures is to make the program easier to read, understand, and debug. The final result is a program that is more reliable and easier to maintain.

The developer must determine what code should be placed in a procedure. Several rules are important to follow when creating procedures in a program; otherwise, the use of procedures might make the program more difficult and more confusing. These rules include:

- The Sub procedure or the Function procedure should perform a single, defined task, such as checking the validity of a specific user input or calculating the cost of a tour on an island. Procedures that perform multiple tasks tend to become large and difficult to design and code.
- A Sub procedure or a Function procedure must perform reasonably substantial processing. It makes little sense to place a procedure call statement in a calling procedure and have the called procedure contain one or two program statements. In such cases, it would be easier and clearer just to place the statements in the calling procedure.
- When deciding whether a set of programming steps should be placed in a Sub procedure or a Function procedure, ask yourself the following questions: 1) Will the program be easier to read and understand if the code is placed in a separate procedure? 2) Does the proposed code perform a single task and does this task require more than three or four programming statements? 3) Can the Sub procedure or Function procedure perform its processing by receiving data as arguments, and by returning data either using the Return statement or by using ByRef arguments?

If the answers to these questions are *yes*, then the code is a good candidate for a procedure within your program.

In the Ocean Tours application, four event handlers are required: 1) Selected Index Change: This event handler is executed when the user selects an island location from a combo box; 2) Find Cost Button: This event handler is executed when the user taps or clicks the btnFindCost Button object; 3) Clear Button: This event handler is executed when the user taps or clicks the btnClear Button object; 4) frmTours Load Event: This event handler is executed when the Windows Form object is loaded.

Within each event handler, the event planning document is used to identify the tasks that must be accomplished. As each of the tasks is identified, you should ask the preceding questions. If it appears that the task should be accomplished in a procedure, the procedure must be included in the event planning document.

Event Planning Document

You will recall that the event planning document is a table that specifies which objects in the user interface will cause events, the action taken by the user to trigger each event, and the event processing that must occur. The event planning document for the program in this chapter must specify two forms and the events that occur for objects on each form. In addition, the tasks that must be accomplished for each event must be identified and decisions must be made for whether the tasks will be accomplished in a Sub or Function procedure. The event planning document for the Ocean Tours Trip Selection program is shown in Figure 7-52 and Figure 7-53.

EVENT PLANNING DOCUMENT

Program Name: Ocean Tours Trip Selection	Developer: Corinne Hoisington	Object: SplashScreen1	Date: June 22, 2015
OBJECT	**EVENT TRIGGER**	**EVENT PROCESSING**	
SplashScreen1_Load	Load	An opening splash screen appears with the company name, version number, and year of copyright	

FIGURE 7-52

EVENT PLANNING DOCUMENT

Program Name: Ocean Tours Trip Selection	Developer: Corinne Hoisington	Object: frmTours	Date: June 22, 2015
OBJECT	**EVENT TRIGGER**	**EVENT PROCESSING**	
cboIsland_SelectedIndexChanged	Select Index	Assign island selection to an Integer SUB (Aruba(), Jamaica(), KeyWest()): Based on the island selection, display a list of the available tours on the island Change Visible property to True for all objects on the form Clear the labels that provide trip information Set the focus on the Number in Party text box	
ArubaTours()	Sub procedure call	Display list of available tours (deep sea fishing, kayaking, scuba, and snorkeling) in list box	
JamaicaTours()	Sub procedure call	Display list of available tours (glass bottom boat, parasailing, snorkeling) in list box	
KeyWestTours()	Sub procedure call	Display list of available tours (deep sea fishing, glass bottom boat, scuba, snorkeling) in list box	

FIGURE 7-53 (continues)

Program Name: Ocean Tours Trip Selection	Developer: Corinne Hoisington	Object: frmTours	Date: June 22, 2015
OBJECT	**EVENT TRIGGER**	**EVENT PROCESSING**	

btnFindCost	Click	FUNCTION (ValidateNumberInParty): Validate that the value in the Number in Party text box is valid
		FUNCTION (ValidateTourSelection): Ensure that the user has selected a tour in the list box
		If the number in party is valid and a tour is selected:
		    Convert number in party to an integer
		    Change selected island index to integer
		    FUNCTION(ArubaFindCost, JamaicaFindCost, KeyWestFindCost):
		        Calculate cost based on island choice
		    Display tour, cost, and length
		Else display error message	

ValidateNumberInParty()	Function procedure call	Set Boolean indicator to False
		Convert number in party to integer
		If conversion valid
		    If number > 0 and < 100
		        Set Boolean indicator to True for valid number
		If conversion not valid
		    Catch format, overflow, and system exceptions
		    Display error message boxes
		    Place focus in Number in Party text box
		    Clear Number in Party text box
		Return Boolean indicator	

ValidateTourSelection()	Function procedure call	Convert tour selection index to integer
		If conversion successful
		    Place selected item string in ByRef variable
		    Set Boolean validity indicator to True
		Else Display error message box
		    Set Boolean validity indicator to False
		Return ocean tour selected index integer	

ArubaFindCost()	Function procedure call	If tour selected is deep sea fishing
		    Set cost to Aruba deep sea fishing for one person
		    Set length to Aruba deep sea fishing
		If tour selected is kayaking
		    Set cost to Aruba kayak for one person
		    Set length to Aruba kayak
		If tour selected is scuba
		    Set cost to Aruba scuba for one person
		    Set length to Aruba scuba
		If tour selected is snorkel
		    Set cost to Aruba snorkel for one person
		    Set length to Aruba snorkel
		Calculate cost of trip: cost * number in party
		Return cost of trip	

FIGURE 7-53 (continues)

Program Name: Ocean Tours Trip Selection	Developer: Corinne Hoisington	Object: frmTours	Date: June 22, 2015
OBJECT	**EVENT TRIGGER**	**EVENT PROCESSING**	

JamaicaFindCost()	Function procedure call	If tour selected is glass bottom boat
		  Set cost to Jamaica glass bottom boat for one person
		  Set length to Jamaica glass bottom boat
		If tour selected is parasail
		  Set cost to Jamaica parasail for one person
		  Set length to Jamaica parasail
		If tour selected is snorkel
		  Set cost to Jamaica snorkel for one person
		  Set length to Jamaica snorkel
		Calculate cost of trip: cost * number in party
		Return cost of trip	

KeyWestFindCost()	Function procedure call	If tour selected is deep sea fishing
		  Set cost to Key West deep sea fishing for one person
		  Set length to Key West deep sea fishing
		If tour selected is glass bottom boat
		  Set cost to Key West glass bottom boat for one person
		  Set length to Key West glass bottom boat
		If tour selected is scuba
		  Set cost to Key West scuba for one person
		  Set length to Key West scuba
		If tour selected is snorkel
		  Set cost to Key West snorkel for one person
		  Set length to Key West snorkel
		Calculate cost of trip: cost * number in party
		Return cost of trip	

btnClear	Click	Set Select Island cbo text to "Select Island Location" Clear text box, list, and labels Hide all objects except Select Island cbo	
frmTours_Load	Load	Set sleeping period to 5000 milliseconds	

FIGURE 7-53 (continued)

Design and Code the Program

After identifying the events and tasks within the events, the developer is ready to create the program. As you have learned, creating the program means designing the user interface and then entering Visual Basic statements to accomplish the tasks specified in the event planning document. As the developer enters the code, she also will implement the logic to carry out the required processing.

Guided Program Development

To design the user interface for the Ocean Tours application and enter the code required to process each event in the program, complete the steps on the following pages:

NOTE TO THE LEARNER

In the following activity, you should complete the tasks within the specified steps. Each of the tasks is accompanied by a Hint Screen. The purpose of the Hint Screen is to indicate where you should perform the activity in the Visual Studio window and to remind you which method to use. If you need further help completing a step, refer to the figure identified by *ref:*.

Guided Program Development

1

- **Create a New Windows Project** Open Visual Studio and then close the Start page. Tap or click the New Project button on the Standard toolbar. Begin a Windows Forms Application project and name the project `Ocean Tours`. Name the Form object `frmTours.vb`.

- **Add a New Item to the Project** Tap or click PROJECT on the menu bar and then tap or click Add New Item on the PROJECT menu *(ref: Figure 7-5)*.

- **Select Splash Screen as the New Item** Select the Splash Screen template. Tap or click the Add button *(ref: Figure 7-6)*.

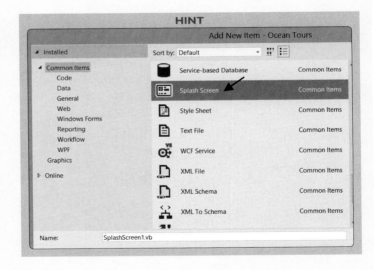

- **Select the Generic Splash Screen**
When the generic splash screen opens,
tap or click the left side of the screen
to select it *(ref: Figure 7-7)*.

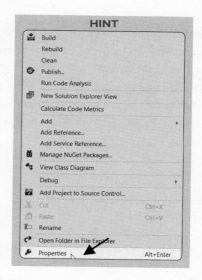

- **Prepare to Set the Contents of the Splash Screen** Press
and hold or right-click the application name Ocean Tours in
the Solution Explorer, and then tap or click Properties on the
shortcut menu to open the Project Designer window
(ref: Figure 7-8).

- **Set the Splash Screen** On the Application tab, scroll down
and tap or click the Splash screen list arrow to change the
setting of (None) to SplashScreen1 *(ref: Figure 7-10)*.

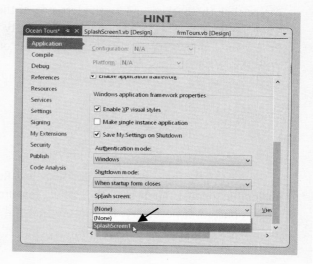

(continues)

- **Add Text to the Splash Screen** To change the text of the splash screen, tap or click the Assembly Information button in the Project Designer window *(ref: Figure 7-11)*.

- **Set the Assembly Information** In the Assembly Information dialog box, change the title to `Ocean Tours` and change the copyright to the current year *(ref: Figure 7-12)*. Tap or click the OK button to close the dialog box. Close the Properties window. The information on the Splash Screen form does not change. The changes appear when the application is executed.

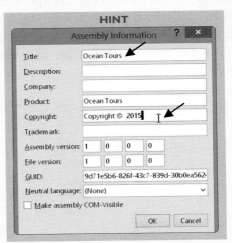

- **Change the Background Image** To customize the picture, tap or click the background on the left side of the splash screen and select the BackgroundImage property in the Properties window. Tap or click the ellipsis button *(ref: Figure 7-13)*.

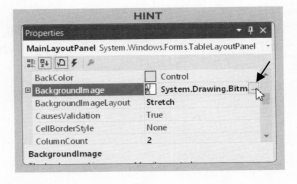

- **Select the Project Resource File** The Select Resource dialog box opens. Tap or click the Project resource file option button, if necessary, and ensure that the Resources. resx file is selected.

- **Select an Image File** Tap or click Import and select the image file Ocean.jpg, which is provided with your data files and is available on CengageBrain.com. Tap or click the OK button in the Select Resource dialog box.

The splash screen is designed (Figure 7-54).

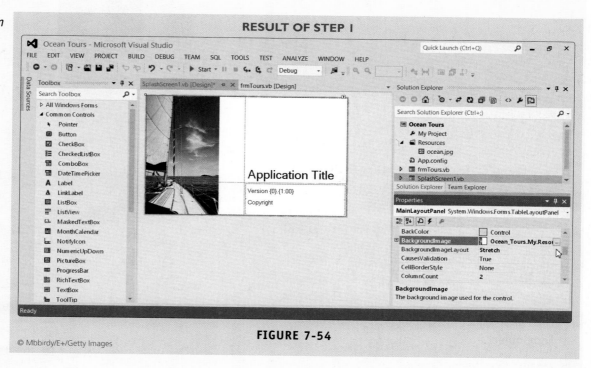

RESULT OF STEP 1

© Mbbirdy/E+/Getty Images

FIGURE 7-54

2

- **Assign a Title to the Form Object** With the Windows Form object selected, change its Text property to `Information on Available Tours`.

- **Add a Background Image** With the Windows Form object selected, tap or click the ellipsis button for the BackgroundImage property. Select the Ocean image in the Select Resource dialog box. Tap or click the OK button in the Select Resource dialog box.

- **Resize the Windows Form Object** Resize the Windows Form object to (700,490) to view the entire image.

(continues)

● **Add a Panel Object** Drag a Panel object from the
Containers category of the Toolbox to the portion of
the Windows Form object not covered by the image. Resize
the Panel object so it covers the white space where no
image is displayed.

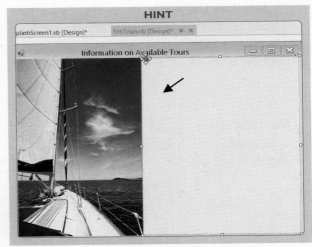

HINT

© Mbbirdy/E+/Getty Images

● **Change the Panel Object's BackColor to
Transparent** In the BackColor property for the
Panel object, tap or click the BackColor property
arrow, tap or click the Web tab if necessary, and
then tap or click Transparent on the Web palette.
Making the panel transparent allows all the objects
placed on the Windows Form object to be visible
but allows you to center and align objects within
the Panel object instead of the entire Windows
Form object.

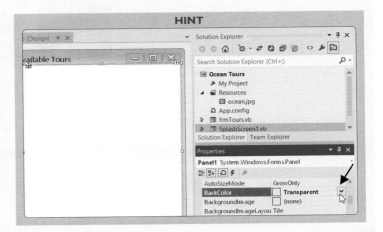

HINT

● **Add a Label and a ComboBox Object** Add a Label object
on the right side of the Form object. Change the Text
property to Ocean Tours Information. Name the
Label lblTitle. Change the font property to Verdana,
Bold, 14 points. Change the BackColor property of the Label
object to LightGray in the Web palette. The location of the
Label object can be (15,14). Add a ComboBox object under
the Label object. The location is (70,70). Name the ComboBox object cboIsland. Change the Text property to
Select Island Location:. Resize the ComboBox
object to see all the text *(ref: Figure 7-20)*. Change the font
size to 11 points.

HINT

- **Add the Terms in the Items Property** Enter the following terms in the Items property of the ComboBox object: `Aruba`, `Jamaica`, and `Key West` on separate lines *(ref: Figure 7-21).*

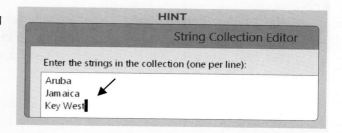

- **Add a Label Object** Drag a Label object from the Visual Basic Toolbox to the Form object. Place the Label object at location (90,119) within the Panel object. Change the Text property to `Number in Party:`. Name the Label object `lblParty`. Change the font size to 11 points.

- **Add a TextBox Object for the Number in Party** Drag a TextBox object from the Toolbox to the Panel object on the Windows Form object. Place the TextBox object at location (266,115). Resize the TextBox object to fit the length of approximately two numbers. Name the TextBox object `txtNumberInParty`. Change the font size to 11 points.

© Mbbirdy/E+/Getty Images

- **Add the Select Ocean Tour Label Object** Drag a Label object from the Toolbox to the Windows Form object. The location is (118,160). Change the Text property to `Select Ocean Tour:`. Name the Label object `lblSelect`. Change the font size to 11 points.

- **Add the Tours ListBox Object** Drag a ListBox object from the Toolbox to the Windows Form object. The location is (121,185). Name the ListBox `lstTours`. Change the font size to 11 points.

- **Add the Find Cost Button Object** Drag a Button object from the Toolbox to the Windows Form object. The location is (20,292). Name the Button object `btnFindCost` and change the Text property to `Find Cost of Tour`. Resize the button until the text is visible.

(continues)

● **Add the Clear Button Object** Drag another Button object from the Toolbox to the Windows Form object. The location is (197,292). Name the Button object `btnClear` and change the Text property to `Clear Form`.

● **Add a Label Object for the Tour Type** Drag a Label object from the Toolbox to the Windows Form object. The location is (115,346). Name the Label object `lblTourType`. Enter 10 Xs for the Text property.

● **Add a Label Object for the Cost** Drag a Label object from the Toolbox to the Windows Form object. The location is (115,370). Name this Label object `lblCost`. Enter 10 Xs for the Text property.

● **Add a Label Object for the Tour Length** Drag a Label object from the Toolbox to the Windows Form object. The location is (115,393). Name this Label object `lblLength`. Enter 10 Xs for the Text property.

● **Change the Font** Select all the objects on the form except lblTitle and change the font to Times New Roman, 11 points. Resize any objects as required so that the text is visible.

● **Set the Visible Properties** Change the Visible property to False for the following objects: lblParty, txtNumberIn-Party, lblSelect, lstTours, btnFindCost, btnClear, lblTourType, lblCost, and lblLength. These objects are not displayed until the island is selected.

● **Set the Accept Button** Tap or click the background of the Windows Form object on its title bar and change the AcceptButton property of the Button object to btnFindCost.

● **Set the Cancel Button** Tap or click the background of the Windows Form object on its title bar and change the CancelButton property of the Button object to btnClear.

Guided Program Development *continued*

The Form object frmTours is designed (Figure 7-55).

RESULT OF STEP 2

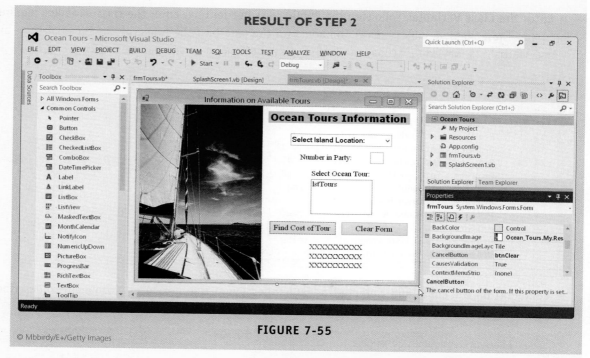

© Mbbirdy/E+/Getty Images

FIGURE 7-55

3

● **Code the Comments** Double-tap or double-click the cboIsland ComboBox object on the frmTours.vb [Design] tab to open the code window and create the cboIsland_SelectedIndexChanged event handler. Close the Toolbox. Tap or click before the first word in Public Class frmTours, and then press the ENTER key to create a blank line. Insert the first four standard comments. Insert the Option Strict On command following the comments to turn on strict type checking.

```
                                HINT
1  ☐ ' Program Name: Ocean Tours Trip Selection
2    | ' Author:       Corinne Hoisington
3    | ' Date:         June 22, 2015
4    | ' Purpose:      The Ocean Tours Trip Selection application determines the
5    | '               ocean tours available and calculates the cost of the tour.
6
7      Option Strict On
```

(continues)

● **Enter the Class Variables** Following the Public Class header line, enter the class variables required for the program. These class variables are: a) The hours for the length of the tours; b) The types of tours available (deep sea fishing, kayaking, scuba, snorkeling, glass bottom boat, and parasailing).

HINT

```
 9  ⊟Public Class frmTours
10
11        ' Class variables
12        Private _intTwoHours As Integer = 2
13        Private _intThreeHours As Integer = 3
14        Private _intFourHours As Integer = 4
15        Private _intEightHours As Integer = 8
16        Private _strDeepSeaFishing As String = "Deep Sea Fishing"
17        Private _strKayaking As String = "Kayaking"
18        Private _strScuba As String = "Scuba"
19        Private _strSnorkeling As String = "Snorkeling"
20        Private _strGlassBottomBoat As String = "Glass Bottom Boat"
21        Private _strParasailing As String = "Parasailing"
```

● **Comment on the cboIsland_SelectedIndexChanged Event Handler** Enter a comment to describe the purpose of the cboIsland_SelectedIndexChanged event handler.

HINT

```
22
23  ⊟    Private Sub cboIsland_SelectedIndexChanged(ByVal sender As System.Object, ByVal e As System.EventArgs) Handles cboIsland.SelectedInde
24            ' This event handler allows the user to enter the island choice
25            ' and then calls subprocedures to place the island activities in the list.
```

● **Code the Sub Procedure Calls to Place the Appropriate Tours in the List Box** When the user selects an island in the cboIsland ComboBox object, the SelectedIndexChanged event is triggered. In that event handler, the island choice indicated by the selected index must be changed to an integer. Then, based on that integer, the appropriate Sub procedure is called to place the correct tours in the lstTours list box. Write the code to obtain the selected index integer, clear the lstTours ListBox object of any previous entries, and then call the appropriate Sub procedure (ref: Figure 7-30).

HINT

```
27            Dim intIslandChoice As Integer
28
29            intIslandChoice = cboIsland.SelectedIndex
30            lstTours.Items.Clear()
31            Select Case intIslandChoice
32                Case 0
33                    ArubaTours()
34                Case 1
35                    JamaicaTours()
36                Case 2
37                    KeyWestTours()
38            End Select
```

• **Set the Visibility and Focus** After the user selects the island location from the ComboBox object and the event handler calls the Sub procedures to load the ListBox object with the correct tours, the objects on the Windows Form object must become visible. In addition, the Label objects for the tour's type, cost, and length must be cleared of the Xs placed in them during design. Finally, the focus should be set on the txtNumberInParty TextBox object. Enter the code to complete this processing.

```
                            HINT
39           ' Make items visible in the window
40           lblParty.Visible = True
41           txtNumberInParty.Visible = True
42           lblSelect.Visible = True
43           lstTours.Visible = True
44           btnFindCost.Visible = True
45           btnClear.Visible = True
46           lblTourType.Visible = True
47           lblCost.Visible = True
48           lblLength.Visible = True
49           ' Clear the labels
50           lblTourType.Text = ""
51           lblCost.Text = ""
52           lblLength.Text = ""
53           ' Set focus on number in party text box
54           txtNumberInParty.Focus()
55
56       End Sub
```

• **Code the Sub Procedures for Aruba Tour Options** After the first event handler is completed, the Sub procedures called by the event handler should be written. The event handler that handles the cboIsland_SelectedIndexChanged event calls three Sub procedures. Code the first referenced Sub procedure, which is called ArubaTours. To do so, tap or click below the End Sub statement for the event handler, press the ENTER key to insert a blank line, and then write the Sub procedure declaration. It begins with the word Private, followed by the word Sub and then the name of the Sub procedure. Press the ENTER key, write a comment that explains the purpose of the Sub procedure, and then write the statements that put the Aruba tours in the lstTours ListBox object *(ref: Figure 7-31)*.

```
                            HINT
57
58 ⊟   Private Sub ArubaTours()
59           ' This procedure fills in the possible ocean tours for Aruba
60           lstTours.Items.Add(_strDeepSeaFishing)
61           lstTours.Items.Add(_strKayaking)
62           lstTours.Items.Add(_strScuba)
63           lstTours.Items.Add(_strSnorkeling)
64
65       End Sub
```

(continues)

● **Code the Sub Procedures for the Jamaica and Key West Tour Options** In a similar manner, write the code for the Jamaica and Key West Sub procedures that place the appropriate tour names in the lstTours ListBox object.

HINT

```
66
67      Private Sub JamaicaTours()
68          'This procedure fills in the possible ocean tours for Jamaica
69          lstTours.Items.Add(_strGlassBottomBoat)
70          lstTours.Items.Add(_strParasailing)
71          lstTours.Items.Add(_strSnorkeling)
72
73      End Sub
74
75      Private Sub KeyWestTours()
76          'This procedure fills in the possible ocean tours for Key West
77          lstTours.Items.Add(_strDeepSeaFishing)
78          lstTours.Items.Add(_strGlassBottomBoat)
79          lstTours.Items.Add(_strScuba)
80          lstTours.Items.Add(_strSnorkeling)
81
82      End Sub
```

● **Initialize the btnFindCost_Click Event and Write the Event Handler Variables** Tap or click the frmTours.vb [Design] tab and then double-tap or double-click the Find Cost of Tour button to create the event handler for the button click event. The first step is to write a comment describing the purpose of the event handler. Then, code the variable declarations for the variables required in the event handler. These variables include: a) Integer variables for the group size, tour choice, island choice, and length of tour; b) Boolean variables to indicate the validity of the number in the party and the tour selection; c) A String variable to contain the name of the selected tour; d) A Decimal variable to contain the total cost of the selected tour. Write the code to create and initialize these variables.

HINT

```
84      Private Sub btnFindCost_Click(ByVal sender As System.Object, ByVal e As System.EventArgs) Handles btnFindCost.Click
85          ' This button event handler determines the cost of the ocean
86          ' tour and displays the tour, the cost, and the length
87
88          Dim intGroupSize As Integer
89          Dim blnNumberInPartyIsValid As Boolean = False
90          Dim blnTourIsSelected As Boolean = False
91          Dim intTourChoice As Integer
92          Dim strSelectedTour As String = ""
93          Dim intIslandChoice As Integer
94          Dim intLengthOfTour As Integer = 0
95          Dim decTotalCost As Decimal
```

- **Validate the User Input** The next steps are to call two Function procedures. The first procedure verifies that the value entered in the txtNumberInParty TextBox object is valid, and the second verifies that a tour was selected. Write the two Function calls for these Function procedures. The ValidateNumberInParty Function procedure returns a Boolean value indicating whether the number entered is valid (True) or not valid (False). The ValidateTourSelection Function procedure returns the number of the tour selected by the user. It also sets a Boolean value in the blnTourIsSelected Boolean variable to indicate if a tour has been selected (true) or not selected (False). This value is set because the blnTourIsSelected variable is passed to the Function procedure ByRef.

HINT

```
97        ' Call a function to ensure the number of people in the party is valid
98        blnNumberInPartyIsValid = ValidateNumberInParty()
99        ' Call a function to ensure a tour was selected
100       intTourChoice = ValidateTourSelection(blnTourIsSelected, strSelectedTour)
```

- **Code the Rest of the btnFindCost_Click Event** Upon return from the procedure calls, the btnFindCost_Click event handler must determine whether the number of people in a party is valid and that a tour was selected. If both are true, the Text property of the txtNumberInParty TextBox is converted to an integer value named intGroupSize. The Function procedures are passed three variables that are needed in the procedures. The variables intTourChoice and intGroupSize are passed by value because the values are not changed in the Function procedures. The variable intLengthOfTour is passed by reference because the value is changed in the Function procedures. The value returned from the Function procedures as the total cost of the tour is assigned to the variable decTotalCost. After the Function procedures are called, the event handler displays the selected tour type, cost, and length. Write the code to implement this processing.

HINT

```
101       ' If number of people and the tour selection are valid, calculate the cost
102       If (blnNumberInPartyIsValid And blnTourIsSelected) Then
103           intGroupSize = Convert.ToInt32(txtNumberInParty.Text)
104           intIslandChoice = cboIsland.SelectedIndex
105           Select Case intIslandChoice
106               Case 0
107                   decTotalCost = ArubaFindCost(intTourChoice, _
108                                             intGroupSize, intLengthOfTour)
109               Case 1
110                   decTotalCost = JamaicaFindCost(intTourChoice, _
111                                             intGroupSize, intLengthOfTour)
112               Case 2
113                   decTotalCost = KeyWestFindCost(intTourChoice, _
114                                             intGroupSize, intLengthOfTour)
115           End Select
116           ' Display the cost of the ocean tour
117           lblTourType.Text = "Tour: " & strSelectedTour
118           lblCost.Text = "Cost: " & decTotalCost.ToString("C")
119           lblLength.Text = "Length: " & intLengthOfTour.ToString() & " hours"
120       End If
121
122   End Sub
```

(continues)

Guided Program Development *continued*

● **Code the ValidateNumberInParty Function Procedure** The next step is to code the ValidateNumberInParty
Function procedure. Tap or click below the btnFindCost_Click event handler and enter the Function procedure declaration. The Function procedure returns a Boolean value that indicates whether the user entered a valid number.
The value must be an integer that is greater than 0 and less than 100. A Try-Catch block is used for the conversion
to an integer operation to catch any invalid data the user entered. Multiple Catch blocks are used to catch specific
exceptions. If an exception occurs, the error message is displayed in a message box, the focus is placed on the
txtNumberInParty TextBox object, and the value in the TextBox object is cleared. Write the code for this Function
procedure *(ref: Figure 7-48)*.

```
                                 HINT
124  ⊟       Private Function ValidateNumberInParty() As Boolean
125                ' This procedure validates the value entered for the number in party
126
127            Dim intPartyNumber As Integer
128            Dim blnValidityCheck As Boolean = False
129            Dim strNumberInPartyErrorMessage As String = _
130                "Please enter the number of people in your party (1-99)"
131            Dim strMessageBoxTitle As String = "Error"
132
133            Try
134                intPartyNumber = Convert.ToInt32(txtNumberInParty.Text)
135                If intPartyNumber > 0 And intPartyNumber < 100 Then
136                    blnValidityCheck = True
137                Else
138                    MsgBox(strNumberInPartyErrorMessage, , strMessageBoxTitle)
139                    txtNumberInParty.Focus()
140                    txtNumberInParty.Clear()
141                End If
142            Catch Exception As FormatException
143                MsgBox(strNumberInPartyErrorMessage, , strMessageBoxTitle)
144                txtNumberInParty.Focus()
145                txtNumberInParty.Clear()
146            Catch Exception As OverflowException
147                MsgBox(strNumberInPartyErrorMessage, , strMessageBoxTitle)
148                txtNumberInParty.Focus()
149                txtNumberInParty.Clear()
150            Catch Exception As SystemException
151                MsgBox(strNumberInPartyErrorMessage, , strMessageBoxTitle)
152                txtNumberInParty.Focus()
153                txtNumberInParty.Clear()
154            End Try
155
156            Return blnValidityCheck
157
158        End Function
```

● **Code the ValidateTourSelection Function Procedure** Tap or click below the ValidateNumberInParty function and enter the ValidateTourSelection Function procedure declaration. This Function procedure ensures that the user selected a tour from the lstTours ListBox object and then returns an integer value for the list selection to the calling procedure. To determine if a tour was selected, the procedure uses a Try-Catch block to convert the selected index value to an integer. If the conversion is successful, a choice was made and the choice is returned. In addition, a Boolean variable in the calling procedure is set to True because the variable was passed ByRef. If the selected index is not converted, the user did not make a choice; an error message box is displayed and the Boolean variable is set to False. One Catch block is used because the only error that uses the ListBox object occurs if the user does not select a tour.

```
                                    HINT
160    Private Function ValidateTourSelection(ByRef blnTour As Boolean, _
161        ByRef strTour As String) As Integer
162        ' This function ensures the user selected a tour
163
164        Dim intOceanTour As Integer
165        Try
166            intOceanTour = Convert.ToInt32(lstTours.SelectedIndex)
167            strTour = lstTours.SelectedItem.ToString()
168            blnTour = True
169        Catch Exception As SystemException
170            ' Detects if tour not selected
171            MsgBox("Select an Ocean Tour", , "Error")
172            blnTour = False
173        End Try
174        Return intOceanTour
175
176    End Function
```

● **Code the ArubaFindCost Function Procedure to Find the Cost of an Aruba Island Tour** Tap or click below the ValidateTourSelection Function procedure and enter the ArubaFindCost Function procedure declaration. The purpose of this Function procedure is to determine the cost of an Aruba tour. Three variables are passed to the function. Two are passed ByVal: the tour selection and the group size. Tour length is passed ByRef. The ArubaFindCost Function procedure uses the tour selection and group size to determine the cost of the tour based on published rates (*ref: Figure 7-51*). It also changes the values in the tour length field for use in the calling procedure. Write the code for the ArubaFindCost Function procedure.

(continues)

Guided Program Development   *continued*

		HINT

```vb
178  Private Function ArubaFindCost(ByVal intTourSelection As Integer, _
179      ByVal intGroupSize As Integer, ByRef intTourLength As Integer) As Decimal
180      ' This function calculates the cost of the tours to Aruba
181
182      Dim decTourCost As Decimal
183      Dim decFinalCost As Decimal
184      Dim decArubaDeepSeaCost As Decimal = 199D
185      Dim decArubaKayakCost As Decimal = 89D
186      Dim decArubaScubaCost As Decimal = 119D
187      Dim decArubaSnorkelCost As Decimal = 89D
188
189      Select Case intTourSelection
190          Case 0
191              decTourCost = decArubaDeepSeaCost
192              intTourLength = _intEightHours
193          Case 1
194              decTourCost = decArubaKayakCost
195              intTourLength = _intTwoHours
196          Case 2
197              decTourCost = decArubaScubaCost
198              intTourLength = _intThreeHours
199          Case 3
200              decTourCost = decArubaSnorkelCost
201              intTourLength = _intFourHours
202      End Select
203      decFinalCost = decTourCost * intGroupSize
204      Return decFinalCost
205
206  End Function
```

● **Code the JamaicaFindCost Function Procedure to Find the Cost of a Jamaica Island Tour** Tap or click below the ArubaFindCost Function procedure and enter the JamaicaFindCost Function procedure declaration. The purpose of this Function procedure is to determine the cost of a Jamaica tour. It uses the same three passed variables as the ArubaFindCost Function procedure. It also uses similar logic and returns the same values. Write the code for the JamaicaFindCost Function procedure.

HINT

```
207
208 ⊟    Private Function JamaicaFindCost(ByVal intTourSelection As Integer, _
209       ByVal intGroupSize As Integer, ByRef intTourLength As Integer) As Decimal
210           ' This function calculates the cost of the tours to Jamaica
211
212         Dim decTourCost As Decimal
213         Dim decFinalCost As Decimal
214         Dim decJamaicaGlassBottomCost As Decimal = 39D
215         Dim decJamaicaParasailCost As Decimal = 119D
216         Dim decJamaicaSnorkelCost As Decimal = 59D
217
218         Select Case intTourSelection
219             Case 0
220                 decTourCost = decJamaicaGlassBottomCost
221                 intTourLength = _intTwoHours
222             Case 1
223                 decTourCost = decJamaicaParasailCost
224                 intTourLength = _intTwoHours
225             Case 2
226                 decTourCost = decJamaicaSnorkelCost
227                 intTourLength = _intThreeHours
228         End Select
229         decFinalCost = decTourCost * intGroupSize
230         Return decFinalCost
231
232     End Function
```

(continues)

● **Code the KeyWestFindCost Function Procedure to Find the Cost of a Key West Island Tour** Tap or click below the JamaicaFindCost Function procedure and enter the KeyWestFindCost Function procedure declaration. The purpose of this Function procedure is to determine the cost of a Key West tour. It uses the same three passed variables as the JamaicaFindCost Function procedure. It also uses similar logic and returns the same values. Write the code for the KeyWestFindCost Function procedure.

HINT

```
234  Private Function KeyWestFindCost(ByVal intTourSelection As Integer, _
235      ByVal intGroupSize As Integer, ByRef intTourLength As Integer) As Decimal
236          ' This function calculates the cost of the tours to Key West
237
238      Dim decTourCost As Decimal
239      Dim decFinalCost As Decimal
240      Dim decKeyWestDeepSeaCost As Decimal = 89D
241      Dim decKeyWestGlassBottomCost As Decimal = 29D
242      Dim decKeyWestScubaCost As Decimal = 119D
243      Dim decKeyWestSnorkelCost As Decimal = 59D
244
245      Select Case intTourSelection
246          Case 0
247              decTourCost = decKeyWestDeepSeaCost
248              intTourLength = _intFourHours
249          Case 1
250              decTourCost = decKeyWestGlassBottomCost
251              intTourLength = _intTwoHours
252          Case 2
253              decTourCost = decKeyWestScubaCost
254              intTourLength = _intThreeHours
255          Case 3
256              decTourCost = decKeyWestSnorkelCost
257              intTourLength = _intThreeHours
258      End Select
259      decFinalCost = decTourCost * intGroupSize
260      Return decFinalCost
261
262  End Function
```

● **Code the Clear Button Click Event** After the Function procedures that are called from the btnFindCost_Click event handler have been coded, the next step is to write the code for the Clear Button click event handler. This event handler must reset the Windows Form object and objects on the form to look the same as when the program starts. This includes resetting the message in the cboIsland ComboBox object, clearing the Number in Party text box and the tours list box, blanking the labels that display the results, and removing all the objects from view except the cboIsland ComboBox object. Display the Design window and then double-tap or double-click the btnClear object to open the btnClear_Click event handler. Write the code for the event handler.

HINT

```
264  Private Sub btnClear_Click(ByVal sender As System.Object, ByVal e As System.EventArgs) Handles btnClear.Click
265        ' This event handler clears the form and resets the form for
266        ' reuse when the user clicks the Clear button.
267
268        cboIsland.Text = "Select Island Location"
269        txtNumberInParty.Clear()
270        lstTours.Items.Clear()
271        lblTourType.Text = ""
272        lblCost.Text = ""
273        lblLength.Text = ""
274        lblParty.Visible = False
275        txtNumberInParty.Visible = False
276        lblSelect.Visible = False
277        lstTours.Visible = False
278        btnFindCost.Visible = False
279        btnClear.Visible = False
280        lblTourType.Visible = False
281        lblCost.Visible = False
282        lblLength.Visible = False
283
284  End Sub
```

● **Code the frmTours_Load Event** The last bit of code to write for the Ocean Tours program is the event handler for the frmTours load event. You will recall that when the application begins, a splash screen opens first. To display the splash screen longer than the default time, you must add a sleep timer. Return to the frmTours.vb [Design] window and double-tap or double-click the Windows Form object. Assuming that you want the splash screen to be displayed for 5 seconds, code the statement to delay program execution for 5000 milliseconds *(ref: Figure 7-16)*.

HINT

```
286  Private Sub frmTours_Load(ByVal sender As System.Object, ByVal e As System.EventArgs) Handles MyBase.Load
287        ' Hold the splash screen for 5 seconds
288
289        Threading.Thread.Sleep(5000)
290
291  End Sub
292
293  End Class
```

(continues)

Code Listing

The complete code for the sample program is shown in Figure 7-56.

```vbnet
 1 ' Program Name: Ocean Tours Trip Selection
 2 ' Author:        Corinne Hoisington
 3 ' Date:          June 22, 2014
 4 ' Purpose:       The Ocean Tours Trip Selection application determines the
 5 '                ocean tours available and calculates the cost of the tour.
 6
 7  Option Strict On
 8
 9 Public Class frmTours
10
11      ' Class variables
12      Private _intTwoHours As Integer = 2
13      Private _intThreeHours As Integer = 3
14      Private _intFourHours As Integer = 4
15      Private _intEightHours As Integer = 8
16      Private _strDeepSeaFishing As String = "Deep Sea Fishing"
17      Private _strKayaking As String = "Kayaking"
18      Private _strScuba As String = "Scuba"
19      Private _strSnorkeling As String = "Snorkeling"
20      Private _strGlassBottomBoat As String = "Glass Bottom Boat"
21      Private _strParasailing As String = "Parasailing"
22
23      Private Sub cboIsland_SelectedIndexChanged(ByVal sender As System.Object, ByVal e As
   System.EventArgs) Handles cboIsland.SelectedIndexChanged, cboIsland.SelectedIndexChanged
24          ' This event handler allows the user to enter the island choice
25          ' and then calls subprocedures to place the island activities in the list.
26
27          Dim intIslandChoice As Integer
28
29          intIslandChoice = Me.cboIsland.SelectedIndex
30          lstTours.Items.Clear()
31          Select Case intIslandChoice
32              Case 0
33                  ArubaTours()
34              Case 1
35                  JamaicaTours()
36              Case 2
37                  KeyWestTours()
38          End Select
39          ' Make items visible in the window
40          lblParty.Visible = True
41          txtNumberInParty.Visible = True
42          lblSelect.Visible = True
43          lstTours.Visible = True
44          btnFindCost.Visible = True
45          btnClear.Visible = True
46          lblTourType.Visible = True
47          lblCost.Visible = True
48          lblLength.Visible = True
49          ' Clear the labels
50          lblTourType.Text = ""
51          lblCost.Text = ""
52          lblLength.Text = ""
53          ' Set focus on number in party text box
54          txtNumberInParty.Focus()
55
56      End Sub
57
58      Private Sub ArubaTours()
59          ' This procedure fills in the possible ocean tours for Aruba
60          lstTours.Items.Add(_strDeepSeaFishing)
61          lstTours.Items.Add(_strKayaking)
62          lstTours.Items.Add(_strScuba)
63          lstTours.Items.Add(_strSnorkeling)
64
65      End Sub
66
67      Private Sub JamaicaTours()
68          'This procedure fills in the possible ocean tours for Jamaica
69          lstTours.Items.Add(_strGlassBottomBoat)
70          lstTours.Items.Add(_strParasailing)
71          lstTours.Items.Add(_strSnorkeling)
72
73      End Sub
74
75      Private Sub KeyWestTours()
76          'This procedure fills in the possible ocean tours for Key West
77          lstTours.Items.Add(_strDeepSeaFishing)
78          lstTours.Items.Add(_strGlassBottomBoat)
79          lstTours.Items.Add(_strScuba)
80          lstTours.Items.Add(_strSnorkeling)
81
82      End Sub
```

FIGURE 7-56 (continues)

```
83
84  ⊟  Private Sub btnFindCost_Click(ByVal sender As System.Object, ByVal e As System.EventArgs) Handles btnFindCost.Click
85          ' This button event handler determines the cost of the ocean
86          ' tour and displays the tour, the cost, and the length
87
88          Dim intGroupSize As Integer
89          Dim blnNumberInPartyIsValid As Boolean = False
90          Dim blnTourIsSelected As Boolean = False
91          Dim intTourChoice As Integer
92          Dim strSelectedTour As String = ""
93          Dim intIslandChoice As Integer
94          Dim intLengthOfTour As Integer = 0
95          Dim decTotalCost As Decimal
96
97          ' Call a function to ensure the number of people in the party is valid
98          blnNumberInPartyIsValid = ValidateNumberInParty()
99          ' Call a function to ensure a tour was selected
100         intTourChoice = ValidateTourSelection(blnTourIsSelected, strSelectedTour)
101         ' If number of people and the tour selection are valid, calculate the cost
102         If (blnNumberInPartyIsValid And blnTourIsSelected) Then
103             intGroupSize = Convert.ToInt32(txtNumberInParty.Text)
104             intIslandChoice = cboIsland.SelectedIndex
105             Select Case intIslandChoice
106                 Case 0
107                     decTotalCost = ArubaFindCost(intTourChoice, _
108                                             intGroupSize, intLengthOfTour)
109                 Case 1
110                     decTotalCost = JamaicaFindCost(intTourChoice, _
111                                             intGroupSize, intLengthOfTour)
112                 Case 2
113                     decTotalCost = KeyWestFindCost(intTourChoice, _
114                                             intGroupSize, intLengthOfTour)
115             End Select
116             ' Display the cost of the ocean tour
117             lblTourType.Text = "Tour: " & strSelectedTour
118             lblCost.Text = "Cost: " & decTotalCost.ToString("C")
119             lblLength.Text = "Length: " & intLengthOfTour.ToString() & " hours"
120         End If
121
122     End Sub
123
124  ⊟  Private Function ValidateNumberInParty() As Boolean
125         ' This procedure validates the value entered for the number in party
126
127         Dim intPartyNumber As Integer
128         Dim blnValidityCheck As Boolean = False
129         Dim strNumberInPartyErrorMessage As String = _
130             "Please enter the number of people in your party (1-99)"
131         Dim strMessageBoxTitle As String = "Error"
132
133         Try
134             intPartyNumber = Convert.ToInt32(txtNumberInParty.Text)
135             If intPartyNumber > 0 And intPartyNumber < 100 Then
136                 blnValidityCheck = True
137             Else
138                 MsgBox(strNumberInPartyErrorMessage, , strMessageBoxTitle)
139                 txtNumberInParty.Focus()
140                 txtNumberInParty.Clear()
141             End If
142         Catch Exception As FormatException
143             MsgBox(strNumberInPartyErrorMessage, , strMessageBoxTitle)
144             txtNumberInParty.Focus()
145             txtNumberInParty.Clear()
146         Catch Exception As OverflowException
147             MsgBox(strNumberInPartyErrorMessage, , strMessageBoxTitle)
148             txtNumberInParty.Focus()
149             txtNumberInParty.Clear()
150         Catch Exception As SystemException
151             MsgBox(strNumberInPartyErrorMessage, , strMessageBoxTitle)
152             txtNumberInParty.Focus()
153             txtNumberInParty.Clear()
154         End Try
155
156         Return blnValidityCheck
157
158     End Function
159
160  ⊟  Private Function ValidateTourSelection(ByRef blnTour As Boolean, _
161         ByRef strTour As String) As Integer
162         ' This function ensures the user selected a tour
163
164         Dim intOceanTour As Integer
165         Try
166             intOceanTour = Convert.ToInt32(lstTours.SelectedIndex)
167             strTour = lstTours.SelectedItem.ToString()
168             blnTour = True
169         Catch Exception As SystemException
170             ' Detects if tour not selected
171             MsgBox("Select an Ocean Tour", , "Error")
172             blnTour = False
173         End Try
174         Return intOceanTour
175
176     End Function
```

FIGURE 7-56 (continues)

```
177
178 ⊟    Private Function ArubaFindCost(ByVal intTourSelection As Integer, _
179         ByVal intGroupSize As Integer, ByRef intTourLength As Integer) As Decimal
180             ' This function calculates the cost of the tours to Aruba
181
182         Dim decTourCost As Decimal
183         Dim decFinalCost As Decimal
184         Dim decArubaDeepSeaCost As Decimal = 199D
185         Dim decArubaKayakCost As Decimal = 89D
186         Dim decArubaScubaCost As Decimal = 119D
187         Dim decArubaSnorkelCost As Decimal = 89D
188
189         Select Case intTourSelection
190             Case 0
191                 decTourCost = decArubaDeepSeaCost
192                 intTourLength = _intEightHours
193             Case 1
194                 decTourCost = decArubaKayakCost
195                 intTourLength = _intTwoHours
196             Case 2
197                 decTourCost = decArubaScubaCost
198                 intTourLength = _intThreeHours
199             Case 3
200                 decTourCost = decArubaSnorkelCost
201                 intTourLength = _intFourHours
202         End Select
203         decFinalCost = decTourCost * intGroupSize
204         Return decFinalCost
205
206     End Function
207
208 ⊟    Private Function JamaicaFindCost(ByVal intTourSelection As Integer, _
209         ByVal intGroupSize As Integer, ByRef intTourLength As Integer) As Decimal
210             ' This function calculates the cost of the tours to Jamaica
211
212         Dim decTourCost As Decimal
213         Dim decFinalCost As Decimal
214         Dim decJamaicaGlassBottomCost As Decimal = 39D
215         Dim decJamaicaParasailCost As Decimal = 119D
216         Dim decJamaicaSnorkelCost As Decimal = 59D
217
218         Select Case intTourSelection
219             Case 0
220                 decTourCost = decJamaicaGlassBottomCost
221                 intTourLength = _intTwoHours
222             Case 1
223                 decTourCost = decJamaicaParasailCost
224                 intTourLength = _intTwoHours
225             Case 2
226                 decTourCost = decJamaicaSnorkelCost
227                 intTourLength = _intThreeHours
228         End Select
229         decFinalCost = decTourCost * intGroupSize
230         Return decFinalCost
231
232     End Function
```

FIGURE 7-56 (continues)

```
233
234  ⊟   Private Function KeyWestFindCost(ByVal intTourSelection As Integer, _
235           ByVal intGroupSize As Integer, ByRef intTourLength As Integer) As Decimal
236               ' This function calculates the cost of the tours to Key West
237
238           Dim decTourCost As Decimal
239           Dim decFinalCost As Decimal
240           Dim decKeyWestDeepSeaCost As Decimal = 89D
241           Dim decKeyWestGlassBottomCost As Decimal = 29D
242           Dim decKeyWestScubaCost As Decimal = 119D
243           Dim decKeyWestSnorkelCost As Decimal = 59D
244
245           Select Case intTourSelection
246               Case 0
247                   decTourCost = decKeyWestDeepSeaCost
248                   intTourLength = _intFourHours
249               Case 1
250                   decTourCost = decKeyWestGlassBottomCost
251                   intTourLength = _intTwoHours
252               Case 2
253                   decTourCost = decKeyWestScubaCost
254                   intTourLength = _intThreeHours
255               Case 3
256                   decTourCost = decKeyWestSnorkelCost
257                   intTourLength = _intThreeHours
258           End Select
259           decFinalCost = decTourCost * intGroupSize
260           Return decFinalCost
261
262       End Function
263
264  ⊟   Private Sub btnClear_Click(ByVal sender As System.Object, ByVal e As System.EventArgs) Handles btnClear.Click
265               ' This event handler clears the form and resets the form for
266               ' reuse when the user clicks the Clear button.
267
268           cboIsland.Text = "Select Island Location"
269           txtNumberInParty.Clear()
270           lstTours.Items.Clear()
271           lblTourType.Text = ""
272           lblCost.Text = ""
273           lblLength.Text = ""
274           lblParty.Visible = False
275           txtNumberInParty.Visible = False
276           lblSelect.Visible = False
277           lstTours.Visible = False
278           btnFindCost.Visible = False
279           btnClear.Visible = False
280           lblTourType.Visible = False
281           lblCost.Visible = False
282           lblLength.Visible = False
283
284       End Sub
285
286  ⊟   Private Sub frmTours_Load(ByVal sender As System.Object, ByVal e As System.EventArgs) Handles MyBase.Load
287               ' Hold the splash screen for 5 seconds
288
289           Threading.Thread.Sleep(5000)
290
291       End Sub
292
293  End Class
```

FIGURE 7-56 (continued)

Summary

In this chapter you have learned to create applications using procedures. The items listed in the table in Figure 7-57 include all the new Visual Studio and Visual Basic skills you have learned in this chapter.

Visual Basic Skills		
Skill	**Figure Number**	**Video number**
Examine the Ocean Tours Application	Figure 7-4	Video 7-1
Add the Generic Splash Screen	Figure 7-5	Video 7-2
Pause the Splash Screen	Figure 7-16	Video 7-3
Place a ComboBox Object on a Form	Figure 7-18	Video 7-4
Use an Assignment Statement to Obtain a SelectedIndex	Page 470	
Create a SelectedIndexChanged Event	Figure 7-26	Video 7-5
Code a Procedure Call and a Sub Procedure	Figure 7-28	
Pass an Argument to a Called Procedure	Figure 7-33	
Pass an Argument by Value	Figure 7-34	
Pass an Argument by Reference	Figure 7-38	
Code a Function Procedure	Figure 7-40	

FIGURE 7-57

Reinforcement activities and resources are available at no additional cost on *www.cengagebrain.com*. Visit *www.cengage.com/ct/studentdownload* for detailed instructions about accessing the resources available at the Student Companion Site.

Knowledge Check

1. What is the name of the property that allows you to place a graphic on the background of the Windows Form object?

2. Write the line of code that would hold frmSplashScreen for approximately six seconds.

3. What is the difference between passing by value and passing by reference?

4. What is the fewest number of arguments you can pass to a Sub procedure?

5. What section of code performs a specific task and does not return a value?

6. What section of code performs a specific task and returns a value?

7. What happens to the variables that were passed by value when you leave a Sub procedure?

8. Name the two types of procedures.

9. How many values can a Function procedure return?

10. Write a Return statement that returns the variable intSpeed.

11. Write the Visual Basic statements declaring a Sub procedure called SeatAvailability that receives one variable called intSeats. The variable intSeats will be changed in the procedure. Write only the first and last lines of the Sub procedure.

12. What is the name of a variable that is passed to a procedure?

13. If you want a copy of a variable passed to a procedure, which way should you pass it?

14. You must have a Return statement in a Function procedure. True or false?

15. You must have a Return statement in a Sub procedure. True or false?

16. When multiple arguments are passed to a procedure, the order is not important. True or false?

17. Which type of exception would be detected if you used the conversion command Convert.ToInt32 to convert a non-integer value?

18. Which type of exception would be detected if you used the conversion command Convert.ToDecimal to try to convert a letter of the alphabet?

19. If you enter a number that is too large for the data type, which type of exception would be detected?

20. When deciding whether a set of programming steps should be placed in a Sub procedure or a Function procedure, what are three questions you should ask?

Debugging Exercises

1. Fix the code:

```
Private Sub btnItemNumber_Click(ByVal sender As System.Object, ByVal e As
System.EventArgs) Handles btnItemNumber.Click
        Dim decCost As Decimal
        Dim intCount As Decimal

        decCost = Convert.ToDecimal(txtCost.Text)
        Inventory(decCost, intCount)
End Sub

Private Sub Inventory(ByVal cost, ByVal count)
        count +=3
        cost *=1.3
End Sub
```

2. Fix the code:

```
Private Sub btnBaseball_Click(ByVal sender As System.Object, ByVal e As
System.EventArgs) Handles btnBaseball.Click
        Dim decHits As Decimal = 190
        Dim decTimesAtBat As Decimal = 428
        Dim decBattingAverage As Decimal

        decBattingAverage = BattingAverage(decHits, decTimesAtBat)
        lblHits.Text = "The batting average is " & decBattingAverage.
        ToString()
End Sub
Private Function BattingAverage(ByVal decHitsCount As Decimal, ByVal
decNumberAtBat)
        Dim decAverageAtBat As Decimal
        decAverageAtBat = decHitsCount / decNumberAtBat
End Function
```

3. Fix the code:

```
Private Sub btnMileage_Click(ByVal sender As System.Object, ByVal e As
System.EventArgs) Handles btnMileage.Click
        Dim decMiles As Decimal = 350D
        Dim decGallons As Decimal = 12.8D
        Dim decMilesPer As Decimal

        decMilesPer = Compute(decMiles, decGallons)
        lblDisplays.Text = "Your MPG is  " & decMiles.ToString()
End Sub
```

Debugging Exercises *continued*

```
Private Sub Compute(ByVal decM As Decimal, ByVal decG) As Decimal
        Dim decMPG As Decimal
        decMPG = decM / decG
        Return MPG
End Function
```

Program Analysis

1. What is the output of the code in Figure 7-58?

```
Private Sub btnSevens_Click(ByVal sender As System.Object, ByVal e As
System.EventArgs) Handles btnSevens.Click
    Dim intCount As Integer
    For intCount = 1 To 7
        CalculateSevens(intCount)
    Next
End Sub

Private Sub CalculateSevens(ByVal intCountValue As Integer)
    Dim intResult As Integer
    intResult = intCountValue ^ 3
    lstAnswer.Items.Add(intResult.ToString())
End Sub
```

FIGURE 7-58

2. What is the output of the code in Figure 7-59?

```
Private Sub btnJoke_Click(ByVal sender As System.Object, ByVal e As System.
EventArgs) Handles btnJoke.Click
    DisplayRiddle()
    DisplayAnswer()
End Sub

Private Sub DisplayAnswer()
    lblAnswer.Text = "Because it has a spring in it"
End Sub

Private Sub DisplayRiddle()
    lblRiddle.Text = "Why should you carry a watch when crossing a
desert?"
End Sub
```

FIGURE 7-59

(continues)

3. What is the output of the code in Figure 7-60?

```
Private Sub btnBedrock_Click(ByVal sender As System.Object, ByVal e As Sys-
tem.EventArgs) Handles btnBedrock.Click
        Dim strFullName As String = "Fred Flintstone"
        Dim strSecondName As String = "Barney Rubble"

        CountLength(strFullName, strSecondName)
        lblEnd.Text = "My favorite was " & strSecondName
End Sub

Private Sub CountLength(ByVal strFullName As String, ByRef strSecondName As
String)
        lblFirst.Text = "The first name has " & strFullName.Length & "
letters."
        lblSecond.Text = "The second name has " & strSecondName.Length & "
letters."
        strSecondName = "Dino"
End Sub
```

FIGURE 7-60

4. What is the output of the code in Figure 7-61?

```
Private Sub btnStrangeFacts_Click(ByVal sender As System.Object, ByVal e As
System.EventArgs) Handles btnStrangeFacts.Click
        Dim intHangerLength As Integer = 44
        Dim intMen As Integer = 2000
        Dim intWomen As Integer = 7000
        Dim intValue As Integer

        intValue = Talk(intMen, intWomen)
        lblResponse.Text = "The couple would say " & intValue & " words a
day"
        AverageHanger(intHangerLength)
  End Sub

Private Sub AverageHanger(ByVal intHanger As Integer)
        lblPhrase.Text = "The average length of a coat hanger when straight-
ened is " & intHanger & " inches."
  End Sub

Private Function Talk(ByVal intM As Integer, ByVal intW As Integer) As Integer
        lblPhrase1.Text = "The average man says " & intM & " words a day"
        lblPhrase2.Text = "The average woman says " & intW & " words a
day"
        Return intM + intW
  End Function
```

FIGURE 7-61

Program Analysis *continued*

5. A program contains the procedure declaration shown in Figure 7-62. Write the Function call statement that assigns the returned value to intCubed and passes a variable named intValue.

```
Private Function Cube(ByVal intNum As Integer) As Integer
      Return intNum * intNum * intNum
End Function
```

FIGURE 7-62

6. A program converts and validates a value entered as the population of a city. Write a statement that passes the variable intBase to a procedure and assigns the return value to a variable named intSolution. Write the code that would declare a variable named intPopulation as an Integer. Allow the user to enter the population of her city in a TextBox object named txtCityPopulation. Convert the value to an integer within a Try block. Write a Try-Catch block with an overflow Catch block first, a format exception Catch block second, and a generic exception last. Each Catch block should display a message box that explains the problem with the user's input.
7. Write the code for a Sub procedure named FindHeight that will calculate a person's height in inches when given the feet and inches. For example, a person who is 5'10" is 70 inches tall. Display the result in a message box.

Complete one or more of the following case programming assignments. Submit the program and materials you create to your instructor. The level of difficulty is indicated for each case programming assignment.

● = Easiest
●● = Intermediate
●●● = Challenging

1

BROADWAY PLAY TICKETS

Design a Windows application and write the code that will execute according to the program requirements in Figure 7-63 and the Use Case Definition in Figure 7-64 on the next page. Before writing the code, create an event planning document for each event in the program. The completed Windows Form object and other objects for the user interface are shown in Figure 7-65 and Figure 7-66 on the next page.

REQUIREMENTS DOCUMENT

Date Submitted: September 24, 2015

Application Title: Broadway Play Tickets Application

Purpose: This Windows application allows a user to select various Broadway plays, seating locations, and the number of tickets. The total cost with tax is computed.

Program Procedures: From a Windows application, a user can select a Broadway play, seats, and the number of tickets, and then calculate the total cost of the tickets.

Algorithms, Processing, and Conditions:
1. The user enters the Broadway play, seat location, and the number of tickets needed. The Broadway play is selected from a ComboBox object. The other objects are not visible until the user selects this option.
2. A different Function procedure will be called for each play to calculate the total cost of the tickets. Another Function will be called to compute the tax, regardless of which play is selected.
3. Two types of seating are available: orchestra and mezzanine.
4. Display the subtotal, tax (12%), and final total of the tickets purchased.

Notes and Restrictions: Validate input by using Try-Catch blocks in separate procedures as needed.

Comments:
1. The program opens with a splash screen that is displayed for approximately five seconds.
2. Obtain images for this program from CengageBrain.com. The name of the picture for the Windows form is Broadway. The name of the picture on the splash screen is SplashBroadway.

FIGURE 7-63

Case Programming Assignments

Broadway Play TIckets (continued)

USE CASE DEFINITION

1. The user views the opening splash screen for approximately five seconds.
2. The user enters the Broadway play, seat location, and the number of tickets needed. The user taps or clicks the Calculate Cost button.
3. The user views the subtotal, tax, and final cost of the tickets.

FIGURE 7-64

© 2014 Cengage Learning

Broadway Play	Ticket Cost
Lion King	Orchestra Seating: $135 Mezzanine Seating: $92
Wicked	Orchestra Seating: $149 Mezzanine Seating: $98
Phantom of the Opera	Orchestra Seating: $128 Mezzanine Seating: $82

FIGURE 7-65

© 2014 Cengage Learning

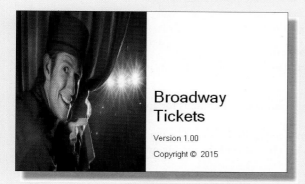

FIGURE 7-66a

© Joshua Blake/Vetta/Getty Images

FIGURE 7-66b

2 • CASH FOR GOLD

Design a Windows application and write the code that will execute according to the program requirements in Figure 7-67 and the Use Case Definition in Figure 7-68 on the next page. Before writing the code, create an event planning document for each event in the program. The completed Windows Form object and other objects in the user interface are shown in Figure 7-69, Figure 7-70, and Figure 7-71 on the next page.

REQUIREMENTS DOCUMENT

Date Submitted: August 11, 2015

Application Title: Cash for Gold Application

Purpose: This Windows application calculates the amount of gold jewelry that can be sold to make a target amount of money or finds the amount of money earned based on the weight of gold jewelry collected at estate sales.

Program Procedures: From a Windows application, the user can select how many ounces of gold must be sold to earn a target amount of money or find the amount earned based on the weight of gold collected.

Algorithms, Processing, and Conditions:
1. The user first selects whether to compute a weight in ounces to reach a goal amount or to compute the amount earned by selling gold jewelry.
2. After the user selects an option, display the necessary objects based on the selection. If the user selects the goal amount, request the target amount the user hopes to earn. If the user chooses to find the amount earned based on the weight of her collected gold, request the weight in ounces.
3. Based on one ounce of gold selling for $1556.65, calculate the weight of gold the user needs to collect to make the goal or calculate the amount of money the collected gold jewelry is worth. Use separate procedures to make the two calculations.
4. Display the result of the calculation on the form.

Notes and Restrictions:
1. A Clear Form button should clear the form.
2. The data the user enters should be validated in Try-Catch blocks in separate procedures as needed.

Comments:
1. The application should begin with a splash screen that holds for approximately four seconds.
2. Obtain images for this program from CengageBrain.com. The name of the picture for the Windows form is Gold. The name of the picture on the splash screen is SplashGold.

FIGURE 7-67

Cash for gold (continued)

USE CASE DEFINITION

1. The user views an opening splash screen for four seconds.
2. The user selects whether to calculate the number of ounces of gold that need to be collected to make her goal amount or find the amount earned based on the weight of the gold collected.
3. The user provides the following information: the target amount she hopes to earn or the ounces of gold collected.
4. The user taps or clicks the Find Target Amount of Gold button or Find Amount Earned button and the result is displayed.
5. The user taps or clicks the Clear Form button to clear the responses.

FIGURE 7-68

FIGURE 7-69

FIGURE 7-71

FIGURE 7-70

3

SAN FRANCISCO SEGWAY TOURS

Design a Windows application and write the code that will execute according to the program requirements in Figure 7-72 and the Use Case Definition in Figure 7-73 on the next page. Before writing the code, create an event planning document for each event in the program. The completed Windows Form object and other objects in the user interface are shown in Figure 7-74 and Figure 7-75 on the next page.

REQUIREMENTS DOCUMENT

Date Submitted:	June 21, 2015
Application Title:	San Francisco Segway Tours Application
Purpose:	This Windows application computes the cost of a Segway tour of San Francisco with different discount coupons.
Program Procedures:	From a Windows application, allow the user to select different Segway tour options, discount any possible coupons, and compute the cost of multiple tickets.
Algorithms, Processing, and Conditions:	1. The user is asked to select a Segway tour from a ComboBox object. The other objects are not visible until the user selects this option.
	2. The user is asked to enter the number of tickets needed in a TextBox object.
	3. One of two Function procedures will be called for the Golden Gate Tour ($79.99) or the Waterfront Tour ($69.99) to compute and pass back the cost of the multiple tickets.
	4. Two discounts are available using a ListBox object: a 10% discount for AAA membership or 15% for military service.
Notes and Restrictions:	1. A Clear Form button should clear the form.
	2. A Try-Catch block in separate procedures will validate the input.
Comments:	1. A splash screen begins this application for five seconds.
	2. Obtain an image for this program from CengageBrain.com. The name of the picture for the Windows form is Segway. The name of the picture on the splash screen is SplashSegway.

FIGURE 7-72

Case Programming Assignments

San Francisco Segway tours (continued)

USE CASE DEFINITION

1. The user views the opening splash screen for five seconds.
2. The user selects whether to purchase Golden Gate or Waterfront tour tickets.
3. The user enters the number of tickets needed and the type of discount, if any.
4. The user taps or clicks the Compute Cost button to display the final cost.
5. The user taps or clicks the Clear Form button to clear the responses.

FIGURE 7-73

© 2014 Cengage Learning

FIGURE 7-74

© Tim E White/Photolibrary/Getty Images

FIGURE 7-75

© Tim E White/Photolibrary/Getty Images

4 ●●

BODY MASS INDEX (BMI) CALCULATOR

Design a Windows application and write the code that will execute according to the program requirements in Figure 7-76. Before designing the user interface, create a Use Case Definition. Before writing the code, create an event planning document for each event in the program.

REQUIREMENTS DOCUMENT

Date Submitted:	October 19, 2015
Application Title:	Body Mass Index (BMI) Calculator Application
Purpose:	This Windows application allows the user to enter a height and weight and computes the user's body mass index.
Program Procedures:	From a Windows form, the user will enter a height and weight using either the imperial or metric system.
Algorithms, Processing, and Conditions:	1. The user first views a Windows application that displays a title, a BMI graphic, a ListBox object to select the imperial or metric system, and labels to enter information for the user's height and weight.
	2. When the user selects imperial or metric and the height and weight, the Compute BMI button can be selected.
	3. A Sub procedure should be called to handle the imperial and metric BMI calculations using the following formulas:
	BMI = (Weight in Pounds / (Height in Inches * Height in Inches)) * 703
	BMI = Weight in Kilograms / (Height in Meters * Height in Meters)
	4. Two Function procedures should be called based on the system selected. Each Function procedure will calculate the BMI and return the Decimal value to the calling procedure. The original procedure will display the result.
Notes and Restrictions:	1. The result should be calculated to the hundredths place.
	2. The input values should be validated by a Try-Catch block.
Comments:	1. An image from the Web should be used for the BMI graphic.
	2. An opening splash screen should be displayed for three seconds.

FIGURE 7-76

5 ●●
TRAILER RENTAL RATES

Design a Windows application and write the code that will execute according to the program requirements in Figure 7-77. Before designing the user interface, create a Use Case Definition. Before writing the code, create an event planning document for each event in the program.

REQUIREMENTS DOCUMENT

Date Submitted:	March 17, 2015
Application Title:	Trailer Rental Rates Application
Purpose:	This application computes the cost to rent a truck, cargo van, or trailer for your move. The application will calculate the total cost, including 8.5% state tax.
Program Procedures:	The user can select the type of rental and the number of days.
Algorithms, Processing, and Conditions:	1. The user first views a Windows form that displays a title, a picture of a moving truck, a ComboBox object requesting the type of rental (truck, $29.95 a day; cargo van, $19.95 a day; or trailer, $14.95 a day), and a TextBox object for the number of days. 2. After the information has been entered, a Sub procedure displays three labels: Subtotal Billing Amount for Your Rental, Taxes for Your Rental, and Final Total. 3. Pass the cost of the rental type and the number of days to a Sub procedure to calculate the rental subtotal. Do not display the amount in this procedure. 4. Another Function procedure should compute the 8.5% tax. Pass that value back to the calling method. 5. Pass the subtotal, tax, and final cost to a Sub procedure to display the results.
Notes and Restrictions:	The input values should be validated in a separate procedure by a Try-Catch block.
Comments:	The picture should be selected from pictures available on the Web.

FIGURE 7-77

6   ●●
CALCULATE YOUR COMMUTE

Design a Windows application and write the code that will execute according to the program requirements in Figure 7-78. Before designing the user interface, create a Use Case Definition. Before writing the code, create an event planning document for each event in the program.

REQUIREMENTS DOCUMENT

Date Submitted:	March 2, 2015
Application Title:	Calculate Your Commute Application
Purpose:	This Windows application computes the yearly cost of commuting to work via car, train, or bus.
Program Procedures:	From a Windows application, the user selects how she commutes to work and then answers questions based on that response to compute the cost of traveling to and from work for one year.
Algorithms, Processing, and Conditions:	1. The user first views a Windows application with a title and a ComboBox object that asks how she commutes — car, train, or bus. The other objects on the form are not visible at this point.
	2. After the user selects the mode of travel, the questions related to that type of travel are displayed immediately.
	3. The following customized questions are displayed based on the user's choice:
	• Car: Daily round trip distance, days worked per month, car's mileage per gallon, cost per gallon of gas, monthly cost of maintenance and insurance, and monthly parking cost.
	• Train: Round trip transit fare and days worked per month.
	• Bus: Round trip transit fare and days worked per month.
	4. After the values have been validated, calculate the cost of commuting for one year for the selected choice.
Notes and Restrictions:	All values that the user enters should be validated.
Comments:	1. The picture shown should be selected from pictures available on the Web.
	2. A splash screen should open the application.

FIGURE 7-78

7 ●●●
BALANCE AN ONLINE BANK STATEMENT

Create a requirements document and a Use Case Definition document and then design a Windows application based on the case project description in Figure 7-79. Before writing the code, create an event planning document for each event in the program.

Your college wants you to write a Windows application that students can use to balance their online bank accounts. This program will be installed on all computers in the student union. The application should allow the user to enter a starting balance and indicate whether the account has a monthly interest rate. Validate the beginning balance to verify that the number is possible. Allow the user to enter checks, ATM cash withdrawals, and deposits. Also, calculate the interest for one month and add the interest amount to the final balance. Users can make multiple debits and deposits and continue until indicating that they are finished making transactions. The interest will be added to the final balance after the transactions are completed. Data validation is needed for all input. An opening splash screen will be displayed as well.

FIGURE 7-79

© 2014 Cengage Learning

Case Programming Assignments

8 ●●● SALARIES FOR COMPUTER OCCUPATIONS

Create a requirements document and a Use Case Definition document and then design a Windows application based on the case project description in Figure 7-80. Before writing the code, create an event planning document for each event in the program.

Create a Windows application that analyzes four computer job titles from the information listed on the U.S. Department of Labor Statistics website at *www.bls.gov*. Search for the U.S. hourly mean wage and annual mean wage for the following occupations: Computer Programmers, Computer System Analysts, Computer and Information Systems Managers, and Computer Software Engineers, Applications. Create a Windows form that has a drop-down list of the four occupations. Based on the user's selection, display the current median hourly pay and yearly pay. Also, project what the pay will be in five years based on a 3% raise per year for each of the present rates.

FIGURE 7-80

Case Programming Assignments

9 ● ● ●
SMARTPHONE GROWTH

Create a requirements document and a Use Case Definition document and then design a Windows application based on the case project description in Figure 7-81. Before writing the code, create an event planning document for each event in the program.

A national digital service provider would like you to create a Windows application that will display the global growth of smartphones. As of 2013, there were 913 million smartphones worldwide. The smartphone market is growing at 22.5 percent per year. Based on this growth rate, create a Sub procedure that calculates and displays the next 10 years of growth in a ListBox object. Also, create a Function procedure that allows the user to enter a year from the next 10 years and then passes back that year's smartphone projection. Validate all entries. An opening splash screen will be displayed as well.

FIGURE 7-81

CHAPTER 8

Using Arrays and File Handling

OBJECTIVES

You will have mastered the material in this chapter when you can:

- Initialize an array

- Initialize an array with default values

- Access array elements using a loop

- Use ReDim to resize an array

- Determine the number of elements in an array using the Length command

- Use the For Each loop

- Initialize two-dimensional arrays

- Read a text file

- Write to a text file

- Calculate depreciation

- Use multiple Form objects

- Access variable objects on other forms

Introduction

You can use Visual Basic to create applications for small businesses or multinational corporations. As programming applications grow in size, the role of organizing, storing, and retrieving large amounts of data becomes vital. This chapter explains how to develop applications that can keep data for later processing, including sorting, calculating, and display.

Chapter Project

In the sample chapter project, a chain of men's retail stores named Trends Menswear requires a Windows application to compute the depreciation of its point of sale registers, sales racks, office computers, and store furniture. **Depreciation** is an accounting term that describes the decline in value of a physical asset over a certain period of time. Most assets lose value due to use, aging, obsolescence, and impairment. Depreciation is an estimate of this declining value and is used for determining taxes and other financial purposes.

Trends Menswear sells business and formal men's attire. The company cannot depreciate the cost of its clothing inventory, but it can claim the depreciated value of its physical assets, such as the point of sale registers and other store equipment. Each store item is assigned a four-character identifying code. A table that lists these items and associated codes is stored in a text file, which is kept on a storage medium such as a USB drive.

When the Windows application for Trends Menswear starts, it opens the text file and fills the Select Inventory Item ListBox object with the item numbers. Before calculating depreciation, the user selects an item and a depreciation method, as shown in Figure 8-1.

FIGURE 8-1

In Figure 8-1, the user taps or clicks the list box arrow to display the items in inventory. After selecting an item, the user can tap or click a radio button to select either the Straight-Line or Double-Declining Balance depreciation method.

In straight-line depreciation, the asset is depreciated by the same amount each year for the life of the asset. In double-declining depreciation, the depreciation is accelerated.

After selecting an item number and method of depreciation, the user taps or clicks the Calculate Depreciation button. The Windows form then displays the product name, the quantity in inventory, and the amount the item is worth over the next five years due to depreciation, as shown in Figure 8-2.

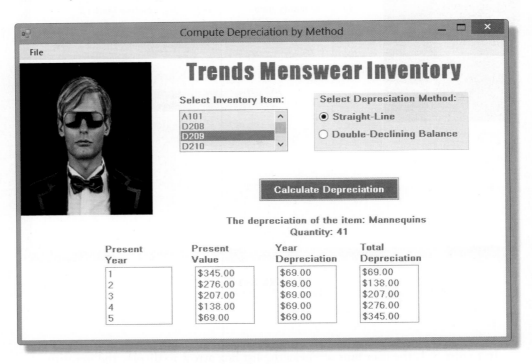

FIGURE 8-2

Trends Menswear purchased the items shown in Figure 8-3 in its first year of business.

Inventory Item	Item Number	Initial Cost	Quantity
Point of Sale Registers	A101	1599.99	12
Store Display Racks	D208	49.99	112
Mannequins	D209	345.00	41
End Cap Displays	D210	118.99	16
Hangers	D211	1.19	1200
Office Computers	E101	629.99	11
Chairs	F310	145.00	32
Sofas	F311	829.99	6

FIGURE 8-3

Each item in Figure 8-3 is depreciated each year for tax reasons. The Internal Revenue Service allows depreciation deductions for five years because the average useful life of these types of items is five years. The items in Figure 8-3 are stored in a text file named inventory.txt. Figure 8-4 shows this file in Notepad. The Windows application opens the inventory.txt text file and reads the information for use in the program.

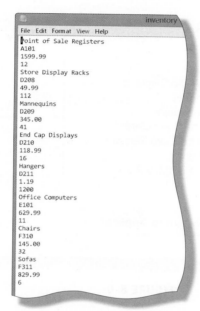

FIGURE 8-4

The Trends Menswear Depreciation application also contains a File menu that displays the following menu items: Display Inventory, Clear, and Exit (Figure 8-5).

FIGURE 8-5

© jens Karlsson/Flickr Select/Getty Images

When the user taps or clicks the Display Inventory menu item, the application opens a second Windows Form object that shows the items in inventory in sorted alphabetical order (Figure 8-6).

FIGURE 8-6

© jens Karlsson/Flickr Select/Getty Images

Introduction to Arrays

After completing Chapters 1 through 7 in this book, you know how to create the user interface for the chapter project, which involves Button, ListBox, Label, and RadioButton objects. The challenge in this chapter is to write code that adds data to the form efficiently and accurately. To do so, you must understand arrays and file handling. The next section provides background on arrays.

Arrays

Every application you have developed thus far involved a limited number of variables and data, but in professional programming projects, applications deal with much larger sets of data that need numerous variables. You have learned that data type variables can store only one value at a time. Therefore, you have not used data types that contain more than one memory location to store more than one value at a time. If you changed a variable's value, the previous value was erased because a typical variable can only store one value at a time. For example, if you wanted to create an application that recorded dinner reservations at a restaurant for named groups with different numbers of people in the groups, you would need a unique variable name for each reservation, as shown in Figure 8-7.

```
5            Dim intBakerReservation As Integer = 4
6            Dim intLopezReservation As Integer = 5
7            Dim intBuckReservation As Integer = 12
8            Dim intChanReservation As Integer = 2
9            Dim intTirrellReservation As Integer = 8
```

FIGURE 8-7

For a large restaurant, you would need to create hundreds of variables to hold hundreds of reservations each night. Having hundreds of variables just to record each night's reservations is impractical and difficult to manage. As you can see, a different kind of variable that can hold more than one value is required.

The solution to developing applications with larger amounts of data is to use an array. An **array** variable is simply a variable that can store more than one value. In fact, an array in Visual Basic can hold more than a million values. Each individual item in an array that contains a value is called an **element**.

Arrays provide access to data by using a numeric **index**, or **subscript**, to identify each element in the array. Using an array, you can store a sequence of values of similar data type. For example, you can store six values of type Decimal without having to declare six different variables. Instead, each of the six values is stored in an individual element of the array, and you refer to each element according to its index within the array. Zero is the index used to reference a value in the first array element. Each subsequent element is referenced by an increasing index value, as shown in Figure 8-8.

decShoeSize(0)	decShoeSize(1)	decShoeSize(2)	decShoeSize(3)	decShoeSize(4)	decShoeSize(5)
9.0	11.5	6.0	7.5	13.0	8.0

FIGURE 8-8

In Figure 8-8, an array named decShoeSize holds six shoe sizes. Each shoe size is stored in an array element, and each element is assigned a unique index. The first value (9.0) is stored in the element with the index of 0. The element is identified by the term decShoeSize(0), which is pronounced "decShoeSize sub zero." The second shoe size (11.5) is stored in the second element of the array, which is referenced as decShoeSize(1). The same scheme is used for all elements in the array.

Initialize an Array

To declare an array in a program, you must include an array declaration statement, which states the name of the array, how many items it can store, and what sort of data it can store. To initialize or declare an array, just as in declaring any other variable, you must reserve the amount of memory that will be needed to store the array. The syntax for declaring an array begins with the word Dim (Figure 8-9).

General Format: Declare an Array

```
Dim intReservations(300) as Integer
```

intReservations assigns the array name

300 is the index or subscript reserving the amount of memory needed – it is the highest numbered index

Integer determines the data type of the entire array

FIGURE 8-9

© 2014 Cengage Learning

The statement in Figure 8-9 declares intReservations as an array of integer variables that holds 301 elements. The first array element is intReservations(0), then intReservations(1), and so on to the last element in the array, intReservations(300). All arrays in Visual Basic 2012 are zero based, meaning that the index of the first element is zero and the indexes increase sequentially by 1. You must specify the number of array elements by indicating the upper-bound index of the array. The upper-bound number specifies the index of the last element of the array. Setting the size of an array is called dimensioning the array.

If you know the values to be placed in each element in the array, you can declare an array by assigning values to each element, as shown in Figure 8-10.

```
13        Dim strNames() As String = {"Baker", "Lopez", "Buck", "Chan", "Tirrell"}
14        Dim intReservations() As Integer = {4, 5, 12, 2, 8}
```

FIGURE 8-10

The data to be placed in each element is contained within curly brackets. An array can be any data type. In Figure 8-10, the first array is a String data type and the second array is an Integer data type. strNames() is an array of String variables that contains five names, with Baker stored in strNames(0), Lopez in strNames(1), and so on. intReservations() is an array of Integer variables that contains five values, with 4 stored in intReservations(0), 5 in intReservations(1), and so on.

These two arrays are **parallel arrays**. Parallel arrays store related data in two or more arrays. The information for one reservation includes strNames(0) for the Baker reservation and the number of people associated with it (4) in intReservations(0). The same subscript is used for the corresponding array elements, as shown in Figure 8-11 and Figure 8-12, which illustrate the arrays created by the code in Figure 8-10.

strNames(0)	strNames(1)	strNames(2)	strNames(3)	strNames(4)
Baker	Lopez	Buck	Chan	Tirrell

FIGURE 8-11

© 2014 Cengage Learning

intReservations(0)	intReservations(1)	intReservations(2)	intReservations(3)	intReservations(4)
4	5	12	2	8

FIGURE 8-12

© 2014 Cengage Learning

Visual Basic determines the size of the array by counting the number of items within the curly brackets. In this case, each array has five elements, and each element has an index number ranging from 0 to 4. The upper-bound index is 4, which specifies the last element of the array. When a number is not used in the declaration statement to state the size of the array, the array is **implicitly sized**, meaning that the number of values is determined at execution. Instead of stating the size, you list the values stored in the array.

Another way to declare an array is to specify its upper-bound index and assign each item of the array one by one, as shown in Figure 8-13. Each sport is assigned to a different element of the strAthlete() array.

HEADS UP

When declaring an implicitly sized array, do not place an upper-bound index in the parentheses following the array name in the declaration. If you do, an error will occur when the array is assigned elements.

```
17          Dim strAthlete(5) As String
18
19          strAthlete(0)  =  "Football"
20          strAthlete(1)  =  "Soccer"
21          strAthlete(2)  =  "Lacrosse"
22          strAthlete(3)  =  "Baseball"
23          strAthlete(4)  =  "Tennis"
24          strAthlete(5)  =  "Hockey"
```

FIGURE 8-13

Initialize an Array with Default Values

When you initialize an array but do not assign values immediately, each element is assigned a default value. The table in Figure 8-14 shows the default value assigned to each data type.

Data Type	Default Value
All numeric data types	0
String data type	Null
Boolean data type	False

FIGURE 8-14

© 2014 Cengage Learning

After the array has been initialized, specific values can be assigned to each element, replacing the default value for each item. You can assign explicit values to the first few elements of the array and allow its remaining elements to be assigned to the default values automatically.

Access Array Elements Using a Loop

Because an array can contain multiple elements, in code you can use a loop to reference each element of an array. Loops can save valuable time when processing a large array because you don't have to write code for each array element. For example, if you were recording the lowest temperature for each day during the month of January to use in later calculations, the code in Figure 8-15 would allow the user to enter all 31 temperatures.

```
26        Dim intDailyTempJanuary(31) As Integer
27        Dim strTemp As String
28        Dim intDays As Integer
29
30        For intDays = 0 To 30
31            strTemp = InputBox("Enter the lowest temperature on January " _
32                & intDays + 1, "Obtain Temperatures")
33            intDailyTempJanuary(intDays) = Convert.ToInt32(strTemp)
34        Next
```

FIGURE 8-15

The array intDailyTempJanuary can hold the low temperature for each of the 31 days in January by using the elements referenced by the subscripts of 0 to 30. The loop counts from 0 to 30 using the variable intDays. The first time through the loop, the temperature obtained in an InputBox is assigned to a String named strTemp. Then, the value in strTemp is converted to an integer and assigned to the element intDailyTempJanuary(0). On each subsequent pass through the loop, the temperature obtained is placed in the next element, moving from intDailyTempJanuary(1) to intDailyTempJanuary(2) and so on until the final value for January 31 is assigned to the array element intDailyTempJanuary(30).

By using a loop in this manner, the program can process items in a large array with a few simple lines.

Array Boundaries

The Visual Basic compiler determines if each subscript is within the boundaries set when you initialized the array. For example, if you initialize an array to contain 31 elements but attempt to reference an element outside that boundary, as shown in Figure 8-16, an exception is produced when the code is executed.

```
37          Dim intDailyTempJanuary(30) As Integer
38          Dim strTemp As String
39          Dim intDays As Integer
40
41          For intDays = 0 To 31
42              strTemp = InputBox("Enter the lowest temperature on January " _
43                  & intDays + 1, "Obtain Temperatures")
44              intDailyTempJanuary(intDays) = Convert.ToInt32(strTemp)
45          Next
```

FIGURE 8-16

The exception occurs when the loop tries to reference an element with the subscript 31. This element does not exist because the array contains 31 elements with an upper-bound index of 30. (Remember that an array's elements always are numbered beginning with zero.) The exception created by the code in Figure 8-16 is an IndexOutOfRangeException (Figure 8-17). A Try-Catch statement can catch this exception, but it is best to stay within the array boundaries of zero and the upper-bound array subscript.

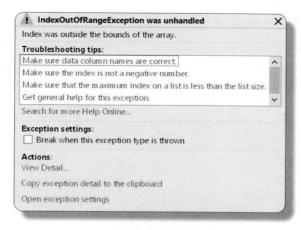

FIGURE 8-17

HEADS UP

A subscript for an array cannot be less than the value 0.

Upper-Bound Index Constant

An array can use a constant value to represent its upper-bound index. By using a constant, the size of several arrays can be specified quickly; as you will learn in the next section, they also can be changed quickly. In Figure 8-18, the arrays strFirstNames() and strLastNames() are sized to hold 41 elements (the indexes are from 0 to 40).

```
Const intUpperBound As Integer = 40
Dim strFirstNames(intUpperBound) As String
Dim strLastNames(intUpperBound) As String
```

FIGURE 8-18

HEADS UP

If you redimension an array to a smaller size and use the Preserve command, you still will lose the items between the original upper-bound array size and the new upper-bound size.

Reinitialize an Array

Although you usually set the number of elements in an array when you declare it, you can alter the size of the array later in the code. Every array in Visual Basic is considered **dynamic**, which means that you can resize it at run time. When you change the number of elements in an existing array, you redimension it. The **ReDim** statement assigns a new array size to the specified array variable. You use a ReDim statement to change the number of elements in an array. The code in Figure 8-19 reinitializes the strEmployees array.

```
Dim strEmployees(50) As String
' Later in the code
ReDim strEmployees(65)
```

FIGURE 8-19

The strEmployees array originally is sized to hold 51 values, but is reinitialized later in the code to hold 66 values. When you use the ReDim statement to redimension the array, all the data contained in the array is lost. If you want to preserve the existing data, you can use the keyword **Preserve**, as shown in Figure 8-20. Preserve resizes the array and retains the data in the elements from 0 through 50.

```
Dim strEmployees(50) As String
' Later in the code
ReDim Preserve strEmployees(65)
```

FIGURE 8-20

Use the Length Property

The Length property of an array contains the number of elements in an array. The code shown in Figure 8-21 displays 51 as the array size.

```
59          Dim strBranchOffices(50) As String
60
61          lblArraySize.Text = "The array size is " & (strBranchOffices.Length)
```

FIGURE 8-21

You can use the Length property in a loop to determine the exact number of iterations needed to cycle through each element in the array. Using the Length property can prevent the program from throwing the IndexOutOfRange exception. In the code in Figure 8-22, the For loop uses the Length property to determine the number of loop iterations.

```
63          Dim intYear(99) As Integer
64          Dim intCount As Integer
65
66          ' Assigns the years from 2001 to 2100 to the elements in the table
67          For intCount = 0 To (intYear.Length - 1)
68              intYear(intCount) = 2001 + intCount
69          Next
```

FIGURE 8-22

In the code in Figure 8-22, intYear.Length is equal to 100 (elements 0 through 99), one more than the array's upper-bound index number. In the For loop, the loop count will run from zero through 99 (intYear.Length – 1), which means the loop will be executed 100 times, once for each element in the array.

Because an array can be resized at anytime, the Length property is useful when you are unsure of an array's size.

Use Arrays

Arrays can be useful in many situations, such as when dealing with large amounts of data and finding totals and averages. For example, the code in Figure 8-23 computes the total yearly income and average yearly income for 10 employees in the warehouse department.

```
71      Dim intYearlySalary(9) As Integer
72      Dim intNumberOfEmployees As Integer
73      Dim intAdd As Integer
74      Dim intTotal As Integer
75
76      ' Allows the user to enter the 10 yearly salaries
77      For intNumberOfEmployees = 0 To (intYearlySalary.Length - 1)
78          intYearlySalary(intNumberOfEmployees) = _
79              InputBox("Enter Salary #" & intNumberOfEmployees + 1, _
80              "Warehouse Dept.")
81      Next
82
83      ' Finds the total amount of salaries entered
84      For intAdd = 0 To (intYearlySalary.Length - 1)
85          intTotal += intYearlySalary(intAdd)
86      Next
87
88      lblDisplayTotalSalary.Text = intTotal.ToString("C2")
89      lblDisplayAverageSalary.Text =_
90      (intTotal / intYearlySalary.Length).ToString("C2")
```

FIGURE 8-23

The reason the value accumulated in the intTotal variable is divided by the Length property is that the intYearlySalary array contains 10 elements. To find the average, you add all the numbers and divide by the number of elements. The line of code that finds the average (line 89) is outside of the loop because the average should be determined once, not repeatedly within the loop.

In the chapter project, the Items property of the lstInventoryId ListBox object must be filled with the inventory item numbers. The inventory item numbers are contained in the _strItemId array. The code in Figure 8-24 places the inventory item numbers in the Items property of the ListBox object. The Length property of the _strItemId array is used to determine the number of iterations in the For loop.

```
43      ' The ListBox object is filled with the Inventory IDs
44      For intFill = 0 To (_strItemId.Length - 1)
45          lstInventoryId.Items.Add(_strItemId(intFill))
46      Next
```

FIGURE 8-24

On line 44, the For loop begins with the intFill variable containing the value 0, which references the first element in the _strItemId array. On each pass through the loop, the value in intFill is incremented by 1 so it references the next element in the array. The loop terminates when the value in intFill is greater than the length of the array minus 1. Recall that the length of the array counts from 1 but the subscript counts from 0. Therefore, the length of the array minus 1 references the last element in the array.

The result of the code in Figure 8-24 is shown in Figure 8-25.

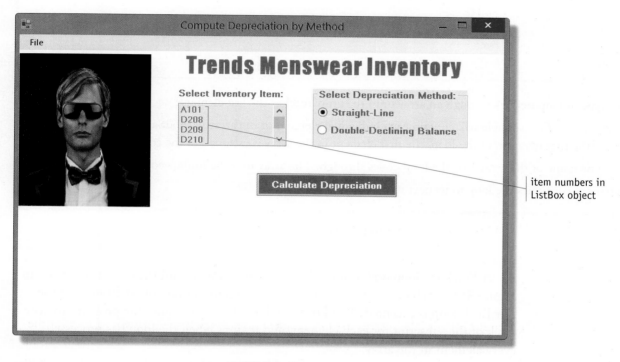

item numbers in ListBox object

FIGURE 8-25

When I use an array in code, I can refer to multiple values by the same name. Does this make my code shorter?

Arrays can shorten and simplify your code, allowing you to create loops that deal efficiently with any number of elements.

CONSIDER THIS

The For Each Loop

Recall from earlier chapters that a loop repeats a process. A special loop designed specifically for arrays is called a **For Each** loop. The loop syntax is shown in Figure 8-26.

General Format: For Each

For Each *Control Variable Name* in *Array Name*

```
` Lines of Code
```

Next

For Each — This type of loop iterates through an array until the array reaches the last element.

Control Variable Name — This variable will contain each individual element of the array without a subscript as the loop is processed. During the first iteration of the loop, the first element in the array is assigned to the control variable.

Array Name( ) — The name of the array that the loop cycles through. The array must be initialized first.

Next — This statement continues the loop to its next iteration.

FIGURE 8-26

A For Each loop cycles through each array element until the end of the array. In Figure 8-27, each element in the array is assigned to the variable strPioneer as the For Each loop is executed. The For Each loop does not require the program to keep track of the subscript for each element, and it stops when the loop has processed every element in the array.

Because each element in the array is assigned to the control variable, the elements and the variable must be the same data type. For example, in Figure 8-27, the array elements and the control variable are both Strings.

```
93      Private Sub btnHistory_Click(ByVal sender As System.Object, ByVal e As System.    ↙
        EventArgs) Handles btnHistory.Click
94
95          Dim strFamousComputerPioneers() As String = {"Pascal", _
96              "Babbage", "Ada", "Aiken", "Jobs"}
97          Dim strHeading As String = "Computer Pioneers:"
98          Dim strPioneer As String
99
100         lstPioneers.Items.Add(strHeading)
101         lstPioneers.Items.Add("")
102
103         For Each strPioneer In strFamousComputerPioneers
104             lstPioneers.Items.Add(strPioneer)
105         Next
106
107     End Sub
```

FIGURE 8-27

When the loop begins, the first element of the strFamousComputerPioneers array is placed in the strPioneer variable and the body of the loop is executed. In the body of the loop, the value in strPioneer is added to the Items property of the lstPioneers ListBox object. On the second iteration of the loop, the second element of the array is placed in the strPioneer variable and the body of the loop is executed again. This looping continues until all elements within the array have been processed.

After the loop processing is complete, the lstPioneers ListBox object displays the output shown in Figure 8-28.

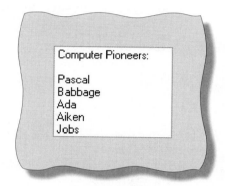

FIGURE 8-28

Scope of Arrays

The scope of an array declared within a procedure is local to that procedure, but an array can be declared as a class-level variable. As with other variables, an array declared as a class-level variable is visible to all procedures within the class. For example, in the chapter project, multiple procedures will use the contents of the arrays that hold the inventory information for Trends Menswear. Therefore, these arrays should be declared as class-level arrays, as shown in Figure 8-29. Later in the chapter, the scope of these variables will be changed so that other classes can access the variables.

```
 9      Public Class frmDepreciation
10
11          ' Class Level Private variables
12          Private _intLifeOfItems As Integer = 5
13          Private _intSizeOfArray As Integer = 7
14          Private _strInventoryItem(_intSizeOfArray) As String
15          Private _strItemId(_intSizeOfArray) As String
16          Private _decInitialPrice(_intSizeOfArray) As Decimal
17          Private _intQuantity(_intSizeOfArray) As Integer
```

FIGURE 8-29

The arrays in Figure 8-29 can be referenced in any procedure following the declaration within the class. Notice that the size of the arrays is determined by the value in the _intSizeOfArray variable, which is declared on line 13.

Pass an Array

An array can be passed as an argument to a Sub procedure or a Function procedure. For example, if you need to find the sum of a salesperson's commissions, you can pass the array that holds the commission amounts to a Sub procedure. The Sub procedure named ComputeDisplayTotal in Figure 8-30 accepts a Decimal array. The For Each loop in this Sub procedure accumulates the sum of the commission amounts.

```
109    Private Sub btnCommission_Click(ByVal sender As System.Object, ByVal e As System. ↙
       EventArgs) Handles btnCommission.Click
110
111        Dim decCommissionAmounts() As Decimal = {1345.99, 7800.16, _
112            5699.99, 3928.09, 1829.45}
113
114        ComputeDisplayTotal(decCommissionAmounts)
115
116    End Sub
117
118    Private Sub ComputeDisplayTotal(ByVal decValueOfCommission() As Decimal)
119
120        Dim decAmount As Decimal
121        Dim decTotal As Decimal = 0
122
123        For Each decAmount In decValueOfCommission
124            decTotal += decAmount
125        Next
126
127        lblTotalCommission.Text = "The Total Commission is " _
128            & decTotal.ToString("C")
129    End Sub
```

FIGURE 8-30

Notice that the array is passed using the ByVal keyword, but with arrays ByVal has a different meaning. Arrays can be passed by value or by reference; however, the ByVal keyword does not restrict a Sub procedure or Function procedure from changing the array's elements. Whether you pass an array by value or by reference, the original array can be accessed and modified within the Sub or Function procedure. When passing arrays using ByVal, the array is not duplicated. If you change the value of any array element in a procedure, the original array is changed.

In Figure 8-31, the decCommissionAmounts array is defined on line 133. The third element is given the value 5699.99. On line 147 in the ChangeValue Sub procedure, the third element in the array, referenced as decValueOfCommission(2), is changed. When the array is displayed in the btnCommission_Click event (line 140), the third element has been changed (see Figure 8-32).

```
131    Private Sub btnCommission_Click(ByVal sender As System.Object, ByVal e As System. ↙
       EventArgs) Handles btnCommission.Click
132
133        Dim decCommissionAmounts() As Decimal = {1345.99, 7800.16, _
134            5699.99, 3928.09, 1829.45}
135        Dim decDisplay As Decimal
136
137        ChangeValue(decCommissionAmounts)
138
139        For Each decDisplay In decCommissionAmounts
140            lstDisplay.Items.Add(decDisplay.ToString("C"))
141        Next
142
143    End Sub
144
145    Private Sub ChangeValue(ByVal decValueOfCommission() As Decimal)
146
147        decValueOfCommission(2) = 4599.99
148
149    End Sub
```

FIGURE 8-31

FIGURE 8-32

Sort an Array

The data in an array often is sorted for an organized display. For example, the telephone white pages are sorted by last name, which makes it easier to search for and locate friends and family members. To sort array contents in Visual Basic, you use a procedure named **Sort**. When the Sort procedure is applied to an array, the lowest value is placed in the first element in the array with an index of zero, the next lowest value is placed in the second element, and so on until the largest value is stored in the highest element of the array. The syntax for the Sort procedure is shown in Figure 8-33.

General Format: Sort Procedure

Array.Sort (ArrayName)

Coding Example:

Dim intAges() as Integer = {16, 64, 41, 8, 19, 81, 23}

Array.Sort(intAges)

After the sort executes, the values in the array are in the order 8, 16, 19, 23, 41, 64, and 81.

FIGURE 8-33

© 2014 Cengage Learning

In the Trends Menswear Inventory Depreciation application, the array _strInventoryItem is declared as a class-level private variable that contains String data, as shown in Figure 8-34. Later the variable will be changed to public to be accessed by a second class. The size of the array is specified by the value in the _intSizeOfArray variable.

```
13      Private _intSizeOfArray As Integer = 7
14      Private _strInventoryItem(_intSizeOfArray) As String
```

FIGURE 8-34

The array is filled with data from a text file in another procedure. The inventory items in the text file are not sorted, but the items should be sorted before being displayed in a ListBox object. Therefore, the array is sorted using the Array.Sort procedure, as shown in Figure 8-35. After sorting, a For Each loop displays the elements in the array in ascending alphabetic (A to Z) order, as shown in Figure 8-36.

```
11          Dim strItem As String
12
13          ' Sorts the _strInventoryItem array
14          Array.Sort(frmDepreciation._strInventoryItem)
15
16          ' Displays the _strInventoryItem array
17          For Each strItem In frmDepreciation._strInventoryItem
18              lstDisplay.Items.Add(strItem)
19          Next
```

FIGURE 8-35

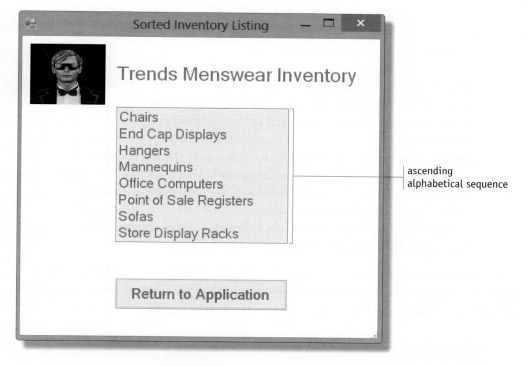

FIGURE 8-36

© Jens Karlsson/Flickr Select/Getty Images

Search an Array

Arrays provide an excellent way to store and process information. Suppose an array holds 5,000 student names in alphabetical order. If you searched for one name in that array, the search could take some time. One search approach is to begin with the first name in index zero and evaluate each name until you find a match. Searching each element in an array is called a **sequential search.** Theoretically, you might have to search 5,000 names before you find a match or discover that the name is not even in the array. For these reasons, a sequential search is not the most efficient way of searching for an element.

If an array is large and requires many repeated searches, you need a more efficient search approach. The **BinarySearch** method searches a sorted array for a value using a binary search algorithm, which searches an array by repeatedly dividing the search interval in half. In an array with the contents shown in Figure 8-37, you could quickly find the value 405 using the BinarySearch method.

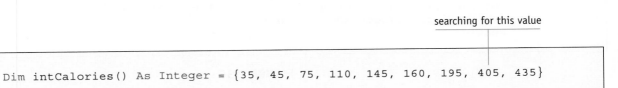

searching for this value

```
165         Dim intCalories() As Integer = {35, 45, 75, 110, 145, 160, 195, 405, 435}
```

FIGURE 8-37

The steps for the BinarySearch method are:

1. Determine the halfway point of the array, which is the number 145 in Figure 8-37. Compare that value first: 145 is less than 405.
2. If the first comparison is not equal to the number being searched, determine whether the value of the search number is less than the middle value. If the search value is less, narrow the search interval to the lower half of the array. Otherwise, narrow the search to the upper half of the array. The search value 405 is greater than the middle value 145, so the process narrows the search to the upper half of the array, which contains 160, 195, 405, and 435.
3. Repeatedly check each interval until the value is found or until the halving process evaluates the entire element list of the array.

The BinarySearch procedure returns the matching index value if the element is found. If the array does not contain the specified value, the method returns a negative integer. The BinarySearch procedure syntax is shown in Figure 8-38.

General Format: BinarySearch Procedure

```
intValue = Array.BinarySearch(arrayname, value)
```

If intValue returns a positive number or zero, a match was found at the subscript number equal to intValue.

If intValue returns a negative number, a match was not found

FIGURE 8-38

© 2014 Cengage Learning

As another example, a user enters the number of calories to consume, and the code in Figure 8-39 determines if the number of calories is found in the intCalories() array. The code also displays the food item index location if it finds a match with the number of calories entered. If the number of calories is not found, a message reports that the food item is not found.

```
165          Dim intCalories() As Integer = {35, 45, 75, 110, 145, 160, _
166              195, 405, 435}
167          Dim strFoods() As String = {"Carrots", "Kiwi", "Egg", "Orange", _
168              "Cola", "Taco", "Yogurt", "Apple Pie Slice", "Raisins"}
169          Dim intSelection As Integer
170          Dim intIndexLocation As Integer
171
172          intSelection = Convert.ToInt32(txtCalories.Text)
173          intIndexLocation = Array.BinarySearch(intCalories, intSelection)
174          If intIndexLocation >= 0 Then
175              lblLocation.Text = "The search item is found in subscript number " _
176                  & intIndexLocation
177              lblFood.Text = strFoods(intIndexLocation)
178          Else
179              lblLocation.Text = "The food item not found"
180          End If
```

FIGURE 8-39

If the calorie value of 405 is entered into the txtCalories TextBox object, the message "The search item is found in subscript number 7" is displayed in lblLocation. The second Label object displays Apple Pie Slice.

Create a Two-Dimensional Array

An array that has a single index or subscript is called a one-dimensional array, but arrays can be multidimensional and hold complex information. An array that has two dimensions has two subscripts. A **two-dimensional array** holds data that is arranged in rows and columns, as shown in Figure 8-40. In other words, two-dimensional arrays store the elements of tables. The array intVal is initialized with three rows and four columns in Figure 8-41 (recall that the values in parentheses specify the highest numbered element).

```
182          Dim intVal(2, 3) As Integer
```

FIGURE 8-40

	column 0	column 1	column 2	column 3
row 0	intVal(0,0)	intVal(0,1)	intVal(0,2)	intVal(0,3)
row 1	intVal(1,0)	intVal(1,1)	intVal(1,2)	intVal(1,3)
row 2	intVal(2,0)	intVal(2,1)	intVal(2,2)	intVal(2,3)

FIGURE 8-41

The table in Figure 8-42 shows the four busiest airports in the United States. The numbers are represented in millions, and identify the number of passengers traveling through each airport each year, according to the Bureau of Transportation Services. The table shows that Atlanta is the busiest airport in the United States, with over 34 million passengers flying through the airport each year. The table has four rows and two columns.

	column 0 2008	column 1 2007	
Atlanta	35	34	**row(0)**
Chicago	28	27	**row(1)**
Dallas	24	23	**row(2)**
Los Angeles	20	19	**row(3)**

FIGURE 8-42

The array declared to hold the contents of the busiest airport table is the same as a one-dimensional array, except for the two subscripts that hold the row and column index values. The declaration statement in Figure 8-43 initializes an array with four rows (0, 1, 2, 3) and two columns (0, 1) named intPassengers.

```
184        Dim intPassengers(3, 1) As Integer
```

FIGURE 8-43

After the array has been initialized, users can enter the values into a TextBox object from the table information or the program can assign the values by using an implicitly sized array, such as the one shown in Figure 8-44.

```
192        Dim intPassengers(,) As Integer = {{35, 34}, {28, 27}, {24, 23}, _
193          {20, 19}}
```

FIGURE 8-44

In the code shown in Figure 8-45, the array representing the busiest U.S. airports is totaled by column to find the number of passengers who flew through the four airports in each of the two years. A nested loop is used to total the two columns of the two-dimensional array. The outer loop controls the column index and the inner loop controls the row index of the array.

```
192        Dim intPassengers(,) As Integer = {{35, 34}, {28, 27}, {24, 23}, _
193            {20, 19}}
194        Dim intTotalColumn As Integer = 0
195        Dim intCol As Integer
196        Dim intRow As Integer
197
198        For intCol = 0 To 1
199            'Resets the total to 0
200            intTotalColumn = 0
201            For intRow = 0 To 3
202                intTotalColumn += intPassengers(intRow, intCol)
203            Next
204            MsgBox("The Sum of Column #" & intCol + 1 & " is " _
205                & intTotalColumn.ToString & " million.")
206        Next
```

FIGURE 8-45

The output for the airport program is shown in Figure 8-46 and Figure 8-47.

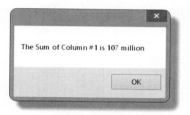

FIGURE 8-46

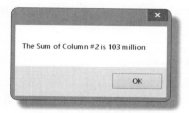

FIGURE 8-47

File Handling

In the applications you created in this book so far, the information entered has originated from assigning data to variables or asking the user to enter data in objects on the form. In many business applications, entering information can be time-consuming if you must enter data for thousands of items. To process data more efficiently, many developers use text files to store and access information for use within an application. Text files have a **.txt** extension. The Windows operating system provides a basic text editor called Notepad that allows you to save files with the .txt extension. A simple text file is called a **sequential file**.

For example, in the chapter project, Trends Menswear's inventory is stored in a text file. By gaining access to that information, the depreciation program can manipulate the data and compute the depreciation for items in the inventory. The text file is available at CengageBrain.com. Visual Basic can access many types of files, including text files, as discussed in this chapter, or various types of databases, which are covered in Chapter 10.

With Visual Basic 2012, the System.IO (input/output) namespace in the .NET Framework provides several classes for working with text files, binary files, directories, and byte streams. The System.IO namespace allows you to create, copy, move, and delete files. The file handler supports all types of data, including both string and numeric data types. The most commonly used classes are FileStream, BinaryReader, BinaryWriter, StreamReader, and StreamWriter.

CONSIDER THIS

Can I read other types of files besides a text file created in Notepad?
The code in this chapter deals specifically with text files created in a text editor such as Notepad, but the System.IO namespace in the .NET Framework provides several classes for working with text files, binary files, directories, and byte streams.

Read a Text File

To open a text file, you need an object available in the System.IO called a **StreamReader**. As its name suggests, this object reads streams of text. You create a StreamReader to provide access to standard input and output files.

To read a file, a variable object is first created for a data type called StreamReader. The prefix for an object is obj in the format used in Figure 8-48.

```
24          Dim objReader As IO.StreamReader
```

FIGURE 8-48

After the object variable is declared, an If statement in the form IO.File.Exists("*filename*") determines if the file is available, as shown in Figure 8-49. The command IO.File.OpenText("*filename*") opens the text file and assigns it to the object variable objReader.

```
31          If IO.File.Exists("e:\inventory.txt") = True Then
32              objReader = IO.File.OpenText("e:\inventory.txt")
33          Else
34              MsgBox("The file is not available. Restart the program when the  ↙
       file is available",,"Error")
35              Close()
36          End If
```

FIGURE 8-49

To read each line of the text file, you use a ReadLine procedure. The first line of data in the text file is assigned to the first element in the array _strInventoryItem (see Figure 8-50).

```
35          _strInventoryItem(intCount) = objReader.ReadLine()
```

FIGURE 8-50

To determine whether the end of the file has been reached, use the Peek procedure of the StreamReader object. The Peek procedure reads the next character in the file without changing position. If the end of the file is reached, the Peek procedure returns the value of −1. You can use a Do While loop to determine if all the lines in the file have been read. When the Peek procedure reaches the end of the file and returns a −1, the Do While loop ends, as shown in Figure 8-51.

```
34          Do While objReader.Peek <> -1
35              _strInventoryItem(intCount) = objReader.ReadLine()
36              _strItemId(intCount) = objReader.ReadLine()
37              _decInitialPrice(intCount) = Convert.ToDecimal(objReader.ReadLine())
38              _intQuantity(intCount) = Convert.ToInt32(objReader.ReadLine())
39              intCount += 1
40          Loop
```

FIGURE 8-51

Before closing the application, be sure to close the file to terminate communications with it, as shown in Figure 8-52.

```
40          objReader.Close()
```

FIGURE 8-52

The Trends Menswear application opens and reads a file named inventory.txt. To read data from a text file, you can complete the following steps:

STEP 1 Open the code window by tapping or clicking the View Code button on the Solution Explorer toolbar. Tap or click inside the frmDepreciation_Load event.

The code window opens and the insertion point appears in the frmDepreciation_Load event handler (Figure 8-53).

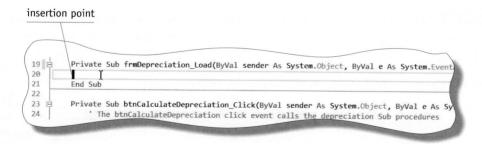

insertion point

```
19    Private Sub frmDepreciation_Load(ByVal sender As System.Object, ByVal e As System.Event
20
21    End Sub
22
23    Private Sub btnCalculateDepreciation_Click(ByVal sender As System.Object, ByVal e As Sy
24          ' The btnCalculateDepreciation click event calls the depreciation Sub procedures
```

FIGURE 8-53

STEP 2   Initialize the variables. Assign an object variable to the IO.StreamReader object. Initialize the StreamReader object by typing `Dim objReader As IO.` An IntelliSense window opens. Select StreamReader. Press enter. Finish declaring the rest of the variable names.

After the objReader object variable is initialized in the IO namespace, IntelliSense opens a listing of IO procedures. The variables are initialized (Figure 8-54).

```
19    Private Sub frmDepreciation_Load(ByVal sender As System.Object, ByVal e As System.EventArg
20
21        ' Initialize an instance of the StreamReader object and declare variables
22        Dim objReader As IO.StreamReader
23        Dim intCount As Integer = 0
24        Dim intFill As Integer
25
26    End Sub
```

FIGURE 8-54

STEP 3   Verify that the inventory.txt data file is available by typing `If IO.` to open an IntelliSense window. Complete the rest of the line using IntelliSense, as shown in Figure 8-55. Assign the objReader variable by typing `objR` and then pressing CTRL + SPACEBAR to complete the variable name. Type `= IO.` to open an IntelliSense window. Type `F`.

The If statement confirms that the data file exists. The objReader is assigned to open the inventory.txt file (Figure 8-55).

IntelliSense list —

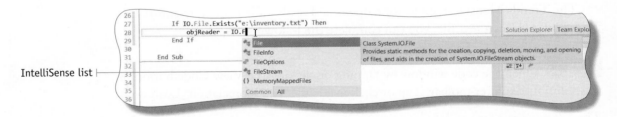

```
26
27        If IO.File.Exists("e:\inventory.txt") Then
28            objReader = IO.F
29        End If
30
31    End Sub
```
Solution Explorer Team Explo

File — Class System.IO.File
FileInfo — Provides static methods for the creation, copying, deletion, moving, and opening
FileOptions — of files, and aids in the creation of System.IO.FileStream objects.
FileStream
MemoryMappedFiles
Common All

FIGURE 8-55

HEADS UP

If your computer's USB drive has a different path, change the drive letter in the path statement.

STEP 4   Select File by typing a period and select OpenText from the IntelliSense list. Type `("e:\inventory.txt")` to access the inventory text file from the USB drive (drive E).

The inventory.txt file is opened on the USB drive (Figure 8-56).

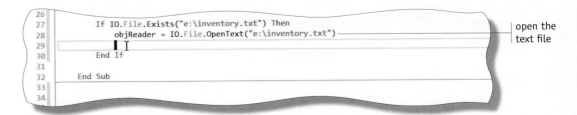

```
26
27        If IO.File.Exists("e:\inventory.txt") Then
28            objReader = IO.File.OpenText("e:\inventory.txt") ——— open the
29                                                                  text file
30        End If
31
32    End Sub
33
34
```

FIGURE 8-56

STEP 5 To read each line of the text file, insert a Do While loop that continues until the Peek procedure returns the value of –1. Specify that the ReadLine() procedure reads each line of the text file. Use the variable intCount to determine the index of each array element.

The code is entered to read inventory item names, item IDs, initial price, and quantity from the text file and assign them to class module-level array variables until the last item of the file is read (Figure 8-57).

```
34          ' Read the file line by line until the file is completed
35          Do While objReader.Peek <> -1
36              _strInventoryItem(intCount) = objReader.ReadLine()
37              _strItemId(intCount) = objReader.ReadLine()
38              _decInitialPrice(intCount) = Convert.ToDecimal(objReader.ReadLine())
39              _intQuantity(intCount) = Convert.ToInt32(objReader.ReadLine())
40              intCount += 1
41          Loop
42
```

read each line of the text file into the appropriate array element

FIGURE 8-57

STEP 6 After the data file has been read, close the file. Insert an Else statement that informs the user if the file cannot be opened and then closes the application.

The object variable objReader file is closed and the Else statement informs the user if the file is not available (Figure 8-58).

if no file is available, inform the user and close the application window

if file was opened, close the file

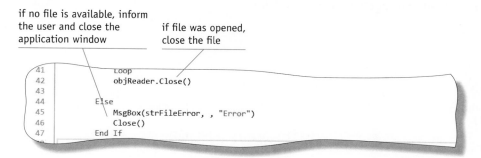

```
41              Loop
42              objReader.Close()
43
44          Else
45              MsgBox(strFileError, , "Error")
46              Close()
47          End If
```

FIGURE 8-58

ONLINE REINFORCEMENT

To view a video of the process in the previous steps, visit CengageBrain.com and navigate to the resources for this title. Tap or click the link for Chapter 8 and then navigate to Video 8-2.

Do I have to access a text file stored on a USB drive?

The text file can be stored on any local computer path or network path. When you select a file using Windows Explorer, Windows 8 has a feature called Copy path that allows you to copy the path where the file is stored. You can then paste that path into your code.

CONSIDER THIS

Write to a Text File

Writing to a text file is similar to reading a text file. The System.IO namespace also includes the **StreamWriter**, which is used to write a stream of text to a file. The following example writes a file of users with their names and logon passwords to a new text file named NewAccounts.txt. Each name and password is written to a separate line in the file. The btnCreateAccount_Click event creates a text file with the new customer information, as shown in Figure 8-59. The Notepad text file named NewAccounts.txt is displayed in Figure 8-60.

```
53    Private Sub btnCreateAccount_Click(ByVal sender As System.Object, ByVal e As System↙
      .EventArgs) Handles btnCreateAccount.Click
54        ' Initialize Variables
55        Dim strCustomerName(5) As String
56        Dim strPassword(5) As String
57        Dim objWriter As New IO.StreamWriter("e:\NewAccounts.txt")
58        Dim intCount As Integer
59
60        For intCount = 0 To (strCustomerName.Length - 1)
61            strCustomerName(intCount) = InputBox("Please enter your name:", "Login ↙
      Information")
62            strPassword(intCount) = InputBox("Please enter a password:", "Password ↙
      Information")
63            If IO.File.Exists("e:\NewAccounts.txt") Then
64                ' Write the file line by line until the file is completed
65                objWriter.WriteLine(strCustomerName(intCount))
66                objWriter.WriteLine(strPassword(intCount))
67            Else
68                MsgBox("The file is not available. Restart the program when ↙
      the file is available",,"Error")
69                Close()
70            End If
71        Next
72
73        ' The file is closed
74        objWriter.Close()
75
76    End Sub
```

FIGURE 8-59

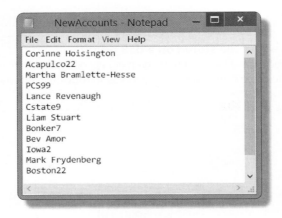

FIGURE 8-60

Compute Depreciation

Depreciation is the decrease in property value and the reduction in the balance sheet value of a company asset to reflect its age and prolonged use. The U.S. Internal Revenue Service states that the life of office equipment is five years for depreciation purposes. The two common ways of computing depreciation are the straight-line method and the double-declining balance method.

The simplest and most common method, **straight-line depreciation**, is calculated by dividing the purchase or acquisition price of an asset by the total number of productive years it can reasonably be expected to benefit the company. This value is called the life of the asset. In the chapter project, each asset in the inventory file has a life of five years. Figure 8-61 shows the formula for computing straight-line depreciation.

```
95          decStraightDepreciation = _decInitialPrice(intItemId) / _intLifeOfItems
```

FIGURE 8-61

To calculate the depreciation for end cap displays in the Trends Menswear program, you can use the straight-line depreciation method shown in Figure 8-62.

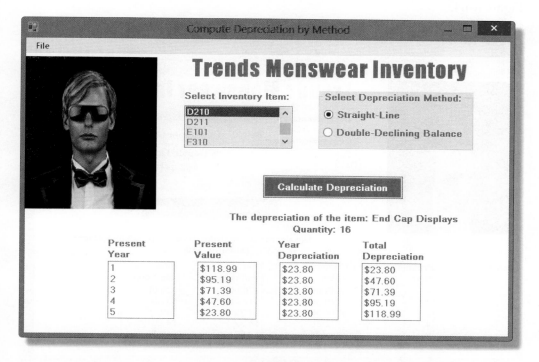

FIGURE 8-62

The double-declining balance depreciation method is like the straight-line method doubled. To use the double-declining balance method, first calculate depreciation using the formula in Figure 8-63. Notice that the price is doubled and divided by the item's life in years. After that asset is depreciated for the first year, subtract the depreciation amount from the initial price for the next year. The resulting value after subtracting the depreciation is used in the formula for each subsequent year.

```
127          ' The loop repeats for the life of the items
128      For intDoublePresentYear = 1 To   intLifeOfItems
129          ' The formula for double-declining depreciation inside the loop to repeat ↙
             the process
130          decDoubleDepreciation = (decDoublePresentYearValue * 2D) / _intLifeOfItems
131          ' Accumulates the total of depreciation
132          decDoubleTotal+ = decDoubleDepreciation
133          ' Displays the depreciation amounts
134      Next
```

FIGURE 8-63

To calculate the depreciation for store display racks in the Trends Menswear program, you can use the double-declining balance depreciation method shown in Figure 8-64.

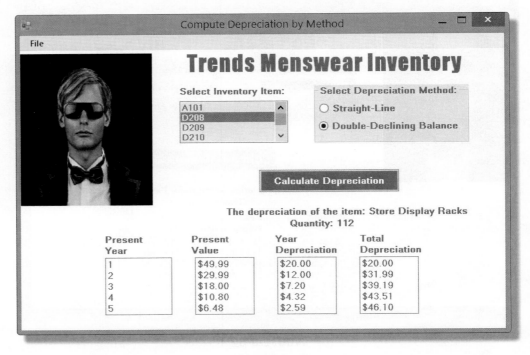

FIGURE 8-64

Use Multiple Form Objects

As program applications become larger, more than one Windows Form object often is needed to display information. Each Windows Form object in your program (Figure 8-65) is associated with a file displayed in the Solution Explorer. For example, the code stored in the frmDepreciation.vb file is displayed in the code window when you tap or click the frmDepreciation.vb tab in the design window.

FIGURE 8-65

Visual Basic 2012 allows you to add multiple Windows Form objects to an application. To add a second Windows Form object to an application, you can complete the following steps:

STEP 1 Tap or click PROJECT on the menu bar, and then tap or click Add Windows Form.

The Add New Item dialog box opens (Figure 8-66).

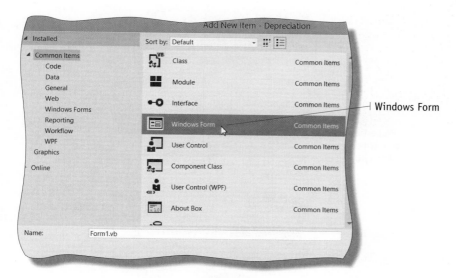

FIGURE 8-66

STEP 2   In the Add New Item dialog box, tap or click Windows Form, and then type `frmDisplayInventory.vb` in the Name text box.

A Windows Form is selected to add as a new item to the Depreciation project. The form is named frmDisplayInventory.vb (Figure 8-67).

Windows Form selected

Windows Form name

Add button

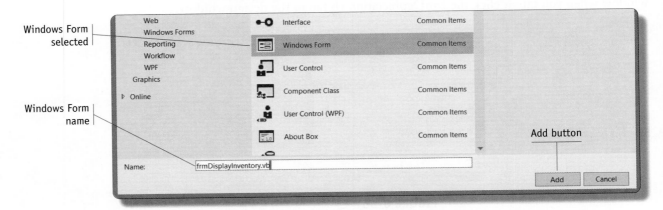

FIGURE 8-67

STEP 3   Click the Add button in the Add New Item dialog box. A second Form object named frmDisplayInventory.vb opens in the Visual Basic 2012 window. In the Properties window, change the Text property of the frmDisplayInventory object to `Sorted Inventory Listing`.

The second Form object opens and its Text property is changed (Figure 8-68).

Properties of new Windows Form object

new Windows Form object

Text property changed

FIGURE 8-68

Choose a Startup Object

Every application begins executing a project by displaying the object designated as the **Startup** object. For the depreciation application, the default Startup object is frmDepreciation.vb. However, you can change the Startup object if you want a different Form object to open first. To begin, press and hold or right-click the project name in Solution Explorer and then tap or click Properties on the shortcut menu. Tap or click the Application tab shown in Figure 8-69, tap or click the Startup form list arrow, and then tap or click the object you want to open when the application starts.

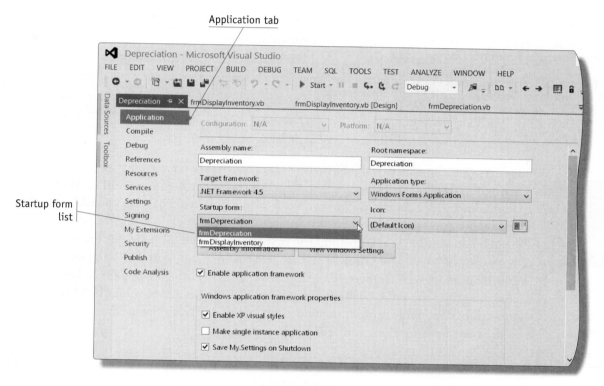

FIGURE 8-69

Create an Instance of a Windows Form Object

Now that you have multiple Windows Form objects in the application, you must write code that opens the Form objects as needed. As you create each Form object, code associated with the Form object creates a class declaration. Figure 8-70 displays the code.

```
96  Public Class frmDepreciation
97
98  End Class
```

FIGURE 8-70

The class frmDepreciation holds the object's properties and the procedures for that class. To display a second or subsequent form, the initial step is to create an **instance** of the Windows Form object. An instance is an object variable that references the second form's class name to access the object's procedures and properties. For example, in the code for the chapter project shown in Figure 8-71, the mnuDisplay_Click event opens when the user taps or clicks the Display Inventory menu item. The tap or click event declares an instance of the second form, which is named frmDisplayInventory. The object variable frmSecond references the instance of the Form object frmDisplayInventory.

```
163     Private Sub mnuDisplay_Click(ByVal sender As System.Object, ByVal e As System.     ↙
        EventArgs) Handles mnuDisplay.Click
164
165         ' The mnuDisplay click event creates an instance of the frmDisplayInventory
166         Dim frmSecond As New frmDisplayInventory
```

FIGURE 8-71

HEADS UP

Command lines placed after the ShowDialog method call are not executed until the second Form object is closed.

After the instance of the Form object is created, another statement must be written to display the instance of the second form. When creating multiple Windows Form objects, Visual Basic allows you to generate two types of forms: **modal** and **modeless**. A modal form retains the input focus while open, and the user cannot switch between Form objects until the first form is closed. You create a modal form with the ShowDialog procedure. In the code example in Figure 8-72, the second Form object, named frmSecond, is displayed using the ShowDialog procedure. The line preceding the ShowDialog() procedure hides the first form using the **Hide** procedure. The Hide procedure removes the first form from the user's screen so that it does not cover up the information it references.

```
167         'Hide this form and show the Display Inventory form
168         Hide()
169         frmSecond.ShowDialog()
```

FIGURE 8-72

The second method used when displaying multiple forms is referred to as a modeless Form object. A modeless form allows you to switch the input focus to another window. The first form stays open when you switch to another form, and lets you use the two forms at the same time. For example, a modeless form is useful for a help window that displays instructions. You create a modeless Form object with the Show procedure, as shown in Figure 8-73. A Hide method is not necessary because both Form objects are displayed at the same time.

IN THE REAL WORLD

Modeless forms are used more often than modal forms in Windows applications.

```
        frmSecond.Show()
```

FIGURE 8-73

Access Variables on Other Forms

When you create multiple Form objects, you might need to access the variable objects used in one form when you are working in another form. In the chapter project, the user can tap or click the Display Inventory menu item to open a second Form object that displays the sorted inventory items. The second form needs to reference the array initialized in the first form's code. You control the availability of a variable by specifying its access level, or **access specifier**. The access level determines what code has permission to read or write to a variable. To access a variable object on a different form, you can declare a class module-level variable with an access specifier other than Private. The access specifier Private determines that the variable can only be used with the class in which it is declared. For example, the variable _intLifeOfItems declared in Figure 8-74 can only be accessed within the class frmDepreciation because it has the access specifier Private.

```
Public Class frmDepreciation

    ' Class Module-Level variable
    Private _intLifeOfItems As Integer = 5
```

FIGURE 8-74

If you want to declare a variable object that can be used in the class where it is declared and in different classes within other Form objects, the variable can be declared using the access specifier Public Shared. A Public Shared variable is shared by all instances of a Form's class. In the chapter project, if you initialize the array of inventory items with the access specifier Public Shared in the frmDepreciation class, as shown in Figure 8-75 on the next page, the Integer _intSizeOfArray and the array _strInventoryItem are now accessible in the second form. By using the Public Shared access specifier, the variable's values are shared across all objects in the depreciation application.

```
13      Public Shared _intSizeOfArray As Integer = 7
14      Public Shared _strInventoryItem(_intSizeOfArray) As String
```

FIGURE 8-75

After the variables are initialized with the access specifier Public Shared, they can be used within a different class on more than one form. To access the shared variable on another form, specify the name of the originating Form object followed by the name of the variable object. In the chapter project, a second Form object named frmDisplayInventory accesses the _strInventoryItem array. To access the array in the second form, the array name must begin with the originating form, frmDepreciation. The originating Form object and the variable name are separated by the dot operator, as shown in Figure 8-76. The array is sorted and displayed on the second Form object.

```
7    Private Sub frmDisplayInventory_Load(ByVal sender As System.Object, ByVal e As System. ↵
     EventArgs) Handles MyBase.Load
8        ' The frmDisplayInventory load event is a second form that
9        ' displays the sorted inventory items
10
11       Dim strItem As String                          originating
12                                                       form name
13       ' Sorts the _strInventoryItem array
14       Array.Sort(frmDepreciation._strInventoryItem)
15
16       ' Displays the _strInventoryItem array
17       For Each strItem In frmDepreciation._strInventoryItem
18           lstDisplay.Items.Add(strItem)
19       Next
20
21   End Sub                                    dot operator     variable name
```

FIGURE 8-76

HEADS UP

In applications that include multiple forms, it is best to declare every variable as Private unless the variable is used in multiple Form objects.

When you type frmDepreciation and the dot operator, IntelliSense displays the names of the shared variables from that Form object (see Figure 8-77).

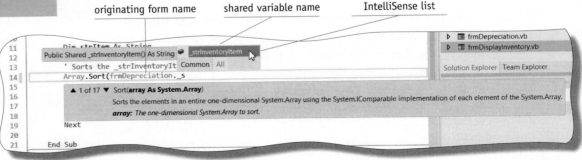

originating form name   shared variable name   IntelliSense list

FIGURE 8-77

After the second form opens, the user can tap or click the Return to Application button (Figure 8-78) to close the second Form object and return to the first Form object, frmDepreciation. The code in Figure 8-79 is executed when the Return to Application button is tapped or clicked. An instance of the first form, frmFirst, is created for frmDepreciation. The second form is hidden and the first form is opened again.

FIGURE 8-78

Jens Karlsson/Flickr Select/Getty Images

Return to Application button

```
23      Private Sub btnReturn_Click(ByVal sender As System.Object, ByVal e As System.
        EventArgs) Handles btnReturn.Click
24          ' This Sub procedure opens the first form
25          Dim frmFirst As New frmDepreciation
26
27          Hide()
28          frmFirst.ShowDialog()
29
30      End Sub
```

FIGURE 8-79

Program Design

The requirements document for the Trends Menswear Inventory Depreciation application is shown in Figure 8-80 on the next page, and the Use Case Definition document is shown in Figure 8-81 on page 577.

REQUIREMENTS DOCUMENT

Date Submitted:	April 14, 2015
Application Title:	Trends Menswear Inventory Depreciation Application
Purpose:	This Windows application opens an inventory data file and computes item depreciation based on the straight-line and double-declining balance methods.
Program Procedures:	A Windows application opens the inventory text file so that the user can select an item and the type of depreciation method. The depreciation is calculated for the five-year life of the inventory item.
Algorithms, Processing, and Conditions:	1. The user first views a Windows application that includes the following: a title; a File menu that includes Display Inventory, Clear, and Exit commands; a ListBox object that displays the inventory item IDs filled from the inventory text file; and a GroupBox object with two RadioButton objects that provide options for straight-line and double-declining balance depreciation methods. A Calculate Depreciation Button object is also available. The Trends Menswear logo is displayed on the left side of the Form object.
	2. After the user selects an item ID and the depreciation method and then taps or clicks the Button object, the selected inventory item and quantity are displayed. ListBox objects display the present year, present value, year depreciation, and total depreciation.
	3. If the user selects the Display Inventory menu item, a second Form object opens and displays the sorted inventory items list. The first Form object closes. The second Form object provides a Return to Application Button object to reopen the first Form object.
	4. The user can select the Clear menu item to clear and reset the first Form object. The user can select the Exit menu item to close the application.
Notes and Restrictions:	The inventory.txt file is located on the USB drive (E:).
Comments:	The image shown in the window should be a picture available on the Web.

FIGURE 8-80

USE CASE DEFINITION

1. The user selects the inventory item ID and the type of depreciation.
2. The user taps or clicks the Calculate Depreciation button to display the selected inventory item and quantity below the button.
3. The depreciation values are displayed for the present year, present value, year depreciation, and total depreciation.
4. The user taps or clicks the Display Inventory menu item to view the sorted inventory items.
5. The user taps or clicks the Clear menu item to clear and reset the form.
6. The user taps or clicks the Exit menu item to close the application.

FIGURE 8-81

© 2014 Cengage Learning

Design the Program Processing Objects

The event planning documents for the Trends Menswear Inventory Depreciation application are shown in Figure 8-82 and Figure 8-83 on page 480.

EVENT PLANNING DOCUMENT

Program Name: Depreciation	Developer: Corinne Hoisington	Object: frmDepreciation	Date: April 14, 2015
OBJECT	**EVENT TRIGGER**	**EVENT PROCESSING**	
frmDepreciation_Load	Load	Open the inventory.txt file from the USB drive; use If...Else statements to handle possible errors when opening the file Assign each line of the text file to array variables Continue to read the text file until all items are assigned If the text file is not available, display a message Fill the ListBox object with the array of inventory item IDs	

FIGURE 8-82 (continues)

© 2014 Cengage Learning

Program Name: Trends Menswear Inventory Depreciation	Developer: Corinne Hoisington	Object: frmDepreciation	Date: April 14, 2015
OBJECT	**EVENT TRIGGER**	**EVENT PROCESSING**	
btnCalculateDepreciation	Click	If the ListBox object and one RadioButton object are selected, call the appropriate Sub procedure based on the depreciation method selected If neither object is selected, display a message reminding the user to make a selection	
StraightLineDepreciation	Called Sub procedure	Make objects visible to display results by calling the MakeObjectsVisible Sub procedure Display the inventory item selected and the quantity of that item Calculate the straight-line depreciation based on the following formula: initial price / life of the item in years Assign the initial price to the present year value In a loop that repeats five times due to the assigned life of the item, accumulate the total depreciation Display the present years in a ListBox object Display the present values in a ListBox object Display the year depreciation in a ListBox object Display the total depreciation in a ListBox object	

FIGURE 8-82 (continues)

Program Name: Trends Menswear Inventory Depreciation	Developer: Corinne Hoisington	Object: frmDepreciation	Date: April 14, 2015
OBJECT	**EVENT TRIGGER**	**EVENT PROCESSING**	
DoubleDecliningDepreciation	Called Sub procedure	Show objects needed for results by calling the MakeObjectsVisible Sub procedure Display the inventory item selected and the quantity of that item Assign the initial price to the present year value In a loop that repeats five times due to the assigned life of the item, calculate the double-declining balance depreciation based on the following formula: initial price * 2 / life of the item in years Accumulate the total depreciation Display the present years in a ListBox object Display the present values in a ListBox object Display the year depreciation in a ListBox object Display the total depreciation in a ListBox object	
MakeObjectsVisible	Called Sub procedure	Change the Visible property of the result objects to true Clear the ListBox objects	
mnuDisplay	Click	Create an instance of the second Form object Hide the first Form object Show the second Form object	
mnuClear	Click	Reset the ListBox SelectedIndex property to −1, clearing the user's selection Set the Checked property of the RadioButton objects to false, clearing the user's selection Change the Visible property of all the result objects to false Clear all the ListBox objects	
mnuExit	Click	Close the application	

FIGURE 8-82 (continued)

EVENT PLANNING DOCUMENT

Program Name: Trends Menswear Inventory Depreciation	Developer: Corinne Hoisington	Object: frmDisplayInventory	Date: April 14, 2015
OBJECT	**EVENT TRIGGER**	**EVENT PROCESSING**	
frmDisplayInventory_Load	Load	Sort the inventory item array Display the inventory item array in sorted order in a ListBox object	
btnReturn	Click	Hide the second Form object Open the first Form object	

FIGURE 8-83

Guided Program Development

To design the user interface for the Trends Menswear Inventory Depreciation application and enter the code required to process each event in the program, complete the steps in this section.

NOTE TO THE LEARNER

In the following activity, you should complete the tasks within the specified steps. Each of the tasks is accompanied by a Hint Screen. The purpose of the Hint Screen is to indicate where you should perform the activity in the Visual Studio window and to remind you which method to use. If you need further help completing a step, refer to the figure identified by *ref:*.

Phase 1: Design the Form

1

• **Create a New Windows Project** Open Visual Studio and then close the Start page. Tap or click the New Project button on the Standard toolbar. Begin a Windows Forms Application project and name the project Depreciation.

• **Name the Form Object** Select the Form object. Change the (Name) property of the Form object to frmDepreciation.

• **Assign a Title to the Form Object** Open the main Form object. Select the Form object and change the Text property to Compute Depreciation by Method.

• **Create the User Interface** Using the skills you have acquired in this course, create the user interface for the frmDepreciation Windows Form object, as shown in Figure 8-84a and Figure 8-84b on the next page.

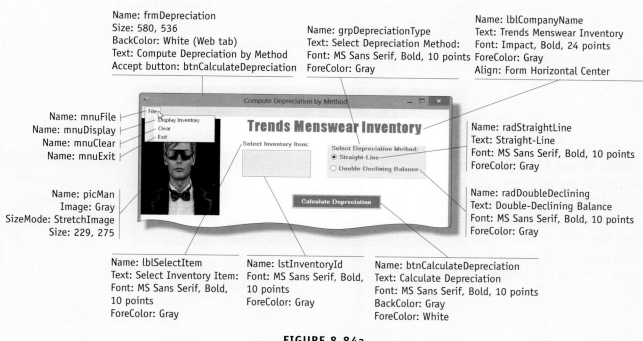

Name: frmDepreciation
Size: 580, 536
BackColor: White (Web tab)
Text: Compute Depreciation by Method
Accept button: btnCalculateDepreciation

Name: grpDepreciationType
Text: Select Depreciation Method:
Font: MS Sans Serif, Bold, 10 points
ForeColor: Gray

Name: lblCompanyName
Text: Trends Menswear Inventory
Font: Impact, Bold, 24 points
ForeColor: Gray
Align: Form Horizontal Center

Name: mnuFile
Name: mnuDisplay
Name: mnuClear
Name: mnuExit

Name: picMan
Image: Gray
SizeMode: StretchImage
Size: 229, 275

Name: radStraightLine
Text: Straight-Line
Font: MS Sans Serif, Bold, 10 points
ForeColor: Gray

Name: radDoubleDeclining
Text: Double-Declining Balance
Font: MS Sans Serif, Bold, 10 points
ForeColor: Gray

Name: lblSelectItem
Text: Select Inventory Item:
Font: MS Sans Serif, Bold, 10 points
ForeColor: Gray

Name: lstInventoryId
Font: MS Sans Serif, Bold, 10 points
ForeColor: Gray

Name: btnCalculateDepreciation
Text: Calculate Depreciation
Font: MS Sans Serif, Bold, 10 points
BackColor: Gray
ForeColor: White

FIGURE 8-84a

jens Karlsson/Flickr Select/Getty Images

(continues)

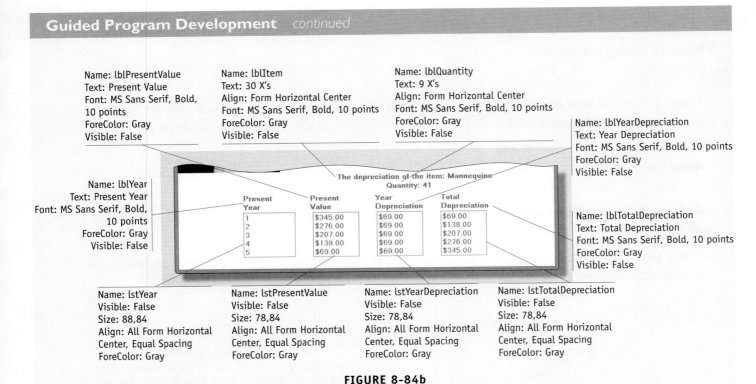

Name: lblPresentValue
Text: Present Value
Font: MS Sans Serif, Bold, 10 points
ForeColor: Gray
Visible: False

Name: lblItem
Text: 30 X's
Align: Form Horizontal Center
Font: MS Sans Serif, Bold, 10 points
ForeColor: Gray
Visible: False

Name: lblQuantity
Text: 9 X's
Align: Form Horizontal Center
Font: MS Sans Serif, Bold, 10 points
ForeColor: Gray
Visible: False

Name: lblYearDepreciation
Text: Year Depreciation
Font: MS Sans Serif, Bold, 10 points
ForeColor: Gray
Visible: False

Name: lblYear
Text: Present Year
Font: MS Sans Serif, Bold, 10 points
ForeColor: Gray
Visible: False

Name: lblTotalDepreciation
Text: Total Depreciation
Font: MS Sans Serif, Bold, 10 points
ForeColor: Gray
Visible: False

The depreciation of the item: Mannequins
Quantity: 41

Present Year	Present Value	Year Depreciation	Total Depreciation
1	$345.00	$69.00	$69.00
2	$276.00	$69.00	$138.00
3	$207.00	$69.00	$207.00
4	$138.00	$69.00	$276.00
5	$69.00	$69.00	$345.00

Name: lstYear
Visible: False
Size: 88,84
Align: All Form Horizontal Center, Equal Spacing
ForeColor: Gray

Name: lstPresentValue
Visible: False
Size: 78,84
Align: All Form Horizontal Center, Equal Spacing
ForeColor: Gray

Name: lstYearDepreciation
Visible: False
Size: 78,84
Align: All Form Horizontal Center, Equal Spacing
ForeColor: Gray

Name: lstTotalDepreciation
Visible: False
Size: 78,84
Align: All Form Horizontal Center, Equal Spacing
ForeColor: Gray

FIGURE 8-84b

2

• **Add a Second Form Object** Tap or click PROJECT on the menu bar, and then tap or click Add Windows Form. In the Add New Item dialog box, tap or click Windows Form. Name the Windows Form object `frmDisplayInventory.vb`. Tap or click the Add button *(ref: Figure 8-67)*.

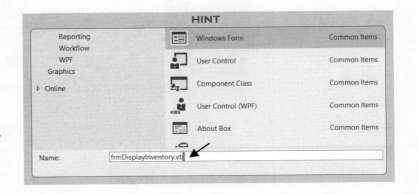

HINT

Reporting	Windows Form	Common Items
Workflow	User Control	Common Items
WPF		
Graphics	Component Class	Common Items
▷ Online	User Control (WPF)	Common Items
	About Box	Common Items

Name: frmDisplayInventory.vb

● **Assign a Title to the Form Object** Open the frmDisplayInventory.vb object. Select the Form object and change the Text property to `Sorted Inventory Listing`.

● **Create the User Interface for the Windows Form Object** Using the skills you have learned in this course, create the user interface for the frmDisplayInventory Windows Form object, as shown in Figure 8-85.

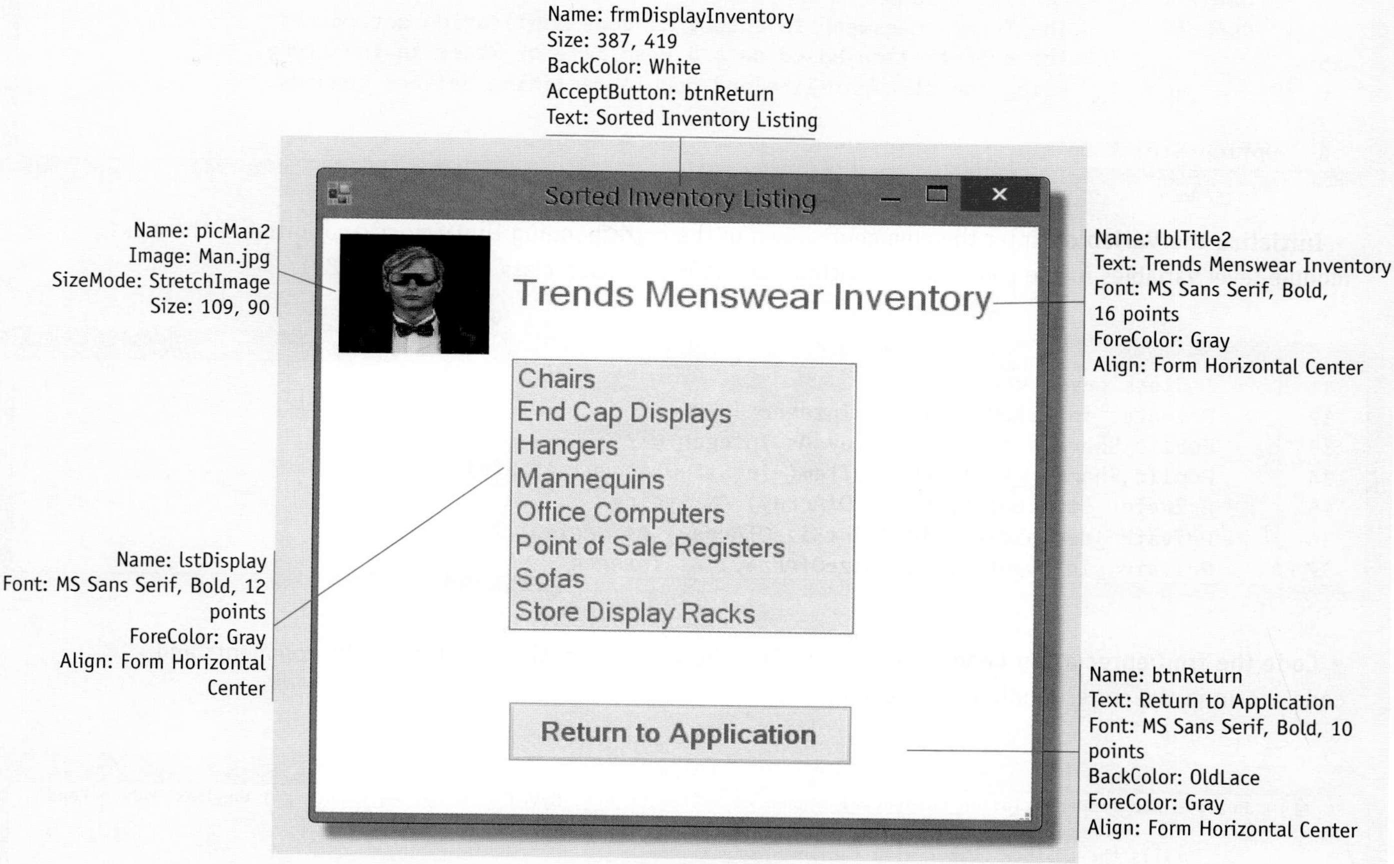

Name: frmDisplayInventory
Size: 387, 419
BackColor: White
AcceptButton: btnReturn
Text: Sorted Inventory Listing

Name: picMan2
Image: Man.jpg
SizeMode: StretchImage
Size: 109, 90

Name: lblTitle2
Text: Trends Menswear Inventory
Font: MS Sans Serif, Bold, 16 points
ForeColor: Gray
Align: Form Horizontal Center

Name: lstDisplay
Font: MS Sans Serif, Bold, 12 points
ForeColor: Gray
Align: Form Horizontal Center

Name: btnReturn
Text: Return to Application
Font: MS Sans Serif, Bold, 10 points
BackColor: OldLace
ForeColor: Gray
Align: Form Horizontal Center

FIGURE 8-85

© Jens Karlsson/Flickr Select/Getty Images

(continues)

Phase 2: Code the Application

3

● **Code the Comments** Tap or click the View Code button to begin coding the application in frmDepreciation.vb. Type the first four standard comments at the top of the code window. Insert the command Option Strict On at the beginning of the code to turn on strict type checking.

HINT

```
1  ⊟ ' Program Name: Trends Menswear Depreciation Windows Application
2    ' Author:        Corinne Hoisington
3    ' Date:          April 14, 2015
4    ' Purpose:       The Trends Menswear Inventory Windows Application determines
5    '                the depreciation based on a 5 year life of items in inventory
6    '                using the straight-line and double-declining balance methods.
7
8    Option Strict On
```

● **Initialize the Variables** Enter the comment shown in the corresponding Hint Screen and initialize the class module-level variables in the code window within the frmDepreciation class *(ref: Figure 8-29).*

HINT

```
11       ' Class Level variables
12       Private _intLifeOfItems As Integer = 5
13       Public Shared _intSizeOfArray As Integer = 7
14       Public Shared _strInventoryItem(_intSizeOfArray) As String
15       Private _strItemId(_intSizeOfArray) As String
16       Private _decInitialPrice(_intSizeOfArray) As Decimal
17       Private _intQuantity(_intSizeOfArray) As Integer
```

● **Code the frmDepreciation Load Event** To initialize the variables of this event, type the comments and code shown in the corresponding Hint Screen.

HINT

```
19  ⊟     Private Sub frmDepreciation_Load(ByVal sender As System.Object, ByVal e As System.EventArgs) Handles MyBase.Load
20          ' The frmDepreciation load event reads the inventory text file and
21          ' fills the Listbox object with the inventory items
22
23          ' Initialize an instance of the StreamReader object and declare variables
24          Dim objReader As IO.StreamReader
25          Dim strLocationAndNameOfFile As String = "e:\inventory.txt"
26          Dim intCount As Integer = 0
27          Dim intFill As Integer
28          Dim strFileError As String = "The file is not available. Restart when the file is available."
```

Guided Program Development   *continued*

- **Code the If...Else Statements** Inside the frmDepreciation_Load event, after the variables are initialized, insert an If statement that validates whether the inventory.txt file exists. The inventory file is opened from the USB drive and assigned to the instance of the StreamReader named objReader. The Do While loop continues to read each item in the file until the file is completed (Peek < > –1). Each line of the file is read and assigned to a unique array subscript by the ReadLine command. The counter intCount increments after each iteration of the loop to increase the subscript number *(ref: Figures 8-55, 8-56, 8-57)*.

```
HINT
30          ' Verify the file exists
31          If IO.File.Exists(strLocationAndNameOfFile) Then
32              objReader = IO.File.OpenText(strLocationAndNameOfFile)
33              ' Read the file line by line until the file is completed
34              Do While objReader.Peek <> -1
35                  _strInventoryItem(intCount) = objReader.ReadLine()
36                  _strItemId(intCount) = objReader.ReadLine()
37                  _decInitialPrice(intCount) = Convert.ToDecimal(objReader.ReadLine())
38                  _intQuantity(intCount) = Convert.ToInt32(objReader.ReadLine())
39                  intCount += 1
40              Loop
41              objReader.Close()
```

- **Fill the ListBox Object** Inside the frmDepreciation load event, a For loop counts from the beginning of the array at the index of 0 until the end of the array is reached. The statement within the loop fills the inventory IDs in the lstInventoryId ListBox object. Because the file might not be found, include an Else statement to inform the user if the file is not available and close the application.

```
HINT
43              ' The ListBox object is filled with the Inventory IDs
44              For intFill = 0 To (_strItemId.Length - 1)
45                  lstInventoryId.Items.Add(_strItemId(intFill))
46              Next
47          Else
48              MsgBox(strFileError, , "Error")
49              Close()
50          End If
51
52      End Sub
```

(continues)

- **Code the btnCalculateDepreciation_Click Event** Tap or click the frmDepreciation.vb [Design] tab.
Double-tap or double-click the Calculate Depreciation Button object. The btnCalculateDepreciation_Click event
opens. If the lstInventoryId ListBox and one of the RadioButton objects have been selected by the user, one
of the depreciation methods is called. A message box is displayed to remind the user to select one of the
objects if they are left blank.

HINT

```
54  Private Sub btnCalculateDepreciation_Click(ByVal sender As System.Object, ByVal e As System.EventArgs) Handles btnCalculateDepreciation.C
55      ' The btnCalculateDepreciation click event calls the depreciation Sub procedures
56      ' Declare variables
57      Dim intSelectedItemId As Integer
58      Dim strMissingSelection As String = "Missing Selection"
59      Dim strSelectDepreciationError As String = "Select a Depreciation Method"
60      Dim strSelectInventoryItemIDError As String = "Select an Inventory Item ID"
61
62      ' If the Listbox and a Depreciation RadioButton object are selected,
63      ' call the depreciation procedures
64      If lstInventoryId.SelectedIndex >= 0 Then
65          intSelectedItemId = lstInventoryId.SelectedIndex
66          If radStraightLine.Checked Then
67              StraightLineDepreciation(intSelectedItemId)
68          ElseIf radDoubleDeclining.Checked Then
69              DoubleDecliningDepreciation(intSelectedItemId)
70          Else
71              MsgBox(strSelectDepreciationError, , strMissingSelection)
72          End If
73      Else
74          MsgBox(strSelectInventoryItemIDError, , strMissingSelection)
75      End If
76
77  End Sub
```

● **Code the StraightLineDepreciation Sub Procedure** Begin a new Sub procedure that calculates the depreciation when the straight-line method is selected. The result objects are displayed in the MakeObjectsVisible Sub procedure. The cost of straight-line depreciation is calculated and displayed in the ListBox objects on the Form object *(ref: Figure 8-61)*.

HINT

```
78
79     Private Sub StraightLineDepreciation(ByVal intItemId As Integer)
80         'This Sub procedure computes and displays the straight line depreciation for the item selected
81         ' Declare variables
82         Dim intStraightPresentYear As Integer
83         Dim decStraightPresentYearValue As Decimal = 0
84         Dim decStraightDepreciation As Decimal
85         Dim decStraightTotal As Decimal
86         Dim strDepreciationItem As String = "The depreciation of the item: "
87         Dim strQuantityMessage As String = "Quantity: "
88
89         ' The procedure MakeObjectsVisible is called to display the Form objects
90         MakeObjectsVisible()
91         ' Display the item and quantity of the selected item
92         lblItem.Text = strDepreciationItem & _strInventoryItem(intItemId)
93         lblQuantity.Text = strQuantityMessage & _intQuantity(intItemId).ToString()
94         ' The formula for straight-line depreciation
95         decStraightDepreciation = _decInitialPrice(intItemId) / _intLifeOfItems
96         decStraightPresentYearValue = _decInitialPrice(intItemId)
97
98         ' The loop repeats for the life of the items
99         For intStraightPresentYear = 1 To _intLifeOfItems
100            ' Accumulates the total of depreciation
101            decStraightTotal += decStraightDepreciation
102            ' Displays the depreciation amounts
103            lstYear.Items.Add(intStraightPresentYear.ToString())
104            lstPresentValue.Items.Add(decStraightPresentYearValue.ToString("C"))
105            lstYearDepreciation.Items.Add(decStraightDepreciation.ToString("C"))
106            lstTotalDepreciation.Items.Add(decStraightTotal.ToString("C"))
107            decStraightPresentYearValue -= decStraightDepreciation
108         Next
109
110     End Sub
```

(continues)

Guided Program Development *continued*

● **Code the DoubleDecliningDepreciation Sub Procedure** Begin a new Sub procedure that calculates the depreciation when the double-declining balance method is selected. The result objects are displayed in the MakeObjectsVisible Sub procedure. The cost of double-declining balance depreciation is calculated and displayed in the ListBox objects on the Form object *(ref: Figure 8-63)*.

HINT

```
111
112  ⊟  Private Sub DoubleDecliningDepreciation(ByVal intItemId As Integer)
113           ' This Sub procedure computes and displays the double declining
114           ' balance depreciation for the item selected
115         Dim intDoublePresentYear As Integer
116         Dim decDoublePresentYearValue As Decimal = 0
117         Dim decDoubleDepreciation As Decimal
118         Dim decDoubleTotal As Decimal
119
120           ' The procedure MakeObjectsVisible is called to display the Form objects
121         MakeObjectsVisible()
122           ' Display the item and quantity of the selected item
123         lblItem.Text = "The depreciation of the item: " & _strInventoryItem(intItemId)
124         lblQuantity.Text = "Quantity: " & _intQuantity(intItemId).ToString()
125         decDoublePresentYearValue = _decInitialPrice(intItemId)
126
127           ' The loop repeats for the life of the items
128         For intDoublePresentYear = 1 To _intLifeOfItems
129             ' The formula for double-declining depreciation inside the loop to repeat the process
130           decDoubleDepreciation = (decDoublePresentYearValue * 2D) / _intLifeOfItems
131             ' Accumulates the total of depreciation
132
133           decDoubleTotal += decDoubleDepreciation
134             ' Displays the depreciation amounts
135           lstYear.Items.Add(intDoublePresentYear.ToString())
136           lstPresentValue.Items.Add(decDoublePresentYearValue.ToString("C"))
137           lstYearDepreciation.Items.Add(decDoubleDepreciation.ToString("C"))
138           lstTotalDepreciation.Items.Add(decDoubleTotal.ToString("C"))
139           decDoublePresentYearValue -= decDoubleDepreciation
140         Next
141     End Sub
```

● **Code the MakeObjectsVisible Sub Procedure** The Form objects that display the results are made visible. The ListBox objects are also cleared.

```
                                    HINT
143    Private Sub MakeObjectsVisible()
144         ' This procedure displays the objects showing the results
145         lblItem.Visible = True
146         lblQuantity.Visible = True
147         lblYear.Visible = True
148         lstYear.Visible = True
149         lblPresentValue.Visible = True
150         lstPresentValue.Visible = True
151         lblYearDepreciation.Visible = True
152         lstYearDepreciation.Visible = True
153         lblTotalDepreciation.Visible = True
154         lstTotalDepreciation.Visible = True
155         ' The previous data is removed
156         lstYear.Items.Clear()
157         lstPresentValue.Items.Clear()
158         lstYearDepreciation.Items.Clear()
159         lstTotalDepreciation.Items.Clear()
160
161    End Sub
```

● **Code the mnuDisplay_Click Event** An instance of the second Form object, frmDisplayInventory, is named frmSecond. The first form is hidden and the second form is opened *(ref: Figure 8-71 and Figure 8-72)*.

```
                                    HINT
163    Private Sub mnuDisplay_Click(ByVal sender As System.Object, ByVal e As System.EventArgs) Handles mnuDisplay.Click
164         ' The mnuDisplay click event creates an instance of the frmDisplayInventory
165         Dim frmSecond As New frmDisplayInventory
166
167         'Hide this form and show the Display Inventory form
168         Hide()
169         frmSecond.ShowDialog()
170
171    End Sub
```

(continues)

Guided Program Development   *continued*

● **Code the mnuClear_Click Event** The mnuClear_Click event clears the Form object for the next set of inputs.

HINT

```
173   Private Sub mnuClear_Click(ByVal sender As System.Object, ByVal e As System.EventArgs) Handles mnuClear.Click
174       ' The mnuClear click event clears and resets the form
175       lstInventoryId.SelectedIndex = -1
176       radStraightLine.Checked = False
177       radDoubleDeclining.Checked = False
178       lblItem.Visible = False
179       lblQuantity.Visible = False
180       lblYear.Visible = False
181       lstYear.Visible = False
182       lstYear.Items.Clear()
183       lblPresentValue.Visible = False
184       lstPresentValue.Visible = False
185       lstPresentValue.Items.Clear()
186       lblYearDepreciation.Visible = False
187       lstYearDepreciation.Visible = False
188       lstYearDepreciation.Items.Clear()
189       lblTotalDepreciation.Visible = False
190       lstTotalDepreciation.Visible = False
191       lstTotalDepreciation.Items.Clear()
192
193   End Sub
```

● **Code the mnuExit_Click Event** The mnuExit_Click event closes the application.

HINT

```
195   Private Sub mnuExit_Click(ByVal sender As System.Object, ByVal e As System.EventArgs) Handles mnuExit.Click
196       ' The mnuExit click event closes the application
197       Application.Exit()
198
199   End Sub
200
201 End Class
```

The frmDepreciation code is completed (Figure 8-86).

RESULT OF STEP 3

```
1   ' Program Name: Trends Menswear Depreciation Windows Application
2   ' Author:       Corinne Hoisington
3   ' Date:         April 14, 2015
4   ' Purpose:      The Trends Menswear Inventory Windows Application determines
5   '               the depreciation based on a 5 year life of items in inventory
6   '               using the straight-line and double-declining balance methods.
7
8   Option Strict On
9   Public Class frmDepreciation
10
11      ' Class Level variables
12      Private _intLifeOfItems As Integer = 5
13      Public Shared _intSizeOfArray As Integer = 7
14      Public Shared _strInventoryItem(_intSizeOfArray) As String
15      Private _strItemId(_intSizeOfArray) As String
16      Private _decInitialPrice(_intSizeOfArray) As Decimal
17      Private _intQuantity(_intSizeOfArray) As Integer
18
19      Private Sub frmDepreciation_Load(ByVal sender As System.Object, ByVal e As System.EventArgs) Handles MyBase.Load
20          ' The frmDepreciation load event reads the inventory text file and
21          ' fills the ComboBox object with the inventory items
22
23          ' Initialize an instance of the StreamReader object and declare variables
24          Dim objReader As IO.StreamReader
25          Dim strLocationAndNameOfFile As String = "e:\inventory.txt"
26          Dim intCount As Integer = 0
27          Dim intFill As Integer
28          Dim strFileError As String = "The file is not available. Restart when the file is available."
29
30          ' Verify the file exists
31          If IO.File.Exists(strLocationAndNameOfFile) Then
32              objReader = IO.File.OpenText(strLocationAndNameOfFile)
33              ' Read the file line by line until the file is completed
34              Do While objReader.Peek <> -1
35                  _strInventoryItem(intCount) = objReader.ReadLine()
36                  _strItemId(intCount) = objReader.ReadLine()
37                  _decInitialPrice(intCount) = Convert.ToDecimal(objReader.ReadLine())
38                  _intQuantity(intCount) = Convert.ToInt32(objReader.ReadLine())
39                  intCount += 1
40              Loop
41              objReader.Close()
42
43              ' The ListBox object is filled with the Inventory IDs
44              For intFill = 0 To (_strItemId.Length - 1)
45                  lstInventoryId.Items.Add(_strItemId(intFill))
46              Next
47          Else
48              MsgBox(strFileError, , "Error")
49              Close()
50          End If
51
52      End Sub
```

FIGURE 8-86 (continues)

(continues)

Guided Program Development *continued*

```
53
54    Private Sub btnCalculateDepreciation_Click(ByVal sender As System.Object, ByVal e As System.EventArgs)
55        ' The btnCalculateDepreciation click event calls the depreciation Sub procedures
56        ' Declare variables
57        Dim intSelectedItemId As Integer
58        Dim strMissingSelection As String = "Missing Selection"
59        Dim strSelectDepreciationError As String = "Select a Depreciation Method"
60        Dim strSelectInventoryItemIDError As String = "Select an Inventory Item ID"
61
62        ' If the Listbox and a Depreciation RadioButton object are selected,
63        ' call the depreciation procedures
64        If lstInventoryId.SelectedIndex >= 0 Then
65            intSelectedItemId = lstInventoryId.SelectedIndex
66            If radStraightLine.Checked Then
67                StraightLineDepreciation(intSelectedItemId)
68            ElseIf radDoubleDeclining.Checked Then
69                DoubleDecliningDepreciation(intSelectedItemId)
70            Else
71                MsgBox(strSelectDepreciationError, , strMissingSelection)
72            End If
73        Else
74            MsgBox(strSelectInventoryItemIDError, , strMissingSelection)
75        End If
76
77    End Sub
78
79    Private Sub StraightLineDepreciation(ByVal intItemId As Integer)
80        'This Sub procedure computes and displays the straight line depreciation for the item selected
81        ' Declare variables
82        Dim intStraightPresentYear As Integer
83        Dim decStraightPresentYearValue As Decimal = 0
84        Dim decStraightDepreciation As Decimal
85        Dim decStraightTotal As Decimal
86        Dim strDepreciationItem As String = "The depreciation of the item: "
87        Dim strQuantityMessage As String = "Quantity: "
88
89        ' The procedure MakeObjectsVisible is called to display the Form objects
90        MakeObjectsVisible()
91        ' Display the item and quantity of the selected item
92        lblItem.Text = strDepreciationItem & _strInventoryItem(intItemId)
93        lblQuantity.Text = strQuantityMessage & _intQuantity(intItemId).ToString()
94        ' The formula for straight-line depreciation
95        decStraightDepreciation = _decInitialPrice(intItemId) / _intLifeOfItems
96        decStraightPresentYearValue = _decInitialPrice(intItemId)
97
98        ' The loop repeats for the life of the items
99        For intStraightPresentYear = 1 To _intLifeOfItems
100           ' Accumulates the total of depreciation
101           decStraightTotal += decStraightDepreciation
102           ' Displays the depreciation amounts
103           lstYear.Items.Add(intStraightPresentYear.ToString())
104           lstPresentValue.Items.Add(decStraightPresentYearValue.ToString("C"))
```

FIGURE 8-86 (continues)

```
105            lstYearDepreciation.Items.Add(decStraightDepreciation.ToString("C"))
106            lstTotalDepreciation.Items.Add(decStraightTotal.ToString("C"))
107            decStraightPresentYearValue -= decStraightDepreciation
108        Next
109
110    End Sub
111
112 ⊟  Private Sub DoubleDecliningDepreciation(ByVal intItemId As Integer)
113        ' This Sub procedure computes and displays the double declining
114        ' balance depreciation for the item selected
115        Dim intDoublePresentYear As Integer
116        Dim decDoublePresentYearValue As Decimal = 0
117        Dim decDoubleDepreciation As Decimal
118        Dim decDoubleTotal As Decimal
119
120        ' The procedure MakeObjectsVisible is called to display the Form objects
121        MakeObjectsVisible()
122        ' Display the item and quantity of the selected item
123        lblItem.Text = "The depreciation of the item: " & _strInventoryItem(intItemId)
124        lblQuantity.Text = "Quantity: " & _intQuantity(intItemId).ToString()
125        decDoublePresentYearValue = _decInitialPrice(intItemId)
126
127        ' The loop repeats for the life of the items
128        For intDoublePresentYear = 1 To _intLifeOfItems
129            ' The formula for double-declining depreciation inside the loop to repeat the process
130            decDoubleDepreciation = (decDoublePresentYearValue * 2D) / _intLifeOfItems
131            ' Accumulates the total of depreciation
132            decDoubleTotal += decDoubleDepreciation
133            ' Displays the depreciation amounts
134            lstYear.Items.Add(intDoublePresentYear.ToString())
135            lstPresentValue.Items.Add(decDoublePresentYearValue.ToString("C"))
136            lstYearDepreciation.Items.Add(decDoubleDepreciation.ToString("C"))
137            lstTotalDepreciation.Items.Add(decDoubleTotal.ToString("C"))
138            decDoublePresentYearValue -= decDoubleDepreciation
139        Next
140
141    End Sub
142
143 ⊟  Private Sub MakeObjectsVisible()
144        ' This procedure displays the objects showing the results
145        lblItem.Visible = True
146        lblQuantity.Visible = True
147        lblYear.Visible = True
148        lstYear.Visible = True
149        lblPresentValue.Visible = True
150        lstPresentValue.Visible = True
151        lblYearDepreciation.Visible = True
152        lstYearDepreciation.Visible = True
153        lblTotalDepreciation.Visible = True
154        lstTotalDepreciation.Visible = True
155        ' The previous data is removed
156        lstYear.Items.Clear()
```

FIGURE 8-86 (continues)

(continues)

```
157        lstPresentValue.Items.Clear()
158        lstYearDepreciation.Items.Clear()
159        lstTotalDepreciation.Items.Clear()
160
161    End Sub
162
163    Private Sub mnuDisplay_Click(ByVal sender As System.Object, ByVal e As System.EventArgs) Handles mnuDisplay.Click
164        ' The mnuDisplay click event creates an instance of the frmDisplayInventory
165        Dim frmSecond As New frmDisplayInventory
166
167        'Hide this form and show the Display Inventory form
168        Hide()
169        frmSecond.ShowDialog()
170
171    End Sub
172
173    Private Sub mnuClear_Click(ByVal sender As System.Object, ByVal e As System.EventArgs) Handles mnuClear.Click
174        ' The mnuClear click event clears and resets the form
175        lstInventoryId.SelectedIndex = -1
176        radStraightLine.Checked = False
177        radDoubleDeclining.Checked = False
178        lblItem.Visible = False
179        lblQuantity.Visible = False
180        lblYear.Visible = False
181        lstYear.Visible = False
182        lstYear.Items.Clear()
183        lblPresentValue.Visible = False
184        lstPresentValue.Visible = False
185        lstPresentValue.Items.Clear()
186        lblYearDepreciation.Visible = False
187        lstYearDepreciation.Visible = False
188        lstYearDepreciation.Items.Clear()
189        lblTotalDepreciation.Visible = False
190        lstTotalDepreciation.Visible = False
191        lstTotalDepreciation.Items.Clear()
192
193    End Sub
194
195    Private Sub mnuExit_Click(ByVal sender As System.Object, ByVal e As System.EventArgs) Handles mnuExit.Click
196        ' The mnuExit click event closes the application
197        Application.Exit()
198
199    End Sub
200
201 End Class
```

FIGURE 8-86 (continues)

● **Code the Comments for the Second Form, frmDisplayInventory** Tap or click the frmDisplayInventory tab to return to Design view. Double-click the Form object to open the code window. Code the comments for the form processing. Code the `Option Strict On` statement.

```
                                    HINT
1 ⊟' The frmDisplayInventory class is opened by frmDepreciation
2 |' and displays the inventory file in sorted order
3
4   Option Strict On
5 ⊟Public Class frmDisplayInventory
```

● **Code the frmDisplayInventory_Load Event** The _strInventoryItem array is sorted. The For Each loop starts at the beginning element and continues until the last item is displayed in the ListBox object *(ref: Figure 8-35)*.

```
                                    HINT
   Private Sub frmDisplayInventory_Load(ByVal sender As System.Object, ByVal e As System.EventArgs) Handles MyBase.Load
        ' The frmDisplayInventory load event is a second form that
        ' displays the sorted inventory items

        Dim strItem As String

        ' Sorts the _strInventoryItem array
        Array.Sort(frmDepreciation._strInventoryItem)

        ' Displays the _strInventoryItem array
        For Each strItem In frmDepreciation._strInventoryItem
            lstDisplay.Items.Add(strItem)
        Next

   End Sub
```

(continues)

Guided Program Development *continued*

● **Code the btnReturn_Click Event** Tap or click the frmDisplayInventory [Design]* tab. Double-click the Return to Application button. Inside the btnReturn Click event, create an instance of the frmDepreciation Form object named frmFirst. Hide the second form and open the first form.

HINT

```
23      Private Sub btnReturn_Click(ByVal sender As System.Object, ByVal e As System.EventArgs) Handles btnReturn.Click
24          ' This Sub procedure opens the first form
25          Dim frmFirst As New frmDepreciation
26
27          Hide()
28          frmFirst.ShowDialog()
29
30      End Sub
31  End Class
```

The frmDisplayInventory code is completed (Figure 8-87).

RESULT OF STEP 4

```
1  ' The frmDisplayInventory class is opened by frmDepreciation
2  ' and displays the inventory file in sorted order
3
4  Option Strict On
5  Public Class frmDisplayInventory
6
7      Private Sub frmDisplayInventory_Load(ByVal sender As System.Object, ByVal e As System.EventArgs) Handles MyBase.Load
8          ' The frmDisplayInventory load event is a second form that
9          ' displays the sorted inventory items
10
11         Dim strItem As String
12
13         ' Sorts the _strInventoryItem array
14         Array.Sort(frmDepreciation._strInventoryItem)
15
16         ' Displays the _strInventoryItem array
17         For Each strItem In frmDepreciation._strInventoryItem
18             lstDisplay.Items.Add(strItem)
19         Next
20
21     End Sub
22
23     Private Sub btnReturn_Click(ByVal sender As System.Object, ByVal e As System.EventArgs) Handles btnReturn.Click
24         ' This Sub procedure opens the first form
25         Dim frmFirst As New frmDepreciation
26
27         Hide()
28         frmFirst.ShowDialog()
29
30     End Sub
31 End Class
```

FIGURE 8-87

Summary

In this chapter you have learned to create a Windows application using arrays and data files. The items listed in the table in Figure 8-88 include all the new Visual Studio and Visual Basic skills you have learned in this chapter.

Visual Basic Skills		
Skill	**Figure Number**	**Video Number**
Examine the Trends Menswear Depreciation Application	Figure 8-1	Video 8-1
Read Data From a Text File	Figure 8-53	Video 8-2
Use Multiple Form Objects	Figure 8-66	Video 8-3

FIGURE 8-88

Learn Online

Reinforcement activities and resources are available at no additional cost on *www.cengagebrain.com*. Visit *www.cengage.com/ct/studentdownload* for detailed instructions about accessing the resources available at the Student Companion Site.

Knowledge Check

1. Using implicit sizing, assign the integers 6, 9, 18, 31, 26, and 17 to an array named intLuckyWinners.

2. Write a statement that assigns the length of an array named strAddressBook to a variable named intAddressCount.

3. What is the upper-bound index of an array whose size is 75?

4. Write a line of code that initializes an array named intEvenNumbers with the first five even numbers, starting with 2.

5. Answer the following questions about the following initialized array:

    `Dim strCityNames(6) as String`

    a. Assign Detroit to the first array location. What is the index number?

    b. Assign Miami to the fourth location in the array. What would the assignment statement look like?

    c. What value does strCityNames.Length have?

    d. How many cities can this array hold?

    e. What would happen if you assigned strCityNames(7) = "Houston"?

6. Can you have a Boolean data type array?

7. Write a line of code that assigns the values Fred, Wilma, and Pebbles to the elements in the array strFlintstones().

8. Which of the three Flintstones in question 7 would be assigned to strFlintstones(1)?

9. What is the lower index of an array?

10. Write a statement that assigns the length of an array named intMovieTimes to intSpan.

11. Write a statement that assigns the elements shown in Figure 8-89 to a two-dimensional array with implicit sizing named intPinNumbers.

1659	2916	9876	3928
1117	9665	5397	4488
1211	0767	2956	2041

FIGURE 8-89

© 2014 Cengage Learning

12. How many elements can be stored in the array in Figure 8-90?

```
Dim decRoomSize(4, 6) As Decimal
```
             FIGURE 8-90

13. Write a statement that assigns the value 12.3 to the last item in the array in question 12.

14. Write a statement that assigns the first line of an opened text file to the first element in an array named strCartoon.

15. Write a statement that opens a text file named E:\accesscodes.txt and assigns the instance of the StreamReader to objReader.

16. Write a Sort statement to sort an array named strStreetNames.

17. If a binary search returns a negative value, what does that mean?

18. What is the default value of the elements in an array called intTopSpeed()?

19. Write the statement that hides the Windows Form object that is currently open in an application.

20. Write the statement that would initialize the variable intFinalExam as a Public Shared class-level variable that can be accessed in other Windows Form objects.

Debugging Exercises

1. Correct the lines of code in Figure 8-91.

```
Dim intJellyBeans() As Integer = (23, 77, 89, 124, 25)
ReDim intJellyBeans(10) As Integer
```
             FIGURE 8-91

2. Correct the line of code in Figure 8-92.

```
Dim strHighwayNumbers() As String = {95, 81, 605, 5}
```
             FIGURE 8-92

(continues)

Debugging Exercises *continued*

3. Rewrite the code shown in Figure 8-93 to fix any errors.

```
Dim strFriends(4) = {"Brea", "Eric", "Daniel", "Ryan", "Brittany"}
```

FIGURE 8-93

4. Rewrite the code shown in Figure 8-94 to fix any errors.

```
objReader = IO.File.OpenText{E:\testresults.txt}
```

FIGURE 8-94

5. Rewrite the code shown in Figure 8-95 to fix any errors.

```
For Each intPulseRate In intHeartRate()
        lstPulse.Items.Add(intHeartRate)
Next
```

FIGURE 8-95

6. What exception would be produced by the code shown in Figure 8-96?

```
Dim intPlaneType(300) As Integer
Dim intCount As Integer

For intCount = 0 To 301
     intPlaneType(intCount)=767
Next
```

FIGURE 8-96

7. Rewrite the code in Figure 8-97 to read each line of a text file into an array named strFordModel.

```
Do While objReader.Peek = -1
     strFordModel(intCount) = objReader.ReadLine()
     intCount += 1
Loop
```

FIGURE 8-97

8. Rewrite the statement in Figure 8-98 to fix the error.

```
Dim intEvenNumbers(4),(8) As Integer
```

FIGURE 8-98

Program Analysis

1. What is the output of the code shown in Figure 8-99?

```
Private Sub btnSuperHero_Click(ByVal sender As System.Object, ByVal e
As System.EventArgs) Handles btnSuperHero.Click

        Dim strName() As String = {"Wonder Woman", "Superman", "Spiderman",
"Green Lantern", "Batman"}

        Array.Sort(strName)
        lblFavorite.Text = "My favorite super hero is " & strName(3)
End Sub
```

FIGURE 8-99

2. What are the values for every element by subscript in the array when the code in Figure 8-100 has been executed?

```
Dim intJellyBeans() As Integer = {23, 77, 89, 124, 25}
intJellyBeans(3) = 59
ReDim intJellyBeans(6)
intJellyBeans(2) = 24
```

FIGURE 8-100

3. What are the values for every element by subscript in the array when the code in Figure 8-101 has been executed?

```
Dim intJellyBeans() As Integer = {23, 77, 89, 124, 25}
intJellyBeans(3) = 59
ReDim Preserve intJellyBeans(6)
intJellyBeans(2) = 24
```

FIGURE 8-101

4. In the array shown in Figure 8-102, what value would be displayed for these lines of code?

```
Dim intInsuranceQuotes() As Integer = {456, 398, 412, 508, 612}
lblResult.Text = "The Insurance Rate is " & _
        (intInsuranceQuotes(intInsuranceQuotes.Length - 1))
```

FIGURE 8-102

(continues)

5. What is the output of the code shown in Figure 8-103?

```
Private Sub frmCompute_Load(ByVal sender As System.Object, ByVal e As System.
EventArgs) Handles MyBase.Load
    Dim intQuantity() As Integer = {17, 22, 3, 7, 51, 27}
    lstResults.Items.Add(intQuantity(3))
    lstResults.Items.Add(intQuantity(1) + intQuantity(3))
    lstResults.Items.Add(intQuantity(2 + 3))
End Sub
```

FIGURE 8-103

6. Write a For Each loop that displays every element of an array named strSongNames in a ListBox named lstDisplay. The loop variable is named strPlay.

7. Write a section of code that declares an array named strStocksOwned initialized with the values in the table in Figure 8-104. Sort the array. Write the contents of the sorted array to a new file named e:\stockportfolio. txt. Close the file when the file has been created with the stock names.

Stocks Owned
Microsoft
Cisco
Coca-Cola
Disney
Exxon
Merck

FIGURE 8-104

© 2014 Cengage Learning

8. Write a For Next loop using the Length command that computes the sum of an array named decMaySales. After the loop, display the average in a Label object named lblAverage with the currency format. Use Length in the formula that computes the average.

Program Analysis *continued*

9. What is the output of the code shown in Figure 8-105?

```
Dim intDoubleArray(3, 2) As Integer
Dim strDisplay As String = " "
Dim intOuter As Integer
Dim intInner As Integer

For intOuter = 0 To 3
    For intInner = 0 To 2
        intDoubleArray(intOuter, intInner) = intOuter + intInner
        strDisplay &= intDoubleArray(intOuter, intInner) & " "
    Next
Next
txtValues.Text = strDisplay
```

FIGURE 8-105

10. Write the code to implicitly size an array named strDay and to determine the day of the week (such as Monday) if the user enters the number 1 into a TextBox object named txtDayOfWeek and the number is converted to an Integer variable named intDay. The day of the week is displayed in a Label object named lblFullDay.
11. An array is declared with the following Dim statement: Dim intSeniorGrades(12,8). After values have been assigned to this array, write a loop named intCount that computes the sum of the seventh row of the array. Assign the sum to intSeniorSum.
12. In the statement lblDisplay.Text = "The result is " & frmInitial.intBloodPressure, what was the name of the original Windows Form object that initialized intBloodPressure?

(continues)

Complete one or more of the following case programming assignments. Submit the program and materials you create to your instructor. The level of difficulty is indicated for each case programming assignment.

●   = Easiest
●●   = Intermediate
●●● = Challenging

1 ●
CLASSIC CAR SHOW

Design a Windows application and write the code that will execute according to the program requirements in Figure 8-106 and the Use Case Definition in Figure 8-107. Before writing the code, create an event planning document for each event in the program. The completed Windows application and other objects in the user interface are shown in Figure 8-108.

REQUIREMENTS DOCUMENT

Date Submitted:	January 24, 2015
Application Title:	Classic Car Show Application
Purpose:	This Windows application determines the total estimated value of classic cars in a car show for insurance purposes.
Program Procedures:	In a Windows application, compute the total value of the classic cars in the car show from data in a text file. The file contains the car model, year, and value of each classic car.
Algorithms, Processing, and Conditions:	1. A Windows application displays a title and image. The application opens a text file named cars.txt from a USB drive (E:).
	2. The program assigns the text file contents to three arrays that hold the model of each car, its year, and the estimated value of the vehicle. The array currently has 11 elements.
	3. When the Compute Inventory button is tapped or clicked, the program computes the total number of classic cars added to the text file so far and the total value of all the classic cars for insurance purposes.
	4. The program displays the names of the classic cars sorted in order of each car model's year.
	5. A File menu is displayed with the menu items Clear and Exit; the Clear item clears the result from the Form object and the Exit item exits the application.
Notes and Restrictions:	Close the opened text file before the program exits.
Comments:	1. The cars.txt file is available on CengageBrain.com.
	2. Obtain an image for this program from CengageBrain.com. The name of the picture on the Windows form is Car.

FIGURE 8-106

Case Programming Assignments

Classic Car Show (continued)

USE CASE DEFINITION

1. The user taps or clicks the Compute Inventory button.
2. The user views the sorted names of the classic cars and the year of each model.
3. The user taps or clicks the Clear menu item to clear the results on the Windows Form object.
4. The user taps or clicks the Exit menu item to close the application.

FIGURE 8-107

© 2014 Cengage Learning

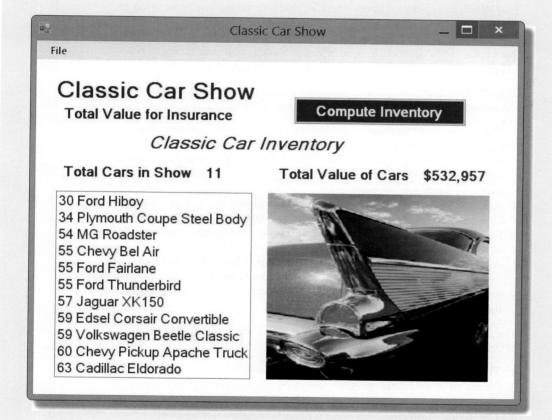

FIGURE 8-108

© Andrea Gingerich/E+/Getty Images

2

U.S. MEDIAN HOME PRICES

Design a Windows application and write the code that will execute according to the program requirements in Figure 8-109 and the Use Case Definition in Figure 8-110. Before writing the code, create an event planning document for each event in the program. The completed Windows application and other objects in the user interface are shown in Figure 8-111.

REQUIREMENTS DOCUMENT

Date Submitted:	January 24, 2015
Application Title:	U.S. Median Home Prices Application
Purpose:	This Windows application opens a text file that lists the median home prices of the 10 largest cities in the United States. The user selects a city and displays the projected median home price in that city for the next five years, given a projected 3 percent increase per year. A menu selection also can show the 10 largest cities and their current median home prices on a second Windows Form object.
Program Procedures:	In a Windows application, a user can view expected 3 percent increases in the median home price for the next five years in any of the 10 largest U.S. cities.
Algorithms, Processing, and Conditions:	1. The user views a Windows application that contains a title, graphic, and a ListBox object displaying the 10 largest cities in the United States. The ListBox object is filled from a text file named cities.txt that is opened and read by the application from the USB drive (drive E:). The text file contains each city name with the current median home price.
	2. After the user selects the city from the ListBox object, and taps or clicks the Compute Expected Growth button, another ListBox object displays the next five years of projected median home prices based on 3 percent increase each year in the selected city.
	3. A File menu displays the Display Median Home Prices, Clear, and Exit menu items. When the user selects the Display Median Home Prices menu item, a second Windows Form object opens and displays the 10 largest U.S. cities and their median home prices.
Notes and Restrictions:	The user must select a city from the ListBox object before the median home price of that city is displayed.
Comments:	1. The cities.txt file is available on CengageBrain.com.
	2. Obtain an image for this program from CengageBrain.com. The name of the picture on the Windows form is Home.
	3. The second Form object displays a Display Cities and Median Home Price button to reopen the initial Form object.

FIGURE 8-109

Case Programming Assignments

U.S. Median Home Prices (continued)

USE CASE DEFINITION

1. The user selects a city to display its next five years of projected median home prices based on 3 percent growth each year and taps or clicks the Compute Expected Growth button.
2. The user selects the Display Median Home Prices menu item to open a second form that displays the current median home prices in the 10 largest U.S. cities.
3. The user selects the Clear menu item to clear the form.
4. The user selects the Exit menu item to exit the application.

FIGURE 8-110

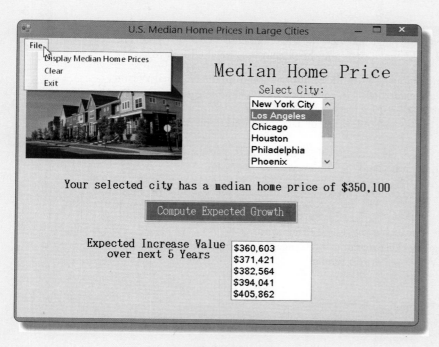

FIGURE 8-111

3 RAINFALL STATISTICS

Design a Windows application and write the code that will execute according to the program requirements in Figure 8-112 and the Use Case Definition in Figure 8-113. Before writing the code, create an event planning document for each event in the program. The completed Windows application and other objects in the user interface are shown in Figure 8-114.

REQUIREMENTS DOCUMENT

Date Submitted:	August 17, 2015
Application Title:	Rainfall Statistics Application
Purpose:	This Windows application uses a text file of annual rainfall totals in Seattle for the years 2000 to 2015 to find the average rainfall and the rainiest year during the period. The user can also select a year within the range to display the total rainfall in inches that year.
Program Procedures:	A Windows application analyzes rainfall totals for the years 2000 to 2015. The user can select a year from the range and view the total rainfall in inches that year. The average rainfall for the range of years and the rainiest year are also displayed.
Algorithms, Processing, and Conditions:	1. The application first opens a text file of information from the National Weather Service. The file is named rain.txt, and it lists the total rainfall amounts in Seattle during the years 2000–2015. 2. The user can select a year in the range of data to view the total rainfall for that year. 3. When the user taps or clicks the Display Statistics button, the average rainfall for the years within the range and the rainiest year are displayed.
Notes and Restrictions:	Use two Sub methods to compute the average rainfall and the year with the most rainfall.
Comments:	1. The rain.txt file is available on CengageBrain.com. 2. Obtain an image for this program from CengageBrain.com. The name of the picture on the Windows form is Rainfall.

FIGURE 8-112

Case Programming Assignments

Rainfall Statistics (continued)

USE CASE DEFINITION

1. From a list box, the user selects a year from the range of 2000 to 2015.
2. The program displays the inches of rainfall for that year.
3. The user taps or clicks the Display Statistics button to view the average rainfall for the years 2000–2015 and the rainiest year in the range.

FIGURE 8-113

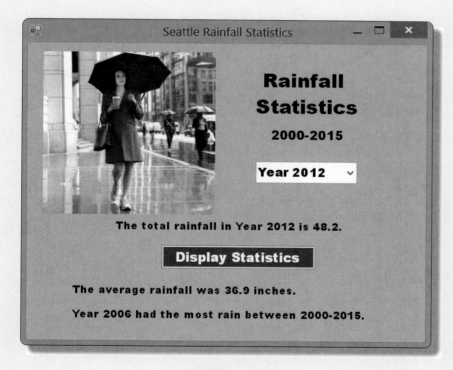

FIGURE 8-114

4 ●●
FINAL AVERAGES FOR SEMESTER

Design a Windows application and write the code that will execute according to the program requirements in Figure 8-115. Before designing the user interface, create a Use Case Definition. Before writing the code, create an event planning document for each event in the program.

REQUIREMENTS DOCUMENT

Date Submitted:	May 17, 2015
Application Title:	Final Averages for Semester Application
Purpose:	This Windows application allows an instructor to enter 13 project scores from a course and compute one student's grade for the semester. The application displays the student's final average for the semester when the two lowest scores are removed from the average. The 11 grades in sorted order and the final average are written to a text file named grades.txt, which is stored on a USB drive (drive E:).
Program Procedures:	In a Windows application, a student's grade is computed after the lowest two project scores are dropped. The results are written to a text file.
Algorithms, Processing, and Conditions:	1. The user views a Windows application that displays a title, a picture of a grade book, and an InputBox function that requests the 13 grades. 2. The program displays the final average for the semester with the two lowest scores dropped. 3. The program saves the sorted 11 grades and the final average to a text file named grades.txt, which is stored on the USB drive (drive E:).
Notes and Restrictions:	The project scores should be between 0 and 100.
Comments:	The image of a grade book should be selected from a picture available on the Web.

FIGURE 8-115

5

PATIENT BLOOD PRESSURE REPORT

Design a Windows application and write the code that will execute according to the program requirements in Figure 8-116. Before designing the user interface, create a Use Case Definition. Before writing the code, create an event planning document for each event in the program.

REQUIREMENTS DOCUMENT

Date Submitted:	February 14, 2015
Application Title:	Patient Blood Pressure Report Application
Purpose:	This Windows application determines which patients have a systolic blood pressure reading that is considered too high.
Program Procedures:	In a Windows application, a text file of patient information named patient.txt is opened. The patients who have a systolic reading above 120 are written to a second text file named consult.txt for consultation. The systolic reading is the first number in blood pressure results.

Algorithms, Processing, and Conditions:

1. Each day, a text file named patient.txt is opened from the USB drive. The patient.txt file contains patient names, ID numbers, and systolic blood pressure results from a lab.
2. An opening graphic and title are displayed on the Windows Form object.
3. A File menu includes options to Display Patient Information, Clear, and Exit. Selecting the Display Patient Information option displays the contents of the patient.txt file on a second Windows Form object.
4. The patient names and systolic blood pressure levels are assigned to an array that holds 16 elements each.
5. Blood pressure systolic levels are tested to check whether the systolic number is above the value 120.
6. All patients who have a systolic level above 120 have their names and systolic results written to a text file named consult.txt on the USB drive. A nurse will contact these patients for further evaluation.
7. The program displays the number of patients who had a systolic level above 120 and the average systolic value of today's patients.

Notes and Restrictions:	n/a

Comments:

1. The patient.txt file is available on CengageBrain.com.
2. An appropriate image for this application should be selected from a picture available on the Web.

FIGURE 8-116

Case Programming Assignments

6 ● ●
WEDDING BAND

Design a Windows application and write the code that will execute according to the program requirements in Figure 8-117. Before designing the user interface, create a Use Case Definition. Before writing the code, create an event planning document for each event in the program.

REQUIREMENTS DOCUMENT

Date Submitted: March 4, 2015

Application Title: Wedding Band Application

Purpose: This Windows application opens a text file that contains song names ordered by popularity, their music genre, and the song length in minutes. The application determines how many songs from the playlist can be performed during the reception and displays the songs to be played. A list of songs in a particular genre can also be displayed.

Program Procedures: In a Windows application, the user can enter the length of the reception and view the songs that will be performed from the playlist. The user can also select a type of music and have the appropriate songs on the playlist displayed in sorted order.

Algorithms, Processing, and Conditions:

1. The application opens and reads the values from a song list named songs.txt, which includes the titles, genres, and lengths of each song. The length of each song is listed in the format *minutes.seconds*. For example, 3.16 represents 3 minutes and 16 seconds.

2. The user can enter the length of the event and tap or click the Show Music List button to display the songs that will be performed from the playlist during the event.

3. The user can tap or click a drop-down list of music genres, select a genre, and display the songs in the playlist from that genre.

4. The user can select the Display Song Set menu item to open a second Form object that provides a choice of displaying the playlist in the current play order or as a sorted song list. The first Form object closes. The second Form object provides a button that the user can tap or click to return to the first Form object.

5. The user can select the Clear menu item to clear and reset the first Form object. The user can also select the Exit menu item to close the application.

Notes and Restrictions: n/a

Comments: The songs.txt file is available on CengageBrain.com.

FIGURE 8-117

7
●●●
SNOW CONE STAND

Create a requirements document and a Use Case Definition document and then design a Windows application based on the case project shown in Figure 8-118. Before writing the code, create an event planning document for each event in the program:

A local summer snow cone stand sells almost 5,000 snow cones per week in 10 flavors and saves this sales data in a text file. Create your own text file for your 10 favorite flavors of snow cones. Develop a Windows application that allows the manager of the stand to record how many snow cones were sold in each of the 10 flavors. The application will compute the total amount of snow cones sold for the week, the most popular flavor, the least popular flavor, and the average number of each flavor sold. Display the name of the snow cone stand within a logo on the Windows form. (Use two parallel arrays to hold the flavors and the amount sold of each flavor. You should use a different procedure for each of the results.)

FIGURE 8-118

© 2014 Cengage Learning

8
●●●
MOST POPULAR GAMES SOLD

Create a requirements document and a Use Case Definition document and then design a Windows application based on the case project shown in Figure 8-119. Before writing the code, create an event planning document for each event in the program:

If necessary, download the text file named games.txt from CengageBrain.com. The file contains the names of the nation's 10 top-selling video games and the domestic sales for each in millions of dollars. Open the text file and assign the contents to an array that identifies each game title. Allow the user to enter a title and determine if it is one of the 10 most popular video games. Display the domestic sales amount for the game if a match is made. Sort the array alphabetically by game title and display the sorted array on a second form. Compute the total amount of money made by the top 10 games and display the total on the second form.

FIGURE 8-119

© 2014 Cengage Learning

Case Programming Assignments

9 ●●● JOB GROWTH IN THE INFORMATION TECHNOLOGY FIELD

Create a requirements document and a Use Case Definition document and then design a Windows application based on the case project shown in Figure 8-120. Before writing the code, create an event planning document for each event in the program:

The U.S. Department of Labor has projected that the Information Technology job sector is growing. Enter the information from the following table into Notepad and save the text file.

Job Title	Jobs in 2015	Jobs Projected for 2020
Computer Developers	857,000	1,181,000
Computer Support	862,000	1,016,000
Systems Analysts	504,000	650,000
Database Administrators	119,000	154,000
Network Administrators	262,000	402,000
IT Managers	205,000	307,000

Calculate the changes in job numbers for each position and display the values. Compute the average number of positions that will be available in these fields each year during the period shown. Fill a ListBox object with the job titles so that the user can select a position and see the number of available jobs for the years 2015 and 2020 on a second form.

FIGURE 8-120

CHAPTER 9

Creating Web Applications

OBJECTIVES

You will have mastered the material in this chapter when you can:

- Create a Web application

- Build a Web form using ASP.NET 4.5

- Set Web form properties

- Use the full screen view

- Add objects to a Web form

- Add a DropDownList object

- Add a Calendar object

- Add a custom table for layout

- Validate data on Web forms

- Use the <br> tag in Visual Basic code

- Use string manipulation methods in the String class

Introduction

Visual Studio allows you to create applications that can run on the Web. Visual Basic 2012 includes ASP.NET 4.5 technology, with which you can create a user interface and a form for a Web application. A **Web form** is a page displayed in a Web browser, such as Internet Explorer and Firefox, and requests data from the user. The Visual Basic tools and techniques you use will be familiar based on what you have learned thus far in this course.

A practical example of a Web application developed using Visual Basic 2012 that can be delivered over the Internet is the project developed in this chapter — a cabin rental Web site that includes a Home page and Reservations page. This chapter project is based on a request from a resort called Big Bear Cabins to create a Web application for guests who want to reserve cabins online. The application displays a Web form that requests the guest's first and last names, email address, cabin selection(s), the number of nights they want to stay, and the check-in date, as shown in Figure 9-1.

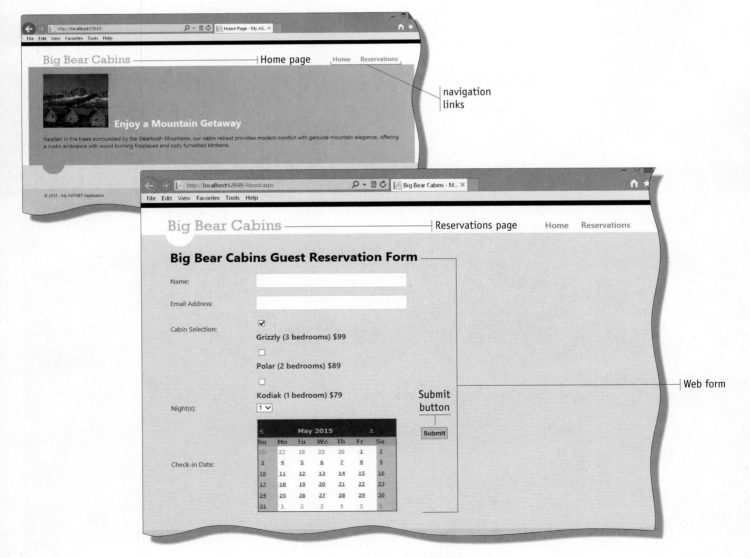

Karl Weatherly/Photodisc/Getty Images

FIGURE 9-1

After the Home page is displayed in a browser, the user can tap or click the Reservations navigation button to complete the form by entering the requested information, and then tap or click the Submit button on the form. The application validates the information the user entered by confirming that the guest entered a name, provided an email address in the correct format, and selected a valid check-in date. If the user makes an error, a message identifies the error, as shown in Figure 9-2.

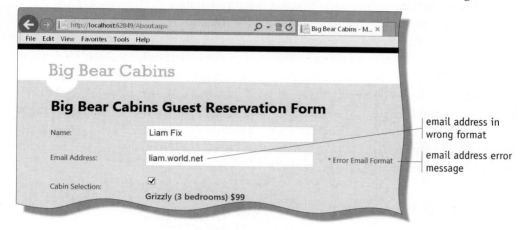

FIGURE 9-2

When the validation is complete, a reservation message is displayed that confirms the reservation information and calculates the total cost of the stay, as shown in Figure 9-3.

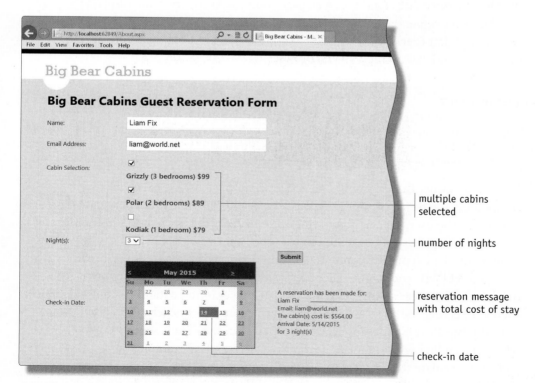

FIGURE 9-3

ONLINE REINFORCEMENT

To view a video of the program execution shown in Figure 9-2, visit CengageBrain.com and navigate to the resources for this title. Tap or click the link for Chapter 9 and then navigate to Video 9-1. Turn on your speakers to listen to the audio walkthrough of the steps.

Create a Web Application

To develop a form such as the one shown in Figure 9-3 on the previous page using Visual Basic, you create a Web application, which is similar to creating a Windows application. When completed, a Visual Basic Web application is displayed as one or more Web pages in a browser.

A Web page that allows users to enter information on a Web form, like the Big Bear Cabins page in this chapter, is considered a **dynamic** Web page because the user enters data and the Web page reacts to the data. In contrast, a Web page that displays information such as text and pictures with no interactivity is called a **static** Web page.

After a Web page is created, the Web page is hosted (placed) on a Web server. A **Web server** is a computer that stores Web documents and makes them available to people on the Internet. When you test your Web application created using Visual Basic 2012, Visual Studio 2012 creates a temporary Web server on your computer so you can view your Web page in a browser. When your Web page is ready for the world to see, it must be placed on an actual Web server.

Active Server Page (ASP.NET 4.5) Platform

The ASP.NET 4.5 technology used with Visual Basic 2012 creates an **active server page (ASP)**. When describing an active server page, developers speak of the server-side computer and the client-side computer. The server-side computer is the Web server that contains the actual active-server page and that will deliver the page to the client-side computer via the Internet. The client-side computer (often referred to as the client) runs the Web browser that requests a Web page from the Web server and displays the page.

An active server page has two primary components: the generated code component that executes on the Web server, and the HTML component that is interpreted and executed by a Web browser.

CONSIDER THIS

What is the purpose of HTML code?
Hypertext Markup Language (HTML) code is a standardized system for tagging text files to achieve font, color, graphic, and hyperlink effects on Web pages displayed in browsers. You can view the HTML code on a Web page using the Internet Explorer browser by clicking View and then Source.

When Visual Basic compiles an active server page using ASP.NET 4.5 technology, the page contains both the server-side code that will operate on data entered by the user, such as computing the total cost of a reservation in the Big Bear Cabins Web application, and the HTML code that will display the page in a Web browser on the client-side computer. When the page is requested by a browser, ASP sends the HTML code to the client requesting the Web page, where the page is displayed. The user can interact with the page by entering data or making selections, such as selecting the check-in date. When the user taps or clicks the Submit button, as in the Big Bear Cabins application for example, the data is sent to the Web server, where the coding within the application is executed. For example, the application code can calculate the total cabin cost and then display it on the Web form.

When you develop an ASP page in Visual Basic, the work you do on the design page to create the user interface will generate the HTML code for the active server page. This code includes the HTML to format and display the page, and might include JavaScript code to perform certain processing, such as ensuring that a text box contains data.

The event handler code that you write in Visual Basic for an event, such as clicking the Submit button, is executed on the Web server. So, in the Big Bear Cabins dynamic Web page, when the user taps or clicks the Submit button, the control returns to the Web server and the event handler code written by the developer is executed. This code can perform calculations and other processing as you have seen in previous chapters. When the event handler code changes an object displayed in the Web page, such as changing the Label object that contains the reservation message, that change immediately is displayed on the Web page.

Create a Web Site with Visual Studio 2012

Visual Studio 2012 introduces a technology for creating Web pages that makes Web page design faster and simpler. A new Web component is now part of ASP.NET 4.5 that dramatically improves designing HTML layout. Microsoft Expression Web, the Web site software that replaces FrontPage, is built into the design portion of ASP.NET, making it easier for designers to open a Visual Basic 2012 Web page in Expression Web without any conversion issues. You can also open an Expression Web page directly in Visual Basic 2012. You do not need Expression Web to work with its Web pages in Visual Basic 2012, but Expression Web has many tools to enhance Web design.

Create a Dynamic Web Site Using Visual Basic

Using Visual Basic 2012 to create a dynamic Web site is similar to creating an interactive Windows application — you drag objects from the Toolbox and place them in a design window to build a form. Some of the Web form objects are different from Windows objects because they are designed for use online. To create a Visual Basic Web project for the Big Bear Cabins application, you can complete the following steps:

> **HEADS UP**
>
> To reopen a saved Visual Basic Web application, open Visual Studio and then tap or click Open Web Site on the FILE menu. Browse to the main project folder to open the Web site.

STEP 1 Start Visual Studio. Tap or click the FILE tab and then tap or click New Web Site.

The New Web Site dialog box opens (Figure 9-4).

New Web Site
dialog box

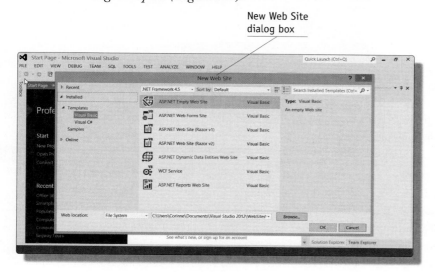

FIGURE 9-4

STEP 2 In the center pane, tap or click ASP.NET Web Forms Site. Name the chapter project application `Cabin` in the Location text box. In Figure 9-5, the Web Site is placed on the e: drive.

The ASP.NET Web Site will be stored on the e: drive (Figure 9-5).

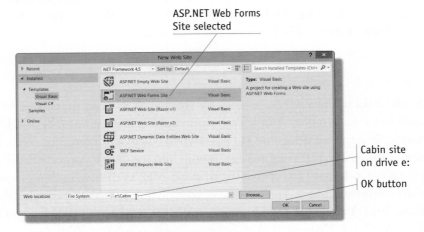

ASP.NET Web Forms Site selected

Cabin site on drive e:

OK button

FIGURE 9-5

STEP 3 Tap or click the OK button in the New Web Site dialog box.

The Web application Design window opens (Figure 9-6). The Default.aspx page is displayed. On the scroll bar at the bottom of the page, the Design button is selected, showing that the Design window is displayed.

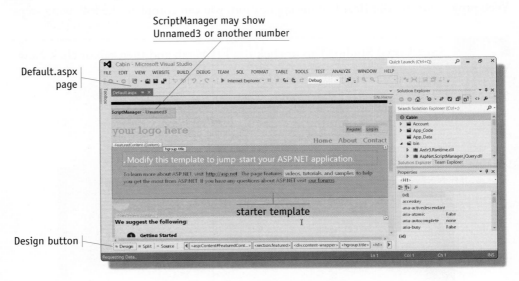

ScriptManager may show Unnamed3 or another number

Default.aspx page

starter template

Design button

FIGURE 9-6

Use a Multipage Starter Template

Visual Basic 2012 provides a starter template to assist you in designing a Web page. The starter template allows you to create a new ASP.NET application with some layout and structure already implemented within it. When you first open the starter template, the Default.aspx page opens, but many other template pages are available with the starter template. Figure 9-7 shows the file named Site.master in the Solution Explorer. The Site.master file is a master page file that provides an overall layout for the site with headers, buttons, and footers. A master page is designed to create a consistent layout for the pages in your application. It defines the look and feel and standard behavior that you want for all of the pages in your Web site. If you change the color or title of the master page, all the pages in the site will reflect that same color and title. First design the master page and then customize the actual pages on the Web site. The Web site in this project has two pages. The default page (Default.aspx) serves as the Home page, which gives the traveler information about the Big Bear Cabins. The Reservations page (About.aspx) provides a reservation form that a traveler can use to make reservations.

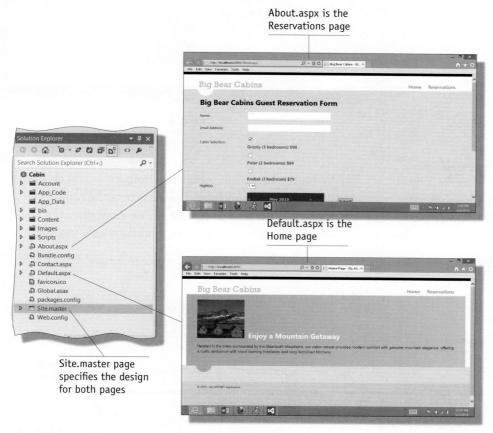

About.aspx is the
Reservations page

Default.aspx is the
Home page

Site.master page
specifies the design
for both pages

FIGURE 9-7

Customize the Master Page

The master page specifies the layout, color, and text that are repeated on the actual Web pages that are displayed by the browser. A master page is basically defined as a nondisplaying page. It contains the information about the layout of the page, which will be used in the creation of body pages. It enables the user to create the layouts of the pages quickly and conveniently across the entire Web site. To change the text on the master page, you can complete the following steps:

STEP 1   In the Solution Explorer window, double-tap or double-click Site.master to open the page.

The Site.master page opens (Figure 9-8).

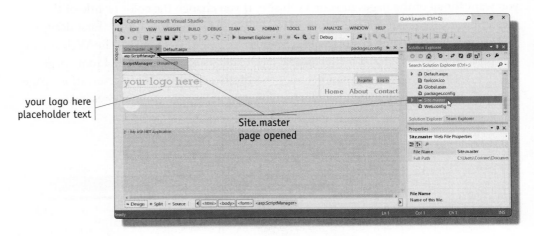

your logo here placeholder text

Site.master page opened

FIGURE 9-8

STEP 2   Tap or click VIEW on the menu bar, point to Toolbars, and then tap or click Formatting. Select the "your logo here" placeholder text at the top of the Site.master page. Type `Big Bear Cabins` to replace the original title. On the Formatting toolbar, tap or click the Font Size box arrow, and then select xx-large.

The title on the Master page changes to Big Bear Cabins. The font size is changed (Figure 9-9).

Font Size box arrow

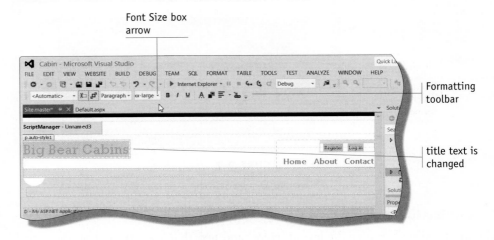

Formatting toolbar

title text is changed

FIGURE 9-9

Can I use the Formatting toolbar to change the color of the text or background?
Yes, when you select text within the Web page you can change the foreground and background color using the Formatting toolbar.

Customize Navigation Links on the Master Template

The Master page has navigation links that play an integral role in making your site easy to use and navigate. By default, the Master site has three links: Home, which connects to the Default.aspx page when tapped or clicked; About, which connects to the About.aspx page when tapped or clicked; and Contact, which connects to the Contact.aspx page. The chapter project has only two pages — Home and Reservations — so the Contact link should be deleted. It also would make more sense for the About link to be renamed Reservations. The site does not need a Register or Log in portion, so these default options will be deleted. To delete the Contact navigational link, rename the second navigational link to Reservations, and delete the Register and Log in tabs, follow these steps:

STEP 1   On the Site.master page, select the text Contact. Press the DELETE key to delete the Contact link. Select the text About in the About link and type `Reservations` to rename the link.

The Contact link is deleted and the About link is renamed Reservations (Figure 9-10).

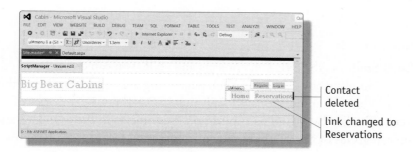

FIGURE 9-10

STEP 2   Tap or click the Register and Log in tabs on the Site.master page.

The Register and Log in tabs of the page are selected (Figure 9-11).

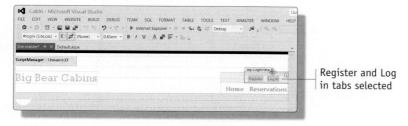

FIGURE 9-11

STEP 3   Press the DELETE key to remove the Register and Log in tabs from the Site.master page.

The Register and Log in tabs are deleted (Figure 9-12).

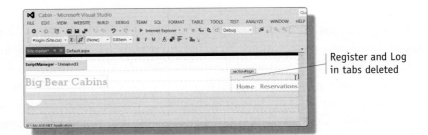

Register and Log in tabs deleted

FIGURE 9-12

Customize the Default Page

After the Site.master page is designed, the content pages in this Web site automatically inherit the changes in the page style and navigation buttons. For example, the Default.aspx page, which serves as the Home page to the Big Bear Cabins site, inherits the font and link changes made when the Master page was customized.

Add Objects to the Web Page

Using Visual Studio's ASP.NET 4.5 objects and code, you can create interactive Web forms. You place objects on the Web page using a Toolbox similar to the one used for Windows applications, though the ASP.NET 4.5 categories of tools are different. The Big Bear Cabins application uses objects in the Standard and Validation categories of the Toolbox shown in Figure 9-13.

Toolbox

Standard category

Validation category

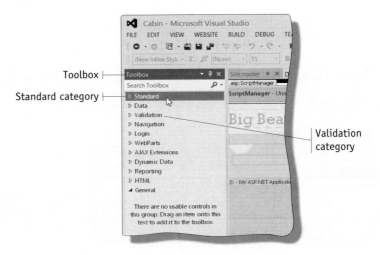

FIGURE 9-13

Toolbox objects unique to Web application objects include Login objects for allowing user access, Navigation objects for creating site maps, and Validation objects for checking Web form input. Some Windows application objects work the same way, but have different object names in the Web environment. For example, in a Windows application you use a PictureBox object to display a picture, but in an ASP.NET 4.5 Web page, you use an Image object. Both the PictureBox object and the Image object place an image into the application, but the Image object needs a URL to specify where the picture resides. The Big Bear Cabins Home page displays a picture, a description, and the address of the Big Bear Cabins.

Add an Image Object to the Default Page

On the Big Bear Cabins Home page (Default.aspx), an image of the Big Bear Cabins is displayed in an Image object on the left side of the page below the navigation buttons. The **Image** object is similar to the PictureBox object in a Windows application. The major difference is where the Image object is stored. Most Web pages reference a picture stored on a Web server connected to the Internet. On an ASP.NET Web form, you do this by specifying the entire URL (Web address) in the ImageUrl property of an Image object. To add an Image object that displays an image stored on a Web server, you can complete the following steps:

STEP 1   Save Site.master. In the Solution Explorer, double-tap or double-click Default.aspx. Notice that the Default.aspx page has inherited the title and Reservations navigation page from the Site.master. Open the Toolbox. Select the text 'Modify this template to jump-start your ASP.NET application.' in the FeaturedContent(Custom) area, and then press the DELETE key.

The Default.aspx page opens and the FeaturedContent area is cleared (Figure 9-14).

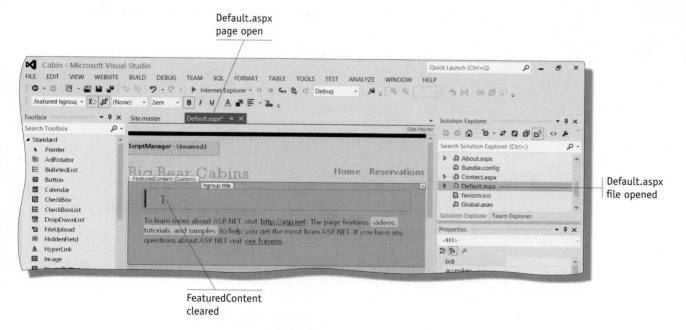

Default.aspx
page open

Default.aspx
file opened

FeaturedContent
cleared

FIGURE 9-14

STEP 2 Double-tap or double-click the Image object in the Standard category of the Toolbox to display it on the Web page in the FeaturedContent area. Resize the object so that it is 175 pixels (width) by 150 pixels (height).

The Image object appears on the Default.aspx page and is resized (Figure 9-15). A placeholder appears in the Image object until you specify a URL or path to an image file.

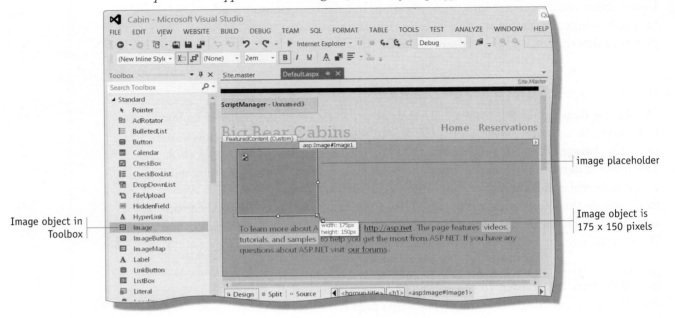

FIGURE 9-15

STEP 3 In the Properties window, name the Image object by entering `picCabins` in its (ID) property. Specify which image to display by entering the Web address `http://delgraphics.delmarlearning.com/CourseTechnology/cabins.jpg` as the ImageUrl property. Press the Enter key. You need Internet connectivity to view the image.

The cabins.jpg image appears in the Image object, replacing the placeholder (Figure 9-16).

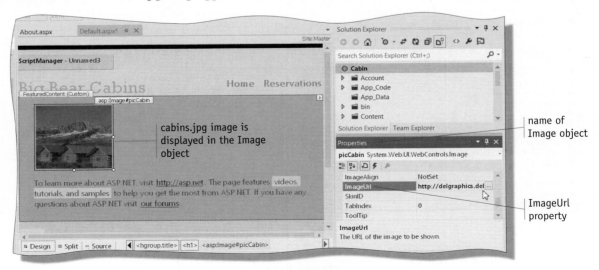

FIGURE 9-16

Enter Text Directly on the Web Page

ASP.NET 4.5 allows you to enter text directly on the Web page without creating labels. You should enter text directly on the page only if the text will not be changed by coded statements. Label objects are useful if you intend to change their contents after the user makes a selection on the Web page and the Web application needs to display a result. If the text is not going to change, type it directly on the page. As you type, use the SPACEBAR to add spaces and align text, and use the ENTER key to start a new line. To enter text directly on a Web page, follow these steps:

STEP 1   Tap or click to the right of the Image object. Add a space using the SPACEBAR and type Enjoy a Mountain Getaway directly on the Default.aspx page.

The text Enjoy a Mountain Getaway appears to the right of the picture (Figure 9-17).

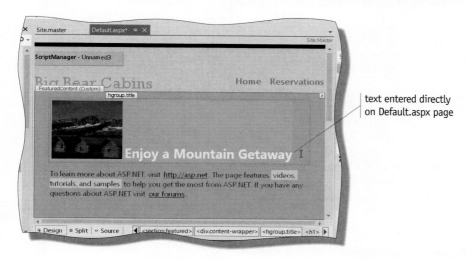

FIGURE 9-17

© Karl Weatherly/Photodisc/Getty Images

STEP 2 To change the vertical alignment, select the text, tap or click the style property in the Properties window, and then tap or click the ellipsis button to the right of the style property to display the Modify Style dialog box. In the Category pane of the Modify Style dialog box, tap or click Block. In the vertical-align drop box, select top.

The style property is changed to top vertical alignment in the Modify Style dialog box (Figure 9–18).

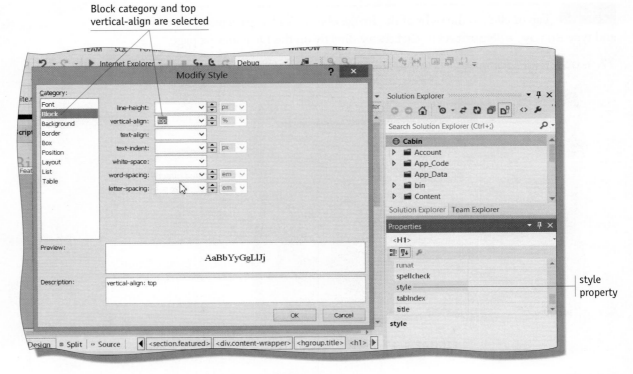

Block category and top
vertical-align are selected

style
property

FIGURE 9-18

STEP 3   Tap or click the OK button, and then tap or click a blank spot to deselect the text.

The typed text is vertically aligned to the top of the FeaturedContent area (Figure 9-19).

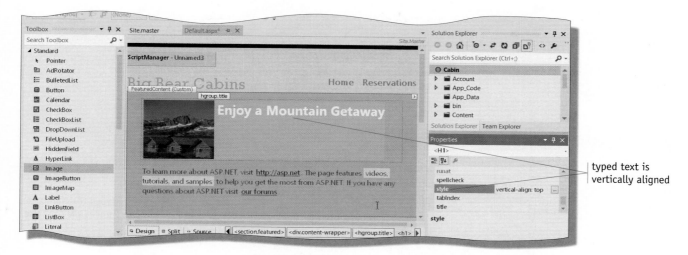

FIGURE 9-19

© Karl Weatherly/Photodisc/Getty Images

STEP 4   Select the text in the placeholder paragraph below the image and press the DELETE key. Change the font size to medium using the Formatting toolbar. Enter the text `Nestled in the trees surrounded by the Beartooth Mountains, our cabin retreat provides modern comfort with genuine mountain elegance, offering a rustic ambiance with wood burning fireplaces and cozy furnished kitchens.`

The text describing the Big Bear Cabins is displayed on the page (Figure 9–20).

FIGURE 9-20

© Karl Weatherly/Photodisc/Getty Images

STEP 5 Select the text in the MainContent area and then press the DELETE key.

The text in the MainContent area is deleted (Figure 9-21).

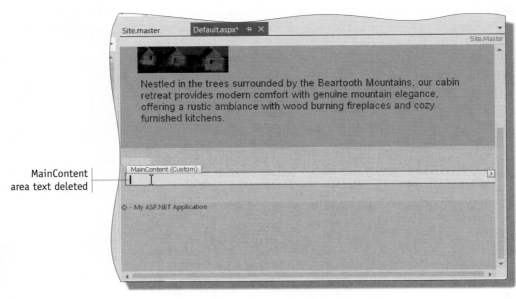

FIGURE 9-21

© Karl Weatherly/Photodisc/Getty Images

Create an ASP Web Form for the Reservations Page

Web pages are often interactive. For example, an online college application has text boxes that can be validated to be sure the information is correct. The Guest Reservation form in the chapter project will request each guest's name, email address, cabin type, the number of nights, and the date of arrival.

Add a Table for Alignment on a Web Form

A table is often used to organize Web site content into columns. On the Reservations page (About.aspx), a table is used to simplify object placement. The Guest Reservation form includes a table with seven rows and three columns filled with TextBox objects, CheckBox objects, a DropDownList object, and a Calendar object. To add a table to the Reservations page to organize form objects, follow these steps:

STEP 1 In the Solution Explorer window, double-tap or double-click About.aspx to create a Web form for the Reservations page. Delete the text in the MainContent area. Tap or click in the MainContent area and type `Guest Reservation Form`. Press ENTER. Delete the Aside Title text area. Tap or click in the paragraph below the MainContact area and delete all the text. Tap or click TABLE on the menu bar, and then tap or click Insert Table. In the Size section of the Insert Table dialog box, change the number of Rows to 7 and the number of Columns to 3.

The Insert Table dialog box opens and the number of rows is changed to seven and the number of columns is changed to three (Figure 9-22).

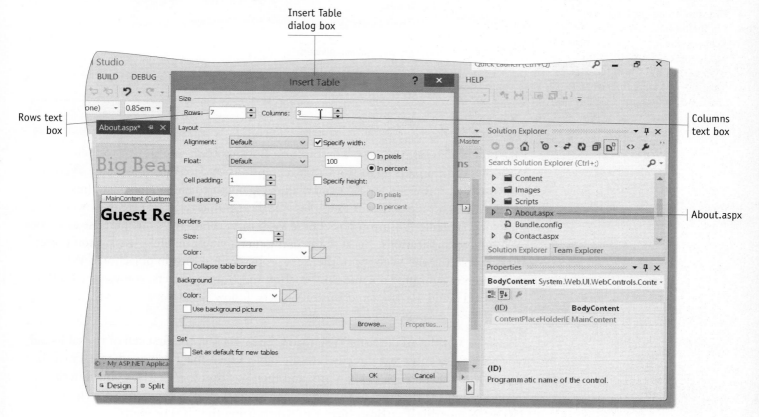

FIGURE 9-22

STEP 2 Tap or click the OK button. To resize the columns, point to a column divider until a two-sided arrow appears. Drag the divider to change the column width. As you drag, a ScreenTip shows the width of the column in pixels. Resize the first column until it is 150 px wide. Resize the second column to 250 px wide.

The table is displayed in the About.aspx page. The column width of the first column is changed to 150 px and the second column is changed to 250 px (Figure 9-23).

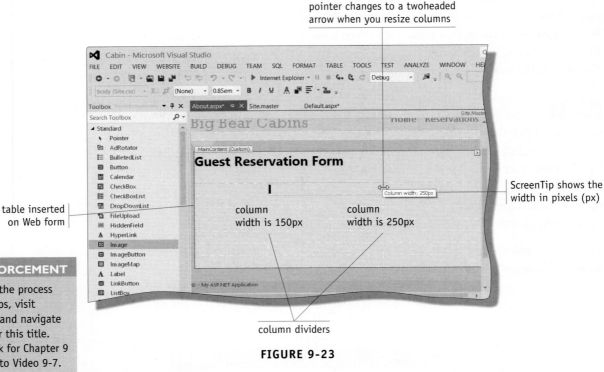

FIGURE 9-23

Add TextBox and Button Objects

Like other Web form objects, TextBox and Button objects are similar to their Windows counterparts apart from a few exceptions. A TextBox object on a Web page usually is provided for data entry, allowing a user to enter a name, address, email address, or zip code, for example. The Text property of a TextBox object, therefore, is blank. A Button object on a Web form serves the same purpose as it does in Windows applications. Because the user generally taps or clicks the Button object after completing the Web form, the Text property for a Button object on a Web form often is Submit. To name the TextBox and Button objects, you use the (ID) property. To add TextBox and Button objects, follow these steps:

STEP 1 On the About.aspx Web form, tap or click in the first cell of the table and type Name: to enter text directly into the table. Open the Toolbox, drag a TextBox object from the Toolbox to the form, and then position the TextBox object in the second cell in the first row of the table. Resize the TextBox object to a width of 250 px. Name this TextBox object txtName using the (ID) property.

Text is typed into the first cell and a TextBox object is placed inside the second cell on the top row of the table (Figure 9–24).

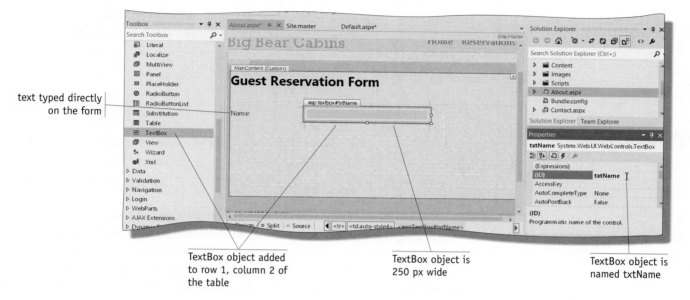

text typed directly on the form

TextBox object added to row 1, column 2 of the table

TextBox object is 250 px wide

TextBox object is named txtName

FIGURE 9-24

STEP 2   In the first cell in the second row of the table, type `Email Address:` to enter text directly into the table. Drag a TextBox object from the Toolbox to the form and then position the TextBox object in the second cell in the second row in the table. Resize the TextBox object to a width of 250 px. Name this TextBox object `txtEmail` using the (ID) property.

Text is typed into the first cell and a TextBox object is placed inside the second cell on the second row of the table (Figure 9–25).

ONLINE REINFORCEMENT

To view a video of the process in the previous steps, visit CengageBrain.com and navigate to the resources for this title. Tap or click the link for Chapter 9 and then navigate to Video 9-8.

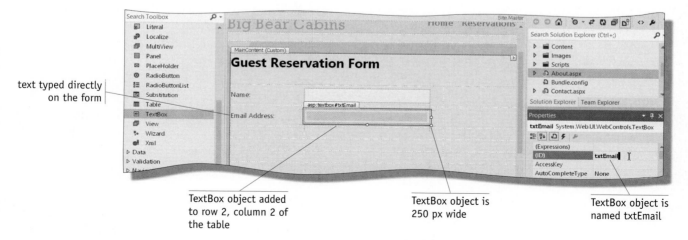

text typed directly on the form

TextBox object added to row 2, column 2 of the table

TextBox object is 250 px wide

TextBox object is named txtEmail

FIGURE 9-25

Add CheckBox Objects

Three CheckBox objects are used in the Guest Reservation form to determine which cabin(s) the guest wants to reserve. The **CheckBox** object allows the user to choose from several options. It is similar to the RadioButton object, except the CheckBox object allows the user to pick more than one option. In contrast, the RadioButton object allows a user to choose only one option from a group of related options. The CheckBox and RadioButton objects work the same in Web, Windows, and Mobile applications

When you name a CheckBox object, you should include the chk prefix in its (ID) property. In addition, you can specify that a check box is selected by default when a form opens. For example, because the Grizzly cabin (3 bedrooms) is the most popular cabin choice at the Big Bear Cabins, the check box for the Grizzly cabin should be selected when the page first is displayed. To specify this setting, change the Checked property of the CheckBox object from False to True.

In the Big Bear Cabins application, the user can select one or more cabins based on an individual or group reservation. For example, as shown in Figure 9-26, a large family might select the Grizzly (3 bedrooms) for the teen children and the Kodiak (1 bedroom) for the parents. RadioButton objects would not work in this example because only one RadioButton object can be selected at the same time within the same group.

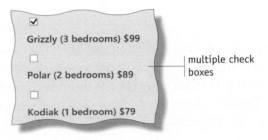

FIGURE 9-26

To place a CheckBox object on a Web form, you can complete the following steps:

STEP 1   In the third row of the table, type `Cabin Selection:` in the first cell. Drag the CheckBox object from the Toolbox to the Web form, and then position it in the third row, second cell.

The CheckBox object is placed on the Web form (Figure 9-27). The placeholder text will remain until you change the Text property. It does not, however, appear on the Web page when the page is displayed in a Web browser.

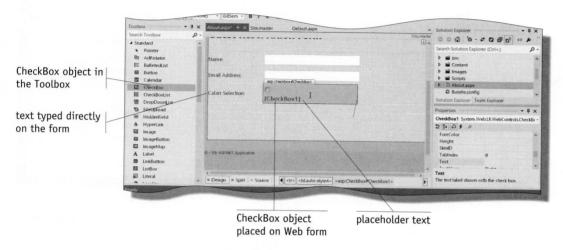

CheckBox object in the Toolbox

text typed directly on the form

CheckBox object placed on Web form

placeholder text

FIGURE 9-27

STEP 2   Name the CheckBox object by tapping or clicking to the right of its (ID) property in the Properties window and then entering `chkGrizzly`. Change the Text property of the CheckBox object to `Grizzly (3 bedrooms) $99`.

The CheckBox object is named chkGrizzly in the (ID) property. After changing the Text property of chkGrizzly, the CheckBox object on the form displays the new text (Figure 9-28).

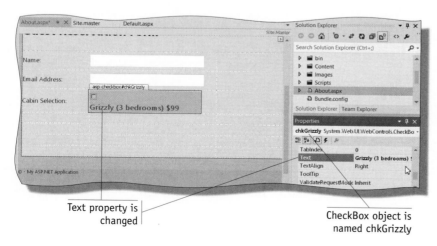

Text property is changed

CheckBox object is named chkGrizzly

FIGURE 9-28

STEP 3 At the Big Bear Cabins, the Grizzly is the most popular cabin. This cabin, therefore, should be checked when the form opens to save time for the user. To select the Grizzly check box, change the Checked property for the object from False to True.

The chkGrizzly CheckBox object appears with a check mark on the form, and the Checked property is set to True (Figure 9-29).

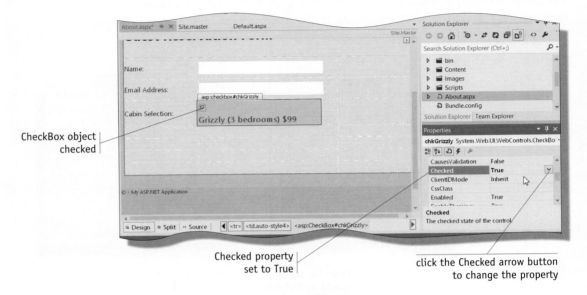

CheckBox object checked

Checked property set to True

click the Checked arrow button to change the property

FIGURE 9-29

STEP 4 In the second column, fourth and fifth rows of the table, add two more CheckBox objects named `chkPolar` and `chkKodiak`, respectively. Change the Text property of the first CheckBox object to `Polar (2 bedrooms) $89` and the second CheckBox object to `Kodiak (1 bedroom) $79`.

Two CheckBox objects are added to the form (Figure 9-30).

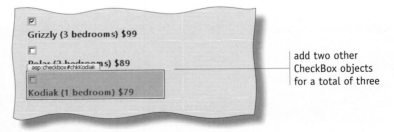

add two other CheckBox objects for a total of three

FIGURE 9-30

Code for CheckBox Objects

After the user selects one or more CheckBox objects representing the cabin selections and taps or clicks the Submit button on the Web form, control returns to the Web server. On the Web server, the event handler for the Submit button can evaluate which CheckBox objects are selected. The code shown in Figure 9-31 determines which CheckBox objects are selected by referring to the Checked property, in the same manner as when RadioButton objects are checked.

```
42              If chkGrizzly.Checked Then
43                  decCabinCost += decGrizzlyCost
44              End If
45              If chkPolar.Checked Then
46                  decCabinCost += decPolarCost
47              End If
48              If chkKodiak.Checked Then
49                  decCabinCost += decKodiakCost
50              End If
```

FIGURE 9-31

In Figure 9-31, the statement on line 42 checks the Checked property for the chkGrizzly check box. If it is checked, the Grizzly Cabin cost is added to the value in the decCabinCost variable. Similarly, if the chkPolar check box is checked, its cabin cost is added to the value in the decCabinCost variable. The same is true for the chkKodiak check box. If all three check boxes are checked, the value in the decCabinCost variable will be the sum of the individual cabin costs for all three cabins.

Add a DropDownList Object

On the Guest Reservation Web form, guests can use a DropDownList object to specify the number of nights they plan to stay. The DropDownList object allows users to select one item from a predefined list. It is similar to the ListBox object used in Windows applications, except that for a DropDownList object, the list of items remains hidden until users tap or click the list arrow button.

After adding a DropDownList object to a form and naming it, you can specify the items you want to display in the list. You often want to order these items alphabetically or numerically for ease of use. The first item in this list appears in the DropDownList object by default. The DropDownList object will not display the items in the list until you run the application and display the Web form in a browser. The user must tap or click the list arrow to view the complete list of items during execution. The prefix for the name (ID) of the DropDownList object in Visual Basic is ddl.

On the Guest Reservation form, a DropDownList object is used to determine the number of nights the guests plan to stay at the cabin. To add a DropDownList object to the Web form, you can complete the following steps:

STEP 1 In the sixth row of the table, type `Night(s):` in the first column. Drag the DropDownList object to the second column of the sixth row. Name the DropDownList object by tapping or clicking to the right of the (ID) property in the object's Properties window and then typing `ddlNights`.

A DropDownList object appears on the Web form and is named ddlNights (Figure 9–32).

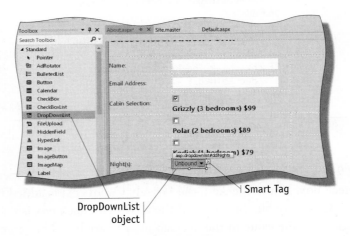

FIGURE 9-32

STEP 2 To fill the DropDownList object with list items, tap or click the Smart Tag on the upper-right corner of the object.

The DropDownList Tasks menu opens (Figure 9–33).

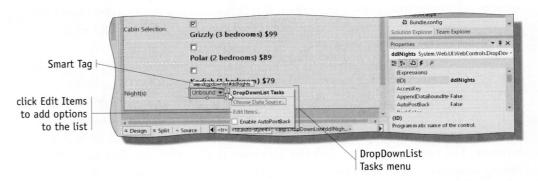

FIGURE 9-33

STEP 3   Tap or click Edit Items on the DropDownList Tasks menu.

The ListItem Collection Editor dialog box opens (Figure 9-34).

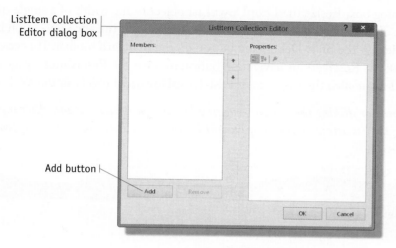

FIGURE 9-34

STEP 4   Tap or click the Add button. In the ListItem Properties pane on the right side of the dialog box, tap or click to the right of the Text property and enter 1.

The number 1 is entered as the first item in the DropDownList object (Figure 9-35).

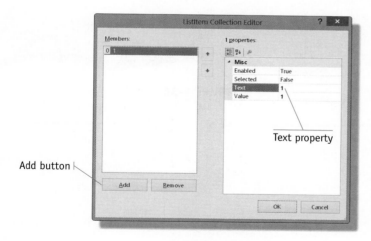

FIGURE 9-35

STEP 5   Tap or click the Add button and enter 2 as its Text property. Repeat this step, entering the numbers 3 through 7 to specify the number of nights users can select in the DropDownList object. Tap or click the OK button in the ListItem Collection Editor dialog box. Resize the DropDownList object to the width of a single digit, if necessary. To view the completed DropDownList object, run the application by tapping or clicking the Start Debugging button on the Standard toolbar. If necessary, tap or click the Reservations navigation button to open the Reservations page in the browser. Tap or click the list arrow on the DropDownList object in the Web page.

After tapping or clicking the Start Debugging button, the browser opens. After tapping or clicking the list arrow on the DropDownList object, the list item contents appear (Figure 9-36).

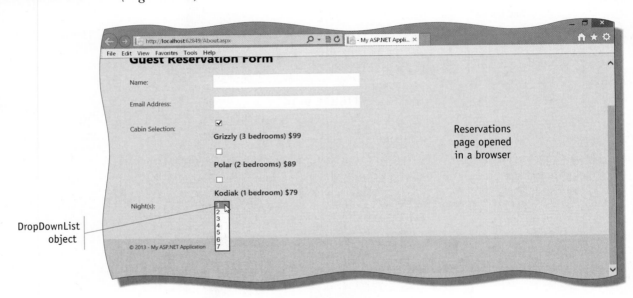

DropDownList object

FIGURE 9-36

Add a Calendar Object

The Guest Reservation form contains a calendar that allows guests to select their arrival date. Visual Basic provides an object to manipulate months, days, and years when specifying information such as reservations, anniversaries, or bill payments. The **Calendar** object is organized by month and displays the number of days in each month as appropriate for the year. For example, March has 31 days and February includes an extra day when the year is a leap year. By default, the Calendar object displays the current month according to the system date and selects the current day when the application is executed. You can use the Calendar object in any type of application, including Windows and Web applications. When creating a Calendar object, use the prefix cld in the name. To place the Calendar object on a Web form, you can complete the following steps:

STEP 1   Close the browser window. In the last row of the table, type `Check-in Date:`. Drag the Calendar object from the Toolbox to the Web form, and then position it on the form. In the (ID) property, name the Calendar object `cldArrival`.

The Calendar object is placed on the Windows form (Figure 9–37).

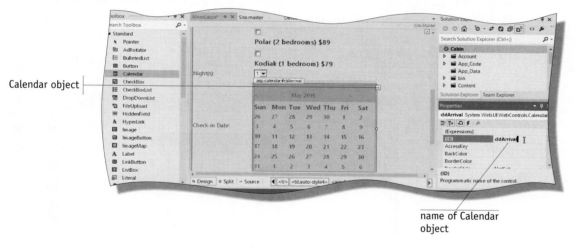

FIGURE 9-37

STEP 2 Select the Calendar object, if necessary, and then tap or click the Smart Tag on the upper-right corner of the Calendar object.

The Calendar Tasks menu opens (Figure 9–38).

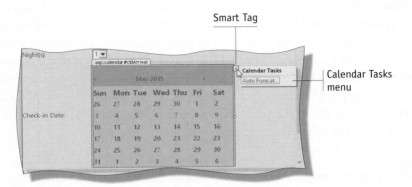

FIGURE 9-38

STEP 3 Tap or click Auto Format on the Calendar Tasks menu. When the AutoFormat dialog box opens, tap or click the Colorful 2 scheme in the Select a scheme list.

The AutoFormat dialog box previews the selected Colorful 2 scheme (Figure 9–39).

ONLINE REINFORCEMENT

To view a video of the process in the previous steps, visit CengageBrain.com and navigate to the resources for this title. Tap or click the link for Chapter 9 and then navigate to Video 9-11.

FIGURE 9-39

Specify a Web Form Title

A Web form displays its title in the title bar of the browser used to view the form. Not all browsers have a title bar, but the title also appears as the title of the MainContent area and as the tab name in the browser. You specify the title bar text for a Web form using the Title property. To change the browser Title property from its default of About Us on the Reservations page to the title, Big Bear Cabins Reservation Form, you can complete the following steps:

STEP 1 Tap or click the OK button to close the AutoFormat dialog box. In the Properties window of the Reservations Web form, tap or click the drop-down box at the top and select DOCUMENT.

DOCUMENT is selected in the Properties window (Figure 9–40).

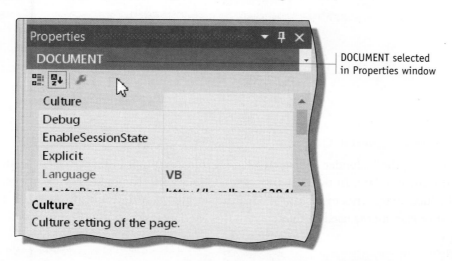

FIGURE 9-40

STEP 2 In the Properties window, scroll until the Title property is visible, and then tap or click in the right column of the Title property. Enter the title Big Bear Cabins with a blank space following the text entry. When the Web page is displayed, the Title property appears in front of the MainContent title.

The title Big Bear Cabins is entered in the Title property of the Properties window. This title will be displayed in front of the MainContent title and on some browsers as the title bar or tab name of the browser for the Reservations page (Figure 9–41).

FIGURE 9-41

Code for a Calendar Object

When using the Calendar object, two dates often are important: the selected date and the current date. In the Visual Basic code that you write in an event handler, you can include statements to reference both the selected date and the current date. The format of statements used to reference these two dates is shown in Figure 9-42.

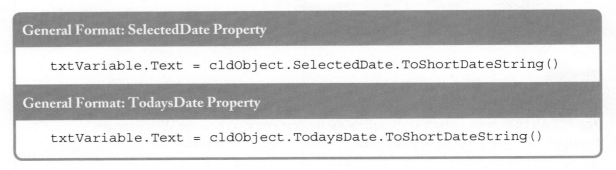

FIGURE 9-42

© 2014 Cengage Learning

In Figure 9-42, the SelectedDate property references the date the user tapped or clicked in the Calendar object. In the general format, the ToShortDateString() procedure changes the date to a String format so it can be displayed in a TextBox object. If you are referencing only the selected date without the need to change it to a string value, the procedure is not required.

Similarly, the current date is referenced by the property TodaysDate.

In the Big Bear Cabins application, it is important to ensure that the date the user selects is equal to or greater than the current date. For a reservation date, a user cannot select a date that has already passed. One of the If statements used in the sample program to test this condition is shown in Figure 9-43.

```
32          If cldArrival.SelectedDate < cldArrival.TodaysDate
33              lblCalendarError.Visible = True
34          Else
35              lblCalendarError.Visible = False
36          End If
```

FIGURE 9-43

In Figure 9-43, the selected date for the cldArrival Calendar object is compared to the current date (TodaysDate) for the cldArrival Calendar object. If the selected date is less than the current date, an error message is displayed; otherwise the error message is not displayed.

If the user does not tap or click a date on the calendar prior to tapping or clicking the Submit button and running the event handler code, the Calendar object automatically returns a date that is less than the current date. Therefore, the If statement on line 32 will detect both the case when the user selects a date less than the current date, and the case when the user does not select a date.

Add Validation Controls

An important part of creating Web forms is validating the data entered in the form to make sure the user has entered reasonable values. Instead of using a series of If statements or other complex code, ASP.NET 4.5 provides built-in validation control objects that compare a form's objects to a set rule using little or no code. The validation control objects check input forms for errors and display messages if users enter incorrect or incomplete responses. Built-in validation control objects include RequiredFieldValidator, which verifies that a required field contains data, and RangeValidator, which tests whether an entry falls within a given range.

Apply a Required Field Validator

The simplest validation control is the **RequiredFieldValidator** object, which finds a specified object to validate and determines whether the object is empty. For example, in the Big Bear Cabins application, the user must enter her first and last name. Otherwise, a reservation cannot be made. The RequiredFieldValidator object reminds the user to complete all required fields. You can customize this reminder by changing the ErrorMessage property, which often is helpful to let users know what they have done incorrectly. If the user enters a value in a field, the RequiredFieldValidator does not display an error message.

In the Big Bear Cabins Guest Reservation form, the first object to validate is the Name TextBox object, which is named txtName. You can add a RequiredFieldValidator object to the Web form that tests txtName to determine if it is empty. If it is, an error message appears reminding the user to enter a first name. After adding the RequiredFieldValidator object, you must specify that it validates the txtName TextBox object.

The prefix used for the RequiredFieldValidator is rfv. To validate a required TextBox object using a RequiredFieldValidator object, follow these steps:

STEP 1 In the Toolbox, hide the Standard tools by tapping or clicking the filled triangle icon next to Standard. Expand the Validation tools by tapping or clicking the open triangle icon next to Validation.

The seven Validation tools are displayed (Figure 9-44).

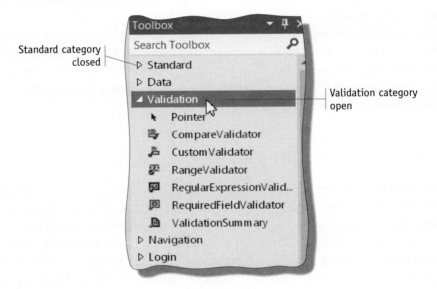

FIGURE 9-44

STEP 2   Drag the RequiredFieldValidator to the right of the Name TextBox object.

The RequiredFieldValidator object is placed to the right of txtName (Figure 9–45).

RequiredFieldValidator
in Validation category

RequiredFieldValidator
added to the form

FIGURE 9-45

STEP 3   Name the RequiredFieldValidator by typing `rfvName` in its (ID) property.

The RequiredFieldValidator object is named rfvName (Figure 9–46).

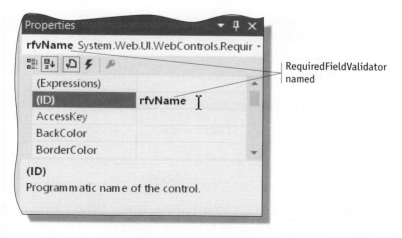

RequiredFieldValidator
named

FIGURE 9-46

STEP 4 To specify that the rfvName RequiredFieldValidator object validates the txtName TextBox object, tap or click to the right of the ControlToValidate property in the Properties window, tap or click the list arrow, and then select txtName.

The ControlToValidate property is set to txtName (Figure 9-47).

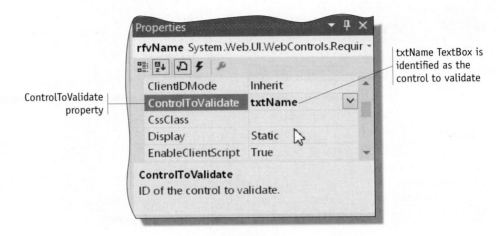

FIGURE 9-47

STEP 5 In the Properties window for the RequiredFieldValidator, change the ErrorMessage property to * Enter Name.

*The ErrorMessage property is changed to * Enter Name (Figure 9-48).*

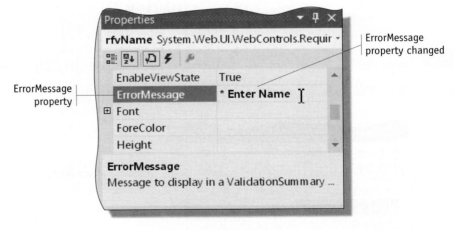

FIGURE 9-48

When the application is run on a Web browser with a Submit button, the error message will be displayed if the Submit button is tapped or clicked and no text has been entered in the txtName text box.

Apply the Range Validator

Another validation control built into ASP.NET 4.5 is the **RangeValidator** control, which tests whether an input value falls within a given range. If you were testing whether a number entered on a Web page was a valid day in a month, the RangeValidator control could test if the day number is between 1 and 31. The RangeValidator control uses the prefix rgv in its name, and the following five properties to complete its validation:

- **ControlToValidate** property contains the name of the object you are validating.
- **MinimumValue** property contains the smallest value in the range.
- **MaximumValue** property contains the largest value in the range.
- **Type** property matches the data type of the value, such as Integer or String.
- **ErrorMessage** property explains to the user what value is requested.

Apply the Compare Validator

Another validation control is the **CompareValidator** object, which you use to compare an object's value with another object or a constant value. The CompareValidator control can also compare the value in one object to the value in another object. In the example shown in Figure 9-49, the user enters a password into a Web form, and reenters the password to confirm that the two passwords are the same. You can use the CompareValidator control to verify that the passwords match.

Enter Password: secret

Confirm Password: secret1

Submit Button   Passwords do not match

FIGURE 9-49

© 2014 Cengage Learning

The CompareValidator uses three properties to complete its validation:

- **ControlToValidate** property contains the name of the object that you are validating.
- **ControlToCompare** property contains the name of the object that you are comparing to the ControlToValidate property.
- **ErrorMessage** property contains a message stating that the value does not match.

In Figure 9-50, four properties are changed to apply the CompareValidator object to verify a password: (ID), ControlToCompare, ControlToValidate, and ErrorMessage. This Figure also shows that the prefix for the CompareValidator object is cmv.

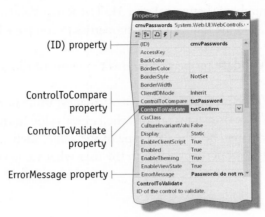

(ID) property

ControlToCompare property

ControlToValidate property

ErrorMessage property

FIGURE 9-50

Apply the Regular Expression Validator

The **RegularExpressionValidator** control confirms whether the user entered data that matches standard formats such as a phone number, email address, URL, zip code, or Social Security number. If the user does not enter the data in the proper format, an error message is displayed. The prefix rev is used for the RegularExpressionValidator control. The RegularExpressionValidator uses three properties to complete its validation:

- **ControlToValidate** property contains the name of the object that you are validating.
- **ErrorMessage** property contains a message stating that the value does not match the valid format.
- **ValidationExpression** property allows the user to select the format for the object.

In the Big Bear Cabins Guest Reservation form, the second TextBox object on the form requests the user's email address. To confirm that the information entered is a possible email address, a RegularExpressionValidator object can test the contents of the Text property of the txtEmail object and verify that it matches the format of a valid email address, which follows the format of *name@domain.com*. To incorporate a RegularExpressionValidator object in a Web page, you can complete the following steps:

STEP 1   Drag the RegularExpressionValidator object from the Toolbox to the right of the Email Address TextBox object in the table.

The RegularExpressionValidator object is placed in the table to the right of txtEmail (Figure 9-51).

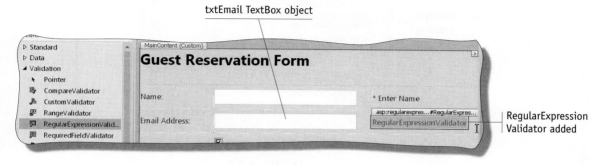

FIGURE 9-51

STEP 2   Name the RegularExpressionValidator by typing `revEmail` in its (ID) property.

The RegularExpressionValidator object is named revEmail (Figure 9-52).

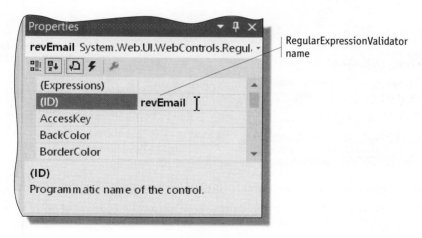

FIGURE 9-52

STEP 3 Tap or click to the right of the ControlToValidate property, tap or click the list arrow, and then tap or click txtEmail.

The ControlToValidate property is set to txtEmail (Figure 9-53).

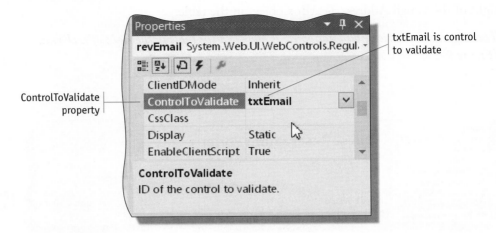

FIGURE 9-53

STEP 4 Change the ErrorMessage property to * Error Email Format.

*The ErrorMessage property is changed to * Error Email Format (Figure 9-54).*

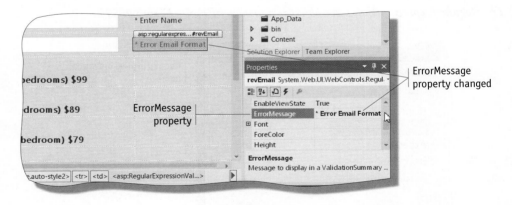

FIGURE 9-54

STEP 5 To set txtEmail to validate that it contains a standard email address, tap or click to the right of the ValidationExpression property, and then tap or click its ellipsis button. In the Regular Expression Editor dialog box, select Internet e-mail address in the Standard expressions list.

The Internet email address is selected as the standard expression to validate (Figure 9–55).

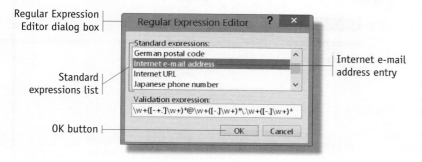

FIGURE 9-55

STEP 6 Tap or click the OK button in the Regular Expression Editor dialog box. Run the application by tapping or clicking the Start Debugging button on the Standard toolbar. Enter a name and an email address without an @ symbol, such as `liam.world.net`, and then press the ENTER key.

An error message appears to the right of the Email Address TextBox object (Figure 9-56). When a valid email address is entered and the ENTER key is pressed again, the error message is removed.

FIGURE 9-56

Apply Multiple Validations

You can apply more than one type of validation control on an object to validate more than one aspect of the data. Often you may want to make a certain control required using the RequiredFieldValidator object, and to check the range using the Range-Validator object. In Figure 9-57 on the next page, a RequiredFieldValidator confirms that the number of hours worked is not left blank, and the RangeValidator verifies that the number entered is between 1 and 60. Each validation control displays an error message if the object does not meet the specified criteria.

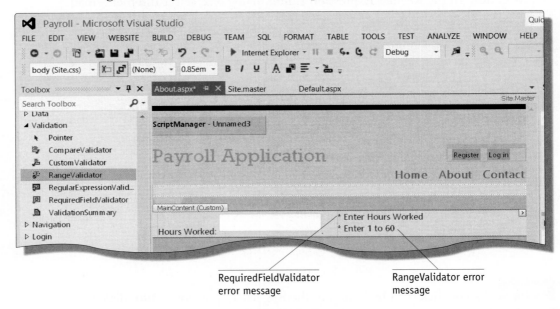

RequiredFieldValidator
error message

RangeValidator error
message

FIGURE 9-57

Display a ValidationSummary Control

Instead of validating data, the **ValidationSummary** control lets you display validation error messages in a single location, creating a clean layout for the Web form. By default, each validation control displays an error message next to the object it validates. On a large or complex form, however, the error messages might interfere with data or other objects. You can use the ValidationSummary object to display all of the error messages in a different place, listing them in a blank area at the top or bottom of the form, for example, where they will appear together when the validation criteria for any control is not met.

To use a ValidationSummary object, drag the object to the location on the Web page where you want the summary to appear. The prefix used for naming the ValidationSummary object is vsm.

CONSIDER THIS

Do I have to set the ControlToValidate property for a validation summary?
The validation summary displays the error messages for all the other validation objects, so you do not have to set the ControlToValidate property. The error message displayed in this control is specified by the ErrorMessage property of each validation control. If the ErrorMessage property of the validation control is not set, no error message is displayed for that validation control.

Use the
 Tag in Visual Basic Code

One HTML tag often used when creating Web pages is the **
** tag, which stands for break; it breaks the text by starting a new line. When you are creating a Web form in Visual Basic, you can use the <br> tag to skip a line before starting a new one in a Label object.

In the Big Bear Cabins chapter project, after the user enters reservation information, a confirmation message is displayed that includes details about the reservation such as the name, email address, cost of the cabins, date, and number of nights (Figure 9-58).

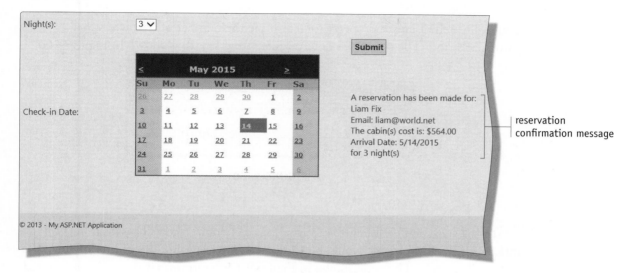

FIGURE 9-58

In Figure 9-58, the message consists of five lines. Based on your screen resolution the text may wrap and you may have six lines. Each of the lines except the last line ends with the <br> tag so that the text that follows will be on the next line. The code to create the message is shown in Figure 9-59.

```
53        strMessage = "A reservation has been made for: " &
54            & strName & "<br>" & "Email: " & strEmail & "<b
55        strMessage &= "The cabin(s) cost is: " _
56            & decCabinCost.ToString("C") & "<br>"
57        strMessage &= "Arrival Date: " _
58            & cldArrival.SelectedDate.ToShortDateString() _
59            & "<br>" & " for " & intNumberOfNights & " nigh
60        lblReservation.Text = strMessage
```

FIGURE 9-59

In Figure 9-59, the message to be displayed is built in the strMessage String variable. On line 53, the first line of the message is placed in the variable. The last item in the string is the <br> tag, which will cause the text that follows to be on the next line. Notice that the tag must be within double quotation marks because it is a string.

The statements on lines 54 and 56 also end with the **
** tag. As a result of the statements in Figure 9-59, a five-line message will be created.

Use String Manipulation Properties and Procedures in the String Class

The String class in Visual Basic has many properties and procedures that allow you to manipulate strings, which you often need to do when developing Web forms. For example, you might want to find the length of the string that the user entered or convert lowercase text to uppercase. The commands discussed in this section work with ASP.NET 4.5 as well as in any Windows or mobile application.

Find String Length

You can use the **Length** property to determine the number of characters in a particular string. The syntax for determining string length is shown in Figure 9-60.

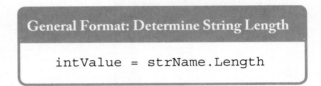

General Format: Determine String Length

```
intValue = strName.Length
```

FIGURE 9-60

© 2014 Cengage Learning

In the statement intLength = "Visual Basic".Length, the value placed in the intLength Integer variable would be 12 because the Length property counts spaces as well as characters. The code shown in Figure 9-61 determines if the zip code entered in the txtZipCode TextBox object has a length of five characters.

```
8        Dim intCount As Integer
9
10       intCount = txtZipCode.Text.Length
11       If intCount <> 5 Then
12           lblError.Text = "You must enter 5 digits"
13       End If
14
```

FIGURE 9-61

If you enter only four digits in the zip code, as shown in Figure 9-62, a message appears reminding you to enter five digits.

FIGURE 9-62

Use the Trim Procedure

When entering information into a TextBox object, the user might accidentally add extra spaces before or after the input string. When that string is used later, the extra spaces might distort the format of the output. To prevent this, Visual Basic provides a procedure named **Trim** to remove spaces from the beginning and end of a string. The syntax for the Trim procedure is shown in Figure 9-63.

> **General Format: Trim Procedure**
>
> ```
> strName = strName.Trim()
> ```

FIGURE 9-63

© 2014 Cengage Learning

In the Big Bear Cabins Guest Reservation form, the user enters a name and an email address. If the user includes spaces before or after the entries, the spaces will appear in the final output. The Trim procedure shown in Figure 9-64 removes extra spaces.

```
26        ' Trim additional spaces that are entered by the user
27        strName = txtName.Text.Trim
28        strEmail = txtEmail.Text.Trim
```

FIGURE 9-64

Convert Uppercase and Lowercase Text

The **ToUpper** and **ToLower** procedures convert a string to all uppercase or all lowercase, respectively. The following syntax in Figure 9-65 shows how to use the ToUpper and ToLower procedures:

> **General Format: UpperCase and LowerCase Procedures**
>
> ```
> strName = strName.ToUpper()
>
> strName = strName.ToLower()
> ```

FIGURE 9-65

© 2014 Cengage Learning

When you compare a string, Visual Basic checks if you entered the word as specified. For example, if you enter YES in response to a question, but the code accepts only yes, the If statement as shown in Figure 9-66 would convert the response of YES to yes. The ToUpper() and ToLower() methods save coding time because all the possible ways to enter a response do not have to be compared.

```
87          If strAnswer.ToLower() = "yes" Then
```

FIGURE 9-66

© 2014 Cengage Learning

Program Design

As you have learned, the requirements document identifies the purpose of the program being developed, the application title, the procedures to be followed when using the program, any equations and calculations required in the program, any conditions within the program that must be tested, notes and restrictions that must be followed by the program, and any other comments that would be helpful to understanding the problem. The requirements document for the Big Bear Cabins Web application is shown in Figure 9-67 and the Use Case Definition is shown in Figure 9-68 on the next page.

REQUIREMENTS DOCUMENT

Date Submitted:	May 3, 2015
Application Title:	Big Bear Cabins
Purpose:	This Web application allows the user to book a reservation at the Big Bear Cabins using a Web form.
Program Procedures:	From a Web application, the user should complete an online reservation form to enter the guest's name, email address, cabin preference, number of nights, and starting date. The total cost of the stay should be calculated and displayed.
Algorithms, Processing, and Conditions:	1. The user must be able to enter the requested reservation information on a Web form. The information should include the guest's name, email address, which cabins they prefer, number of nights, and starting date of the stay. The user can select one or more cabins from the following choices: Grizzly (3 bedrooms) $99, Polar (2 bedroom) $89, and Kodiak (1 bedroom) $79. 2. After entering the reservation information, the user taps or clicks the Submit button. 3. The information entered is validated. 4. The application displays the final cost of the stay.
Notes and Restrictions:	1. Data in the Name TextBox object is required. 2. Data in the Email TextBox object is validated to confirm that it is in an email address format. 3. The Calendar object is checked to confirm that a date is selected and that the selected date is not before the current date. The maximum length of stay is seven nights.
Comments:	Display a picture of the cabins on the Web form.

FIGURE 9-67

USE CASE DEFINITION

1. The Web page opens, displaying the title Big Bear Cabins with a picture as well as TextBox objects to enter the guest's name and email address. A Calendar object is used to select the beginning date of the reservation. A DropDownList object is used to enter the number of nights. The cabin selections are entered with CheckBox objects.
2. User taps or clicks the Submit button.
3. The data entered is checked and validated.
4. If necessary, the user makes corrections and resubmits the data.
5. The application confirms the reservation and displays the final cost of the stay.

FIGURE 9-68

Event Planning Document

You will recall that the event planning document consists of a table that specifies an object in the user interface that will cause an event, the action taken by the user to trigger the event, and the event processing that must occur. The event planning document for the Big Bear Cabins Web application is shown in Figure 9-69.

EVENT PLANNING DOCUMENT			
Program Name: Cabin Web Application	**Developer:** Corinne Hoisington	**Object:** Default.aspx	**Date:** May 3, 2015
OBJECT	**EVENT TRIGGER**	**EVENT PROCESSING**	

btnSubmit	Click	Validate the name to confirm it is not empty
		Validate email address to confirm it is in the email address format
		Trim extra spaces from name and email data
		Blank the reservation message
		If a cabin has not been selected
		    Display a cabin error message
		    If arrival date is not valid
		       Display a calendar error message
		    Else
		    Hide the calendar error message
		Else
		    Hide cabin error message
		    If arrival date is valid
		       Accumulate cabin costs
		       Convert number of nights to Integer
		       Calculate cost of Cabin (total Cabin costs * number of nights)
		       Create the reservation message
		       Display the reservation message
		    Else
		       Display calendar error message	

FIGURE 9-69

Code the Program

After identifying the events and tasks within the events, you are ready to create the program. As you have learned, creating the program means designing the user interface and then entering Visual Basic statements to accomplish the tasks specified on the event planning document. As you enter the code, you also will implement the logic to carry out the required processing.

Guided Program Development

NOTE TO THE LEARNER

In the following activity, you should complete the tasks within the specified steps. Each of the tasks is accompanied by a Hint Screen. The purpose of the Hint Screen is to indicate where you should perform the activity in the Visual Studio window and to remind you which method to use. If you need further help completing a step, refer to the Figure identified by *ref:*.

Guided Program Development

Phase 1: Customize the Master and Home Pages

1

- **Begin the Web Application** Start Visual Studio, and then create a Visual Basic Web Site Application project by tapping or clicking the New Web Site button on the Standard toolbar. In the center pane, click ASP.NET Web Forms Site, if necessary. Enter the project name `Cabin` and store the program on the e: drive (or a network or USB drive of your choice). Tap or click the OK button *(ref: Figure 9-4)*.

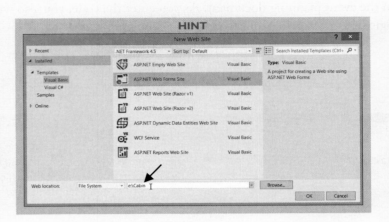

- **Display the Formatting Toolbar** Tap or click VIEW on the menu bar, point to Toolbars, and then tap or click Formatting.

- **Change the Heading on the Site.master Page** In the Solution Explorer, double-tap or double-click the Site.master page. On the page, select the "your logo here" placeholder text. Type `Big Bear Cabins`. Select the typed title. On the Formatting toolbar, change the font size to xx-large.

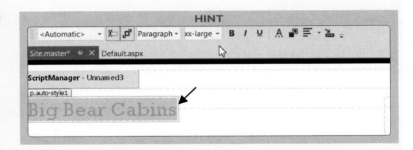

- **Change the Second Navigational Link** On the Site.master page, select the "Contact" text. Press the DELETE key to delete the Contact link. Select the "About" text in the About link and type `Reservations` to rename the link. Tap or click the Register and Log in tabs on the Site.master page. Press the DELETE key to remove the Register and Log in tabs.

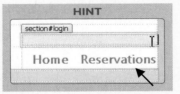

- **Add an Image Object** Save the Site.master and switch to the Default.aspx page. Delete the existing text in the title placeholder in the FeaturedContent area. Double-tap or double-click the Image object in the Standard category of the Toolbox to display it within the Web page in the FeaturedContent area. Resize the object so that it is 175 pixels (width) by 150 pixels (height). Change its ImageUrl property to `http://delgraphics.delmarlearning.com/CourseTechnology/cabins.jpg` *(ref: Figure 9-16)*.

- **Type Directly on the Page** Tap or click to the right of the Image object and type `Enjoy a Mountain Getaway`. Tap or click the ellipsis button of the style property in the Properties window. In the Modify Style dialog box, select the Block category and then select top in the vertical-align box. Tap or click the OK button.

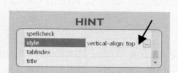

- **Type the Paragraph** Select the text in the paragraph below the image and press the DELETE key. Change the font size to medium using the Formatting toolbar. Enter the text `Nestled in the trees surrounded by the Beartooth Mountains, our cabin retreat provides modern comfort with genuine mountain elegance, offering a rustic ambiance with wood burning fireplaces and cozy furnished kitchens`. Delete the text in the MainContent area *(ref: Figure 9-20)*.

The Default. aspx Web page includes an image and typed text (Figure 9-70).

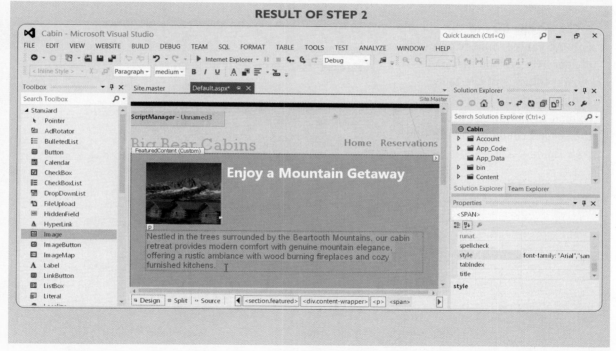

Karl Weatherly/Photodisc/Getty Images

FIGURE 9-70

(continues)

Phase 2: Build the Guest Reservation Web Form

3

● **Insert a Table in the Web Form** In the Solution Explorer, double-tap or double-click the About.aspx file. Delete the text in the MainContent area. Type Guest Reservation Form in the MainContent area. Tap or click TABLE on the menu bar, and then tap or click Insert Table. In the Insert Table dialog box, enter 7 in the Rows text box and 3 in the Columns text box, and then tap or click the OK button to create a table with seven columns and three rows *(ref: Figure 9-22).*

● **Change the Size of the Column Tables** Point to the divider between the first and second columns of the table, and then drag to resize the first column to 150 pixels. Resize the second column to 250 pixels *(ref: Figure 9-23).*

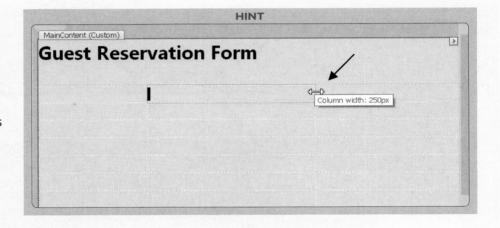

Enter Text and Objects in the Table

● In the first column of the table, enter `Name:`, `Email Address:`, `Cabin Selection:`, `Night(s):`, and `Check-in Date:` in separate rows. In the second column, drag the first TextBox object to the right of the Name title, and then name the TextBox object `txtName` *(ref: Figure 9-24)*.

● Drag the second TextBox object to the right of the Email Address title, and then name the TextBox object `txtEmail` *(ref: Figure 9-25)*.

● Drag a CheckBox object to the right of the Cabin Selection text. Name the CheckBox object `chkGrizzly`. Change the Text property to `Grizzly (3 bedrooms) $99`. Change the Checked property to True *(ref: Figure 9-28)*.

● Drag the second CheckBox object below the first CheckBox object, and then name the CheckBox object `chkPolar`. Change its Text property to `Polar (2 bedrooms) $89`. Drag the third CheckBox object below the second CheckBox object, and then name the third CheckBox object `chkKodiak`. Change its Text property to `Kodiak (1 bedroom) $79` *(ref: Figure 9-30)*.

● Drag a DropDownList object to the right of the Night(s) title. Change the name of the DropDownList object to `ddlNights`. Tap or click the Smart Tag on the DropDownList object, and then tap or click Edit Items. The ListItem Collection Editor dialog box opens. Tap or click the Add button, and then enter the number `1` as the Text property. Tap or click the Add button as necessary to add the numbers `2` through `7`. After adding number `7`, tap or click the Remove button to remove the entry in the Members list, if necessary. Tap or click the OK button *(ref: Figure 9-36)*.

● Drag a Calendar object to the right of the Check-in Date text. Name the Calendar object `cldArrival`. Tap or click the Smart Tag on the Calendar object, and then tap or click Auto Format. Select Colorful 2, and then tap or click OK. *(ref: Figure 9-39)*.

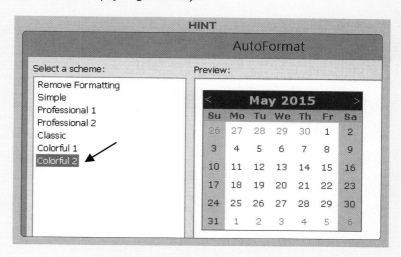

The Guest Reservation Form (About. aspx) includes typed text, text boxes, check boxes, a drop-down list, and a calendar (Figure 9-71).

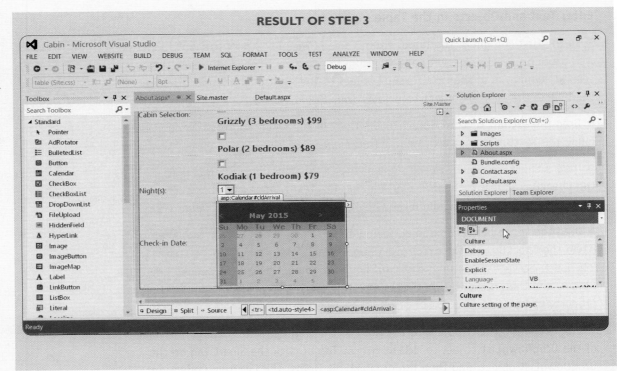

FIGURE 9-71

Phase 3: Add Validation Objects

4

- **Add the Required Validation Objects** In the Toolbox, expand the Validation controls by tapping or clicking the expand icon next to Validation *(ref: Figure 9-44)*.

HINT

- **Validate the Name TextBox Object** Drag the RequiredFieldValidator object onto the Web form to the first row in the third column. Name the Validator Object `rfvName`. Change its ErrorMessage property to `* Enter Name` *(ref: Figure 9-48)*.

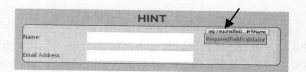

HINT

- **Select the TextBox Object to Validate** In the Properties window for the rfvName object, tap or click the list arrow in the ControlToValidate property and then tap or click txtName *(ref: Figure 9-47)*.

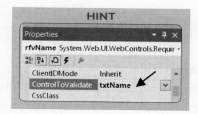

HINT

(continues)

● **Validate the Email TextBox Object** Drag the RegularExpressionValidator object onto the Web form in the second row of the third column. Place the RequiredFieldValidator object to the right of the txtEmail TextBox object. Name the Validator object `revEmail`. Change its ErrorMessage property to `* Enter a Valid Email`. In the Properties window, tap or click the list arrow in the ControlToValidate property and then tap or click txtEmail.

● **Add Regular Expression Validator for Email** Drag the RegularExpressionValidator object below the Email Address field. Name the Validator object `revEmail`. Change its ErrorMessage property to `* Error Email Format`. Tap or click the list arrow in the ControlToValidate property, and then tap or click txtEmail. Tap or click the ellipsis button in the ValidationExpression property. When the Regular Expression Editor dialog box opens, select Internet e-mail address. Tap or click the OK button *(ref: Figure 9-55)*.

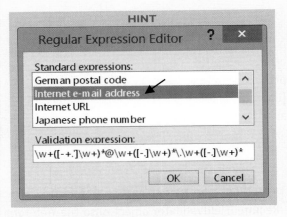

● **Add the Missing Cabin Selection Message** Drag a Label object onto the Web form to the third row in the third column. Place the label in the same row as the Grizzly check box. Name the label `lblCabinError`. Change the Text property to `* Select a Cabin`. Set the Visible property for the label to False.

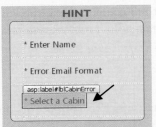

● **Add the Submit Button** Drag a Button object to the last row of the third column to the right of the Calendar object. Change the Button object (ID) property to `btnSubmit`. Change the Text property to `Submit`. Tap or click after the Submit button and press Enter several times until the Submit button is at the top of the cell.

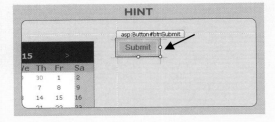

- **Add a Calendar Warning Label** Drag a Label object below the Submit button. Change the (ID) property of the Label object to `lblCalendarError`. Change the Text property to `* Select a valid date`. The warning message is displayed only if a valid date is not selected. Change the Visible property to False.

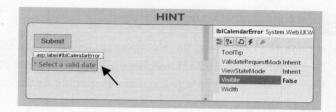

- **Add a Result Label** Drag a Label object below the Submit button and the calendar error Label object. Name the Label object `lblReservation`. Delete any value in the Text property. The lblReservation placeholder with the text [lblReservation] is displayed on the Web form, but will not appear in the actual Web page.

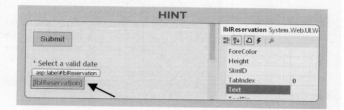

- **Change the DOCUMENT Property** Tap or click the object arrow in the Properties window and then select DOCUMENT. Type `Big Bear Cabins` as the Title property.

The validation objects and messages are part of the Web form (Figure 9-72).

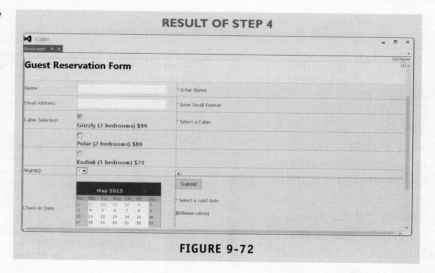

FIGURE 9-72

Guided Program Development   *continued*

Phase 4: Code the Application

5

● **Code the Comments** Double-tap or double-click the Submit button on the form to begin coding the btnSubmit_ Click event in the Web application. Insert the first four standard comments at the top of the code window. Insert the command Option Strict On at the beginning of the code to turn on strict type checking.

HINT

```
btnSubmit                                        ▼  ⚡ Click
 1 ⊟ ' Project:   Big Bear Cabins Online Reservation Form
 2   | ' Author:    Corinne Hoisington
 3   | ' Date:      May 3, 2015
 4   | ' Purpose:   The following Web application will request reservation information
 5   |              for the Big Bear Cabins. This web site will compute
 6   |              the cost of the number of nights and cabin(s) selected.
 7
 8     Option Strict On
```

● **Comment on the btnSubmit Click Event** In the btnSubmit click event, enter a comment that explains the purpose of the click event.

HINT

```
12 ⊟    Protected Sub btnSubmit_Click(ByVal sender As Object, ByVal e As System.EventArgs) Handles btnSubmit.Click
13          ' The btnSubmit Click Event will calculate the cost of the cost of the cabin
14          ' based on the type of cabin selected and the number of nights reserved.
15
```

● **Initialize Variables** Tap or click in the btnSubmit click event and enter the variables used in the application. These variables include String variables for the name and email address; Decimal variables that will contain the cabin costs for the three cabins and the result of the cabin cost calculation; an Integer value for the number of nights the user selects from the drop-down list; and a String variable in which to compose the reservation message.

HINT

```
16          ' Declare and initialize variables
17          Dim decGrizzlyCost As Decimal = 99D
18          Dim decPolarCost As Decimal = 89D
19          Dim decKodiakCost As Decimal = 79D
20          Dim strName As String
21          Dim strEmail As String
22          Dim decCabinCost As Decimal = 0D
23          Dim intNumberOfNights As Integer
24          Dim strMessage As String
25
```

● **Trim the TextBox Object Data** Using the Trim procedure, write the code to remove excess spaces from the data the user entered. Place the trimmed Name from the TextBox object in the strName variable and the trimmed Email address in the strEmail variable *(ref: Figure 9-64)*.

HINT	
26	' Trim additional spaces that are entered by the user
27	strName = txtName.Text.Trim
28	strEmail = txtEmail.Text.Trim

● **Clear the Reservation Message** Write a statement to clear the lblReservations label.

HINT	
29	lblReservation.Text = ""

● **Ensure a Cabin is Selected** Write an If statement that ensures a cabin has been selected. The Checked property of one or more of the CheckBox objects must be true. Use the Not operator to check for all three properties. If the cabin has not been selected, display the cabin error message.

HINT	
30	If Not (chkGrizzly.Checked Or chkPolar.Checked Or chkKodiak.Checked) Then
31	lblCabinError.Visible = True

● **Ensure a Valid Date is Selected** Regardless of whether a valid suite was selected, the program must ensure a valid date was selected. Therefore, if a suite is not selected, write an If statement that ensures the date is valid (that is, the selected date is not less than the current date). If the date is invalid, display the calendar error message; otherwise, do not display the calendar error message.

HINT	
30	If Not (chkGrizzly.Checked Or chkPolar.Checked Or chkKodiak.Checked) Then
31	lblCabinError.Visible = True
32	If cldArrival.SelectedDate < cldArrival.TodaysDate Then
33	lblCalendarError.Visible = True
34	Else
35	lblCalendarError.Visible = False
36	End If
37	Else

(continues)

● **Hide Cabin Message When Cabin is Selected** If a cabin is selected, the cabin error message must be hidden; that is, the cabin error message Visible property must be set to False. Write the statement to set the Visible property to False.

	HINT
30	If Not (chkGrizzly.Checked Or chkPolar.Checked Or chkKodiak.Checked) Then
31	lblCabinError.Visible = True
32	If cldArrival.SelectedDate < cldArrival.TodaysDate Then
33	lblCalendarError.Visible = True
34	Else
35	lblCalendarError.Visible = False
36	End If
37	Else
38	lblCabinError.Visible = False

● **Ensure a Valid Date is Selected** When a cabin has been selected, the program must ensure a valid date was selected. If a cabin is selected and a valid date is selected, the data validity checking is complete and the cabin cost can be calculated. Write a statement to ensure that the selected date is greater than or equal to the current date, and if the date is valid, set the Visible property for the error message to False.

	HINT
39	If cldArrival.SelectedDate >= cldArrival.TodaysDate Then
40	lblCalendarError.Visible = False

● **Determine Total of Cabin Costs** The user can select more than one cabin. For example, one cabin might be for parents and another cabin might be for their children. Therefore, the program must determine if each check box is checked, and if so, the cabin cost per night is accumulated. Write the statements to determine if a suite check box is checked and, if so, to accumulate the Cabin costs in the decCabinCost variable.

	HINT
41	' Calculate the cost of the cabin(s) selected by the user
42	If chkGrizzly.Checked Then
43	decCabinCost += decGrizzlyCost
44	End If
45	If chkPolar.Checked Then
46	decCabinCost += decPolarCost
47	End If
48	If chkKodiak.Checked Then
49	decCabinCost += decKodiakCost
50	End If

● **Calculate Total Cabin Cost** To calculate the total cabin cost, the number of nights selected by the user from the drop-down list must be converted from a String to an Integer. Then, the calculation to determine the total cabin costs (number of nights x cabin cost) must occur. Write the statements to perform these activities.

HINT	
51	`intNumberOfNights = Convert.ToInt32(ddlNights.SelectedItem.Text)`
52	`decCabinCost = intNumberOfNights * decCabinCost`

● **Create the Reservation Message** Write the code to create the reservation message and place it in the strMessage String variable. Then, place the message stored in the strMessage variable in the Text property of the lblReservation Label object *(ref: Figure 9-59)*.

HINT	
53	`strMessage = "A reservation has been made for: " & " " _`
54	`    & strName & " " & "Email: " & strEmail & " "`
55	`strMessage &= "The cabin(s) cost is: " _`
56	`    & decCabinCost.ToString("C") & " "`
57	`strMessage &= "Arrival Date: " _`
58	`    & cldArrival.SelectedDate.ToShortDateString() _`
59	`    & " " & " for " & intNumberOfNights & " night(s)"`
60	`lblReservation.Text = strMessage`

● **Show Calendar Error Message** If the user did not select a valid date for the check-in date, display the calendar error message by changing the Visible property for the error message label to True.

HINT	
61	`        Else`
62	`            lblCalendarError.Visible = True`
63	`        End If`
64	`    End If`
65	`End Sub`
66	`End Class`

Code Listing

The complete code for the sample program is shown in Figure 9-73.

```
1  ⊟ ' Project:  Big Bear Cabins Online Reservation Form
2    ' Author:   Corinne Hoisington
3    ' Date:     May 3, 2015
4    ' Purpose:  The following Web application will request reservation information
5    '           for the Big Bear Cabins. This web site will compute
6    '           the cost of the number of nights and cabin(s) selected.
7
```

FIGURE 9-73 (continues)

```
 8   Option Strict On
 9  ⊟Partial Class About
10       Inherits System.Web.UI.Page
11
12  ⊟    Protected Sub btnSubmit_Click(ByVal sender As Object, ByVal e As System.EventArgs) Handles btnSubmit.Click
13           ' The btnSubmit Click Event will calculate the cost of the cost of the cabin
14           ' based on the type of cabin selected and the number of nights reserved.
15
16           ' Declare and initialize variables
17           Dim decGrizzlyCost As Decimal = 99D
18           Dim decPolarCost As Decimal = 89D
19           Dim decKodiakCost As Decimal = 79D
20           Dim strName As String
21           Dim strEmail As String
22           Dim decCabinCost As Decimal = 0D
23           Dim intNumberOfNights As Integer
24           Dim strMessage As String
25
26           ' Trim additional spaces that are entered by the user
27           strName = txtName.Text.Trim
28           strEmail = txtEmail.Text.Trim
29           lblReservation.Text = ""
30           If Not (chkGrizzly.Checked Or chkPolar.Checked Or chkKodiak.Checked) Then
31               lblCabinError.Visible = True
32               If cldArrival.SelectedDate < cldArrival.TodaysDate Then
33                   lblCalendarError.Visible = True
34               Else
35                   lblCalendarError.Visible = False
36               End If
37           Else
38               lblCabinError.Visible = False
39               If cldArrival.SelectedDate >= cldArrival.TodaysDate Then
40                   lblCalendarError.Visible = False
41                   ' Calculate the cost of the cabin(s) selected by the user
42                   If chkGrizzly.Checked Then
43                       decCabinCost += decGrizzlyCost
44                   End If
45                   If chkPolar.Checked Then
46                       decCabinCost += decPolarCost
47                   End If
48                   If chkKodiak.Checked Then
49                       decCabinCost += decKodiakCost
50                   End If
51                   intNumberOfNights = Convert.ToInt32(ddlNights.SelectedItem.Text)
52                   decCabinCost = intNumberOfNights * decCabinCost
53                   strMessage = "A reservation has been made for: " & "<br>" _
54                       & strName & "<br>" & "Email: " & strEmail & "<br>"
55                   strMessage &= "The cabin(s) cost is: " _
56                       & decCabinCost.ToString("C") & "<br>"
57                   strMessage &= "Arrival Date: " _
58                       & cldArrival.SelectedDate.ToShortDateString() _
59                       & "<br>" & " for " & intNumberOfNights & " night(s)"
60                   lblReservation.Text = strMessage
61               Else
62                   lblCalendarError.Visible = True
63               End If
64           End If
65       End Sub
66   End Class
67
```

FIGURE 9-73 (continued)

Summary

In this chapter you have learned to create an online Web application using ASP.NET 4.5. The items listed in the table shown in Figure 9-74 include all the new Visual Studio and Visual Basic skills you have learned in this chapter.

Visual Basic Skills		
Skill	**Figure Number**	**Video Number**
Examine the Big Bear Cabin Application	Figure 9-1	Video 9-1
Create a Visual Basic Web Project	Figure 9-4	Video 9-2
Change Text on the Master Page	Figure 9-8	Video 9-3
Rename Navigation Buttons	Figure 9-10	Video 9-4
Add an Image Object on the Web Page	Figure 9-14	Video 9-5
Enter Text Directly on the Web Page	Figure 9-17	Video 9-6
Add a Table for Alignment on a Web Form	Figure 9-22	Video 9-7
Add a TextBox Object	Figure 9-24	Video 9-8
Add a CheckBox Object	Figure 9-27	Video 9-9
Add a DropDownList Object	Figure 9-32	Video 9-10
Add a Calendar Object to a Web Form	Figure 9-37	Video 9-11
Specify a Web Form Title	Figure 9-40	Video 9-12
Write Code for Check Box Objects	Page 637	
Write Code for a Calendar Object	Page 644	
Validate TextBox Object Using a RequiredFieldValidator Object	Figure 9-45	Video 9-13
Validate the Range Using a RangeValidator Object	Page 649	
Validate Two Objects with the CompareValidator Object	Page 649	
Validate Data Using a RegularExpressionValidator Object	Figure 9-51	Video 9-14
Validate Data Using Multiple Validations	Page 653	
Display a ValidationSummary Control	Page 654	
Use the Tag in Visual Basic Code	Page 654	
Use the String Length Property	Page 656	
Use the Trim Procedure	Page 657	
Convert Uppercase and Lowercase Text	Page 657	

FIGURE 9-74

Learn Online

Reinforcement activities and resources are available at no additional cost on *www.cengagebrain.com*. Visit *www.cengage. com/ct/studentdownload* for detailed instructions about accessing the resources available at the Student Companion Site.

Knowledge Check

1. In an active server page, what computer executes the event handler code you write in Visual Basic 2012?

2. Name five Web sites that incorporate Web forms and state the purpose of each Web form (such as to enter customer information for purchasing an item). Do not list any sites that were mentioned in this chapter.

3. What is the extension of an ASP Web page?

4. When you test a Web application, the page opens in a(n) _____.

5. A Web page or Web site is hosted on a(n) _____ _____.

6. A Web site that allows you to enter information is considered a(n) _____ Web page.

7. In a Windows application, each object has a (Name) property. In a Web application, each object has a _____ property, which is similar to the (Name) property.

8. Write a line of code that would display the date selected by the user in the TextBox shown in Figure 9-75.

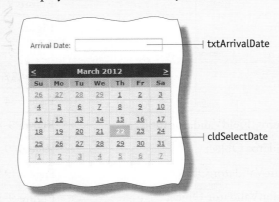

FIGURE 9-75

9. In the ListBox object shown in Figure 9-76, write the lines of code that would display in a Label named lblSizeDisplay "You have selected size: Large" if the user selects "L".

FIGURE 9-76

10. Explain the major difference between CheckBox and RadioButton objects.

11. What is the name of the property that assigns the object name to the validation control?

12. Which control validator confirms that the user enters the constant value of 17.1?

13. Which control validator checks if a value is between 6 and 30?

14. Which control validator confirms that a TextBox object is not left blank?

15. Write a line of code that would convert strResponse to all lowercase letters.

16. Write a line of code that would assign the length of a string named strCompany to the variable intSizeOfCompanyName.

17. Write a line of code that would display in a Label object named lblDisplayBirthday the date a user selected from a Calendar object named cldBirthdate.

18. How does the Image object in ASP.NET differ from an image in a Windows application?

19. In the browser window shown in Figure 9-77, name the type of validation and list any changes that were made in the Properties window.

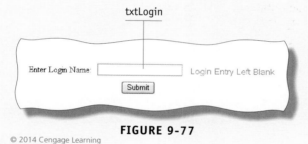

FIGURE 9-77

© 2014 Cengage Learning

20. What is the name of the page that serves as a template for the pages that are actually displayed in the browser?

1. Fix the error(s) in the following line of code.

```
decVideoTitle = strVideoTitle(Text.Length)
```

2. Fix the error(s) in the following lines of code.

```
If (chkSpeedingTicket.Checked) = True Then
decSpeedingTicket += 120
End If
```

(continues)

3. What will be contained in the Text property of the lblResult Label object after executing the following code?

```
Dim strPhrase As String
strPhrase = " Live long"
strPhrase += " and prosper "
strPhrase = strPhrase.Trim()
lblResult.Text=strPhrase
```

4. What is the output of the following code?

```
Dim strPhrase As String
strPhrase = "Shut the front door"
lblResult.Text= "Count =" & strPhrase.Length
```

5. Write the output that would be displayed in the Info label after the following statements are executed.

```
lblInfo.Text = "Home Address: " & "<br>" & "3506 Wards Rd" & "<br>" &
"Lynchburg, VA 24502"
```

Program Analysis

1. Name each of the property changes that are required in the Properties window for a Range Validator in order to validate that a TextBox named txtDeductibleRange contains a value in the range 12.50 up to and including 500.00. Display an error message that states "Please enter an acceptable deductible between 12.50 and 500".

2. Write a Visual Basic statement that displays the length of a variable named strSentence in a Label object named lblStringLength.

3. Write the section of code that would display a list of services in a Label object named lblService if the user selects any of the corresponding CheckBoxes shown in Figure 9-78.

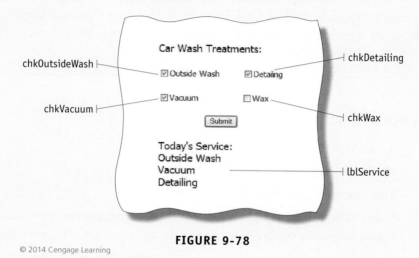

FIGURE 9-78

© 2014 Cengage Learning

Case Programming Assignments

Complete one or more of the following case programming assignments. Submit the program and materials you create to your instructor. The level of difficulty is indicated for each case programming assignment.

●   = Easiest
● ●   = Intermediate
● ● ●   = Challenging

1 ●
GO CAMPING

Design a Web application for a camper rental application. Write the code that will execute according to the program requirements shown in Figure 9-79 and the Use Case Definition document shown in Figure 9-80 on the next page. Before writing the code, create an event planning document for each event in the program. The completed Web page is shown in Figure 9-81 on page 682.

REQUIREMENTS DOCUMENT

Date Submitted:	August 11, 2015
Application Title:	Go Camping Web Application
Purpose:	This Web application allows the user to rent a camper.
Program Procedures:	From a Web application, the user completes an online reservation form to select the type of camper, the number of days to rent the camper, starting date, and mileage.
Algorithms, Processing, and Conditions:	1. The user must be able to enter the requested reservation information on a Web form. The information should include their name, whether the user wants a compact RV ($65 a day) or large RV ($85 a day), the number of days (max 10 days), the start date, and the mileage ($30 for every 100 miles traveled).
	2. After entering the reservation information, the user clicks the Submit button.
	3. The information entered is validated.
	4. The application displays the final cost of the camper rental that has been selected.
Notes and Restrictions:	1. Data validation controls should be used. The name is validated to confirm that it is not left blank.
	2. The calendar object must have a date selected that is later than the current date.
	3. The number of nights must be 3 to 10 nights.
	4. A user may reserve only one camper.

FIGURE 9-79 (continues)

Go Camping (continued)

Comments:	1. Display a picture of a camper on the Web form. An image URL can be located on a search engine such as Bing or Google.
	2. Place the image and title on the Site.master page. Delete the navigational links to make a single page.

FIGURE 9-79 (continued)

© 2014 Cengage Learning

USE CASE DEFINITION

1. The Web page opens, displaying a picture of a camper, one TextBox object to request a name, two RadioButton objects to select a camper, a DropDownList object displaying the length of the rental (3-10 nights), a Calendar object to select the start date, a TextBox object to request mileage, and a Submit button.
2. The user enters the information, makes the appropriate selections, and taps or clicks the Submit button.
3. Validation controls check the data.
4. The application displays the final cost of the camper rental.

FIGURE 9-80

© 2014 Cengage Learning

Case Programming Assignments

Go Camping *(continued)*

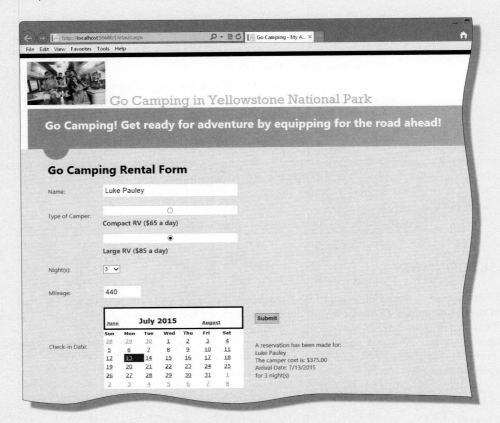

FIGURE 9-81

Hola Images/Getty Images

2

ONLINE CLASS REGISTRATION

Design a Web application and write the code that will execute according to the program requirements shown in Figure 9-82 and the Use Case Definition document shown in Figure 9-83 on the next page. Before writing the code, create an event planning document for each event in the program. The completed Web page is shown in Figure 9-84 on the next page.

REQUIREMENTS DOCUMENT

Date Submitted:	July 31, 2015
Application Title:	Online Class Registration Web Application
Purpose:	This Web application allows a new student to register for an online class at a local college.
Program Procedures:	From a Web application, the user should enter their first name and last name to create an email address in the format: asuka.satou@ravencollege.edu, with the first and last name in lowercase letters.
Algorithms, Processing, and Conditions:	1. The user must be able to enter their first name and their last name. 2. The user must select an online course from a DropDownList object with the following choices: Accounting 212, Information Technology 101, English 112, and History 111. 3. The user clicks the Submit button. 4. The information entered is validated. 5. The application displays the department and the new email address in the format first name, dot, last name (all lowercase) @ sign, ravencollege.edu.
Notes and Restrictions:	Data validation tools should be used. The first and last names are validated to confirm that they are not left blank.
Comments:	1. The email address will be displayed in lowercase letters. 2. Place the title and image on the Site.master page. Display a picture of an online student on the Web form. An image URL can be located on a search engine such as Bing or Google. Delete the navigational links.

FIGURE 9-82

Case Programming Assignments

Online Class Registration (continued)

USE CASE DEFINITION

1. The Web page opens, displaying the title, two TextBox objects to enter the user's name, a DropDownList object for selecting the online course, and a Submit button.
2. User enters their first name and last name.
3. User selects the online course.
4. User taps or clicks the Submit button.
5. Validation controls check that the data was entered.
6. The application displays the online course and the email address.

FIGURE 9-83

© 2014 Cengage Learning

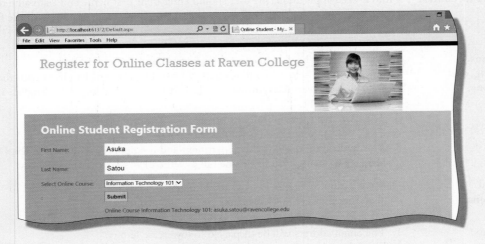

FIGURE 9-84

Goldmund Lukic/Vetta/Getty Images

3

SET YOUR GOLF TEE TIME

Design a Web application and write the code that will execute according to the program requirements shown in Figure 9-85 and the Use Case Definition document in Figure 9-86 on the next page. Before writing the code, create an event planning document for each event in the program. The completed Web page is shown in Figure 9-87 on the next page.

REQUIREMENTS DOCUMENT

Date Submitted:	January 4, 2015
Application Title:	Set Your Golf Tee Time Web Application
Purpose:	This Web application allows the user to sign up online for a golf tee time and date.
Program Procedures:	From a Web application, the user should select a tee time and date.
Algorithms, Processing, and Conditions:	1. The Web site has two pages. The Home page provides information about the golf course. The second page allows users to sign up for a tee time. 2. The Web form should include the name of the golfer requesting the tee time, the possible times, and a calendar to select a date. 3. After the selection is entered, the user clicks the Submit button. 4. The information entered is validated.
Notes and Restrictions:	1. Data validation controls should be used. 2. No optional service is required. 3. A drop-down list control displays tee times on the half hour and hour from 8 am to 2 pm. 4. The golf date must be later than the current date.
Comments:	Display a golf picture representing the golf course on the Web form.

FIGURE 9-85

(continues)

Case Programming Assignments

Set Your Golf Tee Time (continued)

USE CASE DEFINITION

1. The Web page opens, displaying an opening information page about the golf course, a picture representing the golf course, a TextBox object requesting the golfer's name, a DropDownList object requesting the tee time, a Calendar object to select the date, and a Submit button.
2. User clicks the Submit button.
3. Validation controls check the data.
4. The application displays the name, tee time, and date for the golf outing.

FIGURE 9-86

© 2014 Cengage Learning

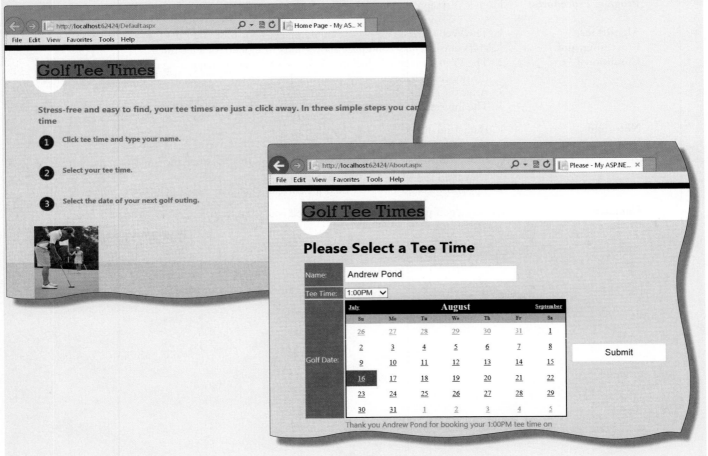

FIGURE 9-87

Noel Hendrickson/Digital Vision/Getty Images

4 •• HELP DESK

Design a Web application and write the code that will execute according to the program requirements shown in Figure 9-88. Before writing the code, create an event planning document for each event in the program. Create a Use Case Definition document for the application.

REQUIREMENTS DOCUMENT

Date Submitted:	February 22, 2015
Application Title:	Help Desk Web Application
Purpose:	This Web application allows college staff to fill in a Web form requesting help from a computer help desk.
Program Procedures:	From a Web application, the user should enter their name, email address, lab number (1–15), computer station number (1–30), the operating system (DropDownList object with two options), and a large TextBox object to describe the problem in order to create a work ticket for the help desk.
Algorithms, Processing, and Conditions:	1. The user must be able to enter information about the requested computer repair on a Web form. The user will enter their first and last name, email address, phone number, lab number (1–15), computer station number (1–30), the operating system (DropDownList object with the choices of (Windows 8 or Windows 7), and a large TextBox object to describe the problem in order to create a work ticket for the help desk. 2. After the information is entered, the user can click the Submit button. 3. The information entered is validated. 4. The application displays a help desk work ticket below the Submit button.
Notes and Restrictions:	1. Data validation tools should be used. The first and last names are validated to confirm that they are not left blank. 2. The email address is checked to verify that it conforms to the proper email format. 3. The phone number is checked to verify that it conforms to a U.S. phone number. 4. The lab number and computer number are to be validated to confirm they are within the proper ranges.
Comments:	Display a picture representing your school logo on the Web form.

FIGURE 9-88

5 ●●
LIL CUCCI'S PIZZERIA

Design a Web application that calculates the cost of pizza according to the prices listed in Figure 9-89. The Home page opens with a picture and information about the great homemade pizza pies. The Order page provides an order form and displays the final price. Write the code that will execute according to the program requirements shown in Figure 9-90 on the next page. Before writing the code, create an event planning document for each event in the program. Create a Use Case Definition document for the application.

Pizza Size	Cost
Small	$7.99
Medium	$9.99
Large	$12.99
Extra Large	$15.99
Each Extra Topping (Cheese Included)	$0.99

FIGURE 9-89

© 2014 Cengage Learning

Lil Cucci's Pizzeria (continued)

REQUIREMENTS DOCUMENT

Date Submitted:	July 24, 2015
Application Title:	Lil Cucci's Pizzeria Web Application
Purpose:	This Web application allows a customer to fill out a pizza order form.
Program Procedures:	From a Web application, the user should enter their name, address, and phone number. They also should select the size pizza they would like to order and the toppings. The final cost of the order will be displayed.
Algorithms, Processing, and Conditions:	1. The Web site has two pages. The Home page promotes the pizzeria. The Order page displays an order form. 2. The user must be able to enter information to order a pizza using a Web form. The user will enter their first and last name, address, phone number, the size of the pizza from a DropDownList object and CheckBoxes displaying pizza topping choices (at least six kinds of toppings). 3. After the information is entered, the user clicks the Submit button. 4. The information entered will be validated. 5. The application displays the final cost of the pizza order and a message that the pizza will be delivered in 45 minutes.
Notes and Restrictions:	1. Data validation tools should be used. The first and last names are validated to confirm that they are not left blank. 2. The phone number is checked to ensure that it conforms to a U.S. phone number.
Comments:	A picture of a pizza will be displayed on the Web form.

FIGURE 9-90

6 ●●
THE VILLAGE BIKE SHOP

Design a Web application and write the code that will execute according to the program requirements shown in Figure 9-91. Before writing the code, create an event planning document for each event in the program. Create a Use Case Definition document for the application.

REQUIREMENTS DOCUMENT

Date Submitted: January 4, 2015

Application Title: The Village Bike Shop Web Application

Purpose: This Web application allows the user to reserve rental bikes online.

Program Procedures: From a Web application, the user should enter their name, address, and phone number. They also should select the number of hours to rent a bike, the type of bike, and the number of bikes to rent. The final cost of the rental will be displayed.

Algorithms, Processing, and Conditions:
1. The user must be able to view a graphic of a bicycle, a DropDownList object with the number of hours (1–8), a calendar requesting the date the bike is being reserved, the type of bike (beach cruiser, road, or mountain), and a TextBox object indicating the quantity (check to make sure the number is between 1 and 12).
2. After the information is entered, the user taps or clicks the Submit button.
3. The information entered will be validated.
4. The application will display a summary of their reservation. Beach cruisers are $5 per hour, road bikes are $6 per hour, and mountain bikes are $7.50 per hour per bike. The total cost will be displayed for the total reservation with the date.

Notes and Restrictions:
1. Data validation tools should be used. The range of the quantity ordered is to be 1–12.
2. The name, address, and phone number must be present.
3. The phone number must conform to a U.S. phone number.

Comments: A picture of a bicycle will be shown on the Web form.

FIGURE 9-91

7 ●●● RE-CREATE AN ONLINE FORM

Create a requirements document and a Use Case Definition document, and then design a Web application, based on the case project shown in Figure 9-92.

Find an online form on the Internet you would like to re-create that has varied objects such as a label, radio button, check box, text box, and drop down list objects. Use a similar layout of the existing web site and at least eight objects on the form to display your own version of the web site for practice. Validate the form using validation objects as needed.

FIGURE 9-92

© 2014 Cengage Learning

8 ●●● MOORE'S LAW

Create a requirements document and a Use Case Definition document, and then create a Web application, based on the case project shown in Figure 9-93.

Create a Web application that displays Moore's Law, which states that the computing power or the number of transistors within the same silicon processor doubles every 18 months. In other words, computing speed doubles every 18 months. As shown in the following table, allow the user to enter the current average speed in GHz and display the next 15 years of projected speed. Use the validation controls to make sure the entry is filled in and that the decimal entered is between 1.0 and 10.0.

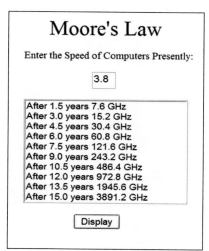

FIGURE 9-93

© 2014 Cengage Learning

9 •••
JAVA SHOP

Create a requirements document and a Use Case Definition document, and then create a Web application, based on the case project shown in Figure 9-94.

To speed up the ordering process, a local coffee shop will allow customers to order their coffee on a touch screen while standing in line. The Web application will display the cost of the coffee. Allow the customer to enter their first name, display a DropDownList object with five coffee flavors, and allow the user to select the size of the coffee: Tall, Grande, and Vente. Prices for these sizes are shown in the table below. Use validation controls. The coffee shop also provides options such as a double shot, flavored syrups, whipped cream, and soy milk for 49 cents each. Display the person's name and order with the purchase price with a 6.5% sales tax.

Size	Price
Tall	$2.59
Grande	$3.09
Vente	$3.59

FIGURE 9-94

CHAPTER 10

Incorporating Databases with ADO.NET

OBJECTIVES

You will have mastered the material in this chapter when you can:

- Understand database files

- Connect to a database using ADO.NET 4.5

- Use multiple database types

- Connect Form objects to the data source

- Bind database fields to the Windows Form object

- Access database information on a Windows Form object

- Add a record

- Delete a record

- Select records from a list

- Program beyond the Database Wizard

- Create the OleDbDataAdapter object

Introduction

As you have learned, information used in Visual Basic 2012 can originate from any source, including data entered into objects such as a TextBox, data assigned within the code, or data read from a text file. Large applications often need to connect to the data required in business today. Businesses store huge volumes of data in databases, and information technology must manage this data and perform database operations such as change, add, and delete. It also must retrieve the database information for viewing and decision making. Increasingly, developers use Visual Basic 2012 to connect to databases and allow users to perform these operations and more. Within the Visual Studio environment, applications can connect to a variety of database sources through the data access technology of ADO.NET.

Chapter Project

In the sample chapter project, the Urban Gardens Association requires a Windows application to access their Garden database, which documents the local urban gardeners, the names of their gardens, and their spring planting costs.

The information in the Garden database is stored as a Microsoft Access database. By placing the information in a simple-to-use Windows application, the staff of the Urban Gardens Association can easily view, update, and delete local urban garden information. By accessing the Urban Gardens Windows application, the entire staff can determine the local urban gardeners, their urban garden locations, and spring planting costs.

The Urban Gardens Windows application loads the present urban gardens from a Microsoft Access 2013 database named Garden.accdb, which is stored on a USB drive. When the Windows form opens, it displays the first record, which indicates the first urban garden, as shown in Figure 10-1.

HEADS UP

The new LINQ database commands are featured in Appendix E. LINQ (Language Integrated Query, pronounced "link") is one of the new features provided with Visual Basic 2012 and .NET Framework 4.5. LINQ makes it easy to query data using SQL (Structured Query Language) commands within the Visual Basic code window.

Move next   Move last
button   button

FIGURE 10-1

© i love images/Getty Images

The user can use the navigation toolbar at the top of the Windows form to continue through the rest of the urban garden information. The Windows form displays each of the 16 records that currently are saved in the Gardener table, which was created using Microsoft Access 2013, as shown in Figure 10-2.

FIGURE 10-2

The Garden.accdb database also can be updated to include new urban gardeners. The user can tap or click the Add new button on the navigation toolbar at the top of the Windows form to open a blank record. Figure 10-3 shows a new record entered into the Windows form to represent a new gardener in the local area named Eric Matthews. After entering the record, the user can add the record to the database by tapping or clicking the Save Data button on the navigation toolbar. The original Access database is permanently updated.

FIGURE 10-3

© i love images/Getty Images

A user also can change the Garden.accdb Access database by deleting records using the Windows form interface. The user can delete a record by tapping or clicking the Delete button on the navigation toolbar. Tapping or clicking the Delete button removes the record currently displayed in the Windows form. For example, if Tracy Tirrell moves from the area, the record of Tracy's garden needs to be removed from the Access database. The user tap or clicks the buttons on the navigation toolbar to access Tracy's garden record, and then taps or clicks the Delete button shown in Figure 10-4 to permanently remove any record of Tracy's garden.

FIGURE 10-4

© i love images/Getty Images

TextBox objects are not the only objects that can be used to display database data. In Figure 10-5, a ComboBox object is used to display the gardener's name, which is stored in the Gardener Name field. When a field such as Gardener Name is displayed in a ComboBox object, the user can tap or click the ComboBox arrow to display a list of the values in the field. The user then can tap or click a name in the Gardener Name field list to navigate directly to the individual record for the selected name. For example, the user can view the garden of Ramona Coveny by selecting Ramona Coveny from the ComboBox object for the Gardener Name field as shown in Figure 10-5.

FIGURE 10-5

© i love images/Getty Images

The Urban Gardens Association intends to keep close tabs on the spring planting costs because most of the funding comes from an urban renewal state grant. A Total Planting Cost button allows the user to compute the total cost of spring planting for the records within the database. Figure 10-6 shows the Urban Gardens form after the Total Planting Cost button has been tapped or clicked. A total of $8,608.95 currently is allocated in the Garden database.

FIGURE 10-6

© i love images/Getty Images

Database Files

A **database** is a collection of related information stored in a structured format. Common examples of business databases include a customer list, product information, mailing list, or reservation system. A database organizes data in **tables**. A table is a collection of data about a specific topic, such as a listing of local urban gardens for the Urban Gardens Association. Using a separate table for each topic means that you store that data only once, which makes a database efficient and reduces data-entry errors.

The chapter project creates a user interface that accesses the data from the Urban Gardens Association's database, which is named Garden.accdb. The Garden database contains a table shown in Figure 10-2 on page 695 that contains the local urban gardens. A table structures data into rows and columns. Each row is referred to as a **record**. A record in a table contains information about a person, product, or other entity.

Each record in the Gardener table in the Garden database contains information about a local urban garden. In Figure 10-7, the selected record shows all the information about Irene Wheeler's urban garden.

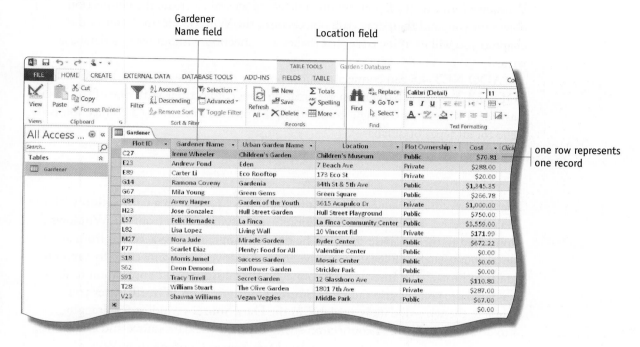

FIGURE 10-7

Each record begins with the Plot ID, which is a unique number that identifies each city garden plot and can be used only once. The Plot ID is contained in the Plot ID field. Each column in a table is referred to as a **field**. A field contains a specific piece of data within a record. For example, in the Gardener table, the column listing the location of each urban garden is the Location field. Each column in the table is a field and displays data such as the names of the gardeners, locations, whether the land is owned by the city or privately owned, and the spring planting cost.

Each table in a relational database must contain a unique value. Therefore, no two gardeners in the Garden database are assigned the same Plot ID. A unique field is an identifier that represents the **primary key** for the table. The Plot ID is the primary key for the Gardener table in the Garden database. A primary key is used in relational databases to avoid problems such as duplicate records and conflicting values in fields.

Connect to a Database Using ADO.NET

To support databases using Visual Basic 2012, a library called ActiveX Data Objects works within all Windows, Office, and Web applications. The current version, ADO.NET 4.5, allows the developer to create, administer, and manipulate almost any type of database. ADO.NET 4.5 can open a connection to a database and can disconnect from that database.

Visual Studio provides tools to connect an application to data from many sources, such as databases, Web services, and objects. If you are using ADO.NET 4.5 in Visual Basic 2012, you often do not need to create a coded connection for the Windows form. Instead, you can use a database wizard to create the connection object for you, and then drag data objects onto the Windows form. Later in the chapter, you will examine code that makes a connection without using a database wizard.

ADO.NET 4.5 can connect to most popular database systems such as Oracle, SQL, and Access. Whether you are creating data connections with one of the Visual Basic data wizards or coding a connection, the process of defining a connection is the same for all types of databases.

Establish a Database Connection

The first step in accessing database information is to establish a **connection** with the database source. You create a connection by specifying a path from the Windows application to the database source. The database source can be accessed from any digital source such as a local hard drive, network drive, or a connection to a remote database through the Internet. To connect a Visual Basic 2012 application to data in a database, you can use the **Data Source Configuration Wizard**. After you complete the wizard, data is available in the **Data Sources** window for dragging onto a Windows form. A connection string contacts the data source and establishes a connection with the database using the Data Source Configuration Wizard. The wizard uses the Fill method to fill a DataSet object with table rows and columns from a selected table within a database. A **DataSet** object is a temporary cache storage for data retrieved from a data source. The DataSet object is a major component of the ADO.NET 4.5 architecture.

For the Urban Gardens chapter project, a Windows application must connect to the Access database table named Gardener in the Garden.accdb database. To connect to the database using the Data Source Configuration Wizard, you can complete the following steps:

STEP 1 Create a Windows application named Urban Gardens. Name the form `frmGarden`. Change the Text property to `Urban Gardening`. Resize the form to a size of `780, 530`. Change the BackColor property to White on the Web tab. An image representing one of the local gardeners named Garden.jpg is available with your Data Files. Place a PictureBox object on the left side of the window. Name the PictureBox object `picGarden`. Change the Size property to `255,160`. Make the location `24,30`. Using the Image property, import the Garden.jpg image for the PictureBox object. Change the SizeMode to StretchImage. On the right side of the form, place a Label object named lblTitle. Change the Text property to `Urban Gardens`. Make the Font property Script MT, Bold, size 40, and the ForeColor property Green on the Web tab. Change the Location property of the lblTitle Label object to `300,65`. Close the Toolbox, and then tap or click PROJECT on the menu bar.

The Windows form is created and the Data menu is opened (Figure 10-8).

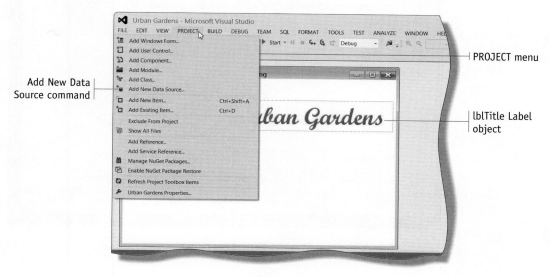

FIGURE 10-8

STEP 2   Tap or click Add New Data Source on the PROJECT menu.

The Data Source Configuration Wizard window opens requesting the Data Source Type (Figure 10-9).

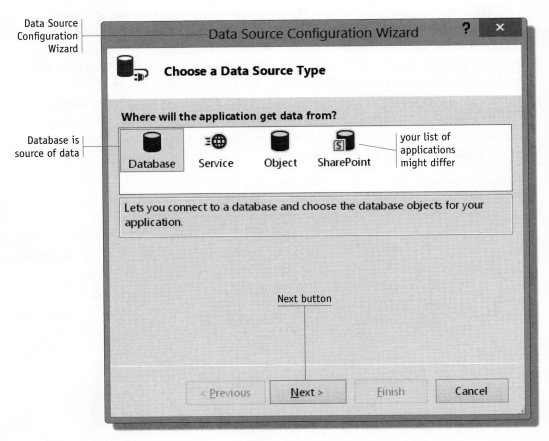

FIGURE 10-9

STEP 3   In the Choose a Data Source Type dialog box, tap or click Database, and then tap or click Next. In the Choose a Database Model dialog box, tap or click Dataset, and then tap or click Next.

After selecting the Dataset option and tapping or clicking the Next button, the Choose Your Data Connection dialog box opens (Figure 10–10).

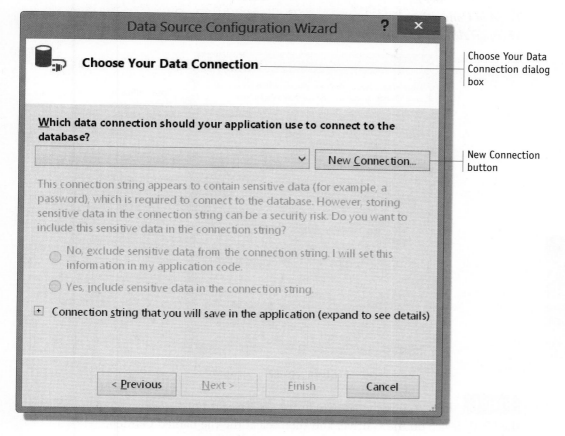

FIGURE 10-10

STEP 4 Tap or click the New Connection button. In the Add Connection dialog box, tap or click the Change button to select the data source.

After the New Connection button is tapped or clicked, the Add Connection dialog box opens. After tapping or clicking the Change button, the Choose Data Source dialog box opens (Figure 10–11).

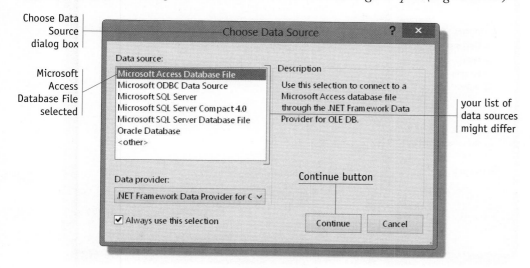

FIGURE 10-11

STEP 5 In the Choose Data Source dialog box, select Microsoft Access Database File because the Garden database is an Access database. Tap or click the OK button.

The Add Connection dialog box reopens (Figure 10-12). The Data source appears as Microsoft Access Database File.

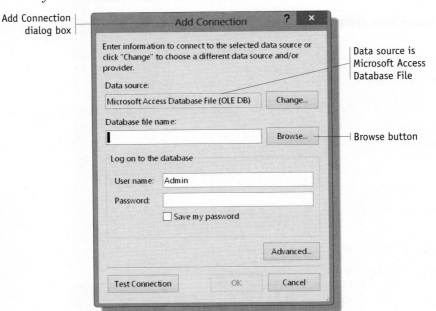

Add Connection dialog box

Data source is Microsoft Access Database File

Browse button

FIGURE 10-12

STEP 6 Tap or click the Browse button to the right of Database file name. Select the USB device on the E drive, and then select the file named Garden.

The Access database file Garden on the USB E drive is selected (Figure 10–13). The files and folders on your USB drive might be different from those shown here.

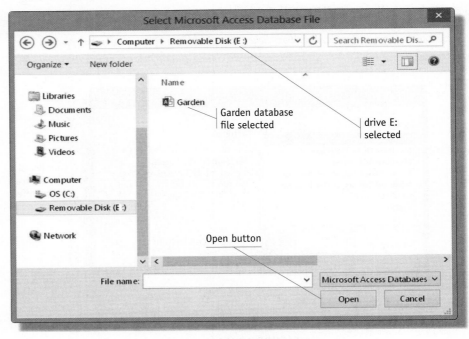

Garden database file selected

drive E: selected

Open button

FIGURE 10-13

STEP 7 Tap or click the Open button.

The Add Connection dialog box reopens (Figure 10–14).

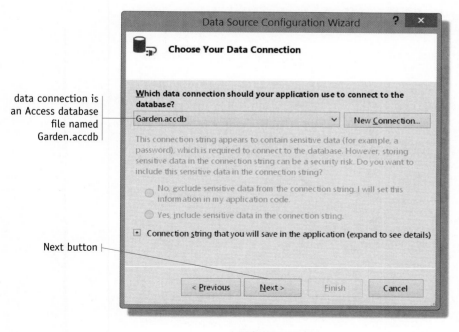

FIGURE 10-14

STEP 8 Tap or click the OK button in the Add Connection dialog box.

The Choose Your Data Connection dialog box opens to confirm the database file you are using (Figure 10–15).

FIGURE 10-15

STEP 9   Tap or click the Next button.

A reminder dialog box opens stating that the connection uses a local data file that is not in the current project (Figure 10–16). The dialog box also asks if you want to copy the file to your project. You do not want to add data and update the copied database. It is best to update the original database file.

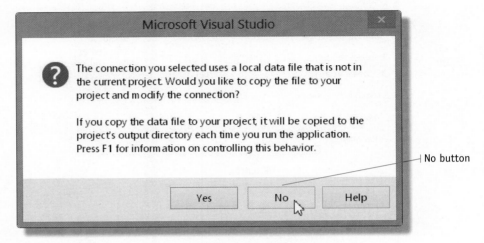

FIGURE 10-16

STEP 10 Tap or click the No button, and then tap or click the Next button. When the Choose Your Database Objects dialog box opens, select which database objects you want in the DataSet. Tap or click the expand icon next to the Tables option. Tap or click the Gardener check box to select that table. A connection is made from the Visual Basic application to the Gardener table within the Garden.accdb database.

After the expand icon is tapped or clicked to display the tables available, the Gardener check box is checked (Figure 10-17).

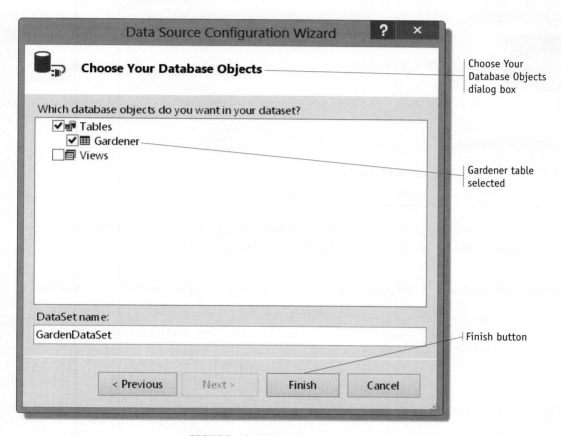

FIGURE 10-17

STEP 11   Tap or click the Finish button. Tap or click GardenDataSet.xsd to select the DataSet.

The dialog box closes, and a connection to the Gardener table is made. The Solution Explorer displays the DataSet named GardenDataSet.xsd (Figure 10-18).

GardenDataSet added to program

FIGURE 10-18

© i love images/Getty Images

After a connection is established, you can design programs using the open connection and retrieve and manipulate the data accessed with the database file.

If I move my Access database file to a different path, how do I change that path within the Visual Basic application?
In the Solution Explorer, tap or click the App.Config file to view the code for the database file path. In the line that begins with connectionString, you can view the path of the database file. You can change the path if you have moved the database to a different location, for example from drive E: to drive C:.

IN THE REAL WORLD

You also can configure a connection string to store a user name and password for a secure database. Many business databases are password protected.

ONLINE REINFORCEMENT

To view a video of the process in the previous steps, visit CengageBrain.com and navigate to the resources for this title. Tap or click the link for Chapter 10 and then navigate to Video 10-2.

Connect Form Objects to the Data Source

After a connection is created to an existing data source, the DataSet can provide the application with the ability to interact with the database. The DataSet temporarily stores the data in the application while you work with it. After you have configured a DataSet with the Data Source Configuration Wizard, the next step is to load the DataSet with the data stored in the database. After the DataSet is filled with the table information, the data can be displayed on the Windows form. Loading the DataSet string is called **data binding**. Data binding allows you to display each field as an object on the form. You can complete data binding by dragging the fields on the form or by coding. To view the data available in the source database, you can complete the following steps:

STEP 1   In the Garden project window, point to the Data Sources tab on the left side of the window. If the Data Sources tab is not visible, tap or click VIEW on the menu bar, tap or click Other Windows, and then tap or click Data Sources.

The Data Sources tab is selected (Figure 10-19).

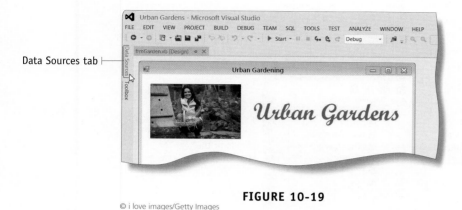

Data Sources tab

FIGURE 10-19

© i love images/Getty Images

STEP 2   Tap or click Data Sources to view the database sources.

A DataSet named GardenDataSet is displayed showing a connection to the Gardner table (Figure 10–20).

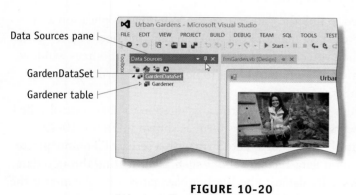

Data Sources pane

GardenDataSet

Gardener table

FIGURE 10-20

© i love images/Getty Images

STEP 3   Tap or click the expand icon for the Gardener table to expand the list of field names within the table. Each bindable field item in the Data Sources window can be placed on the Windows Form object.

The fields of the Gardener table are displayed (Figure 10–21). Each field is displayed by default with an icon that designates each database item as a TextBox object.

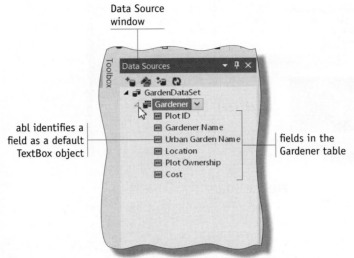

abl identifies a field as a default TextBox object

Data Source window

fields in the Gardener table

FIGURE 10-21

Bind Database Fields to the Windows Form

After a connection is created to link the database to the Windows application and the data source displays the existing field objects, you can drag the field objects to the Windows Form object. When you drag field objects from the Data Sources window, Visual Studio automatically creates a **databinding** to populate the form by binding the form object to the DataSet information.

After the first field item is placed on the form, a navigation toolbar control called the **BindingNavigator** appears on the Windows form as shown in Figure 10-22. The BindingNavigator control consists of a ToolStrip with a series of ToolStripItem objects for most of the common data-related actions such as navigating through data, adding data, and deleting data. By default, the BindingNavigator control contains the standard buttons shown in Figure 10-22.

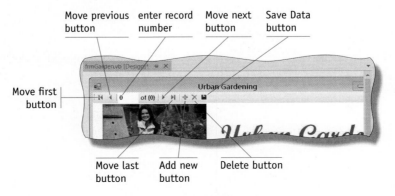

Move previous button   enter record number   Move next button   Save Data button

Move first button

Move last button   Add new button   Delete button

FIGURE 10-22

© i love images/Getty Images

The first four arrow navigation buttons on the BindingNavigator control allow the user to move throughout the data in the associated table and to interact with the records. A user also can type the record number directly in the text box to navigate quickly to the associated record. The Add new button inserts a new row to add a new record to the original database table. The Delete button permanently deletes the current record displayed in the Windows form from the database table. The Save Data button saves any changes made on the current form such as changing the spelling of a field item or updating the cost. If a record is added or deleted, the Save Data button must be tap or clicked to save the change to the original database table.

The BindingNavigator appears when the first table field is bound to the Windows form. To bind each database field to the Windows form object, follow these steps:

STEP 1   Select the Plot ID field in the Data Sources window. Drag the Plot ID field to the Windows Form object below the PictureBox object.

The Plot ID field is placed on the Windows form (Figure 10-23). The Plot ID TextBox object is now bound to the data in the table. A navigation toolbar called a BindingNavigator control automatically is added to the top of the Windows Form object. A GardenDataSet, GardenBindingSource, GardenTableAdapter, TableAdapterManager, and GardenBindingNavigator appear in the component tray and bind the database data to the Windows Form object.

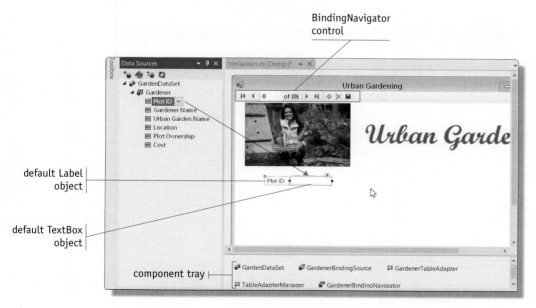

FIGURE 10-23

STEP 2 Drag the rest of the field objects from the Data Sources window to the Windows form. Select all the field labels and field TextBox objects and change the font size to 10 points. Use the formatting tools on the FORMAT menu to equally distribute the bound objects. You can select the Label and the TextBox objects separately to move them independently of each other. Use the layout shown in Figure 10-24.

All of the field objects are placed on the Windows form and formatted to align with one another (Figure 10-24).

formatted field
objects

FIGURE 10-24

STEP 3   Run the application by tapping or clicking the Start Debugging button on the Standard toolbar to fill the Windows Form object with the data from the Gardener table. Use the Move next button on the navigation toolbar to move through the records. Tap or click the Move last button to display the last record.

The Windows form opens with the data in the first record filling the TextBox objects. The Move next button on the navigation toolbar is tapped or clicked to view records. The last record is displayed (Figure 10-25).

last record
displayed

FIGURE 10-25

© i love images/Getty Images

Add Records

By running the application, the user can view every record within the database. For the Urban Gardens application, the Windows form can allow the user to update the database by adding new gardeners. To add a new record to the database table, you can follow these steps:

STEP 1   If necessary, tap or click the Start Debugging button on the Standard toolbar to run the Urban Gardens application.

The Windows form opens, displaying the first record (Figure 10-26).

FIGURE 10-26

© i love images/Getty Images

STEP 2   Tap or click the Add new button to add a new record to the database table.

A blank record opens displaying 17 as the record number in the navigation toolbar (Figure 10–27).

17ᵗʰ record displayed   Add new button

FIGURE 10-27

© i love images/Getty Images

STEP 3 Add a new record by typing the Plot ID W77. Type the rest of the information as displayed in Figure 10-28. After the record is complete, tap or click the Save Data button on the BindingNavigator control to save the new record to the original database.

After the new record is typed into the Windows form, the Save Data button is tapped or clicked to add it to the original database table (Figure 10–28).

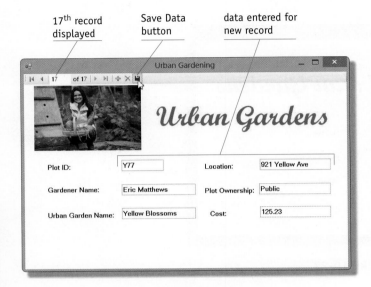

17th record displayed   Save Data button   data entered for new record

© i love images/Getty Images

FIGURE 10-28

Delete Records

In the Urban Gardens application, users might need to remove information for a gardener if they are no longer part of the Urban Gardeners Association. To delete an existing record in the database table, follow these steps:

STEP 1 If necessary, tap or click the Start Debugging button on the Standard toolbar to execute the Urban Gardens application.

The Windows form opens displaying the first record (Figure 10-29).

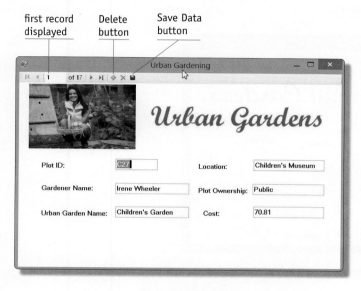

first record displayed   Delete button   Save Data button

FIGURE 10-29

STEP 2   Use the navigation buttons to move to Tracy Tirrell's record. Her garden record should be deleted because she is moving from the area. Tap or click the Delete button on the BindingNavigator control to delete her record from the database table. Tap or click the Save Data button to remove the record from the original database.

After the Delete button is tapped or clicked, Tracy Tirrell's record is deleted from the Windows form and William Stuart's record is displayed (Figure 10-30). Notice that the database now has 16 records instead 17 records.

16 records in the database

one record has been deleted

© i love images/Getty Images

FIGURE 10-30

Select Records from a List

By default, the Data Sources window displays each table item as a TextBox object, but Visual Basic 2012 allows you to change the default TextBox object to another Toolbox object of your choice. In Figure 10-31, when Plot ID is selected in the Data Sources window, a list arrow appears to the right of the field. When the list arrow is tapped or clicked, a listing of common Toolbox objects is displayed. The Customize option lets you select other Toolbox objects not already listed. For example, you can select Customize to add a MaskedTextBox instead of the default TextBox option if you are including a phone number or zip code.

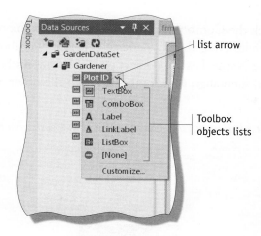

FIGURE 10-31

In Figure 10-30, the only way to navigate through the records is to use the BindingNavigator control or enter a record number, but a quicker way to move directly to a particular record is to select that record from a ComboBox object. For example, in Figure 10-5 on page 697, the gardener's name is displayed in a ComboBox object. The user taps or clicks the list arrow to view the items in the Gardener Name list, and then taps or clicks a last name. The record matching the selected gardener's name is displayed immediately. To change the Toolbox object type, you can complete the following steps:

STEP 1 Select the Gardener Name Label and TextBox objects on the Windows form. Press the DELETE key to delete the Gardener Name objects from the Windows form. Select the Gardener Name table field in the Data Sources window and then tap or click its list arrow.

The Gardener Name objects are deleted from the Windows Form object (Figure 10-32). The Last Name field in the Data Sources window displays a list of possible Toolbox object selections.

FIGURE 10-32

STEP 2   Tap or click the ComboBox object from the Toolbox object listing for the Gardener Name field. Drag the Gardener Name field ComboBox object to the original location of the Name TextBox object on the Windows Form object. Change the font size to 10 and then align the ComboBox with the other objects on the Windows Form.

The Gardener Name ComboBox object is placed on the Windows Form object (Figure 10-33).

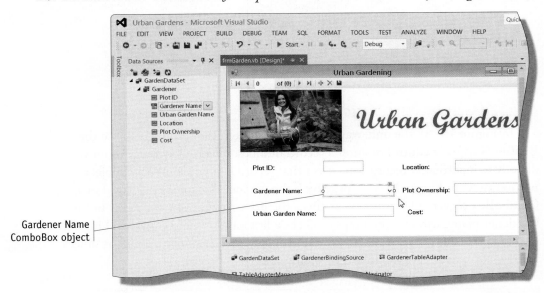

Gardener Name
ComboBox object

FIGURE 10-33

© i love images/Getty Images

STEP 3   To fill the ComboBox object with the names of the gardeners, the ComboBox object must be bound to the Gardener Name field. To bind the items to the ComboBox object, select the Gardener Name object on the Windows form and tap or click the Action tag on the Gardener Name ComboBox object.

The ComboBox Tasks menu appears (Figure 10-34).

Action tag

Use Data Bound
Items check box

ComboBox
Tasks menu

FIGURE 10-34

© i love images/Getty Images

STEP 4   Tap or click the Use Data Bound Items check box on the ComboBox Tasks menu. The Data Binding Mode list is displayed. Tap or click the Data Source list arrow under Data Binding Mode, and then select GardenerBindingSource to connect the table to the ComboBox object. Next, tap or click the Display Member list arrow and then select Gardener Name. Tap or click the Value Member list arrow and then tap or click Gardener Name in the list. Do not change the Selected Value entry.

The ComboBox object is now bound to the Gardener Name field in the Gardener table (Figure 10-35).

FIGURE 10-35

© i love images/Getty Images

STEP 5 Tap or click the Start Debugging button on the Standard toolbar to run the application. After the Windows form opens, tap or click the list arrow on the Gardener Name ComboBox object.

The Gardener Name ComboBox object displays the gardeners' names (Figure 10-36).

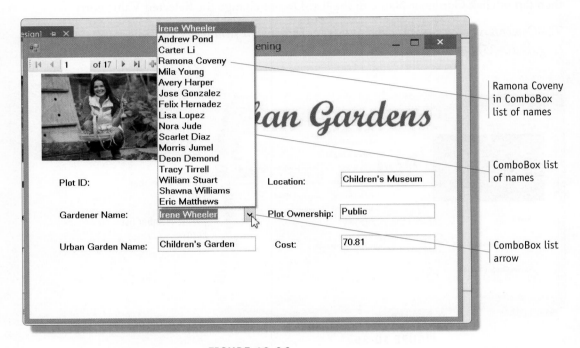

FIGURE 10-36

STEP 6   Tap or click Ramona Coveny to move directly to the record containing the information for Ramona Coveny's urban garden.

The application navigates directly to the selected record (Figure 10-37).

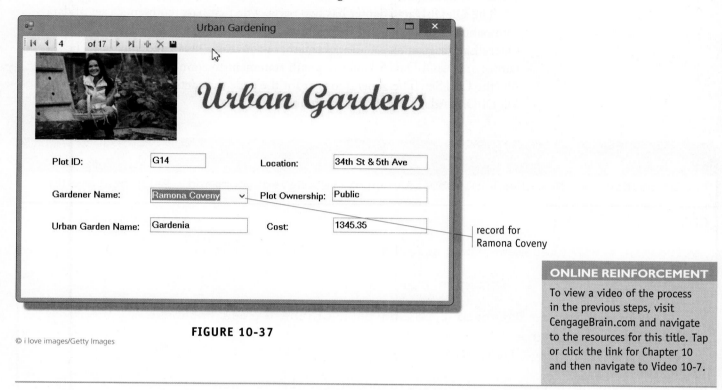

FIGURE 10-37

© i love images/Getty Images

Program Beyond the Database Wizard

Although the Database Wizard allows you to view, update, and delete records from a database, often other operations such as calculating an average or determining how many records meet a certain criteria will need to be programmed. For example, in the chapter project, the Urban Gardens Association would like to use a Button object on the Urban Gardens Windows form to compute the total cost of spring planting. The Urban Gardens Association then can calculate and track their present allocation of spring planting funds for seeds and fertilizer. Code must be written to handle that specific request.

Can I add a Try-Catch statement to confirm that the database is available?
In the Form Load event, you can add this code:

```
Try
        GardenerTableAdapter.Fill(Me.GardenDataSet.Gardener)
Catch
        MsgBox("The database is not on the USB")
End Try
```

CONSIDER THIS

Create the OleDbDataAdapter Object

The Database Wizard creates a bridge between the DataSet and the database that contains the data. The bridge that carries the database table information is called an **OleDbDataAdapter**.

The OleDbDataAdapter has two parts. The first part represents a set of data commands programmed using a SQL Select command. **SQL** stands for Structured Query Language, and is the language that communicates with databases. The second part of an OleDbDataAdapter is a path statement to connect to the database that fills the DataSet. The general format for the code that defines the two parts of the OleDbDataAdapter is shown in Figure 10-38.

General Format: OleDbDataAdapter

```
Dim odaName As New OleDb.OleDbDataAdapter(SQL Select command, Path statement)
```

Code:

```
'strSql is a SQL statement that selects all the fields from the'
Gardener table
Dim strSql As String = "SELECT * FROM Gardener"

'strPath provides the database type and path of the Garden database
Dim strPath As String = "Provider=Microsoft.ACE.OLEDB.12.0 ;" _
& "Data Source=e:\Garden.accdb"

Dim odaGarden As New OleDb.OleDbDataAdapter(strSql, strPath)
```

The SQL statement assigned to strSQL("SELECT * FROM Gardener") is a query statement that requests that the entire table named Gardener is opened for use by the application. The * symbol represents the wildcard symbol, which means all fields with the table are available.

The Path statement assigned to strPath("Provides-Microsoft.ACEOLEDB.12.0 ;"& "Data Source-e:\Garden.accdb") has two portions. The first portion represents the database source. Microsoft.ACE.OLEDB12.0 assigns the drivers needed to create a connection to an Access database. The second portion represents the path of where the database resides.

An instance of the OleDbDataAdapter is assigned to the variable odaGarden. The prefix oda is used for an OleDbAdapter.

FIGURE 10-38

Fill a DataTable Object

After the OleDbDataAdapter makes a connection to the database, a **DataTable** is needed to hold the data that is retrieved from that connection. The DataTable is a crucial object in the ADO.NET 4.5 library. The DataSet used in the Database Wizard is a collection of DataTable objects. The DataTable is initialized using the dat prefix.

After the DataTable is initialized, it must be filled using the **Fill** command with the data from the selected table. When the DataTable is filled, the appropriate tables and columns are created for the table data. As soon as you connect to the database and fill the DataTable object, the next statement should disconnect the application from the database. To keep the maximum number of connections available, you should keep connections open only as long as necessary. By using the database in disconnected form, the system resources of the computer and network are not overloaded. To disconnect from the database, use the **Dispose** command.

The code in Figure 10-39 can be executed in a program without using the Database Wizard or you can run the wizard to access the data. The code opens a connection to the Gardener table in the Garden.accdb Access database on the USB drive. A DataTable named datCost is initialized. The DataTable datCost is then filled with the data from the Gardener table. The Dispose procedure closes the connection for the datCost DataTable.

```
22   Private Sub btnCost_Click(sender As Object, e As EventArgs) Handles btnCost.Click
23       ' strSq1 is a SQL statement that selects all the fields from the
24       ' Gardener table
25
26       Dim strSql As String = "SELECT * FROM Gardener"
27
28       'strPath provides the database type and path of the Garden database
29       Dim strPath As String = "Provider=Microsoft.ACE.OLEDB.12.0 ;" & "Data Source=e:\Garden.accdb"
30       Dim odaGarden As New OleDb.OleDbDataAdapter(strSql, strPath)
31       Dim datCost As New DataTable
32       Dim intCount As Integer
33       Dim decTotalCost As Decimal = 0D
34
35       ' The DataTable name datCost is filled with the table data
36       odaGarden.Fill(datCost)
37       'The connection to the database is disconnected
38       odaGarden.Dispose()
```

FIGURE 10-39

After the DataTable is created, commands can access the data stored in its rows and columns. The number of rows or columns in the DataTable can be computed with the **Count** property. In a DataTable named datCost, the code entered with IntelliSense in Figure 10-40 determines the number of rows in the DataTable object. The Gardener table contains 16 rows numbered 0 to 15.

```
46          Dim intNumberOfRows As Integer
47          intNumberOfRows = datCost.Rows.Count
```

FIGURE 10-40

The number of rows in the code in Figure 10-40 is equal to the number of records in the DataTable object. You can also compute the number of columns in a DataTable by entering the code in Figure 10-41.

```
49          Dim intNumberOfColumns As Integer
50          intNumberOfColumns = datCost.Columns.Count
```

FIGURE 10-41

The DataTable object can also be used to access individual fields within a database by using the Rows procedure. For example, if you wanted to determine the first value in the Cost field for the first record, the field name "Cost" can be used with the DataTable Rows procedure. In Figure 10-42, the variable decFirstValue is assigned to the first record's cost.

```
52          Dim decFirstValue As Decimal
53          decFirstValue = Convert.ToDecimal(datCost.Rows(0)("Cost"))
```

FIGURE 10-42

In Figure 10-42, the first argument for the Rows procedure (0) references the first row (row zero) in the data table, which is the first record in the table. The entry in the second parentheses ("Cost") identifies the field within the first row.

In the original database shown in Figure 10-2 on page 695, if datCost represents the DataTable for the Gardener table, the first field value for the field Cost is assigned to decFirstValue. The value 70.81 is assigned to the variable decFirstValue in Figure 10-42.

Using the Rows method and the field name, you also can compute the sum or average of the entire spring planting cost values for all the records in the table. In the chapter project, when the user taps or clicks a button on the Windows Form object, the event handler for the button tap or click computes the total cost of spring planting for all the urban gardens. To code a connection with a database and compute the sum, you can complete the following steps:

STEP 1   Download the original Access database file Garden.accdb again to overwrite any data you added or deleted from the database. Open the Urban Gardens Windows application. Add a Button object named `btnCost` to the Windows Form object and change the Text property to `Total Planting Cost`. Change the font size to 12 and the ForeColor property to Green. Set the Size property for the button to `238, 35` and center the Button object horizontally across the form. Add a Label object below the Button object named `lblTotalPlantingCost` with the Text property of 23 "X's" and center the text. Change the font size to 12 points. Set the Visible property for the lblTotalPlantingCost Label object to False because the X's should not be displayed when the program begins.

A Button object and Label object are added to the Windows Form object (Figure 10–43).

FIGURE 10-43

STEP 2   Double-tap or double-click the Total Planting Cost button to create the btnCost_Click event handler. To initialize the OleDbDataAdapter, enter the code shown in Figure 10-44 inside the click event. The first variable, strSql, is assigned the SQL statement that queries all the fields in the Gardener table. The second variable, strPath, is assigned the database driver for Access and the path to the Garden.accdb file. The third variable, odaGarden, is an instance of the OleDbDataAdapter.

Inside the btnCost_Click event, the variables are initialized for the OleDbDataAdapter (Figure 10-44).

```
22    Private Sub btnCost_Click(sender As Object, e As EventArgs) Handles btnCost.Click
23        ' strSq1 is a SQL statement that selects all the fields from the
24        ' Gardener table
25
26        Dim strSql As String = "SELECT * FROM Gardener"
27
28        'strPath provides the database type and path of the Garden database
29        Dim strPath As String = "Provider=Microsoft.ACE.OLEDB.12.0 ;" & "Data Source=e:\Garden.accdb"
30        Dim odaGarden As New OleDb.OleDbDataAdapter(strSql, strPath)
```

FIGURE 10-44

STEP 3   After the first three variables are initialized, initialize the rest of the variables needed for the Button object event handler. An instance named datCost is initialized to represent the DataTable object. The intCount variable is used to count through a For loop. The last variable, decTotalCost, will contain the total amount of the spring planting costs.

The rest of the variables are initialized (Figure 10-45).

```
31        Dim datCost As New DataTable
32        Dim intCount As Integer
33        Dim decTotalCost As Decimal = 0D
```

FIGURE 10-45

STEP 4   Continuing inside the btnCost_Click event handler, enter the code shown in Figure 10-46 to fill the DataTable with the contents of the Gardener table. In the next line of code, use the Dispose method to close the connection.

The DataTable is filled and the connection is disconnected (Figure 10–46).

```
35          ' The DataTable name datCost is filled with the table data
36          odaGarden.Fill(datCost)
37          'The connection to the database is disconnected
38          odaGarden.Dispose()
```

FIGURE 10-46

STEP 5   Enter the code shown in Figure 10-47 to create a For loop to increment through each record in the Gardener table. Because the rows are numbered 0 to 15, the upper range is one less than the numbers of rows in the table, making 16 records. The value in each Cost field is added to the value in the decTotalCost variable.

The total spring planting cost is computed in the For loop (Figure 10–47).

```
39          For intCount = 0 To datCost.Rows.Count - 1
40              decTotalCost += Convert.ToDecimal(datCost.Rows(intCount)("Cost"))
41          Next
```

FIGURE 10-47

STEP 6   Enter the code shown in Figure 10-48 to display the total spring planting cost.

The total cost is displayed (Figure 10–48).

```
42          lblTotalPlantingCost.Visible = True
43          lblTotalPlantingCost.Text = "The Total Planting Cost is " & decTotalCost.ToString("C")
44      End Sub
45
46  End Class
```

FIGURE 10-48

HEADS UP

You can use the process described beginning in Figure 10-43 on page 727 with or without using a database wizard.

ONLINE REINFORCEMENT

To view a video of the process in the previous steps, visit CengageBrain.com and navigate to the resources for this title. Tap or click the link for Chapter 10 and then navigate to Video 10-8.

Program Design

The requirements document for the Urban Gardens application is shown in Figure 10-49, and the Use Case Definition document is shown in Figure 10-50.

REQUIREMENTS DOCUMENT

Date Submitted: February 22, 2015

Application Title: Urban Gardens Application

Purpose: This Windows application opens a Windows form showing an Access database with data about local urban gardens. The data can be viewed, updated, and deleted. The application also computes the total cost of spring planting for all urban gardens.

Program Procedures: In a Windows application, the Garden Access database file is opened and the user can view, add, and delete records as needed. The total cost of planting is calculated.

Algorithms, Processing, and Conditions:
1. The user first views a Windows application that loads an existing Access database table that includes fields for the Plot ID, Gardener Name, Urban Garden Name, Location, Plot Ownership (public or private), and the Cost. A navigation toolbar appears at the top of the Windows form, allowing the user to move from record to record. The Windows form also includes a title and gardening image.
2. The user can tap or click the Add new button on the navigation toolbar to add a new gardener. The record is saved when the user taps or clicks the Save Data button on the navigation toolbar.
3. The user can tap or click the Delete button on the navigation toolbar to delete a gardener's record. The record is permanently deleted when the user taps or clicks the Save Data button on the navigation toolbar.
4. The user can tap or click the Total Planting Cost button to compute the total cost of spring planting.

Notes and Restrictions: The Access database named Garden.accdb file is located on the USB drive on the E drive.

Comments:
1. The Garden.accdb file is available on CengageBrain.com.
2. Obtain an image for this program from CengageBrain.com. The name of the picture on the Windows form is Garden.

FIGURE 10-49

USE CASE DEFINITION

1. The user views the Access database information about local urban gardens.
2. The user taps or clicks the Add new button to add gardeners and taps or clicks the Save Data button to permanently save the new gardener to the original database.
3. The user taps or clicks the Delete button to delete an urban gardener and taps or clicks the Save Data button to permanently delete the record from the original database.
4. The user taps or clicks the Total Planting Cost button to display the total cost of spring planting.

FIGURE 10-50

Event Planning Document

The event planning document for the Urban Gardens Windows application is shown in Figure 10-51.

EVENT PLANNING DOCUMENT

Program Name: Urban Gardens Windows Application	Developer: Corinne Hoisington	Object: frmGarden	Date: February 22, 2015
OBJECT	**EVENT TRIGGER**	**EVENT PROCESSING**	
frmGarden	Load	Fill the DataSet object using the Data Source Configuration Wizard	
btnCost	Click	Initialize the OleDbDataAdapter with the type of database and path statement Fill the data table Disconnect the database For each record in the database: Add each record's cost to the total cost Display the total planting cost	

FIGURE 10-51

Guided Program Development

NOTE TO THE LEARNER

In the following activity, you should complete the tasks within the specified steps. Each of the tasks is accompanied by a Hint Screen. The purpose of the Hint Screen is to indicate where you should perform the activity in the Visual Studio window and to remind you which method to use. If you need further help completing a step, refer to the figure identified by *ref:*.

Guided Program Development

Phase 1: Design the Form

1

● **Create a New Windows Project** Open Visual Studio and then close the Start page. Tap or click the New Project button on the Standard toolbar. Begin a Windows Forms Application project and name the project Urban Gardens.

● **Name the Form Object** Select the Windows Form object. In the Solution Explorer, rename Form1.vb to frmGarden.vb.

● **Title the Form Object** Select the Windows Form object and change the Text property to Urban Gardening.

● **Build the Top Portion of the Windows Form Object** Using the skills you have learned in this course, complete the top portion of the Windows Form object. For detailed specifications, see Figure 10-8 on page 701.

The top of the form is completed (Figure 10-52).

RESULT OF STEP 1

FIGURE 10-52

© i love images/Getty Images

• **Create a Connection Using the Data Source Configuration Wizard** In the Urban Gardens project window, tap or click PROJECT on the menu bar, and then tap or click Add New Data Source on the PROJECT menu *(ref: Figure 10-8)*.

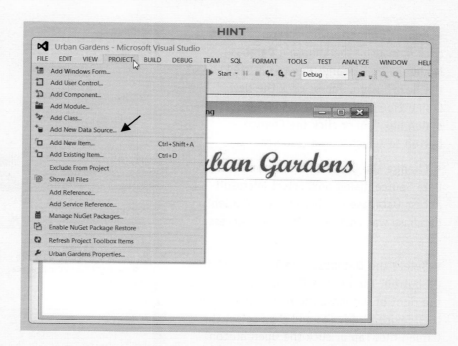

• **Choose the Data Source** If necessary, select Database in the "Where will the application get data from?" group in the Data Source Configuration Wizard dialog box. Tap or click the Next button.

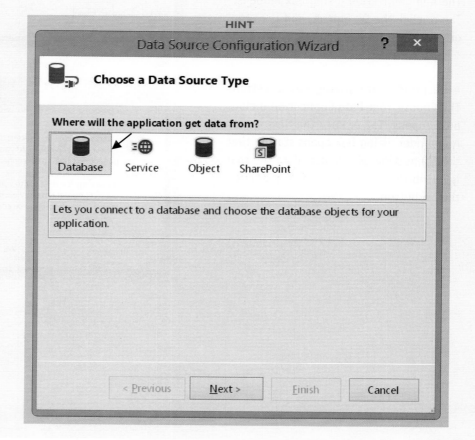

(continues)

Guided Program Development *continued*

● **Add a Connection** If necessary, tap or click Dataset in the Choose a Database Model dialog box and then tap or click the Next button. Tap or click the New Connection button. In the Add Connection dialog box, tap or click the Change button to select the data source.

● **Change the Data Source** In the Change Data Source dialog box, select Microsoft Access Database File because the Garden database was created in Microsoft Access.

● **Select the Database File** Tap or click the OK button. Tap or click the Browse button to the right of Database file name. Select the USB device in drive E: and then select the Garden file. Tap or click the Open button. The Add Connection dialog box reopens. Tap or click the OK button, and then tap or click the Next button.

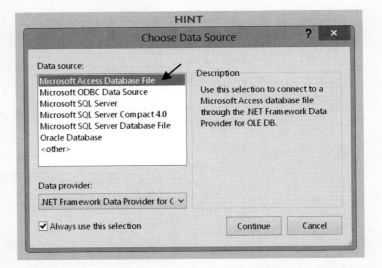

● **Respond to the Dialog Box Question** The Choose Your Data Connection dialog box reopens. Tap or click the Next button. A reminder dialog box opens stating that the connection uses a local data file that is not in the current project. Tap or click the No button.

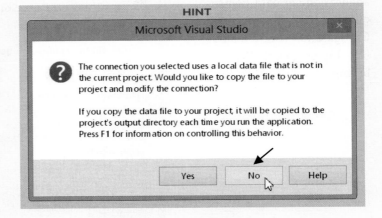

Guided Program Development *continued*

- **Save the Connection String** The next dialog box opens requesting which connection your application should use. Tap or click the Next button.

HINT

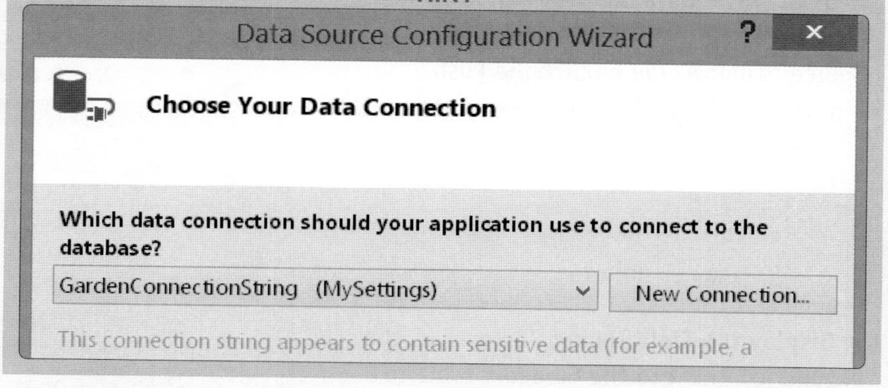
Data Source Configuration Wizard
Choose Your Data Connection
Which data connection should your application use to connect to the database?
GardenConnectionString (MySettings)
New Connection...
This connection string appears to contain sensitive data (for example, a

- **Connect to the Gardener Table** The Choose Your Database Object dialog box opens. Tap or click the expand icon next to the Tables option. Tap or click the Gardener check box to select the Gardener table. Tap or click the Finish button.

HINT

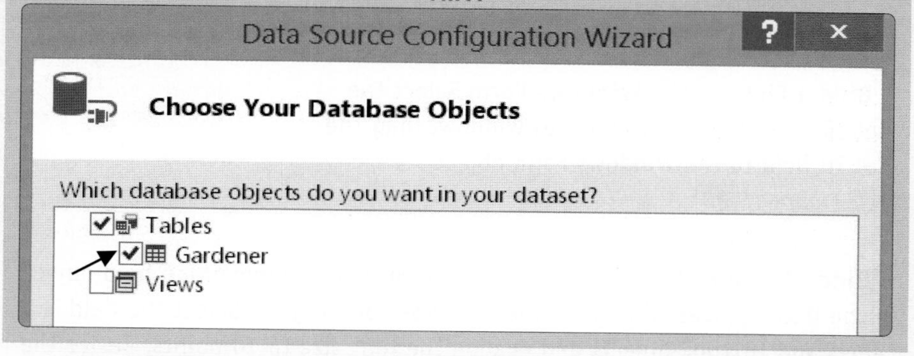
Data Source Configuration Wizard
Choose Your Database Objects
Which database objects do you want in your dataset?
Tables
Gardener
Views

The GardenDataSet is displayed in the Solution Explorer (Figure 10-53).

RESULT OF STEP 2

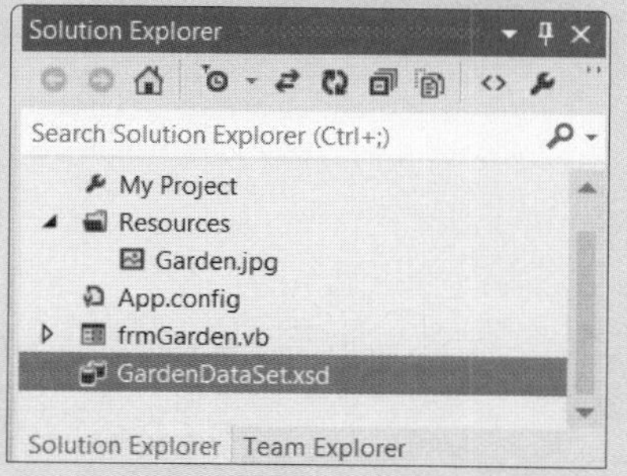
Solution Explorer
Search Solution Explorer (Ctrl+;)
My Project
Resources
Garden.jpg
App.config
frmGarden.vb
GardenDataSet.xsd
Solution Explorer
Team Explorer

FIGURE 10-53

(continues)

Guided Program Development *continued*

3

● **Display the Data Sources Window** Tap or
click Data Sources to display the Data
Sources window. Tap or click the Push
Pin icon to pin the Data Sources window.

● **Display the Field Names** Tap or click the
expand icon next to the Gardener table to
expand the listing of the field names within the table.

● **Bind a Field to the Windows Form** Select the
Plot ID field in the Data Sources window. Drag the
Plot ID field to the Windows Form object
(ref: Figure 10-23).

● **Bind All the Fields to the Windows Form** Drag the remaining field objects
in the Data Sources window to the Windows Form object. Select the field
Labels and TextBox objects and change the font size to 10 points. Resize the
Label and TextBox objects. Use the formatting tools on the FORMAT menu to
equally distribute the bound objects. Use the layout shown in Figure 10-54.

- **Add a Button Object** Add a Button object to the Windows form named `btnCost` with the Text property changed to `Total Planting Cost`. Change the font size to 10 points and the ForeColor property to Green. Add a Label object named `lblTotalPlantingCost` with the Text property of 30 X's. Change the font size to 14 points and bold. Change the ForeColor property to Green. Center the Label object on the form (see Figure 10-54 for layout).

The Windows Form object is designed (Figure 10-54).

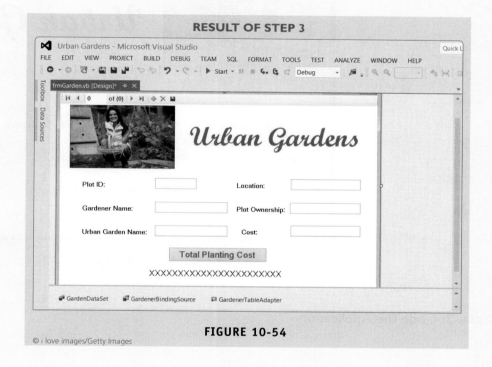

© i love images/Getty Images

FIGURE 10-54

(continues)

Guided Program Development   *continued*

4

- **Execute the Application to Load the Database Data** Tap or click the Start Debugging button on the Standard toolbar to run the application. The data fills the Windows form.

- **Use the Navigation Toolbar** With the application running, navigate through the database records. Add a record, and then delete a record.

The Windows form is designed and the database is connected to the application (Figure 10-55).

RESULT OF STEP 4

© i love images/Getty Images

FIGURE 10-55

Phase 2: Code the Application

5

- **Code the Comments** Tap or click the View Code button on the Solution Explorer toolbar to begin coding the application. Type the first four standard comments at the top of the code window.

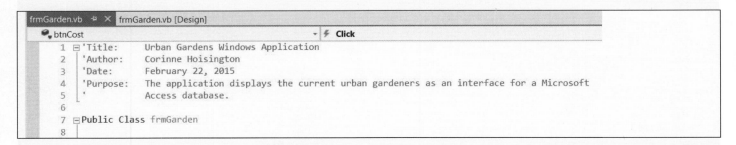

```
1 ⊟'Title:     Urban Gardens Windows Application
2  'Author:    Corinne Hoisington
3  'Date:      February 22, 2015
4  'Purpose:   The application displays the current urban gardeners as an interface for a Microsoft
5  '           Access database.
6
7 ⊟Public Class frmGarden
8 |
```

• **Comment the Code Created by the Database Wizard** The Data Source Configuration Wizard creates two Sub methods. Enter the comments in the first line of the first Sub method as shown in the adjacent Hint Screen.

```
 7  Public Class frmGarden
 8
 9      Private Sub frmGarden_Load(sender As Object, e As EventArgs) Handles MyBase.Load
10          'TODO: This line of code loads data into the 'GardenDataSet.Gardener' table. You can move, or remove it, as needed.
11          Me.GardenerTableAdapter.Fill(Me.GardenDataSet.Gardener)
12
13      End Sub
14
15      Private Sub GardenerBindingNavigatorSaveItem_Click(sender As Object, e As EventArgs) Handles GardenerBindingNavigatorSaveItem.Click
16          Me.Validate()
17          Me.GardenerBindingSource.EndEdit()
18          Me.TableAdapterManager.UpdateAll(Me.GardenDataSet)
19
20      End Sub
```

• **Code the OleDbDataAdapter for the btnCost_Click Event** Double-tap or double-click the Total Planting Cost button in the Design window to create the btnCost_Click event handler. To initialize the OleDbDataAdapter, enter the code in the adjacent Hint Screen inside the click event. The first variable, strSql, is assigned the SQL statement that queries all the fields in the Gardener table. The second variable, strPath, is assigned the database driver for Access and the path to the Garden.accdb file. The third variable, odaGarden, is an instance of the OleDbDataAdapter (*ref: Figure 10-44*).

```
22      Private Sub btnCost_Click(sender As Object, e As EventArgs) Handles btnCost.Click
23          ' strSql is a SQL statement that selects all the fields from the
24          ' Gardener table
25
26          Dim strSql As String = "SELECT * FROM Gardener"
27
28          'strPath provides the database type and path of the Garden database
29          Dim strPath As String = "Provider=Microsoft.ACE.OLEDB.12.0 ;" & "Data Source=e:\Garden.accdb"
30          Dim odaGarden As New OleDb.OleDbDataAdapter(strSql, strPath)
```

• **Fill the DataTable Object** Inside the btnCost_Click event, after initializing the OleDbDataAdapter, initialize an instance named datCost to represent the DataTable object. Declare the intCount variable for use in counting through a For loop. Initialize the last variable, decTotalCost, which will contain the total of the planting costs. Write the statement to fill the DataTable with the contents of the Gardener table. Code the Dispose method to close the open connection.

```
31          Dim datCost As New DataTable
32          Dim intCount As Integer
33          Dim decTotalCost As Decimal = 0D
34
35          ' The DataTable name datCost is filled with the table data
36          odaGarden.Fill(datCost)
37          'The connection to the database is disconnected
38          odaGarden.Dispose()
```

(continues)

Guided Program Development *continued*

• **Calculate and Display the Sum of the Spring Planting Costs** Write a For loop statement to increment the count for each record in the Gardener table. Because the rows number 0 to 15, the upper range is one less than the numbers of rows in the table, making 16 records. Write the code within the loop to add the value in each Cost field to the value in the decTotalCost variable. Write the code to display the total spring planting costs in the lblTotalPlantingCost Label object, including making the Label object visible.

```
39              For intCount = 0 To datCost.Rows.Count - 1
40                  decTotalCost += Convert.ToDecimal(datCost.Rows(intCount)("Cost"))
41              Next
42              lblTotalPlantingCost.Visible = True
43              lblTotalPlantingCost.Text = "The Total Planting Cost is " & decTotalCost.ToString("C")
44          End Sub
45
46      End Class
```

The code is completed (Figure 10-56).

RESULT OF STEP 5

```
1  'Title:     Urban Gardens Windows Application
2  'Author:    Corinne Hoisington
3  'Date:      February 22, 2015
4  'Purpose:   The application displays the current urban gardeners as an interface for a Microsoft
5  '           Access database.
6
7  Public Class frmGarden
8
9      Private Sub frmGarden_Load(sender As Object, e As EventArgs) Handles MyBase.Load
10         'TODO: This line of code loads data into the 'GardenDataSet.Gardener' table. You can move, or remove it, as needed.
11         Me.GardenerTableAdapter.Fill(Me.GardenDataSet.Gardener)
12
13     End Sub
14
15     Private Sub GardenerBindingNavigatorSaveItem_Click(sender As Object, e As EventArgs) Handles GardenerBindingNavigatorSaveItem.Click
16         Me.Validate()
17         Me.GardenerBindingSource.EndEdit()
18         Me.TableAdapterManager.UpdateAll(Me.GardenDataSet)
19
20     End Sub
21
22     Private Sub btnCost_Click(sender As Object, e As EventArgs) Handles btnCost.Click
23         ' strSq1 is a SQL statement that selects all the fields from the
24         ' Gardener table
25
26         Dim strSql As String = "SELECT * FROM Gardener"
27
28         'strPath provides the database type and path of the Garden database
29         Dim strPath As String = "Provider=Microsoft.ACE.OLEDB.12.0 ;" & "Data Source=e:\Garden.accdb"
30         Dim odaGarden As New OleDb.OleDbDataAdapter(strSql, strPath)
31         Dim datCost As New DataTable
32         Dim intCount As Integer
33         Dim decTotalCost As Decimal = 0D
34
35         ' The DataTable name datCost is filled with the table data
36         odaGarden.Fill(datCost)
37         'The connection to the database is disconnected
38         odaGarden.Dispose()
39         For intCount = 0 To datCost.Rows.Count - 1
40             decTotalCost += Convert.ToDecimal(datCost.Rows(intCount)("Cost"))
41         Next
42         lblTotalPlantingCost.Visible = True
43         lblTotalPlantingCost.Text = "The Total Planting Cost is " & decTotalCost.ToString("C")
44     End Sub
45
46  End Class
```

FIGURE 10-56

Summary

In this chapter you have learned to create a Windows application using database files and ADO.NET 4.5. The items listed in the table in Figure 10-57 include all the new Visual Studio and Visual Basic skills you have learned in this chapter.

Visual Basic Skills		
Skill	**Figure Number**	**Video Number**
Examine Urban Gardens	Figure 10-1	Video 10-1
Connect to the Database Using the Data Source	Figure 10-8	Video 10-2
View the Data Available in the Source Database	Figure 10-19	Video 10-3
Bind Each Database Field to the Windows Form Object	Figure 10-23	Video 10-4
Add a New Record to the Database Table	Figure 10-26	Video 10-5
Delete an Existing Record in the Database Table	Figure 10-29	Video 10-6
Change Toolbox Object Type	Figure 10-32	Video 10-7
Code a Connection with a Database and Compute the Sum	Figure 10-43	Video 10-8

FIGURE 10-57

Learn Online

Reinforcement activities and resources are available at no additional cost on *www.cengagebrain.com*. Visit *www.cengage.com/ct/studentdownload* for detailed instructions about accessing the resources available at the Student Companion Site.

Knowledge Check

1. ADO.NET 4.5 can only connect to local databases stored on a USB drive. True or false?

2. Define ADO.

3. Define SQL.

4. What is the name of a unique field that must be present in each relational database?

5. Name three types of databases that can connect with ADO.NET 4.5.

6. What is a DataSet object?

7. Does a row in a database table represent a record or a field?

8. Name five types of objects that can be dragged from a data field in the Data Sources window to the Windows Form object without using the Customize option.

9. What is the object name of the navigation toolbar?

10. When you add a record to a database using the Add new button on the navigation toolbar, the record is not added to the original database. What action must take place to add the record to the original data source?

11. How many records does the database table named SouthernStates displayed in Figure 10-58 contain?

APPROXIMATE POPULATION OF THE SOUTHERN STATES PROJECTED FOR 2025			
AutoNumber	**State Name**	**State Capital**	**Population**
1	Florida	Tallahassee	20,066,000
2	Georgia	Atlanta	10,962,000
3	South Carolina	Columbia	4,574,000
4	North Carolina	Raleigh	9,916,000
5	Virginia	Richmond	8,165,000
6	Alabama	Montgomery	5,224,000
7	Louisiana	Baton Rouge	5,111,000
8	Tennessee	Nashville	7,249,000
9	West Virginia	Charleston	1,864,000
10	Mississippi	Jackson	3,413,000
11	Kentucky	Lexington	4,314,000

Source: http://www.census.gov/population/projections/state/stpjpop.txt

FIGURE 10-58

12. In the table in Figure 10-58 on the previous page, name the field labels.

13. For the table in Figure 10-58, write a statement that references the North Carolina state capital city and assign the value to the strCapitalCity variable.

14. What properties under the Data Binding Mode must you set when you bind a ComboBox object to a Windows form?

15. What procedure places data in the Data Table?

16. What command disconnects a database connection?

17. Write a line of code to initialize a String variable named strOrder to a Select SQL statement that would select all the fields from a table named Coffee.

18. Which wildcard symbol is used in a Select statement?

19. What does the wildcard symbol mean in the Select statement?

20. Write the statement that would fill a DataTable object named datCoins if an instance of the OleDbDataAdapter is named odaCollection.

Debugging Exercises

1. The code shown in Figure 10-59 is designed to increment through each row in a database table. Correct the error in the code.

```
For intRecordCount = 0 To datInventory.Rows.Count
     ' Processing statements
Next
```

FIGURE 10-59

2. Correct the line of code shown in Figure 10-60:

```
strNumberOfRows = datCityName.Rows.Count
```

FIGURE 10-60

3. Rewrite the code shown in Figure 10-61 correctly:

```
strNumberOfRows = Convert.ToString(datCityName.Rows(5)(City))
```

FIGURE 10-61

Program Analysis

1. Write a command that assigns an Access database named usedcarparts.accdb and a path located on the E drive to a string named strConnect for use later in an instance of an OleDbDataAdapter.

2. Consider the database table named BaseballStadiums shown in Figure 10-62. If the instance of the DataTable is named datStadium, what value would the statement in Figure 10-63 assign to the variable intCount?

Stadium Number	Stadium Name	Location	Team
203	Dodgers Stadium	Los Angeles, CA	Dodgers
304	Petco Field	San Diego, CA	Padres
425	Wrigley Field	Chicago, IL	Cubs
509	Camden Yards	Baltimore, MD	Orioles
698	Fenway Park	Boston, MA	Red Sox
756	Citi Field	New York City, NY	Mets

FIGURE 10-62

© 2014 Cengage Learning

```
intCount = datStadium.Rows.Count
```

FIGURE 10-63

3. Using the database table in Figure 10-62, what value would be assigned to strTeamName in the code in Figure 10-64?

```
strTeamName = Convert.ToString(datStadium.Rows(3)("Team"))
```

FIGURE 10-64

4. Using the database table in Figure 10-62, what value would be assigned to strLocation in the code in Figure 10-65?

```
strLocation = Convert.ToString(datStadium.Rows(1)("Location"))
```

FIGURE 10-65

5. Using the database table in Figure 10-62, what value would be assigned to intNumber in the code in Figure 10-66?

```
intNumber = datStadium.Columns.Count
```

FIGURE 10-66

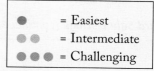

Case Programming Assignments

Complete one or more of the following case programming assignments. Submit the program and materials you create to your instructor. The level of difficulty is indicated for each assignment.

● = Easiest
●● = Intermediate
●●● = Challenging

1 ●
YARD SALE LISTINGS

Design a Windows application and write the code that will execute according to the program requirements in Figure 10-67 and the Use Case Definition in Figure 10-68. Before writing the code, create an event planning document for each event in the program. The completed Windows application and other objects in the user interface are shown in Figure 10-69.

REQUIREMENTS DOCUMENT

Date Submitted: October 30, 2015

Application Title: Yard Sale Listings Application

Purpose: This Windows application opens an Access database with 16 listings for yard sales this Saturday. The data in the database can be viewed, updated, and deleted. The application can be used by a customer looking for local yard sales each week.

Program Procedures: In a Windows application, the Access database file is opened and the user can view, add, and delete records as needed.

Algorithms, Processing, and Conditions:

1. The user first views a Windows application that loads an existing Access database table named YardSale that includes the Yard Sale ID, Yard Sale Owner, and Location. A navigation toolbar appears at the top of the Windows form, allowing the user to move from record to record. The Windows form also includes a title and an image.

2. The user can tap or click the Add new button on the navigation toolbar to add a new yard sale. The record is saved when the user taps or clicks the Save Data button on the navigation toolbar.

3. The user can tap or click the Delete button on the navigation toolbar to delete a yard sale. The record is permanently deleted when the user taps or clicks the Save Data button on the navigation toolbar.

Notes and Restrictions: The Sales.accdb file is located on the USB drive on the E drive.

Comments:

1. The Sales.accdb file is available on CengageBrain.com.
2. Obtain an image for this program from CengageBrain.com. The name of the picture on the Windows form is Yard.

FIGURE 10-67

(continues)

Case Programming Assignments

Yard Sale Listings (continued)

USE CASE DEFINITION

1. The user views the Access database information displaying yard sales and their locations.
2. The user taps or clicks the Add new button to add a new yard sale and taps or clicks the Save Data button to save the item to the original database.
3. The user taps or clicks the Delete button to delete a yard sale and permanently deletes the record from the original database by tapping or clicking the Save Data button.

FIGURE 10-68

© 2014 Cengage Learning

FIGURE 10-69

© David Sacks/Lifesize/Getty Images

2 HUMANE SOCIETY ADOPTIONS

Design a Windows application and write the code that will execute according to the program requirements in Figure 10-70 and the Use Case Definition in Figure 10-71 on the next page. Before writing the code, create an event planning document for each event in the program. The completed Windows application and other objects in the user interface are shown in Figure 10-72.

REQUIREMENTS DOCUMENT

Date Submitted: April 22, 2015

Application Title: Humane Society Adoptions Application

Purpose: This Windows application opens an Access database with 20 dogs that are available at the Humane Society. The data in the database can be viewed, updated, and deleted. The application can be used for marketing the available dogs and changes weekly based on dog availability.

Program Procedures: In a Windows application, the Access database file is opened and the user can view, add, and delete records as needed.

Algorithms, Processing, and Conditions:
1. The user views a Windows application that loads an existing Access database table that includes the Dog Tag, Dog Type, Color, and Age.
2. A navigation toolbar appears at the top of the Windows form, allowing the user to move from record to record. The Windows form also includes a title and a graphic image.
3. The user can tap or click the Add new button on the navigation toolbar to add a dog to the database. The record is saved when the user taps or clicks the Save Data button on the navigation toolbar.
4. The user can tap or click the Delete button on the navigation toolbar to delete a dog. The record is permanently deleted when the user taps or clicks the Save Data button on the navigation toolbar.
5. The user can tap or click a list arrow to move directly to a dog record.

Notes and Restrictions: The Dogs.accdb file is located on the USB drive on the E drive.

Comments:
1. The Dogs.accdb file is available on CengageBrain.com.
2. Obtain an image for this program from CengageBrain.com. The name of the picture on the Windows form is Dog.

FIGURE 10-70

(continues)

Case Programming Assignments

Humane Society Adoptions (continued)

USE CASE DEFINITION

1. The user views the Access database information displaying images of the dogs that are available for adoption at the Humane Society.
2. The user taps or clicks the Add new button to add a dog and taps or clicks the Save Data button to save the item to the original database.
3. The user taps or clicks the Delete button to delete a dog from the database and permanently deletes it from the original database by tapping or clicking the Save Data button.
4. The user can tap or click a list arrow to display the dogs to move directly to a dog's record.

FIGURE 10-71

FIGURE 10-72

3

CURRENCY CONVERSION

Design a Windows application and write the code that will execute according to the program requirements in Figure 10-73 and the Use Case Definition in Figure 10-74. Before writing the code, create an event planning document for each event in the program. The completed Windows application and other objects in the user interface are shown in Figure 10-75.

REQUIREMENTS DOCUMENT

Date Submitted:	August 1, 2015
Application Title:	Currency Conversion Application
Purpose:	This Windows application opens an Access database with five currency conversion values in a Windows form. The values are for inventory goods at a store. The data in the database can be viewed, updated, and deleted. The application also computes the total value of the inventory in stock.
Program Procedures:	In a Windows application, the Access database file is opened and the user can view, add, and delete records as needed.
Algorithms, Processing and Conditions:	1. The user first views a Windows application that loads an existing Access database table, which includes the currency abbreviation, the currency name, and the conversion against a single U.S. dollar. A navigation toolbar appears at the top of the Windows form, allowing the user to move from record to record. The Windows form also includes a title and a graphic image.
	2. The user can tap or click the Add new button on the navigation toolbar to add a new currency to the database. The record is saved when the user taps or clicks the Save Data button on the navigation toolbar.
	3. The user can tap or click the Delete button on the navigation toolbar to delete a currency type. The record is permanently deleted when the user taps or clicks the Save Data button on the navigation toolbar.
	4. The user can tap or click the Compute Total Value of Inventory Button object to compute the total value of the store's inventory.
Notes and Restrictions:	1. The Currency.accdb file is located on the USB drive on the E drive.
	2. Open the database and update the current conversions. Visit *www.xe.com/ucc* to research the amount equivalent to $1 U.S. in the currency from other countries and enter that value in the same database table.
Comments:	1. The Currency.accdb file is available on CengageBrain.com.
	2. Obtain an image for this program from CengageBrain.com. The name of the picture on the Windows form is Money.

FIGURE 10-73

(continues)

Case Programming Assignments

Currency Conversion (continued)

USE CASE DEFINITION

1. The user views the Access database information displaying the currency conversion against the U.S. dollar.
2. The user taps or clicks the Add new button to add a new currency and taps or clicks the Save Data button to save the item to the original database.
3. The user taps or clicks the Delete button to delete the currency and permanently deletes the record from the original database by tapping or clicking the Save Data button.

FIGURE 10-74

© 2014 Cengage Learning

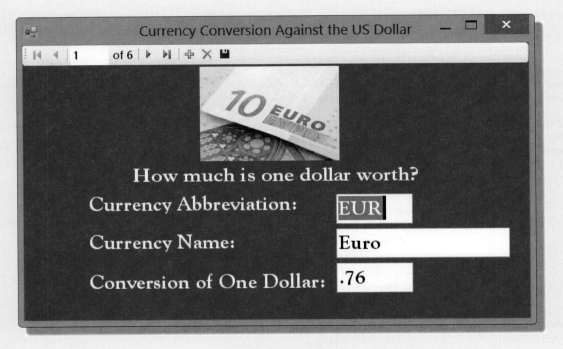

FIGURE 10-75

© yorkfoto/E+/Getty Images

Case Programming Assignments

4 •• SPORTS LEAGUE BASEBALL TEAM

Design a Windows application and write the code that will execute according to the program requirements in Figure 10-76. Before designing the user interface, create a Use Case Definition. Before writing the code, create an event planning document for each event in the program.

REQUIREMENTS DOCUMENT

Date Submitted: May 13, 2015

Application Title: Sports League Baseball Team Application

Purpose: This Windows application opens an Access database with 22 boys and girls ages 12–14 who are playing in the National Sports League co-ed championship. The data in the database can be viewed, updated, and deleted in the Windows form. The application computes in three separate counts the number of team members who are 12, 13, or 14 years old and calculates the average age of the team.

Program Procedures: In a Windows application, the Access database file is opened and the user can view, add, and delete records as needed. The total of each age in the database also can be displayed.

Algorithms, Processing, and Conditions:
1. The user first views a Windows application that loads an existing Access database table that includes the player number, first name, last name, parent's name, address, city, state, zip, telephone, and age. A navigation toolbar appears at the top of the Windows form, allowing the user to move from record to record. The Windows form also includes a title and a graphic image.
2. The user can tap or click the Add new button on the navigation toolbar to add a new player to the team. The record is saved when the user taps or clicks the Save Data button on the navigation toolbar.
3. The user can tap or click the Delete button on the navigation toolbar to delete a team player. The record is permanently deleted when the user taps or clicks the Save Data button on the navigation toolbar.
4. The user can tap or click the Ages Button object to compute the total number of team members who are 12, 13, or 14 years old. The user also can compute the average age of the team.

Notes and Restrictions:
1. The LittleLeague.accdb file is located on the USB drive on the E drive.
2. Use a Try-Catch statement to catch an exception if the file is not available.

Comments: The LittleLeague.accdb file is available on CengageBrain.com.

FIGURE 10-76

5 •• COLLEGE MAJORS

Design a Windows application and write the code that will execute according to the program requirements in Figure 10-77. Before designing the user interface, create a Use Case Definition. Before writing the code, create an event planning document for each event in the program.

REQUIREMENTS DOCUMENT

Date Submitted: March 9, 2015

Application Title: College Majors Application

Purpose: This Windows application opens an Access database with 36 college majors in a Windows form. The data in the database can be viewed, updated, and deleted. The application also computes the total number of students attending the college. The user can select a major from a combo box list and the application displays the percentage of students participating in that major.

Program Procedures: In a Windows application, the Access database file is opened and the user can view, add, and delete records as needed. The total student population and percent of students in a particular major also can be displayed.

Algorithms, Processing, and Conditions:

1. The user first views a Windows application that loads an existing Access database table that includes the department, college major, and the number of students in that major. A navigation toolbar appears at the top of the Windows form, allowing the user to move from record to record. The Windows form also includes a title and a graphic image.
2. The user can tap or click the Add new button on the navigation toolbar to add a new major to the college. The record is saved when the user taps or clicks the Save Data button on the navigation toolbar.
3. The user can tap or click the Delete button on the navigation toolbar to delete a major. The record is permanently deleted when the user taps or clicks the Save Data button on the navigation toolbar.
4. The user can tap or click the Find Total button object to compute the total number of students presently in majors.
5. The user can select the college major from a combo box list and the application will display the percentage of students at the college participating in that major.

Notes and Restrictions: The College.accdb file is located on the USB drive on the E drive.

Comments:
1. The College.accdb file is available on CengageBrain.com.
2. Use a graphic image you obtain from the Web.

FIGURE 10-77

Case Programming Assignments

6 ●●
KID-FRIENDLY STOCKS

Design a Windows application and write the code that will execute according to the program requirements in Figure 10-78. Before designing the user interface, create a Use Case Definition. Before writing the code, create an event planning document for each event in the program.

REQUIREMENTS DOCUMENT

Date Submitted: August 17, 2015

Application Title: Kid-Friendly Stocks Application

Purpose: This Windows application opens an Access database in a Windows form with 16 child-centered stocks selected for an investment portfolio. The data in the database can be viewed, updated, and deleted. The application also computes the total investment made in the portfolio and lists the name of the stocks with the selected rating, which have been entered into the database.

Program Procedures: In a Windows application, the Access database file is opened and the user can view, add, and delete records as needed. The total portfolio investment is calculated.

Algorithms, Processing, and Conditions:
1. The user first views a Windows application that loads an existing Access database table that includes the stock symbol, the name of the stock, the price per share, number of shares, and the earning potential rating. A navigation toolbar appears at the top of the Windows form, allowing the user to move from record to record. The Windows form also includes a title and graphic image.
2. The user can tap or click the Add new button on the navigation toolbar to add a new stock purchase. The record is saved when the user taps or clicks the Save Data button on the navigation toolbar.
3. The user can tap or click the Delete button on the navigation toolbar to delete a stock purchase. The record is permanently deleted when the user taps or clicks the Save Data button on the navigation toolbar.
4. The user can select the stock symbol using the list arrow on a ComboBox object to move directly to the record needed.
5. The user can tap or click the Compute Total Investment Button object to compute the total worth of stock owned.
6. The stock ratings list includes Exceptional, High, Average, and Low, and can be selected by the user. The application will display all the stock names in the selected rating in a ListBox object.

Notes and Restrictions:
1. The KidFriendlyStocks.accdb file is located on the USB drive on the E drive.
2. Update the stock values in the Access database to their current values.

Comments:
1. The KidFriendlyStocks.accdb file is available on CengageBrain.com.
2. Use a graphic image you obtain from the Web.

FIGURE 10-78

Case Programming Assignments

7 ●●●
CALORIES CONSUMED

Create a requirements document and a Use Case Definition document, and then design a Windows application based on the case project shown in Figure 10-79. Before writing the code, create an event planning document for each event in the program.

A nutritionist often has patients create a food diary to see the amount of calories consumed each day. Create an Access database with the following fields: an item number as an AutoNumber field, food consumed, and number of calories. On the Web, research the amount of calories each food contains. Enter calorie data into the database of all food and beverages consumed in one day (at least 12 items). Develop a Windows application that displays the Access database table of calories consumed in one day. The application will compute the total number of calories consumed. The Department of Health estimates the average requirement of a daily calorie intake is 1,940 calories per day for women and 2,550 for men. The application should request whether the user is a male or female. When the total number of calories is displayed, the percentage of calories consumed above or below the recommended daily calorie intake also should be shown.

FIGURE 10-79

Case Programming Assignments

8 ●●● GRADUATION PARTY EVENT

Create a requirements document and a Use Case Definition document, and then design a Windows application based on the case project shown in Figure 10-80. Before writing the code, create an event planning document for each event in the program.

> Create an Access database that holds the invitation information for 15 people you would like to invite to a graduation party. The main table should have a primary key and include AutoNumber, first name, last name, address, city, state, zip code, and phone number fields for each family invited. Create a Windows form that will display the families who are invited to the graduation party. Include a field in the database that also requests the number who RSVP for the party. This number will be added to the Windows form as you receive RSVP responses. Compute the total amount of people attending the party.

FIGURE 10-80

Case Programming Assignments

9 ●●●
ADDRESS BOOK

Create a requirements document and a Use Case Definition document, and then design a Windows application based on the case project shown in Figure 10-81. Before writing the code, create an event planning document for each event in the program.

Create an Access database with the following information about 12 of your friends: first name, last name, address, city, state, zip, and age. Create a database that uses a ComboBox object for last names. Compute and display the average age of your friends. Use an image and allow users to add and delete friends from the database.

FIGURE 10-81

CHAPTER 11

Multiple Classes and Inheritance

OBJECTIVES

You will have mastered the material in this chapter when you can:

- Use the TabIndex property

- Edit input, including MaskedTextBox, TextBox, and ComboBox objects

- Describe the three-tiered program structure

- Understand a class

- Create a class

- Instantiate an object

- Pass arguments when instantiating an object

- Write a class constructor

- Call a procedure in a separate class

- Code a base class and a subclass to incorporate inheritance

- Call procedures found in a base class and a subclass

- Write overridable and overrides procedures

- Create and write a comma-delimited text file

Introduction

In previous chapters you have learned that a class is a named group of program code. Within a class such as Form1, you can define attributes, Sub procedures, and Function procedures. The classes you have used thus far have either been generated by the design feature of Visual Basic or were used from a library of classes supplied by Visual Studio 2012. In this chapter, you will define a class in code and will develop the code in the class to help complete the chapter project.

When you define classes, you have the option of using a feature called inheritance, which is common to object-oriented programming languages such as Visual Basic. Inheritance allows one class, called a subclass, to use attributes and procedures defined in another class, called a base class.

Finally, when you define your own classes, you have the opportunity to design a three-tiered structure for your program so it is more reliable, more robust, and more easily understood. The sample program in this chapter uses the three-tiered program structure.

Chapter Project

The sample chapter project features the College Registration Costs window displayed in Figure 11-1.

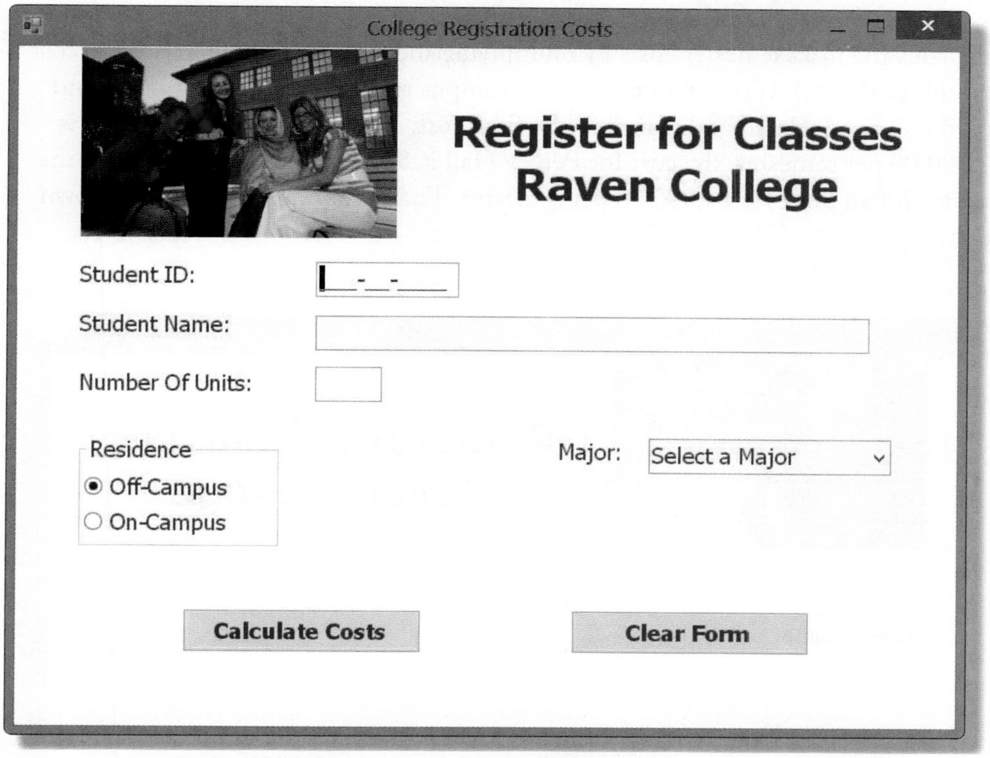

FIGURE 11-1

© Purestock/Getty Images

In the window shown in Figure 11-1, a student or a worker assisting the student enters the student ID number, the student name, and the number of units for which the student is registering. The user also identifies whether the student is living off campus or on campus, identifies the housing and board an on-campus student is using, and identifies the student's major.

Then, when the user taps or clicks the Calculate Costs button, the application calculates the total semester costs by multiplying the number of units times the cost per unit ($450.00). If the student is an on-campus resident, the cost for room and board also is calculated and placed in the final cost. The cost for Cooper Dorm is $2,900.00 per semester, the cost for Percey Hall is $3,400.00 per semester, and the cost for Julian Suites is $4,000.00 per semester. The total semester costs are shown below the buttons (Figure 11-2).

FIGURE 11-2

© Purestock/Getty Images

The user is required to enter valid values for each of the items on the registration form. If the user does not enter a value or enters an invalid value, such as a nonnumeric value in the Number of Units text box, a message box is displayed to prompt the user to enter a valid value (Figure 11-3).

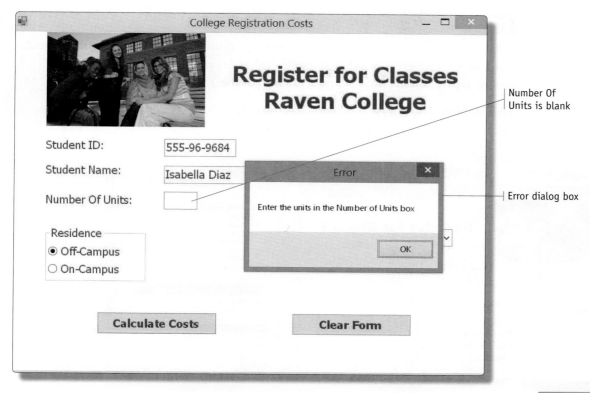

Number Of
Units is blank

Error dialog box

FIGURE 11-3

© Purestock/Getty Images

In Figure 11-3, the user failed to enter the number of units, so the message box directs the user to enter the number.

In addition to calculating the total semester costs, this program creates a log on disk for the students whose costs have been calculated. This log is kept as a text file. The program must write records in the text file as students use the program.

ONLINE REINFORCEMENT

To view a video of the program execution shown in Figure 11-1, visit CengageBrain.com and navigate to the resources for this title. Tap or click the link for Chapter 11 and then navigate to Video 11-1. Turn on your speakers to listen to the audio walkthrough of the steps.

Use the TabIndex Property in the User Interface

The user interface in the College Registration Costs program does not contain any objects that you have not seen in previous programs. However, the program does implement a new property that users often find useful.

When users enter data into a Windows Form object, they usually enter the data in sequence on the form. For example, in Figure 11-2, the user can enter the Student ID first, followed by the Student Name, then the Number of Units, and so on. Often, users prefer to press the TAB key to move the insertion point from one object on the Windows Form object to the next. To specify the sequence of objects that will be selected when the user presses the TAB key, you use the TabIndex property. To implement the TabIndex property for the Windows Form object in Figure 11-2, you can complete the steps on the next page:

STEP 1   Select the object that will be selected when program execution begins. In the example, the selected object will be the txtStudentID MaskedTextBox object. Scroll in the Properties window until the TabIndex property is visible and then double-tap or double-click the right column of the TabIndex property.

The TabIndex property for the MaskedTextBox object is selected (Figure 11–4).

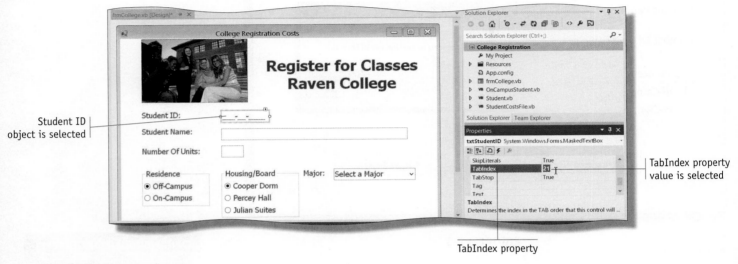

© Purestock/Getty Images

FIGURE 11-4

STEP 2   Type 1 and then press the ENTER key.

The value 1 in the TabIndex property of an object indicates that the object will be selected when the program begins execution (Figure 11–5). When program execution begins, the insertion point will be located in the txtStudentID MaskedTextBox object.

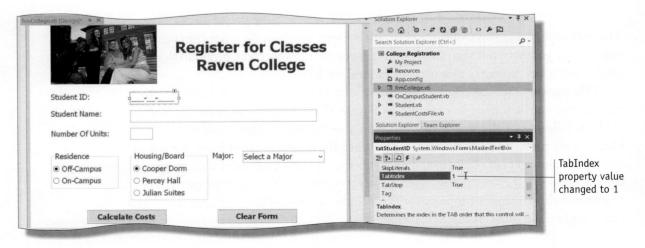

© Purestock/Getty Images

FIGURE 11-5

STEP 3   Select the object that should be selected when the user presses the TAB key. In the sample program, the txtStudentName TextBox object should be selected. Double-tap or double-click the right column of the TabIndex property for the txtStudentName TextBox object, type 2, and then press the ENTER key.

The TabIndex value for the txtStudentName object is set to 2 in the Properties window (Figure 11-6). When the user enters the Student ID value and presses the TAB key, the insertion point will be in the Student Name text box. Using these same techniques, you can continue to identify objects on the Windows Form object that will be selected when the user presses the TAB key.

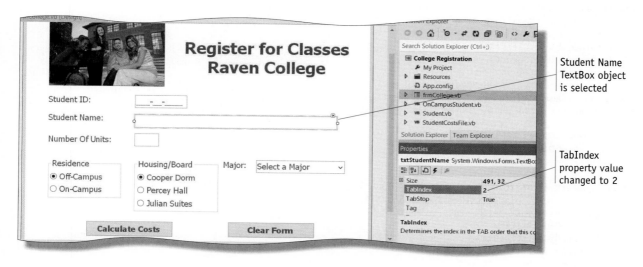

FIGURE 11-6

© Purestock/Getty Images

Edit Input Data

Like other applications in this book, the data that users enter in the College Registration Costs program must be checked to ensure its validity. When the user clicks the Calculate Costs button, the following items must be checked:

1. Student ID: The student ID object is a masked text box, and the mask is for the Social Security number in the same layout, so the mask ensures that the user can enter only numbers. However, the Social Security mask does not ensure that the user enters all nine numbers. Therefore, a check must be included in the program to require the user to enter all nine numeric digits.
2. Student Name: The program must ensure that the user enters characters in this TextBox object. In addition, spaces cannot be entered instead of actual alphabetic characters.
3. Number of Units: The user must enter a numeric value from 1 through 24 for the number of units the student is taking.
4. Major: The user must select a major from the list in the Major ComboBox object.

ONLINE REINFORCEMENT

To view a video of the process in the previous steps, visit CengageBrain.com and navigate to the resources for this title. Tap or click the link for Chapter 11 and then navigate to Video 11-2.

The code to implement these editing requirements is shown in Figure 11-7.

```
17          Dim objOnCampusStudent As OnCampusStudent
18          Dim InputError As Boolean = False
19
20          ' Is student ID entered properly
21          If txtStudentID.MaskFull = False Then
22              MsgBox("Enter your Student ID in the Student ID box", , _
23                  "Error")
24              txtStudentID.Clear()
25              txtStudentID.Focus()
26              InputError = True
27              ' Is student name entered properly
28          ElseIf txtStudentName.TextLength < 1 Or _
29                  txtStudentName.Text < "A" Then
30              MsgBox("Enter your name in the Student Name box", , "Error")
31              txtStudentName.Clear()
32              txtStudentName.Focus()
33              InputError = True
34              ' Is number of units entered properly
35          ElseIf Not IsNumeric(txtNumberOfUnits.Text) Then
36              MsgBox("Enter the units in the Number of Units box", , _
37                  "Error")
38              txtNumberOfUnits.Clear()
39              txtNumberOfUnits.Focus()
40              InputError = True
41              ' Has 1-24 units been entered
42          ElseIf Convert.ToInt32(txtNumberOfUnits.Text) < 1 _
43                  Or Convert.ToInt32(txtNumberOfUnits.Text) > 24 Then
44              MsgBox("Units must be 1 - 24", , "Error")
45              txtNumberOfUnits.Clear()
46              txtNumberOfUnits.Focus()
47              InputError = True
48              ' Has a major been selected
49          ElseIf cboMajor.SelectedIndex < 0 Then
50              MsgBox("Please select a major", , "Error")
51              cboMajor.Focus()
52              InputError = True
53          End If
```

FIGURE 11-7

In Figure 11-7, on line 18, a Boolean variable named InputError is defined and given the value False. This variable will be set to a value of True if an error is found in the editing statements. If any input area contains an error, the registration costs will not be calculated.

The editing checks are completed within an If...Else If statement. Because of the checks in this statement, each of the fields must contain valid data before the next field is checked; for example, until the Student ID field contains valid data, the Student Name field is not checked. This approach ensures that each field will contain valid data before the registration costs are calculated.

To ensure that the Student ID masked text box contains all nine numeric digits, the MaskFull property is tested, as shown in Figure 11-8.

```
20        ' Is student ID entered properly
21        If txtStudentID.MaskFull = False Then
22            MsgBox("Enter your Student ID in the Student ID box", , _
23                "Error")
24            txtStudentID.Clear()
25            txtStudentID.Focus()
26            InputError = True
```

FIGURE 11-8

The MaskFull property identifies whether all digits have been entered into the mask. For the Student ID, if all nine numeric digits have been entered into the masked text box, the property will be true; otherwise, the property will be false. If the MaskFull property is false, a message box will be displayed that directs the user to enter the student ID in the Student ID box. In addition, the masked text box is cleared, the focus is placed in the masked text box, and the InputError Boolean variable is set to True, indicating an error occurred.

If the Student ID field is correct, the next check is to ensure that the Student Name text box contains data. The Else...If statement to check the Student Name text box is shown in Figure 11-9.

```
28        ElseIf txtStudentName.TextLength < 1 Or _
29                txtStudentName.Text < "A" Then
30            MsgBox("Enter your name in the Student Name box", , "Error")
31            txtStudentName.Clear()
32            txtStudentName.Focus()
33            InputError = True
```

FIGURE 11-9

The If statement tests whether the length of the data in the text box is less than 1 and whether the first character entered is less than the letter A. If the length is less than 1, no data was entered in the text box. If the first character is less than A, then either a space or a special character was entered as the first character, both of which are invalid. If either of these conditions is true, a message box appears and instructs the user to enter a student name, the text box is cleared, focus is placed back on the Student Name text box, and the InputError Boolean variable is set to True.

If the Student Name text box contains valid data, the Number of Units TextBox object is checked to ensure that it contains a numeric value from 1 through 24. To make this check, two If statements are required: one to check for numeric data (line 35 in Figure 11-10) and one to ensure that the value is 1 through 24 (lines 42-43 in Figure 11-10). If either of these tests finds an error, a message box is displayed again, the TextBox object is cleared, the focus is placed in the text box, and the InputError variable is set to True.

```
34              ' Is number of units entered properly
35          ElseIf Not IsNumeric(txtNumberOfUnits.Text) Then
36              MsgBox("Enter the units in the Number of Units box", , _
37                  "Error")
38              txtNumberOfUnits.Clear()
39              txtNumberOfUnits.Focus()
40              InputError = True
41              ' Has 1-24 units been entered
42          ElseIf Convert.ToInt32(txtNumberOfUnits.Text) < 1 _
43                  Or Convert.ToInt32(txtNumberOfUnits.Text) > 24 Then
44              MsgBox("Units must be 1 - 24", , "Error")
45              txtNumberOfUnits.Clear()
46              txtNumberOfUnits.Focus()
47              InputError = True
```

FIGURE 11-10

The last data-editing step is to ensure that the user selected a major in the Major ComboBox object (Figure 11-11).

```
48              ' Has a major been selected
49          ElseIf cboMajor.SelectedIndex < 0 Then
50              MsgBox("Please select a major", , "Error")
51              cboMajor.Focus()
52              InputError = True
53          End If
```

FIGURE 11-11

As you have learned, when testing for a selection in a ComboBox object, the SelectedIndex property will contain the value −1 if a selection has not been made, and will contain the index value of the selected entry if a selection has been made. If the SelectedIndex property is less than zero, then a selection has not been made, so a message box displays an error message, the focus is placed on the ComboBox object, and the InputError Boolean variable is set to true.

If all tests are passed, the processing to compute the registration costs and other processing can occur.

Program Structure Using Classes

In previous programs, the Form class has been the basis of the program. It presented the user interface and has contained the Visual Basic statements that have processed data the user entered. In some programs, multiple procedures have been included in the class to complete the required processing.

When programs become larger and more complex, often you will divide the necessary processing into classes. This can have several benefits:

- The program is easier to read, understand, and maintain.
- A class can be used in more than one program for the same purpose. For example, the Button class that is used to create buttons in the user interface is used each time a Button object is placed on the Windows Form object.
- The processing accomplished in a class is separated from other classes, making the program easier to maintain and less prone to error.
- Variables defined in one class can be hidden from processing in other classes, so there is less likelihood of programming errors. Controlling the use of these variables (often called attributes or properties) by other classes reduces the inadvertent or purposeful inappropriate use of the attributes.

The concept of separating processing and hiding data within specific classes is called **encapsulation**, and is a major contributor to reliable and robust programs. Encapsulation is one of the fundamental principles of object-oriented programming. Encapsulation wraps related data and functions into a single entity.

Why should I use encapsulation?

- Encapsulation gives maintainability, flexibility, and extensibility to your code.
- Encapsulation provides a way to protect data from accidental corruption by keeping portions of the code in separate classes.
- Encapsulation hides information within an object.

When developing programs with multiple classes, a starting point for determining what classes should appear in a program is the three-tiered program structure. This structure specifies that a program is divided into three separate tiers: Presentation, Business, and Persistence (see Figure 11-12).

Presentation Tier	Business Tier	Persistence Tier
User Interface, Forms	Logic, Calculations	Data Storage (Files and Databases)

FIGURE 11-12

© 2014 Cengage Learning

The **presentation tier** contains the classes that display information for the user and accept user input. In many programs, the presentation tier consists of one or more forms and the objects placed on the forms. In a Web application, the presentation tier is the Web form and Web page that appear to the user. In addition, the processing in the presentation tier ensures that valid data is entered into the program for processing in the business tier.

The **business tier** contains the logic and calculations that must occur to fulfill the requirements of the program. The class(es) in the business tier generally use data entered by users and data obtained from storage to perform the logic and calculations. The business tier is named for the fact that it implements the "business rules" required for the application.

The **persistence tier**, sometimes called the **data access tier**, contains the code required to read and write data from permanent storage. Data that is stored in a file or database on disk often is called persistent data because it remains after the program is terminated.

When designing a program using the three-tiered approach, a primary rule is that classes in the presentation tier can communicate only with classes in the business tier. They never can communicate with classes in the persistence tier. In the same manner, classes in the persistence tier cannot communicate with classes in the presentation tier.

By following this rule, a program is much easier to maintain if changes must be made. For example, if a program currently writes data to a text file, such as in the College Registration Costs program in this chapter, and a decision is made to write the data in a database instead, only the class(es) in the persistence tier must be examined and changed. The user interface classes should have nothing to do with how data is stored. Therefore, the developer can be confident that if the correct changes are made to the persistence classes, the program will run properly regardless of the processing in the presentation classes.

Similarly, the business classes need not be concerned with how the data is obtained or stored. While the business classes will decide what data is needed and what data should be written to storage, only the persistence classes will actually read or write data.

This same thinking holds true for the separation of the business and presentation tiers. The classes in the business tier, where the logic and calculations occur, should not have to be concerned with the functionality of the user interface, nor should the user interface classes be concerned with how the data is manipulated by the business classes.

By placing classes in one of the three tiers depending on each class's function, the program becomes much easier to design, develop, and maintain.

Sample Program Classes

The College Registration Costs program in this chapter uses the three-tiered approach. The classes in each of the tiers are as follows:

1. Presentation tier: The presentation tier contains the frmCollege class. This class displays the user interface in a Windows Form object and edits the user input data to ensure its validity.

2. Business tier: The business tier contains two classes: the Student class and the OnCampusStudent class. The Student class contains data for each registered student and calculates the registration costs for some students. The OnCampusStudent class is used for registered students who live in on-campus residence halls.

3. Persistence tier: The persistence tier consists of one class, StudentCostsFile, which creates and writes the Student Costs File.

Create a Class

The class in the presentation tier, the frmCollege class, is created when the new Windows application is started. The other classes are created using the technique shown in the following steps:

STEP 1   With Visual Studio open and a new Windows Application project started, press and hold or right-click the project name in the Solution Explorer window and then point to Add on the shortcut menu.

The shortcut menu is displayed (Figure 11-13). When you point to the Add menu item, the Add submenu also is displayed.

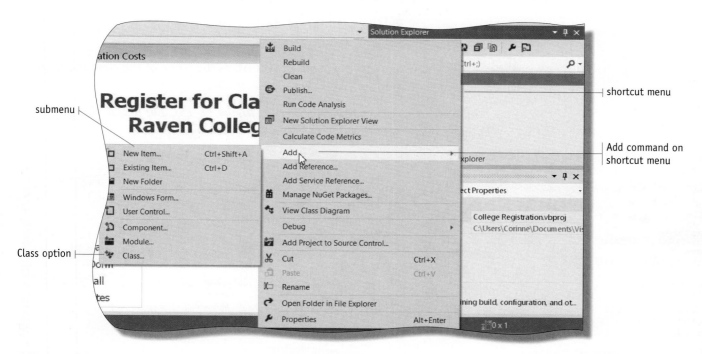

FIGURE 11-13

STEP 2   Tap or click Class on the Add submenu.

The Add New Item dialog box is displayed (Figure 11-14). Class is selected as an installed template in the middle pane.

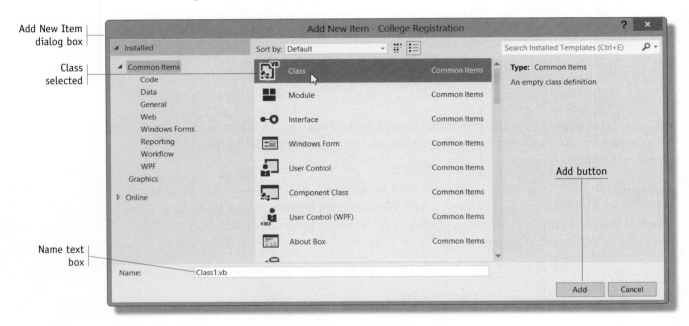

FIGURE 11-14

STEP 3   In the Name text box, type `Student` as the name of the class and then tap or click the Add button.

Visual Studio creates a new class called Student (Figure 11-15). The class is identified in the Solution Explorer window. The code window is opened for the class.

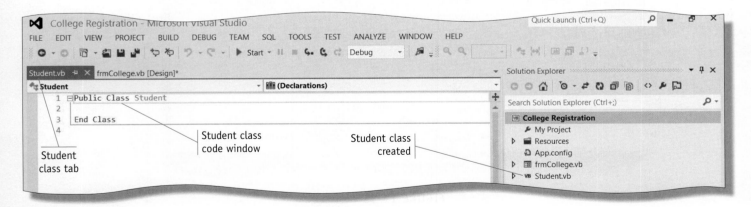

FIGURE 11-15

STEP 4   Using the same techniques, create the OnCampusStudent class and the StudentCostsFile class.

The Solution Explorer window now shows the four classes for the program: OnCampusStudent, frmCollege, Student, and StudentCostsFile (Figure 11-16). To select a class and display its code window, double-tap or double-click the class name in the Solution Explorer.

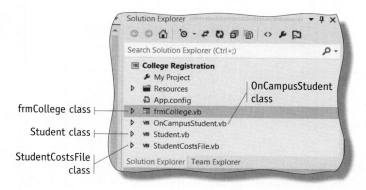

frmCollege class

OnCampusStudent class

Student class

StudentCostsFile class

FIGURE 11-16

ONLINE REINFORCEMENT

To view a video of the process in the previous steps, visit CengageBrain.com and navigate to the resources for this title. Tap or click the link for Chapter 11 and then navigate to Video 11-3.

Code Classes

After the classes have been defined, you must write the code for each class. You can write code for each class using the same techniques you have used for previous programs. Before beginning, however, you must consider how classes communicate so you can write the correct code.

Instantiate a Class and Class Communication

As you have learned, the code in a class acts as a template for an object. For example, when you drag the Button .NET component from the Toolbox to the Windows Form object, the Button object is created, or instantiated, based on the code in the Button class. Properties of the Button object, such as the text shown in the button, are processed using the code in the Button class.

Similarly, whenever you define a class in your Visual Basic program, you must instantiate an object based on that class in order for the processing within the object to take place. To instantiate an object, you can use the New statement, as shown in Figure 11-17.

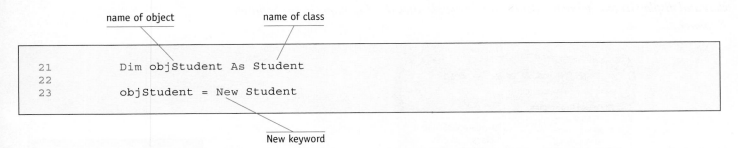

```
name of object            name of class

21        Dim objStudent As Student
22
23        objStudent = New Student
```

New keyword

FIGURE 11-17

In Figure 11-17, the Dim statement on line 21 specifies a variable named objStudent that will contain the address of the Student object when it is created. The name of the class from which the object will be instantiated (Student) must follow the As keyword. As you have learned previously, an object name begins with the prefix obj.

The assignment statement on line 23 creates the new object from the Student class and places the address of the object in the variable called objStudent. The keyword New must follow the equal sign, followed by the name of the class. Once the object is created, public procedures, public variables or attributes, and properties of the object can be referenced by other objects within the project.

A single statement also can be used to create an object, as shown in Figure 11-18.

```
25        Dim objStudent As New Student
```

FIGURE 11-18

The Dim statement on line 25 in Figure 11-18 both creates a variable to hold the address of the object (objStudent) and instantiates the object by using the keyword New followed by the name of the class.

The technique shown in Figure 11-17 is more widely used because the variable can be defined in the variables section of the code and the object is not instantiated until it is needed.

Constructors in New Instantiated Classes

When a class is instantiated into an object using the New keyword, a special procedure called a constructor is executed in the class. The **constructor** prepares the object for use in the program. The code in the constructor executes before any other code in the object. In addition to processes that are automatically completed by the constructor, the user can choose to write code for the constructor as well.

If the developer writes no code for a class constructor, Visual Basic automatically generates any processing that must be accomplished to prepare the object for use. The developer can include a constructor with no executing code, as shown in Figure 11-19.

```
 1  Public Class Student
 2
 3      Sub New()
 4          'Constructor for Student class
 5
 6          'If required, initializing statements go here
 7
 8      End Sub
 9
10  End Class
```

FIGURE 11-19

Note in Figure 11-19 that the constructor begins with the statement Sub New(). No name is required for the constructor — the New keyword identifies the Sub procedure as the constructor.

Because the code in the constructor executes before any other code in the object, it is a good location to place initializing code statements that prepare the object for execution.

Pass Arguments When Instantiating an Object

When you instantiate an object, data often must be passed to the object. For example, in the College Registration Costs program, the user enters the Student ID, Student Name, and other data into the user interface form. The Student object requires this data in order to calculate the registration costs and cause the StudentCostsFile object to write the required text file. If an object requires data when it is instantiated, the data can be passed as part of the instantiation code. For example, to pass the Student ID, the Student Name, the Major, and the Number of Units from the Form object to the Student object when the Student object is instantiated in the Form object, the statement in Figure 11-20 can be used.

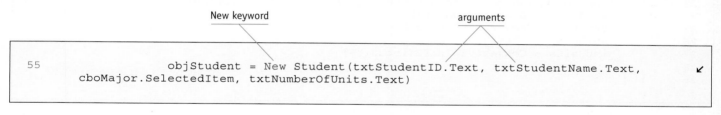

```
                      New keyword                              arguments

55                    objStudent = New Student(txtStudentID.Text, txtStudentName.Text,      ↙
              cboMajor.SelectedItem, txtNumberOfUnits.Text)
```

FIGURE 11-20

In Figure 11-20 on the previous page, the assignment statement that is specified in the Form class uses the New keyword in a manner similar to that shown in Figure 11-17 on page 772, except that arguments are included within the parentheses following the New keyword. Notice that the format of the arguments for the New statement is identical to the format used when passing arguments to a procedure, as you saw in Chapter 8. In Figure 11-20, the values in the txtStudentID Text property, the txtStudentName Text property, the cboMajor.SelectedItem property, and the txtNumberOfUnits Text property are passed to the instantiated object.

In the Student class, the New statement must be written with corresponding arguments; that is, the "signature" of the instantiating statement (Figure 11-20) must be the same as the constructor heading in the class. The New statement for the Student class is shown in Figure 11-21.

```
12    Sub New(ByVal strStudentID As String, ByVal strStudentName As String, ByVal         ⤦
      strMajor As String, ByVal intUnits As String)
```

FIGURE 11-21

Note in Figure 11-21 that the arguments for the New statement in the Student class match up to the arguments in the instantiation statement in Figure 11-20. The arguments are passed ByVal, which you recall means a copy of the value is passed to the instantiated object but the original value is not used.

Once the object is instantiated and the arguments are passed, the constructor can use the values in the arguments to set the values in variables within the class. The code in Figure 11-22 illustrates the assignment statements in the constructor to set the value of the variables defined in the Student class to the values passed from the calling object by the statement in Figure 11-21.

```
12    'Class variables                                                                    ⤦
13    Private _strStudentID As String
14    Private _strStudentName As String
15    Private _strMajor As String
16    Private _intUnits As Integer
17
18    Sub New(ByVal strStudentID As String, ByVal strStudentName As String, _
19            ByVal strMajor As String, ByVal intUnits As String)
20        ' This subprocedure is a constructor for the Student class. It is
21        ' called when the object is instantiated with arguments
22
23        'The following code assigns the arguments to class variables
24        _strStudentID = strStudentID
25        _strStudentName = strStudentName
26        _strMajor = strMajor
27        _intUnits = Convert.ToInt32(intUnits)
28
29    End Sub
```

FIGURE 11-22

In the constructor shown in Figure 11-22, the assignment statements on lines 24 through 27 place the values passed from the instantiation statement into the variables defined in the Student class (lines 13 through 16). When the object based on the Student class is instantiated, the constructor code ensures that the variables in the object contain data entered by the user.

Notice that the variables in the Student class are defined with Private access. Generally, when using multiple classes within a program, variables (also called attributes) should not be available to code within other classes of the program. Classes can reference attributes within another class only if the class that contains the attributes allows it. You will learn techniques for such access later in this chapter, but attributes should usually be defined with Private access.

Call a Procedure in a Separate Class

Most of the time, separate classes in a program contain procedures that must be executed. For example, in the College Registration Costs program, the Student class must contain a procedure that calculates the registration costs. This procedure is shown in Figure 11-23.

```
16      Private _intUnits As Integer
17      Private _decCost As Decimal
18      Private _decCostPerUnit As Decimal = 450D
 .
 .
 .
35      Function ComputeCosts() As Decimal
36          ' This function computes the registration costs, and
37          ' returns the registration costs
38
39          _decCost = _intUnits * _decCostPerUnit
40
41          Return _decCost
42
43      End Function
```

FIGURE 11-23

In Figure 11-23, the ComputeCosts function in the Student class multiplies the number of units (_intUnits) times the cost per unit (_decCostPerUnit) to determine the cost (_decCost). The cost then is returned as a decimal value to the calling class by the Return statement on line 41.

You might ask why the statement on line 39 cannot be included in the Form class that calls the Student class instead of calling the ComputeCosts function in the Student class. The short answer is that it could be. However, when designing larger and more robust programs, it is important to keep the tasks of each class separate.

In this case, the presentation tier of the three-tiered structure, represented by the Form object, should have no knowledge of how student registration costs are calculated. In the sample program of this chapter, the calculation is a simple multiplication statement. In the future, the calculation of registration costs might involve multiple lookups in a database, complex calculations based on major, in-state or out-of-state residence, and so on. The presentation class(es) should have nothing to do with these processes; the Student class should be the class in the program that knows how to perform all student activities. Therefore, even when the calculation is simple, as in the sample program, these tasks should be contained within the correct class.

To call the ComputeCosts procedure in the Student object, a statement in the Form object must identify both the object and the procedure within the object. The statement on lines 75–76 calls the ComputeCosts procedure, as shown in Figure 11-24.

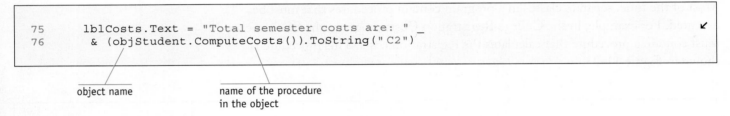

```
75      lblCosts.Text = "Total semester costs are: " _
76        & (objStudent.ComputeCosts()).ToString("C2")
```

object name   name of the procedure
                     in the object

FIGURE 11-24

On line 76 in Figure 11-24, the statement objStudent.ComputeCosts() identifies the objStudent object from Figure 11-17 on page 772 and the ComputeCosts procedure from Figure 11-23 on the previous page, separated by the dot operator (.). The statement says, "Pass control to the ComputeCosts procedure found in the objStudent object." The ComputeCosts procedure is a Function procedure, and the value returned from the procedure call is converted to a string and then assigned to the Text property of the lblCosts Label object so it can be displayed in the Windows Form object (see Figure 11-2 on page 760).

In this section, you have seen the entire process for creating a class, instantiating a class, and calling a procedure in a class. This process is fundamental when designing larger and more robust programs.

Inheritance

In the College Registration Costs program, the Student object contains student information from the Form object and performs calculations for the student. A student living on campus is a specialized student whose costs include housing and board. Therefore, the cost calculation for the on-campus student is different from that for an off-campus student. In addition, the On-Campus Student object must include Boolean indicators for the type of housing selected.

If the student lives off campus, a Student object will be instantiated, and if the student lives on campus, an On-Campus Student object will be instantiated. Because the Student and On-Campus Student objects contain some different attributes and their cost calculations are different, logically they could be separate objects. Visual Basic and other object-oriented programming languages offer an alternative, however. This alternative is inheritance.

Inheritance allows one class to inherit attributes and procedures from another class. For example, the Student object contains the Student ID, the Student Name, the Major, and the Number of Units. These same values are required for the on-campus student. In addition, the On-Campus Student object contains indicators for the housing selected. By using inheritance, the attributes of the Student object can be used by the On-Campus Student object as well. Inheritance is the ability to use all of the functionality of an existing class and extend those capabilities without rewriting the class (Figure 11-25).

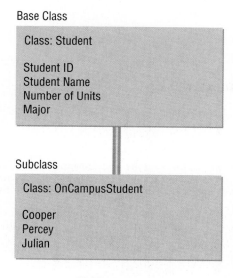

Base Class

Subclass

FIGURE 11-25
© 2014 Cengage Learning

In Figure 11-25, the Student class contains the Student ID, Student Name, Number of Units, and Major attributes. Because the OnCampusStudent class inherits from the Student class, the OnCampusStudent class can reference the Student ID variable in the Student class as if that variable were defined in the OnCampusStudent class. This is true of the other Student class variables as well. As you can see, the OnCampusStudent class inherits the attributes it can use from the Student class, and then defines the unique attributes it requires as well.

In the example in Figure 11-25, the Student class is called the **base class**. The OnCampusStudent class is called the **subclass**. The subclass can use attributes from the base class as if those attributes were defined in the subclass.

The code for the attributes in the Student base class and the OnCampusStudent subclass is shown in Figure 11-26.

```
 1 ' Class:         Student
 2 ' Developer:     Corinne Hoisington
 3 ' Date:          August 29, 2015
 4 ' Purpose:       This business class for a registering college student
 5 '                calculates the semester costs for tuition. It also causes the
 6 '                student costs file to be written.
 7
 8 Option Strict On
 9
10 Public Class Student
11
12     'Class variables
13     Protected _strStudentID As String
14     Protected _strStudentName As String
15     Protected _strMajor As String
16     Protected _intUnits As Integer
17     Protected _decCost As Decimal
18     Protected _decCostPerUnit As Decimal = 450D
19
20     Dim objStudentCostsFile As StudentCostsFile
```

FIGURE 11-26a

```
 1 ' Class:         OnCampusStudent
 2 ' Developer:     Corinne Hoisington
 3 ' Date:          August 29, 2015
 4 ' Purpose:       This business class for registering an on-campus college
 5 '                student calculates the semester costs, including tuition
 6 '                and housing. It also causes the student costs file to be written.
 7
 8 Option Strict On
 9
10 Public Class OnCampusStudent
11     Inherits Student
12
13     ' Class variables
14     Private _Cooper As Boolean
15     Private _Percey As Boolean
16     Private _Julian As Boolean
17
18     Dim objStudentCostsFile As StudentCostsFile
```

FIGURE 11-26b

After the usual comment statements for the Student class, the variables required for the Student class are declared. You can see that the string variables for Student ID, Student Name, and Major are declared, together with an integer variable for the Number of Units. In addition, the _decCost Decimal variable will contain the result of the calculation, and _decCostPerUnit is a Decimal variable that contains the fixed cost per unit (450D) used in the calculation for semester costs.

Note that the variables in the Student class are declared with Protected access. Protected means statements in the subclasses of the base class can reference the variable as if the referencing statement were declared in the base class instead of the subclass. Statements outside the base class and the subclasses, however, cannot reference the variables.

In the OnCampusStudent subclass, the Class statement on line 10 includes the Inherits entry on line 11. This required entry indicates that the OnCampusStudent class inherits from the Student class. Any subclass must include the Inherits entry to indicate the class from which it inherits.

The three Boolean variables required in the subclass are declared, but no declarations are made for Student ID, Student Name, or the other variables declared in the Student base class. These variables can be used as if they are part of the OnCampusStudent subclass.

Why should I use inheritance?

• Inheritance provides a clear model structure that is easy to understand without much complexity.

• Inheritance enables you to create new classes that reuse, extend, and modify the behavior defined in other classes.

• Using inheritance manages code by dividing it into parent and child classes.

CONSIDER THIS

Constructors

Both the base class and the subclass must have constructors. The code for the base class constructor and the subclass constructor is shown in Figure 11-27 and Figure 11-28.

BASE CLASS CONSTRUCTOR

```
22      Sub New(ByVal strStudentID As String, ByVal strStudentName As String, _
23           ByVal strMajor As String, ByVal intUnits As String)
24          ' This subprocedure is a constructor for the Student class. It is
25          ' called when the object is instantiated with arguments
26
27          'The following code assigns the arguments to class variables
28          _strStudentID = strStudentID
29          _strStudentName = strStudentName
30          _strMajor = strMajor
31          _intUnits = Convert.ToInt32(intUnits)
32
33      End Sub
```

FIGURE 11-27

SUBCLASS CONSTRUCTOR

```
20      Sub New(ByVal StudentID As String, ByVal StudentName As String, _
21           ByVal Major As String, ByVal Units As String, _
22           ByVal Cooper As Boolean, ByVal Percey As Boolean, _
23           ByVal Julian As Boolean)
24          ' This subprocedure is a constructor for the Student class. It is called when
25          ' instantiated with arguments
26
27          MyBase.New(StudentID, StudentName, Major, Units)
28
29          'The following code assigns the arguments to class variables
30          _Cooper = Cooper
31          _Percey = Percey
32          _Julian = Julian
33
34      End Sub
```

FIGURE 11-28

In the constructor for the Student base class, the Student ID, Student Name, Major, and Number of Units are passed when the object is instantiated. The constructor places the Student ID, Student Name, and Major in string variables, and converts the Number of Units to an integer.

In the constructor for the OnCampusStudent subclass, the Student ID, Student Name, Major, Number of Units, and the Boolean indicators for Cooper, Percey, and Julian are passed by the instantiating statement. The required first statement in the subclass constructor is the MyBase.New statement (line 27 in Figure 11-28 on the previous page). This statement calls the code in the base class (Student) constructor and executes it. Therefore, when the subclass is instantiated, both the base class and subclass constructors are executed.

In Figure 11-28, after the base class constructor is executed, the OnCampusStudent constructor places the Boolean indicators in variables so they can be tested in the class processing.

Again, it should be emphasized that the Student ID, Student Name, Major, and Number of Units variables are available to the OnCampusStudent subclass even though these variables are not declared within the class. They are available because of inheritance.

Inheritance and Procedures

When using inheritance, the subclass can use the procedures within the base class as well as its variables. Between the base class and the subclass, five different techniques can be used for referencing and calling a procedure from an outside class such as a Form class. After the base class and the subclass have been instantiated, the following techniques are available:

Base Class:

1. Call a named procedure in the base class.
    Example: `objBaseClass.RegularBaseClassFunction()`

2. Call an Overridable procedure in the base class.
    Example: `objBaseClass.OverridableBaseClassFunction()`

Subclass:

1. Call an Overridable procedure in the subclass.
    Example: `objSubClass.OverridableBaseClassFunction()`

2. Call a named procedure in the subclass.
    Example: `objSubClass.RegularSubClassFunction()`

3. Call a base class procedure in the subclass.
    Example: `objSubClass.RegularBaseClassFunction()`

Each of these methods is explained in the following sections.

Call a Named Procedure in the Base Class

A Sub procedure or a Function procedure in the base class can be called from another class in the manner you have seen previously. Thus, if a base class contains a Function procedure called RegularBaseClassFunction, another class can call the function using the statement objBaseClass.RegularBaseClassFunction(), where objBaseClass is the instantiated base class object and RegularBaseClassFunction is the name of the Function procedure.

An example of the code for this process is shown in Figure 11-29.

FORM CLASS

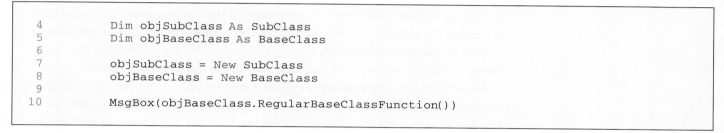

```
4          Dim objSubClass As SubClass
5          Dim objBaseClass As BaseClass
6
7          objSubClass = New SubClass
8          objBaseClass = New BaseClass
9
10         MsgBox(objBaseClass.RegularBaseClassFunction())
```

FIGURE 11-29a

BASE CLASS

```
3      Function RegularBaseClassFunction() As String
4          Return "Regular base class function"
5      End Function
```

FIGURE 11-29b

FIGURE 11-29c

In Figure 11-29a on the previous page, the objBaseClass object is instantiated on line 8 of the Form class. The statement on line 10 in Figure 11-29a calls the RegularBaseClassFunction in the objBaseClass object. When the function returns the text value, the value is displayed in the message box in Figure 11-29c. The process shown in Figure 11-29 is the normal process for calling a procedure in another class.

Call an Overridable Procedure in a Base Class

When a procedure is written in the base class, the procedure will perform its assigned processing. Sometimes, the subclass might require basically the same task to be completed, but with some differences in how it is accomplished. For example, in the College Registration Costs sample program, the Student base class procedure determines the costs by multiplying the number of units times the cost per unit. In the OnCampusStudent subclass, the costs are calculated by multiplying the number of units times the cost per unit and then adding the housing/board costs.

Even though the process accomplishes the same task of computing costs, the calculations are different. When a task is accomplished in a different manner in a base class than in a subclass, the procedure can have the same name in both the base class and the subclass, but if the procedure in the subclass is called, it overrides the procedure in the base class. If the procedure in the base class is called, it is executed as a normal procedure call, as shown in Figure 11-30.

FORM CLASS

```
4          Dim objSubClass  As SubClass
5          Dim objBaseClass  As BaseClass
6
7          objSubClass  = New SubClass
8          objBaseClass  = New BaseClass
9
10         MsgBox(objBaseClass .OverridableBaseClassFunction ())
```

FIGURE 11-30a

BASE CLASS

```
7      Overridable Function OverridableBaseClassFunction() As String
8          Return "Overridable base class function"
9      End Function
```

FIGURE 11-30b

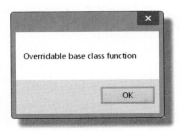

FIGURE 11-30c

Notice in Figure 11-30b that the keyword Overridable precedes the Function keyword. Overridable means a subclass can contain a procedure with the same procedure name as that in the base class. If the procedure in the subclass is called (in other words, SubClassName.ProcedureName), then it is executed even though it has the same name as the procedure in the base class. In Figure 11-30a, however, the procedure named OverridableBaseClassFunction in the base class is called from the Form class, so that procedure is executed.

Call an Overridable Procedure in a Subclass

In Figure 11-31, a call is made to the OverridableBaseClassFunction that is defined in the subclass. Notice in Figure 11-31c that the Function name in the subclass is preceded by the Overrides keyword, which indicates the function in the base class will be overridden by the function in the subclass when the latter function is called.

FORM CLASS

```
4        Dim objSubClass As SubClass
5        Dim objBaseClass As BaseClass
6
7        objSubClass = New SubClass
8        objBaseClass = New BaseClass
9
10       MsgBox(objSubClass.OverridableBaseClassFunction())
```

FIGURE 11-31a

BASE CLASS

```
7    Overridable Function OverridableBaseClassFunction() As String
8        Return "Overridable base class function"
9    End Function
```

FIGURE 11-31b

SUBCLASS

```
8    Overrides Function OverridableBaseClassFunction() As String
9        Return "Overrode the base class overridable function"
10   End Function
```

FIGURE 11-31c

FIGURE 11-31d

In Figure 11-31b on the previous page, the function defined on line 7 of the base class is called OverridableBaseClassFunction, and the name is preceded by the Overridable keyword. In Figure 11-31c, the function with the same name on line 8 of the subclass overrides the function in the base class. As a result, when the subclass function is called (line 10 of the Form class in Figure 11-31a), the subclass message appears in the message box.

Call a Named Procedure in the Subclass

As with any other public procedure in a class, a named procedure in a subclass can be called (Figure 11-32).

FORM CLASS

```
4        Dim objSubClass As SubClass
5        Dim objBaseClass As BaseClass
6
7        objSubClass = New SubClass
8        objBaseClass = New BaseClass
9
10       MsgBox(objSubClass.RegularSubClassFunction())
```

FIGURE 11-32a

SUBCLASS

```
4    Function RegularSubClassFunction() As String
5        Return "Regular subclass function"
6    End Function
```

FIGURE 11-32b

FIGURE 11-32c

The example in Figure 11-32 is a straightforward procedure call to a procedure in another class.

Call a Base Class Procedure in the Subclass

The last common procedure call involving inheritance occurs when a procedure in the base class is called by referencing the subclass, as shown in Figure 11-33.

FORM CLASS

```
4          Dim objSubClass As SubClass
5          Dim objBaseClass As BaseClass
6
7          objSubClass = New SubClass
8          objBaseClass = New BaseClass
9
10         MsgBox(objSubClass.RegularBaseClassFunction())
```

FIGURE 11-33a

BASE CLASS

```
3      Function RegularBaseClassFunction() As String
4          Return "Regular base class function"
5      End Function
```

FIGURE 11-33b

FIGURE 11-33c

In Figure 11-33 on the previous page, the procedure call statement in the Form class (line 10 in Figure 11-33a) calls a procedure that is not even in the subclass. Nonetheless, the regular base class function is executed because when a procedure is called that is not in the class specified in the call statement, Visual Basic will move up to the base class to see if the procedure is located there. If so, the procedure in the base class is executed.

Inheritance can be a relatively complex subject that has more ramifications than you have learned in this chapter. Nonetheless, this beginning knowledge of inheritance will serve you well as you continue your education in programming and development.

Persistence Classes

As you learned earlier in this chapter, the persistence tier in an application is sometimes called the data access tier. It contains classes that are involved in saving and retrieving data stored on a permanent storage medium such as a hard disk or a USB drive. A typical persistence class is the StudentCostsFile class in the College Registration Costs sample program in this chapter. This class is concerned with performing all tasks required for the Student Costs file. In the sample program, this processing consists of writing the file as a text file and saving it on a USB drive. Other processing might be required for this file in the future, including the retrieval of the text file or converting the text file into a database file. Generally, any required processing of the Student Costs file should be carried out by the StudentCostsFile class.

To define the StudentCostsFile class, you must write comments, variables, and a constructor, as you have seen earlier in this chapter. The code to define the StudentCostsFile class is shown in Figure 11-34.

```
 1  ' Class:        Student Costs File
 2  ' Developer:    Corinne Hoisington
 3  ' Date:         August 29, 2015
 4  ' Purpose:      This class represents the Student Costs File. The WriteRecord
 5  '               procedure writes a comma-delimited student costs file that
 6  '               contains the Student ID, Student Name, Major,
 7  '               and Student Costs.
 8
 9 Option Strict On
10
11 Public Class StudentCostsFile
12
13
14     ' Class variables
15     Private _strStudentID As String
16     Private _strStudentName As String
17     Private _strMajor As String
18     Private _decStudentCosts As Decimal
19
20     Sub New(ByVal StudentID As String, ByVal StudentName As String, _
21             ByVal Major As String, ByVal Costs As Decimal)
22         ' This sub procedure is the constructor for the StudentCostsFile
23         ' class.
24
25         'The following code assigns the arguments to class variables
26         _strStudentID = StudentID
27         _strStudentName = StudentName
28         _strMajor = Major
29         _decStudentCosts = Costs
30
31     End Sub
```

FIGURE 11-34

In Figure 11-34, the typical comments are followed by the declaration of the variables used in the class. Notice that each of the variables is declared with Private access so they cannot be referenced by code in any other class within the program.

Following the variable declarations is the constructor procedure, as identified by the keyword New. Within the constructor, the code on lines 26–29 sets the values in the variables to the values passed to the StudentCostsFile class when it is instantiated.

Comma-Delimited Text Files

The Student Costs file is a comma-delimited text file, which means a comma separates each field in a record in the file, as shown in Figure 11-35.

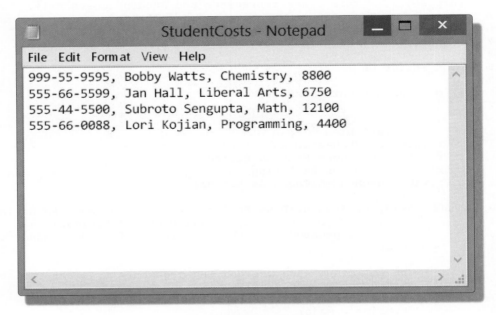

FIGURE 11-35

Notice in Figure 11-35 that a comma appears at the end of each field, but no comma is displayed at the end of the record. A comma-delimited text file is commonly used because it can be read into programs such as Microsoft Excel and Microsoft Access to import the data into the application.

In Chapter 8, you learned to use a StreamWriter to write a stream of text to a file. To create the file shown in Figure 11-35, a record that contains the Student ID, the Student Name, the Major, and the Costs must be added to the file each time new registration costs are calculated for a student. Because you do not know how many records will be placed in the file during the registration process, a StreamWriter must be created that can append, or add, records to the file. Because a record contains four fields, the first three of which are followed by a comma, a Write statement must be used so that a new line is not created in the file each time part of a record is written to the disk. The code to accomplish this processing is shown in the WriteRecord Sub procedure in Figure 11-36.

```
33      Sub WriteRecord()
34          ' This subprocedure opens the StudentCosts output text file and then
35          ' writes a record in the comma-delimited file
36
37          Dim strNameandLocationOfFile As String = "e:\StudentCosts.txt"
38
39          Try
40              Dim objWriter As IO.StreamWriter = _
41                  IO.File.AppendText(strNameandLocationOfFile)
42
43              objWriter.Write(_strStudentID & ",")
44              objWriter.Write(_strStudentName & ",")
45              objWriter.Write(_strMajor & ",")
46              objWriter.WriteLine(_decStudentCosts)
47              objWriter.Close()
48
49          Catch ex As Exception
50              MsgBox("No device available - program aborted", , "Error")
51              Application.Exit()
52
53          End Try
54
55      End Sub
```

FIGURE 11-36

In Figure 11-36, the Dim statement on line 37 declares a string that contains the name and location of the file to be written. A Try-Catch block is created on line 39 because if a USB drive is not located on drive E, an exception will be thrown. The Catch statement on line 49 catches the exception, displays a message box containing an error message, and exits the application.

Assuming no exception occurs, the Dim statement on lines 40–41 declares the objWriter as an IO.StreamWriter. The identification of the IO.StreamWriter indicates that the writer will append text to the file. Appending the text means writing the next record in the file following the last record in the file; that is, the records accumulate in the file as it is written.

The Write procedure calls on lines 43–45 write the Student ID, the Student Name, and the Major in the record, each followed by a comma. The WriteLine procedure call on line 46 writes the Student Costs in the record and places a line return in the file so the next record can be written. Finally, the Close procedure call on line 47 closes the file.

Program Design

As you have learned, the requirements document identifies the purpose of the program being developed, the application title, the procedures to be followed when using the program, any required equations and calculations, any conditions that must be tested, notes and restrictions that must be followed by the program, and any other comments that would be helpful to understanding the problem. The requirements document for the College Registration Costs application is shown in Figure 11-37.

REQUIREMENTS DOCUMENT

Date Submitted:	August 29, 2015
Application Title:	College Registration Costs
Purpose:	This Windows application allows a user to enter student registration information for Raven College and then calculates the student registration costs.
Program Procedures:	In a Windows application, the user enters the student ID, student name, and number of units (credits), selects an off-campus or on-campus resident status, selects housing and board if resident status is on-campus, and then selects a major. When the user clicks a button, the application calculates the semester costs and records the information in a log file.
Algorithms, Processing, and Conditions:	1. The user first enters the student ID, student name, and number of units.
	2. The user selects either off-campus residence or on-campus residence. If on-campus residence is selected, the user indicates the housing/board selection (Cooper Dorm, Percey Hall, or Julian Suites). The user then selects the student's major from a list.
	3. When the user clicks a button, the program calculates the semester costs and writes a log file.
	4. A Clear Form button should be available to clear the form and place the insertion point in the Student ID text box.
	5. The course cost is $450.00 per unit.

FIGURE 11-37 (continues)

6. The formula to calculate semester course costs is the number of units times the cost per unit.

7. If the student is an on-campus resident, the following housing/board costs must be added to the course costs: Cooper Dorm, $2,900.00 per semester; Percey Hall, $3,400.00 per semester; Julian Suites, $4,000.00 per semester.

8. The log file is a text file that contains the Student ID, the Student Name, the Major, and the semester costs. It should be a comma-delimited file.

Notes and Restrictions:

1. The student ID must be a complete Social Security number.

2. The student name cannot be left blank and must begin with an alphabetic character.

3. The number of units must be a numeric value of 1 through 24.

4. A major must be selected. The majors available are Biology, Business, Chemistry, Programming, Fine Arts, Liberal Arts, Mathematics, Physics, Sociology, and Theology.

5. The housing/board selections should not be displayed in the window unless the user selects the on-campus resident status.

6. When the user clicks the button to calculate costs and the program determines that an error occurred during data entry, a message box is displayed and the user must enter valid data before continuing.

7. Off-campus residency is the default selection; if a student is an on-campus resident, Cooper Dorm is the default selection.

Comments:

1. Obtain an image for this program from CengageBrain .com. The name of the picture is College.

2. The program should use a three-tier structure with presentation, business, and persistence classes.

FIGURE 11-37 (continued)

The Use Case Definition for the application is shown in Figure 11-38.

USE CASE DEFINITION

1. The user enters the student ID, the student name, and the number of units.
2. If necessary, the user selects off-campus or on-campus resident status using radio buttons. If on-campus residency is selected, the housing/board choices are displayed. If necessary, the user selects the housing/board choice.
3. The user selects a major from a list.
4. The user clicks the Calculate Costs button.
5. The program calculates and displays the semester costs, including the cost of housing/board if appropriate.
6. The program writes a log of the student registration costs.
7. If necessary, the user clicks the Clear Form button to clear the form of data and place the insertion point in the Student ID text box.

FIGURE 11-38

© 2014 Cengage Learning

Design the Program Processing Objects

You will recall that an event planning document is a table that specifies which objects in the user interface will cause events, the action taken by the user to trigger each event, and the event processing that must occur. In addition, an event planning document is required for each object in the program that is called from another object. The event planning documents for the College Registration Costs program are shown in Figure 11-39 through Figure 11-42 on page 795.

EVENT PLANNING DOCUMENT

Program Name: College Registration Costs	Developer: Corinne Hoisington	Object: frmCollege	Date: August 29, 2015
OBJECT	**EVENT TRIGGER**	**EVENT PROCESSING**	

btnCalculateCosts	Tap or click	Declare Student object
		Declare OnCampusStudent object
		Declare Boolean Input Error indicator
		If student ID mask is not full
		    Display message box with error message
		    Clear student ID masked text box
		    Place focus on student ID masked text box	

FIGURE 11-39 (continues)

OBJECT	EVENT TRIGGER	EVENT PROCESSING

		Set input error indicator to true
		Else If student name text length < 1 or first character in text box less than "A"
		  Display message box with error message
		  Clear student name text box
		  Place focus on student name text box
		  Set input error indicator to true
		Else If number of units is not numeric
		  Display message box with error message
		  Clear number of units text box
		  Place focus on number of units text box
		  Set input error indicator to true
		Else If number of units is not 1-24
		  Display message box with error message
		  Clear number of units text box
		  Place focus on number of units text box
		  Set input error indicator to true
		Else If major selected index < 0
		  Display message box with error message
		  Place focus on major combo box
		  Set input error indicator to true
		End If
		If no input error
		  If off-campus radio button checked
		    Instantiate student object with arguments
		    Set costs label visible property to true
		    Call student compute costs procedure
		    Display student costs
		  Else
		    Instantiate on-campus student object with arguments
		    Set costs label visible property to true
		    Call on-campus student compute costs procedure
		    Display student costs
		End If

FIGURE 11-39 (continues)

OBJECT	EVENT TRIGGER	EVENT PROCESSING
radOnCampus Radio Button	Selected	Make housing/board group visible
radOffCampus Radio Button	Selected	Make housing/board group not visible
btnClearForm	Tap or click	Clear student ID masked text box Clear student name text box Clear number of units text box Set major combo box selected index to −1 Set major combo box text property to "Select a Major" Set off-campus radio button checked property to true Set Cooper radio button checked property to true Set housing/board group visible property to false Set costs label visible property to false Place focus on student ID masked text box

FIGURE 11-39 (continued)

EVENT PLANNING DOCUMENT

Program Name: College Registration Costs	Developer: Corinne Hoisington	Object: objStudent (Student class)	Date: August 29, 2015
OBJECT	**EVENT TRIGGER**	**EVENT PROCESSING**	
New (student id, student name, major, units)	Class constructor	Set student ID equal to passed student ID Set student name equal to passed student name Set major equal to passed major Convert number of units passed to Integer	
ComputeCosts	Function procedure call	Cost = units * cost per unit Instantiate WriteStudentRecord object Write the student record Return the cost	

FIGURE 11-40

EVENT PLANNING DOCUMENT

Program Name: College Registration Costs	Developer: Corinne Hoisington	Object: objOnCampusStudent (OnCampusStudent class)	Date: August 29, 2015
OBJECT	**EVENT TRIGGER**	**EVENT PROCESSING**	
New(student ID, student name, major, units, Cooper Boolean, Percey Boolean, Julian Boolean)	Class constructor	Call base class constructor (student ID, student name, major, units) Set Cooper Boolean to passed Cooper Boolean Set Percey Boolean to passed Percey Boolean Set Julian Boolean to passed Julian Boolean	

ComputeCosts	Function procedure call	If Cooper housing
		    Set housing cost = Cooper cost
		Else If Percey housing
		    Set housing cost = Percey cost
		Else If Julian housing
		    Set housing cost = Julian cost
		End If
		Cost = (units * cost per unit) + housing cost
		Instantiate objStudentCostsFile object
		Write the student record
		Return the cost	

FIGURE 11-41

EVENT PLANNING DOCUMENT

Program Name: College Registration Costs	Developer: Corinne Hoisington	Object: objStudentCostsFile (StudentCostsFile class)	Date: August 29, 2015
OBJECT	**EVENT TRIGGER**	**EVENT PROCESSING**	
New(student ID, student name, major, costs)	Class constructor	Set student ID equal to passed student ID Set student name equal to passed student name Set major equal to passed major Set costs equal to passed costs	
WriteRecord	Function procedure call	Define stream writer for append text file Write student ID with comma Write student name with comma Write major with comma Write costs with line return Close text file	

FIGURE 11-42

Guided Program Development

To design the user interface for the College Registration Costs application and enter the code required to process each event in the program, complete the steps in this section.

Phase 1: Design the Form

1

- **Create a New Windows Project** Open Visual Studio and then close the Start page. Tap or click the New Project button on the Standard toolbar. Begin a Windows Forms Application project and name the project `CollegeRegistrationCosts`.

- **Name the Form Object** Select the Form object. Change the (Name) property of the Form object to `frmCollege`.

- **Assign a Title to the Form Object** With the frmCollege object selected, change the Text property to `College Registration Costs`.

- **Change the Form Class Name** In the Solution Explorer window, press and hold or right-click Form1.vb, select Rename on the shortcut menu, and change the class name to `frmCollege.vb`.

(continues)

● **Create the User Interface** Using the skills you have acquired in this course and referencing the requirements document in Figure 11-37 on pages 790-791, create the user interface for the frmCollege object, as shown in Figure 11-43. The heading is Tahoma font, bold, 24 points. All other fonts are Tahoma, regular, 12 points.

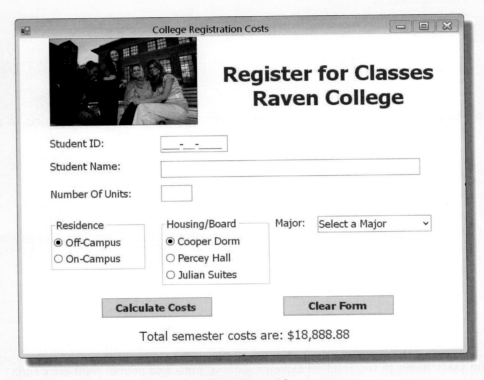

FIGURE 11-43

© Purestock/Getty Images

Phase 2: Code the Application

2

● **Open the Calculate Costs Button Event Handler** On the Windows Form object in the Design window, double-tap or double-click the Calculate Costs Button object.

● **Enter Comments and Option Strict On** Enter the common comments for the frmCollege class. Include the Option Strict On statement.

```
                                          HINT
1  ' Program:      College Registration Costs
2  ' Developer:    Corinne Hoisington
3  ' Date:         August 29, 2015
4  ' Purpose:      This program calculates the registration costs for a college
5  '               student. It also records the costs in a text file.
6
7  Option Strict On
8
9  Public Class frmCollege
```

● **Enter Comments and Define the Variables for the Calculate Costs Button Event Handler** Below the event handler introductory code, write the comments and then define the variables required for the button event handler. The variables include the two object variables for the Student and OnCampusStudent objects and the Boolean input error indicator *(ref: Figure 11-17)*.

```
                                          HINT
11  Private Sub btnCalculateCosts_Click(ByVal sender As System.Object, ByVal e As System.EventArgs) Handles btnCalculateCosts.Click
12      ' This Calculate Costs button click event handler edits the
13      ' registration(costs) form to ensure it contains valid data.
14      ' Then, after passing control to the business class, it displays the cost.
15
16      Dim objStudent As Student
17      Dim objOnCampusStudent As OnCampusStudent
18      Dim InputError As Boolean = False
```

● **Enter the If...ElseIf Statement to Check the Input Data** Enter the code to check the input data, as documented in the program requirements document *(ref: Figure 11-7)*.

	HINT
20	`' Is student ID entered properly`
21	`If txtStudentID.MaskFull = False Then`
22	`    MsgBox("Enter your Student ID in the Student ID box", , _`
23	`        "Error")`
24	`    txtStudentID.Clear()`
25	`    txtStudentID.Focus()`
26	`    InputError = True`
27	`    ' Is student name entered properly`
28	`ElseIf txtStudentName.TextLength < 1 Or _`
29	`        txtStudentName.Text < "A" Then`
30	`    MsgBox("Enter your name in the Student Name box", , "Error")`
31	`    txtStudentName.Clear()`
32	`    txtStudentName.Focus()`
33	`    InputError = True`
34	`    ' Is number of units entered properly`
35	`ElseIf Not IsNumeric(txtNumberOfUnits.Text) Then`
36	`    MsgBox("Enter the units in the Number of Units box", , _`
37	`        "Error")`
38	`    txtNumberOfUnits.Clear()`
39	`    txtNumberOfUnits.Focus()`
40	`    InputError = True`
41	`    ' Has 1-24 units been entered`
42	`ElseIf Convert.ToInt32(txtNumberOfUnits.Text) < 1 _`
43	`        Or Convert.ToInt32(txtNumberOfUnits.Text) > 24 Then`
44	`    MsgBox("Units must be 1 - 24", , "Error")`
45	`    txtNumberOfUnits.Clear()`
46	`    txtNumberOfUnits.Focus()`
47	`    InputError = True`
48	`    ' Has a major been selected`
49	`ElseIf cboMajor.SelectedIndex < 0 Then`
50	`    MsgBox("Please select a major", , "Error")`
51	`    cboMajor.Focus()`
52	`    InputError = True`
53	`End If`

- **Enter the Code to Call the Appropriate Function Procedure in the Appropriate Object** If the input data is correct, enter the code to instantiate the Student class object or the OnCampusStudent class object and then call the ComputeCosts function in the appropriate object. Be sure to include the correct arguments for the New statement for each new object *(ref: Figure 11-20)*.

HINT

```
54          ' If no input error, process the registration costs
55        If Not InputError Then
56            If radOffCampus.Checked Then
57                objStudent = New Student(txtStudentID.Text, _
58                    txtStudentName.Text, Convert.ToString(cboMajor.SelectedItem), _
59                    txtNumberOfUnits.Text)
60                lblCosts.Visible = True
61                lblCosts.Text = "Total semester costs are: " _
62                    & (objStudent.ComputeCosts()).ToString("C2")
63            Else
64                objOnCampusStudent = New OnCampusStudent(txtStudentID.Text, _
65                    txtStudentName.Text, Convert.ToString(cboMajor.SelectedItem), _
66                    txtNumberOfUnits.Text, radCooperDorm.Checked, _
67                    radPerceyHall.Checked, radJulianSuites.Checked)
68                lblCosts.Visible = True
69                lblCosts.Text = "Total semester costs are: " _
70                    & (objOnCampusStudent.ComputeCosts()).ToString("C2")
71            End If
72        End If
73    End Sub
```

- **Write the Code for the Off-Campus Radio Button CheckedChanged Event** Write the code to hide the HousingBoard Group.

HINT

```
75    Private Sub radOffCampus_CheckedChanged(ByVal sender As System.Object, ByVal e As System.EventArgs) Handles radOffCampus.CheckedChar
76        ' This event handler is executed when the Off Campus radio
77        ' button is selected. It hides the Housing/Board radio buttons
78
79        grpHousingBoard.Visible = False
80
81    End Sub
```

- **Write the Code for the On-Campus Radio Button CheckedChanged Event** Write the code to make the HousingBoard Group visible.

HINT

```
83    Private Sub radOnCampus_CheckedChanged(ByVal sender As System.Object, ByVal e As System.EventArgs) Handles radOnCampus.CheckedChang
84        ' This event handler is executed when the On Campus radio button
85        ' is selected. It makes the Housing/Board radio buttons visible
86
87        grpHousingBoard.Visible = True
88
89    End Sub
```

(continues)

● **Write the Code for the Clear Form Button** Write the code to clear the form and place the focus on the Student ID text box, as defined in the event planning document (*ref: Figure 11-39*).

The frmCollege code is completed (Figure 11-44).

```
1  ⊟' Program:      College Registration Costs
2   ' Developer:    Corinne Hoisington
3   ' Date:         August 29, 2015
4   ' Purpose:      This program calculates the registration costs for a college
5   '               student. It also records the costs in a text file.
6
7   Option Strict On
8
9  ⊟Public Class frmCollege
10
11 ⊟    Private Sub btnCalculateCosts_Click(ByVal sender As System.Object, ByVal e As System.EventArgs) Handles btnCalculateCosts.Click
12          ' This Calculate Costs button click event handler edits the
13          ' registration(costs) form to ensure it contains valid data.
14          ' Then, after passing control to the business class, it displays the cost.
15
16          Dim objStudent As Student
17          Dim objOnCampusStudent As OnCampusStudent
18          Dim InputError As Boolean = False
19
20          ' Is student ID entered properly
21          If txtStudentID.MaskFull = False Then
22              MsgBox("Enter your Student ID in the Student ID box", , _
23                  "Error")
24              txtStudentID.Clear()
25              txtStudentID.Focus()
26              InputError = True
27              ' Is student name entered properly
28          ElseIf txtStudentName.TextLength < 1 Or _
29                  txtStudentName.Text < "A" Then
30              MsgBox("Enter your name in the Student Name box", , "Error")
31              txtStudentName.Clear()
32              txtStudentName.Focus()
33              InputError = True
34              ' Is number of units entered properly
35          ElseIf Not IsNumeric(txtNumberOfUnits.Text) Then
36              MsgBox("Enter the units in the Number of Units box", , _
37                  "Error")
38              txtNumberOfUnits.Clear()
39              txtNumberOfUnits.Focus()
40              InputError = True
41              ' Has 1-24 units been entered
42          ElseIf Convert.ToInt32(txtNumberOfUnits.Text) < 1 _
43                  Or Convert.ToInt32(txtNumberOfUnits.Text) > 24 Then
44              MsgBox("Units must be 1 - 24", , "Error")
45              txtNumberOfUnits.Clear()
46              txtNumberOfUnits.Focus()
47              InputError = True
48              ' Has a major been selected
49          ElseIf cboMajor.SelectedIndex < 0 Then
50              MsgBox("Please select a major", , "Error")
51              cboMajor.Focus()
52              InputError = True
53          End If
54          ' If no input error, process the registration costs
55          If Not InputError Then
56              If radOffCampus.Checked Then
```

FIGURE 11-44 (continues)

```vbnet
 57                     objStudent = New Student(txtStudentID.Text, _
 58                         txtStudentName.Text, Convert.ToString(cboMajor.SelectedItem), _
 59                         txtNumberOfUnits.Text)
 60                     lblCosts.Visible = True
 61                     lblCosts.Text = "Total semester costs are: " _
 62                         & (objStudent.ComputeCosts()).ToString("C2")
 63                 Else
 64                     objOnCampusStudent = New OnCampusStudent(txtStudentID.Text, _
 65                         txtStudentName.Text, Convert.ToString(cboMajor.SelectedItem), _
 66                         txtNumberOfUnits.Text, radCooperDorm.Checked, _
 67                         radPerceyHall.Checked, radJulianSuites.Checked)
 68                     lblCosts.Visible = True
 69                     lblCosts.Text = "Total semester costs are: " _
 70                         & (objOnCampusStudent.ComputeCosts()).ToString("C2")
 71                 End If
 72             End If
 73         End Sub
 74
 75   ⊟     Private Sub radOffCampus_CheckedChanged(ByVal sender As System.Object, ByVal e As System.EventArgs) Handles radOffCampus.CheckedChanged
 76             ' This event handler is executed when the Off Campus radio
 77             ' button is selected. It hides the Housing/Board radio buttons
 78
 79             grpHousingBoard.Visible = False
 80
 81         End Sub
 82
 83   ⊟     Private Sub radOnCampus_CheckedChanged(ByVal sender As System.Object, ByVal e As System.EventArgs) Handles radOnCampus.CheckedChanged
 84             ' This event handler is executed when the On Campus radio button
 85             ' is selected. It makes the Housing/Board radio buttons visible
 86
 87             grpHousingBoard.Visible = True
 88
 89         End Sub
 90
 91
 92   ⊟     Private Sub btnClearForm_Click(ByVal sender As System.Object, ByVal e As System.EventArgs) Handles btnClearForm.Click
 93             ' This event handler is executed when the user clicks the
 94             ' Clear Form button. It resets all objects on the user interface.
 95
 96             txtStudentID.Clear()
 97             txtStudentName.Clear()
 98             txtNumberOfUnits.Clear()
 99             cboMajor.SelectedIndex = -1
100             cboMajor.Text = "Select a Major"
101             radOffCampus.Checked = True
102             radCooperDorm.Checked = True
103             grpHousingBoard.Visible = False
104             lblCosts.Visible = False
105             txtStudentID.Focus()
106
107         End Sub
108     End Class
```

FIGURE 11-44 (continued)

(continues)

3

● **Create the Classes Required for the Remainder of the Program** Press and hold or right-click the name of the project (CollegeRegistrationCosts) in the Solution Explorer, point to Add on the shortcut menu, and then tap or click Class on the shortcut menu. Add the Student.vb class. Use the same technique to add the OnCampusStudent.vb class and the StudentCostsFile.vb class *(ref: Figure 11-13)*.

HINT

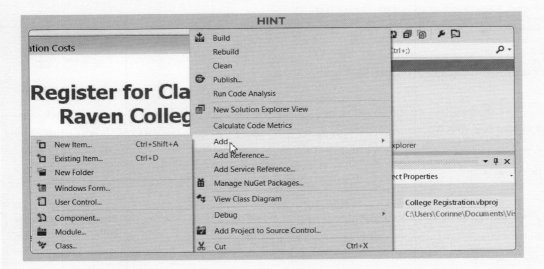

● **Enter Comments and Option Strict On for the Student Class** Display the Student class code window. Enter the common comments for the Student class. Include the Option Strict On statement.

HINT

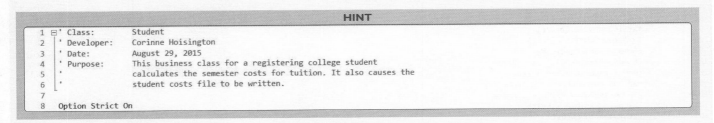

```
1  ⊟' Class:       Student
2   ' Developer:   Corinne Hoisington
3   ' Date:        August 29, 2015
4   ' Purpose:     This business class for a registering college student
5   '              calculates the semester costs for tuition. It also causes the
6   '              student costs file to be written.
7
8    Option Strict On
```

● **Define the Class Variables for the Student Class** Define the class variables for the Student class, including the declaration for the StudentCostsFile object. Remember that the variables should be declared with Protected access because they are used in the OnCampusStudent subclass.

HINT

```
12        'Class variables
13        Protected _strStudentID As String
14        Protected _strStudentName As String
15        Protected _strMajor As String
16        Protected _intUnits As Integer
17        Protected _decCost As Decimal
18        Protected _decCostPerUnit As Decimal = 450D
19
20        Dim objStudentCostsFile As StudentCostsFile
```

● **Write the Student Class Constructor** Write the code for the Student class constructor based on the requirements shown in the event planning document *(ref: Figure 11-21)*.

HINT

```
22    Sub New(ByVal strStudentID As String, ByVal strStudentName As String, _
23            ByVal strMajor As String, ByVal intUnits As String)
24        ' This subprocedure is a constructor for the Student class. It is
25        ' called when the object is instantiated with arguments
26
27        'The following code assigns the arguments to class variables
28        _strStudentID = strStudentID
29        _strStudentName = strStudentName
30        _strMajor = strMajor
31        _intUnits = Convert.ToInt32(intUnits)
32
33    End Sub
```

(continues)

● **Write the Code for the ComputeCosts Overridable Function Procedure** Write the code to calculate the cost, instantiate the object for the StudentCostsFile class, call the procedure to write the file, and return the cost.

HINT

```
35      Overridable Function ComputeCosts() As Decimal
36          ' This function computes the registration costs, writes a record
37          ' in the student costs file, and returns the registration costs
38
39          'Calculate cost
40          _decCost = _intUnits * _decCostPerUnit
41
42          'Write the student record
43          objStudentCostsFile = New StudentCostsFile(_strStudentID, _
44              _strStudentName, _strMajor, _decCost)
45          objStudentCostsFile.WriteRecord()
46
47          'Return the calculated cost
48          Return _decCost
49
50      End Function
51
52  End Class
```

The Student class code is completed (Figure 11-45).

```
1    ' Class:        Student
2    ' Developer:    Corinne Hoisington
3    ' Date:         August 29, 2015
4    ' Purpose:      This business class for a registering college student
5    '               calculates the semester costs for tuition. It also causes the
6    '               student costs file to be written.
7
8    Option Strict On
9
10   Public Class Student
11
12       'Class variables
13       Protected _strStudentID As String
14       Protected _strStudentName As String
15       Protected _strMajor As String
16       Protected _intUnits As Integer
17       Protected _decCost As Decimal
18       Protected _decCostPerUnit As Decimal = 450D
19
20       Dim objStudentCostsFile As StudentCostsFile
21
22       Sub New(ByVal strStudentID As String, ByVal strStudentName As String, _
23               ByVal strMajor As String, ByVal intUnits As String)
24           ' This subprocedure is a constructor for the Student class. It is
25           ' called when the object is instantiated with arguments
26
27           'The following code assigns the arguments to class variables
28           _strStudentID = strStudentID
29           _strStudentName = strStudentName
30           _strMajor = strMajor
31           _intUnits = Convert.ToInt32(intUnits)
32
33       End Sub
34
35       Overridable Function ComputeCosts() As Decimal
36           ' This function computes the registration costs, writes a record
37           ' in the student costs file, and returns the registration costs
38
39           'Calculate cost
40           _decCost = _intUnits * _decCostPerUnit
41
42           'Write the student record
43           objStudentCostsFile = New StudentCostsFile(_strStudentID, _
44               _strStudentName, _strMajor, _decCost)
45           objStudentCostsFile.WriteRecord()
46
47           'Return the calculated cost
48           Return _decCost
49
50       End Function
51
52   End Class
```

FIGURE 11-45

(continues)

4

● **Enter Comments and Option Strict On for the OnCampusStudent Class** Display the OnCampusStudent class code window. Enter the common comments for the OnCampusStudent class. Include the Option Strict On statement and the Inherits statement, which indicates that the OnCampusStudent class inherits from the Student class.

HINT

```
 1 ⊟' Class:        OnCampusStudent
 2  ' Developer:    Corinne Hoisington
 3  ' Date:         August 29, 2015
 4  ' Purpose:      This business class for a registering an on-campus college
 5  '               student calculates the semester costs, including tuition
 6  '               and housing. It also causes the student costs file to be written.
 7
 8  Option Strict On
 9
10 ⊟Public Class OnCampusStudent
11     Inherits Student
12
```

● **Define the Class Variables for the OnCampusStudent Class** Define the class variables for the OnCampusStudent class, including the declaration for the StudentCostsFile object. The variables should be declared with Private access.

HINT

```
13     ' Class variables
14     Private _Cooper As Boolean
15     Private _Percey As Boolean
16     Private _Julian As Boolean
17
18     Dim objStudentCostsFile As StudentCostsFile
```

● **Write the OnCampusStudent Class Constructor** Write the code for the OnCampusStudent class constructor based on the requirements shown in the event planning document *(ref: Figure 11-28)*.

HINT

```
19
20 ⊟   Sub New(ByVal StudentID As String, ByVal StudentName As String, _
21            ByVal Major As String, ByVal Units As String, _
22            ByVal Cooper As Boolean, ByVal Percey As Boolean, _
23            ByVal Julian As Boolean)
24       ' This subprocedure is a constructor for the Student class. It
25       ' is called when instantiated with arguments
26
27       MyBase.New(StudentID, StudentName, Major, Units)
28
29       'The following code assigns the arguments to class variables
30       _Cooper = Cooper
31       _Percey = Percey
32       _Julian = Julian
33
34     End Sub
```

● **Write the Code for the ComputeCosts Overriding Function Procedure** Write the code to define the variables, determine the housing/board cost, calculate the semester cost, instantiate the object for the StudentCostsFile class, call the procedure to write the file, and return the semester cost.

HINT

```
35
36          Overrides Function ComputeCosts() As Decimal
37              ' This function computes the registration costs, writes a record
38              ' in the student costs file, and returns the registration costs
39
40              'Define variables
41              Dim HousingCost As Decimal
42              Const cdecCooperHousingCost As Decimal = 2900D
43              Const cdecPerceyHousingCost As Decimal = 3400D
44              Const cdecJulianHousingCost As Decimal = 4000D
45
46              'Calculate the cost
47              If _Cooper Then
48                  HousingCost = cdecCooperHousingCost
49              ElseIf _Percey Then
50                  HousingCost = cdecPerceyHousingCost
51              ElseIf _Julian Then
52                  HousingCost = cdecJulianHousingCost
53              End If
54
55              _decCost = (_intUnits * _decCostPerUnit) + HousingCost
56
57              'Write the student record
58              objStudentCostsFile = New StudentCostsFile(_strStudentID, _
59                  _strStudentName, _strMajor, _decCost)
60              objStudentCostsFile.WriteRecord()
61
62              'Return the calculated cost
63              Return _decCost
64
65          End Function
66
67      End Class
```

The OnCampusStudent class code is completed (Figure 11-46).

```
1  ' Class:        OnCampusStudent
2  ' Developer:    Corinne Hoisington
3  ' Date:         August 29, 2015
4  ' Purpose:      This business class for registering an on-campus college
5  '               student calculates the semester costs, including tuition
6  '               and housing. It also causes the student costs file to be written.
7
8   Option Strict On
9
10 Public Class OnCampusStudent
11     Inherits Student
12
13     ' Class variables
14     Private _Cooper As Boolean
15     Private _Percey As Boolean
16     Private _Julian As Boolean
17
18     Dim objStudentCostsFile As StudentCostsFile
19
20     Sub New(ByVal StudentID As String, ByVal StudentName As String, _
21             ByVal Major As String, ByVal Units As String, _
22             ByVal Cooper As Boolean, ByVal Percey As Boolean, _
23             ByVal Julian As Boolean)
24         ' This subprocedure is a constructor for the Student class. It
25         ' is called when instantiated with arguments
26
27         MyBase.New(StudentID, StudentName, Major, Units)
28
29         'The following code assigns the arguments to class variables
30         _Cooper = Cooper
31         _Percey = Percey
32         _Julian = Julian
33
34     End Sub
35
36     Overrides Function ComputeCosts() As Decimal
37         ' This function computes the registration costs, writes a record
38         ' in the student costs file, and returns the registration costs
```

FIGURE 11-46 (continues)

```
39
40          'Define variables
41          Dim HousingCost As Decimal
42          Const cdecCooperHousingCost As Decimal = 2900D
43          Const cdecPerceyHousingCost As Decimal = 3400D
44          Const cdecJulianHousingCost As Decimal = 4000D
45
46          'Calculate the cost
47          If _Cooper Then
48              HousingCost = cdecCooperHousingCost
49          ElseIf _Percey Then
50              HousingCost = cdecPerceyHousingCost
51          ElseIf _Julian Then
52              HousingCost = cdecJulianHousingCost
53          End If
54
55          _decCost = (_intUnits * _decCostPerUnit) + HousingCost
56
57          'Write the student record
58          objStudentCostsFile = New StudentCostsFile(_strStudentID, _
59              _strStudentName, _strMajor, _decCost)
60          objStudentCostsFile.WriteRecord()
61
62          'Return the calculated cost
63          Return _decCost
64
65      End Function
66
67  End Class
```

FIGURE 11-46 (continued)

5

● **Enter Comments and Option Strict On for the StudentCostsFile Class** Display the StudentCostsFile class code window. Enter the common comments for the StudentCostsFile class. Include the Option Strict On statement.

HINT

```
1  ' Class:       Student Costs File
2  ' Developer:   Corinne Hoisington
3  ' Date:        August 29, 2015
4  ' Purpose:     This class represents the Student Costs File. The WriteRecord
5  '              procedure writes a comma-delimited student costs file that
6  '              contains the Student ID, Student Name, Major,
7  '              and Student Costs.
8
9  Option Strict On
10
11 Public Class StudentCostsFile
12
```

(continues)

- **Define the Class Variables for the StudentCostsFile Class** Define the class variables for the StudentCostsFile class. The variables should be declared with Private access.

HINT

```
14        ' Class variables
15        Private _strStudentID As String
16        Private _strStudentName As String
17        Private _strMajor As String
18        Private _decStudentCosts As Decimal
```

- **Write the StudentCostsFile Class Constructor** Write the code for the StudentCostsFile class constructor based on the requirements shown in the event planning document.

HINT

```
19
20        Sub New(ByVal StudentID As String, ByVal StudentName As String, _
21                ByVal Major As String, ByVal Costs As Decimal)
22            ' This sub procedure is the constructor for the StudentCostsFile
23            ' class.
24
25            'The following code assigns the arguments to class variables
26            _strStudentID = StudentID
27            _strStudentName = StudentName
28            _strMajor = Major
29            _decStudentCosts = Costs
30
31        End Sub
```

● **Write the Code for the WriteRecord Sub Procedure** Write the code to define the variable. Then, in a Try-Catch block, declare an IO StreamWriter, write the comma-delimited record in the file, and close the file *(ref: Figure 11-36)*.

HINT

```
33    Sub WriteRecord()
34        ' This subprocedure opens the StudentCosts output text file and then
35        ' writes a record in the comma-delimited file
36
37        Dim strNameandLocationOfFile As String = "e:\StudentCosts.txt"
38
39        Try
40            Dim objWriter As IO.StreamWriter = _
41                IO.File.AppendText(strNameandLocationOfFile)
42
43            objWriter.Write(_strStudentID & ",")
44            objWriter.Write(_strStudentName & ",")
45            objWriter.Write(_strMajor & ",")
46            objWriter.WriteLine(_decStudentCosts)
47            objWriter.Close()
48
49        Catch ex As Exception
50            MsgBox("No device available - program aborted", , "Error")
51            Application.Exit()
52
53        End Try
54
55    End Sub
56
57 End Class
```

The *StudentCostsFile* class code is completed (Figure 11-47).

```
1  ' Class:       Student Costs File
2  ' Developer:   Corinne Hoisington
3  ' Date:        August 29, 2015
4  ' Purpose:     This class represents the Student Costs File. The WriteRecord
5  '              procedure writes a comma-delimited student costs file that
6  '              contains the Student ID, Student Name, Major,
7  '              and Student Costs.
8
9  Option Strict On
10
11 Public Class StudentCostsFile
12
13
14     ' Class variables
15     Private _strStudentID As String
16     Private _strStudentName As String
17     Private _strMajor As String
18     Private _decStudentCosts As Decimal
```

FIGURE 11-47 (continues)

(continues)

```
19
20    Sub New(ByVal StudentID As String, ByVal StudentName As String, _
21              ByVal Major As String, ByVal Costs As Decimal)
22        ' This sub procedure is the constructor for the StudentCostsFile
23        ' class.
24
25        'The following code assigns the arguments to class variables
26        _strStudentID = StudentID
27        _strStudentName = StudentName
28        _strMajor = Major
29        _decStudentCosts = Costs
30
31    End Sub
32
33    Sub WriteRecord()
34        ' This subprocedure opens the StudentCosts output text file and then
35        ' writes a record in the comma-delimited file
36
37        Dim strNameandLocationOfFile As String = "e:\StudentCosts.txt"
38
39        Try
40            Dim objWriter As IO.StreamWriter = _
41                IO.File.AppendText(strNameandLocationOfFile)
42
43            objWriter.Write(_strStudentID & ",")
44            objWriter.Write(_strStudentName & ",")
45            objWriter.Write(_strMajor & ",")
46            objWriter.WriteLine(_decStudentCosts)
47            objWriter.Close()
48
49        Catch ex As Exception
50            MsgBox("No device available - program aborted", , "Error")
51            Application.Exit()
52
53        End Try
54
55    End Sub
56
57 End Class
```

FIGURE 11-47 (continued)

Summary

In this chapter you have learned to create multiple classes using the three-tier program structure and to incorporate inheritance into your program. The items listed in the table in Figure 11-48 include all the new Visual Studio and Visual Basic skills you have learned in this chapter.

Visual Basic Skills		
Skill	**Figure Number**	**Video Number**
Examine the College Registration Costs Program	Figure 11-1	Video 11-1
Set the TabIndex Property	Figure 11-4	Video 11-2
Edit Input Data	Figure 11-7	
Code the MaskFull Property	Figure 11-8	
Code the TextBox TextLength Property	Figure 11-9	
Create a Class	Figure 11-13	Video 11-3
Instantiate a Class	Figure 11-17	
Code a Class Constructor	Figure 11-19	
Pass an Argument when Instantiating an Object	Figure 11-20	
Call a Procedure from Another Class	Figure 11-24	
Write Code for Inheritance	Figure 11-26	
Code Base Class and Subclass Constructors	Figure 11-27 and Figure 11-28	
Call and Code Procedures for Inheritance	Figure 11-29 through Figure 11-33	
Code a Persistence Class	Figure 11-34	
Write a Comma-Delimited Text File	Figure 11-36	

FIGURE 11-48

© 2014 Cengage Learning

Learn Online

Reinforcement activities and resources are available at no additional cost on *www.cengagebrain.com*. Visit *www.cengage.com/ct/studentdownload* for detailed instructions about accessing the resources available at the Student Companion Site.

Knowledge Check

1. If the TextLength property of a TextBox object is less than 1, what does that tell you?

2. What property is used to ensure that the user has entered all digits in a MaskedTextBox object?

3. What property can you use to specify the sequence of objects that will be selected when the user presses the TAB key?

4. What are the names of the three tiers in a three-tiered program structure? What occurs in each of the three tiers?

5. In a three-tiered program structure, which tiers are allowed to communicate with each other?

6. Identify the three steps to create a new class in a Visual Basic program.

7. Write the code to instantiate the objEmployee object based on the Employee class.

8. When is a class constructor executed?

9. Write the code to instantiate the objVehicle object based on the Vehicle class and to pass the following values to the object: Color, Model, Engine. Write the New statement in the Vehicle class.

10. Write a statement to call the ComputeDiscount procedure in the objDiscountItem object.

11. Explain the benefits of using separate classes in a program.

12. Complete the following sentence: Inheritance allows one class to inherit _____ and _____ from another class.

13. Describe the difference between a base class and a subclass when using inheritance.

14. What entry must be included in the Class statement of a subclass?

15. What is the first statement that must be coded in a subclass constructor?

16. What is an overridable procedure? Why is it used?

17. In a class, can an attribute be referenced that is not defined in the class? How is this attribute reference resolved?

18. What is a comma-delimited text file?

19. When an IO.StreamWriter is created, what does the IO.File.AppendText entry mean?

20. What is the difference between the Write procedure and the WriteLine procedure in the IO.StreamWriter class?

Debugging Exercises

1. The code in Figure 11-49 executes when a button is tapped or clicked on a Windows Form object. Identify what will happen when a single error occurs. What happens if two errors occur at the same time? What happens if three errors occur at the same time? How can this code be repaired?

```
20          Dim InputError As Boolean = False
21
22          If txtSocialSecurity MaskFull = False Then
23              MsgBox("Enter your Student ID in the Student ID box", , _
24              "Error")
25              txtSocialSecurity.Clear()
26              txtSocialSecurity Focus()
27              InputError = True
28          End If
29
30          If txtLastName TextLength < 1 Or txtLastName Text < "A" Then
31              MsgBox("Enter your name in the Student Name box", , "Error")
32              txtLastName.Clear()
33              txtLastName.Focus()
34              InputError = True
35          End If
36
37          If Not IsNumeric(txtNumberOfDependents.Text) Then
38              MsgBox("Enter the units in the Number of Units box", , _
39               "Error")
40              txtNumberOfDependents.Clear()
41              txtNumberOfDependents Focus()
42              InputError = True
43          End If
```

FIGURE 11-49

(continues)

2. Examine the following code and make any corrections required.

CALLING CLASS

```
62  Dim objSubClass As New SubClass(txtLastName, _
63      txtNumberOfDependents)
```

OBJSUBCLASS

```
4  Sub New(ByVal LastName)
```

3. Correct the following code.

```
4  Dim objStoreName As StoreName
5  StoreName = New StoreName
```

4. Referencing Exercise 3 above, correct the following statement:

```
22  lblStoreAddress = GetAddress.objStoreName
```

Program Analysis

1. What is the output of the code in Figure 11-50?

```
33 Sub WriteRecord()
34     ' This subprocedure opens the StudentCosts output text file and then
35     ' writes a record in the comma-delimited file
36
37     Dim strNameandLocationOfFile As String = "E:\StudentCosts.txt"
38
39     Try
40         Dim objWriter As IO.StreamWriter = _
41             IO.File.AppendText(strNameandLocationOfFile)
42
43         objWriter.Write(_strStudentID & ",")
44         objWriter.Write(_strStudentName & ",")
45         objWriter.Write(_strMajor & ",")
46         objWriter.WriteLine(_decStudentCosts)
47         objWriter.Close()
48
49     Catch ex As Exception
50         MsgBox("No device available - program aborted", , "Error")
51         Application.Exit()
52
53     End Try
54 End Sub
```

FIGURE 11-50

2. Analyze the code in Figure 11-51a, Figure 11-51b, and Figure 11-51c. What is the output of the code?

```
17          Dim objCustomer As Customer
18          Dim objInternetCustomer As InternetCustomer
19
20          objCustomer = New Customer
21          objInternetCustomer = New InternetCustomer
22
23          MsgBox.Show(objInternetCustomer.CustomerFunction())
```

FIGURE 11-51a

```
1 Public Class Customer
2
3     Function CustomerFunction() As String
4         Return "Customer function"
5     End Function
6
7     Overridable Function OverridableCustomerFunction() As String
8         Return "Overridable customer function"
9     End Function
10
11
12 End Class
13
```

FIGURE 11-51b

```
1 Public Class InternetCustomer
2     Inherits Customer
3
4     Function InternetCustomerFunction() As String
5         Return "Internet customer function"
6     End Function
7
8     Overrides Function OverridableCustomerFunction() As String
9         Return "Overrode the customer overridable function"
10     End Function
11
12 End Class
13
```

FIGURE 11-51c

(continues)

3. Analyze the code in Figure 11-52a, Figure 11-52b, and Figure 11-52c. What is the output of the code?

```
17          Dim objCustomer As Customer
18          Dim objInternetCustomer As InternetCustomer
19
20          objCustomer = New Customer
21          objInternetCustomer = New InternetCustomer
22
23          MsgBox.Show(objInternetCustomer.InternetCustomerFunction())
```

FIGURE 11-52a

```
1 Public Class Customer
2
3     Function CustomerFunction() As String
4         Return "Customer function"
5     End Function
6
7     Overridable Function OverridableCustomerFunction() As String
8         Return "Overridable customer function"
9     End Function
10
11
12 End Class
13
```

FIGURE 11-52b

```
1 Public Class InternetCustomer
2     Inherits Customer
3
4     Function InternetCustomerFunction() As String
5         Return "Internet customer function"
6     End Function
7
8     Overrides Function OverridableCustomerFunction() As String
9         Return "Overrode the customer overridable function"
10     End Function
11
12 End Class
13
```

FIGURE 11-52c

4. Analyze the code in Figure 11-53a, Figure 11-53b, and Figure 11-53c. What is the output of the code?

```
17          Dim objCustomer As Customer
18          Dim objInternetCustomer As InternetCustomer
19
20          objCustomer = New Customer
21          objInternetCustomer = New InternetCustomer
22
23          MsgBox.Show(objInternetCustomer.OverridableCustomerFunction())
```

FIGURE 11-53a

```
1 Public Class Customer
2
3      Function CustomerFunction() As String
4          Return "Customer function"
5      End Function
6
7      Overridable Function OverridableCustomerFunction() As String
8          Return "Overridable customer function"
9      End Function
10
11
12 End Class
13
```

FIGURE 11-53b

```
1 Public Class InternetCustomer
2      Inherits Customer
3
4      Function InternetCustomerFunction() As String
5          Return "Internet customer function"
6      End Function
7
8      Overrides Function OverridableCustomerFunction() As String
9          Return "Overrode the customer overridable function"
10      End Function
11
12 End Class
13
```

FIGURE 11-53c

(continues)

5. Analyze the code in Figure 11-54a, Figure 11-54b, and Figure 11-54c. What is the output of the code?

```
17          Dim objCustomer As Customer
18          Dim objInternetCustomer As InternetCustomer
19
20          objCustomer = New Customer
21          objInternetCustomer = New InternetCustomer
22
23          MsgBox.Show(objCustomer.OverridableCustomerFunction())
```

FIGURE 11-54a

```
1 Public Class Customer
2
3     Function CustomerFunction() As String
4         Return "Customer function"
5     End Function
6
7     Overridable Function OverridableCustomerFunction() As String
8         Return "Overridable customer function"
9     End Function
10
11
12 End Class
13
```

FIGURE 11-54b

```
1 Public Class InternetCustomer
2     Inherits Customer
3
4     Function InternetCustomerFunction() As String
5         Return "Internet customer function"
6     End Function
7
8     Overrides Function OverridableCustomerFunction() As String
9         Return "Overrode the customer overridable function"
10     End Function
11
12 End Class
13
```

FIGURE 11-54c

Complete one or more of the following case programming assignments. Submit the program and materials you create to your instructor. The level of difficulty is indicated for each case programming assignment.

● = Easiest
●● = Intermediate
●●● = Challenging

1 ●
MOBILE DEVELOPER'S CONFERENCE REGISTRATION

Design a Windows application and write the code that will execute according to the program requirements in Figure 11-55 and the Use Case Definition in Figure 11-56 on the next page. Before writing the code, create an event planning document for each event in the program. The completed Windows Form object and other objects in the user interface are shown in Figure 11-57 on the next page.

REQUIREMENTS DOCUMENT

Date Submitted: February 28, 2015

Application Title: Mobile Developer's Conference Registration

Purpose: This Windows application allows a visitor to the Mobile Developer's conference to register for the meeting.

Program Procedures: In a Windows application, the user enters the visitor's corporation ID, first and last name, and the number of days the visitor will be attending. The user selects whether a pre-conference course is being attended and selects the course if necessary. The user then clicks a button. The application calculates the costs for attending the conference and records the information in a log file.

Algorithms, Processing, and Conditions:
1. The user first enters the visitor's corporation ID, first and last name, and number of days to attend.
2. The user selects whether the visitor will attend a pre-conference course (Pre-Conference Android Track or Windows Store Track) and then selects the course if necessary (for example, Mobile Security, Mobile Design, or Mobile Databases).
3. When the user clicks a button, the program calculates the costs for attending the conference and writes a log file.
4. A Clear Form button should be available to clear the form and place the insertion point in the Corporation ID text box.
5. The conference cost is $350.00 per day. The minimum number of days is 1, and the maximum number of days is 4.
6. The formula to calculate conference costs is number of days times the cost per day.
7. If the visitor chooses to attend one of the pre-conference courses, it will cost $675.00. This cost should be added to the conference cost.
8. The log file is a text file that contains the Corporation ID, the First Name, the Last Name, the pre-conference course taken, and the total conference costs. If no pre-conference course is taken, the field should contain no data for it in the text file record. The file should be a comma-delimited file.

FIGURE 11-55 (continues)

(continues)

Case Programming Assignments

Notes and Restrictions:

1. The corporation ID must be five numeric digits in length.
2. The first name and the last name cannot be left blank and must begin with an alphabetic character.
3. The number of days must be a numeric value of 1 through 4.
4. The pre-conference course selections should not be displayed in the window unless the user selects a type of pre-conference course.
5. When the user clicks the button to calculate costs and the program determines that an error occurred during data entry, a message box should be displayed and the user must enter valid data before continuing.
6. No pre-conference course is the default value.

Comments:

1. Obtain an image for this program from CengageBrain.com. The name of the picture is Mobile.
2. The program should use a three-tiered structure with presentation, business, and persistence classes.

FIGURE 11-55 (continued)

© 2014 Cengage Learning

USE CASE DEFINITION

1. The user enters the visitor's corporation ID, first name, last name, and the number of days the visitor will attend the conference.
2. If necessary, the user selects a type of pre-conference course and then selects a course.
3. The user clicks the Calculate Costs button.
4. The program calculates and displays the conference costs, including the pre-conference course cost, if appropriate.
5. The program writes a log of the conference registration costs and other information.
6. If necessary, the user clicks the Clear Form button to clear the form and place the insertion point in the Corporation ID text box.

FIGURE 11-56

© 2014 Cengage Learning

(continues)

Case Programming Assignments

Mobile Developer's Conference Registration *(continued)*

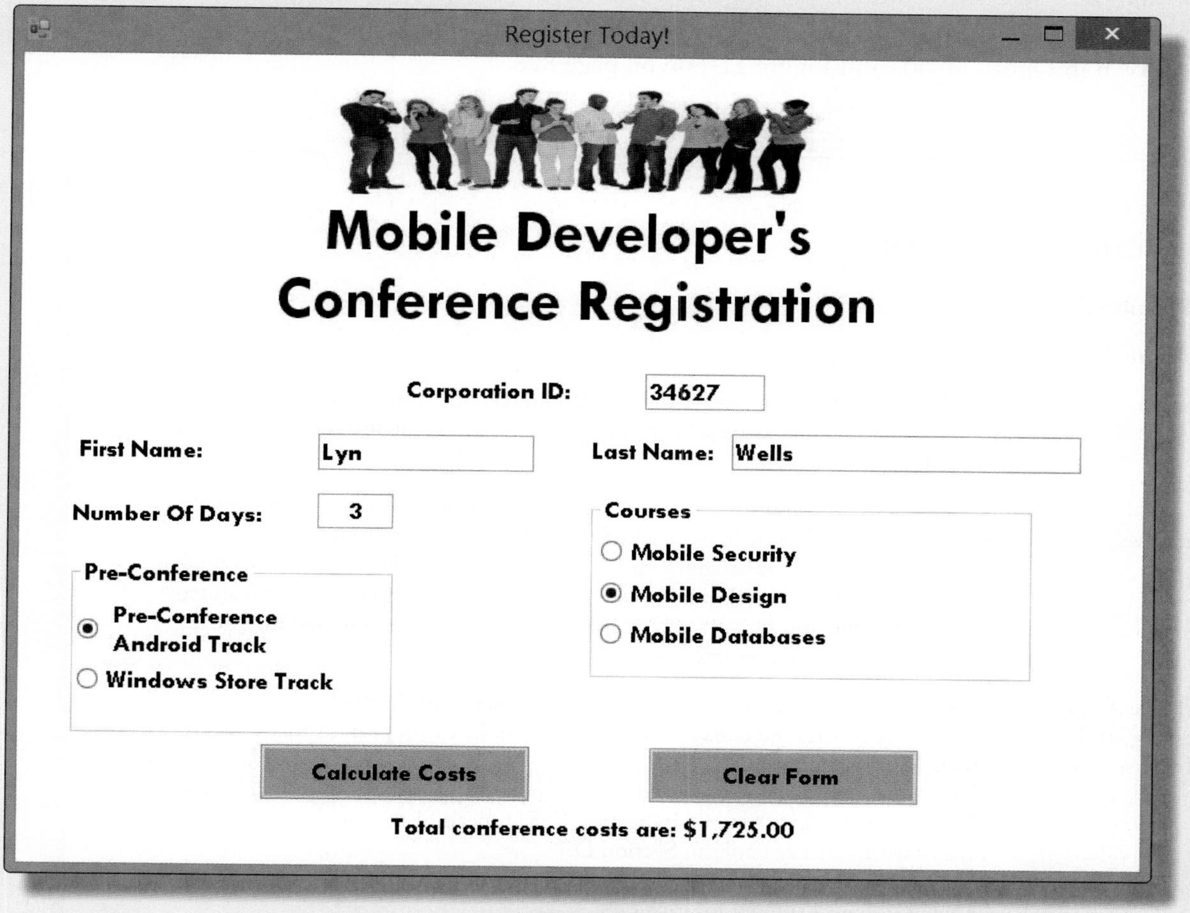

FIGURE 11-57

2 HISTORY LIBRARY INVENTORY

Design a Windows application and write the code that will execute according to the program requirements in Figure 11-58 and the Use Case Definition in Figure 11-59. Before writing the code, create an event planning document for each event in the program. The completed Windows Form object and other objects in the user interface are shown in Figure 11-60a and Figure 11-60b on page 828.

REQUIREMENTS DOCUMENT

Date Submitted: February 28, 2015

Application Title: History Library Inventory

Purpose: This Windows application allows the user to enter a book into a history library inventory. When all books have been entered, the program identifies the number of books entered for each type.

Program Procedures: From a Windows application, a user enters an ISBN, title, and author(s) of a book. The user also identifies the book as a U.S. history book, a European history book, or a world history book. The program identifies the shelf area where the selected book is stored, based on the type of book. A log is kept of all inventory entries and is stored on disk. When the user finishes entering the inventory, the program identifies the number of books the user entered for each type.

Algorithms, Processing, and Conditions:
1. The user enters the ISBN, the title, and the author(s) of the book.
2. The user identifies the book as a U.S. history book, a European history book, or a world history book.
3. Based on the type of book selected, the program displays the book's shelf location. (U.S. history books are stored in Section F, European history books in Section A, and world history books in Section D.)
4. When the user indicates that all books have been entered, the program displays the number of books entered for each type.
5. In a comma-delimited text file, the program keeps a log of all books entered. The file should contain the ISBN, the book title, and the author(s).

Notes and Restrictions: Validate data that the user enters using accepted standards.

Comments:
1. Obtain an image for this program from CengageBrain.com. The name of the picture is Library.
2. The program should use a three-tiered structure with presentation, business, and persistence classes.

FIGURE 11-58

(continues)

Case Programming Assignments

History Library Inventory (continued)

USE CASE DEFINITION

1. The user views the opening screen.
2. The user enters the ISBN, the book title, and the book author(s).
3. The user selects the book category.
4. The user clicks the Enter Book button to enter the book into the inventory.
5. The program displays the shelf location; it also writes a record in the inventory text file.
6. To enter another book, the user clicks the New Book button.
7. When finished, the user clicks the Inventory Entry Complete button.
8. The program displays the number of books entered by category.

FIGURE 11-59

© 2014 Cengage Learning

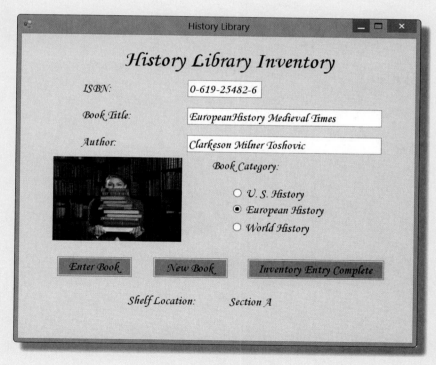

FIGURE 11-60a

© Dougal Waters / Photodisc / Getty Images

Case Programming Assignments

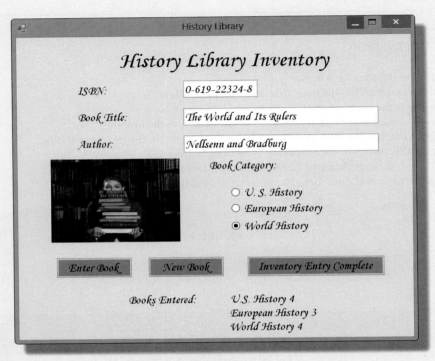

FIGURE 11-60b

Case Programming Assignments

3
MOBILE PHONE DATA PLANS

Design a Windows application and write the code that will execute according to the program requirements in Figure 11-61 and the Use Case Definition in Figure 11-62 on the next page. Before writing the code, create an event planning document for each event in the program. The completed Windows Form object and other objects in the user interface are shown in Figure 11-63 on the next page.

REQUIREMENTS DOCUMENT

Date Submitted: July 18, 2015

Application Title: Mobile Phone Data Plans

Purpose: This Windows application calculates the costs of data plans for mobile phones.

Program Procedures: From a Windows application, a buyer selects a data plan. The buyer also can elect to add a mobile hotspot to tether multiple devices. A buyer is either in the store or buying over the Internet. The program calculates the cost of the phone and mobile hotspot purchased.

Algorithms, Processing, and Conditions:
1. The buyer enters her last name, street address, and zip code. If buying over the Internet, the buyer also enters an email address.
2. The buyer selects a data plan from a list of plans.
3. The user can select a type of hotspot from a list.
4. Based on the plan and hotspot selections, the program calculates the total cost.
5. The total cost for an in-store purchase must include 7.75% sales tax.
6. An Internet sale generates a shipping charge of $28.00 to mail the phone.
7. The types of data plans and their costs are 1 GB, $30; 2 GB, $50; 4 GB, $70; and unlimited, $120. A mobile hotspot costs an additional $20.
8. Write a comma-delimited text file to record each sale. The text file should contain the user's last name, zip code, phone choice, hotspot choice, and total cost.

Notes and Restrictions:
1. Validate data that the user enters using accepted standards.
2. In-store is the default type of buyer.
3. The Email Address label and text box are not displayed unless the user is an Internet buyer. An Internet buyer must enter an email address.

Comments: The program should use a three-tiered structure with presentation, business, and persistence classes.

FIGURE 11-61

(continues)

Case Programming Assignments

Mobile Phone Data Plans (continued)

USE CASE DEFINITION

1. The user views the opening screen.
2. The user enters her last name, street address, and zip code.
3. The user selects an option from the data plan list. If desired, the user can select a hotspot for an extra cost. The user selects either In-Store or Internet as the type of buyer. An Internet buyer must enter an email address.
4. The user clicks the Calculate Cost button.
5. The program displays the cost of the sale.
6. The program writes a record of the sale in a text file.

FIGURE 11-62

© 2014 Cengage Learning

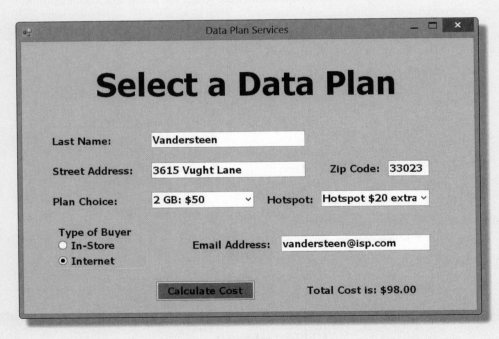

FIGURE 11-63

© 2014 Cengage Learning

Case Programming Assignments

4 ●●
BANK ACCOUNT PROJECTION

Design a Windows application and write the code that will execute according to the program requirements in Figure 11-64. Before designing the user interface, create a Use Case Definition. Before writing the code, create an event planning document for each event in the program.

REQUIREMENTS DOCUMENT

Date Submitted:	July 14, 2015
Application Title:	Bank Account Projection
Purpose:	This Windows application calculates and displays the expected values of different types of bank accounts held for one year by current customers of Tenth Street Regional Bank.
Program Procedures:	In a Windows application, a user enters her name and current account number, selects one of five types of accounts, and then enters the amount to be placed in the account. The program calculates the projected value of the account after one year, assuming that the user makes no other deposits or withdrawals.

Algorithms, Processing, and Conditions:

1. The user enters her name and current account number.
2. The user identifies the type of account being considered. The types of accounts are Regular Savings, Checking, 1-year CD, 2-year CD, and 5-year CD.
3. The user enters the amount to be deposited. The minimum amount is greater than $1,000.00.
4. When the user clicks a button, the program calculates and displays the value of the account after one year.
5. The value of the account is based on the following: Regular Savings, 1.75% interest; Checking, $25.00 per month service charge; 1-year CD, 1.85% interest; 2-year CD, 2.30% interest; 5-year CD, 2.37% interest.
6. A comma-delimited text file is kept for each account inquiry. The text file contains the account number, the amount to be deposited, and the type of account selected.
7. The user can tap or click a button to clear the form.

Notes and Restrictions:

Validate data that the user enters using accepted standards.

Comments:

1. Use the Web to find an appropriate image for the user interface.
2. The program should use a three-tiered structure with presentation, business, and persistence classes.

FIGURE 11-64

5

APP STORE PURCHASE

Design a Windows application and write the code that will execute according to the program requirements in Figure 11-65. Before designing the user interface, create a Use Case Definition. Before writing the code, create an event planning document for each event in the program.

REQUIREMENTS DOCUMENT

Date Submitted:	August 16, 2015
Application Title:	App Store Purchase
Purpose:	This Windows application calculates the costs of apps from the App Store.
Program Procedures:	In a Windows application, a user selects one of five apps to purchase from a list. The user enters the buyer's credit card number and expiration date, and identifies whether the buyer is a student. The program calculates the cost of the app. It also keeps a log of purchases.
Algorithms, Processing, and Conditions:	1. The user enters the buyer's credit card number and expiration date. 2. The user identifies the app the buyer is purchasing. 3. The five software packages and their prices are: Speed Up the Internet, $1.99; A Writer's Writer, $0.99; Distance Personnel Management, $2.99; Email Photo Manager, $4.99; Keyboard SpeedLearner, $1.99. 4. For each package, a discount applies if the buyer is a student. The discounts are: Speed Up the Internet, 6%; A Writer's Writer, 8%; Distance Personnel Management, 8%; Email Photo Manager, 5%; Keyboard SpeedLearner, 2%. 5. After entering the information, the user can tap or click the Final Total button to determine the amount to be charged to the credit card. 6. The user can tap or click a button to clear the form. 7. The program writes a comma-delimited text file to keep track of all software purchases. The text file contains the credit card number, the name of the app purchased, the discount amount, and the total amount. 8. At any time, the user can tap or click the Daily Total button to have the program calculate and display the amount of sales that have been recorded in the text file.
Notes and Restrictions:	Validate data that the user enters using accepted standards.
Comments:	1. Use the Web to find an appropriate image for the user interface. 2. The program should use a three-tiered structure with presentation, business, and persistence classes.

FIGURE 11-65

6 ●●
USED CAR INVENTORY

Design a Windows application and write the code that will execute according to the program requirements in Figure 11-66. Before designing the user interface, create a Use Case Definition. Before writing the code, create an event planning document for each event in the program.

REQUIREMENTS DOCUMENT

Date Submitted:	July 21, 2015
Application Title:	Used Car Inventory
Purpose:	This Windows application allows the user to add cars to the inventory of a used car dealer named Car Cruiser. The program displays the sticker price for each car based on discounts, and allows the user to display the entire inventory.
Program Procedures:	In a Windows application, a user enters the vehicle number, make, model, year, mileage, and standard price for a used car that is being placed in the inventory of the used car dealer. In addition, the user selects the car's color from a list of colors and indicates whether the vehicle is a convertible. The program creates the sticker price for the car and writes a record for the car in the inventory text file.
Algorithms, Processing, and Conditions:	1. The user enters the vehicle number, make, model, year, mileage, and standard price for a used car being placed in inventory.
	2. The user selects the car color from a list of 17 common car colors, including black, dark gray, and red.
	3. The user indicates whether the car is a convertible.
	4. The program calculates the sticker price for the car on the used car lot.
	5. If the car is black, a 15% discount is applied to the standard price to determine the sticker price. If the car is dark gray, a 21% surcharge is added to the standard price to determine the sticker price. If the car is red, a 9% surcharge is added to the standard price to determine the sticker price. For all other cars, the standard price and the sticker price are the same.
	6. If the car is a convertible, a 26% surcharge is added to the sticker price calculated in step 5 to determine the total sticker price.
	7. After the user enters all the data and clicks a button, the sticker price is displayed.
	8. When the button is tapped or clicked, the program also writes a comma-delimited text file that records the new entry into the inventory. The record includes the vehicle number, make, model, year, mileage, and sticker price.
	9. At any time, the user can tap or click the Display Inventory menu item on the File menu to display the records in the inventory text file. In a separate window, the vehicle number, make, model, year, mileage, and sticker price should be displayed in a list for every car in the inventory.
Notes and Restrictions:	Validate data that the user enters using accepted standards.
Comments:	1. Use the Web to find an appropriate image for the user interface.
	2. The program should use a three-tiered structure with presentation, business, and persistence classes.

FIGURE 11-66

7 •••
NAIL SALON APPOINTMENTS

Create a requirements document and a Use Case Definition document and then design a Windows application based on the case project shown in Figure 11-67. Before writing the code, create an event planning document for each event in the program.

The Nirvana Nail Salon has asked you to create its new appointment system. The salon provides manicures and pedicures to customers. The salon needs to know the name of each customer and the date and time of each customer's appointment. (*Hint:* For the date, consider using the DateTimePicker object or the Calendar object.) Customers who are Nirvana members receive a 20% discount on a full manicure, which is normally $25.00. Pedicures are also available for $32.00; Nirvana members receive a 25% discount on a pedicure. All appointments should be made on the hour from 8 AM to 7 PM. The following specials are available with manicures at an additional price: Gel Nails ($39.99); Paraffin Treatment ($15.00); French Manicure ($3.99); Spa Treatment ($19.99). For pedicures, the following specials can be added: Design Nail ($2.99); Spa Treatment ($19.99). When customers make an appointment, they should be told the total price of the services during the call. The owners of the nail salon would like to be able to view the list of appointments at any time.

FIGURE 11-67

Case Programming Assignments

8 ●●●
FISHING BOAT ORDERS

Create a requirements document and a Use Case Definition document and then design a Windows application based on the case project shown in Figure 11-68. Before writing the code, create an event planning document for each event in the program.

Your friend operates a charter fishing boat. She offers both full-day and half-day excursions. She receives a variety of requests for handling the fish that her customers catch, and has determined prices for each type of request:

- Prepare individual filets and ship them to a given address. Filets are $9.25 per pound, and shipping charges are $3.89 per pound.
- Freeze the fish and ship the order to a given address. The fish is $8.75 per pound, and shipping charges are $5.95 per pound.
- Prepare filets and instruct a taxidermist to mount the fish. Ship the order to a given address. Filets are $9.25 per pound, and shipping charges are $3.89 per pound. The taxidermist charges a flat fee of $675.00 plus $85.00 per pound.
- Prepare the fish filets and donate them to a local charity. The charge for donation is $2.00 per pound.

Your friend has asked you to develop an application that can help her keep track of her orders. When she enters an order, she wants to be able to tell her customer the price at the same time. She also would like to be able to view all her orders and the dates they are due to ship.

FIGURE 11-68

Case Programming Assignments

9 ●●● A COMMUNITY APPLICATION

Create a requirements document and a Use Case Definition document and then design a Windows application based on the case project shown in Figure 11-69. Before writing the code, create an event planning document for each event in the program.

> You have been asked to locate computer users on your campus or within your community, determine an application they need, and then write the application. Work with your users to develop and implement the application.

FIGURE 11-69

CHAPTER 12 (ENRICHMENT CHAPTER)

Windows Store Apps

OBJECTIVES

You will have mastered the material in this chapter when you can:

- Describe a Windows Store app

- Describe a touch-first app

- Understand the Windows Store Application Life Cycle

- Get a free Windows developer license

- Create a Windows Store app

- Customize a splash screen

- Add an image to a page

- Add TextBlock, TextBox, and ComboBox objects

- Code a Windows Store app

- Run a Windows Store app in a simulator

- Analyze the code

- Run a performance analysis

- Package an app

- Certify an app

- Publish an app

- Monetize an app

Introduction

A Windows Store app is a new type of application that runs on Windows 8 devices and can be developed using a Windows 8 computer with Visual Studio 2012. Unlike traditional desktop Windows applications, a Windows Store app has a single chromeless window that fills the entire screen with menus or minimize/maximize buttons by default. ("Chromeless" means the window displays no controls such as ribbons or toolbars.) Visual Studio Windows Store apps provide programming support for developers to create innovative program solutions that take advantage of an improved user interface. In addition, Windows Store apps target multiple devices with Visual Basic code similar to that used in traditional Windows applications. Windows Store apps can support horizontal and vertical layouts to create a customized experience across a variety of form factors and display sizes. These apps work with a variety of input sources, including touch, pen, mouse, and keyboard.

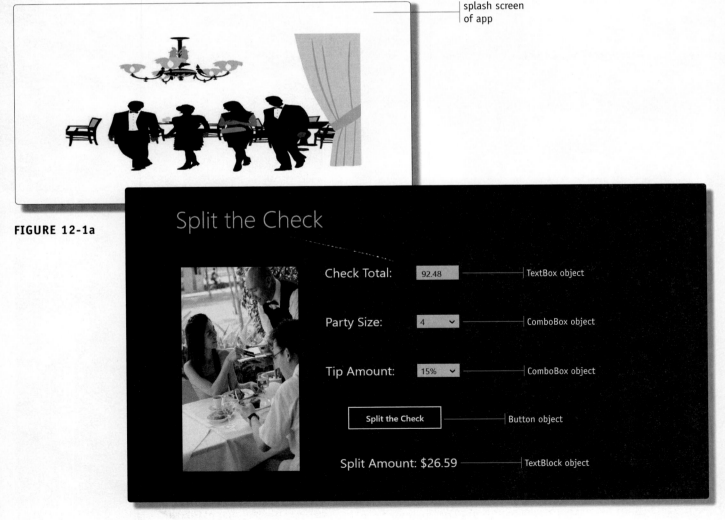

FIGURE 12-1a

FIGURE 12-1b

To see a practical example of a Windows Store app developed using Visual Basic 2012 for a Windows 8 device, you can use the sample chapter project, which is called Split the Check. This app helps a group of diners split a restaurant tab. The Split the Check app opens with the splash screen shown in Figure 12-1a. After the splash screen closes, the main form fills the screen and asks the user to fill in the information from her restaurant check. After the user enters the amount of the restaurant bill, enters the number of diners, and selects a 10, 15, or 20 percent tip, the Split the Check app displays the amount each diner should pay, as shown in Figure 12-1b.

ONLINE REINFORCEMENT

To view a video of the program execution shown in Figure 12-1, visit CengageBrain.com and navigate to the resources for this title. Tap or click the link for Chapter 12 and then navigate to Video 12-1. Turn on your speakers to listen to the audio walkthrough of the steps.

Windows Store Apps

When you install an app from the Windows Store on a Windows 8 device (Figure 12-2), it appears as a **tile** on the Start screen. Free and paid apps are distributed through the Windows Store; paid apps range in cost from $1.49 to $999.99. After an app is installed from the Windows Store, a tile representing the app is displayed on the Start screen and the Apps screen. In previous versions of Windows, applications were represented by icons instead of tiles. In their default form, tiles are simple opaque rectangles or squares arranged on the Start screen in a grid. Tiles on the Start screen are connected to people, apps, folders, photos, and websites.

FIGURE 12-2

Free and paid apps can be acquired in the Windows Store as an app package. An **app package** has the file extension .appx and contains a manifest and other files that are part of the app. Some Windows Store apps require programming access to user resources such as the Documents library or other devices such as a printer. These apps must declare that they require such access. When you submit an app you have developed to the Windows Store, it is checked to ensure that the declared capabilities match the app description.

Touch-First Interface

You have learned throughout this text that the user interface is important to the design and function of a program. Windows 8 computers and smartphones changed how a user interacts with a device because of the introduction of immersive touch. Windows 8 and subsequent versions of the Windows operating system are designed to be **touch-first**, meaning that while traditional inputs such as keyboard and mouse are still supported, other input methods such as touch and finger gestures are the primary interaction with the user interface. Notice the 10 touch points on the Windows 8 Start screen shown in Figure 12-3. Most Windows 8 computers have a 10-point multitouch display with a larger track pad, both of which are designed for better interaction with the features of Windows Store Apps.

Use a Touch Screen

Windows users who have computers and other devices with touch screens can interact with the screen using gestures. A **gesture** is a motion you make on a touch

FIGURE 12-3

screen with the tip of one or more fingers. Touch screens are convenient because they do not require a separate device for input. Table 12-1 presents common ways to interact with a touch screen.

Table 12–1 Touch Screen Gestures

Motion	Description	Common Uses
Tap	Quickly touch and release one finger one time.	Activate a link. Press a button. Run an app.
Double-tap	Quickly touch and release one finger two times.	Run a program or app. Zoom in (make the screen contents larger) at the location of the double tap.
Press and hold	Press and hold one finger until an action occurs.	Display a shortcut menu (immediate access to allowable actions). Activate a mode enabling you to move an item with one finger to a new location.
Drag	Press and hold one finger on an object and then move the finger to the new location.	Move an item around the screen. Scroll.
Swipe	Press and hold one finger and then move the finger horizontally or vertically on the screen.	Select an object. Swipe from edge to display a bar such as the Charms bar, App bar, and Navigation bar.
Stretch	Move two fingers apart.	Zoom in (make the screen contents larger).
Pinch	Move two fingers together.	Zoom out (make the screen contents smaller).

© 2014 Cengage Learning

Windows Store

The Windows Store is an online store where you shop for Windows 8 apps. From the Start screen, visit the Windows Store to browse and download apps for recipes, photos, sports, news, and other content. Some apps are free; others are available for a fee. Once you install an app from the Windows Store, you own it and can use the app on up to five devices, whether it was free or purchased.

IN THE REAL WORLD

Tiles can deliver content even when their apps are not running by using a feature called **Live Tiles**. With Live Tiles, one glance at your Start screen tells you the weather in your hometown, the latest national news, or when someone likes your Facebook post, all updated in real time.

A **Windows Store app** is an app sold in the Windows Store; it runs on Windows 8 devices such as ultrabooks, tablets, and smartphones. Windows Store apps run in a single window that fills the screen by default. Because they are designed to run on Windows 8, the apps work with a variety of input sources, including touch, pen (stylus), mouse, and keyboard. Instead of traditional icons, some Windows Store apps use Live Tiles that can display notifications. You can write Windows Store apps in a variety of languages, such as Visual Basic and C# with XAML, C++ with XAML or DirectX, and JavaScript with HTML/CSS. This chapter creates a Windows Store app using a Windows 8 computer with Visual Studio 2012, the Visual Basic language, and XAML, pronounced *Zamel*. **XAML** (Extensible Application Markup Language) is a markup language that simplifies the layout of a user interface for a .NET Framework application. You use Visual Basic to code the events and XAML to design the user interface for the Windows Store app.

The Windows Store makes your apps available to millions of customers around the world. You write your app once and set the price in your local currency, and the Windows Store offers the app in a worldwide marketplace that supports more than 100 languages. Consider writing your app in multiple languages to increase your worldwide audience and sales.

Windows Store Application Life Cycle

Windows Store apps differ from Windows applications in several ways, ranging from how they are deployed to how they run. The Windows Store Application Life Cycle describes the different experiences that a user has with an app. Users acquire your app from the Windows Store as an app package. After the app is installed and launched, Windows displays a splash screen for the app. While the splash screen is displayed, the app is registering event handlers and setting up any custom user interface it needs for loading. After the app is run, the user may choose to **suspend** the app. When the user stops using the app or when Windows enters a low power state, the app is suspended. Most apps stop running when the user stops using them. In a traditional Windows application, the upper-right corner of the window displays Minimize, Maximize, and Close buttons that the user can tap or click to change how the window is displayed or closed. Windows Store apps typically are displayed on a full-sized screen that does not close, but is suspended while the user performs other tasks. The recommended way to close a Windows Store app is to touch or click the top-center area of the screen and drag the app toward the bottom of the screen. When you let go, the app closes.

Get a Free Windows Developer License

Visual Studio 2012 does not allow anyone to create a Windows Store app without a developer license. A developer license for Windows Store apps lets you install, develop, test, and evaluate apps before the Windows Store tests and certifies them. Developer licenses are free, and you can acquire as many as you need if you already have a Microsoft account. By default, developer licenses that you acquire using a Microsoft account must be renewed every 30 days. When you create your first Windows Store app, you can sign up for a free developer's license. You will need a separate individual ($49) or company ($99) Windows Store developer account to publish an app to the Windows Store. This fee is waived for students who sign up for a Windows Store developer student account at *dreamspark.com*.

Before the Windows Store accepts your Windows app, you must package and certify it according to certain rules. The app is checked to confirm that it functions properly and is virus-free. Prohibited app content includes adult topics, discrimination, illegal activities, slanderous speech, and excessive profanity.

If my developer's license expires, how do I renew it?

After you have a project open, you can renew your license by completing the following steps:

• Tap or click PROJECT on the menu bar.

• Tap or click Store on the PROJECT menu.

• Tap or click Acquire Developer License.

• Tap or click the I Agree button in the Developer License dialog box.

• Follow the rest of the steps to sign up for the account.

(margin) CONSIDER THIS

Create a Windows Store App

When you install Visual Studio 2012 on a Windows 8 computer, the developer tools used to create a Windows Store app are included automatically. If you install Visual Studio 2012 on a Windows 7 computer, the Windows Store app development tools cannot be installed. Visual Studio 2012 includes templates that provide a starting point to help you create Windows Store apps. To create a new Visual Basic Windows Store app project and create a developer's license, take the following steps:

STEP 1 Tap or click the New Project button on the Standard toolbar. Tap or click Windows Store in the left pane.

Visual Studio opens the New Project window (Figure 12–4). If you are using Windows 7, you will not see the Windows Store templates listed because you need Windows 8 to develop a Windows Store app. Windows Store is highlighted in the left pane and the types of Windows Store projects you can create using Visual Basic are listed in the middle pane.

Windows Store displayed on Windows 8 computers

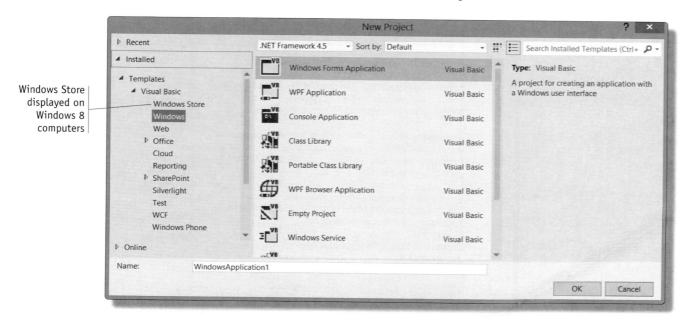

FIGURE 12-4

STEP 2   If necessary, tap or click Blank App (XAML) Visual Basic in the middle pane. Type the project name `Split the Check` in the Name text box.

Blank App (XAML) is selected in the middle pane and the app's name is displayed in the Name text box (Figure 12-5). By selecting Blank App (XAML), you are specifying that you want to create a single-page project for a Windows Store app that has no predefined controls or layout.

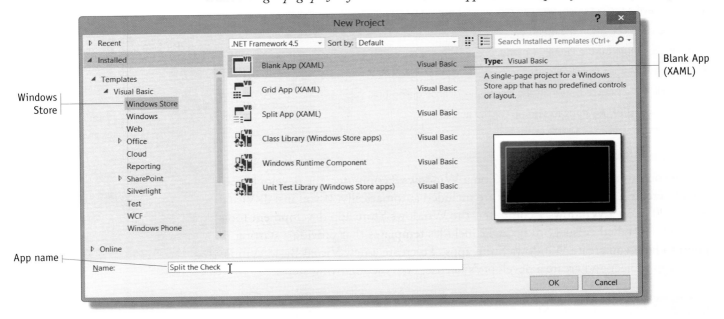

FIGURE 12-5

STEP 3   Tap or click the OK button in the New Project window. If you have not created a developer's license, the Developer License dialog box opens.

Visual Studio creates a new app. The Developer License dialog box opens (Figure 12-6). The project name is displayed in the title bar of the Visual Studio window.

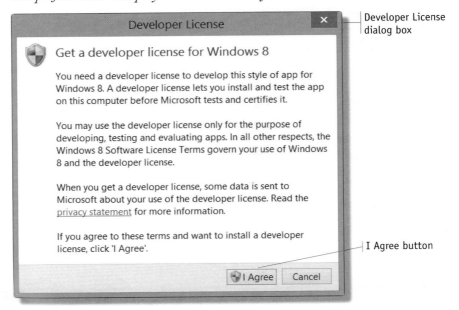

FIGURE 12-6

STEP 4   Tap or click the I Agree button in the Developer License dialog box. Your computer connects to the Microsoft License server using an Internet connection.

The Sign in Developer License dialog box opens, requesting your Microsoft account information (Figure 12-7).

FIGURE 12-7

STEP 5   Type your Microsoft account name and password in the appropriate text boxes. If you do not have an account, tap or click the Sign up now link and follow the steps. Tap or click the Sign in button.

After you sign in with your Microsoft account, the Developer License dialog box opens with a confirmation message displaying an expiration date (Figure 12-8). Your expiration date will not be the same as the one in Figure 12-8.

FIGURE 12-8

STEP 6 Tap or click the Close button in the Developer License dialog box.

The Split the Check app code editor opens (Figure 12-9).

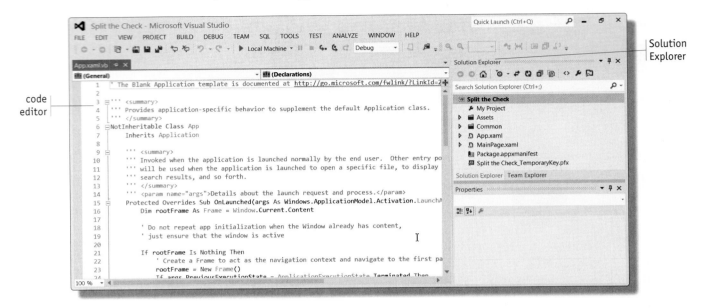

code editor

Solution Explorer

FIGURE 12-9

ONLINE REINFORCEMENT

To view a video of the process in the previous steps, visit CengageBrain.com and navigate to the resources for this title. Tap or click the link for Chapter 12 and then navigate to Video 12-2.

Windows Store Solution Explorer Files

The Blank App template does not have a predefined layout, but many files are automatically created within the Solution Explorer file structure. Any Visual Basic Windows Store app has the same initial files in the Solution Explorer as those shown in Figure 12-10.

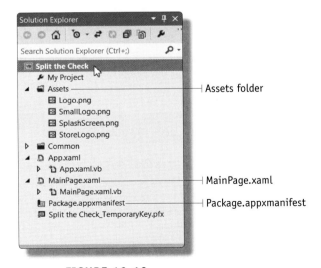

Assets folder

MainPage.xaml

Package.appxmanifest

FIGURE 12-10

- In the Assets folder:
  - o A set of large and small logo images (Logo.png and SmallLogo.png) are displayed on the Start screen. When a tile is displayed, Windows uses the Logo. png file. A splash screen (SplashScreen.png) appears when your app starts.
  - o An image (StoreLogo.png) represents your app in the Windows Store.
- XAML design and code files are included for the app (App.xaml and App. xaml.vb).
- A start page (MainPage.xaml) and an accompanying code file (MainPage. xaml.vb) run when your app starts.
- A manifest file (Package.appxmanifest) includes information that describes your app and lists the files that your app contains. This file contains all of the configuration, settings, and declarations for your application. You can refer to this file for almost everything related to your app running on a Windows 8 device.
- A file ending with TemporaryKey.pfx contains the keyfile related to your developer's license.

Replace the MainPage File

In the Solution Explorer, the MainPage.xaml file is based on the Blank Page template. You should delete MainPage.xaml because its code contains only a minimal amount of functionality. To create the Split the Check app, a template named Basic Page replaces the Blank Page template. The Basic Page template can adapt to different layouts and adds helper classes that increase functionality. This template includes a title and a Back button control in the layout. To replace MainPage.xaml with the Basic Page template, you can take the following steps:

STEP 1 In the Solution Explorer, tap or click MainPage.xaml. Press the DELETE key.

A confirmation message opens and confirms that MainPage.xaml will be deleted permanently (Figure 12-11).

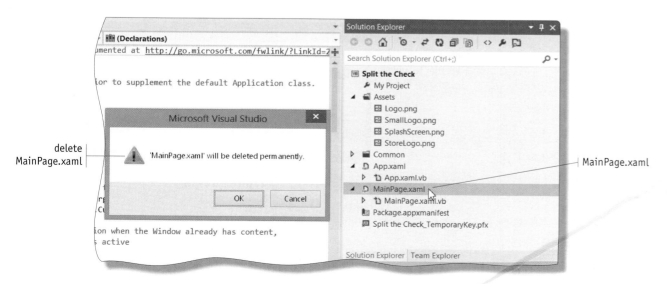

FIGURE 12-11

STEP 2 Tap or click the OK button to permanently delete MainPage.xaml. Tap or click PROJECT on the menu bar, and then select Add New Item. In the left column, tap or click Windows Store. In the middle pane, tap or click Basic Page. Type `MainPage.xaml` in the Name text box.

The Add New Item – Split the Check dialog box opens; the Windows Store Basic Page template is renamed as MainPage.xaml (Figure 12-12).

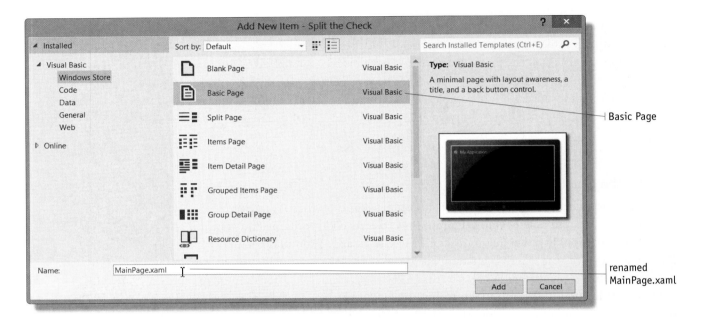

FIGURE 12-12

STEP 3 Tap or click the Add button.

A Microsoft Visual Studio dialog box opens and asks whether to add missing files (Figure 12-13).

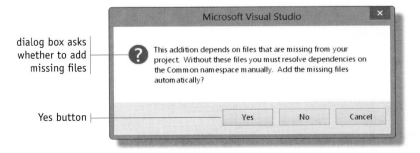

FIGURE 12-13

STEP 4 Tap or click the Yes button. When the new page shows an error in the designer, tap or click the Local Machine button in the toolbar to run the app.

The new page shows an error in the designer until you build the helper classes it needs. A gray splash screen is displayed briefly with an X in the center. After tapping or clicking the Local Machine button, the app displays the start page with the title My Application in full-screen mode (Figure 12-14).

My Application

Windows Store app runs in full screen

FIGURE 12-14

STEP 5 Tap or click the Stop Debugging button in the toolbar.

The Basic Page template named MainPage.xaml opens in Visual Studio. Files for several utility classes are added to your project in the Common folder (Figure 12-15).

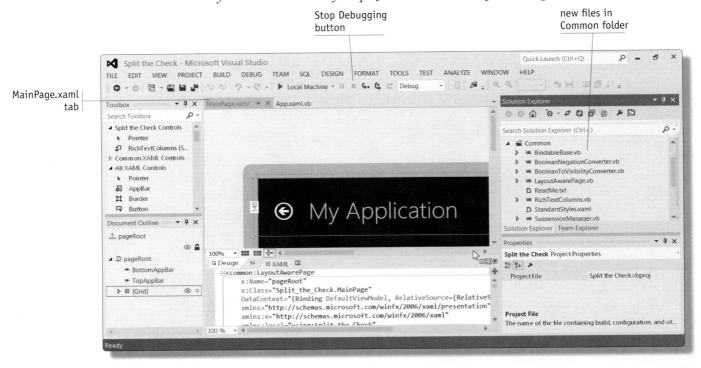

FIGURE 12-15

HEADS UP

If you leave the default name for the Basic Page template, BasicPage1.xaml, the project will not build correctly.

Customize the Splash Screen

When you execute the app, a splash screen is displayed briefly with a gray background, as specified in the app's manifest files. The X in the center of the page is defined by SplashScreen.png in the Assets folder. Every Windows Store app must have a splash screen that consists of a background color and a splash screen image. In the chapter project, the background color for the splash screen is set to white and an image named SplashScreen.png is displayed. Windows Store apps display the splash screen immediately when the user launches an app to provide visual interest while app resources are initialized behind the scenes. As soon as your app is ready for interaction, Windows dismisses the splash screen.

You customize the splash screen using the Manifest Designer, which is found in the Package.appxmanifest file. The image displayed on a splash screen must be 620 x 300 pixels and should use the transparent PNG file format. You can convert image files in Microsoft Paint to the appropriate size and PNG file format if necessary. Microsoft recommends that the splash screen not display advertisements or multiple images. The background color of the splash screen can be changed to common colors such as white, green, and blue, or to hexadecimal colors in a format such as #46A46B. To change the image of the splash screen in the Assets folder and customize the color using the Manifest Designer, complete the following steps:

STEP 1   Scroll in the Solution Explorer and double-tap or double-click the Package.appxmanifest file.

The Package.appxmanifest tab opens, displaying the properties of the app's deployment package in the Manifest Designer (Figure 12-16).

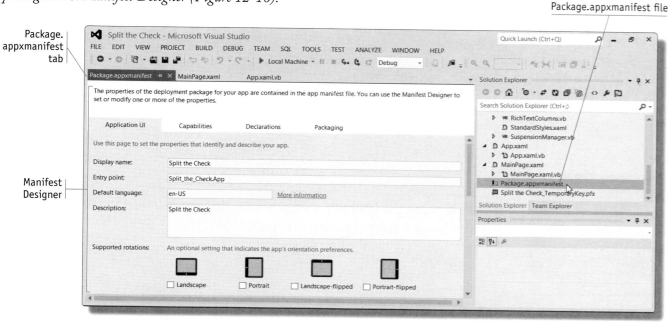

FIGURE 12-16

STEP 2   Scroll down to view the Splash Screen section in the Manifest Designer.

The Splash Screen section is displayed in the Manifest Designer (Figure 12-17).

FIGURE 12-17

STEP 3   Type white in the Background color text box of the Manifest Designer.

The background color for the splash screen is set to white (Figure 12-18).

white entered as
Background
color

FIGURE 12-18

STEP 4   Open the USB folder that contains the student Data Files for Chapter 12. In the Solution Explorer, expand the Assets folder, if necessary. To replace the blank splash screen file, drag the SplashScreen.png file from the USB folder to the Assets folder until a plus sign pointer appears. Release the mouse button.

A Destination File Exists dialog box opens (Figure 12-19).

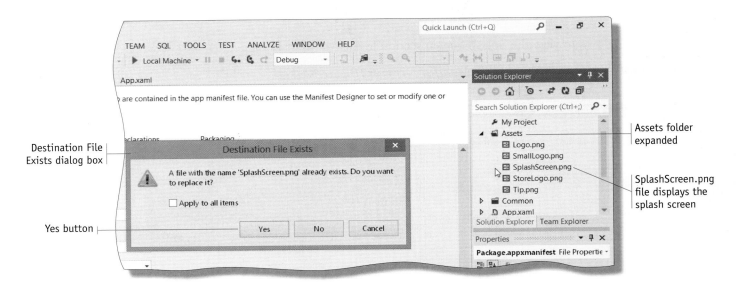

Destination File
Exists dialog box

Yes button

Assets folder
expanded

SplashScreen.png
file displays the
splash screen

FIGURE 12-19

STEP 5   Tap or click the Yes button.

The original SplashScreen.png file in the Assets folder is replaced with the file from the USB drive.

Change the Page Title

By default, the MainPage.xaml page is titled My Application. The title appears in a TextBlock object. Each object in Windows Store app development has properties. These properties are similar to those in Windows applications, but a new feature called a **property marker** is displayed in the Properties window to the right of each property value. The property marker is a small box symbol that you can tap or click to open a property menu. The Text property marker is green to indicate that it is set to a resource. To change the page title, you can complete the following steps:

STEP 1   Close the Package.appxmanifest tab. Tap or click the Yes button if necessary to save changes to Package.appxmanifest. Collapse the Assets folder in the Solution Explorer. Tap or click the My Application TextBlock object at the top of MainPage.xaml. Scroll to the Text property in the Properties window.

With the TextBlock object selected, the Properties window displays the Text property of the object (Figure 12-20).

ONLINE REINFORCEMENT

To view a video of the process in the previous steps, visit CengageBrain.com and navigate to the resources for this title. Tap or click the link for Chapter 12 and then navigate to Video 12-3.

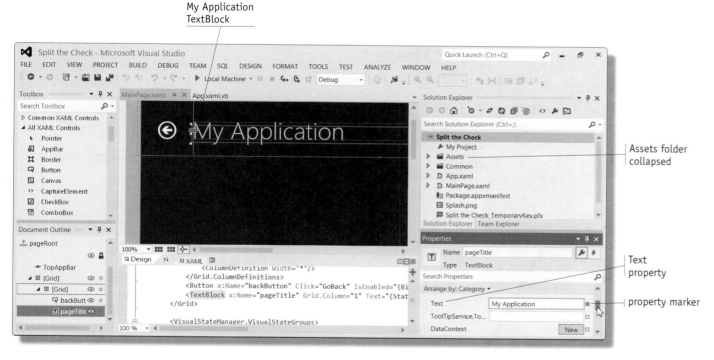

My Application
TextBlock

Assets folder collapsed

Text property

property marker

FIGURE 12-20

STEP 2 Tap or click the property marker (green box symbol) for the Text property of the TextBlock object.

The property menu opens for the Text property (Figure 12-21).

property menu

Edit Resource

property marker

FIGURE 12-21

STEP 3 Tap or click Edit Resource on the property menu. Type Split the Check in the Value text box.

The value for the Text property is entered (Figure 12-22).

Edit Resource dialog box

Value is changed

Text property

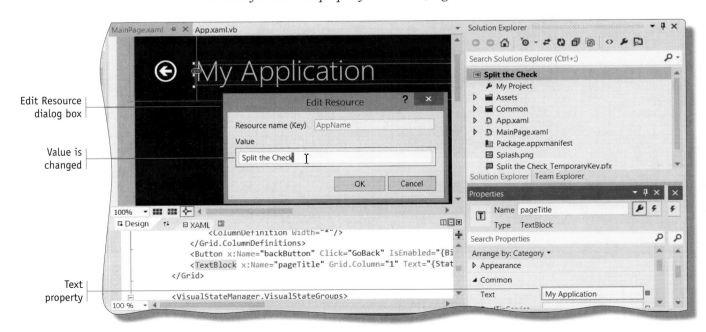

FIGURE 12-22

STEP 4   Tap or click the OK button in the Edit Resource dialog box.

The pageTitle TextBlock object is updated (Figure 12–23).

page title
changes

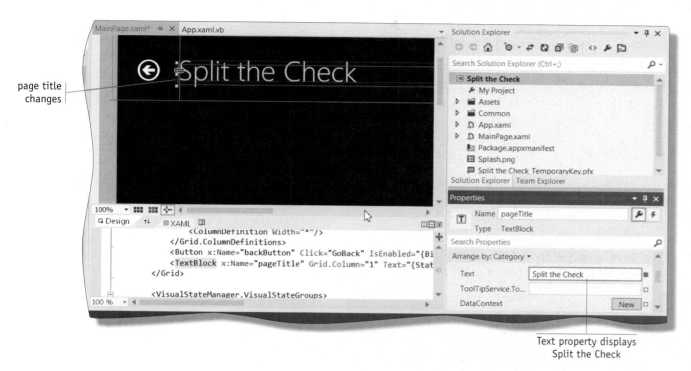

Text property displays
Split the Check

FIGURE 12-23

Add an Image

A Toolbox is available so you can drag and drop objects onto the design surface of each page. Similar objects that are available in Windows applications, such as an Image object, are also provided in the Toolbox of Windows Store apps. Before you place an image on a page within a Windows Store app, the image file must be placed in the Assets folder in the Solution Explorer. To add an image to the start page of an app, you can complete the following steps:

STEP 1   Open the USB folder that contains the student Data Files. In the Solution Explorer, expand the Assets folder. To add the Tip.png file to the Assets folder, drag the Tip.png file to the Assets folder until a plus sign pointer appears, and then release the mouse button.

The Tip.png file appears in the Assets folder in the Solution Explorer (Figure 12-24).

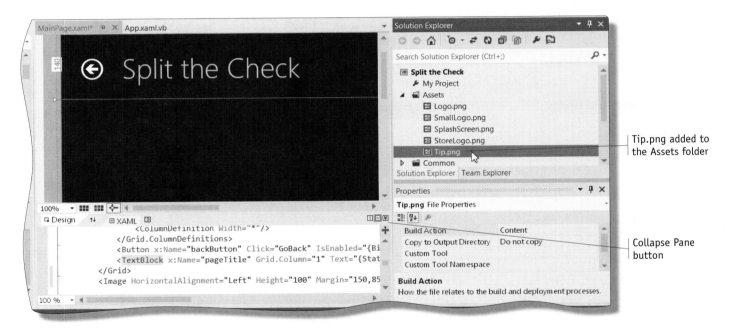

FIGURE 12-24

STEP 2 Tap or click the Collapse Pane button to hide the XAML code. If necessary, open the Toolbox by tapping or clicking VIEW on the menu bar and then tapping or clicking Toolbox. Tap or click Common XAML Controls on the Toolbox. Drag the Image object to MainPage.xaml. Type `picTip` in the Name property of the Image object.

An image named picTip is displayed on the MainPage.xaml page (Figure 12-25).

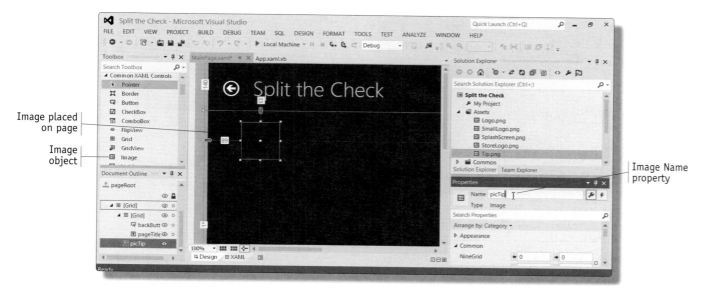

FIGURE 12-25

STEP 3 Tap or click the arrow to the right of the Source property.

The images in the Assets folder are displayed in the Source list (Figure 12-26).

FIGURE 12-26

STEP 4 Tap or click Tip.png in the Source list.

The Tip.png image from the Assets folder is displayed in MainPage.xaml (Figure 12-27).

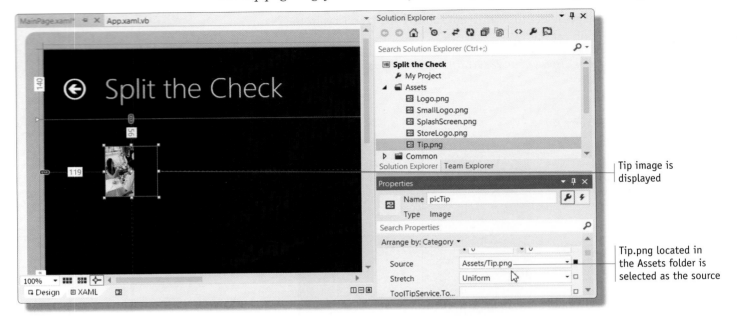

Tip image is displayed

Tip.png located in the Assets folder is selected as the source

FIGURE 12-27

STEP 5 Expand the Layout property in the Properties window. Type 275 in the Width property text box and 500 in the Height property text box.

The width and the height properties are changed and the image is resized (Figure 12-28).

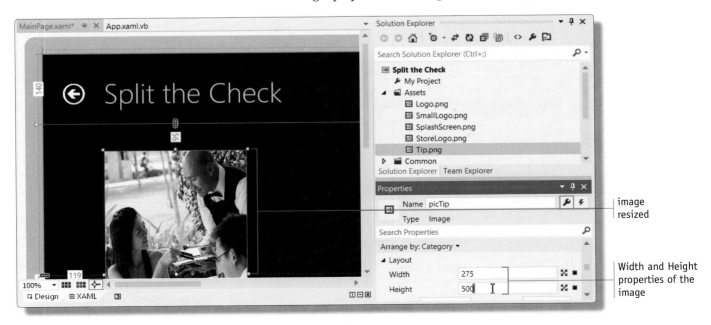

image resized

Width and Height properties of the image

FIGURE 12-28

Add TextBlock Objects

In Windows applications, a Label object displays text in the Windows form. Similarly, a TextBlock object displays text in a Windows Store app page. To add TextBlock objects to the page, you can complete the following steps:

STEP 1   Collapse the Assets folder. Drag the TextBlock object from the Toolbox to MainPage.xaml until a red snap line appears to align the TextBlock object with the top of the image.

The TextBlock object is aligned with red snap lines to the top of the Image object (Figure 12-29).

FIGURE 12-29

© Asia Images Group/Getty Images

STEP 2   Type `lblCheck` in the Name property of the TextBlock object. Type `Check Total:` in the Text property. Scroll down and expand the Text category. Type `30 px` in the FontSize property to the right of the FontFamily property set as Global User Interface.

The TextBlock object is displayed on the page with the text Check Total: and a font size of 30 px (Figure 12-30).

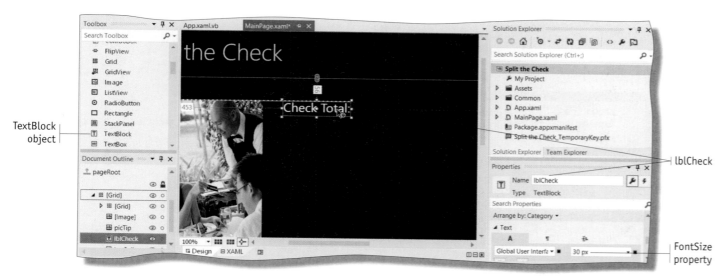

FIGURE 12-30

© Asia Images Group/Getty Images

STEP 3 Drag another TextBlock object from the Toolbox to MainPage.xaml until a red snap line appears to align the object with the left edge of the previous TextBlock object. Type `lblParty` in the Name property of the TextBlock object. Type `Party Size:` in the Text property. Type `30 px` in the FontSize property.

The second TextBlock object is displayed with the text Party Size: and a font size of 30 px (Figure 12-31).

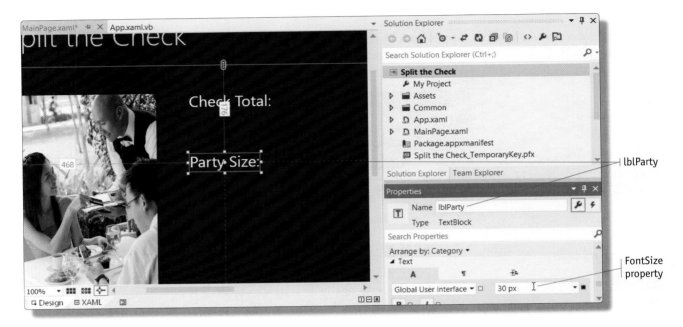

lblParty

FontSize property

FIGURE 12-31

STEP 4 Drag a third TextBlock object to MainPage.xaml until a red snap line appears to align the object with the left edges of the previous TextBlock objects. Type `lblTip` in the Name property of the TextBlock object. Type `Tip Amount:` in the Text property. Type `30 px` in the FontSize property.

The third TextBlock object is displayed with the text Tip Amount: and a font size of 30 px (Figure 12-32).

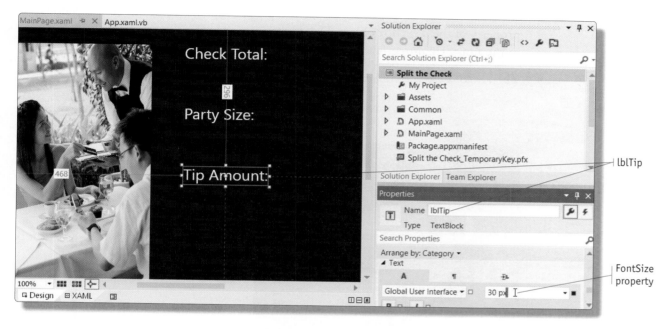

FIGURE 12-32

Add a TextBox Object

When the Split the Check app runs, the user first enters the check total that will be split among a group of diners. A TextBox object is necessary to accept the user's input. To add a TextBox object, you can complete the following step:

STEP 1   Drag a TextBox object from the Toolbox to MainPage.xaml until a red snap line appears to align the object with the top of the first TextBlock object. Resize the TextBox object until the width is 100 pixels. Type `txtCheck` in the Name property of the TextBox object. Delete the text in the Text property. Type `20 px` in the FontSize property.

The TextBox object is displayed with a font size of 20 px (Figure 12-33).

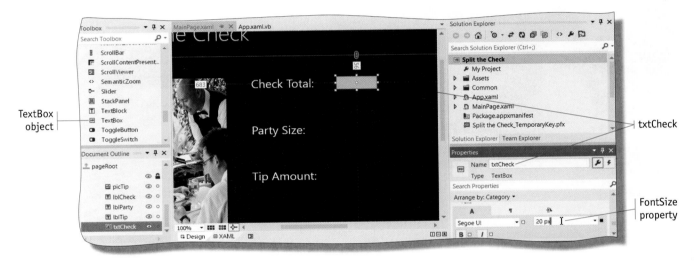

FIGURE 12-33

Design Concepts for Touch

The emergence of touch-based smartphones, tablets, and ultrabooks has changed how users interact with their devices. With touch, you can enlarge and shrink each image to view and edit picture files, use gestures to sign in to your device instead of typing a password, or create a short message service (SMS) message by tapping the screen. Using touch is silent and less distracting than typing on a keyboard, but if the design is not functional, touch can be frustrating for the user. As you add touch interactive controls, consider that each control needs to be large enough for touch. Microsoft recommends that touch controls should be at least 40 × 40 pixels and that closely adjacent controls should have at least 5 pixels separating them. Touch controls should not be placed near the edges of the touch screen because the edges are sometimes beveled and less sensitive to touch. The edges can also be very difficult to touch accurately.

A well-designed app should use the common controls in the Windows Store Apps Toolbox. Most common controls are designed to support an effective touch experience. If necessary, the app can use well-implemented custom controls that are designed to support easy targeting and interactive manipulation. For example, in the Split the Check app, the user could either type the size of the party splitting the check or select it from a ComboBox object. (ComboBox objects are listed in the Common Controls category of the Toolbox.) Lengthy text input is especially difficult using touch, so acceptable default text values can greatly simplify tasks.

Add ComboBox Objects

After the user enters the check total, the next step is to enter the size of the party (2–10) and the tip amount (10%, 15%, or 20%). Two ComboBox objects are necessary to accept the user's touch or mouse input for the size of the party and the tip amount. To add multiple ComboBox objects, you can complete the following steps:

STEP 1 Drag a ComboBox object from the Toolbox to MainPage.xaml until a red snap line appears to align the object with the top of the Party Size: TextBlock object. Resize the ComboBox object to a width of 100 pixels. Type cboPartySize in the Name property of the ComboBox object. Type 20 px in the FontSize property. Tap or click the ellipsis button to the right of the Items property.

The Object Collection Editor: Items dialog box opens so you can add the items to display in the ComboBox object (Figure 12-34).

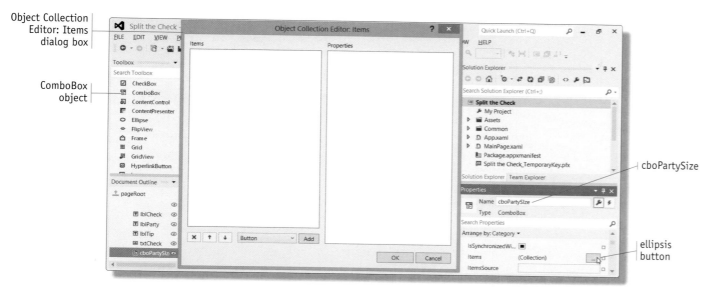

FIGURE 12-34

STEP 2   Tap or click the Button arrow and then tap or click ComboBoxItem at the bottom of the Object Collection Editor: Items dialog box. Tap or click the Add button and then type 2 in the Content text box in the right Properties pane. Tap or click the Add button and then type 3 in the Content text box in the right Properties pane. Repeat this step to add each of the numbers 4 through 10 as options in the Content text box.

The Object Collection Editor: Items dialog box shows the options to display in the cboPartySize ComboBox object (Figure 12-35).

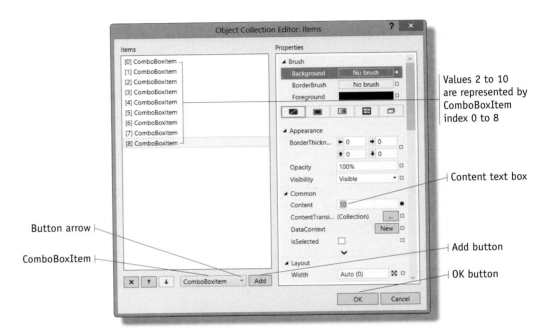

FIGURE 12-35

STEP 3   Tap or click the OK button to close the dialog box. Drag another
ComboBox object from the Toolbox to MainPage.xaml until a red snap line appears
to align the object with the top of the Tip Amount: TextBlock object. Resize the
ComboBox object to a width of 100 pixels. Type `cboTip` in the Name property of
the ComboBox object. Type `20 px` in the FontSize property.

The second ComboBox object is displayed on MainPage.xaml (Figure 12-36).

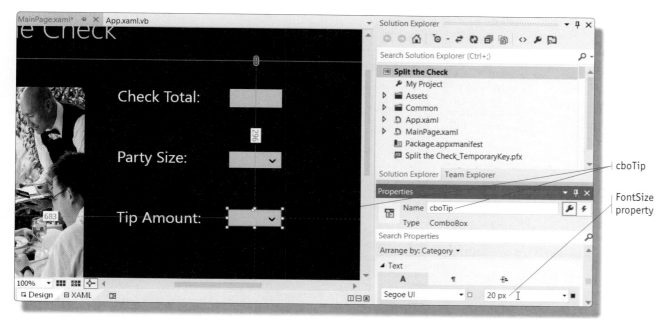

FIGURE 12-36

STEP 4   Tap or click the ellipsis button to the right of the Items property for cboTip. Tap or click the Button arrow and then tap or click ComboBoxItem in the Object Collection Editor: Items dialog box. Tap or click the Add button. Type 10% in the Content text box in the right Properties pane. Tap or click the Add button and then type 15% in the Content text box in the right Properties pane. Tap or click the Add button and then type 20% in the Content text box in the right Properties pane.

The Object Collection Editor: Items dialog box shows the options to display in cboTip (Figure 12-37).

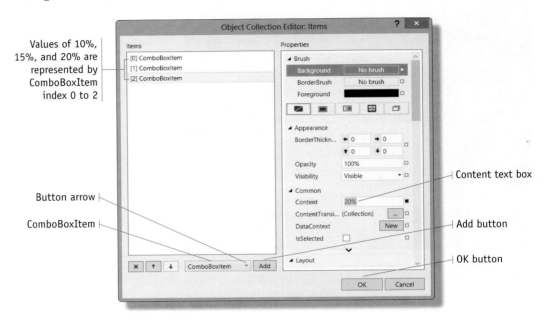

Values of 10%, 15%, and 20% are represented by ComboBoxItem index 0 to 2

Button arrow

ComboBoxItem

Content text box

Add button

OK button

FIGURE 12-37

STEP 5   Tap or click the OK button to close the Object Collection Editor: Items dialog box.

The ComboBox object named cboTip contains three tip amounts.

Add a Button Object

One of the most common events in many apps occurs when a user taps or clicks a Button object to launch an event handler in the code. When the user taps or clicks the Button object in the Split the Check app, the app displays the amount each diner will pay for their share of the check with the tip included. Remember to make user interface elements such as a button large enough for a fingertip to contact. To add a Button object and TextBlock object, you can complete the following steps:

STEP 1   Drag a Button object from the Toolbox to MainPage.xaml below the Tip Amount: TextBlock and cboTip ComboBox objects. Resize the Button object to a width of 225 pixels. Type `btnSplit` in the Name property of the Button object. Type `Split the Check` in the Content property of the Button object. Type `20 px` in the FontSize property of the Text category.

The Button object is displayed on the page (Figure 12-38).

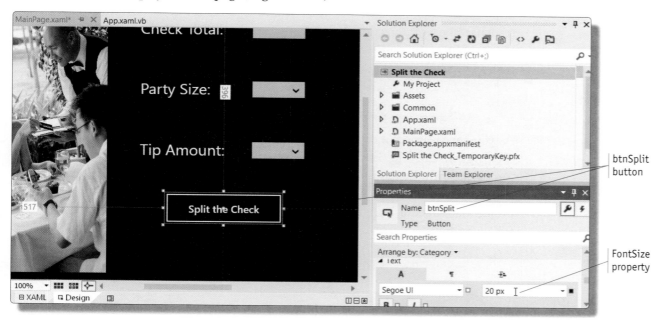

FIGURE 12-38

© Asia Images Group/Getty Images

STEP 2   Drag a TextBlock object from the Toolbox to MainPage.xaml and align it with the left edge of the Button object. Type `lblResult` in the Name property of the TextBlock object. Delete the text TextBlock in the Text property. Type `30 px` in the FontSize property.

The lblResult TextBlock object is displayed at the bottom of the page (Figure 12-39).

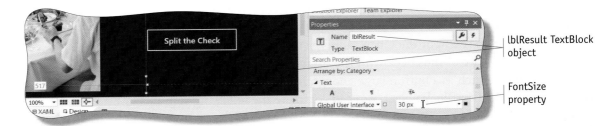

FIGURE 12-39

© Asia Images Group/Getty Images

Code a Windows Store App

The Visual Basic code for Windows Store apps is similar to the code for a Windows application. For example, you write code to handle events that take place in response to user interaction. When a user interacts with Windows 8 Store apps, any touch, mouse, and pen/stylus interactions are received, processed, and managed as pointer input.

Enter Visual Basic Code for Event Handling

As you have learned, most processing in an event-driven program occurs when the user triggers an event. In the Split the Check app, the user taps or clicks the Button object with the mouse, stylus/pen, or fingertip after entering the check total, party size, and tip amount. The code is identical to that in a Windows application project developed using Visual Basic. You can create the event handler using the following steps:

STEP 1   Double-tap or double-click the Split the Check Button object. Type the
introductory comments for the event and then type the Option Strict On statement.
Tap or click within the btnSplit_Click event.

*The code window is displayed on the MainPage.xaml.vb tabbed page (Figure 12-40).
The code in the window is generated by Visual Studio. This code identifies the Basic Page
template code and a click event handler, which is the code that executes when an event is
triggered by touch, a mouse click, or a tap from a stylus. The insertion point appears in the
btnSplit_Click event handler.*

MainPage.xaml.vb
tab

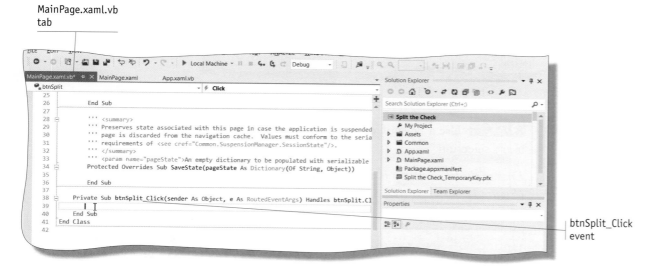

btnSplit_Click
event

FIGURE 12-40

STEP 2   Initialize the variables for the app.

The variables are initialized in the btnSplit_Click event handler (Figure 12-41).

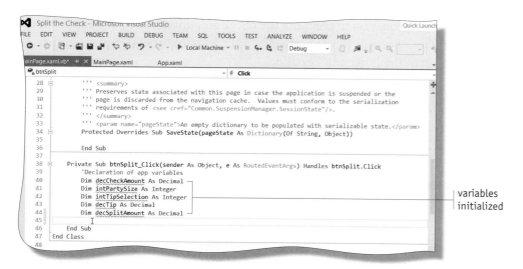

variables
initialized

FIGURE 12-41

STEP 3 Convert the TextBox and ComboBox objects and assign them to variables.

Each of the user's selections is assigned to a variable. The SelectedIndex property of cboPartySize has the value of 2 added to the index value. The index of the first ComboBox object is assigned to 0, so if the user selects the corresponding party size of 2, the value of 2 must be added to the index (Figure 12-42).

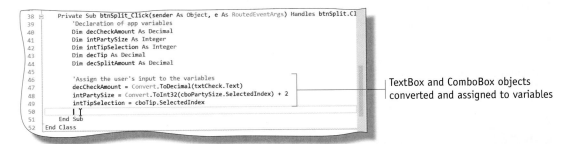

```
38    Private Sub btnSplit_Click(sender As Object, e As RoutedEventArgs) Handles btnSplit.Cl
39        'Declaration of app variables
40        Dim decCheckAmount As Decimal
41        Dim intPartySize As Integer
42        Dim intTipSelection As Integer
43        Dim decTip As Decimal
44        Dim decSplitAmount As Decimal
45
46        'Assign the user's input to the variables
47        decCheckAmount = Convert.ToDecimal(txtCheck.Text)
48        intPartySize = Convert.ToInt32(cboPartySize.SelectedIndex) + 2
49        intTipSelection = cboTip.SelectedIndex
50
51    End Sub
52 End Class
```

TextBox and ComboBox objects converted and assigned to variables

FIGURE 12-42

STEP 4 Use a Select Case statement to assign a tip decimal value based on the user's selection.

Each of the tip selections is assigned to a decimal value using a Select Case statement (Figure 12-43).

```
50        'Assign the tip
51        Select Case intTipSelection
52            Case 0
53                decTip = 0.1D
54            Case 1
55                decTip = 0.15D
56            Case 2
57                decTip = 0.2D
58        End Select
59
60    End Sub
61 End Class
```

Select Case determines tip percentage based on index of ComboBox object

FIGURE 12-43

STEP 5 Enter an equation to compute the check amount added to the tip amount divided by number of people in the party. The split amount for each person in the party is displayed in the lblResult TextBlock.

The equation and result are coded to compute the split amount of the total check amount with tip added (Figure 12-44).

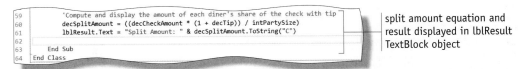

```
59        'Compute and display the amount of each diner's share of the check with tip
60        decSplitAmount = ((decCheckAmount * (1 + decTip)) / intPartySize)
61        lblResult.Text = "Split Amount: " & decSplitAmount.ToString("C")
62
63    End Sub
64 End Class
```

split amount equation and result displayed in lblResult TextBlock object

FIGURE 12-44

Package and Market an App

After you complete the design and coding process, you can access the Windows Store and package your Windows Store app for distribution by using Visual Studio. You can use the Windows Store as the primary way to sell your apps or otherwise make them available.

Customize the App Logos

Before your app is tested and published, you must customize the logos that initially appear as placeholder images. The image file named Logo.png in the Assets folder is displayed as a Windows tile on the Start screen. You can use an optional file, WideTile.png, for a full-sized Windows tile. The Logo.png file in the Assets folder is used when an application list is shown in Windows 8. The third logo, represented by the image file named StoreLogo.png, is used for marketing the app in the Windows Store. Users will see this icon when deciding which new apps to add to their device. An unprofessional icon indicates a poor application to most users. Before uploading the app to the Windows Store, you must replace the three placeholder logos with actual image files to pass Microsoft app certification. The three logos need to be an exact size. Logo.png must be 150 × 150 pixels, SmallLogo.png must be 30 × 30 pixels, and StoreLogo.png must be 50 × 50 pixels.

When designing the images for your app logos, consider adding your app's name in the image or having Windows overlay the name on top of the image. By default, Logo.png appears on the Start screen (Figure 12-45) as a gray tile that displays the name of the app and a white X as a placeholder for an actual image.

Split the Check app tile appears on Start screen without an image by default

FIGURE 12-45

You can copy your customized logos and replace the placeholder image logo files in the Assets folder. To replace the placeholder images with the three logos you need to display on the tile and in the Windows Store, you can take the following steps:

STEP 1 Open the USB folder that contains the student Data Files for Chapter 12. In the Solution Explorer, expand the Assets folder. To replace the blank logo files named Logo.png, SmallLogo.png, and StoreLogo.png, drag the Logo.png, SmallLogo.png, and StoreLogo.png files to the Assets folder until a plus sign pointer appears, and then release the mouse button.

A Destination File Exists dialog box opens (Figure 12-46).

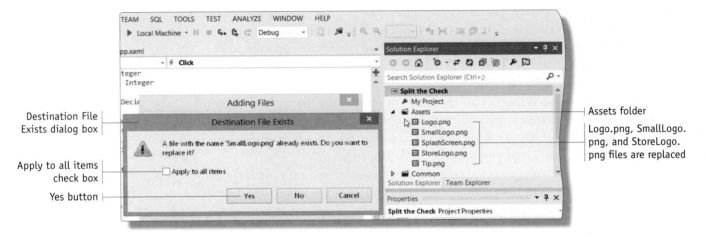

FIGURE 12-46

STEP 2 Tap or click the Apply to all items check box in the Destination File Exists dialog box. Tap or click the Yes button.

The three original placeholder files in the Assets folder are replaced with the files from the USB drive (Figure 12-47).

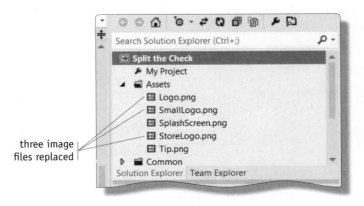

FIGURE 12-47

STEP 3   Tap or click the Save All button on the toolbar, and then tap or click Save in the Save Project dialog box. Tap or click the Start Debugging button to run the app on the local machine. (If a Local Machine button appears instead of the Start Debugging button, tap or click the Local Machine button.) Test the program and close the app. Press the WINDOWS key to view the Start screen. Scroll to the right, if necessary, to view the app logo tile for the Split the Check app on the Start screen.

The app logo is displayed on the Start screen (Figure 12–48).

Windows tile displays Split the Check logo image

FIGURE 12-48

Test the App

Before the world views your app, you want to make sure everything works perfectly. You can run the app on your local machine, on the built-in simulator within Visual Studio, or on a remote machine. By default, your app runs on the local machine, as shown in Figure 12-49.

FIGURE 12-49

Windows Store apps are displayed on a full screen and respond to user touch and hardware events such as screen rotations. The Visual Studio **simulator** for Windows Store apps is a desktop application that simulates a Windows Store app. It enables a developer on a single machine to run applications and simulate common touch and rotation events. When you run an app in the simulator, you can choose the physical screen size and resolution that you want to emulate. Before you publish a Windows Store app, ensure that the app logo and splash screen will be displayed correctly on a variety of devices that have different screen resolutions. To run an app in the simulator, you can follow these steps:

STEP 1 Tap or click the arrow to the right of the Start Debugging button (or the Local Machine button) on the Standard toolbar.

Simulator is selected as the device on which the app will be tested during the debugging process (Figure 12-50).

FIGURE 12-50

STEP 2 Tap or click Simulator.

The simulator opens and briefly displays a splash screen (Figure 12-51). When the splash screen closes, the main page of the app opens (Figure 12-52).

Start Debugging button with Simulator selected

splash screen appears in the simulator

FIGURE 12-51

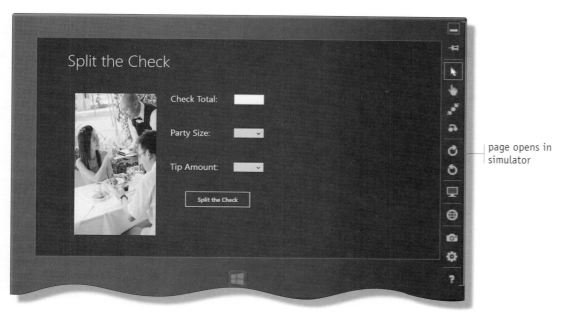

page opens in
simulator

FIGURE 12-52

© Asia Images Group/Getty Images

STEP 3 Tap or click the Rotate clockwise (90 degrees) button on the right side of
the simulator.

The simulator rotates the main page of the app 90 degrees (Figure 12-53).

Rotate clockwise (90
degrees) button

FIGURE 12-53

© Asia Images Group/Getty Images

STEP 4 Tap or click the Change resolution button on the right side of the simulator.

Seven different resolution sizes are displayed in the Change resolution listing (Figure 12-54).

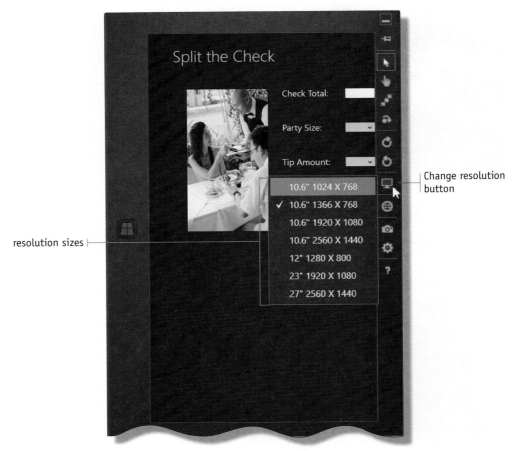

FIGURE 12-54

© Asia Images Group/Getty Images

STEP 5   Tap or click the Send Windows key button on the side of the simulator.
Scroll if necessary to view the Split the Check app tile.

The Start screen displays the Split the Check app tile (Figure 12–55).

Send Windows key button

FIGURE 12-55

© A-Digit/Getty Images

IN THE REAL WORLD

The Microsoft Windows Simulator offers a Copy screenshot tool that can take active screenshots of the app while it is running. You can capture a screenshot of your app for submission to the Windows Store. When you submit an app to the Windows Store, you must include screenshots of the app while it is running.

STEP 6   Press and hold or right-click Microsoft Windows Simulator on the taskbar, and then tap or click Close window.

The Microsoft Windows Simulator closes.

Analyze the Code

Visual Studio 2012 features a code analysis tool that can examine your code for a set of common defects and violations of good programming practice. Part of the process of submitting an app to the Windows Store involves certification by Microsoft testers. Validating your code prior to submission gives your app the best chance of passing certification. To test a completed app in the Run Code Analysis tool, you can complete these steps:

STEP 1   Tap or click ANALYZE on the menu bar, and then tap or click Run Code Analysis on Split the Check.

A Code Analysis pane opens on the right side of the Visual Studio window. After several seconds, the Code Analysis pane lists any detected issues. If you have errors, you can search the Help files for assistance to correct each issue (Figure 12-56).

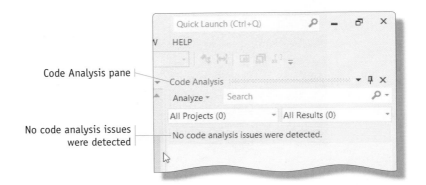

FIGURE 12-56

STEP 2   Tap or click the Close button on the Code Analysis pane.

The Code Analysis pane closes.

Performance Testing

Another tool to help ensure that your app performs well is the built-in Visual Studio Performance Analysis tool. The **Performance Analysis tool** records data about the app's performance and execution. You can then view this data as a chart. You can also determine if you have any performance bottlenecks that affect your app. For example, if you were connecting to a database and a Performance Analysis graph showed an extreme spike in the system resources, you might want to change the way your app accesses the database. To test a completed app in the Performance Analysis tool, you can complete these steps:

STEP 1   Tap or click the MainPage.xaml tab. Tap or click ANALYZE on the menu bar, and then tap or click Start Performance Analysis. The simulator opens, the splash screen is displayed, and then the main page opens. Run the app with any test data and tap or click the Split the Check button to complete the execution. Press and hold or right-click the simulator button on the taskbar, and then tap or click Close window to close the simulator.

After the app runs and the tool is closed, a Sample Profiling Report opens (Figure 12-57). Notice that on a 100-point scale, the blue line representing CPU usage was low throughout the execution, which means that the app performs well.

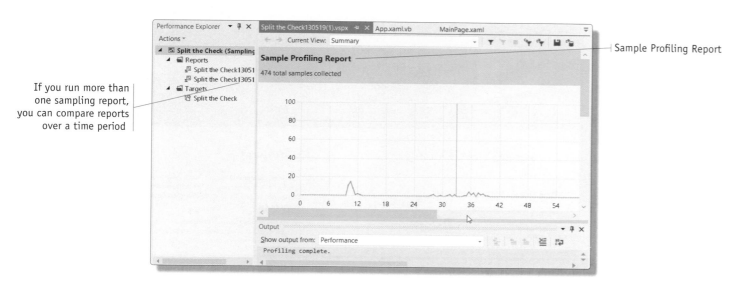

FIGURE 12-57

STEP 2   Close the tab for the Performance Analysis tool (Split the Check######. vspx). The ###### symbols represent different numbers for each Sample Profiling Report that is run.

The Performance Analysis tab is closed.

Open a Windows Store Developer Account

When you created your first app, you used your Microsoft account to acquire a 30-day developer's license. You must also set up a Windows Store developer account to reserve an app name and submit your app to the Windows Store. The Windows Store requires a credit card to open a developer account, even if you have a registration code that offsets the registration fee. The credit card is used to confirm your identity. (Recall that *dreamspark.com* provides students with a free registration code.) The Windows Store offers two types of developer accounts: individual accounts for $49 a year and company accounts for $99 a year. To open a Windows Store developer account, you can complete the following step:

STEP 1   Tap or click PROJECT on the menu bar, tap or click Store, and then tap or click Open Developer Account.

A website opens so you can complete the registration information (Figure 12–58).

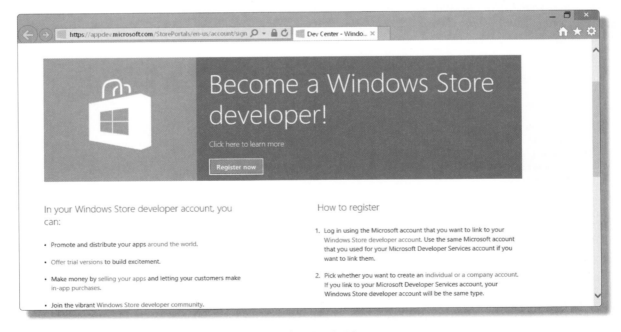

FIGURE 12-58

Reserve an App Name

Before packaging and posting your app in the Windows Store with your developer's account, you must reserve a unique name for the app on the dashboard of the Windows Store. The dashboard is where you submit a new app, see how your current apps are doing, and get information to help plan your next app. You can reserve a Windows Store app name for one year. An app's name makes an initial impression to customers about its purpose, so you should select a name that captures customers' interest. To reserve an app name, you can complete the following steps:

STEP 1 Tap or click PROJECT on the menu bar, tap or click Store, and then tap or click Reserve App Name.

The Windows Store Dashboard website opens. After you log in to your account, the dashboard opens to begin the process of reserving a name for your app (Figure 12-59).

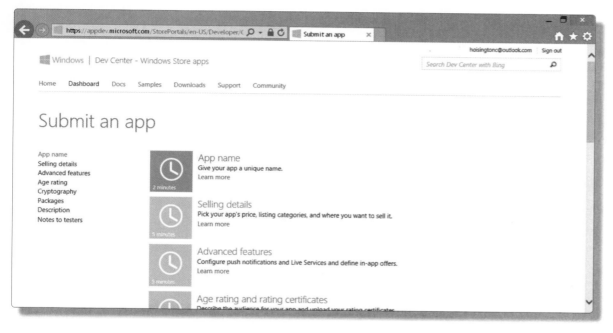

FIGURE 12-59

STEP 2   For the Split the Check app, verify that the app is named Split the Check with Tip.

This name is unique and reserved for one year (Figure 12–60).

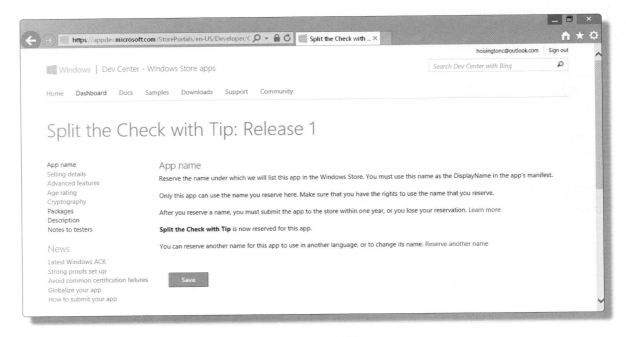

FIGURE 12-60

Package an App

Before you submit your app to the Windows Store, be sure to have the information in Table 12-2 ready. Even if the action is optional, make sure you include everything so your app is well represented in the Windows Store.

Prepare for Submitting an App

Action	Details
Reserve an App Name	Using the dashboard, reserve a unique app name that is 256 characters or less.
Plan a Price Tier	Create a plan for your free or paid app. Consider adding free trials or in-app purchases.
Select a Market	Decide which languages will be available for your app and the countries where it will be sold.
Select a Category	Each app requires a category such as productivity or games. After selecting the category, you must also select a subcategory.
Declare App as Accessible	When you declare your app as accessible, you agree that it is accessible to all users, including those with disabilities. For example, this means you have tested the app with high-contrast mode and with a screen reader.
Post Minimum System RAM	Determine the minimum amount of RAM memory necessary to run the app.
State Age Rating	Age ratings include suitability for ages 3+, 7+, 12+, and 16+.
Write Description	Each app can be marketed within the Windows Store with a description of 10,000 characters or less.
Add Keywords	Optional – You can use up to seven keywords to describe your app.
Add Copyright and Trademark	Add copyright and trademark information (200 characters or less).
Market with Promotional Images	Optional – Post up to four images.
Market with Screenshots	Optional – Post up to eight screenshots of the app while it is running, with a description of 200 characters or less for each screenshot.
Post an App Website & Support Contact	Optional – Post a URL for the app.

TABLE 12-2

You can submit your app to the Windows Store by completing the following steps:

STEP 1   Tap or click PROJECT on the menu bar, tap or click Store, and then tap or click Create App Packages.

The Create Your Packages dialog box asks if you want to build packages to upload to the Windows Store (Figure 12-61).

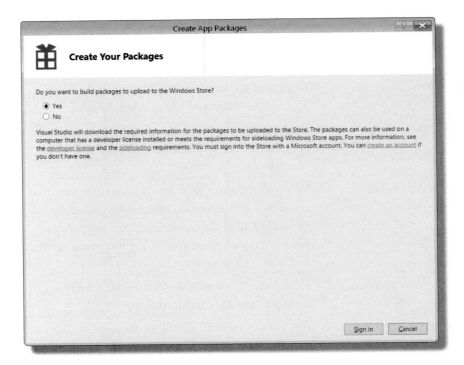

FIGURE 12-61

STEP 2   Tap or click Yes, and then click the Sign In button.

You can submit an app for which you have reserved a name. You must sign into your Windows Store developer account to continue (Figure 12-62).

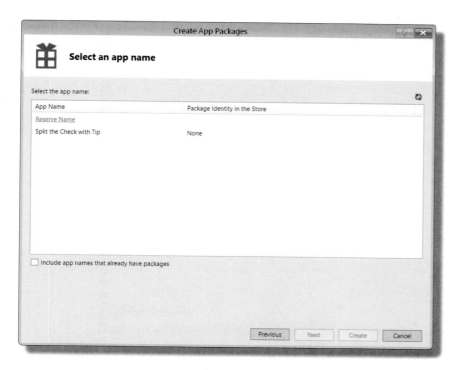

FIGURE 12-62

STEP 3   Tap or click the Create button.

The version of the app submission is displayed as Version 1.0.0.0 (Figure 12-63).

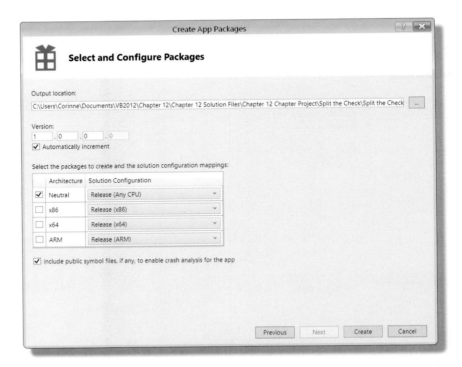

FIGURE 12-63

At this point, your app is tested by the Windows Store with the Windows App Certification kit to obtain a **test certificate**. All app packages that Visual Studio generates are signed with a test certificate. When you create a package, Visual Studio generates a folder that includes the signed package. The certificate (.cer) file is included in the app; this file contains a public key that signs the package for approval to the Windows Store. If your app has errors, the Windows Store generates a report that explains how to fix your app. The certification process takes several minutes (Figure 12-64), and it checks for programming errors as well as keyboard and touch input best practices. The process also ensures that the app launches within five seconds, image assets are the correct size, placeholders have been replaced, the app is not a security risk, and that your app meets other additional requirements listed in the dashboard.

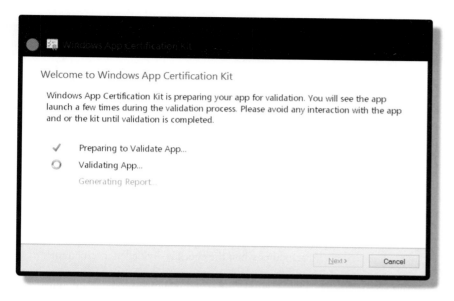

FIGURE 12-64

Submit an App

After you have reserved the app's name, set up a payout account, built the app's package, and tested the app with the Windows App Certification kit, the app is ready for submission. By opening the Windows Store dashboard, you can submit the app with selling details to supply information such as your app's price, category, markets, age ratings, and description.

Monetize a Windows Store App

Creating a business model for monetizing an app is vital if you want to make money in the Windows Store. Like the Apple Store and Google Play Android Marketplace, Windows Store apps that generate less than $25,000 in sales pay the app developer 70 percent of those sales. After the app generates its first $25,000 in sales, the fee for subsequent revenue increases to 80 percent in the Windows Store. As you plan your apps, think about which business model makes the most sense for you and build your app to support your financial plans. You can adjust your pricing or business model later if you decide to make changes. Consider the following business models for monetizing your app:

- Collect the full price of the app before download.
- Offer free trials or limited versions of the app and state that a paid full version is available.
- Sell content, other apps, or new app functionality (such as unlocking the next level of a game) from within the app.
- Create an income stream from advertisements within the app.

Program Design

The requirements document for the Split the Check app is shown in Figure 12-65, and the Use Case Definition document is shown in Figure 12-66.

REQUIREMENTS DOCUMENT

Date Submitted: April 19, 2015

Application Title: Split the Check App

Purpose: This Windows Store app calculates the amount due from each diner when the check is divided at a restaurant.

Program Procedures: The Windows Store app requests the check amount, party size, and tip percentage, and then computes the correct amount that each diner should contribute to pay the check and tip.

Algorithms, Processing, and Conditions:
1. The user views a splash screen, and then the main page opens.
2. The user enters the check amount, party size (2-10), and tip percentage (10%, 15%, 20%), and then taps or clicks a Button object.
3. The split amount is displayed in a TextBlock object.

Notes and Restrictions: The input can be entered by touch or by a keyboard and mouse.

Comments: The image shown in the window should be a picture available on the web.

FIGURE 12-65

© 2014 Cengage Learning

USE CASE DEFINITION

1. The user enters the check amount, number in party, and tip percentage.
2. The user taps or clicks the Split the Check button to display the split amount each diner should pay.

FIGURE 12-66

© 2014 Cengage Learning

Design the Program Processing Objects

The event planning document for the Split the Check app is shown in Figure 12-67.

EVENT PLANNING DOCUMENT			
App Name:	**Developer:**	**Object:**	**Date:**
Split the Check	Corinne Hoisington	MainPage.xaml	July 19, 2015
OBJECT	**EVENT TRIGGER**	**EVENT PROCESSING**	
btnSplit	Tap or click	Convert the user input Calculate the split amount with tip Display the split amount	

FIGURE 12-67

Guided Program Development

To fine-tune the user interface in the Split the Check app and enter the code required to process each event in the program, complete the following steps to create the program shown in Figure 12-1a and Figure 12-1b on page 838.

NOTE TO THE LEARNER

In the following activity, you should complete the tasks within the specified steps. Each of the tasks is accompanied by a Hint Screen. The purpose of the Hint Screen is to indicate where you should perform the activity in the Visual Studio window and to remind you which method to use. If you need further help completing a step, refer to the figure identified by *ref:*.

Guided Program Development

Phase 1: Design the Form

1

● **Create a New Windows Store App** Open Visual Studio and then close the Start page. Tap or click the New Project button on the Standard toolbar. Begin a Windows Store App project as a Blank App and name the project `Split the Check`. If necessary, create a free developer's license (*ref: Figure 12-05*).

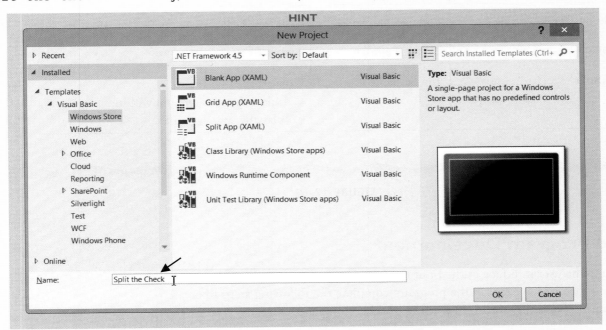

● **Delete MainPage.xaml** Delete MainPage.xaml in the Solution Explorer.

● **Add a New MainPage.xaml** Tap or click PROJECT on the menu bar, and then tap or click Add New Item. In the left column, tap or click Windows Store. In the middle pane, tap or click Basic Page. Type `MainPage.xaml` in the Name text box (*ref: Figure 12-12*).

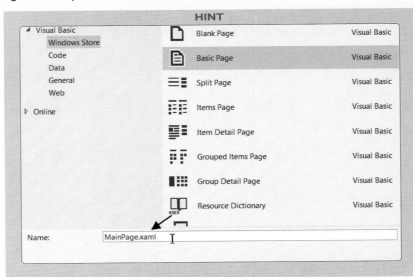

Guided Program Development   *continued*

● **Customize the Splash Screen** Double-tap or double-click Package.appxmanifest. Under Splash Screen, type white for the Background color. Copy the SplashScreen.png file provided with your Data Files to overwrite the placeholder image with the same name in the Assets folder in the Solution Explorer (*ref: Figure 12-19*).

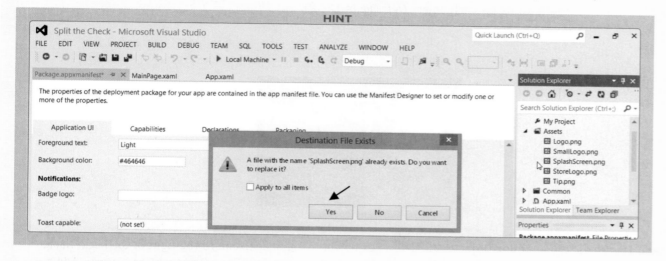

● **Change the Page Title** Select the title My Application on MainPage.xaml. Change the text by tapping or clicking the property marker to the right of the Text property. Tap or click Edit Resource in the property menu and then type Split the Check in the Value text box of the Edit Resource dialog box. Tap or click the OK button (*ref: Figure 12-22*).

● **Add an Image Object** Drag the Tip.png file provided with your Data Files to the Assets folder in the Solution Explorer. Tap or click the Collapse Pane button. Drag the Image object from the Toolbox below the page title on Main-Page.xaml. Name the Image object picTip. Tap or click the arrow to the right of the Source property and select Tip.png. To resize the image, change the Width property to 275 and the Height property to 500 (*ref: Figure 12-28*).

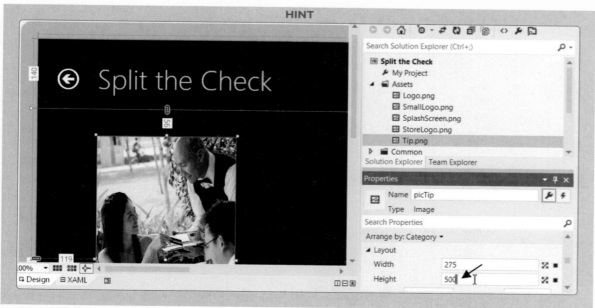

(continues)

● **Add TextBlock Objects** Add three TextBlock objects to MainPage.xaml. Name the first TextBlock object `lblCheck` and name the text `Check Total:`. Name the second TextBlock object `lblParty` and name the text `Party Size:`. Name the third TextBlock object `lblTip` and name the text `Tip Amount:`. Change the FontSize property to `30` px for each object (*ref: Figure 12-32*).

● **Add TextBox and ComboBox Objects** Add a TextBox object to MainPage.xaml to the right of lblCheck. Name the TextBox object `txtCheck` with the Text property cleared and the FontSize property set to `20` px. Add a ComboBox object named `cboPartySize` to the right of lblParty. Change the FontSize property to `20` px. Tap or click the ellipsis to the right of the Items property. Change the Button object to a ComboBoxItem. Tap or click the Add button, and then type `2` in the Content text box. Repeat the process until the values 3 through 10 are added as ComboBoxItems. Add another ComboBox object named `cboTip` to the right of lblTip. Change the FontSize property to `20` px. Tap or click the ellipsis to the right of the Items property. Change the Button object to a ComboBoxItem. Tap or click the Add button, and then type `10%` in the Content text box. Repeat the process to add `15%` and `20%` as ComboBoxItems (*ref: Figure 12-36*).

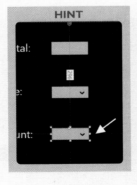

- **Add a Button and TextBlock Objects** Add a Button object named `btnSplit` with the Content property set to `Split the Check` and the FontSize property set to `20 px`. Add a TextBlock object at the bottom named `lblResult` with a cleared Text property and the FontSize property changed to `30 px` (*ref: Figure 12-39*).

The MainPage.xaml design is completed (Figure 12-68).

FIGURE 12-68

© Asia Images Group/Getty Images

Phase 2: Code the Application

- **Code the Comments** Double-tap or double-click the btnSplit Button object to begin coding the application in MainPage.xaml.vb. Type the first four standard comments at the top of the code window. Insert the command `Option Strict On` at the beginning of the code to turn on strict type checking.

- **Initialize the Variables** Enter the code shown in the corresponding Hint Screen and initialize the variables in the code window within the btnSplit_Click event (*ref: Figure 12-41*).

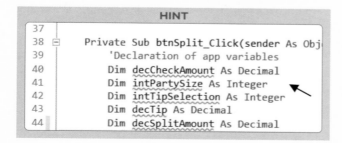

```
HINT
37
38   Private Sub btnSplit_Click(sender As Obj
39       'Declaration of app variables
40       Dim decCheckAmount As Decimal
41       Dim intPartySize As Integer
42       Dim intTipSelection As Integer
43       Dim decTip As Decimal
44       Dim decSplitAmount As Decimal
```

(continues)

- **Convert the Input to Numeric Values** To convert the input from the TextBox and ComboBox objects to numeric values, type the code shown in the corresponding Hint Screen. The value of 2 is added to cboPartySize to match the party size (*ref: Figure 12-42*).

```
                                    HINT
46            'Assign the user's input to the variables
47            decCheckAmount = Convert.ToDecimal(txtCheck.Text)
48            intPartySize = Convert.ToInt32(cboPartySize.SelectedIndex) + 2
49            intTipSelection = cboTip.SelectedIndex
```

- **Code the Select Case Statement** Inside the btnSplit_Click event, after the variables are initialized and converted to numeric values, insert a Select Case statement that assigns the appropriate tip amount of .1D, .15D, or .2D, based on the selected index of the ComboBox object (*ref: Figure 12-43*).

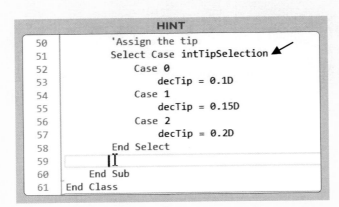

```
                                    HINT
50                  'Assign the tip
51                  Select Case intTipSelection
52                      Case 0
53                          decTip = 0.1D
54                      Case 1
55                          decTip = 0.15D
56                      Case 2
57                          decTip = 0.2D
58                  End Select
59
60          End Sub
61      End Class
```

- **Compute and Display the Split Amount** To compute the tip, the check amount must be added to the tip amount (check amount multiplied by tip percentage) and divided by the number in the party. The lblResult TextBlock displays the split amount (*ref: Figure 12-44*).

The btnSplit_Click event code is completed (Figure 12-69).

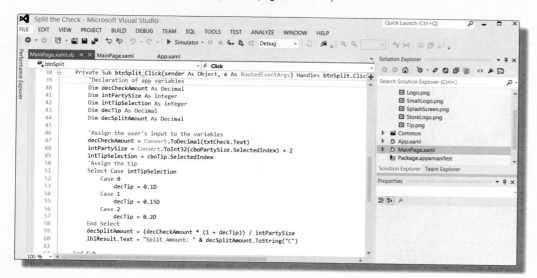

FIGURE 12-69

3

- **Add Three Logo Image Files** Open the USB folder that contains the student Data Files for Chapter 12. In the Solution Explorer, expand the Assets folder. Drag the Logo.png, SmallLogo.png, and StoreLogo.png files to the Assets folder until a plus sign pointer appears. Release the mouse button. Tap or click the Apply to all items check box in the Destination File Exists dialog box. Tap or click the Yes button (*ref: Figure 12-46*).

- **Run the Program** After you make changes to a program, you should save and run it to ensure that your changes work properly and are correct. Also, test the app using the simulator (*ref: Figure 12-52*).

(continues)

● The splash screen opens briefly in the simulator, and then the main page of the app opens, as shown in Figure 12-70.

FIGURE 12-70

© Asia Images Group/Getty Images

Code Listing

The complete code for the sample program is shown in Figure 12-71.

```vb
1  ' Program:      Split the Check Windows Store App
2  ' Developer:    Corinne Hoisington
3  ' Date:         July 19, 2015
4  ' Purpose:      This app calculates each diner's share of a restaurant check with the tip included.
5
6  Option Strict On
7  ' The Basic Page item template is documented at http://go.microsoft.com/fwlink/?LinkId=234237
8
9  ''' <summary>
10 ''' A basic page that provides characteristics common to most applications.
11 ''' </summary>
12 Public NotInheritable Class MainPage
13     Inherits Common.LayoutAwarePage
14
15         ''' <summary>
16         ''' Populates the page with content passed during navigation.  Any saved state is also
17         ''' provided when recreating a page from a prior session.
18         ''' </summary>
19         ''' <param name="navigationParameter">The parameter value passed to
20         ''' <see cref="Frame.Navigate"/> when this page was initially requested.
21         ''' </param>
22         ''' <param name="pageState">A dictionary of state preserved by this page during an earlier
23         ''' session.  This will be null the first time a page is visited.</param>
24         Protected Overrides Sub LoadState(navigationParameter As Object, pageState As Dictionary(Of String, Object))
25
26         End Sub
27
28         ''' <summary>
29         ''' Preserves state associated with this page in case the application is suspended or the
30         ''' page is discarded from the navigation cache.  Values must conform to the serialization
31         ''' requirements of <see cref="Common.SuspensionManager.SessionState"/>.
32         ''' </summary>
33         ''' <param name="pageState">An empty dictionary to be populated with serializable state.</param>
34         Protected Overrides Sub SaveState(pageState As Dictionary(Of String, Object))
35
36         End Sub
37
38     Private Sub btnSplit_Click(sender As Object, e As RoutedEventArgs) Handles btnSplit.Click
39         'Declaration of app variables
40         Dim decCheckAmount As Decimal
41         Dim intPartySize As Integer
42         Dim intTipSelection As Integer
43         Dim decTip As Decimal
44         Dim decSplitAmount As Decimal
45
46         'Assign the user's input to the variables
47         decCheckAmount = Convert.ToDecimal(txtCheck.Text)
48         intPartySize = Convert.ToInt32(cboPartySize.SelectedIndex) + 2
49         intTipSelection = cboTip.SelectedIndex
50         'Assign the tip
51         Select Case intTipSelection
52             Case 0
53                 decTip = 0.1D
54             Case 1
55                 decTip = 0.15D
56             Case 2
57                 decTip = 0.2D
58         End Select
59         decSplitAmount = (decCheckAmount * (1 + decTip)) / intPartySize
60         lblResult.Text = "Split Amount: " & decSplitAmount.ToString("C")
61
62     End Sub
63 End Class
```

FIGURE 12-71

Summary

In this chapter you have learned to create a Windows Store app that runs on a Windows 8 device. The items listed in the table in Figure 12-72 include all the new Visual Studio and Visual Basic skills you have learned in this chapter. Video 12-1 demonstrates the complete program execution.

Visual Basic Skills		
Skill	**Figure Number**	**Video Number**
Examine the Split the Check App	Figure 12-1	Video 12-1
Create a Windows Store App	Figure 12-4	Video 12-2
Customize a Splash Screen	Figure 12-16	Video 12-3
Add an Image	Figure 12-24	Video 12-4

FIGURE 12-72

Learn Online

Reinforcement activities and resources are available at no additional cost on *www.cengagebrain.com*. Visit *www.cengage.com/ct/studentdownload* for detailed instructions about accessing the resources available at the Student Companion Site.

Knowledge Check

1. Describe how a Windows Store app is displayed differently from a Windows application.

2. Instead of icons, Windows Store apps are launched by tapping or clicking _____.

3. What is the file extension of an app package in the Windows Store?

4. What does *touch-first* mean when using Windows Store apps?

5. How many touch points does a Windows 8 device typically have?

6. Windows Store apps can be written in which programming languages?

7. What does XAML stand for?

8. In the chapter project, which language was used to create the design and which language was used to code the events?

9. How do you close a Windows Store app?

10. What is the file name and extension in the Solution Explorer that displays the start page of the app?

11. What is the purpose of the TemporaryKey.pfx file in the Solution Explorer?

12. In the chapter project, why was the initial Blank Page MainPage.xaml file deleted and replaced with a Basic Page template?

13. In which file can you change the background color of the splash screen?

14. What is the name of the green square symbol used in the Text property of a TextBlock object?

15. Instead of running an app on the local machine when tapping or clicking the Start Debugging button, what other options do you have?

16. What is the name of the tool that records data about the app's execution?

17. What is the cost of an individual or company Windows Store developer's license if you are not a student?

18. For a Windows Store app that generates less than $25,000 in sales, what percentage of sales does the developer receive?

19. Name four business models for monetizing an app.

20. An app must launch within how many seconds to become certified?

Debugging Exercises

1. Which four placeholder image files in the Assets folder must be replaced with actual images?

2. When you submit an app to be certified, the Assets folder is approved if the four images are the correct size. Using the same order you listed the images in response to the previous question, list their correct sizes.

Program Analysis

1. The chapter project used a Select Case conditional statement. Rewrite the Select Case statement as If… Else conditional statements.

2. Using the Performance Analysis tool, run your own local test of the chapter project and take screenshots of your results.

3. Using the Code Analysis tool, run your own local test of the chapter project and take screenshots of your results.

Case Programming Assignments

Complete one or more of the following case programming assignments. Submit the program and materials you create to your instructor. The level of difficulty is indicated for each assignment.

●	= Easiest
●●	= Intermediate
●●●	= Challenging

1 ●
FAHRENHEIT TO CELSIUS CONVERSION

Design a Windows Store app and write the code that will execute according to the program requirements in Figure 12-73 and the Use Case Definition in Figure 12-74 on the next page. Before writing the code, create an event planning document for each event in the program. The completed Windows Store app and other objects in the user interface are shown in Figure 12-75a and Figure 12-75b on the next page.

REQUIREMENTS DOCUMENT

Date Submitted:	January 1, 2015
Application Title:	Fahrenheit to Celsius Conversion App
Purpose:	This Windows Store app opens with a splash screen and allows a user to convert a Fahrenheit temperature to a Celsius temperature.
Program Procedures:	From the start page on the screen, the user should enter a Fahrenheit temperature, and the equivalent Celsius temperature should be displayed.
Algorithms, Processing, and Conditions:	1. A blue splash screen is displayed; it includes an image named SplashScreen.png.
	2. The user must be able to enter the Fahrenheit temperature on the first page.
	3. After the user taps or clicks the Compute Celsius Temperature button, the Celsius temperature is displayed.
Notes and Restrictions:	1. All placeholder images must be replaced.
	2. The temperature should be displayed with one value to the right of the decimal point.
	3. Research the formula for the conversion.
Comments:	Obtain images for this app from CengageBrain.com. The pictures are provided in the Chapter 12\Temperature App folder and are named Logo.png, SmallLogo.png, SplashScreen.png, StoreLogo.png, and Temperature.png.

FIGURE 12-73

(continues)

Case Programming Assignments

Fahrenheit to Celsius Conversion (continued)

USE CASE DEFINITION

1. The user enters the Fahrenheit temperature.
2. The app displays the converted Celsius temperature.

FIGURE 12-74

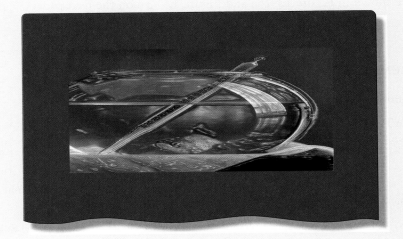

FIGURE 12-75a

FIGURE 12-75b

2

COLLEGE TUITION CALCULATOR

Design a Windows Store app and write the code that will execute according to the program requirements in Figure 12-76 and the Use Case Definition in Figure 12-77 on the next page. Before writing the code, create an event planning document for each event in the program. The completed Windows Store app and other objects in the user interface are shown in Figure 12-78a and Figure 12-78b on the next page.

REQUIREMENTS DOCUMENT

Date Submitted: December 14, 2015

Application Title: College Tuition Calculator App

Purpose: This Windows Store app displays a splash screen briefly. An app page opens in which the user enters a number of credit hours and whether he is a state resident. The tuition for the semester is displayed.

Program Procedures: From the app, the user enters the number of credit hours for the semester and state residency status.

Algorithms, Processing, and Conditions:
1. A black splash screen is displayed; it includes an image named SplashScreen.png.
2. The user must be able to enter the number of semester credits on the first page and select a state residency status from the ComboBox object (in state or out of state).
3. After the user taps or clicks the Compute Tuition button, the tuition is displayed.

Notes and Restrictions:
1. All placeholder images must be replaced.
2. The tuition is $304.77 per credit hour for out-of-state students and $168.33 for in-state students.

Comments: Obtain images for this app from CengageBrain.com. The pictures are provided in the Chapter 12\Tuition App folder and are named Logo.png, SmallLogo.png, SplashScreen.png, StoreLogo.png, and Tuition.png.

FIGURE 12-76

(continues)

College Tuition Calculator (continued)

USE CASE DEFINITION

1. The user enters the number of credits for a semester.
2. The user selects in-state or out-of-state residency from a ComboBox object.
3. The user taps or clicks the Compute Tuition button.
4. The app displays the total tuition costs.

FIGURE 12-77

© 2014 Cengage Learning

FIGURE 12-78a

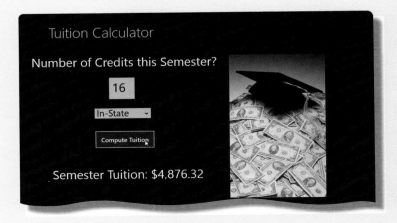

FIGURE 12-78b

Case Programming Assignments

3 ● PAINT CALCULATOR

Design a Windows Store app and write the code that will execute according to the program requirements in Figure 12-79 and the Use Case Definition in Figure 12-80 on the next page. Before writing the code, create an event planning document for each event in the program. The completed Windows Store app and other objects in the user interface are shown in Figure 12-81a and Figure 12-81b on the next page.

REQUIREMENTS DOCUMENT

Date Submitted:	July 19, 2015
Application Title:	Paint Calculator App
Purpose:	This Windows Store app displays a splash screen briefly. An app page opens in which the user enters the linear width in feet of each of the four walls in a room and the height in feet of the ceiling. The app displays the amount of paint needed to paint the room. The amount is rounded to the nearest whole gallon.
Program Procedures:	From the first page of the app, the user enters the number of linear feet of each wall and the ceiling height to compute the amount of paint needed.
Algorithms, Processing, and Conditions:	1. A red splash screen is displayed; it includes an image named SplashScreen.png. 2. The user must be able to enter the linear feet of each of the four walls and the ceiling height. 3. After the user taps or clicks the How many gallons of paint? button, the needed number of gallons is displayed. The amount is rounded to the nearest whole gallon.
Notes and Restrictions:	1. All placeholder images must be replaced. 2. The formula for the needed amount of paint is (perimeter of room * ceiling height)/350. On average, one coat of one gallon of paint will cover 350 square feet.
Comments:	Obtain images for this app from CengageBrain.com. The pictures are provided in the Chapter 12\Paint App folder and are named Logo.png, Paint.png, SmallLogo.png, SplashScreen.png, and StoreLogo.png.

FIGURE 12-79

(continues)

Case Programming Assignments

Paint Calculator (continued)

USE CASE DEFINITION

1. The user enters the linear feet of each of four walls and the ceiling height.
2. The user taps or clicks the How many gallons of paint? button.
3. The app displays the amount of paint needed for the room. The amount is rounded to the nearest whole gallon.

FIGURE 12-80

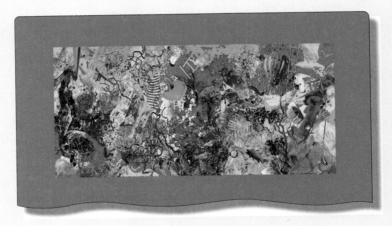

FIGURE 12-81a

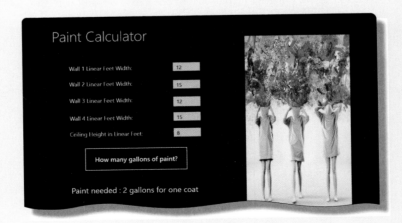

FIGURE 12-81b

Case Programming Assignments

4 ●●
NAUTICAL MILES CONVERSION

Design a Windows Store app and write the code that will execute according to the program requirements in Figure 12-82. Before writing the code, create a Use Case Definition and event planning document for each event in the program.

REQUIREMENTS DOCUMENT

Date Submitted:	January 6, 2015
Application Title:	Nautical Miles Conversion App
Purpose:	Nautical miles are different from road miles (statute miles) due to the curvature of the earth on the sea. This app allows you to convert nautical miles into statute miles.
Program Procedures:	From the first page of the app, the user enters the number of nautical miles to convert to statute miles.
Algorithms, Processing, and Conditions:	1. A coordinating-color splash screen is displayed; it includes an image named SplashScreen.png. 2. The user must be able to enter the number of nautical miles her boat has covered. 3. After the user taps or clicks the Convert to Statute Miles button, the number of statute miles covered is displayed.
Notes and Restrictions:	1. All placeholder images must be replaced. An image is needed for the main page. Select a background color that matches the image used in the splash screen. 2. The formula for converting nautical miles to statute miles is nautical miles * 1.15. 3. Display the result two places past the decimal point.
Comments:	Locate images from the web and resize them to the multiple sizes necessary for a Windows Store app. Use Paint or a similar program to resize the images.

FIGURE 12-82

Case Programming Assignments

5 ●● TARGET HEART RATE

Design a Windows Store app and write the code that will execute according to the program requirements in Figure 12-83. Before writing the code, create a Use Case Definition and event planning document for each event in the program.

REQUIREMENTS DOCUMENT

Date Submitted:	March 21, 2015
Application Title:	Target Heart Rate App
Purpose:	When you exercise, your heart rate increases proportionately with the intensity of the exercise. Your target heart rate can be calculated as 80 percent of your maximum heart rate based on your age.
Program Procedures:	From the opening page in the app, the user enters her age. A cardio image is displayed. The user can then tap or click the Maximum Heart Rate button or the Target Heart Rate button to display the results.
Algorithms, Processing, and Conditions:	1. A coordinating-color splash screen is displayed. 2. The user must be able to enter her age. 3. After the user taps or clicks the Maximum Heart Rate button, her maximum heart rate is displayed based on her age. 4. After the user taps or clicks the Target Heart Rate button, her target heart rate is displayed based on her age.
Notes and Restrictions:	1. The formula for maximum heart rate is 220 – user's age. 2. The formula for target heart rate is (220 – user's age) * 80%. 3. Use more than one font color on MainPage.xaml.
Comments:	Locate images from the web and resize them to the multiple sizes necessary for a Windows Store app. Use Paint or a similar program to resize the images.

FIGURE 12-83

6

PRESCRIPTION GLASSES

Design a Windows Store app and write the code that will execute according to the program requirements in Figure 12-84. Before writing the code, create a Use Case Definition and event planning document for each event in the program.

REQUIREMENTS DOCUMENT

Date Submitted:	January 6, 2015
Application Title:	Prescription Glasses App
Purpose:	An online store for prescription glasses displays a sale screen in a Windows Store app that promotes single-vision frames for $79. Other options can be added with tax to compute the final cost.
Program Procedures:	From the first page of the app, the user can make selections in optional check boxes and then tap or click the Total with Online Tax button to compute the final total.
Algorithms, Processing, and Conditions:	1. A coordinating-color splash screen is displayed. 2. A message states that basic single-vision frames are on sale for $79 and instructs the user to check the following add-on options. 3. The user can check optional add-ons such as Reading Bifocal Lenses for $49, Progressive Lenses for $69, Scratch-free Protective Coating for $39, and Anti-glare Coating for $29. 4. After the user taps or clicks the Total with Online Tax button, an 8 percent tax is added to the subtotal and displayed.
Notes and Restrictions:	1. All placeholder images must be replaced. An image is needed for the main page. Select a background color that matches the image used in the splash screen. 2. Display the result as currency.
Comments:	Locate images from the web and resize them to the multiple sizes necessary for a Windows Store app. Use Paint or a similar program to resize the images.

FIGURE 12-84

7

● ● ●

AIRPORT RESTAURANT

Based on the following problem definition, complete the Airport Restaurant app. The restaurant allows patrons to order their meals from tablet devices mounted in each booth. Before writing the code, create an event planning document for each event in the program.

The Gourmet Burger restaurant in an airport terminal allows patrons to order from Windows tablets. The basic cost of a burger with lettuce, tomato, and onion is $7.99. The following toppings are $0.99 each: cheddar cheese, mushrooms, ham, and jalapeños. The user must be able to select the preceding toppings from one Rectangle control. The following toppings are $1.99 each: bacon, avocado, chili, and gruyere cheese. The user must be able to select the preceding toppings from a second Rectangle control. Each person types her name and selects what she wants on her burger. The app displays the total price after 12 percent tax is applied. Only one burger can be ordered at a time. Locate images for the app online.

8 ●●●
MY THREE BEST RECIPES

Create your own app with three buttons on the left side of the screen that display your favorite recipes. Click a button to display a recipe's ingredients list, directions, and cooking time. Before writing the code, create an event planning document for each event in the program. Locate images for the app online.

9 ●●●
CREATE YOUR OWN APP

Create your own app based on an idea that your instructor approves. Before writing the code, create an event planning document for each event in the program. Locate images for the app online.

APPENDIX A

Unicode

The 256 characters and symbols that are represented by ASCII and EBCDIC codes are sufficient for English and western European languages (see Figure A-1 on the next page), but do not provide enough characters for Asian and other languages that use different alphabets. Further compounding the problem is that many of these languages use symbols, called ideograms, to represent multiple words and ideas. One solution to the problem of accommodating universal alphabets is Unicode. Unicode is a 16-bit coding scheme that can represent all the world's current, classic, and historical languages in more than 65,000 characters and symbols. In Unicode, 30,000 codes are reserved for future use, such as ancient languages, and 6,000 codes are reserved for private use. Existing ASCII coded data is fully compatible with Unicode because the first 256 codes are the same. Unicode is implemented in several operating systems, including Windows 7, Windows Vista, Windows XP, Mac OS X, and Linux. To view a complete Unicode chart, see www.unicode.org.

UNICODE KEYBOARD CHARACTERS

Decimal	Hexadecimal	Octal	Binary	Character
32	20	040	00100000	
33	21	041	00100001	!
34	22	042	00100010	"
35	23	043	00100010	#
36	24	044	00100100	$
37	25	045	00100101	%
38	26	046	00100110	&
39	27	047	00100111	'
40	28	050	00101000	(
41	29	051	00101001	)
42	2A	052	00101010	*
43	2B	053	00101011	+
44	2C	054	00101100	,
45	2D	055	00101101	–
46	2E	056	00101110	.
47	2F	057	00101111	/
48	30	060	00110000	0
49	31	061	00110001	1
50	32	062	00110010	2
51	33	063	00110011	3
52	34	064	00110100	4
53	35	065	00110101	5
54	36	066	00110110	6
55	37	067	00110111	7
56	38	070	00111000	8
57	39	071	00111001	9
58	3A	072	00111010	:

FIGURE A-1 (continued)

Decimal	Hexadecimal	Octal	Binary	Character
59	3B	073	00111011	;
60	3C	074	00111100	<
61	3D	075	00111101	=
62	3E	076	00111110	>
63	3F	077	00111111	?
64	40	100	01000000	@
65	41	101	01000001	A
66	42	102	01000010	B
67	43	103	01000011	C
68	44	104	01000100	D
69	45	105	01000101	E
70	46	106	01000110	F
71	47	107	01000111	G
72	48	110	01001000	H
73	49	111	01001001	I
74	4A	112	01001010	J
75	4B	113	01001011	K
76	4C	114	01001100	L
77	4D	115	01001101	M
78	4E	116	01001110	N
79	4F	117	01001111	O
80	50	120	01010000	P
81	51	121	01010001	Q
82	52	122	01010010	R
83	53	123	01010011	S
84	54	124	01010100	T
85	55	125	01010101	U
86	56	126	01010110	V

FIGURE A-1 (continued)

Decimal	Hexadecimal	Octal	Binary	Character
87	57	127	01010111	W
88	58	130	01011000	X
89	59	131	01011001	Y
90	5A	132	01011010	Z
91	5B	133	01011011	[
92	5C	134	01011100	\
93	5D	135	01011101	]
94	5E	136	01011110	^
95	5F	137	01011111	]
96	60	140	01100000	,
97	61	141	01100001	a
98	62	142	01100010	b
99	63	143	01100011	c
100	64	144	01100100	d
101	65	145	01100101	e
102	66	146	01100110	f
103	67	147	01100111	g
104	68	150	01101000	h
105	69	151	01101001	i
106	6A	152	01101010	j
107	6B	153	01101011	k
108	6C	154	01101100	l
109	6D	155	01101101	m
110	6E	156	01101110	n
111	6F	157	01101111	o
112	70	160	01110000	p
113	71	161	01110001	q

FIGURE A-1 (continued)

Decimal	Hexadecimal	Octal	Binary	Character
114	72	162	01110010	r
115	73	163	01110011	s
116	74	164	01110100	t
117	75	165	01110101	u
118	76	166	01110110	v
119	77	167	01110111	w
120	78	170	01111000	x
121	79	171	01111001	y
122	7A	172	01111010	z
123	7B	173	01111011	{
124	7C	174	01111100	|
125	7D	175	01111101	}
126	7E	176	01111110	~
127	7F	177	01111111	DEL

FIGURE A-1 (continued)

The My Namespace

Rapid application development (RAD) uses a number of tools to help build graphical user interfaces that would normally take a large development effort. One of the Visual Basic RAD tool innovations introduced in the 2005 version and continued with the 2012 version is the **My** namespace. The My namespace provides a shortcut to several categories of information and functionality and is organized so that you can use IntelliSense to find code elements you use often. Microsoft created the My namespace to make it easier to execute common code patterns that you use when developing .NET applications. By providing a shortcut to the most commonly used .NET Framework Class Library classes and methods, the My namespace helps you retrieve settings and resources that your application requires.

The My namespace feature provides rapid access to the classes and methods through the My classes shown in the table in Figure B-1.

Object	Allows Access to
My.Application	The application information and its services such as name, version, log, and current directory.
My.Computer	The host computer and its resources, and services. My.Computer provides access to a number of very important resources including My.Computer.Network, My.Computer. FileSystem, and My.Computer.Printers.
My.Forms	All the forms in the current project.
My.Request	The current Web request.
My.Resources	The resource elements.
My.Response	The current Web response.
My.Settings	The configuration settings of the user and application level. This object enables great personalization without writing many lines of code.

FIGURE B-1 (continues)

Object	Allows Access to
My.User	The security context of the current authenticated user. The My.User object analyzes the user at runtime, which assists security issues.
My.WebServices	The XML Web services referenced by the current project. Consuming Web services is a necessary ability for modern Web applications.

FIGURE B-1 (continued)

Coding Examples

My is a wrapper that makes accessing the advanced features of .NET easier. For example, you can use the class **My.Application** to determine the version of the current application by using the line of code shown in Figure B-2. Figure B-3 shows the dialog box that displays the version number. You often need to know the latest version of the application to determine whether the application is in final form.

```
MsgBox(My.Application.Info.Version.ToString())
```

FIGURE B-2

FIGURE B-3

The **My.Application** class also can be used to display the current setting of the culture of a computer. Figure B-4 shows the code you can use to display the culture, which is the language that the computer has been assigned in the language settings. In Figure B-5, the culture is set to English – United States.

```
MsgBox(My.Application.Culture.ToString())
```

FIGURE B-4

FIGURE B-5

Another class called **My.Computer** can return information about the computer on which the application is deployed, as determined at run time. The My.Computer class provides properties for manipulating computer components such as audio, the clock, the keyboard, and the file system. The My.Computer class can play .wav files and system sounds using the Audio object. You can use the My.Computer.Audio.Play and My.Computer.Audio.PlaySystemSound methods to play .wav sound files and system sounds. The code shown in Figure B-6 plays a .wav file named beachmusic.wav.

```
My.Computer.Audio.Play("C:\beachmusic.wav")
```

FIGURE B-6

A .wav file also can be played in the background when a file named AudioPlayMode.Background is specified, as shown in Figure B-7.

```
My.Computer.Audio.Play("C:\blues.wav", _
          AudioPlayMode.Background)
```

FIGURE B-7

The My.Computer class can access the Clipboard and show what is temporarily stored in the system buffer. For example, if you copied the phrase, "Examples of the My.Computer Class", the phrase would be stored in the Clipboard system buffer of the computer. Use the code shown in Figure B-8 to display the contents of the Clipboard in a dialog box as shown in Figure B-9.

```
MsgBox(My.Computer.Clipboard.GetText())
```

FIGURE B-8

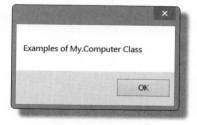

FIGURE B-9

The My.Computer class can access an object that provides properties for displaying the current local date and time according to the system clock by entering the code shown in B-10. Figure B-11 on the next page shows the dialog box that displays the system date and time.

```
MsgBox(My.Computer.Clock.LocalTime.ToString())
```

FIGURE B-10

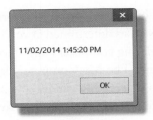

FIGURE B-11

Another My.Computer class determines the current state of the keyboard, such as which keys are pressed, including the CAPS LOCK or NUM LOCK key. The code shown in Figure B-12 provides a true result if the CAPS LOCK key has been pressed. Figure B-13 shows the dialog box that displays the result.

```
MsgBox(My.Computer.Keyboard.CapsLock.ToString())
```

FIGURE B-12

FIGURE B-13

The My.Computer.Mouse class allows you to determine the state and hardware characteristics of the attached mouse, such as the number of buttons or whether the mouse has a wheel. The code shown in Figure B-14 determines if the mouse has a wheel, and Figure B-15 shows the dialog box that displays the result.

```
MsgBox(My.Computer.Mouse.WheelExists.ToString())
```

FIGURE B-14

FIGURE B-15

The My.Computer.Network class interacts with the network to which the computer is connected. For example, if the code in Figure B-16 is entered in the code window, the result would be true, as shown in Figure B-17, if the computer is connected to an intranet or Internet network.

```
MsgBox(My.Computer.Network.IsAvailable.ToString())
```

FIGURE B-16

FIGURE B-17

You can use the My.Computer.Network class to ping another computer. Ping is a basic network function that allows you to verify a particular IP address exists and can accept requests. Ping is used diagnostically to ensure that a host computer you are trying to reach is operating. The code shown in Figure B-18 determines if the IP address is active, and the dialog box shown in Figure B-19 displays the result.

```
MsgBox(My.Computer.Network.Ping("71.2.41.1"))
```

FIGURE B-18

FIGURE B-19

The My.Computer.Screen object can be used to determine many properties of the screen connected to the computer system. You can determine the properties of each monitor attached to the computer system, including the name, the brightness of the screen, and the working area size. The number of bits per pixel can be determined by the code shown in Figure B-20. In a digitized image, the number of bits used to represent the brightness contained in each pixel is called bits per pixel. Bits per pixel is a term that represents the brightness of the screen resolution. Figure B-21 shows the result of the code.

```
MsgBox(My.Computer.Screen.BitsPerPixel.ToString())
```

FIGURE B-20

FIGURE B-21

The My.Computer.Screen class also can display the current resolution of the user screen, as shown in Figures B-22 and B-23 on the next page.

```
MsgBox(My.Computer.Screen.Bounds.Size.ToString())
```

FIGURE B-22

FIGURE B-23

Another class called **My.User** allows you to gather information about the current user. The code example in Figure B-24 shows how to use the **My.User.Name** property to view the user's login name. An application uses Windows authentication by default, so **My.User** returns the Windows information about the user who started the application, as shown in Figure B-25.

```
MsgBox(My.User.Name)
```

FIGURE B-24

FIGURE B-25

The My namespace also provides a simpler way of opening multiple forms in the same project by using the My.Forms object. If the project includes more than one form, the code shown in Figure B-26 opens a second form named Form2.

```
My.Forms.Form2.Show()
```

FIGURE B-26

APPENDIX C

Naming Conventions

The table in Figure C-1 displays the common data types used in Visual Basic 2012 with the recommended naming convention for the three-character prefix preceding variable names of the data type.

Data Type	Sample Value	Memory	Range of Values	Prefix
Integer	48	4 bytes	−2,147,483,648 to +2,147,483,647	int
Double	5.3452307	8 bytes	−1.79769313486232E308 to +1.79769313486232E308	dbl
Decimal	3.14519	16 bytes	Decimal values that may have up to 29 significant digits	dec
Char	'?' or 'C'	2 bytes	Single character	chr
String	"The Dow is up .03%"	Depends on number of characters	Letters, numbers, symbols	str
Boolean	True or False	Typically 2 bytes; depends on implementing platform	True or False	bln

FIGURE C-1

The table in Figure C-2 displays the less common data types used in Visual Basic 2012 with the recommended naming convention for the three-character prefix preceding variable names of the data type.

Data Type	Sample Value	Memory	Range of Values	Prefix
Byte	7	1 byte	0 to 255	byt
Date	April 22, 2014	8 bytes	0:00:00 (midnight) on January 1, 0001 through 11:59:59 PM on December 31, 9999	dtm
Long	345,234,567	8 bytes	$-9,223,372,036,854,775,808$ to $+9,223,372,036,854,775,807$	lng
Object	Holds a reference	4 bytes (32-bit) 8 bytes (64-bit)	A memory address	obj
Short	16,567	2 bytes	$-32,768$ to $32,767$	shr
Single	234,654.1246	4 bytes	$-3.4028235E+38$ to $-1.401298E-45$ for negative values and $1.401298E-45$ to $3.4028235E+38$ for positive values	sng

FIGURE C-2

Form Object Naming Conventions

The table in Figure C-3 displays the prefix naming conventions for Form objects. The three-letter prefixes used before variables names especially are helpful when you use IntelliSense.

Object Type	Prefix	Object Type	Prefix
Button	btn	ListBox	lst
Calendar	cld	MenuStrip	mnu
CheckBox	chk	NumericUpDown	nud
ComboBox	cbo	PictureBox	pic
CompareValidator	cmv	RadioButton	rad
DataGrid	dgd	RangeValidator	rgv
DateTimePicker	dtp	RegularExpressionValidator	rev
DropDownList	ddl	RequiredFieldValidator	rfv
Form	frm	TextBox	txt
GroupBox	grp	ValidationSummary	vsm
Label	lbl		

FIGURE C-3

Note: **Boldface** page numbers indicate key terms.

JUDGES
Canada
J	Justice
JA	Justice of Appeal
JJ	Justices
CJ	Chief Justice

United Kingdom
LJ	Lord Justice
MR	Master of the Rolls

CASELAW REPORTERS
Canada
AR	Alberta Reports
BCDLA	British Columbia Decisions, Labour Arbitration
BCLR	British Columbia Law Reports
BLR	Business Law Reports
CBR	Canadian Bankruptcy Reports
CCC	Canadian Criminal Cases
CCEL	Canadian Cases on Employment Law
CCLT	Canadian Cases on the Law of Torts
CELR	Canadian Environmental Law Reports
CPR	Canadian Patent Reporter
CTC	Canada Tax Cases
DLR	Dominion Law Reports
DTC	Dominion Tax Cases
Ex CR	Canada Law Reports: Exchequer Court of Canada
FC	Federal Court Reports
FTR	Federal Trial Reports
LAC	Labour Arbitration Cases
NBR	New Brunswick Reports
Nfld & PEIR	Newfoundland and Prince Edward Island Reports
NSR	Nova Scotia Reports
OLR	Ontario Law Reports
OLRB Rep	Ontario Labour Relations Board Reports
OR	Ontario Reports
OTC	Ontario Trial Cases
OWN	Ontario Weekly Notes
PPSAC	Personal Property Security Act Cases
Sask R	Saskatchewan Reports
SCR	Supreme Court Reports
WWR	Western Weekly Reports

United Kingdom
AC	Appeal Cases
All ER	All England Reports
App Cas	Appeal Cases
Ch D	Chancery Division
ER	English Reports
HL Cas	House of Lords Cases
KB	King's Bench
LR	Law Reports
Lloyds Rep	Lloyd's Law Reports
QB	Queen's Bench
WLR	Weekly Law Reports

United States
F	Federal Reporter
F Supp	Federal Supplement
NE	Northeastern Reporter
NY	New York Reports
P	Pacific Reporter
So	Southern Reporter
WL	Westlaw

Quicklaw Databases
BCJ	British Columbia Judgments
OJ	Ontario Judgments
YJ	Yukon Judgments

Australia and New Zealand
CLR	Commonwealth Law Reports
SR (NSW)	State Reports (New South Wales)
Qd R	Queensland Reports

STATUTES
Canada
RRO	Revised Regulations of Ontario
RSC	Revised Statutes of Canada
RSA	Revised Statutes of Alberta
RSBC	Revised Statutes of British Columbia
RSM	Revised Statutes of Manitoba
RSN	Revised Statutes of Newfoundland
RSNB	Revised Statutes of New Brunswick
RSNWT	Revised Statutes Northwest Territories
RSNS	Revised Statutes of Nova Scotia
RSO	Revised Statutes of Ontario
RSPEI	Revised Statutes of Prince Edward Island
RSQ	Revised Statutes of Quebec
RSS	Revised Statutes of Saskatchewan
RSY	Revised Statutes of Yukon
SOR	Statutory Orders and Regulations

United Kingdom
Vict	Victoria
Cha	Charles

United States
USC	United States Code

PERIODICALS
Berkeley Tech LJ	Berkeley Technology Law Journal
Can Bar Rev	Canadian Bar Review
Cornell LQ	Cornell Law Quarterly
Osgoode Hall LJ	Osgoode Hall Law Journal

Managing the Law

The Legal Aspects of Doing Business

Mitchell McInnes
Faculty of Law, The University of Western Ontario

Ian Kerr
Faculty of Law, Common Law Section, University of Ottawa

J. Anthony VanDuzer
Faculty of Law, Common Law Section, University of Ottawa

Chi Carmody
Faculty of Law, The University of Western Ontario

Foreword *by*

Madam Justice Eileen E. Gillese
Ontario Court of Appeal

Prentice
Hall

Toronto

National Library of Canada Cataloguing in Publication Data

Managing the law: the legal aspects of doing business/Mitchell McInnes ... [et al.]

Includes index
ISBN 0-13-012767-1

1. Commercial law—Canada. I. McInnes, Mitchell
KE919.M35   2003   346.71'07   C2002-901184-1

0-13-012767-1

Vice President, Editorial Director: Michael J. Young
Acquisitions Editor: Kelly Torrance
Marketing Manager: Deborah Meredith
Developmental Editor: Maurice Esses
Production Editor: Marisa D'Andrea
Copy Editor: Elaine Freedman
Production Coordinator: Janette Lush
Page Layout: Bill Renaud
Photo Research: Cheryl Freedman
Art Director: Mary Opper
Interior and Cover Design: Anthony Leung
Cover Image: Mike Hamel, Masterfile

1 2 3 4 5   07 06 05 04 03

Printed and bound in the United States of America.

Photo Credits
p. 1: © NCC/CCN; p. 31: PhotoDisc; p. 52: © Dick Hemingway; p. 74: PhotoDisc; p. 95: www.adventures.com, The Great Canadian Adventure Company; p. 100: © Dick Hemingway; p. 122: PhotoDisc; p. 141: Courtesy of Saskatchewan Property Management Corporation; p. 160: PhotoDisc; p. 182: PhotoDisc; p. 210: © Dick Hemingway; p. 231: PhotoDisc; p. 252: © M.E. Menagh, Photo Co-ordinator, Traffic Services, Toronto Police Service; p. 277: © Dick Hemingway; p. 299: © Dick Hemingway; p. 322: Prentice Hall Archives; p. 374: Corbis/Magma; p. 403: © Dick Hemingway; p. 425: Canadian Press CP; p. 447: © Dick Hemingway; p. 472: Prentice Hall Archives; p. 495: © Dick Hemingway; p. 520: Prentice Hall Archives; p. 545: PhotoDisc; p. 571: PhotoDisc; p. 594: Canadian Press MTLP.

Alison, Kate, Ben, and *Sam*—for patiently understanding the need for summers, weekends, and evenings to be spent at the office;

Eta, Morley, Sheryl, and *Karen*—gratitude continually pours forth for your constant love and support;

Jodie—without whose constant indulgence and support my contribution to this book would not have been possible; and *Taylor* and *Eli*—for putting up with their father's frequent absences to work on this project, mostly without complaint;

Daphne and *Ian*—with every best wish.

Mitchell McInnes, PhD (Cambridge), LLM (Cambridge), LLB (Alberta), BA (Alberta), of the Bar of Alberta, Associate Professor

Mitchell McInnes has spent nearly 15 years providing business people with risk management guidance, particularly in the areas of contract, tort, property, and trusts. Mitchell is an editor of the *Canadian Business Law Journal* and has published over 60 papers in leading journals, including the *Canadian Bar Review*, the *Cambridge Law Journal*, and the *Law Quarterly Review*. He has also published and co-authored several important books on law, including *Cases and Materials on the Law of Torts*, 5th Edition (Scarborough: Carswell, 2000), *Restitution: Developments in Unjust Enrichment* (Sydney: Law Book Company, 1996), and the forthcoming Butterworths publication, *The Law of Unjust Enrichment and Restitution*. His work has been relied upon at all levels of courts, including the Supreme Court of Canada and the High Court of Australia.

Mitchell has received numerous awards for excellence in teaching, including the University of Western Ontario's highest teaching honour, the Edward G. Pleva Award. He has been recognized on several occasions by *Maclean's* magazine as one of Canada's leading university professors. He previously taught at the University of Melbourne and Deakin University in Australia, and clerked at the Supreme Court of Canada. He currently teaches at the University of Western Ontario.

Ian R. Kerr, PhD (Western), MA (Western), LLB (Western), BA Hons (Alberta), BSc (Alberta), of the Bar of Ontario, Associate Professor

As Canada Research Chair in Ethics, Law, and Technology, Ian Kerr is Canada's leading authority on how legal and ethical issues intersect with electronic commerce. Ian plays a significant role in the development of national and international model laws in e-commerce, privacy policy, digital copyright policy, and the delivery of government services online. He has advised various Canadian agencies on legal policy for online activities, and is a Canadian delegate to the United Nations' Special Working Group on e-Commerce, a project of the United Nations Commission on International Trade Law. Ian is also a member of the Corporate/Commercial Law Group and acts as special counsel in technology law to Ottawa-based law firm Nelligan O'Brien Payne LLP.

With his background in philosophy, technology, and private law, Ian has published numerous articles and papers and has edited and contributed to several books and journals on the legal implications of doing business online, including the *Electronic Commerce Research Journal* and the *Canadian Business Law Journal*. He has also contributed scholarly articles and chapters in several books on a range of other subjects, including contract law, the philosophy of law, ethics and information, and cyberspace law. Ian previously taught law, philosophy, and new media at the University of Western Ontario. He has won four awards for his teaching. He now teaches at the Faculty of Law, University of Ottawa, where he has co-designed a new graduate program in law and technology.

J. Anthony VanDuzer, LLM (Columbia), LLB (Ottawa), BA (Queen's), of the Bar of Ontario, Associate Professor

J. Anthony VanDuzer has taught and practised extensively in the area of corporate and commercial law for nearly 20 years. He has published over 40 articles and papers. Tony has also written and edited several significant books on business law, including *Russia and the International Trading System* (St. Petersburg: St. Petersburg State University Press, 2000), one of the first books on post-Soviet Russia and the international trading system; *The Law of Partnerships and Corporations* (Concord: Irwin, 1997); and *Merger Notification in Canada* (with Albert Gourley, Toronto: CCH Canadian, 1994). Over the past decade, he has often been called on to advise Canadian government agencies and organizations on business and trade law issues. He has worked with international development agencies in delivering technical assistance related to business and trade law in Russia, China, the Ukraine, Georgia, Bulgaria, Bosnia, Vietnam, Kyrgyzstan, and the countries of the Caribbean Community.

Tony is a senior fellow at the University of Ottawa's Centre on Governance and an associate at the Centre for Trade Policy and Law, an institute jointly established by the University of Ottawa Faculty of Law and the Norman Paterson School of International Affairs at Carleton University. In 2002, he was appointed to the Academic Advisory Council to the Deputy Minister for International Trade. He formerly taught multinational management for the University of Ottawa's Executive MBA program and currently teaches a variety of business law subjects at the University of Ottawa's Faculty of Law.

Chi Carmody, SJD (Georgetown), LLM (Michigan), LLB (Ottawa), BJour (California State University, Northridge), BA Hons (Toronto), of the Bars of Ontario and New York, Assistant Professor

Chi Carmody practised law in Toronto before undertaking graduate work in international law and international trade law in 1996. In addition to teaching public international law, international trade law, international business transactions, contracts, and various other business law subjects, he has interned with the Appellate Body Secretariat of the World Trade Organization in Geneva, worked as a core team member of the Cambodian Law and Development Project with the University of Michigan, and lectured at Georgetown University Law Center in Washington, DC and the Université Montpellier I in France.

Chi is contributor to and general editor of *Trilateral Perspectives on International Law* (American Society of International Law, 2002), and is author of the forthcoming Oxford University Press publication, *Remedies and the WTO Agreement*. He is a former editor of several legal publications, including the Canada Law Book's *Employment Bulletin* and the University of Ottawa's *Ottawa Law Review*. Chi teaches in the Faculty of Law at the University of Western Ontario and lectures occasionally at Western's Richard Ivey School of Business.

Law is both visible and invisible. The visible part, the one that most of us focus on, takes place in the Canadian courts. It involves gavels and robes and formal decisions. The invisible part, however, is much larger and more pervasive. It contains our understanding of what is permissible and what is not. It is the complex web of rules and principles that provides the structure for human interaction and that governs almost every important aspect of our lives. The more clearly we understand these rules and principles, the more harmonious our interactions.

Life on the bench has confirmed my long-held belief that if people understand the law, they will work and live within its structure. An important question therefore arises: how can the vast and complex body of law be made accessible to the non-lawyer? *Managing the Law: The Legal Aspects of Doing Business* provides an admirable response. Its genius lies in its scope and in its style. It achieves a rare balance by being comprehensive without being encyclopedic. Furthermore, it presents material in a manner that is both accessible and engaging. The authors have avoided the dense, formal, legalistic style often found in books of this sort. But at the same time, they have not sacrificed substance for the sake of simplification.

Earlier in my career, I came to appreciate the challenges involved in preparing a business law text. I therefore later encouraged my colleagues Mitchell McInnes and Ian Kerr to build an author team capable of creating a textbook that would allow a new generation of students to easily grasp the legal aspects of doing business. To my great satisfaction, Mitchell and Ian persuaded Tony VanDuzer and Chi Carmody to join them in this project. The authors are well recognized as passionate teachers and effective educators.

Managing the Law is written in an intelligent style for university and college students. Its primary aim is to teach them to think like business managers. It achieves that goal by instilling an understanding of the essential rules and principles that govern modern commerce. Through a combination of innovative techniques and interactive learning tools, students are trained to effectively manage legal risk.

Teaching law to non-lawyers is challenging. *Managing the Law* draws students into the law and encourages them to actively participate in their own education. The comprehensive set of supplementary materials available to instructors supports that exercise. Indeed, my personal pleasure in writing this foreword comes from the knowledge that the authors, through *Managing the Law*, will contribute to great teaching and effective learning beyond their own classrooms.

Madam Justice Eileen E. Gillese
Ontario Court of Appeal
Toronto, Ontario

Brief Contents

Table of Contents

Preface

Managing the Law: The Legal Aspects of Doing Business equips students with the conceptual tools and intellectual skills they need to identify, assess, and manage the legal risks that arise in doing business. Students who study this text will gain a basic understanding of:

- the function of law
- the structure of the Canadian legal system
- the specific areas of the law that are especially important to business

Students will also acquire the ability to:

- identify legal problems that arise in business and apply basic legal principles to them
- formulate opinions on important socio-legal issues that affect business
- critically evaluate legal arguments put forth by others
- devise arguments and present them persuasively

Training students "to think like lawyers" (to use a favourite phrase of law professors) has long been the main purpose of law courses, even those designed for business students. This book certainly provides valuable insight into the way in which lawyers and judges think. It primary goal, however, is quite different. The aim of *Managing the Law* is to help students learn how "to think like successful business people." Its key concept is risk management. Business people should know enough about the law to identify legal issues and arrange their affairs to avoid difficulties. Moreover, they should know enough about the law to recognize when it is appropriate to obtain expert advice from the legal profession. Success in the business world often depends on thoughtful delegation.

We wrote this book with this goal firmly in mind. As a result, *Managing the Law: The Legal Aspects of Doing Business* differs from other textbooks in two important ways. First, it is a book for business students, not law students. *Managing the Law* provides a thorough and current picture of the legal rules that are relevant in the business world. It does not sacrifice important information for the sake of simplicity. But at the same time, it does not overwhelm the business student with unnecessary detail or impenetrable jargon. The tone is intelligent and student-friendly. The text is accessible and comprehensible.

Second, the text focuses on risk management in both its choice and presentation of material. Legal topics are chosen for their relevance to the commercial context and are presented in a manner that fosters the development of effective risk-management skills. Through the extensive use of discussion boxes, review exercises, cases and problems, and video cases, *Managing the Law* draws students into the business law world and requires them to actively resolve practical problems, even if that involves recognizing the need for a lawyer's assistance.

Business students, like Canadians in general, are a diverse group. They come from a variety of backgrounds in terms of personal characteristics, past qualifications, and professional aspirations. Some are new Canadians; others have long-established roots. Some are embarking on post-secondary education for the first time; others are engaged in advanced degrees. Some have little experience in the business world; others are retraining after successful careers. Some are seeking a generalized education; others are more focused on a particular career. This book is appropriate for them all.

Law texts are invariably dense and uninviting, not only in substance and language but also in appearance. Business law texts are often no different. In contrast, we have specifically designed *Managing the Law* with the full breadth of its target audience in mind. It is visually engaging. Its use of colour, boxes, icons, figures, and layout draws readers in and provides them with room to breathe intellectually.

Managing the Law has also been designed to be used in any course that deals with legal issues in a "business context," using that term broadly. Consequently, it is appropriate for students who are studying the legal aspects of accounting, business administration, commerce, finance, management, marketing, or office administration.

ORGANIZATION

Managing the Law is divided into five parts.

- **PART ONE: Introduction to Business Law** consists of one unit.

  Unit I opens with a discussion of why business people should study law. In doing so, it explains the core concept of risk management. It then sketches the essential features of the Canadian legal system, including:
  - the nature of law
  - branches of law
  - sources of law
  - the court system
  - mechanisms for resolving legal disputes

- **PART TWO: Private Law Regulation of Business** is divided into four units.

  Unit II comprises eight chapters dealing with contracts. Because of the significance of enforceable agreements in the commercial context, separate chapters are devoted to each of the following:
  - formation of contracts
  - consideration and privity
  - terms and representations
  - contractual defects
  - discharge and breach
  - remedies

  The final chapters of Unit II focus on two particularly important types of contracts:
  - sales of goods
  - negotiable instruments

  Unit III consists of three chapters on tort law. The focus again is on risk management in the business world. We introduce such key concepts as vicarious liability and liability insurance, and we examine important business torts, such as deceit and defamation. The final chapter deals with the tort of negligence, with a special emphasis on professional negligence that arises in the commercial matters.

  Unit IV has three chapters on the law of property. The discussion, as always, places the reader at the heart of practical problems in business law. The examination of personal property, for instance, centres on the institution of bailment and how insurance can be used to manage legal risks.

  Unit V, consisting of two chapters, is special. It provides an introduction to business law in the digital age. In separate chapters, it deals with:
  - knowledge-based businesses and intellectual property rights
  - electronic commerce

- **PART THREE: Methods of Carrying on a Business** is divided into two units. The three chapters in **Unit VI** examine various types of business organizations—sole proprietorships, partnerships, corporations, agency relationships, joint ventures, and franchises—and highlights the principles of risk management.

  Unit VII addresses specific decisions that affect business. Its two chapters focus on issues arising from:
  - secured transactions
  - bankruptcy and insolvency

- **PART FOUR: Public Law Regulation of Business** consists of one unit divided into two chapters. **Unit VIII** moves the discussion out of the purely private realm and into the world of public regulation and international relations. The first chapter examines how Canadian governments regulate commercial conduct through, for example, competition law, consumer protections laws, and environmental protection laws. The second chapter looks at issues that affect business conducted in the global economy. In addition to explaining the traditional rules that underlie international sales, it also outlines how Canadian businesses are affected by international trade organizations and agreements, such as the WTO, GATT, and NAFTA.

■ **PART FIVE: Employment Law** consists of one unit, **Unit IX**, which comprises two chapters. The first focuses on individual employment, highlighting risk management at all stages of the employee–employer relationship from pre-employment matters (such as advertising and hiring) to post-employment matters (such as dismissal and severance packages). The second chapter focuses on organized labour. It includes a discussion of collective agreements, grievances, and industrial conflicts.

Taken together, those five parts provide a thorough examination of the legal issues that generally affect Canadian businesses. At the same time, we have organized the material to offer instructors flexibility in matching the book to their course designs. Recognizing that time is usually tight in business law courses, we have adopted a modular approach in organizing the chapters and units. After covering the introductory Chapter 1 and the core material on contracts in Chapters 2 to 7, instructors can feel free to cover the remaining units and chapters in the order that best suits their needs.

FEATURES

Students learn effectively when they are interested, enthusiastic, and engaged. Therefore, we designed this text to encourage students to participate actively, rather than merely read passively. A number of features ensure that the materials are both accessible and stimulating.

■ **OBJECTIVES.** Each chapter opens with a list of 10 objectives, which stress key issues and highlight risk-management skills that students should aim to develop. By providing a roadmap at the beginning of each chapter, the objectives help students read and understand the material more efficiently and more effectively.

■ **KEY TERMS.** Key terms are boldfaced where they are defined in the body of the text. They are also restated with their definitions in the margins.

■ **OTHER MARGINALIA.** To help students in their initial reading and later review of chapters, we have summarized and highlighted important issues in the margins of the text.

■ **DISCUSSION BOXES.** Each chapter contains at least one instance of each of five distinct types of discussion boxes. These boxes provide instructors with additional opportunities to stimulate critical thinking and engage students in classroom debate. With the exception of the Case Briefs, each discussion box ends with Questions for Discussion. (Model answers are provided in the *Instructor's Manual*.) Each type of box fulfills a specific teaching goal.

  ■ **Case Brief** boxes illustrate how the courts have formulated and applied legal rules in specific business contexts. They also introduce students to many leading cases in the common law system.

  ■ **Business Decision** boxes ask students to respond as business people to common legal problems. Designed to foster the development of sound commercial judgment, they focus less on purely legal concepts and more on practical matters that influence decisions in the commercial world.

  ■ **Business Law in Action** boxes illustrate how legal rules apply in particular commercial contexts and ask students to use their knowledge and skills to resolve additional issues or alternative scenarios.

OBJECTIVES

After completing this chapter, you should be able to:

1. Explain why it is important for business people to study law.
2. List four basic strategies for managing risks.
3. Provide a general definition of the word "law."
4. Explain two meanings of the term "civil law" and three meanings of the term "common law."
5. List four areas of public law and three areas of private law. Pro

CASE BRIEF 17.1

Rudder v Microsoft (1999) 47 CCLT (2d)

Microsoft Network (MSN) provides online information services to members of its network. The plaintiffs were two Canadian law students who had entered into an online contract to receive MSN's services. They started a lawsuit in Ontario against MSN when they believed that they

The court terms of the that said, "I a any terms n print. Such a only the ter

BUSINESS DECISION 7.1

Expectation Damages and Reliance Damages

As a music promoter, you hired Ursula to perform a piano concert in exchange for $5000. Based on your experience in the music business, you expected to personally receive a net profit of $7000 from the concert. Ursula received full payment when she signed the contract, but

reluctantly c py. Not only occurred, yo

Questio

1. Assuming contract,

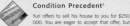

BUSINESS LAW IN ACTION

Condition Precedent[5]

Yuri offers to sell his house to you for $250 000. You are eager to accept that offer, but you do not want to completely commit yourself to the purchase until you are sure that you can sell your own cottage for at least $200 000. You and Yuri therefore agree on the terms that would govern the sale of Yuri's house,

of the contra your obligatio occurs imme a buyer for yo Yuri and he Furthermore, in 30 days, y

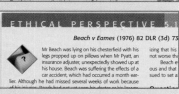

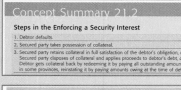

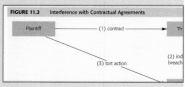

- **You Be the Judge** boxes ask students to respond as judges to legal problems that commonly arise in the business world. They are designed to give students insight into legal thought processes.

- **Ethical Perspective** boxes ask students to assess morally contentious business law scenarios. They compel students to place both business considerations and legal concerns into a larger social context, and to appreciate that alternative solutions often pull in different directions. These boxes are particularly effective in generating classroom discussions.

- **CONCEPT SUMMARIES.** Most chapters contain at least one concept summary. Presented in tabular form, they provide succinct and easily understood reviews of difficult concepts and rules. Many compare and contrast related areas of law.

- **FIGURES.** Most chapters contain at least one figure. Diagrams and drawings illustrate and clarify important concepts, contribute to the visual appeal of the book, and further draw students into the material.

- **CHAPTER SUMMARIES.** Each chapter ends with a chapter summary, which reviews the important concepts of the chapter. These summaries help prepare students for the end-of-chapter exercises.

- **REVIEW QUESTIONS.** Twenty review questions appear at the end of each chapter. Some ask students to define and explain key concepts and terms. Others ask them to respond to short problems. The review questions can be discussed in class or assigned to students for independent study. (Model answers are provided in the *Instructor's Manual*.)

- **CASES AND PROBLEMS.** Each chapter concludes with 12 cases and problems (except for Chapter 1, which has six). These exercises vary in both length and difficulty. They are ideally suited to classroom discussion, but can also be assigned to students for independent study. (Model answers are provided in the *Instructor's Manual*.)

- **CANADIAN CASE STUDIES.** A special Canadian Case Study, associated with a CBC video segment, is provided at the ends of Units 3, 4, 6, 8, and 9. These case studies can be completed even without viewing the accompanying videos. (The videos are available to instructors on cassettes.) With or without the videos, these cases readily lend themselves to classroom discussion. (Model answers are provided in the *Instructor's Manual*.)

- **ANNOTATED WWWEBLINKS.** Each unit concludes with a list of annotated Web links, grouped by topic, which make it easier for students to further explore selected legal issues.

- **LIST OF ABBREVIATIONS.** For convenience, an Explanation of Citations and a List of Abbreviations are provided on the inside of the cover.

SUPPLEMENTS

We have carefully prepared resources to aid instructors in presenting lectures, fostering class discussion, and administering examinations.

- **INSTRUCTOR'S MANUAL.** The *Instructor's Manual* is designed to enhance the organization and presentation of course materials. It includes model answers for all of the questions that appear in the discussion boxes, review questions, cases and problems, and video case studies. Where appropriate, the answers also explain the pedagogic purpose of their associated questions. The manual also provides case briefs for every judicial decision that is mentioned in the text or its footnotes. It also includes teaching tips that instructors might find useful in tailoring the textbook to their particular needs, along with additional teaching suggestions on related topics not explicitly discussed in the book.

- **INSTRUCTOR'S RESOURCE DISK.** To complement the manual, a special *Instructor's Resource Disk* is available. It contains:
  - An electronic version of the *Instructor's Manual*.
  - Acrobat versions of all the figures and Concept Summary boxes that appear in the textbook.
  - PowerPoint slides for each chapter that can be used in electronic form to present materials in class or in printed form to guide the preparation of new lecture notes.

- **TEST ITEM FILE.** The *Test Item File* provides over 1550 questions that can be used for tests and examinations For each chapter, the file contains: (i) 30 multiple-choice questions, (ii) 15 true-false questions, and (iii) 15 short essay questions. Each question is accompanied by a model answer, cross-referenced to the relevant section of the text, ranked according to its level of difficulty, and identified by skill type as either recall or applied.

- **PEARSON EDUCATION CANADA TESTGEN.** The *Pearson Education Canada TestGen* is a special computerized version of the *Test Item File* that enables instructors to view and edit the existing questions, add questions, generate tests, and print the tests in several formats. Powerful search and sort functions make it easy to locate questions and arrange them in any order. TestGen also enables instructors to administer tests on a local area network, have the tests graded electronically, and have the results prepared in electronic or printed reports. Issued on a CD-ROM, the TestGen is compatible with Windows or Macintosh operating systems.

- **CBC/PEARSON EDUCATION CANADA VIDEO LIBRARY FOR BUSINESS LAW.** The CBC and Pearson Education Canada have combined their expertise in educational publishing and global reporting to create special video support for the text. The library consists of five video segments from the CBC programs *Venture* and *MarketPlace*. Each segment supplements a Canadian Case Study in the book.

- **COMPANION WEBSITE (www.pearsoned.ca/mcinnes).** The Electronic Study Guide section of the *Companion Website* includes 30 self-test questions for each chapter. (The questions do not duplicate any of those in the *Test Item File*.) Students can try the questions, send the answers to the electronic grader, and receive instant feedback. The Electronic Study Guide also includes one Internet exercise per chapter, which requires students to use their computer-research skills to analyze and resolve a business law problem. The General Resources section of the *Companion Website* provides an online Glossary, direct links to the Websites described at the end of each unit of the textbook, and the videos that supplement the Canadian Case Studies. The Instructor Resources section of the *Companion Website* will link instructors to Pearson Education Canada's protected Instructor Central site where they can download the same supplements that are available on the *Instructor's Resource Disk*.

ACKNOWLEDGMENTS

We wish to thank a number of people who were instrumental in the production of this book.

Madam Justice Eileen Gillese of the Court of Appeal for Ontario played a critical role, in her former capacity as Dean of Law at the University of Western Ontario, in conceiving the project and bringing the parties together.

Several members of Pearson Education's team made vital contributions. Maurice Esses expertly steered the work through its various stages of development. Marisa D'Andrea efficiently guided the book through production. Elaine Freedman copyedited the work with care. Michael Young provided vision. Kelly Torrance brought tremendous enthusiasm to her role as acquisitions editor. And Steve Iacovelli will long be remembered for his energy and humour.

The Faculties of Law at the University of Western Ontario and the University of Ottawa each provided a stimulating and supportive environment in which to work. Amy Jacobs, of the University of Western Ontario, provided invaluable secretarial assistance.

A number of students at these institutions served as research assistants: Goldie Bassie, Marcus Bornfruend, Alasdair Federico, Robert Gazdag, Heather Gray, Vanessa Gruben, Greg Hagen, Brett Harrison, John Hoben, Andrew Huzzar, Nikiforos Iatrou, Carole Johnson, Kathryn Kirkpatrick, Cherolyn Knapp, Corey Levin, Trevor McGowan, Michelle McLean, Bernard Sandler, Jek-Hui Sim, Peter Shears, and Katie Warfield.

Our special thanks go to Mysty Clapton, who was involved in the entire book and whose editorial contributions as a research assistant are truly inestimable.

The focus, content, and style of this book reflect the comments—often challenging and always insightful—that we received from external reviewers. We are grateful to each of the following for providing formal reviews of different parts of the manuscript:

Howard A. Baker	(*Competition Bureau of Canada, Department of Justice*)
Dale Brawn	(*Laurentian University*)
Richard Cregan	(*Dalhousie University*)
George Cummins	(*Memorial University*)
Maureen Donnelly	(*Brock University*)
Ray Harvey	(*British Columbia Institute of Technology*)
John Harrison	(*University of Manitoba*)
Peter Holden	(*Capilano College*)
Ivan Ivankovich	(*University of Alberta*)
Donna Koziak	(*Athabasca University*)
Garth Maguire	(*Okanagan College*)
W. Ming Song	(*Capilano College*)
David Purvis	(*Sir Sandford Fleming College*)
Karen Reschke	(*Athabasca University*)
Manfred Schneider	(*University of Toronto*)
N. John Stroud-Drinkwater	(*British Columbia Institute of Technology*)
Kenneth Thornicroft	(*University of Victoria*)
Don Valeri	(*Douglas College*)

Mitchell McInnes
Ian Kerr
Tony VanDuzer
Chi Carmody

A Great Way to Learn and Instruct Online

The Pearson Education Canada Companion Website is easy to navigate and is organized to correspond to the chapters in this textbook. Whether you are a student in the classroom or a distance learner you will discover helpful resources for in-depth study and research that empower you in your quest for greater knowledge and maximize your potential for success in the course.

Companion Website

[**www.pearsoned.ca/mcinnes**]

Prentice Hall

Jump to... http://www.pearsoned.ca/mcinnes   Home | Search | Help | Profile

Companion Website

Home >

Companion Website

Managing the Law: The Legal Aspects of Doing Business, by McInnes, Kerr, VanDuzer, and Carmody

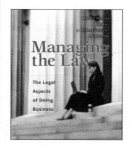

Electronic Study Guide

The modules in this section provide students with tools for learning course material. These modules include:

- Multiple-Choice Questions
- Short Essay Questions
- True-False Questions
- Internet Research Exercises

Students can send answers to the grader and receive instant feedback on their progress through the Results Reporter. Model answers and references to the textbook are provided to ensure that students take advantage of all available resources to enhance their learning experience.

Updates and Other Resources

The modules in this section are designed for students and instructors alike. These modules include:

- Online Glossary
- Web Destinations
- CBC Videos

Instructor Resources

This section includes a link to our protected Instructor Central site where instructors will find the following items to facilitate teaching:

- Instructor's Manual
- Figures and Concept Summary boxes from the book
- PowerPoint Slides

Table of Statutes

Note: The page numbers at the end of each entry refer to pages in this book.

Table of Cases

Note: The page numbers at the end of each entry refer to pages in this book.

1 The Legal System and Risk Management

CHAPTER OVERVIEW

OBJECTIVES

After completing this chapter, you should be able to:

1. Explain why it is important for business people to study law.
2. List four basic strategies for managing risks.
3. Provide a general definition of the word "law."
4. Explain two meanings of the term "civil law" and three meanings of the term "common law."
5. List four areas of public law and three areas of private law. Provide examples that demonstrate how each one of those areas is relevant to business people.
6. Explain how federalism is related to the division of powers.
7. Describe the *Canadian Charter of Rights and Freedoms* and provide several examples of how it can help or hurt a business.
8. Explain the historical development of equity. Briefly explain the relationship between law and equity today.
9. Outline the court structure in Canada. Explain the nature of a court hierarchy, the doctrine of precedent, and the rule of law.
10. Identify the general advantages and disadvantages of formal litigation. List three alternatives to formal litigation. Identify the general advantages and disadvantages of each of those alternatives.

Law is essential to any society. It both reflects and shapes the ways in which people interact. As we will see in this textbook, it can affect a person even before birth (can you sue someone for injuries that you suffered as a fetus?) and even after death (what happens to your property after you are gone?). It also governs the most important issues that arise in between: the freedom to choose how to live, the right to marry, the ability to care for children, the obligation to pay taxes, and so on.

The law, not surprisingly, is enormous. As a whole, it cannot be studied in a single course. Indeed, as a whole, it cannot be mastered in an entire lifetime. Therefore, we have to make choices. We must examine some topics and leave others to the side. To a large extent, those choices depend upon our reason for studying law in the first place.

WHY STUDY LAW?

We therefore begin with the obvious question. Why should you, as a business student, study law? The answer turns on an equally obvious fact—businesses exist primarily to make money. The goal is to maximize gains and minimize losses. Of course, there are many factors in that equation: hard work, natural talent, good luck, and so on. But for the most part, success and failure are the results of choices. A business must choose, for example, a product, a price, a location, and a marketing strategy. And every one of those *business* choices has *legal* consequences. Some consequences are profitable; others are financially disastrous. The difference between winning and losing in the business world often depends upon the ability to make the right choices from a legal perspective. That fact suggests, in general terms, both *why* you should study law and *which* parts of the law you should study.

It is important to realize that the law can both hurt *and* help. Many people think of laws only in terms of prohibitions and punishments. For example, if you break the rule against murder, you may be sent to jail. But the law can also allow you to do things that you could not otherwise do. Generally speaking, for instance, I am entitled to ignore my promises. I can stay home and read even if I agreed to meet you at the movies. Beyond the fear of making you angry, there is nothing that compels me to keep my word. In the business world, however, that sort of behaviour simply cannot be tolerated. If I promise to provide widgets to your factory, you may act on the assumption that I will deliver. For instance, you may hire extra staff or promise to resell the widgets to someone else. You therefore need some way of holding me to my word. Your best bet is to persuade me to enter into a *contract*. As we will see in the next chapter, a contract is a legal concept that allows people to create *enforceable* promises. In that situation, you would not have to worry (as much) that I might ignore my promise.

Risk Management

risk management is the process of identifying, evaluating, and responding to the possibility of harmful events

Throughout this book, we will see a number of other ways in which businesses can positively benefit from the law. Much more often, however, we will be concerned about avoiding losses. The main theme of our discussion is that legal education plays a critical role in *risk management*. **Risk management** is the process of identifying, evaluating, and responding to the possibility of harmful events. Business Law in Action 1.1 provides a simple example.

Risk Management

One of your ex-employees is hoping to join another company. She has asked you to write a reference letter on her behalf. She obviously does not know that you have a very low opinion of her, largely because you believe that she stole money from your business. Furthermore, since the company that she wants to join is one of your best customers, you are tempted to write a candid letter.

Question for Discussion

1. Will you write a reference for your ex-employee? If so, what will it say?

Unless you know something about the law of torts, you are not in a position to answer those questions properly. You need to identify, evaluate, and respond to the legal risks involved.

- *Identification*: If you accuse your ex-employee of theft, she may sue you for defamation because your statement would cause a reasonable person to think less of her. You need to be concerned about *liability*, about actually being held legally responsible. But you also need to be concerned about the possibility of being sued. As we will discuss later in this chapter, litigation is time consuming and expensive, even when you win.

- *Evaluation*: Having identified the risk of being sued for defamation, you may decide that a candid letter would nevertheless be legally acceptable. Your allegations may be true. Even if they are not, you may be justified in sharing your suspicions with the other company. Furthermore, you may believe that the arguments in your favour are strong enough to discourage your former employee from suing you.

- *Response*: Finally, having identified and evaluated the risks, you need to formulate a response. You have several options. You can refuse to write a letter. You can write a letter that does not mention your suspicions. Or you can write a letter that accuses your former employee of theft. The choice is still yours. Significantly, however, you are now in a position to make an informed decision. A basic understanding of the law makes you a better business person.

Note that we are talking about risk *management*. There are potential costs associated with nearly every form of behaviour, and that includes doing nothing at all. A business probably cannot exist, and certainly cannot profit, unless it is willing to take some chances. The goal therefore is not necessarily to eliminate risks; it is to *manage* them. The appropriate strategy depends upon the circumstances.

- *Risk avoidance*: Some risks are so serious that they should be avoided altogether. An automobile that regularly explodes upon impact should be removed from the market. Aside from issues of morality, the financial costs of being held liable will probably outweigh any sales profits.[1]

  risk avoidance eliminates a risk altogether

- *Risk reduction*: Some risks can be reduced to an acceptable level through precautions. For example, a bank that lends $500 000 to a manufacturer realizes that the loan may not be repaid if the economy goes into reces-

  risk reduction limits a risk to an acceptable level

---

[1] *Grimshaw v Ford Motor Co* 119 Cal App 3d 757 (1981).

sion. The bank can, however, protect itself by requiring the business to grant a *mortgage* over its factory. In that case, if the bank does not get its money, it may at least get the property.

- *Risk shifting*: Risk management often has both a front end and a back end. Suppose an Internet service provider is concerned that its equipment may be inadequate. There is a danger that its system will crash and that some of its customers will claim compensation for the losses that they suffer as a result. The company has at least two options.

- It could buy new equipment to minimize the possibility of a problem occurring in the first place. That would involve a form of risk reduction.

- It could continue using its old equipment, but take steps to ensure that someone else pays for any losses that do occur. For example, it could write an *exclusion clause* into the standard form contract that it requires its customers to sign.[2] Or it could purchase an *insurance policy* that would require an insurance company to compensate customers that suffer losses. Those tactics *shift* the burden of the risk onto other people. Each option also carries costs of its own. An exclusion clause might frighten away potential customers and an insurance policy can be expensive to buy.

- *Risk acceptance*: It is sometimes appropriate to simply accept a risk. Imagine a dairy farm that operates alongside a golf course. It is possible that a wild shot could hit a cow, and that the golf course could be held responsible for the resulting injuries. Nevertheless, if the likelihood of such an accident is small, the club might decide to do nothing at all. It certainly would not close the course to avoid the risk altogether. It might also find that the costs of reducing the risk by erecting a large safety net, or shifting the risk by buying an insurance policy, are too high. The most sensible approach might be to hope for the best and pay for any cattle that are hurt.

Risk management does not require you to become a lawyer. Quite often, however, it does require you to hire a lawyer. As a business person, you need to know enough about the law to recognize potential problems. In some situations, you will be able to resolve those problems yourself, preferably by taking steps to avoid them in the first place. But in other situations, it makes sense to call in an expert. Although lawyers' fees can be quite high, you may end up paying much more in the long run if you do not seek professional advice at the outset. Compared to the cost of losing a lawsuit or watching a deal collapse, a lawyer's bill is usually a bargain. In fact, many businesses now have *in-house counsel*. Instead of hiring lawyers from time to time as the need arises, a company may create its own permanent legal department. While that option creates an additional expense, it also provides more efficient risk protection. Lawyers will be on hand not only to resolve legal problems, but also to help identify them.

AN INTRODUCTION TO THE LEGAL SYSTEM

In the chapters that follow, we will examine various areas of law, including contract, tort, and property. But first, we must discuss the Canadian legal system

[2] An exclusion clause restricts or eliminates a person's normal right to sue. See Chapter 4.

as a whole. We can do so quite quickly. While it is important for business people to understand the basic structure of the courts, for instance, most of the details can be left to the lawyers.

The Nature of Law

What are laws? Most people would say that they are rules. That may be true, but it is also clear that not every rule is a law. Sometimes that point is obvious. For example, there is a rule against moving a bishop horizontally across a chess board, but there certainly is not any law to that effect. Sometimes, however, it is much more difficult to determine whether a rule is also a law. Consider Ethical Perspective 1.1.

ETHICAL PERSPECTIVE 1.1

Rules and Laws

While fishing from a lakeshore, I saw a canoeist tip his boat and fall into the water. Although he screamed for help for over 20 minutes, I did nothing at all. My motor boat was nearby, and I could have easily rescued him, but I preferred to continue fishing. Was there any rule that required me to get involved? Assuming that the canoeist drowned, can I be held legally responsible?

Most people would agree that I was required to rescue the canoeist, especially since I could have done so safely and easily. However, that rule may exist only in *morality*, and not in *law*. According to an old American case, I could not be held legally responsible even if I had rented the boat to the deceased when I knew that he was drunk.[3] A Canadian court would undoubtedly decide otherwise in the same circumstances today.[4] But if I did not have a business rela-

tionship with the canoeist, the answer would be less clear. The courts traditionally drew a distinction between moral obligations and legal obligations, and generally said that there was no duty to rescue in law. Recently, however, Canadian judges have begun to adopt a different attitude. Consequently, while we now know that there is sometimes both a moral duty *and* a legal duty to rescue, we do not know exactly when that is true.

Questions for Discussion

1. How would you, as a business person, decide when to follow a moral rule, even if you were not obligated to do so by a legal rule?

2. Does your answer depend entirely upon morality? Are there also important business consequences to acting morally or immorally?

Ethical Perspective 1.1 demonstrates that it is occasionally difficult to distinguish between moral obligations and legal obligations. However, it also points us toward a workable definition of the word "law." Although philosophers have debated the issue for thousands of years, it is sufficient for our purposes to say that a **law** is a rule that can be enforced by the courts. If I merely broke a moral obligation by refusing to rescue the canoeist, then I might be punished, but only through public opinion. Colleagues might stop talking to me, and newspapers might print unflattering articles. However, if I also broke a legal obligation, then I would have more serious things on my mind. Depending on the precise nature of the legal obligation, a court might decide to put me in jail or require me to compensate the victim's family for his death.

a **law** is a rule that can be enforced by the courts

[3.] *Osterlind v Hill* 160 NE 301 (Mass 1928).

[4.] *Crocker v Sundance Northwest Resorts Ltd* (1988) 51 DLR (4th) 321 (SCC). That case is discussed in Chapter 12.

A Map of the Law

civil law systems trace their history to ancient Rome

a jurisdiction is a geographical area that uses the same set of laws

common law systems trace their history to England

Even after it has been distinguished from other types of rules, the law remains an enormous topic. To make sense of it all, we need to organize it into different parts. There are many ways of doing so. In Canada, for example, it is necessary to distinguish between *civil law* and *common law*.[5] **Civil law** systems trace their history to ancient Rome. Since the Roman Empire covered almost all of Europe, the vast majority of countries in that continent are still under that system of law. The only civil law *jurisdiction* in Canada, however, is Quebec, which initially borrowed its law from France. (Although it has many different meanings, **jurisdiction** in this situation refers to a geographical area that uses the same set of laws.) **Common law** systems trace their history to England. Consequently, most jurisdictions that were settled by English colonists continue to use the common law. That is true of the rest of Canada, as well as such jurisdictions as Australia, New Zealand, and most of the United States.[6] Since there are significant differences between civil law systems and common law systems, there are also significant differences between the law that applies in Quebec and the law that applies in the rest of this country. In this book, we will concentrate on the Canadian laws that apply outside of Quebec.

Within Canada's common law system, we can further organize legal rules on the basis of the topics that they address. Although it does not cover every possibility, Figure 1.1 represents some of the most important areas that we will discuss in this book.

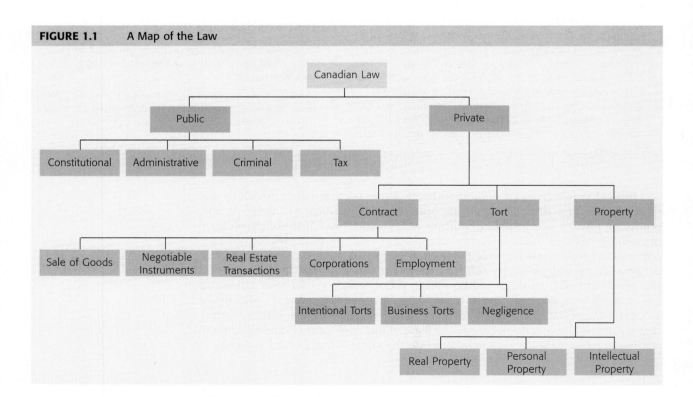

FIGURE 1.1   A Map of the Law

---

[5] There are other systems of law as well, such as Aboriginal law and Islamic law.

[6] The exception in the United States is Louisiana. Like Quebec, it was settled by France and therefore uses a civil law system.

Public Law

Figure 1.1 shows that the major division is between *public law* and *private law*. **Public law** is concerned with governments and the ways in which they deal with their citizens. It includes:

- constitutional law
- administrative law
- criminal law
- tax law

Constitutional law provides the basic rules of our political and legal systems. It determines who is entitled to create and enforce laws, and it establishes the fundamental rights and freedoms that Canadians enjoy. We will discuss the Constitution in more detail in a later part of this chapter.

In the past 50 years, Canadians have grown to expect more and more from their elected officials. To manage the workload, governments regularly *delegate* or *assign* responsibility to a variety of agencies, boards, commissions, and tribunals. **Administrative law** is concerned with the creation and operation of those bodies. It has a profound impact on business. For instance, a human rights tribunal may decide that a corporation discriminated against women by paying them less than it paid men for work of similar value. If so, the company may be ordered to pay millions of dollars in compensation.[7] Even if a particular business never becomes involved in that sort of landmark case, it probably has to deal, in the normal course of operations, with a number of administrative bodies. There are literally hundreds. Figure 1.2 lists a sampling of federal, provincial (or territorial), and municipal bodies that regularly affect business.[8]

public law is concerned with governments and the ways in which they deal with their citizens

constitutional law provides the basic rules of our political and legal systems

administrative law is concerned with the creation and operation of administrative agencies and tribunals

FIGURE 1.2	**Administrative Bodies**
Federal	
Canadian Radio-television and Telecommunications Commission	regulates broadcasting and telecommunications systems
National Energy Board	regulates pipelines, energy development, and trade in the energy industry
Canadian International Trade Tribunal	investigates possible violations of international trade regulations
Competition Tribunal	resolves disputes under the *Competition Act*
Provincial or Territorial	
Workers' Compensation Board	promotes workplace safety and rehabilitates and compensates injured workers
Labour Relations Board	assists in the resolution of labour disputes
Environmental Appeal Board	assists in the resolution of environmental disputes
Professional Society (eg Law Society of Alberta)	regulates and licenses the practice of a particular profession (eg law)

(continued)

[7.] *Bell Canada v Canadian Telephone Employees Association* (2001) 199 DLR (4th) 664 (FC CA).

[8.] This list is not exhaustive. Some bodies serve more than one function. Note that, below the federal level, the name of a particular body may vary from place to place.

FIGURE 1.2	*(continued)*
Municipal	
Zoning and Planning Board	regulates the use of land
Building and Inspections Department	regulates and licenses building projects
Licence Division	regulates and licenses business operations

criminal law deals with offences against the state

Criminal law deals with offences against the state. In other words, it is concerned with people who break rules that are designed to protect society as a whole. For instance, if you punch me, you have committed a *tort* because you have done something wrong to me personally. However, you have also committed a *crime* because you have done something wrong to the entire community. Even if I am not particularly upset about being hit, society may want to discourage and punish your behaviour. Consequently, the police and the prosecutor may bring you to court even if I would prefer to drop the matter. Although we tend to think of criminals as violent individuals, it is important to know that crime can happen in the business world as well.

- *White-collar crimes*, as the name suggests, are committed by people in suits. A manager who steals money from the petty cash drawer is a white-collar criminal.
- A crime can even be committed by a company itself. A *corporate crime* occurs, for instance, when a used car dealership adopts a policy of rolling back the odometers on its vehicles. That company is guilty of fraud.[9]

tax law is concerned with the rules that are used to collect money for the purposes of public spending

To operate, the various branches of government, such as Parliament, administrative bodies, and courts, require a great deal of money. **Tax law** is concerned with the rules that are used to collect money for public spending. This is an area of great interest to the business community.

Private Law

private law is concerned with the rules that apply in private matters

Although we will occasionally discuss public law, our focus is on *private law*. **Private law** is concerned with the rules that apply in private matters. Both parties in a private dispute are usually private *persons*, either individuals or organizations like corporations. For instance, your theatre company might sue me if I failed to perform a play as promised. However, private law can also apply to the government. First, it is possible for a private person to sue a public body.[10] Suppose that the municipal government carelessly forgot to inspect the foundations of your house while it was being built. If your basement later develops cracks, you could sue the construction company for providing shoddy work, but you could also sue the city for its failure to enforce its own building regulations.[11] The government is also subject to the private law when it enters into private transactions, such as when a government contractually agrees to purchase paper from a store.

---

[9] *R v Waterloo Mercury Sales Ltd* (1974) 49 DLR (3d) 131 (Alta Dist Ct). Corporate crime is discussed in Chapter 19.

[10] And vice versa. If you accidentally burned down city hall, the municipal government could sue you.

[11] *Neilson v City of Kamloops* (1984) 10 DLR (4th) 641 (SCC).

Private law is usually divided into three main parts:

- the law of contracts
- the law of torts
- the law of property

The **law of contracts** is concerned with the creation and enforcement of agreements. For business people, this is a tremendously important area of law. Business is based on transactions, and the law of contracts governs virtually every one of them. For instance, even if we limit ourselves to the headings in Figure 1.1, we can see that contracts are involved in: (i) the *sale of goods*, such as cows and computers, (ii) the use of *negotiable instruments*, such as cheques, (iii) *real estate transactions*, such as the purchase of land, (iv) the operation of *corporations*, and (v) the *employment* relationship that exists between a business and its workers. We will see many more examples throughout this book.

the law of contracts is concerned with the creation and enforcement of agreements

We have defined a crime as a public wrong, or an offence against society as a whole. A **tort**, in contrast, is a private wrong, or an offence against a particular person. Like the law of contracts, the law of torts covers a great deal of territory. For the purposes of discussion, we will split the category into three: (i) *intentional torts*, such as assault and false imprisonment, (ii) *business torts*, such as deceit and conspiracy, and (iii) *negligence*, which covers most situations in which one person carelessly hurts another.

a tort is a private wrong

As the name suggests, the **law of property** governs the acquisition, use, and disposition of property. The discussion is once again divided into three main parts: (i) *real property*, which involves land and things that are attached to land, (ii) *personal property*, which involves things that can be moved from one place to another, and (iii) *intellectual property*, which involves things that consist of original ideas, such as patents and copyrights. All three forms of property are important in business. Every company owns personal property; the vast majority have interests in real property; and a growing number rely heavily on intellectual property. There are also several areas of law that deal with all forms of property. Two important examples will reappear throughout this text: (i) *succession*, which deals with the distribution of property after people die, and (ii) *trusts*, which deals with a situation in which one person holds property on behalf of another.

the law of property governs the acquisition, use, and disposition of property

Overlap

Before leaving this section, we must stress that different areas of law can overlap. There are at least two possibilities.

- First, a single event can trigger more than one set of rules. We have already mentioned one example. If you punch me, you may commit both a crime and a tort. Other illustrations are more common in the business world. For instance, if you hire lawyers who provide poor work and bad advice, you may have the option of suing them for both breach of contract (because they did not fulfill your agreement) and the tort of negligence (because they carelessly caused you to suffer a loss).[12]

- Second, some situations involve various types of laws. For example, an employment relationship is based on a contract between the employer and the employee. Nevertheless, the parties should also have some knowledge of administrative law (in case a company discriminates against ethnic minorities), criminal law (in case a boss sexually harasses an employee), and tort law (in case one worker injures another).

---

12. *Central Trust Co v Rafuse* (1986) 31 DLR (4th) 481 (SCC).

Sources of Law

In the last section, we organized laws according to topics. In this section, we organize them according to sources. Broadly speaking, there are three sources:

- the Constitution
- legislation
- the courts

As we will see, not all laws are created equal. Some are more important than others.

The Constitution

the Constitution is the document that creates the basic rules for Canadian society, including its political and legal systems

any law that is inconsistent with the Constitution is of no force or effect

The most important source of law is the **Constitution**. This document creates the basic rules for Canadian society, including our political and legal systems.[13] The fact that it provides the foundations for everything else has two significant consequences. First, every other law in the country must be compatible with it. Section 52 of the Constitution states: "The Constitution of Canada is the supreme law of Canada, and any law that is inconsistent with the provisions of the Constitution is, to the extent of the inconsistency, of no force or effect."

Second, the Constitution is *very* difficult to change. It is one thing to tinker with the rules that govern the enforcement of contracts. It is a far more serious matter to alter the fundamental rules of Canadian society. Most laws can be changed by a legislature or by a court. The Constitution is different—it can be changed only through a special *amending formula*. This requires the consent of Parliament plus the legislatures of at least two-thirds of the provinces that represent at least 50 percent of the country's population. Not surprisingly, Constitutional amendments are rare.

Constitutional amendments are rare

Division of Powers   Many parts of the Constitution are important to business people. We will look at two. The first concerns the *division of powers*.[14] To understand that concept, it is necessary to appreciate that Canada is a **federal** country because it has two levels of government.[15]

Canada is a federal country because it has two levels of government

- *Federal*: The Parliament of Canada, which is located in Ottawa, governs the country as a whole. It is composed of two parts. The House of Commons consists of members of Parliament (MPs), who are elected from every province and territory. The Senate consists of senators, who are appointed to their jobs. Since Canada began life as a British colony and is still part of the British Commonwealth, the Queen of England remains our head of state.[16] In reality, the country is run by the political party that has the most MPs. The leader of that party is the prime minister.

- *Provincial and Territorial*: In addition to electing members of Parliament to represent them nationally in Ottawa, Canadians also elect politicians to represent them within their own provinces and territories.[17] The

---

[13.] Schedule B to the *Canada Act 1982*, (UK) 1982, c 11. Although our current Constitution came into force in 1982, it is virtually identical to the *British North America Act*, which contained Canada's first Constitution in 1867. The most notable feature of the new Constitution is that it includes the *Charter of Rights and Freedoms*.

[14.] Chapter 23 examines the division of powers as it affects business regulation in Canada.

[15.] A province or territory can create a third level of government, a municipality.

[16.] Since she is seldom in Canada, the Queen is represented by the Governor General.

[17.] Provinces and territories do not have senators.

elected body, or *legislature*, is usually called the Legislative Assembly.[18] And for the most part, each of the 13 legislatures is similar to Parliament. Once again, even though the official head of state is the Queen, power really is held by the party with the most elected members, whose leader is the premier.[19]

Wherever you live in Canada, you are subject to two sets of laws: federal and provincial (or territorial). With respect to any particular issue, however, there is generally only one law. Our system would not work very well, for instance, if Parliament required you to drive on the right side of the road at the same time that your legislature required you to drive on the left. Sections 91 and 92 of the Constitution create a **division of powers**, stating the areas in which each level of government can create laws. Concept Summary 1.1 lists some areas that are particularly important to business people. Note the last item on the left side of the chart. The federal government has the **residual power**, the power over everything that is not otherwise mentioned. Consequently, Parliament now has authority over a number of topics that did not exist when our original Constitution was written in 1867, such as telecommunications and air travel.

the division of powers states the areas in which each level of government can create laws

the residual power gives the federal government authority over everything that is not specifically mentioned

Concept Summary 1.1

Division of Powers

FEDERAL	PROVINCIAL OR TERRITORIAL
criminal law	property and civil rights (eg contracts, torts)
taxation	direct taxation to raise money for provincial purposes
unemployment insurance	corporations with provincial objects
banks	the creation of municipalities
bankruptcy and insolvency	matters of a local or private nature within a province
money	
negotiable instruments (such as cheques)	
international and interprovincial trade and commerce	
navigation and shipping	
copyright	
any matter that is not exclusively given to the provinces	

A government sometimes tries to create a law outside of its own area. When it does so, it acts ***ultra vires***, which literally means "beyond the power." As a result of section 52 of the Constitution (which we quoted earlier), such laws are "of no force or effect." In other words, they are not really laws at all. In one famous case, the federal government tried to create a law that prohibited people from importing or manufacturing margarine. It did so to protect the dairy industry from competition. The Supreme Court of Canada found that that law was partially invalid.[20] The federal government was entitled to ban the *importation* of margarine because it had authority over international and inter-

an *ultra vires* law is beyond the power of the government and therefore is invalid

---

18. There is some variation. Newfoundland, for instance, has a House of Assembly.

19. In her absence, the Queen is represented by a lieutenant governor in each province and a commissioner in each territory.

20. *Reference Re Validity of s 5(a) of the Dairy Industry Act (Canada)* [1949] 1 DLR 433.

provincial trade. It could not, however, ban the *manufacture* of margarine. Because a province has authority over "property and civil rights," it can regulate the production or sale of margarine within its own borders.

the *Charter of Rights and Freedoms* protects basic rights and freedoms

Charter of Rights and Freedoms

Traditionally, as long as a government acted within the scope of its power (or *intra vires*), its laws were generally valid. Since 1982, however, the situation has been much different. In that year, the *Canadian Charter of Rights and Freedoms* was written into the Constitution.[21] As its name indicates, the *Charter* was introduced to protect basic rights and freedoms. Although a large number are included in the document, we quote three that are especially important to business people.

Fundamental Freedoms

2   Everyone has the following fundamental freedoms:
 (a) freedom of conscience and religion;
 (b) freedom of thought, belief, opinion and expression, including freedom of the press and other media of communication;
 (c) freedom of peaceful assembly; and
 (d) freedom of association.

Mobility Rights

6   (1) Every citizen of Canada has the right to enter, remain in and leave Canada.

 (2) Every citizen of Canada and every person who has the status of a permanent resident of Canada has the right
  (a) to move to and take up residence in any province; and
  (b) to pursue the gaining of a livelihood in any province....

Equality Rights

15 (1) Every individual is equal before and under the law and has the right to the equal protection and equal benefit of the law without discrimination and, in particular, without discrimination based on race, national or ethnic origin, colour, religion, sex, age or mental or physical disability.

 (2) Subsection (1) does not preclude any law, program or activity that has as its object the amelioration of conditions of disadvantaged individuals or groups including those that are disadvantaged because of race, national or ethnic origin, colour, religion, sex, age or mental or physical disability.

any law that is inconsistent with the *Charter* is of no force or effect

Since the *Charter* is part of the Constitution, any law that is inconsistent with it is "of no force or effect." From a business perspective, the result can be quite dramatic. A few examples demonstrate that point.

- To protect Christian beliefs, Parliament created a law that required most stores to close on Sundays. That law was declared invalid because it discriminated against non-Christians.[22] It violated their freedom of religion under section 2(a).
- Alberta created a law that prohibited law firms in that province from creating partnerships with law firms in other provinces. That law was declared invalid because it prevented lawyers from working in different parts of the country.[23] It violated mobility rights under section 6(2).

[21.] Schedule B to the *Canada Act 1982*, (UK) 1982, c 11.
[22.] *R v Big M Drug Mart Ltd* (1985) 18 DLR (4th) 321 (SCC).
[23.] *Black v Law Society of Alberta* (1989) 58 DLR (4th) 317 (SCC).

- British Columbia passed a law that prevented people who were not Canadian citizens from practising law in that province. That law was declared invalid because it discriminated against people on the basis of their national origin.[24] It violated their right to equality under section 15(1).

Although many of its rights and freedoms are quite broad, the *Charter* is also subject to several restrictions.

- *Government action*: Section 32(1) of the *Charter* states that the document applies to "Parliament" and "the legislature ... of each province." Consequently, its rights and freedoms have full effect only if a person is complaining about the government's behaviour.[25] The *Charter* does not directly apply to disputes involving private parties. For instance, the right to freedom of expression that is found in section 2(b) does not entitle a union to picket a private corporation.[26] Interestingly, the Supreme Court of Canada has said that private law should be developed in a way that is consistent with *Charter* values.[27] It is not yet clear exactly what that means.

  the *Charter* applies only to government action

  the *Charter* generally does not apply against private parties

- *Corporations*: The *Charter* generally does not apply *against* private corporations. It may not apply in *favour* of them either. It depends on the circumstances. For example, section 2(b) refers to "everyone," while section 15(1) refers to "every individual." A company is a kind of "person," but it is not an "individual." As a result, it enjoys freedom of expression, but not the right to equality.[28]

  some parts of the *Charter* do not apply in favour of corporations

- *Reasonable limits*: Section 1 of the *Charter* states that the rights and freedoms are subject to "such reasonable limits prescribed by law as can be demonstrably justified in a free and democratic society." The Constitution therefore recognizes that it is occasionally acceptable to violate a person's rights. In one famous case, the Supreme Court of Canada held that a shop owner's freedom of expression was infringed by a law that prevented him from selling violent pornography.[29] However, the judges also held that society was justified in banning that sort material because it is degrading, dehumanizing, and harmful to women. The law was therefore enforceable and the shop owner was prohibited from selling the offending material.

  the rights and freedoms contained in the *Charter* are subject to reasonable limits

- *Notwithstanding clause*: Section 33 may allow Parliament or a legislature to create and enforce a law "notwithstanding" the fact that it violates the *Charter*.[30] In practice, however, the notwithstanding clause is almost

  governments can sometimes create and enforce laws that violate the *Charter* by using the notwithstanding clause

---

[24.] *Andrews v Law Society (British Columbia)* (1989) 56 DLR (4th) 1 (SCC).

[25.] In this situation, "government" refers to Parliament, the legislatures, and other organizations that are closely controlled by the government, including the police and community colleges, but not universities and hospitals.

[26.] *RWDSU Local 580 v Dolphin Delivery Ltd* (1986) 33 DLR (4th) 174 (SCC).

[27.] *Dobson v Dobson* (1999) 174 DLR (4th) 1 (SCC).

[28.] Although "everyone" includes both people and corporations, not all of the freedoms listed in section 2 are available to companies. For instance, while a corporation has a need to express itself, it cannot have a religious belief. Its employees can, however, hold religious beliefs, which is why Sunday closing laws can be declared invalid, as discussed above.

[29.] *R v Butler* (1992) 89 DLR (4th) 449 (SCC).

[30.] The notwithstanding clause applies only to some of the rights and freedoms listed in the *Charter*. Parliament or a legislature can override section 2 (fundamental freedoms) or section 15 (equality rights), for instance, but not section 6 (mobility rights). Furthermore, the notwithstanding clause can be used for only five years at a time. At the end of that period, the clause must be re-applied. That rule ensures that significant constitutional rules are re-examined on a regular basis.

never used.[31] The section requires the government to expressly declare that it is overriding fundamental rights and freedoms. And that sort of declaration is usually bad politics—it tends to upset voters.

We have seen that two parts of the Constitution are especially important to business: the division of powers and the *Charter*. By way of review, consider Case Brief 1.1.

Irwin Toy Ltd v Quebec (Attorney General) (1989) 59 DLR (4th) 577 (SCC)

Quebec created a law that generally prohibited advertisements aimed at pre-teens. Irwin Toys wanted to advertise its products on television. It argued that the law was unconstitutional because: (i) it dealt with television, which is a federal matter, rather than a provincial matter, and (ii) it violated the *Charter*'s freedom of expression.

Division of powers: The Supreme Court of Canada agreed that the federal Parliament has authority over telecommunications as part of its residual power. However, the Court also said that the disputed law only affected television in an indirect or incidental way. The province's goal was not to regulate broadcasters; it was to regulate advertisers. And since

the regulation of advertisements is a provincial matter, the law was acceptable under the division of powers.

Charter of Rights and Freedoms: The Supreme Court of Canada agreed that the disputed law violated freedom of expression under section 2(b) of the *Charter*. After all, it prevented the toy company from using television to tell children about its products. However, the Court also held that the province was justified in placing restrictions on the ability to advertise. Society has an interest in protecting young children from commercial exploitation. Furthermore, the ban was reasonable. For instance, it only applied to children under 13 years of age.

Legislation

legislation is law that is created by Parliament or a legislature

The Constitution is the first source of law; *legislation* is the second. **Legislation** is law that is created by Parliament or a legislature. The most important examples are *statutes*, or *acts*. The *Criminal Code*, for example, is the federal statute that determines the types of behaviour that are crimes.[32] And every jurisdiction in Canada has an act that allows companies to be created.[33]

The Legislative Process   As a matter of risk management, it is important to understand how legislation is created. That may seem surprising. After all, when we talk about risk management, we are usually worried about laws that already exist. Sometimes, however, the best strategy is to either prevent the creation of a law or make sure that it is written in a way that causes as little trouble as possible.

We briefly describe the process that is used to create a statute in Parliament. The same basic procedure applies in the provincial and territorial legislatures.[34]

[31.] Exceptions do exist. For instance, the notwithstanding clause was used in Quebec in the 1980s to protect a law that allowed only French to be used on outdoor signs.

[32.] RSC 1985, c C-46.

[33.] The usual name is the *Business Corporations Act*, the *Corporations Act*, or the *Companies Act*. Those statutes are examined in Chapters 18 and 19.

[34.] There are some differences. For instance, there is no need for Senate approval at the provincial or territorial level. Furthermore, while royal assent is given by the Governor General at the federal level, it is given by the lieutenant governors in the provinces and by the commissioners in the territories.

- *First reading*: A proposal for a new law or an amendment to an old one is presented in the House of Commons as a *bill*.[35] That is usually just a formal introduction. The MPs almost always agree, without any debate, to send the bill on to the next step. However, even at this early stage, it is possible for business people to have some effect. For example, although they cannot introduce bills into Parliament themselves, they can *lobby*, or encourage their MPs to do so.

- *Second reading*: Some time later, the bill is brought back into the House of Commons. The MPs then have a chance to argue for or against it. Since the entire process is open to the public, some of those arguments may be based on comments that the MPs received from members of the public, including business people. If the bill once again has the support of most of the MPs, it can eventually go on to the next stage. In the meantime, however, it is sent to a legislative committee for detailed study, which may involve inviting business people to make comments.

- *Third reading*: After the bill has passed through the committee, it returns to the House of Commons for a final debate and vote by the MPs. If it still has majority support, it is sent on to the Senate.

- *Senate approval*: The same three-stage process is repeated in the Senate. Business people can try to exert influence there as well. In practice, however, the Senate is less powerful than the House of Commons, largely because its members are appointed rather than elected. In a democracy, power primarily rests with the people who are chosen directly by the public.

- *Royal assent*: If the bill is passed through the Senate, it requires one last formality. Since the head of state in Canada is technically the Queen, a bill does not become a law until it receives *royal assent*, which is Her Majesty's approval. That approval is given on her behalf by the Governor General.

Subordinate Legislation and Municipalities   It is impossible for Parliament and the legislatures to constantly monitor all of their legislation to make sure that it is effective and up to date. Therefore, statutes often set up a basic structure but allow someone else (such as a government minister, a commission, or a tribunal) to create specific rules without the need to go through the entire legislative process. Those regulations are known as **subordinate legislation**.[36] For example, Parliament created the Canadian Radio-television and Telecommunications Commission (CRTC) and gave it the power to regulate broadcasting in Canada.

subordinate legislation are rules that are created with the authority of Parliament or the legislature

One of the most important types of subordinate legislation involves *municipalities*. The Constitution is concerned with only two levels of government: federal and provincial (or territorial). However, a third level is needed. For instance, neither Parliament nor the legislature will decide whether cats can roam free in a particular town. That decision must be made locally. The Constitution gives the provinces the power to create **municipalities**, which are towns and cities. And when a province creates a municipality, it gives that new body the authority to pass **by-laws**, which are a type of subordinate legislation. Although municipalities are the lowest level of government, their impact on business can be significant. Among other things, by-laws are used to license

a municipality is a town or city

a by-law is a type of subordinate legislation that is created by a municipality

---

[35.] Occasionally, a bill is introduced in the Senate, rather than the House of Commons.

[36.] There are various types of subordinate legislation, including regulations, by-laws, statutory instruments, ordinances, and Orders-in-Council. The appropriate one depends on the circumstances.

businesses, impose some sorts of taxes, plan commercial developments, and regulate parking. City hall is a powerful place.

The Courts

The third source of laws are the *courts*. In this section, we are concerned with situations in which judges deal with laws they have created themselves.

Before we begin, however, it is important to note that judges also have a vital role to play in connection with the other two sources of law. By itself, the Constitution or a statute is simply words on a page. Furthermore, those words are often quite vague. What does the *Charter* mean, for instance, when it says that every individual is entitled to the equal protection of the law "without discrimination based on race, national or ethnic origin, colour, religion, sex, age or mental or physical disability"? Since that phrase says nothing at all about sexual orientation, is it possible to fire a person from a job because he is gay? No. The Supreme Court of Canada has *interpreted* section 15 as prohibiting such discrimination.[37] You can never be sure what a law means until a judge says what it means. Nevertheless, it is also true that our legal system is based on the concept of **parliamentary supremacy**. While judges are required to interpret constitutional and statutory documents, they must also obey them.

> the concept of parliamentary supremacy requires the courts to obey the Constitution and elected officials

Law and Equity   "Common law" is a confusing term because it sometimes refers to a particular type of court. However, it has at least two other meanings.

- *Systems*: We previously used the term "common law" to refer to legal systems that can be traced to England, and compared the common law system that operates throughout most of Canada to the civil law system that Quebec borrowed from France.[38]

- *Sources*: Within a common law system, the term "common law" can also be used in a more specific way to refer to rules that are created by judges rather than by legislators or the drafters of the Constitution. Most of the rules in contract, for instance, are common law rules because they were developed by the courts. Statutes apply only to certain small areas of contract. The law of taxation, in contrast, is almost completely based on statutes. For the most part, judges simply interpret and apply the legislation.

- *Courts*: If we limit our discussion to judge-made rules, we can use the phrase "common law" in an even more specific way. England traditionally had two sets of courts: the *courts of law* and the *courts of equity*. Lawyers sometimes still talk about the "common law" when referring to rules developed in the first type of court, and about "equity" when referring to rules developed in the second type of court.

Figure 1.3 uses a diagram to explain the various meanings of the term "common law."

---

[37] *Vriend v Alberta* (1998) 156 DLR (4th) 385 (SCC).

[38] "Civil law" is another confusing phrase. It often refers to a legal system that can be traced to ancient Rome. However, within a common law system, it can also refer to private law rather than public law. For example, when Canadian lawyers talk about "civil litigation," they are usually referring to cases involving contracts or torts.

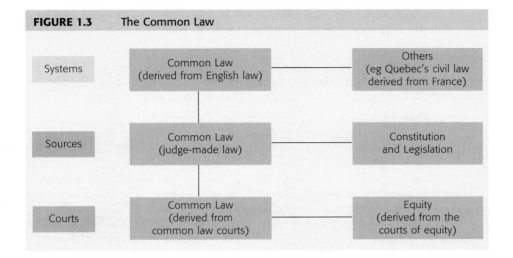

FIGURE 1.3   The Common Law

The legal system that developed in England originally had only one type of court. And the rules and procedures that were used in those *courts of law* were often rigid and harsh. At the same time, however, the king (or queen) was seen as the ultimate source of law. Consequently, when people were unhappy with decisions they received in court, they could ask the king for relief. Not surprisingly, the king was too busy to deal with all of those *petitions* personally. He therefore asked the *chancellor*, who was his legal and religious adviser, to act on his behalf. As the number of petitions continued to increase, the chancellor asked other people to act on his behalf. The chancellor and the people under him eventually became recognized as a separate court that was known as the *court of equity* (or the *court of chancery*).

That name reflects the way in which the new court originally decided cases. The king, the chancellor, and the chancellor's men simply did what they believed was right. Unlike the courts of law, they were much less concerned with rigid rules and much more concerned with justice. In other words, their decisions were based on **equity**, which, in a general sense, means fairness.

equity is, in a general sense, fairness

Equity continues to play an important role in our legal system. However, it is much different from when it was first created. Two changes are especially significant.

- *The nature of equity*: The concept of equity no longer allows judges to decide cases simply on the basis of fairness. Like the courts of law, the courts of equity eventually developed and applied a consistent set of rules. Equity may still be slightly more flexible than law. But for the most part, those two systems are different only because they occasionally apply different rules. For instance, if I break a contract by refusing to transfer a house to you, the law says that you are only entitled to the *monetary value* of that house, not the property itself. Equity, however, may be willing to grant *specific performance* and force me to actually transfer the house to you.

equity no longer allows judges to decide cases simply on the basis of fairness

- *One set of courts*: Initially, the courts of law and the courts of equity were completely separate. They occupied different buildings, they used different judges, they heard from different lawyers. At the end of the nineteenth century, however, the two court systems were joined into one.

the courts of law and the courts of equity are now joined

Consequently, every Canadian court is now a court of law *and* a court of equity. The same judges apply both sets of rules.[39]

The Court Structure Although our legal system no longer has separate courts for law and equity, it does have a variety of courts. In this section, we describe five. First, however, we need to briefly explain three concepts:

- the court hierarchy
- the doctrine of precedent
- the rule of law

The first concept is the easiest. To say that the courts are in a **hierarchy** means that they are arranged according to importance. One court is on top, some are in the middle, and several are on the bottom.

The courts at the bottom are *trial courts*. There is a single judge and sometimes a jury.[40] The person who makes the complaint is the **plaintiff** or, in a criminal case, the **Crown** (the government). The complaint is made against the **defendant** or, as the person is sometimes called in a criminal case, the **accused**. The parties are normally represented by lawyers. In most circumstances, witnesses testify and provide evidence. The parties themselves may be witnesses. A criminal case ends in a *conviction* if the Crown proves *beyond a reasonable doubt* that the accused is guilty. That is a very high standard. If it is not met, then the accused is *acquitted*. Outside of criminal law, it is only necessary to prove a case on a *balance of probabilities*. The plaintiff has to show that its version of the events is *probably* true.

The higher courts are *appeal courts*, or *appellate courts*. An **appeal court** decides whether a case was correctly decided at trial. For the most part, however, it does so in a limited way. It usually deals only with the law. There is a strong presumption that the facts were properly settled at trial. For that reason, appeal courts do not take evidence from witnesses. They hear arguments only from the parties or their lawyers. The party who is attacking the lower court judgment is the **appellant**; the other party is the **respondent**. An appeal either can be *allowed*, if the trial judgment was wrong, or *dismissed*, if the trial judgment was right. It is sometimes possible to appeal the decision of an appeal court. For instance, if you are unhappy with the result that you received in a trial, you can usually appeal it to the Court of Appeal. And if you are unhappy with the decision that you receive from that court, you may be able to appeal it to the Supreme Court of Canada.

The second concept is more complicated. The **doctrine of precedent** requires a court to follow any other court that is above it in a hierarchy.[41] We can demonstrate that idea by taking a few examples from Figure 1.4.

- Since it is at the top of the entire court structure, the Supreme Court of Canada is not required to obey any other court.[42] (However, it is required to obey the Constitution and legislation.)

Margin notes:

the court hierarchy arranges the courts according to importance

the plaintiff or the Crown is the person who makes the complaint

the defendant or the accused is the person against whom the complaint is made

an appeal court decides whether a case was correctly decided at trial

the appellant is the party who attacks the lower court judgment

the respondent is the party defending the lower court judgment

the doctrine of precedent requires a court to follow any other court that is above it in a hierarchy

---

[39] If there is any inconsistency, the equitable rules apply.

[40] In Canada, juries are seldom used in private law cases. They are usually limited to criminal cases, where the accused can generally choose between either a judge alone or a judge and a jury. The judge is responsible for finding the law and the jury is responsible for finding the facts.

[41] Lawyers sometimes refer to that doctrine by the Latin *stare decisis*, which means "to stand by decided matters."

[42] Until 1949, it was possible for Canadians to send their appeals to the Judicial Committee of the Privy Council in England, which the Supreme Court of Canada was therefore required to obey.

FIGURE 1.4   Structure of Canadian Courts

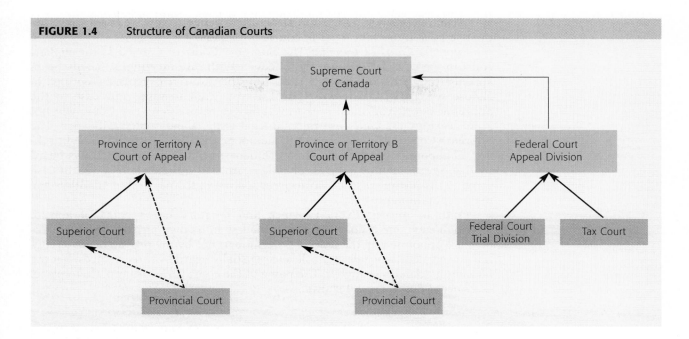

- The Superior Court of Province A must obey both the Court of Appeal in that province and the Supreme Court of Canada. Those courts stand above it in the *same* court hierarchy. They are connected by the *same* set of lines.

- However, the Superior Court in Province A does *not* have to obey the Court of Appeal in Province B.[43] Those courts are not part of the same hierarchy. They are not connected by the same set of lines. That does not mean, however, that judges *never* rely on decisions from other jurisdictions.[44] Suppose that a trial judge in Edmonton has a difficult case. Neither the Alberta Court of Appeal nor the Supreme Court of Canada has decided one like it. That judge is allowed to look elsewhere for help. Help may be found in the Ontario Court of Appeal, in a trial judgment from Brandon, or perhaps in a decision from Singapore. Those sorts of authorities are not *binding*, but they may be *persuasive*.

Third, the **rule of law** states that disputes should be settled on the basis of laws, not personal opinions. The concept of a hierarchy and the doctrine of precedent support the rule of law by requiring judges to follow the courts above them. That system has a number of benefits, one of the most important being consistency. For instance, the Supreme Court of Canada recently decided that a mother cannot be sued for carelessly injuring her child before birth.[45] If that issue arises again in Kamloops, Windsor, or Charlottetown, it must be resolved in the same way. That sort of consistency also creates another important benefit: respect for the legal system. Even if you disagree with the trial judge's decision in one of those cities, you can be confident that it was based on law, not the judge's personal preference.

the **rule of law** states that disputes should be settled on the basis of laws, not merely personal opinions

---

[43.] Nor does it have to obey the Appeal Division of the Federal Court.

[44.] Similarly, the doctrine of precedent does not prevent a judge from finding help in a *lower* court. For instance, although the Supreme Court of Canada is not *bound* by the decision of a trial judge in Saskatoon, it might find it to be highly *persuasive*.

[45.] *Dobson v Dobson* (1999) 174 DLR (4th) 1 (SCC).

We have considered the court structure in general. Now we briefly describe the five most important types of courts in Canada.

Supreme Court of Canada: The Supreme Court of Canada is the highest court in the country. It is not a trial court. With rare exceptions, it only hears appeals from other appellate courts.[46] Furthermore, it is generally entitled to choose which appeals it will hear.[47] If you want to take your case to the Supreme Court, you must seek *leave* and get permission. The Court will not grant leave unless your case raises a legal issue of national significance. The Supreme Court of Canada has nine members: the Chief Justice and eight others, all appointed by the federal government. Appeals are almost always heard by five, seven, or nine *justices*, or judges. An odd number is required in case some of the justices *dissent*, or disagree, on the outcome. In that situation, the majority opinion prevails.

Court of Appeal: Every province and territory has a court of appeal. Although each one is concerned with the law in its own jurisdiction, its members are appointed by the federal government, not by the provincial or territorial government. Appeals at this level are usually heard by three justices, but the number is sometimes higher. The name of the court varies from place to place, as Concept Summary 1.2 shows.

Concept Summary 1.2

Court Names

PROVINCE OR TERRITORY	SUPERIOR COURT	APPEAL COURT
Alberta	Queen's Bench	Court of Appeal
British Columbia	Supreme Court	Court of Appeal
Manitoba	Queen's Bench	Court of Appeal
New Brunswick	Queen's Bench	Court of Appeal
Newfoundland	Supreme Court, Trial Division	Supreme Court, Court of Appeal
Northwest Territories	Supreme Court	Court of Appeal
Nova Scotia	Supreme Court	Court of Appeal
Nunavut	Court of Justice	Court of Appeal
Ontario	Superior Court	Court of Appeal
Prince Edward Island	Supreme Court, Trial Division	Supreme Court, Appeal Division
Quebec	Superior Court	Court of Appeal
Saskatchewan	Queen's Bench	Court of Appeal
Yukon	Supreme Court	Court of Appeal

Superior Court: The federal government also appoints judges to the superior court in each province and territory. The main job of the superior courts is to hear trials. However, they also occasionally hear appeals from lower courts. The names vary across the country, as Concept Summary 1.2 shows.

Provincial Court: The provincial governments appoint the members of the provincial courts. These are also trial courts. Although the details vary from place to place, they generally deal with four types of cases: (i) small claims,

---

[46] It occasionally hears *references*, which occurs when the federal government asks for an opinion as to whether a statute is constitutionally valid.

[47] Some exceptions exist for criminal cases.

which are private disputes involving small amounts of money (usually between $1000 and $10 000); (ii) family matters, such as support payments; (iii) youth matters, such as young offenders and neglected children; and (iv) most criminal cases. More serious trials are usually moved up to a superior court. That is true, for instance, of private claims involving large amounts of money and criminal cases involving such crimes as murder. Decisions in the provincial courts can be appealed to the superior court or, in some circumstances, directly to the court of appeal.

Federal Court: The federal government appoints the members of three specialized courts that deal only with matters that affect the federal government.[48] The Tax Court allows a person to dispute the government's demand for the payment of a tax. The Trial Division of the Federal Court hears trials concerning such matters as copyright, bills of exchange, and telecommunications. The Appeal Division of the Federal Court hears appeals from its own Trial Division and from the Tax Court.

As a review of this section, consider how you would answer the questions in You Be the Judge 1.1.

YOU BE THE JUDGE 1.1

Court Structure

Oscar Reynes has sued the company that owns the Alberta Fire, a professional soccer team. Due to an administrative error, the team sold 20 000 tickets to a game even though its stadium only contains 10 000 seats. A riot erupted in the stands as fans fought with each other and with the police. Twelve people were killed, and many more were severely injured. Although Oscar did not attend the game and did not personally know anyone who did, he watched the entire spectacle on television. He claims that he has suffered psychological distress as a result of the incident.

As a member of the Court of Queen's Bench in Alberta, you heard Oscar's trial in Edmonton. You are convinced that he has, in fact, suffered emotional harm as a result of watching the riot. You are also convinced that the soccer club acted carelessly by selling too many tickets. However, you are not sure if the defendant is legally responsible for the plaintiff's injury. On the one hand, neither the Supreme Court of Canada nor the Alberta Court of Appeal has discussed that precise issue. On the other hand, several other courts in the country have dealt with very similar cases. Both the Supreme Court of British Columbia and the Saskatchewan Court of Appeal *have* imposed liability. In contrast, both the Superior Court in Quebec and the Ontario Court of Appeal *have refused* to impose liability.

Questions for Discussion

1. Are any of those precedents binding on you? If not, are any of them relevant?
2. Given that consistency is one of the goals of our legal system, what can be done to make the law the same across the country?

Litigation and Alternative Dispute Resolution

People often think that legal disputes must be resolved through formal litigation. However, most lawyers will tell you to go to court only as a last resort. There are several reasons for that advice.

- First, litigation is a lottery. The results are not entirely predictable. The doctrine of precedent is designed to create consistency, but sometimes there are not any binding authorities on point. And sometimes, the judge

litigation is a lottery

---

48. The Federal Court's role in the government's regulation of business is discussed in Chapter 23.

simply gets it wrong. Furthermore, even if the law is clear, the facts may be in dispute. The judge may not believe you or may think that your witnesses are lying.

litigation is time consuming and expensive

- Second, formal litigation is time consuming and expensive. It is not unusual for a case to drag on for more than a decade, as it winds its way through a trial and perhaps two appeals. During that time, important members of a company are pulled away from the office to give evidence and to advise the lawyers. Needless to say, lawyers' fees and other costs quickly add up.[49]

litigation tends to be fatal to a relationship

- Third, formal litigation tends to be fatal to a relationship. The courts provide an adversarial process that creates winners and losers. Within fairly generous boundaries, each party is allowed, and even encouraged, to attack the other. Not surprisingly, the parties may not be willing to do business with each other after that experience.

litigation can have indirect costs such as bad publicity

- Fourth, formal litigation can have indirect costs. For example, since court proceedings are open to the public, they may be reported in the media. Depending on the circumstances, a corporation may actually be more concerned about bad publicity than about being held liable.

There are other disadvantages to formal litigation. One of the most important is illustrated in Business Decision 1.1. What would you do in that situation?

BUSINESS DECISION 1.1

Disadvantages of Formal Litigation

Your company, which sells books and CDs over the Internet, was recently brought to a standstill for three days as a result of a computer virus that infected your system. The overall cost of that incident, including the loss of sales and the expense involved in repairing your equipment, is about $750 000. After some investigation, you discovered that the virus was sent to you by a hacker in Whitehorse. As is common in this type of situation, that hacker is a high-school student who lives with his parents.

Further investigations and a brief discussion with your lawyer revealed additional information.

The precedents consistently state that a hacker in this type of situation is legally responsible for the damage that has been caused.

Experience suggests that this type of litigation tends to be quite expensive because of the technical nature of the evidence. Furthermore, your investigations indicate that while the boy is remarkably lazy and unlikely to ever make much of his life, he is also very knowledgeable about computers. In fact, he has threatened to "create as much trouble as possible" if he is sued.

Parents are generally not liable for their children's behaviour. Consequently, although the hacker was living at home when he sent the virus, he is the only person who could be sued. You could not bring an action against his mother or father.

Questions for Discussion

1. Should you sue the boy?
2. From a risk management perspective, what is the major argument against doing so?

alternative dispute resolution (ADR) is any process that allows the parties to settle an argument without a binding court order

Fortunately, litigation is not the only option. In fact, it is becoming less common. Businesses are increasingly relying on *alternative dispute resolution* techniques. **Alternative dispute resolution (ADR)** is any process that allows

---

[49.] A court usually awards *costs*, by requiring the losing party to pay some of the winning party's expenses. However, court-awarded costs rarely cover all of those expenses. And for the loser, the situation is even worse. It must pay for all of its expenses and some of the winner's.

the parties to settle an argument without a binding court order. We can look at three possibilities:

- negotiation
- mediation
- arbitration

A **negotiation** is a discussion that leads to the settlement of a dispute. Although the parties may use their lawyers, they are not required to do so. Negotiation has many advantages. It tends to be quicker, less complicated, and less expensive than litigation. It often helps the parties to remain on good terms with each other. It allows business people to take advantage of their own bargaining skills. And since it is a private procedure, it can be used to avoid bad publicity. However, the process also has limitations and dangers. First, since negotiation requires co-operation, it may not be possible if a dispute has already turned ugly. Second, the parties may not have equal bargaining power, especially if one is inexperienced and unrepresented by a lawyer. Having fewer resources and less information, that person may not be capable of securing a fair settlement and may, indeed, be exploited. Third, if a dispute concerns a loss that is covered by an insurance policy, the insured party must let the insurance company take control of the negotiations. If that party attempts to settle the matter itself, it may lose the benefits of the policy. Finally, there is no guarantee of success. Negotiations may collapse and a dispute may remain unresolved. If so, the effort put into the negotiations will be largely wasted.

Mediation is a process in which a neutral person, called a *mediator*, helps the parties reach an agreement. The important point is that mediation is *non-binding*. The mediator brings the parties together, listens to their arguments, outlines the issues, comments on each side's strengths and weaknesses, and suggests possible solutions. But the mediator does *not* give a decision, and the parties are *not* required to obey any orders. In that sense, mediation is unlike formal litigation, but like negotiation. It has many of the same benefits, limitations, and dangers as negotiations, except that it also provides the parties with a neutral perspective.

Arbitrations, in contrast, look more like court proceedings. **Arbitration** is a process in which a neutral third person, called an *arbitrator*, imposes a decision on the parties. Accordingly, the fundamental difference between arbitration and mediation is that an arbitrator's decision is almost always *binding*. The parties must obey it.[50] Indeed, it is common for the parties to agree beforehand that the arbitrator's decision, unlike a trial judgment, cannot even be appealed. This finality is one of the benefits of arbitration. There are others. Like negotiation and mediation, it tends to be quicker, more private, less expensive, and less adversarial than formal litigation. Furthermore, arbitrators often have more expertise than judges. The government selects people to become judges for a variety of reasons. Once those people are *on the bench* (have become judges), they generally hear every type of case. Sometimes they have a great deal of experience in an area; sometimes they have none at all. Arbitrators, in contrast, are selected by the parties to a particular dispute precisely because they do have expertise in the area. A professor of contract law may be chosen to decide whether an agreement is valid, or a person with an extensive background in employment relations may be asked to resolve a labour dispute.[51]

negotiation is a discussion that leads to the settlement of a dispute

mediation is a process in which a neutral person, called a mediator, helps the parties reach an agreement

arbitration is a process in which a neutral third person, called an arbitrator, imposes a decision on the parties

---

[50.] If necessary, the winning party can obtain a court order that enforces the arbitrator's decision.

[51.] As we will see in Chapter 24, arbitration is particularly important in international business.

There are two more important things to know about alternative dispute resolution.

some contracts require the use of ADR

- ADR is *permitted* in almost every kind of case. For instance, it is quite common in family law and is sometimes even used in criminal matters. In the business context, however, ADR may be *required*. Many contracts expressly state that any disagreements *must* be settled through negotiation, mediation, or arbitration, rather than through formal proceedings. That is especially true in such fields as construction and international trade.

various forms of dispute resolution can sometimes be used in the same case

- Various forms of dispute resolution may be used in the same case. Suppose that I agreed to manufacture and deliver a computer component to you. You are willing to pay for the component when it arrives, but insist that the price should be reduced because it does not work as well as expected. We might try to negotiate a settlement. If that fails, we might seek help from a mediator. If that also fails, we might send our dispute to an arbitrator. And if I am unhappy with that decision, I might appeal it to a court (unless I had agreed that the arbitration was final and binding).

Chapter Summary

The study of law is important to business because of the need for risk management. Risk management is the process of identifying, evaluating, and responding to the possibility of harmful events. Depending on the circumstances, a business can pursue various strategies for risk management, including risk avoidance, risk reduction, risk shifting, and risk acceptance.

A law is a rule that can be enforced by the courts. It is important to distinguish laws from other types of rules, including rules of morality. With the exception of Quebec, Canada is a common law country because its legal system was adopted from England. Canadian law can be divided into public law and private law. Public law is concerned with governments and the ways in which they deal with people. Examples of public law include constitutional law, administrative law, criminal law, and tax law. Constitutional law provides the basic rules of our legal system. Administrative law is concerned with the creation and operation of administrative bodies. Criminal law deals with offences against the state. And tax law is concerned with the rules that are used to collect money for public spending. Private law is concerned with the rules that apply in private matters. Examples include contract law, tort law, and property law. The law of contracts is concerned with the creation and enforcement of agreements. The law of torts is concerned with private wrongs. And the law of property governs the acquisition, use, and disposition of property.

The three sources of law are: the Constitution, Parliament and the legislatures, and the courts. The most important is the Constitution, which is the document that creates the basic rules for Canadian society. Section 52 of that document says that any law that is inconsistent with the Constitution is "of no force or effect." Canada is a federal country because it has two levels of government: federal and provincial or territorial. Sections 91 and 92 of the Constitution create a division of powers by stating the areas in which each level of government can create laws. A government that tries to create a law outside of its own area acts *ultra vires*. The *Canadian Charter of Rights and Freedoms* is a part of the Constitution that protects basic rights and freedoms. Although many of its provisions are quite broad, the *Charter* is also subject to several restrictions. It applies only against government behaviour; it may not apply in favour of corporations; it is subject to reasonable limits; and some of its sections can be overridden by the notwithstanding clause.

Legislation is law that is created through the authority of Parliament or a legislature. As a matter of risk management, it is sometimes possible for business people to affect the creation of a law during the legislative process. Subordinate legislation, which is law that is created by someone on behalf of Parliament or the legislature, is important to municipalities.

Parliamentary supremacy requires that the courts obey the Constitution and elected officials. Nevertheless, in some areas, the courts do have the authority to create laws. Historically, there were two court systems: courts of law and courts of equity. Equity was developed in response to the harsh nature of law. Today, there is only one court system. Every Canadian judge applies both legal rules and equitable rules. While those rules are still sometimes different, the concept of equity no longer allows judges to decide cases simply on the basis of fairness.

Canadian courts are arranged in a hierarchy. Trial courts are at the bottom. The person who makes the complaint at trial is the plaintiff or, in a criminal case, the Crown. The other party is the defendant or, in a criminal case, the accused. Appeal courts are at the top of the hierarchy. An appeal court decides whether a case was correctly decided at trial. The parties in an appeal are called the appellant and the respondent. The doctrine of precedent requires a court to follow any court that is above it in a hierarchy. The rule of law states that disputes should be settled on the basis of laws rather than personal opinions. The hierarchy of the courts and the doctrine of precedent support the rule of law by requiring judges to follow the courts above them.

There are four ways of resolving legal disputes. Formal litigation in the court system is quite common, but has several significant disadvantages. It is unpredictable; it is time consuming and expensive; it is often fatal to business relationships; and it can have a number of indirect costs, such as bad publicity. Business people are therefore increasingly using alternative dispute resolution (ADR) techniques. ADR is a process that allows the parties to settle an argument without a binding court order. A negotiation is a discussion between the parties that may lead to the settlement of a dispute. Mediation is a process in which a mediator helps the parties reach an agreement. Arbitration is a process in which an arbitrator imposes a decision upon the parties. The major difference between mediation and arbitration is that arbitration is normally binding on the parties.

Review Questions

1. Briefly define the term "risk management." Why is risk management important in the business world and how is it related to the study of law?

2. What are the three steps that are involved in risk management? Illustrate your answer with an example.

3. "The only sensible way to manage a risk is to avoid it." Explain whether that statement is accurate.

4. What is "in-house counsel"? Identify an advantage and a disadvantage to in-house counsel.

5. Are there any moral obligations that are not also legal obligations? Prove your answer by providing an example.

6. Explain two meanings of the term "civil law" and three meanings of the term "common law."

7. What is the difference between public law and private law? Can the government ever be involved in a private law case?

8. What is administrative law? Explain how it is relevant to business.

9. What is the difference between white-collar crime and corporate crime?

10. Briefly outline three areas of private law. Provide an example of each that is important to business.

11. What is the significance of section 52 of the Constitution?

How is that section related to the concept of *ultra vires* legislation?

12. "Since Canada is a *federal country*, the Constitution provides for a *division of powers*." Explain the meaning of that statement, focusing on the italicized terms.

13. Briefly explain how the introduction of the *Canadian Charter of Rights and Freedoms* changed Canadian constitutional law. Did it increase or decrease the grounds upon which laws can be declared invalid?

14. Describe four restrictions to the application of the *Charter*.

15. What is the difference between legislation and subordinate legislation? Explain how those concepts are related to the operation of municipalities.

16. Define the term "parliamentary supremacy." How does that concept affect a judge's ability to decide a case?

17. Explain the historical difference between law and equity. Are law and equity still separate systems of law?

18. Describe the doctrine of precedent. Explain how it is related to the court hierarchy and to the rule of law.

19. List four disadvantages to resolving a legal dispute through formal court proceedings.

20. Define the term "alternative dispute resolution." Name three forms of ADR and identify some advantages and disadvantages of each.

Cases and Problems

1. The Nagatomi Corporation is Canada's largest manufacturer of farm machinery. It specializes in custom-designing equipment to meet its customers' individual needs. Inga Raimani operates a farm in the foothills of Alberta. Because the terrain in the area is quite uneven in places, she cannot use a standard harvesting machine. Unfortunately, the custom-built harvester that she has used for the past 23 years was destroyed in a fire last winter. Immediately after the accident, she contacted Nagatomi and ordered a replacement. She stressed to the sales representative that she absolutely needed the machine by the first day of September. The parties drafted a contract, which contained the following provisions:

   (5) The Nagatomi Corp shall deliver the unit by the last day of August of the current year.
   (6) Inga Raimani shall pay the full price of $150 000 before delivery.
   (9) In the event that payment is not received by the last day of August of the current year, Inga Raimani shall lose the right to demand possession of the machine and the Nagatomi Corp shall have the right to sell the machine to another customer. If the machine is re-sold to another customer, Inga Raimani shall compensate the Nagatomi Corp for any expenses or losses that it incurs as a result.

   By the middle of August, Nagatomi contacted Inga and informed her that the machine was ready for delivery. At that point, however, she informed the company that she did not have $150 000 and that she was unable to obtain a bank loan. She explained that her financial situation had been badly damaged by a number of health problems and by a sharp increase in the cost of farm supplies. But she also further explained that her crop was particularly good and that she would easily be able to pay the full price, with interest, *after* the harvest. She therefore pleaded with the company to deliver the machine first and to accept payment later.

   Nagatomi realizes that Inga cannot harvest her crop without the machine. It also realizes, in light of her recent problems, that she would probably be forced into bankruptcy if she could not bring in the harvest. At the same time, however, it knows that it is not under any legal obligation to deliver the machine before payment. Furthermore, it has received an order from a farmer in Colorado for a custom-built harvester with exactly the same specifications as Inga's. That harvester does not need to be delivered until the end of next summer.

   Is Nagatomi under any obligation to deliver the machine to Inga? Does it have a legal obligation? A moral obligation? Even if it does not have any obligation, should it agree to Inga's proposal? What factors influence your answer?

2. Rabby Industries Ltd manufactures computer software. Late last year, it launched Budget Smart, a program that allows users to manage their finances from their home computers. It shipped 1 000 000 units to stores around Canada. As a result of an extensive advertising campaign and favourable reviews in the media, sales have been very good. About 600 000 units have already been sold, and the rest are moving quickly from store shelves. Recently, however, Rabby's engineers discovered a problem. After 18 months in use, the program causes damage to some types of home computers. At this point, the full extent of the problem remains unknown. For instance, it is not clear which types of systems will be affected. It is clear, however, that in at least some situations, the defect will irreversibly erase the entire hard drive, and all of the computer's information will be lost.

   Rabby has not yet received any customer complaints. The company knows, however, that the situation will soon change. It is therefore concerned about a number of things. It is distressed by the thought of damaging customers' computers. It is worried that it might be forced into bankruptcy if it is held liable in a large number of cases. And it is worried that it might even be financially ruined by a small number of claims. Since it is still a relatively new company in a highly competitive field, it could be wiped out by bad publicity.

   Discuss Rabby's situation from a risk management perspective. Explain the process of risk management and identify several responses that the company might consider.

3. After years of feeling politically neglected and abused by the federal government, the voters of a particular province elected a government that was committed to eventually forming a new country. Although the government of that province is not yet ready to declare its independence, it has decided to take steps in that direction. For instance, it recently enacted a statute that creates a new system of money. The premier believes that the people of her province will develop an even greater sense of pride if they have their own bills and coins to spend. Is that legislation valid? Explain your answer.

4. As a result of a number of scandals, the federal government has become extremely sensitive to criticism. Parliament therefore has recently added a section to the Criminal Code that makes it a crime to criticize the prime minister's behaviour. Because of concerns about freedom of speech, that section was written to ensure that the new law does *not* apply to individuals. It applies only to corporations and similar types of organizations. The company that owns *Picayune*, a political magazine, believes that the new provision is unconstitutional. Is it correct? Explain your answer.

5. Because skateboarding is a particularly dangerous activity, the Ontario government recently created the *Skateboarding Liability Act*. Its purpose is to force certain people to take responsibility for their own risky behaviour. The relevant sections of the statute state:

12. No action shall be brought against the owner or operator of a licensed skateboarding park for any injuries that are suffered as a result of a skateboarding accident.
13. This act only applies to adults and does not affect the rights of minors. A minor is any person who is under the age of 18 at the time of an accident.
14. This act does not apply if an injury is suffered as a result of the gross negligence of the owner or operator of a skateboarding park.

Anna Eagles recently sued the Concrete Wave Skateboarding Corporation for catastrophic injuries she suffered as a result of an accident at one of their outdoor parks. The evidence indicates that she visited the park very early one morning and slipped on a wet patch. The parties agree that the wet patch was a small puddle that was created by a light rain shower the night before. They also agree that Concrete Wave was negligent (that is, careless), but not grossly negligent (that is, extremely careless) in failing to remove the water before the park opened.

The defendant proved that Anna was 18 at the time of the accident and therefore argued that the *Skateboarding Liability Act* prevented her from suing. Anna, on the other hand, argued that a Canadian court can ignore a statute if it would lead to an unfair result. The trial judge accepted the plaintiff's position. She was influenced by a number of factors.

Anna is now a paraplegic with enormous medical bills.

Concrete Wave is a large company with a great deal of money and full insurance coverage.

If Anna had suffered the same injuries before her eighteenth birthday, she would be entitled to sue the defendant. Furthermore, Anna is somewhat immature. While she does not have any sort of mental disability, it is quite clear that she was "young for her age" at the time of the accident. Her lawyer made a compelling argument that she was in need of the same sort of protection that the statute gives to people who are, say, 17.

The *Skateboarding Liability Act* has not yet been considered by any other judge in Ontario. However, in a similar case in another province, the trial judge ignored a virtually identical statute and held in favour of the plaintiff. The court of appeal in that province upheld that decision.

Has the trial judge in this case done anything wrong?

6. You operate a small lawn-care business. You have a staff of eight workers, which you employ from the beginning of April to the end of October of each year. You own several pieces of equipment, which you store in a large shed at the back of your property. Although that equipment is vital to your business, it is not insured. As a result of several incidents in the past, insurance companies have classified you as high risk. Therefore, you cannot afford insurance. As an alternative form of protection, however, you bought a combination burglar alarm/fire detector from the Sentinel Corporation, Canada's largest security company.

In mid-October, the security system was smashed, your storage shed was vandalized, and all of your equipment was stolen. The police have indicated that there is virtually no chance of recovering the goods. You have explained to Sentinel that you believe that the theft would not have occurred if the intruder alarm had worked properly. Although the evidence quite clearly points in that direction, Sentinel has taken the position that the device did not prevent the theft because you did not use it properly.

The dispute is complicated by several factors.

Since winter is approaching, you do not need to replace your equipment immediately. However, if you are unable to do so by the beginning of the next season, your business will be in serious jeopardy and might even be wiped out altogether. Due to a backlog of cases, court officials have told you that you probably could not get a trial date before June.

If you won your case at trial, you would probably receive compensation for all of your losses. On the other hand, if you lost, you would not receive any compensation. As usual, litigation offers an all-or-nothing solution. At the same time, you realize that you could operate your business with less equipment. Consequently, you might be satisfied if Sentinel agreed to provide compensation for at least 70 percent of your losses.

Your primary goal is to receive money from Sentinel. However, you also believe that an important principle is involved. After the theft, you discovered that Sentinel has a reputation for: (i) occasionally selling shoddy equipment, and (ii) using its size to force dissatisfied customers into accepting small and confidential payments. Ideally, you would like to defeat Sentinel in court as a way of publicizing its unethical tactics.

And finally, assuming that you are able to save your business, you will once again need security equipment. As a result of the theft, insurance coverage will be even more expensive than before. Furthermore, although there are a number of local security companies, their prices tend to be higher than Sentinel's because they deal in smaller volumes. Consequently, despite your current problems, you would probably want to do business with Sentinel again.

What type of dispute resolution techniques will you use to resolve your dispute with Sentinel? What are the advantages and disadvantages to each of the various options?

WWWeblinks

General Legal Web Sites

Access to Justice Network
www.acjnet.org

This educational resource has a searchable database and numerous links to a variety of legal topics.

Best Guide to Canadian Legal Research
legalresearch.org/

This guide offers strategies and techniques for Canadian legal research, links to a number of online research tools, and access to statutory materials arranged by jurisdiction.

Canadian Legal Information Institute
www.canlii.org

This information resource, created by the Federation of Law Societies of Canada, provides a searchable database and links to court Web sites and legislative materials arranged by jurisdiction.

CANLAW—The Canadian Legal Network
www.canlaw.net/canlaw/

This network provides access to online Canadian legal resources. Besides accessing information through the searchable database, visitors can access legal information by topic.

Department of Justice Canada
canada.justice.gc.ca/

This Web site offers a range of information related to the Canadian justice system. Besides providing information on the department's programs and services, the site contains links to other legal resources.

JURIST Canada
jurist.law.utoronto.ca/

JURIST provides links to Web sites developed by Canadian law teachers for courses on such topics as contracts, labour, and property law. It also offers access to a variety of national and international research resources.

National Library of Canada—Canadian Legal Information by Subject
www.nlc-bnc.ca/caninfo/ep034.htm#34

This site offers links to a number of Web sites on a wide variety of legal topics. Some links are organized by jurisdiction.

Introduction to the Legal System

Canada's Legal Tradition
www.pch.gc.ca/csp-pec/english/about/law/index.htm

This Web site, prepared by the Department of Canadian Heritage, offers information on Canada's legal tradition, including descriptions of the distinction between common law and civil law, the distinction between public law and private law, sources of law, and the division of powers.

Canada's System of Justice
canada.justice.gc.ca/en/dept/pub/just/index.html

This comprehensive Web site contains information on the goals, sources, and operation of the Canadian justice system. It also gives an overview of the procedure used in civil and criminal cases.

Constitution Act, 1867
laws.justice.gc.ca/en/const/index.html

The *Constitution Act, 1867* creates the basic rules for Canadian society, including our political and legal systems. Sections 91 and 92 create a division of powers by listing the areas in which each level of government can create laws.

Charter of Rights and Freedoms
laws.justice.gc.ca/en/charter/index.html

The *Charter* is the part of the Constitution that protects basic rights and freedoms, such as fundamental rights, mobility rights, and equality rights.

Guide to the *Canadian Charter of Rights and Freedoms*
www.pch.gc.ca/ddp-hrd/canada/guide/index_e.shtml

The Department of Canadian Heritage offers a section-by-section guide to the *Canadian Charter of Rights and Freedoms* at this site, with the aim of increasing understanding of the *Charter* and heightening awareness of its importance in daily life, including potential use by business.

Canada's Court System
canada.justice.gc.ca/en/dept/pub/trib/index.html

This link to the Department of Justice Web site gives an overview of Canada's court system. It describes the different types of courts and their administration.

Canadian Legislation
www.legis.ca/en/

Legislation is law that is created by Parliament or by a legislature. This site offers links to statutes, regulations, and legislative information for every jurisdiction in Canada.

Guide to Making Federal Acts and Regulations

canada.justice.gc.ca/en/jus/far/Index.htm

This guide provides a detailed description of the federal legislative process that is used to create a statute in Parliament.

Canadian Foundation for Dispute Resolution

www.cfdr.org/

This non-profit organization combines the efforts of corporations and law firms to promote the alternative resolution of business disputes. Its site provides information and links to other alternative dispute resolution resources.

Draft Policy on Dispute Resolution

canada.justice.gc.ca/en/ps/drs/reglement.html

This draft policy from the Department of Justice outlines the commitment of the federal government to promote alternative methods of dispute resolution. The site lists the federal government's goals and suggests steps to increase access to justice.

2 The Nature and
Creation of Contracts

CHAPTER OVERVIEW

Intention to Create
  Legal Relations

Offer

The Nature of an Offer
Invitation to Treat
Communication of an Offer
The Life of an Offer

Acceptance

Acceptance by Promise
Acceptance by Performance

OBJECTIVES

After completing this chapter, you should be able to:

1. Identify three essential elements of most contracts.
2. Outline the situations in which people generally do or do not have an intention to create legal relations.
3. Distinguish between an offer and an invitation to treat.
4. Explain five ways by which an offer may cease to exist.
5. Explain the effect of a firm offer.
6. Outline the role of offer and acceptance in the tendering process.
7. Explain how the courts resolve a battle of the forms.
8. Distinguish between bilateral contracts and unilateral contracts, and explain the difference between acceptance by promise and acceptance by performance.
9. Explain whether an offer can ever be accepted by conduct or by silence.
10. Describe the postal rule and explain when it will apply.

Most people are unaware of the vast number of contracts they enter into every day. Consider your acquisition of this textbook. You may have found it, borrowed it, or received it as a gift; but most likely you bought it. Try to recall that transaction. At that time, did you know that you were creating a contract? Did you realize that your conduct generated a number of legal rights and obligations?

You may have had a choice in how you purchased this book. You probably bought it from your university or college bookstore, but you also may have bought it directly from the publisher via telephone, fax, or the Internet. Or you may have acquired a used copy from a former student. In any event, you probably paid with cash, a credit card, or a debit card. Those, however, were not the only possibilities. For example, if you bought this book from a former student, you may have acquired it in exchange for a set of computer disks. Or if you were industrious, you may have convinced the owner of a bookstore to give you a copy in exchange for your promise to work a weekend at the store.

a **contract** is an agreement that creates rights and obligations that can be enforced in law

Whichever option you used, you presumably became party to a **contract**. You and the other person entered into an agreement that created rights and obligations that can be enforced in law. You were able to enter into that agreement, in part, because you both experienced a **meeting of the minds**. You shared a mutual agreement to enter into an enforceable transaction on a particular basis.[1] And the most obvious feature of that contract is that it involved a mutual **exchange of value**. You both gave up something as part of the deal.[2] You provided, say, cash in return for the book, while the other person provided the book in return for cash.

a **meeting of the minds** is a mutual agreement to enter into a legal transaction on a particular basis

an **exchange of value** occurs when the parties each give up something

It is important to realize that a contractual relationship can continue even after there has been an exchange of value. Indeed, one reason for entering into a contract may be to reserve some rights and obligations for the future. Therefore, the choices you made when entering into the transaction can be important.

contracts limit future choices

For example, if you paid with a promise to work in the bookstore, you limited your options for the future. You will have to spend your weekend stocking shelves. Or consider what would happen if your book becomes unglued during the semester, and pages fall out. If you bought this book "as is" from a used book seller, you might not have any remedy. The situation would be different, however, if you purchased it from a bookseller who offered a "satisfaction or money back" guarantee. You would enjoy the right to a refund. Having already given the guarantee, the bookseller no longer has a choice about returning your purchase price. The law of contract would require them to do so. As an aside, consider why some booksellers are willing to give such guarantees. While they presumably value freedom of choice as much as you do, they also recognize that guarantees generate goodwill and increase the price that customers are willing to pay. By limiting their choices in the future, booksellers hope to attract more business.

contracts are practically invisible when the future unfolds as expected

Fortunately, textbooks seldom come unglued. That fact raises an important point about the operation of contracts. Because the book that you bought almost certainly is of satisfactory quality, the seller's guarantee will probably never be enforced. As with most contracts, many rights and duties lie quietly beneath the surface while the future unfolds as the parties expected. In that sense, contract law represents the pathology of commerce. Legal issues usually arise only if a commercial relationship becomes unhealthy.

However, it is dangerous to assume that ignorance is bliss and that business people do not really need to know about the law. While it is true that most con-

---

[1.] Lawyers sometimes refer to this as *consensus ad idem*, or "agreement on that previously mentioned."

[2.] Lawyers sometimes refer to this as *quid pro quo*, or "something for something."

tracts are performed without problems, it is also true that many of the problems that do arise are the result of the parties' failure to carefully consider the legal implications of their actions. Bear this in mind as you read the rest of this unit. Most of the cases that you will encounter are unusual precisely because they went to court. People need the help of a judge only when something has gone terribly wrong. By knowing your rights and obligations, you can almost always avoid that situation.

Even when something does go wrong, it may be preferable from a business perspective to avoid the court system. We discussed that proposition in Chapter 1. While a clear understanding of your legal rights and obligations allows you to litigate more effectively, it may be better to resolve a dispute informally. Legal proceedings tend to signal the end of a relationship. The long-term benefits of retaining a healthy commercial relationship are often more important than winning a particular dispute.

We now turn to more specific matters. There are three essential elements to the creation of most contracts:

1. The parties must have an *intention to create legal relations*
2. They must reach a mutual agreement through the process of *offer* and *acceptance*
3. They must enter into a bargain by each giving *consideration*

We will discuss the first two elements in this chapter and the third in Chapter 3.

Before beginning, we need to dispel a common misunderstanding about contracts. You may have noticed that the preceding list did not refer to the *writing* of a contract. In fact, most contracts do not have to be written in order to be enforceable. In Chapter 5, we will discuss some exceptions to that rule. At the same time, we will also consider other factors that may render a contract ineffective, such as *illegality* and *lack of capacity*.

INTENTION TO CREATE LEGAL RELATIONS

A contract will not arise without an **intention to create legal relations.** The parties must have intended to create a legally enforceable agreement. To decide that issue, a court asks whether a "reasonable person" would have believed that the parties intended to enter into a contract.[3] Note that that test is *objective* rather than *subjective*. The judge is concerned with what a reasonable person would have thought, not necessarily with what the parties themselves actually thought. There are two reasons for that rule. First, a test of subjective intentions would be difficult to apply because a person could easily lie at trial. Second, an important goal of the law of contracts is to protect reasonable expectations. If you and I enter into an apparent contract for the sale of widgets, I will reasonably expect to receive those widgets even if, during the sale negotiations, you secretly planned to keep them for yourself. Furthermore, on the basis of my reasonable expectation, I may have arranged to resell the widgets to someone else, who may have arranged to sell them to yet another person, and so on. The business world could not function smoothly unless people were entitled to rely on outward appearances.

*an **intention to create legal relations** arises if a reasonable person would believe that the parties intended to create a legally enforceable agreement*

[3.] The concept of a "reasonable person" is discussed in detail in Chapter 12.

The presence or absence of an intention to create legal relations is usually obvious. A reasonable person simply ignores unrealistic and exaggerated proposals. For instance, a lecturer's sarcastic promise to pay $5000 for a correct response in class cannot be taken at face value. To further simplify matters, the courts usually presume that an intention to create legal relations exists in a commercial context, but not between friends or family members.[4] However, those presumptions can be *rebutted*, or disproved. For example, a business person may be able to convince a judge that while a commercial agreement was contained in a formal document, it *was not* really intended to be legally binding.[5] Likewise, a son may be able to persuade a judge that while his mother's promise to pay his tuition at business school was given within a family setting, it really *was* intended to create contractual obligations.[6] The most difficult cases arise when social relations and commercial transactions mix. How would you decide the case in You Be the Judge 2.1?

YOU BE THE JUDGE 2.1

Fobasco Ltd v Cogan (1990) 72 OR (2d) 254 (HCJ)

When major league baseball came to Toronto in 1976, Eddie Cogan bought eight season's tickets in a prime location—field level, behind first base. At that time, he agreed to sell four of his tickets to Fobasco Ltd, a company owned by his friend and business associate, David Fingold. David, in turn, gave the tickets away to Fobasco Ltd's prospective customers to drum up business. Although that arrangement lasted for many years, Eddie decided in 1986, around the same time that the Blue Jays became contenders and shortly before they moved into SkyDome, that he would prefer to sit next to his own sons rather than Fobasco Ltd's clients. He told his old friend that their arrangement was at an end. David was upset because he could not otherwise get good seats to the games. He therefore sued for breach of contract, claiming that Eddie had contractually agreed to sell tickets to Fobasco Ltd on an annual basis.

Questions for Discussion

1. Would a reasonable person believe that the parties had entered into contractual relations? Or did they merely have a social arrangement?

2. While contracts generally do not need to be written to be effective, do you believe that the lack of writing in this case is significant? What if the parties, as businessmen, normally put all of their contracts into writing?

3. If you believe that a contract should be recognized, should Eddie be required to make tickets available to Fobasco Ltd forever?

OFFER

The Nature of an Offer

an offer is an indication of a willingness to enter into a contract on certain terms

an offeror is a party who is offering to enter into a contract

an offeree is a party who is entitled to accept or reject an offer to enter into a contract

The parties must have more than an intention to create legal relations. They must also enter into a mutual agreement through the process of offer and acceptance. An **offer** is an indication of a willingness to enter into a contract on certain terms. The party who offers to enter into a contract is called the **offeror**. The party who is entitled to accept or reject the offer is called an **offeree**.

Great care must be taken in making offers because a contract comes into existence as soon as an offer is accepted. At that point, both parties become

---

[4] *Balfour v Balfour* [1919] 2 KB 571 (CA).

[5] *Rose & Frank Co v JR Crompton & Rose Ltd* [1923] 2 KB 261 (CA).

[6] *Jones v Padavatton* [1969] 2 All ER 616 (CA).

obligated to fulfill the promises contained in the agreement. And once a contract comes into existence, neither party acting alone can alter its contents or bring it to an end.

Consider the dangers that can arise from making an offer. Suppose that you sent a message to your class Web site offering to sell your cars. If 10 people simultaneously show up at your door wanting to buy a vehicle, are you contractually obliged to honour 10 contracts even though you have only two cars to sell? The courts recognize that it would be impractical if every proposal could be classified as an offer that is capable of being transformed into a contract. Therefore, judges have developed careful guidelines for deciding which types of statements qualify as offers. They have also placed limits on how long statements can function as offers.

Invitation to Treat

The courts classify some statements not as offers but rather as *invitations to treat*. An **invitation to treat** is an indication of a willingness to receive an offer. In other words, it is an invitation for others to make an offer. In such circumstances, the person who responds to the invitation is the offeror, and the person who initially presents the invitation is the offeree.

an **invitation to treat** is an indication of a willingness to receive an offer

The distinction between an offer and an invitation to treat depends on an objective test. A court will ask how a reasonable person would interpret a particular statement in the circumstances. Would it be reasonable to believe that the party making the statement was exposing itself to the risk of becoming immediately bound to a contract if it received an acceptance? Or would it be more reasonable to believe that the party was simply indicating that it might be willing to accept an offer if it received one that it liked?

Those questions are often difficult to answer. Fortunately, the courts tend to apply certain presumptions. Most significantly, they usually say that the display of an item on a store shelf, even if it carries a price tag, is a mere invitation to treat.[7] Similarly, a statement placed in a newspaper advertisement or catalogue is usually not an offer. There is a very good reason for those presumptions. Recall our example in which 10 people see your advertisement and they all want to buy a car. If your ad is classified as an offer, you might be held liable to fulfill 10 contracts, even though you have only two cars to sell. However, if your ad is classified as an invitation to treat, each response is an offer, which you are free to accept or reject. The presumptions regarding advertisements and displays generally protect business people from overexposing themselves. There are exceptions to those presumptions. An advertisement may be considered an offer if a reasonable person would read it that way. That may be true, for example, if it expressly indicates that a limited number of items are available while supplies last. Your ad therefore might be an offer if it said, "Cars for sale. $10 000 each. First come. First served." In that situation, you would not be in danger of being bound to an unmanageable number of contracts.[8]

[7.] *Pharmaceutical Society of Great Britain v Boots Cash Chemists (Southern) Ltd* [1953] 1 QB 401 (CA).

[8.] Business people occasionally try to take advantage of that rule by advertising items they do not have to sell in the hopes of attracting customers who can be persuaded, once they are in the store, to buy other items. In most jurisdictions, such practices, known as "bait and switch," are prohibited by statute: *Competition Act*, RSC 1985 c C-34, s 52 (Can); *Fair Trading Act*, SA 1998 c F-1.05, s 9 (Alta); *Trade Practices Act*, RSBC 1996 c 457, s 2 (BC); *Trade Practices Inquiry Act*, RSM 1987 c T110, s 2 (Man); *Trade Practices Act*, RSN 1990 c T-7, s 5 (Nfld); *Consumer Services Act*, RSNS 1989 c 94, s 6(1)(c) (NS); *Business Practices Act*, RSO 1990 c B.18, s 2 (Ont); *Business Practices Act*, RSPEI 1988 c B-7, s 2 (PEI); *Competition Protection Act*, RSQ c P-40.1, ss 224-225 (Que); *Consumer and Commercial Affairs Act*, RSS 1988 c C-29.2, s 8 (Sask).

Communication of an Offer

A statement is not an offer unless it is communicated and received *as* an offer. The issue is not as simple as it might appear. Suppose the directors of a company decide during a meeting to offer a $10 000 bonus to a long-serving secretary in exchange for her early retirement. The directors ask the secretary to type the hand-written notes of their meeting. In doing so, she learns of the proposed bonus, completes the task at hand, and promptly tenders her resignation. She is probably not entitled to the bonus payment. The minutes of the meeting were communicated to her, not as a contractual offer, but rather as a typing assignment. In those circumstances, the reasonable person would not believe that the directors intended to be bound by their communication.[9]

However, as long as a proposition is communicated and received as an offer, it usually does not have to take any particular form.[10] It may be contained in a written document. For example, if you buy a television from a department store on credit, you will probably be asked to complete a lengthy application that contains countless terms and conditions. That is your offer to the store. Alternatively, an offer may be made verbally. For example, if you go to a restaurant and say, "A cheeseburger and a milkshake, please," you are offering to enter into a contract for the purchase of a meal. An offer may even be inferred from conduct alone. For example, if you enter a barber shop, sit silently in the chair, and get a trim, you have offered, and the barber has accepted, a contract to cut your hair.[11]

The Life of an Offer

An offer does not necessarily survive until it is accepted. There are several ways in which an offer may cease to exist even though it has not been transformed into a contract:

- revocation
- lapse of time
- death or insanity
- rejection
- counter offer

Revocation

Revocation occurs if the party who made an offer withdraws it. The offeror is the master of the offer and is generally entitled to revoke it at any time.[12] As a matter of risk management, however, there is some need for caution. Revocation is not effective unless it is reasonably communicated to the offer-

---

[9] *Blair v Western Mutual Benefit Association* [1972] 4 WWR 284 (BC CA).

[10] In Chapter 5, we will discuss situations in which a contract must be written to be enforceable.

[11] If the parties to a contract do not stipulate a price, the courts may require the purchaser to pay a reasonable price.

[12] Generally, an offeror can communicate revocation in the same way that it communicated the offer. For instance, if the offer appeared in a newspaper advertisement, the revocation can appear there as well.

ee. Until that occurs, the offer remains open, and the offeree can create a contract through acceptance.

Firm Offers   Although the basic rules regarding revocation are quite simple, two types of situations call for special attention. The first involves a **firm offer,** which occurs when the offeror promises to hold an offer open for acceptance for a certain period. Do not be misled by the terminology. A firm offer is not very firm at all. As a general rule, the offeror can revoke it at any time. The reason, as Ethical Perspective 2.1 shows, turns on the fact that a firm offer is not contained in a contract and therefore is not enforceable in law. Nevertheless, as you read that case, consider how you, as a business person, would act in such circumstances.

a **firm offer** occurs when the offeror promises to hold an offer open for acceptance for a certain period

ETHICAL PERSPECTIVE 2.1

Dickinson v Dodds (1876) 2 Ch D 463 (CA)

George Dickinson was one of several people interested in buying a piece of land from John Dodds. On Wednesday, John wrote to George, offering to sell the property and promising to hold that offer open until Friday morning. While George was considering his options on Thursday, he learned that John was negotiating with another potential buyer. George immediately tried to find John to accept the offer. Although George failed to locate John that night, he did manage to leave a letter of acceptance with John's mother-in-law. Moreover, he caught up with John the next morning and expressed his desire to buy the property. By that time, however, George had learned from a third party that the land had already been sold to someone else. George sued John for failing to fulfill his promise to keep the offer open.

The lawsuit failed. The court held that John's promise was unenforceable because it was entirely *gratuitous*. He had not received anything of value in exchange for his promise to hold his offer open until Friday.

Questions for Discussion

1. Do you approve of John's behaviour? What do you think of the fact that the law allowed him to break his promise? Is the legal rule pertaining to firm offers morally acceptable?

2. Although firm offers are revocable, most successful business people honour such promises. What reasons might motivate them to do so?

Despite the general rule, a firm offer *cannot* be revoked if the offeror's promise was placed under *seal* or if the offeree paid for the right to accept within a certain period.[13] For example, if you think that you might want to buy a particular piece of land in the future, but are not prepared to commit yourself to that transaction just yet, you might try to purchase an *option* from the owner. An **option** is a contract in which the offeror receives something of value in exchange for a binding promise to hold an offer open for acceptance for a specific period. That option would accomplish two things. First, it would allow you and the offeror, at some point in the future, to create a contract for the sale of land. Second, it would immediately create an entirely separate contract requiring the offeror to wait while you decided whether to buy the land. As you might expect, one must take special care in granting options. Consider the situation in Business Decision 2.1.

an **option** is a contract in which the offeror receives something of value in exchange for a binding promise to hold an offer open for acceptance for a specific period

---

13. We discuss seals in Chapter 3.

BUSINESS DECISION 2.1

The Granting of Options

ABC Corporation is investigating the possibility of developing a shopping mall in a certain neighbourhood. To do so, it will need to buy your land. It will also need to obtain zoning approval for its proposal. Although you have offered to sell your property for $100 000, ABC Corporation does not want to incur any obligations to you unless its zoning application is allowed. However, it also knows that other companies may offer to buy your land to develop their own projects. It therefore wants to buy an option under which you will hold your offer open for 90 days.

Questions for Discussion

1. Will you grant the option? If so, on what terms?
2. How does the existence of other prospective buyers affect your decision?
3. How will your expectations about the future market value of your land affect your decision?

---

a tender is an offer to undertake a project on particular terms

Tenders   The second special situation involving the revocation of offers is more complicated. It is also very important in the business world. Suppose that a city wants a new library built. It will probably call for *tenders*. A **tender** is an offer to undertake a project on particular terms. In calling for tenders, the city issues an invitation to treat and promises to award the project to the company that submits the best offer. However, the city needs some assurance that the offers will remain open while it considers them. If the general rule applied, the city might be disappointed because each bidder would be entitled to withdraw its offer any time before acceptance—a very disruptive possibility. A court will probably find a way of ensuring that the offer in each tender remains open while the city makes its decision.

To do so, a court can find that the bidding process immediately creates a special contract between the city and each company that submits an offer.[14] Thus, the city's call for tenders serves two purposes.

1. It constitutes an offer to enter into a special contract, called "Contract A," to hold a fair tendering process in exchange for the submission of an irrevocable bid.
2. It also constitutes an invitation to treat to receive offers to enter into a contract, called "Contract B," for the construction of the library.

A company's tender also serves two purposes.

1. It constitutes acceptance of the city's offer to enter into a fair and irrevocable tendering process under Contract A.
2. It also constitutes an offer to enter into a contract for the construction of the library under Contract B.

There will be many Contract As—one for each company that submits a tender to the city, but only one Contract B—between the city and the company that submits the winning tender. Concept Summary 2.1 illustrates this view of the tendering process.

[14.] *R v Ron Engineering & Construction (Eastern) Ltd* (1981) 119 DLR (3d) 267 (SCC).

Concept Summary 2.1

The Tendering Process

STAGES	CONTRACT A (Contract to Enter Process)	CONTRACT B (Contract to Build Library)
Call for Tender by City to Company	offer by city to hold a fair tendering process	invitation to treat issued by city
	⇕	⇕
Submission of Tender by Company to City	acceptance by company of offer	offer by company to build library
		⇕
Award of Project by City to Company		acceptance by city of offer

Lapse of Time

An offeror is entitled to limit the lifespan of an offer, possibly by stating that acceptance must occur by a specific date. That is almost always true with an option. But even if no time period is stated, an offer is only open for a "reasonable period." In deciding what constitutes a reasonable period, a court will look at many factors, including the subject matter of the proposed contract, the nature of the agreement, the volatility of the market, and the usual practice in the industry. An offer to sell farmland in a financially depressed region may be open for many weeks; an offer to sell shares in a wildly fluctuating market may be open for mere hours.

an offer is revoked on the lapse of time

Death or Insanity

It is often said that an offer is automatically revoked if either the offeror or the offeree dies. A dead person does not have the capacity to enter into a contract, and there cannot be a meeting of the minds if only one person is alive. An exception may apply, however, if the proposed contract does not call upon the affected party to personally perform. For example, that may be true if the offer pertains to the sale of land rather than the performance of a concert. In that situation, the offeree may communicate acceptance to the deceased offeror's estate, or the deceased offeree's estate may communicate acceptance to the offeror.[15] The same analysis generally holds true for insanity.

an offer is usually revoked if one of the parties dies or becomes insane

Rejection

Rejection occurs when the offeree refuses an offer. An offer is terminated once it is rejected. Suppose that Bruno offers to sell his business to Helga for $100 000. If she says, "No, thank you, I'm not interested," the offer is dead. And because it is dead, Helga cannot later accept it if she changes her mind and decides that she really would like to buy the business after all. Unless Bruno repeats his initial offer, Helga must make an offer to him and hope that he accepts it.

rejection occurs when the offeree refuses an offer

[15.] In this context, "estate" refers to the person representing the interests of the deceased.

Counter Offer

A similar rule applies to *counter offers*. A **counter offer** occurs when an offeree responds to an offer by indicating a willingness to enter into a contract, but on different terms. A counter offer has the effect of rejecting an existing offer and creating a new one. Consequently, as Concept Summary 2.2 shows, a counter offer causes the parties to switch roles.

Concept Summary 2.2

Offer and Counter Offer

EVENT	PARTY A	PARTY B
Offer	Offeror ——————————→	Offeree
Counter Offer	Offeree ←——————————	Offeror

To create a contract, an offer must be *entirely* accepted. Any attempt to accept in modified terms constitutes a counter offer. Returning to our previous example, suppose that Helga responded to Bruno's offer by saying, "You've got yourself a deal, but I can pay only $50 000." Her statement is a counter offer. It kills Bruno's offer to sell for $100 000 and replaces it with her own offer to buy at $50 000. If Bruno rejects Helga's offer, she cannot revive his initial offer by saying, "Okay, I'll pay the full $100 000." If she wants the business, she must hope that Bruno repeats his original offer. He may do so expressly or implicitly by responding to her counter offer by saying something like, "No, I won't take less than $100 000."

Because the general rule regarding counter offers may be harsh, the courts sometimes characterize an offeree's statement as a harmless inquiry rather than a counter offer. Therefore, if Helga had said, "I'd love to buy your business, but I'm just wondering if you'd take $50 000 for it," she might be able to persuade a judge that even if Bruno had said "No," his original offer would still be open for acceptance.

Judges also try to avoid the general rule regarding counter offers in cases involving a *battle of the forms*. A **battle of the forms** occurs when each party claims to have entered into a contract on the basis of its own standard form document. A business often prepares a complicated contractual form, containing many terms, which it will insist upon using for every transaction. This only makes sense, as it would be too difficult and expensive to constantly negotiate new contracts.[16] Problems arise if both parties insist upon using their *own* forms and if those forms contain *different* terms. To decide which contractual form, if either, applies, a judge will consider several factors, including the usual practice in the industry, past dealings between the parties, the precise sequence of events, and the forms, if any, that the parties actually signed. Consider the example in Business Law in Action 2.1.

---

16. Problems can also arise if only one party uses a standard form contract. Corporations often try to use such documents to force complicated and harsh terms on its customers. That problem is addressed in Chapter 4.

BUSINESS LAW IN ACTION 2.1

Battle of the Forms

For years, Vendor Inc has been selling widgets to you without any problems. During that time, it developed a standard form document, which it uses to offer its goods for sale. That document contains a clause that allows unsatisfactory goods to be returned for a refund within 7 days. You also developed a standard form document, which you use for accepting offers of sale. That document, however, contains a clause that allows unsatisfactory goods to be returned for a refund within 21 days. In fact, most businesses that buy and sell widgets use a 21-day return period. You and Vendor purport to create a contract for the sale of 5000 widgets. As always, you each use your own form and, as always, neither of you realizes that those forms have different terms. If, after 10 days, the widgets break and you want your money back, are you entitled to a refund?

Strictly speaking, because it did not exactly match the terms of Vendor's offer, your document seems to be a counter

offer rather than an acceptance. And if there has been no offer and acceptance, there cannot be a contract. Nevertheless, since the agreement is *executed* (already performed) rather than *executory* (not yet performed), and since you both reasonably believed that a contract existed, a judge might be persuaded to find that a contract was created. For example, if Vendor signed and returned a copy of your document before shipping the widgets, the judge might hold that Vendor agreed to the terms contained in your counter offer, especially since those terms reflect industry practice.[17] In some situations, however, it will simply not be possible to save the transaction, and you will be without a contractual remedy for the defective goods.

Questions for Discussion

1. What does this example demonstrate about the need to carefully read every document that affects your business?
2. How can you avoid the sort of difficulties that arise in this case?

ACCEPTANCE

In discussing acceptance, it is important to distinguish two situations:

- acceptance by promise
- acceptance by performance

Acceptance by Promise

Many contracts are *bilateral*. A **bilateral contract** occurs when a promise is exchanged for a promise. The offer consists of the offeror's promise to do something; the acceptance consists of the offeree's promise to do something. Therefore, when the contract comes into existence, both parties have promises to fulfill. Suppose, for example, that you offer to sell your car for $7500. To accept your promise to transfer ownership of the vehicle, I promise to pay the price. As Figure 2.1 illustrates, we have a bilateral contract. That would be true whether we expected to complete the exchange immediately or next week.

a **bilateral contract** occurs when a promise is exchanged for a promise

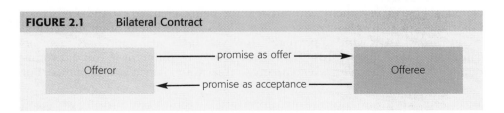

FIGURE 2.1   Bilateral Contract

---

17. *Butler Machine Tool Co v Ex-cell-O Corp* [1979] 1 All ER 695 (CA).

acceptance occurs when an offeree agrees to enter into the contract proposed by the offeror

We can define the element of acceptance even more precisely. **Acceptance** occurs when an offeree agrees to enter into the contract proposed by the offeror. Acceptance generally has to be communicated to the offeror. It must be unequivocal and it must correspond precisely with the terms of the offer. If the offeree changes the terms, it does not create an acceptance but rather a counter offer, as we saw in the last section. An acceptance must also be a *response* to an offer. For that reason, no contract is formed if I send you a letter that says, "I will sell you my car for $5000," at the same time that you send me a letter that says, "I will buy your car for $5000." This situation is sometimes described as a "cross-offer"—each letter contains an offer and neither contains an acceptance. Therefore, there is no meeting of the minds.

Words

a bilateral contract is usually accepted through words

acceptance must be communicated in a way that was required or permitted by the offeror

Acceptance usually occurs through written or spoken words. The offeror, as master of the offer, can dictate how those words must be communicated. It is possible to insist that acceptance be communicated to a particular location or provided in a particular form. For example, if an offeror states that "acceptance *must* be sent in writing to my office," a contract is not formed if acceptance is communicated orally or if it is sent to the offeror's home. Often, however, the offeror does not impose any restrictions, and the offeree can accept by any reasonable means. If so, it is usually best to avoid complications by responding in kind, for example, by providing written acceptance to a written offer. It may be possible, however, to use any equally effective method, for example, by responding to a faxed offer with a telephoned acceptance.

Conduct

a bilateral contract may be accepted by conduct

In some circumstances, an offer may be accepted by conduct. Suppose that I offer $5000 in exchange for your promise to develop a software program for me. If you accept, you will probably say, "Yes," either orally or in writing. However, you might also nod agreeably and silently shake my hand. A reasonable person would likely interpret your conduct as acceptance.

Silence

a bilateral contract cannot be accepted by silence alone

While acceptance may occur without words if the offeree acts in a certain way, silence alone cannot be acceptance. That rule can be very important. An unscrupulous company may send goods to you along with a note that says, "Unless you inform us that you do not want to purchase these things, you will be charged for them." Generally speaking, you will not be required to pay, even if you completely ignore the offer.[18]

The courts developed that basic rule. Some jurisdictions also have statutes that discourage businesses from foisting goods on unsuspecting consumers. In Ontario, for example, the *Consumer Protection Act* allows recipients of unsolicited goods to use them without fear of being charged.[19] And in British Columbia, the *Consumer Protection Act* allows the recipient of an unsolicited credit card to use it without paying.[20] However, those rules apply only to *unsolicited* goods and credit cards. The situation may be different if you did something in the past that allows a company to treat your silence as acceptance. For

---

[18.] *Felthouse v Bindley* (1862) 142 ER 1037 (Ex Ch).

[19.] RSO 1990, c C-31, s 36.

[20.] RSBC 1996, c 69, s 47.

example, by joining a book club, you may enter into a contract that requires you to pay for a monthly selection unless you return it within a specified time. In such circumstances, your acceptance of the book will consist of your silence *plus* your earlier promise to abide by your agreement with the company. The result may be the same if you regularly accept goods from a company and pay for them.

Many people now order goods electronically. In response to the public's overwhelming interest in electronic commerce, many companies have automated their purchasing and shipping departments. These automated systems allow companies to silently receive and process orders. Their computers do all of the talking. Business Law in Action 2.2 reveals some of the contractual issues that can arise as a result.

BUSINESS LAW IN ACTION 2.2

Can Computers Accept Contractual Offers?

In 1997, Neuromedia Inc launched Shallow Red online. Shallow Red, known among computer experts as a *bot* or *software agent*, is software that operates through Web pages to answer basic questions about Neuromedia's products. It can interact with people or other bots to exchange information and engage in operations that look very much like negotiations leading to the creation of contracts. We will soon reach the point where bots can initiate and complete transactions autonomously, without human intervention. In fact, the aim of intelligent software technology is to allow transactions to take place without the need for human traders to review or even be aware of them.

Suppose you are interacting with Shallow Red online, believing that it is a human being somewhere in Canada. You offer to buy a software program that you need quickly for a certain price. Shallow Red accepts and promises delivery within two weeks. After three weeks of waiting for the software, you call Neuromedia to complain. They say that Shallow Red was unable to detect that you were ordering from Canada and that Neuromedia Inc does business only in the United States. They argue that there was no contract because Neuromedia Inc itself was silent, and silence does not amount to acceptance.

Questions for Discussion

1. How would you argue that your offer was indeed accepted?
2. Should computers be allowed to contractually accept offers?

Source: For further information on Shallow Red and other bots, see <www.botspot.com>.

Acceptance at a Distance

Special problems can occur when people do not deal face to face. Practically speaking, contracts cannot always be created in person. Business people often deal with each other across vast distances. And even when they are neighbours, they may not have the time or inclination to arrange a mutually convenient meeting. Furthermore, individual consumers are increasingly entering into transactions and paying bills not only through the mail, but also over the telephone or by various electronic means, such as ATMs and the Internet.

Two issues arise when parties deal with each other at a distance. First, if the lines of communication break down, it is necessary to decide whether a contract was formed. Suppose that an insurance company, in exchange for a certain payment, offers to protect your business against the risk of property damage. As required by the offer, you mail your letter of acceptance and a cheque to the insurer. The letter is lost in the postal system and never arrives. If your property is later damaged by a flood, do you have insurance coverage? Is the insurer liable even though it never received your letter?

Second, even if the lines of communication work properly, it may be necessary to determine where and when a contract was formed. Returning to the previous example, suppose that your business is located in Alberta, but that the insurance company is located in Manitoba. Assume that the insurance company is required to pay a fee to the Government of Manitoba if a contract is formed there, but not if it is formed in Alberta. Where was your contract formed? Is the insurer liable for the fee?

The General Rule   The law in this area is complicated, partly because the courts have not yet decided how to deal with many of the newer forms of technology, such as portable pagers and the Internet. In broad terms, the courts have used a pair of rules for many years. First, the **general rule** states that acceptance by *instantaneous communication* is effective when and where it is received by the offeror. There is a historical point worth emphasizing here. The general rule was formulated when people generally conducted business face to face. In such circumstances, we say that there is **instantaneous communication** because the interaction between the parties involves little or no delay. Since the general rule was initially formulated, the courts have held that many forms of communication, including the telephone and the fax machine, are instantaneous.[21]

We can illustrate the general rule governing instantaneous communications with our previous example. Suppose that while you are in Alberta, you telephone your insurer located in Manitoba and accept its offer of coverage. Your acceptance takes effect when and where it is received. Your contract is therefore formed in Manitoba when your insurer hears you say, "I accept." However, if your statement was inaudible because you happened to be driving through a tunnel while talking on your cell phone, a contract would not be formed. Acceptance is effective only when and where the offeror *actually* receives it.

The Postal Rule   The general rule works well for instantaneous communications. It can cause problems, however, for *non-instantaneous communications*. A **non-instantaneous communication** is one that involves a substantial delay between the offeree's transmission and the offeror's receipt, such as when a letter is mailed or a package is sent by courier.[22]

Significantly, the courts refuse to rigidly classify communications as instantaneous or non-instantaneous. Even if a form of communication *appears* to be instantaneous, it may be considered non-instantaneous if, in the circumstances, it involves a substantial delay between transmission and receipt. For example, although a fax is usually received without delay, not every faxed communication is considered instantaneous. A judge would consider the parties' objective intentions, usual business practices, and the fairness of placing the risk on one person rather than the other. Therefore, if an offer states that "acceptance must be conveyed by means of instantaneous communication no later than Friday," you should not fax an acceptance letter at 11:59 pm on that day. If you know that the offeror's office always closes for the weekend at 5:00 pm, and that no one will be there to receive a late-night fax, your communication is not really instantaneous. It will not be effectively received until Monday morning. Given the circumstances, the acceptance would be late, and a contract would not be formed.

Consider why the courts draw a distinction between instantaneous and non-instantaneous communications. If a non-instantaneous acceptance was effective only when and where it was actually received, the offeree would be

---

the **general rule** states that acceptance by instantaneous communication is effective when and where it is received by the offeror

an **instantaneous communication** is any form of communication in which there is little or no delay in the interaction between the parties

a **non-instantaneous communication** is any form of communication that involves a substantial delay between transmission and receipt

---

[21.] The rule that applies to e-mail is discussed in Chapter 17.

[22.] *Nova Scotia v Weymouth Sea Products Ltd* (1983) 149 DLR (3d) 637, affd 4 DLR (4th) 314 (NS CA).

required to frequently check with the offeror in order to know whether a contract was formed. And until the receipt of the acceptance was confirmed, the offeree would be reluctant to perform the contract. Suppose I mail a letter from Saskatoon accepting your offer to pay me $5000 to deliver a series of lectures in Charlottetown. Unless I can be sure that we have a contract as soon as I put my letter in the mailbox, I will hesitate to book a flight, even if air fare will be much more expensive if I delay. I would be afraid that if I bought a ticket today, you might revoke your offer tomorrow before receiving my acceptance. If so, I would have a ticket to Charlottetown and no real reason to go there.

For those reasons, the general rule does not apply to non-instantaneous forms of communication. Instead, according to the **postal rule**, an acceptance that is communicated in a non-instantaneous way is effective where and when the offeree sends it. Continuing with our example, a contract is formed in Saskatoon as soon as I drop my acceptance letter into the mailbox, even though you will not receive that letter in Charlottetown for several days.

> the postal rule states that an acceptance that is communicated in a non-instantaneous way is effective where and when the offeree sends it

By holding that my acceptance takes effect as soon as I send it, rather than when you receive it, the postal rule prevents you from revoking your offer while my letter is in the postal system. After all, you cannot revoke an offer that I have already accepted. In fact, the postal rule may work against you in an even stranger way. As long as the judge believes that I actually sent the letter, a contract can be formed between us even if my letter is lost in the mail and never reaches you.

Notice that the postal rule imposes certain risks upon you as the offeror. Until you actually receive a clear acceptance or rejection from me, you cannot be sure if a contract has been created. There are, however, ways around the postal rule. First, you could carefully draft your business proposals to ensure that they are invitations to treat rather than offers. If so, any replies that you receive will be offers seeking your acceptance rather than acceptances of your offer. You remain in control of the process. Second, even if you make an offer and are willing to receive acceptance by mail, you are entitled, as master of the offer, to eliminate the postal rule. You could, for example, say that a letter of acceptance is effective only when and where you actually receive it. You would therefore not be bound by an acceptance letter that was lost in the mail.

> the postal rule merely is a default rule—it can be eliminated by the offeror

We emphasize one more point about the postal rule. It applies only to acceptances. It does not apply to an offer, a revocation, a rejection, or a counter offer. An offer or a revocation is effective only when and where it is actually received by the offeree. And a rejection or counter offer is effective only when and where it is received by the offeror. Consider the situation in Business Law in Action 2.3.

BUSINESS LAW IN ACTION 2.3

The Postal Rule

On June 1, Maria sent you a letter offering to sell her watch for $50. On June 3, she sent another letter that supposedly revoked her offer. On June 5, you received Maria's offer and immediately put an acceptance letter into a mailbox. On June 7, you received Maria's revocation letter. And on June 9, she received your acceptance letter.

Question for Discussion

1. Assuming that the usual rules apply, do you and Maria have a contract?

The rules in this area are somewhat complicated. By way of review, consider Concept Summary 2.3.

Concept Summary 2.3

Communication Rules

RULES GOVERNING INSTANTANEOUS COMMUNICATIONS (GENERAL RULE)	
Type of Communication	**Effective**
• offer by offeror	• when and where received by offeree
• revocation by offeror	• when and where received by offeree
• rejection by offeree	• when and where received by offeror
• counter offer by offeree (who becomes the offeror)	• when and where received by initial offeror (who becomes the offeree)
• acceptance by offeree	• when and where received by offeror
RULES GOVERNING NON-INSTANTANEOUS COMMUNICATIONS (POSTAL RULE)	
Type of Communication	**Effective**
• offer by offeror	• when and where received by offeree
• revocation by offeror	• when and where received by offeree
• rejection by the offeree	• when and where received by offeror
• counter offer by offeree (who becomes the offeror)	• when and where received by initial offeror (who becomes the offeree)
• acceptance by offeree	• when and where sent by offeree

Acceptance by Performance

a **unilateral contract** occurs when an act is exchanged for a promise

an offeree accepts a unilateral contract through performance

no contract exists unless and until the offeree performs

the offeror is the only one who has an outstanding obligation under a unilateral contract

We have discussed bilateral contracts in which a promise is exchanged for a promise. One party offers to do something in the future, and the other party accepts by similarly promising to do something in the future. The rules are different for *unilateral contracts*. A **unilateral contract** occurs when an act is exchanged for a promise. In that situation, the offeror promises to pay a reward to anyone who performs a particular act. As Figure 2.2 illustrates, the offeree accepts by actually performing its part of the agreement. Note two things about unilateral contracts. First, no contract exists unless and until the offeree performs. Second, if the offeree performs and the contract is created, the offeror is the only one who has an outstanding obligation.

FIGURE 2.2	Unilateral Contract

For example, suppose that I offer to pay $100 to anyone who finds and returns my lost cat. At that point, we do not have a contract, and you are not required to look for her. However, a contract may be created if and when you bring her home to me. If so, you will not be obligated to do anything more, but I will be expected to pay the reward. Note that we said that a unilateral contract *may* be created if you return my cat to me. That will be true only if you acted with the *intention of accepting* my offer. If you did not, we did not have a meeting of the minds, and there is no contract. Perhaps you had not seen my offer but returned my cat out of the goodness of your heart. Although your actions took the proper form for acceptance, they were not performed in *response* to my offer.[23] Therefore, you are not entitled to the reward.

Case Brief 2.1 provides a famous illustration of a unilateral contract.

an offeree must perform with the intention of accepting an offer

CASE BRIEF 2.1

Carlill v Carbolic Smoke Ball Co [1893] 1 QB 256 (CA)

In the 1890s, England was plagued by two related phenomena: an influenza epidemic and quack medicine. The Carbolic Smoke Ball Co was one of many companies that tried to capitalize on the country's ill health. It produced a hand-held gadget that, when squeezed, emitted a small cloud of carbolic acid dust. The company claimed that if one inhaled the dust regularly, it would prevent a long list of ailments ranging from diphtheria and bronchitis to snoring and sore eyes. As part of its marketing ploy, it published an advertisement that offered to pay £100 to any person who contracted influenza while using the Carbolic Smoke Ball. Mrs Carlill saw the ad, bought the product, and used it as directed. When she later came down with the flu, she claimed to be entitled to £100. The company refused to pay. It said that there was no contract because she had not told them that she had accepted their offer and was using their product.

The Court, undoubtedly put off by the company's unsavoury practices, rejected that argument. It held that the contract was unilateral and that the company, as offeror, had implicitly dispensed with the usual need for the communication of acceptance. Consequently, Mrs Carlill, as offeree, effectively accepted the offer by using the product as directed. As a result, she was entitled to collect £100.

The courts generally prefer bilateral contracts over unilateral contracts.[24] Bilateral contracts provide more protection. Neither party has to worry about wasting time and expense. The offeree knows that if it performs, it will be entitled to the offeror's performance, and *vice versa*. In contrast, a unilateral contract might operate unfairly. Consider a twist on the facts of *Carbolic Smoke Ball*. The company said that it would pay £100 to anyone who caught the flu despite using the device three times a day for two weeks. What if Mrs Carlill had gone to the trouble and expense of buying and using the ball three times a day for 13 days, but just as she was about to complete the treatment, a company representative knocked on her door and said, "Sorry, the deal's off"? Acceptance of a unilateral offer is not effective until the stipulated act is completed, and, as we saw earlier, an offeror is generally free to revoke an offer any time before acceptance. Consequently, it might appear that Mrs Carlill could not collect the reward even if she became sick after continuing to use the smoke ball.

courts prefer to find bilateral contracts rather than unilateral contracts

A court would struggle to avoid that result. It would want to give Mrs Carlill an opportunity to inhale the dust for one more day and claim the money if she became sick. Its approach to the problem might be quite complex. For example, a judge might hold that the company's notice actually contained offers for *two* unilateral contracts. The main contract would involve the company's promise to pay £100 to anyone who became sick despite using the smoke ball. The other contract would involve the company's promise to not revoke its offer once a customer began using the device.[25]

---

23. *R v Clarke* (1927) 40 CLR 227 (Aust HC).

24. *Dawson v Helicopter Exploration Co* [1955] 5 DLR 404 (SCC).

25. *Errington v Errington* [1952] 1 KB 290 (CA).

Chapter Summary

A contract is an agreement that creates rights and obligations that can be enforced in law. The formation of a contract usually requires three things: an intention to create legal relations, a meeting of the minds, and an exchange of value. The first two requirements were discussed in this chapter; the third is considered in the next chapter.

The courts presume an intention to create legal relations in commercial contexts but not in family or social settings. However, these presumptions can be rebutted.

A meeting of the minds occurs through the process of offer and acceptance. Not every statement regarding a proposed transaction is an offer. The courts will not recognize a contract if a reasonable person would have interpreted the parties' communications as involving mere inquiries or invitations to treat.

Contractual offers must be communicated and received as offers. An offer may be made orally, in writing, or through conduct. The life of an offer is usually limited. To create a contract, acceptance must occur before the offer is terminated. An offer can be brought to an end through revocation, lapse of time, death or insanity, rejection, or counter offer. A counter offer creates a new offer in which the person who originally was the offeree becomes the offeror. The process of offer and acceptance requires special attention in the case of an option, a tender, or a battle of the forms.

A bilateral contract occurs when a promise is exchanged for a promise. Acceptance arises when an offeree agrees to enter into the contract proposed by the offeror. Acceptance usually occurs through words, but it may also occur through conduct. Mere silence generally cannot be acceptance, but silence may be sufficient if it is coupled with other factors. In any event, acceptance must be unequivocal and correspond precisely with the terms of the offer. Generally, it must be communicated to the offeror. With instantaneous forms of communication, acceptance is effective and a contract is formed when and where the communication is received by the offeror. The same is not true for non-instantaneous forms of communication, where acceptance occurs when and where it is sent, whether it is received or not. The general rule and the postal rule can be altered or eliminated by the offeror. The offeror, as master of the offer, can set special rules for acceptance.

A unilateral contract occurs when performance is exchanged for a promise. The offeree accepts by performing its part of the agreement. No contract exists unless and until the offeree performs. And if the offeree performs and the contract is created, the offeror is the only one who has an outstanding obligation. The courts generally prefer bilateral contracts over unilateral contracts.

Review Questions

1. What is meant by the term "meeting of the minds"? How is it significant to the formation of contracts?

2. What is meant by the term "exchange of value"? How is it significant to the formation of contracts?

3. What risks are associated with offers? Describe two techniques by which the courts reduce those risks.

4. Describe a principle that the courts often apply to commercial agreements but not to agreements between family members.

5. Why do the courts generally rely upon an objective test rather than a subjective test when deciding contractual issues?

6. In what sense is an offeror the "master of the offer"? What special powers does the master of the offer enjoy?

7. Distinguish between an offer and an invitation to treat. Give an example of each. How does the distinction help to promote commercial activity?

8. Briefly discuss the commercial and ethical implications of revoking a firm offer.

9. Explain how options operate. Why is an option enforceable, whereas a firm offer is not?

10. Describe how the tendering process works. Explain the two types of contracts that are involved.

11. Briefly discuss the factors that a court will consider to determine whether an offer has been open for a reasonable period of time. Why do you think these factors are important? Give an example of a situation where these factors come into play.

12. Explain when and why death or insanity will result in the termination of an offer.

13. What is the effect of rejecting an offer? Why do you think the rule is set up this way? If you change your mind after rejecting an offer, what could you do to revive the transaction?

14. What is a counter offer? What effect does a counter offer have on an offer?

15. Describe the problems that arise from a "battle of the forms."

16. What is the difference between a bilateral contract and a unilateral contract? How is each type of contract accepted?

17. Can an offer ever be accepted through the offeree's silence? Why or why not?

18. What is the difference between instantaneous and non-instantaneous forms of communication? How is that difference relevant to the formation of contracts?

19. What is the postal rule? Why have the courts created it?

When does it apply?

20. Can an offer of a unilateral contract be revoked while the offeree is in the process of performing the stipulated act of acceptance? Why or why not?

Cases and Problems

1. Susan and Hector, long-time friends, go to the races together. They each place a Sweep Six bet, which requires predicting the winning horse in each of six consecutive races. After the third race, Susan and Hector realize that they had both picked the first three winners, but they also realize that they had chosen different horses for the remaining races. Therefore, to maximize their individual chances of success, they each promise that if they win, they will split the jackpot evenly with the other person. Hector's horse loses the next race, but Susan's wins. Susan's predictions for the fifth and sixth race also prove accurate, and the track awards her $500 000. Susan claims that she can avoid paying Hector because there had not been an intention to create legal relations. What arguments can you make for and against her claim?

2. In the hope of drawing customers to its store, Wild Ed's Stereo Shop places the following advertisement in Friday's newspaper.

** ONE TIME ONLY **
If you are one of the first three customers through **Wild Ed's** doors tomorrow morning, a 36" colour television, normally priced at $2000, is yours for only $500!!!

Don't **miss** this amazing opportunity.

Olga camps outside Wild Ed's store on Friday night to get this great bargain on a television. Unfortunately, although Olga is the only customer there when the doors open on Saturday morning, Wild Ed confesses that he does not really have any televisions to sell. He does, however, direct her to a line of full-priced stereos. Olga is not amused. Although newspaper advertisements are generally considered invitations to treat, suggest reasons why a reasonable person might interpret Wild Ed's ad as an offer.

3. The city of Darlington, which wishes to build a new recreational centre, places an advertisement in a local newspaper requesting that contractors submit tenders. The newspaper advertisement states that tenders must be received by 4:00 pm on June 15 and that tenders are irrevocable after they have been received by the city. Ronaldo is

among the contractors who submit tenders. At 4:15 on June 15, however, he realizes that he had miscalculated the expenses that would be involved in the project and that his bid consequently is grossly understated. He telephones the city and asks it to remove his tender from consideration. Even though the city has yet to select the winning tender, it rejects Ronaldo's request and informs him that it will select his bid if that bid offers to build the recreation centre for the lowest price. Explain whether Ronaldo will be able to revoke his bid.

4. Following a grisly murder, the police department offered to pay a $5000 reward for information leading to the conviction of the responsible party. Sandra, a shadowy underworld figure, knew that the crime had been committed by her rival, Maurice. She accordingly went to the police station and provided information that eventually led to his life imprisonment. She was delighted to have Maurice out of the way, but was even more excited when she later learned of the police department's reward offer. Although she had not known of that offer when she provided the incriminating evidence, she now seeks to collect the $5000. Is she entitled to the money? Explain your answer.

5. Jake owns several cash registers, which he rents out. Three years ago, he entered into a written contract with Emily under which he allowed her to rent one of his cash registers for one year in exchange for $5000. At the end of that year, the parties entered into another contract on precisely the same terms. When that second contract came to an end, Jake wrote to Emily saying, "If I do not hear from you to the contrary, I'll assume that you'll take the cash register for a third year at a price of $5000." Emily did not reply to Jake's message, but she did use his cash register all of last year. He now wishes to be paid. Is Emily liable for the third year's rent? Did the parties have a contract last year? Give your reasons.

6. Ahmad owned Regent Arms, an apartment block in downtown Vancouver, which he wished to sell. He knew that Felicity, a real estate developer, was interested in such properties. Therefore, on Thursday, he faxed this offer to her: "I will sell Regent Arms to you for $5 000 000. If you wish to accept this offer, please do so as soon as possible. I promise that I will not make a similar offer to anyone else while you are considering this proposal." Felicity was very interested in the offer but received it just as she was about to leave for a meeting in Medicine Hat. When she returned on the following Monday, she immediately faxed a letter purporting to accept Ahmad's offer. He replied that since

he had not heard from her earlier, he had sold Regent Arms to another party on Saturday. Felicity now claims that because Ahmad had done nothing to communicate the revocation of his offer, his offer was still open for acceptance when she sent her fax to him. Is she correct? Has the offer lapsed or been revoked? Explain the arguments that Ahmad and Felicity might make if their dispute went to court.

7. On June 1, Elsa mails a letter to Ivan offering to buy a painting from him for $100 000. He receives that letter on June 8 and on the same day mails a letter rejecting her offer. The next day, however, he changes his mind and contacts her by telephone to accept her offer. By June 15, however, when Elsa receives Ivan's letter, she has decided that she no longer wants to go through with the deal. Applying the rules summarized in Concept Summary 2.1 to each step of these negotiations, determine if and when the parties formed a contract.

8. On October 15, Olaf mails a letter in Winnipeg offering to sell widgets to Simone. The next day, before Simone receives Olaf's offer, he sends another letter from Winnipeg revoking his offer. Simone receives Olaf's offer letter in Kelowna on October 21 and immediately sends a letter of acceptance. The next day, she receives Olaf's revocation letter in Kelowna. Applying the rules summarized in Concept Summary 2.1, determine if, when, and where the parties formed a contract.

9. Ten years ago, Edgar's daughter, Tina, married Hussein. Because the young couple could not afford to buy a house by themselves, Edgar placed a down payment of $90 000 on a home and told his daughter and son-in-law that they could live in the house and that if they paid monthly mortgage instalments of $1000 until the mortgage was satisfied, he would transfer the clear title into their name. Unfortunately, Tina and her parents recently had a falling out. Although Tina and Hussein have regularly paid the monthly mortgage instalments and wish to continue doing so until the mortgage is paid off (which they predict will occur in about seven years), Edgar has purportedly revoked his offer and stated that he intends to pay the remaining mortgage instalments and permanently live in the house himself. Did the parties act with an intention to create legal relations? Was the contract proposed by Edgar's initial offer a bilateral contract or a unilateral contract? Have Tina and Hussein fully accepted Edgar's offer? If not, can Edgar revoke his offer? If it was a unilateral contract, were Tina and Hussein obligated to pay the full mortgage once they began to make instalment payments?

10. Five years ago, Arvid and Dora were involved in an amorous relationship while they studied business together at college. Since that time, they have gone their separate ways and have moved to separate cities, but they are still intimate on those rare occasions when their paths cross. Unfortunately, while Arvid's business has flourished, Dora's has floundered and she has fallen on hard times. Last month, Arvid wrote to Dora to offer her a job with his company. The relevant portion of his letter stated, "Given all that we have been through together and given the generous salary that I am offering, I just know that you'll accept. I'm considering the deal done and I'll begin setting up an office for you tomorrow." Arvid's letter did not mention that his offer was also motivated partly by a secret desire to rekindle their old romance into a permanent and stable relationship. When Dora received the letter, she decided to definitely take the job and began making arrangements to join Arvid's company. She did not, however, inform her old friend of that decision. She wanted to surprise him by simply appearing at his door the next week. However, three days later, her own company received an unexpected financial grant from the federal government. At that point, she reconsidered her earlier decision to work for Arvid and telephoned him to say that she would not be joining him after all. Because he had already spent a considerable amount of money preparing for Dora's arrival and because he was upset that she spurned his offer, Arvid reacted angrily. He insisted that a contract had been created and that she was his employee. Is he correct? Did Arvid act with an intention to create legal relations? Does it necessarily matter that both Arvid and Dora firmly believed that they had formed an enforceable agreement? Has there been valid acceptance?

11. Ekaterina owned a farm in a remote region of Saskatchewan, which she had been trying to sell for several years. In late November, Rasheed faxed her an offer to purchase the property for $50 000 and asked that she quickly reply by fax or telegram. Two weeks later, Ekaterina responded with a letter that stated that, by coincidence, another person had recently expressed interest in the farm and that, in the circumstances, she would sell for not less than $60 000. Her message stated that if that price was satisfactory, the deal "could be completed immediately," and suggested January 1 as a closing date. Ekaterina's letter also asked Rasheed to reply by telephone or e-mail to avoid delay. A week later, Ekaterina's letter was delivered to Rasheed's house. As he was abroad on business, his wife, Naima, opened it in his absence. Without Rasheed's authorization, Naima immediately sent a telegram to Ekaterina, stating that Rasheed would return in 10 days and asking that the offer be held open until that time. The telegram also indicated that Rasheed had earlier expressed interest in the property and stated that if he purchased the farm, he would not require the land until March, as it would not be possible to commence farming operations until the spring. Ekaterina did not reply to that telegram. Ten days later, Rasheed returned from abroad and promptly e-mailed Ekaterina to accept her offer to sell the farm for $60 000. She replied that she had sold the property to a third party the previous day and that her offer consequently was no longer open. Rasheed believes that since his acceptance was communicated before he was informed of the sale to the third party, a contract was formed between himself and Ekaterina. Is he correct? Was Ekaterina's offer still open when Rasheed purported to accept it? What factors would a judge consider in deciding that issue?

12. Nostromo Corporation has its headquarters in Edmonton but operates throughout Canada. A branch office in Halifax sent a letter to Conrad, a prospective customer in Nova Scotia, offering to sell widgets. The offer stated, "Acceptance should be made by return mail." Conrad sent a fax to Nostromo Corp's head office in Edmonton pur-

portedly accepting the offer. He then entered into a sub-contract with a third party, under which he agreed to resell the widgets that he expected to receive from Nostromo Corp. Conrad was subsequently disappointed, however, when the company stated that it did not recognize his acceptance and refused to deliver the widgets to him. (As a result, he was forced to breach his contract with the third party.) Was a contract formed between Nostromo Corp and Conrad? Specifically, was Conrad entitled to accept by fax rather than by mail? Was he entitled to deliver his acceptance to the home office in Edmonton rather than the branch office in Halifax? How would a judge likely interpret the passage quoted from the company's offer? Was there any commercially compelling reason for the branch operation to insist upon acceptance by mail? Was there any commercially compelling reason for the branch operation to insist upon acceptance to the office in Halifax?

3 Consideration and Privity

CHAPTER OVERVIEW

Consideration
Sufficient and Adequate
  Consideration
Past Consideration
Pre-existing Obligation
Promises Enforceable without
  Consideration

Privity of Contract
Assignment
Trusts
Statute
Employment

OBJECTIVES

After completing this chapter, you should be able to:

1. Explain the nature of consideration and the role it plays in the formation of contracts.
2. Describe past consideration and explain why it cannot support a contract.
3. Distinguish between: (i) pre-existing public duties, (ii) pre-existing contractual obligations owed to a third party, and (iii) pre-existing contractual obligations owed to the same party.
4. Describe the nature and effect of a seal.
5. Define promissory estoppel and identify its four requirements.
6. Describe the concept of privity of contract and explain its relationship to the concept of consideration.
7. Distinguish between equitable assignments and statutory assignments and explain how assignments provide an exception to the privity of contract rule.
8. Explain how a trust can be used to create an apparent exception to the privity of contract rule.
9. Identify two types of statutes that provide exceptions to the privity of contract rule.
10. Explain when and why employees will be entitled to enforce exclusion clauses that are contained in contracts to which they are strangers.

In Chapter 2, we looked at some of the ingredients necessary to the formation of a contract: intention to create legal relations, offer, and acceptance. In this chapter, we examine another: *consideration*. As we will see, "consideration" refers to the thing that each party provides under a contract. This is critical—unless consideration exists on both sides of a bargain, the courts will usually not enforce the parties' agreement.

We will also examine the concept of *privity of contract*. Consideration, offer and acceptance, and intention to create contractual relations are required for the formation of a contract. "Privity of contract" refers to an individual's relationship to a contract, identifying who can sue or be sued under an agreement.

CONSIDERATION

The main goal of contract law is to enforce bargains. And as business people know, a bargain involves more than an offer and an acceptance. It also involves a *mutual exchange of value*. Without that sort of exchange, a contract usually cannot exist. Suppose I offer to give you a computer, and you simply agree to receive it. I have made a **gratuitous promise**—I did not receive anything of legal value in exchange for it. I have promised to give you something, but you have not promised to do anything in return. Consequently, while you will be entitled to keep the computer if I actually give it to you, you cannot force me to fulfill my promise if I still have the thing in my hands. Because we did not have a bargain, we did not have a contract. And because we did not have a contract, I can change my mind.

a bargain involves a mutual exchange of value

a gratuitous promise is a promise for which nothing of legal value is given in exchange

The creation of a contract therefore generally depends on an exchange of value. *Consideration* must be provided by both parties. While that term is notoriously difficult to define, **consideration** is generally said to exist when a party either gives or promises to give a benefit to someone else *or* suffers or promises to suffer a detriment to itself.[1] Consideration must move *from* each side of a contract but not necessarily *to* the other side. For example, you and I will have a contract if I promise to give $5000 to your brother, and you promise to give a car to my sister. In that situation, it is enough that we have both promised to provide a benefit to *someone*; we did not have to promise to provide benefits to each other.

consideration is generally said to exist when a party either gives or promises to give a benefit to the other party or suffers or promises to suffer a detriment to itself

consideration must move from each side of a contract but not necessarily to the other side

The idea of consideration is quite broad and does not usually cause any problems. Nevertheless, difficulties do occasionally arise. Therefore, it is important to examine the concept of consideration in detail.

Sufficient and Adequate Consideration

A contract must be supported by *sufficient consideration*. **Sufficient consideration** has value from a legal perspective. Suppose that, in exchange for my promise to give you a computer, you promise to provide me with "love and affection." We do not have a contract. Whatever value we may place on "love and affection," that sort of thing has no value at all from a legal perspective. Judges do, however, place value on just about everything else, such as a promise to refrain from smoking, drinking, and swearing.[2] The reason for this rather surprising attitude is not entirely clear. It probably arises from the fact that during the nineteenth century, when many of the rules in law of contract

sufficient consideration has value from a legal perspective

[1.] *Currie v Misa* (1875) LR 10 Ex 153 (HL).

[2.] *Hamer v Sidway* 27 NE 256 (1891 NY CA).

were created, judges generally wanted to avoid becoming involved in intimate matters.[3]

Although consideration must be sufficient, it does not have to be *adequate*. **Adequate consideration** has essentially the same value as the consideration for which it is exchanged. For example, if I promise to give you a computer worth $5000, and you promise to give up smoking, drinking, and swearing for a year, it would seem that I have made a very bad bargain. In economic terms, I will be giving up far more than you will be providing in return. Nevertheless, we probably have a contract, and it is unlikely that a judge will save me from my own foolishness. Because the law presumes that people are able to look after their own interests, it generally allows them to decide what price they will demand under a contract.[4]

Forbearance to Sue

For business people, the difference between sufficient consideration and adequate consideration is particularly important in the context of *forbearance to sue*. **Forbearance to sue** is a promise not to pursue a lawsuit. Because lawsuits are expensive and unpredictable, very few are actually decided by judges. In the vast majority of cases, the parties settle their dispute out-of-court. They often enter into a contract for that purpose. The plaintiff promises not to bring the matter into court, and the defendant agrees to pay less money than it allegedly owed. If the plaintiff's action would have succeeded in court, there is consideration on both sides of the contract. The plaintiff surrendered the right to claim full damages, and the defendant paid money.[5] But what if it is later discovered that the plaintiff would have lost the case if it had gone to court? In that situation, it might appear that the plaintiff did not give consideration. After all, it merely agreed not to pursue a lawsuit that it would have lost. Nevertheless, a judge would likely hold the parties to their agreement. As you read You Be the Judge 3.1, consider the possible reasons for enforcing such contracts. Also consider the importance of receiving advice from a lawyer before agreeing to forbear on a possible action.

consideration must be sufficient but not adequate

adequate consideration has essentially the same value as the consideration for which it is exchanged

forbearance to sue is a promise to not pursue a lawsuit

YOU BE THE JUDGE 3.1

Forbearance to Sue[6]

Igor works as a stockbroker for a company. Following procedures that he remembered reading in the company's official policy, he purchased $100 000 worth of shares on instructions from a client. Unfortunately, despite Igor's repeated

demands, the client refused to pay for those shares. Worse yet, during that time, the value of the shares dropped by 60 percent. Eventually, the company took control of the account, sold the shares for $40 000, and threatened to sue Igor for $60 000. In the company's view, the whole fiasco was his fault. Igor vigorously denied liability, but he was worried that a lawsuit would

(continued)

[3.] As Chapter 2 explained, the courts generally assume that there is no intention to create legal relations between family members and close friends.

[4.] However, as Chapter 5 will explain, when one party exercises an unfair advantage over the other, the courts may become concerned about the inadequacy of consideration. For example, if a con artist tricks a senior citizen into trading her home for his essentially worthless share certificates, a judge may strike down the parties' agreement because it is grossly unfair.

[5.] The term "damages" refers to the money that the court may order the defendant to pay to the plaintiff. Chapter 7 discusses damages.

[6.] The facts are based on *Stott v Merit Investments Inc* (1988) 48 DLR (4th) 288 (Ont CA).

(continued)

damage his professional reputation. He was also unable to find the policy document that he had relied on. Consequently, he agreed to pay $50 000 in exchange for the company's promise to drop the matter. Two weeks later, however, before actually making the payment, Igor located the lost document. It proved that he could not be held liable in the circumstances.

Questions for Discussion

1. Can the company force Igor to pay the $50 000? Did he incur a contractual obligation to do so? Did the company provide consideration in exchange for his promise?

2. Even if the company did not actually have a valid claim against Igor, is it true to say that it gave nothing of value when it agreed to drop its lawsuit against him?

3. As a matter of policy, why are the courts eager to find the existence of a contract, even if the underlying claim is invalid? If they refused to do so, would it ever make sense for a party to forbear? Consider the general consequences that would follow from such an approach.

In some situations, the courts will not enforce forbearance agreements, especially if the party that threatened to sue did not honestly believe that it had a valid claim in the first place. Case Brief 3.1 provides a remarkable illustration.

CASE BRIEF 3.1

Moss v Chin (1994) 120 DLR (4th) 406 (BC SC)

Mr Chin ran down Mrs Moss at a pedestrian crosswalk. Because she suffered severe brain damage, her interests were represented by the Public Trustee. The Public Trustee sued Mr Chin in the tort of negligence and claimed, among other things, the cost of Mrs Moss's future medical expenses. Over time, as negotiations between the parties progressed, Mrs Moss's physical condition deteriorated, and she eventually died. The Public Trustee, however, hid that fact from Mr Chin and convinced him to settle the lawsuit for a certain amount of money.

Mr Chin later learned that he had paid for future medical expenses for a woman who was already dead. He convinced a judge to set aside the settlement contract and refund the money that had been paid. Although the courts generally uphold settlement agreements, the judge said that the Public Trustee could not enforce an agreement that it created dishonestly.

Past Consideration

Because the law views a contract as a bargain, consideration must be provided by both sides. There must also be **mutuality of consideration**. Each party must provide consideration *in return* for the other party's consideration.

The requirement of mutuality is important to the idea of *past consideration*. **Past consideration** consists of something that a party did *prior* to the contemplation of a contract. In such circumstances, there is no mutuality. The past consideration is not provided in return for the other party's consideration. And for that reason, past consideration is not really consideration at all. It therefore cannot support a contract.

Sometimes it is difficult to determine whether something is past consideration. Consider these two situations. First, suppose you were planning to build a golf course in a windy area and consequently required unusually heavy sand for its traps. You offered to pay $5000 to anyone who put you in touch with an appropriate supplier. By coincidence, Abdul, a business associate who knew about your proposed golf course, had sent you a letter the *previous day* that contained precisely the information that you needed. When you eventually received

mutuality of consideration requires that each party provide consideration *in return* for the other party's consideration

past consideration consists of something that a party did *prior* to the contemplation of a contract

past consideration cannot support a contract

his letter a week later, you told him to come by your office to collect the $5000. By the time that he arrived, however, you had changed your mind about the money. Although he would be upset, he had no right to enforce your promise. One reason is that his letter merely provided *past consideration*—it was written *before* you even proposed the contract.[7]

Now suppose that instead of making a general offer to pay $5000, you said to Abdul personally, "I'd like you to set me up with an appropriate supplier." After a day of investigation, he reported back with the relevant information. You responded by saying, "Great work! I'll pay you $5000 for your efforts. Come by tomorrow for the cash." When he arrived, however, you told him that you had changed your mind. It might appear that he would again be disappointed by the past consideration rule. After all, he provided the information *before* you expressly promised to pay $5000 for it. A court, however, would view the matter differently. A reasonable person would interpret your request for Abdul's help as an offer to pay him for his services. A judge would therefore require you to pay a "reasonable price."[8] A judge would also find that your *subsequent* promise to pay $5000 merely provided evidence as to a price that was reasonable. (If you had not subsequently promised $5000, the judge would determine the value of Abdul's services after considering all of the circumstances.) In other words, although the terms of the contract were not entirely settled at the outset, there was a sufficient meeting of the minds. And on that view, Abdul's actions were good consideration rather than past consideration. They were provided *in return* for your implicit promise that he would be rewarded for his efforts.[9] They were part of a bargaining process.

The rule on past consideration may produce results that seem at odds with basic notions of fairness and morality. Consider the situation in Ethical Perspective 3.1.

ETHICAL PERSPECTIVE 3.1

Past Consideration[10]

While strolling on a beach, you discover Heena unconscious and face down in the water. You pull her ashore, administer first aid, and bring her back to life. Shaken, but grateful, she promises to pay you $500 every year for the remainder of your life. However, when you attempt to collect the first payment, she states that she has changed her mind and refuses to pay anything.

Questions for Discussion

1. Does Heena have a moral obligation to pay any money to you? Does she have a legal obligation to do so?
2. Leaving aside the rule governing past consideration, do you believe that Heena should be required to pay anything to you?

---

7. *Eastwood v Kenyon* (1840) 113 ER 482 (CA). As we saw in Chapter 2, there is another reason why Abdul could not enforce your promise. His purported acceptance did not occur *in response* to your offer. He sent the information to you only by coincidence.

8. Lawyers sometimes refer to the reasonable price for services as *quantum meruit*, or "as much as its worth."

9. *Lampleigh v Braithwait* (1615) 80 ER 255 (KB).

10. The facts are based on *Webb v McGowin* 168 So 2d 196 (Ala CA 1935).

Pre-existing Obligation

Because past consideration is no consideration at all, an act that was *actually performed* before a contract was proposed cannot provide consideration for that agreement. But can a contract be supported by a *promise* to fulfill a **pre-existing obligation**, that is, an obligation that existed, but was not actually performed, before the contract was contemplated?

We must distinguish three types of pre-existing obligations:

- a pre-existing public duty
- a pre-existing contractual obligation owed to a third party
- a pre-existing contractual obligation owed to the same party

a pre-existing obligation is an obligation that existed, but was not actually performed, before the contract was contemplated

Pre-existing Public Duty

A person who owes a *pre-existing public duty* cannot rely upon that obligation as consideration for a new contract. For example, firefighters and police officers who are called to your office during an emergency cannot sell their services to you under a contract. One reason is that when they became public servants, they already promised to help people like you in times of need. Therefore, they do not have anything more that they can offer as part of a new agreement. An even stronger reason, which is not tied to the idea of past consideration, is that it would be against *public policy* to allow public servants to take advantage of your misfortune by charging for their services. It would also be undesirable if public servants were tempted to pass by poor citizens and enter into lucrative contracts with wealthy citizens.

good consideration cannot be based on public duty

However, by becoming a public servant, a person does not promise to protect citizens around the clock. For example, after police officers finish their shifts, they can generally do as they please. They are certainly not required to guard your house during their vacations, even if you are worried that thieves might be lurking in the area. If you want that type of protection, you have to pay for it. Judging from the illustration in Business Decision 3.1, such contracts are becoming more common.

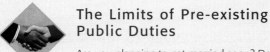

BUSINESS DECISION 3.1

The Limits of Pre-existing Public Duties

Are you planning to get married soon? Do you expect to receive cash-filled envelopes as wedding presents? If so, consider the case of Lazarus Kiriakidis and Christine DePoce of Toronto.

Like many couples, Kiriakidis and DePoce expected to receive gifts of money from their guests. While they were planning their wedding, however, they learned that armed robbers had entered two wedding receptions in the previous year and had made off with about $100 000 in cash. Kiriakidis and DePoce therefore decided to protect them-

selves, their guests, and their wedding presents by hiring two off-duty police officers, at about $45 an hour each, to act as private guards.

Because police officers do not have a pre-existing obligation to guard wedding receptions, they are able to provide consideration when entering into contracts for such services.

Question for Discussion

1. Identify situations in which a business might consider hiring off-duty police officers.

Source: Based in part on "Here comes the bride — and armed guards," *The Globe and Mail*, July 13, 1998.

Pre-existing Contractual Obligation Owed to Third Party

We have seen that a promise to perform a pre-existing *public duty* is not good consideration for a new contract. In contrast, a promise to perform a pre-existing obligation that previously arose under a *contract with a third party* can be good consideration for a new contract. That rule is often important in business, as Case Brief 3.2 shows.

good consideration can be based on a pre-existing contractual obligation owed to a third party

---

CASE BRIEF 3.2

Pao On v Lau Yiu Long [1980] AC 614 (PC)

The plaintiff bought 4 200 000 shares from a company called Fu Chip. Under the terms of that agreement, the plaintiff promised Fu Chip that it would not resell more than 60 percent of those shares within one year. Resale of a larger number of the shares would hurt Fu Chip's financial situation. The plaintiff later realized, however, that it might suffer a financial loss itself if, for some reason, the value of the shares dropped. It would be required to retain the shares while their value declined. The plaintiff therefore approached the defendants, who were the majority shareholders in Fu Chip, and persuaded them to enter into a separate, *indemnification* contract.[11] Under that agreement, the plaintiff promised to honour its earlier sale contract with Fu Chip, and the defendants promised to compensate the plaintiff for any loss

that it suffered as a result. The plaintiff therefore used the same consideration twice. It separately promised both the defendants and Fu Chip (which, as a stranger to the indemnification contract, was classified as a *third party* to that agreement) that it would not resell 60 percent of the shares within one year.

As feared, the value of the shares dropped, and the plaintiff claimed indemnification under its contract with the defendant. The defendants argued that the plaintiff had merely promised to fulfill the first (sale) contract and had not provided good consideration for the second (indemnification) contract. The court, however, held that the plaintiff's promise to perform the contractual obligation that it already owed to Fu Chip (the third party) was good consideration for its later contract with the defendants.

In one sense, there is an advantage to using the same consideration for two different contracts. Despite promising to do only one thing, you may be able to extract valuable promises from two different parties. However, there is also a danger in that sort of arrangement. Suppose a classical quartet agrees with a promoter to perform a concert in exchange for $15 000. The quartet subsequently persuades a music publisher, under a separate contract, to pay $20 000 for the right to record the concert. If all goes well, the quartet will receive $15 000 from the promoter *and* $20 000 from the publisher, even though it essentially did only one thing. However, if the quartet refuses to perform, it will be held liable to both the promoter *and* the publisher, even though it essentially failed to do only one thing.

Pre-existing Contractual Obligation Owed to the Same Party

We have seen that a promise to perform a pre-existing obligation that previously arose under a contract with a *third party* can be good consideration for a new contract. But what if the pre-existing obligation arose under an earlier contract with the *same party* that is on the other side of the new contract? Perhaps surprisingly, a different rule applies in that situation. The courts usually hold

good consideration usually cannot be based on a pre-existing contractual obligation owed to the same party

---

11. Indemnification consists of compensating a party for a loss that it suffers.

that the *same* person cannot be required to pay twice for the same benefit. If a promise is merely repeated, it does not provide anything new. Furthermore, the courts want to prevent a person from threatening to breach one contract in order to get the other party to enter into a second contract at a higher price. The leading case is discussed in Case Brief 3.3.

CASE BRIEF 3.3

Gilbert Steel Ltd v University Construction Ltd (1976) 67 DLR (3d) 606 (Ont CA)

The plaintiff contractually agreed to sell several shipments of steel to the defendant at a set price. After that agreement was partially fulfilled, the plaintiff's own supplier raised its prices. The defendant then promised to pay the plaintiff a higher price for the remaining shipments of steel. The plaintiff delivered the rest of the steel, but the defendant refused to honour its promise to pay the extra amount. The defendant argued that the plaintiff had already promised to deliver the steel under the initial contract and therefore did not provide anything in exchange for the later promise of the higher price.

The court agreed. It held that the defendant was not required to pay the extra price because it had not received anything new in exchange for its promise to do so.

The court's analysis may seem appropriate in *Gilbert Steel*, but it does not sit so well in other situations. Parties sometimes fail to appreciate the effort and expense that will be involved in the performance of their contract. If so, they may genuinely agree that the terms of their original contract should be revised to ensure that the deal benefits both of them, especially if they want to develop and maintain goodwill. Successful business people often recognize that a small sacrifice in the short term can lead to larger benefits in the long term. For those reasons, many scholars argue that a party's promise to revise the terms of a contract should sometimes be enforceable if the revision accurately reflects an unexpected change in circumstances. That argument was accepted in England and may eventually be adopted in Canada as well.[12]

In the meantime, there are other ways in which Canadian business people can avoid the rule in *Gilbert Steel*. First, they can use the process of *novation* to discharge their initial contract and enter into a new agreement that includes a higher price.[13] Second, they can agree that something new is to be done in exchange for the extra price. For example, in *Gilbert Steel*, the plaintiff could have promised to deliver either somewhat more steel or the same amount of steel somewhat earlier. Third, as we will discuss in the next section, the defendant's promise in *Gilbert Steel* would have been binding, despite the lack of any new consideration from the plaintiff, if it had been made under *seal*. And finally, as previously suggested, business people can simply ignore the rule in *Gilbert Steel*. They may be unaware of it. And even if they are aware of it, they may realize that financial success in the long run sometimes requires flexibility in the short run.

Concept Summary 3.1 lists the general rules regarding pre-existing obligations and consideration.

[12.] *Williams v Roffey Bros & Nicholls (Contractors) Ltd* [1990] 1 All ER 512 (CA).

[13.] The concept of novation is discussed in Chapter 6.

Concept Summary 3.1

Pre-Existing Obligations and Consideration

Situation	Can a pre-existing obligation generally provide consideration for a new contract?
Pre-existing public duty	No
Pre-existing contractual obligation owed to third party	Yes
Pre-existing contractual obligation owed to same party	No

Promises Enforceable without Consideration

Generally speaking, a promise is enforceable only if it is contained in a contract that is supported by consideration. That rule, however, is subject to two major exceptions:

- seals
- promissory estoppel

We begin, however, by considering another common situation, in which one party promises to forgive a debt.

Promise to Forgive an Existing Debt

Occasionally, a *creditor* (someone to whom a debt is owed) promises to accept less than full payment from a *debtor* (someone who owes a debt). Generally speaking, that promise is unenforceable unless it is supported by fresh consideration. However, that view often conflicts with the commercial realities of the business world.

Suppose you lend me $100 000, which I promise to repay in cash on June 1. To keep things simple, assume that the loan is interest free. When the repayment date arrives, however, I honestly explain that I do not have that much money. You therefore promise to discharge my debt if I pay $70 000. I comply, but after receiving $70 000, you insist that I still owe $30 000. And as a matter of law, you are correct. Because I gave nothing in exchange for your promise to discharge my debt for a mere $70 000, your promise is unenforceable.[14]

Arguably, however, I *did* give consideration for your promise to forgive $30 000 of my original debt. Although I initially *promised to pay* $100 000, my *actual payment* of $70 000 probably provided a new benefit to you. If you had not accepted it, you would have been put to the trouble and expense of suing me. Furthermore, if my financial situation continued to deteriorate, I might have declared bankruptcy. If so, you would have been required to share my assets with my other creditors and therefore might have received far less than $70 000.[15]

Traditionally, judges rejected that argument and held that a creditor generally is not bound by a promise to accept anything less than full payment from a debtor. There are some exceptions to that rule. First, a promise to accept a smaller sum is enforceable if it is placed under *seal*. Second, a promise to accept less money is enforceable if the debtor gives something new in exchange for it. Returning to our earlier example, I might have promised to give you $70 000

a promise by a creditor to accept less than full payment from a debtor is generally unenforceable

---

14. *Foakes v Beer* (1884) 9 App Cas 605 (HL).

15. Bankruptcy is discussed in Chapter 22.

plus a vehicle that I own. Or I might have promised to pay $70 000 on May 31 instead of $100 000 on June 1. If you agreed to that arrangement, you effectively bought one day for $30 000. Perhaps most surprisingly, your promise might even be enforceable if I promised to pay $70 000 by *cheque* instead of $100 000 in *cash*.[16]

In addition to those judicially created exceptions, an important statutory exception exists in many parts of Canada. Several jurisdictions have legislation that allows a debt to be extinguished upon payment of lesser amount.[17] Section 16 of the *Mercantile Law Amendment Act* of Ontario is typical.[18]

> "Part performance of an obligation either before or after breach thereof when expressly accepted by the creditor or rendered in pursuance of an agreement for that purpose, though without any new consideration, shall be held to extinguish the obligation."

Significantly, that provision requires *part performance*—part of the debt must have been paid. Therefore, it would apply if you *actually received* $70 000 from me. However, if you merely received my *promise* to pay that amount, you could change your mind and insist upon full payment any time before I handed over the $70 000.

Seals

A **seal** is a mark that is placed upon a written contract to indicate a party's intention to be bound by the terms of that document, even though the other party may not have given consideration. The essential purpose of a seal is to draw the parties' attention to the importance of the occasion and to ensure that they appreciate the seriousness of making an enforceable promise outside the usual bargaining process. Accordingly, before you affix your seal to a document, you should carefully reflect on the fact that you may be agreeing to do something for nothing.

The process of placing a seal on a document is subject to a loose rule and a strict rule. On the one hand, the seal need not take any particular form. Historically, a seal was applied by pressing an insignia (usually of a family crest or a coat of arms) into a drop of hot wax on a document. While the usual practice today is to affix a red adhesive wafer to a document, it is also acceptable to simply write the word "seal" on the paper. On the other hand, the courts insist that the seal must be applied at the time that a party signs the document. It is not sufficient, for example, to use a form that already has the word "seal" written on it or to add the word "seal" after the fact.[19]

*a **seal** is a mark that is placed on a written contract to indicate a party's intention to be bound by the terms of that document, even though the other party may not have given consideration*

Promissory Estoppel

To explain the concept of *promissory estoppel*, we need to first define the term "estoppel."[20] **Estoppel** is a rule that precludes a person from disputing or retracting a statement that they made earlier. In a variety of situations, a court

*an **estoppel** is a rule that precludes a person from disputing or retracting a statement that they made earlier*

---

16. *Foot v Rawlings* (1963) 37 DLR (2d) 695 (SCC). But see *D & C Builders v Rees* [1965] 3 All ER 837 (CA).

17. *Judicature Act*, RSA 1980, c J-1, s 13(1) (Alta); *Law and Equity Act*, RSBC 1996, c 253, s 43 (BC); *Mercantile Law Amendment Act*, RSM 1987, c M120, s 6 (Man); *Judicature Act*, RSNWT 1988, c J-1, s 40 (NWT); *Judicature Act* (Nun), SNWT 1998, c 34, s 37 (Nun); *Queen's Bench Act*, RSS 1978, Q-1, s 45(7) (Sask); *Judicature Act*, RSY 1986, c 96, s 25 (Yuk).

18. *Mercantile Law Amendment Act*, RSO 1990, c M-10.

19. *Royal Bank of Canada v Kiska* (1967) 63 DLR (2d) 582 (SCC).

20. The term is derived from the Latin word meaning "to stop" or "to prevent."

may hold that a person is "estopped" from unfairly denying the truth of a prior statement if the person to whom the statement was made relied on it. For example, suppose you trick me into building a house on your property by saying that the land is mine. When I complete the project, the law will not allow you to unfairly assert your ownership in the property. You will be estopped from denying the truth of your earlier statement that I owned the land. I therefore may be entitled to keep the property along with the house.[21]

Traditionally, the concept of estoppel applied only to statements regarding *past* or *present* facts.[22] More recently, however, it has been applied to statements regarding *promises* and *future* facts as well. **Promissory estoppel** is a doctrine that prevents a party from retracting a promise that another party has relied upon. That doctrine therefore creates an important exception to the general rule that only enforces promises that were acquired in exchange for consideration. Case Brief 3.4 discusses the decision that established the modern principle of promissory estoppel.

promissory estoppel is a doctrine that prevents a party from retracting a promise that the other party has relied upon

---

CASE BRIEF 3.4

Central London Property Ltd v High Trees House Ltd [1947] KB 130 (KB)

The defendant leased an apartment block in London, England from the plaintiff. The lease began in 1937 and was to run for 99 years, at a yearly charge of £2500. The defendant intended to rent out the individual apartments to other tenants. However, it became apparent after World War II began that the defendant could not rent out enough apartments to cover its obligations under the main lease. The plaintiff was sympathetic and therefore promised that it would reduce the rent to £1250 per year. That was a gratuitous promise because the defendant did not give any consideration in exchange for it. The parties proceeded on that basis for several years. By 1945, however, the war had ended, and the building was fully occupied. The plaintiff then brought an action to determine: (i) whether it could charge the original rent of £2500 in future years, and (ii) whether it could recover as back rent the amount that it had allowed the defendant to not pay during the war.

The court held that while original rent could be reinstated in *future years*, the plaintiff was estopped from retracting its promise that it would only charge half rent during the war. In other words, for the *past years*, the plaintiff's promise was enforceable even though it was not supported by consideration.

As Case Brief 3.4 shows, the doctrine of promissory estoppel will apply only if four requirements are met.

the representor must clearly indicate that it will not enforce its legal rights against the representee

1. The *representor* (the party making the promise) must clearly indicate that it will not enforce its legal rights against the *representee* (the party receiving the promise). Therefore, promissory estoppel will not apply if, for example, one party is simply slow in collecting money that it is owed. Accepting late payment is not the same thing as clearly saying that future payments need not be made on time or that they need not be made at all.[23]

the representee must rely upon the statement in a way that would make it unfair for the representor to retract its promise

2. The representee must *rely* upon the statement in a way that would make it unfair for the representor to retract its promise. For example, the representee might have re-arranged its business plans because of the promise. However, if the promise was not relied upon in any way, then it is not enforceable.

21. *Willmott v Barber* (1880) 15 Ch D 96.

22. *Jorden v Money* (1854) 5 HL Cas 185 (HL).

23. *John Burrows Ltd v Subsurface Surveys Ltd* (1968) 68 DLR (2d) 354 (SCC).

3. The representee must not be guilty of *inequitable behaviour*. This means that the doctrine of promissory estoppel does not apply, for example, if the representee unfairly pressured the representor into making the statement. [24]

the representee must not be guilty of inequitable behaviour

4. The representor's statement must be made in the context of an *existing legal relationship*. Although American courts use the similar doctrine of "injurious reliance" to *create* rights, Canadian courts usually hold that promissory estoppel can be used only to *vary* existing rights. (As lawyers in this country sometimes say, promissory estoppel can be used as a shield, but not as a sword.) Consequently, unless a legal relationship already exists between the parties, our courts will not enforce a gratuitous promise even if the representee has relied upon it.[25]

the representor's statement must be made in the context of an existing legal relationship

If these four requirements are met, the representor cannot assert its original rights with respect to the *past*. However, that party may be allowed to enforce its original rights in the *future* if it gives reasonable notice of its intention to do so. As we saw, this occurred in *High Trees*. That possibility does not exist, however, if it would result in an unfair hardship for the representee.

promissory estoppel can usually be brought to an end through reasonable notice

PRIVITY OF CONTRACT

Consideration is necessary for the *creation* of a contract. The concept of *privity of contract* is different. It identifies the people who can be involved in the *enforcement* of a contract. Nevertheless, we address it in this chapter because it is closely tied to the idea of consideration.

It is often important to ask who can enforce a contract or have a contract enforced against them. In a simple two-party situation, each party enjoys the right to enforce the agreement against the other. Suppose, for example, that you agree to sell your car to me for $5000. You can sue me if I fail to pay the money, and I can sue you if you fail to transfer the car.

Complications can arise, however, if the facts involve a *stranger*. A **stranger** is someone who did not participate in the creation of the contract. Suppose you agreed to transfer your car to me if I paid $5000 to your sister. If I get the vehicle but refuse to pay the price, the real complaint lies with your sister. She is the one who suffers from my broken promise. Can she compel me to fulfill the contract that I made with you?

a stranger is someone who did not participate in the creation of the contract

A court would probably answer "no." A contract is used to distribute benefits and burdens *amongst the parties*. The last part of that sentence is important. You and I cannot impose an obligation on someone who is not part of our agreement. Likewise, someone who is not part of our agreement generally cannot take advantage of it. Those rules are reflected in the *privity of contract* doctrine. **Privity of contract** refers to the relationship that exists between the individuals who create a contract. Only those people are *parties* to the agreement, and in most situations, only parties can sue or be sued on the contract.[26]

the privity of contract doctrine refers to the relationship that exists between the individuals who create a contract

Although the two concepts are technically distinct, the privity of contract doctrine is often expressed in terms of the consideration doctrine. That approach emphasizes the bargaining aspect of contracts and says that, generally speaking, only a person who has provided something of value can sue or be

generally speaking, only parties can sue or be sued on a contract

---

[24.] *D & C Builders Ltd v Rees* [1965] 3 All ER 837 (CA).

[25.] *Maracle v Travelers Indemnity Co of Canada* (1991) 80 DLR (4th) 652 (SCC); compare *Re Tudale Exploration Ltd v Bruce* (1978) 20 OR (2d) 593 (HCJ).

[26.] *Dunlop Pneumatic Tyre Co Ltd v Selfridge & Co Ltd* [1915] AC 847 at 853 (HL).

sued on the contract. Returning to our illustration, we can see why your sister cannot compel me to fulfill my promise. Although she expected to take the benefit of that promise, she did not bargain for it. She gave nothing in return for my agreement to pay $5000. If you are surprised by that result, consider what might happen if *you* tried to enforce my promise against me. You provided consideration when you promised to transfer the car to me. You therefore have the right to sue me *in theory*. But *in practice*, I might be able to persuade a court that I do not have to pay the money to you either.[27] After all, I was supposed to pay $5000 to your sister rather than to you. Why should you now be able to demand payment from me?

As our discussion suggests, the privity of contract rule sometimes seems unfair. A number of common law jurisdictions around the world, including one in Canada, have therefore abolished that doctrine.[28] In those places, a stranger who was intended to enjoy the benefit of a promise can generally enforce it. Other jurisdictions rely on narrower and less dramatic ways of occasionally avoiding the harsh consequences of the privity doctrine. We will examine a number of those exceptions and apparent exceptions:

- assignment
- trusts
- statutes
- employment[29]

As we do so, note the business contexts in which these issues arise and the ways in which business people can prevent problems from arising in the first place.

Assignment

assignment is a process in which a contractual party transfers its rights to a third party

A business person who wants to allow a stranger to enforce a contract will usually use an *assignment*. **Assignment** is a process in which a contractual party transfers its rights to a third party. The contractual party who assigns its rights is called the **assignor**; the stranger to whom the contractual rights are assigned is called the **assignee**; and the original contracting party against whom the assigned rights can be enforced is called the **debtor**. In effect, as Figure 3.1 illustrates, the assignee steps into the assignor's shoes to enforce the promise against the debtor.

the **assignor** is the contractual party who assigns its contractual rights

the **assignee** is the stranger to whom the contractual rights are assigned

the **debtor** is the original contracting party against whom the assigned right can be enforced

Assignment often provides the best way to avoid the harsh consequences of the privity doctrine. The process is, however, quite complex. This section merely provides a basic overview of assignments. A business person who is faced with a complicated assignment issue should consult a lawyer.

Equitable Assignments

an **equitable assignment** is an assignment that was traditionally enforced by the courts of equity

We start with the fact that the assignment can occur either as an *equitable assignment* or as a *statutory assignment*. An **equitable assignment** is an assignment that was traditionally enforced by the courts of equity, which we discussed in Chapter 1. It is usually possible to make an equitable assignment of a

---

[27.] *Woodar Investment Development Ltd v Wimpey Construction UK Ltd* [1980] 1 WLR 277 (HL).

[28.] *Contracts (Rights of Third Parties) Act 1999*, c 31 (UK); *Law Reform Act*, SNB 1993, c L-1.2, s 4 (NB).

[29.] Several other exceptions to the privity doctrine are examined in other chapters: promises that run with the land (Chapter 13), negotiable instruments (Chapter 9), and agency (Chapter 20).

FIGURE 3.1   Assignment of Debt

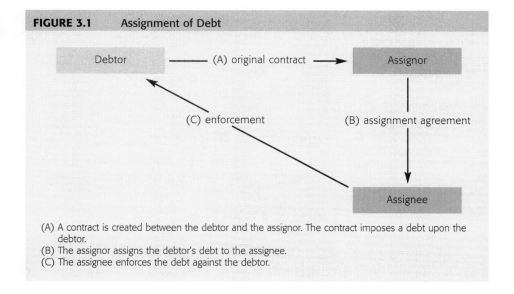

(A) A contract is created between the debtor and the assignor. The contract imposes a debt upon the debtor.
(B) The assignor assigns the debtor's debt to the assignee.
(C) The assignee enforces the debt against the debtor.

contractual right, although there are some exceptions. First, the parties to a contract can agree that their rights are non-assignable. Furthermore, the courts sometimes refuse to allow an assignment on policy grounds. For example, contracts for matrimonial support cannot be assigned.

In some respects, the process involved in an equitable assignment is very simple. No particular documents are required, and the assignment can even be completed orally. As a matter of risk management, however, it is best to use a written document whenever possible to avoid complications and disputes.

A valid assignment does not depend on the debtor's consent. Nevertheless, if you are an assignee, there are several reasons why you should provide *notice* of the assignment to the debtor as soon as possible. A debtor has to pay a debt only once. Consequently, if it pays the assignor before receiving notice from you, you cannot demand a second payment for yourself. (You can, however, sue the assignor.) A similar danger occurs if the assignor improperly assigns the same debt to you and then to another person. If that person is unaware of your assignment, it is entitled to payment if it provides the debtor with notice before you do. And again, since the debtor has to pay only once, you could not demand a second payment for yourself. (You could, however, sue the assignor.)

Taking Subject to the Equities There is another reason why you should give notice as soon as possible. An assignment is **subject to the equities**, which means that the debtor can generally use the same defences and counterclaims against the assignee that it could have used against the assignor. Nevertheless, it is important to draw a distinction between: (i) defences and counterclaims that arose out of the *same contract* that is the subject of assignment, and (ii) defences and counterclaims that arose out of *other transactions* between the debtor and the assignor.

The debtor can *always* rely on the first category of defences and counterclaims against the assignee. However, the debtor can rely on the second category of defences and counterclaims only if its transaction with the assignor occurred *before* it received notice from the assignee. Those rules are rather complex. The examples in Business Law in Action 3.1 and 3.2 help to illustrate them.

an equitable assignment should, but need not, be made in writing

an assignee should secure its rights by providing notice to the debtor as soon as possible

subject to the equities means that the debtor can generally use the same defences and counterclaims against the assignee that it could have used against the assignor

BUSINESS LAW IN ACTION 3.1

Equities Arising from the Assigned Contract

In January, Stetson Construction agreed to build a cottage in May in exchange for Ahmad's promise that he would pay $60 000 in August. Since Stetson needed money up front to buy supplies, it assigned its rights to you in March for $55 000. You immediately notified Ahmad of the assignment.

After you gave notice, Stetson broke its contract with Ahmad by using inadequate materials in the construction of the cottage. As a result, Ahmad was required to spend $40 000 to hire another contractor to repair the problem. It is now September.

Question for Discussion

1. If you bring an action against Ahmad under the equitable assignment, how much will you probably be able to collect?

BUSINESS LAW IN ACTION 3.2

Equities Arising from Other Transactions

Citron Used Cars sold a vehicle to White Stationery Inc for $7000. When White failed to pay the purchase price, Citron assigned its contractual right to recover that money to you. White later delivered $5000 worth of paper products to Citron under a separate contract. Citron has not yet paid that price.

Questions for Discussion

1. How much would you be entitled to collect from White if you gave notice *before* Citron became indebted to White for the receipt of the paper products?
2. How much would you be able to collect from White if you gave notice *after* Citron became indebted to White for the receipt of the paper products?

Although equitable assignments of contractual rights are quite flexible, they can also create problems for the assignee. Most significantly, if it wants to sue the debtor, the assignee may have to include the assignor as a party to that action.[30] That may be difficult to do, however, if the assignor is no longer available. For example, the assignor may have been a company that ceased to exist after it made the assignment.

Statutory Assignments

a statutory assignment is an assignment that conforms with the requirements of a statute

Because of the problems associated with equitable assignments, legislation has been introduced across Canada that creates an alternative form of assignment.[31] A **statutory assignment** is an assignment that conforms with the requirements of a statute.

While they generally follow the same principles as equitable assignments, statutory assignments are subject to three special requirements.

---

[30] The assignor is included in the action as a co-plaintiff if it is willing to co-operate with the assignee, or as a co-defendant if it is not.

[31] *Judicature Act*, RSA 1980, c J-1, s 21(1) (Alta); *Law and Equity Act*, RSBC 1996, c 253, s 36 (BC); *Law of Property Act*, RSM 1987, c L-90, s 31 (Man); *Conveyancing and Law of Property Act*, RSO 1990, c C-34, s 53(1) (Ont); *Judicature Act*, RSNB 1973, c J-2, s 31 (NB); *Judicature Act*, RSN 1990, c J-4, s 103 (Nfld); *Judicature Act*, RSNS 1989, c 240, s 43(5) (NS); *Choses in Action Act*, RSS 1978, c 11, s 2 (Sask). The legislation in Manitoba and Saskatchewan is slightly broader in scope; the discussion in the text focuses on the position in the other common law jurisdictions.

1. While an equitable assignment may be oral, a statutory assignment must be *written*.
2. While notice to the debtor is merely advisable under an equitable assignment, *written notice* is required for a valid statutory assignment.
3. Unlike an equitable assignment, a statutory assignment must be *absolute* at the time that it is created. An assignment is not absolute if it is *conditional*, for example, because it depends on some uncertain event in the future. That situation would arise if the assignor continues to deliver goods to the debtor on credit and therefore alters the amount of the debt. Nor is an assignment absolute if it is *incomplete*, for example, because it covers only part of a debt. That situation would arise if the assignor assigned $3000 of a $5000 debt to the assignee.

> a statutory assignment must be in writing, supported by written notice, and absolute

A statutory assignment is simply an alternative to an equitable assignment. Consequently, even if the requirements of the statute are not met, an assignment can still be effective in the equitable sense. In fact, equitable assignments are sometimes preferred for that very reason. For example, the assignor may intend to have ongoing transactions with the debtor, with the result that the amount of debt will vary from time to time. If so, an assignment of the right to receive payment from the debtor would be conditional. The assignment would therefore have to be equitable, rather than statutory.

Assignments by Operation of Law

Equitable and statutory assignments arise from the assignor's intention. Other types of assignment, however, occur by operation of law. The best examples involve bankruptcy and death. When a contractual party becomes bankrupt, all of its rights and liabilities are placed under the administration of *trustee in bankruptcy*.[32] When a person dies, all of their contractual rights and liabilities are placed under the administration of a *personal representative*. In either event, the assignee has the responsibility of collecting and paying the person's debts. For reasons that are explained in the next section, however, the assignee is not required to satisfy obligations of a *personal* nature that were owed by the bankrupt or the deceased.

> assignment occurs by operation of law in cases of bankruptcy and death

Vicarious Performance

So far we have discussed the assignment of contractual *rights*. We have not considered the assignment of contractual *obligations*. In fact, contractual obligations cannot be assigned. The general rule is that a party must personally perform. That is clearly true if the party's personal skills are essential to the fulfillment of the contract. For example, if a Broadway producer hires a famous actress to star in a production, she is not entitled to send her understudy to play the role. The contract is intended to secure *her* services.

> some contractual obligations cannot be assigned

In many situations, however, *vicarious performance* is allowed. **Vicarious performance** occurs when a contractual party arranges to have a stranger perform its obligations. That is possible if the contractual party's personal skills are not essential to performance. For instance, if you enter into a contract with a house builder, you cannot reasonably expect that individual to *personally* undertake the work alone. It is clear that the contractor will use employees or subcontractors. However, vicarious performance is not a form of assignment. The obligation to build the house remains on the builder. Consequently, if the house

> vicarious performance occurs when a contractual party arranges to have a stranger perform its obligations

---

32. The process of bankruptcy is discussed in detail in Chapter 22.

is defective because the employees or subcontractors were careless, you will still sue the builder.[33]

Trusts

a trust occurs when one person administers property on behalf of another

the trustee is the person who holds the property on behalf of the other

the beneficiary is the person on whose behalf the property is held

An apparent exception to the privity doctrine involves the equitable concept of the *trust*. A **trust** occurs when one person holds property on behalf of another. The person who holds the property is the **trustee**, and the person for whom the property is held is the **beneficiary**. For example, suppose that an elderly couple want to provide for their grandchildren's education but are afraid that the money may be wasted. They therefore give the money to a trustee, who will sensibly spend the money on the grandchildren's behalf. The trustee may, for example, pay for their tuition or accommodation while they are at school.

A trust can be used to avoid the consequences of the privity doctrine. A person who enters into a contract as a trustee obtains the other party's contractual promise on behalf of the beneficiary of the trust. Consequently, although it did not personally enter into the contract, the beneficiary is entitled to enforce that promise. Figure 3.2 illustrates that situation.

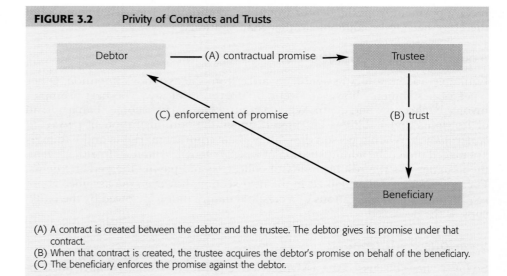

FIGURE 3.2   Privity of Contracts and Trusts

(A) A contract is created between the debtor and the trustee. The debtor gives its promise under that contract.
(B) When that contract is created, the trustee acquires the debtor's promise on behalf of the beneficiary.
(C) The beneficiary enforces the promise against the debtor.

The trust was once commonly used to avoid the privity doctrine. Today, however, the courts demand clear proof that the contractual promise really was intended to be held on trust. Case Brief 3.5 illustrates both the general nature of trusts and the courts' attitude toward their use in the avoidance of the privity doctrine.

---

[33] The builder, in turn, may have a contractual action against the workers. Moreover, as we will discuss in Chapter 12, you may have actions in tort against both the builder and the workers.

CASE BRIEF 3.5

Vandepitte v Preferred Accident Insurance Co [1933] AC 70 (PC)

Mr Berry purchased liability insurance coverage for his vehicle from the defendant insurance company. That insurance policy was contained in a standard form document and was said to cover not only Mr Berry but also anyone driving his car with his consent.

While driving her father's car with his consent, Jean Berry caused an accident that injured the plaintiff, Alice Vandepitte. Mrs Vandepitte sued the defendant insurance company and argued that the insurer was liable for Jean's actions under the terms of her father's policy. In response, the defendant company argued that while Jean fell within the wording of that policy, she was not a party to the insurance contract and therefore had no rights under the policy. And if that was true, then the defendant could not be compelled to compensate

Mrs Vandepitte for the injuries that she sustained as a result of Jean's careless driving.

In response to that argument, Mrs Vandepitte claimed that Jean *was* made a party to the contract by way of a trust. On that view, Mr Berry purchased the insurance policy from the defendant not only for himself but also on trust for his daughter. He therefore held the defendant's promise to provide insurance coverage on behalf of himself *and* his daughter.

The Privy Council recognized the possibility of such an arrangement. It held, however, that the plaintiff had not established that Mr Berry actually intended to acquire insurance coverage on trust for his daughter. While earlier cases simply assumed the existence of that intention, the court here insisted on clear proof of the fact. Canadian courts continue to follow that stricter approach.

Statute

Because the privity doctrine often creates injustice, the legislatures have created a number of true exceptions that allow strangers to enforce promises. The clearest illustrations arise in the context of insurance contracts. For example, *Vandepitte v Preferred Accident Insurance Co* would be decided differently today because legislation has been introduced throughout Canada that allows people like Jean Berry to enforce insurance contracts made for their benefit.[34] Similar provisions have been introduced for life insurance.[35] The primary purpose of a life insurance policy is to benefit someone who is not a party to that contract, usually a grieving family member. It would be grossly unfair if an insurance company could invoke the privity doctrine and refuse to make payment to that person after an insured party died.

statutes often create broad exceptions to the privity doctrine

Employment

The same reasoning has led the courts to create exceptions to the privity doctrine in other situations. Judges, however, proceed more cautiously than legislators, and the judicial exceptions are much narrower in scope. The clearest

34. *Insurance Act*, RSA 1980, c I-5, s 320 (Alta); *Insurance Act*, RSBC 1996, c 226, s 159 (BC); *Insurance Act*, RSM 1987, c I-40, s 258 (Man); *Insurance Act*, RSNB 1973, c I-12, s 250 (NB); *Automobile Insurance Act*, RSN 1990, c A-22, s 26 (Nfld); *Insurance Act*, RSNWT 1988, c I-4, s 28 (NWT); *Insurance Act*, RSNS 1989, c 231, s 133 (NS); *Insurance Act*, RSNWT 1988, c I-4, s 151 (Nun); *Insurance Act*, RSO 1990, c I-8, s 258 (Ont); *Insurance Act*, RSPEI 1988, c I-4, s 240 (PEI); *Saskatchewan Insurance Act*, RSS 1978, c S-26, s 210 (Sask); *Insurance Act*, RSY 1986 c 91, s 153 (Yuk).

35. *Insurance Act*, RSA 1980, c I-5, s 264 (Alta); *Insurance Act*, RSBC 1996, c 226, s 53 (BC); *Insurance Act*, RSM 1987, c I-40, s 172 (Man); *Insurance Act*, RSNB 1973, c I-2, s 156 (NB); *Life Insurance Act*, RSN 1990, c L-14, s 26 (Nfld); *Insurance Act*, RSNWT 1988, c I-4, s 93 (NWT and Nun); *Insurance Act*, RSNS 1989, 231, s 197 (NS); *Insurance Act*, RSO 1990, c I-8, s 195 (Ont); *Insurance Act*, RSPEI 1988, c I-4, s 143 (PEI); *Saskatchewan Insurance Act*, RSS 1978, c S-26, s 157 (Sask); *Insurance Act*, RSY 1986, c 91, s 97 (Yuk).

example arises in the employment context. When a company agrees to do work for a customer, it is usually obvious that the actual task will be performed by the company's employees. Furthermore, the contract that is created between the customer and the company may include an exclusion clause that expressly says that the customer cannot sue either the company *or* its employees if something goes wrong.[36] However, if the employees do perform carelessly, the customer may sue them in tort and argue that they cannot rely upon the contractual exclusion clause. After all, they were not parties to that contract.

Recently, the Supreme Court of Canada held that employees may be entitled to rely upon an exclusion clause that was created for their benefit, even though they lack privity of contract. In *London Drugs Ltd v Kuehne & Nagel International Ltd*, Iacobucci J said that an exception to the privity doctrine exists if two conditions are met.[37] First, it must have been clear from the outset that the employees would perform work under the contract. Second, the employees must have been acting in the course of their employment when the accident occurred. In reaching that conclusion, the judge was particularly influenced by the practical reality of the situation. As is typically true, it was clear in *London Drugs* that both the company and the customer expected that the former's employees would be protected by the exclusion clause if something went wrong. It would be grossly unfair, especially to the hapless employees, if the customer was later allowed to act against that expectation.

[36.] Exclusion clauses are discussed in Chapter 4.

[37.] (1992) 97 DLR (4th) 261 (SCC). See also *Fraser River Pile & Dredge Ltd v Can-Dive Services Ltd* (1999) 176 DLR (4th) 257 (SCC).

Chapter Summary

Consideration is an essential element in the formation of most contracts. Because the law of contract is based on the concept of a bargain, gratuitous promises are generally not enforced. There must be an exchange of consideration between the parties. The bargain between the parties need not be a good one; as long as there is an exchange of value, a contract will be created. Consideration must be sufficient but it need not be adequate. An important application of the rules governing the sufficiency and adequacy of consideration arises in the context of forbearance to sue.

Past consideration is no consideration at all because it fails to satisfy the requirement of mutuality. Good consideration can be based on a pre-existing contractual obligation owed to a third party. However, good consideration cannot be based on a pre-existing public duty and usually cannot be based on a pre-existing contractual obligation owed to the same party.

As a general rule, a creditor's promise to accept less than full payment from a debtor is not binding. That rule is, however, subject to several exceptions.

A promise may be enforceable even if it is not supported by consideration if it was placed under seal or if it falls under the doctrine of promissory estoppel. In Canada, the doctrine of promissory estoppel is used to vary existing contractual rights but not to create new ones.

The doctrine of privity of contract is closely associated with the doctrine of consideration. A person who has not provided consideration and who is not a party to a contract generally cannot sue or be sued on the contract.

The privity of contract doctrine is subject to several exceptions and apparent exceptions. A stranger to a contract can enforce a contractual promise that has been assigned to it. An assignment of a contractual right may be either equitable or statutory and may arise either from the assignor's intention or by operation of law. A beneficiary can enforce a contractual promise acquired on its behalf by a trustee. In a number of situations, statutes allow strangers to enforce contractual rights created for their benefit. Likewise, the courts have recently allowed employees to take advantage of exclusion clauses that are contained in contracts for which they have not provided consideration and with respect to which they lack privity.

Review Questions

1. What is a gratuitous promise? Can such a promise support a contract?

2. Is it possible for a person to enter into an enforceable contract without receiving any benefit from the agreement?

3. How and why do the courts distinguish between the "adequacy" and the "sufficiency" of consideration?

4. What is a forbearance agreement? Why do the courts generally uphold such agreements? Are such agreements supported by consideration?

5. What is the requirement of mutuality? How is it related to the bargain theory of contract?

6. What is past consideration? In light of the bargaining process that underlies a contract, explain why judges hold that past consideration is no consideration at all.

7. "There is a difference between past consideration on the one hand and on the other hand a promise that indicates the reasonable price for work that was previously performed under a contract." Explain the meaning of that statement. Provide an example to illustrate your answer.

8. Explain why a pre-existing public duty cannot be good consideration under a new contract. Does your explanation rely entirely on the doctrine of consideration, or does it also include other factors?

9. "Good consideration usually cannot be based on a pre-existing contractual obligation owed to the same party." Describe three ways by which business people can avoid that rule. What commercial reasons might motivate them to do so?

10. Suggest reasons why good consideration for a new contract can be based on a pre-existing contractual obligation that is owed to a third party, but cannot be based on a pre-existing contractual obligation that is owed to the same party that is involved in the new agreement.

11. List and briefly describe the non-statutory exceptions to the general rule that payment of a lesser sum does not discharge a debt of a larger amount.

12. In your province or territory, does legislation ever allow you to discharge a debt by paying your creditor a lesser amount than you actually owe to it?

13. What is the effect of sealing a contractual document?

14. Describe the doctrine of promissory estoppel. What does it mean to say that promissory estoppel can be used to vary, but not create, contractual rights? Give examples to illustrate your answer.

15. Explain the relationship between the requirement of consideration and the privity of contract doctrine.

16. "The process of assignment undermines the privity of contract doctrine." Discuss the extent to which that statement is true.

17. Explain why it would be undesirable if contractual parties were free to assign contractual obligations, even though contractual rights generally can be assigned. Illustrate your answer with examples. Discuss the extent to which the doctrine of vicarious performance provides an exception to the general rule precluding assignment of contractual obligations.

18. Explain how a trust can be used to avoid the consequences of the privity of contract doctrine.

19. Explain the circumstances in which an employee may be entitled to rely upon an exclusion clause contained in an employer's contract.

20. Why do you think judges allow employees to take advantage of exclusions clauses to which they are strangers? Give at least two reasons for your answer.

Cases and Problems

1. On Maria's eighteenth birthday, her uncle Juan said to her, "I still think that you're too young to be driving, but I promise that when you turn 21, I'll buy a car for you. All I want from you in return is your love and affection." He then wrote down his words and, being something of a show-off, applied his seal using hot wax and his family insignia. Despite the fact that Maria, who was desperate for a car, was particularly adoring toward her uncle for the next three years, Juan refused to honour his promise when she turned 21. Can Maria get the car? Did she provide consideration in exchange for Juan's promise?

2. While Emily was on holidays, her neighbour, Francesco, noticed that her roof was badly damaged by a hailstorm and became concerned that it might leak in the next rainstorm. Consequently, he paid a roofing contractor to repair the roof at a cost of $2000. When Emily returned home, she was very grateful for Francesco's intervention and promptly promised to reimburse him for his expenses. Before actually making payment, however, she changed her mind and now refuses to fulfill her promise. Is Francesco entitled to enforce his neighbour's promise? Did the parties enter into an enforceable agreement?

3. Hardy Construction Ltd contractually agreed to build an office complex for Schtick Corp. Under the terms of that contract, Hardy Construction would incur a financial penalty if it failed to complete the project on schedule. Hardy Construction hired Laurel Electric Co as a subcontractor to install wiring in the building. The terms of that subcontract required payment of $50 000 on completion. Laurel Electric began work immediately but later discovered that it had honestly underestimated the cost of performance. Accordingly, it approached Hardy Construction and stated that unless it was promised an additional $20 000, it simply would not be able to complete the job. Hardy Construction realized: (i) that it could not possibly find a replacement for Laurel Electric on such short notice, and (ii) that any delay in completion of the project would trigger the penalty provision contained in its contract with Schtick Corp. Hardy Construction consequently agreed to Laurel Electric's request. Nevertheless, although Laurel Electric subsequently completed its performance on schedule, Hardy Construction refuses to pay more than $50 000. Does it have a right to do so in law? Regardless of its legal position, why might Hardy Construction consider honouring its promise to pay an extra $20 000? Explain whether you believe that the law should more closely reflect business practice.

4. Jacques was indebted to Rumana for $5000, plus 15 percent interest per annum, which he was required to pay in cash in monthly installments of $400. Jacques, however, was unhappy with that arrangement and asked Rumana if she would be willing to lower the interest rate to 12 percent in exchange for his promise to pay monthly installments of $600 in a series of post-dated cheques. Although she initially agreed to that proposal, Rumana later insisted that Jacques comply with the terms of their original agreement. Is she entitled to do so? Identify two arguments that Jacques could present in response to the suggestion that he provided no consideration for Rumana's promise to abide by the revised repayment schedule.

5. Tyrell Corp owed $10 000 to Deckard Investigations Ltd for past services in locating former employees. Under the terms of the parties' contract, Tyrell was required to make installment payments of $500 on the first day of each month. If Tyrell was late on any single installment, Deckard was entitled to demand immediate payment of the entire outstanding amount. Tyrell made the first two payments on schedule but then fell into a habit of making payment in the middle of the month. For 10 consecutive months, Deckard silently received the late payments without objection. On the basis of that silence, Tyrell re-arranged its finances on the assumption that Deckard would always accept late payment. However, when Tyrell attempted to make a late payment for the eleventh month in a row, Deckard invoked the acceleration clause contained in the parties' contract and demanded immediate payment of $4000. Tyrell proves that it will suffer a hardship if it is now required to completely live up to the terms of the original agreement. It therefore insists that Deckard be precluded from doing so by the doctrine of promissory estoppel. Identify the most obvious reason why that argument will fail.

6. The Blacksox Baseball Club and Roark Designs Corp con-

ducted extensive negotiations concerning the development of a new ball park. During those negotiations, the owner of the Blacksox said to the owner of Roark, "Look, we both know that this stadium will eventually be built. The lawyers will have to work out the details, and of course nothing will be official until we sign a formal contract. But as far as I'm concerned, we might as well get started. I can promise you right now that if you draft the plans, we'll pay you $100 000 for your efforts." Roark spent a considerable amount of time and money preparing a blueprint for a new stadium. Unfortunately, the entire proposal collapsed when, through no fault of either the Blacksox or Roark, the local government denied zoning approval for the project. Roark nevertheless insists that the Blacksox abide by the promise made by their president. Will the doctrine of promissory estoppel assist Roark in that regard?

7. Julio Cruz and Ingrid Forsberg were married more than a year ago. On the wedding day, Julio's father, Mr Cruz, and Ingrid's mother, Mrs Forsberg, entered into a contract that was intended to provide financial support for the young couple. Mr Cruz promised to pay $5000 to the couple on their first anniversary. In exchange, Mrs Forsberg promised to pay $4000 to the couple on the same day. Nevertheless, on the couple's first anniversary, neither Mr Cruz nor Mrs Forsberg was willing to honour their promises. Does a contract exist in these circumstances? If so, who are the parties to that contract? If a contract does exist, what consideration was provided in support of it? Who provided that consideration? Are Julio and Ingrid entitled to compel their parents to pay the promised amounts?

8. Everlast Tire Co, which manufactures automobile tires, sold a shipment of tires to Automotive Wholesaler Inc. Under the terms of that contract, Automotive Wholesaler was allowed to resell the tires below the price suggested by Everlast if: (i) the sub-buyer was a business in the car industry, and (ii) the sub-buyer promised not to resell below the price suggested by Everlast. Automotive Wholesaler then sold the tires to AJ's Used Cars Ltd. Under the terms of that contract, AJ's, which was engaged in the car industry as a used car dealer, promised Automotive Wholesaler that it would not resell the tires below the price suggested by Everlast. AJ's also promised Automotive Wholesaler that if it broke that promise, it would pay $100 to Everlast for each tire that was sold below the manufacturer's suggested price. In fact, AJ's did sell 10 tires to individual customers at prices that were well below the price suggested by Everlast. Everlast now argues that it is entitled to recover $1000 from AJ's. Is that true? If not, does the result seem fair? And if not, what are the simplest means by which Everlast could have arranged the resale of its tires so that it would be able to enforce the promise that AJ's made to Automotive Wholesaler?

9. Ann agreed to provide a car to Bruno in exchange for his promise to pay $8000 to her sister, Claire. Ann actually delivered the vehicle as promised, but Bruno refuses to pay any money to Claire. Is Claire entitled to compel Bruno to honour his undertaking? If not, does Ann have the right to recover the $8000 from Bruno? Is there anything that Ann can now do that would allow Claire to enforce Bruno's promise?

10. HAL Data Co delivered an expensive computer to Northeast Storage Ltd for safekeeping. The parties' contract contained this clause:

    Northeast Storage Ltd undertakes to use skill and care in the handling of all goods left with it for storage purposes. However, Northeast Storage Ltd shall not be held liable for more than $40 with respect to damage and loss, howsoever caused, to any goods left with it for storage purposes.

    Ivan, an employee of Northeast Storage, carelessly damaged the computer that HAL Data had left with Northeast Storage. Repairs to the computer will cost about $5000. HAL Data would like to recover that amount from either Northeast Storage or Ivan. Is Northeast Storage protected by the clause? Was that company entitled to allow its employee to handle HAL Data's computer, or was the storage company required to perform its contractual obligation by itself? If Northeast Storage was entitled to allow Ivan to handle the computer, is Ivan precluded by the doctrine of privity from taking advantage of the exclusion clause?

11. Hank and Dale Gribble were twin brothers who could not have been more different. Hank was an established personal trainer who led an exceptionally healthy lifestyle, whereas Dale had never worked a day in his life, smoked cigarettes and drank alcohol constantly, and ate fast food on a daily basis. Dale's doctor recently told him that if he did not change his ways, he would have a heart attack before his thirty-fifth birthday. Needless to say, Hank was extremely worried about his brother. He begged his brother to join a gym, but Dale refused to pay the outrageous fees. Hank was so troubled that he offered to be Dale's personal trainer and nutritionist for three nights per week in exchange for Dale's promise to quit smoking, drinking, and eating poorly. Hank was so sure he could make a difference in Dale's life that he promised to give up a week's wages to the Heart and Stroke Foundation (HSF) if Dale was not under 300 pounds by the end of the month. Dale was tired of listening to Hank nag, so he agreed to the arrangement.

    True to his word, Dale met with Hank three nights a week, but by the end of the first month, Dale was still well over 300 pounds. Coincidentally, Peggy, the area co-ordinator

    of the local HSF, overheard the brothers' initial agreement while working out one day. Since that time, she followed Dale's progress closely, and knew when the brothers did not meet their 300-pound goal. She approached Hank and asked him to make the contribution that he promised, but he refused. Hank claims that the agreement between him and Dale is unenforceable for lack of consideration. Is he correct? Can Dale enforce the agreement between him and his brother? Can Peggy enforce the agreement between Hank and Dale? Explain your answers.

12. Busy Conference Centre (BCC) owed Delish Catering Company $5000 for a conference Delish catered two weeks before. Delish, in turn, owed $3000 to Fresh Food Suppliers Inc (FFS). The owners of FFS refused to deliver any more produce to Delish until it received payment in full. Delish offered to assign $3000 of its accounts receivable from BCC to FFS, but FFS would only agree to the assignment if it was in writing. Without consulting a lawyer, Fern, a representative from Delish, wrote up the following agreement:

    For value received, the undersigned hereby assigns and transfers to Fresh Food Suppliers the right to $3000 that shall be due the undersigned from Busy Conference Centre under a contract for services rendered. Signed under seal this 23rd day of June 2002.

    Fern M. Dupelle

    In the week following the assignment, Delish broke a new contract with BCC by forgetting to cater an important business meeting. As a result, BBC was required to spend $5000 to hire another caterer to fill in at the last minute. In the interest of their ongoing business relationship, Delish and BCC agreed to settle the matter by balancing the $5000 accounts receivable with the $5000 liability under the catering contract. The day after reaching the settlement, BCC received notice from FFS concerning the $3000 assignment. BCC and Delish have both refused to make payment. FSS plans to use the written agreement to prove that there is a valid assignment under provincial statute. Will that argument succeed? Why or why not? How should FSS argue its case and against whom?

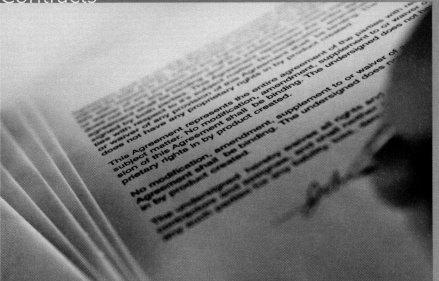

4 Representations and Terms

OBJECTIVES

After completing this chapter, you should be able to:

1. Identify pre-contractual and contractual statements.
2. Distinguish misrepresentations from other false statements made during contractual negotiations.
3. Identify the various circumstances when silence might amount to misrepresentation.
4. Explain the differences between innocent, fraudulent, and negligent misrepresentation.
5. Describe the legal effects of innocent, fraudulent, and negligent misrepresentation.
6. Outline the rules associated with proving the existence of express terms.
7. Summarize and apply the various judicial approaches to interpreting express terms.
8. Discuss when, how, and why a court might imply a term into a contract.
9. Describe the nature of ticket contracts.
10. Outline the advantages and disadvantages of standard form agreements.

We have considered how a contract is formed. Now we will consider the actual contents of a contract. To do this, we will examine the legal effect of statements made or adopted by parties in connection with their contracts. First, we will investigate statements made by the parties during the negotiation of a contract. Second, we will consider what happens when those statements turn out to be false. Third, we will consider how terms—provided both by the parties themselves and by legislators and courts—can be incorporated into a contract and how those terms will be understood. Fourth, we will consider the importance of standard form agreements in consumer transactions.

PRE-CONTRACTUAL AND CONTRACTUAL STATEMENTS

Because the communication of an offer and its acceptance can be accomplished in a number of ways, it is often difficult to assess the statements made during contract negotiations. Some contracts are made in writing, others are made orally, and a few arise through the parties' conduct. Written contracts can take the form of a signed document with a seal, or they can be much less formal, possibly a note or a letter or an order form. Since contracts can be made through different forms and different combinations of communication, it is sometimes difficult to identify which of the parties' statements are part of the actual contract and exactly how those statements should be understood. In other words, how does one identify the terms of a particular contract?

Determining which communications are part of a contract involves a process of elimination. We begin with the fact that not every statement communicated by a party during the negotiation process is a *contractual term*. A **contractual term** is a provision in an agreement that creates a legally enforceable obligation. By nature, it is a *promissory statement*. The person who makes it voluntarily agrees to do something in the future. Not every statement made during contract negotiations is promissory. Therefore, we must distinguish contractual terms, which are promissory, from *pre-contractual representations*, which are not. A **pre-contractual representation** is a statement one party makes by words or conduct with the intention of inducing another party to enter into a contract. By definition, it does not impose a contractual obligation. Although a pre-contractual representation may induce the creation of a contract, it does not form part of that contract. Figure 4.1 illustrates some of the differences between contractual terms and pre-contractual representations.

contracts can be made through the combination of different forms of communication

a **contractual term** is a provision in an agreement that creates a legally enforceable obligation

a **pre-contractual representation** is a statement one party makes by words or conduct with the intention of inducing another party to enter into a contract

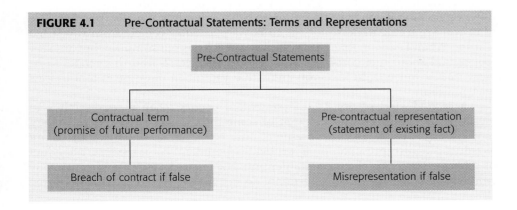

FIGURE 4.1   Pre-Contractual Statements: Terms and Representations

Pre-Contractual Statements

Contractual term (promise of future performance)

Pre-contractual representation (statement of existing fact)

Breach of contract if false

Misrepresentation if false

MISREPRESENTATION

The distinction between contractual terms and pre-contractual representations is especially important if a statement turns out to be untrue. If a non-contractual statement is false, we say that one of the parties has made a *misrepresentation*. When a contractual statement turns out to be false, we say that one of the parties is in *breach of contract*. That distinction is important because misrepresentation and breach of contract have different legal effects. Pre-contractual representations may result in a form of legal liability, such as actionable misrepresentation, but not in an action for breach of contract. In this section we will focus on misrepresentation.[1]

The Nature of Misrepresentation

A **misrepresentation** is a false statement of fact that induces the recipient to enter into a contract. As with other types of representations, it may induce a contract, but it does not form part of that agreement.

A misrepresentation is an incorrect statement of *existing* fact. It is false when it is made. In contrast, a contractual term is not meant to describe an existing state of facts, but rather it provides a promise of *future* performance. Given its promissory nature, a contractual term cannot be false when it is given. Nor can a breach of contract occur as soon as such a promise is made. A breach occurs only when one of the parties fails to perform precisely as promised.

Misstatement of Fact

Not every misstatement during pre-contractual negotiations is a misrepresentation. A misrepresentation occurs only if the speaker claimed to state a *fact*. That requirement occasionally creates difficulties because people sometimes communicate a number of non-factual statements during the negotiation process. For example, they sometimes state their own *opinions*. An **opinion** is the statement of a belief or judgment. For example, a person offers an opinion when they estimate the potential future revenue of an income-earning property. Opinions can range from carefree speculations to deliberate assessments based on a substantial body of evidence.

A personal opinion is not usually a misrepresentation even if it is inaccurate. Nevertheless, there are risks involved in offering opinions. If you state an opinion in a way that leads me to think that it *must* be true, a court may find that your statement includes not only an opinion but also an implied statement of fact that can be treated as a misrepresentation. That is true especially if you are known to have expertise in the subject of your opinion. It is also risky to offer an opinion if you have no reason to believe that it is actually true. Suppose that you are trying to persuade me to buy a particular vehicle from your used car lot. When I explain that I know nothing about gas consumption but am very concerned about fuel costs, you say, "I think that you'll find this model to be very thrifty, indeed." In fact, you know that the car in question is a notorious gas guzzler.

A second kind of non-factual statement occurs when a party claims to describe its **future conduct** or that of some third party. Such statements are not usually treated as misrepresentations. However, a statement of future conduct *is* a misrepresentation if it is made fraudulently or if the future conduct is described in terms of a present intention. For instance, to persuade me to buy your farm, you might say, "I certainly do not intend to sell the neighbouring

a misrepresentation is a false statement of fact that induces the recipient to enter into a contract

a misrepresentation is an incorrect statement of existing fact

to prove misrepresentation, one must be able to demonstrate that the speaker claimed to state some fact

an opinion is the statement of a belief or judgment

a personal opinion is not usually treated as a misrepresentation

a non-promissory statement as to a party's future conduct is not usually treated as a misrepresentation

---

[1.] We consider the remedies for breach of contract in Chapter 7.

land to Herb's Waste Management Company." That statement contains a indication of your *present* state of mind, and if it is inaccurate, it may be classified as a fraudulent misrepresentation.

People sometimes discuss the law during pre-contractual negotiations.[2] A misrepresentation does not arise merely because you inaccurately describe a particular *law itself*. We all are presumed to know the law. However, the court may find a misrepresentation if you inaccurately describe the *consequences of a law*, because those consequences are treated as a matter of fact rather than law. Suppose you are trying persuade me to buy your land. It is not a misrepresentation if you incorrectly tell me that zoning laws do not apply to the property. That is a matter of law. However, it may be a misrepresentation if you inaccurately tell me that zoning approval has been granted and that I therefore would be able to develop the land. That is a matter of fact.[3]

> a misrepresentation may arise from a statement regarding the consequences of a law, but not an inaccurate statement about a law itself

Concept Summary 4.1 shows that expressions of opinion, descriptions of future conduct, and statements of law—even when they are inaccurate and induce the creation of contracts—are not normally treated as misrepresentations. To prove misrepresentation in those circumstances, a party must prove that the speaker implicitly claimed to state some fact. It is often difficult to tell when a factual statement has been made. Consider the cases in Business Law in Action 4.1 and 4.2.

Concept Summary 4.1

Types of Pre-Contractual Statements Inducing Contracts

Non-factual statements (not actionable as misrepresentation)	Factual statements (actionable as misrepresentation)
Opinion based on speculation	Expert opinion
Description of another's future intent	Description of one's present intent
Statement of law	Statement of legal consequences

BUSINESS LAW IN ACTION 4.1

Statement of Fact or Opinion?[4]

An agent of Relax Realtors Inc is negotiating with a prospective purchaser of a strip mall. The purchaser is content with the building, price, zoning restrictions, and closing date. The only unresolved issue is that one of the current tenants in the mall has a 10-year lease, which will remain in effect even if the building is sold. The purchaser is reluctant to enter into a relationship with an unknown tenant for that length of time and therefore asks the real estate agent a series of questions about the tenant. In response, the real estate agent describes the person as "a most desirable tenant" and says only good things about the tenant. Taking these statements on faith, the purchaser decides to buy the strip mall. Six months after completing the real estate transaction, the purchaser finds out that the tenant's rent has been in arrears for several months. Upon further review of the financial statements given to the purchaser by the realtor, they discover that this was not the first time that the tenant had been in arrears.

Question for Discussion

1. Was Relax Realtor's description of the leaseholder as "a most desirable tenant" a statement of fact or opinion? Explain your answer.

---

2. Compare *Rule v Pals* [1928] 2 WWR 123 (Sask CA) and *Graham v Legualt* [1951] 3 DLR 423 (BC SC).

3. *Hopkins v Butts* (1967) 65 DLR (2d) 711 (BC SC).

4. *Smith v Land & House Property Corp* (1885) 28 ChD 7 (CA).

BUSINESS LAW IN ACTION 4.2

Statement of Fact or Future Conduct?[5]

During negotiations over a share purchase agreement, Tom states that he is willing to invest in the Unlucky Insurance Co only if it plans to: (i) open an office in Vancouver, and (ii) make him the company's medical consultant in that city before year-end. Unlucky Insurance Co agrees to Tom's conditions. Tom purchases the shares. Year-end comes, but the company has not fulfilled Tom's wishes. He sues for misrepresentation.

Question for Discussion

1. Was Unlucky Insurance Co's agreement to do business in Vancouver, with Tom as its consultant, a misrepresentation or merely a misstatement about its future conduct? Explain your answer.

Silence as Misrepresentation

parties generally are not required to disclose materials facts during pre-contractual negotiations

Difficulty can arise if a party remains silent on a particular issue. As a general rule, parties are not required to disclose material facts during pre-contractual negotiations, no matter how unethical non-disclosure may be. For example, the director of a corporation who knows certain facts that will increase the value of that company's shares in the very near future need not disclose those facts to a shareholder who is negotiating to sell shares to the director.[6] There are, however, at least four occasions when the failure to speak will amount to misrepresentation:

- when silence would distort a previous assertion
- when the contract requires a duty of utmost good faith
- when a special relationship exists between the parties
- when a statutory provision requires disclosure

an undisclosed change affecting the accuracy of a previous representation is a misrepresentation

When Silence Would Distort a Previous Assertion   A party's silence sometimes has the effect of falsifying previously true statements. When a change in circumstances affects the accuracy of an earlier representation, the party that made that statement has a duty to disclose the change to the other party. Failure to do so amounts to a misrepresentation.

Silence also distorts a previous representation if the whole truth is not told. Despite the right to remain silent, a party cannot give a *partial* account if the unspoken words would substantially alter the meaning of the actual statement, even if the actual words are literally true. Suppose you take your cotton shirts to the dry cleaner. You are asked to sign a claim ticket, which, the cleaner tells you, "excludes liability for damage caused to silk and crushed velvet during the dry cleaning process." That is true. But the ticket *also* excludes liability for any other damage to any kind of fabric. The half-truth is a misrepresentation.[7]

a half-truth may be a misrepresentation

When the Contract Requires a Duty of Utmost Good Faith   By their very nature, some contracts require a party to make full disclosure of the material facts. These are known as *contracts of utmost good faith*. The requirement of utmost good faith arises when one party is uniquely situated to know the material facts. For example, insurance rates are determined by calculating the likelihood of a

some contracts require a duty of utmost good faith

---

5. *International Casualty Co v Thomson* (1913) 11 DLR 634 (SCC).

6. *Prudential Insurance Co Ltd v Newman Industries Ltd* [1981] Ch 257.

7. *Curtis v Chemical Cleaning and Dyeing Co Ltd* [1951] 1 KB 805.

ETHICAL PERSPECTIVE 4.1

Misrepresentation and Silence[8]

Like practically every kid he grew up with, Johnny Grievor had always wanted to be a firefighter. There was only one problem. He was functionally blind in his left eye. Knowing that the city of Ottawa would not hire him if it knew about his visual impairment, Grievor applied to be a firefighter without disclosing his disability. He also remained silent about the fact that he had arranged a stand-in to take the required medical examination. On the basis of his résumé and the results of the medical taken by his stand-in, the city offered Grievor a position.

One day, while responding to a fire alarm, the fire truck that Grievor was driving collided with a van, killing two people. A short time later, the fire chief received an anonymous call indicating that Grievor was blind in his left eye. As a result, the city encouraged his resignation and subsequently had charges pressed against Grievor under the *Criminal Code*. Although he had resigned from the fire department, Grievor argued that the city was nonetheless obliged to pay his legal fees because the criminal charges stemmed from an event that took place while he was working. The city

claimed misrepresentation and argued that it therefore was not responsible for Grievor's legal fees even though the employment contract contained a clause requiring the city to pay for "any and all damages or claims for damages or injuries or accidents done or caused by [him] during the performance of [his] duties."

The court held that the failure to disclose his visual impairment amounted to a misrepresentation that *would have* justified Grievor's dismissal. However, because the city never terminated his contract, opting to accept his resignation instead, the city was obliged to pay his legal fees.

Questions for Discussion

1. Do you agree that Grievor had a duty to disclose his disability? Would these facts have given rise to misrepresentation if Grievor had not used a stand-in to pass his medical examination? Explain your answer.

2. Do you agree that the city should be required to pay Grievor's legal fees? What if circumstances were different and money was owing to the families of the car crash victims? Should the city be required to pay the families if Grievor cannot? Explain your answer.

specific kind of loss actually occurring. To assess the risk of insuring against that event, an insurance company needs to know a number of facts about the party seeking insurance. Since that party alone possesses full knowledge of the relevant facts, good faith requires the disclosure of all information associated with the risk so that the insurer can make an informed decision to accept or reject coverage. A failure to disclose all pertinent information, or any changes in previously supplied information, is usually treated as a misrepresentation.

When a Special Relationship Exists Between the Parties   When the relationship between two parties is one of trust, or when one of the parties has some other form of special influence over the other, a duty of disclosure may arise. Suppose your accountant is selling her cottage. If she sells it to a stranger, she is not obliged to disclose information about its structural defects if the purchaser does not ask the relevant questions. But she cannot remain silent if she is selling it to you. Because you would otherwise trust her on the basis of your special relationship, she has to fully disclose all material facts, whether or not you asked questions about the building's structure.

When a Statutory Provision Requires Disclosure   Some statutes require the disclosure of material facts in a contractual setting.

- Insurance legislation in many provinces contains statutory conditions that are deemed to be part of every insurance contract and must be printed on every policy. One condition requires the disclosure of perti-

---

8. *Ottawa (City) v Ottawa Professional Fire Fighters* (1985) 52 OR (2d) 129 (Div Ct).

nent information by those seeking insurance. Otherwise, the contract cannot be enforced.[9]

- Some financial officers have a duty to disclose material facts. If a director or officer of a corporation fails to disclose that they are a party to a material contract or have a material interest in a person who is party to a material contract, a court can set aside the contract.[10] The same holds true for some Crown corporations.[11] A similar disclosure requirement arises in the securities law.[12]

- Many provinces have legislation regulating the formation of domestic contracts. If a party failed to disclose significant assets or significant liabilities that existed when the domestic contract was made, the court can set aside the agreement or a provision in it.[13]

Inducement

actionable misrepresentation requires the deceived party to prove that the false statement induced the contract

For a statement to be actionable as misrepresentation, the deceived party must prove that the false statement induced the contract. In other words, the statement must produce a misunderstanding in the mind of its recipient that entices that person to enter into the agreement. The statement does not have to be the only inducing factor. A party can claim relief for misrepresentation even if other factors were also influential. However, a statement is not an inducement if its recipient conducts an independent inquiry as to its truth. After all, if the recipient does not rely on the truth of the statement, how can the statement induce the contract? If a false statement does not affect the recipient's decision even though it was intended to do so, it is not actionable as a misrepresentation.

What happens when the recipient of a false representation has an opportunity to test its accuracy, but fails to do so? Should that failure to investigate preclude a claim of misrepresentation?

YOU BE THE JUDGE 4.1

Failure to Investigate a Misrepresentation[14]

Hurd saw Redgrave's advertisement for the sale of a suburban residence and a share in a local law practice. Hurd requested information about the earning potential of the practice. Redgrave indicated that the annual income of the practice was £400. In support of that claim, he produced business summaries from the previous three years indicating receipts of about £200 per year. When asked about the source of the remaining income,

Redgrave produced boxes of papers and letters relating to additional business and allowed Hurd to inspect all of the accounts at his leisure. Although given the opportunity to do so, Hurd never bothered to inspect the documents. Relying instead on Redgrave's representations, Hurd agreed to buy the house and practice for £1600. Shortly after moving in, Hurd realized that the practice was utterly worthless.

Questions for Discussion

1. From a business perspective, do you think that it was

(continued)

---

9. For example, *Insurance Act*, RSBC 1996, c 226, s 126 (BC); RSO 1990, c I.8, s148 (Ont).

10. For example, *Bank Act*, SC 1991, c 46, s 206 (Can); *Credit Unions and Caisses Populaires Act, 1994*, SO 1994, c11, s 148 (Ont); *The Credit Union Act, 1985*, SS 1985, c C-45.1, s 74 (Sask).

11. *Financial Administration Act*, RSC 1985, c F-11, s 118 (Can).

12. *Securities Act*, RSO 1990, c S.5, s 75 (Ont); RSA 1981 c S-6.1, s 119 (Alta); RSBC 1996, c 418, s 85 (BC); RSM 1989, c S50, ss 50, 72 (Man).

13. For example, *Family Law Act*, RSO 1990, c F.3, s 56 (Ont); SNWT 1997, c 18, s 8 (NWT).

14. *Redgrave v Hurd* (1881) 20 Ch D 1 (CA).

(continued)

reasonable for Hurd to rely on Redgrave's representations about the income earning potential of the practice?

2. If you were the judge, would you allow Hurd to claim mis-

representation even though he did not bother to inspect the documents?

3. Would your decision be any different if Redgrave intentionally deceived Hurd and buried the actual accounts in boxes of irrelevant documents?

The Legal Consequences of Misrepresentation

There are two possible consequences of an actionable misrepresentation. The deceived party may receive:

- the remedy of rescission
- the right to damages

Rescission is the only *contractual* consequence of misrepresentation.

Rescission

Rescission is the cancellation of a contract with the aim of restoring the parties, to the greatest extent possible, to their pre-contractual state. It can be done by the parties or, if necessary, through the courts. However, it is often difficult to know in advance whether a court will grant rescission because it is a *discretionary remedy*, one that is not available *as of right*. The remedy is awarded on the basis of the court's judgment about what is best according to the rules of reason and justice.[15]

The remedy of rescission is often accompanied by an order for *restitution*. **Restitution** involves a giving back and taking back on both sides. Suppose you manufacture snowboards and need to order a steady supply of waterproof paints. A supplier represents that it has waterproof paints to sell but insists that you agree to purchase four shipments over the next two years to take advantage of the special rate. You agree to those conditions, requisition a cheque, and send it to the supplier. When the first shipment arrives, you discover that the paint is not waterproof and is therefore useless to you. You ask for your money back, but the supplier refuses. Assuming that the shipments of paint are worth thousands of dollars, it might be wise to seek an order of rescission from the courts rather than to simply announce your desire to disregard the contract. In this instance, merely setting aside the contract will not suffice. Since you transferred thousands of dollars in reliance on the supplier's representation that the paint is waterproof, you want your money back. Likewise, the supplier will not provide a refund unless you return the truckload of paint so that it can be resold. Consequently, the appropriate remedy will include an order for restitution. The supplier will be compelled to give back your money, and you will be compelled to give back the paint. By ordering restitution, the court restores both of you to your pre-contractual states.

The victim of a misrepresentation may be barred from rescission in certain circumstances. First, that is true if the misled party *affirmed* the contract. **Affirmation** occurs when the misled party declares an intention to carry out the contract or otherwise acts as though it is bound by it. To continue the earlier example, suppose you discover that the first shipment of paint is not waterproof but do nothing about it. Six months pass, and the next shipment arrives.

rescission is the cancellation of a contract by the court with the aim of restoring the parties, to the greatest extent possible, to their pre-contractual state

rescission is a discretionary remedy

restitution involves a giving back and taking back on both sides

affirmation occurs when the misled party declares an intention to carry out the contract or otherwise acts as though it is bound by it

---

15. *Wrights Canadian Ropes Ltd v Minister of National Revenue* [1946] 2 DLR 225 (SCC).

You then complain that neither shipment contained waterproof paint. Although the six-month *lapse of time* is not necessarily an affirmation, it certainly provides evidence that you affirmed the contract.[16]

courts are unlikely to grant rescission when restitution is not possible

Second, rescission may be barred if restitution is impossible. If the parties cannot be substantially returned to their pre-contractual positions, a court is reluctant to grant rescission. The more that has been done under the contract, the less likely a court is to grant rescission. To further continue our example, if you used a substantial portion of the paint supply before discovering that it was not, in fact, waterproof, restitution is not possible in a strict sense. You cannot give the paint back, so rescission may not be available either.

courts are unlikely to grant rescission when the rights of third parties are affected

Third, rescission may be unavailable if it would affect a third party. In this case, it is the rights of a third party that make restitution impossible. Suppose you buy a strip mall on the basis of certain representations about its earning potential. You lease portions of the mall to tenants but are unable to earn enough to pay down your mortgages on the building, let alone make anywhere near the profits you were promised. If you seek an order for rescission against the vendor of the mall, you would probably fail. The tenants have acquired a right to occupy the premises. Those third-party rights therefore preclude the court from forcing the vendor to give back your purchase price in exchange for an empty shopping mall.

Damages

damages are an award of money by a court that is intended to redress a wrongful event

Damages are an award of money by a court that is intended to redress a wrongful event. Note that damages are *not* a contractual consequence of misrepresentation. The victim of a misrepresentation can seek damages from a court only if the misrepresentation was either *fraudulent* or *negligent* in nature. In those cases, the deceived party's right to sue for damages flows not from the law of contract but from the law of tort. Tort law is based on the principle that "a person who by his or her fault causes damage to another may be held responsible."[17] Tort law is a separate topic and will be addressed in Unit III.

Types of Misrepresentation

The law distinguishes between three types of misrepresentation:

- innocent misrepresentations
- fraudulent misrepresentations
- negligent misrepresentations

The rules are somewhat different for each.

Innocent Misrepresentation

an innocent misrepresentation is a statement a person makes carefully and without knowledge of the fact that it is false

An **innocent misrepresentation** is a statement a person makes carefully and without knowledge of the fact that it is false. If the speaker is innocent of any fraudulent or negligent conduct, the general rule is that the deceived party is not entitled to recover damages. The only legal remedy available for innocent misrepresentation is rescission, and rescission is available only when there is a substantial difference between what the deceived party had bargained for and what was, in fact, obtained.

---

[16] *Leaf v International Galleries* [1950] 2 KB 86 (CA).

[17] *Canadian National Railway v Norsk Pacific Steamship* (1992) 91 DLR (4th) 289 (SCC).

Negligent Misrepresentation

Even a person who acts honestly may *carelessly or unreasonably* make a statement that is inaccurate and induces the creation of a contract. Such statements are known as **negligent misrepresentations**. Until recently, the law did not distinguish between innocent misrepresentations and negligent misrepresentations. Consequently, both can support the remedy of rescission. However, the courts have now recognized that a negligent misrepresentation may also amount to a tort that supports an award of damages.[18]

a **negligent misrepresentation** is a false, inducing statement made in an unreasonable or careless manner

Fraudulent Misrepresentation

The worst kind of misrepresentation is a *fraudulent misrepresentation*. A **fraudulent misrepresentation** occurs when a person makes a statement they know is false *or* that they have no reason to believe is true *or* that is reckless.[19] The courts are especially willing to rescind contracts that are induced by fraud. A fraudulent misrepresentation also supports an action for the tort of deceit.[20]

a **fraudulent misrepresentation** occurs when a person makes a statement they know is false *or* that they have no reason to believe is true *or* that is reckless

Concept Summary 4.2

Types of Misrepresentation and Their Legal Effect

	Elements of proof	Available remedies
Innocent misrepresentation	• false statement of fact or misleading silence • inducing contract	• rescission of contract
Negligent misrepresentation	• false statement • made in an unreasonable or careless manner • inducing a contract • causing a loss that is not always sufficiently remedied by rescission	• rescission of contract • damages in tort
Fraudulent misrepresentation	• false statement or misleading silence • made without honest belief in its truth • made with intent to induce contract • inducing contract • causing a loss not always sufficiently remedied by rescission	• rescission of contract • damages in tort

CONTRACTUAL TERMS

Having considered pre-contractual statements, we can now turn to statements that are actually part of an agreement. Unlike representations and misrepresentations, contractual terms arise from statements that actually impose obligations under the contract. We will consider two types of contractual terms:

- those expressed by the parties
- those implied by a court or statute

Express Terms

An **express term** is a statement made by one of the parties that a reasonable person would believe was intended to create an enforceable obligation.

an **express term** is a statement made by one of the parties that a reasonable person would believe was intended to create an enforceable obligation

---

[18.] Chapter 12 covers the tort of negligent misrepresentation.

[19.] *Derry v Peek* (1889) 14 App Cas 337 (HL).

[20.] Chapter 11 covers the tort of deceit.

Proof of Express Terms

When the contract is formed on the basis of an oral agreement, it is first necessary to determine what words were actually spoken. That is primarily a question of evidence. Written contracts produce different difficulties. For example, what if the formation of a contract involves the exchange of several conflicting documents? Which of the written provisions prevail?[21] Perhaps even more difficult is the situation that arises when a combination of written and spoken words are used during the formation of a contract. Which words best reflect the intentions of the parties? We consider each of these situations.

It is often difficult to prove the terms of a contract that was created orally. When an agreement is unwritten and unwitnessed, it usually comes down to a determination of whose account seems most credible. Still, most contracts do not have to be written. As long as there is no formal writing requirement and all of the other conditions of contract formation have been met, oral agreements are binding. Nevertheless, as a matter of risk management, it is usually a good idea for a business person to "get it in writing." Aside from issues of proof, the writing process encourages the parties to contemplate the terms more carefully.

If an agreement is written, oral evidence generally cannot be used to add to, subtract from, qualify, or vary the terms of the document.[22] That is known as the *parol evidence rule*. **Parol evidence**, in this context, refers to evidence that is not contained within the written contract. Knowledge of that rule is an important element of risk management. Business people often sign a written agreement on the assurance that some of its terms will not be enforced, or on the assurance that certain items discussed during negotiations are part of the deal even though they are not mentioned in the document. One should be extremely suspicious about such assurances. The parol evidence rule generally means that they are unenforceable.

There are several exceptions to the parol evidence rule. Parol evidence is admissible:

- to rectify or fix a *mistake* in a contractual document
- to prove that a contract was *never really formed* or is somehow *defective*
- to resolve *ambiguities* in the document
- to demonstrate that a document does not contain the parties' *complete agreement*

There is one other way around the parol evidence rule. This requires characterizing a statement that does not appear in the written agreement as a *collateral contract*, which stands independently beside the main contract. **A collateral contract** is a separate agreement one party makes in exchange for the other party's agreement to enter into the main contract. Suppose you want to buy oil of a certain quality. The seller's standard written contract contains a clause indicating that it *does not* warrant the quality of its oil.[23] You therefore offer to enter into a contract for the purchase of oil under the seller's standard form contract, but only if the seller enters into a collateral contract that *does* warrant the quality of the oil. You have avoided the parol evidence rule. The seller's promise regarding the quality of the oil is still inadmissible under the main contract. Nevertheless, it is enforceable as a separate agreement.

risk management suggests that agreements should be put in writing

parol evidence is evidence that is not contained within the written contract

the parol evidence rule generally precludes a court from enforcing assurances that are not contained in the written document

a collateral contract is a separate undertaking one person makes to another in consideration of that other person's entry into a formal contract

---

[21.] In Chapter 2, we discussed the possibility of the "battle of forms."

[22.] *Goss v Lord Nugent* (1833) 110 ER 713 at 715.

[23.] *LG Thorne & Co Pty Ltd v Thomas Borthwick & Sons (A'asia) Ltd* (1956) 56 SR (NSW) 81 at 94.

Concept Summary 4.3

Exceptions to the Parol Evidence Rule

Parol evidence is admissible to rectify a mistaken contractual document
Parol evidence is admissible to prove that a contract was never formed or is defective
Parol evidence is admissible to resolve contractual ambiguities
Parol evidence is admissible to demonstrate an incomplete agreement
Parol evidence rule is not applicable to collateral contract

Interpretation of Express Terms

Even if the parties agree on particular terms and write them into a document, they may disagree on the interpretation of those words if a dispute arises. Consider Business Law in Action 4.3.

BUSINESS LAW IN ACTION 4.3

Contractual Interpretation

It was Julia's twenty-fifth birthday, and she was about to be married to Robert. About an hour before the ceremony, Julia seemed a bit tense. To ease her through the event, Robert's wealthy mother, Fiona, handed Julia a one-page document, which contained the offer: "If you promise to go through with this today, I promise to pay you $1 000 000 on your thirty-fifth birthday, as long as the two of you do not remarry." Julia smiled and signed the document. She knew that the offer was a serious one. Despite the fact that Julia marched down the aisle with-

out a second thought, the marriage lasted only five years. Shortly after Julia's thirtieth birthday, Robert divorced her and went to "find himself" somewhere in the Himalayas.

Three years later, Robert found himself back in his hometown, slightly older and wiser. One night, while out with some of his friends, Robert saw a woman from across the bar and fell in love with her on the spot. It was Julia. After nearly two years of cautious, exclusive dating, they decided that they would get married again. Three weeks after exchanging their vows, Julia turned 35. Julia approached Fiona about her contractual promise to pay $1 000 000. Fiona refused to pay, arguing that Julia and Robert had breached the terms of the agreement.

Julia and Fiona agree that the contract contains the term "as long as the two of you do not remarry." However, they each have a different view of what that means. The term is **ambiguous**, having more than one plausible meaning. That is quite common. A great deal of contractual litigation turns on differences in interpretation. In resolving such disputes, the courts ask how a reasonable business person in the parties' position would have interpreted the relevant clause. Nevertheless, the issue can still be difficult. For the purposes of discussion, we can continue with the case.

> an ambiguous term has more than one plausible meaning

Fiona would likely take a **literal approach** to the words in the document and stress their *ordinary meaning*. She would argue that the contract plainly stated payment was due only if Julia and Robert did not remarry. By divorcing and then marrying each other again, they broke that condition.

> The literal approach assigns words their ordinary meaning

Julia would interpret the contract somewhat differently. She would take a *contextual approach*. The **contextual approach** goes beyond the four corners of the document by looking at the parties' intentions and their circumstances. Julia would argue that her mother-in-law's motive was to make sure that she and Robert got married and stayed married *to each other*. On that view, the term "as long as the two of you do not remarry" was meant to discourage Robert and

> the contextual approach goes beyond the four corners of the document by looking at the parties' intentions and their circumstances

Julia from marrying *other* people. And since they were married to each other on Julia's thirty-fifth birthday, they fell within the meaning of the contract.

Which of those two approaches is more plausible? If you are inclined to side with Fiona, you should also consider the *golden rule* of interpretation. According to the **golden rule**, words will be given their plain, ordinary meaning unless to do so would result in absurdity.[24] If we were to adopt a strict, literal reading of the term "so long as the *two* of you do not remarry," a strange result would follow. We would be forced to conclude that Julia should be paid even if she abandoned Robert and married someone else, as long as Robert remains unmarried on Julia's thirty-fifth birthday. Given Fiona's intention at the time she made the offer, such an interpretation would seem absurd. In this case, the golden rule suggests that we avoid a strict, literal interpretation.

Another possible reason for finding against Fiona is the *contra proferentem* rule. The **contra proferentem rule** ensures that the meaning least favourable to the author will prevail. That rule is justified by the fact that the author is in the best position to construct a term in a clear and unambiguous manner.

the **golden rule** says that words will be given their plain, ordinary meaning unless to do so would result in absurdity

the *contra proferentem* rule ensures that the meaning least favourable to the author will prevail

Implied Terms

Even if the parties carefully write out their agreement, that document may not contain all of the relevant terms. A contract may contain both express terms and *implied terms*. An **implied term** arises by operation of law, either through the common law or under a statute.

an **implied term** arises by operation of law, either through the common law or under a statute

Terms Implied by a Court

Unlike representations and express terms, implied terms do not arise from the parties themselves. They are inserted into a contract by the law. And since people are generally entitled to create their own agreements, a court will normally not imply a term unless it is necessary to implement the parties' presumed intentions. An implied term is "necessary" in this context if: (i) it is an obvious consequence of the parties' agreement, or (ii) business efficacy requires it.

Those two criteria often overlap. Suppose you are in the business of leasing equipment. A customer returns some leased equipment to you on time but in damaged condition. What if your contract did not expressly say anything about the condition of the equipment? That sort of term was presumably intended by both parties. After all, the whole point of a rental agreement is that the thing must be returned at the end of the lease. Consequently, a court will imply a term that requires the equipment to come back in the same condition in which it went out, subject to reasonable wear and tear.[25]

Courts are usually careful to imply a term only if it is reasonable to do so. That does not mean that a court will imply a term simply because it is reasonable or would improve the contract. Courts are not generally in the business of rewriting people's contracts. However, if a particular way of doing business has evolved over time into a generally accepted practice, that custom may be incorporated into a contract as long as it is not inconsistent with the parties' express agreement. Returning to the example, you rent equipment to a business that frequently leases the same kind of equipment. You can enforce the terms that are habitually used in such circumstances even though you never expressly mentioned them.[26]

a court will normally not imply a term unless it is necessary to implement the parties' presumed intentions

customary terms may be implied into an agreement

---

24. *Suncor Inc v Norcen Int Ltd* (1988) 89 AR 200 (QB).

25. *Con-force Prods Ltd v Luscar Ltd* (1982) 27 Sask R 299 (QB).

26. *British Crane Hire Corp Ltd v Ipswich Plant Hire Ltd* [1975] QB 303.

The courts sometimes imply a term on the basis of a contract's legal characteristics. Certain kinds of agreements, by their very nature, involve certain obligations, even if the parties did not intend them. The Supreme Court of Canada, for example, has held that an employment contract contains a term that requires the employer to provide reasonable notice before dismissing the employee, even if a contract is silent on the issue or even if the agreement expressly says that the employee can be dismissed without notice.[27]

a court may imply a term on the basis of a contract's legal characteristics

Terms Implied by Statute

Terms are often implied by statute. In Chapter 8, we will see several examples that arise under the *Sale of Goods Act*. Manitoba, the Northwest Territories, and the Yukon all have consumer protection acts, which imply a term that the goods being sold are new and unused, unless otherwise described.[28] In Alberta, Prince Edward Island, and Saskatchewan, legislation implies a term that farm machinery that is being sold is well designed and will function properly.[29] Whenever a statute implies a term into a contract, the term is incorporated without judicial intervention. If a dispute comes before the courts, the term is treated as if the parties expressly created it. In some cases, however, a statutory term will not apply if the parties have expressly excluded it.

Standard Form Agreements

The terms of many business transactions are dictated by *standard form agreements*. **Standard form agreements** are mass-produced documents usually drafted by the party in an economic position to offer certain terms on a "take-it-or-leave-it" basis. Standard form agreements are most often used for transactions that occur over and over again. A bank, for instance, does not want to negotiate a completely new contract every time it lends money to a customer. As a matter of risk management, it is better to use a model that has been refined over the years to avoid difficulties. Furthermore, it would be time consuming and expensive to allow each customer to negotiate new terms. And that additional cost would translate into higher interest rates. The same general principles apply to any business that enters into similar agreements on a repetitive basis.

standard form agreements are mass-produced documents usually drafted by a party who is in an economic position to offer those terms on a "take-it-or-leave-it" basis

There is a downside to standard form agreements. Such contracts are often so long and complex that few customers actually read and understand them. Furthermore, because they tend to be offered on a take-it-or-leave-it basis, customers have no realistic opportunity to bargain for better terms. How many times have you come across these sorts of agreements? Like most people, you probably do not even pretend to read them. You simply sign your name at the bottom. In a sense, you are at the mercy of the other party. If you refuse to accept to the standard terms, you cannot purchase the goods or services in question.

One type of term that customers are often required to accept in standard form agreements seeks to protect the other party from various sorts of legal liability. These are known as **exclusion clauses**, or *limitation clauses*, or *waivers*. For example, a company that is in the business of providing thrill-seekers with an adventure might try to use an exclusion clause to avoid lawsuits initiated by

exclusion clause is a contractual term that seeks to protect one party from various sorts of legal liability

---

[27.] *Machtinger v HOJ Industries* (1992) 91 DLR (4th) 491 (SCC). Employment contracts are discussed in Chapter 25.

[28.] RSM 1987, c C200, s 58 (Man); RSNWT 1988, c C-17 s 70 (NWT); RSY 1986, c 31, s 58 (Yuk).

[29.] *Farm Implements Act*, SA 1982, c F-4-1 (Alta); *Farm Implements Act*, RSPEI 1988, c F-4 (PEI); *Agricultural Implements Act*, RSS 1978, c A-10 (Sask).

customers who are accidentally injured during an adventure. Such a term is perfectly legitimate if these three things can be demonstrated:

- First, the term must have been drafted in clear, *unambiguous language*. If an exclusion clause is ambiguous, it will be interpreted as strictly and literally as possible and will be accorded the meaning least favourable to its author.

- Second, the party against whom the exclusion clause is meant to operate must be given *reasonable notice* of the term and its effect.

- Third, it must be shown, by signature or otherwise, that the party against whom the exclusion clause is meant to operate *agreed* that the exclusion clause is part of the contract.

Although an exclusion clause will not be invalidated merely because of an inequality of bargaining power, the courts will take into account any such imbalance when determining whether the weaker party *truly* agreed to incorporate the clause into the contract.

Ticket Contracts

terms should be brought to the customer's notice when the contract is made or beforehand

Standard form agreements sometimes take the form of a ticket or receipt. As a business person, you might try to incorporate certain terms, including exclusion clauses, into your contract by having them printed on the back of a ticket you issue to your customers. Whether that is valid depends on how those terms are presented. As with exclusion clauses, the general rule is that the terms must be brought to the customer's notice either before or when the contract is made. As usual, the question is not whether the customer actually read those terms, but whether they were given *reasonable notice*. If the reasonable person would not have known about the printing on the back of the ticket, then the customer probably will not be bound by those terms. On the other hand, if the customer knew that the back of the ticket contained terms, those terms will be incorporated into the contract, even if the customer chose not to read them.

Standard Form Agreements

Friedrich has a small book store in Fredericton. Having decided to broaden his horizons, he registered the Internet domain name <www.friedrichsbooks.ca> and hired a Web design consultant to help him set up his page for e-commerce. Because he will now be offering books for sale worldwide, Friedrich wants to be sure that his standard purchase contract includes several key terms. In particular, he would like to have a "no refund" policy and a requirement that all payments are to be made in Canadian currency. Friedrich's consultant has offered him a choice of three design layouts for an electronic catalogue that would be the equivalent of 19 pages in a paper document.

The first layout is a very long, one-page catalogue. Rather than having page breaks signifying the end of each paper page equivalent, the customer scrolls through the electronic catalogue by clicking on the scroll bar. The "no refund" policy

and the Canadian currency requirement are found somewhere in the middle of the catalogue. At the bottom of the catalogue is an electronic order form, which allows the customer to enter the desired book titles. Once the customer has completed the form, all that is left to do is click on the "order now" button, at which point the purchase request is sent to Friedrich electronically. With this layout, the customer has the opportunity to view the "no refund" policy and the Canadian currency requirement but could, accidentally or on purpose, miss them entirely and place an order without being aware of those terms.

The second layout has a much more elegant design. It has the appearance of an all-in-one page design, but the entire catalogue is accessible from a single screen and does not require the customer to scroll through the document. Instead, access to all of the same text is available through hyperlinks. By clicking on specific icons, the customer can *(continued)*

(continued)

choose which information to view. One icon in this layout is labeled "terms & conditions." If the customer clicks on it, the "no refund" policy, Canadian currency requirements, and other key terms appear on the screen. Another icon is the "order now" button. Customers can access it whether they have clicked on the terms and conditions hyperlink or not.

The third layout is similar to the second except that it is more cumbersome. It requires customers to click on the "terms & conditions" icon. It also requires them to answer "yes" when asked, "Have you read the terms and conditions and do you agree to them?" Once they have done so, they are then required to answer "yes" a second time when asked,

"Are you sure?" That mechanism makes it virtually impossible for customers to place orders without being aware of the existence of Friedrich's terms and conditions.

Questions for Discussion

1. Which of these layouts will ensure that Friedrich's terms will be incorporated into the contract? Explain your answer.

2. From a business perspective, which layout would you recommend to Friedrich? Why?

3. Are there any other terms that Friedrich should incorporate into the standard contract to help the success of his new worldwide business venture?

Signed Forms

As a general rule, people who sign a standard form agreement are bound by all of the terms expressed in it, even if they have not actually read or understood the contract. Although that rule may seem harsh, there is a rationale for it. By signing a document, a customer indicates a willingness to be bound by its terms; the party on the other side of the agreement is entitled to rely on that appearance.

Many standard form agreements are, however, extremely long and complicated. A judge therefore may apply an exception to the general rule if the customer is required to quickly sign the document without enjoying a reasonable opportunity to study its terms. In such circumstances, there is a heavy onus on the party relying on the document to prove that the customer was given reasonable notice of its relevant terms. That exception prevents a more powerful party from burying onerous or unusual terms in the small print of a difficult document.

> a person who signs a standard form agreement is generally bound by all of the terms expressed in it

CASE BRIEF 4.1

Tilden Rent-a-Car Co v Clendenning (1978) 83 DLR (3d) 400 (Ont CA)

While filling out a car rental application at the Vancouver airport, Mr Clendenning was asked by the rental agent whether he wanted to purchase collision insurance for an additional, modest fee. After agreeing to pay extra, Clendenning was handed a complicated rental contract. Being in a hurry, he signed the document without reading it. The rental agent neither asked him to read the contract nor mentioned that it included an unusual term that excluded insurance coverage if the driver had consumed *any* amount of alcohol.

During the rental period, Clendenning got into an accident and damaged the vehicle. He admitted to drinking a small quantity of alcohol that day, but it was unclear exactly how much he had consumed. Not having read the agreement, Clendenning was unaware of the term that excluded coverage if *any* alcohol was consumed. That term did not appear on the face of the contract; but it was found on the back in small print. Clendenning claimed he was led to believe that the insurance provided complete coverage. Tilden, on the other hand, argued that Clendenning's signature was sufficient to bind him to the terms of the contract. Tilden also claimed that Clendenning's previous dealings with Tilden provided him with ample opportunity to read the terms of the contract despite the fact that he signed it that day in a hurry.

The Court of Appeal held that Clendenning's signature did *not* represent a true acceptance of the terms in the contract. Because the relevant term was onerous and unusual, Tilden was required to provide Clendenning with reasonable notice of it as well as a reasonable opportunity to understand and appreciate what he was signing.

Standard form agreements such as the one signed by Mr Clendenning are often complex documents containing clauses drafted in confusing legal language and typeset in fine print. Standard form agreements often contain several *boilerplate* provisions that give rise to various legal consequences. Boilerplate provisions often allocate the legal risks incurred by people doing business and therefore play a crucial role in determining the nature of the relationship between contracting parties, including their potential liabilities to each other and to third parties. The appendix to this chapter contains a survey of some significant boilerplate provisions.

Chapter Summary

Not every statement made during pre-contractual negotiations becomes a contractual term. Pre-contractual representations are assertions of fact made with the intention of inducing another party to enter into a contract, though they form no part of the contract. Contractual terms, on the other hand, are provisions in an agreement that create legally enforceable obligations. If necessary, a court will determine whether a statement is a representation or a term, based on what a reasonable person would have understood the statement to mean with respect to the party's intentions.

A misrepresentation is a false pre-contractual statement that induces the recipient of the statement to enter into a contract. Inaccurate expressions of opinion, descriptions of future conduct, and statements of law are normally not treated as misrepresentations. To prove misrepresentation in those circumstances, a party must prove that the speaker implicitly claimed to state some fact. Silence can amount to misrepresentation if: (i) remaining silent distorts a previous assertion, (ii) the contract requires the utmost good faith, (iii) a special relationship exists between the parties requiring disclosure, or (iv) a statutory provision requires disclosure.

For a false statement to be actionable misrepresentation, the deceived party must be able to prove that it induced the contract. The two possible consequences of an actionable misrepresentation are: (i) the remedy of rescission, and (ii) the right to damages. The remedy of rescission usually coincides with restitution, requiring a giving back and taking on both sides. Its aim is to return the parties to their pre-contractual state. Rescission may be barred if: (i) the misled party ultimately affirms the contract, (ii) restitution is not possible, or (iii) a third party's rights are affected. Damages are an award of money meant to compensate the loss suffered by the misled party due to the misrepresentation. They are available in some circumstances under the law of tort.

An innocent misrepresentation involves a statement made carefully and without knowledge that it is false. A negligent misrepresentation is a false statement made in an unreasonable or careless manner. A fraudulent misrepresentation is made without any belief in its truth or with reckless indifference. All three types of misrepresentation can give rise to rescission. Only fraudulent and negligent misrepresentation can give rise to tort damages.

An express term, whether oral or written, is a statement intended to create a legally enforceable obligation. When an agreement has been reduced to writing, the parol evidence rule states that oral evidence is inadmissible to vary or qualify the written contract unless it will: (i) help rectify a mistaken document, (ii) determine whether a contract is defective, (iii) resolve contractual ambiguities, or (iv) demonstrate an incomplete agreement. Parol evidence can also be used to demonstrate the existence of a collateral contract.

Courts use several approaches to resolve business disputes over the interpretation of contractual terms. The literal approach assigns words their ordinary meaning. The contextual approach takes into account the parties' intentions, as well as the surrounding circumstances. The golden rule suggests that words be given their plain meaning unless doing so would result in absurdity. Courts imply a term only if it is necessary to implement the parties' presumed intentions. Some statutes imply certain terms into particular types of contract.

Standard form agreements are mass-produced documents drafted by the party who is in an economic position to offer those terms on a take-it-or-leave-it basis. A person who signs a standard form agreement is generally bound by its terms, whether or not they ever read or understood those terms. Courts require that the existence of onerous or unusual terms in a standard form agreement be brought to the attention of the other party to be effective.

Review Questions

1. Distinguish between a pre-contractual representation and a contractual term, giving examples of each. Why is that distinction important?

2. Define "misrepresentation" in your own words. Can a statement be a misrepresentation if neither party is aware that the statement is false? What must one be able to demonstrate to prove misrepresentation?

3. What is the difference between a misrepresentation and a breach of contract?

4. Name three types of false statements that are often made during the course of negotiations that are not misrepresentations. Give an example of each.

5. Provide examples of the four circumstances in which the failure to speak will amount to misrepresentation.

6. What are two possible legal consequences of an actionable misrepresentation? Which of those possibilities provides a contractual remedy?

7. What is meant by the term "rescission"?

8. List three circumstances that may preclude the victim of a misrepresentation from seeking restitution. Why is restitution unavailable in these circumstances?

9. What is an express term? Why is it sometimes difficult to determine the meaning of an express term?

10. What is meant by the term "parol evidence"?

11. Why is it important for business people to know and understand the parol evidence rule?

12. When is a contractual term ambiguous? Describe how courts resolve disputes over ambiguous terms.

13. What is the difference between the literal approach and contextual approach to contractual interpretation?

14. State and explain the golden rule of interpretation.

15. State and explain the *contra proferentem* rule.

16. What is an implied term?

17. When will a court find that a contract contains an implied term? When will a court be reluctant to do so?

18. Briefly describe the significance of the standard form agreement in modern commercial transactions.

19. When is it irrelevant that a standard form agreement was signed?

20. When might it be appropriate for a business to design and use a ticket contract? What is the general rule about such agreements?

Cases and Problems

1. Seymour is a supplier of custodial cleaning products. While negotiating a contract to sell a crate of floor wax, Seymour makes the following statements. Categorize each statement as: (i) a pre-contractual representation, (ii) a mere opinion, (iii) a contractual term, or (iv) a collateral contract. Give reasons for your answer and describe the legal effect of each statement.

   a. "This floor wax is the best made anywhere in the world."
   b. "I personally truly believe this floor wax is the best made anywhere in the world."
   c. "Studies have shown that this floor wax is the best made anywhere in the world."
   d. "If, after trying this floor wax, you don't agree that it is unquestionably the best made anywhere in the world, I'll come polish your floors myself for a month."
   e. "If, after trying this floor wax, you don't agree that it is unquestionably the best made anywhere in the world, I'll eat my hat."

2. Alex is planning a group-hiking expedition in the Canadian Rockies. He decides that the group will need to hire a guide since most of its members are not experienced hikers. Alex approaches the owner of Roma's Hiking Village and asks her to supply an experienced guide. Because all of her local guides are already booked, Roma recommends her friend Dima. Dima is a well-known Himalayan trekker who happens to be visiting Canada. When Alex inquires whether Dima is qualified to lead a group through the Canadian Rockies, Roma replies, "He's no slouch. In my opinion he is the best trekker in the Himalayas." On the basis of her recommendation, Alex enters into a contract to hire Dima. It turns out that Dima had never toured the area and was unable to locate the campsite on two of the four days of the trip. Upon their return, Alex demands his money back. Roma refuses, arguing that she never held Dima out as someone who was familiar with the particular area. Do you think that Alex will be successful in proving that Roma made a material misrepresentation that induced the contract?

3. Ziggy purchased some farmland and a small farmhouse with the aim of growing tobacco. After a very successful first season, he realized that he should insure his business. He contacted Farmers Choice Insurance Ltd. Simone, a broker for Farmers Choice, appraised Ziggy's farm and set up the policy. Ziggy paid for the entire year's insurance upfront. Two months after the policy took effect, a fire destroyed the entire crop. Although the cause of the fire

could not be determined, Ziggy put in a claim for the damage incurred. After its investigation, Farmers Choice refused to pay Ziggy's insurance claim, stating that it was previously unaware of these facts:

a. Ziggy had suffered a previous loss by fire.
b. Ziggy's wife had previously been convicted of fraud and had served time in a penitentiary.
c. A fire insurance policy issued by another insurance company had previously been cancelled prior to its expiration date.
d. Ziggy's wife admittedly had enemies and there was therefore a danger of arson.
e. Ziggy was a chronic alcoholic and, although never proven, it was suspected that the previous fire had been caused by a still exploding in Ziggy's basement.

Simone admits that she did not specifically ask Ziggy any questions pertaining to those facts. Will Farmers Choice be able to avoid its contract with Ziggy altogether? Should the original contract stand even if no payment is to be made on this particular claim?

4. Navinder decided to list her summer cottage for sale at a price of $130 000. Nancy, a prospective purchaser, asked Navinder whether she knew anything about its current market value. Navinder indicated that although it had not recently been appraised, the cottage was originally built for $50 000 on land for which she paid $25 000. She indicated that a professional builder had made a number of improvements to the cottage, thereby increasing its value. These included a second-storey loft with two bedrooms and a new bathroom. Navinder stated that the addition added $25 000 to the resale value of the cottage. She also mentioned that a professional landscaper had been hired at a cost of $2500 to finish the property and that she had purchased one acre of undeveloped land on either side of the property at a total cost of $30 000. On that basis, Navinder claimed that the cottage was worth $132 500. Although Nancy loved everything about the cottage, she was somewhat skeptical of Navinder's valuation. Nancy hired Al's Appraisals to determine the value of the property. Al provided a written appraisal at $129 750. Nancy decided to buy the cottage at the listed price. A few months later, Nancy's insurance company reappraised the house for insurance purposes at $82 000. Nancy was astounded. She hired a third appraiser, who provided a detailed report proving beyond the shadow of a doubt that the entire property was worth no more than $85 000. Can Nancy successfully sue Navinder for misrepresentation? Is there any other possible legal means for Nancy to recoup her losses?

5. Antonio and Susanna have decided to leave the big city. They arrange to purchase a large country inn from Jay Jonah Investments Inc. According to the terms of their contract, Antonio and Susanna agree to transfer ownership of their house in the city and to pay Jay Jonah Investments an additional monthly mortgage of $2000 for 24 months in exchange for the country inn. Several months after the deal closed, Antonio and Susanna learned that the representations made about the potential earnings of the country inn were clearly false. They therefore refuse to make any further mortgage payments. In the meantime, Jay Jonah had demolished their house to build a condomini-um complex. Assuming that Antonio and Susanna can prove that they were induced to contract by misrepresentation, what remedy do you think that a court should grant?

6. Mac's Machines Ltd, an importer of high-tech German industrial equipment, had an ongoing shipping arrangement with Take Care Tankers Inc. According to Clause 4 of Take Care Tankers' standard form agreement:

"Subject to express instructions in writing given by the customer, Take Care Tankers reserves to itself complete freedom in respect of means, routes, and procedures to be followed in the handling and transportation of the goods."

Although the parties had done business before on several occasions, a representative from Mac's telephoned Take Care Tankers to request that a particular shipment of machines be stored below deck. Although the machines were usually transported in waterproof plastic containers that were amenable to deck transportation, the shipment in question was packaged in wooden crates and was therefore susceptible to rust if left on deck. The shipping manager at Take Care Tankers assured the Mac's representative over the phone that the special arrangement would be no problem. Despite that promise, the shipment was inadvertently stored on deck. During the voyage, the crate fell overboard, and the machines were lost at sea. On the basis of the telephone call, Mac's claims that Take Care Tankers was not merely negligent but also in breach of contract. Relying on Clause 4 of its standard form agreement, Take Care Tankers claims that the oral assurances made over the telephone were not part of the contract. Leaving aside the issue of negligence, apply your understanding of the parol evidence rule to determine how a court would resolve the contract issue in this case.

7. Sperry Rand makes farm machinery. To promote its products, Sperry published a sales brochure that includes the following representations:

You'll fine-chop forage to one centimetre season after season! You'll harvest over 45 tonnes per hour with ease. Under test conditions, the big New Holland harvesters have harvested well over 60 tonnes per hour. And Micro-Shear cutting action gives you a choice of crop fineness—from one to six centimetres.

Induced by the brochure, John decided to buy one of Sperry's machine from a third-party dealer. As a result of the failure of the machine to live up to its description in the brochure, John lost his entire season's crop. Aiming to recover damages for breach of contract, John attempted to sue the dealership. Unfortunately the dealership had gone bankrupt. John decided that he would try to sue Sperry Rand. Assume that his contract with the dealership excluded any possible tort liability against Sperry Rand. Does John have a contractual remedy against Sperry? Is the parol evidence rule relevant to your determination?

8. Paula's Pets has developed a standard form agreement for its employees. Having had problems in the past with employee absenteeism, Paula's Pets has included a term in its employment contracts stating that an employee shall not miss more than five work days per year subject to

statutory holidays, illness, and the like. Another clause in the agreement provides for a leave of absence in the case of a death in the family:

> All full-time employees of Paula's Pets are entitled to a compassionate leave of absence for the bereavement of a loved family member.

Randall, a full-time employee, decided to take a week off work after his dog was hit and killed by a train. In response to the employer's charge of absenteeism, Randall stated that his employment contract provides for a compassionate leave for "the bereavement of a loved family member." Randall believed that this included his dog; his employer claimed that the contractual term applies only to human family members. Using the various approaches to interpretation, build the best possible argument in favour of each interpretation.[30]

9. Clinton was 14 years old when his mother entered into a written agreement with the county library on his behalf. According to the agreement, Clinton would obtain full borrowing privileges and his mother would become "responsible for any fines, loss or damage occasioned by the use of the library card." Shortly after Clinton lost his library card, a stranger used it to borrow more than 30 items. Those items were never returned. The county library issued a bill to Clinton's mother for $1570, the replacement value of those items. Do you think Clinton's mother should have to pay? How might the library have better managed its affairs?

10. The Upper Crust Academy, an exclusive boarding school, has inserted the following clause into its standard form agreement.

> The parents of _____ hereby authorize the Principal to ensure that said child shall receive a proper social and academic education in accordance with the highest standards of personal conduct and that said child will be kept free from danger while in the custody of Upper Crust Academy.

Like everyone else whose child attended the academy, Manjunath's parents signed the agreement. One evening, Manjunath was returned to the academy by the local police after he was found stealing pylons off the street. In addition to the mischief he caused in the streets, Manjunath was in breach of the curfew rule at the academy. After unsuccessfully attempting to contact Manjunath's parents by phone, the principal decided to sentence Manjunath to 20 hours of peeling potatoes in the academy kitchen to dissuade him from repeating such inappropriate behaviour. When his parents found out that the potato peeling had caused Manjunath to develop unsightly calluses on his hands, they quickly removed their darling son from the academy. The principal of the academy responded by issuing a bill for the remainder of the year's tuition plus an additional fee for boarding. The academy claims that the disciplinary action taken by the principal was within its contractual rights. Manjunath's parents dis-

agree. Given that the agreement makes no specific mention of discipline, how could the principal persuade a court to side with the academy? Explain your reasoning.

11. Abby ordered a new boat through Sporto Yachts Ltd. After a delay of 15 months, the manufacturer finally delivered the boat to Sporto. Although Abby was initially impressed with the boat, his attitude changed after the dealer told him that the manufacturer was demanding an additional payment of $28 155 over the original purchase price. Realizing that his vigorous protest was not helping and worried that he would not otherwise be able to embark on his long-planned journey, Abby paid the additional amount. Once he got possession of the boat, he sued Sporto for the return of the extra payment.

Sporto defended the additional fee on the basis of a "price change" clause in the original purchase agreement. That clause said that since the boat manufacturer reserved the right to change its price, Abby was liable pay the additional amount to the dealer upon delivery of the vessel. That clause allowed Abby to terminate the sale, but it also said that if Abby accepted delivery, he was required to pay the higher amount. Although Abby had been given a copy of the agreement, he claims that he never noticed the clause, which was buried in the fine print on the flip side of the document. He remembers that on the day he signed the contract, there was a line of people at Sporto's counter. According to Abby, there really was no time to read it over. In any event, the salesperson actually dissuaded him from reading it, indicating that the fine print on the back pertained only to the warranty and not to the cost of the boat. Does Abby stand a chance of getting his money back? How might management at Sporto Yachts have avoided this dispute?

12. Achmed was about to buy a used car. The used car dealer showed him a flashy red four-door sedan. Achmed explained to the dealer that he had very few preferences about the colour or model; his only concern was the car's safety record. The dealer reassured him by saying that he only sells reconditioned cars that are perfectly safe. Achmed expressed specific concerns about the brakes. The dealer told Achmed that his mechanic had replaced the brakes on all four wheels just two days before. After taking the car for a short test drive, Achmed agreed to buy it. The dealer presented Achmed with a standard form agreement containing this clause:

> It is agreed by both parties that there is no representation, warranty, collateral agreement, or condition affecting this agreement other than as expressed herein in writing.

Achmed read through the document and signed it. Two weeks later, Achmed was badly injured in an accident after his brakes failed. Achmed's insurance company had the car inspected by a mechanic who was willing to testify that there was no way the brakes had recently been redone and that the brakes could not possibly have been in a safe condition two weeks earlier. On that basis, Achmed sued the used car dealer. Is there any way for Achmed to win, despite having read, understood, and signed the entire agreement clause?

Appendix 4A

Boilerplate Terms

Standard form agreements often include a number of *boilerplate terms.* A **boilerplate term** is a standard provision that can be reused in various contractual settings in a virtually unchanged form. Boilerplate clauses often help to provide a framework for commercial agreements. Without them, many of the parties' substantive rights that are contained in an agreement would have little meaning. Lawyers have come to rely on boilerplate terms to satisfy clients who require contracts to be drafted in a hurry at as little expense as possible. Because they play such an important role in many business transactions, we will briefly consider some of the more common types of boilerplate terms:

- exclusion clauses
- *force majeure* clauses
- confidentiality clauses
- arbitration clauses
- jurisdiction clauses
- entire agreement clauses

Exclusion Clauses

Many standard form agreements contain exclusion clauses, terms that are designed to protect one party from various sorts of legal liability. (An example of an exclusion clause is on the following page.) Exclusion clauses may be perfectly legitimate as long as they meet the certain requirements. See the section on exclusion clauses in this chapter.

A difficult question arises if the party trying to rely on an exclusion clause acted in a way that deprived the other party of substantially the whole benefit of a contract. Suppose you own a factory and enter into a contract with a security company to patrol your building on a regular basis. The security company's standard form contract excludes liability against "burglary, theft, fire, or any other cause." Although these are the very things that you are seeking to avoid in your decision to hire security, you figure that the low monthly fee makes the risk of agreeing to exclude liability seem reasonable. While making the required rounds one day, the security guard decides to light a small fire, which eventually burns out of control and destroys your entire factory. Should the security company be able to take advantage of the exclusion clause, even though it failed to perform the fundamental term of the contract—to secure, rather than to destroy, your factory? To allow the security company to rely on the clause seems unjust, since it was the security company's misperformance of the contract that ultimately deprived you of its entire benefit.

The Supreme Court of Canada has held that an exclusion clause should generally be enforced according to its true meaning, even if the party relying on the exclusion clause has failed to live up to its end of the bargain and thereby deprived the other party of substantially the whole benefit to be obtained under the contract. However, it also held that an exclusion clause will not be enforced if it is "unconscionable" or if it would be "unfair or unreasonable" to enforce the exclusion clause.[31]

[31.] *Hunter Engineering Co v Syncrude Canada Ltd* (1989) 57 DLR (4th) 421 (SCC).

Exclusion Clause
The Great Canadian Adventure Company

The Great Canadian Adventure Company:

I, _____, hereby acknowledge and agree that in my participation in adventure activities by The Great Canadian Adventure Company:

1. I will not hold The Great Canadian Adventure Company, its officers, directors and employees responsible for any injury, death, accident, illness, delay, personal loss, personal property damage or other loss sustained by me and hereby release The Great Canadian Adventure Company, its officers, directors and employees due to any cause whatsoever, including without limitation, negligence on the part of The Great Canadian Adventure Company or its employees. I further agree to indemnify The Great Canadian Adventure Company and its employees for any and all legal fees (on a solicitor and his own client basis) or costs which may be incurred in defending any lawsuit or claim I may bring against them.

2. AND I DO HEREBY ACKNOWLEDGE AND AGREE THAT:

   (a) I will participate in adventure activities entirely at my own risk. Participation in any outdoor activity and travel in natural, outdoor environments involve inherent risks, dangers and hazards. These risks may include, but are not limited to: natural disasters, forces of nature, weather conditions, rugged or steep terrain, avalanches, rock fall, slippery footing, water, isolation from medical facilities, difficult evacuation, equipment failure, mechanical breakdown, human error and accidents. These and other risks may cause serious injury, illness, death, personal property damage or personal losses.

   (b) That this Waiver of all Claims, Release from Liability and Assumption of Risk is binding on myself, my heirs, my executors, administrators, personal representatives and assigns.

   (c) That the term "adventure activities" as used in the Waiver of all Claims, Release from Liability and Assumption of Risk includes without limiting the generality of that term, training sessions, programmes and events that are in any way authorized, sanctioned, organized or operated by The Great Canadian Adventure Company.

   (d) I understand that by signing this release I may be forever prevented from suing or otherwise claiming against The Great Canadian Adventure Company, its officers, directors and employees for certain loss or damages, whether for property loss or personal injury, that I may sustain while participating in adventure activities.

   (e) I understand that the included itinerary is a general guideline of what can be expected on my adventure trip, but is NOT a contract. Factors such as weather conditions, mechanical breakdown, flight cancellations, medical emergencies, political unrest, natural disasters or other uncontrollable circumstances can alter my trip.

   (f) I will not hold The Great Canadian Adventure Company responsible for extra costs incurred by me which include, but are not limited to: extra meals, personal costs, or rebooking of commercial transportation in the event of unforeseen or uncontrollable circumstances.

I confirm that I have carefully read this agreement and understand its terms as acknowledged by my signature below.

Dated at _____ on _____, 20___. Participant's Name:_____
Participant's Signature:_____

Witness's Name:_____ Witness's Signature:_____

* Minors, under 18 years old, must have parent or legal guardian witness the form. Note: All participants in your party are required to read and sign a waiver before a booking/reservation can be confirmed. All waiver forms must be witnessed and dated. Any participants under 18 years old must also have their parent or legal guardian sign the waiver.

a *force majeure* clause aims to protect the parties when part of the contract cannot be performed because of some event that is outside their control

Force Majeure Clauses

Another way for the parties to limit their potential liability is through the use of a *force majeure* clause. *Force majeure* literally means a superior or irresistible force, such as a flood, stormy weather, or war. A ***force majeure* clause** aims to protect the parties when part of the contract cannot be performed because of some event that is outside of their control and could not have been prevented by their exercise of due care. Sound risk-management principles dictate the use of such clauses. Unlike exclusions clauses, which ought to be drafted as narrowly as possible, an effective *force majeure* clause will be drafted as broadly as possible to include as many unpredictable events as are imaginable.

```
Force Majeure Clause
O'Brien's Encyclopedia of Forms[32]
Where the Seller is unable to make delivery of any portion of the Items
covered by this contract due to a labour dispute, accident, fire, war,
government regulation or any cause whatsoever beyond the control of the
Seller, the Seller shall not be liable for such liability to make deliv-
ery if, within a reasonable time, it notifies the Buyer by prepaid post
of the cause of such inability and that the contract for the undelivered
portion of the Items is cancelled or that it will make delivery of such
Items at a future date to be named in the notice of and the Buyer may
within _____ days after the date of mailing such notice, notify the
Seller by prepaid post that it will accept the delivery of the Items pur-
suant to the terms of the Seller's notice or cancel the undelivered por-
tion of the contract but upon the Buyer's failure to so notify the Seller
the undelivered portion shall be cancelled.
```

Confidentiality Clauses

a confidentiality clause prevents disclosure of certain information about the agreement to third parties

In many business transactions, one or both parties want to prevent the disclosure of certain information to third parties. Business people generally do not want competitors or other customers to learn about such things as payment schedules, business operations, or trade secrets. When confidential treatment is warranted, the parties might chose to include a **confidentiality clause**. Unlike the *force majeure* clause, an effective confidentiality provision should be drafted narrowly to apply to only specific, limited information. A good confidentiality clause requires that materials be expressly designated as confidential by the party seeking confidential treatment and that the other party to the agreement have a sufficient time to register objections. It provides that information is presumed not to be confidential and that the burden lies with the party seeking confidential treatment to justify such treatment.

[32] *O'Brien's Encyclopedia of Forms: Commercial and General*, 11th ed looseleaf vol 4 (1998) 39.21–39.22.

```
Confidentiality Clause

Liblicense, Yale University Library

<www.library.yale.edu/~llicense/index.shtml>

It is understood and agreed by the parties that specific reports and
other disclosures required by this agreement, and any changes which may
be effected thereto, are considered by both parties to be sensitive. Such
information will not be disclosed by either party to third persons except
as may be required by law.
```

Arbitration Clauses

Parties often recognize that future disputes about the terms of an agreement could result in costly litigation. To avoid having to litigate such disputes, they sometimes insert an **arbitration clause** into a contract.[33] Arbitration clauses outline who should act to resolve the dispute and what method of arbitration should be used. Business people should consider these features of arbitration clauses:

- First, like exclusion clauses, a well-drafted arbitration clause is drafted in a clear, straightforward manner. By keeping the clause simple, one reduces the risk of hindering the arbitration process.

- Second, an effective arbitration clause stipulates how the expenses incurred in the course of arbitration are to be divided.

- Third, the clause determines, in advance, the number, qualifications, and role of the arbitrators.

- Fourth, an effective clause settles the procedural aspects of the arbitration, including the order in which the parties will present their case and the amount of time allowed for each presentation.

- Fifth, a well-constructed clause ensures that any information discussed at the arbitration will be kept confidential.

- Sixth, the clause contemplates whether the parties will require written reasons in support of the decision and whether there are avenues of appeal available to the parties.

Most of these details may not be specifically enumerated in the arbitration clause itself. They are often prescribed by reference to a document external to the contract, such as a set of rules or guidelines published by some arbitration institute.

an arbitration clause outlines who should act to resolve a dispute and what method of arbitration should be used

---

[33.] Arbitration was discussed in Chapter 1; arbitration clauses will be discussed in Chapter 24.

> Arbitration Clause
>
> BC International Commercial Arbitration Centre
>
> All disputes arising out of or in connection with this contract, or in respect of any legal relationship associated therewith or derived therefrom, shall be referred to and finally solved by arbitration under the rules of the British Columbia International Commercial Arbitration Centre. The appointing authority shall be the British Columbia International Commercial Arbitration Centre. The case shall be administered by the British Columbia International Commercial Arbitration Centre in accordance with its "Procedures for Cases under BCICAC Rules." The place of the arbitration shall be Vancouver, British Columbia, Canada.

Jurisdiction Clauses

a jurisdiction clause predetermines the locale of the court and whose law will apply in the event of a legal dispute between the parties

Parties that are not interested in arbitration as an alternative method of dispute resolution might still decide that it is worthwhile to contemplate where the court battle will take place, should there be one. A **jurisdiction clause** predetermines the locale of the court and whose law will apply in the event of a legal dispute between the parties. Such a clause is especially useful for situations where the parties are not governed by the same jurisdiction. If a business has a centralized structure, based in a single jurisdiction, it is usually wise to insert a jurisdiction clause.[34] Such a clause will help to ensure that those involved in the litigation process, whether as lawyers or witnesses, are not required to travel to other jurisdictions to sue or be sued.

> Jurisdiction Clause
>
> Typical Web Site
>
> This user agreement is governed by the laws of the Province of Ontario, Canada. You hereby consent to the exclusive jurisdiction and venue of courts in Middlesex County, Ontario, Canada in all disputes arising out of or relating to the use of this Web site. Use of this Web site is unauthorized in any jurisdiction that does not give effect to all provisions of these terms and conditions, including, without limitation, this paragraph.

Entire Agreement Clauses

an entire agreement clause is a provision stating that the entire agreement between the parties is contained within the four corners of the contract

When parties to a contract negotiate both orally and in writing, it is sometimes difficult to know which communications are to be incorporated as terms of the contract. One way to avoid uncertainty is to use an *entire agreement clause*. An **entire agreement clause** is a provision stating that the entire agreement between the parties is contained within the four corners of the contract. Such a clause ensures that none of the exceptions to the parol evidence will operate to defeat the written document. The principles of risk management therefore require business people to determine whether the standard forms they are signing contain an entire agreement clause. If so, they must ensure that every single aspect of the agreement is captured in the written document.

[34.] We discuss that situation in Chapter 24.

```
Entire Agreement Clause

O'Brien's Encyclopedia of Forms[35]

This Agreement constitutes the entire agreement between the Lessor and
Lessee and the Lessee acknowledges that there are no promises, induce-
ments, representations, collateral warranties, warranties, conditions,
options or terms, oral or written, express or implied or otherwise, made
by or on behalf of the Lessor or operating in favour of the Lessee with
respect to any aspect of the Equipment (including, without limitation,
its condition, design, capabilities, operation, use, suitability, fit-
ness, durability, quality, merchantability, or history (e.g., new, used,
reconditioned) or with respect to the appropriate treatment of this
Agreement or payments to be made pursuant thereto for the Lessee's
accounting or tax purposes, other than as may be expressly stated in this
Agreement.
```

APPENDIX 4A SUMMARY

Standard form agreements often include a number of boilerplate terms, which can be reused in various contractual settings. Exclusion clauses seek to protect one party from various sorts of legal liability. To be effective, they must be drafted in unambiguous language; the party against whom the exclusion clause is meant to operate must be given reasonable notice; and both parties must agree that the clause is part of the contract. *Force majeure* clauses aim to protect the parties from events beyond their control. Confidentiality clauses prevent disclosure of certain information to third parties. Arbitration clauses outline who should act to resolve a dispute and what method of arbitration should be used. Jurisdictional clauses predetermine the locale of the court and whose law will apply in the event of a legal dispute between the parties. Entire agreement clauses state that the entire agreement between the parties is contained within the contract, preventing the assertion of oral terms.

[35] *O'Brien's Encyclopedia of Forms: Commercial and General,* 11th ed looseleaf vol 4 (1998) 39.21–39.22.

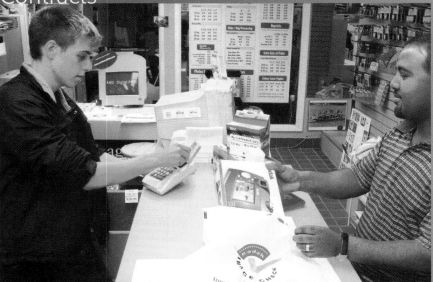

5 Contractual Defects

CHAPTER OVERVIEW

Incapacity to Contract
Personal Incapacity
Business Corporations
Associations
Indian Bands and Native Persons
Public Authorities

Absence of Writing
Statute of Frauds

Mistake
General Principles
Mistakes Preventing the Creation of Contracts
Mistakes Rendering Impossible the Purpose of the Contract
The Doctrine of Frustration
Documents Mistakenly Signed

Illegality
Agreements Prohibited by Statute
Common Law Illegality
The Doctrine of Public Policy

Unfairness During Bargaining
Duress
Undue Influence
Unconscionable Transactions

OBJECTIVES

After completing this chapter, you should be able to:

1. Identify six types of parties that lack capacity or have limited capacity to contract.
2. Distinguish between voidable and enforceable contracts with a minor.
3. Explain what it means for a corporation to act beyond its capacity.
4. Outline the types of contracts that must be evidenced in writing, state the basic writing requirements that must be proved, and summarize the legal effect of non-compliance.
5. Distinguish between mistakes affecting the creation of contracts and mistakes rendering the purpose of a contract impossible.
6. Explain the doctrine of frustration and its effect.
7. Summarize the traditional factors that courts take into account in determining whether an agreement is illegal.
8. Discuss the doctrine of public policy and its effect.
9. Define duress of goods and economic duress.
10. Distinguish between undue influence and unconscionable transactions, and identify when a presumption is created in each case.

Not every apparent contract achieves its intended effect—some contracts are defective. There are several types of contractual defects. One is the result of the absence of a formal requirement, such as a signature. Another is caused by events that invalidate a party's consent to contract. For example, one party may be mistaken about the fundamental terms of the contract or pressured into accepting an offer. An agreement may be considered defective if it conflicts with public policy or if it is illegal. Contractual defects are particularly significant because they often provide one of the parties with a defence when the other party commences a lawsuit. For example, if a party is unduly pressured into signing a document and is later sued for breach of the agreement, that party can avoid liability by claiming that the contract was defective.

In this chapter we survey six different contractual defects and their legal consequences:

- incapacity
- absence of writing
- mistake
- frustration
- illegality
- unfairness during bargaining

INCAPACITY TO CONTRACT

A person cannot enter into a contract unless they have the legal power to give consent. For example, although a 10-year-old may be able to read, understand, and sign a contractual document, the child may not be bound by that agreement. The same is true for adults who, for some other reason, lack the ability to consent. To protect specific groups of people, the law has drawn a distinction between those who have the *capacity* to contract and those who do not. **Capacity** is the legal power to give consent. Sometimes the question of capacity depends on a person's ability to understand the nature and consequences of their acts. At other times it does not.

capacity is the legal power to give consent

We will consider six groups of persons who may have no capacity or only limited capacity to create a contract:

- minors
- mentally disabled persons
- intoxicated persons
- corporations
- associations
- Indian bands and Native persons
- public authorities

Personal Incapacity

Minors

The law distinguishes between *minors* and those said to have reached *the age of majority*. The **age of majority** is the age at which a person is held fully accountable in law. Those who have not reached the age of majority are **minors**. The law does not try to decide on a case-by-case basis whether a

age of majority is the age at which a person is held fully accountable in law

minors are people who have not reached the age of majority

minor is capable of entering into a contract. Instead, it says that everyone under the age of majority lacks capacity. In some jurisdictions, including Alberta, Saskatchewan, and Ontario, the age of majority is 18 years.[1] In other provinces, including Newfoundland, New Brunswick, and British Columbia, it is 19 years.[2] Though perhaps overprotective in some instances, the law's approach shields minors from exploitation and the consequences of their own inexperience. It is therefore important for businesses that transact with minors to understand how the law operates.

contract is voidable if the minor is entitled to avoid the legal obligations that it created

Some contracts are *voidable* at the minor's option. A contract is **voidable** if the minor is entitled to avoid the legal obligations that it created. Note an important legal subtlety here. *Some* contracts with minors are voidable; not *every* contract with a minor is void at the outset. If a contract is voidable, the minor may elect to avoid contractual liability. If so, they are relieved of all future liabilities under the contract. However, the minor may also choose to carry out the contract, making the obligations binding.

A minor who wants to avoid contractual liability should do so as soon as possible. Suppose a 15-year-old boy rents stereo equipment for a year. If he elects to avoid the contract after two months, he cannot be sued for the other ten. He can, however, be sued for the rent that accumulated before he avoided the agreement. Furthermore, if there is a substantial delay, a court may say that the boy *affirmed* the contract and therefore lost the right to avoid it. Finally, once a person reaches the age of majority, they must decide, within a reasonable time, whether they want to void a contract that they created as a minor.

The ability to avoid certain contracts does not mean that a minor can take the benefit of a contract and then cancel it with impunity. Minors who elect to avoid contracts must give back any benefits that they received under them.

enforceable contracts, which deal with necessaries, cannot be avoided by minors

There are some contracts that a minor cannot avoid—**enforceable contracts**. Minors are generally bound by contracts for such necessary goods and services as food, clothing, education, medical treatment, and legal advice, which are to their benefit.[3] That rule is based on the need to ensure that people are willing to sell the necessities of life to minors. Consequently, a minor who contracts for such goods or services can be forced to pay a reasonable price, but not necessarily the price stated in the contract, as long as they do not already have access to the necessity.

contract of employment is binding if, viewed as a whole, it is to the minor's benefit

Like contracts for necessaries, a contract of employment is binding if, viewed as a whole, it is to the minor's benefit. This point is important to any business that employs minors. To ensure that such a contract is enforceable, the employer must make sure that the contract is not unreasonably harsh to the minor. That does not mean that none of the terms can be to the minor's disadvantage. After all, there can be no contract unless the minor provides some consideration, either in the form of conferring a benefit or suffering some detriment.

Mental Incapacity

a person may lack capacity because of a deficient intellect

Regardless of age, a person may also lack capacity because of a deficient intellect. We need to distinguish two situations. First, if a court has declared a person to lack mental capacity, their contracts are *void* and cannot be enforced at all. Second, even if there is no court declaration, a person may still be considered

---

[1.] *Age of Majority Act*, RSA 1980, c A-4, s 3 (Alta); *Age of Majority Act*, RSS 1978, c A-6, s 2 (Sask); *Age of Majority and Accountability Act*, RSO 1990, c A.7 (Ont).

[2.] *Age of Majority Act*, RSNB 1972, c 5, s 2 (NB); *Age of Majority Act*, RSBC 1979, c 5, s 7 (BC).

[3.] Goods that are considered "necessaries" are usually enumerated by statute: *Sale of Goods Act*, RSPEI 1988, c S-1, s 4 (PEI); RSM 1987, c S10, s 4 (Man).

mentally incompetent. If so, their contracts are *voidable*, just as in the case of a minor. They can avoid the agreement within a reasonable time of becoming competent. There is, however, an important difference between mental incapacity and minority. A minor's contract is voidable even if the other party was unaware of the age issue. In contrast, the contract of a person with a mental incapacity is voidable only if the other party should have recognized the problem.

In the absence of a judicial declaration of mental incompetence, it is sometimes difficult to tell if a person is incapacitated. A person may obviously lack capacity because of extreme age or because of some kind of impairment in mental function. Often, however, it requires a careful examination of the circumstances, which may be further complicated by the fact that an incapacitated adult may later regain capacity. As a matter of risk management, employees should be trained to identify potential problems.

Despite the general rules, like a minor, a person who enters into a contract while suffering from a mental incapacity is liable to pay a reasonable price for necessaries of life.

Intoxication

The rules for drunkenness are similar to those for mental incapacity. An otherwise capable person may enter into a contract while intoxicated. That agreement is voidable if two conditions are met. First, the person must have been so drunk that they could not know or appreciate what they were doing. Second, the other contractual party must have been alerted to that fact. Often, the courts are as much concerned with the possibility of fraud or unfairness as they are with the issue of incapacity. To set aside a contract, the intoxicated party must make a prompt election to avoid it once sober. A failure to do so will be taken as affirmation of the agreement. Case Brief 5.1 illustrates one court decision.

drunkenness may result in a voidable contract

C A S E   B R I E F   5.1

McLaren v McMillan (1907) 5 WLR 336 (Man KB)

John McLaren had been drinking heavily throughout the day. Shortly after sundown, he was approached by a horse trader named McMillan, who offered him a share in a pony called Silver Coin. After stumbling outside the bar to examine the horse, McLaren expressed satisfaction and signed the relevant documents. When he became sober the next morning, he tried to get out of the deal. Although he vaguely remembered having signed something and also remembered a different transaction that he made with some

other cowboy, McLaren tried to withdraw from the bargain with McMillan. McMillan refused.

The court recognized that intoxication could give rise to a contractual defect. However, it held that drunkenness is not a ground for setting the contract aside if it merely "causes excitement" without producing an excessive state of inebriation. Since McLaren's state of intoxication only darkened his ability to reason without actually depriving him of the ability to reason altogether, he was not entitled to avoid the contract.

Business Corporations

Corporations are treated as legal persons.[4] The law distinguishes between *chartered corporations* and *statutory corporations*. In the context of contractual

---

[4.] Corporations and other types of business organizations are considered in detail in Chapter 18 and Chapter 19.

chartered corporations are treated the same as individuals who have reached the age of majority

statutory corporations have limited contractual capacity

a corporation lacks the capacity to contract when it acts *ultra vires*

capacity, **chartered corporations** are treated the same as individuals who have reached the age of majority. If a chartered corporation enters into contracts in breach of its charter, its charter may be forfeited, but the contracts made in breach of the corporate charter will still be binding. **Statutory corporations**, on the other hand, have a more limited contractual capacity. Because they are statutory creations, their capacity to contract is limited by the powers given to them through legislation. If a statutory corporation attempts to contract in a manner that exceeds its statutory powers, it acts *ultra vires*, literally "beyond the authority." When a corporation acts *ultra vires*, it lacks the capacity to contract. Those agreements consequently are unenforceable. Generally, the question is whether the purported transaction is in line with the legal objects and purposes of the corporation. To understand the importance of this, read Business Decision 5.1.

BUSINESS DECISION 5.1

Drafting Articles of Incorporation

Reva is named a director of a statutory corporation. While drafting the constitutional documents of the corporation, she and the other directors enter into a discussion about how best to characterize its objects. According to its current business plan, the corporation will focus exclusively on the business of constructing the exterior of buildings. For this reason, one of the directors Ling recommends the following characterization: "To carry on in the business of pouring concrete foundations and erecting building

exteriors." Reva expresses concerns about Ling's characterization and counters with the suggestion of a much broader description: "To carry on in the business of construction."

Questions for Discussion

1. Assume that you are also on the board of directors. In what sense is the capacity issue relevant to your decision about whether to adopt the recommendation made by Reva or Ling?

2. What are the advantages and disadvantages of Reva's broader statement of the objects of the corporation?

Associations

associations are usually unincorporated business organizations that lack contractual capacity

Capacity issues arise more frequently with another type of business structure— *associations*. **Associations** are usually unincorporated business organizations, including private clubs, charities, and religious societies. Although they share some features with corporations, most associations do not enjoy independent legal existence and are thus incapable of contracting. Therefore, some provinces have legislation that gives contractual capacity to associations involved in such activities as education, religion, and charity. Trade unions may also be given capacity.[5] Those statutes define an association's capacity in much the same way as a statutory corporation's constitution. If an association attempts to contract outside of those limits, it lacks capacity, and its agreement is ineffective.

Because an association generally lacks capacity, one of its members may enter into a contract for its benefit. Significantly, it is that individual member who becomes liable under the agreement. Unlike corporate officers and directors, individuals cannot escape liability by pleading that they were merely contracting on the association's behalf. On the other side of the bargain, if your business intends to contract with someone who claims to act on behalf of an

---

[5.] Trade unions are examined in Chapter 26.

association, you can manage risk by ensuring that the association has capacity or that the individual personally has the resources to perform the obligations.

Indian Bands and Native Persons

One kind of unincorporated association that *does* have legal capacity is an *Indian band*. According to the *Indian Act*, an **Indian band** is a body of Native people whose land and money are held by the Crown.[6] Nevertheless, despite the Crown's role, Indian bands have contractual capacity in much the same way as corporations.[7] They can sue or be sued.

an **Indian band** is a body of Native people whose land and money is held by the Crown

The same is not always true, however, for individual Native persons who qualify as "Indians" under the Act. Unless they leave their band areas and become "enfranchised," they have a limited capacity to contract. For instance, property on a reservation cannot be used as security for a credit transaction, nor can it be transferred to an outside party without the Crown's consent.

Public Authorities

Many contracts are created on a daily basis by public authorities at the federal, provincial, and municipal levels. Generally speaking, a public authority acting on behalf of a governmental body has the capacity to contract independent of any specific statutory authority to do so.[8] The only limit on a particular official's capacity to contract is the *Constitution Act, 1867*. As we saw in Chapter 1, the Constitution creates a division of powers between the federal government and the provinces and municipalities. As long as a federal, provincial, or municipal public authority's action is consistent with that division of powers, it has contractual capacity.

a public authority acting on behalf of a government generally has contractual capacity

ABSENCE OF WRITING

At one time, a contract would be legally recognized only if it took the form of a deed. Now it is not necessary to place a seal onto a document or to have the document signed by both parties for it to be recognized as a contract. For most contracts, there are no formal requirements. However, certain types of contracts must be *evidenced* in writing. That requirement first arose as a result of an old piece of English legislation—the *Statute of Frauds*.[9]

certain types of contracts must be *evidenced* in writing

Statute of Frauds

The *Statute of Frauds* required some contracts to be evidenced in writing as a way of reducing the risk of perjury, or lying in legal proceedings. The requirement was intended to discourage people from falsely claiming the existence of oral contracts. Whatever merit it originally had, that rationale is less persuasive today. Electronic and paper documents can now be produced, altered, and reproduced with a few clicks of a mouse. For that reason and others, many

the *Statute of Frauds* required some contracts to be evidenced in writing

---

[6.] RSC 1985, c 1-5, s 2 (Can).

[7.] *Wewayakum Indian Band v Canada and Wawayakai Indian Band* [1992] 42 FTR 40 (FC TD).

[8.] PW Hogg *Liability of the Crown* 2d ed (1989) at 161-62.

[9.] 1677 (29 Cha 2) c3.

jurisdictions have amended their legislation.[10] And some jurisdictions, like British Columbia and Manitoba, have repealed the Statute altogether. As electronic commerce continues to expand, it can be assumed that the issue will be examined even more broadly.

Despite such law reform, risk management still requires understanding the *Statute of Frauds*, even for businesses in British Columbia and Manitoba. After all, a company in Kamloops or Brandon may enter into a contract with a party in another jurisdiction where the Statute is still in force. We will therefore discuss:

- the types of contracts that must be evidenced in writing
- the basic writing requirements that must be proved
- the legal effect of non-compliance

Types of Contracts That Must Be Evidenced in Writing

Only certain types of contracts fall under the *Statute of Frauds*. In Chapter 8, we will examine the circumstances in which an agreement for the *sale of goods* must be evidenced in writing. For now, we can look at three other types of contracts.[11]

- guarantees
- contracts for the sale of an interest in land
- contracts not to be performed within a year

a guarantee is a contractual promise by a third party, called a *guarantor*, to satisfy a debtor's obligation if that debtor fails to do so

Guarantees   The Statute applies to *guarantees*. A **guarantee** is a contractual promise by a third party, called a *guarantor*, to satisfy a debtor's obligation if that debtor fails to do so.[12] For example, you may apply for overdraft protection that allows you to withdraw more than your bank account actually contains, in effect, a bank loan. The bank may refuse that arrangement unless you find a third party (such as your parent or your spouse) to guarantee repayment.

an indemnity is an unconditional promise to assume another's debt completely

The guarantor gives a *conditional* promise, and is required to discharge the debt only if you fail to do so. A guarantee can be distinguished from an *indemnity*. An **indemnity** is an *unconditional* promise to assume another's debt completely. To continue with our example, if your spouse promises to indemnify the bank for your overdraft, the bank is entitled to collect payment from your spouse as soon as the overdraft amount becomes due, even if the bank has not bothered to ask you for payment first. An indemnity therefore is not a promise to answer for another's debt. It is a promise to assume another's debt altogether.

the *Statute of Frauds* may apply to contracts of guarantee but not to contracts of indemnity

In many provinces, the *Statute of Frauds* applies to contracts of guarantee but not to contracts of indemnity. Consequently, the bank will not be able to demand payment from the guarantor unless that agreement was evidenced in writing. However, a bank may be able to enforce an indemnity even if the agreement was entirely oral. In British Columbia, the judicial distinction between guarantee and indemnity has been abolished.

[10.] England, New Zealand, and Western Australia have all amended the original requirements under the *Statute of Frauds*. Law reform has been recommended in other provinces, including Ontario and Newfoundland. See Ontario Law Reform Commission *Report on the Amendment of the Law of Contract* (1987) c 5; M Bridge "The *Statute of Frauds* and the Sale of Land Contracts." (1986) 64 Can Bar Rev 58.

[11.] Most provincial statutes require writing in other circumstances, including: (i) ratifications of contracts made by minors upon reaching age of majority, (ii) promises by executors or administartors to be personally liable for the debts of a testator or intestate, (iii) contracts made upon consideration of marriage, (iv) assignment of express trusts, (v) creation of trusts of land, and (vi) leases or agreements to lease land for a term exceeding three years.

[12.] Guarantees are examined in Chapter 21.

Contracts for the Sale of an Interest in Land Contracts for the sale of an interest in land are unenforceable unless they are evidenced in writing.[13] It is sometimes difficult to distinguish contracts that concern an interest in land from others that do not. Consider the example in You Be the Judge 5.1.

YOU BE THE JUDGE 5.1

Van Berkel v De Foort [1933] 1 WWR 125 (Man CA)

Van Berkel entered into an oral agreement that permitted De Foort to cut and remove a crop of wild hay from his land in exchange for a promise to pay $500 upon removal of the crop. De Foort had intended to use the hay to feed his dairy cattle. In the early part of the autumn that year, De Foort decided to give up the dairy business altogether. No longer having any need for wild hay, De Foort simply left the crop on the land to spoil. Van Berkel sued for breach of contract. De Foort attempted to escape liability by pleading the *Statute of Frauds*. He claimed that the contract concerned the sale of an interest in land and was therefore unenforceable since it was not evidenced in writing.

Questions for Discussion

1. Do you think that the contract entered into by Van Berkel and De Foort was a contract for the sale of an interest in land?

2. Should De Foort be able to walk away from his contractual obligations simply on the basis of this formal defect?

Other cases are more clear-cut. For example, a contract to repair a building need not be evidenced in writing, nor must an agreement for room and board. On the other hand, a long-term lease of land clearly must be evidenced in writing.

Contracts Not to Be Performed Within a Year Contracts that are not to be performed within a year of their creation are unenforceable unless they are evidenced in writing. This extends the writing requirement to all sorts of agreements of indefinite duration regardless of their subject matter. Because the Statute applies so broadly, it can catch parties by surprise. Contrary to their expectations, they may not have an enforceable agreement. The courts therefore tend to interpret this part of the Statute quite narrowly. For instance, they usually say that a contract is not caught if it could *possibly* be performed within one year. And sometimes they go to great lengths to enforce oral agreements, notwithstanding the existence of the Statute.

contracts that are not to be performed within a year of their creation are unenforceable unless they are evidenced in writing

Writing Requirements

If a contract falls within the Statute, the court must decide if the writing requirement was satisfied.

Form and Content of the Note or Memorandum

Either the contract must be in writing or there must be a note or memorandum that provides evidence of it. The document does not have to take any particular form, but has to: (i) provide evidence of the essential elements of the contract (such as the parties' names, the subject matter of the agreement, and the price), and (ii) be signed by the party against whom the agreement is being enforced. The courts are often lenient. For instance, they sometimes allow the signature requirement to be satisfied by a name on letterhead or an invoice. Furthermore,

either the agreement must be in writing or there must be a note or memorandum that provides evidence of it

---

[13.] The sale of interests in land is discussed in Chapter 14.

they are sometimes satisfied by the combined effect of several documents, even if they do not expressly refer to each other.[14]

Effect of Non-Compliance   The *Statute of Frauds* renders some contracts *unenforceable* unless they are sufficiently evidenced in writing. Such contracts therefore cannot support an action for breach of contract. If one party does not perform, the other cannot demand a remedy. This does not mean that their agreement is entirely irrelevant. Their contract is not void; it is merely unenforceable. It can therefore be used to pass property and may provide a defence. Suppose that someone pays $5000 to you as a down payment under an oral contract for the sale of land. A down payment acts as part of the purchase price, but it also provides an incentive to perform. If the payor does not go through with the deal, the payee can keep the money. Now suppose that the other party refuses to complete the transaction. Although your contract is unenforceable, it still provides a valid explanation as to why you do not have to repay the $5000.

> unenforceable contracts still have legal effect and can provide a legal defence

This discussion of the *Statute of Frauds* suggests two things for risk management. First, some types of contracts *must* be evidenced in writing to be enforceable. Second, to avoid the uncertainty and debate that oral agreements can create, *all* contracts should be written whenever possible.

MISTAKE

We have examined incapacity and the absence of writing. A third kind of contractual defect arises from *mistakes*.

General Principles

Contracts are based on agreements. However, anyone involved in business knows that people sometimes are mistaken about their agreements.

> one kind of mistake prevents the creation of a contract

- Some mistakes occur when an error affects the basic process of contract formation. When that happens, the mistake may negate the existence of an agreement between the parties. And without an agreement, there cannot be a contract.

> another kind of mistake makes it impossible for the object of the contract to be achieved

- Other mistakes make it impossible for the object of the contract to be achieved. Here, the mistake does not affect the process of contract formation but rather pertains to the very existence of the contract's subject matter. In that case, the contract may be defective.

Mistakes Preventing the Creation of Contracts

Two types of mistakes prevent the creation of a contract:

- mistaken identity
- mistake as to subject matter

Mistaken Identity   Many business relationships are based on trust and reliability. People are more willing to invest in institutions that are known to be reliable. Financial institutions are more willing to lend money or give credit to people who have a history of paying their debts. Therefore, a mistake about corporate or personal identity may become a contractual issue. Fly-by-night

---

[14.] *Harvie v Gibbons* (1980) 109 DLR (3d) 559 (Alta CA).

operations often try to confuse potential customers by using logos similar to recognized brand names. Imposters try to pass themselves off as legitimate business persons. When the innocent party eventually realizes its mistake, it may try to avoid the contract on the basis of its mistake. The situation is even more difficult if the con artist obtains goods under the contract and then resells them to a third party. The person who was duped under the first transaction may try to recover the goods from the third party on the basis of the mistake.

Sometimes that approach succeeds; sometimes it does not. The courts are required to weigh the interests of the seller against those of the innocent purchaser. Mistaken identity will therefore not render a contract defective unless: (i) the mistake was known to the other contractual party, and (ii) the mistake was *material*. A **material mistake** is one that matters to the mistaken party in an important way.

a material mistake is one that matters to the mistaken party in an important way

Mistake about Subject Matter   Some mistakes put the parties at cross-purposes and therefore prevent the formation of a contract. This often occurs when the parties are mutually mistaken about the subject matter of an agreement. Suppose you are an exotic-rug importer. Anticipating huge sales at a trade show in the autumn, you contact a foreign supplier during the summer. You agree to purchase a quantity of rugs to be shipped to Canada from Calcutta on a ship called *Racinante*. You believe that that ship is scheduled to arrive in October. However, neither you nor the seller know that there are, in fact, two ships from Calcutta called *Racinante*, one scheduled to arrive in October, the other in late December. The seller, not knowing about the earlier ship, arranges for the rugs to be carried on the later one. By the time the rugs arrive in December, they are no good to you. Your trade show has come and gone. You are entitled to reject the rugs without payment since the mistake was, in the circumstances, material. The seller was offering rugs on one date, but you were trying to accept them on another. The mutual mistake about the *Racinante* prevented a true agreement or the creation of a contract.[15]

Mistakes Rendering Impossible the Purpose of the Contract

Even if a mistake does not pertain to the process of contract formation, it may be relevant if it makes the contract impossible to perform. We will consider one possibility and another related scenario:

- mistake about existence of the subject matter
- frustration

Mistake about Existence of the Subject Matter

The parties' mistake may render the contract impossible to perform. In this situation, both parties make the *same* mistake, which is usually based on a false assumption. Suppose you agree to lease your beach house to me for the summer. We draft a contract, sign it, and exchange keys for money. The next day, however, we learn that the house had been completely destroyed by a fire a week earlier. Consequently, when we created our contract, we both made the same mistake—we believed that the house existed and that our agreement could be performed. The contract is therefore defective. You have to return my money, and I have to return your keys. And neither one of us can sue to enforce the deal.

a common mistake about the existence of the contract's subject matter may render the agreement ineffective

---

15. *Raffles v Wichelhaus* (1864) 159 ER 375.

However, a common mistake about the existence of the subject matter of a contract does not *always* prevent the enforcement of the agreement. A business should therefore protect itself by inserting into the contract a *force majeure*, or "irresistible force," clause, which states which party bears the hardship if the subject matter of the contract is destroyed or if some other unexpected event occurs. The affected party should then arrange insurance against the potential loss.

The Doctrine of Frustration

We have considered situations involving a mistake about an *existing fact*. Sometimes, however, the parties may make a mistake about the *future*. Even if they are fully informed when they create their contract, subsequent events may make it impossible for them to perform as anticipated.

Going back to our earlier example, I agree to rent your beach house for the summer. We create a contract and exchange keys for money. At that time, the building is in excellent shape. During the spring, however, it is completely destroyed by a fire. I could still occupy the empty lot for the summer, but that is not what we had in mind. The purpose of our agreement has been *frustrated* by an unexpected occurrence.[16] A contract is **frustrated** when some event makes performance impossible or has the effect of radically undermining its very purpose.

The doctrine of frustration, like the law of mistake, tries to strike a fair balance between the parties. Ultimately, however, it requires a decision about who will bear the risk of a loss. In some situations, the parties themselves supply the answer.

- The doctrine of frustration applies only if neither party is responsible for the relevant event. If one party is responsible, then that party bears the loss. For instance, I would not be entitled to a refund if I carelessly burned the beach house down during the first night of my stay.

- Even if neither party is at fault, they may have agreed that one of them would bear the risk of loss. For instance, you may have inserted a *force majeure* clause into our agreement. If so, I could not demand a refund of the rent even though the house is gone.

If the parties themselves cannot settle the issue in some way, a judge must do so. First, however, we must draw a distinction between provinces that use the common law rules and those that have legislation on point.[17] Common law jurisdictions use an all-or-nothing rule. A purchaser can recover *all* of its contractual payments if it has not received *any* benefit from the seller. However, if the purchaser has received *some* benefit, it cannot recover *any* payments. In neither event can the seller actually demand payment from the purchaser, even if the seller incurred substantial expenses under the agreement.

In other jurisdictions, the effect of the legislation turns upon the existence of a contractual payment or a benefit.

- If the purchaser paid an advance or a deposit under the contract, the court has a discretion to divide that money between the parties as it sees

a mistake may be made about the future

a contract is frustrated when some event makes performance impossible or radically undermines the purpose behind the agreement

[16.] A contract is not frustrated merely because it becomes more expensive or somewhat more difficult to perform. For instance, our agreement would still be effective even if, because of heavy rains, you were required to spend a considerable amount of money cleaning up the house to make it fit for habitation during the summer.

[17.] Legislation has been enacted in Alberta, British Columbia, Manitoba, Newfoundland, New Brunswick, Ontario, and Prince Edward Island.

fit. Consequently, if the seller incurred some expense under the contract, it may be entitled to retain an appropriate amount as compensation. In other circumstances, the purchaser may be entitled to a complete refund.

- If the purchaser received some benefit from the seller, the seller is entitled to either retain money that it has received or make a fresh claim for compensation against the purchaser. That compensation, however, cannot exceed the value of the benefit.

- If the purchaser neither paid money nor received a benefit under the contract, the entire burden of the frustrating event falls on the seller. In that situation, the seller cannot claim compensation, regardless of how much expense it incurred under the agreement.[18]

Documents Mistakenly Signed

Another type of mistake occurs when a person signs a contractual document in error. As a general rule, that sort of mistake is irrelevant. A person is usually bound by a signature, even if they did not read the document. The other party is normally entitled to assume that a signature represents an acceptance of the agreement. There are, however, exceptions to that rule. As we saw in Chapter 4, unusual or onerous terms are not binding unless they are reasonably drawn to the attention of the person who signed the contract. There is another exception—*non est factum*.

Non est factum, literally "this is not my deed," allows the mistaken party to avoid any obligations under the contract. The plea is available only if there is a *radical difference* between what a person signed and what that person thought they were signing. That may happen if the document was presented as a sale of land, when it actually was a purchase of shares. In contrast, the doctrine does not apply if the difference is merely a matter of degree. Consequently, a signatory cannot plead *non est factum* simply because they were mistaken about the quantity of goods that were sold under the contract. Furthermore, the doctrine cannot be used by someone who carelessly failed to understand the document. That important point is illustrated in Case Brief 5.2.

non est factum literally means "this is not my deed"

CASE BRIEF 5.2

Saunders v Anglia Building Society [1970] 3 All ER 961 (HL)

Mrs Gallie was 78 years old. Wally Parkin was her nephew. She had expressed her intention to name Wally as the heir to her estate. One day, Wally came over with his buddy Lee and asked her to sign a document. Because her glasses were broken and her spare pair was not handy, she did not read the document. Wally led her to believe that the document would fulfill her intention of granting the estate to him upon her death. On that basis, she signed the document. In fact, the document had a very different effect. Among other things, it immediately assigned £3000 to Lee, who took the money and used it for his own purposes. Mrs Gallie asked the court to declare the assignment defective on the basis of the plea of *non est factum*.

Fearing the consequences of extending the doctrine too far, the House of Lords said that *non est factum* must be carefully limited. It therefore held that Mrs Gallie's carelessness prevented her from relying on the plea. She could have read the document. The fact that her spare glasses were not handy did not excuse her from doing so.

[18.] An exception exists in British Columbia, where the seller can claim compensation for half of its expenses.

ILLEGALITY

illegal agreements are expressly or implicitly prohibited by statute

A contract may be ineffective because it violates the law. There are several variations on that theme. **Illegal agreements** are expressly or implicitly prohibited by statute and are therefore void. Other agreements, though not strictly prohibited, come into conflict with a common law rule or offend public policy. They too are often unenforceable.

Agreements Prohibited by Statute

the purpose of a regulatory statute is not to punish individuals for wrongdoing but rather to regulate their conduct through an administrative regime

Most statutes that prohibit particular types of agreements are *regulatory* in nature. The purpose of a **regulatory statute** is not to punish individuals for wrongdoing but rather to regulate their conduct through an administrative regime. For example, there are statutes that prohibit the sale of apples that have not been graded in accordance with provincial regulations.[19] Other statutes require licences to be obtained prior to engaging in certain kinds of transactions. Often it is unclear whether the object of a particular statute is to prohibit certain conduct outright or merely to exact a fee from those who contract in contravention of the statute. The proper construction of the legislative intent of the statute is important. If the object of a particular statute is interpreted as prohibiting certain conduct, an agreement that contravenes the statute is illegal and therefore unenforceable. However, if the legislative intent is merely to impose a fee or some other form of penalty, the court will not usually interfere with the contract.

Common Law Illegality

the common law is unwilling to recognize agreements that are contrary to public policy

Some agreements are illegal even if they do not contravene a particular statute. The common law is unwilling to recognize agreements that are contrary to public policy. For example, a mobster may hire a thug to kill a politician. If the thug decides instead to take the money and run, the mobster cannot sue for breach of contract. The same is true of any agreement that is aimed at committing a crime or a tort, such as that in Business Law in Action 5.1.

BUSINESS LAW IN ACTION 5.1

Illegality and Public Policy

Sid Suntan decided to launch a new line of sunblock products. Although his company has an excellent reputation for its merchandise and has developed goodwill in the skating and snowboarding community, Sid was concerned that he could not compete with the leading lotion producer because it was too well known. Trying to level the playing field, Sid decided to run a smear campaign against the leading lotion. He hired Lady Sneerwell Inc as his media consultant. A junior representative from Lady Sneerwell, enthusiastic to recruit Sid

Suntan as a new client to the firm, agreed on behalf of the company to run a false and disparaging ad campaign against the competition. He asked Sid Suntan for the firm's usual $10 000 retainer fee. Sid provided cash. The junior representative returned to the firm and began working on the campaign. Three weeks later, after consulting with a senior executive and learning that such an ad campaign could expose the advertising firm to a defamation lawsuit, the junior representative contacted Sid Suntan to repudiate the deal. Sid was furious and demanded the return of his $10 000 retainer. Since three weeks of work had been put

(continued)

[19.] *Kingshott v Brunskill* [1953] OWN 133 (CA).

(continued)

into the campaign, the matter was referred to Lady Sneerwell's legal department.

After reviewing the rules on illegality, the legal department refused to return the retainer. First, the three weeks spent on the campaign itself was sufficient to justify keeping the retainer fee. Second, the legal department believed that the common law would not recognize a contract to commit the tort of defamation. Consequently, Sid Suntan would have no legal means by which to compel the return of the $10 000.

Questions for Discussion

1. Do the rules on illegality and public policy seem fair to you? Why?
2. What if Sid had changed his mind immediately after providing the cash and before Lady Sneerwell Inc had done any work?

The common law will not recognize several other types of agreement, including those that are damaging to a country's safety or foreign relations, that interfere with the administration of justice, that promote corruption, and that promote sexual immorality. Each type of agreement is contrary to public policy.

The Doctrine of Public Policy

It may seem odd that a court can strike down a contract simply because it is contrary to public policy. After all, the law of contract is intended to facilitate stable and predictable business relationships by allowing people to freely enter into whatever bargains they choose. The notion of public policy, however, is notoriously vague. It may also allow judges to make or unmake contracts on the basis of their own personal views as to what is best for society. Public policy, according to an old saying, becomes "an unruly horse" if it is let out of the barn.

Covenants in Restraint of Trade

An agreement may be ineffective on the grounds of public policy if it contains a *covenant in restraint of trade*. A **covenant in restraint of trade** is a contractual term that *unreasonably restricts* one party's liberty to carry on a trade, business, or profession in a particular way. Such covenants often require a person to: (i) trade or *not* trade with someone in particular, or (ii) work for someone in particular or, at least, *not* work for anyone else. In its most unreasonable form, a broadly drafted restraint of trade provision comes close to slavery. In that situation, the covenant will be presumed contrary to public policy unless the party seeking to enforce it can demonstrate that the restriction is reasonable. However, even if an unacceptable provision is struck down, the rest of the contract may remain.

Many restrictive covenants are perfectly reasonable and therefore not contrary to public policy. Suppose you are thinking about buying a convenience store. You may legitimately insert a provision into the contract that prevents the current owner from opening or operating another convenience store within a six-block radius. That provision merely ensures that the current owner does not steal all of your expected customers. It would be different, however, if the contract prohibited the current owner from operating another convenience store *anywhere* in Canada. A convenience store in another neighbourhood, let alone another city, does not create a threat to your business. The contractual term would therefore be an unreasonable restraint of trade, contrary to public policy, and hence ineffective.

Restraint of trade clauses are often found in employment contracts. The employer requires its employees to promise not to use trade secrets or process-

a **covenant in restraint of trade** is a contractual term that *unreasonably restricts* one party's liberty to carry on a trade, business, or profession in a particular way

a covenant in restraint of trade may be presumed contrary to public policy unless the party seeking to enforce it can demonstrate that the restriction is reasonable

some restrictive covenants are reasonable and therefore not contrary to public policy

restraint of trade clauses are often found in employment contracts

es that they acquire during their employment in any other business capacity. The restraint is enforceable if it is reasonable, but ineffective if it is unreasonable. As a matter of risk management, employers should draft such provisions as narrowly as possible to maximize the likelihood of enforcement.

UNFAIRNESS DURING BARGAINING

As we saw in the discussion on incapacity, weaker parties are not always required to complete their agreements. If a disadvantaged party is pressured into an agreement or placed in an unfair position during the bargaining process, the contract may be ineffective. Indeed, the courts occasionally even bend normal contractual rules to achieve fair results. For example, a court might go out of its way to find a defect in the contract formation process.

We conclude this chapter with a brief examination of three types of unfair bargaining:

- duress
- undue influence
- unconscionable transactions

Duress

duress of person refers to physical violence or the threat of violence

duress of goods occurs when one person seizes or threatens to seize another person's goods to force that person to create a contract

economic duress arises when a person enters into a contractual arrangement after being threatened with financial harm

Duress of person refers to physical violence or the threat of violence against a person or that person's loved one. If a contract is the product of duress, it is *voidable*. The innocent party may choose not to perform and recover any payments they made under the agreement. Similar rules apply to *duress of goods*. **Duress of goods** occurs when one person seizes or threatens to seize another person's goods to force that person to create a contract. The innocent party can avoid the contract if they can show that the pressure was practically irresistible.

Fortunately, the courts seldom hear cases involving duress of person or of goods. Unscrupulous business people do, however, occasionally resort to a more subtle form of pressure—*economic duress*. **Economic duress** arises when a person enters into a contractual arrangement after being threatened with financial harm. For example, a contractual party, claiming that the cost of performance is higher than expected, indicates that it will not fulfill its obligations unless it receives additional money.

Economic duress is more difficult to determine than duress of person or duress of goods. It is always wrong to put a gun to someone's head; it is not always wrong to exert economic pressure over them. Indeed, that sort of thing regularly happens in the business world. As Case Brief 5.3 illustrates, the courts look at several factors before determining that a pressure was a threat.

- Economic pressure is more likely to be considered illegitimate if it was made in *bad faith*. It is one thing for a party to honestly say that it cannot perform without more money; it is another to apply pressure on someone simply because they are vulnerable.
- The victim of the pressure must show that they *could not have reasonably resisted*. Sometimes, it is reasonable to resist by bringing the matter to court; sometimes the situation requires a much quicker response.
- The courts are more sympathetic if the victim started *legal proceedings promptly* after the effects of the pressure passed.
- The courts are more likely to become involved if the victim *protested* when presented with the pressure. However, a failure to protest is not

necessarily fatal if that course of conduct was obviously futile in the circumstances.

- A contract is more likely to be considered voidable if the victim *succumbed to the pressure without legal advice*; otherwise, agreement to a contractual proposal tends to look more like a sound business decision.

CASE BRIEF 5.3

North Ocean Shipping Co v Hyundai Construction Ltd [1978] 3 All ER 1170 (CA)

Desperately needing a new ship, North Ocean Shipping contracted with Hyundai Construction to build one for a specified price in American dollars. After the value of that currency plunged, Hyundai said that it would not complete the project unless it received an additional payment. It made that threat knowing that North Ocean urgently needed a ship to fulfill several other contractual commitments. North Ocean paid, but then sued to recover its money.

The English Court of Appeal held that Hyundai's conduct went beyond mere commercial pressure. It amounted to economic duress. The coercion effectively negated North Ocean's apparent consent to the additional payment. Moreover, North Ocean did not later affirm the new arrangement, but rather sued to recover its money.[20]

Undue Influence

Even if the elements of common law duress cannot be established, relief may be available under such equitable principles as *undue influence*. **Undue influence** is the use of any form of oppression, persuasion, pressure, or influence—short of actual force, but stronger than mere advice—that overpowers the will of a weaker party and induces an agreement. Cases involving undue influence are usually one of two types: where the parties are in a *fiduciary relationship*, and where there is no special relationship between the parties. Figure 5.1 illustrates the differences.

undue influence is the use of pressure to overpower the will of a weaker party and induce an agreement

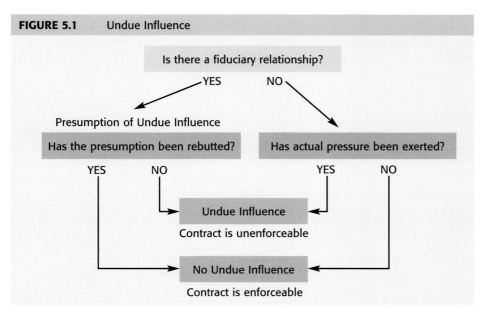

FIGURE 5.1   Undue Influence

[20.] The Supreme Court of Canada approved and adopted this approach in *RE Lister Ltd v Dunlop Canada Ltd* [1982] 135 DLR (3d) 1 (SCC).

a fiduciary relationship is a relationship in which one person is in a position of dominance over the other

A **fiduciary relationship** is one in which one person is in a position of dominance over the other. That power imbalance usually exists in a relationship that is based on trust or confidence. Fiduciary relationships generate a special kind of duty that requires the more powerful party to subordinate its personal interests in favour of the weaker party. Whenever parties in a fiduciary relationship enter into a business transaction, there is good reason to suspect undue influence on the part of the more powerful party. For this reason, the law imposes a *presumption of undue influence* whenever a fiduciary is involved in a transaction.

the law imposes a *presumption of undue influence* whenever a fiduciary is involved in a transaction

Not every transaction involving a fiduciary is defective, and the presumption of undue influence can be rebutted. If the fiduciary can prove that the transaction was fair, the contract will stand. Often, the best tactic for a fiduciary is to ensure that the other party receives independent legal advice before entering into the agreement.

the presumption of undue influence can be rebutted

undue influence must be proven when the parties do not share a fiduciary relationship

The second type of undue influence scenario arises when there is no special relationship between the parties. In such a case, there will be *no presumption* of undue influence. The party seeking relief from such a contract must prove that undue pressure was applied. When a business is not in a position of domination, it will be much harder for the other party to have the transaction set aside for undue influence. As a matter of risk management, a business can avoid that possibility by refraining from bullying tactics and, in appropriate circumstances, by suggesting independent legal advice.

Unconscionable Transactions

an unconscionable transaction is an agreement that no right-minded person would ever make and no fair-minded person would ever accept

Equity also provides relief from *unconscionable transactions*. An **unconscionable transaction** is characterized by its one-sidedness. It is an agreement that no right-minded person would ever make and no fair-minded person would ever accept. The weaker party must prove: (i) that there was an **improvident bargain**, one that was made without proper regard to the future, and (ii) that there was an inequality in the bargaining position of the two parties. (Figure 5.2 distinguishes the differences.) If those elements are satisfied, the court presumes that the transaction was unconscionable. The stronger party must then rebut the presumption of unconscionability. Even if the contract does not provide a benefit for the weaker party, the agreement may stand if the stronger party shows that the bargaining process was fair after all. As usual, the risk can be managed, most notably by ensuring that a customer receives independent legal advice. Ethical Perspective 5.1 illustrates the problem.

an improvident bargain is a bargain made without a regard to one's future

Several provinces have legislation governing unfair transactions. Some is preventive, using such devices as disclosure requirements or "cooling-off" periods to reduce the risk of a stronger party taking advantage of a weaker one.[21] Other statutes prohibit the use of particular unfair terms, such as exclusion or forfeiture clauses.[22] Still other statutes give the court a broad discretion to render harsh or unconscionable agreements ineffective, typically in legislation regulating money lending institutions and insurance companies.[23]

[21.] *Consumer Protection Act*, RSBC 1996, c 69, s 11 (BC); RSM 1987, c C200, s 62(1) (Man); RSO 1990, c C31 s 21 (Ont); *Direct Sellers Act*, RSNB 1973, c D-10, s 17 (NB).

[22.] *Consumer Protection Act*, RSM 1987, c C200, s 58 (Man); RSO 1990, c C31, s 34 (Ont); *Sale of Goods Act*, RSBC 1996, c 410, s 20 (BC).

[23.] *Money Lenders Act*, RSNS 1989, c 289, s 3 (NS); *Unconscionable Transactions Act*, RSA 1980, c U-2, s 2 (Alta); *Insurance Act*, RSO 1990, c I.8 (Ont); RSPEI 1988, c I-4, s 92 (PEI); RSNWT 1988, c I-4, s 46 (NWT).

FIGURE 5.2   Unconscionability

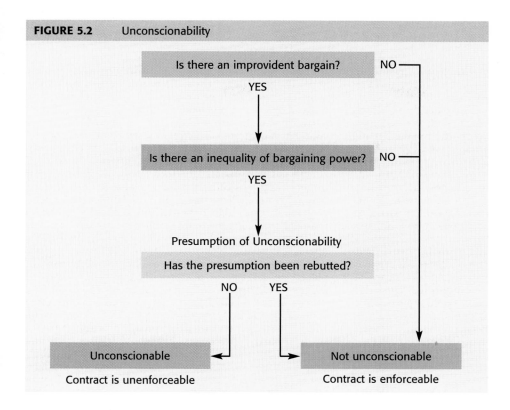

ETHICAL PERSPECTIVE 5.1

ETHICAL PERSPECTIVE 5.1

Beach v Eames (1976) 82 DLR (3d) 736 (Ont Co Ct)

Mr Beach was lying on his chesterfield with his legs propped up on pillows when Mr Pyatt, an insurance adjuster, unexpectedly showed up at his house. Beach was suffering the effects of a car accident, which had occurred a month earlier. Although he had missed several weeks of work because of his injuries, Beach had not yet seen his doctor or his lawyer, nor had he consulted with his own insurance agent.

Pyatt quickly and accurately sized up the situation. He knew that Beach had limited education and modest mental abilities. He also knew that Beach trusted him. Pyatt seized the opportunity and offered to settle, for a payment of $500, any potential claims that Beach might enjoy under his insurance policy. Beach agreed and signed the document, not real-

izing that his injuries might be worse than he suspected but not worse than Pyatt suspected.

Beach eventually realized that his injuries were very serious and that he had agreed to a very bad deal. He therefore sued to set aside the settlement contract.

Questions for Discussion

1. Did the insurance adjuster do anything wrong or was he just doing his job? Explain.

2. If you owned the insurance company, how would you respond to this incident?

3. If you were the judge in this case, how would you respond to this incident?

Chapter Summary

A contract may be defective due to: (i) incapacity, (ii) absence of writing, (iii) mistake, (iv) frustration, (v) illegality, and (vi) unfairness during bargaining.

A contract cannot normally be created by a person who lacks the legal power of consent. With the exception of a limited class of contracts concerning employment and the purchase of necessaries, a minor's contracts are voidable. Similarly, an agreement created by a mentally incapacitated adult may be set aside. Intoxicated persons who seek to avoid contractual liability can only do so if they can prove that they were incapable of knowing or appreciating what they were doing, and that the other party was aware of this incapacity. A statutory corporation, unlike a chartered corporation, has a limited contractual capacity. If a statutory corporation attempts to contract in a manner that exceeds its statutory powers, it lacks the capacity to contract. Although associations are generally incapable of contracting, some provinces have enacted legislation that enables associations involved in specific purposes to enter into contracts. Generally, a public authority acting within its powers has the capacity to contract independent of any specific statutory authority to do so.

The *Statute of Frauds* requires the party seeking to enforce such contracts as guarantees, contracts for the sale of an interest in land, and contracts not to be performed within a year, to adduce evidence in the form of a written and signed memorandum or note.

A mistake can interfere with the parties' attempt to reach an agreement or make it impossible for the object of the contract to be achieved. A mistake of identity or a material mistake about the terms of a contract may preclude its formation if the mistake is known to the other party. A material mistake about the subject matter of a contract may also negate consent. A common mistake about the existence of the subject matter renders it impossible for a contract to be fulfilled and will sometimes operate as a defence. A mistaken assumption that one or both parties make about the future can result in frustrating a contract. A contract is frustrated when some event occurs that makes further performance of the contract impossible or radically undermines its very purpose.

Illegal agreements are those that are expressly or implicitly prohibited by statute. Illegal agreements, along with other agreements that come into conflict with a common law rule or public policy, are often unenforceable. An example of an agreement that conflicts with public policy is a covenant in restraint of trade, which is enforceable only if it is reasonable.

When a party is pressured into an agreement or placed in an unfair position during the bargaining process, the agreement may be defective. Economic duress arises when a party enters into a contractual arrangement after being threatened with financial harm. Undue influence occurs when pressure is exerted by a stronger party to overpower the will of a weaker party and thereby induce an agreement. The law imposes a rebuttable presumption of undue influence whenever a fiduciary is involved in a transaction. The presumption is usually rebutted if the stronger party shows that the weaker party had the opportunity to seek independent advice. An unconscionable transaction is an agreement that no right-minded person would ever make and no fair-minded person would ever accept. Although it is generally up to the parties to make their own bargains, courts will interfere if a contract was the result of duress, undue influence, or unconscionability.

Review Questions

1. What is meant by the term "contractual capacity"?

2. Why are some contracts entered into by a minor voidable? What is an election, and when must it be made?

3. Give examples of contracts that will be enforced even if a person has not attained the age of majority.

4. Compare the legal effect of a contract entered into by a mentally disabled adult and a contract entered into by a minor.

5. Describe a situation that would lead a court to allow an intoxicated person to avoid contractual liability.

6. Explain how the contractual capacity of a chartered corporation differs from that of a statutory corporation.

7. Why must a business person be particularly careful when contracting with or on behalf of an association?

8. Do Indian bands have the legal capacity to contract? Under what circumstances do Native persons have the capacity to contract? Explain.

9. What is the difference between a guarantee and an indemnity?

10. Does the *Statute of Frauds* have effect throughout Canada? Briefly explain the rationale for the writing requirement.

11. Outline the writing requirements typically stipulated by a *Statute of Frauds*.

12. If a contract does not comply with the *Statute of Frauds*, making it unenforceable, does it follow that the agreement has no legal effect? Explain your answer.

13. Outline the difference between mistakes preventing the

creation of contracts and mistakes that make it impossible for the object of a contract to be achieved. Provide examples of each.

14. How might a case of mistaken identity provide a contractual defence?

15. Explain the doctrine of frustration. What are its effects?

16. What is the difference between common law and statutory approaches to the doctrine of frustration?

17. Explain why the plea of *non est factum* is part of the law of mistake.

18. What is a restrictive covenant? How is it relevant to the doctrine of public policy?

19. Outline three bases upon which a court might set aside an unfair contract. Is there a common thread underlying the rationale in each?

20. Explain the basic characteristics of a fiduciary relationship. Give examples.

Cases and Problems

1. Erin had always been independent. Shortly before her seventeenth birthday, she moved out of her parents' house and bought a used car, which she needed for her fledgling chocolate-covered-cranberry enterprise. She agreed to pay $15 000 for the car, $5000 as a down payment and the rest in monthly instalments over one year. She used the car mostly to make deliveries and to pick up supplies. After she drove the car for three months, the bearings burnt out. Since Erin was in a position to hire a delivery person, she decided that she no longer wanted the car. Having studied the basics of contract law in high school, Erin attempted to return the vehicle to the car dealership, claiming that she had elected to avoid the contract. The dealership refused, having received an opinion from its lawyer that a contract for necessaries is enforceable against a minor. Erin replied that the car was not a necessary, and that the contract was therefore not enforceable. Do you think that Erin will be permitted to avoid her contract with the dealership? Give reasons to support your position.

2. Elwood is a pig farmer who is known to enjoy a drink or two. One day in July, after a weekend of particularly heavy drinking, he staggered into the office of Pork Bellies of America and offered to sell all of his piglets. He promised to deliver them in October, as soon as they were fattened up. Hank, Pork Bellies' purchasing agent, saw that Elwood was extremely drunk, but decided to write up the contract anyway since the price was a fair one. After the deal was signed, Hank and Elwood went to the neighbourhood saloon to play darts and have lunch. The next day, after sobering up, Elwood was reminded about their agreement. In fact, over the course of the next two weeks, Hank and Elwood ran into each other on a number of occasions. Each time, Hank mentioned the deal, and Elwood acknowledged it. In September, the price of pork nearly doubled. Consequently, Elwood sent Pork Bellies of America a registered letter saying that he would not be delivering the pigs. He had decided to sell them to someone else at a higher price. Pork Bellies has sued Elwood. Will the court allow Elwood to avoid contractual liability? Give reasons to support your position.

3. Michel is a 22-year-old man who has been declared mentally incompetent. He can barely read or write and has an IQ of 41. Nevertheless, he executed a deed of conveyance transferring his proprietary interest in his late father's farm to his stepmother, Paula, in exchange for a small annual payment. Without providing much in the way of detail, Michel told his legal guardian about signing the papers and giving them to Paula. Michel's guardian quickly made an application to the court to set aside the deed and the agreement. The guardian freely admits that the price agreed to is fair and that Paula was not intent on fraud. Is the agreement between Paula and Michel enforceable? Would your answer be different if Paula were not related to Michel and did not know about his condition?

4. The general manager of Nunzio's Kosher Pizzeria has hired you to wash dishes in the evening. On your third shift, you are finally introduced to Nunzio. He seems like a nice guy as he welcomes you aboard. You are paid weekly by a cheque drawn from the account of a numbered company called 551999 Alberta Ltd. Nunzio's name is one of the two signatures on the cheques. Things go well for the first two months. Then you are not paid for three weeks in a row. The following week, the pizzeria is shut down. After finding out that the numbered company has gone bankrupt, you see your lawyer about suing Nunzio personally. After reviewing the corporate records, your lawyer tells you that there has been a mistake of identity—your employment contract was with the numbered company, but Nunzio is neither an officer or shareholder in that company. What does your lawyer mean by mistaken identity, and how will it apply in your case?

5. Fedor's law firm represents the Hole-In-One Mini Donuts Co. While doing some legal work for the company, Fedor discovers that the Hole-In-One no longer owns any assets. Rodya and Philka, the two corporate shareholders, verbally assure Fedor that they will not only answer for the legal fees already incurred by the corporation but will also take responsibility for any and all future charges. Although Fedor accepts this proposal, he does not require it to be put into writing. On the faith of their promise, the law firm continues to do work for the corporation. Fedor sends another bill to Hole-In-One, knowing full well that the corporation is unable to pay. Shortly thereafter, Fedor commences an action against Rodya and Philka. The defendants claim that

their promise is unenforceable because it was not in writing. How would you respond to that argument?

6. Several years back, Golden Joe's Geology bought a 1000-acre package of land in the Northwest Territories. When he purchased the property, Joe was sure to purchase the mineral rights as well. For years, Joe spent his summers panning for gold on the property. Recently, quite by accident, Joe discovered that his land is at the heart of a potentially lucrative diamond stash. Joe is overjoyed and has decided to sell his property so that he can retire to a tropical locale. He has agreed to sell the property and mineral rights to Prospectus Prospecting, which will invest the money needed to mine and process the diamonds. The agreement is drawn up and signed by both parties, and everyone is satisfied. However, when the actual land transfer is about to take place, it is discovered that the Crown grant of property to Joe has been substantially revoked. As a result, the land available for sale is in fact reduced by 90 percent. Is Joe still entitled to performance of the contract with Prospectus? Explain why or why not. As a prudent business manager, could Joe have better protected himself against such a possibility? Explain how.

7. Joel retires because of an injury at work. He and his wife, Samuriti, meet with a representative of his former employer's pension department to discuss disability benefits. The company's pension plan provides Joel with a choice. He can receive a monthly pension, which would be payable to his wife after his death. Or if his wife waives her right to a survivor's pension, he can opt to receive a larger monthly payment now. For Samuriti, English is a second language. She indicates this to the company manager, who encourages her to go ahead and read the waiver anyway. The manager explains very briefly that the form simply allows them to get more money now rather than having to wait to collect it. Samuriti tries her best to read the document but does so with little understanding. Not realizing that her signature would in any way affect her future, Samuriti signs the document. It is her impression that she is merely signing Joel's policy as a witness. Joel dies a few months later. Samuriti's lawyer brings an action for a declaration that the waiver is unenforceable. Does Samuriti have a good case? How might a better manager in the pensions office have handled this matter?

8. While Lamont attended university as an anthropology student, he received students loans totalling $25 000. At that time, he dealt with the Regal Bank. After finishing school, he moved away without advising the bank and without ever arranging to make payments on his student loans. The government had guaranteed the loan under the *Canada Student Loans Act*. The Regal Bank filed a claim to recover Lamont's debt from the government. In turn, the government went to court and obtained a judgment against Lamont. Because of the judgment, Lamont is unable to collect any income tax refunds until the debt is discharged. Lamont decides to appeal the decision and asks a clever friend at law school to help out with his case. According to Lamont's clever friend, regulation 10(1) of the *Canada Student Loans Regulations* requires all student loan agreements to include a clause requiring payment of the outstanding balance in the event that the student defaults on a loan. Lamont's agreement with the Regal Bank contained

no such clause. Therefore, according to Lamont's clever friend, the loan agreement is illegal. Will the court find Lamont's loan agreement to be unenforceable? Summarize what you believe will be the court's reasoning.

9. Edmond is the first mate on an old fishing trawler in Nova Scotia. Go Fish Inc has just purchased and outfitted a new vessel and wants to hire Edmond as its captain. The president of Go Fish Inc offers Edmond the job and, as an inducement, gives him a $10 000 loan. According to the terms of their arrangement, $3000 of the loan will be forgiven once Edmond as captain completes the new vessel's maiden voyage. Two days after the maiden voyage, Edmond suffers a long-term disability and is told that he might not be able to sail ever again. He phones his boss to tell her that he cannot continue to fulfill his part of the bargain. The ship continues to sail without him. Go Fish Inc wonders whether it can recover the $10 000 loan and an additional sum from Edmund for breach of contract. Your business consulting firm is contacted by Go Fish Inc to provide advice. What advice will you give? How might the business manager at Go Fish Inc have avoided having to seek your advice?

10. Mind Games Inc hires CompuNerd to overhaul its entire computer network for a flat fee of $350 000. Marinka, Mind Games Inc's general manager, stresses that the computer upgrades must be finished by the end of July so that there is enough time for Mind Games Inc to complete a large consulting project before its fall deadline. Marinka explains to CompuNerd that a failure to meet these deadlines would cause Mind Games Inc severe financial hardship. From the start, the computer overhaul seems jinxed. Due to several delays, the software upgrades are not quite half finished by the beginning of August. Bernie, the nerd in charge of the upgrades, meets with Marinka that afternoon. He claims that the delays were unavoidable and that CompuNerd is running into unexpected costs. He insists on renegotiating their agreement to include additional payment for "time and materials." He threatens Marinka by saying that, unless she agrees to the new terms, he will reduce his staff by half. Marinka realizes that such a reduction would mean that the computer upgrades would not be completed for two additional months. Finding herself in a serious bind, Marinka reluctantly agrees to alter the terms of the original flat-fee contract to include additional payment for time and materials. But after the job is finished, Mind Games Inc pays only the originally agreed upon amount. CompuNerd sues to recover the amount owing under the renegotiated terms. Marinka asks you to determine whether Mind Games Inc is obligated to pay the additional amount. How did you arrive at your conclusion?

11. Coby and Maya immigrate to Canada. Unlike her doctor husband, Maya speaks no English and misses her friends and family terribly. She becomes depressed. Her husband, Coby, prescribes an antidepressant in ever-increasing dosages. Eventually, the couple separates. Maya continues to take her medication. They enter into a separation agreement whereby Coby pays Maya support, but the monthly sum barely covers her rent and living expenses. During divorce proceedings, Maya claims that she was forced into the separation agreement by her overbearing husband and

that she was heavily sedated at the time. What is the legal basis of her claim? What must her husband prove to ensure that the separation agreement contract is enforceable?

12. One cold November day, Gertrude and Kenny Crowchild are called into a meeting with the regional manager of Big Bucks Bank of Canada. The bank manager makes it quite clear that if the Crowchilds refuse to pay off their outstanding business debts on their family farm, they will lose the farm. They suggest one way to do so would be to consider a second mortgage. The Crowchilds are told to seek financial advice before deciding. Optimistic that his business will soon pick up, Kenny is ready to meet the bank's demands. Gertrude is initially reluctant and wants to get a second opinion. After many heated discussions in private, Kenny eventually convinces Gertrude that the mortgage is a necessary evil. The next day, without seeking independent legal advice, the Crowchilds cosign a second mortgage at prime rate and secure the mortgage with the family farm. Five years later, the Crowchilds divorce. Gertrude contests the validity of the second mortgage, alleging that the bank coerced her and Kenny into an unconscionable transaction, and that her husband had exerted undue influence in convincing her to cosign the mortgage. Did Gertrude's relationship with her husband have any bearing on their contract with the bank? Is the bank responsible for the pressure exerted by Kenny Crowchild over his former wife?

6 Breach and Discharge

CHAPTER OVERVIEW

OBJECTIVES

After completing this chapter, you should be able to:

1. Explain the nature and effect of a discharged contract.
2. Discuss the manner in which a contract may be discharged by performance.
3. Describe the circumstances in which a contract can be discharged if a party has not performed in a timely manner.
4. Explain the difference between a condition subsequent, a true condition precedent, and a condition precedent.
5. Explain the difference between rescission, accord and satisfaction, and release.
6. Explain the difference between a variation and a novation.
7. Describe the circumstances under which a contractual right is waived.
8. Discuss three situations in which a contract may be discharged by operation of law.
9. Describe the differences between conditions, warranties, and intermediate terms. Explain the situations in which a contract may be discharged for breach.
10. Describe three different types of breach.

We have considered the formation of contracts, the contents of contracts, and the ways in which contracts may be defective. We will now finish our general discussion of contracts by examining the end of the contractual process. In this chapter, we will examine the ways in which a contract may be brought to an end. In the next, we will examine the remedies that may be available to the innocent party if a contract is brought to an end by a wrongful act.

A business person is often keenly interested in knowing whether a contract has been brought to an end. Suppose that a manufacturer contractually agrees to deliver 500 widgets to a business. Do the manufacturer's obligations come to an end after it delivers the 500th item? If the purchaser wants more widgets, does the manufacturer have to supply them? What if some of the widgets that have been delivered are defective? Is the manufacturer obligated to repair or replace them? To answer those questions, we must examine the discharge of contracts.

As we saw in Chapters 4 and 5, some contracts come to an end when they are voided or rescinded. Most contracts, however, are brought to an end through discharge. **Discharge** means that the parties are relieved of the need to perform in the future. We will look at a number of ways in which a contract can be discharged. (See Figure 6.1 on p. 124.) Some involve performance; others reflect the parties' agreements or intentions; still others arise by operation of law; and one particularly important type of discharge occurs when one party wrongfully fails to perform as expected.

> discharge means that the parties are relieved of the need to perform in the future

DISCHARGE BY PERFORMANCE

When parties enter into a contract, they generally assume that everything will go well. And, in fact, the most common method of discharge is **performance**, which is the fulfillment of the obligations that were imposed by a contract. Once the parties have satisfied their obligations, they have nothing more to do under the contract.

> performance is the fulfillment of the obligations that were imposed by the contract

In some situations, however, it may be difficult to determine whether proper performance has occurred. This usually arises because of the general rule that requires the parties to perform *exactly* as the contract stipulated. Any deviation from the terms of the contract, however small, is considered a breach, rather than performance, and will entitle the innocent party to a remedy.

> the parties generally must perform exactly as the contract stipulated

Time of Performance

Notwithstanding the general rule that requires strict compliance with the terms of a contract, the courts usually hold that **time is not of the essence**. In other words, even if a contract states that performance must occur by a particular date, a party may be entitled to perform late. However, if it does so, it can be held liable for losses that the other party suffers as a result of the delay. For example, suppose that I contractually agree to deliver a vehicle to you by June 1. Although our agreement stipulated that date, I may be allowed to discharge our contract by delivering on June 8. But if I do so, I may be required to compensate you for the fact that you had to rent a car for a week.

> time is not of the essence in most situations

In some situations, however, time *is* of the essence. If so, late performance can be refused, in which case the contract will not be discharged by performance. For example, time is of the essence if the parties agree to that fact, either expressly or implicitly. Furthermore, even if time is not initially of the essence, a party can insist upon timely performance by giving reasonable notice that performance must occur by a specific date. Finally, even if the parties do not agree on a specific time or date, the courts will find that performance must

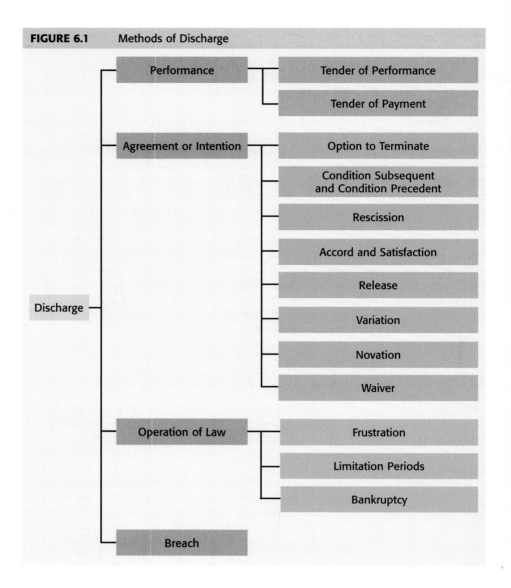

FIGURE 6.1 Methods of Discharge

occur within a reasonable time, having regard to all of the circumstances, including the subject matter of the contract. For example, a contract dealing with perishable goods or a volatile market may require the parties to act promptly.

Tender of Payment

Most contracts require a payment of money by at least one of the parties. We have all satisfied that sort of obligation on many occasions, usually without giving it much thought. However, business people should be aware of some very specific rules that govern payments.

First, the debtor has the primary obligation of locating the creditor and *tendering*, or offering, payment, even if the creditor has not asked for it. The tender must be reasonable. It cannot occur at an inconvenient time or under

a debtor is obliged to reasonably tender payment

inconvenient circumstances. However, a reasonable tender has to be made only once. If such a tender is rejected, the debtor still has to pay the debt but can wait for the creditor to come by. Furthermore, interest does not accrue on a payment once a reasonable tender has been made, even if that tender is improperly rejected. Likewise, if the parties' dispute eventually goes to trial, a judge may punish a creditor who improperly rejected a reasonable tender by holding that party liable for the debtor's costs of litigation.

Second, unless a contract says otherwise, a creditor can insist on receiving *legal tender*. **Legal tender** is a payment that is offered in the form of notes (bills) and coins to a certain value.[1] Consequently, a creditor generally does not have to accept payment by way of a cheque or electronic debit. Nor does it have to accept payment from a disgruntled or idiosyncratic customer who tries to pay a large debt with an enormous bag of pennies. A creditor does not even have to make change—the debtor must provide exactly the correct amount of money. However, creditors usually waive the strict requirements regarding legal tender and happily receive any acceptable form of payment. As a precaution, however, a business person who intends to pay by anything other than a precise amount of legal tender should provide for that possibility in the contract.

Third, despite the usual rule, a debtor does not have to actually tender payment if it would obviously be refused. Consequently, if the creditor indicates beforehand that it intends to reject payment, the debtor does not have to waste time on a useless gesture.

Tender of Performance

Many of the same principles apply when a contract requires the provision of goods or services rather than money. For instance, while the party who owes the obligation is required to properly tender performance, it only has to do so once. Furthermore, that party is discharged of its duty to perform if the other party renders performance impossible. For example, the owner of a parcel of land may refuse to allow a building contractor onto the work site. In that situation, the innocent party is entitled to begin a lawsuit immediately to recover *damages*. **Damages**, which is the amount of money that the court may order the defendant to pay to the plaintiff, are discussed in Chapter 7.

A tender is usually effective only if the goods or services conform precisely with terms of the contract. Occasionally, a party can be discharged from further obligations if it provides *substantial performance*.[2] **Substantial performance** generally conforms with the contract but is defective or incomplete in some minor way. In deciding whether substantial performance has occurred, a court will consider such factors as the nature of the defect and the difference between the contract price and the cost of curing the defect. For example, many building contracts state that payment is due only once construction is completed. Nevertheless, if a builder leaves a work site without having installed, say, several door knobs, it will likely be discharged from its obligations and will be entitled to payment. The innocent party, however, will be entitled to deduct the cost of having the door knobs installed by another company.

legal tender is a payment that is offered in the form of notes (bills) and coins to a certain value

an obligation to provide goods or services must be performed in much the same way as an obligation to pay money

damages is the amount of money that the court may order the defendant to pay to the plaintiff

substantial performance generally conforms with the contract but is defective or incomplete in some minor way

---

[1] *Currency Act*, RSC 1985, c C-52, s 8 (Can). In terms of coinage, legal tender consists of up to $40 in two-dollar coins, $25 in one-dollar coins, $10 in quarters or dimes, $5 in nickels, and 25¢ in pennies.

[2] *H Dakin & Co Ltd v Lee* [1916] 1 KB 566 (CA).

DISCHARGE BY AGREEMENT

In some situations, one or both parties can discharge a contract even though it was not fully performed. That type of discharge can occur in several ways.

Option to Terminate

an **option to terminate** is a contractual provision that allows one or both parties to discharge a contract without the agreement of the other

When creating a contract, the parties can insert an **option to terminate**, which allows one or both of them to discharge the contract without the agreement of the other. That sort of provision is often found in employment contracts. Each party may be permitted to end the relationship on, say, two-months' notice.[3] In principle, however, an option to terminate can be inserted into any type of contract.

Options to terminate are frequently subject to restrictions. For example, a party may be entitled to terminate only after giving reasonable notice that it intends to do so. Similarly, the contract may require the party that exercises the option to compensate the other party for the losses that it suffered as a result of the early termination.

Condition Subsequent and Condition Precedent

a **condition subsequent** is a contractual term that states that the agreement will be terminated if a certain event occurs

When creating a contract, the parties can also insert a **condition subsequent**, a contractual term that states that the agreement will be terminated if a certain event occurs. A condition subsequent is different from an option to terminate because it does not have to be exercised by either party to be effective. Under a condition subsequent, a contract may be automatically discharged as soon as the relevant event happens. For example, the contract represented by a ticket to an open-air concert may state that the musicians' obligation to perform is discharged in the event of rain. If so, the contract will probably also entitle the disappointed ticket holder to a refund or a ticket to another event.

a **true condition precedent** is a contractual term that states that an agreement will come into existence only if and when a certain event occurs

A contract that is subject to a condition subsequent exists until it is discharged by the occurrence of the relevant event. It is also possible, however, to make a contract subject to a true condition precedent. A **true condition precedent** is a contractual term that states that an agreement will come into existence only if and when a certain event occurs.[4] Suppose that you and I want to deal in a certain type of weapon, but we are concerned that such a contract may be illegal. We can settle the terms of the agreement but state that our contract will actually be created only if it receives government approval. In that situation, we would not have a contract and therefore would not be violating the law if government approval was refused.

Strictly speaking, a condition subsequent is a contractual term that causes an existing contract to come to an end upon the occurrence of a specified event, whereas a true condition precedent is a contractual term that allows a contract to come into existence only once a specified event occurs. Unfortunately, Canadian courts also use the term "condition precedent" to refer to a contract that is *formed* immediately, but that does not have to be *performed* until later or perhaps at all. As we will see in Chapter 14, that type of condition precedent is very common in contracts for the sale of land. Consider the example in Business Law in Action 6.1.

[3.] As discussed in Chapter 25, if an employment contract does not contain such a provision, the courts will allow the contract to be terminated on "reasonable notice."

[4.] *Pym v Campbell* (1856) 119 ER 903 (KB).

BUSINESS LAW IN ACTION 6.1

Condition Precedent[5]

Yuri offers to sell his house to you for $250 000. You are eager to accept that offer, but you do not want to completely commit yourself to the purchase until you are sure that you can sell your own cottage for at least $200 000. You and Yuri therefore agree on the terms that would govern the sale of Yuri's house, but state that the performance of that contract is conditional on your ability to find a buyer for your cottage within 30 days.

Although the relevant term of your agreement will be called a "condition precedent," it will not affect the *existence* of the contract between you and Yuri. It will merely *suspend* your obligations to perform. In other words, your contract occurs immediately, but unless and until you are able to find a buyer for your cottage, you do not have to pay $250 000 to Yuri and he does not have to transfer his house to you. Furthermore, if you cannot find a buyer for your cottage within 30 days, your contract with Yuri will be discharged.

Questions for Discussion

1. Why would you want to enter into such an agreement?
2. Why would Yuri agree to such an agreement?

Note two more things about the type of condition precedent discussed in the last exercise. First, because a contract exists from the outset, Yuri is not entitled to sell his house to another person during the 30-day period. If he does, he will be in breach of his contract with you. After all, he has only one house to sell and has already agreed to sell it to you. To avoid that problem, Yuri should have insisted on another contractual term that would have required you to sell your cottage, or otherwise obtain the purchase price for his house, more quickly (say, within three days) if he received interest from another prospective purchaser. That sort of term would have allowed Yuri to entertain other offers, while still providing you with some security.

Second, while a condition precedent may suspend the *primary* obligations under an existing contract, one or both parties may have *subsidiary* obligations that they are required to perform right away. For example, while you would not have to pay the purchase price for Yuri's house immediately, you probably would have to make a reasonable effort to satisfy the condition precedent by finding a purchaser for your cottage. If you failed to do so, you could be held liable for a breach of that subsidiary obligation.[6]

Concept Summary 6.1 shows the differences between conditions subsequent, true conditions precedent, and conditions precedent.

Concept Summary 6.1

Conditions Subsequent, True Conditions Precedent, and Conditions Precedent

Type of Condition	Time of Creation of Contract	Effect of Condition
Condition subsequent	Immediate	Discharge of existing contract
True condition precedent	If and when condition is satisfied	Creation of contract
Condition precedent	Immediate	Suspension of primary obligations

[5.] *Wiebe v Bobsein* [1986] 1 WWR 270 (BC CA).

[6.] *Dynamic Transport Ltd v OK Detailing Ltd* (1978) 85 DLR (3d) 19 (SCC).

Rescission

Options to terminate, conditions subsequent, and conditions precedent are ways in which the parties can agree, *when initially creating a contract*, that their obligations will be discharged in certain circumstances. The same sort of agreement can also be reached *after a contract has been created*.

First, we must distinguish between *executory contracts* and *executed contracts*. A contract is **executory** from a particular party's perspective if that party has not fully performed its obligations. A contract is **executed** from a particular party's perspective if that party has fully performed its obligations.

If a contract is executory on both sides, it can be discharged through *rescission*. **Rescission** occurs when the parties agree to bring their contract to an end.[7] That agreement may be express or implied. For example, if neither party performs under a contract for a very long time, a court may infer that they agreed to abandon it. Similarly, the parties can enter into a new contract that necessarily implies the discharge of an earlier one. Suppose I agree to sell my car to you for $5000. If, before executing that agreement, we enter into another contract that calls upon me to deliver my car and my boat to you in exchange for $7500, the second contract necessarily implies the rescission of the first. After all, we both know that I have only one car to sell.

As Chapter 3 explained, an agreement is usually enforceable only if it is supported by *consideration*. Each party must either provide a benefit or suffer a detriment. If an executory contract is rescinded, that requirement is easily satisfied. Each party suffers a detriment by giving up the right to insist upon performance of the original contract.

*a contract is **executory** from a particular party's perspective if that party has not fully performed its obligations*

*a contract is **executed** from a particular party's perspective if that party has fully performed its obligations*

rescission occurs when the parties agree to bring a contract to an end

Accord and Satisfaction

The situation is more difficult if one party has fully performed, or *executed*, the contract. In that case, a mere agreement to discharge a contract may be unenforceable for lack of consideration. The party that has not performed cannot suffer a detriment by giving up the right to insist upon performance. After all, the other party has already performed. Consider the case in You Be the Judge 6.1.

YOU BE THE JUDGE 6.1

Accord and Satisfaction

Miles and Sudevi entered into a contract. He agreed to repair her roof and she promised to drill a water well on his farm. Miles immediately fulfilled his obligation by repairing Sudevi's roof. Sudevi later discovered, however, that contrary to her initial assumption, Miles's farm is situated on rock rather than sand. She also realized that she did not have the type of equipment required to drill a well through rock. Miles took pity on her and generously agreed to simply discharge their contract.

Questions for Discussion

1. Did Sudevi provide consideration in exchange for Miles's agreement to discharge the contract? Could she provide consideration by releasing Miles from his obligation to repair her roof?

2. Is Miles required to honour his promise to discharge the contract?

[7.] This use of the term "rescission" must be distinguished from the way in which "rescission" was discussed in Chapter 4. In this context, the word refers to a *bilateral*, or two-party, agreement to discharge a contract. In the context of contracts induced by fraud, misrepresentation, or mistake, the same word refers to a *unilateral*, or one-party, decision by the innocent party to terminate a contract.

The agreement to discharge the original contract in the last exercise would have been enforceable if there had been accord and satisfaction. **Accord and satisfaction** occurs when a party gives up its right to demand contractual performance in return for some new benefit. "Accord" refers to the parties' new agreement; "satisfaction" to the new consideration provided by the party that is relieved of the need to perform the original contract. Suppose that Miles's second agreement with Sudevi (the accord) required her promise to build a water tank on his property (the satisfaction). If so, he could not require Sudevi to perform the original contract. In effect, by promising to build a water tank, she bought the right to not drill the well.

accord and satisfaction occurs when a party gives up its right to demand contractual performance in return for some new benefit

Release

The parties can agree to discharge a contract without fresh consideration if they enter into a *release*. A **release** is an agreement under seal to discharge a contract. As we saw in Chapter 3, a seal serves as a substitute for consideration. As a result, an agreement can be enforceable even if it is not supported by an exchange of value.

a release is an agreement under seal to discharge a contract

Variation

Parties usually use an accord and satisfaction or a release when they want to terminate a contractual relationship. In some situations, however, they may want to retain their agreement, but in a modified form. **Variation** involves an agreement to alter the terms of an existing contract.

variation involves an agreement to vary the terms of an existing contract

A variation requires the consent of both parties as well as fresh consideration from both. That requirement is usually satisfied as each party either abandons rights under the original terms of the contract or assumes new obligations under the modified terms of the contract.

Suppose that Stefan and Nicole enter into a contract under which he promises to cut her lawn 20 times during the summer, and she agrees to pay a lump sum of $2000 at the end of the season. However, spring arrives unusually late, and Nicole's lawn will not require as much attention as expected. The parties might agree to vary their contract by requiring Stefan to perform only 15 times and requiring Nicole to pay only $1500. If so, Stefan provides consideration by suffering the detriment of giving up the right to $500 and Nicole provides consideration by suffering the detriment of giving up the right to lawn care on five occasions.

Novation

Variation can be used to introduce small changes to an existing contract. However, if the parties want to introduce substantial changes that go to the root of their agreement, they can use *novation*. Generally speaking, **novation** is a process by which one contract is discharged and another is introduced in its place.

novation is a process by which one contract is discharged and another is introduced in its place

The new contract may differ from the old one because it imposes significantly different obligations on the same parties. Suppose that Lucy initially agrees to sell an apartment building to Ricardo. If she later discovers that she is unable to perform that contract, she might offer to sell a condominium complex instead. If Ricardo agrees to that proposal, the parties could discharge their original agreement for the apartment building and replace it with a new agreement for the condominium complex.

Usually, however, novation involves a substitution of parties rather than obligations. The Supreme Court of Canada has defined novation as "a *trilateral* agreement by which an existing contract is extinguished and a new contract is brought into being in its place."[8] In that situation, the parties under the new contract essentially adopt the rights and liabilities that existed under the old contract. Consider Business Law in Action 6.2.

BUSINESS LAW IN ACTION 6.2

Novation

Rainbow Developments bought a large parcel of land on which to build a shopping centre. To finance that project, it borrowed $500 000 from First National Bank. As security for that loan, Rainbow gave First National a mortgage over the land. Unfortunately, Rainbow later experienced financial difficulties and was forced to sell its land to you. You and Rainbow agree that you should effectively step into its shoes.

Question for Discussion

1. Assuming that First National is willing to let you take Rainbow's place, describe the process that should be used.

There are several things to note about novations. First, a novation cannot occur unless all the affected parties consent to the new arrangement. In Business Law in Action 6.2, First National could not be forced to create a mortgage with you on the same terms as its earlier mortgage with Rainbow. Second, whether new obligations or new parties are introduced, the consideration that supports the agreement to discharge the old contract is the original parties' willingness to release their rights under that agreement. Third, although novation can be achieved either expressly or implicitly, as a matter of risk management, the agreement should always be clearly written.

Waiver

We have seen a number of situations in which the parties agree to discharge their contractual obligations. In each instance, the agreement is enforceable only if it is supported by consideration or a seal. However, a promise to discharge or suspend a contractual obligation may be enforceable even without consideration or a seal.

waiver occurs when a party abandons a right to insist on contractual performance

Waiver occurs when a party abandons a right to insist on contractual performance.[9] There are several points to note. First, waiver does *not* require consideration or a seal. It operates as an exception to the general rule that the courts will not enforce gratuitous promises. Second, waiver does not have to take any particular form. It can be either written or oral, express or implied. Third, because waiver allows a contractual party to obtain a benefit without providing anything in return, the courts require clear evidence that the other party intended to waive its rights. Fourth, although the cases are somewhat inconsistent, the better view is that waiver is effective only if the party who received the waiver relied upon it. And finally, a party can retract its own waiver if it gives reasonable notice of its intention to do so *and* if retraction is unfair to the other party. Case Brief 6.1 illustrates these rules.

[8.] *National Trust Co v Mead* (1990) 71 DLR (4th) 488 at 500 (SCC).

[9.] Waiver is similar to the concept of promissory estoppel, which we examined in Chapter 3. Some commentators suggest that the main difference between the two is simply jurisdictional. Waiver was developed by the courts of law, and promissory estoppel was developed by the courts of equity.

CASE BRIEF 6.1

Maritime Life Assurance Company v Saskatchewan River Bungalows Ltd (1994) 115 DLR (4th) 478 (SCC)

Maritime Life Assurance (MLA) sold an insurance policy to Saskatchewan River Bungalows (SRB) on the life of Mr Fikowski. The contract required that the premium (that is, the price) be received at the insurer's head office in Halifax by July 26 each year. In 1984, SRB sent a cheque for the premium on July 24, but it was lost in the mail. At that point, the insurer was entitled to terminate the policy for non-payment. Nevertheless, it sent a number of notices that offered to accept late payment. By February 1985, however, it ran out of patience and sent a letter stating that the policy had been cancelled. In April, SRB collected its mail for the first time in many months and finally became aware that MLA had not received the cheque for the premium. It then waited another three months before delivering a replacement

cheque. Unfortunately, by that time, Mr Fikowski had fallen ill and died soon after. SRB then claimed a benefit under the life insurance policy and argued that MLA had waived its right to timely payment because it had not insisted on strict performance under the contract.

The Supreme Court of Canada held that MLA had implicitly waived its right to timely payment when it offered to accept late payment. However, the Court also held that MLA was entitled to retract its waiver. Furthermore, because SRB received notice that the policy was cancelled at the same time that it received the insurer's earlier offer to accept late payment (April 1985), it had not relied upon that offer. Consequently, MLA was not required to give reasonable notice of its intention to retract its waiver. The result was that SRB could not collect a benefit under the life insurance policy when Mr Fikowski died.

DISCHARGE BY OPERATION OF LAW

We have examined contracts that are discharged by performance or by agreement of the parties. However, a contract may also be discharged by operation of law. In this section, we will briefly consider three situations in which that frequently happens:

- frustration
- lapse of limitation period
- bankruptcy

Frustration

As Chapter 5 explained, a contract is *frustrated* when it becomes impossible to perform or when the circumstances change so much that performance would be something much different than the parties initially expected. One result of frustration is that the parties are, as a matter of law, discharged from performing any remaining obligations.

frustration discharges a contract

Lapse of Limitation Period

The need to perform a contractual obligation can also be displaced by the passage of time. **Statutes of limitation** require a party who has suffered a breach of contract to sue within a certain period, usually six years. There are two main reasons for that legislation. First, the courts do not want to deal with claims if the evidence is old and unreliable. Second, it is unfair to hold the threat of a lawsuit over a person's head for a very long time.

statutes of limitation require a party who has suffered a breach of contract to sue within a certain period

Technically speaking, a contract is not discharged if a person fails to sue within the required time. That person is simply prevented from starting legal proceedings. There are, however, exceptions to that rule. Most significantly, the right to sue may be revived, even after the lapse of the limitation period, if the party that broke the contract acknowledges that it is still liable.[10] It might do so by paying part of its outstanding debt. Consider Ethical Perspective 6.1.

ETHICAL PERSPECTIVE 6.1

Limitation Periods

Twelve years ago, you entered into a contract with Estevan Flooring Inc for the installation of a hardwood dance floor in your tavern. Estevan Flooring completed the work and delivered a bill for $7500. Unfortunately, your tavern had fallen on hard times and you were able to pay only $2500. In the circumstances, the owner of Estevan Flooring saw little point in suing you for the rest of the money. In the past two years, however, your tavern has enjoyed tremendous business and has prospered financially. Estevan Flooring therefore

has asked you for the remaining $5000, plus interest. It has done so despite being informed by its lawyer that the statutory limitation period has expired.

Questions for Discussion

1. Will you pay the remainder of the bill that you initially received from Estevan Flooring?
2. Is your decision based strictly on legal considerations? Is it influenced by commercial considerations? By moral considerations? To what extent do those different considerations overlap?

Bankruptcy

bankruptcy may result in the discharge of contractual obligations

Bankruptcy is discussed at length in Chapter 22. Here, it is enough to note that a bankrupt debtor is discharged from outstanding contractual obligations *if* the bankruptcy was caused by misfortune rather than by misconduct.[11]

DISCHARGE BY BREACH OF CONDITION

a breach occurs whenever a party does not perform precisely as promised

Finally, a contract may be discharged if one of the *terms*, or promises, that it contains is broken. As we saw in the discussion on discharge by performance, a contract must be strictly performed. Consequently, a **breach** occurs whenever a party does not perform precisely as promised. However, not every breach will result in the discharge of a contract.

Types of Terms

a term is a condition if the innocent party would be substantially deprived of the expected benefit of the contract in the event of breach

According to the traditional approach, the law distinguishes between two types of contractual terms. First, a term is a **condition** if the innocent party would be substantially deprived of the expected benefit of the contract in the event of

---

[10] *Limitations Act*, RSA 1980, c L-15.1, s 9 (Alta); *Limitation of Actions Act*, RSBC 1996, c 266, s 5(5) (BC); *Limitations Act*, RSM 1987, c L150, s 9 (Man); *Limitations Act*, RSNB 1973, c L-8, s 11 (NB); *Limitations Act*, RSNS 1989, c 258, s 6(1) (NS); *Limitations Act*, RSO 1990, c L-15, s 51(1) (Ont); *Statute of Limitations*, RSPEI 1988, c S-7, s 6 (PEI); *Limitations Act*, RSS 1978, c L-15, s 7 (Sask).

[11] *Bankruptcy and Insolvency Act*, RSC 1985, c B-3, s 175 (Can).

breach.[12] For example, if a rental company delivers a minivan, instead of a large moving truck as it promised, the customer receives something much different than it expected. Furthermore, given the serious consequences of the company's breach, it would be unfair to require the customer to carry on with the contract by accepting the vehicle and paying for it, even at a reduced price. Since the customer is deprived of the essence of what it expected to receive, it should not be required to uphold its end of the bargain. Consequently, the customer enjoys an option. It can choose to discharge the contract and claim damages for the losses that it suffered as a result of the breach. Or it can choose to continue on with the contract and merely claim damages for the losses that it suffered because it received a minivan instead of a large moving truck. Breach of a condition does not automatically discharge a contract. Nor can a party generally bring a contract to an end simply by breaching a condition. The right of discharge lies with the innocent party.

> breach of a condition generally provides the innocent party with the option of discharging the contract

> breach of a condition does not automatically discharge a contract

Second, a term is a **warranty** if the innocent party would *not* be substantially deprived of the expected benefit of the contract in the event of breach. Suppose that a rental company properly delivers a large moving truck but, contrary to its promise, the radio receives AM signals, rather than FM signals. Given the relatively insignificant nature of that breach, it is fair to require the customer to carry on with the contract. It is, after all, still receiving the essence of what it expected to receive. Consequently, a breach of warranty does *not* provide the innocent party with the option of discharging the contract. Although that party can claim damages for any losses that it suffered as a result of the breach, it must continue on with the contract.

> a term is a **warranty** if the innocent party would *not* be substantially deprived of the expected benefit of the contract if that term is breached

> breach of a warranty does *not* provide the innocent party with the option of discharging the contract

While the courts generally continue to follow the traditional approach, they have recently recognized that some contractual terms cannot be treated so simply. Historically, it was thought that all terms could be classified, as soon as a contract was formed, as either (i) conditions, which support the right of discharge if breached, or (ii) warranties, which do not. That view can lead to unfair or inconvenient results. It is sometimes clear that the breach of a particular term will, or will not, substantially deprive the innocent party of the expected benefit of a contract. But often, a seemingly important term may be breached in a trivial way, or a seemingly unimportant term may be breached in a significant way. For example, the courts have occasionally held that date of shipment is a condition of a contract, and that if goods are shipped one day earlier or later than agreed, the innocent party is entitled to discharge the contract, even if it did not suffer a loss as a result of the breach.[13] That result may be difficult to justify, especially if the innocent party discharges the contract only because it wanted a way out of a contract that it realized was unprofitable.

To avoid that sort of situation, the courts now recognize a third type of term that applies when the consequences of a breach are not obvious at the outset. A term is **intermediate** if, depending upon the circumstances, the innocent party may or may not be substantially deprived of the expected benefit of the contract in the event of breach.[14] As you would expect, the innocent party may or may not have the right to discharge the contract if an intermediate term is breached. The existence of that right depends upon whether the breach *in fact* substantially deprived that party of the expected benefit of the agreement. In that sense,

> a term is **intermediate** if, depending upon the circumstances, the innocent party may or may not be substantially deprived of the expected benefit of the contract in the event of breach

---

12. We must be careful to distinguish "condition" as it is used in this context from the same word as it was used in the context of "conditions subsequent" and "conditions precedent."

13. *Bowes v Shand* (1877) 2 App Cas 455 (HL).

14. Lawyers sometimes use "innominate term" instead. That type of term is innominate, or unnamed, because it is not named either a "condition" or a "warranty."

intermediate terms are "wait-and-see" terms. Case Brief 6.2 provides an excellent example.

CASE BRIEF 6.2

Hong Kong Fir Shipping Co v Kawasaki Kisen Kaisha Ltd [1962] 2 QB 26 (CA)

The plaintiff owned a ship that it chartered, or rented, to the defendant for two years. A term of that contract required the plaintiff to provide a "seaworthy" vessel. The contract also stated that if the ship was out of service for repairs during the life of the agreement, the defendant would be entitled to extend the duration of the contract accordingly. In fact, the ship was out of commission for most of the first seven months of the contract because its engines required extensive repairs. The defendant therefore claimed that it discharged the agreement on the basis of the plaintiff's breach of condition. The plaintiff, however, denied that it had breached a condition. Indeed, it claimed that the defendant had breached a condition of the contract when it tried to discharge the agreement.

The English Court of Appeal held for the plaintiff. It said that the seaworthiness term could be breached in a variety of ways, some serious and others trivial. For example, a ship might be unseaworthy either because its hull is irreparably pierced or because its toilets do not work quite right. The disputed term therefore was classified as an intermediate term, which would support a right of discharge only if its breach substantially deprived the defendant of the expected benefit of the agreement. And in the circumstances, the court held that, although the vessel required extensive repairs during the initial part of the contract, the defendant could still enjoy the essence of the agreement. As a result, the defendant was liable for a breach of contract on the basis that it wrongfully claimed to discharge the agreement.

Concept Summary 6.2 shows the basic differences between conditions, warranties, and intermediate terms.

Concept Summary 6.2

Conditions, Warranties, and Intermediate Terms

Type of Term	Effect of Breach on Innocent Party	Rights of Innocent Party
Condition	substantially deprived of benefit of contract	discharge contract and claim damages *or* continue with contract and claim damages
Warranty	not substantially deprived of benefit of contract	continue with contract and claim damages
Intermediate	depending upon circumstances—may or may not be substantially deprived of benefit of contract	depending upon seriousness of breach— discharge contract and claim damages *or* continue with contract and claim damages

It is often difficult to distinguish between conditions, warranties, and intermediate terms. The parties can expressly state that breach of a certain term will or will not support a right of discharge. A statute may also classify a term as either a condition or a warranty.[15] Usually, however, a judge must decide the matter by examining all of the circumstances. In essence, the court asks whether the parties, as reasonable people, would have intended to allow the innocent party to bring the contract to an end in the situation that happened. In doing so, the judge may be influenced by the portion of the total performance that is defective, the likelihood that the breach will be repeated in the future if the contract calls for performance by instalments, and the seriousness of the breach to the innocent party.

---

[15]. That is true under the *Sale of Goods Act*, which is discussed in Chapter 8.

As a matter of risk management, note that uncertainty regarding the classification of terms often creates the sort of dilemma that arose in *Hong Kong Fir Shipping*. You may believe that the other party breached the contract in a way that allows you to discharge the agreement and sue for damages. But if you are wrong about that, *you* may commit a breach that allows the other party to discharge the contract and sue *you* for damages. Consequently, in a doubtful case, you should seek legal advice before attempting to discharge a contract for breach. You should also be aware that even your lawyer may not be able to predict how a judge will interpret the situation. Business Decision 6.1 illustrates that difficulty.

BUSINESS DECISION 6.1

Discharging for Breach

You wanted to operate a live-bait kiosk during a week-long fishing competition at Lake Katenben. Although you expected to sell some of the worms to recreational anglers, you assumed that most of your sales would be to the competitors. You entered into a contract with LJ, a local farmer, which required him to deliver 10 kilograms of worms to you each morning at 3:00 am for the seven days that the fishing competition was scheduled to run. LJ properly performed on the first day, but he did not deliver the second day's bag of worms until 9:30 am. Although you were able to sell a small portion of the second day's shipment to recreational anglers, you sold nothing to the competitive anglers, who had all left the dock before sunrise.

You are in a dilemma. One the one hand, you know that if you miss another day of trade with the competitive anglers,

you will probably not earn a profit during the week-long competition. You also know that if you discharge your contract with LJ, you can arrange an alternative supply of worms without difficulty. On the other hand, you are worried that if LJ's single late delivery does not really justify discharge, you will be liable to him in breach of contract.

Questions for Discussion

1. Should you attempt to discharge your contract with LJ?

2. Would it be relevant that LJ's breach was caused by his difficulty in finding 10 kilograms of worms on the second night? What if his breach was caused by the fact that he was involved in an automobile accident at 2:00 am while driving to deliver the load of worms to you?

3. Would it be relevant if the competition lasted one month rather than one week?

Types of Breach

Whether it applies to a condition, a warranty, or an intermediate term, a breach can occur in three ways:

- defective performance
- anticipatory breach
- self-induced impossibility

Defective Performance

Most breaches take the form of *defective performance*. **Defective performance** occurs when a party fails to properly perform an obligation due under a contract. That idea is quite broad. It includes a complete lack of performance. For example, a photographer may entirely fail to attend a wedding that he was expected to film. It also includes a relatively trivial departure from the terms of a contract. For example, a wedding photographer may use 49 rolls of film, rather than 50 as promised.

defective performance occurs when a party fails to properly perform an obligation due under a contract

Anticipatory Breach

anticipatory breach occurs when a party indicates in advance, by words or conduct, that it does not intend to fulfill an obligation when it falls due under a contract

Defective performance applies to an obligation that is due. An *anticipatory breach* arises before an obligation is to be performed. **Anticipatory breach** occurs when a party indicates in advance, by words or conduct, that it does not intend to fulfill an obligation when it falls due. Generally, the same rules apply to an anticipatory breach as to other types of breach. For example, depending upon the seriousness of the situation, the breach may or may not entitle the innocent party to discharge the contract. And even if an anticipatory breach is serious enough to support discharge, a contract will not actually be brought to an end unless the innocent party chooses to do so. As an English judge poetically said, "An unaccepted repudiation is like a thing writ in water and of no value to anybody."[16]

The innocent party is entitled to seek relief *immediately* if there is an anticipatory breach. There is no need to wait until the time when the obligation was to be performed. Suppose you enter into a contract to rent a cottage for the summer months. If the landlord contacts you in February and states that the premises will not be available, you do not have to wait until June before suing.

If an anticipatory breach is serious enough to support discharge, the innocent party should carefully consider whether it wants to exercise that option. Once a decision is made, it cannot later be changed. Furthermore, if the innocent party chooses to insist upon performance instead of discharging the agreement, it may later regret that decision. To understand why, consider Business Law in Action 6.3.

Anticipatory Breach

You own a farm that produces vegetables. You enter into a contract with Claudette, an independent trucker, which requires her to collect a tonne of potatoes from you on June 1 for delivery to a market. On May 1, however, you contact Claudette and inform her that, due to labour problems, your potatoes will not be available for collection until June 30.

Although Claudette could discharge the contract and sue for damages at that point, she decides to insist upon per-

formance. On May 15, your labour problems unexpectedly disappear. Your potatoes will be available on June 1 after all. A week later, however, Claudette's truck develops engine problems that necessitate month-long repairs. Consequently, when she does not arrive to collect your potatoes on June 1, you can sue her for breach of contract.

Question for Discussion

1. As a matter of risk management, what lesson can you learn from Claudette's experience?

Self-Induced Impossibility

a contract cannot be discharged on the basis of self-induced impossibility

As we saw in Chapter 5, a contract is discharged for frustration if, through no fault of either party, it becomes impossible to perform. However, if the impossibility is caused by one of the parties, then that party will be held liable for breach. Suppose that I agree to deliver a specific cord of firewood to you by January 1. If I burn that wood in my own fireplace during December, I have made the contract impossible to perform. Consequently, you will be entitled to discharge our contract and claim damages from me.

[16.] *Howard v Pickford Tool Co* [1951] 1 KB 417 at 421 *per* Asquith LJ (CA).

The Effect of Discharge

It is important to understand the consequences of discharge. In Chapters 4 and 5, we examined contracts that were rescinded or voided. In those situations, the contract is wiped out altogether, as if it never existed. The effect of discharging a contract for breach is quite different. The parties are merely relieved of the need to perform their primary obligations in the future. For example, once the contract in *Hong Kong Fir Shipping* was discharged, the owner no longer had to provide a seaworthy ship, and the charterer no longer had to pay for the use of the ship. Discharge does not, however, wipe out the contract altogether. The agreement survives for the purposes of contractual liability. Returning to *Hong Kong Fir Shipping*, the owner would have to rely on the contract to sue the charterer for damages. Similarly, if the contract contained an exclusion clause that limited the charterer's liability, that clause would have effect since the contract would still be alive for that purpose.[17]

discharge merely relieves the parties of the need to perform primary obligations in the future

Factors Affecting the Right to Discharge

Even if a contract is breached in a way that would normally support a right of discharge, that right may be lost if, for example, the innocent party chooses to continue with the agreement. Discharge may also be impossible if the party in breach provided a benefit that the innocent party cannot return. In that situation, the innocent party must perform its own obligations under the contract and be content with a claim for damages. Suppose that a lawn-care company breaches a contract by spreading an inferior grade of fertilizer on your lawn. Because the fertilizer cannot be returned, you do not have the option of discharging the contract. You can, however, claim damages for the fact that you received an inferior product.

the right to discharge may be lost in some circumstances

[17.] Exclusion clauses were examined in Chapter 4.

Chapter Summary

A contract may be discharged by performance if both parties completely or substantially fulfill their obligations. Time is usually not of the essence, but it may be in some circumstances. A tender of payment or performance must be reasonable, but once done, it need not be repeated. Payment and performance do not have to be tendered if a tender would clearly be rejected.

   A contract may be discharged by agreement in a number of ways.

1. A contract may contain an option to terminate that allows one or both parties to bring that contract to an end without the agreement of the other.
2. A contract may be discharged on the basis of a condition subsequent. Moreover, a contract that is subject to a "condition precedent" does not exist unless and until the specified event occurs.
3. An executory contract can be rescinded if both parties agree to do so. Each party provides consideration by releasing the other from the obligation to perform the original contract.
4. A partially executed contract may be discharged by accord and satisfaction. If so, the party that has yet to fully perform must provide new consideration.
5. A contract may be discharged by a release if the parties make an agreement under seal to terminate the contract.
6. The terms of a contract may be subject to variation if each party provides consideration for the alterations.
7. A contract may be discharged and replaced with a new contract under the process of novation. If so, consideration for the new contract consists of the parties' agreement not to enforce the terms of the original contract.
8. Performance of a contractual obligation may be waived by the party that was not required to perform the obligation.

   A contract can be discharged by law if it is frustrated

or if a contractual party becomes bankrupt. Similarly, although the passage of time does not technically discharge a contract, it may prevent a party from suing for breach of contract.

A contract may be discharged for breach of a condition, a warranty, or an intermediate term. Classification of a term generally depends on whether a breach substantially deprives the innocent party of the expected benefit of the contract. The innocent party is entitled to discharge a contract only if the breached term is a condition or an intermediate term that has resulted in a substantial deprivation. A term may be breached through: (i) defective performance of an obligation that has fallen due, (ii) anticipatory breach of an obligation that has yet to fall due, or (iii) self-induced impossibility.

Review Questions

1. Briefly explain the effect of discharging a contract.
2. Explain the meaning of the term "time is of the essence." Is time of the essence under most contracts? If time is of the essence under a particular contract, what happens if performance does not occur on schedule?
3. Will a contractual party ever be relieved of the obligation to tender performance?
4. What is legal tender? How is the concept of legal tender relevant to the issue of discharge by performance?
5. Explain the term "substantial performance." Can a contract be discharged on the basis of substantial performance? If so, does the failure to tender complete performance give rise to any consequences?
6. Explain the operation of a condition subsequent.
7. Explain the operation of a condition precedent.
8. Explain the operation of a condition precedent that merely suspends the performance, rather than the creation, of a contract.
9. Explain the difference between rescission, accord and satisfaction, and release. Why does the issue of consideration cause problems for accord and satisfaction but not for rescission or release?
10. Explain the difference between variation and novation. Why does the issue of consideration cause problems for variation but not for novation?
11. Does the process of waiver require consideration?
12. If a contract is discharged by operation of law as a consequence of the lapse of a limitation period, can the right to sue for breach of contract ever be revived?
13. What test do the courts use to distinguish between conditions, warranties, and intermediate terms?
14. Why does the breach of a condition support the right to discharge?
15. Why does the breach of a warranty not support the right to discharge?
16. When will the breach of an intermediate term support the right to discharge?
17. What is an anticipatory breach? How does it differ from a normal breach?
18. Describe the circumstances in which a breach will arise from self-induced impossibility. How do those circumstances differ from circumstances involving frustration?
19. If a contract is discharged for breach of a condition, does that contract completely cease to exist?
20. Under what circumstances will the right to discharge be lost even if there has been a breach of a condition?

Cases and Problems

1. Anastasia entered into a contract with Rufus to purchase a stereo. Under the terms of that agreement, she was required to pay the total price of $755 in cash on July 15, and he was required to deliver the stereo after receiving payment. Although she failed to pay on time, Anastasia went to Rufus's house on July 18 and handed him eight $100 bills. Rufus refused the payment and insisted that he was discharging the contract on the basis of Anastasia's breach. Was Rufus justified in doing so? If Anastasia had tendered the same payment on July 15, would Rufus have been required to accept it? Explain your answer.

2. Elda entered into an employment contract with the Blacksox Baseball Club to sell food at a concession stand during the team's home games. One term of the contract stated: "The employer agrees to pay to the employee $200 per game plus a 10 percent commission on food sales." Another term of the contract stated: "This agreement shall not be binding if, for whatever reason, fan attendance is so low as to render the employee's services unnecessary." After a promising start to the season, the Blacksox team went into a prolonged losing streak, during which attendance dropped by 60 percent. At that point,

the team asked Elda to hand in her uniform and told her that her contract was terminated. She is very upset because she was relying on that job to pay for this year's school tuition. Did the Blacksox organization have the right to terminate the contract? Explain your answer.

3. Miles Jones offered to sell his house to Irene Lukey for $200 000. Irene was inclined to accept the offer, but before entirely committing herself to the sale, she wanted to ensure that she would be able to obtain government planning approval to replace the existing house with an apartment complex. Miles, however, was not willing to entirely suspend his search for a buyer while Irene negotiated with the government. The parties therefore signed a document that contained this clause.

> "Miles Jones agrees to sell his house to Irene Lukey for $200 000. Completion of the sale is conditional upon Ms Lukey's ability to obtain planning approval within 30 days. Prior to the completion of the sale, Mr Jones is entitled to negotiate with other prospective buyers. In the event that Mr Jones receives an offer of at least $200 000 from another prospective buyer, Ms Lukey shall have three days after receiving notice of that fact to remove the condition from this agreement. If the condition is not removed within that period, Mr Jones shall have the right to complete a sale with another prospective buyer."

Irene's negotiations with the government proceeded smoothly, and she expected to receive planning approval within four days of having signed the agreement with Miles. However, two days after signing the agreement, Miles contacted Irene and informed her that he had sold his property to another buyer. When Irene accused him of breaching their contract, he replied that a contract would not arise under the document that they had signed unless and until she received planning approval. Consequently, in the absence of a binding contract, he felt entitled to sell the house to another buyer. Is he correct? Explain.

4. Dennis and Carmen entered into a contract under which he agreed that, in one week's time, he would pay $10 000 in exchange for her motorcycle. Three days later, however, he contacted her and said, "Look, as it turns out, my financial situation isn't as strong as I thought it was. I wonder if you'd be willing to just call off our agreement?" She replied, "Fine. You keep the money and I'll keep the motorcycle." After considering the matter further, however, Carmen called him back and said that she wanted the contract to be performed as initially planned. Dennis refuses to comply. In fact, he insists that the contract no longer exists. Is he correct? If the parties' contract did come to an end, explain the process that was used to achieve that result.

5. Rabby Computer Inc agreed to design a networking system for Pendulum Publishing Ltd. The contract called for Pendulum to pay $50 000 after Rabby completed its performance. However, when Rabby finished designing the system, Pendulum stated that it could not afford to pay that amount of money in cash. Pendulum therefore asked Rabby if it would agree to discharge the contract upon receipt of $35 000. Although Rabby initially agreed to the proposal, it later insisted upon full payment. It did so before it actually received any money from Pendulum. Is Pendulum entitled to have the contract discharged if it pays $35 000? Would your answer be different if Rabby had promised under seal that he would discharge the contract upon receipt of $35 000? Would your answer be different if Rabby had initially agreed to discharge the contract in exchange for $35 000 plus a set of encyclopedias from Pendulum? Explain your answers.

6. On May 21, the Bremen Bread Co agreed to purchase flour from Lausanne Granary Inc. The contract called for Lausanne to deliver a tonne of flour to Bremen every Monday for a year. The contract also stated that time was of the essence with respect to the delivery dates. From the outset, however, there were problems. During the first two months of the contract, Lausanne delivered the flour twice on a Monday, four times on a Tuesday, once on a Wednesday, and once on a Thursday. After the eighth week, Bremen informed Lausanne that it was discharging the contract for breach of a condition. In response, Lausanne argued that Bremen was precluded from doing so because it had already accepted late delivery on six occasions without a word of complaint. Did Lausanne breach the contract? If so, was Bremen entitled to rely upon that breach? If Bremen cannot complain of the defective nature of Lausanne's past performance, must it also accept late deliveries in the future? Explain your answers.

7. Ten years ago, Stanislav purchased a car from his co-worker Kerri for $10 000. The full purchase price was supposed to be paid on delivery. However, Stanislav paid only $2000 when Kerri delivered the car to him, and he has not paid anything since. For many years, Kerri did not mention the matter because she did not want to create an unpleasant situation in her workplace. Recently, however, when she retired from her job, she notified Stanislav that she wanted to be paid the remaining part of the purchase price plus interest. He replied, "I know that I still owe at least $8000 to you, but I also know that there is some law that prevents you from claiming it anymore." Is he correct? Is Kerri now entitled to receive any money? Explain your answers.

8. Aimee, a music producer, purchased a vehicle from Eddie's Fine Cars Inc. To save money, Eddie drafts the sales contracts himself rather than relying on the expertise of a lawyer. Because Aimee is very particular about her music, she insisted that her contract with Eddie include the following term: "It is a condition of this contract that all the extras in the vehicle shall be in good working order. More specifically, Eddie's Fine Cars Inc warrants that the air conditioning and the stereo are as good as new." After taking possession of the car, however, Aimee discovered that the CD player operates at an improper speed, with the effect that songs are heard in ¾ time. She also realized that she overpaid for the vehicle. Consequently, she wants to return it to Eddie for a full refund. Is she entitled to do so? Would your answer be different if the sales contract had been drafted in precisely the same terms by a team of lawyers? Explain your answers.

9. Bettini entered into a contract with the Vancouver Opera Company under which he agreed to perform for the company twice a month for one year. A term in the contract required Bettini to arrive in Vancouver at least three days

before each performance to attend rehearsals. As a seasoned professional, however, he believed that he did not need that much rehearsal and he therefore arrived only one day before his first scheduled performance. The director of the opera company was furious and tried to discharge the agreement on the basis that Bettini had committed a serious breach of the contract. Was the director entitled to do so? Would your answer be the same if Bettini had arrived as scheduled for the first 10 performances, but had arrived only one day before the eleventh? Would your answer be different if Bettini was not a seasoned professional, but rather a novice? Explain your answers.

10. Ivan entered into a contract with Poe Paperback Inc, a small publishing company, to write a mystery novel in exchange for $5000. Under the terms of the contract, Ivan was to deliver a manuscript to Poe within 18 months. However, after three weeks of staring hopelessly at a blank computer screen, Ivan reached the conclusion that he had developed an irreparable writer's block and that he would not be able to produce the promised novel. He sent a letter to Poe that said, "I am terribly sorry, but I will have to withdraw from our contract. Since you have not made any payments to me yet, I cannot imagine that you have any objections and I will assume that my proposal is acceptable to you." Ivan received no response from Poe. After another 12 months, however, he suddenly found the inspiration to write a brilliant mystery novel in the space of two weeks. He then entered into negotiations with Christie Mysteries Ltd, a large publishing company, to sell the completed manuscript for $100 000. At that point, Poe contacted Ivan and insisted that the book belonged to them. Ivan, however, insists that he was relieved of his contractual obligations to Poe. Did Ivan breach his contract with Poe? If so, describe the nature of the breach. If there was a breach of contract, is Poe entitled to rely upon it and to seek legal relief from Ivan? Explain.

11. Gerry and Harlan both have lawn-care businesses. For a number of years, they agreed to take care of each other's clients for a two-week period while the other took a family vacation. Seven years ago, while Harlan was away, Gerry fully performed his part of the agreement. That same summer, just as Gerry was about to leave for his vacation, Harlan fell off his riding lawn mower and broke his leg. Harlan was no longer able to perform under their arrangement and, although Gerry was upset to miss his vacation, he agreed to discharge their contract and do his own maintenance. Harlan was uncomfortable about being indebted to Gerry, so he proposed a number of solutions to clear the debt:

- He offered to have his young son, Jeb, complete the work. Gerry, however, was not confident that the quality of Jeb's work would meet his high standards. Gerry thanked Harlan for his offer, but told him that he would do the work himself.

- Harlan offered to pay Gerry market value for his earlier work, but Gerry told him not to give it another thought.

- Harlan also tried to give Gerry three bags of top-of-the-line fertilizer, but it was not the brand Gerry liked to use, so he politely declined the offer.

Harlan decided he had done what he could to fulfill his obligations, so he gave up trying.

For many years, Gerry and Harlan maintained the same arrangement. This past summer, the day before leaving for his vacation, Gerry told Harlan that he intended to take an extended four-week holiday, but expected that Harlan would not charge anything more under their agreement on account of the incident that had happened seven years earlier. Harlan acknowledged his indebtedness to Gerry and agreed to work one extra week, but simply refused to do Gerry's lawn maintenance for two additional weeks on such short notice. Gerry is furious at Harlan's refusal and insists that he will sue Harlan if Harlan does not perform. Is Harlan legally obligated to perform under the seven-year-old agreement? Would Gerry succeed in court? Give reasons for your answer.

12. Dolores Van de Laer and her husband, Harry, recently had an in-ground pool constructed in their backyard. To protect their seven children, they hired Ruth, a certified lifeguard, to teach the family proper swimming techniques and basic rescue procedures. From the beginning, Ruth had difficulty keeping the older children in line while she assisted the younger ones. She complained to Dolores and Harry, and even though they spoke to the children, the situation did not improve. After a few lessons, Ruth told the Van de Laer's that she could not take it anymore and that she had arranged to have her friend Kirk, also a certified lifeguard, replace her as their swimming instructor. Dolores and Harry grudgingly agreed to the new arrangement. They soon discovered that Kirk was great with all of the children and that he was also experienced at pool maintenance. Neither Dolores nor Harry had much luck keeping the pool's pH balanced, so they instructed Kirk to take over that responsibility as well.

Later that summer, Kirk bumped into Ruth at a friend's pool party. When she asked how the job was going, Ruth was surprised to learn that Kirk was disappointed with the pay. Ruth had thought the pay was quite good, but apparently the Van de Laer's were paying Kirk $50 less per week than they had promised Ruth. When Kirk learned this, he was outraged that the Van de Laer's had taken advantage of him. The next day, before beginning the lesson, Kirk spoke with Dolores and demanded to receive the money she owed him under the original agreement with Ruth. Additionally, he asked for an extra $25 dollars per week as payment for the pool maintenance. Dolores refused to pay Kirk any extra money. She claims that the original agreement with Ruth was discharged by agreement and that a new one with different rights and obligations was created with Kirk. Kirk, however, argues that there was a novation and that he adopted the same rights and obligations that existed under the old contract. Analyze each party's argument. Do you think Kirk is entitled to more money? Explain your answer.

7 Contractual Remedies

CHAPTER OVERVIEW

Damages

Expectation Damages
Reliance Damages
Nominal Damages
Liquidated Damages
Punitive Damages

Equitable Relief

Specific Performance
Injunctions

Exclusion Clauses

Unjust Enrichment

OBJECTIVES

After completing this chapter, you should be able to:

1. Define the term "damages" and explain why the courts will generally award only damages for a breach of contract.
2. Describe expectation damages and explain how they are calculated.
3. Describe how courts deal with the problems of "cost of cure" and "intangible losses."
4. Explain two important limitations on the availability of expectation damages.
5. Explain the nature of reliance damages and distinguish them from expectation damages.
6. Describe nominal damages and punitive damages and explain how they are calculated.
7. Distinguish liquidated damages from penalties.
8. Describe specific performance and injunctions and explain when they are awarded.
9. Explain how exclusion clauses apply under contracts that are discharged for breach.
10. Describe the cause of action in unjust enrichment and the remedy of restitution, and explain when those concepts are applicable.

One or more remedies may be available if a contract is breached. As we saw in Chapter 6, if the breach substantially deprives the innocent party of the benefit it expected to receive under the agreement, that party is usually entitled to discharge the contract. Other remedies may also be available, whether or not a contract is discharged for breach. Figure 7.1 outlines the possibilities we will discuss.

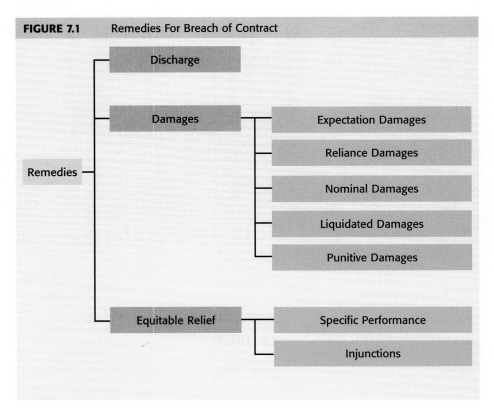

FIGURE 7.1   Remedies For Breach of Contract

DAMAGES

damages is an award of money that is intended to cure a wrongful event, such as a breach of contract

the innocent party is usually entitled to receive only the monetary value of the thing it expected to get under the contract

In the vast majority of cases, the remedy for a breach of contract is *damages*. **Damages** is an award of money that is intended to cure a wrongful event, such as a breach of contract. The nature of that remedy needs to be stressed. Except in rare cases, the plaintiff is *not* entitled to receive the *exact thing* it expected to get under the agreement. It is only entitled to the *monetary value* of that thing. For example, if I agree to sell my car to you but later break my promise after you have paid the price, you are probably not entitled to get the car itself. Rather, you are entitled to the monetary value of that car.

There are several reasons why courts usually award only monetary damages for a breach of contract. First, the courts of law historically did not have the authority to compel a defendant to do anything other than pay money.[1] Second, contracts traditionally were seen as commercial arrangements between

---

[1.] In contrast, the courts of equity did have the authority to compel a defendant to do other things. As we discuss below, those courts can still award *specific performance* and *injunctions* instead of monetary damages. The difference between courts of law and courts of equity was explained in Chapter 1.

business people. And even today, money is usually the only thing that matters in the commercial world. Consequently, there is no need to award any other sort of remedy. Third, especially in the business world, it would often be inconvenient to award something other than monetary damages. Returning to our earlier example, suppose that I am a used car dealer and that I agreed to sell a specific car to you. What would happen if, as a result of my breach, you could sue me and demand the delivery of that particular vehicle? It could be several years before our dispute was resolved. And in the meantime, I would not be able to deal with the car. I would have to set it aside in case you won the case. An efficient economy, however, requires the free flow of goods and value.

Expectation Damages

Within the broad category of damages, there are many different *measures of relief*, or ways in which the courts can calculate the amount of money that the plaintiff is entitled to recover from the defendant. The most common measure of relief in contract law is *expectation damages*. **Expectation damages** represent the monetary value of the benefit that the plaintiff expected to receive under the contract.

expectation damages represent the monetary value of the benefit that the plaintiff expected to receive under the contract

That definition contains an important idea. Expectation damages are *forward-looking* because they are intended to place the plaintiff in the position that it expected to be in *after* the contract was properly performed. In contrast, compensatory damages in tort law (discussed in Unit 3) are *backward-looking* because they are intended to place the plaintiff in the position that it was in *before* the defendant acted wrongfully (for instance, by making a defamatory statement or carelessly causing an accident). Consider the difference.

expectation damages are *forward-looking* because they are intended to place the plaintiff in the position that it expected to be in *after* the contract was properly performed

- Backward-looking damages are easily justified. They allow the plaintiff to recover the value of something, such as a favourable reputation or an unbroken leg, that it previously possessed but lost as a result of the defendant's wrongful act.

- Forward-looking damages go further. They allow the plaintiff to recover the value of something that it never previously possessed, but merely expected to receive under its contract with the defendant. Nevertheless, forward-looking damages can be justified in contract law. The business world operates largely on the basis of credit, which is a promise to do something in the future. Such a promise is valuable only if the person who receives it can be confident that it will be fulfilled. Expectation damages therefore provide an assurance that if a promise is not fulfilled, the innocent party will at least be able to recover the monetary value of that promise.

As Figure 7.2 shows, expectation damages are calculated as the value of the benefit that the plaintiff expected to receive under the contract *minus* the value of the costs that it expected to incur. Suppose that you agree to pay $5000 for a computer that is really worth $7000. You expect to make a profit of $2000.

FIGURE 7.2   Calculation of Expectation Damages

| Expectation Damages | = | expected benefits under the contract | − | costs under the contract |

Consequently, if the vendor breaches the contract by refusing to deliver the computer, and if you have not yet paid the price, you will be entitled to receive $2000 in cash. And if you pay the entire price before the breach occurs, you will be entitled to $7000 in cash. In either event, you are entitled to enjoy the profit of $2000.

The examples in You Be the Judge 7.1 and 7.2 will help you understand how expectation damages are calculated. As you work through them, ask yourself these two questions. How much did the plaintiff *expect* to have at the end of the contract? How much does the plaintiff *actually* have after the defendant's breach? Expectation damages should equal the difference between those two numbers.

YOU BE THE JUDGE 7.1

Calculation of Expectation Damages

Jose agreed to sell a widget to Maria for $5000. Although she made a down payment of $4000, he refused to deliver the widget because he discovered that it was really worth $7500. Assuming that Jose's refusal amounts to a breach of contract,

Maria will be entitled to recover expectation damages of $6500.

Questions for Discussion

1. As a judge, how would you arrive at that conclusion?
2. Does that conclusion seem fair?

YOU BE THE JUDGE 7.2

Calculation of Expectation Damages

Jose agreed to sell a widget to Maria for $5000. Although she made a down payment of $4000, he refused to deliver the widget. He did so despite the fact that the widget was really worth only $1000. Assuming that Jose has breached the contract, Maria

will not be entitled to recover any expectation damages. (However, she may be entitled to restitution, as explained at the end of this chapter.)

Questions for Discussion

1. As a judge, how would you arrive at that conclusion?
2. Does that conclusion seem fair?

As we have seen, it is usually fairly easy to calculate expectation damages. In some situations, however, the exercise is much more difficult. We will consider five issues:

- difficulty of calculation
- cost of cure or loss of value
- intangible losses
- remoteness
- mitigation of damages

Difficulty of Calculation

expectation damages are usually available even if they are very difficult to calculate

Expectation damages are usually available even if they are very difficult to calculate. The courts will do the best they can, even if the evidence is inconclusive.

In one famous case, the defendant breached a contract by depriving the plaintiff of an opportunity to win a beauty contest.[2] While the plaintiff's actual chance of winning the contest was highly speculative, the court awarded expectation damages based on its best guess as to how she would have fared in the competition.

Cost of Cure or Loss of Value

Sometimes, it is difficult to decide exactly what the plaintiff expected to receive from the defendant. For example, there often is a question as to whether the plaintiff expected to receive a *service* or the *value of the end-product* of that service. Consider the illustration in Case Brief 7.1.

CASE BRIEF 7.1

Groves v John Wunder Co (1939) 286 NW 235 (Minn CA)

The plaintiff rented a piece of land to the defendant for $105 000. The defendant was entitled to operate a sand and gravel mine on that property, but it was also required to level the ground when the lease expired. After removing a great deal of sand and gravel, the defendant left huge craters on the property. It did so for economic reasons. It would have cost $60 000 to level the land. But even if the land was level, it would have been worth only $12 000.

The plaintiff claimed that expectation damages should

be measured by the *cost of cure*. It argued that it expected to receive a level piece of land at the end of the lease and that it was therefore entitled to receive the amount of money that would be required to put the land into that condition. In response, the defendant claimed that expectation damages should be measured by the *loss of value*. It argued that what the plaintiff really expected to receive under the contract was land worth $12 000.

The court agreed with the plaintiff and awarded $60 000 in expectation damages.

That result may seem surprising, especially when you learn that the plaintiff did not actually use the damages that it received from the defendant to level the land.[3] Nevertheless, the court's decision may be justifiable. The defendant's promise to level the land was part of the price that it agreed to pay in exchange for the right to mine sand and gravel from the property. If the plaintiff had known that the land would be left with huge craters, it probably would have insisted on a different deal. For instance, instead of asking for $105 000 plus level land, it might have just asked for $165 000.

The courts often follow the approach taken in *Groves v John Wunder Co*. They are most likely to do so if the plaintiff has a legitimate interest in having the work done or if the plaintiff has actually already spent money curing the defendant's defective performance.[4] However, judges usually refuse to calculate expectation damages on a "cost of cure" basis if the difference between the cost of cure and the benefits of the cure are unreasonably large. For example, in a recent English case, the defendant breached a contract by building a swimming pool to a depth of six feet six inches, rather than seven feet six inches. The cost of curing that defect was £22 000. The value of the swimming pool, however, was the same in either event. The evidence also indicated that the defendant's

damages may be awarded for cost of cure or for loss of value, depending on the circumstances

---

[2] *Chaplin v Hicks* [1911] 2 KB 786 (CA).

[3] The plaintiff is generally entitled to spend its damages as it chooses.

[4] *Nu-West Homes Ltd v Thunderbird Petroleum Ltd* (1975) 59 DLR (3d) 292 (Alta CA).

breach did not make the pool any more dangerous for diving. The court therefore refused to award expectation damages on a "cost of cure" basis.[5]

Intangible Losses

an intangible loss is a loss that does not have any apparent economic value

Expectation damages are also difficult to calculate when the plaintiff suffers an intangible loss as a result of the defendant's breach. An **intangible loss** is a loss that does not have any apparent economic value. Examples include the anger, frustration, sadness, or disappointment that may occur when a promise is broken.

Historically, the courts generally refused to award damages for intangible losses. As we discussed earlier, contracts were seen as commercial arrangements between business people who were concerned with financial matters rather than hurt feelings. Furthermore, the courts did not traditionally feel comfortable assigning dollar figures to personal emotions. What is the monetary value of your sense of disappointment if a car rental company delivers a mini-van instead of the sporty convertible that it had promised?

expectation damages are sometimes awarded for intangible losses

Recently, however, the courts have started to recognize that "peace of mind" is one of things that a person may expect to receive under a contract. As a result, while the cases are somewhat inconsistent, expectation damages have been awarded for the disappointment that was caused when a holiday was ruined and for the distress that was caused when a beloved pet dog was suffocated to death during air travel.[6] However, the courts still refuse to compensate a person for the humiliation or dejection they may feel as a result of being unfairly fired from a job.[7]

Remoteness

a loss is remote if it would be unfair to hold the defendant responsible

The plaintiff cannot recover expectation damages for *every* loss that it suffers after the defendant's breach. The loss must have been *caused* by the breach as a matter of fact. Furthermore, the loss must not be *remote* from the breach. A loss is **remote** if it would be unfair to hold the defendant responsible for it.

a loss is not remote if the defendant either should have known, or actually did know, that that sort of loss might occur if the contract was breached

A loss is *not* remote if the defendant either *should have known* or *actually did know* that that sort of loss might occur if the contract was breached. That test has two parts.

- First, liability may be imposed if *a reasonable person would have known* that the plaintiff's loss might result from a breach. That is true even if the plaintiff did not draw the defendant's attention to that possibility.
- Second, liability may be imposed if the *defendant actually knew* that the plaintiff's loss might result from the breach. That is true even if a reasonable person would not normally have expected such a loss.

Case Brief 7.2 illustrates the two parts of the remoteness test.

[5] *Ruxley Electronics & Construction Ltd v Forsyth* [1996] 1 AC 344 (HL). The court did, however, award £2500 for "loss of amenity" or "intangible loss."

[6] *Jarvis v Swan Tours Ltd* [1973] QB 233 (CA); *Newell v Canadian Pacific Airlines Ltd* (1976) 74 DLR (3d) 574 (Ont Co Ct).

[7] *Wallace v United Grain Growers Ltd* (1997) 152 DLR (4th) 1 (SCC). Exceptionally, however, an ex-employee may recover "punitive damages." We consider that possibility later.

CASE BRIEF 7.2

Victoria Laundry (Windsor) Ltd v Newman Industries Ltd [1949] 2 KB 528 (CA)

The defendant agreed to deliver a boiler to the plaintiff on June 5. When the contract was created, the defendant knew in a general sense that the plaintiff operated a laundry, but it did not know of the specific nature of the plaintiff's business. The defendant broke the contract by delivering the boiler 20 weeks late. As a result of that breach, the plaintiff suffered two types of losses. First, it lost £16 per week because it was unable to perform ordinary laundry operations, such as cleaning and pressing shirts. Second, it lost £262 per week because it was unable to obtain a highly lucrative and highly unusual dyeing contract from the government.

The defendant's breach caused both types of losses. Liability therefore turned on the issue of remoteness. Even though the plaintiff had not specifically mentioned the possibility of the first type of loss when the contract was created, the defendant was liable for £16 per week in expectation damages. The court held that any reasonable person, even without being told, would have known that that type of loss might occur. In contrast, the court held that the second type of loss was remote. Because the government contract was highly unusual, a reasonable person would not have known about it without being told. And furthermore, the plaintiff had not told the defendant about it. The plaintiff therefore could not recover the additional £262 per week.

Remoteness is a principle of fairness. Note that it is applied when the parties created their contract, not when the defendant committed the breach or when the judge hears the case. Before entering into a contract, a party will consider all of the costs potentially associated with the agreement, including the risk of being held liable as a result of committing a breach. As that risk increases, the party will ask for a higher price. And at some point, the risk will become too much and the party will refuse to enter into the contract altogether. The party can only be expected to make that calculation on the basis of information that it *should know* or that it *does know*. It would be unfair to impose liability for a loss that it could not have predicted.

Victoria Laundry provides a good example of this. It was fair to impose liability for £16 per week because the defendant must have realized that if it broke its promise, the plaintiff would be unable to conduct its ordinary laundry business. However, the defendant had no way of knowing that its breach might cause the plaintiff to lose the government contract. And if it had known of the possibility of being held liable for £262 per week, it almost certainly would have demanded a higher price from the plaintiff.

As a matter of risk management, the lesson is clear. Before entering into a contract, you should make sure that the other party is aware of any unusual losses that you might suffer as a result of its breach. The other party may demand a higher price or even refuse to enter into the agreement.[8] But if you do not draw attention to the possibility of an unusual loss, you will not be able to recover expectation damages if that loss occurs.

remoteness is a principle of fairness

Mitigation of Damages

Even if remoteness is not a problem, the plaintiff is prevented from recovering damages to the extent that it unreasonably failed to *mitigate* a loss.[9] **Mitigation**

mitigation occurs when the plaintiff takes steps to minimize the losses that result from the defendant's breach

---

[8.] The other party could enter into the contract at a lower price, but insist on the insertion of an "exclusion clause." Exclusion clauses are discussed later in this chapter.

[9.] *Asamera Oil Corp v Sea Oil & General Corp* (1978) 89 DLR (3d) 1 (SCC).

occurs when the plaintiff takes steps to minimize the losses that result from the defendant's breach. Consider the example in Business Law in Action 7.1.

BUSINESS LAW IN ACTION 7.1

Mitigation of Damages

Manfred agreed to deliver a shipment of potato chips to you each week for a year. If he had fulfilled that promise, you would have been able to earn a net profit of $1000 per week by reselling the chips in your convenience store. Unfortunately, Manfred breached the contract by refusing to make any deliveries. Instead of ordering the same number of chips from someone else, you simply complained for the next 52 weeks. At the

end of the year, you brought a claim against Manfred for $52 000 in expectation damages.

Questions for Discussion

1. Assuming that your loss is not remote, is Manfred liable for all of your loss?
2. Assuming that you could have arranged an alternative supply of chips within three weeks of the breach, how much will you receive in damages?

Business Law in Action 7.1 illustrates four more points about mitigation.

- First, lawyers sometimes say that there is a "duty to mitigate." In fact, there is not really a *duty* in the sense of something that *must* be done. The plaintiff is not required to mitigate. However, failing to do so is a poor business decision. As we saw, you are unable to recover damages for losses that you could have mitigated.

- Second, the plaintiff is responsible only for taking *reasonable* steps to mitigate a loss. The plaintiff is not precluded from recovering expectation damages simply because it failed to adopt an unreasonably difficult, inconvenient, or risky way of minimizing the loss that resulted from the defendant's breach.

- Third, damages are denied *only to the extent that* the plaintiff unreasonably failed to mitigate. Although you did not take any steps toward mitigation, you are still entitled to $3000 in damages. You would have suffered that loss even if you had acted reasonably.

- Fourth, the plaintiff can recover the costs associated with mitigation. For example, if you had spent $500 arranging the alternative supply of chips within three weeks, you would have been entitled to $3000 in lost profits, plus $500 as the cost of mitigation.

Reliance Damages

Expectation damages are the usual remedy for a breach of contract. In some situations, however, other types of damages may be awarded. *Reliance damages* are the most common alternative. **Reliance damages** represent the monetary value of the expenses that the plaintiff wasted under a contract.

In one sense, reliance damages are the opposite of expectation damages. If you ask for expectation damages, you are saying, "Give me what I expected to get. Put me in the position that I would have been in if the contract had been properly performed." However, if you ask for reliance damages, you are saying, "Give me what I lost. Put me in the position that I would have been in if I had not wasted resources under this contract." Expectation damages look forward in an attempt to fulfill a contract; reliance damages look backward in an attempt to undo the effects of a contract.

reliance damages represent the monetary value of the expenses that the plaintiff wasted under a contract

The plaintiff is generally entitled to recover either expectation damages or reliance damages, but not both. Expectation damages represent the benefit that the plaintiff expected to receive under the contract; reliance damages represent the costs that it expected to incur. If the plaintiff wants the benefits, it must be willing to pay the costs. As a result, the plaintiff should sometimes carefully consider which measure of damages is preferable.[10] Business Decision 7.1 provides an illustration.

BUSINESS DECISION 7.1

Expectation Damages and Reliance Damages

As a music promoter, you hired Ursula to perform a piano concert in exchange for $5000. Based on your experience in the music business, you expected to personally receive a net profit of $7000 from the concert. Ursula received full payment when she signed the contract, but told you a week later that she was not willing to perform. You

reluctantly cancelled the concert. You are now doubly unhappy. Not only did you pay $5000 for a piano recital that never occurred, you were also deprived of your expected revenue.

Question for Discussion

1. Assuming that Ursula's behaviour constitutes a breach of contract, will you claim expectation damages or reliance damages?

Reliance damages are subject to an important limitation. They can be awarded only to the extent that a contract is *not unprofitable*.[11] The plaintiff therefore cannot claim reliance damages to escape the consequences of having entered into a bad bargain. It must bear responsibility for having made a poor deal. While that rule may seem complicated, it can be easily illustrated. Consider Ethical Perspective 7.1.

reliance damages are available only to the extent that a contract is not unprofitable

---

ETHICAL PERSPECTIVE 7.1

Reliance Damages and Bad Bargains[12]

You agreed to pay $14 000 to Anwar in exchange for a shipment of steel. Although you provided $5000 as a down payment, he refused to deliver the goods. You sue for breach of contract. At trial, the evidence indicates that you had entered into a bad bargain. Although you agreed to pay $14 000, the steel was really worth only $11 000. If the contract had been fully performed, you would have suffered a net loss of $3000.

Because you did not expect to earn a profit under the contract, you cannot recover any expectation damages.

Moreover, although you paid $5000 under the contract, you can recover reliance damages only to the *extent* that your contract was *not unprofitable*. Since you would have suffered a net loss of $3000 if the contract had been performed, you can recover only $2000 in reliance damages. In effect, you are responsible for the $3000 that you expected to lose as a result of entering into a bad bargain.[13]

Questions for Discussion

1. Does that result seem fair to you?
2. Suggest a reason why the courts have adopted that rule.

---

[10] The plaintiff is entitled to sue for both expectation damages and reliance damages. However, if it successfully proves that the defendant committed a breach of contract, the plaintiff must tell the trial judge which measure of relief it wants to receive.

[11] *Bowlay Logging Ltd v Domtar Ltd* (1982) 135 DLR (3d) 179 (BC CA).

[12] *Bush v Canfield* 2 Conn 485 (1818).

[13] We will examine the cause of action in unjust enrichment later in this chapter. When we do so, return to Ethical Perspective 7.1 and calculate the amount of money you would be entitled to receive as restitution rather than as expectation damages or reliance damages.

Nominal Damages

nominal damages symbolically indicate that the plaintiff technically suffered a wrong when the defendant failed to fulfill a promise

If the plaintiff proves that a contract was broken, but cannot prove that it suffered any loss as a result that breach, the court may award *nominal damages*. **Nominal damages** symbolically indicate that the plaintiff technically suffered a wrong when the defendant failed to fulfill a promise. Because they are merely symbolic, nominal damages are awarded in very small amounts, such as $10.

It is usually a bad idea to bring an action to recover nominal damages. Judges do not like to waste time on trivial matters. If a court believes that the plaintiff did not have a legitimate reason for suing the defendant, it may require the plaintiff to pay the costs associated with the trial. And the value of those costs will be much greater than the value of the nominal damages that the plaintiff is entitled to receive from the defendant.

Liquidated Damages

liquidated damages represent a genuine attempt to estimate the value of the loss that may occur as a result of a breach

At the time of creating a contract, the parties may want to ensure that they will not be caught up in a complicated and expensive lawsuit if a dispute arises in the future. They may also want to provide each other with an incentive to perform properly. To accomplish those goals, they may state that *liquidated damages* shall be paid if there is a breach. **Liquidated damages** represent a genuine attempt to estimate the value of the loss that may occur as a result of a breach. If the contract is in fact breached, the innocent party is entitled to recover the liquidated amount, even if that amount turns out to be more than the loss that it actually suffered. Liquidated damages also work the other way. The innocent party is usually entitled to recover only the liquidated amount, even if it suffered a larger loss as a result of the breach.

a penalty requires a party to pay an exorbitant amount if it breaches the contract

Liquidated damages must be distinguished from *penalties*. A **penalty** requires a party to pay an exorbitant amount if it breaches the contract. Unlike liquidated damages, a penalty is not a genuine attempt to estimate the loss that may be caused by a broken promise. It is merely an attempt to coerce the performance of an agreement. While the courts enforce liquidated damages, they do not enforce penalties. If a contract contains a penalty clause, the court will ignore it and calculate damages in the usual way.

Punitive Damages

punitive damages are intended to punish the defendant

Damages are usually intended to compensate the plaintiff for a loss. *Punitive damages*, however, have a different purpose. **Punitive damages** are intended to punish the defendant. Consequently, if the defendant has done something that the court thinks deserves punishment, the plaintiff may be entitled to recover both compensatory damages (either expectation damages or reliance damages) *and* punitive damages.

Punitive damages are often misunderstood. There is a popular perception, based on American movies and news programs, that punitive damages are awarded very often and in very large amounts. In fact, Canadian courts take a much narrower view of the matter. In this country, punitive damages are available for a breach of contract only in exceptional circumstances. The Supreme Court of Canada has said that two conditions generally must be met.[14] First, the defendant must not only commit a breach of contract, but also act in a "harsh,

---

[14.] *Whiten v Pilot Insurance Co* (2002) 209 DLR (4th) 257 (SCC); compare. *Royal Bank of Canada v W Got & Associates Electric Ltd* (1999) 178 DLR (4th) 385 (SCC).

vindictive, reprehensible and malicious" manner. Second, in committing that breach of contract, the defendant must have also committed another independently actionable wrong, such as a tort. Those requirements can be satisfied only in very unusual circumstances. In one famous example, a professional hockey team broke its contract with a player by refusing to allow him to visit a physician for treatment of an injury.[15] In that situation, the team: (i) breached its contract, (ii) in a morally reprehensible way, and (iii) in a way that also created the tort of negligence. The player was therefore entitled to both compensatory damages and punitive damages.

Concept Summary 7.1 shows the types of damages we have just discussed.

Concept Summary 7.1

Contractual Damages

Type	Purpose
Expectation damages	Place the plaintiff in the position it would have enjoyed if the contract had been performed
Reliance damages	Compensate the plaintiff for the costs it incurred in reliance upon the contract
Nominal damages	Symbolically indicate that the defendant breached its promise to the plaintiff
Liquidated damages	Enforce the parties' estimate of the loss that the plaintiff would suffer if the defendant breached the contract
Punitive damages	Punish the defendant for breaching the contract in an outrageous way

EQUITABLE RELIEF

As we discussed earlier, a person who suffers a breach of contract usually receives monetary damages. In most situations, that sort of remedy is adequate. Suppose that a car dealer breaks a promise by refusing to deliver a particular vehicle to you. If you are limited to monetary damages, you will not receive that specific car. But with the money that you recover from the defendant, you can buy another car that is virtually identical. Furthermore, by limiting you to monetary relief, the law allows the car dealer to carry on with business as usual. He does not have to hold onto the disputed vehicle while your lawsuit slowly works its way through the court system. In some situations, however, money is not enough. The courts of equity therefore developed other types of remedies.

Specific Performance

The most important type of equitable relief is *specific performance*. **Specific performance** occurs when the court orders the defendant to fulfill a contractual obligation to do something.[16] Note that the plaintiff does not just receive the monetary value of the defendant's promise; it receives the actual performance of that promise.

It is sometimes said that specific performance, like other equitable remedies, is *discretionary*. The plaintiff does not have a *right* to receive it simply

specific performance occurs when the court orders the defendant to fulfill a contractual obligation to do something

---

[15.] *Robitaille v Vancouver Hockey Club Ltd* (1981) 124 DLR (3d) 228 (BC CA).

[16.] If the defendant refuses to obey the court's order, it can be held in *contempt of court*, and therefore be subject to a fine, or imprisoned.

specific performance is a discretionary remedy

because the defendant breached the contract. The court has to be convinced that specific performance would be *appropriate* in the circumstances. That discretion is, however, exercised on the basis of settled rules. For example, a judge will not order the defendant to specifically perform a promise unless the plaintiff came to court with "clean hands." The plaintiff has dirty hands if, for instance, it somehow took advantage of the defendant. Specific performance will also be refused if it would create a hardship for the defendant, or if the plaintiff unreasonably delayed in bringing the lawsuit.

Specific performance depends on four other factors:

- adequacy of damages
- mutuality
- judicial supervision
- personal services

specific performance is available only if monetary damages would provide an inadequate remedy

The first limitation is the most important. Specific performance is awarded only if monetary damages would provide an *inadequate* remedy. In our earlier example, you could not get specific performance against the car dealer because monetary damages were sufficient for your purposes. You could use those damages to buy a virtually identical vehicle from someone else. The situation would be different, however, if the specific car that the dealer promised to deliver was unique, and if you had a legitimate reason for wanting to receive that car in particular. For instance, you might be entitled to specific performance if your contract with the dealer concerned John Lennon's infamous psychedelic Rolls Royce.

Specific performance is rarely awarded for contracts that deal with goods, such as cars. However, the courts were traditionally willing to award specific performance almost every time that someone agreed to sell land. Every piece of land was thought to be unique, with the result that monetary damages would never allow the plaintiff to buy a substitute from someone else. That general rule was modified in a recent case when the Supreme Court of Canada said that, in the modern world, "[r]esidential, business and industrial properties are all mass produced much in the same way as other consumer goods."[17] Consequently, if the plaintiff wants specific performance of a promise to transfer land, it has to prove that it really does have a substantial interest in receiving that property.

mutuality means that specific performance can be awarded to a party only if it could also be awarded against that same party

The requirement of *mutuality* provides a second important limitation on the availability of specific performance. **Mutuality** means that specific performance can be awarded *to* a party only if it could also be awarded *against* that same party. It would be unfair to award specific performance to one party, but only monetary damages to the other. For example, the courts generally will not award specific performance *against* an infant. Consequently, they also generally will not award specific performance *to* an infant. If a person who enters into a contract with an infant cannot be assured of getting anything more than monetary damages, it should not be compelled to give anything more in return.

specific performance generally will not be awarded if such an order would require ongoing judicial supervision

Third, specific performance generally will not be awarded if it would require ongoing *judicial supervision*. Judges want to resolve disputes once and for all. They do not want the parties repeatedly coming to court. Furthermore, they are not willing to constantly monitor a situation to ensure that the defendant is behaving properly. For those reasons, the courts may refuse to order specific performance of a promise to keep a grocery store in operation.[18]

[17.] *Semelhago v Paramadevan* (1996) 136 DLR (4th) 1 (SCC).

[18.] *Co-Operative Insurance v Argyll Stores Ltd* [1998] AC 1 (HL).

Finally, the courts generally will not order specific performance of a promise to perform a *personal service*. For example, an actress will not be compelled to appear in a movie even if she promised to do so. Aside from the fact that specific performance would require ongoing judicial supervision, it would also create something close to slavery.

the courts generally will not order specific performance of a promise to perform a personal service

Injunctions

Specific performance compels a person to fulfill a contractual obligation to *do something*. An *injunction* usually operates in the opposite direction. That term is used in a variety of ways. For now, we will say that an **injunction** occurs when the court orders the defendant to *refrain from doing something* that is prohibited by the contract. Suppose that you enter into an agreement with a manufacturer that allows you to sell its product in only one province. If you try to conduct sales in other provinces, the manufacturer can obtain an injunction to prevent you from doing so.

an **injunction** occurs when the court orders the defendant to refrain from doing something that is prohibited by the contract

The same rules generally govern specific performance and injunctions. For example, neither type of remedy is available if monetary damages are sufficient to protect the plaintiff's interests. There are, however, some differences. The courts are much more willing to award injunctions than specific performance. The primary reason is clear. Specific performance involves a *positive undertaking*, which is a promise to *do something*. An order that compels a person to do something greatly limits freedom of choice. While a person is doing one thing, it cannot do anything else. In contrast, an injunction involves a *negative undertaking*, which is a promise to *not do something*. And an order that prevents a person from doing one thing is not particularly intrusive. The person remains free to do anything else.

the courts are more willing to award injunctions than specific performance

That difference between the two types of equitable remedies creates an interesting tension in some situations. As we saw, the courts generally refuse to order specific performance of a promise to provide personal services. For example, a court will not compel an actress to appear in a movie. However, it may impose an injunction to prevent her from breaching a contractual promise to *not* perform for anyone else. Consider the decision in Case Brief 7.3.

CASE BRIEF 7.3

Warner Bros Pictures Inc v Nelson [1937] 1 KB 209

Early in her career, Bette Davis entered into a contract with Warner Bros, a movie studio. That agreement contained both positive and negative undertakings. Positively, Davis promised to act in the studio's films. Negatively, she promised not to act in anyone else's films. By 1937, Bette Davis had enjoyed considerable success in such movies as *Of Human Bondage* with Leslie Howard, *The Petrified Forest* with Humphrey Bogart, and *Dangerous*, for which she won an Academy Award. At that point, she evidently decided that her contract with the studio did not offer enough money for

a someone of her stature. She therefore wanted to work elsewhere at a higher rate of pay.

Warner Bros did not seek specific performance of Davis's positive promise to perform in its movies. And, indeed, the court said that such an order would not have been granted. The studio did, however, obtain an injunction with respect to the actress's negative promise not to appear in anyone else's movies. The court held that if Davis wanted to appear on film during the life of her contract with Warner Bros, she had to work for the studio. The court also held, however, that she was free to earn a living in other ways if she chose.

Although the court awarded an injunction in *Warner Bros Pictures Ltd v Nelson*, it also stressed that that type of remedy is subject to an important restriction. An injunction will not be granted if it would compel the defendant to choose between working for the plaintiff and not working at all. That rule is seen in Case Brief 7.4.

CASE BRIEF 7.4

Page One Records Ltd v Britton [1968] 1 WLR 157 (Ch D)

The defendants, four young English musicians who played under the name of *The Troggs*, had a hit song in 1966 with "Wild Thing." Several years earlier, they had signed a contract with the plaintiff. Under the terms of that agreement, the defendants gave a positive promise to employ the plaintiff as their manager and a negative promise to not employ anyone else in that capacity. Unfortunately, the relationship between the parties deteriorated, and the group decided that it could no longer work with the plaintiff. The plaintiff sought an injunction preventing *The Troggs* from hiring anyone else to act as their manager.

The court refused to grant an injunction for several reasons. Most significantly, the judge recognized that an injunction would effectively prevent the defendants from earning a living. Unlike Bette Davis, who apparently could make money from doing things other than acting, the members of *The Troggs* were really only employable as musicians. Furthermore, they could work as musicians only if they had the services of a manager. Consequently, an injunction would essentially require them to choose between working with the plaintiff and not working at all. The court refused to require them to make that choice.

EXCLUSION CLAUSES

an exclusion clause excludes or limits liability in the event of breach

Before completing our discussion of contractual remedies, we must note that the parties can generally agree on whatever terms they want. That freedom includes the ability to preclude remedies that would normally be available for breach of contract. We have already seen that the parties can agree to *liquidated damages* (but not *penalties*). They can also insert an *exclusion clause* into their contract. An **exclusion clause** excludes or limits liability in the event of breach. The clause may apply to certain types of breach. For example, the parties can agree that liability will arise if a promise is intentionally broken, but not if it is carelessly broken. Or the clause may limit the amount of damages that are available. For example, the parties can agree that an action cannot be brought for more than $500. In either event, an exclusion clause can apply even if the parties' contract has been discharged for breach.

Although exclusion clauses serve several useful purposes, they can also produce unfair results, especially when they are contained in *standard form contracts*. As we saw in Chapter 4, the courts and legislatures have addressed that problem in a number of ways. For example, an exclusion clause is strictly enforced against the party that drafted it. As a result, a sign in a restaurant that excludes liability for "lost and stolen clothes" may not protect the restaurateur if a diner's briefcase is stolen. Likewise, an exclusion clause is effective only if it is drawn to the other party's attention before the contract is created. And finally, an exclusion clause will not apply to a loss that is caused by a fundamental breach if the effect of it would be unconscionable or unfair.

UNJUST ENRICHMENT

If an agreement is broken, the innocent party usually complains about the breach of contract and asks for damages, specific performance, or an injunction. In some situations, however, that party may bring an action in *unjust enrichment* to ask for *restitution*. The rules for unjust enrichment and restitution are quite complex. We will consider them briefly.

Unjust enrichment is a cause of action that requires proof of three elements:

- an enrichment to the defendant
- a corresponding deprivation to the plaintiff
- the absence of any juristic reason for the defendant's enrichment[19]

The remedy for unjust enrichment is always *restitution*. **Restitution** requires the defendant to give back the enrichment that it received from the plaintiff. We earlier said that expectation damages allow the plaintiff to demand, "Give me what I expected to get," and that reliance damages allow the plaintiff to demand, "Give me what I lost." Following the same pattern, we can now say that restitution allows the plaintiff to demand, "Give me what you received from me."

We must stress one point about the relationship between the law of contract and the law of unjust enrichment. Unjust enrichment *cannot* be claimed if the parties' transaction is governed by an enforceable contract. Unjust enrichment therefore can be used if there *never was* a contract between the parties. For example, if I mistakenly pay $1500 in rent to you, rather than to my landlord, there is no contract between us and I can demand restitution from you. Unjust enrichment can also be used if an apparent contract between the parties is either *void* because its terms are uncertain, or *unenforceable* because it is not in writing.[20] Finally, unjust enrichment can be used if a valid contract has been *discharged* on the basis of a breach.

Since the law of unjust enrichment is a very complicated, a business person should consult a lawyer whenever a problem arises in that area. As Case Brief 7.5 demonstrates, however, an action for unjust enrichment is sometimes much better than an action for breach of contract.

unjust enrichment is a cause of action that requires proof of an enrichment to the defendant, a corresponding deprivation to the plaintiff, and the absence of any juristic reason for the defendant's enrichment

restitution requires the defendant to give back the enrichment that it received from the plaintiff

---

[19] *Pettkus v Becker* (1980) 117 DLR (3d) 257 (SCC).

[20] *Clarke v Moir* (1987) 82 NSR (2d) 183 (NS CA); *Deglman v Guaranty Trust Co of Canada* [1954] 3 DLR 785 (SCC). As we saw in Chapter 5, most contracts do not have to be written.

CASE BRIEF 7.5

Boomer v Muir (1933) 24 P 2d 570 (Cal DC)[21]

The plaintiff agreed to build a dam for the defendant in exchange for a price that it later realized was well below market value. The plaintiff worked on the project and received a number of payments during the first 18 months of the contract. However, as the project neared completion, the defendant refused to honour its obligation to supply materials. The plaintiff discharged the contract on the basis of that breach.

At that point, the plaintiff had an option. It could have claimed expectation damages under the cause of action in breach of contract. However, because it had entered into a bad bargain, that choice was relatively unappealing. In light of the payments that the defendant had already made, the plaintiff would have only received an additional $20 000.

The plaintiff therefore claimed restitution in unjust enrichment for the value of the construction services that it had rendered:

- the defendant was *enriched* because it had received the value of the plaintiff's services,
- the plaintiff suffered a *corresponding deprivation* because it had supplied the services, and
- there was *no juristic reason* why the defendant should be able to retain the value of the plaintiff's services if it was unwilling to perform its own obligations under the contract.

Significantly, once the plaintiff established the cause of action in unjust enrichment, it was entitled to restitution of the *actual value* of its services. Because the plaintiff's claim was not breach of contract, its remedy was not limited by the terms of its contract with the defendant. Consequently, after taking into account the payments that the defendant had already made, the court awarded $257 000 to the plaintiff. That was $237 000 more than it expected to receive under the contract.

[21.] See also *Lodder v Slowey* [1904] AC 442 (PC); *Komorowski v Van Weel* (1993) 12 OR (3d) 444 (Ont Gen Div).

Chapter Summary

If a contract is breached, the innocent party may be entitled to a variety of remedies. If the breach is serious, the innocent party may be allowed to discharge the contract. Whether or not a contract is discharged for breach, the innocent party may be entitled to damages.

Expectation damages allow the innocent party to recover the monetary value of the benefit that it expected to receive under the contract. The calculation of expectation damages is complicated if the plaintiff claims the cost of cure or the value of intangible losses. Expectation damages are subject to two important restrictions: remoteness and mitigation. Instead of expectation damages, the innocent party may be entitled to reliance damages, which allow it to recover the monetary value of expenses that it wasted in reliance upon the contract. Reliance damages are available only to the extent that the contract was not unprofitable. The courts will enforce a contractual term regarding liquidated damages, but they will not enforce a penalty. If the innocent party did not suffer any loss as a result of a breach, the court may award nominal damages.

Punitive damages are occasionally awarded to punish the defendant.

Equitable remedies are sometimes available for a breach of contract. Specific performance occurs when the court orders the defendant to fulfill a contractual obligation to do something. An injunction occurs when the court orders the defendant to refrain from doing something that is prohibited by the contract. Specific performance and injunctions are subject to special limitations.

Even if a contract has been discharged for breach, an exclusion clause contained in that contract may continue to limit the defendant's liability.

In some situations, it may be possible to sue for unjust enrichment rather than breach of contract. The cause of action in unjust enrichment requires proof that: (i) the defendant received an enrichment, (ii) the plaintiff suffered a corresponding deprivation, and (iii) there was an absence of any juristic reason for the defendant's enrichment. The remedy for unjust enrichment is always restitution.

Review Questions

1. What are "damages"?
2. How are expectation damages calculated?
3. In what sense do expectation damages compensate the plaintiff? Why is it desirable to award damages based on expectations?
4. What is the difference between "loss of value" and "cost of cure" damages? Present arguments for and against cost of cure damages.
5. What problems are associated with the calculation of damages for intangible losses?
6. How does the concept of remoteness relate to the general theory of expectation damages?
7. Under what circumstances will damages be considered remote and therefore unavailable?
8. Briefly outline the rules regarding mitigation of loss.
9. Do the rules governing mitigation seem fair to you? Is there any justification for requiring the plaintiff to minimize the losses that are caused by the defendant's breach?
10. How do reliance damages differ from expectation damages?
11. Can a party escape the consequences of a bad bargain by claiming reliance damages rather than expectation damages?
12. What are nominal damages? How are they calculated? What purpose do they serve?
13. "The recovery of nominal damages does not always mean that the plaintiff comes out ahead." Discuss the accuracy of that statement.
14. What are liquidated damages? How do they differ from penalties? Are liquidated damages recoverable? Are penalties recoverable?
15. What are punitive damages? How are they calculated? Under what circumstances are they available? What purpose do they serve?
16. Explain the main reason why the courts prefer to award monetary damages rather than specific performance.
17. Under what circumstances will a court order specific performance?
18. Why are the courts more willing to grant injunctions than specific performance?
19. When will the courts allow a party to bring a claim in unjust enrichment?
20. Define the term "restitution." How does restitution differ from expectation damages and reliance damages?

Cases and Problems

1. Redwood Inc, which owned a parcel of land that contained dense forests, entered into a contract with Bunyon Corp. Bunyon was required to cut and remove the trees from a 100-acre area. In exchange, Redwood was required to pay $150 000 and provide trucks to Bunyon to transport the cut logs from the work site. After Bunyon had cleared about 50 acres, Redwood breached a condition of the contract by failing to provide a sufficient number of trucks. Bunyon therefore discharged the contract for breach and claimed damages. At trial, the evidence indicated that Bunyon had entered into a bad bargain. It had cleared about half of the designated area and had received $75 000 in payment from Redwood. In doing so, however, Bunyon had actually incurred $300 000 in expenses. That amount represented the true market value of the services rendered and was not at all attributable to incompetence or mismanagement. If Bunyon claimed expectations damages, what amount of money should it have received? If Bunyon claimed reliance damages, what amount of money should it have received? Is there any other basis upon which Bunyon could claim relief? If so, what amount of money would it receive?

2. Pacific Guano Ltd wanted to mine phosphate on Ocean Island in the south Pacific. The small population of that island formed the Ocean Island Residents Co (OIRC) and entered into an agreement with Pacific Guano. Under the terms of that contract, Pacific Guano received the right to extract unlimited quantities of phosphate from the island for 20 years in exchange for its promises to pay $20 000 000 and to undertake an extensive reforestation project at the end of the 20-year term. Shortly after signing the contract, the members of the OIRC, which consisted of all the residents of Ocean Island, permanently resettled to another nearby island. Pacific Guano carried out its mining operations and paid $20 000 000. However, at the end of the lease, it refused to replant the property and left the island resembling a lunar landscape. The reforestation project that the contract required would have cost about $3 000 000, but it would have improved the value of the land by only $600 000. Is the OIRC entitled to recover $3 000 000 as cost of cure damages? Leaving aside the legal rules, do you think that the OIRC *should* be able to recover $3 000 000 as cost of cure damages? If, at the time of forming the contract, the OIRC had known that

Pacific Guano would not reforest the land as promised, would the OIRC have entered into the same contract? Explain your answers.

3. Classique Cars Ltd rents out limousines for $200 per day, almost invariably to people arranging wedding parties. It is one of several companies to do so. On one occasion, Classique found that it was over-booked and did not have enough limousines to meet its rental obligations. It therefore called Adam, with whom it had entered into a rental contract a week earlier, and informed him that he would not be provided with a vehicle. Adam responded by informing Classique for the first time that he did not want a limousine for a wedding party. He needed the car to film a scene in a movie that he was directing. Adam also told Classique that if he did not receive a limousine, the filming schedule for his movie would be set back one day at a cost of $50 000. If Adam sues Classique, identify two reasons why he may not be entitled to recover $50 000 in expectation damages.

4. For the return flight home to Halifax from a prestigious European dog show, Connie wanted her prizewinning Scottish terrier, Thistle, to travel with her in the first class section of the plane. As she explained to the airline representatives, in addition to Thistle's value as a show dog, he was the only family she had and meant the world to her. Safeway Airlines, however, had a strict policy against carrying animals in the passenger compartments. Connie, who was terribly concerned about the welfare of Thistle, offered to purchase the entire first class section of the airplane so that the dog could travel with her. Much to her disappointment, the airline representatives refused her offer, but assured her that Thistle would arrive safely in Halifax. Sadly, upon arriving at the Halifax airport, it was discovered that Thistle had suffocated to death in the cargo compartment of the Safeway Airlines plane.

Connie had purchased Thistle two years before for $750. She had originally purchased the dog as a companion, but soon discovered that Thistle's delightful disposition was perfect for showing. By all accounts, Thistle was expected to earn a considerable amount in prize money. Connie is deeply distressed about the loss of her beloved pet and feels that she should be compensated for the loss of Thistle's companionship. Is she entitled to recover damages? If so, how would you characterize and calculate those damages?

5. Paolo owns an apartment complex in a poor area of town. The building contains a large number of identical apartments. Because demand is low, there are always several empty apartments. Paolo leased an apartment to Dhalia for one year at a rent of $1000 per month. After two months, however, Dhalia broke the lease, moved out, and refused to pay the remaining rent. The next day, Paolo convinced Xavier to live in the apartment that Dhalia had occupied. In doing so, did Paolo mitigate the loss that resulted from Dhalia's breach? Would your answer be the same if Dhalia had introduced Xavier to Paolo? What if Dhalia had introduced Xavier to Paolo only because she was moving out? In answering those questions, place yourself in Paolo's position and ask whether Xavier's contract really made up for the loss that Dhalia caused when she broke her lease.

6. Jane agreed to purchase a yacht from Ted for $100 000. Payment of the money and delivery of the boat were both scheduled to occur on May 31. On May 28, however, Ted telephoned Jane and told her he had decided to keep the yacht for himself. Jane was annoyed with Ted but had no difficulty in buying a virtually identical boat from someone else at the same price on May 29. Nevertheless, she still believes that Ted behaved badly and insists that he should be held accountable. If she sued him for breach of contract, would she win? If so, explain the type of damages that she would receive. From Jane's perspective, is there any danger in bringing such a claim?

7. The Maple Leaf Mall is home to about 30 stores. The shopping centre's largest and greatest attraction was the AllMart, which provided a significant commercial benefit to the nearby, smaller businesses. AllMart had a 25-year lease with the Mall, which contained this term:

> AllMart agrees to keep the premises open for trade during the usual hours of business in the shopping centre and to maintain the store's appearance in keeping with the high quality standards of all stores in the Maple Leaf Mall.

Ten years after signing the lease, RWB Enterprises Inc, the corporation that owned AllMart, decided to downsize its operations to increase the profitability of the chain. To achieve that end, RWB closed some of the less profitable stores, which included the Maple Leaf location. The owners of the Maple Leaf Mall asked AllMart to keep its doors open until the Mall was able to secure a replacement tenant. They also offered to reduce the rent until a suitable replacement was found. Despite these incentives, RWB refused to stay open and quickly removed all of its inventory. The shopping centre and its other tenants felt the immediate impact of the AllMart closure. The owners of the Maple Leaf Mall have decided to take the matter to court. They are seeking specific performance of the contractual term to keep the premises open for trade. Will they succeed? Explain the factors that a judge would consider when deciding the matter. Do the owners of the Maple Leaf Mall have an alternative to specific performance under the circumstances?

8. For many years, Conor worked part time at Liam's Irish Pub and Restaurant while he attended college. When Conor graduated and received a diploma in hotel and restaurant management, Liam, the owner, asked him to stay at the restaurant full time. He offered to pay Conor the going rate for a waiter. Liam also said that if Conor helped with management, he would leave the restaurant to him in his will. Conor accepted that proposal. So, in addition to his regular shifts waiting tables, for which he was paid, Conor also did the following:

- he learned and eventually took over the restaurant's bookkeeping and payroll
- he ordered the restaurant and pub's supplies
- he assisted with the general maintenance and upkeep of the restaurant
- he hired and trained new employees
- he often helped out behind the bar when the pub was short-staffed

That arrangement went on for about five years until, tragically, Liam was killed in an automobile accident. Despite his promise, Liam failed to include Conor in his will. Conor has decided to sue Liam's estate and wants to seek specific performance to have the oral agreement between himself and Liam enforced. As you will recall from Chapter 5, however, Liam and Conor's contract relating to land is unenforceable for want of writing. Can you think of another basis upon which Conor could recover the value of his services from Liam's estate? Explain.

9. In September, Marcy's Department Store placed an order with Fuego Toys Inc for the upcoming holiday season. While it is difficult to predict which toys will be popular with children, both parties expected that the Squiggles line of giggling squirrels would be among the market leaders. Marcy's therefore agreed to buy 50 000 Squiggles at $20 each. From that stock, the department store expected to earn a gross profit of $1 000 000 by charging $40 per item. Marcy's was concerned, however, because it knew that Fuego's overseas manufacturing operations were experiencing labour difficulties. Marcy's therefore persuaded Fuego to insert the following clause into the contract.

> Fuego Toys Inc promises to deliver 50 000 Squiggles to Marcy's Department Store by 15 December. If Fuego is unable to meet that obligation, it will pay liquidated damages of $40 for each Squiggle that it is unable to deliver on schedule.

As the holiday season drew closer, the Squiggles fad grew much more dramatically than the parties had anticipated. By mid-December, their market value reached $100 per item. Unfortunately, Fuego's overseas labour problems also grew unexpectedly. As a result, it was unable to deliver any Squiggles to Marcy's. Furthermore, it was impossible for Marcy's to obtain an alternative source of Squiggles so close to the holidays. Assuming that Marcy's paid the purchase price at the time of signing the contract, how much can it recover in damages? Explain your answer.

10. Five years ago, Vladimir Ulyanov, a professional hockey player, signed a contract with the Rebels Hockey Club, which contained these terms:

(a) Vladimir Ulyanov agrees to perform for the Rebels Hockey Club and not to perform for any other hockey club for the duration of this contract.
(b) This contract shall run for 10 years from the date of signing.
(c) The Rebels Hockey Club agrees to pay Vladimir Ulyanov a base salary of $6 000 000 per year for the duration of this contract.

Last year, the Rebels hired a new coach, who changed the club's style of play by focusing far more on intimidation and far less on skill. Vladimir, a highly talented, but slightly built, player, wants no part of the new approach and has signed a contract to play with a rival team. The Rebels have brought an action against him for breach of contract.

The team argues that monetary damages would not be an adequate remedy because: (i) no amount of money would allow them to hire another player of Vladimir's calibre, (ii) it is impossible to accurately predict the loss of merchandising and ticket revenue that would be caused by Vladimir's defection to a rival team. In response, Vladimir says that his only employment prospects outside of professional hockey lie in the food service industry, and that if he is required to take a job in a restaurant, his annual income would drop from $6 000 000 to $25 000. Will a court order specific performance against Vladimir? Will a court order an injunction against Vladimir? What do you believe would be a fair result in this case?

11. Daphne purchased fire insurance for her home from Pontius Insurance Co. Several years later, her house was destroyed by fire, and she asked Pontius to pay $250 000, which was the value of her home. After a brief investigation, Pontius realized that the claim was legitimate and that Daphne was legally entitled to that money. However, it also realized that she was in psychologically vulnerable state and that if she was threatened, she might withdraw her claim. Pontius therefore contacted Daphne and falsely told her that its investigators had found evidence that strongly suggested that she had committed arson to collect money under her insurance policy. Pontius's tactic backfired. Daphne did not retract her claim. Instead, she instructed her lawyer to sue Pontius for as much money as possible. Is there any chance that she is entitled to collect more than $250 000? Why or why not?

12. Tele-planet Inc entered into a contract with the government of Ruvutu, an island nation in the south Atlantic, to construct a telecommunications centre. The project was to be completed by Tele-planet in Canada and then shipped in segments to Ruvutu by June 1. As Tele-planet was told at the time of entering into the agreement, the government of Ruvutu intended to use the centre for, amongst other things, broadcasting commercial television signals to neighbouring countries. Tele-planet, however, breached its contractual obligations by failing to deliver on schedule. In fact, it did not ship the components until late November. After the government of Ruvutu received the components, it brought an action against Tele-planet for expectation damages of $1 000 000, the amount of money it initially expected to earn between June and November by using the telecommunications centre to broadcast commercial television signals. In response, Tele-planet insisted that Ruvutu suffered no loss as a result of the breach. That argument was based on the fact that, during June, Ruvutu was engaged in a brief, but destructive, war with a neighbouring island. During the skirmish, the enemy destroyed almost all of Ruvutu's existing telecommunication devices. Accordingly, Tele-planet claims that Ruvutu actually benefited from the late delivery because the telecommunications centre would have been destroyed during the war if it had been delivered on schedule. How would you expect a judge to resolve those arguments?

8 Special Contracts:
Sale of Goods

CHAPTER OVERVIEW

OBJECTIVES

After completing this chapter, you should be able to:

1. Explain why a knowledge of the *Sale of Goods Act* is important for risk management.
2. Define the term "sale of goods" and explain when it applies.
3. Outline the rules that determine when property and risk pass under a sale of goods.
4. Summarize the rules that the Act implies with respect to the seller's title to sell.
5. Summarize the rules that apply when goods are sold on the basis of a sample.
6. Explain the extent to which the Act requires goods to match their description. Explain the difference between "merchantability" and "fitness for an intended purpose."
7. Describe the rules that the Act implies with respect to delivery and payment.
8. Outline the situations in which an action for the price is available and explain how that sort of action is different from a claim for damages under a breach of contract.
9. Explain the difference between a lien and a stoppage in transit, and describe the situations in which each can apply.
10. Explain when the seller can exercise a right of repossession.

We have completed our basic examination of contracts. Before leaving the topic, however, we will look at several types of contracts that are subject to special rules. We will discuss a number of these in other chapters, including leases, mortgages, insurance, agency, electronic commerce, and employment. In this chapter and the next, we will briefly consider two types of special contracts that are especially important in the business context: *sales of goods* and *negotiable instruments*.

THE *SALE OF GOODS ACT*

The Canadian economy was traditionally based on the sale of tangible (physical) goods, like beaver pelts, timber, oil, and grain. Recently, that situation has started to change. We are beginning to depend much more on intangible things, like information and services. The sale of goods nevertheless remains vitally important. First, as individual consumers, we will always need to buy things like food and clothing. Second, many businesses in this country continue to deal primarily in goods, either buying or selling things like bicycles, apples, and cows. Third, even those businesses that do focus on information occasionally find it necessary to participate in the sale of goods. For example, although accountants are paid to provide analysis and advice, they cannot do so without first buying calculators, computers, and pens.

the sale of goods remains vitally important to the Canadian economy

Because sale of goods contracts are so significant, they are governed by a special statute, the *Sale of Goods Act*. Interestingly, that statute was initially introduced as a *codification*. Over several hundred years, judges had developed a large number of rules that applied when goods were sold. They did this to ensure the smooth flow of commerce. Business people do not want to spend time or money in court. They want clear and comprehensive laws that allow them to quickly deal with potential problems and get on with the job of making money. With that same goal in mind, the British Parliament transferred, or *codified*, the judge-made rules into the *Sale of Goods Act* in 1893. Since then, all of the common law jurisdictions in Canada have adopted virtually identical legislation.[1]

the *Sale of Goods Act* is a codification of judge-made rules

The history of the Act continues to be significant. Judges never intended to force contractual parties into certain types of agreements. They merely wanted to provide *default rules* that would apply if the parties did not deal with particular issues themselves. The general concept of freedom of contract meant the parties were usually free to make up different rules if they wished. That generally remains true today. While some exceptions do exist, the *Sale of Goods Act* is typically intended to fill in gaps. Goods can be bought and sold quickly because the parties do not have to negotiate and agree on a long list of terms. The Act does much of that work for them. At the same time, however, the Act also gives parties the freedom to create contracts with different terms, which better serve their purposes.

the *Sale of Goods Act* generally only provides default rules

---

[1.] *Sale of Goods Act*, RSA 1980, c S-2 (Alta); *Sale of Goods Act*, RSBC 1979, c 370 (BC); *Sale of Goods Act*, RSM 1987, c S10 (Man); *Sale of Goods Act*, RSNB 1973, c S-1 (NB); *Sale of Goods Act*, RSN 1990, c S-6 (Nfld); *Sale of Goods Act*, RSNWT 1988, c S-6 (NWT); *Sale of Goods Act*, RSNS 1989, c 408 (NS); *Sale of Goods Act*, RSO 1990, c S-1 (Ont); *Sale of Goods Act*, RSPEI 1988, c S-1 (PEI); *Sale of Goods Act*, RSS 1978, c S-1 (Sask); *Sale of Goods Act*, RSY 1986, c 154 (Yuk). Because the statutes are almost identical, references in this text will be made to the Ontario legislation. A table of concordance, which provides a comparative listing of section numbers for all of the statutes, can be found in GHL Fridman *Sale of Goods in Canada* 4th ed (1997) at 3-5.

the *Sale of Goods Act* affects the issue of risk management

It is important to understand how the *Sale of Goods Act* affects risk management. Because the Act provides default rules, a contract may include terms that the parties did not even discuss. Suppose you sell a conveyor belt to a mining company that is involved in a large and expensive project. If the belt is defective and causes the mining operation to shut down for several weeks, you may be held responsible for an enormous loss. Whether or not you were aware of the fact, your contract with the mining company may have included a condition that the conveyor belt was of *merchantable quality* or *fit for its intended purpose*. And if one of those conditions was breached, you might be liable for, say, $500 000 even though you only charged $500 for the belt. Knowledge of the *Sale of Goods Act* is therefore critically important. You cannot effectively manage a risk unless you are at least aware of it. If you are buying or selling goods, you should know the rights and obligations that the statute implies. And if you are unwilling to accept those rights and obligations, you should either walk away from the deal or persuade the other party to adopt different terms. If you do enter into a contract, you should use your knowledge of the Act to ensure that you are properly covered by insurance.

A SALE OF GOODS

a sale of goods is a contract whereby the seller transfers or agrees to transfer the property in goods to the buyer for a money consideration called the price

The *Sale of Goods Act* applies only to a *sale of goods*. It defines a **sale of goods** as "a contract whereby the seller transfers or agrees to transfer the property in goods to the buyer for a money consideration, called the price."[2] We stress four points.

- the Act applies only to a *sale*
- the Act applies only to a sale of *goods*
- the Act applies only to a sale of goods for *money*
- the Act is sometimes enforceable only if the contract is *evidenced in writing*

a sale occurs if the buyer obtains ownership in the goods as soon as the contract is created

an agreement to sell occurs if the buyer does not obtain ownership of the goods until some time after the contract is created

First, the Act applies only to a *sale*. That term covers two situations: *sale* and *agreement to sell*. A **sale** occurs if the buyer obtains ownership in the goods as soon as the contract is created. An **agreement to sell** occurs if the buyer does not obtain ownership of the goods until some time after the contract is created. For example, the buyer may agree to purchase a car that has not yet been manufactured or a bicycle that has not yet been separated out from an inventory of several dozen bikes. However, a sale of goods does *not* occur if the buyer is not intended to eventually obtain ownership. Consequently, the Act does not apply, for instance, if goods are leased (because ownership is not transferred); if they are given as a gift (because there is no contract); or if they are provided as security for a loan (because ownership is not transferred for the purpose of a sale).[3] And, as usual, the courts are guided by the substance, rather than the form, of a transaction. Consequently, the parties cannot turn a lease into a sale simply by calling it "an agreement to sell."[4]

goods include tangible things that can be moved

Second, the Act applies only to a sale of *goods*. Goods include tangible things that can be moved.[5] These include cars, books, pigs, and crops that will

---

[2] *Sale of Goods Act* s 21(1).

[3] The Act is not excluded merely because goods are sold on credit. For instance, when goods are sold under a *conditional sales contract*, the buyer obtains possession immediately, but the seller retains ownership until the full price is paid. The Act nevertheless applies because the ultimate purpose of that transaction is to transfer property in exchange for money.

[4] *Helby v Matthews* [1895] AC 471 (HL).

[5] *Sale of Goods Act* s 1(1).

be harvested from the land. It does not include land or things that have already been attached to land, such as houses and fences, as those things are not moveable. Nor does the definition of "goods" include things that are not tangible. For that reason, the Act does not apply to the sale of trademarks, shares, debts, or negotiable instruments.[6] And finally, services are not caught by the legislation. A difficult question often arises, however, when goods are sold together with services. In such circumstances, a judge must determine whether the essence of the contract was the performance of a service on the one hand or the transfer of property on the other.[7] Although the courts are not always consistent in their approach, Case Brief 8.1 provides a common illustration.

CASE BRIEF 8.1

Gee v White Spot Ltd (1987) 32 DLR (4th) 238 (BC SC)

Mr Gee developed botulism after eating a meal at the defendant's restaurant. Claiming that the food he had purchased fell within the definition of "goods," he sued for damages under the *Sale of Goods Act*. The restaurant responded by arguing that the contract was really based on services, that is, the preparation of the meal.

The judge stressed that a contract does not have to deal exclusively with goods to fall within the Act. He then found in favour of Mr Gee for two main reasons. First, he held that a customer's primary purpose in ordering a meal in the restaurant is not to receive the services of a cook and a waiter, but rather to receive the food itself. Second, the judge was influenced by the fact that consumers like Mr Gee are better protected from defective goods if they are allowed to sue under the *Sale of Goods Act*.

Third, the Act applies only if the buyer provides consideration in the form of money. It does not apply if the parties simply trade goods, say, a car for a boat. However, the buyer does not have to pay entirely with cash. First, "money" includes both cash and other forms of payment, such as cheques and credit cards, that allow the seller to receive cash. Second, the Act may apply even if the buyer pays with money and goods. For example, you may purchase a new bicycle by paying $200 and trading in your old bike. That transaction would be considered a sale of goods.

the Act applies only to a sale for money

Finally, a sale of goods is sometimes enforceable only if it is *evidenced in writing*. That requirement is limited in several ways. First, it applies only in some jurisdictions and only if the price is over a specific amount.[8] Second, a lack of writing does not mean that a contract is invalid, but rather that a court will not enforce it. And third, the rule does not apply if the buyer: (i) accepts part of the goods, (ii) pays part of the price, or (iii) provides something "in earnest." The first two exceptions are straightforward. The third occurs when the buyer gives something valuable, other than part of the purchase price, to make the agreement binding. That is an ancient idea that is seldom used today.

a sale of goods sometimes is enforceable only if it is evidenced in writing

---

[6.] Those things are intangible even though they can be *represented* by something tangible, such as a share certificate.

[7.] As we will see, one of the Act's most important functions is that it implies a number of terms regarding quality. Even if a contract involves services rather than goods (so that the Act does not apply), the courts may imply similar terms. For example, in *Maple Leaf Construction v Maloney*, a contract to build a tennis court was not a sale of goods, but it did contain an implied condition as to quality: *Maple Leaf Construction (1978) Ltd v Maloney* (1987) 34 BLR 93 (Man QB).

[8.] The dollar value varies: $50 (Alberta, Newfoundland, Northwest Territories, Nunavut, and Saskatchewan), $40 (Nova Scotia), $30 (Prince Edward Island), and $1000 (Yukon). There is no writing requirement in Manitoba, New Brunswick, or Ontario. And in British Columbia, executory (unperformed) contracts for more than $20 are unenforceable unless they are evidenced in writing, according to the *Consumer Protection Act*, RSBC 1996, c 65, s 12.

PASSING OF PROPERTY

property passes when the ownership or title in goods is transferred from the seller to the buyer

If a contract involves a sale of goods, the Act implies a number of terms. A particularly important one is concerned with the *passing of property*. **Property passes** when the ownership or title in goods is transferred from the seller to the buyer. At that point, the property stops belonging to the seller and starts belonging to the buyer. Significantly, however, there is often a difference between *property* and *possession*. The seller may still possess the goods, in the sense of having physical control over them, even though the buyer has become the owner. Likewise, the buyer may obtain possession of the goods even though the seller is still the owner. As we will see, that separation of ownership and possession can cause considerable problems.

risk passes with property, unless the parties otherwise agree

risk is any loss or damage that may occur to the goods

The passing of property is important for several reasons. It may affect the remedies that are available if a contract is breached.[9] It may also be important if one party becomes bankrupt. Suppose you pay for goods that the seller promises to deliver in a week. If the seller declares bankruptcy before doing so, you will want to prove that you already acquired ownership in the goods. Otherwise, they may form part of the seller's bankrupt estate, and you will have to share them with the other creditors.[10] The passing of property is most important, however, because the Act states that *risk* passes with property unless the parties otherwise agree.[11] **Risk** is any loss or damage that may occur to the goods. Consequently, the party who bears the risk suffers the loss if, for example, goods are destroyed in a fire or stolen by a thief. From a risk management perspective, the lesson is clear. If you are buying valuable goods, you should make sure that you have an insurance policy that protects your investment from the moment that the property passes to you.

The Act provides rules for determining when property and risk pass under five situations.[12] We will quote each rule and follow it with a brief illustration.

> RULE 1 Where there is an unconditional contract for the sale of specific goods in a deliverable state, the property in the goods passes to the buyer when the contract is made and it is immaterial whether the time of payment or the time of delivery or both is postponed.

BUSINESS LAW IN ACTION 8.1

Passing of Property—RULE 1

After closing a major deal and earning your first $1 000 000 in business, you decide to reward yourself by buying something special. You therefore visit Clouseau's Jewellery store, pick out a diamond, and agree to buy it for $50 000. However, because you want to go straight to the gym afterwards, you persuade Clouseau to place the diamond in his safe. You promise that you will pick it up the next morning when you bring in the purchase price. Unfortunately, Clouseau's store is burglarized that night, and the thief makes off with the diamond.
(continued)

[9.] In particular, the seller may bring *an action for the price* if property has passed.

[10.] As we will discuss under the heading "repossession," different rules may apply if a buyer becomes bankrupt after receiving title, but before paying the price. The seller may be protected from the buyer's bankruptcy.

[11.] *Sale of Goods Act* s 21. Business people often use certain types of contracts that allocate property and risk in different ways. As we will see in Chapter 24, that is true for bills of lading, as well as CIF and FOB contracts.

[12.] *Sale of Goods Act* s 19.

(continued)

Because there was an unconditional sale of a specific item that was already in a deliverable state, the property and the risk passed to you as soon as the contract was made. It is irrelevant that Clouseau still had possession of the diamond and that you had not yet paid the price. Consequently, the theft is your problem. You are still required to pay $50 000 to Clouseau, even though he no longer has the diamond. To protect yourself, you should have bought an insurance policy from an insurer at the same time that you bought that diamond from the jeweller.

RULE 2 Where there is a contract for the sale of specific goods and the seller is bound to do something to the goods for the purpose of putting them into a deliverable state, the property does not pass until such thing is done and the buyer has notice thereof.

BUSINESS LAW IN ACTION 8.2

Passing of Property—RULE 2

Assume the same facts as before, except that you agree to pay $50 000 for a particular diamond on the condition that Clouseau recut it. He agrees, estimates that the job will take between one and two weeks, and says that he will call you when he is finished. Eight days later, Clouseau recuts the diamond, places it in his safe, and leaves a reminder for himself to call you the next day. However, before he can call you, his store is burglarized, and the thief makes off with the diamond.

There was a sale of goods that required Clouseau to do something to put the diamond into a "deliverable state," that is, to put it into a condition that would require you to accept it under the contract. Consequently, property did not pass to you. While Clouseau had re-cut the diamond, he had not yet notified you. The theft is therefore his problem. You do not have to pay the purchase price, and unless he had insurance, he will suffer the loss.[13]

RULE 3 Where there is a contract for the sale of specific goods in a deliverable state but the seller is bound to weigh, measure, test or do some other act or thing with reference to the goods for the purpose of ascertaining the price, the property does not pass until such act or thing is done and the buyer has notice thereof.

BUSINESS LAW IN ACTION 8.3

Passing of Property—RULE 3

Assume the same facts as in Business Law in Action 8.1, except that you leave the diamond with Clouseau so that he can weigh it to determine its exact price. After doing so, he calls and tells you that the diamond is ready to be collected. Before you can get to his store, however, it is burglarized, and a thief makes off with the diamond.

There was a sale of goods that required Clouseau to do something to determine the price of the diamond. Consequently, property did not pass to you immediately. It did, however, pass as soon as Clouseau weighed the diamond *and* notified you of that fact. The theft is therefore your problem. Unless you bought insurance for the diamond, you will have to pay $50 000 to Clouseau for nothing.

---

[13] If you already paid the purchase price, you would be able to recover it from Clouseau either under the contract or under an action for unjust enrichment, as explained in Chapter 7.

RULE 4 When goods are delivered to the buyer on approval or "on sale or return" or other similar terms, the property therein passes to the buyer,

(i)   when the buyer signifies approval or acceptance to the seller or does any other act adopting the transaction;

(ii)   if the buyer does not signify approval or acceptance to the seller but retains the goods without giving notice of rejection, then if a time has been fixed for the return of the goods, on the expiration of such time, and, if no time has been fixed, on the expiration of a reasonable time; what is a reasonable time is a question of fact.

BUSINESS LAW IN ACTION 8.4

Passing of Property—RULE 4

Assume the same basic facts, except that Clouseau allows you to take a diamond away on a trial basis because you are not sure that you really want to buy it. He is hoping that you will be persuaded to finalize the sale once your friends see the item and express their envy. Ten days later, a thief breaks into your house and steals the diamond.

More information is required to determine who will bear the loss of the diamond. Property would have passed if you had told Clouseau that you had chosen to keep the diamond or if you had done something that was inconsistent with his ownership of it (such as having it set into your own ring). Property also would have passed if you had agreed to return the diamond within three days, or if ten days was more than a reasonable length of time.

RULE 5

(i)   Where there is a contract for the sale of unascertained or future goods by description and goods of that description and in a deliverable state are unconditionally appropriated to the contract, either by the seller with the assent of the buyer, or by the buyer with the assent of the seller, the property in the goods thereupon passes to the buyer, and such assent may be expressed or implied and may be given either before or after the appropriation is made.

(ii)   Where in pursuance of the contract the seller delivers the goods to the buyer or to a carrier or other bailee (whether named by the buyer or not) for the purpose of transmission to the buyer and does not reserve the right of disposal, the seller shall be deemed to have unconditionally appropriated the goods to the contract.[14]

BUSINESS LAW IN ACTION 8.5

Passing of Property—RULE 5

Assume the same basic facts, except that Clouseau does not have an appropriate diamond in stock. You therefore pay $50 000, and he agrees to obtain a diamond from his dealer, which he will then deliver to you within a month. A week later, Clouseau receives an appropriate diamond from his supplier. He places it in his safe with the intention of delivering it to your office the next day. Unfortunately, his store is burglarized that night, and the thief makes off with the diamond.

Because there was a sale of unascertained goods, property would pass to you only after Clouseau obtained *and*

unconditionally appropriated a particular diamond to your contract. The courts have interpreted that requirement narrowly. Unconditional appropriation occurs only if the seller has lost the ability to use the goods for any purpose other than fulfilling the buyer's contract. Very often, that happens only when the goods are actually delivered to the buyer. Consequently, although the courts are somewhat inconsistent, the stolen diamond was probably *not* unconditionally appropriated to your contract.[15] After all, Clouseau could have changed his mind overnight and ordered another diamond for you. If so, property did not pass and the theft is his problem, not yours.

---

14. Bailees are discussed in Chapter 15.

15. If Clouseau's actions *do* amount to unconditional appropriation, the court would probably find that you had given your "assent" (agreement) beforehand when you asked him to obtain an appropriate diamond.

Concept Summary 8.1 reviews the rules regarding the passing of property.

Concept Summary 8.1

Passing of Property—Default Rules

Type of Contract	Property Passes
RULE 1: an unconditional contract for the sale of specific goods that are already in a deliverable state	• at the time of the contract, even if delivery and payment occur later
RULE 2: a contract for specified goods that requires the seller to do something to put the goods into a deliverable state	• when the seller has done that thing *and* the buyer has been notified
RULE 3: a contract for specified goods that requires the seller to do something to the goods (such as weigh, measure, or test them) in order to determine the price	• when the seller has done that thing *and* the buyer has been notified
RULE 4: a delivery of goods "on sale or return"	• when the buyer has signified approval *or* adopted the transaction *or* retained the goods beyond a reasonable time
RULE 5: a contract for unascertained or future goods by description	• when goods of that description, that are in deliverable state, are unconditionally appropriated to the contract by one party with the other party's assent

Before leaving the issue of property passing, note two more points.

- First, it bears repeating that the Act merely provides default rules. The parties are generally entitled to override the Act and adopt other rules for the passing of property and risk.[16] Suppose that you take possession of a specific diamond after promising to pay $50 000 to Clouseau. According to RULE 1, property has passed to you even though he has not yet received any money. However, if Clouseau is worried about your ability to pay, he might insert a *retention of title* clause into your contract that specifically says that he will continue to own the diamond until you have paid the full price. Otherwise, if you became bankrupt, he might lose the jewel *and* he might not be paid in full.

- Second, even if property has passed to the buyer, the risk is still on the seller if that party creates a loss by improperly delaying delivery.[17] Suppose that Clouseau agrees to deliver a specific diamond to you on Monday. He carelessly forgets to do so and the diamond is stolen early Tuesday morning. Although property passed to you under RULE 1 when the contract was made, he bears the risk of the loss. The theft is his problem.

TERMS IN CONTRACTS OF SALE

The *Sale of Goods Act* implies a number of terms in addition to the rules that determine the passing of property. We will look at three types:

[16.] *Sale of Goods Act* s 18.

[17.] *Sale of Goods Act* s 21. Likewise, a party who possesses goods that are owned by someone else can be held responsible as a "bailee" for wrongfully causing those goods to be damaged or lost. We will examine bailees and bailors in Chapter 15.

- terms regarding the seller's title to sell
- terms regarding the nature of the goods themselves
- terms regarding delivery and payment

Before we do so, we will repeat several points that we made in Chapter 7. There are generally two categories of contractual terms: *conditions* and *warranties*. Conditions are more important than warranties. If a condition is breached, the innocent party substantially loses the expected benefit of the contract. That party therefore usually has the option of either continuing on with the contract and suing for damages *or* discharging the contract and suing for damages. That choice has to be made promptly, and once it is made, it cannot be changed. In contrast, the benefit of a contract is not substantially lost if there is merely a breach of a warranty. Consequently, the innocent party never has the option of discharging the contract. The only remedy is to carry on with the agreement and sue for damages. The *Sale of Goods Act* adopts those rules. Some of the implied terms under the Act are classified as conditions, while others are classified as warranties.[18]

Title to Sell

there is an implied condition that the seller has title to sell

When you are buying goods, you want some assurance that the seller actually has *title to sell*. A person who does not actually own the goods cannot normally transfer ownership to you.[19] You may end up paying for nothing; or worse, you may commit a tort by attempting to buy property that belongs to someone else.[20] The Act therefore implies a condition that the seller either has the right to sell the goods or will have the right to do so when the time comes to pass property.[21]

there are implied warranties that the buyer will receive clear title

Similarly, you normally want some assurance that the seller is the *only* person who has an interest in the goods. Even if the seller is the owner, you do not want to buy property that is, for instance, the subject of a mortgage in favour of a third party. The Act therefore implies warranties that the buyer will receive clear title.

Nature of the Goods

The Act implies a number of conditions dealing with the goods themselves.

- goods sold by description must match that description
- goods sold by sample must correspond with the sample
- goods must be of merchantable quality
- goods must be fit for their intended purpose

---

18. The parties are, however, generally free to use their own rules rather than the default rules provided in the Act.

19. Lawyers often use the phrase *"nemo dat quod non habet,"* which means "no one can give what they do not have." There are some exceptions to that rule. For example, the *Sale of Goods Act* says that a buyer who possesses goods, but who has not yet obtained ownership from the seller, can sell the property to an innocent person who was unaware of the seller's rights. The same basic rule applies to a seller who has possession of goods but no longer owns them. Those rules are intended to protect innocent people who honestly believe that they dealing with property owners.

20. We will examine the tort of conversion in Chapter 10.

21. *Sale of Goods Act* s 13.

Description

The Act implies a condition that goods sold by description must match that description.[22] Suppose you want to buy a stereo that can hold six CDs. You see such a product advertised on a Web site and place an order. When the equipment arrives, however, you discover that it can hold only three CDs. The seller has breached a condition, and you are entitled to reject the goods and discharge the contract.

goods sold by description must match their description

Note that the term "description" refers to the *identity* of goods rather than to their *quality*. Consequently, there would not be a breach of contract (at least not under this heading) if the stereo you received could hold six CDs but was not as loud as you had hoped. You still received an item that matched its description: a six-CD stereo.

description refers to identity, rather than quality

Note also that goods can be sold by "description" even if a sale occurs in person. Suppose you bought a stereo from a store rather than over the Internet. There were 20 identical boxes on a shelf and you picked one. You could still discharge the contract for breach of a condition if you got home and discovered that the stereo did not really hold six CDs as the box had promised. You relied on the description of the goods even though you also selected one particular box for yourself.

goods can be sold by description even if a sale occurs in person

Sample

A special set of conditions applies if goods are sold by *sample*. A **sale by sample** occurs when the parties agree to deal in goods that correspond to a particular specimen. Suppose after seeing a circular saw being demonstrated in a hardware store, you read a brochure about that tool and tell the salesperson that you want to buy 10 units for your construction company. Four rules will apply to the sale.[23]

a **sale by sample** occurs when the parties agree to deal in goods that match a particular specimen

- First, if you bought by description as well as by sample, the store is required to deliver goods that correspond to both the description *and* the sample. Consequently, the saws must be the same kind that was demonstrated *and* they must have the features that were listed in the brochure.

- Second, the store must deliver saws that are of the same *quality* as the sample. Consequently, you would be able to discharge the contract if they did not cut as quickly or as accurately as the saw that was used in the demonstration.

- Third, the store must give you a *reasonable opportunity to compare* the saws to the one that was used during the demonstration.

- Fourth, the saws would have to be free from any defect that would make them *unmerchantable* and could not have been discovered by a *reasonable examination*. Consequently, you will have a strong incentive to inspect the saws when they are delivered. If they later turn out to be defective, you will not be able to complain if you could have discovered those defects at the outset. However, you are only expected to conduct a *reasonable* inspection. You would not have to take the saws apart or perform complicated tests on them.

---

22. *Sale of Goods Act* s 14.
23. *Sale of Goods Act* s 14, 16(2).

Merchantable Quality

The general rule in sales is ***caveat emptor***: "let the buyer beware." Therefore, unless the seller made specific promises, you cannot complain if you are disappointed by the goods that you bought. The law expects you to be responsible for yourself. If you want to be protected from defective goods, you should either inspect them before you enter into a contract or pay the seller to guarantee their quality. At the same time, however, the law recognizes that those options are not realistic in many circumstances. Suppose you visit a major electronics store to buy a new computer for your office. You will probably not have much opportunity to actually inspect or test a specific unit before taking it away. Furthermore, the store will probably be reluctant to draft a new contract that reflects your particular needs or concerns. It will want to use the standard document that it uses for all of its sales. For those reasons, to protect buyers like you, the *Sales of Goods Act* creates certain exceptions to the general rule of *caveat emptor*.[24]

First, the Act implies a condition that goods are of a *merchantable quality* if they are purchased by description from someone who normally deals in those sorts of goods. That rule requires three comments.

- First, goods are **merchantable** if a reasonable person would buy them without a reduction in price despite knowing their imperfections. Goods do not have to be perfect to be merchantable. Returning to our example, a reasonable person might pay the full price for a computer even if a couple of pads on the keyboard are a bit sticky. However, no sensible person would pay full price for a computer with a cracked hard drive. Note that the implied condition can apply to both manufactured goods (such as computers) and natural products (such as milk). It can also apply to both new and used goods, although the expected quality of used goods is often lower. And finally, the implied condition can apply to both the quality of the goods themselves and such things as their labelling and packaging.[25]

- Second, the implied condition applies only if the *seller normally deals* in those sorts of goods. Consequently, a requirement of merchantability would arise if you bought a computer from an electronics store, but not if you bought it from me. I am not in the business of selling computers.

- Third, the implied condition of merchantability does not cover *defects that the buyer should have noticed* if they examined the goods. Although the cases are somewhat inconsistent, it appears that the buyer is not actually required to conduct an examination. But if an inspection does occur, the seller is no longer responsible for problems that the buyer should have noticed. The seller does remain liable, however, for defects that could not have been discovered even with a reasonable examination. Consequently, if you spent 40 minutes thoroughly inspecting a computer without noticing any defects, you would still be able to discharge the contract if you later discovered that the machine overheats if it is left running for more than six hours.

Fit for Intended Purposes

The requirement of merchantability is concerned with quality: the goods must not be defective. In some situations, the Act also implies a condition that goods must be *fit for their intended purpose*. Although those two requirements often overlap, they are different. Even if goods are not defective, they may not be

[24.] *Sale of Goods Act* s 15.
[25.] *Sale of Goods Act* s 1(1).

suitable for the buyer's needs. For example, a computer is not defective simply because it does not have a DVD player. However, it is not fit for your purpose if you require a DVD player for use in your marketing business.

Although the implied condition of fitness is potentially very useful, it applies only in certain circumstances.

the implied condition of fitness for a purpose applies only in certain circumstances

- First, the *seller must normally deal* in the sorts of goods that the buyer purchased.

- Second, the *buyer must rely on the seller's skill or judgment* in selecting goods for a particular purpose and the *seller must be aware* of that fact. The buyer does not have to expressly mention a purpose that is obvious. It can be assumed that a personal computer will be used for word processing at least part of the time. However, the buyer does have to stipulate less obvious purposes. For instance, if you are relying on the seller to select a computer that is capable of operating a small Internet business, you must say so. Indeed, as a matter of risk management, you should specify your purpose whenever there is any doubt.

- Third, the implied condition does not apply if the buyer purchases goods on the basis of a *trade name*, rather than relying on the seller's judgment. The condition is intended to protect someone who relies on a vendor's skill and experience in selecting appropriate goods. Consequently, if you simply tell a store that you want a specific model of computer, you cannot later complain if that machine does not suit your needs. You made the choice for yourself. However, the implied condition is not barred every time you mention a trade name. The court has to decide whether you were relying on your own judgment or whether you were seeking the store's advice as to the suitability of a particular product.

Exclusion Clauses

The implied conditions and warranties that we have considered impose substantial burdens. For that reason, a person who sells goods will often try to avoid those obligations by writing an *exclusion clause* into the contract.[26] As a general rule, the Act allows the parties to exclude or vary any of the implied terms.[27] At the same time, however, the courts and the legislatures are skeptical of exclusion clauses and use several techniques to limit their availability. First, some jurisdictions statutorily prevent sellers from introducing exclusion clauses in contracts with individual consumers.[28] Second, judges read exclusion clauses very narrowly. For instance, a clause that excludes "all implied *warranties*" does not affect the Act's implied *conditions*. Third, an exclusion clause will not be enforced if it would be unfair or unconscionable.[29]

Delivery and Payment

The Act also implies a number of terms dealing with *delivery* and *payment*.

- First, unless the parties otherwise agree, *delivery and payment should occur concurrently*.[30] The buyer should take possession of the goods at

delivery and payment should generally occur at the same time

---

26. We examined exclusion clauses in Chapter 4.

27. *Sale of Goods Act* s 53.

28. See Chapter 23.

29. See Chapter 5.

30. *Sale of Goods Act* s 27.

the same time that the seller receives the money. Very often, however, the parties agree that delivery and payment will be separated, such as when goods are bought with a cheque. The buyer may get the property immediately, even though the seller has to wait for payment from the bank.

<table>
<tr><td>time of delivery is normally a condition

time of payment is normally a warranty</td></tr>
</table>

- Second, although the Act is rather vague, the courts tend to find that the *time of delivery is a condition*, whereas the *time of payment is a warranty*.[31] Consequently, the buyer may be able to discharge the contract if delivery is late, whereas the seller may have to settle for damages if payment does not occur promptly. The parties are entitled to stipulate when payment and delivery must occur. If they fail to do so, the contract must be performed within a "reasonable time." As always, the courts determine the "reasonableness" in light of all of the circumstances.[32]

delivery normally occurs at the seller's place of business

- Third, *delivery normally occurs at the seller's place of business*, unless the parties agree to some other arrangement.

the seller must deliver goods that conform with the contract

- Fourth, there is an implied condition that the *seller will deliver goods that conform with the contract*. That requirement is quite broad. For example, you are entitled to reject a shipment of peas if you ordered carrots. Similarly, if you ordered 50 cartons of peas for $500, you do not have to accept more or less. If the seller delivers 48 cartons of peas, you have the option of either rejecting them all *or* paying at the reduced price of $480. And if the seller delivers 52 cartons, you have the option of rejecting them all *or* accepting 50 at the price of $500 *or* accepting them all and paying at the contract rate of $520.

Concept Summary 8.2 presents a review of the terms that are implied under the Act.

Concept Summary 8.2

Implied Terms—Default Rules

Title to Sell	• condition that the seller has title to sell • warranty that the buyer will receive clear title
Nature of the Goods	• condition that goods sold by description will match that description • condition that goods sold by sample will match the sample in quality *and* that the buyer will have reasonable opportunity to compare the goods to the sample *and* that the goods are free from unmerchantable defects • condition that goods are of a merchantable quality if they are purchased by description from someone who normally deals in such goods • condition that goods will be fit for their intended purpose if the buyer relies on the skill or judgment of a seller who normally deals in such goods
Delivery and Payment	• delivery and payment shall be concurrent • condition that delivery will occur on time and warranty that payment will occur on time • delivery will occur at the seller's place of business • condition that seller will deliver goods that conform with the contract

[31] *Sale of Goods Act* s 11.
[32] *Sale of Goods Act* s 54.

REMEDIES

If there is a breach of a contract for the sale of goods, several remedies may be available. The *Sale of Goods Act* provides a number of special remedies for an unpaid seller.[33] However, it also allows the parties to use the general remedies that we saw in the last two chapters.

General Remedies

First, the innocent party generally has the right to discharge a contract if there has been a breach of a *condition*. Suppose that you agree to pay $50 000 to Nordic Furniture for the delivery of five oak desks to your office on June 1. You will be able to discharge the contract if, for instance, Nordic delivers desks on June 10 (late delivery), or if it delivers the wrong number of desks (wrong quantity) or pine desks (failure to correspond to description) or desks that topple over (unmerchantable and unfit for intended purpose). If you do discharge the contract, you will not have to pay the price, and if you already paid the price, you will be able to recover it. In other circumstances, the seller would have the right to discharge the agreement. For instance, Nordic would be able to bring the contract to an end if, contrary to the usual rule, the time of payment was a condition, which you breached by failing to provide $50 000 on June 1 (late payment).

Second, the innocent party always has the right to claim compensatory damages. That is normally the only remedy that is available if there is a breach of a *warranty*. However, if there is a breach of a *condition*, the innocent party usually has the ability to discharge the contract in addition to claiming damages. In other words, that party can treat the term as either a condition (discharge plus damages) or a warranty (damages alone). Sometimes, however, that option is lost.[34] The Act states that a condition *must* be treated as a warranty:

- if the contract is not severable (in other words, if delivery is not made in instalments) and if the buyer has accepted at least some of the goods, or
- if property in specific goods has already passed to the buyer.

In any event, the general purpose of compensatory damages is to put the innocent party in the same financial position that it would have enjoyed if the contract had been properly performed. Consider the case in You Be the Judge 8.1.

> a contract can be discharged for breach of a condition
>
> damages can be claimed for a breach of either a condition or a warranty

YOU BE THE JUDGE 8.1

Compensatory Damages and the *Sale of Goods Act*

The town of Noix holds an annual, one-day Nut Festival, which attracts a large number of tourists. Helene, who operates a restaurant in Noix, contacted Ranjit, who owns a dry goods supply company, and ordered 50 kilograms of walnuts. As she explained to him, she intended to devote her entire menu during the festival to dishes prepared with walnuts. She paid $2500, and Ranjit promised to deliver the goods on May 30. Ranjit delivered on time, but the nuts were almost all mouldy. As she was entitled to do, Helene rejected them on the ground that

(continued)

[33.] This section discusses remedies that may be available for a breach of contract. Note that a contractual party may occasionally be entitled to rely on a different cause of action. For instance, it may be possible to rescind a contract that was induced by a misrepresentation (Chapter 4), or sue for damages under the torts of deceit (Chapter 11) or negligence (Chapter 12).

[34.] *Sale of Goods Act* s 12.

(continued)

they were unfit for their intended purpose. They would have made her customers sick. Unfortunately, given the circumstances, Helene was unable to arrange an alternative supply of nuts and therefore was forced to remain closed during the festival. She consequently lost $10 000 in net profits from that day.

Question for Discussion

1. How much will Helene receive in damages from Ranjit? Explain how you reached that decision.

Third, as we saw in Chapter 7, the courts will enforce a contractual term for *liquidated damages*.[35] The parties are allowed to agree in advance that a certain amount will be paid if their agreement is breached. In the context of sale of goods, the most important illustration of that rule concerns *deposit*s. A **deposit** is a sum of money that the buyer pays when entering into a contract and that the seller is allowed to keep if the contract is not performed. Suppose that you promise to pay within one week for a television that is worth $1000. The store clerk may demand a deposit of $100. If you return within a week and pay the remaining $900, you will be allowed to take the television home. But if you fail to pay the outstanding balance, the store will be entitled to keep the television *plus* the $100.

a deposit is a sum of money that the buyer pays when entering into a contract and that the seller is allowed to keep if the contract is not performed

Fourth, in exceptional circumstances, a court may award *specific performance* of a contractual promise.[36] However, as we saw in Chapter 7, that remedy is available only if monetary damages would be inadequate. As a result, a buyer will not be entitled to specific performance unless the goods in question are special or unique, such as a family heirloom or a priceless painting.

a court may award specific performance in exceptional circumstances

Special Remedies for the Seller

An unpaid seller has a number of special remedies under the Act. We will consider four:

- an action for the price
- a lien
- stoppage in transit
- repossession

Action for the Price

The *Sale of Goods Act* states that the seller can sometimes bring an *action for the price*.[37] An **action for the price** occurs when the seller sues the buyer for the price of the goods. To help you understand how that type of action is different from a claim for damages under a breach of contract, consider Ethical Perspective 8.1.

an action for the price occurs when the seller sues the buyer for the price of the goods

---

[35] However, the courts will not enforce a *penalty*, which is an amount of money that is completely out of proportion to the consequences of a breach.

[36] *Sale of Goods Act* s 50.

[37] *Sale of Goods Act* s 47.

ETHICAL PERSPECTIVE 8.1

Action for the Price and Expectation Damages

You own a used car dealership. One afternoon in late September, Conchita came onto your lot. She explained that she had moved to town to study for a business degree and that she needed a small vehicle for shopping. She looked at a number of cars before settling on a particular convertible. Because you were concerned about her financial circumstances, you persuaded her to sign a contract that required her to pay the full price of $8000 on October 1, even though she would not actually take possession of the car until October 4.

On September 29, however, Conchita informed you that she had dropped out of school because she needed to return home to care for a sick relative. She also asked if you would consider letting her out of the contract. You told her that you would think about it overnight. Later that same day, Logan wandered onto the lot and offered to pay $7000 for the same convertible.

You have three main options. First, you could simply release Conchita from the contract. She would not pay anything, and you could sell the car to Logan. Second, you could rely on the Act and bring an action for the price against Conchita: she would have to pay $8000, and you would have to deliver the car to her. Third, you could discharge your contract with Conchita and sue her for damages. Under the normal rules, you would be entitled to recover only $1000 from her. As Chapter 7 explained, if you sue for damages, you are expected to mitigate (or minimize) your loss. You could do so by selling the car to Logan. And in that situation, you would lose only $1000 as a result of Conchita's breach, since you would have sold the car for $7000 instead of $8000.

Questions for Discussion

1. Which of those three options would you choose? Why?
2. Is it fair that you have the ability to force Conchita to pay for a car that she no longer wants? Would your answer be different if you could not find anyone else to buy that particular vehicle?

Although the action for the price is an important remedy, it is available in only two situations: (i) if property has already passed to the buyer, or (ii) regardless of whether or not property has passed, if the contract requires payment to be made on a certain day and the buyer fails to do so.

Lien

The Act allows the seller to exercise a *lien* in some circumstances.[38] A **lien** occurs when a person retains possession of something until another person fulfills an obligation. In the context of sale of goods, the seller may have the right to hold the goods until the buyer pays the price. That right can arise whether or not property has already passed.[39] It can also arise even if the time of payment is a warranty rather than a condition. In that case, while the seller cannot discharge the agreement if it does not receive the price on time, it may be able to hold onto the goods until the money is paid.

The right to exercise a lien is limited in several ways. First, a lien requires possession. Consequently, once the buyer legitimately takes control of the goods, the seller loses the right to apply a lien. Second, the seller normally cannot exercise a lien if the buyer enjoys credit under the contract. Suppose that you agree to deliver furniture to Leon on February 14, even though the contract does not require him to pay until October 31. You could not enforce a lien on Valentine's Day. You would have to deliver the goods and then wait until Halloween for the

a lien occurs when a person retains possession of something until another person fulfills an obligation

---

[38] *Sale of Goods Act* s 39.

[39] Technically, the seller cannot exercise a lien unless property has passed. A person cannot have a lien over their *own* goods. However, a seller can exercise a similar right to *withhold delivery* if property has not passed and if payment has not been received: *Sale of Goods Act* s 38(2).

insolvency occurs when a person is unable to meet their debts as they become due

money.[40] The situation would be different, however, if Leon became *insolvent* before February 14.[41] **Insolvency** occurs when a person is unable to meet its debts as they become due. In that case, the Act allows a lien to be exercised, even if goods were sold on credit. However, sometimes it is dangerous for a seller to use a lien in such circumstances, as Business Decision 8.1 shows.

BUSINESS DECISION 8.1

Seller's Lien and Insolvency

You agree to sell 100 dictionaries to Erykah, who operates a small bookstore. Under the terms of that agreement, you are required to deliver the dictionaries on July 31, and she is required to pay $5000 before October 15. You know that she intends to eventually resell the books for $75 each.

On July 29, you hear a rumour that Erykah has experienced severe financial difficulties and has stopped paying her debts. For the next two days, you unsuccessfully try to contact her to determine if that rumour is true.

When July 31 arrives, you find yourself in a dilemma.

You do not know whether you should deliver the books as promised.

Questions for Discussion

1. Explain the dilemma. What will happen if you deliver the books and later learn that Erykah is insolvent? What will happen if you refuse to deliver the books and later learn that the rumour was false, and that Erykah was not insolvent?

2. How will you resolve the dilemma? As you continue to read through the rest of this section on remedies, consider your other options.

Stoppage in Transit

stoppage in transit occurs when an unpaid seller instructs a carrier to not deliver goods to a buyer

The remedy of *stoppage in transit* is similar to a lien, but it is even more remarkable.[42] It can be exercised even if the seller no longer has property *or* possession. **Stoppage in transit** occurs when an unpaid seller instructs a carrier to not deliver goods to a buyer. Suppose that you agree to sell a bull to Festus. Under the terms of that contract, you are required to send the animal to him by train, and he is required to pay $7500 when it arrives. During the course of the trip, however, you learn that Festus has become insolvent. In that situation, the Act allows you to contact the train company and prevent it from delivering the bull as initially directed. You can also demand that Festus pay within a reasonable time.[43] If he does so, he will be entitled to the bull. If not, you are free to sell the animal to another buyer and claim damages from Festus for any loss that his breach caused.[44]

Like a lien, stoppage in transit cannot be exercised if the buyer has already acquired possession of the goods.[45] Furthermore, it can only be exercised if the

---

[40.] A lien can be exercised, however, if the time for credit has *expired*. Consequently, if you agreed to deliver some of the furniture on Valentine's Day and the rest on New Year's Eve, you would not have to make the second delivery if Leon failed to pay the price on Halloween.

[41.] The idea of insolvency will be discussed in Chapter 22.

[42.] *Sale of Goods Act* ss 42-44. Stoppage in transit is no longer much used. Many people believe that it unfairly favours the seller over the buyer's other creditors. Furthermore, payment today is very often made by way of bankers' confirmed credits. Consequently, there is less danger that the seller will be unpaid.

[43.] If the goods are "perishable," the seller can resell them immediately without first demanding payment from the buyer: *Sale of Goods Act* s 46(3).

[44.] The same right of resale arises in connection with a lien and (presumably) with a repossession.

[45.] The right of stoppage in transit is also lost if a "document of title" (such as a *bill of lading*, which we will consider in Chapter 24) is transferred to the buyer, who then uses that document to sell the goods to a third party who is unaware of any stoppage: *Sale of Goods Act* s 45.

buyer has actually become insolvent. Consequently, the dilemma that we saw in Business Decision 8.1 can again arise.

Repossession

Section 81.1 of the *Bankruptcy and Insolvency Act* provides the most remarkable remedy of all. A seller is sometimes entitled to *repossess* goods from a buyer. That right may be available even though the buyer already obtained property *and* possession. The remedy of repossession is, however, limited to very narrow circumstances. It can be used only if:

- the goods are purchased for use in the buyer's business (and not for personal use)
- the seller delivers the goods to the buyer without receiving full payment
- the buyer becomes bankrupt or insolvent
- the seller provides written notice to the buyer's trustee in bankruptcy, within 30 days after delivery, that the goods are being repossessed
- the goods remain in the buyer's possession, have not been resold to an innocent third party, and are in the same condition as when they were delivered

a seller is sometimes entitled to repossess goods from a buyer

The effect of repossession is significant. Rather than being forced to bring an action and stand in line with the buyer's other creditors, the seller is allowed to recover the goods and simply walk away from the purchaser's financial problems.[46]

Concept Summary 8.3 reviews the extraordinary remedies that may be available to an unpaid seller of goods.

Concept Summary 8.3

Special Remedies for Unpaid Sellers

Remedy	Nature
Action for price	The seller is entitled to sue for price of the goods, even if that price exceeds the damages arising from the buyer's breach
Lien	The seller is entitled to retain possession of the goods until payment is made, even if property has passed to the buyer
Stoppage in transit	The seller is entitled to prevent a carrier from delivering the goods to the buyer, even if property has passed to the buyer
Repossession	The seller is entitled to recover possession of the goods from the buyer, even though property and possession have passed to the buyer

---

[46.] Special remedies apply in favour of farmers, fishermen, and aquaculturists: *Bankruptcy and Insolvency Act*, RSC 1985, c B-3, s 81.2 (Can).

Chapter Summary

Sale of goods contracts are governed by a special statute called the *Sale of Goods Act*. That Act supplies default rules that apply unless the parties have agreed otherwise. A knowledge of the Act is therefore necessary for the purposes of risk management.

The Act applies only to a sale of goods. There must be a sale that transfers property from the seller to the buyer. The contract must substantially deal with goods rather than services. The buyer must provide money as consideration. In some jurisdictions, some sale of goods contracts must be evidenced in writing.

The Act provides a number of default rules regarding the passing of property. The passing of property is important for several reasons. First, it may affect the remedies that are available to the parties. Second, it may allow one party to avoid financial complications if the other party becomes insolvent. And third, the party who has the property usually also bears the risk.

The Act implies several default terms. Some terms are conditions, and others are warranties. There is an implied condition that the seller has title to sell and an implied warranty that the buyer will receive clear title. There is an implied condition that goods sold by description must match their description. A number of conditions may apply if goods are sold by sample: (i) the goods must correspond to the sample, (ii) the buyer must be given a reasonable opportunity to inspect the bulk and compare it to the sample, and (iii) the goods must be merchantable. If goods are sold by description, there may be an implied condition that the goods are merchantable or fit for their intended purpose. Implied conditions or warranties can sometimes be avoided through exclusion clauses.

The Act implies a number of terms regarding delivery and payment. As a general rule, delivery and payment should occur at the same time. Time of delivery is normally a condition, but time of payment is normally a warranty. Delivery should usually occur at the seller's place of business. The seller must deliver goods that conform with the contract.

In addition to allowing general contractual remedies, the Act provides a number of special remedies for unpaid sellers. If property has passed, or if the buyer has not paid on a fixed date as required by the contract, the seller can bring an action for the price. A seller is generally entitled to enforce a lien to retain possession of goods until full payment is made. If the buyer is insolvent, the seller can exercise a right of stoppage in transit to recover goods that are in the possession of a third-party carrier. Even if the buyer has received possession and property, the seller can sometimes exercise a right of repossession if the buyer is insolvent or bankrupt.

Review Questions

1. Briefly explain why knowledge of the *Sale of Goods Act* is important for managing risk.

2. Define a "sale" according to the Act. Does a lease qualify as a sale? Does a gift? Explain your answers.

3. Define "goods" according to the Act. Can a transaction ever fall under the Act if one party provides services? Explain your answer.

4. Can a sale of goods occur if I trade my bicycle to you for a stereo? Explain your answer.

5. When, if ever, does a sale of goods have to be evidenced in writing in your jurisdiction?

6. Briefly explain three reasons why the passing of property is important.

7. "As a general rule, the risk in specific goods that are already in a deliverable state does not pass to the buyer until the seller has received the price." Is that statement correct? Explain your answer.

8. "As a general rule, if the seller has agreed to do something (such as repair or weigh) specific goods, property does not pass to the buyer until delivery actually occurs." Is that statement correct? Explain your answer.

9. Describe a contract that is "on sale or return." When does property normally pass under that sort of contract?

10. Explain the significance of the concept of "unconditional appropriation" under a contract for unascertained goods. When does unconditional appropriation occur?

11. Outline the terms that the Act implies with respect to the seller's title to sell. Are those terms conditions or warranties? What is the practical difference between a condition and a warranty?

12. The Act implies a term that goods must correspond to their "description." Does that requirement apply to both the identity and the quality of goods? Can goods be bought by description if the buyer selects a particular item off a store shelf?

13. Define the term "sale by sample." Why should the buyer always inspect goods that are sold by sample?

14. What is meant by the phrase *caveat emptor*? Why is it important to a sale of goods contract? Does the Act entirely eliminate the need to be concerned with that phrase?

15. When are goods considered "merchantable"? Can imperfect goods be merchantable? Outline the situations in which the Act implies a term of merchantability.

16. When are goods considered "fit for their intended purpose"? Explain three limitations on the rule that goods must be fit for their intended purpose.

17. "According to the Act, delivery and payment must always occur at the same time. Furthermore, a contract can always be discharged if either delivery or payment is late." Are those statements true? Explain your answers.

18. The Act allows a court to impose a remedy that occurs under the general law of contract. Outline four possibilities.

19. When will the seller be able to bring an action for the price? How does that type of action differ from an action for damages under a breach of contract?

20. Summarize the differences between a lien, a stoppage in transit, and a repossession. Why might it be true to say that repossession is the most remarkable of those remedies?

Cases and Problems

1. Celebrity Sports Inc (CSI) holds an annual celebrity softball game, which involves hockey players, politicians, and movie stars. Because of the nature of the event, a large part of CSI's profits come from merchandising. In particular, it has traditionally made a great deal of money from souvenir programs, which feature biographies and photographs of the people who play in the game. After its old publisher went out of business, CSI entered into an agreement with Page One Ltd (POL) to produce the programs. The relevant portion of that contract states:

> POL shall provide whatever services are necessary to produce 20 000 programs, each consisting of 44 pages. Those programs shall contain biographies and colour photographs of every player. CSI agrees to pay $15 000 for POL's services.

Although POL produced the appropriate number of programs, the pages appeared in reverse order due to a printing error. As a result, the programs were unmerchantable and unfit for their intended purpose. CIS therefore wants to bring an action under the *Sale of Goods Act.* POL, however, argues that the Act does not apply because the contract was for services. Did the parties have a contract for the sale of goods? Explain your answer.

2. Because she and her partner were unable to conceive a child naturally, Miranda Lopez visited Dr Omar Korn, a fertility expert. He suggested artificial insemination using semen collected from a donor. She agreed, and three weeks later, after Dr Korn had obtained semen from an anonymous donor, Mrs Lopez underwent an artificial insemination procedure. In exchange, she paid $1500. The procedure was unfortunately a failure. First, Mrs Lopez did not become pregnant. She does not, however, wish to sue Dr Korn on that basis. As he had explained to her at the outset, there was a chance that the semen would fail to fertilize an egg. Second, Mrs Lopez contracted HIV. The evidence indicates the man who donated the semen carried the virus, which was passed on to Mrs Lopez as a result of the procedure. Mrs Lopez wants to sue Dr Korn under the *Sale of Goods Act* because the semen that he provided was unmerchantable and unfit for its intended purpose. Did the parties enter into a contract for the sale of goods? Explain your answer.

3. Over the course of many years, Reliable Accounting Inc and Porteau Furnishings Ltd had entered into a number of contracts. Reliable had purchased desks and chairs from Porteau, and Porteau had purchased financial advice from Reliable. Recently, Reliable required new office furniture for two temporary members of staff. Unfortunately, as a result of certain financial difficulties, it did not have a great deal of money in its general account. It persuaded Porteau to grant a lease of two new desks in exchange for free accounting services during the next tax season. The desks were delivered, but they were useless. Due to poor workmanship, they collapsed whenever a computer was placed on them. Reliable wants to sue Porteau for supplying unmerchantable goods under the *Sale of Goods Act.* Did the parties enter into a sale of goods? Give two reasons for your answer.

4. Manon, a pig farmer, brought a number of animals to market for sale. Max surveyed them and told Manon that he was looking for a stud pig that he could use for breeding. Manon pointed to Herman who, she said, had a proud history of successfully fathering large litters of healthy piglets. Although Max agreed to purchase Herman, Manon suggested that he call his insurance company first. She explained that she once paid a high price for a stud hog only to lose the animal to disease a short time later. Max, who was thankful for the advice, called his insurance company and arranged to have Herman covered at 3:00 pm that same day. Manon and Max then entered into a contract that contained this clause:

> The buyer agrees to purchase the pig named Herman at 3:00 pm on this day. The price shall be determined on the basis of the pig's weight and the prevailing market rate.

After the parties signed the contract, Manon discovered that her scales were broken. Max therefore agreed to leave Herman with her so that she could borrow another set of scales and determine the purchase price. Manon did so, but before she could contact Max and tell him the price, an unidentified vandal opened Herman's pen and let the pig escape. Despite a long search, Herman has not been found. Manon has sued for the price, but Max refuses to pay for a pig that he says he never owned. Is Manon entitled to the money? Explain your answer.

5. Three days before Vera was scheduled to start university,

she visited Paragraphs Bookshop in search of a good dictionary. Although the salesperson showed her a number of options, Vera was most intrigued by the enormous, 20-volume *Canadian Comprehensive Dictionary*. She hesitated in buying it only because it was priced at $525. The manager of Paragraphs Bookshop therefore agreed to let her take the set home for one week "on sale or return." Four days later, Vera decided to buy the volumes. She therefore stamped her name, in very small letters, on the back cover of the first volume. She intended to return to Paragraphs Bookshop the next day to pay for the set. Before she did so, however, her father unexpectedly presented her with another copy of the *Canadian Comprehensive Dictionary* as a gift. Vera was delighted at the prospect of saving $525 and therefore took the first copy of the set back to the book store. The manager, however, refused to accept it and insisted that Vera was required to pay the purchase price. Was the manager entitled to do this? Explain your answer.

6. Auric Bond was seeking a safe investment for $100 000 that he had inherited from his parents. He contacted Goldcomp Inc, a company that dealt in precious metals. Goldcomp presented a standard form contract to Auric. The relevant portion of that document said:

> Gold is one of the safest investments available, and Goldcomp makes every effort to ensure that your investment is protected as it grows. Goldcomp holds a large amount of gold bullion in its guarded vault. Once you have paid the purchase price, an appropriate percentage of that gold will be allocated to you, and you will receive a certificate verifying your ownership of that gold. You can, at any time, take physical delivery of your purchase by providing Goldcomp with seven days' notice.

Auric agreed to those terms, paid $100 000 to Goldcomp, and received a certificate stating that he was the owner of a certain amount of gold.

Goldcomp recently became bankrupt. Its debts exceed it assets by a 10:1 ratio. Furthermore, it was recently discovered that Goldcomp never actually separated its gold into separate bundles for Auric or its other customers. All of its gold sat in an undifferentiated mass in its vault. Auric has given seven-days' notice under the agreement, but because of its bankruptcy, Goldcomp has not delivered any gold to him. In the circumstances, Auric can sue Goldcomp for breach of contract. However, if he does so, he will simply obtain a personal judgment and will have to share Goldcomp's meagre assets with the other creditors. He would be lucky to get $10 000 under that approach. Auric therefore wants to argue that he can take possession of $100 000 worth of gold on the basis that he already has property or ownership in it. Will that argument be successful? Explain your answer.

7. Asbury Motors Inc deals in used cars. Among its stock was a Cadillac that it had accepted as part of a trade-in sale with Rosalita. (Rosalita has since disappeared.) Bruce wandered onto Asbury's lot, surveyed the vehicles, and bought the Cadillac for $10 000. Three months later, however, the police appeared at Bruce's house and confiscated the car. They explained to him that they were returning it to its real owner, Clarence, from whom Rosalita had stolen it about nine months earlier. Bruce contacted Asbury Motors and demanded a refund. While the manager was sympathetic to his situation, she pleaded her innocence and honestly explained that she had no idea that the Cadillac had been stolen. She also claimed that Bruce was not entitled to a full refund because he had already accepted the car. Can Bruce recover $10 000 from Asbury Motors? Explain your answer.

8. Kerasic Lumber Inc agreed to sell planks to Chios Home Supply Ltd. The parties' contract contained the following paragraph:

> Kerasic Lumber will deliver 1000 redwood planks to Chios Home Supply on June 1. Chios Home Supply will pay $7 per plank for a total contract price of $7000. Each plank shall be: (i) 3 centimetres thick, (ii) between 30 and 35 centimetres wide, and (iii) between 3 metres and 3.1 metres in length.

On June 1, Kerasic Lumber delivered 1020 planks to Chios Home Supply. Each plank fell within the terms of the contract with respect to width and length, but about half of the planks were between 3.2 and 3.3 centimetres thick. Chios Home Supply rejected the goods and refused to pay the purchase price. Its motivation for doing so turned on the fact that it had discovered that it could buy the goods from another supplier at a lower price. Kerasic has sued under the contract. As part of its claim, it is able to prove that the planks were free from defects and were entirely fit for Chios's purposes. Will Kerasic win? Provide two reasons for your answer.

9. Woltz Homes Ltd was building a new house. As the project neared completion, the company's manager, Jack, realized that he needed glue to install the carpet. Jack therefore visited Khartoum Flooring and spoke to a salesperson named Tom. When Jack explained what he needed, Tom confessed that he was new to the job and admitted that he could not provide much help. In response, Jack said that he knew what he was looking for and simply asked Tom to take him to the right section of the store. Tom did so, and Jack picked up a large bucket of glue. Tom offered to open the bucket, but Jack said, "No need. This is the stuff that I'm after." Before Jack paid, Tom asked him to sign a contract, which was standard practice for all sales at Khartoum Flooring. That document contained a paragraph that said, "This sale shall not be affected by any warranties that may be implied by statute or law." When Jack got back to the work site and opened the bucket, he discovered that the glue was crystallized and therefore useless. He returned the bucket to Khartoum Flooring, but the store refused to provide a refund or a substitute. The store's owner insists that: (i) Jack has to take responsibility for the fact that he declined the opportunity to inspect the glue before buying it, and (ii) the exclusion clause contained in the sale contract negates any terms that might be implied by the *Sale of Goods Act*. Is he correct? Explain your answer.

10. Arnold was in training for a bodybuilding competition. Unfortunately, because he worked erratic hours as a plumber, he often found it impossible to exercise in a gym. He therefore devised a number of weight-training

programs that he could perform at his own home. Six weeks before the date of the competition, however, he realized that he could not win unless he increased the size and definition of his back muscles. He therefore contacted Jungle Jim Playsets and ordered "The Mountaineer." The Mountaineer is marketed as a combination play station and swing set for children between the ages of 3 and 12. It appealed to Arnold because it features a long bar that is about six feet off the ground. After installing The Mountaineer in his backyard, Arnold began to use that bar for doing chin-ups. To maximize the difficulty of that exercise, he used a belt to strap heavy weights to himself. Two weeks before the competition, The Mountaineer collapsed on Arnold as he was doing a series of chin-ups. Arnold weighs 255 pounds and, at the time of the accident, had an additional 200 pounds strapped to himself. Although he did not suffer any serious injuries, Arnold has complained to Jungle Jim Playsets. He believes that he is entitled to either a refund or replacement equipment because The Mountaineer did not perform as he had expected. Is he correct? Explain your answer.

11. After upgrading his film studio, Werner agreed to sell his old equipment to Isabelle, a young director who wanted to film a movie beginning on May 1. The equipment consisted of a number of cameras and related items that were valued at $250 000. The parties signed a contract on March 1 that contained this paragraph:

> The seller agrees to deliver the equipment to the buyer's residence on or before April 30. The buyer agrees to pay the purchase price of $250 000 on April 15. The seller will remain the owner of the equipment until full payment has been received or the equipment is delivered to the buyer, whichever is earlier.

On April 15, Isabelle explained to Werner that she would not be able to pay the price for at least two months. However, she also insisted that she required the equipment by April 30 to begin filming her own movie on May 1. Werner indicated that he was reluctant to hand the equipment over until he received full payment. On April 30, Isabelle repeated her demand. Having done some legal research, she also told Werner that time of delivery was a condition of a contract, and that he could be held liable for any losses that she suffered as a result of late delivery. She also told him that the equipment was already hers because the property in it passed as soon as they signed their agreement. Is she correct? Does the equipment already belong to her? Is Werner required to deliver the equipment before receiving the purchase price? If Werner wants to sue for the purchase price, is he entitled to do so? Explain your answers.

12. Solstar Inc manufactures cellular telephones. In July, it agreed to sell 10 000 units to Buy-Lo, a discount department store. The contract required delivery to occur on September 1 at Buy-Lo's store. It also required payment to be made in full on September 15. In late August, shortly before Solstar intended to ship the goods, its manager, Emily, heard a rumour that Buy-Lo had become insolvent and was no longer able to pay its debts. She therefore told the foreman in Solstar's warehouse to not ship the goods as planned. Due to a clerical error, however, the goods were sent to an independent trucking company for delivery to Buy-Lo. When Emily learned of that, she instructed her assistant, Jeremy, to contact the trucking company and demand that the shipment be returned to Solstar. Was she entitled to do so? What should Solstar do if Emily's request does not reach the trucking company until after the goods are delivered to Buy-Lo? What additional facts do you need to know to answer those questions? Explain your answers.

9 Special Contracts:
Negotiable Instruments

CHAPTER OVERVIEW

OBJECTIVES

After completing this chapter, you should be able to:

1. Explain why it is often more dangerous to pay with cash than with a negotiable instrument.

2. Summarize five requirements that a document must satisfy before it will fall within the *Bills of Exchange Act*.

3. Explain how a cheque works by describing the events that occur between: (i) the drawer and the payee, (ii) the drawer and the drawee, and (iii) the drawee and the payee.

4. Distinguish between overdrawn cheques and countermanded cheques.

5. Describe the process of certification, and explain how it affects the rights of the parties to a cheque.

6. Distinguish between a bill of exchange and a cheque.

7. Explain how a promissory note operates.

8. Describe the requirements for the negotiation of: (i) a bearer instrument, and (ii) an order instrument.

9. Summarize seven forms of endorsement and explain how each form affects the issue of liability.

10. Distinguish between: (i) immediate parties, (ii) holders, and (iii) holders in due course; and between (i) personal defences, (ii) defect in title defences, and (iii) real defences.

In Chapter 8, we saw that contracts dealing with the sale of goods are governed by special rules that are intended to make the business world operate efficiently. The same is true for contracts that take the form of *negotiable instruments*. Even if you are not familiar with that term, you certainly are familiar with the underlying concept. In fact, when you pay for something with a cheque, you are dealing with a negotiable instrument.

There are many different ways of making payments. Sometimes it is easiest to use cash.[1] The simplest way of buying a cup of coffee is to hand over, say, $1.25 in coins. Cash, however, can be inconvenient and dangerous. It is inconvenient because it is bulky. The price of a cup of coffee easily fits into your pocket, but the price of a car does not. More significantly, cash is dangerous because it is usually impossible to recover if it is lost or stolen. The essential feature of cash is that it is *currency*. A $20 bill is valuable in itself—it does not simply represent a right to acquire something else that is valuable. Furthermore, a person can become the owner of cash by honestly paying for it. Suppose that I steal $10 000 from your wallet. My dishonesty prevents me from becoming the owner of that money. However, if I use that cash to buy a stereo from a storekeeper who was unaware of the theft, you no longer own the money; the storekeeper does.[2] Consequently, you cannot retrieve it from her. You can sue me, but like many thieves, I may have disappeared or I may be so poor that I am not worth suing. As a matter of risk management, the lesson of that story is clear. Never carry more cash than you are prepared to do without.

There are other ways of making payments that are more convenient and less dangerous than cash. For instance, credit cards and debits cards can be used. In this chapter, we will discuss negotiable instruments. **A negotiable instrument** consists of a contract that contains an obligation to pay money. Suppose that you buy a car from a dealership. A contract is created—you are required to pay the price, and the dealer is required to transfer the car to you. But *how* will you pay the price? It would be foolish for you to carry $20 000 in cash from your bank to the car lot.[3] At the same time, however, the dealer wants something more than your simple promise under the sale agreement. You therefore write out a cheque for $20 000. That cheque is a *new* contract. You have promised that $20 000 will be paid to whoever presents that piece of paper to your bank. Consequently, if your bank refuses to honour the cheque, the dealer can sue you either on the sale contract *or* on the cheque itself.[4] The second option is usually preferable. It is easier to prove the existence of a negotiable instrument than the existence of a sales contract.

cash is often inconvenient and dangerous

a negotiable instrument consists of a contract that contains an obligation to pay money

---

[1] In fact, as we saw in Chapter 6, unless the parties have otherwise agreed, a creditor is entitled to receive payment in *legal tender*, that is, cash.

[2] The law allows the storekeeper to become the owner of the $10 000 because it wants cash to flow freely. If the storekeeper was required to determine if I actually owned the $10 000 that I gave her, the business world would grind to halt. Every cash purchase would involve a long, expensive, and perhaps impossible process of proving ownership of the coins and bills that the buyer offered. Different rules apply to things other than money. As we saw in Chapter 8, the general rule is *nemo dat quod non habet*, "no one can give what they do not have." Consequently, if I stole your car and traded it to my neighbour for her boat, you would probably be entitled to recover the value of the car from her, even if she had acted honestly.

[3] It might be equally foolish for the dealership to accept cash. If that money was lost or stolen before it could be deposited in a bank, the dealership would suffer the loss. The dealership would be in a safer position if you paid by cheque. If that cheque was lost or stolen, the dealer could ask you to provide another one: *Bills of Exchange Act*, RSC 1985, c B-4, s 155 (Can). In exchange, it would have to indemnify you for any loss that might occur because of the existence of two cheques.

[4] Your obligation to pay $20 000 under the sales contract was *conditionally discharged* when you gave the cheque to the dealership. When your bank refused to honour that cheque, however, your obligation under the sales contract was revived.

Understandably, most people do not realize that a cheque is a type of contract.[5] Many of the rules that normally govern contracts do not apply in the same way to negotiable instruments. We note three important differences.

- Like all contracts, a cheque is enforceable only if it is supported by *consideration*. Something of value must be given in exchange for it. However, the requirement of consideration is more easily satisfied in the case of a cheque. As Chapter 3 explained, consideration normally cannot consist of a promise to perform an obligation that is already owed to the same party. However, that rule does not apply to a cheque.[6] In our previous example, the dealership's promise to transfer a car to you acted as consideration twice: first for the sale contract and then for your cheque.

- Normally, a contract can be enforced only by someone with *privity*. Chapter 3 explained that a stranger, someone who did not participate in the creation of the agreement, cannot sue on it. Nevertheless, anyone who holds a cheque can sue on it. Suppose that the dealership in our earlier example coincidentally owed $20 000 to the *Daily Bugle* for a newspaper advertisement. Instead of cashing your cheque and using that money to pay its bill, the dealer might simply sell your cheque to the newspaper. The *Daily Bugle* could then sue you on the cheque, even though it was not originally a party to that contract.

- Contractual obligations can generally be *assigned* to a stranger. As we saw in Chapter 3, however, assignment is a cumbersome process.[7] Furthermore, a person who receives a contractual right through an assignment takes it *subject to the equities*. The assignee cannot be in a better position than the assignor. Assume that the dealership assigned its rights under the *sales contract* to the *Daily Bugle*. If the newspaper sued you for the price, you could use any defence that you could have used against the dealership. Suppose that the dealer breached the contract by selling you a car that required $5000 in repairs. If the purchase price was $20 000, you would only have to pay $15 000 to the newspaper. The situation might be different, however, if the dealership sold your *cheque* to the *Daily Bugle*. The most remarkable thing about a negotiable instrument is that, depending on the circumstances, it can improve as it is passed from one person to the next. Consequently, the newspaper might be able to recover $20 000 from you even though your car was defective. You would have to sue the dealership for breach of contract if you wanted to be paid $5000 for the repairs.

Thus, a negotiable instrument represents a compromise between a simple contract and money. A negotiable instrument is more valuable than a simple contract because, like money, it is *negotiable*. It can be easily transferred from one party to another in a way that may remove any defects. The *Daily Bugle* acquired clear title to the cheque that you had given to the car dealership, just as the storekeeper became the owner of the cash that I had stolen from you in our earlier example. At the same time, however, a negotiable instrument is not actually money. It is a contract that is intended to eventually result in the

---

5. Although this section refers to cheques, the same observations generally apply to other types of negotiable instruments as well.

6. *Bills of Exchange Act* s 52. The Act also presumes that consideration was given by every person whose signature appears on a negotiable instrument: s 57(1).

7. For instance, an assignee normally is required (as a matter of risk management, if not as a matter of law) to give notice of an assignment to a debtor. That requirement does not apply to a negotiable instrument.

payment of money. Consequently, it carries the major risk that is associated with every contract: non-performance. While it is often much better to sue on a negotiable instrument than on a simple contract, enforcement is ultimately necessary in either event. And if a cheque is created by a person who simply does not have any assets, it may be a worthless piece of paper.[8] Coins and bills, in contrast, are never worthless. They have value in themselves.

THE *BILLS OF EXCHANGE ACT*

The subjects of this chapter and the previous one have many similarities. Negotiable instruments and sales of goods both involve contracts that are critically important in the business world. Furthermore, because of the need for commercial certainty, both have been *codified*. As you will recall, when the British Parliament introduced the *Sale of Goods Act* in 1893, it adopted the rules that judges had developed over many years. The legislature's aim was to ensure that the economy ran smoothly. The same process occurred for negotiable instruments. In 1882, the British Parliament enacted the *Bills of Exchange Act*, which formally adopted rules that judges had developed over several centuries. The legislature's intention was to increase economic efficiency by providing business people with a comprehensive set of rules regarding non-monetary payments. The Canadian Parliament once again followed the British model and introduced its own *Bills of Exchange Act* in 1890.[9] With a few exceptions, that statute has hardly changed in more than a century.

the *Bills of Exchange Act* is a codification of judge-made rules

Although both statutes were motivated by similar concerns, they are quite different in some ways. The most important difference is that the *Bills of Exchange Act* is much less flexible than the *Sale of Goods Act*. The *Sale of Goods Act* is a relatively simple statute that provides default rules. The parties are generally free to pick and choose among those rules and, even if they accept some and reject others, their contract can still fall within the Act. The *Bills of Exchange Act* is a much longer and more complicated statute. Furthermore, as we will see in the next section, it contains a large number of rules that a contract *must* satisfy. If those requirements are not met, the Act does not apply. That difference arises because a sale of goods normally involves only two parties, whereas negotiable instruments are designed to be freely transferred among many people. Consequently, there is an even greater need for certainty with negotiable instruments. If I did not participate in the creation of a cheque, for instance, I may not be willing to buy it unless I can be assured, by simply looking at that piece of paper, that it is valuable.

the *Bills of Exchange Act* is inflexible because negotiable instruments are designed to be freely transferred among many people

TYPES OF NEGOTIABLE INSTRUMENTS

There are many varieties of negotiable instruments. Share certificates, for instance, are sometimes placed into that category. The *Bills of Exchange Act*, however, applies only to three types of negotiable instruments: *cheques*, *bills of exchange*, and *promissory notes*. We will look at each of those separately. But

---

[8.] Interestingly, as we shall see, a cheque may be valuable even if the person who wrote it is penniless. It may be possible to collect money from anyone who *endorsed* the cheque.

[9.] *Bills of Exchange Act*, 45 & 46 Vict, c 61. Sales of goods are a provincial matter, but negotiable instruments are a federal matter. Consequently, while each province and territory has its own *Sale of Goods Act*, there is only one *Bills of Exchange Act*, which applies across the country.

first, we can summarize the five requirements that must always be met before the Act will apply.[10] Note how each requirement serves the goal of certainty that we just discussed. A negotiable instrument must tell a complete story. A business person cannot be expected to look behind it.

- First, although most contracts can be created orally, a negotiable instrument must be *signed* and *written*. The reason is obvious. A promise cannot be clearly passed from one person to the next unless it is in writing.

- Second, the *parties* must be clearly identified. It must be possible to immediately determine who is required to make the payment. That information is important when the time comes to "cash" the instrument. However, it is also useful in deciding whether to buy a document in the first place. A cheque that is created by a con artist who holds an account at a bank that is in the process of collapsing is probably not worth the paper it is written on.

- Third, the contract must involve an obligation to pay a *certain sum of money*. The obligation must deal entirely with the payment of money, not with such things as the delivery of goods or the performance of services. It also must be possible to calculate the amount of money by simply looking at the document itself. Consequently, while a negotiable instrument may involve the payment of interest, it cannot, for instance, require the payment of "a reasonable price" or "any money that may be won in a lottery."

- Fourth, the *time of payment* must be clearly stated. A person buying a negotiable instrument must be able to determine precisely when that piece of paper can be turned into cash.

- Fifth, the contract must contain an *unconditional obligation*. For instance, if a person paid the price of a car with a cheque, that document could not require payment to be made "if the buyer is satisfied with the vehicle." As always, it must be possible for a person who buys a negotiable instrument to immediately know exactly what it is receiving.

Cheques

The most common form of negotiable instrument is a *cheque*. A **cheque** is created when a person orders a bank to pay a specific amount of money to someone.[11] Suppose that Hank Quinlan, an accountant, bought an oak desk from Anna Schmidt for $5000. Hank did not have any money in his pocket but he did have a chequing account at the Bank of Edmonton. He gave Anna the cheque in Figure 9.1, which shows that: (i) Hank is the *drawer*, (ii) the Bank of Edmonton is the *drawee*, and (iii) Anna is the *payee*. The **drawer** is the person who "draws," or creates, the cheque. The **drawee** is the bank that is ordered to pay the money. And the **payee** is the person who is entitled to receive the money from the bank.

To appreciate the effect of that cheque, you must understand the relationships that exist between the parties.

- *Hank and Anna*: There are two contracts between Hank and Anna. The first is the sale of goods agreement; the second is the cheque itself. By

---

a negotiable instrument must be signed and written

the parties must be clearly identified

the contract must involve an obligation to pay a certain sum of money

the time of payment must be clear from the document itself

the contract must contain an unconditional obligation

a cheque is created when a person orders a bank to pay a specific amount of money to someone

the drawer is the person who "draws," or creates, the cheque

the drawee is the bank that is ordered to pay the money

the payee is the person who is entitled to receive the money from the bank

---

[10.] A document that does not meet those requirements may still be a valid contract, but it does not fall under the *Bills of Exchange Act*.

[11.] The term "bank" includes some credit unions and trust companies: *Bills of Exchange Act* s 164. If an instrument is not drawn on a bank, it cannot be a cheque, but it may be a bill of exchange. By

FIGURE 9.1   Cheque

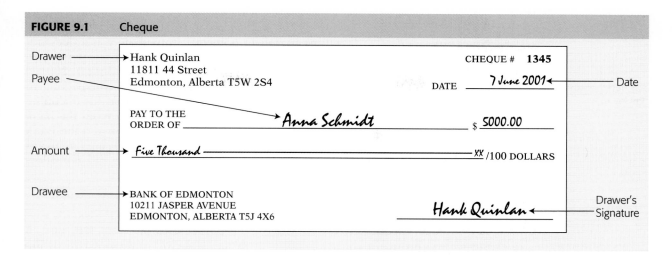

writing that cheque, Hank tried to fulfill his obligation under the sales contract by ordering the Bank of Edmonton to pay $5000 to Anna.

- *Hank and the Bank of Edmonton*: Hank has a contractual relationship with the Bank of Edmonton. When he opened his chequing account at the bank, he exchanged a large number of promises. For example, he agreed to allow the bank to *debit* his account—withdraw money from it—whenever he wrote a cheque.[12] In exchange, the bank promised to *honour*, or pay, cheques that Hank wrote, as long as they appeared in the correct form and he had enough money in his account. Hank ordered the bank to fulfill that promise when he wrote the cheque to Anna. Assuming that everything went well, the bank honoured that cheque, paid $5000 to Anna, and deducted that same amount from Hank's account. If the bank improperly refused to pay $5000 to Anna when she presented the cheque to it, it could be held liable to Hank for breach of contract.[13]

- *Anna and the Bank of Edmonton*: Anna does *not* have a relationship with the Bank of Edmonton. She is a stranger to the agreement that exists between Hank and the bank. Consequently, she could not sue the bank if it refused to pay $5000 to her. If she wanted that money, she would have to sue Hank, either on the cheque or on the sales contract.

Most cheques operate smoothly. However, there are five possible complications:

- postdated cheques
- staledated cheques
- overdrawn cheques
- countermanded cheques
- certification

[12.] That statement is not entirely accurate. When money is deposited into an account, the bank almost always becomes the owner of the bills and coins that it received. In exchange, it gives its contractual promise to repay a similar amount when the depositor asks for it. Consequently, in our example, the Bank of Edmonton would not actually withdraw any *money* from Hank's account after cashing his cheque. Rather, it would simply reduce the amount that it owed to him.

[13.] For the sake of simplicity, we assume that Anna personally took Hank's cheque to the Bank of Edmonton for payment. She could have *endorsed* that cheque to her own bank and allowed it to collect the money on her behalf. We will discuss *endorsements* later.

Postdated Cheques

Sometimes, a drawer is willing to deliver a cheque immediately, but does not want it to be cashed until later. Assume that while Hank and Anna entered into their sales contract on June 1, 2001, he *postdated* the cheque to June 7, 2001.[14] A **postdated cheque** is dated in the future. Perhaps Hank was expecting to receive payment from a client on June 3 that would ensure that his chequing account held at least $5000.[15] Anna could not receive payment from the bank until June 7. According to the contract that exists between Hank and the Bank of Edmonton, the bank is allowed to debit his account only if it acts in accordance with his instructions. And in this case, his instructions did not allow Anna to be paid before June 7.

Staledated Cheques

A postdated cheque causes problems if the payee seeks payment too soon. A *staledated* cheque, in contrast, causes problems if the payee seeks payment too late. A cheque is **staledated** when the payee does not seek payment within a reasonable time. Suppose that Anna did not present the cheque to the Bank of Edmonton until June 7, 2002, a whole year later. The bank would probably refuse payment. Banks normally will not honour a cheque that is presented more than six months after the date that appears on it. In that case, Anna would be forced to sue Hank for the $5000, either on the cheque or on the sales contract.[16]

Overdrawn Cheques

A cheque is **overdrawn** when the drawer's account does not hold enough money to satisfy it completely. Some people use the term "NSF," or "not sufficient funds." That would occur in our example if Hank's chequing account did not contain at least $5000 when Anna presented his cheque for payment. At that point, the Bank of Edmonton would have an option. It would almost certainly refuse to honour the cheque, in which case Anna would sue Hank for non-payment.[17] However, the bank could treat Hank's overdrawn cheque as his request for a loan, pay $5000 to Anna, and then seek repayment from Hank. Interestingly, that would be true even if the bank failed to realize that Hank's account was overdrawn and paid Anna by mistake.

Countermanded Cheques

As a general rule, a bank can deal with a customer's money only if it has that person's authorization. That rule is important whenever there is a *countermand*. A **countermand** occurs when a customer orders a bank to refuse payment on a cheque.[18] This is also known as a *stop payment order*. Returning to our example, assume that Hank noticed that the desk was badly damaged after he took it home. If Anna had not yet cashed his cheque, he might contact the Bank of

---

[14.] *Bills of Exchange Act* s 26(d).

[15.] Postdated cheques are often used if a contract requires instalment payments. For example, if you lease a car for six months, you may be asked for a series of postdated cheques: one for January 1, one for February 1, and so on.

[16.] Although a bank may not honour a cheque that is presented more than six *months* after its date, the payee usually has six *years* to sue the drawer. Statutes of limitation say that contracts, including cheques, become unenforceable only after that time: Chapter 6.

[17.] If Hank knew, when he wrote the cheque, that his account did not contain sufficient funds, he could be charged with the crime of false pretences: *Criminal Code*, RSC 1985, c C-46, s 362(4) (Can).

[18.] *Bills of Exchange Act* s 167.

Edmonton and tell it to stop payment. After all, if he intends to return the desk to Anna, he does not want her to have his money. By countermanding the cheque, Hank would remove the bank's authority to deal with his account. And since the bank would not be willing to give its own money to Anna, it would not pay her $5000 when she presented the cheque.

The ability to countermand a cheque can be very useful. In practice, however, it is limited by two factors.

- First, a bank will not normally accept a countermand unless the drawer gives that order in person and unless the cheque in question is fully described (including the date, the payee, and the amount). Banks require that level of detail because they do not want to stop payment on a cheque incorrectly.

- Second, many bank contracts include a term that allows a bank to debit a customer's account if a countermanded cheque is honoured by mistake. Otherwise, the bank may have to sue the payee if it wants to recover a payment that it made by mistake.[19]

Also note that a cheque is automatically countermanded if the bank is notified that the drawer has died before the payee receives payment.[20]

Certified Cheques

Although a cheque is a special kind of contract, it is still a *promise* to pay. And as always, a promise may or may not be kept. Consequently, there is no guarantee that a cheque will actually be cashed. The cheque may be countermanded by the drawer or dishonoured by the drawee. The best way to avoid those problems is through *certification*.[21] **Certification** occurs when a drawee bank promises to honour a cheque.[22] It normally does so by stamping the word "certified" and the date on the front of the cheque. It then deducts the appropriate amount from the drawer's account, places those funds in a "suspense account," and uses them to honour the cheque when it is presented for payment.

certification occurs when a drawee bank promises to honour a cheque

A cheque can be certified by the payee (or holder). Assume that after receiving the cheque from Hank, Anna presented it to the Bank of Edmonton for certification. Perhaps she was travelling to Calgary and felt safer carrying a certified cheque rather than $5000 cash. More commonly, however, a cheque is certified by the drawer. For example, if she was concerned about Hank's ability to pay, Anna might have required him to certify his cheque before giving it to her as payment for the desk.

a cheque can be certified by either the payee or the drawer

Whether a cheque is certified by the payee or by the drawer, the consequences are basically the same. Although the law is not entirely clear, the courts generally treat certification as "something equivalent to money."[23] We can see the effects of that rule by continuing on with our example.

- A bank normally owes an obligation only to its own customer. However, once the Bank of Edmonton certified Hank's cheque, it also owed an

the bank owes an obligation to the payee under a certified cheque

---

19. In that case, the bank would sue for restitution under the action in unjust enrichment: *Barclays Bank v WJ Simms, Son & Cooke (Southern) Ltd* [1980] QB 677. We discussed that cause of action in Chapter 7. The bank could not sue in contract because it does not have a contract with the payee.

20. *Bills of Exchange Act* s 167(b).

21. The *Bills of Exchange Act* does not refer to certification. That procedure is based on American banking law rather than the English statute that the Canadian Parliament copied.

22. Banks charge a fee for certification.

23. *Centrac Inc v CIBC* (1994) 120 DLR (4th) 765 at 768 (Ont CA).

obligation to Anna. In effect, it promised her that it would honour the cheque. If it later broke that promise, it could be sued by Anna.

■ By certifying the cheque, the Bank of Edmonton assured Anna that it would not later dishonour that instrument on the ground that Hank's account was *overdrawn*. A bank normally will not certify a cheque until after it has transferred funds from the drawer's account into a suspense account. But Anna could demand payment even if the bank certified the cheque in the mistaken belief that Hank's account held enough funds. A bank cannot hide behind its own error; it must fulfill its promise.

■ Certification also assured Anna that Hank's cheque could not be *countermanded*. A drawer is normally entitled to issue a stop payment order any time before a cheque is cashed. However, since certification is treated as "something equivalent" to payment, Hank lost the right to countermand the cheque once the Bank of Edmonton certified it.[24] The bank would have to pay Anna even if Hank objected.[25]

> a certified cheque cannot be dishonoured on the ground that the drawer's account is over-drawn

> a certified cheque generally cannot be countermanded

Bills of Exchange

A **bill of exchange** is created when one person orders another person to pay a specific amount of money to a third person. Suppose that Marisa Figo, who operates a manufacturing plant in Winnipeg, bought a shipment of steel from Olaf Bregstein, an industrialist in Sweden. Although that contract was made on March 1, 2001, the parties agreed that the purchase price of $100 000 was not due until September 1, 2001. Marisa arranged for payment to be made through the Red River Trust Company, with which she held a line of credit.[26] She issued the bill of exchange shown in Figure 9.2.

That bill of exchange looks very similar to a cheque. In fact, a cheque is simply a special type of bill of exchange. The major difference between them is that a cheque *must* be drawn on a bank, while a bill of exchange *may* be drawn on a bank *or* on anyone else. We can quickly describe the parties in this case. Marisa was the *drawer* because she ordered money to be paid from one person to another. The Red River Trust Company was the *drawee* because it was ordered by one person to pay money to another. And Olaf was the *payee* because he was intended to receive the money eventually.

We can understand how a bill of exchange works by examining Figure 9.2.

> a bill of exchange is created when one person orders another person to pay a specific amount of money to a third person

> a cheque is a special type of bill of exchange that must be drawn on a bank

> a bill of exchange *may* be drawn on a bank *or* on anyone else

■ Marisa used a basic pre-formatted bill of exchange and filled in the relevant blanks. In effect, she ordered the Red River Trust Company to pay $100 000 to Olaf. Marisa then gave the bill to Olaf. Olaf was not entitled to receive payment immediately, since the parties' contract said that payment for the steel was not due until September 1. Marisa therefore made sure that Olaf could not receive the money from the Red River Trust Company any earlier. Although she created the bill on March 1, she expressly stated that payment was due "*Six Months* AFTER DATE."

---

24. *Maubach v Bank of Nova Scotia* (1987) 62 OR (2d) 220 (CA). Exceptionally, a bank may allow a certified cheque to be countermanded if the drawer is willing to provide *indemnification* by promising to provide compensation to the bank if it is sued by the payee.

25. An exception may occur when a cheque is certified by the drawer. If the drawer returns the cheque to the bank, the bank will cancel it and return the funds from the suspense account to the chequing account. However, once the drawer actually delivers the cheque to the payee, countermand is no longer possible.

26. A line of credit is an amount of money that an institution is willing to lend to a person from time to time.

FIGURE 9.2   Bill of Exchange

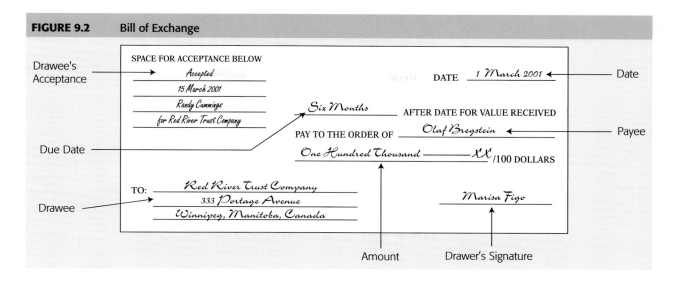

- Olaf could have simply kept the bill until September 1. However, he wanted some assurance that he would actually receive $100 000 on that date. He therefore presented the bill to the Red River Trust Company on March 15.

- The Red River Trust Company had two options when it received the bill from Olaf. It could have indicated that it was not prepared to pay $100 000 on September 1. It would have done so, for instance, if Marisa's line of credit was limited to $50 000. In that case, the trust company would have *dishonoured* the bill, and Olaf would have been entitled to sue Marisa for immediate payment.[27] In this case, however, it appears that Marisa's line of credit was large enough to satisfy the bill. The Red River Trust Company therefore indicated that it was willing to *honour* the bill when it came due. Randy Cummings, an authorized signing agent for the trust company, *accepted* the bill.[28] **Acceptance** occurs when the drawee promises to pay a bill. Randy did so by writing "*Accepted*," the date of acceptance, and his signature on the bill, and then returning the document to Olaf.[29] At that point, the trust company became the *acceptor* rather than simply the drawee.

- Acceptance of a bill is very similar to certification of a cheque. Once the drawee has accepted a bill, it can be sued by the payee for failing to make payment on the due date. Furthermore, once a bill is accepted, the drawer loses control of it. Consequently, after March 15, the Red River Trust Company was required to pay $100 000 to Olaf on September 1, *and* Marisa lost the ability to cancel the bill.

- Assuming that everything went as planned, Olaf presented the bill to the Red River Trust Company on September 1 and received $100 000. The trust company then required Marisa to repay that amount (undoubtedly with interest).

acceptance occurs when the drawee promises to pay a bill

[27.] *Bills of Exchange Act* s 81. Note that Olaf could sue Marisa immediately, even though the bill was not due until September 1.

[28.] Marisa also could have asked the Red River Trust Company to accept the bill before she delivered it to Olaf.

[29.] *Bills of Exchange Act* s 38. Note two things about Randy's acceptance. First, he signed "*for the Red River Trust Company.*" If he had not used those words, he might have been personally liable as the acceptor. Second, strictly speaking, acceptance only requires the acceptor's signature: s 35(2). However, additional information is usually added to avoid difficulties.

Note four more things about bills of exchange.

a bill of exchange is a contract

- A bill of exchange, like a cheque, is a contract. Therefore, it is not enforceable unless it is supported by consideration. In this case, Olaf gave consideration for Marisa's bill when he promised to deliver steel to her. That fact is indicated by the phrase "FOR VALUE RECEIVED" that appears on the bill.

a bill of exchange may be a demand draft, a sight draft, or a time draft

- A cheque *must* be payable "on demand."[30] In other words, the drawer must order the drawee to make payment as soon as the payee presents the cheque.[31] A bill of exchange *may* be payable on demand, in which case it is called a *demand draft*. However, it can also be a *sight draft*. This is like a demand draft, except that the payee is not entitled to receive any money until three days after the bill has been presented to the drawee. And finally, as in our example, a bill of exchange can be a *time draft*, which is payable only on a future date. Although Marisa's bill was dated March 1, Olaf could not obtain payment until "*Six Months* AFTER DATE." The date of payment therefore would be September 1.

a bill of exchange may be used to transfer funds or create credit or both

- A bill of exchange is usually used for one of two purposes. Both are seen in our example. First, a bill of exchange can be used, like a cheque, to safely transfer funds. Second, because a bill does not have to be payable on demand, it can be used to easily extend credit. In this case, Olaf gave Marisa credit for half of a year. He was not entitled to receive $100 000 until September 1, even though her debt under the sales contract arose on March 1.

a bill of exchange is usually only used in special circumstances

- Bills of exchange were traditionally much more common than cheques. Today, however, the situation is reversed. Bills are usually used only in special circumstances, such as international trade between large business enterprises. In our example, Olaf agreed to deliver $100 000 worth of steel from Sweden to Winnipeg.

Promissory Notes

A cheque or a bill of exchange normally involves an *order* between *three* parties: the drawer instructs the drawee to transfer money to the payee. A *promissory note* is usually a *promise* between *two* parties. A **promissory note** is created when one person gives another person a written promise to pay a specific amount of money.[32] The person who is intended to receive the money is once again called the *payee*. The person who creates the instrument is called the *maker*.

a **promissory note** is created when one person gives another person a written promise to pay a specific amount of money

the person who is intended to receive the money is called the payee

the person who creates the instrument is called the maker

Suppose that on May 1, 2001, Rita Perez agreed to deliver a shipment of sleds to John Chang for $50 000. Because John did not have enough cash to cover the purchase price immediately, Rita agreed to accept instalment payments. The parties assumed that John would be able to pay for the sleds as he resold them in his sporting goods store during the next winter. John therefore gave Rita the promissory note shown in Figure 9.3.[33]

[30.] *Bills of Exchange Act* s 165.

[31.] A post-dated cheque is payable on demand, but the payee cannot demand payment before the date that appears on the cheque.

[32.] *Bills of Exchange Act* s 176(1).

[33.] Although payment was postponed under the promissory note, Rita could have received payment immediately if she had sold the note to a third party. That third party, as the holder of the note, would have been entitled to receive $50 000, plus 10 percent interest, from John starting on November 1.

FIGURE 9.3   Promissory Note

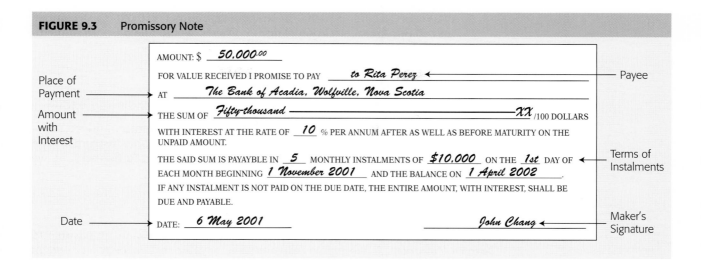

Examining Figure 9.3 will help us understand promissory notes.

■ Although there is no drawee under a promissory note, the document indicated that Rita was entitled to collect the money at the Bank of Acadia in Wolfville, Nova Scotia. John presumably had an account there. If the note did not say anything about the place of payment, Rita could have collected the money at John's office.

■ A promissory note is almost always used as a credit instrument. In this case, John was allowed to postpone payment for the sleds. As usually occurs with credit transactions, the promissory note required payment *with interest*. John promised to pay $50 000 *plus* 10 percent interest.

promissory notes often require the payment of interest

■ Like a cheque or a bill of exchange, a promissory note can be payable as a lump sum. However, notes are often payable in *instalments*. That was true in our case. John promised to pay $10 000 per month beginning in November of 2001, and to pay the remaining amount on April 1, 2002. As a matter of risk management, John should have made sure that a short receipt was written on the note each time that an instalment was paid. For instance:

promissory notes are often payable in instalments

$10 000 received in part payment
Rita Perez (1 November 2001)

Without that sort of notation, John might have been forced to make the same payment twice. Assume that Rita received $10 000 on November 1, and then sold the note to an innocent third party. If the payment to Rita was not indicated on the note itself, the third party could probably require John to pay the November instalment again. To encourage commercial transactions, the law usually allows a third party to take a negotiable instrument at face value.

■ An *acceleration clause* is often found in promissory notes. An **acceleration clause** states that the entire amount of a promise becomes due immediately if a single instalment is not paid on time. There is one in the last line of the pre-formatted note that John used. The explanation for an acceleration clause is quite simple. Suppose that John failed to pay the November instalment in a way that made it clear to Rita that the other instalments would fail as well. Without an acceleration clause, she

an acceleration clause states that the entire amount of the promise becomes due immediately if a single instalment is not paid on time

could sue for only $10 000 in November, another $10 000 in December, and so on. An acceleration clause, however, would allow her to immediately claim the entire $50 000 plus interest.

NEGOTIATION

We have focused on situations in which the payee receives money under a negotiable instrument. However, we have also seen that a negotiable instrument can be *negotiated*, that is, transferred from one party to another. In this section, we examine the process of negotiation.

Methods of Negotiation

The process of negotiation depends on whether an instrument is payable to *bearer* or to *order*. A negotiable instrument is payable to **bearer** if any person who holds it is entitled to receive payment. A bearer instrument can arise in several ways. We can use the promissory note in Figure 9.3 for illustration.

- John could have made the note payable "*to Rita Perez or bearer*" or simply "*to bearer*."
- John could have left the name of the payee blank.[34]
- John could have made the note payable to a fictitious person, such as "*to Sherlock Holmes*," or to a non-person, such as "*to cash*."[35]
- Although the note in Figure 9.3 is an order note, it would have become a bearer note if Rita had delivered it to someone else after *endorsing* it with her signature and nothing more: "*Rita Perez*."[36] The note would then remain a bearer instrument unless some later party turned it back into an order instrument by using a *special endorsement*. (We will examine endorsements shortly.)

The important point is that a bearer instrument can be negotiated by the simple delivery, or physical transfer, of the document. An endorsement is unnecessary.

A negotiable instrument is payable to **order** if the party that is entitled to receive payment is named. For example, the note in Figure 9.3 provides an example because the note is payable "*to Rita Perez*."[37] An order instrument cannot be negotiated unless it is *endorsed and delivered* to a new party. Suppose that Rita wanted to negotiate the note to her sister, Carmen. She could not do so by simply giving that piece of paper to her.[38] She would also have to endorse it by at least signing her name on the back: "*Rita Perez*."

Margin notes:

a negotiable instrument is payable to bearer if any person who holds it is entitled to receive payment

a bearer instrument can be negotiated by delivery alone

a negotiable instrument is payable to order if the party entitled to receive payment is named

an order instrument can be negotiated by endorsement and delivery

---

[34] In that situation, Rita could have filled in her own name: *Bills of Exchange Act* ss 30, 31.

[35] *Bills of Exchange Act* s 20(5).

[36] *Bills of Exchange Act* s 66(5). It appears that an instrument that starts as a bearer instrument (for instance, if John made the note "*to bearer*") always remains a bearer instrument: s 20(3).

[37] The note also would have been payable to order if John had written "*to the order of Rita Perez*" or "*to Rita Perez or order*." Note that the cheque in Figure 9.1 and the bill of exchange in Figure 9.2 are also order instruments.

[38] An order instrument that is delivered but not endorsed may create an equitable assignment. In that case, however, the person who receives the instrument does not receive any special benefits under the Act: *Aldercrest Developments Ltd v Hamilton Co-Axial (1958) Ltd* (1973) 37 DLR (3d) 254 (SCC).

Liability

In this section, we will consider several types of endorsements. Before doing so, however, we will briefly discuss how negotiation can affect liability. Staying with Figure 9.3, we assume this series of events.

- John Chang made a promissory note payable "*to Rita Perez.*"

- Rita changed that order note into a bearer note by simply signing her name on it before delivering it to her sister, Carmen.

- Carmen sold the note to Vlad Hlinka in exchange for a car. Because the note had become a bearer instrument, Carmen was able to negotiate it to Vlad by simply giving it to him. Vlad changed the instrument back into an order note by delivering it to his business associate, Enya McCall, along with the following endorsement: "*Vlad Hlinka – Pay to Enya McCall.*"

- Enya asked John to make payment under the note.

Those events are represented in Figure 9.4.

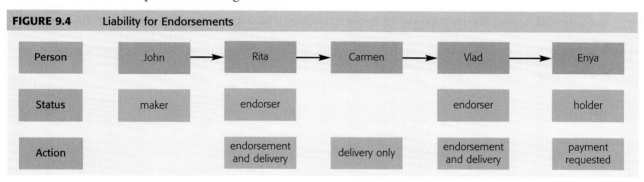

FIGURE 9.4	Liability for Endorsements			
Person	John	Rita	Carmen	Vlad	Enya
Status	maker	endorser		endorser	holder
Action		endorsement and delivery	delivery only	endorsement and delivery	payment requested

The primary liability under a promissory note falls on the maker.[39] In this case, John had the initial obligation to pay Enya. One of the most interesting features of a negotiable instrument, however, is that an endorser may also be held liable. As a general rule, a person who provides an endorsement promises people who later acquire the instrument that it will be paid.[40]

- As a result of that rule, Enya might receive full payment even if John was unable to pay a cent. She could sue everyone who endorsed the note: Rita and Vlad. Rita could be held liable even though she did not have any direct contract with Enya. Her responsibility would arise entirely from the fact that she endorsed the note. However, Enya could *not* sue Carmen.[41] Although Carmen negotiated the note to Vlad, she did so when it was in bearer form. She was therefore able to transfer it to him by delivery alone. And since she did not endorse the note, she did not promise that it would be paid.

- An endorser who is held liable can sometimes sue a person who negotiated the instrument at an earlier time. Assume that Enya collected payment from Vlad. He might be able to shift that loss to either Carmen or Rita.

[39.] The rules discussed in this section generally apply to cheques and bills of exchange as well. Under a cheque, the drawer has the primary liability. Under a bill, the primary liability falls on the drawer at first. However, if a bill is accepted, then the drawee/acceptor has the primary liability: *Bills of Exchange Act* s 186.

[40.] *Bills of Exchange Act* s 132.

[41.] *Bills of Exchange Act* s 136(2).

- Unlike Enya, Vlad could sue Carmen even though she did not endorse the note. There are two possibilities. First, the Act would allow Vlad to sue Carmen if she gave him an instrument that: (i) was not genuine, (ii) she had no right to transfer, or (iii) she knew was worthless.[42] On our facts, it is unlikely that any of those requirements could be met. Second, Vlad might be able to sue Carmen on the basis of their sales contract if, in exchange for his car, she had promised that she would pay the note if asked to do so.

- Vlad could sue Rita because she endorsed the note before he acquired it.

as a general rule, a person who provides an endorsement promises people who later acquire the instrument that it will be paid

- Now, assume that Enya collected payment from Rita rather than Vlad. Rita could *not* in turn sue Vlad. Although he endorsed the note, he did so *after* she did. A person who wants payment on an instrument must look to an *earlier* party. Consequently, since John was unable to pay, Rita would probably suffer the eventual loss in this case.

The ability to demand payment from an endorser is very important. It is, however, subject to an important limitation. Liability generally cannot be imposed on an endorser unless that person received a *notice of dishonour*.[43] A **notice of dishonour** consists of a statement that the person who was primarily liable on the instrument failed to pay. Note these other things about a notice of dishonour.

a notice of dishonour consists of a statement that the person who was primarily liable on the instrument failed to pay

- Notice normally must be given very quickly—usually within one business day.[44]

- Notice does not normally have to be in writing, but it must clearly identify the instrument in question.[45]

- Notice must be given by a holder who wants payment from an endorser. Enya, for example, should have given notice to Vlad and Rita as soon as John refused to pay. Notice must also be given by one endorser who wants payment from another. Vlad, for example, should have given notice to Rita as soon as Enya asked him to pay.

- If notice is not properly given, an endorser is discharged and cannot be held liable on the instrument.

- Notice is not required, however, if: (i) the endorser cannot be reached through a reasonable effort, or (ii) the endorser waived the need for notice, for instance, by writing "notice of dishonour unnecessary" beside a signature.[46]

From a risk management perspective, the lesson is clear. If the person who is primarily liable under an instrument is unable to pay, you must give notice as soon as possible to everyone you might want to sue. If you fail to do so, your rights may be lost.

---

[42] *Bills of Exchange Act* s 173.

[43] *Bills of Exchange Act* s 95. Since the primary liability for an *accepted* bill of exchange falls on the acceptor, the notice requirements apply to the drawer as well as the endorsers.

[44] *Bills of Exchange Act* s 96. A delay may be excused if the circumstances were beyond a person's control: s 104. Furthermore, a notice that is sent through the postal system only has to be mailed by the next day: s 102(2). And finally, notice is deemed to have been given even if it is lost in the postal system: s 103.

[45] *Bills of Exchange Act* s 97. A much more formal notice, called a protest, must be given if an instrument is drawn, payable, or accepted in Quebec or outside of Canada: ss 108-125. As a matter of risk management, one should always give notice in writing, which is easy to prove.

[46] *Bills of Exchange Act* s 105.

Forms of Endorsement

Several types of endorsement are allowed under the *Bills of Exchange Act*. We will consider seven:

- special endorsement
- identifying endorsement
- qualified endorsement
- conditional endorsement
- accommodation endorsement
- general endorsement
- restrictive endorsement

To better understand each of those possibilities, we return to Figure 9.1 and assume that the following parties dealt with the cheque that Hank Quinlan drew on his account at the Bank of Edmonton: (i) Anna Schmidt, (ii) Jed Leland, (iii) Michael O'Hara, (iv) Isabel Minafer, (v) Elsa Bannister, (vi) Harry Lime, and (vii) Susana Vargas. Figure 9.5 shows the endorsement that each person placed on the cheque.

FIGURE 9.5   Endorsements on a Cheque

Anna Schmidt — Pay to Mike O'Hara

Jed Leland—Anna Schmidt hereby identified

Mike O'Hara — pay to Isabel Minafer without recourse

Isabel Minafer — Pay to Harry Lime if he takes me to Vienna

Elsa Bannister — Guarantor for I. Minafer

Harry Lime

Susana Vargas—for deposit only

Special Endorsement

Hank made the cheque payable to Anna. After receiving it, she added a *special endorsement*.[47] She did so by signing her name on the back of the cheque and by indicating that the money should be paid to Mike O'Hara. Once Mike obtained the cheque from Anna, he replaced her as the only person who was entitled to receive payment.

Identifying Endorsement

Before Mike received the cheque from Anna, however, Jed Leland added an *identifying endorsement*. Presumably, Mike was reluctant to buy the cheque from Anna because he did not personally know her. Jed, however, knew both parties and was willing to assure Mike that Anna was indeed the payee.

[47.] *Bills of Exchange Act* s 66(3).

Significantly, Jed could not be held liable as a normal endorser. He could only be held liable if the person who negotiated the cheque to Mike was not really Anna Schmidt.

Qualified Endorsement

After receiving the cheque from Anna, Mike transferred it to Isabel Minafer under a *qualified endorsement*.[48] By stating that his endorsement was "without recourse," Mike indicated that he was not willing to be held liable if the cheque was later dishonoured. Consequently, if Susana Vargas was eventually unable to receive payment from Hank's account at the Bank of Edmonton, she could not sue Mike.

Conditional Endorsement

A cheque must contain an unconditional obligation. Hank, for instance, could not have drafted the cheque payable to "*Anna Schmidt if she takes me to Vienna.*" That order would be conditional on the trip. An endorsement, however, can be conditional.[49] In this case, Isabel has endorsed the cheque "*to Harry Lime if he takes me to Vienna.*" Consequently, if Isabel was later sued on her endorsement, she could in turn sue Harry if he did not take her to Vienna.

Accommodation Endorsement

Before Isabel actually delivered the cheque to Harry, Elsa Bannister added an *accommodation endorsement*.[50] Presumably, Harry was concerned that if he ever tried to sue Isabel on her endorsement, she might not have enough money to pay. Elsa was therefore persuaded to sign as "*Guarantor for I Minafer.*" That endorsement is called an "accommodation" because it accommodated, or helped, Isabel's effort to negotiate the cheque to Harry. It is also called "anomalous" because it is unusual. A person normally uses an endorsement to negotiate an instrument that they own. In this case, however, Elsa was not trying to transfer her own property. Instead, she was assisting in the transfer of Isabel's property. Elsa nevertheless could be held liable as an endorser.

General Endorsement

After Harry received the cheque from Isabel, he added his *general* (or *blank*) *endorsement*.[51] By simply writing his signature and nothing more, Harry transformed the cheque from an order instrument into a bearer instrument.

Restrictive Endorsement

Finally, after Susana received the cheque from Harry, she added her *restrictive endorsement*.[52] By writing "*for deposit only,*" Susana prevented the instrument from being negotiated any further. The cheque could be used only to pay funds into Susana's bank account. As a matter of risk management, that sort of endorsement provides good protection against theft.

---

[48] *Bills of Exchange Act* s 33(a).

[49] *Bills of Exchange Act* s 65. The Act also indicates that later parties can assume that the condition was fulfilled.

[50] *Bills of Exchange Act* ss 54, 130.

[51] *Bills of Exchange Act* s 66.

[52] *Bills of Exchange Act* s 67.

DEFENCES

Contractual rights can generally be assigned from one party to another. For better or worse, however, the assignee simply steps into the assignor's shoes. Most significantly, the assignee acquires the contract *subject to the equities*. If sued by the assignee, the debtor can rely on any defence that it could have used against the assignor.

A negotiable instrument is a type of contract. It is, however, a special type of contract. As a result of the process of negotiation, the rights under an instrument can be easily transferred *and* they can be improved as they are transferred. Consequently, a defence that could have been used against a payee may not be available against a person who received the instrument by way of negotiation. In this section, we will consider several defences and discover when they apply. The issue of defences is quite complicated. To simplify the discussion, we will use the cheque that appears, front and back, in Figure 9.6. As you can see, it appears that: (i) Iman Khan drew a cheque for $9000 on her account at the Island National Bank in favour of Felix Sobers, (ii) Felix Sobers specially endorsed the cheque to Janet Botham, (iii) Janet Botham specially endorsed the cheque to Waqar Akram, and (iv) Waqar Akram now wants payment.

FIGURE 9.6   Defences

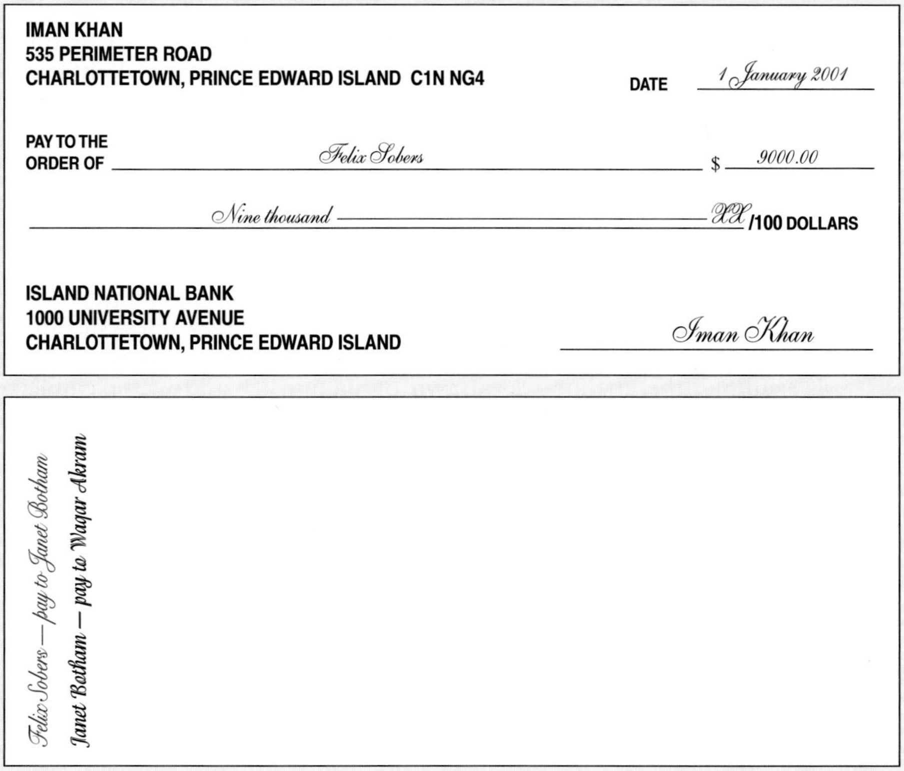

IMAN KHAN
535 PERIMETER ROAD
CHARLOTTETOWN, PRINCE EDWARD ISLAND C1N NG4   DATE   *1 January 2001*

PAY TO THE
ORDER OF _____ *Felix Sobers* _____ $ ___ *9000.00* ___

_____ *Nine thousand* _____ *XX*/100 DOLLARS

ISLAND NATIONAL BANK
1000 UNIVERSITY AVENUE
CHARLOTTETOWN, PRINCE EDWARD ISLAND   *Iman Khan*

Felix Sobers — pay to Janet Botham
Janet Botham — pay to Waqar Akram

Types of Parties

To discuss defences, we need to identify three types of parties: (i) *immediate parties*, (ii) *holders*, and (iii) *holders in due course*.

- **Immediate parties** are parties who dealt directly with each other. In our case, there are three sets of immediate parties: Iman and Felix, Felix and Janet, and Janet and Waqar.

- A **holder** is a person who has possession of a negotiable instrument.[53] In our example, Waqar is the holder. Depending upon the circumstances, he may also be a holder in due course.

- A **holder in due course** is a person who acquired a negotiable instrument under specific conditions.[54] While those conditions are complex, we can summarize them. Note that they all relate to honesty. Only an honest person deserves the special treatment that the Act gives to a holder in due course.

  - The instrument must be *supported by value*, that is, consideration. Interestingly, Waqar could be a holder in due course even if he did not personally give consideration. It would be enough if someone before him gave consideration for the cheque.[55]

  - The holder must have taken an instrument that was *complete and regular on its face*. An instrument is not complete if an important part is left blank. That would be true if, for instance, Waqar received a cheque that did not state an amount.[56] And an instrument is not regular if it looks suspicious. That would be the case, for instance, if the cheque contained obvious erasures or alterations.

  - The holder must have acquired the instrument *without notice of any previous dishonour*. Consequently, Waqar would not be a holder in due course if, for example, he knew or strongly suspected either that the Island National Bank had already refused to honour the cheque or that Iman had countermanded it.

  - The holder must have taken the instrument in *good faith* and *without notice of any defect* in the title of the person who negotiated it. Waqar therefore would not be a holder in due course if, for instance, he knew or strongly suspected that Iman had been forced or tricked into drawing the cheque, or that Janet had forged Felix's endorsement.

  - The holder must have acquired the instrument *before it was overdue*.[57] As we have seen, an instrument may be due at different times.[58] In our example, the cheque was drawn on January 1 and was payable on demand. As a result, Waqar might not be a holder in due course if he received the document from Janet on May 23. There is usually some-

---

[53.] *Bills of Exchange Act* s 2.

[54.] *Bills of Exchange Act* s 55. Unless there is evidence to the contrary, the Act assumes that every holder is a holder in due course: s 57(2).

[55.] *Bills of Exchange Act* s 53. Unless there is evidence to the contrary, the Act presumes that every person who signs an instrument gave value: s 57(1).

[56.] Interestingly, the holder of an instrument generally has the right to fill in any blanks: *Bills of Exchange Act* s 30.

[57.] *Bills of Exchange Act* s 69.

[58.] A bill of exchange or promissory note that is payable on a specific day, rather than on demand, is due on that day.

thing suspicious about a cheque that has not been cashed for almost six months.[59]

Note that every person who acquires an instrument *after* a holder in due course, and who is not involved in any fraud or illegality, is also considered a holder in due course.[60]

There are three types of defences that are available under the Act: (i) *personal defences*, (ii) *defect in title defences*, and (iii) *real defences*. The availability of each type of defence depends on the type of party involved. Concept Summary 9.1 presents a general overview.

Concept Summary 9.1

Parties and Defences

	Personal Defences	Defect in Title Defences	Real Defences
Immediate Party	✓	✓	✓
Holder	✗	✓	✓
Holder in Due Course	✗	✗	✓

Personal Defences

If an action occurs between two immediate parties, the defendant can use any type of defence, including a *personal defence*. As the name suggests, a **personal defence** is one that affects the parties themselves rather than the instrument. Assume that Waqar presented the cheque to the Island National Bank for payment, but left empty-handed because Iman's account did not contain enough money. He could sue Janet on the cheque because she endorsed it. In response, however, she could raise any defence that arose from her dealings with him. We can consider two common examples.

> a **personal defence** is one that affects the parties themselves, rather than the instrument

- Janet could *set-off* any debt that Waqar owed to her. Suppose that she negotiated the cheque to him because he sold her a car for $9000. A few days later, she sold him a boat for $5000, but he failed to pay. If Waqar sued Janet on the cheque, she could admit liability, set-off the price of the boat, and pay only $4000.

> set-off

- Janet could also rely on a *failure of consideration*.[61] For instance, if the car that Waqar sold to her was defective and required $3000 in repairs, she could admit liability, plead breach of contract, and pay only $6000. After all, she expected to receive a car worth $9000 but received one worth only $6000.

> failure of consideration

Defect in Title Defences

Defect in title defences are available against an immediate party *and* against a simple holder. A **defect in title defence** occurs when an instrument is obtained improperly. It is different from a personal defence because it affects the instrument itself.

> a **defect in title defence** occurs when an instrument is obtained improperly

---

[59.] A promissory note that is payable on demand is not overdue simply because a reasonable length of time has passed: *Bills of Exchange Act* s 182. That is because a promissory note, unlike a bill or cheque, is normally used to extend credit.

[60.] *Bills of Exchange Act* s 56.

[61.] If consideration was *never* given in exchange for the cheque, that instrument would be entirely unenforceable.

Suppose that Waqar is a holder, but not a holder in due course, because he received the cheque from Janet when it was overdue.[62] Further suppose that the Island National Bank refused to honour the cheque because Iman's account was overdrawn. Waqar could sue Iman as the drawer of the cheque. If he did so, however, she could avoid liability by proving any of the following defect in title defences.

fraud or duress

- Iman would not have to pay Waqar if she initially drafted the cheque as a result of Felix's *fraud* or *duress*.[63] Perhaps Felix tricked her, or threatened her with a beating unless she created the instrument. In that situation, Felix did not obtain good title to the cheque. And since Waqar was not a holder in due course, he did not obtain good title either.

illegal consideration

- Likewise, Iman would not have to pay Waqar if she issued the cheque to Felix in exchange for *illegal consideration*. That would be the case if, for instance, Felix promised to deliver drugs to her.

drunk or insane

- Felix's title also would have been defective if he knew, or should have known, that Iman was *drunk* or *insane* when she drafted the cheque.[64] Once again, that defect would affect Waqar as well.

absence of delivery

- A defect in title can occur when there is an *absence of delivery*. Suppose that Iman completed the cheque as it appears in Figure 9.6, but never actually gave it to Felix. If he took it from her desk without her permission, he would obtain a defective title, as would Waqar.[65]

no authority

- If Iman gave the cheque to Felix with instructions to fill in $7000 as the amount, he would have obtained a defective title if he instead made the cheque out for $9000. He had *no authority* for what he actually did.

discharged or renounced

- Finally, Waqar would have received a defective title if the cheque that he acquired from Janet had been *discharged* or *renounced*.[66] Suppose, for instance, that after Iman issued the cheque to Felix, he wrote her a note that said, "You don't really owe this money to me. I therefore won't ask for payment." He nevertheless gave the cheque to Janet, who in turn sold it to Waqar. Because of Felix's renunciation, Iman would not have to pay Waqar. To be safe, of course, she should have asked Felix to return the cheque to her as soon as he renounced his rights.[67]

[62.] To simplify the situation, assume that Janet received the cheque as a gift from Felix. Since she would not be a holder in due course in the examples that follow, Waqar could not become a holder in due course by obtaining the cheque from her: *Bills of Exchange Act* s 56.

[63.] *Bills of Exchange Act* s 55(2). Fraud is usually a defect in title defence. However, it may be a real defence if it amounts to *non est factum* (literally, "this is not my deed"). As we saw in Chapter 5, that defence is available in very limited circumstances. It might work in our case, for instance, if Iman, who was illiterate, infirm, or blind, was tricked into signing the cheque because she thought she was being asked for her autograph.

[64.] Insanity normally creates a defect in title defence. However, it can also lead to a real defence if the person was legally declared to be mentally incompetent: *Bills of Exchange Act* s 46(1).

[65.] There was a defect in title because Iman did not deliver a *completed* instrument. However, she would have a real defence if she did not deliver the cheque *and* if that instrument was *incomplete*. Perhaps Felix stole it from her desk, filled in the amount (which she had left blank), and gave it to Janet, who sold it to Waqar. In that case, Waqar could not demand payment from Iman, even if he was a holder in due course.

[66.] *Bills of Exchange Act* ss 139, 141.

[67.] As a matter of risk management, a cheque that has been honoured should have "paid" written on its face. A mere holder cannot sue on a cheque that has been discharged. However, a holder in due course *can* sue on a discharged or cancelled cheque, as long as that fact is not apparent from the instrument itself: *Bills of Exchange Act* s 141. Suppose that Felix was allowed to keep the cheque even though he had been paid. If Waqar later became a holder in due course, he could force Iman to pay again if the cheque had not been stamped "paid."

Real Defences

A holder in due course cannot be defeated by personal defences or defect in title defences. That person has to worry only about *real defences*. A **real defence** occurs when an instrument is fundamentally flawed. Such a defence is *real* in the sense that it affects the *res*—the thing—itself. It does not simply concern a personal matter between the parties or a defect in one party's title to an instrument.

a **real defence** occurs when an instrument is fundamentally flawed

Assume that Waqar is a holder in due course and that the Island National Bank has refused to honour the cheque. If Waqar sought payment from someone else, he might be met by a real defence. We have already seen that *fraud* or *duress*, *drunkenness* or *insanity*, *absence of delivery*, and *discharge or renunciation* can lead to either a defect in title defence or a real defence, depending on the circumstances. We also need to consider three more possibilities.

- Iman would not have to pay if she created the cheque when she was a *minor*.[68] Waqar could, however, demand payment from either Felix or Janet, on the basis of their endorsements, if they were adults.[69]

  minor

- A *material alteration* may create a real defence.[70] Suppose that Felix changed the amount of the cheque from $9000 to $29 000 after he received it from Iman. The effect of that alteration would depend on Felix's skills as a con artist.

  material alteration

  - If the alteration *was not* apparent to the naked eye, Waqar could enforce the cheque against Iman but only for the original amount of $9000. However, he could also enforce the cheque against Felix or Janet for $29 000. Felix would be liable for that amount because he was the wrongdoer. Janet would be fully liable because she chose to add her endorsement to the cheque *after* it was altered. She therefore promised to pay $29 000.

  - If the alteration *was* apparent to the naked eye, Waqar could not enforce it against Iman at all. However, for the reasons that we just discussed, he could enforce it against Felix or Janet for $29 000.

  Note one more thing about alterations. Look carefully at the cheque in Figure 9.6 and compare it to the cheque in Figure 9.1. As you can see, Iman was sloppy in a way that Hank was not. She left spaces in the cheque that allowed Felix to easily alter the amount. Assume that the Island National Bank honoured the cheque and paid $29 000 to Waqar. Normally, the bank could only debit $9000 from Iman's account because that was the only amount that she authorized. However, since the alteration in this case was caused by Iman's carelessness, the bank could take $29 000 from her account. As a matter of risk management, you should always follow Hank's lead and draft instruments in a way that prevents fraud.

- *Forgery* is a real defence that can be used against a holder in due course. Suppose that someone stole the cheque from Felix, forged his endorsement, and then transferred the instrument to Janet. Although the rules that would apply in that case are complex, the main points can be stated briefly.[71]

[68] Although Iman could not be liable to anyone on the cheque, she could be held liable to Felix on the sales contract if he provided her with *necessary* goods or services, as discussed in Chapter 5.

[69] *Bills of Exchange Act* s 47. The same rules apply if a contract is drafted by a corporation that does not have the capacity to incur liability under a negotiable instrument.

[70] *Bills of Exchange Act* ss 144, 145.

[71] *Bills of Exchange Act* s 48, 49.

- A person whose signature is forged generally cannot be held liable. Consequently, if the bank refused to honour the cheque, Waqar could not sue Felix.

- Similarly, a person who signed an instrument *before* a forgery occurred generally cannot be held liable. Consequently, Waqar would also be unable to sue Iman.

- However, a person who signed an instrument *after* a forgery occurred generally can be held liable. Consequently, Waqar could demand payment from Janet, even if she did not know that Felix's signature had been forged. By adding her own endorsement, she promised to pay in any event.

- If the Island National Bank honoured the cheque and paid Waqar, it would have debited Iman's account for $9000. Iman could recover that money from the bank, but only if she promptly notified the bank after learning about the forgery.[72]

- If the bank honoured the cheque, it could recover the amount that it paid from either Waqar (because he received the money) or Janet (because she endorsed the cheque after the forgery), but only if it notified them within a reasonable time after it learned of the forgery.

The effect of these rules can be summarized. The person who committed the forgery should bear the loss. However, that sort of person often disappears or does not have enough money. Therefore, the loss usually falls on the first person who endorsed the instrument after the forgery, in this case, Janet.

CONSUMER BILLS AND NOTES

The *Bills of Exchange Act* has changed very little since it was enacted over 100 years ago. The only substantial alteration was introduced in 1970 to protect consumers. The problem that Parliament wanted to avoid is illustrated in Business Law in Action 9.1.

BUSINESS LAW IN ACTION 9.1

Consumer Bills and Notes

Christine used a promissory note to buy $10 000 worth of aluminum siding for her house from Noel's Exteriors Inc. Noel, however, never delivered the goods. In fact, he disappeared altogether. Because Noel was an immediate party, Christine could have relied on his breach of contract if he had sued her on the note. Furthermore, she could have sued him on the sales contract for damages. In the circumstances, that action would have been a waste of time and money.

To make matters worse, Noel sold the note to Mastiff Financing Ltd, which was a holder in due course. When Mastiff sued Christine, she did not have any defence to its claim. Most significantly, since Mastiff was not an immediate party to her, it did not take the instrument subject to the equities. Consequently, Christine could not argue that Noel never delivered the siding. She therefore had to pay $10 000 to Mastiff, even though she received nothing in return.

---

[72] If an *endorser's* signature had been forged, Iman would have to give notice within one year. If her own signature, as the *drawer*, had been forged, Iman would have to notify the bank within "a reasonable time."

In response to that problem, Parliament added a series of sections to the Act to provide some protection to consumers.[73] The new provisions apply to *consumer instruments* only. A **consumer instrument** is a bill of exchange, cheque, or promissory note that is used by a consumer to buy goods or services from a business on credit. Note three things about that definition. First, the instrument must be used for *credit* purposes. That requirement is satisfied by a promissory note, and by a bill of exchange or cheque that is postdated at least 31 days. Second, the instrument must be used to purchase goods or services from a business person. And third, the instrument must be given by a "consumer," that is, someone who intends to use the purchase for personal, rather than business, purposes.

The front of a consumer instrument must be marked with the words "consumer purchase." The effect of those words is dramatic. Any person, including a holder in due course, who acquires a properly marked consumer instrument takes it subject to the equities. Consequently, if that person sues on the instrument, the consumer can use almost any defence that it could have used against the original seller. The situation is more complicated if an instrument is not properly marked.

- A holder in due course who acquires an instrument without notice that it was used for a consumer purchase does not take it subject to the equities. Consequently, it can be defeated only by a real defence.

- In the hands of any other sort of person, however, an unmarked consumer instrument is void.

- A seller who fails to properly mark a consumer instrument can be fined or imprisoned. The same is true for people who transfer unmarked instruments that they know were used for consumer purchases.

a consumer instrument is a bill of exchange, cheque, or promissory note that is used by a consumer to buy goods or services on credit

a properly marked consumer instrument is acquired subject to the equities

---

[73.] *Bills of Exchange Act* ss 188–192.

Chapter Summary

A negotiable instrument is a special kind of contract that contains an obligation to pay money. The process of negotiation requires the modification of several general contractual principles, including consideration, privity, and assignment. The *Bills of Exchange Act* codifies the rules for three types of negotiable instruments: cheques, bills of exchange, and promissory notes.

The Act will not apply unless an instrument satisfies five basic requirements. A negotiable instrument must: (i) be written and signed, (ii) clearly identify the parties, (iii) contain an obligation to pay a specific sum of money, (iv) clearly state a time of payment, and (v) contain an unconditional obligation. Those requirements are intended to create the level of certainty that is necessary for the process of negotiation.

A cheque is created when a person orders a bank to pay a specific amount of money to someone. It has three parties: (i) the drawer is the person who "draws," or creates, the cheque, (ii) the drawee is the bank that is ordered to pay money, and (iii) the payee is the person who is entitled to receive the money from the bank. Although most cheques operate smoothly, complications can arise if a cheque is: (i) postdated, (ii) staledated, (iii) overdrawn, (iv) countermanded, or (v) certified.

A bill of exchange is created when one person orders another person to pay a specific amount of money to a third person. A bill may be payable: (i) on demand, (ii) on sight, or (iii) on a specific date. A bill may be accepted by the drawee before it is due. If so, the drawee becomes an acceptor and must honour the bill when it is presented for payment.

A promissory note is created when one person gives another person a written promise to pay a specific amount of money. A promissory note is generally different from a cheque or a bill because: (i) it contains a promise rather than an order, and (ii) it involves two parties, rather than three. A promissory note: (i) is often payable with interest, (ii) is often payable in instalments, and (iii) often contains an acceleration clause.

Negotiation involves the transfer of an instrument from one party to another. A bearer instrument is payable to whoever holds it. It can be negotiated by delivery alone. An order instrument is payable to a named person. It can be negotiated by endorsement and delivery. The primary liability for an instrument is on the drawer in the case of a cheque, the drawer or acceptor in the case of a bill, and the maker in the case of a note. However, liability can usually also be imposed on any person who endorsed the instrument. An endorsement usually creates a promise to pay. There are seven main types of endorsement: (i) special, (ii) identifying, (iii) qualified, (iv) conditional, (v) accommodation, (vi) general, and (vii) restrictive.

For the purposes of defences, there are three types of parties: (i) immediate parties, (ii) holders, and (iii) holders in due course. There are three types of defences: (i) personal defences, which are available against immediate parties, (ii) defect in title defences, which are available against immediate parties and holders, and (iii) real defences, which are available against immediate parties, holders, and holders in due course.

Review Questions

1. If a negotiable instrument is used to pay for goods, the parties usually enter into two separate contracts. Describe those contracts.

2. Briefly compare the rules that apply to negotiable instruments with the general contractual rules that govern the issues of consideration and privity.

3. What is the main advantage of receiving the negotiation of an instrument rather than the assignment of a contract?

4. Why does the *Bills of Exchange Act* require an instrument to be written and signed?

5. "A cheque becomes staledated only when the statutory limitation period lapses." Is that statement correct? Explain your answer.

6. What options does a bank have if a customer writes a cheque on an overdrawn account?

7. What is a "stop payment order"? How is such an order given?

8. "The drawee owes the payee an obligation to honour a valid cheque." Is that statement ever correct? If so, when?

9. Is a drawee bank required to honour a certified cheque if the drawer's account is overdrawn or if there has been a countermand? Explain the policy that underlies your answer.

10. Which party has the ability to accept a bill of exchange? What is the effect of acceptance from that party's perspective? What is the effect of acceptance from the perspective of the drawer and the payee?

11. Explain the difference between: (i) a demand draft, (ii) a sight draft, and (iii) a time draft.

12. If you make a promissory note that is payable in instalments, what precaution should you take after you pay each instalment? What is the potential result of not adopting that precaution?

13. What is the purpose of an acceleration clause?

14. What is the danger of receiving an instrument in bearer form? Explain how you can protect yourself against that danger once you have received the instrument?

15. Explain the requirements for negotiating: (i) a bearer instrument, and (ii) an order instrument.

16. What risk do you normally assume when you endorse a negotiable instrument?

17. What is a notice of dishonour? When must it be given? What are the consequences of not giving a notice of dishonour?

18. Briefly describe a holder in due course. What types of defences are available against a holder in due course? Why is a holder in due course given special treatment under the *Bills of Exchange Act*?

19. "When creating a negotiable instrument, you should always ensure that you use all of the space that is available for the amount." Is that good advice? Explain your answer.

20. List and briefly explain four types of defences that may act as either defect in title defences or real defences.

Cases and Problems

1. Every year for a decade, Chamique gave an expensive birthday gift to her friend Ahmad. Last year, she gave him a diamond ring; the year before, a stereo. This year, however, she found that she was too busy with work to actually spend time shopping for a present, so she drafted a cheque for $5000 and gave it to Ahmad. Ahmad accepted it, but later told Chamique that he was hurt that she did not make more of an effort. Chamique became very upset herself and placed a stop payment order on the cheque before Ahmad cashed it. Since the bank will not honour the cheque, Ahmad wants to sue Chamique on the instrument. Is he entitled to do so? Give the best reason for your answer.

2. Gilles, who is 16 years old but looks much older, bought a snowboard from Eva's Sporting Goods. He paid the $750 price with a promissory note that was payable in three monthly instalments of $250 each. Eva stamped the words "consumer purchase" on the note at the time of the sale. Unfortunately, the board was stolen the first time that Gilles took it to the mountains. He believes that he should no longer be required to pay for something that he no longer enjoys. Not surprisingly, Eva has a different opinion. She believes that Gilles got what he wanted and that he is liable to pay the full price. Is Gilles liable on the note? Explain your answer.

3. Bibi, a lawyer, provided legal advice to Bjorn on a small matter. When he asked her for her fee, she said, "Oh, just pay whatever you think is appropriate." Although the evidence indicates that the reasonable value of Bibi's work was $2500, Bjorn gave her a cheque on February 14 for $15 000. Bibi slipped it into her desk without even looking at the amount. The cheque sat there until December, when Bibi presented it to the drawee bank for payment. The bank refused to honour it, however, because Bjorn's account was overdrawn. Bibi then telephoned Bjorn personally and asked him for payment of $15 000. He refused, claiming that he was temporarily insane when he drafted the cheque: "You should have known that I was on the verge of a complete mental collapse and that I was madly—if irrationally—in love with you. Why else would I give you a cheque for that much money on Valentine's Day? You certainly didn't earn $15 000." And indeed, the evidence indicates that Bjorn was quite obviously insane when he drafted the cheque. Bibi wanted nothing more to do with Bjorn, but she did want the money. Therefore she sold the cheque to the Bergman Collection Agency, which was entirely unaware of Bjorn's argument when it purchased the instrument from Bibi. Bergman has since learned of Bjorn's argument, but claims that it is entitled to payment as a holder in due course. Is that correct? Explain your answer.

4. The Leduc Black Gold Company regularly retained the services of Jamaal Raheem, a geologist. On one occasion, it asked him to provide an opinion as to whether there was oil beneath a particular piece of land near Lethbridge, known as the "pronghorn project." After conducting a number of tests, he suggested that the area *might* be suitable for drilling. When Leduc asked for Jamaal's fee, he replied, "Look, just promise to take care of me if this project ever comes through." The next day, Leduc gave Jamaal a document that was entitled "Promissory Note" and was signed by Leduc's president on behalf of the company. That document said:

    > The Leduc Black Gold Company promises that it will pay a reasonable fee to Jamaal Raheem if the pronghorn project becomes profitable. Payment shall be made six months after production at the well begins.

    Has Leduc created a promissory note under the *Bills of Exchange Act*? Give three reasons for your answer.

5. On May 1, Alexa drew a bill of exchange for $25 000 on her line of credit at the People's Trust Company. The bill was payable to Svend on October 26. On June 1, Svend took the bill to the trust company. Audrey, a clerk, ensured that Alexa's credit was in good standing and wrote the following on the bill: "Accepted, October 26, Alexa Ulianov [signature]." At that point, which party was primarily liable for paying the bill on October 15?

6. The Hamilton Steel Company drew a cheque for $50 000 on its account at the Bank of Ontario. The cheque was payable to Elmore Hudson, who was the president of the company. Two weeks later, however, Elmore left his position with Hamilton Steel and established his own company. To promote that new business, he asked Aldercrest Advertising Inc to prepare a number of billboards. Aldercrest was owned by Elmore's good friend Lila Ming.

When Lila asked Elmore how he wanted to pay for her services, he said, "I'm at the airport and I'm about to leave for a much-needed vacation. But I know that you still have a key to my house. If you let yourself into my place and look in my desk, you'll find a cheque for $50 000 that I received from Hamilton Steel. I haven't done a thing with it yet. Take it. You now own everything that it represents." Lila followed Elmore's instructions, obtained the cheque, and presented it for payment at the Bank of Ontario. The bank, however, refused to honour the instrument because Hamilton Steel had issued a stop payment order on it. The evidence indicates that while Hamilton Steel owed $50 000 to Elmore, he owed $40 000 to the company on a loan that became repayable once he left to start his own business. Explain the rights, if any, that Lila has against Hamilton Steel.

7. Eloise Marchant agreed to lend $100 000 to Miguel Cervantes, a business associate. She gave him a cheque for that amount that she drew on her account at the Bank of Saskatoon. He promised to repay her within one year with 10 percent interest. A week later, Miguel went to the bank and asked the manager to certify the instrument that he had received from Eloise. The manager, who was new to the job, failed to notice that Eloise's account held only $40 000. He certified the cheque and returned it to Miguel. Three days later, Miguel returned to the bank and demanded payment. At that point, the bank manager finally realized his error and refused to honour the cheque. Explain the rights and liabilities that arise between the various parties.

8. After opening up her first bank account, Chloe sat around with her friends one evening, playing with her new cheques. As a joke, she made a cheque for $10 000 payable to "Superman." At the end of the evening, Chloe simply threw that cheque into a trash can. During the evening, Simon, who works as a janitor in Chloe's apartment building, found the cheque and put it in his pocket. A few days later, he gave it to Ivan in exchange for car engine. Ivan presented the cheque to Chloe' bank, which honoured the instrument and debited $10 000 from Chloe's account. Chloe has sued the bank on the basis that it disposed of her money without her authority. She insists that it must pay $10 000 to her. Is she correct? Explain your answer.

9. In late January, Kurtz Enterprises purchased office supplies from Kilgore Equipment. It paid with a promissory note for $25 000 that was made to the order of Kilgore Equipment and was due on September 1. In June, Kilgore specially endorsed the note and sold it to Willard Financial Inc. On September 1, Willard tried to claim $25 000 from the maker only to discover that Kurtz Enterprises had disappeared. Over the next week, the president of Willard discussed the situation with her lawyer and accountant. On September 8, she contacted Kilgore Equipment and demanded payment. She took the position that Kilgore was liable on the basis of its endorsement. Is she correct? Explain your answer.

10. Dr Gaius, a veterinarian, bought a large shipment of med-

icine from George Taylor, who operated a medical supply company. Payment was made by way of a promissory note for $50 000, which was payable to Taylor in five equal monthly instalments beginning on August 15. Because Taylor doubted Dr Gaius's financial security, he required her to arrange for another signature to be added to the instrument. Dr Gaius persuaded her friend Cornelius McDowall to sign the back of the document alongside the words: "I will pay the debt if Dr Gaius cannot." The note also contained an acceleration clause. On the morning of August 15, Taylor telephoned Dr Gaius and reminded her that the first instalment of $10 000 was due. Using information that she had previously received from him, she deposited that amount into his bank account. In the early afternoon on the same day, Taylor sold the note to Kym Heston, who was unaware that Dr Gaius had already made the first payment. Not surprisingly, when Heston requested payment later that same day, Dr Gaius objected on the basis that she had already paid $10 000 to Taylor. Heston is sympathetic and points out that she had also been conned by Taylor, who had since disappeared. Nevertheless, having bought the note from Taylor, Heston wants payment. Is she entitled to any money? If so, when and from whom?

11. Earl Tetley worked as a payroll clerk for Tinwings Inc. Over the course of several months, he defrauded the company of about $250 000. His plan was simple. He drafted cheques, on behalf of the company, that were payable to people who had recently quit or been fired from Tinwings. He then forged the payees' blank endorsements and presented the cheques to the drawee, the Bank of Manitoba. The bank honoured the cheques, paid the money to Earl, and debited Tinwings's account. Tinwings eventually discovered that scheme. Although it normally would have contacted the police immediately, it hesitated to do so because Earl was the company president's nephew. Tinwings therefore agreed that it would keep the situation quiet as long as Earl repaid the money with interest within 18 months. After a year and a half, however, Earl had made only a token repayment of $5000. Earl has since been convicted and imprisoned for his fraud. Without any other option, Tinwings has now sued the Bank of Manitoba. The company argues that since the endorsements on the cheques were forged, the bank had no authority to debit its account. Is that correct? Explain your answer.

12. Marlon bought a delivery van for his business from Tanita for $20 000. Half of the purchase price was paid with cash, and the other half with a cheque that was payable to bearer. After meeting with Marlon, Tanita took the subway back to her office. Unfortunately, she forgot her purse, which contained both the cash and the cheque that she had received from Marlon, on the subway. After several days of frantic phone calls, it became clear to Tanita that the person who picked up her purse did not intend to return it. Has Tanita necessarily suffered a $20 000 loss? What should she do to minimize the damage? What should Marlon do?

WWWeblinks

Contract Law

www.duhaime.org/ca-con1.htm

This page provides an introduction to various areas of contract law, including offer and acceptance, privity, mistake, misrepresentation, breach, and remedies. The site also offers summaries of leading case law.

JURIST Canada—Contracts

jurist.law.utoronto.ca/cour_pgs.htm

The JURIST Web site features links to course pages developed by Canadian law teachers. They include materials relevant to the study of contract law.

CataLaw—Contract and Remedy Law

www.catalaw.com/topics/Contract.shtml

This Canadian site provides a comprehensive and searchable index of legal links related to contract and remedy law in Canada, Australia, the United Kingdom, and the United States.

CanadaLegal.com

www.canadalegal.com/search.asp?a=42&n=100

This Web site provides access to articles and newsletters prepared by Canadian law firms related to contract law. The links are arranged by jurisdiction.

Contracts Canada

contractscanada.gc.ca/en/index.html

This site offers information on how the federal government conducts business with its suppliers, including government purchasing and government contacts.

Misrepresentation and Consumer Fraud

www.rochongenova.com/certifi1.html

This page provides case briefs for recent Canadian cases involving misrepresentation and consumer fraud.

Industry Canada Consumer Information

strategis.ic.gc.ca/sc_consu/consaffairs/engdoc/oca.html

This Web site provides information to consumers on such matters as recalls, consumer law, and awareness.

Interpretation of Terms

www.cmg.ca/Contractinterpretation.htm

This page provides a rough-and-ready guide to the interpretation of contractual terms with an eye to future arbitration.

Signed and Unsigned Consumer Contracts

qsilver.queensu.ca/law/bala/law120/mar22?01c.htm

This page examines the relevant case law with regard to both signed and unsigned standard form agreements. It also discusses the practical considerations involved in using ticket contracts and signed forms in business transactions.

Online Contracting

www.worldlaw.com/kaboom.htm

This site contains the 1999 article "Kaboom!! How to blow all your profits using crummy contracts on the Internet," which explores many issues concerning the creation of online contracts, including contractual incapacity and other defects.

Ontario *Statute of Frauds* RSO 1990, c S-19

www.e-laws.gov.on.ca/DBLaws/Statutes/English/90s19_e.htm

This Statute is representative of provincial legislation that sets out the types of contracts that must be evidenced in writing.

Contracting Online

www.bbburn.com/pmart11.htm

This site contains a 2001 article "Contracting online," which explores issues of contracting online, including contract formation, writing requirements, and statutory changes.

British Columbia *Frustrated Contract Act*, RSBC 1996, c 166

www.qp.gov.bc.ca/statreg/stat/F/96166_01.htm

This Act applies to contracts that are discharged by reason of the application of the doctrine of frustration.

Canada *Bills of Exchange Act*, RSC 1985, c B-4

laws.justice.gc.ca/en/B-4/index.html

The federal *Bills of Exchange Act* sets out the rules governing three types of negotiable instruments: cheques, bills of exchange, and promissory notes.

10 Introduction to Torts and Intentional Torts

CHAPTER OVERVIEW

OBJECTIVES

After completing this chapter, you should be able to:

1. Describe the nature of liability insurance, and explain why it is important to business people.
2. Describe the concept of vicarious liability, and explain how it affects business people.
3. Outline the types of remedies that are generally available in tort law.
4. Describe two important types of alternative compensation schemes, and explain why they have been created.
5. Explain the general nature of intentional torts, and define "intention" as it applies to those torts.
6. Describe the torts of assault and battery, and describe a situation in which battery presents a particular danger for business people.
7. Explain the tort of false imprisonment, and describe how a business can protect itself against liability.
8. Outline the extent to which tort law protects privacy interests.
9. Describe the tort of trespass to land, and explain when a business is entitled to prohibit people from coming onto its premises.
10. Outline the torts that protect the possession of chattels, and explain the dangers that arise when stolen goods are bought by mistake.

There are two main sources of obligations in private law. In Unit II, we looked at contracts. In this unit, we look at *torts*. The discussion is split into three main parts. In this chapter, we consider intentional torts; in the next, we consider several miscellaneous torts that often affect business people; and in the third, we consider negligence, which is the most important tort. First, however, we will look at a number of matters that affect all torts.[1]

INTRODUCTION TO TORT LAW

You certainly heard the word "contracts" before you began this course, but you may not have heard the word "tort." "Tort" is derived from the French word *"tort,"* which means wrong, which came from the Latin word *"tortus,"* which means twisted or crooked. While it is difficult to precisely define the term, a **tort** generally consists of a failure to fulfill a private obligation that was imposed by law.

It is important to understand that the obligation in tort law is *private* rather than *public*.

- A private obligation, which is sometimes called a *civil* obligation, is owed to a particular person.[2] If something goes wrong, that person usually sues for damages.

- In contrast, a public obligation, which normally takes the form of a *criminal* obligation, is owed to society as a whole. If something goes wrong, the government prosecutes an action on behalf of the entire community. And if the court believes that the accused person is guilty, it can impose punishment, such as a fine or imprisonment.

Private obligations and public obligations can overlap. For instance, if you physically attack me, you may commit both a tort (for which I could sue) *and* a crime (for which you could be prosecuted). Concept Summary 10.1 illustrates the differences between tort law and criminal law.

*a **tort** generally consists of a failure to fulfill a private obligation that was imposed by law*

tort law and criminal law often overlap

Concept Summary 10.1

Tort Law and Criminal Law

	Private law or public law?	Which parties are involved in the obligation?	Who are the parties to the action if that obligation is broken?	What is the usual remedy?
Tort Law	private law	the defendant owes an obligation to the plaintiff	the plaintiff sues the defendant	compensatory damages
Criminal Law	public law	the accused owes an obligation to society	the government prosecutes the accused	punishment (such as a fine or imprisonment)

It is also important to understand how torts differ from contracts.

- Contractual obligations are generally *created voluntarily*. A party does not have to act in a particular way unless it *agreed* to do so. That is one reason

contractual obligations are created voluntarily and therefore usually cause few problems

---

[1.] In this introduction to tort law, we will introduce the names of several torts that will be discussed later in this unit.

[2.] As we will see in Chapter 18, the legal definition of a "person" generally includes a corporation.

why most contracts are performed without any difficulties: the parties know their obligations in advance and therefore can plan to fulfill them.

- In contrast, obligations in tort law are not created voluntarily—they are *imposed by law*. You may have to fulfill a tort obligation even if you did not agree to do so, and even if you are completely unaware of it. For that reason, tort law may take you by surprise. Suppose that you buy supplies from someone who appears to own them. If it turns out that the goods were actually stolen, you may be held liable to their real owner under the tort of conversion, even though you acted honestly.

tort obligations are imposed by law and often take business people by surprise

Liability Insurance

liability insurance is a contract in which an insurance company agrees, in exchange for a price, to pay damages on behalf of a person who incurs liability

a duty to defend requires the insurance company to pay the expenses associated with lawsuits brought against the insured party

Because torts can occur unexpectedly, risk management is especially important. Business people should know enough about tort law to predict potential problems and to develop strategies for avoiding liability. They should also protect themselves with *liability insurance*.[3] **Liability insurance** is a contract in which an insurance company agrees, in exchange for a price, to pay damages on behalf of a person who incurs liability. Figure 10.1 provides an illustration. Liability insurance also includes a *duty to defend*. A **duty to defend** requires the insurance company to pay the expenses associated with lawsuits brought against the insured party.[4] That is significant. The costs of litigation can be very high, even if you win your case.

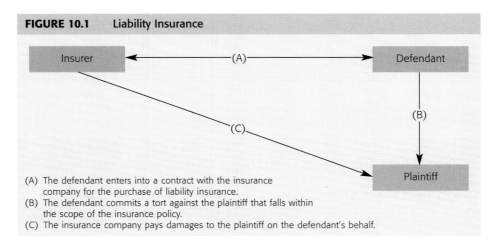

FIGURE 10.1   Liability Insurance

(A) The defendant enters into a contract with the insurance company for the purchase of liability insurance.
(B) The defendant commits a tort against the plaintiff that falls within the scope of the insurance policy.
(C) The insurance company pays damages to the plaintiff on the defendant's behalf.

the compensatory function tries to ensure that people are fully compensated when they wrongfully suffer a loss

the tortfeasor is a person who commits the tort

the deterrence function tries to discourage people from committing torts by threatening to hold them liable for the losses they cause

Liability insurance creates an interesting tension within tort law. On the one hand, it contributes to the *compensatory function* of torts. The **compensatory function** tries to ensure that people are fully compensated when they wrongfully suffer a loss. A **tortfeasor**, who is a person who commits a tort, may not personally have enough money to pay damages. If so, the victim will not receive complete compensation unless the tortfeasor has insurance. But on the other hand, liability insurance undermines the *deterrence function* of tort law. The **deterrence function** tries to discourage people from committing torts by threatening to hold them liable for the losses that they cause. People have little reason to be afraid, however, if they know that their insurance companies

---

3. There are also other types of insurance, which are considered in Chapter 15.
4. *Scott v Wawanesa Mutual Insurance Co* (1989) 59 DLR (4th) 660 (SCC).

will pay if something goes wrong. Perhaps for that reason, studies suggest that tort law has surprisingly little deterrent effect.[5]

Liability insurance plays an important role in tort law.[6] It is important to understand, however, that liability insurance policies do not usually cover *all* torts. Case Brief 10.1 provides a recent illustration.

CASE BRIEF 10.1

Non-Marine Underwriters, Lloyd's of London v Scalera (2000) 185 DLR (4th) 1 (SCC)

The plaintiff, a young teenager, worked in a corner store that was located at the end of a city bus line. The defendant, a bus driver, sexually abused her on a number of occasions. She later sued him for battery. He claimed coverage under his liability insurance policy. His insurance company rejected his claim, however, by pointing to a clause in that contract that excluded coverage for injuries inflicted through "intentional or criminal acts."

The Supreme Court of Canada held that the defendant was not protected by his insurance policy because he had committed the tort of battery with the intention of injuring the plaintiff. As a result, the plaintiff's chances of recovering full damages was reduced. While the insurance company was wealthy, the defendant was not.

Vicarious Liability

Liability insurance is always a good idea, especially for any business that has employees. The reason involves the doctrine of *vicarious liability*. **Vicarious liability** occurs when an employer is held liable for a tort that was committed by an employee. As Ethical Perspective 10.1 shows, the idea of holding one person responsible for another person's actions raises difficult ethical issues.

vicarious liability occurs when an employer is held liable for a tort that was committed by an employee

---

ETHICAL PERSPECTIVE 10.1

Bazley v Curry (1999) 174 DLR (4th) 45 (SCC)

The defendant was a charitable organization that operated a residential care facility for emotionally troubled children. It employed a number of people, including a man named Curry, to act as substitute parents (for example, by bathing children and putting them to bed at night). Although the defendant conducted a reasonably thorough investigation before hiring Curry, it failed to discover that he was a pedophile. Sadly, Curry sexually assaulted a number of children, including the plaintiff, within the

defendant's facilities. The plaintiff sued the defendant organization on the basis that it was vicariously liable for Curry's actions.

The Supreme Court of Canada held that an employer is vicariously liable for both: (i) acts that it authorized an employee to do, and (ii) other closely connected acts. On the facts of the case, the Court found that Curry's actions fell within the second category.[7] While recognizing that the employer certainly did not want its employees to sexually abuse the

(continued)

[5.] M Trebilcock & D Dewees "The Efficacy of the Tort System and Its Alternatives: A Review of Empirical Evidence" (1992) 30 Osgoode Hall LJ 57.

[6.] It is also possible to purchase insurance for liabilities arising outside of tort. For example, a company may obtain coverage for liabilities arising through breach of contract.

[7.] It is often difficult to determine whether an employee's tort fell within the second branch of the test. On the same day that it held the employer responsible in *Bazley v Curry*, the Supreme Court of Canada refused to impose vicarious liability in a similar case: *Jacobi v Griffiths* (1998) 174 DLR (4th) 71.

(continued)
children, the Court held that the nature of the employer's operation significantly increased the risk of wrongdoing.

Questions for Discussion

1. Is it fair to impose liability on an employer that acted reasonably?
2. Why should an innocent person be responsible for someone else's wrongs?

The doctrine of vicarious liability may be justified on a number of grounds.

- First, it serves the compensatory function of tort law because it allows the plaintiff to claim damages from both an employee (who may not have any money) and an employer (which is more likely to have money or, at least, liability insurance).

- Second, vicarious liability may serve the deterrence function of tort law by providing employers with an incentive to avoid unusually hazardous activities and to hire the best people available.

- Third, as a matter of fairness, it may be appropriate to require a business to take responsibility for the losses that its activities create, even if those losses are caused by employees who misbehave.

It is important to note several other points about vicarious liability. First, an employer is not liable *every time* an employee does something wrong. As the Supreme Court of Canada stressed in *Bazley v Curry*, an employer is not vicariously liable if an employee's tort occurred completely outside of the employment relationship or if the employee "was on a frolic of his own."

Second, an employer may be held vicariously liable for employees, but not for *independent contractors*. Consequently, as a matter of risk management, it is sometimes preferable for a business to have work performed by an independent contractor rather than by an employee.[8] While it is often difficult to distinguish between those two types of workers, the courts are more inclined to find that a person is an employee if: (i) the employer generally controls what is done, how it is done, when it is done, and where it is done, (ii) the worker uses the employer's equipment and premises, (iii) the worker is paid a regular wage or salary rather than a lump sum at the end of each project, and (iv) the worker is integrated into the employer's business and is not in their own business.

Third, vicarious liability does not relieve the employee of responsibility. Rather, it allows the plaintiff to sue both the employer *and* the employee, and to recover all or some of its damages from either defendant. Furthermore, if the employer actually pays damages to the plaintiff, it is usually entitled to claim that amount from the employee. In practice, however, employers seldom do so. Aside from the fact that an employee is unlikely to have much money, employers usually realize that morale would drop if employees were worried about being held liable.

Fourth, an employer may be both *vicariously liable* and *personally liable* in the *same situation*. Vicarious liability occurs if the employer is responsible for an *employee's tort*. Personal liability occurs if the employer is responsible for its *own tort*. Business Law in Action 10.1 provides an illustration.

---

an employer is not vicariously liable if an employee commits a tort completely outside the scope of employment

the doctrine of vicarious liability applies to employees but not to independent contractors

vicarious liability does not relieve the employee of responsibility

an employer may be held liable both vicariously and personally

---

[8.] Chapter 25 considers the distinction between employees and independent contractors in detail.

BUSINESS LAW IN ACTION 10.1

Vicarious Liability and Personal Liability

You suffer a serious injury after falling out of a chairlift at a ski resort. The evidence indicates that the accident was caused by the fact that the lift was carelessly operated by Alberto, an employee of the resort. The evidence also indicates that the resort failed to properly train Alberto.

Liability could arise in three ways. First, Alberto might be *personally* liable, under the tort of negligence, because he carelessly operated the chairlift. Second, the resort might be *vicariously* liable because it was Alberto's employer. Third, the resort might also be *personally* liable, under the tort of negligence, because it carelessly failed to train its employee.

Questions for Discussion

1. Why should you sue both Alberto and the resort?
2. Who would pay for your injuries if: (i) Alberto alone was held liable, (ii) both Alberto and the resort were held liable, and (iii) the resort alone was held liable?

Figure 10.2 summarizes our discussion of vicarious liability. It assumes that the only tort was committed by the employee.

FIGURE 10.2   Vicarious Liability

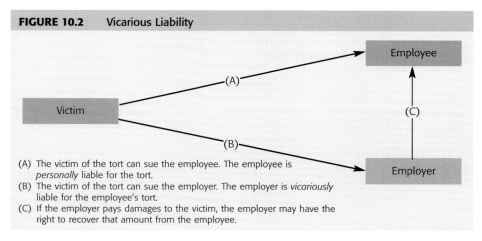

(A) The victim of the tort can sue the employee. The employee is *personally* liable for the tort.
(B) The victim of the tort can sue the employer. The employer is *vicariously* liable for the employee's tort.
(C) If the employer pays damages to the victim, the employer may have the right to recover that amount from the employee.

Remedies

The victim of a tort usually receives compensatory damages. Other remedies may be available as well. There is, however, no need for a detailed discussion here as we examined many of the same issues in Chapter 7 when we looked at remedies for breach of contract.

Compensatory Damages

Compensatory damages are the standard remedy in both contract and tort. In either situation, the defendant is required to pay the monetary value of the losses that it caused the plaintiff to suffer. There is, however, a significant difference between contract and tort. In contract, the court usually awards *expectation damages*. As Chapter 7 explained, expectation damages are *forward-looking* because they are intended to place the plaintiff in the position that it expected to be in *after* the contract was properly performed. In contrast, compensation in tort is *backward-looking* because it is intended to place the plaintiff in the position that it enjoyed *before* the defendant acted wrongfully.

Why does contract look forward while tort looks back? The difference is largely due to the source of the obligation. In contract, the defendant voluntarily

compensatory damages require the defendant to pay the monetary value of the losses it caused the plaintiff to suffer

compensation in contract generally looks forward; compensation in tort generally looks backward

agreed to do something in the future. It is therefore required to fulfill that promise, either through performance or through the monetary value of performance. The law says, "You promised to do something. Now do it."[9] In tort, however, an obligation is not created voluntarily. It is imposed by law. The defendant therefore cannot be forced to improve the plaintiff's position. It can only be required to repair the harm that it caused. The law says, "You should not have done something. Now undo it."

The distinction between compensation in contract and tort is especially important whenever it is possible for the plaintiff to sue the defendant in both contract *and* tort. The plaintiff can recover damages for only one of those actions, even if both are successful, and will choose whichever option provides the most money.[10] To more fully understand these issues, consider You Be the Judge 10.1.

YOU BE THE JUDGE 10.1

Compensation in Tort and Contract[11]

Pippa agreed to buy a pizzeria from David. During the negotiations that led up to that contract, David said a number of things about the restaurant's profitability. If those statements had been true, Pippa would have received a net profit of $80 000 on her investment. In fact, as David knew, the business was actually far less profitable than he had said. As a result of relying on David's statement, Pippa lost $65 000 on the purchase.

David admits that he is guilty of both: (i) a breach of contract (because his promises were untrue), and (ii) the tort of deceit (because he lied to Pippa). The parties simply want

you, as the judge, to determine how much money Pippa is entitled to receive in damages.

Questions for Discussion

1. How much money would be required to place Pippa in the position that she would have enjoyed if the contract had turned out as expected?
2. How much money would be required to place Pippa in the position that she would have enjoyed if she had not entered into the contract?
3. Given that the plaintiff ultimately can recover for either breach of contract or tort, but not both, how much will she receive?

---

a loss is remote if it would be unfair to hold the defendant responsible for it

Chapter 7 explained how expectation damages in contract are limited by the principles of *remoteness* and *mitigation*. A loss is **remote** if it would be unfair to hold the defendant responsible for it. Consequently, damages may not be available even if the defendant's breach caused the plaintiff to suffer a loss. The same rule generally applies in tort law. The courts ask whether a reasonable person in the defendant's position would have realized that a particular activity might cause the sort of harm that the plaintiff suffered.[12] Suppose that one of your employees develops a rare disease after coming into contact with rat urine. You might not be liable even if you carelessly allowed rats to run loose in your warehouse. A judge once held that a reasonable person would recognize the danger of *rat bites*, but not *rat urine*.[13]

There is an important limitation on the remoteness principle. The concept

---

9. As we saw in Chapter 7, the plaintiff occasionally is entitled to *specific performance*. If so, the defendant must actually perform the promised act.

10. *Central Trust Co v Rafuse* (1986) 31 DLR (4th) 481 (SCC).

11. *Goldstar Management Ltd v Varvis* (1995) 175 AR 321 (QB).

12. *Overseas Tankship (UK) Ltd v Morts Dock and Engineering Co Ltd*, *The Wagon Mound (No 1)* [1961] AC 388 (PC).

13. *Tremain v Pike* [1969] 3 All ER 1303.

of remoteness applies to most types of torts, but not to intentional torts. People who intentionally do wrong do not deserve any leniency.[14]

The principle of *mitigation* also limits damages in both contract and tort. In either event, compensation cannot be recovered for a loss that the plaintiff unreasonably failed to mitigate. **Mitigation** occurs when the plaintiff takes steps to minimize the losses that result from the defendant's breach. Suppose that a customer was bitten by a rat that you negligently allowed to run around your warehouse. You advised her to get a tetanus shot, but she refused. As a result, she developed lockjaw and was unable to work for eight months. If she had received a tetanus shot, she would have missed only three days of work. Your liability will be limited to three days of lost income if the court believes that the plaintiff's decision to refuse the tetanus shot was unreasonable.[15]

the remoteness rules do not apply to intentional torts

mitigation occurs when the plaintiff takes steps to minimize the losses that result from the defendant's breach

Punitive Damages

Punitive damages may be awarded in addition to compensatory damages. **Punitive damages** are intended to punish the defendant. As we saw in Chapter 7, punitive damages are available far less often in Canada than in the United States. A tortfeasor in this country will be punished only if it acted in a harsh, vindictive, high-handed, reprehensible, or malicious way. For example, punitive damages have been awarded against an elderly doctor who committed the tort of battery on a young woman by refusing to give her drugs unless she had sex with him, against a reform school that committed the tort of negligence by failing to fire a predatory employee who sexually abused a young inmate, and against a land developer who committed the tort of trespass to land by cutting down trees on a neighbouring lot to enhance the view from its own property.[16]

punitive damages are intended to punish the defendant

Nominal Damages

Nominal damages can be awarded for *some* torts. **Nominal damages** symbolically recognize that the defendant committed a tort, even though the plaintiff did not suffer any loss. Since nominal damages are merely symbolic, they are awarded in very small sums, say, $10. Furthermore, because they are usually awarded only if the plaintiff did not suffer any loss, they are generally restricted to torts that are actionable *per se*. Most torts (such as negligence) occur only if the defendant inflicted a loss upon the plaintiff. However, some torts (such as the intentional torts) occur as long as the defendant acted wrongfully. They are therefore actionable *per se*, that is, in themselves, rather than being actionable upon proof of a loss.

nominal damages symbolically recognize that the defendant committed a tort even though the plaintiff did not suffer any loss

a tort is actionable per se *if it does not require proof of the plaintiff's loss*

Injunctions

An *injunction* may be available for a tort, just as it may be available for a breach of contract. An **injunction** occurs when a court orders the defendant not to commit a tort or to reverse the effects of a tort that has been committed. For example, if you commit the tort of nuisance by operating a foul-smelling pig farm in a residential area, you may be told to relocate your business to a rural area. If you refuse to do so, you may be punished for contempt of court.

an injunction occurs when a court orders the defendant not to commit a tort or to reverse the effects of a tort that has been committed

---

[14.] *Bettel v Yim* (1978) 88 DLR (3d) 543 (Ont Co Ct).

[15.] *McAuley v London Transport Executive* [1957] 2 Lloyds Rep 500 (CA).

[16.] *Norberg v Wynrib* (1992) 92 DLR (4th) 449 (SCC) ($10 000 in punitive damages); *Roose v Hollett* (1996) 139 DLR (4th) 161 (NS CA) ($35 000 in punitive damages); *Horseshoe Bay Retirement Society v SIF Development Corp* (1990) 66 DLR (4th) 42 (BC SC) ($100 000 in punitive damages).

Alternative Compensation Schemes

It is important to appreciate that tort law is not the only source of compensation. In fact, in recent years, the number of *alternative compensation schemes* has increased considerably. An **alternative compensation scheme** is a system that allows a person who has suffered an injury to receive compensation without bringing an action in tort. Two such systems are especially important:

- workers' compensation
- no-fault insurance

Because job-related injuries are so common, workers' compensation schemes exist across the country. While the details vary among jurisdictions, the basic ideas are always the same. A fund is established with compulsory contributions from employers. Workers who are injured on the job are usually prevented from suing in tort. They are, however, entitled to receive compensation from the fund without having to prove that anyone has wrongfully caused their injuries. That system is much quicker and much easier than tort law.

The second major type of alternative compensation scheme applies to injuries that are caused by automobile accidents. Several provinces have adopted some form of no-fault system.[17] In Manitoba and Quebec, for example, victims of traffic accidents cannot sue in tort, but they are entitled to receive compensation from the scheme without having to prove that another driver was at fault. Other provinces have enacted less extensive schemes. In British Columbia, the right to no-fault benefits exists in addition to the right to sue in tort. And in Saskatchewan and Ontario, the no-fault system prevents an action in tort unless the victim's losses are especially serious.

There are two main reasons for the rise of alternative compensation schemes.

- First, tort law provides compensation only if a person is injured as a result of a *wrongful* act. From the victim's perspective, however, the physical and financial consequences of being injured are the same, even if an injury occurs *innocently*. Consequently, it is sometimes desirable to allow that person to collect compensation regardless of fault.
- Second, tort law is inefficient. Since it is based on an adversarial system in which lawyers compete on behalf of clients, it requires a great deal of time and expense. Studies suggest that less than one-third of all the money involved in the tort system is actually used for compensating injuries.[18] Because alternative compensation schemes operate on a no-fault basis, there is far less need for costly investigations and lengthy disputes.

While alternative compensation schemes have many advantages, they also have a major disadvantage. They provide compensation more often, but they also provide less of it. In tort law, the plaintiff is usually entitled to recover the full value of a loss. In alternative compensation schemes, however, the level of compensation is almost always capped. Since such schemes include many more claimants, they would quickly go broke if they provided full compensation for every loss.

an alternative compensation scheme is a system that allows a person who has suffered an injury to receive compensation without bringing an action in tort

workers' compensation schemes allow people who suffer job-related injuries to receive compensation without proving fault under the tort system

automobile accident compensation schemes allow people who have suffered traffic-related injuries to receive monetary assistance without proving fault under the tort system

alternative compensation schemes provide relief more often, but in smaller amounts

[17] For a useful summary of automobile accident compensation schemes, see AM Linden & LN Klar *Canadian Tort Law* 11th ed (1999) at 754-7.

[18] Ontario Ministry of Financial Institutions *Ontario Task Force on Insurance, Final Report* (1986) at 66.

INTENTIONAL TORTS

Having completed our introductory discussion, we will now examine specific torts, starting with several *intentional torts* that are important to business:

- assault and battery
- false imprisonment
- invasion of privacy
- trespass to land
- interference with chattels

Intentional torts generally involve intentional, rather than merely careless, conduct.[19] "Intentional," however, has an unusual definition. It is enough if the defendant knew that a particular act would have particular consequences. The plaintiff does *not* have to prove that the defendant intended either to cause harm or commit a tort. For example, if you build a fence on my property, you commit the intentional tort of trespass to land, even if thought that the land belonged to you. It is enough that you knew that your actions would result in a fence being constructed on *that* piece of ground. The courts have adopted that broad definition of "intention" because they want to protect the interests that I have in myself and in my property. From a risk management perspective, the lesson is clear. Before acting in a particular way, you should know as much as possible about the consequences of doing so.

intentional torts involve intentional, rather than merely careless, conduct

Assault and Battery

Although they are often discussed together, *assault* and *battery* are separate torts. An **assault** occurs when the defendant intentionally causes the plaintiff to reasonably believe that offensive bodily contact is imminent. There are several important points in that definition.

assault occurs when the defendant intentionally causes the plaintiff to reasonably believe that offensive bodily contact is imminent

- First, the tort is not based on physical contact. It is based on a reasonable belief that such contact will occur. The tort is designed to keep the peace by discouraging people from alarming others. As a result, you may commit an assault by swinging your fist at me, even if you do not actually make contact. In contrast, if you punch me from behind, you do not commit the tort of assault if I did not know that the blow was coming (although you do commit the tort of battery).

- Second, it is enough if the plaintiff *reasonably believed* that bodily contact would occur. As a result, you may commit an assault by pointing a gun in my direction, even if the gun is not really loaded. I would only have to prove that a reasonable person would have thought that a gunshot was possible.

- Third, the plaintiff must have believed that bodily contact was *imminent*. Although that requirement is rather vague, you probably would not commit an assault if you threatened to kick me two weeks from today. Something more immediate is necessary.

[19.] Confusingly, Canadian courts occasionally say that an intentional tort can consist of either intentional *or* careless conduct: *Cook v Lewis* [1952] 1 DLR 1 (SCC). Our discussion, however, can be limited to intentional acts. The intentional torts are also characterized by a requirement of *directness*—the plaintiff's injury must flow naturally from the defendant's conduct and must not depend upon the intervention of some outside factor. That requirement is complicated, but it seldom creates problems in practice. There is no need to explore it in this book. See L Klar *Tort Law* 2nd ed (1996) at 26-9.

- Fourth, an assault can occur even if the plaintiff was not frightened. It is enough that the defendant threatened some form of *offensive contact*. For example, you may commit an assault by swinging your fist at me, even if I know that you are far too small to do any harm.

People seldom sue for assault alone. It seldom justifies the trouble and expense of litigation. A claim for assault is usually joined with a claim for *battery*. A **battery** consists of offensive bodily contact.[20] There are several points to note about this definition.

battery consists of offensive bodily contact

- First, the requirement of "bodily contact" is not strictly applied. It is enough if the defendant causes something, such as a knife or a bullet, to touch the plaintiff. It is also enough if the defendant makes contact with the plaintiff's clothing or with something that the plaintiff is holding.

- Second, not every form of contact is offensive. Normal social interaction is allowed. Consequently, you do not commit a battery if you gently brush past me in a crowded elevator or if you tap my shoulder to get my attention. At the same time, however, contact may be offensive even if it is not harmful. Consequently, you will commit a battery if you kiss me despite my objections. You may even commit a tort if your actions are highly beneficial. Case Brief 10.2 provides a dramatic illustration.

CASE BRIEF 10.2

Malette v Shulman (1990) 67 DLR (4th) 321 (Ont CA)

A woman suffered horrendous injuries in a traffic accident and was taken unconscious to a hospital. The attending surgeon realized that she would die unless she received a blood transfusion. However, he also knew that the woman's purse contained a card that identified her as a Jehovah's Witness and that she objected to such treatment. The surgeon decided to administer the transfusion anyway. The procedure was successful and the woman recovered. Nevertheless, while she was grateful to be alive, she sued the doctor for battery.

The plaintiff was awarded $20 000 for the mental distress that she suffered as a result of receiving the transfusion. It was irrelevant that the defendant acted in her best interests and that he probably saved her life. Although the court accepted that a physician can usually presume that a person would want to receive full treatment, it also stressed the patient's right to control her own body. Accordingly, since there was no reason to doubt the authenticity of the card, the defendant could not act contrary to the plaintiff's wishes.

Understanding the tort of battery is especially important for businesses that control crowds or remove rowdy customers. Bouncers and security personnel often injure patrons whom they eject from taverns, concerts, and sporting events. Given the doctrine of vicarious liability and the need for risk management, such employees should be carefully trained. Case Brief 10.3 serves as a warning.

---

[20] A person who commits the tort of battery often commits a crime at the same time.

CASE BRIEF 10.3

Vasey v Wosk's Ltd [1988] BCJ No 2089 (SC)

The plaintiff was escorted out of a bar after becoming drunk and belligerent. Once outside, he struck one of the bouncers from behind. In retaliation, that bouncer knocked him to the ground with a kick to the head. Another bouncer then climbed on top of the plaintiff and punched him in the face for about five minutes. The plaintiff suffered a number of injuries and consequently sued the company that owned the bar.

The court held that the bar's employees were entitled to use reasonable force to remove the obnoxious customer from the premises. It further held that the plaintiff was partially to blame for the disturbance because he had struck one of the bouncers from behind. However, it also held that the employees used excessive force. It therefore allowed the plaintiff to recover compensation for the losses that he suffered, minus a reduction of 30 percent to reflect the fact that he had provoked the attack. The bouncers were held personally liable and the company that owned the bar was held vicariously liable.

False Imprisonment

False imprisonment occurs when a person is confined within a fixed area without justification. An actual prison is not necessary. The tort can be committed if a person is trapped in a car, locked in a room, or set adrift in a boat. But in any event, the confinement must be complete. The defendant does not commit a false imprisonment if it obstructs one path while leaving a reasonable alternative open, or if the plaintiff can easily escape.

The tort of false imprisonment is not committed if the plaintiff agreed to be confined. *Consent* is a complete defence to all intentional torts. Consequently, bus passengers cannot complain if the driver refuses to make an unscheduled stop. A company that operates a mine is generally entitled to leave a worker underground until the end of a shift.[21] And a traveler at an airport may be detained to be searched. The same rule may apply to a customer in a store, at least if the store gave advance warning. Likewise, although a false imprisonment can be committed by wrongfully detaining someone's valuable property, the tort does not arise if the plaintiff agreed to that arrangement. Consequently, a person cannot remove a vehicle from a car park without paying the appropriate fee.

An imprisonment is false only if it is done *without authority*. That statement raises an important question for business people. When is there authority to make an arrest? Unfortunately, the law is complicated and somewhat unsettled. However, the courts generally apply these rules.

- A *police officer* may arrest anyone who is reasonably suspected of: (i) being in the act of committing a crime, or (ii) having committed a *serious* crime in the past.[22] If that test is satisfied, the police officer does no wrong, even if the person who was arrested was actually innocent.

- The rules are much narrower, however, for *private citizens*—including *security guards*. People may be arrested only while they are *actually committing* crimes.[23] If, in fact, no crime was being committed, the

> a false imprisonment occurs when a person is confined within a fixed area without justification

> the tort of false imprisonment is not committed if the plaintiff agreed to be confined

> consent is a complete defence to all intentional torts

> an imprisonment is not false unless it is done without authority

---

[21.] *Herd v Weardale Steel, Coal & Coke Co Ltd* [1915] AC 67 (HL).

[22.] *Criminal Code*, RSC 1985, c C-46, s 495 (Can).

[23.] *Criminal Code*, RSC 1985, c C-46, s 494 (Can); *Hayward v FW Woolworth Co Ltd* (1979) 98 DLR (3d) 345 (Nfld SC TD). A private citizen may also arrest a person who is reasonably believed to have committed a crime *and* who is being chased by a police officer. If that test is satisfied, the citizen will not be liable in tort, even if no crime had actually been committed.

arrest is unjustified. And whoever made the arrest may be held liable in tort, even if they acted honestly and reasonably. The law generally favours a customer's freedom of movement over a store's desire to protect its property.

It is therefore dangerous for a business to instruct a security guard to detain a suspected shoplifter. That danger is heightened by the fact that false imprisonment can occur without physical force. The tort can certainly be committed if a person is handcuffed or locked in a room. However, it can also be committed if a person is *psychologically* detained, as when an innocent shopper agrees to accompany a security guard to a back room to avoid public embarrassment.[24] In that type of case, a judge has to decide whether the plaintiff acted voluntarily or under compulsion.

a false imprisonment can arise from psychological detention

As Business Decision 10.1 illustrates, the rules for false imprisonment may place a business person in a difficult position.

BUSINESS DECISION 10.1

False Imprisonment and Detention by Security Guards

Terrence works as a security guard in your music store. He notices that Martin, who has been caught shoplifting in the past, is clutching his jacket closed. While Terrence strongly suspects that Martin is attempting to steal a CD, he also knows that the young man's father is a lawyer who specializes in tort law. He asks for advice.

You have several options.

- You could tell Terrence to let Martin to walk away, possibly with a stolen CD.
- You could tell Terrence to ask Martin to follow him into a back room for the purposes of questioning. If Martin was

shoplifting, you have no need to worry. But if he was not, he may sue you and Terrence for false imprisonment.

- You could tell Terrence to contact the police. If the investigating officers believed that Martin was committing a crime, they could arrest him. If Martin was not actually shoplifting, the police would be protected as long as they acted on reasonable grounds. Furthermore, Martin probably could not sue you or Terrence because you did not personally detain him.[25]

Questions for Discussion

1. Which option will you adopt?
2. If you adopt the third option, do you believe that Martin will still be in the store when the police arrive?

Similar problems arise when a customer tries to leave a restaurant without paying the full bill. As a general rule, a restaurant cannot detain a customer to force payment. A refusal to pay is usually a breach of contract but not a crime. Detention can therefore lead to a false imprisonment.[26] It is normally safer to simply sue the customer for the price of the meal.

Even a business person who is authorized to make an arrest should not use more force than is necessary. In most situations, the customer should be given an opportunity to surrender peacefully. And in any event, the arrested person should be turned over to the police as soon as possible.

---

24. *Chaytor v London, New York & Paris Assoc of Fashion Ltd* (1961) 30 DLR (2d) 527 (Nfld SC TD).

25. You and Terrence might be held liable if you directed the police to arrest Martin, rather than simply present the facts and allow them to make their own decision: *Valderhaug v Libin* (1954) 13 WWR 383 (Alta CA).

26. *Bahner v Marwest Hotel Ltd* (1969) 6 DLR (3d) 322 (BC SC); *Perry v Fried* (1972) 32 DLR (3d) 589 (Nfld SC TD).

Invasion of Privacy

Tort law protects your physical well-being through the actions in assault, battery, and false imprisonment. However, it does not provide as much protection for your privacy. There is no separate action for *invasion of privacy*. There are several reasons for that omission. The courts want to support freedom of expression and freedom of information. They find it difficult to define the concept of privacy in a way that strikes a fair balance between the parties. And they find it difficult to calculate compensatory damages for the kinds of harm, such as embarrassment, that an invasion of privacy usually causes.

there is no separate action for invasion of privacy

That is not to say that tort law does not provide any protection at all. Privacy is *indirectly* protected by several torts.

privacy is indirectly protected by several torts

- A photographer who sneaks onto someone's property to obtain candid pictures commits the tort of *trespass to land*.[27]

- An employee who publishes embarrassing details about their employer's private life may be held liable for *breach of confidence*.[28]

- A company that makes unauthorized use of a celebrity's image to sell its own products may commit the tort of *misappropriation of personality*.[29]

- A newspaper that ignores a judge's instructions and publishes the name of a police officer who had been sexually assaulted during an undercover investigation may commit the tort of *negligence*.[30]

Furthermore, the courts may be in the process of developing a new tort of invasion of privacy. For example, an Ontario judge imposed liability upon a couple who, as part of a petty feud, installed a surveillance camera that continuously monitored their neighbours' backyard. While recognizing that the law generally does not prohibit one person from watching another, the judge held that an intentional invasion of privacy will not be permitted.[31] Similarly, although the decision in Case Brief 10.4 was decided under Quebec's civil law and therefore is not directly applicable in Canada's other jurisdictions, it may also signal a new direction in the protection of privacy interests. If so, it will mean that certain types of businesses will have to change the way they operate.

the courts may be in the process of developing a special tort of invasion of privacy

CASE BRIEF 10.4

Aubry v Éditions Vice-Versa Inc (1998) 157 DLR (4th) 577 (SCC)

A photographer took a picture of a young woman sitting on the steps of a building in Montreal. When the photograph was published in an arts magazine, the young woman was teased by her school friends. She then brought an action against the photographer and the magazine for invasion of privacy.

A majority of the Supreme Court of Canada awarded $2000 to the young woman. It said that a balance must be struck, in light of the circumstances of each case, between the right to privacy and the right to freedom of expression. On the facts, the plaintiff's right was stronger, partially because she was identifiable and therefore should have been asked for her consent. The court was also influenced by the fact that the plaintiff was the primary subject of the photograph. She was not simply part of a larger image of a building or a crowd.

---

[27] The tort of trespass to land is considered later in this chapter.

[28] *Stephens v Avery* [1988] Ch 449. The action for breach of confidence is examined in Chapter 16.

[29] *Athans v Canadian Adventure Camps Ltd* (1977) 80 DLR (3d) 583 (Ont HCJ).

[30] In *LR v Nyp* (1995) 25 CCLT (2d) 309 (Ont Gen Div), the court was anxious to protect sexual assault victims from embarrassment by preserving their privacy. The tort of negligence is considered in Chapter 12.

[31] *Lipiec v Borsa* (1996) 31 CCLT (2d) 294 (Ont Gen Div).

several provinces have enacted legislation to protect privacy

Because the courts are moving slowly in this area, several provinces have legislation to protect privacy interests.[32] While those statutes vary from jurisdiction to jurisdiction, they generally impose liability if a person "wilfully" violates another's privacy by doing something that it knows to be wrong. The definition of "privacy" has been left open so that the courts have the flexibility needed to respond to different types of situations. Case Brief 10.5 illustrates the statutory action.

CASE BRIEF 10.5

Hollinsworth v BCTV [1999] 6 WWR 54 (BC CA)

The plaintiff entered into a contract with the defendant, Look International Enterprises (LIS), to have a hairpiece surgically attached to his scalp. Under the terms of that contract, LIS was allowed to videotape the procedure for instructional purposes only. Seven years later, without the plaintiff's knowledge, LIS allowed a television station to use the videotape during a news feature on hair grafts. When the station's reporter asked if the patient had consented to such use, LIS wrongly said, "Yes." The plaintiff suffered great embarrassment as a result of the broadcast. He sued both LIS and the television station under British Columbia's *Privacy Act*.

The court awarded damages of $15 000 against LIS for its "willful" invasion of privacy. The plaintiff's claim against the television station failed, however, because the station had not acted "wilfully." Given the information that its reporter had received from LIS, the station believed that the plaintiff had consented to the use of the videotape.

Trespass to Land

a trespass to land occurs when the defendant improperly interferes with the plaintiff's land

A **trespass to land** occurs when the defendant improperly interferes with the plaintiff's land. Interference can take several forms. A trespass is obviously committed if a vandal sneaks onto someone's property. However, the tort can also arise quite innocently. That is true, for instance, if I kick a ball into your yard (even if I do not walk onto your property to retrieve the ball), or if a lawn care company mistakenly cuts your grass instead of your neighbour's. If that seems surprising, remember our earlier discussion of "intention." It is enough if I intended to do the act, even if I did not intend to do wrong or to cause damage. The law wants to protect property interests. As the old saying goes, "A man's home is his castle."

a tort is not committed by a person who has authority to be on a property

The tort is not committed, however, by a person who has legal authority to be on a property. For example, police officers are entitled to enter premises under a search warrant. Likewise, a number of other public officials, such as building inspectors and meter readers, may do whatever is reasonably necessary to carry out their duties.

More significantly for our purposes, a trespass does not occur merely because a customer walks into a place of business during regular hours. Under normal circumstances, it is assumed that the business *consented* to the intrusion—indeed, it implicitly *invited* the customer onto the property. However, a business can usually revoke its consent, as long as it does not violate human rights legislation (for example, by excluding a person on racial grounds).[33]

---

32. *Privacy Act*, RSBC 1996, c 373 (BC); *The Privacy Act*, RSM 1987, c P125 (Man); *Privacy Act*, RSN 1990, c P-22 (Nfld); *Privacy Act*, RSS 1978, c P-24 (Sask).

33. The business will not always be able to revoke its consent. For example, a customer who has paid to attend a baseball game and has not broken any of the conditions attached to his ticket cannot be ejected merely because he refuses to show his ticket to an attendant during the game: *Davidson v Toronto Blue Jays Baseball Ltd* (1999) 170 DLR (4th) 559 (Ont Gen Div).

Consequently, the owner of a shopping mall is not required to allow mall employees to set up a picket line on its premises as part of a labour dispute.[34] Similarly, the owner of a racetrack may exclude a highly successful gambler.[35] And once a business has revoked its consent, a customer who remains on its property becomes a trespasser. If the customer still refuses to leave, the business may use reasonable force to eject them. However, as we discussed under the tort of battery, it should be very careful when doing so.

The usual remedy for a trespass to land is compensation for the harm that it caused. However, a court may also award nominal damage if there was no loss, or punitive damages if the defendant's conduct was shockingly bad. Furthermore, if the defendant's wrong is ongoing, the plaintiff may be entitled to an injunction to stop the trespass. For example, if a company constructs a billboard on a person's land without permission, the judge will likely demand that it be torn down. In some circumstances, however, the courts are faced with a difficult choice between protecting the plaintiff's property interests and avoiding economic waste. In deciding whether to grant an injunction, a judge will consider a number of factors, including the defendant's motivation for committing the wrong, the extent to which monetary damages would adequately protect the plaintiff, and the costs associated with removing the trespass. How would you decide the case in You Be the Judge 10.2?

YOU BE THE JUDGE 10.2

Trespass to Land and Injunctions

Vista Inc, a real estate developer, built a 20-storey apartment complex. Unfortunately, as a result of an innocent error, a corner of the building extends two metres onto the neighbouring lot, which is owned by Paolo. Vista admits that it committed the tort of trespass and it is willing to either pay compensatory damages or buy the affected land from Paolo. Paolo, however, insists that he should be able to exercise complete control over his property. He therefore wants an injunction to prevent Vista's ongoing trespass. To do so, Vista would have to tear down a substantial part of its building.

Questions for Discussion

1. Would you grant the injunction?
2. Would your answer be different if the cost of removing the trespassing portion of the apartment complex was $50 000? What if it was $5 000 000?
3. Would your answer be different if Paolo suffered no financial loss as a result of the trespass? What if, for some reason, he suffered a substantial loss of $50 000 or $5 000 000? What if he was simply very upset that his rights had been infringed?
4. Would your answer be different if Vista had committed the trespass on purpose? What if Vista knew at the outset that it was committing a tort but was confident that, even if Paolo noticed the trespass, a court would award only nominal damages for the minor infringement?

Interference with Chattels

Tort law protects not only land, but also *chattels*. **Chattels** are moveable forms of property, such as horses, books, and cars. The rules are quite complicated, largely because the courts have developed a number of torts to protect chattels. We will outline the most important of those torts:

chattels are moveable forms of property

---

34. *Harrison v Carswell* (1975) 62 DLR (3d) 68 (SCC). In some provinces, legislation now allows picketing in such circumstances: for example, *Petty Trespasses Act*, RSM 1987, c P-150 (Man).

35. *Russo v Ontario Jockey Club* (1987) 46 DLR (4th) 359 (Ont HCJ).

- trespass to chattels
- conversion
- detinue

Concept Summary 10.2 lists the essential features of those torts.

Concept Summary 10.2

Intentional Interference with Chattels

Tort	Basis of the Tort	General Remedy
trespass to chattels	defendant's interference with chattels in plaintiff's possession	compensation for loss
conversion	defendant's interference with chattels in plaintiff's possession —serious enough to justify forced sale	forced sale of chattel from plaintiff to defendant
detinue	defendant's failure to return chattels that plainiff has right to possess	compensation for loss or return of chattels

trespass to chattels occurs when the defendant interferes with chattels in the plaintiff's possession

Trespass to chattels occurs when the defendant interferes with chattels in the plaintiff's possession. The element of interference is satisfied if the defendant damages, destroys, takes, or uses the plaintiff's goods. There may even be a trespass if the defendant merely touches the plaintiff's property, at least if that property is, for example, a priceless painting that requires protection.[36] As a general rule, the remedy for trespass to chattels is compensatory damages.[37] Consequently, if you completely destroyed my car, you would be required to pay the vehicle's market value. In contrast, if you merely damaged my car, you would be required to pay either for the value that it lost or for its repairs, whichever is less.

conversion occurs when the defendant interferes with the plaintiff's chattels in a way that is seriousness enough to justify a forced sale

The tort of **conversion** occurs when the defendant interferes with the plaintiff's chattels in a way that is serious enough to justify a forced sale. That may be true if the defendant takes, detains, uses, buys, sells, damages, or destroys the plaintiff's property. If so, the defendant will be required to buy the item by paying the market value that the chattel had at the time of the tort. In exchange for that payment, the defendant acquires the property.

The main difficulty with the tort of conversion is that there is no clear test for determining whether a particular defendant's actions are serious enough to justify a forced sale. The courts consider all of the facts, including:

- the extent to which the defendant exercised ownership or control over the chattel
- the extent to which the defendant intended to assert a right that was inconsistent with the plaintiff's right to the property
- the duration of the defendant's interference
- the expense and inconvenience caused to the plaintiff[38]

Conversion is clearly committed if a thief steals my property or if a vandal destroys it. The tort may also occur if you habitually use my umbrella without my permission, but not if you use it only once because you were caught in a downpour.[39]

[36.] JG Fleming *The Law of Torts* 9th ed (1998) at 59.

[37.] In exceptional cases, the plaintiff may receive nominal damages or punitive damages.

[38.] W Prosser "The Nature of Conversion" (1957) 42 Cornell LQ 168 at 174.

[39.] *Canadian Orchestraphone Ltd v British Canadian Trust Co* [1932] 2 WWR 618 (Alta CA).

Once again, the tort may be committed even if the defendant did not intend to do anything wrong. It is enough, for instance, that you intended to exercise control over my property, even if you thought that you were entitled to do so. That rule presents a particular danger for business people. As a matter of risk management, it means that you should use every reasonable effort to ensure that you buy goods from people who are actually entitled to sell them. And even that may not be enough to protect you from liability. Ethical Perspective 10.2 illustrates the rules.

ETHICAL PERSPECTIVE 10.2

Conversion and Innocent Purchasers[40]

John stole a herd of cattle from Katherine and sold the animals to you for $50 000. Before you paid, you checked the cattle and noticed that they were not branded. You also asked John about the herd and were convinced that he owned the animals. Unfortunately, he has disappeared, and Katherine has sued you for conversion. You protest that you had acted honestly.

While an unsuspecting buyer or seller of goods is sometimes protected by a special defence, a court would probably hold you liable for conversion. In buying the cattle and treating them as your own, you seriously interfered with Katherine's rights. Consequently, you would have to pay her $50 000, which was the market value of the animals. Note that while you will be entitled to keep the herd, you have now paid $100 000 for it. You could try to recover $50 000 from John, but he has disappeared, as rogues often do.

Questions for Discussion

1. Are the rules for conversion fair?
2. Why do you think that the law of conversion is so strict?

The tort of **detinue** occurs when the defendant fails to return a chattel that the plaintiff is entitled to possess. The word "detinue" is derived from the old French word "*detenue*," which means detention. Because the tort is based on a wrongful detention, the plaintiff is normally required to demand possession of the property before bringing an action. That requirement is removed, however, if the demand would obviously be refused. The fact that detinue consists of a wrongful detention also affects the remedies that may be available to a plaintiff. First, the tort comes to an end as soon as the defendant returns the property to the plaintiff. At that point, the plaintiff is normally limited to compensation for losses that it suffered during the detention, as well as for any harm done to the item. Second, if the property has not been returned by the time of trial, the plaintiff can ask the court to compel the defendant to do so.[41] The court usually gives the defendant the option of either giving the property back or paying damages. However, the judge may require the property to be returned if it is special or if damages would not satisfy the plaintiff.

Detinue is the only tort that generally allows a court to order the defendant to return a chattel to the plaintiff. However, if I take your property, you may be entitled to exercise a right of *recaption* on your own. **Recaption** occurs when a party takes its own property back. It should be done very carefully. While you may be entitled to recover your property, you cannot use unreasonable force in doing so. If you are overly aggressive, you may end up committing a tort, such as battery.

detinue occurs when the defendant fails to return a chattel that the plaintiff is entitled to possess

a person who has committed the tort of detinue may be ordered to return the property to the plaintiff

recaption occurs when a party takes its own property back

---

40. *Nilsson Bros Inc v McNamara Estate* [1992] 3 WWR 761 (Alta CA).

41. That option does not exist under trespass to chattels or conversion. Those torts generally only support monetary damages.

Chapter Summary

A tort generally consists of a failure to fulfill a private obligation that was imposed by law. It is important to distinguish between tort and crimes. Torts involve private obligations; crimes involve public obligations. It also is important to distinguish between torts and contracts. Torts generally involve obligations imposed by law; contracts generally involve obligations that the parties voluntarily create for themselves.

Liability insurance is a contract in which an insurance company agrees, in exchange for a price, to pay damages on behalf of a person who incurs liability. It is critically important in tort law, especially in the business context. Liability insurance furthers tort law's compensatory function, but undermines its deterrence function.

Even if an employer did nothing wrong, it may be held vicariously liable for a tort committed by its employee.

The victim of a tort usually receives compensatory damages. Compensation in tort looks backward. It is intended to place the plaintiff in the position that that party enjoyed before the tort occurred. It is not available for losses that are remote or for losses that the plaintiff failed to mitigate. In unusual situations, a court may award punitive damages or nominal damages, or impose an injunction.

The tort system does not provide compensation to people whose injuries are innocently caused. It is also expensive and inefficient. Therefore, alternative compensation schemes have been introduced in some jurisdictions for some purposes.

Intentional torts involve intentional conduct. It is enough if the defendant knew that particular conduct would have particular consequences. The plaintiff does not have to prove that the defendant intended either to cause harm or commit a tort.

Several types of intentional torts may be committed against a person. An assault occurs when the defendant intentionally causes the plaintiff to reasonably believe that offensive bodily contact is imminent. A battery consists of offensive bodily contact. False imprisonment occurs when a person is confined within a fixed area without justification. There is no intentional tort of invasion of privacy. The courts may, however, be in the process of developing one. A number of other torts indirectly protect privacy interests.

There are several types of intentional torts that may be committed against a person's property. Trespass to land occurs when the defendant improperly interferes with land that the plaintiff possesses. Trespass to chattels occurs when the defendant interferes with chattels that the plaintiff possesses. Conversion occurs when the defendant interferes with the plaintiff's chattels in a way that is serious enough to justify a forced sale. Detinue occurs when the defendant fails to return goods that the plaintiff has the right to possess. In some circumstances, a person may be entitled to recover property by recaption.

Review Questions

1. What is a tort? How does a tort differ from a crime? How are tort obligations different from contractual obligations?

2. What is the role of liability insurance in tort law? Does liability insurance serve the functions of tort law?

3. What is the difference between "vicarious liability" and "personal liability"?

4. When will an employer be held vicariously liable for torts committed by its employees? When will an employer be held vicariously liable for torts committed by its independent contractors?

5. How does the vicarious liability of an employer affect the personal liability of an employee?

6. Are compensatory damages calculated in the same way in both tort and contract? Explain your answer.

7. What are "alternative compensation schemes"? From the perspective of an injured person, how are such schemes more favourable than tort law? How are they less favourable?

8. In what sense do the intentional torts require intentional conduct? Is tort law's definition of "intention" fair? Explain your answer.

9. Explain the difference between assault and battery. Describe a situation in which there is an assault but not a battery. Describe a situation in which there is a battery but not an assault.

10. "A business person is at liberty to use any amount of force to remove an undesirable customer." Is that statement true? As a business person, what factors would you consider before removing a customer from your place of business?

11. Does a false imprisonment always occur when people are detained against their wishes? If not, list situations in which the tort is not committed despite a detention.

12. Do police officers, security guards, and private citizens have the same rights when it comes to arresting criminals and suspected criminals? Explain the special dangers that arise when a business person arrests a suspected shoplifter.

13. Is it generally possible for a restaurant owner to arrest a person who refuses to pay the full amount of a bill? Explain your answer.

14. Does tort law recognize a special claim for invasion of privacy? Explain your answer.

15. Describe how privacy statutes generally operate.

16. List four ways in which tort law indirectly protects privacy.

17. When will a court impose an injunction to stop a continuing trespass to land?

18. Explain the special dangers that the tort of conversion presents when a business person buys chattels.

19. Describe the special remedy that is available for detinue but not for trespass to chattels or conversion?

20. What is a "right of recaption"?

Cases and Problems

1. Rick, who operates a tavern, hired Ugarte to work as a bouncer. As Rick was leaving early one evening, he drew Ugarte's attention to a table of rowdy drinkers that included a woman named Ilsa. Rick, knowing that his employee had a tendency to violently overreact to stressful situations, instructed Ugarte to refrain from using physical force if the situation got out of hand. As the hours passed, however, Ilsa and her friends grew increasingly obnoxious, and Ugarte grew increasingly agitated. Ugarte eventually snapped and attempted to forcibly remove Ilsa. In the course of doing so, he pushed her down a flight of stairs, and she suffered extensive injuries. While it is quite clear that Ugarte committed the tort of battery against Ilsa, she has little interest in suing him because she knows that he is virtually penniless. Rick, in contrast, is widely known to have a great deal of money. Is there any way that Ilsa can sue Rick? Explain your answer.

2. Mei, who works in a car factory, was seriously injured as a result of a tort that was committed by Tom, a fellow employee. Is Mei entitled to sue Tom in tort for compensatory damages? If not, is she entitled to receive compensation from any other source? Explain your answer.

3. Stella is a frail, elderly woman. She was awakened at 5:00 am by her neighbour, Stanley, whom she heard shouting. She angrily got dressed, went next door, and loudly banged on his front door. Stanley opened the door and rudely asked Stella what she wanted. When she told him that he was making too much noise, he told her to mind her own business and began to shut his door. At that point, Stella raised a baseball bat that she had brought with her and said, "Lucky for you that I went to bed early last night. Otherwise, I'd hit you with this thing right now." Stanley snorted, "As if you could do any harm," and shut his door. After discussing the incident with his buddies the next day, Stanley decided to bring a tort action against Stella as a matter of principle. Has Stella committed an intentional tort? If so, what damages would Stanley likely receive?

4. During an office party, Sonny saw his friend Fredo standing near the railing of a stairwell. Wanting to scare Fredo as a joke, Sonny sneaked up and gave him a gentle push from behind. Unfortunately, while Sonny had intended to grab his friend to prevent him from falling over the railing, he lost his grip on Fredo's jacket. Fredo fell forward, tumbled over the railing, and suffered severe injuries when he hit the landing below. Angry over the incident, Fredo has ended the friendship and insists that Sonny should have to pay his medical bills. Sonny feels bad about the situation but insists that since he never intended to do any harm, he should not be held responsible. Can Sonny be held liable to Fredo for an intentional tort? Explain your answer.

5. The Oxbridge Rowing Association (ORA) arranged to hold a race on the river running through the city of Camford. It received the city's permission to use a section of the riverbank to erect a grandstand and charge an admission fee to the public. On the day of the race, the ORA, with the city's permission, used a barricade to block off a section of the footpath that normally allowed the public to stroll along the riverbank. Shortly before the race was to start, Regina, a member of the ORA, noticed that Henley, who was in the regular habit of strolling along the river in the morning, was climbing over the barricade. Regina explained the situation to Henley and informed him that a detour had been set up that would allow members of the public to walk along another portion of the riverbank. Henley objected, saying that he wanted to follow his usual route. When he tried to press forward, Regina politely but firmly stood her ground. At that point, Henley declared, "You have no right to hold me here. I will stand here all day if you force me to do so, but mark my words, I will get through eventually." Regina responded by saying, "You can stand there if you want to, or you can use the detour if you want to, but I will not let you through until the race is over." True to her word, Regina continued to block Henley's way until the race finished. At that point, she stepped aside and allowed him to proceed along his usual route. Henley has now sued Regina for false imprisonment. He insists that she detained him when she would not allow him to walk where he wanted to walk. Is he correct? Explain your answer.

6. As part of a promotional campaign, the Blacksox Baseball Club ran an advertisement in a local newspaper that featured a picture of about three dozen fans who were cheering wildly at a recent home game. In one corner of the picture, a man and a woman were hugging and kissing, apparently delighted with their team's success. The man's wife, however, knew better. When she saw the photo, she realized that her husband had resumed an affair with a woman he had promised to never see again. Angry that the Blacksox had exposed his infidelity, the man wants to sue the organization for invasion of privacy. Assuming that no relevant conditions were attached to the ticket that the man had purchased, and assuming that the relevant

events occurred in Alberta, can he successfully bring an action against the team on the basis of an intentional tort? Explain your answer.

7. Indira, an employee of Speedit Delivery Service, left a package at the front door of 57 Rollingwood Drive. In fact, she was supposed to leave it at the front door of 75 Rollingwood Drive. Late that night, when Anton arrived home at 57 Rollingwood Drive, he tripped over the box and suffered serious injuries. Is he entitled to sue for an intentional tort? If so, whom should he sue? Explain your answer.

8. Elaine and Latka each operate a stall in a market. During a particularly busy day, Elaine noticed that she had nearly run out of coins. She normally walked to a nearby bank to obtain change. However, since business was so brisk, she did not want to leave her stall unattended for long. She went to Latka's stand to ask if she could borrow his vehicle. He was out for lunch, but she noticed that he had left his car keys under his counter. While she did not really know Latka very well, Elaine assumed that he would not mind if she borrowed his car for a few minutes. When she returned, however, Latka was furious to learn that she had taken his car without permission. Has Elaine committed an intentional tort? If so, which one? Explain the remedy that Latka may receive.

9. Basil, who operated a small hotel in Banff, was excited to learn that the town had been chosen to host a major conference of environmentalists during the off-season. At that time of year, most of his rooms were usually vacant. The event's organizers announced that they would visit hotels on a particular day to decide where to lodge delegates during the conference. Basil consequently spent a great deal of time and money improving his facilities. Unfortunately, his neighbour, Sybil, noticed his preparations. Shortly before the organizers were scheduled to arrive in town, and while Basil was temporarily away on business, Sybil constructed a shed out of biologically hazardous and non-recyclable materials. She acted purely out of spite. She wanted to upset the environmentalists and ensure that Basil's hotel was not chosen for the conference. Her ploy worked. The organizers were thoroughly offended by the sight of the structure. Consequently, while they were otherwise impressed with Basil's facilities, they refused to award a contract to him. Basil is very upset with Sybil, especially since he discovered that she intentionally had constructed much of the building on his property. Has Sybil committed an intentional tort? If so, what remedies are available to Basil?

10. Felicity and Oscar formerly operated a travel agency together. As a result of an unpleasant disagreement over the future of the business, however, Oscar brought the relationship to an end. While he was willing to leave the shop premises to Felicity, he took a number of items, including a tank full of goldfish. Although she is happy to get along without most of those items, she is very upset about the goldfish because she loves them dearly. Oscar agrees that the fish belong to Felicity, but he refuses to return them to her. Has Oscar committed any intentional torts? Which tort should Felicity use? Explain your answer.

11. Madeleine sees Hugh stealing her car. Because she does not know who he is or where he lives, she realizes that she would have little chance of successfully suing him in tort. She also realizes that if she does not act immediately, she may lose her car permanently. What can Madeleine do?

12. Mary operates a convenience store. Much to her dismay, it has become a hangout for teenagers. She hired Frank to act as a security guard between the hours of 3:00 and 5:00 pm, when the store is at its busiest. Mary noticed that a young woman named Shelley, whom she had previously suspected of shoplifting, was acting suspiciously. She notified Frank, who approached Shelley and said in a loud voice and an accusing tone, "Come here. I've got a few questions to ask you." Shelley realized that Frank was acting on instructions from his employer and shouted over his shoulder at Mary, "If you've got a problem, come over here and speak to me yourself! I'll smack you silly!" At that point, Frank lunged at Shelley in an attempt to determine whether she was concealing stolen goods in her jacket. He grabbed her arm, but she managed to wrestle free and run out of the store. A number of Shelley's classmates saw the fracas and later teased her about it. Angry that Frank and Mary had humiliated her, Shelley returned to the street outside the store later that night and threw a garbage can through the shop window. Discuss the intentional torts that the parties may have committed.

11

Miscellaneous Torts
Affecting Business

CHAPTER OVERVIEW

Intimidation

Interference with Contractual
  Relations

Conspiracy

Deceit

Occupiers' Liability
Common Law Rules
Statutory Rules

Nuisance
Defences to Nuisance
Remedies for Nuisance

The Rule in *Rylands v
  Fletcher*

Defamation
Defences to Defamation
Remedies for Defamation

OBJECTIVES

After completing this chapter, you should be able to:

1. Explain the two ways in which a business can commit the tort of intimidation.
2. Distinguish between direct inducement to breach of contract and indirect inducement to breach of contract.
3. Describe the tort of conspiracy and explain the risks that arise when two or more companies plot together against another business.
4. Outline the elements of the tort of deceit.
5. Use the tort of deceit to explain the difference between compensation in tort and compensation in contract.
6. Explain the rules that apply to occupiers' liability in your province or territory.
7. Outline the range of situations in which the courts may impose liability on a business for committing the tort of nuisance.
8. Describe the elements of the rule in *Rylands v Fletcher* and explain how that tort involves strict liability.
9. Explain why businesses are frequently in danger of committing the tort of defamation.
10. Describe the three main defences to the tort of defamation.

In Chapter 10, we began our consideration of tort law by examining several intentional torts that commonly affect business people. In this chapter, we continue our discussion by looking at a number of torts that are also important in the business context:

■ intimidation

■ interference with contractual relations conspiracy

■ deceit

■ occupiers' liability

■ nuisance

■ the rule in *Rylands v Fletcher*

■ defamation

Because we are considering a large number of topics in this chapter, we cannot examine every issue in great detail. As always, our primary goal is to identify situations in which business people should think carefully about risk management. Note that a number of other tort-like actions, such as breach of confidence and breach of fiduciary duty, are examined later in this book.

INTIMIDATION

The tort of *intimidation* is concerned with unethical business practices. **Intimidation** occurs when the plaintiff suffers a loss as a result of the defendant's threat to commit an unlawful act against either the plaintiff or a third party. As that definition suggests, the tort of intimidation has two branches, which are represented in Figure 11.1.

intimidation occurs when the plaintiff suffers a loss as a result of the defendant's threat to commit an unlawful act against either the plaintiff or a third party

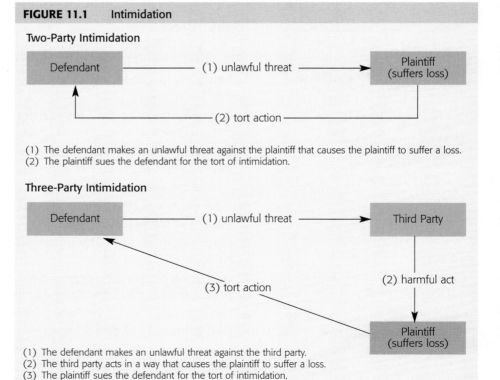

FIGURE 11.1   Intimidation

Two-Party Intimidation

(1) The defendant makes an unlawful threat against the plaintiff that causes the plaintiff to suffer a loss.
(2) The plaintiff sues the defendant for the tort of intimidation.

Three-Party Intimidation

(1) The defendant makes an unlawful threat against the third party.
(2) The third party acts in a way that causes the plaintiff to suffer a loss.
(3) The plaintiff sues the defendant for the tort of intimidation.

- **Two-party intimidation** occurs when the defendant directly coerces the plaintiff into suffering a loss. For example, the manager of a supermarket might use threats of physical violence to frighten the owner of a small convenience store into closing down.

- **Three-party intimidation** occurs when the defendant coerces a third party into acting in a way that hurts the plaintiff. In the leading case of *Rookes v Barnard*, the plaintiff was an employee of an airline.[1] The defendant, a trade union, was angry with him as a result of a labour dispute. The union threatened the airline with an illegal strike unless it fired the plaintiff. The plaintiff successfully sued the defendant after the airline gave in to that pressure and fired him.

two-party intimidation occurs when the plaintiff is directly coerced into suffering a loss

three-party intimidation occurs when the defendant coerces a third party into acting in a way that hurts the plaintiff

Whether intimidation involves two or three parties, the basic rules remain the same. First, the plaintiff must prove that the defendant threatened to commit an unlawful act, such as a crime, a tort, or even a breach of contract.[2] Second, the tort does not occur unless the threatened party submitted to the intimidation. For example, the plaintiff would not have won in *Rookes* if the airline had ignored the union's threat. Third, as long as the other elements of the tort are established, there is no need to prove that the defendant intended to hurt the plaintiff. For instance, intimidation may occur even if the tortfeasor was motivated by a desire to benefit itself, rather than injure the plaintiff.

INTERFERENCE WITH CONTRACTUAL RELATIONS

One of the most effective ways of gaining an advantage over a competitor in the business world is to hire away its best workers or otherwise prevent those people from performing their jobs, especially in professions and industries that employ highly skilled personnel. However, that tactic can trigger the tort of *interference with contractual relations*. As its name suggests, **interference with contractual relations** occurs when the defendant disrupts a contract that exists between the plaintiff and a third party. Figure 11.2 illustrates its two main possibilities:

interference with contractual relations occurs when the defendant disrupts a contract that the plaintiff has with another party

- direct inducement to breach of contract
- indirect inducement to breach of contract

---

[1] *Rookes v Barnard* [1964] AC 1129 (HL).

[2] It is not clear if two-party intimidation can ever be based on the defendant's threat to break a contract with the plaintiff. The courts have sometimes said that the plaintiff should resist that sort of pressure by simply suing for breach of contract. That tactic is not possible in a three-party situation since the plaintiff cannot sue on a contract that exists between the defendant and the third party. Furthermore, the Supreme Court of Canada has indicated that a threat to break a contract is not intimidation in either a two-part or a three-party situation if the defendant reasonably believed that such a threat was lawful: *Central Canada Potash Co v Saskatchewan* (1978) 88 DLR (3d) 609 (SCC).

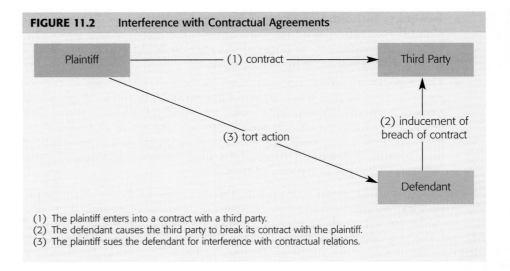

FIGURE 11.2   Interference with Contractual Agreements

(1) The plaintiff enters into a contract with a third party.
(2) The defendant causes the third party to break its contract with the plaintiff.
(3) The plaintiff sues the defendant for interference with contractual relations.

a direct inducement to breach of contract occurs when the defendant directly persuades a third party to break its contract with the plaintiff

A **direct inducement to breach of contract** occurs when the defendant directly persuades a third party to break its contract with the plaintiff. Liability requires four factors.

- First, the defendant must have *known about the contract* that existed between the third party and the plaintiff. The defendant does not, however, have to know all of the details.

- Second, the defendant must have *intended to cause* the third party to breach that contract. However, the defendant does not have to intend to hurt the plaintiff. The tort may be committed even if the defendant was motivated by a desire to benefit itself.

- Third, the defendant must have *actually caused* the third party to break its contract with the plaintiff. For instance, the defendant might hire the third party in a way that makes it impossible for that person to work for the plaintiff. The issue is much more difficult, however, if the defendant simply *informed* the third party about the advantages and disadvantages of working for the plaintiff. In that situation, the judge will ask whether the defendant actually *encouraged* the third party to commit a breach of contract.

- Fourth, the plaintiff must have suffered a *loss* as a result of the defendant's conduct. In most cases, that requirement is satisfied by the fact that the third party did not perform its contract with the plaintiff.

Note that in addition to suing the defendant in *tort* for inducing breach of contract, the plaintiff can also sue the third party in *contract* for the actual breach. However, the plaintiff cannot recover full damages under both actions.[3] Finally, if the defendant's conduct is particularly outrageous, the plaintiff may be entitled to recover punitive damages, as well as compensatory damages, under the tort.

Case Brief 11.1 illustrates the rules for inducing breach of contract.

[3.] We discussed the possibility of concurrent actions in tort and contract in Chapter 10.

CASE BRIEF 11.1

Lumley v Gye (1853) 118 ER 749 (QB)

An opera singer named Johanna Wagner agreed to sing for one season with the plaintiff's company, Her Majesty's Theatre. The defendant persuaded Miss Wagner to break that contract by offering to pay her a higher fee to sing with his company, the Royal Italian Opera. The plaintiff suffered a financial loss as a result of losing Miss Wagner's services. Therefore he sued the defendant for inducing breach of contract.

The court upheld the claim. The defendant knew about Miss Wagner's agreement with the plaintiff and intentionally persuaded her to break that contract. The defendant therefore was liable to compensate the plaintiff for the losses that occurred when the diva failed to honour her contract. Furthermore, in another case arising from of the same facts, the court awarded an injunction to prevent Miss Wagner from singing for the defendant's company.[4]

As we have seen, a tort may be committed if the defendant *directly* interferes with a contract that exists between the plaintiff and a third party. A tort can also be committed through *indirect* interference. An **indirect inducement to breach of contract** occurs when the defendant indirectly persuades a third party to break its contract with the plaintiff.[5] For example, the defendant may physically prevent the third party from going to work or steal tools that the third party needs to perform the contract with the plaintiff. Liability depends upon the same four factors that we have discussed *plus* proof that the defendant's actions were themselves *unlawful*.[6] Consequently, the tort may be committed if the defendant illegally detains the third party or steals that person's tools. But the tort is not committed if, for instance, a union (the defendant) calls a legal strike that causes a company (the third party) to breach its contract with a customer (the plaintiff).

an indirect inducement to breach of contract occurs when the defendant indirectly persuades a third party to break its contract with the plaintiff

CONSPIRACY

One person is generally entitled to use lawful actions to economically hurt another.[7] Curiously, however, those same lawful actions may be tortious if they are undertaken by *several people*. The tort of **conspiracy** usually occurs when two or more defendants agree to act together with the primary purpose of causing a financial loss to the plaintiff. The lesson is clear. While the law generally condones aggressive competition between individuals, its sense of fair play may be offended if several people conspire against another.

conspiracy usually occurs when two or more people agree to act together with the primary purpose of causing the plaintiff to suffer a financial loss

The tort of conspiracy is hard to establish. The courts are reluctant to find that the defendants co-operated for the *primary purpose* of hurting the plaintiff. For example, in one recent case, a number of people organized a consumer boycott of a paper company's products to draw attention to Aboriginal land claims.[8] Although the company lost a lot of money when many of its customers were persuaded to buy elsewhere, its tort action against the boycott organizers

---

4. *Lumley v Wagner* (1852) 42 ER 687 (Ch D).

5. *DC Thompson & Co Ltd v Deakin* [1952] Ch 646 (CA).

6. Note that the defendant must have intended to induce a breach of contract, even if it did not intend to hurt the plaintiff.

7. *Allen v Flood* [1898] AC 1 (HL). Chapter 23 discusses statutes controlling unfair business practices that improperly affect competition.

8. *Daishowa Inc v Friends of the Lubicon* (1998) 158 DLR (4th) 699 (Ont Gen Div).

failed. The court held that the protestors' main purpose was not to hurt the company, but rather to raise public awareness of a political issue.

The tort of conspiracy raises difficult issues, both legally and ethically. Consider Ethical Perspective 11.1.

ETHICAL PERSPECTIVE 11.1

Conspiracy to Injure Plaintiff by Lawful Means

Do the rules governing the tort of conspiracy make sense from an ethical or legal point of view?

Questions for Discussion

1. Should a single person, acting alone, be entitled to intentionally hurt another person's business interests, as long as lawful means are used? What arguments can be made for and against the current law?

2. If it is ethically permissible for one person, acting alone, to intentionally harm another person's economic interests, why should the situation be any different merely because several people act together to achieve the same result? Is the plaintiff more vulnerable if it is targeted by a single, but enormous, multinational corporation, rather than two small local businesses?

We have seen that conspiracy is hard to prove if the defendants injured the plaintiff by acting in an otherwise *lawful* way. The rules are different if the defendants injured the plaintiff by conspiring to perform an *unlawful* act. For instance, they might agree to commit a tort, or to violate the *Criminal Code*, labour relations legislation, or licensing regulations.[9] In that situation, the court does not have to be satisfied that the defendants' *primary purpose* was to hurt the plaintiff. It is enough if the defendants *should have known* that their actions might have that result.[10]

DECEIT

The law also encourages ethical behaviour in the business world through the tort of *deceit*.[11] **Deceit** occurs if the defendant makes a false statement, which it knows to be untrue, with which it intends to mislead the plaintiff, and which causes the plaintiff to suffer a loss.[12] There are four parts to that definition.

First, the defendant must make a *false statement*. That requirement is easily met if the defendant says or writes something that is positively untrue. However, it may also be satisfied in other ways.

- The defendant may be held liable for a *half-truth*. For example, if I am selling my business to you, I may present figures representing gross profits as if they reflect net profits.

- The defendant may be held liable for *failing to update information*. For example, if I am selling my business to you, I may provide information that is accurate when I give it, but that later becomes inaccurate because of a dramatic change in the market. If that change happens before our

deceit occurs if the defendant makes a false statement, which it knows to be untrue, with which it intends to mislead the plaintiff, and which causes the plaintiff to suffer a loss

for deceit to occur, the defendant must make a false statement

---

[9.] If the unlawful act also constitutes a separate tort, such as deceit, the plaintiff can bring an action in that tort, without relying on the tort of conspiracy.

[10.] *Canada Cement LaFarge Ltd v BC Lightweight Aggregate Ltd* (1983) 145 DLR (3d) 385 (SCC).

[11.] Chapter 4 discussed how the concept of fraud or deceit is important in the law of contract. For example, it may allow one party to rescind an agreement.

[12.] *Derry v Peek* (1889) 14 App Cas 337 (HL).

deal closes, I may have to tell you about it. If I do not, my silence may amount to a representation that the circumstances have stayed the same.

- The general rule in the commercial world is *caveat emptor*: "let the buyer beware." Consequently, the seller is usually not obligated to volunteer information. The buyer is responsible for asking questions and making investigations. There are, however, exceptions to that rule. For instance, if I am selling a house to you, I am required to warn you about hidden defects that make the building dangerous or unfit for habitation. If I fail to do so, I may be held liable for silently deceiving you.

The lesson is clear. As a matter of risk management, business people must not only avoid lying; they must also avoid creating the wrong perception.

Second, the defendant must *know*, at the time of making a statement, that it is false. It is enough if the defendant acted recklessly, without regard to the truth. But it is not enough if the defendant was merely careless.[13]

Third, the defendant must make the statement with the *intention of misleading* the plaintiff. The statement does not have to made directly to the plaintiff. However, the court must be satisfied that the defendant intended to deceive the plaintiff, or at least was substantially certain that the plaintiff would be misled. Suppose that you and I are involved in complex commercial negotiations. I may be liable for deceit if I make a false statement to your banker with the intention of tricking you into signing a contract.

Fourth, the plaintiff must suffer a *loss* as a result of *reasonably relying* upon the defendant's statement. The plaintiff's reliance is "reasonable" if a reasonable person might have reacted to the defendant's statement in the same way. That rule has several consequences.

- The defendant's statement normally has to refer to a *past or present fact*. Liability is usually not possible if the defendant offered an opinion, predicted the future, or made the sort of boastful claim (called a "puff") that salespeople often make. Reasonable people do not rely on those kinds of statements.

- Occasionally, however, a statement of fact may be *implied* by an opinion, a prediction, or a puff. Suppose that I persuade you to buy my car by lying: "This little miser will go 300 kilometres between fill-ups." A court might find that my prediction includes a statement of existing fact regarding the vehicle's current rate of gas consumption.

In terms of remedies, it is important to remember that we are dealing with a tort, rather than a breach of contract. As we saw in You Be the Judge 10.1, that means that compensatory damages look backward, rather than forward. The plaintiff is entitled to be put into the position that it would have enjoyed if the defendant had not lied, not into the position that it would have enjoyed if the defendant's statement had been true. Suppose that I tricked you into buying an apartment complex from me for $600 000. The building is actually worth $500 000. But if my deceitful statement had been true, it would have been worth $750 000. In tort, you are entitled to $100 000, not $250 000.

for deceit to occur, the defendant must know that the statement is false

for deceit to occur, the defendant must intend to mislead the plaintiff

for deceit to occur, plaintiff must suffer a loss as a result of reasonably relying upon the defendant's statement

OCCUPIERS' LIABILITY

The tort of **occupiers' liability** requires an occupier of premises to protect visitors from harm.

occupiers' liability requires an occupier of premises to protect visitors from harm

---

13. Chapter 12 discusses how the plaintiff may be held liable under the tort of negligence as a result of carelessly making a false statement.

an occupier is any person who has substantial control over premises

a visitor is any person who enters onto premises

premises include more than land

- An **occupier** is any person who has substantial control over premises. Note that the critical element is *control*, not *ownership*. A tenant, for instance, can control an apartment without owning it.
- A **visitor** is any person who enters onto premises. We will discuss different types of visitors later.
- **Premises** include more than land. Apartments and offices certainly count, but occasionally, so do elevators, vehicles, ships, trains, and airplanes. The scope of occupiers' liability is therefore quite wide and potentially very dangerous for business people.[14] Although there has been a sharp rise in electronic commerce, most businesses still occupy premises that are visited by customers, suppliers, sales representatives, cleaners, government officials, trespassers, and so on. If one of those visitors trips over a step, slips on spilled food, falls through a decrepit floorboard, crashes into a plate-glass window, or is beaten by another visitor, the business may be held liable as result of being the occupier.

The law of occupiers' liability is complicated, partly because it differs between jurisdictions. Legislation has been enacted in some places, but not others. We will therefore separately consider:

- the common law rules (which were made by judges)
- the statutory rules (which were made by legislators)

Common Law Rules

the traditional common law rules are based on categories of visitors and obligations

The traditional common law rules are based a system of categories. Broadly speaking, there are four types of visitors:

- *trespassers*, who do not have permission to enter the premises (for example, burglars)
- *licensees*, who have permission to enter the premises, but who do not further the occupier's economic interests (for example, social guests)
- *invitees*, who have permission to enter the premises and who further the occupier's economic interests (for example, business customers)
- *contractual entrants*, who enter into a contract to use the premises, rather than to receive services that are offered on the premises (for example, hotel guests, but not restaurant diners)

Historically, a different obligation was owed to each type of visitor:

- an occupier was not allowed to *intentionally or recklessly injure* a trespasser (for example, by setting a trap for burglars)
- an occupier was required to protect a licensee from *hidden dangers* that were *actually known* to the occupier
- an occupier was required to take reasonable care to protect an invitee from *unusual dangers* that the occupier *knew or should have known* about
- an occupier owed a contractual obligation to a contractual entrant to make sure that the premises were as *safe as reasonably possible*

---

14. The law of occupiers' liability is not restricted to the business world. Any person who controls premises (including residential premises) falls within the tort.

There are a number of problems with that traditional system.

- First, it can lump together different types of people. For example, a person who breaks into an office is a trespasser, but so is a child who curiously wanders onto a construction site. It seems unfair that the occupier should not have to do more for the child than for the criminal.

- Second, it is often difficult to distinguish between the different categories. That is especially true for licensees and invitees. For example, does a visitor to a municipal library or a provincial park provide an economic benefit to the occupier?[15] Should the visitor's ability to recover compensation for a loss depend upon the answer to that narrow question?

- Third, a visitor's status may change from one moment to the next. For example, a customer who refuses a request to leave a store is transformed from an invitee into a trespasser.

- Fourth, it often is difficult to decide whether a danger is *hidden* or *unusual*. Does an icy parking lot during a Canadian winter satisfy either requirement?[16]

Business Law in Action 11.1 illustrates some of those difficulties.

BUSINESS LAW IN ACTION 11.1

Common Law Categories of Occupiers' Liability[17]

In the course of describing the law of occupiers' liability, a judge once posed this question. "A canvasser who comes onto your premises without your consent is a trespasser. Once he has your consent, he is a licensee. Not until you do business with him is he an invitee. Even when you have done business with him, it seems rather strange that your duty towards him should be different when he comes to your front door than when he goes away. Does he change his colour in the middle of the conversation?"

Questions for Discussion

1. Does the judge believe that it is possible to determine the precise moment when a person changes from a trespasser into a licensee and then into an invitee?

2. If your answer to the last question was "no," then how do courts actually decide cases? Might they intuitively decide an appropriate result and then characterize the plaintiff in a way that achieves that result?

Because of those difficulties, the jurisdictions that still use the common law rules have modified them.[18] They have generally moved away from categorizing visitors and toward increasing the occupier's obligations.

the traditional common law rules have been modified

- First, an occupier must do more than simply refrain from intentionally or recklessly hurting a trespasser. The law now uses a duty of *common humanity* that strikes a balance between the parties.[19] The occupier's obligations are determined by a number of factors, including:

---

15. *Nickell v City of Windsor* (1926) 59 OLR 618 (CA); *Coffyne v Silver Lake Regional Park Authority* (1977) 75 DLR (3d) 300 (Sask QB).

16. Compare *Francis v IPCF* (1993) 136 NBR (2d) 215 (QB) and *Waldick v Malcolm* (1991) 83 DLR (4th) 114 (SCC).

17. *Dunster v Abbott* [1953] 2 All ER 1572 at 1574 *per* Lord Denning (CA).

18. Newfoundland, the Northwest Territories, Nunavut, Saskatchewan, and the Yukon.

19. *Veinot v Kerr-Addison Mines Ltd* (1975) 51 DLR (3d) 533 (SCC).

- the age of the trespasser
- the reason for the trespass
- the nature of the danger that caused the injury
- the occupier's knowledge of that danger
- the occupier's cost of removing that danger

- Second, licensees and invitees are now generally treated the same. An occupier must protect them both from *unusual* dangers. Previously, a licensee was only protected from *hidden* dangers.[20]
- Third, the courts in Newfoundland have gone even further. An occupier in that province is required to use *reasonable care* toward all *lawful* visitors.[21]

Statutory Rules

the statutory rules substantially simplify and broaden the common law rules

Because of the problems associated with the common law rules, six provinces have enacted legislation to govern occupiers' liability.[22] Although the statutes vary somewhat between jurisdictions, the basic principles are the same. We note the most important differences between the common law and the legislation.

- First, the common law generally applies only to dangers that are created by the *condition* of the premises. The legislation also applies to *activities* that occur on the premises. For example, under a statute, the occupier of a campsite can be held liable not only for failing to remove a rotten tree that collapsed on a visitor, but also for failing to prevent one drunken guest from attacking another.
- Second, as a general rule, the standard of care no longer depends upon a visitor's classification. Nor are special distinctions drawn between, say, hidden or unusual dangers. An occupier must use *reasonable care*, which depends upon a number of factors:
  - the potential danger to the visitor
  - the occupier's cost of removing the danger
  - the purpose of the visit
  - the nature of the premises

  There are special exceptions to that general rule in some provinces.

  - In Alberta, an occupier is not required to protect adult trespassers from danger. It is merely prohibited from wilfully or recklessly hurting them. In contrast, reasonable care must be take to protect child trespassers that the occupier knows, or ought to know, are on the property.
  - Likewise, an occupier in Ontario or Prince Edward Island does not have to use reasonable care to protect some types of trespassers. It

---

[20.] There may still be a slight difference. It may be that a licensee can only sue for a danger that the occupier *knew* about, while an invitee can also sue for a danger that the occupier *should have known* about: *Yelic v Gimli (Town)* (1986) 33 DLR (4th) 248 (Man CA).

[21.] *Stacey v Anglican Church of Canada (Diocesan Synod of Eastern Newfoundland and Labrador)* (1999) 182 Nfld & PEIR 1 (Nfld CA).

[22.] *Occupiers' Liability Act*, RSA 1980, c O-3 (Alta); *Occupiers' Liability Act*, RSBC 1996, c 337 (BC); *Occupiers' Liability Act*, RSM 1987, c O 8 (Man); *Occupiers' Liability Act*, SNS 1996, c 27 (NS); *Occupiers' Liability Act*, RSO 1990, c O.2 (Ont); *Occupiers' Liability Act*, RSPEI 1988, c O-2 (PEI). New Brunswick has gone even further by doing away with a separate tort of occupiers' liability altogether: *Law Reform Act*, SNB 1993, c L-1.2, s 2. In that province, the courts simply use the general tort of negligence, which is discussed in Chapter 12.

is enough to simply refrain from intentionally hurting them. A similar rule applies in Manitoba, but only to trespassing snowmobilers.

- Third, the statutes generally allow an occupier to avoid liability by issuing a warning. For example, the occupier of a ski resort might conspicuously post signs that state:

AS A CONDITION OF USING THESE FACILITIES, YOU
ASSUME ALL RISK OF PERSONAL INJURY, DEATH OR
PROPERTY LOSS RESULTING FROM ANY CAUSE WHATSOEVER.[23]

An occupier's liability may also be affected by other statutes.[24]

- Fourth, under the common law, a landlord generally cannot be held liable for injuries that a person suffers while visiting a tenant. The primary reason is that a landlord has ownership, but not control, over the premises and therefore is not an occupier. A different rule applies under the legislation. A landlord may be liable to a visitor if it fails to make repairs under its lease with the tenant. For example, a landlord may be held responsible if a tenant's guest falls in a stairwell due to the absence of a handrail.[25]

NUISANCE

The tort of *nuisance* also involves land. Generally, a **nuisance** occurs when the defendant unreasonably interferes with the plaintiff's use and enjoyment of its own land.[26] There is a tension between the way in which the defendant wants to use *its* property and the way in which the plaintiff wants to use *its* property. The courts have a great deal of flexibility in resolving a dispute between neighbours.[27]

A nuisance occurs if the defendant *interferes* with the plaintiff's use of its land. Interference can happen in a variety of ways. Simple cases involve *physical damage* to the plaintiff or its property. For instance:

- the defendant's factory may emit chemical particles that drift with the wind and destroy the paint on the plaintiff's building, or
- the defendant's construction project may create a heavy vibration that cracks the foundations of the plaintiff's store.

A nuisance can also occur if the defendant creates a smell or a sound that *impairs the enjoyment* of the plaintiff's property. For instance:

- the defendant may operate a pig farm that causes a stench to waft over the plaintiff's outdoor café, or
- the blaring music from the defendant's nightclub may keep nearby residents awake at night.

Margin notes:

a nuisance occurs when the defendant unreasonably interferes with the plaintiff's use and enjoyment of its own land

physical damage

impairment of enjoyment

[23.] Chapter 4 discussed exclusion clauses.

[24.] For example, innkeepers in Ontario need to take less care than usual: *Innkeepers Act*, RSO 1990, c I7.

[25.] *Zavaglia v MAQ Holdings Ltd* (1986) 6 BCLR (2d) 286 (CA).

[26.] Our discussion is limited to the tort of *private nuisance*. There is also the less important tort of *public nuisance*. A public nuisance occurs when the defendant commits the crime of common nuisance against the public, but creates a special loss for the plaintiff: *Criminal Code*, RSC 1985, c C-46, s 180(2) (Can). That tort can arise, for instance, if the defendant creates a hazard on a street that not only interferes with the general public's right to use that roadway, but also causes the plaintiff to be injured in a traffic accident: *Ryan v Victoria (City)* (1999) 168 DLR (4th) 513 (SCC).

[27.] Strictly speaking, it is not necessary for *both* parties to have an interest in land. While the plaintiff can sue only if its land is affected, the defendant does not have to commit the nuisance from its own property. In practice, however, most nuisance cases arise between neighbours.

a non-intrusive nuisance may occur through various forms of interference

It may even be possible to commit a *non-intrusive* nuisance, without causing anything to travel onto the plaintiff's property. For instance:

- the defendant may install a sewer system on its own property that drains water *from* the plaintiff's land in a way that damages the foundations of the plaintiff's building, or
- the defendant may operate a brothel that brings traffic and criminals close to the plaintiff's home.

Note, however, that certain types of activities generally will *not* support a claim in nuisance. For instance, it is unlikely that a tort is committed if:

- the defendant builds something on its own property that ruins the plaintiff's view of a lake or reduces the amount of sunshine that enters the plaintiff's house, or
- the defendant paints its building a colour that reduces the market value of the plaintiff's house.[28]

interference is not a nuisance unless it is unreasonable

A nuisance occurs only if the defendant's interference is *unreasonable*. In deciding that issue, the courts look at a number of factors. The most important is the nature of the interference. The defendant's conduct is almost always considered unreasonable if it causes substantial *physical damage*. In contrast, the courts are less likely to hold the defendant liable if it merely *impairs the enjoyment* of the plaintiff's property, especially if the defendant's interference is *non-intrusive*. Beyond that, the courts also consider:

- the *nature of the neighbourhood* (for example, the smell of livestock may be reasonable in the country but not in the city)
- the *time and day* of the interference (for example, construction sounds that are reasonable at noon on a weekday may be unreasonable late at night or on the weekend)
- the *intensity and duration* of the interference (for example, a barking dog or a foul odour may have to be tolerated if it occurs occasionally, but not if it is nearly constant)
- the *social utility* of the defendant's conduct (for example, the late night sound of screeching tires may be reasonable if it is caused by an ambulance, but not if it is caused by drag racing)
- the defendant's *motivation* (for example, the sound of a gun may be reasonable if it occurs in the course of normal activities, but not if it is made to terrify the plaintiff's foxes and ruin his breeding business)[29]

Defences to Nuisance

There are several defences to the tort of nuisance, but they are generally interpreted very narrowly.[30] The courts are reluctant to allow the defendant to escape liability despite unreasonably interfering with the plaintiff's property. The defence of *statutory authority* provides a good example. **Statutory authority** means that the defendant caused a nuisance while acting under legislation.

statutory authority means that the defendant caused a nuisance while acting under legislation

---

[28.] It may be different if the defendant *intentionally* annoys or hurts the plaintiff.

[29.] *Hollywood Silver Fox Farm v Emmett* [1936] 2 KB 468 (QB).

[30.] For example, the plaintiff cannot complain if it *consented* to the defendant's activity. However, consent usually requires proof that the plaintiff encouraged the defendant's activity, not that it merely failed to complain.

Significantly, that defence applies only if the defendant's nuisance was an *inevitable result* of the statutorily authorized activity. Business Decision 11.1 illustrates that rule.

BUSINESS DECISION 11.1

Nuisance and the Defence of Statutory Authority[31]

Legislation allowed the Town of Sepsis to build a sewage system that conformed with industry standards. Such systems usually use pipes that are between 1 metre and 1.5 metres in diameter. In the course of construction, the mayor of Sepsis decided, for financial reasons, to use 1-metre pipes. Several months after the project was completed, the town received a lot of rain. While the system generally performed quite well, it backed up in one neighbourhood and pumped raw sewage into your restaurant. As a result, you were required to replace all of your kitchen equipment, which had been ruined by the mess. The evidence indicates that the problem was caused by the fact that the pipes were too narrow to accommodate the rainfall. It also indicates that the problem would not have occurred if 1.5-metre pipes had been used.

Since litigation is expensive, you do not want to sue the Town of Sepsis unless there is a good chance that you will win your case. How would you make that decision?

Questions for Discussion

1. Did Sepsis commit the tort of nuisance?
2. If Sepsis did commit the tort, could it nevertheless avoid liability by pleading the defence of statutory authority? Given the legislation and the evidence, was a nuisance inevitable?

Before leaving the issue of defences, note that the defendant is not relieved of liability merely because the nuisance already existed when the plaintiff arrived in the neighbourhood. For instance, a physician can complain that the noise from a factory disrupts his practice, even though the person who previously occupied his building was not affected by that sound.[32]

Remedies for Nuisance

The most common remedies for nuisance are compensatory damages and injunctions. The usual rules regarding compensation apply and do not have to be repeated here. Injunctions are more complicated. A judge will usually grant one to stop a nuisance. For example, the defendant may be required to close a chemical plant that is emitting noxious fumes, or it may be ordered to refrain from dumping pollution into a river. Occasionally, however, the court may exercise its discretion to refuse an injunction. That is clearly true if the nuisance causes relatively little damage to the plaintiff and if damages can provide an adequate remedy. It may also be true if an injunction would create an intolerable hardship for the defendant or, more importantly, for the community as a whole. Consequently, if a town's entire economy revolves around a single factory, a judge would be reluctant to grant an injunction that would have the effect of closing that factory. Finally, the courts sometimes award both compensatory damages and an injunction. The damages take care of past losses, and the injunction prevents harm in the future.

the primary remedies for nuisance are compensatory damages and injunctions

---

[31.] *Tock v St John's (City) Metropolitan Area Board* (1989) 64 DLR (4th) 620 (SCC); *Ryan v Victoria (City)* (1999) 168 DLR (4th) 513 (SCC).

[32.] *Sturges v Bridgman* [1895] AC 587 (HL).

THE RULE IN *RYLANDS v FLETCHER*

the rule in *Rylands v Fletcher* states that the defendant can be held strictly liable for a non-natural use of land if something escapes from its property and injures the plaintiff

The rule in *Rylands v Fletcher* is a third tort that deals with land.[33] The **rule in Rylands v Fletcher** states that the defendant can be held strictly liable for its non-natural use of land if something escapes from its property and injures the plaintiff. We need to examine three aspects of that rule.

the defendant must have made non-natural use of its land

First, the defendant must have made a *non-natural use* of its land. Courts have interpreted this in two ways. Some courts say that it refers to any use of land that creates a *special* danger; others say that the defendant must create a *special and unusual* danger. Judges have recently preferred the second interpretation.[34] As a result, the defendant cannot be held liable simply because it installs a gas appliance in its building, or deliberately starts a fire to burn away scrub grass in the normal course of its farming operations. While those activities are non-natural, they are not unusual. It is therefore irrelevant that they endangered the plaintiff. However, the tort may be committed if the defendant collects an unusual amount of water in a reservoir, or stacks fireworks in a store display. Those activities are not only especially dangerous; they are also unusual.

the plaintiff must be injured by something that escaped from the defendant's land

Second, something associated with a non-natural use must *escape* from the defendant's land and cause the plaintiff to suffer a loss. For instance, water may break through a reservoir and flood a neighbour's house, or explosives may ignite in a store, shoot onto the sidewalk, and injure a pedestrian. The need for an escape may create problems if the plaintiff suffers an injury *on the defendant's property*. A spectator who is hit by flying debris at a racetrack may not be able to use *Rylands v Fletcher* since nothing *left* the defendant's premises. It would not be surprising, however, if a judge ignored the requirement of an escape in that situation to avoid an unfair result.

most torts are based on some form of fault

liability in *Rylands v Fletcher* is strict

liability may be avoided by use of a defence

Third, most torts are based on some form of *fault*. The defendant is usually liable only if it intentionally, or at least carelessly, caused the plaintiff's injury. The rule in *Rylands v Fletcher*, in contrast, is *strict*. The defendant may be held liable even though it acted as carefully as possible. Strict liability does not, however, mean that liability is imposed *every time* there is a non-natural use, an escape, and an injury. A defence may be available in exceptional circumstances. For example:

- the plaintiff may have *consented* to the defendant's non-natural use of its land
- the escape may have been caused by a *third party* or a *natural force* (such as a tornado or an earthquake) that the defendant could not have guarded against
- the plaintiff's injury may have been the *inevitable result* of an activity that the defendant was *statutorily authorized* to do

Those defences, however, are difficult to prove. Consequently, business people should learn an important lesson from the rule in *Rylands v Fletcher*. They should take special precautions whenever they use land in a non-natural way.

We have seen four torts that involve the use of land. We discussed trespass to land in Chapter 10 and occupiers' liability, nuisance, and the rule in *Rylands v Fletcher* in this chapter. Concept Summary 11.1 shows the most important features of those torts.

---

[33] *Rylands v Fletcher* (1868) LR 3 HL 330.

[34] *Tock v St John's (City) Metropolitan Area Board* (1989) 64 DLR (4th) 620 (SCC).

Concept Summary 11.1

Concept Summary 11.1

Torts Involving the Use of Land

Tort	Basis of Liability
occupiers' liability	the defendant, who is the occupier of premises, fails to take adequate precautions to protect the plaintiff, who is visiting those premises
nuisance	the defendant unreasonably interferes with the plaintiff's use and enjoyment of its own land
rule in *Rylands v Fletcher*	the defendant uses its land in a non-natural way with the result that something escapes and injures the plaintiff
trespass to land	the defendant intentionally interferes with the plaintiff's land

DEFAMATION

Communication is essential to the success of any business. However, it also creates the risk of *defamation*. **Defamation** occurs when the defendant makes a false statement that could lead a reasonable person to have a lower opinion of the plaintiff.[35]

The defendant's statement is defamatory only if a reasonable person would have thought that it referred to the plaintiff. That requirement is quite broad.

- First, it can be satisfied even if the defendant did not *intend* to refer to the plaintiff. The purpose of the tort is to protect reputations. It is therefore enough if a reasonable person would have *thought* that the defendant was referring to the plaintiff. Reputations are often hurt by mistake.

- Second, a claim for defamation can be made by any sort of *living person*. As we will see in Chapter 18, the term "person" refers not only to human beings, but also to things like corporations.

- Third, defamation may be difficult to prove if the defendant made a statement about a *group of individuals*. Each person must prove that the statement can be reasonably interpreted as referring to them *personally*. That is unlikely if the group is large and if the statement is a generalization. Consequently, I probably could not sue you for saying, "All lawyers are crooks!"

To test your understanding of those rules, consider You Be the Judge 11.1.

defamation occurs when the defendant makes a false statement that could lead a reasonable person to have a lower opinion of the plaintiff

the defamatory statement must reasonably be understood as referring to the plaintiff

YOU BE THE JUDGE 11.1

Defamation of Groups and Organizations

During a music industry trade show in Moncton, Layla mentioned to her friend Derek that she wanted to purchase a certain type of keyboard. He responded by saying, "Well, I wouldn't buy from those clowns in Edmonton. The company is on the verge of bankruptcy, and the people who work there are morons. If you ever got a thing from them—and that's a mighty big *if*—it'd be a piece of garbage."

The type of keyboard Layla wanted is manufactured by 12 different companies. Domino Music Inc is the only one
(continued)

---

35. Some parts of defamation have been modified by legislation. Nevertheless, the most important issues are governed by the common law rules that are discussed in the text.

(continued)
that is located in Edmonton. Derek is being threatened with litigation by: (i) Domino Music Inc, (ii) Eric, who has been an employee of Domino for 10 years, and (iii) the personal representative for Duane, who recently died, but who worked for Domino when Derek made his statement.

Questions for Discussion

1. Is Domino Music Inc entitled to sue for defamation? Explain your answer.
2. Is Eric entitled to sue for defamation? Explain your answer.
3. Is Duane's personal representative entitled to sue for defamation on Duane's behalf? Explain your answer.

slander is a defamatory statement that is spoken

libel is a defamatory statement that is written

almost any uncomplimentary comment can be considered defamatory

Lawyers sometimes draw a distinction between *slander* and *libel*. **Slander** is a defamatory statement that is spoken; **libel** is a defamatory statement that is written. While that distinction is important for technical reasons in some parts of Canada, the general rule is that defamation can occur through any sort of communication, including spoken words, written documents, gestures, photographs, and puppet shows.

Almost any uncomplimentary statement can be defamatory, as long as it could hurt a person's reputation. You will defame me if you suggest, for example, that I am incompetent, racist, lazy, dishonest, infected with a communicable disease, or involved in criminal activity. Furthermore, even a seemingly harmless statement may be defamatory once it is considered in context. For example, although I would not normally be defamed if you said that I sold pork chops, it might be different if I own a kosher deli.

defamation requires publication

publication occurs when a statement is communicated to a third party

There cannot be defamation without *publication*. **Publication** occurs when a statement is communicated to a third party. Remember that the tort is concerned with the protection of reputations. If I say something uncomplimentary to you in private, I may hurt your feelings or upset you, but I cannot damage your reputation, because it is based on what *other people* think of you. The rule about publication can, however, work in your favour. A new tort may occur every time that a statement is *repeated*. Consequently, if I write a defamatory book about you, I commit a tort when I deliver the manuscript to my publisher. But my publisher may also commit a tort against you when it sells the book to the public.

Defences to Defamation

The tort of defamation is broadly interpreted. In some situations, however, the defendant will not be held liable even though it published a statement that hurt the plaintiff's reputation. We will briefly look at three important defences to the tort of defamation:

- justification
- privilege
- fair comment

justification occurs if the defendant's statement is true

Justification occurs if the defendant's statement is true. Note that the statement must *actually* be true. The defendant will not avoid liability simply because it *honestly believed* that the statement was true. Note also that the defendant has the burden of proof. Once the plaintiff satisfies the requirements that we discussed, a judge will assume that the defendant's uncomplimentary statement was false. The defendant must prove otherwise.

a privilege is immunity from liability

The courts want people to speak freely on important issues. Consequently, they sometimes grant a *privilege*. A **privilege** is immunity from liability. It takes two forms. First, an *absolute privilege* provides complete immunity. It applies even if the defendant knowingly made a false statement for a malicious purpose. That defence is available only when the law needs to encourage people to communicate without *any* fear of being sued. It is therefore usually limited to statements made:

- during parliamentary proceedings
- between high government officials who are dealing with government business
- by a judge, lawyer, litigant, or witness in the context of legal proceedings
- between spouses

The second form of the defence is *qualified privilege*. Rather than being limited to specific situations, it may apply whenever: (i) the defendant has a legal, moral, or social obligation to make a statement, and (ii) the statement is made to someone who had a similar duty or interest in receiving it. Both of those elements must be satisfied. Consequently, a qualified privilege may be recognized if:

- a manager makes an unfair statement about a former employee to the personnel director of a company that is considering hiring that individual—but not if the manager makes the same statement to a friend during idle gossip, or
- a department store discreetly posts a notice instructing its employees not to accept cheques from a customer who is wrongly suspected of fraud—but not if the notice is large enough to be noticed by other customers, who have no interest in the matter.[36]

The defence of qualified privilege is also limited to statements that the defendant made in good faith. It is not available if the defendant knew that its statement was untrue or if the defendant was motivated by some malicious purpose.

The defence of *fair comment* is intended to encourage useful debate on significant social issues. A **fair comment** is an honest expression of an opinion regarding a matter of public importance. That defence has several requirements.

a fair comment is an honest expression of an opinion regarding a matter of public importance

- First, it is intended to protect *informed opinions*. The defendant has to prove that a reasonable person would have interpreted the statement as an opinion based on fact, rather than as a fact. Consequently, the defence may apply if a newspaper columnist accurately describes a politician's behaviour and suggests that "the leadership of this country is morally corrupt"—but not if that statement is made without the support of any background information.[37]
- Second, the defendant's opinion must concern an issue of *public interest*, such as a cultural, religious, or political matter. Consequently, while it is possible to criticize the public activities of poets, priests, and politicians, the defence does not allow personal attacks on their private lives.
- Third, a comment is not "fair" unless it was *honestly held*.[38] But as long as that requirement is met, the defendant may be protected even if its statement was highly critical and very damaging.
- Finally, the defence of fair comment is not available if the defendant acted *maliciously*.

---

[36] *Pleau v Simpson-Sears Ltd* (1977) 75 DLR (3d) 747 (Ont CA).

[37] The background information may be expressed or implied.

[38] That requirement creates difficulties for letters to the editor that are printed in newspapers. The Supreme Court of Canada has held that a newspaper is entitled to use the defence of fair comment only if the publisher honestly shares the opinion that is contained in such a letter: *Cherneskey v Armadale Publishers Ltd* (1978) 90 DLR (3d) 321 (SCC). That is a very narrow rule. As a result, several provinces have legislation that allows a newspaper to use the defence as long as an honest person could have held the opinion in question, even if the publisher did not: *Defamation Amendment Act*, RSA 1980, c D 6, s 9 (Alta); *Defamation Act*, RSM 1987, c D20, s 9 (Man); *An Act to Amend the Defamation Act*, SNB 1980, c 16, s 8.1(1) (NB); *Libel and Slander Act*, RSO 1990, c L.12, s 24 (Ont).

Remedies for Defamation

The usual remedy for defamation is compensation. Punitive damages may also be awarded if the defendant's conduct was particularly outrageous.[39] And in truly exceptional circumstances, a court may impose an injunction to prevent a person from even making a statement—but only if it is clear that the statement would be defamatory. In most situations, judges are reluctant to restrict freedom of speech in that way.

[39.] *Hill v Church of Scientology of Toronto* (1995) 126 DLR (4th) 129 (SCC).

Chapter Summary

In this chapter, we examined eight torts that are particularly important for business people.

Intimidation occurs when the plaintiff suffers a loss as a result of the defendant's threat to commit an unlawful act against either the plaintiff or a third party. Two-party intimidation occurs when the defendant directly coerces the plaintiff into suffering a loss. Three-party intimidation occurs when the defendant coerces a third party into acting in a way that hurts the plaintiff.

Interference with contractual relations occurs when the defendant disrupts a contract that exists between the plaintiff and a third party. A direct inducement to breach of contract occurs when the defendant directly persuades a third party to break its contract with the plaintiff. An indirect inducement to breach of contract occurs when the defendant indirectly persuades a third party to break its contract with the plaintiff.

Conspiracy usually occurs when two or more defendants agree to act together with the primary purpose of causing a financial loss to the plaintiff. The conspiring parties can be held liable even if their actions are otherwise lawful. However, the courts are more willing to impose liability if the defendants acted in an otherwise unlawful way.

Deceit occurs if the defendant makes a false statement, which it knows to be untrue, with which it intends to mislead the plaintiff, and which causes the plaintiff to suffer a loss.

The law of occupiers' liability requires an occupier of premises to protect visitors from harm. Some provinces and territories rely on the traditional common law rules. Others rely upon occupiers' liability statutes.

Nuisance occurs when the defendant unreasonably interferes with the plaintiff's ability to use and enjoy its own land. The defence of statutory authority may protect a defendant from liability, but it has been narrowly interpreted by the courts. The courts often award injunctions to stop or prevent nuisances.

The rule in *Rylands v Fletcher* states that the defendant may be held strictly liable for its non-natural use of land if something escapes from its property and injures the plaintiff.

Defamation occurs when the defendant makes a false statement that could lead a reasonable person to have a lower opinion of the plaintiff. Liability may be avoided through the defences of justification, privilege, and fair comment.

Review Questions

1. The courts sometimes say that the tort of intimidation cannot be based on a threat to commit a breach of contract. Why does that apparent rule apply to two-party intimidation, but not to three-party intimidation?

2. "It is not enough for the plaintiff to prove that the defendant acted in an intimidating way. The plaintiff also has to show that the defendant's intimidation was effective." Explain the extent to which that statement is true.

3. "A company is in danger of committing a tort every time it hires a person away from a rival company." Explain the extent to which that statement is true.

4. Which tort is easier to prove: direct inducement to breach of contract or indirect inducement to breach of contract? Explain your answer.

5. Why is it usually difficult to prove the tort of conspiracy if the defendants' actions were otherwise *lawful*? Is the situation different if the defendants' actions are otherwise *unlawful*? Explain your answer.

6. It is sometimes said that the tort of deceit requires a statement of fact. How is a statement of fact different from an opinion, a prediction, or a puff? Why is a statement of fact necessary?

7. In terms of remedies, why is it important that deceit is a tort rather than a breach of contract?

8. Why are almost all businesses potentially in danger of committing the tort of occupiers' liability?

9. Describe the main problems created by the common law's traditional approach to occupiers' liability. How have Canadian courts improved that tort?

10. Explain the general approach of occupiers' liability legislation. In what ways are the statutory rules significantly different from the common law rules?

11. What factors do the courts consider in deciding whether the defendant has committed the tort of nuisance? What is the most important factor?

12. Explain why the defence of statutory authority seldom applies in an action for nuisance.

13. What remedies are available for the tort of nuisance. How does a judge decide which remedy to award in any particular case?

14. What do the courts mean when they say that a person can be held liable under the rule in *Rylands v Fletcher* only if there has been a "non-natural use" of land? Why is the meaning of that term important?

15. Why is the rule in *Rylands v Fletcher* considered a strict liability tort?

16. Explain three defences that may be available against the rule in *Rylands v Fletcher.*

17. Why is publication critically important to the tort of defamation? Why do I not commit the tort of defamation if, in the course of a private conversation, I wrongly accuse you of some horrible crime?

18. Explain the defences of absolute privilege and qualified privilege. Outline the situations in which those defences will apply.

19. Describe the defence of fair comment. Why is that defence especially important to businesses like newspapers, magazines, and television broadcasters?

20. Briefly describe the remedies that may be available for the tort of defamation.

Cases and Problems

1. The federal government operated a program under which it leased land to Aboriginal Canadians. It entered into one such lease with David Cardinal, a member of the River Valley Band. Shortly afterwards, however, several other members of that band began to harass Cardinal by using their trucks to block access to that property, allowing their cattle to stray onto the land, and, despite his repeated objections, hunting on his land. Cardinal believes that they did so to frighten him into terminating his lease with the government. If that happened, the other members of the band would be able to lease the land for themselves. When he confronted them with that allegation, one of their group replied, "We haven't done anything wrong. But if you can't stand the heat, maybe you should just get out of the kitchen!" Does Cardinal have a cause of action in intimidation? Do you have enough information to answer that question?

2. DeJohnette Developments was in the process of building a recording studio. It agreed to purchase about $5 000 000 worth of sound equipment from Peacock Electronics Inc. Jarrett Koln, who custom-builds sound equipment, heard that DeJohnette was planning a new recording studio. Koln did not know that DeJohnette had already entered into a contract with Peacock. He sent a letter to DeJohnette that said:

> You should not, under any circumstances, buy equipment from Peacock. Although that company has been

around for years, the quality of its merchandise is vastly inferior compared to mine.

DeJohnette knew that Koln was correct. Recent studies had shown that Peacock's equipment was second rate. DeJohnette nevertheless honoured its contract with Peacock and refused to buy from Koln. Peacock, however, is upset that Koln jeopardized its agreement with DeJohnette. Can Peacock successfully sue Koln for inducing breach of contract? Provide several reasons for your answer.

3. The cement-manufacturing business is a cut-throat industry. For many years, a small number of large companies, including Ash Inc and Izzy Supplies Ltd, have enjoyed a virtual monopoly. They have strongly resisted the emergence of new competitors. Two years ago, Roxel Corp attempted to break into the business. Because of certain technological advances that it had developed, Roxel was able to produce a much better product than was currently available in the market. Although Roxel's product was initially available only in the Atlantic provinces, Ash and Izzy were worried that their profits might drop sharply if Roxel became successful and expanded across the country. They therefore agreed to sell their own cement in the Maritimes at a drastically reduced price. That agreement had two effects: (i) it allowed Ash and Izzy to maintain their traditional share of the market across the country, and (ii) it incidentally drove Roxel out of the cement business. The agreement

between Ash and Izzy was unlawful under the *Competition Act* because it involved regional price discrimination. Can Roxel successfully sue Ash and Izzy for the tort of conspiracy? Explain your answer.

4. The directors of Sol-Go Inc publicly declared that their company intended to develop a high-speed commuter rail system between Ottawa and Toronto that would operate on solar power. Wei Chang, who was interested in investing in solar-powered modes of transportation, contacted the company and asked whether government approval for the plan had been granted. She received a letter that stated, "Although government approval has not yet been received, we can assure you that it is forthcoming. Our application has met all government requirements." Satisfied with that answer, Wei bought $50 000 worth of shares in Sol-Go. She was very disappointed several weeks later when she read in a newspaper that the government had rejected the company's application on the ground that the proposed project failed to extend beyond Ottawa to Montreal. When Wei contacted the directors of Sol-Go, they honestly assured her that, at the time of writing their previous letter, they believed that government approval would be granted. They also pointed out to her that while the proposed commuter project had fallen through, several other projects had done unexpectedly well, and that the value of her shares consequently was still $50 000. Is Sol-Go liable to Wei Chang for the tort of deceit? Provide several reasons for your answer.

5. The Alkabe Corporation owned a large piece of land on which it planned to develop a shopping mall. When the starting date of that project was delayed, the company erected a one-metre-high fence around the site and posted a notice: "ABSOLUTELY NO TRESPASSING." The site nevertheless became a very popular play area for local children. A number of young teens created a large ramp that they used for jumping their bikes. Alkabe learned of that fact, but it took no steps to stop the children from playing on the site. Some time later, Jyoti, a 13-year-old, was seriously injured when she flipped her bike while racing over the ramp. Would Alkabe be held liable for the tort of occupiers' liability under the traditional common law rules? Assuming that the accident occurred in the jurisdiction in which you live, will the Alkabe Corporation be held liable for the tort of occupiers' liability? Explain your answer.

6. Big Nickel Metals Inc has operated a steel plant in Sudbury for a number of years and employs 5000 residents of that town (out of a total workforce of about 65 000). One of the main pieces of equipment in the plant is a 720-tonne press that is used to produce sheet metal. Denari Inc recently purchased an unused building across the street from the plant and converted it into a condominium complex for senior citizens. Immediately after opening that complex, however, Denari was flooded with complaints from its tenants because of the noise that was produced by Big Nickel's press. The manager of Big Nickel is sympathetic to that complaint, and has offered to refrain from using the press between midnight and dawn. However, he has also indicated that the press is essential to the operation of the plant and that without it, his company would have to lay off almost all of its employees. The manager of Denari, in response, has said that the seniors living in his

complex are very upset by the noise from the press, regardless of when it is operated. He has also shown that a number of units in the condominium complex remain empty, even though there is generally a great demand for such accommodation in Sudbury. Those vacancies are caused by the noise produced by Big Nickel. The resulting loss of revenue to Denari is estimated to be $50 000, and that amount is expected to rise by $10 000 for every month that the press continues in operation. Can Denari Inc successfully sue Big Nickel Metals Inc for nuisance? If so, what remedy will the plaintiff receive? Explain your answer.

7. The Putrescible Food Company operates a plant that processes and packages a wide variety of foods, including meats and vegetables. In the course of doing so, it generates a large amount of waste product. It has long been in the habit of burying that waste in a ravine that is located just inside the boundary of its property. (A residential district is situated on the other side of the ravine.) As the company knew might happen, the buried waste has generated methane gas. On the basis of its scientists' tests, however, Putrescible Foods believed that the pit was deep enough to prevent the gas from seeping out. Nevertheless, in a recent accident, an invisible cloud of that gas did drift out of the ravine, across the company's property, and into the nearby residential district. Alonzo suffered terrible injuries after striking a match to light a cigar. The flame from the match ignited the cloud of gas and caused a fireball that engulfed him. At the time of the accident, Alonzo was standing on a public street in front of his house. Which of the torts, if any, that we have discussed in this chapter provides him with the best possibility of successfully suing the Putrescible Food Company? Explain your answer.

8. Cherry Bomb Music Inc operates an office on the tenth floor of a building. Cougar Dance Studio occupies the office on the floor below. Cherry Bomb installed a sophisticated security system to protect its premises. Nevertheless, an unidentified person deactivated the security system late one night and broke into Cherry Bomb's office looking for CDs to steal. Since there were none to be found, the trespasser went on a rampage. Among other acts of vandalism, the trespasser flushed a large firecracker down a toilet that was located within Cherry Bomb's office. The explosion caused the water pipe to break, with the result that Cougar Dance Studio suffered severe water damage. Cougar has sued Cherry Bomb under the rule in *Rylands v Fletcher*. Will that action be successful? Provide two reasons for your answer.

9. Slabel Books Inc published an unauthorized biography of the late Jackie Rogers Jr. While fully documenting Jackie's remarkable artistic abilities, the book also attempted to reveal the darker side of the genius. In doing so, however, it made a number of inaccurate statements, including one suggesting that Jackie lip-synched in concert on those frequent occasions when he was too heavily drugged to remember lyrics. Jackie's widow is outraged by those false allegations and intends to bring an action in defamation to clear her deceased husband's name. Will she succeed? Explain your answer.

10. Tony Twist was a professional hockey player with the Quebec Nordiques and the St Louis Blues. During his

career, he was known as an enforcer—while playing in the NHL for a decade, he amassed only 10 goals, but over 1100 minutes in penalties. Todd McFarlane is the publisher of a number of comic books. One of those publications, *Spawn*, features a vicious gangster named Antonio Twistelli, who also goes by the nickname of "Tony Twist." The real Tony Twist's mother became very upset when she discovered that such a character shared her son's name. She was worried that *Spawn* would lead people to think badly of her boy. McFarlane insists that he did not base his comic book villain on any real person and argues that if he wanted to borrow a hockey player's name, he would have called the gangster Wayneatelli Gretzkytello. Can the real-life Tony Twist successfully sue McFarlane for defamation? What test would a court apply in these circumstances?

11. Mary Tran graduated with a business degree three years ago. She began working almost immediately as a financial analyst for Marshall James Inc, an investment-consulting company. After starting that job, she contacted the bank that had carried her student loan to settle the details of her debt and arrange a repayment schedule. The bank informed her that her debt had been assigned to Financial Debt Recovery Ltd (FDR). When she contacted FDR, she was told that she would be required to make monthly payments of $1000. She was also told that she would be required to pay "a substantial amount" of interest. She asked for details about the outstanding amount, but FDR refused to provide that information. Tran therefore said that she would not begin making payments until she knew how much she owed in total. Under the terms of the loan contract that she had originally signed with the bank, she was entitled to do so.

Tran heard nothing more from FDR for several weeks. She then began to receive telephone messages that threatened her with serious violence unless she immediately paid a $2000 "loan transfer fee." Although her loan contract did not require the payment of such a fee, she complied with FDR's demand out of fear for her life. FDR also called John Molloy, the managing partner of Marshall

James, and said: (i) that Tran was actively seeking employment elsewhere, and (ii) that Tran had a criminal record for fraud. Both of those statements were entirely untrue, but they were told in such a convincing way that Molloy believed them. As a result, Molloy followed FDR's advice and terminated Tran's employment with Marshall James Inc. If FDR's allegations had been true, Molloy's actions would have been justified. On the true facts, however, they amounted to a breach of contract. Tran found a position with another firm some time later, but at a much lower rate of pay. She has suffered a $50 000 loss as result of changing jobs.

Tran bears no ill will toward Molloy or Marshall James Inc because she realizes that they were tricked by FDR. She does, however, want to sue FDR. Describe three torts that we discussed in this chapter that Tran could use against FDR.

12. Weston Properties Inc owned a business complex. Prime Advertising Ltd signed a 10-year lease to occupy 80 percent of it. That lease granted Prime the exclusive right to place its logo on the front of the building. Two years later, Weston leased part of the remaining space in the complex to an abortion clinic. Prime strenuously objected on the basis that its business was damaged by the clinic's controversial nature. In particular, it was upset that its corporate logo invariably appeared in news photos of protests that opposing pro-choice and pro-life groups staged in front of the clinic. Prime asked Weston to terminate the clinic's lease, but that request was rejected. Prime therefore decided to relocate its own business to another building. The president of the Imperial Development Corp learned of the situation and aggressively offered to lease space in its complex to Prime. Prime accepted that offer, left Weston's building, and signed a lease with Imperial. Weston commenced two lawsuits. It successfully sued Prime in breach of contract for failing to honour the 10-year lease it had signed. It then sued Imperial for the tort of inducing breach of contract. Will Weston win that case as well? Explain your answer.

12 Negligence

OBJECTIVES

After completing this chapter, you should be able to:

1. Describe the nature and function of the concept of a duty of care.

2. Explain the term "reasonable foreseeability," and explain the ways in which that concept is relevant to the tort of negligence.

3. Explain why policy considerations are important to the duty of care, especially in the context of claims for negligent statements.

4. Describe the reasonable person, and explain how that person is relevant to the standard of care.

5. Outline the special considerations that arise when a court decides whether a professional has acted carelessly.

6. Outline the nature and function of the but-for test.

7. Explain how the concept of remoteness helps courts to decide "thin skull" cases and cases involving intervening acts.

8. Briefly describe the defence of contributory negligence.

9. Explain why and how the courts have limited the defence of voluntary assumption of risk.

10. Outline the scope of the defence of illegality.

In this chapter, we finish our discussion of torts by examining the most important tort of all: negligence. In non-legal terms, that word usually means "carelessness." Its legal meaning is much the same. The **tort of negligence** determines whether the defendant can be held liable for carelessly causing the plaintiff to suffer a loss or injury. That issue can arise in numerous ways: a manufacturer may produce a beverage that makes a consumer sick; an investment counsellor may provide bad advice that leads a client to purchase worthless stocks; a golfer may hit an errant shot that cracks a spectator's skull; a builder may construct a defective bridge that collapses on a motorist's vehicle; an employer may write an inaccurate report that prevents an employee from receiving a promotion; and so on.

the tort of negligence determines whether the defendant can be held liable for carelessly causing injury to the plaintiff

The tort of negligence requires the plaintiff to prove that the defendant:

- owed a *duty of care*, in that it was required to act carefully toward the plaintiff
- *breached the standard of care* by acting carelessly
- *caused harm* to the plaintiff

Even if the plaintiff proves those three elements, the defendant may be able to avoid liability by proving a defence. Three possibilities are especially important. The defendant may show that at least one of these defences existed:

- the plaintiff's injury was caused by its own *contributory negligence*
- the plaintiff *voluntarily assumed the risk* of being injured by the defendant
- the plaintiff was injured while engaged in some form of *illegal* behaviour

Those elements are represented in Figure 12.1.

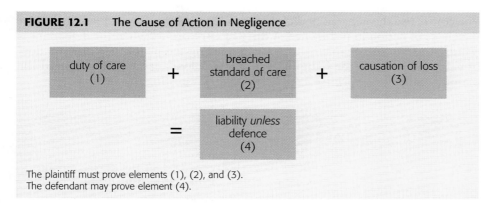

FIGURE 12.1   The Cause of Action in Negligence

duty of care (1) **+** breached standard of care (2) **+** causation of loss (3)

= liability *unless* defence (4)

The plaintiff must prove elements (1), (2), and (3).
The defendant may prove element (4).

Before examining those elements, we must discuss two preliminary matters. First, people sometimes talk about *professional negligence*. That phrase is misleading because it suggests that there is a separate tort by that name. In fact, the term "professional negligence" simply refers to negligence that is committed by a professional person, such as a banker, a lawyer, or an accountant.[1] However, it *is* true that the cause of action in negligence is flexible enough to reflect different types of situations. For example, the standard of care always requires the defendant to act as a reasonable person would act *in similar circumstances*. The precise content of that requirement therefore depends upon the circumstances. An architect who is drafting plans for an office tower must

there is no separate tort of professional negligence

[1.] Chapter 19 explains how a professional may also be held liable on other grounds, such as breach of contract and breach of fiduciary duty.

act much more carefully than a child who is playing street hockey. And in that way, the idea of "professional negligence" makes sense. It refers to the special considerations that shape the general cause of action in negligence when it is applied to professional people. The topic of professional negligence is discussed later in this chapter.

Second, the law of negligence contains a tension between two important values. On the one hand, in order to compensate people who suffer injuries, the courts want a wide scope of liability. On the other hand, the courts recognize that the imposition of liability sometimes actually hurts society. If a business had to fully compensate every person whom it injured, it might not be able to afford to carry on. Admittedly, in some situations, that would be a good thing. An especially hazardous industry that produces few social benefits perhaps should be shut down. In other situations, however, it may be in society's best interests to protect certain types of activities from liability. For example, it is quite difficult to successfully sue a physician, largely because judges do not want to discourage doctors from practising in risky areas, such as obstetrics.[2] The tension between the desire to provide compensation and the desire to encourage socially useful activities appears in all areas of tort law. It is particularly noticeable in negligence, however, because that cause of action is so flexible. It is not much of an exaggeration to say that a judge, with a bit of ingenuity, can often reasonably find for either the plaintiff or the defendant. The actual decision frequently depends on which interests the judge finds more compelling. As we discuss the action in negligence, note how the courts view the societal role of different types of business activities.

courts must strike a balance between compensating people who suffer injuries and facilitating socially desirable activities

DUTY OF CARE

The courts use the concept of *duty of care* to control the scope of liability under the cause of action in negligence. A **duty of care** occurs when the defendant is required to use reasonable care to avoid injuring the plaintiff. Without a duty of care, there cannot be liability, even if the defendant carelessly injured the plaintiff. Ethical Perspective 12.1 provides an interesting illustration.

*a **duty of care** occurs when the defendant is required to use reasonable care to avoid injuring the plaintiff*

ETHICAL PERSPECTIVE 12.1

Duty of Care[3]

The Supreme Court of Canada has held that a pregnant woman does not owe a duty of care to her unborn child. Consequently, if a pregnant woman carelessly causes a traffic accident that results in damage to her unborn child, that child cannot sue in negligence even if it is later born with a disability.

Interestingly, the same rule does *not* apply between an unborn child and other people. Anyone, except a mother, can owe a duty of care. For example, if a father carelessly causes a child to suffer an injury before birth, he can be held liable if

that child is later born with a disability. Furthermore, everyone, including a mother, can be held liable for carelessly causing an injury to a child *after* it is born.

The rule that denies the existence of a duty of care between a pregnant woman and her unborn child reflects the Court's attempt to strike a balance between the desirability of providing compensation for the injured child and the desirability of protecting the woman's freedom of action. Because nearly everything that a woman does can affect her unborn child, it has been argued that a duty of care would unfairly require her to be on guard for nine months.

(continued)

2. *Reibl v Hughes* (1980) 114 DLR (3d) 1 (SCC); *ter Neuzen v Korn* (1995) 127 DLR (4th) 577 (SCC).
3. *Dobson v Dobson* (1999) 174 DLR (4th) 1 (SCC).

(continued)

Questions for Discussion

1. Has the Supreme Court of Canada struck a fair balance?
2. From a legal and moral perspective, should a pregnant woman be entitled to carelessly injure her unborn child? When answering those questions, consider that the mother would usually want to be held liable to her injured child. More precisely, she would want her child to be able to recover compensatory damages from her insurance company.

Test for Determining the Existence of Duty of Care

A duty of care is required for an action in negligence. But how does a judge decide when to impose such a duty? Traditionally, there was no general answer—a duty of care was restricted to certain types of relationships, such as innkeeper and traveller, lawyer and client, railway company and passenger, surgeon and patient. A plaintiff could win only if it fell within one of those relationships. Eventually, however, the courts replaced those individual categories with a single test. A duty of care can now be recognized any time that certain conditions are met. Case Brief 12.1 discusses one of the most famous cases in our legal system.

CASE BRIEF 12.1

Donoghue v Stevenson [1932] AC 562 (HL)

The plaintiff, Mrs Donoghue, visited a café with a friend. Her friend bought her a bottle of ginger beer that the defendant had manufactured. After drinking some of the beverage, the plaintiff poured the remainder into her glass. She then noticed that the bottle contained, along with ginger beer, a decomposed snail. The event made her sick, and she sued the defendant for carelessly allowing a snail to get into the drink.

The issue before the court was whether a manufacturer owes a duty of care to a person who consumes, but did not personally buy, a particular product. Lord Atkin said "yes."

> You must take reasonable care to avoid acts or omissions which you can reasonably foresee would be likely to injure your neighbour. Who, then, in law is my neighbour? The answer seems to be—persons who are so closely and directly affected by my act that I ought reasonably to have them in contemplation as being so affected when I am directing my mind to the acts or omissions which are called in question.

That decision is important to business people for two reasons. First, it created a general test for determining the existence of a duty of care. It is no longer necessary to bring a case within one of the traditional categories. Second, it established that a manufacturer can be held liable to any consumer. Manufacturers therefore have to worry not only about the people who buy their products, but also about the people who use their products. We will discuss the second point later.

Based on *Donoghue v Stevenson*, the Canadian courts have developed a two-part test for the creation of a duty of care.[4]

- First, it must have been *reasonably foreseeable* that the plaintiff could be injured by the defendant's carelessness.

- Second, there must not be any compelling *policy* reasons for refusing to impose a duty of care on the defendant.

> the existence of a duty of care is based on reasonable foreseeability and policy

---

[4] *Neilsen v Kamloops (City)* (1984) 10 DLR (4th) 641 (SCC).

Reasonable Foreseeability

the reasonable foreseeability test is objective

The reasonable foreseeability test is *objective*. The issue is not whether the defendant *personally knew* that its activities might injure the plaintiff. It is whether a *reasonable person* in the defendant's position would have recognized that possibility. That test is intended to strike a balance between the parties. It would be unfair to deny compensation simply because the defendant was unaware of a danger. The plaintiff should not be disadvantaged by the defendant's lack of awareness. But at the same time, it would be unfair to hold the defendant liable for *every* injury that it creates, even those that were unforeseeable. A person cannot take precautions against a hidden danger. Similarly, it is difficult to arrange liability insurance for an unpredictable event. To better understand the reasonable foreseeability test, consider Business Decision 12.1.

the defendant cannot be held liable for carelessly injuring the plaintiff unless it was reasonably foreseeable that such an injury might occur

BUSINESS DECISION 12.1

Reasonable Foreseeability and Risk Management[5]

Hermes Holdings Ltd sold a piece of land to Mercury Developments Inc for $500 000. Mercury intended to build a shopping mall on that property. To do so, however, it needed certain documents to be delivered to a government office by December 31. If it failed to do so, it would not be able to proceed with its project and it would suffer a loss of $1 000 000. Hermes still had possession of those documents. Mercury therefore told it to send them to the government office by courier.

Hermes contacted your courier company. You agreed to deliver an envelope to the government office by December 31 in exchange for $10. Hermes did not, however, tell you what the envelope contained, nor that Mercury would suffer an enormous loss if delivery was late. Unfortunately, because you were very busy, you did not actually deliver the envelope until January 3.

Hermes is not particularly concerned about the late delivery. Mercury, however, is very upset. Your carelessness cost it $1 000 000. Nevertheless, you probably would not be held liable. A reasonable person in your position might not have appreciated the consequences of late delivery.

Questions for Discussion

1. Why would it be unfair to hold you liable if Mercury's loss was not reasonably foreseeable?

2. If the situation had been fully explained to you at the outset, would you still have charged only $10? Would it make good business sense to expose yourself to the risk of $1 000 000 in damages in exchange for such a small price?

Policy Considerations

a duty of care will not be imposed if it is against policy

The test for a duty of care has two parts. Even if the plaintiff's injury was *reasonably foreseeable*, the defendant cannot be held liable if there are compelling *policy reasons* for refusing to impose a duty of care. We can look at two prominent examples.

- As we saw in Ethical Perspective 12.1, a pregnant woman is not liable for injuring her unborn child. The Supreme Court of Canada decided that it would be unfair to substantially restrict a woman's behaviour for nine months.

there is no general duty to rescue

- Similarly, there is no general *duty to rescue*. For instance, I can stand by while a child drowns, even if I could easily prevent that death. Once again, the courts want to protect my freedom of choice. If the law *prohibits* me from doing one thing (such as shooting a gun), I am still free to do anything else. However, if the law *requires* me to do something (such as rescue a child), I cannot do anything else at the same time.

---

5. *BDC Ltd v Hofstrand Farms Ltd* (1986) 26 DLR (4th) 1 (SCC).

Consequently, the courts will not impose a duty to rescue in the absence of a *special relationship*. I am therefore required to rescue my *own* child. More significantly for business people, a duty to rescue may also be imposed if the defendant received a financial benefit from its relationship with the plaintiff. Consequently, a tavern may be expected to ensure that a drunken customer gets home safely.[6]

a duty to rescue may be imposed in special relationships

Negligent Statements   The courts sometimes refuse to impose a duty of care if they are afraid of "opening the floodgates" by allowing too many people to sue in negligence. In the business context, the best example concerns *negligent statements*. The Canadian economy is increasingly based on the supply of information and advice, rather than on the production of physical goods. Inevitably, some of the statements that are made by professionals (such as financial advisers, business consultants, lawyers, stockbrokers, and bankers) will be inaccurate. And inevitably, consumers and clients will suffer as a result. The law of negligence must strike a balance between the need to compensate people who are hurt by negligent statements and the need to protect businesses from the potentially disastrous consequences of being held liable.

negligent statements present special dangers that generally do not apply to negligent actions

Special rules are needed because *careless statements* are different from *careless actions* in at least three ways.

- Since the dangers associated with physical conduct are usually obvious, the need for precaution is normally clear as well. You know that if you swing a baseball bat in a crowded room, you may hurt someone. In contrast, because the risks associated with statements are often hidden, the need for care is usually less apparent. Consequently, people tend to speak loosely, especially in social settings.

- "Words are more volatile than deeds."[7] In most situations, the risk created by a careless action is limited in time and space. Drunk drivers pose a real threat, but generally only for the motorists and pedestrians in their path. Furthermore, they will likely be stopped once the first accident occurs. In contrast, if a duty of care exists for a careless statement, there is a possibility of "liability in an indeterminate amount for an indeterminate time to an indeterminate class."[8] Suppose that a financial report that was created for personal purposes is mistakenly distributed to the public. If it contains inaccurate information, many people may later rely upon it and suffer financial loses when they make bad investments.

- Careless actions usually result in property damage or personal injuries. A negligent driver may crash through your fence or run you down. Careless statements, however, usually result in *pure economic losses*, that is, financial losses that are not tied to any property damage or personal injuries. For example, if you follow your stockbroker's negligent advice and make a poor investment, you will simply lose money. And significantly, the law is more reluctant to provide compensation for pure economic losses, than for property damage or personal injuries.[9] Some things are more important than others.

---

[6] *Jordan House Ltd v Menow & Honsberger* (1973) 38 DLR (3d) 105 (SCC).

[7] *Hedley Byrne & Co v Heller & Partners Ltd* [1963] 2 All ER 575 at 602 (HL).

[8] *Ultramares Corp v Touche* 255 NY 170 (CA 1931).

[9] That is true whether a pure economic loss is caused by careless words or by careless conduct. In contrast, the courts generally do not feel the need to apply special rules if the defendant's careless statement causes the plaintiff to suffer property damage or physical injury. In one case, a model suffered physical injuries as a result of falling off a stage while following a director's instructions: *Robson v Chrysler Corp (Canada)* (1962) 32 DLR (2d) 49 (Alta CA).

For those reasons, Canadian courts apply special rules when deciding whether to recognize a duty of care if the defendant's *careless statement* caused the plaintiff to suffer a *pure economic loss*.[10] Case Brief 12.2 discusses a simplified version of a leading case.

CASE BRIEF 12.2

Hercules Management Ltd v Ernst & Young (1997) 146 DLR (4th) 577 (SCC)

The defendant was an accounting firm that prepared audited financial statements for a company. Those statements were required by statute and were intended to allow shareholders to supervise the management of the company. The plaintiff, who was one of the shareholders in the company, claimed that the defendant carelessly prepared those statements. He also claimed that he suffered pure economic losses after relying upon inaccurate information that they contained. More specifically, he argued that the statements caused him to continue his investment in the company, which later went broke.

The Supreme Court of Canada applied the two-part test for a duty of care. The first part required proof that it was *reasonably foreseeable* that the plaintiff would suffer a loss by relying upon the defendant's statement. A duty of care is more likely to be imposed with respect to a statement if:

- the defendant possessed, or claimed to possess, *special knowledge*—it is often reasonable to rely upon information that is provided by an apparent expert
- the statement was communicated on a *serious occasion*—it is often reasonable to rely upon information that is provided during a business meeting, but not during an informal party
- the defendant's statement was made in response to *an inquiry*—a person who is specifically asked for information should realize that the answer may be relied upon
- the defendant received a *financial benefit* in exchange for the statement—reasonable people do not usually pay for information unless they intend to rely upon it
- the defendant communicated a *statement of fact*, or an *opinion or prediction based on fact*, rather than a purely personal opinion—it is often reason-

able to rely upon a professional evaluation of certain stocks, but not upon a prediction as to the outcome of a horse race

However, a duty of care is less likely to be imposed if:

- the defendant issued a *disclaimer* along with its statement—a reasonable person does not generally rely upon a statement if the speaker was unwilling to assume responsibility

Given the facts of the case, including the lack of a disclaimer, the Court held that it was reasonably foreseeable that the plaintiff would reasonably rely upon the defendant's statement.

At the second stage of the duty of care analysis, however, the Court was worried about "indeterminate liability." The defendant prepared the statements for a specific purpose—to allow shareholders to monitor the management of the company. It did not intend for those statements to be used as investment advice by people like the plaintiff.[11] The Court was also worried that the fear of widespread liability would cause businesses in the defendant's position to substantially increase their prices to offset the risk of being held responsible. The Court therefore held, *on policy grounds*, that a duty of care will be recognized only if:

- the defendant knew that the plaintiff, either individually or as a member of a defined group, might rely upon the statement
- the plaintiff relied upon that statement for its intended purpose

Because he was a shareholder, the plaintiff was a member of an identifiable class. He did not, however, use the statement for its intended purpose. He used it as investment advice, rather than for management of the company. The defendant therefore did not owe a duty of care to the plaintiff.

---

[10] The courts are more willing to impose liability if the defendant's inaccurate statement was intentional rather than merely careless. In this section, we are discussing the law of *negligent statements*. However, as Chapter 11 explained, liability can also be imposed under the tort of *deceit* if the defendant intentionally misled the plaintiff.

[11] Financial statements may be relied upon for many reasons by many types of people, including creditors, customers, competitors, and employees.

As a business person, you should learn three important lessons from Case Brief 12.2. First, you should be very careful about providing information and advice. Second, if you do not wish to be held liable for your statements, you should clearly disclaim responsibility. Third, you should be careful about relying on statements made by others. While you may be entitled to compensation, your claim may also be rejected on policy grounds.

BREACH OF THE STANDARD OF CARE

The first element of the cause of action in negligence requires the plaintiff to prove that the defendant owed a duty of care. The second element requires the plaintiff to prove that the defendant *breached the standard of care*. The **standard of care** tells the defendant how it should act. It is **breached** when the defendant acts less carefully.

The standard of care is based on the **reasonable person test**—the defendant must act in the same way that a reasonable person would act in similar circumstances. The reasonable person is a *fictional character*. One judge provided this description.

> I shall not attempt to formulate a comprehensive definition of "a reasonable man."... I simply say that he is a mythical creature of the law whose conduct is the standard by which the Courts measure the conduct of all other persons.... He is not an extraordinary or unusual creature; he is not superhuman; he is not required to display the highest skill of which anyone is capable; he is not a genius who can perform uncommon feats, nor is he possessed of unusual powers of foresight. He is a person of normal intelligence who makes prudence a guide to his conduct. He does nothing that a prudent man would not do and he does not omit to do anything that a prudent man would do. He acts in accord with general and approved practice. His conduct is guided by considerations which ordinarily regulate the conduct of human affairs.[12]

The reasonable person test gives the courts a great deal of flexibility in deciding whether the defendant acted carelessly. Although it is impossible to list all of the relevant factors, we can identify some important ones.

- The reasonable person test is generally *objective*. It does not make allowances for the defendant's *subjective*, or personal, characteristics. For example, I cannot avoid liability by simply proving that I did my best. I may be held liable even though my carelessness was caused by the fact that I suffer from a mental disability.[13] The courts are more concerned to provide compensation to my victims than to show sympathy for my shortcomings. Nevertheless, judges do lower the standard of care somewhat for children. A child is generally not required to act like a reasonable adult.[14] It is enough to act like a reasonable child of similar age, intelligence, and experience.[15]

the **standard of care** tells the defendant how it should act

the standard of care is **breached** when the defendant acts less carefully

the **reasonable person test** requires the defendant to act in the same way that a reasonable person would act in similar circumstances

the reasonable person test is very flexible

[12] *Arland v Taylor* [1955] 3 DLR 358 *per* Laidlaw JA (Ont CA).

[13] I might be able to avoid liability, however, if my mental disability was so severe that I effectively had no control over my actions: *Buckley v Smith Transport Ltd* [1946] 4 DLR 721 (Ont CA) (the defendant caused a traffic accident because he believed that his vehicle was being operated by remote control). Likewise, I might be able to avoid liability if I suffer from a severe physical disability. The law does not expect me to see if I am blind. It does, however, require me to recognize my limitations and to avoid dangerous activities, such as driving.

[14] The rule is different if a child participates in an adult activity, like driving a boat.

[15] *McEllistrum v Etches* (1956) 6 DLR (2d) 1 (SCC). There are relatively few cases in this area, largely because there is seldom anything to be gained from suing a child. Furthermore, parents are not *vicariously liable* for their children's torts unless a statute says otherwise: *Parental Responsibility Act*, SM 1996, c 61 (Man). They may, however, be held personally liable for failing to properly supervise their children.

- The reasonable person takes precautions against *reasonably foreseeable risks*. Notice that the test does not refer to "probable" or "likely" risks. As long as it is not fanciful, something may be reasonably foreseeable even if it is unlikely to occur. A 1-in-100 or 1-in-1000 chance may be sufficient. At the same time, however, there is no need to take precautions against unforeseeable risks. The reasonable person does not guard against every conceivable danger.

- The reasonable person is influenced by both the *likelihood of harm* and the *potential severity of harm*. Greater care is required if the chance of injury is 90 percent rather than 10 percent. Likewise, greater care is required if the relevant injury is death rather than a light bruise.

- The reasonable person is more likely to adopt *affordable precautions*. For example, a taxi company that regularly carries children should certainly pay $50 for tamper-proof door locks. But it does not have to spend an enormous sum by purchasing the safest vehicles on the market.

- The reasonable person may act in a way that has great *social utility*, even though it creates a risk. For instance, it is sometimes appropriate for an ambulance driver to speed through a red light to save a dying patient.

- The standard of care requires the defendant to act as the reasonable person would act "in similar circumstances." Consequently, less care is required during emergencies. The *sudden peril doctrine* states that even a reasonable person may make a mistake under difficult circumstances.

Professional Negligence

a professional must act as a reasonable professional would act in similar circumstances

Professionals, such as lawyers, physicians, accountants, bankers, architects, stockbrokers, financial advisers, and engineers, are held to the same basic standard of care that we have described. They must act as a reasonable person would act in similar circumstances. In this context, however, the courts pay special attention to four factors.

First, it is not enough for a professional person, while engaged in a professional activity, to meet the standard that would be applied if a layperson performed the same task. A professional must act as the *reasonable professional* would act in similar circumstances.

- Professional people must live up to the training that they received or claim to have received. The last part of that sentence is important: if people claim to have special expertise, they cannot avoid liability by later confessing that they lied about their qualifications.

- Even within the same profession, more may be expected of a specialist than of a generalist. For example, an accountant who specializes in a particular area must perform to a higher level when acting within that area than an accountant who does not claim to have the same expertise.

- Special allowances are *not* made for beginners. Even an inexperienced professional must conform to the standard of a reasonably competent and experienced professional.

Those rules are based on the reasonable expectations that people have about professionals.

the standard of care is not based on hindsight

Second, by the time a case gets to trial, it is often easy to say what the defendant could have done to avoid injuring the plaintiff. It would be unfair, however, to judge the defendant's actions in *hindsight*. That is especially significant in scientific or technical fields, where knowledge often develops very quickly. The standard of care is therefore based on information that was reasonably available to the defendant at the time of the accident.[16]

Third, a professional who follows an *approved practice* cannot generally be held liable. Consequently, the standard of care is usually met if the defendant either complies with requirements established by a professional organization or does what other professionals in the same field normally do. But sometimes, an approved practice is itself careless. A court can reach that conclusion, however, only if the relevant activity can be judged by common sense and does not involve technical or complex matters. Case Brief 12.3 illustrates those rules.[17]

a professional who follows an approved practice generally cannot be held liable

---

CASE BRIEF 12.3

ter Neuzen v Korn (1995) 127 DLR (4th) 577 (SCC)

The defendant physician artificially inseminated the plaintiff in 1985. Tragically, he used infected semen and the plaintiff contracted HIV. She sued him in negligence and argued that he carelessly failed to realize that HIV could be transmitted through artificial insemination. In response, the defendant argued that, at the time of the procedure, it was not generally known that HIV could be transmitted in that way.

The Supreme Court of Canada held that the defendant had not breached the standard of care:

[C]ourts do not ordinarily have the expertise to tell professionals that they are not behaving appropriately in their field.... As a general rule, where a procedure involves difficult or uncertain questions of medical treatment or complex, scientific or highly

technical matters that are beyond the ordinary experience and understanding of a judge or jury, it will not be open to find a standard medical practice negligent. On the other hand, as an exception to the general rule, if a standard practice fails to adopt obvious and reasonable precautions which are readily apparent to the ordinary finder of fact, then it is no excuse for a practitioner to claim that he or she was merely conforming to such a negligent common practice.

The facts fell into the first category. When the procedure was performed in 1985, HIV was poorly understood, even by leading scientists. The court therefore could not decide that the practice that was being used by a respectable body of physicians—including the defendant—was careless.

Fourth, carelessness is different from mere *errors of judgment*. The former can result in liability; the latter cannot. A professional does not have to be perfect. As long as the defendant's mistake is one that a reasonable professional might make, the standard of care is not breached. For example, a surgeon will not be held liable for incorrectly choosing one procedure over another if a reasonable physician might have done the same.

a mere error of judgment does not breach the standard of care

Product Liability

Like professional negligence, the topic of product liability falls within the general action in negligence. However, it also requires special attention.

Product liability can occur when a person is injured by a product. As we saw in Chapters 6 and 8, the victim may be entitled to sue for breach of contract. If so, liability is *strict*. In other words, the plaintiff does not have to prove that the defendant acted carelessly. It is enough that the contract was broken in a way that caused harm. Sometimes, however, the parties are not linked

product liability can occur when a person is injured by a product

---

[16.] *Walker Estate v York Finch General Hospital* (2001) 198 DLR (4th) 193 (SCC).

[17.] Although the case brief involves a claim for medical malpractice, the same principles also apply in other professional contexts.

together by a contract. If so, the consumer must rely upon the law of negligence. While the action in negligence is certainly useful, it depends, as always, upon proof that the plaintiff's injury was caused by the defendant's *carelessness*. In Canada, product liability is not strict.[18]

The courts almost always find that a duty of care was owed to a person who was injured by a defective product, whether that person was the purchaser, a consumer, or simply a bystander. Liability therefore usually turns on the standard of care. We divide that discussion into three parts:

- manufacture
- design
- failure to warn

Manufacture

liability may be imposed for careless manufacture

The courts usually impose liability if the defendant carelessly *manufactured* a product that injured the plaintiff. *Donoghue v Stevenson*, which we discussed in Case Brief 12.1, is the classic case. Mr Stevenson was required to compensate Mrs Donoghue because he negligently allowed a snail to crawl into a bottle of ginger beer.

Design

liability may be imposed for a careless design

The courts are more cautious if the plaintiff's injury was caused by the *design*, rather than the *manufacture*, of a product. A manufacturing defect usually affects only a few items. Not every bottle of Mr Stevenson's ginger beer contained a decomposed snail. A design defect, in contrast, usually affects every item that is produced. For instance, if a system of headlights is poorly designed, *every* vehicle that uses that system will create a danger. The courts are therefore more concerned about imposing a tremendous burden on the defendant. In the headlights case, the judge demanded proof that the product's disadvantages outweighed its advantages.[19] He carefully balanced the probability and severity of harm against the difficulty and expense of using an alternative design.

Warning

liability may be imposed for a careless failure to warn

Even if a product is carefully designed and manufactured, liability may arise if consumers are not reasonably *warned* about its dangers. For instance, ladders should carry stickers that caution people against using them on slippery surfaces, just as some electrical appliances should alert people to the risk of electrocution in water. Several more points should be noted.

- The nature and extent of the warning depends upon the circumstances. Greater care is required if the danger is severe or if the consumers are unsophisticated. Less care is required if the risk is marginal or if the product is invariably sold to professionals who are specially trained to use it. And no warning at all is required if a danger is obvious. People are assumed to realize, for instance, that knives cut and matches burn.
- A warning is usually needed only for a product's intended use. Sometimes, however, a warning may be required for a use that is unintended, but foreseeable. Model glue is not meant to be sniffed, but manufacturers realize that their product is often abused.

[18.] In contrast, product liability *is* strict in the United States. The plaintiff does not have to prove that the defendant was *careless*.

[19.] *Rentway Canada Ltd v Laidlaw Transport Ltd* (1989) 49 CCLT 150 (Ont HCJ).

- A warning may be required even though the manufacturer discovers the danger *after* the product has been sold. In that situation, it should take reasonable steps to contact consumers and, if necessary, to recall the dangerous items.

- A warning may be required not only by a manufacturer, but also by someone who sells, distributes, or installs a product. The key question is whether the defendant knew, or should have known, of the danger.

- In some situations, the defendant can avoid liability if it provided a warning to a *learned intermediary*. The law in this area is complicated. For our purposes, it is enough to know that the rule may apply if a product is always sold to a professional rather than directly to the intended consumer. Breast implants, for instance, are not bought off store shelves. They are supplied to physicians, who then insert them into patients. If a manufacturer does not warn a doctor, it may be held liable if the implants later rupture inside a woman.[20]

CAUSATION OF HARM

The third element of the cause of action in negligence is *causation of harm*. The defendant will not be held liable, even if it owed a duty of care and breached the standard of care, unless its carelessness caused the plaintiff to suffer a loss.[21] Although causation can be a difficult issue, we will only highlight the basic principles. The reason is simple. From a risk-management perspective, much can be done to avoid liability under the first two stages of the negligence action. But once a business has come under a duty of care and has acted carelessly, there is relatively little that it can do to avoid causing harm. Its carelessness either will or will not hurt somebody.

the defendant will not be held liable unless its carelessness caused the plaintiff to suffer a loss

The issue of causation is usually decided by the *but-for test*. The **but-for test** requires the plaintiff to prove that it would not have suffered a loss but for the defendant's carelessness. It is based on a simple question, "If the defendant had not acted carelessly, would the plaintiff have still suffered the same loss?" If the answer is "yes," the defendant cannot be held liable. If the answer is "no," the defendant may be held liable. To better understand that test, consider the Concept Summary 12.1 and answer the questions in You Be the Judge 12.1.

the but-for test requires the plaintiff to prove that it would not have suffered a loss but-for the defendant's carelessness.

Concept Summary 12.1

The But-For Test

Question	Answer	Result
But-for the defendant's carelessness, would the plaintiff have suffered the same loss?	Yes—the plaintiff would have suffered the same loss even if the defendant had not acted carelessly.	The defendant cannot be held liable.
	No—the plaintiff would not have suffered the same loss if the defendant had not acted carelessly.	The defendant may be held liable.

---

[20] *Hollis v Dow Corning Corp* (1995) 129 DLR (4th) 609 (SCC).

[21] As we have already seen, that loss may take many forms. The plaintiff may sustain a physical injury, property damage, or a pure economic loss.

YOU BE THE JUDGE 12.1

The But-For Test[22]

A man went to a hospital complaining of stomach pain. The doctor on duty believed that there was nothing seriously wrong with the patient and simply told him to go home and sleep. The man later died of arsenic poisoning. His widow has shown that the doctor: (i) owed a duty of care to her husband, and (ii) carelessly failed to realize that her husband's stomach pains were due to arsenic poisoning.

Questions for Discussion

1. Will the doctor be held liable if the evidence indicates that the man would have lived if he had received proper diagnosis and treatment?

2. Will the doctor be held liable if the evidence indicates that the man's arsenic poisoning was so serious that he could not have been saved even if he had been properly diagnosed?

---

the plaintiff generally has to prove all of the elements of the tort of negligence, including causation, on a balance of probabilities

the law generally adopts an all-or-nothing approach to the issue of liability

the plaintiff has to prove only that the defendant's carelessness was a cause of his loss

defendants who cause different injuries are only liable accordingly

defendants who combine to cause a single injury may be held jointly and severally liable

court may refuse to use the but-for test if it would lead to an unfair result

There are several other things to note about causation of harm. First, the plaintiff generally has to prove all of the elements of the tort of negligence, including causation, on a *balance of probabilities*.[23]

Second, the law generally adopts an *all-or-nothing* approach. If there is at least a 51 percent chance that the defendant's carelessness caused the plaintiff's loss, then the court will award damages for *all* of that loss. In contrast, if there is less than a 51 percent chance that the defendant's carelessness caused the plaintiff's injury, then the court will not award damages for *any* of that loss.

Third, the plaintiff has to prove only that the defendant's carelessness was *a cause*—not necessarily *the only cause*—of a loss. Suppose that my back pain was caused mostly by poor posture but partly by your causing me to fall off my bike. I may be entitled to receive 100 percent of my damages from you.[24]

Fourth, if *different defendants* cause the plaintiff to suffer *different injuries*, then each one is responsible accordingly. For example, if you break my arm, and Mary breaks my leg, you can be held liable only for my arm and she can be held liable only for my leg.

Fifth, the situation is more complicated if *different defendants* create a *single injury*. Suppose that you are injured after slipping on my neighbour's sidewalk while leaving my party. You lost your balance and fell only because: (i) I secretly drugged your drinks, *and* (ii) my neighbour, Shannon, failed to shovel her sidewalk. Shannon and I will be held *jointly and severally liable*. That means that you can recover all of your damages from her, *or* all of your damages from me, *or* some of your damages from each of us. The choice is yours. As between ourselves, Shannon and I are responsible in proportion to our share of the blame. Suppose that the court said that she was 30 percent to blame and that I was 70 percent to blame. If you recovered all of your damages from Shannon, she could demand 70 percent of that money from me.

Sixth, a court may reject the but-for test if it would lead to an unfair result. Suppose that you and I went hunting with Akbar. When you made a rustling sound in a bush, he and I both turned and shot because we carelessly mistook you for a bird. You were hit by a single bullet, but you have no way of knowing whose. The but-for test seems to suggest that neither Akbar nor I will be held

---

[22] *Barnett v Chelsea & Kensington Hospital Mgmt Committee* [1969] 1 QB 428.

[23] The courts generally require proof on a *balance of probabilities* in *private law*. In contrast, they require proof *beyond a reasonable doubt* in *criminal law*. The criminal standard is much harder to satisfy. If there is a chance that a person can be sent to jail, rather than merely forced to pay damages, the courts want to be as sure as possible that punishment is deserved.

[24] *Athey v Leonati* (1996) 140 DLR (4th) 235 (SCC).

liable. You cannot prove on a balance of probabilities (that is, at least 51 per-cent) that he fired the relevant shot. Nor can you prove on a balance of proba-bilities (that is, at least 51 percent) that I fired the relevant shot. For each of us, there is only a 50 percent chance. A court, however, would probably hold both us liable and allow you to recover all of your damages from either one or both.[25] Although it has not yet been applied in Canada, Business Law in Action 12.1 shows how some American courts have tried to avoid the but-for test in even more complex situations.

BUSINESS LAW IN ACTION 12.1

Causation and Market Share Liability[26]

For many years, a drug called EFT was pre-scribed to pregnant women to prevent mis-carriages. EFT was, in fact, carcinogenic. The plaintiff, who had taken the drug and developed cancer, wanted compensation from the responsible party. The evidence indicated, however, that the pills that she had consumed could have been man-ufactured by any one of several pharmaceutical companies, all of which had acted carelessly.

The plaintiff could not satisfy the but-for test against any single manufacturer. The court nevertheless held *all* of the companies liable to the plaintiff in proportion to their share of the market. Company A, which held 40 percent of the EFT market, was liable for 40 percent of the plaintiff's damages; Company B, which held 25 percent of the market, was liable for 25 percent of the damages; and so on.

Unlike the other rules that we have seen, the concept of *market share liability* does not allow the plaintiff to recov-er 100 percent of her damages from any single defendant. Each defendant is liable only for its proportionate share of the market.

Questions for Discussion

1. Is the concept of market share liability fair to manufactur-ers? Should Company C, which held only 5 percent of the market, be liable at all? Bear in mind that there is a 95 per-cent chance that it did not produce the pills that the plain-tiff consumed.

2. Is the concept of market share liability fair to the plaintiff? What if three companies each had 33 percent of the mar-ket, but one of those companies has ceased to exist? Should the plaintiff only be able to recover 66 percent of her damages, even though the other two companies had also acted negligently?

Remoteness

Even if the defendant caused the plaintiff to suffer a loss, liability will not be imposed if that loss was too *remote* from the careless conduct. A loss is **remote** if it would be unfair to hold the defendant responsible for it. We already exam-ined that concept in connection with breach of contract in Chapter 7 and inten-tional torts in Chapter 10. We can now add a few more points.

In negligence, the basic issue is whether the *type of harm* that the plaintiff suffered was a *reasonably foreseeable* result of the defendant's carelessness. As always, the phrase "reasonably foreseeable" does not mean "probable" or "likely." It simply refers to a possibility that is not far-fetched. Furthermore, if the *type of harm* that the plaintiff suffered was reasonably foreseeable, it is irrel-evant that the *manner in which it occurred* was not. To understand that distinc-tion, consider Case Brief 12.4.

loss is **remote** if it would be unfair to hold the defendant responsible for it

25. *Cook v Lewis* [1952] 1 DLR 1 (SCC).

26. *Sindell v Abbott Industries* 607 P 2d 924 (Cal 1980).

CASE BRIEF 12.4

Hughes v Lord Advocate [1963] AC 837 (HL)

The defendant's employees had been working in a manhole. They left the cover off the manhole when they went for lunch. They also left a paraffin lamp nearby. A young boy crawled down the manhole with the lamp. He was badly burned when the lamp fell and exploded. The explosion occurred because vapours escaped from the lamp and were ignited by the flame. The court held that that series of events was entirely unforeseeable. It nevertheless imposed liability because the *type* of injury that the plaintiff suffered, a burn, was reasonably foreseeable. It did not matter that the source of that burn was a bizarre accident rather than direct contact with the lamp's flame, as might have been expected.

a thin skull case occurs if the plaintiff was unusually vulnerable to injury

The remoteness principle is used to resolve *thin skull* cases. **A thin skull** case occurs if the plaintiff was unusually vulnerable to injury. In a literal example, suppose that I am injury-prone because my skull is very thin. If you carelessly hit me on the head with a stick, are you responsible for all of my losses? What if a normal person would not have suffered any injury? What if a normal person would have suffered a minor injury, but not one as serious as mine? The law tries to strike a balance between its desire to compensate me and its desire to treat you fairly. You are *not* responsible at all if a normal person would not have suffered *any* harm. But you are fully responsible for *all* of my losses if it was *reasonably foreseeable* that a normal person would have suffered *some* damage.[27] For instance, if your carelessness would have bruised a normal person, I can fully recover for the fact that I also suffered brain damage.[28]

the defendant is generally liable for all of the plaintiff's losses if it was reasonably foreseeable that a normal person might suffer some loss

the courts traditionally have not recognized a thin wallet principle

Significantly for business people, the courts traditionally refused to apply a *thin wallet* principle. In other words, the defendant was not responsible for the fact that the plaintiff suffered to an unusual extent because it was poor. More recently, however, the courts have begun to suggest that the defendant may be fully liable if it was reasonably foreseeable that the plaintiff's poverty would cause it to suffer more than usual.[29] Business Law in Action 12.2 explores those issues.

BUSINESS LAW IN ACTION 12.2

Remoteness and Thin Wallets[30]

You had a contract with Acme Goods Ltd to carry several loads of widgets between Vancouver and Halifax. Unfortunately, Darva carelessly caused an accident that destroyed your truck. You therefore needed to use another vehicle to fulfill your agreement with Acme. The purchase price for a replacement was $100 000, but you

(continued)

---

27. The same principles could apply, for example, if I drive a type of vehicle that is unusually vulnerable to damage in an accident: *Oke v Weide Transport Ltd* (1963) 41 DLR (2d) 53 (Man CA).

28. While the thin skull doctrine may hold the defendant fully liable for the plaintiff's injury, damages are reduced if the plaintiff's skull was not only thin but also *crumbling*. In other words, the plaintiff is denied compensation to the extent that his condition was so fragile that he eventually would have suffered the same injury, even without the defendant's carelessness. In that situation, the defendant merely caused the plaintiff's injury to happen sooner than expected. The defendant is therefore only liable for accelerating the plaintiff's loss.

29. *Alcoa Minerals of Jamaica v Broderick* [2000] 3 WLR 23 (PC).

30. *The Dredger Liesbosch v SS Edison* [1933] AC 449 (HL).

(continued)

were unable to buy one because you did not have immediate access to that much money and because your credit rating is very poor. Consequently, you were forced to lease a truck. You were able to afford that option because you could periodically meet the rental charge after being paid for each delivery of cargo. That option, however, eventually cost you $150 000, which is $50 000 more than the purchase price of a truck.

Assuming that Darva is liable in negligence, you are entitled to compensation for your losses. However, you might recover only $100 000, rather than $150 000. Even though the loss of your truck was reasonably foreseeable, a court might say that Darva is not responsible for the fact that you suffered to an unusual extent because of your own financial problems.

Questions for Discussion

1. Would it be fair if the court rejected the thin wallet principle in your case? Explain your answer.
2. The courts historically accepted the thin skull principle but rejected the thin wallet principle. What does that contrast say about the law's attitude toward personal injuries on the one hand and economic losses on the other? Which sort of harm is considered more important?

The remoteness principle is also used to deal with *intervening acts*. An **intervening act** is an event that occurs *after* the defendant's carelessness and that causes the plaintiff to suffer an additional injury. Suppose that you carelessly broke my leg. A week later, I suffered a broken arm, either because I foolishly ran down stairs on crutches or because I was hit by a car in my physician's parking lot. In either event, you are *factually responsible* for my broken arm. After all, but-for your initial negligence, I would not have been using crutches, nor would I have been visiting my physician. The crucial question, however, is whether you are *legally responsible* or whether, in light of the intervening act, my broken arm is too *remote*. A judge would ask if it was reasonably foreseeable that your initial carelessness would result in my later injury. As usual, that test may be flexible enough to allow a judge to decide my case on policy grounds. Bearing that in mind, how would you decide the dispute in You Be the Judge 12.2?

an **intervening act** is an event that occurs after the defendant's carelessness and that causes the plaintiff to suffer an additional injury

YOU BE THE JUDGE 12.2

Remoteness and Intervening Acts[31]

Shogun Gardens, a Japanese restaurant, specializes in teppanyaki cuisine, in which a chef prepares food on a hot skillet at the customer's table. For the safety of its patrons, the restaurant installed the best fire sprinkler system available. That system was automatically activated after a chef carelessly allowed oil to accumulate and ignite at one of the tables. The system quickly and effectively extinguished the flame. However, in doing so, it emitted a hissing sound. An unidentified customer mistook the sound of the sprinkler for the sound of a leaking gas line and hysterically shouted, "Everybody out! This place is going to blow!" Another customer named Aki was trampled during the stampede that followed.

Shogun Gardens admits that its employee was negligent in causing the fire that triggered the sprinkler system. It insists, however, that the actions of the panic-stricken customer, which were idiotic by any account, amounted to an intervening act. It therefore argues that Aki's injuries are too remote from its chef's carelessness to be recoverable. Do you agree?

Questions for Discussion

1. To what extent are you influenced by the desire to allow Aki to recover compensation for his losses? Bear in mind that the person who started the stampede has not been identified and therefore cannot be sued.
2. To what extent are you influenced by the desire to ensure that Shogun Gardens is not penalized for installing a state-of-the-art sprinkler system?
3. To what extent are you influenced by the fact that the intervening act was idiotic? Would your decision be any different if it was not merely idiotic, but rather a deliberate attempt to start a stampede?

[31.] *Bradford v Kanellos* (1973) 40 DLR (3d) 578 (SCC).

DEFENCES

The plaintiff is usually entitled to compensatory damages once the court is satisfied that there was: (i) a duty of care, (ii) a breach of the standard of care, and (iii) the causation of harm. Occasionally, however, the defendant can avoid liability, at least in part, by proving a defence. We will briefly consider the three most important defences:

- contributory negligence
- voluntary assumption of risk
- illegality

Contributory Negligence

contributory negligence occurs when a loss is caused partly by the defendant's carelessness and partly by the plaintiff's own carelessness

The most important defence is *contributory negligence*. **Contributory negligence** occurs when a loss is caused partly by the defendant's carelessness and partly by the plaintiff's own carelessness. In deciding whether the plaintiff is guilty of contributory negligence, the courts generally use the same factors that they use when deciding whether the defendant breached the standard of care: foreseeability of harm, likelihood of injury, severity of harm, and so on. The cases tend to fall into three groups. Contributory negligence can arise if the plaintiff:

- unreasonably steps into a dangerous situation (as when a sober person accepts a ride from drunk, who then drives into a wall)
- unreasonably contributes to the creation of an accident (as when a passenger in the back of an open bed truck is thrown to the ground while carelessly standing up at the same time that the driver turns a corner too quickly)
- unreasonably contributes not to the creation of an accident, but to the damage that it causes (as when a passenger in a carelessly driven car suffers unusually severe head injuries after refusing to wear a seatbelt)

modern legislation allows for apportionment in cases of contributory negligence

Contributory negligence was traditionally a complete defence. If it applied, the plaintiff could not recover *any* damages. That rule was often unfair. The plaintiff could be denied compensation even though the defendant's carelessness played a much bigger role in causing an injury. Consequently, modern legislation allows for *apportionment*.[32] A court can assign responsibility for the plaintiff's loss between the parties and award damages accordingly. Suppose that you broke your wrist and suffered $10 000 in damages after falling over a package that I carelessly dropped onto the sidewalk. The evidence indicates that you were 25 percent responsible because you did not watch where you were going. A judge could reduce your damages by 25 percent and require me to only pay $7500.

Although judges can apportion the blame between the parties in whatever way is appropriate, they usually place contributory negligence at less than 30

[32.] *Contributory Negligence Act*, RSA 1980, c C-23 (Alta); *Negligence Act*, RSBC 1979, c 298 (BC); *Tortfeasors and Contributory Negligence Act*, RSM 1987 c T90 (Man); *Contributory Negligence Act*, RSN 1990, c C-33 (Nfld); *Contributory Negligence Act*, RSNB 1973, c C-19 (NB); *Contributory Negligence Act*, RSNS 1989, c 95 (NS); *Contributory Negligence Act*, RSNWT 1988, c C-18 (NWT and Nun); *Negligence Act*, RSO 1990, c N.1 (Ont); *Contributory Negligence Act*, RSPEI 1988, c C-21 (PEI); *Contributory Negligence Act*, RSS 1978, c C-31 (Sask); *Contributory Negligence Act*, RSY 1986, c 32 (Yuk).

percent. A court is normally reluctant to further reduce the amount of compensation that is available to the plaintiff, especially since the defendant often has liability insurance.

Voluntary Assumption of Risk

The defence of **voluntary assumption of risk** applies if the plaintiff freely agreed to be exposed to a risk of injury. Unlike contributory negligence, *volenti*, as it is sometimes called, remains a complete defence. If it applies, the plaintiff cannot recover *any* damages. The courts therefore interpret it very narrowly. The defendant has to prove that the plaintiff expressly or implicitly agreed to be exposed to both the physical *and* the legal risk of injury. The last part of that test is not satisfied unless the plaintiff agreed to give up the right to sue the defendant for negligence.[33] Consequently, that defence rarely succeeds.

the defence of voluntary assumption of risk applies if the plaintiff freely agreed to be exposed to a risk of injury

Although it is quite narrow, the defence may be an important tool for risk management. The best way of proving the voluntary assumption of risk is to show that the plaintiff signed an *exclusion clause*. We examined exclusion clauses in Chapter 4. Again, we stress that they must be drawn to a customer's attention. Case Brief 12.5 demonstrates the importance of doing so.

CASE BRIEF 12.5

Crocker v Sundance Northwest Resorts Ltd (1988) 51 DLR (4th) 321 (SCC)

The defendant organized an event in which contestants raced down a snow-covered mountain on inner tubes. Before being allowed to compete, the plaintiff was presented with a form that released the defendant from liability for negligence. Although the plaintiff signed that document, he had not read it, nor had it been explained to him. He was later injured after being thrown from his tube during the race. He sued the defendant on the basis that it carelessly allowed him to compete even though he was obviously very drunk. The defendant responded by pleading the *volenti* defence.

The Supreme Court of Canada held that the plaintiff had not voluntarily assumed the risk of injury.

[T]he waiver provision in the entry form was not drawn to the plaintiff's attention... he had not read it, and, indeed, did not know of its existence. He thought he was simply signing an entry form. In these circumstances [the defendant] cannot rely upon the waiver clause in the entry form.

The Court did, however reduce the plaintiff's damages by 25 percent to reflect his own contributory negligence.

Illegality

A court may refuse to award damages if the plaintiff suffered a loss while participating in an *illegal act*. Like voluntary assumption of risk, however, illegality is unpopular with the courts because it is a complete defence. Unlike contributory negligence, it does not allow for the apportionment of liability. Consequently, the courts have interpreted it very narrowly. Case Brief 12.6 considers the leading case.

a court may refuse to award damages if the plaintiff suffered a loss while engaged in an illegal act

---

33. *Dubé v Labar* (1986) 27 DLR (4th) 653 (SCC).

CASE BRIEF 12.6

Hall v Hebert (1993) 101 DLR (4th) 29 (SCC)

The plaintiff and the defendant went out for a night of drinking and driving. The defendant stalled his car and allowed the plaintiff to try to start it. The plaintiff lost control of the vehicle, drove it off a steep embankment, and suffered serious injuries. He claimed that the defendant was negligent in allowing him to drive while drunk. In response, the defendant argued that the plaintiff was injured while he was engaged in the illegal act of drunk driving.

While reducing the plaintiff's damages by 50 percent to reflect his own contributory negligence, the Supreme Court of Canada rejected the defence of illegality. It held that that defence applies only when the plaintiff attempts to use the tort system in a way that would undermine the integrity of the law. And that occurs only if the plaintiff tries to either profit from his illegal act or avoid a criminal penalty. The defence does not apply if, as in *Hall v Hebert*, the plaintiff merely seeks compensation for the injuries that were caused by the defendant's negligence.

Chapter Summary

Negligence is the most important tort. It requires proof of three elements: (i) a duty of care, (ii) a breach of the standard of care, and (iii) the causation of harm.

A duty of care requires the defendant to use reasonable care to avoid injuring the plaintiff. A duty will be imposed if: (i) it was reasonably foreseeable that the defendant's carelessness might hurt the plaintiff, and (ii) there are no compelling policy reasons for refusing to impose a duty. Policy considerations are especially important when the courts are afraid of "opening the floodgates" by allowing too many people to sue in negligence. In the business context, the best example concerns negligent statements.

The defendant cannot be held liable unless it breached the standard of care, which is based on the reasonable person test. A court must ask whether the defendant acted as a reasonable person would have acted in similar circumstances. That test is flexible and allows the courts to consider all of the circumstances of a case. Judges use special considerations in applying the standard of care in a case of professional negligence or product liability.

The defendant cannot be held liable unless its carelessness caused the plaintiff to suffer a loss. Causation is usually decided by the but-for test. Causation normally has to be established on a balance of probabilities, but once it is, the courts generally adopt an all-or-nothing approach to the issue of liability. The plaintiff merely has to prove that the defendant's carelessness was *a* cause of a loss. If two or more defendants combine to inflict a single injury on the plaintiff, they may be held jointly and severally liable. Even if the defendant caused the plaintiff to suffer a loss, liability will not be imposed if that loss was too remote from the breach of the standard of care. The remoteness principle is used to resolve cases involving thin skulls and intervening acts.

Even if the plaintiff proves duty, breach, and causation, the court may limit or deny liability if the defendant establishes a defence. Damages may be reduced if the plaintiff was guilty of contributory negligence. Damages may be denied entirely if the plaintiff either voluntarily assumed the risk of injury or was engaged in an illegal activity at the time of the accident. The last two defences, however, are interpreted very narrowly by the courts.

Review Questions

1. Although tort law is generally concerned with striking a balance between the desire to provide compensation and the desire to protect socially useful activities from liability, that issue is particularly important in the context of the tort of negligence. Why?

2. How does the element of reasonable foreseeability ensure that potential defendants are treated fairly? In the business context, how does it affect risk management?

3. Does the tort of negligence include a general duty to rescue? Provide one explanation for your answer.

4. List the ways in which negligent actions are different from negligent statements.

5. When will a court recognize a duty of care for a negligent statement?

6. Do the courts rely upon an objective test or a subjective test when they apply the standard of care? Provide one explanation for your answer.

7. Summarize the factors that a judge considers in deciding whether the defendant breached the standard of care.

8. Will a court find that professionals breached the standard of care if they complied with an approved practice? Explain your answer.

9. "Causation is determined on a balance of probabilities in an all-or-nothing manner." What does that statement mean?

10. Explain the concept of joint and several liability. How does it arise in the context of the issue of causation?

11. Is the but-for test always applied to resolve the issue of causation? Illustrate your answer with an example.

12. Explain the concept of market share liability. When and why does it arise? Does it apply in Canadian law?

13. What is the basic test for resolving the issue of remoteness? Must the plaintiff prove that a reasonable person would have foreseen both the type of harm that occurred *and* the manner in which it occurred?

14. Describe the thin skull and thin wallet concepts. Are those concepts applied in Canadian law?

15. When will an intervening act cause a court to find that the plaintiff's loss is too remote?

16. What is the main reason why Canadian courts prefer the defence of contributory negligence to the defences of voluntary assumption of risk and illegality?

17. Outline three situations in which the defence of contributory negligence can arise.

18. What factors will a judge consider in deciding whether a plaintiff was guilty of contributory negligence?

19. Outline the steps a business should take to ensure that it will be protected by the defence of voluntary assumption of risk.

20. In general terms, when will the defence of illegality succeed?

Cases and Problems

1. Maya, who was seven months pregnant, was involved in a snowmobiling accident with Escobar. Although he came away unscathed, his snowmobile suffered light damage. However, while Maya's snowmobile was unmarked, she suffered moderate injuries as a result of the collision. Two months later, Maya delivered Juan, who was born with a mental disability. The medical evidence suggests that Juan's condition was caused by the accident. Discuss the various actions that might be brought between the parties. What if the accident was caused by Maya's carelessness? What if it was caused by Escobar's carelessness? Your answers should focus on the issue of duty of care.

2. Corpshill Ltd, an advertising agency, worked on behalf of several clients, including Power-Ease Inc, a manufacturer of garden tools. Power-Ease asked Corpshill to place a large number of advertisements in newspapers and magazines. As was customary in the business, the agency paid for the advertisements itself and later billed the client for the

expense, which amounted to $100 000. Before doing so, however, Corpshill requested the National Royal Bank (Natroy) to provide a credit rating for Power-Ease. Natroy responded with a letter that stated that Power-Ease's credit was "good for the job." However, that letter also stated that since Natroy was not being paid for providing its opinion, it was responding "without responsibility." Unfortunately, Natroy carelessly failed to check the facts before providing its opinion. Power-Ease was actually in very poor financial condition and in fact subsequently went bankrupt. Consequently, there is no chance that Corpshill will ever receive payment from Power-Ease. Corpshill therefore has sued Natroy for negligent statement. Will it succeed? Explain your answer.

3. The Blacksox Baseball Club, a professional baseball team, plays its home games at Dotcom Park, which it built 15 years ago in a predominantly residential area. Initially, the close proximity of the ballpark to neighbouring houses

caused no problem, primarily because home runs were never hit out of the stadium. Recently, however, that situation has changed due to the combination of increasingly poor pitching and rampant steroid use amongst batters. The Blacksox and their opposition now hit an average of three home runs per game. Furthermore, a home run clears the stadium walls and enters a neighbouring yard about once every three games. One of those long balls, hit by a Blacksox player, recently cracked Abner's skull as he sat reading a book in his backyard. As a result of that injury, he has sustained losses of about $250 000. The Blacksox organization has admitted that it owed a duty of care to Abner, but insists that neither it nor its player breached the standard of care. Do you agree? What factors are important in resolving that issue?

4. Renata owns an importing business. She sought legal advice regarding the possibility of obtaining government approval to enter into a particular contract to purchase widgets from a company in Peru. Because her regular lawyer, a specialist in trade law, was away on vacation, she brought her file to Franz, whom she found in the telephone book. Although Renata did not know it, Franz was not really a lawyer. While he had attended two years of law school, he never graduated and he never passed the bar exam. Furthermore, although he is a distinguished looking 50-year-old, he only recently began to hold himself out as a lawyer. Franz prepared the necessary documents but, because he failed to read the governing statute carefully, he did not instruct Renata to place her corporate seal on them. Renata's application was consequently rejected by the government, and she lost the $75 000 profit that she expected to earn under her contract with the Peruvian company. She has sued Franz, claiming that her loss was caused by his professional negligence. He has responded by arguing that since he was not really a lawyer, he was not really a professional and therefore could not be held to a professional standard of care. He also has argued that even if he can be treated as a professional, he never claimed to have special expertise in the area of trade law and therefore should not be expected to fulfil the standard that would be applied to Renata's regular lawyer. Will either of those arguments succeed?

5. In February 1983, Pia entered the hospital for a simple operation. During that procedure, she received a blood transfusion. Although the operation was entirely successful, Pia was diagnosed with HIV several years later. The blood she had received had come from Everett, a carrier of HIV. He had donated that blood to the Canadian Red Cross Society (CRCS) at a blood donor clinic in January 1982. When it became well known that HIV can be transmitted through blood, the CRCS started using a detailed questionnaire to prevent people in high-risk groups from making donations. Because of his lifestyle, Everett would have fallen into one of those groups. At the time of donation in January 1982, however, there was very little medical information available about HIV, and there was no reasonable basis for believing that it could be spread through blood transfusions. The CRCS therefore did not take any steps to screen out potentially harmful donors. Pia sued Everett and the CRCS in negligence shortly after learning that she was infected. Sadly, both Pia and Everett have since died of AIDS. Pia's widower has nevertheless continued the lawsuit against the CRCS. He claimed that the CRCS was careless in allowing a person of Everett's lifestyle to donate blood. Would that claim succeed? Explain your answer.

6. Mindy was gently riding her horse on a quiet country road. Unexpectedly, Robert and Riley coincidentally passed her at the same time on their motorcycles, one on either side. Her horse panicked and threw her to the ground, causing her to suffer severe injuries. She has incurred $80 000 in medical expenses as a result. She has sued both Robert and Riley. In response, however, each defendant has argued the following proposition: "I didn't cause the accident. But-for my admittedly careless act of speeding on a country road, Mindy still would have been injured. The noise from the other guy's motorcycle alone was enough to scare her horse." Will that argument succeed? For what amount, if any, will Robert be held liable? For what amount, if any, will Riley be held liable? Explain your answer.

7. For many years, the Acme Gum Company sold a product that it called "aspargum," a low-calorie gum made from asparagus and other ingredients. Although aspargum never enjoyed great success in the market, it did prove very popular with a small number of people. Clint was one such person. He chewed aspargum almost daily for nearly two decades. Several years ago, however, aspargum was taken off the market when it was discovered to cause several forms of cancer, including mouth cancer. Clint was recently diagnosed with mouth cancer and has sued Acme. Acme admits that it owed a duty of care to Clint, and that it had carelessly sold a product that it should have known was carcinogenic. It insists, however, that Clint's cancer was not caused by the aspargum but by the cigarettes, which he smoked over the same period. In fact, the evidence indicates that there is a 60 percent chance that the cancer was caused by the aspargum and a 40 percent chance that it was caused by smoking. Assuming that Clint's damages are valued at $1 000 000, how much should he actually receive? Should Acme's liability be reduced to $600 000 to reflect the possibility that the cancer was caused by cigarettes? Explain your answer.

8. Generus Inc is a manufacturer of no-frills products. Until recently, it sold "loobster," an imitation of lobster meat made primarily out of fish entrails. Christian suffered a permanently paralyzing infection after eating a package of loobster. As a result, he no longer is able to work as one of the world's leading heart surgeons and consequently will lose $2 000 000 per year in income over the next 30 years. Generus has admitted: (i) that it owed a duty of care to Christian, and (ii) that it had carelessly allowed fish entrails to sit for several days in the hot sun before tossing them into the batch of loobster that produced the package that Christian bought. However, it insists that it should not be liable for all of Christian's losses. It argues that loobster is aimed at the very low end of the market and that it was entirely unforeseeable that someone with Christian's wealth would buy such cheap food. Will Generus' argument succeed? Explain your answer.

9. Claire brought her truck to Darius's garage for repairs. In

the course of the job, Darius carelessly punctured the gas tank. Fuel leaked onto the floor of his garage and was ignited when he carelessly threw a cigarette butt away. When he noticed the small blaze, he was in the process of carrying a heavy piece of equipment over to the truck. He instructed Claire, who was waiting for her vehicle, to use a nearby fire extinguisher. Unfortunately, she panicked. Instead of grabbing the fire extinguisher, she tried to douse the small, but rapidly growing, flame by throwing snow on it. Her effort was unsuccessful and within a short time, her entire truck was destroyed. Darius has admitted liability, but he insists that Claire was contributorily negligent and should shoulder part of the blame for the damage. Is he correct? Explain your answer.

10. Alcoa Vending Inc operates a fleet of hot-dog stands. Those stands allow Alcoa's employees to cook and sell hot dogs and other meals from portable carts. Although most of the carts are moved from time to time to attract the largest number of customers, one stand has been in almost continuous operation for several years on the side-walk outside of a hockey arena. Broderick owns a house across the street from the arena. The evidence indicates that the fumes from Alcoa's hot-dog cart have corroded the paint on his house and the shingles on his roof. When he first noticed that damage four years ago, he obtained an expert opinion that suggested that the damage would cost $20 000 to repair. Broderick did not have enough money to undertake those repairs, but he did sue Alcoa immediately. The trial date for that action has finally arrived. However, due to general inflation and sharp increase in the cost of appropriate roofing shingles, it would now cost $90 000 to properly repair Broderick's house. Assuming that Broderick can establish a cause of action in negligence against Alcoa, will he be entitled to receive $20 000 or $90 000? Explain your answer.

11. Miranda, a 17-year-old student from Moose Jaw, was a thrill seeker. She had always wanted to try bungee jump-ing. Consequently, while vacationing in Vancouver with friends, she built up her courage by drinking six shots of vodka and went to a theme park operated by X-treme Adventures Inc. When she arrived, she was asked to pay a fee of $20 and to sign a contract that contained the fol-lowing clause.

I am over eighteen (18) years of age and I have read this form in its entirety. I understand that bungee jumping is a dangerous sport and I am aware that by participating in this activity, I may suf-fer some form of physical injury.

Miranda signed the contract. As she was about to make her jump, an employee of X-Treme Adventures instructed her to hold her arms straight out to her sides while she was falling. In the excitement of the event, however, Miranda ignored that advice. Furthermore, due to the employee's carelessness, the bungee cord was a bit too long. As a result, Miranda fell too far, hit her head on a rock, and suffered a spinal injury that has left her paralyzed from the waist down. She has sued X-Treme Adventures. In response, the defendant has argued:

(i) Miranda's damages should be reduced on the ground that she was contributorily negligent because: (a) she failed to hold her arms out as instructed, (b) she lied about her age, and (c) she attempted the jump while under the influence of alcohol;

(ii) Miranda's claim should fail entirely because she had voluntarily assumed the risk of injury by signing the contract; and

(iii) Miranda's claim should fail entirely because she was engaged in the illegal activity of under-aged drinking at the time of the jump.

Will any of those defences succeed? Explain your answer.

12. Jordan is a notoriously irresponsible drunk. As a result, Bora, who owns a tavern, adopted a rule that allowed Jordan to buy beer only if he was accompanied by anoth-er adult. Recently, however, Jordan wandered into Bora's bar alone and depressed that his fortieth birthday was upcoming. Bora was sympathetic, largely because he was going through a mid-life crisis of his own. He agreed to sell beer to Jordan. Three hours and ten bottles later, howev-er, Jordan became drunkenly obnoxious. Bora soon ran out of patience and tossed him into the street. As Jordan wandered down the street, in the general direction of his apartment, he was run down by Selma. While she was nor-mally a cautious driver, her attention had been distracted because she was talking on her cell phone. Jordan wants to sue both Bora and Selma in negligence. Will he fully recover from either or both of those parties? Explain your answer.

WWWeblinks

Introduction to Tort Law

CanadaLegal.com
www.canadalegal.com/search.asp?a=36&n=100

This Web site provides links, arranged by jurisdiction, to tort and negligence articles and newsletters prepared by Canadian law firms.

JURIST Canada—Torts
jurist.law.utoronto.ca/cour_pgs.htm#Torts

The JURIST Web site features links to course pages developed by Canadian law teachers. They include materials relevant to the study of tort law.

Legal Information Institute—Tort Law
www.law.cornell.edu/topics/torts.html

This site provides an overview of tort law from an American perspective and links to federal and state legislative materials and case law.

The Functions of Tort Law
www.law.newcastle.edu.au/teaching/torts/linden2.htm

The article featured on this Web site examines the functions of tort law, including compensation, deterrence, education, psychological function, market deterrence, and ombudsman.

Economica Ltd
www.economica.ca/articles.htm

Economica Ltd is a consulting firm that provides litigation support in personal injury and fatal accident actions. Its Web site features articles on the economics of personal injury and damage assessment.

Intentional Torts

New Brunswick *Trespass Act*, RSNB 1983, c T-11.2
www.gov.nb.ca/acts/acts/t-11-2.htm

The New Brunswick *Trespass Act* sets out the rules governing trespass to land and describes the penalties for conviction of a trespass offence.

Nuisance

Tort Law—Nuisance
www.duhaime.org/nuis.htm

This page introduces the law of nuisance and offers an overview of the available defences and remedies.

Defamation

Canadian Internet Law Resource Page—Torts
aix1.uottawa.ca/~geist/torts.html

This site includes an index of articles, case law, and other resources concerned with defamation on the Internet.

Manitoba *Defamation Act*, RSM 1987, c D20
www.gov.mb.ca/chc/statpub/free/pdf/d020.pdf

The Manitoba *Defamation Act* is representative of provincial defamation legislation. It sets out the defences and damages available under the tort.

Tort Law—Defamation
www.duhaime.org/ca-defam.htm

This page offers an overview of the main principles of the law of defamation and describes the special defences available to the defendant of this tort action, such as qualified privilege and fair comment.

Negligence

Ontario *Negligence Act*, RSO 1990, c N-1
192.75.156.68/DBLaws/Statutes/English/90n01_e.htm

The Ontario *Negligence Act* is representative of provincial apportionment legislation, which allows for apportionment of damages between wrongdoers in cases of contributory negligence.

Tort Law—Negligence
www.duhaime.org/ca?negl.htm

This page provides an introduction to the law of negligence and focuses on the reasonable forseeability test.

BUSINESS TRICKS: CONSPIRING AGAINST COMPETITORS

To help create a robust economy, Canadian law encourages businesses to engage in competitive activities, even if one business causes economic harm to another. For instance, as long as they are telling the truth, business people can generally tell the world that a competitor's product or service is inferior or inadequate. On the other hand, statements that are untrue may lead to liability for defamation. Along similar lines, an individual business person can generally act in a way that benefits their business and hurts a competitor's. However, if two or more business people agree to act together in the same way, they may commit the tort of conspiracy. Consider the case of *Meditrust v Shoppers Drug Mart*.

Meditrust Healthcare Inc is a mail-order pharmacy created in 1992 by entrepreneur Norman Paul. It threatened to revolutionize the pharmacy industry in two ways. First, Meditrust charged a $5 dispensing fee, which was about half of what other drugstores were charging at that time. Second, and more distressing to the industry, a mail-order system of drug dispensing would eliminate the need for customers to visit drug stores. That was cause for alarm in a retail industry that collected an average of $700 to $750 in front-store sales per year from each shopper who waited for prescriptions to be filled. Paul claimed that Meditrust posed such a serious threat that executives of Shoppers Drug Mart led an industry-wide conspiracy to destroy Meditrust and to eliminate it as a competitor in the Canadian retail pharmacy industry.

According to Paul, Shoppers Drug Mart conspired with other pharmacies by participating in a number of activities that were aimed at ruining his business. For example, all Ontario pharmacies threatened to stop ordering from suppliers that continued to do business with Meditrust. Also, the members of the retail pharmacy industry, including Shoppers Drug Mart, supported the production of a video by the Canadian Pharmaceutical Association that described the alleged limitations of mail-order pharmacies. That video was sent to managers of employee benefit programs. The most significant activity, however, was the publication of a damaging letter, written under a false name. A letter from the "Society for Concerned Pharmacists" appeared in 1996 shortly after Paul released a public offering to convince investors to buy shares in Meditrust. That letter was sent to five newspapers and three investment bankers. The society, which claimed to have over 6000 members across Canada, criticized Meditrust's business plan and in effect concluded that Meditrust had limited prospects for success. Paul believes that the statements made in the letter caused investors to have a lower opinion of Meditrust.

After hiring a private investigator, Paul traced the letter back to Shoppers Drug Mart's vice president of public affairs, Arthur Konviser. It turned out that the address on the letter was the address of a mailbox rental company. Paul's investigator found evidence in the rental company's trash that linked the Society's mailbox rental to Konviser's secretary, Gloria Anderson. When a *Globe and Mail* reporter questioned Konviser, he denied any knowledge of the Society for Concerned Pharmacists. However, Konviser later admitted that the opposite was true. According to the Shoppers Drug Mart's statement of defence, Konviser was involved in both preparing and distributing the letter. There was no evidence to suggest that other members of the retail pharmacy industry, outside of Shoppers Drug Mart, were involved in the preparation of the letter. The statement of defence went on to say, however, that the letter made no impact on Meditrust: "Meditrust's business imploded under its own weight, burdened by bad management and a business plan that was perhaps doomed from the beginning." But Norman Paul disagrees. He claims that, as a result of the damage caused by the letter, investors were not interested in dealing with a business shrouded with bad publicity. Consequently, he suffered a considerable loss in the subsequent public sale of Meditrust.

Meditrust is suing Shoppers Drug Mart, among others, for $120 million. As part of that claim, Meditrust must show that it suffered damages as a result of Shoppers Drug

Mart's actions. In a preliminary motion, Shoppers Drug Mart asked a judge to dismiss a large part of Meditrust's claim on the basis that there was no evidence that Meditrust suffered any losses. Justice Molloy held that under the tort of conspiracy, Meditrust could recover only with respect to losses on the public offering. This means that if Meditrust recovers any damages at all, those damages will compensate Meditrust for the losses caused by the letter from the Society for Concerned Pharmacists.

QUESTIONS TO CONSIDER

1. What does Meditrust have to prove to make out its conspiracy claim against Shoppers Drug Mart? Do you think it will succeed? Why?

2. Assuming that Meditrust cannot make out the conspiracy claim, and leaving aside any other possible remedies under the *Competition Act*, what alternative claims, if any, does Meditrust have in private law?

3. Assuming that Meditrust can make out the conspiracy claim with respect to the public offering, how would you calculate its losses?

4. Does it seem fair to you that a business engaging in "dirty business tricks" can escape liability if the plaintiff company cannot show any losses? Why?

Sources: <www.cbc.ca/business/programs/venture/onventure/101700.html>; *Meditrust v Shoppers Drug Mart* (2001) 15 BLR (3d) 221 (Ont Gen Div); J Deverell "Shoppers Drug hit with lawsuit" *Toronto Star* (April 8, 1997) E1, E8.

Video Resource: "Trash Talk (Dirty Business Tricks)," *Venture* # 760, October 17, 2000.

13 Real Property: Interests and Leases

CHAPTER OVERVIEW

OBJECTIVES

After completing this chapter, you should be able to:

1. Name three types of estates, and explain how they differ from one another.
2. Describe the process of expropriation, and explain why it often creates ethical issues.
3. Distinguish between co-ownership and joint tenancy, and explain why one is often preferred in the business world.
4. Explain the nature of condominium ownership.
5. Define "easement," and explain how that type of interest can be created.
6. Distinguish between dominant tenements and servient tenements, and name two types of interests for which that distinction is important.
7. Outline the situations in which it is possible to enforce a restrictive covenant against a person who did not participate in its creation.
8. Distinguish between different types of leases on the basis of how long they last.
9. Outline the basic difference between an assignment and a sublease.
10. Define "quiet possession," and explain two ways in which a landlord can break that type of covenant.

real property includes land and anything attached to land

In this chapter, we begin our discussion of *real property*. Generally speaking, **real property** includes land and anything attached to land (such as fences and buildings).[1] Lawyers historically went much further and viewed real property rights in terms of the "giant carrot theory," which held that a person who owned a particular piece of land also owned the air up to the heavens and the ground down to the centre of the Earth. The modern approach, however, does not go that far. A landowner can control only the airspace to a reasonable height. While that test is rather vague, it does mean, for instance, that you can complain about a crane swinging over your property, but not about a plane flying safely overhead. Similarly, although there are few cases in the area, a landowner can control the ground only to a reasonable depth beneath the surface.

Despite those limitations, property rights remain critically important to Canadian business, even as our economy continues to move away from its traditional focus on natural products (like wheat and oil) to new forms of wealth (like ideas and information). Although a lot of commerce can now be conducted through computers from anywhere in the world, the vast majority of businesses still rely on real property. An Internet bookseller, for instance, requires a warehouse to store its products and probably at least one office for its personnel. Furthermore, just as a private residence is often a person's most valuable asset, real property often represents the largest part of a business's total wealth.

It is therefore important that you have a basic understanding of real property. However, real property is a notoriously large and complex body of law, which contains a number of specialized areas. For the purposes of risk management, many of those details can be left to the experts. A business person is not required, for instance, to know how to draft a long-term commercial lease. Lawyers are available for that purpose. From a business perspective, it is enough to appreciate the possibilities and to recognize the need for outside assistance.

This chapter is divided into two parts. The first summarizes the most important types of interests in land. The second describes the essential elements of leasing agreements. Chapter 14 continues the discussion of real property by explaining the process involved in the sale of real property. It also provides an overview of mortgages. Chapter 15 examines personal property.

INTERESTS IN LAND

an **interest in land** is a right that a person can enforce with respect to a particular piece of land

In this section, we consider different types of **interests in land**, that is, rights that a person can enforce with respect to a particular piece of land. Note that we are discussing rights to property *itself*. This is important. Suppose that you buy a football stadium from me. Two sets of rights and obligations are created.

- First, you and I have a contract. Significantly, we are the only people affected by that agreement. It does not impose rights or obligations on anyone else in the world. Consequently, if I break my promise to transfer the land, I am the only person whom you can sue in contract. Likewise, if you fail to pay the price, I cannot demand the money from anyone other than you.

- Second, once I transfer the property, the stadium belongs to you. If I continue using it for my own purposes, you can get a court order to evict me.

[1] Land is called "real" property because the owner can recover the *res* (which is Latin for "thing") itself. If someone wrongfully takes your house, the law will evict them and allow you to regain possession. Other types of property are called "personal," because the courts usually will not allow you to recover the thing itself. If someone steals your cow, the law will probably only require the thief to pay you the monetary value of the animal. See Chapter 10.

Even more significantly, you can exercise the same rights against *anyone else* who interferes with your property rights. That is because property rights are good against the *whole world*, not just the person from whom they are acquired.[2]

property rights are good against the whole world—not just the person from whom they were acquired

Estates in Land

The most significant interests in land are called *estates*. An **estate** is an exclusive right to possess a property for a period of time. We will consider three varieties:

- the fee simple
- the life estate
- the leasehold estate

an estate is an exclusive right to possess land for a period of time

Fee Simple

A **fee simple** is the largest package of rights that a person can hold in land. Although it technically does not amount to absolute ownership, it comes very close.[3] Consequently, if you enjoy the fee simple in a particular property, you are entitled to possess it for an indefinite duration. You can sell it, lease it, or give it away tomorrow, or you can keep it until you die. And if you do hang on to it for the rest of your life, you are entitled to give it away upon your death. Furthermore, you can generally use or abuse the land however you want. You can maintain it in pristine condition, or you can clear it down to scorched earth.

a fee simple is the largest package of rights that a person can hold

Although your rights under a fee simple are very broad, they are subject to several important limitations. We mention three.

- First, as we saw in Chapter 11, whenever you possess land, you must avoid committing torts like occupiers' liability, nuisance, and the rule in *Rylands v Fletcher*. For instance, if you live in a residential suburb, you cannot operate a pig farm in your backyard. The stench would create a nuisance for your neighbours.

- Second, your use of the land is subject to various forms of regulation. For instance, governments are increasingly creating regulations to prevent people from using their property in ways that hurt the *environment*.[4] Furthermore, every municipality in Canada uses *zoning and planning* regulations to control the types of activities that occur within certain areas. For example, you probably cannot build a casino on your land if a school is located next door.

- Third, your property may be *expropriated*. **Expropriation** occurs when the government takes property for a public purpose, such as the construction of a new bridge or the widening of a highway. You will be enti-

expropriation occurs when the government takes property for a public purpose

---

[2.] That is also true for personal property, which we will discuss in Chapter 15. For instance, as Chapter 10 showed, you can use the tort of conversion against *anyone* who substantially interferes with your car. The entire world must respect your property rights in that vehicle.

[3.] Every piece of the land in Canada is ultimately owned by the Crown, that is, the government. For practical purposes, however, it is generally safe to treat the person with the fee simple as the owner. The Crown's interest is usually relevant only if that person dies without disposing of the property by will *and* without leaving behind any relatives to whom it can be given under *intestacy legislation*. Intestacy means that a person has died without a "testament," or will. In that case, the Crown will take control of the land.

[4.] Environmental regulations are discussed in Chapter 23.

tled to compensation, but you cannot insist upon keeping the land. Similarly, even if the government does not expropriate a section of your land, it may exercise a right to build a sewer system underground or run telephone wires overhead. Expropriation can be particularly controversial in some situations. Consider Ethical Perspective 13.1.

ETHICAL PERSPECTIVE 13.1

Expropriation

Molly lives in a house in Come-by-Chance, Newfoundland, which her family has occupied for six generations. She was recently notified by the provincial government that her property was required for the purpose of constructing a natural gas pipeline that would substantially contribute to the region's economy. She insisted that she would never sell her ancestral home, but was told that she had no choice in the matter. While sympathetic to Molly's situation, the government noted several factors that identified her land as the only suitable place for the pipeline. For instance, her land was located near the gas well and the refinery. Furthermore, other nearby areas were especially vulnerable to environmental damage. The government also assured Molly that she would receive fair compensation. She tearfully insists that no amount of money could ever replace her home.

Question for Discussion

1. Is expropriation ethical? On what grounds do you base your answer?

Life Estate

a **life estate** entitles a person to exclusive possession of a property for the duration of a particular life

A *life estate* is similar to a fee simple, but it carries fewer rights. As the name suggests, a **life estate** entitles a person to exclusive possession of a property for the duration of a particular life. The relevant life usually belongs to the person who holds the estate, but it can also belong to someone else. Suppose that I hold the fee simple in a property and agree to sell a life estate to you. We might agree that the land is yours until you die *or* we might agree that your interest will exist only while my brother is alive. In either event, you will lose control of the property once the relevant life ends. At that time, I will regain control. In most instances, the property will simply come back to me, or to my estate if I have already died, by way of a **reversion**. Alternatively, if I transfer my reversionary interest to someone else, that person will take the property as a **remainder**.

a **reversion** occurs when the property returns to the person who holds the fee simple

a **remainder** occurs when the property goes to a third party who was selected by the person who holds the fee simple

waste occurs when a property is changed in a way that significantly affects its value

The rights under a life estate are limited in another important way. A person with a fee simple is generally free to use or abuse the property. However, while someone with a life estate is normally entitled to profits that are generated by the property, that person cannot commit an act of *waste*. **Waste** occurs when a property is changed in a way that significantly affects its value. That includes, for example, digging pits and cutting down trees. A person with a life estate who commits an act of waste can be held liable to the person who holds the reversion or remainder. The rule against waste, however, normally applies only to acts and not to omissions. Consequently, if you purchase a life estate from me, you cannot demolish a building without my permission, but you are not required to spend money to keep that building in good condition.

Life estates are often useful in family situations.[5] Suppose that you hold the

---

5. In the family context, life estates are sometimes imposed as a matter of law. For example, a woman was historically entitled upon her husband's death to *dower*, which was a life interest in one-third of any real property in which he held a fee simple. Because of problems associated with that rule, dower has been abolished in Canada and replaced with a variety of even more extensive statutory rights. See B Ziff *Principles of Property Law* 3d ed (2000) at 171-4.

fee simple in a residential property that you share with your younger sister, who has a disability. While you want your younger brother to eventually inherit that house, you also want to ensure that your sister always has a place to live after you are gone. Consequently, you draft a will that leaves the fee simple to your brother, but that also carves out a life estate for your sister. Upon your death, she will enjoy the use of the property for the rest of her life (assuming that she does not predecease you) and then the land will go to your brother (or his estate if he has died by that point). In the business world, however, life estates tend to be unattractive. Consider Business Law in Action 13.1.

BUSINESS LAW IN ACTION 13.1

Life Estates in the Business Context

You are looking for a house in which you can both live and operate an accounting business. After weeks of searching, you find an attractive possibility. After negotiating with the owner, however, you realize that you cannot afford to purchase the fee simple. The owner offers two options: (i) a three-year lease, or (ii) a life estate. You are torn between those two possibilities. While you are quite sure that you will want the premises for more than three

years, you are not sure that you will want to remain there permanently. The current owner then correctly explains that if you ever wanted to relocate to another building, you could sell your life estate to a third party.

Question for Discussion

1. Practically speaking, would it be easy to find a buyer of your life estate if you ever decided to relocate? Explain your answer.

Leasehold Estate

A **leasehold estate** occurs when a person has exclusive rights to a property for a specific period of time. A lease is like a fee simple or a life interest because it carries the right of exclusive possession. But a lease is also different because it is not defined by a life. A person with a fee simple can retain the property for life and then dispose of it upon death. A person with a life estate can retain the property during the relevant lifetime. A person with a lease can retain the property for only a specific block of time. That block may be long or short—a day or a century, for instance. It may be limited to a single term, or it may be automatically renewed if neither party objects. But in any event, the duration of the lease is established at the outset. It does not depend upon the length of any particular life. We will discuss leases in the last section of this chapter.

Concept Summary 13.1 reviews the main differences between a fee simple, a life estate, and a lease.

a leasehold estate occurs when a person has exclusive rights to a property for a specific period of time

Concept Summary 13.1

Fee Simple, Life Estate, and Lease

Type of Estate	Nature and Duration of Estate
fee simple	right to exclusive possession during own life *and* right to dispose of property upon death
life estate	right to exclusive possession during relevant life *but no* right to dispose of property upon death
lease	right to exclusive possession during specified period

Shared Ownership

To this point, we have assumed that an estate—whether a fee simple, a life interest, or a lease—is owned by only one person. However, ownership can also be shared among several people. It is therefore important to distinguish *individual ownership* and *shared ownership*. For the purposes of discussion, suppose that there is a large piece of land for sale.

- If you buy the east half and I buy the west half, we *do not* share ownership. Rather, the single piece of land is divided in two, and we each become the *individual* owner of a separate piece. I can put a fence around my property to keep you out, and you can do the same to me.

- In contrast, if we act together and buy *undivided interests* in a single piece of land, we *do* share ownership. We are both owners of the *same* property. Neither one of us can put a fence around any part of the land to keep the other out.[6]

There are two important types of shared ownership:

- joint ownership (or *joint tenancy*)
- co-ownership (or *co-tenancy* or *tenancy in common*)

Joint ownership occurs when two or more people share *exactly* the same interests in a property. Consequently, if you and I are joint tenants with two other people, we each have a 25 percent interest.[7] The most significant feature of a joint tenancy is the *right of survivorship*. The **right of survivorship** means that upon death, a joint tenant's interest automatically passes to the remaining joint tenants. For instance, if I die first, my interest must pass to you and the others—I cannot give it away to anyone else. You and the other joint tenants will then each have a 33 percent interest in the property. That process can be repeated until the last surviving joint tenant takes the whole property.

Co-ownership also occurs when two or more people share an undivided interest in a property. However, there are at least two important differences between co-ownership and joint ownership.

- Co-owners do not have to have *exactly* the same interests. Assume, once again, that you and I share ownership with two other people. While our shares must be undivided, in the sense that none of us can assert individual rights over any particular piece of ground, they do not have to be equal. For instance, I may own a 70 percent interest, while you and the other co-owners each enjoy 10 percent interests.[8]

- More significantly, co-owners do not enjoy the right of survivorship. Consequently, if I die first, you and the other co-owners will not automatically acquire my interest. I can, for instance, leave my share to a friend, who would then become a co-owner along with you and the others.

The differences between co-tenancy and joint tenancy may affect the type of ownership that you choose for your business. Consider Business Decision 13.1.

---

[6] You and I can use a contract to change the rule between ourselves. For instance, we may agree that while we share ownership of the whole property, you can put a fence around the east part, and I can put a fence around the west part.

[7] Each of us is therefore generally entitled to 25 percent of the profits from the land. That rule applies to profits that are received from a *third party* (for example, by renting the property to an outsider). It might be different, however, if one of us earns profits through our own labour (for example, by harvesting raspberries).

[8] I am therefore entitled to 70 percent of the general profits, while you and the others each get 10 percent.

Choice of Shared Ownership

You and your partner have enjoyed great success over the years in a variety of business ventures. As you both near an early retirement at age 60, you decide to enter into one last project. Together you obtain a 75-year lease over a parcel of land on the outskirts of town. You do so with the intention of developing a theme park.

Questions for Discussion

1. Should your shared ownership take the form of a co-tenancy or a joint tenancy?

2. What if the other person was your "partner" in the sense of being the person with whom you have shared an intimate, monogamous, cohabitational relationship for four decades?

3. What if the other person is your "partner" in the sense of being the person with whom, in a purely professional capacity, you have made a great deal of money? Assume that you also have a "partner" of the other sort, with whom you have produced five children.

Joint tenants can avoid the right of survivorship through the process of *severance*.[9] **Severance** occurs when a joint tenant deals with the property in a way that is inconsistent with joint ownership. Suppose that you jointly owned a cottage along with my sister and me. You then sold your interest to your brother. You are no longer an owner of any kind. Furthermore, while your brother is *some* kind of owner, he is *not* a joint tenant with my sister and me. He does not have *exactly* the same interest as us, since he acquired his rights after we acquired ours. Consequently, while my sister and I are still joint tenants with respect to each other, we are co-tenants with respect to your brother. The right of survivorship can be lost in other ways as well. Case Brief 13.1 provides a dramatic example.

severance occurs when a joint tenant deals with the property in a way that is inconsistent with joint ownership

Schobelt v Barber (1966) 60 DLR (2d) 519 (Ont HC)

William and Marjorie Barber, a married couple, were joint tenants of a piece of land. After murdering his wife, William claimed the entire property through the right of survivorship. Marjorie's sister, however, argued that he should not be able to profit from his own wrongdoing. She insisted that she should be entitled to inherit Marjorie's interest as the next-of-kin.

The judge effectively agreed with Marjorie's sister. While William was entitled to acquire his wife's interest by right of survivorship, he was also required to hold it on behalf of her sister. Accordingly, in the end, William and his sister-in-law held the property as tenants in common.

Although the procedures vary between jurisdictions, it is usually possible to bring either form of shared ownership to an end through the process of *partition*. (The parties in Case Brief 13.1 presumably did so.) **Partition** occurs when there is a division of either the property or its sale proceeds. The parties may agree among themselves as to who gets what. But if they cannot do so, they

partition occurs when there is a separation of the property or its sale proceeds

---

[9.] The law tries to avoid the right of survivorship by assuming, in the absence of evidence to the contrary, that property held under shared ownership is subject to a tenancy in common, rather than a joint tenancy.

can ask a judge to resolve the matter. The courts generally have a broad discretion in deciding whether to physically divide the land, sell the land and divide the proceeds, or refuse relief altogether.

Condominiums

It is sometimes possible to have both individual ownership *and* shared ownership. The most common example involves *condominiums*. A **condominium** exists when several people share ownership of some parts of a building, while individually owning other parts.[10] Although the legislation varies considerably across the country, the basic arrangement is always the same.[11] A building is divided into a number of separate units, plus a variety of common areas (such as hallways, stairwells, parking lots, and tennis courts). The separate units are usually residential, but they may also be used for commercial purposes, such as restaurants and shops. If you purchase a unit in a condominium, you receive three sets of rights.

- First, you receive individual ownership of that particular unit. Your rights closely resemble those of a fee simple, except that you do not have the exclusive right to possess a piece of ground, as well as a portion of the earth beneath and the sky above. Instead, you have a "flying fee." In other words, while you do have a large bundle of rights, they apply only to the specific unit that is held in the air by the other parts of the building.

- Second, you and the other individual unit owners share ownership of the common areas as tenants in common. As a result, subject to any more specific rules or arrangements that may be created, you can all use those common areas, such as the pool.

- Third, as you can see, a condominium is a small community. And like other communities, it requires decisions to be made and enforced. For those reasons, it will have a *condominium corporation*, which is a non-profit organization that manages the complex. As the owner of a separate unit, you are entitled to vote on matters concerning the corporation, such as the creation of bylaws and the election of directors. You are also required to pay condominium fees, which are effectively the community's tax.

Non-Possessory Interests in Land

We have examined several property interests that provide a right to possession. Canadian law also recognizes a number of *non-possessory* interests in land. In other words, a person may have rights in a property, without being able to actually possess that property. We will briefly discuss three important possibilities:

- easements
- restrictive covenants
- mineral leases

---

[10] The word "condominium" is derived from the Latin words meaning "joint" (*com*) and "control" (*dominium*).

[11] *Condominium Property Act*, RSA 1980, c C-22 (Alta); *Condominium Act*, RSBC 1996, c 64 (BC); *Condominium Act*, RSM 1987, c C-170 (Man); *Condominium Property Act*, RSNB 1973, c C-16 (NB); *Condominium Act*, RSN 1990, c C-29 (Nfld); *Condominium Act*, RSNWT 1988, c C-15 (NWT and Nun); *Condominium Act*, RSNS 1989, c 85 (NS); *Condominium Act*, SO 1998, c 19 (Ont); *Condominium Act*, RSPEI 1988, c C-16 (PEI); *Condominium Property Act*, RSS 1978, c C-26 (Sask); *Condominium Act*, RSY 1986, c 28 (Yuk).

Easements

An **easement** is a right to use a neighbour's land. Most easements are positive. For instance, you might let me drive across you property to reach a road, or periodically drain my water reservoir onto your land. While less common, an easement can also be negative. For instance, you might be prohibited from constructing a building that would deprive my house of sunlight, or from cutting down a line of trees that protects my fields from wind erosion.

As our examples suggest, an easement can exist only between neighbours. While our properties do not necessarily have to be touching, they do have to be reasonably close together. I must be able to show that I have the **dominant tenement**—the property that benefits from the easement, and that you have the **servient tenement**—the property that accommodates the easement. As long as those requirements are met, an easement can **run with the land**. That means that it can apply even if different people acquire possession of the affected properties.

An easement can be created in several ways.

- *Express*: The simplest method is for the parties to expressly agree upon the creation of an easement. For example, before selling part of my land to you, I might insist that our contract recognize my right to swim in the pond that will be located on your part of the property.

- *Implied*: An easement can also arise by necessary implication. For instance, I might buy a section of your land without realizing that my new property is completely cut off from the highway. In that situation, the courts will presume, unless there is evidence to the contrary, that we silently agreed that I would be allowed to drive across the remaining section of your property to reach the highway.

- *Prescription*: The law traditionally allowed an easement to be acquired by *prescription*, even if there was no agreement between the parties.[12] Prescription exists in only some jurisdictions in Canada.[13] Although the rules vary between them, the basic idea is the same. An easement by **prescription** is created if land is used in a particular way, for a long time (usually 20 years), without secrecy, without objection, and without permission. Suppose that I have openly used a portion of your backlot for a compost heap for many years. You have done nothing about it. The law may now recognize an easement that provides me with the right to continue dumping on your property.[14]

- *Statutory*: Statutes often give utility companies and similar organizations the right to bury television cables, dig sewers, and so on. The telephone company can, for instance, run wires over your yard even if its office is not located nearby. Although such rights are often called *public easements* or *statutory easements*, they are not true easements because there is no dominant tenement.

an **easement** is a right to use a neighbour's land

easements can be positive or negative

a **dominant tenement** is a property that benefits from an easement

a **servient tenement** is a property that accommodates an easement

an easement can run with the land

an easement by **prescription** is created if land is used in a particular way, for a long time, without secrecy, without objection, and without permission

---

[12.] In this context, "prescription" is derived from an old English word meaning "establishment of a claim."

[13.] Prescription is generally abolished in those jurisdictions that use a *land titles* system of registration. The aim of that system, which is discussed in Chapter 14, is to provide documents which make it clear, at all times, what interests exist in each particular piece of land. Interests that arise by operation of law tend to frustrate that goal because they are hidden from view.

[14.] While less common, a *possessory interest* may be acquired through the similar process of *adverse possession*. If I openly take possession of your land and continuously treat it as my own for a long time (usually 20 years), I may become the owner of that property if you fail to assert your rights against me. Once again, that doctrine has generally been modified or abolished in those parts of the country that use the land title system of registration.

a **licence** is permission to act in a way that would otherwise be prohibited

An easement must be distinguished from a mere *licence*. A **licence** is permission to act in a way that would otherwise be prohibited. For example, if your property is located close to a stadium, I might persuade you to allow me to park on your lawn while I attend a football game. Unlike an easement, a licence is not an interest in land, it does not run with the property, and it can be revoked at any time (subject to any contractual rights that may exist between the parties). Furthermore, because a licence is not an easement, it does not require the existence of dominant and subservient tenements.

Restrictive Covenants

a **restrictive covenant** is a promise to use piece of land in a way that benefits one property and burdens another

An easement must be distinguished from a *restrictive covenant*. A **restrictive covenant** is a promise to use a piece of land in a way that benefits one property and burdens another. It is like an easement because it requires a dominant tenement and a servient tenement. In other respects, however, it is quite different. First, while an easement can sometimes arise through prescription, a restrictive covenant can only be created by agreement. Second, a restrictive covenant never allows me to use your land. It merely limits how you can use your own property.[15]

Enforcement is the most difficult issue concerning restrictive covenants. Suppose that I own several business chains, including one that rebuilds abandoned vehicles. You own a large piece of land, which you use in part to operate a florist shop. You are willing to sell half of that property to me, but you are concerned that I might behave in a way that scares off your customers and hurts the value of your land. Consequently, when drafting the sale contract, we insert two *covenants*, which are promises that are written and placed under seal. Under the first, I promise that I will repaint the buildings on my part of the land every two years. Under the second, I promise that I will not use my premises as an autobody shop. Are those promises enforceable? What if one or both of us later sell our properties—you to Miguel and me to Janet? The answers to those questions depend upon: (i) the identity of the parties, and (ii) the nature of the covenant. We consider the three situations shown in Figure 13.1.

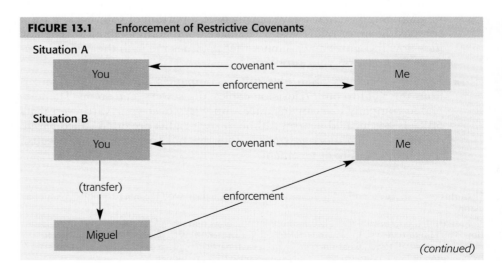

FIGURE 13.1   Enforcement of Restrictive Covenants

Situation A

Situation B

(continued)

---

[15] That limitation cannot be immoral or against public policy. For example, the courts will not enforce a promise that discriminates against people on the grounds of race or religion.

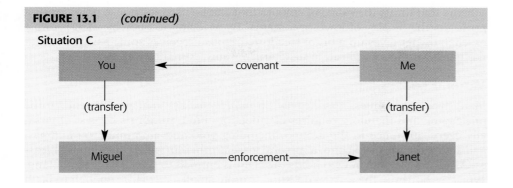

FIGURE 13.1   *(continued)*

Situation C

- *Situation A*: If we both still own the properties, you can sue me if I break either promise. You are entitled to damages if my breach creates a loss. I might also be forced, through specific performance or an injunction, to actually fulfill my promises.

- *Situation B*: Now assume that while you sold your property to Miguel, I still retained mine. A potential problem arises. As we saw in Chapter 3, a contract can usually be enforced only by someone with *privity*, who was a party to the original agreement. However, as we also saw, that rule has exceptions. Perhaps most significantly, contractual *benefits* can generally be *assigned*. Consequently, as long as the original covenants were intended to run with the land, Miguel can sue me if I break either promise.

- *Situation C*: What if you sold your property to Miguel and I sold my property to Janet? If she refused to paint the buildings or if she opened an autobody shop, could Miguel sue her? This situation appears to be similar to the last one, but there is an additional complication. It is generally possible to assign contractual *benefits*, but not contractual *obligations*. The courts are reluctant to impose a burden upon a person simply because they bought a piece of land. Consequently, in deciding whether Janet is caught by the covenants, a judge would look at several factors.[16]

  - Janet may be bound by a *negative* covenant, but not by a *positive* one. She could be *prevented* from doing something, but she could not be *required* to do something else. Accordingly, while she could be restrained from opening an autobody shop, she could not be compelled to paint her buildings.

  - Janet will not be bound unless, as the original parties, we intended our covenants to *run with the land* so as to benefit the dominant tenement. That might be true if our agreement was intended to protect the value of your property, whoever owned it.

  - Janet will not be bound by a covenant unless she either received her property as a gift or had notice of the covenant before she bought the land. A court will have little sympathy for her if she received the property for free. But it will protect her from a hidden covenant if she actually paid for the property.

Restrictive covenants are sometimes used to control entire areas of a city. In that situation, they are called **building scheme covenants**. For example, when creating a new residential neighbourhood, a land developer may create a

a building scheme covenant is a collection of restrictive covenants that are used to control the development of entire areas

16. *Tulk v Moxhay* (1848) 41 ER 1143 (Ch).

scheme that limits the range of colours that can be used for house paint, or that prohibits the display of lawn ornaments. By agreeing to obey by such promises, each owner gives up a bit of freedom, but also receives some assurance that the neighbourhood will retain its character and its market value.

Mineral Leases

Many types of business rely heavily on *mineral leases*. That phrase tends to be misleading and therefore requires clarification. First, **minerals** consist of virtually every substance in the ground, including gold and aluminum, oil and gas, and sand and gravel. Second, a mineral lease is different from other types of leases. As usual, the person who holds the right is entitled to possess a piece of land. Typically, however, the area in question is quite small—just large enough to facilitate the mining operation. After all, the aim of a **mineral lease** is to allow one person to extract and retain something of value from another person's property.

There are two more important things to note about mineral leases.

- Most mineral leases are acquired from the government, even if the fee simple to the affected property belongs to someone else. All of the land in Canada starts with the Crown, which can then distribute it through *grants*. Grants historically included mineral rights. Since the 1880s, however, the government has *reserved* those rights by keeping them for itself. As a result, depending upon where you live in this country, you probably do not have the right to sell the valuable deposits that lie beneath your property. The government does.

- A mineral lease is similar to *profit à prendre*. A **profit à prendre** is a right to take something valuable away from another person's property.[17] That sort of right can apply not only to minerals, but also to other natural things, like blueberries and moose. Significantly, like a mineral lease, a *profit à prendre* is an interest in land, but not an automatic right to the things in question. Consequently, if you buy a *profit à prendre* with respect to the trees on my property, the timber does not belong to you until you actually harvest it from my land.

LEASES

We have already seen that a lease is an estate in land that creates an exclusive right to possession. However, given the significant role that leases play in the modern business world, it is necessary to look at them in detail.[18]

A lease, or a *tenancy* as it is sometimes called, is a property interest created by contract. Therefore, the usual contractual requirements must be satisfied, including intention to create legal relations, offer and acceptance, and consideration. In addition, while most contracts can be created orally, some leases must be put into print. The legislation varies from jurisdiction to jurisdiction, but the basic rule is that a lease must be evidenced in writing unless it is for three years or less.[19] Although an oral lease for a longer period is valid, it is

---

minerals consist of virtually every substance contained in the ground

a mineral lease allows one person to extract and retain something of value from another person's property

a profit à prendre is a right to take something valuable away from another person's property

a lease is a property interest created by contract

some leases must be evidenced in writing

[17.] The term "*à prendre*" is derived from French and means "a right to take."

[18.] In this chapter, we are only concerned with leases of land. As we will see in Chapter 15, it is also possible to lease other types of property.

[19.] *Law and Equity Act*, RSBC 1979, c 224 as am by RSBC 1985, c 10, s 7 (BC); *Statute of Frauds*, RSNB 1973 c S-14, s 7 (NB); *Statute of Frauds*, RSNS 1989, c 442, s 3 (NS); *Statute of Frauds*, RSO 1990, c S.19, ss 1-3 (Ont); *Statute of Frauds*, 1677 (Eng) c 3, ss 1-2 (Alta, Nfld, NWT, Nun, PEI, Sask, Yuk). In Manitoba, the English *Statute of Frauds* has been repealed by RSM 1987, c F-158.

generally unenforceable and therefore can be ignored by either party.[20] (As a general rule, to reduce the danger of uncertainty and litigation, you should put *all* of your contracts into writing.) Because a lease is created by contract, there must be a mutual agreement between two parties: the *landlord* and the *tenant*. The **landlord** is the person with an interest in land who agrees to allow someone else to take possession.[21] The **tenant** is the person who receives the right to possess the property.

Duration

When a fee simple or a life estate is created, there is no way of knowing exactly how long it will last. The relevant life may continue for decades or end the next day. The maximum duration of a lease, however, must be definite. Consequently, it would not be possible to create a lease that would last "until the Maple Leafs next win the Cup."[22] There are several possibilities.

- *Fixed-term tenancy*: A **fixed-term tenancy** exists when it is possible at the outset to determine when the tenancy will end. The parties may actually specify a date, such as "December 31, 2020." Alternatively, if they do not know a specific date at the outset, they may provide a formula that is capable of generating one, such as "the last day of Ramadan in 2020." Even if they initially agreed to a fixed term, the parties can enter into new lease at the end of the old one. And even if they do not create a new fixed-term lease, a *periodic tenancy* may arise if the tenant remains in possession and the landlord accepts rent at regular intervals.

- *Periodic tenancy*: A **periodic tenancy** is also for a fixed period, but it is automatically renewed at the end of each term unless one of the parties provides *notice to quit*. You are probably most familiar with that type of lease, since it is generally used for residential tenancies. The basic term of the lease can be for any length of time. A week, a month, and a year are the most common options. As a general rule, the length of the term mirrors the intervals at which the tenant pays rent. The length of the term usually also mirrors the notice period. Consequently, to terminate a monthly lease, you must provide one clear month's notice.[23] A yearly tenancy, however, normally only requires six months' notice.[24]

- *Tenancy at will:* A **tenancy at will** exists if there is no set term and either party can terminate the lease at any time. Because there is no definite duration, it is sometimes said that a tenancy at will is not really leasehold estate. Nevertheless, there is at least an implicit agreement between the parties and the tenant is liable to pay rent. Tenancies at will most often arise when the owner of a property allows a potential purchaser to

the **landlord** is the person with an interest in land who agrees to allow someone else to take possession

the **tenant** is the person who receives the right to possess the property

a lease must be for a definite duration

a **fixed-term tenancy** exists when it is possible at the outset to determine when the tenancy will end

a **periodic tenancy** is for a fixed period and is automatically renewed at the end of each term unless one of the parties provides notice of termination

a **tenancy at will** exists if there is no set term and either party can terminate the lease at any time

---

[20.] An exception may be created by part performance if the tenant is actually in possession *and* has paid rent.

[21.] Although the landlord typically holds the fee simple in the property, it is also possible for a person with a life estate, or even an earlier lease, to grant a new lease. That last possibility is called a *sublease* and it is discussed below.

[22.] The *maximum* duration must be definite, but a tenancy may end earlier. Therefore it would be possible to have a lease "for 999 years or until the Maple Leafs next win the Cup."

[23.] Note that the period is one *clear* month's notice. For example, if you want to vacate the premises at the end of July, you must give notice by the end of June. If you wait until the first day of July, your lease will continue until the end of August. A longer notice period is required under a residential lease.

[24.] In New Brunswick, Nova Scotia, and Prince Edward Island, the notice period is only three months.

move in before the sale is finalized, or when a tenant remains on the premises with the landlord's consent after the end of a lease.[25]

- *Tenancy at sufferance*: A **tenancy at sufferance** occurs when a tenant continues to possess the premises at the end of a lease *without* the landlord's permission. In that situation, there is not really a lease because the parties do not even have an implied agreement. Indeed, if the tenant does not vacate the property within a reasonable time after being asked to do so, it commits the tort of trespass (as discussed in Chapter 10) and the landlord can take steps to have the tenant forcibly removed. While there is no obligation to pay "rent" (because there is no tenancy), the person in possession is required to pay compensation for the use and occupation of the property.[26]

a tenancy at sufferance occurs when a tenant continues to possess the premises at the end of a lease without the landlord's permission

Assignments and Subleases

As a tenant, you may find that you do not want to occupy the premises for the full length of your lease. Perhaps you have been transferred to another city and no longer require an apartment. Perhaps your business has fallen on hard times and you no longer can afford to rent a warehouse. You have several options.

- You might persuade your landlord to terminate the lease early. That is unlikely to happen, however, unless you also introduce the landlord to a new tenant.

- Even if you cannot escape your lease, you might be able to *assign* it. As we saw in Chapter 3, an **assignment** occurs when you transfer your contractual rights to a third party. That third party (the *assignee*) would step into your shoes (at least for some purposes) and become the tenant. That possibility is subject to limitations.

  an assignment occurs when a contractual party transfers its rights to a third party

  - Although contractual rights can generally be assigned, your lease may either prohibit an assignment or require your landlord's consent (which, your lease may also say, cannot be withheld "unreasonably").[27] Such provisions are very common. Landlords want control over the people who occupy their premises.

  - Second, an assignment would not necessarily include all of the terms in the lease. The assignee would only be bound by the *real covenants*. **Real covenants** include promises that are directly related to the land (like the obligation to pay rent or repair the premises), but not merely personal obligations (like the landlord's promise to buy goods from your warehouse).

    real covenants include promises that are directly related to the land, but not merely personal obligations

  - Third, an assignment would not necessarily protect you from liability. If your assignee did not fulfill the lease, the landlord could normally demand relief from you. You could ask your landlord to release you

---

[25] However, if the landlord continues to receive rent from the tenant at regular intervals, a court may recognize the creation of a periodic tenancy, with the result that notice must be given in a timely manner to terminate the new lease.

[26] If the landlord does accept "rental" payments, a court may recognize the implied creation of a periodic tenancy.

[27] To protect tenants, some jurisdictions have legislation to that effect unless the parties expressly say otherwise. *Landlord and Tenant Act*, RSM 1987, c L70, s 22 (Man); *Landlord and Tenant Act*, RSNB 1973, c L-1, s 11 (NB); *Commercial Tenancies Act*, RSNWT 1988, c C-10, s 11 (NWT and Nun); *Commercial Tenancies Act*, RSO 1990, c L.7, s 23 (Ont); *Landlord and Tenant Act*, RSPEI 1988, c L-4, s 12 (PEI); *Landlord and Tenant Act*, RSS 1978, c L-6, s 13 (Sask); *Landlord and Tenant Act*, RSY 1986, c 98, s 11 (Yuk).

from responsibility, but it would probably refuse. You should therefore ensure that your assignment requires the assignee to honour the lease *and* to compensate you for any money that you may have to pay to the landlord.

- Fourth, an assignment must cover the entire term of a lease. If it falls short, even by one day, then it cannot be an assignment—but it may be a *sublease*.

- A **sublease** occurs when a tenant grants a lease to a third party.[28] In that case, the third party would not step into your shoes. You would continue to be the tenant under the original lease, but you would also be a landlord under the sublease. Your sublease might apply to the whole property or to just one section of it. Similarly, it might contain the same terms as the original lease, but it need not do so. Once again, however, the original lease may prohibit subleasing or require you to obtain your landlord's consent.

a **sublease** occurs when a tenant grants a lease to a third party

Commercial Leases

Generally speaking, there are two types of leases: *commercial* and *residential*. We will focus on the former, and discuss the latter briefly at the end of this chapter.

Standard Covenants

A **commercial lease** occurs when premises are rented for a business purpose. Although some modifications have been introduced by statute or by the common law, the basic contractual rules apply, and the parties are generally free to set their own terms. Consequently, depending upon the circumstances, a commercial lease may consist of a book-length document (for the long-term lease of an office tower) or little more than a simple handshake (for temporary use of a patch of ground as a souvenir kiosk along a parade route). Nevertheless, certain *covenants*, or promises, are standard.

a **commercial lease** occurs when premises are rented for a business purpose

One covenant is the tenant's obligation to pay *rent*. The parties will normally set the rent in advance and possibly, in the case of a long-term lease, also agree on a mechanism for calculating occasional increases.[29] However, even if there is no express agreement on a price, the law will normally require the payment of a "reasonable" amount. Significantly, the obligation to pay rent is generally independent of the other terms in the lease. Consequently, the tenant usually cannot withhold rent simply because the landlord has failed to fulfill a promise to repair the premises. The tenant must bring a separate action for that breach.

the obligation to pay rent is generally independent of the other terms in the lease

A covenant for **quiet possession** prohibits the landlord from interfering with the tenant's enjoyment of the premises.[30] That covenant can be broken in a number of ways.

a covenant for **quiet possession** prohibits the landlord from interfering with the tenant's enjoyment of the premises

- The landlord may be unable to grant an effective lease, for example, because the property is still occupied by another tenant.

---

[28] It is often difficult to distinguish between an assignment and a sublease. There is no magic in words. A court will base its decision on the substance of the transaction, rather than the language that the parties used.

[29] Common mechanisms include a percentage of the tenant's business profits, the market value of the square footage, or reference to an arbitrator.

[30] A landlord is, however, entitled to inspect the premises occasionally for signs of damage and abuse.

- The landlord may disturb the tenant's use of the premises, for example, by allowing carbon monoxide to seep up from a parking lot, or by using a jackhammer that causes an intolerable amount of noise and vibration.

- While the landlord is not responsible for another tenant's *wrongful* behaviour, it may be liable for granting a lease with an incompatible use, for example, by allowing a bowling alley to operate directly over a relaxation clinic.

Depending upon the circumstances, a court may respond to a breach of a covenant for quiet possession in various ways.

- awarding an injunction requiring the landlord to remedy the interference,

- allowing the tenant to discharge the lease and recover compensatory damages, or

- allowing the tenant to have a reduction in rent.

neither party has a general obligation to repair the premises

As a general rule, a landlord is under no obligation to *repair or maintain* the premises before or during a lease. However, if the property is in *very poor* condition, there may be a breach of the covenant for quiet possession. Nor is the tenant generally responsible for fixing or replacing things that are broken or worn as a result normal wear and tear, such as fallen fence posts or threadbare carpets. The tenant is, however, responsible for any damage that it intentionally or negligently causes. It is also required to treat the premises in a "tenant-like manner" by doing things like unplugging blocked toilets.[31] Because neither party has extensive obligations under the common law, commercial leases almost always impose additional responsibilities concerning repair and maintenance. It is in no one's interest to allow the property to become completely run down.

the tenant does not have a general obligation to pay taxes or insurance on a property

Unless the parties otherwise agree, the landlord is required to pay the *taxes* associated with a property. And while neither party is generally obliged to obtain *insurance* over the premises, the landlord normally does so to protect its investment. In some cases, the lease will shift that expense to the tenant. And as a matter of risk management, the tenant should, in any event, obtain insurance coverage for the things that it stores on the premises and for any damage that it may cause to outsiders. For instance, a fire may not only destroy the contents of the rental unit, it may also spread to a neighbouring property.

Remedies

A commercial lease is created by contract and therefore supports the usual contractual remedies if there is a breach. We already referred to several options in Chapter 7, including compensatory damages, injunctions, and discharge. There are also several special forms of relief that may be available to a landlord if the tenant commits a serious breach. We can mention two.

eviction or right of re-entry allows a landlord to resume possession of the premises

forfeiture occurs when a tenant loses its interest in a property

- *Eviction*: If the tenant commits a serious breach, such as not paying the rent, the landlord may be entitled to exercise a right of **eviction** (sometimes called a **right of re-entry**) to resume possession of the premises before the end of the lease. That remedy often creates hardship for the tenant because it results in a **forfeiture**—the tenant loses its interest in the property. Consequently, even if a tenant has committed a serious breach, a court may grant relief from forfeiture by allowing that person to make amends and to retain possession of the property. Each jurisdiction has detailed legislation regarding evictions.

[31.] *Warren v Keen* [1954] 1 KB 15 (CA).

- *Distress*: If a tenant is not evicted for nonpayment, it may be subject to the remedy of *distress*. **Distress** occurs when the landlord seizes the tenant's belongings and sells them to pay the rent. Once again, each jurisdiction has detailed legislation on point.

distress occurs when the landlord seizes the tenant's belongings and sells them in order to pay the rent

Finally, it is important to note that some of the rules that normally govern contractual remedies may not apply to commercial leases. As we discussed in Chapter 7, a person who suffers a breach of contract can claim *expectation damages* for the benefit it should have received under the agreement. Those damages are reduced, however, to the extent that the plaintiff unreasonably failed to *mitigate* a loss. Suppose that I agreed to buy a car from you for $9000. I later refuse to go through with that deal when I learn that the car is worth only $6000. It seems that your expectation damages are $3000, which was your expected profit. However, you will only be entitled to $2000 if I can prove that you could have resold the car to someone else for $7000. You are responsible for the other $1000 because you unreasonably failed to mitigate that loss by selling the car to a third party.

That same rule may not apply to commercial leases. Although the cases are inconsistent, the Supreme Court of Canada has suggested that if a tenant wrongfully vacates the premises, the landlord can sometimes let the premises sit empty and recover the value of the rent that would have been paid over the entire tenancy.[32] Does that seem fair? How would you respond to the dispute in You Be the Judge 13.1?

YOU BE THE JUDGE 13.1

Commercial Leases and Mitigation

Archer Holdings Ltd owns a shopping centre in a suburban area. Although a number of smaller shops rent space in the mall, the "anchor" (that is, the main tenant) is Bainsbury Foods, a grocery store. Bainsbury signed a lease with Archer for a fixed term of 15 years. Business was brisk for the first 12 months, but after a downturn in the economy, Bainsbury began to lose a lot of money as a result of operating in that particular location. Consequently, two years into the lease, it removed its stock and equipment, transferred its employees to other outlets, and closed its doors in Archer's mall.

Archer has resumed control of the vacated space, but has made no effort to find another anchor. The evidence indicates that, despite the downturn in the economy, a replacement tenant could be found if the landlord was willing to reduce the rent by 25 percent. Bainsbury admits that it breached the contract, but insists that it should not be responsible for 13 years of full rent on a property that it no longer occupies.

Question for Discussion

1. Do you agree with Bainsbury's argument? Explain your answer.

Residential Leases

Although it shares the same basic purpose as a commercial lease, a *residential lease* is different in some respects. A **residential lease** provides a place to live. The law therefore has much more incentive to become involved in the landlord-tenant relationship. It may be acceptable to allow two businesses to freely

a residential lease provides a place to live

[32.] *Highway Properties Ltd v Kelly Douglas & Co* (1971) 17 DLR (3d) 710. Damages are reduced, however, to the extent that the landlord does in fact limit its loss by renting the property to a third party.

negotiate the terms of their agreement. It seems unfair and unrealistic, however, to expect a residential tenant to do the same. In that situation, there is likely a great difference in bargaining power between the parties, especially when accommodation is scarce. Almost by definition, a residential tenant has limited resources. People with large amounts of money usually buy, rather than rent, so that their payments create an investment. Consequently, every jurisdiction in Canada has extensive legislation that regulates residential tenancies by requiring some terms, prohibiting others, providing mechanisms for resolving disputes, and so on.[33]

It is impossible for us to consider that legislation in detail.[34] We can, however, note several important ways in which residential leases differ from commercial leases.

- *Termination*: In the commercial context, it is usually possible to terminate a periodic tenancy by giving notice equal to the length of one term. Residential notice periods, however, tend to be much longer, for example, 60 or 90 days for a monthly lease. Likewise, in the residential context, a periodic tenancy may automatically arise at the end of fixed-term lease unless notice was given.

- *Rental rates*: Commercial parties are generally free to agree upon any price. Residential leases, in contrast, are governed by rent control mechanisms that prevent landlords from gouging tenants.

- *Distress*: A commercial landlord may be entitled to seize and sell a tenant's belongings if rent is not paid. However, that right usually is not available against a residential tenant.

- *Repair and maintenance*: Unlike a commercial landlord, a residential landlord has a statutory obligation to repair and maintain the property.

- *Mitigation*: Although a commercial landlord may be relieved of the need to mitigate when a tenant wrongfully vacates a property, a residential landlord is generally required to take reasonable steps to minimize the losses that result from a breach.

---

[33] *Residential Tenancies Act*, SA 1991, c R-15.3 (Alta); *Residential Tenancy Act*, RSBC 1996, c 406 (BC); *Residential Tenancies Act*, SM 1990-91, c 11 (Man); *Residential Tenancies Act*, SNB 1975, c R-10.2 (NB); *Residential Tenancies Act*, 2000, SN 2000, c R-14.1 (Nfld); *Residential Tenancies Act*, RSNWT 1988, c R-5 (NWT and Nun); *Residential Tenancies Act*, RSNS 1989, c 401 (NS); *Tenant Protection Act 1997*, SO 1997, c 24 (Ont); *Rental of Residential Property Act*, SPEI 1988, c 58 (PEI); *Residential Tenancies Act*, RSS 1978, c R-22 (Sask); *Landlord and Tenant Act*, RSY 1986, c 98 (Yuk).

[34] See C Bentley *et al*, *William & Rhodes Canadian Law of Landlord and Tenant*, 6th ed loose-leaf (1988).

Chapter Summary

Real property includes land and things attached to land. A defining feature of property interests is that they are generally enforceable against the whole world and not merely against the person from whom they are acquired.

An estate in land involves the right to exclusive possession. A fee simple entitles a person to exercise rights over a piece of property for life and to dispose of it after death. A life estate lasts only as long as the relevant life—upon death, the property either reverts to the person from whom it was obtained or passes as a remainder to someone else. A lease provides the right to exclusive possession and therefore qualifies as an estate in land. However, its duration is not measured by anyone's life—a lease must be for a definite duration.

Ownership in a piece of land can be shared between two or more people. With co-ownership, two or more people share an undivided interest in a property. With joint ownership, two or more people share exactly the same interests in a property. Joint ownership includes the right of survivorship. Joint ownership can be turned into co-ownership through the process of severance. Shared ownership can be brought to an end through the process of partition. In a condominium, several people share ownership of some parts of a building, while individually owning other parts.

An easement is a right to use a neighbour's land. An easement must exist between two neighbouring properties—the dominant tenement and the servient tenement. An easement may be created expressly or implicitly. In some jurisdictions, it can also be created through prescription. A statutory or public easement is not really an easement because it does not require a dominant tenement. A licence is permission to act in a way that would otherwise be prohibited, but it is neither an easement nor an interest in land.

A restrictive covenant is a promise to use property in a way that benefits the dominant tenement and burdens the servient tenement. A restrictive covenant can be created only by agreement. The enforcement of a covenant depends upon: (i) the identity of the parties, and (ii) the nature of the covenant.

A mineral lease allows a person to extract and retain minerals from another person's property. It is similar to a *profit à prendre*.

A lease (or tenancy) is contractually created between the landlord and the tenant. Its maximum duration must be definite. A fixed-term tenancy exists when it is possible at the outset to determine when the tenancy will end. A periodic tenancy is also for a fixed period, but it is automatically renewed at the end of each term unless one of the parties provides notice to quit. A tenancy at will exists when there is no set term and either party can terminate the lease at any time. With a tenancy at sufferance, a tenant continues to possess the premises at the end of a lease without the landlord's permission. The parties do not really have a lease because they do not have an agreement.

A tenant can sometimes assign its rights under a lease to a third party, who then becomes the tenant. A tenant may also sublease a property. If so, that person remains a tenant under the original lease, but also becomes a landlord under the sublease. Many leases either prohibit assignments and subleases or require the landlord's consent.

With a commercial lease, premises are rented for a business purpose. The parties are generally free to negotiate the terms. Some promises or covenants, however, are standard. If a tenant breaks a commercial lease, the landlord may be entitled to use the special remedies of eviction and distress. In some situations, a landlord can claim contractual relief without the need to mitigate its losses.

A residential lease provides a place to live. Every jurisdiction in Canada has extensive legislation regulating residential tenancies. They all require some terms, prohibit others, and provide mechanisms for resolving disputes.

Review Questions

1. Provide a basic definition of "real property."

2. As a general rule, against whom are property rights enforceable?

3. "A private person who owns a piece of land has complete control over that property." Is that statement true? Provide three illustrations in support of your answer.

4. Outline the difference between a reversion and a remainder.

5. Explain why life estates are generally unattractive in a commercial context.

6. Describe the right of survivorship. Explain when and how it applies. Describe two ways in which that right can be brought to an end.

7. Explain the process of partition. Provide an example of when it would be desirable to use that process.

8. What is a "flying fee"?

9. What does it mean to say that an interest "runs with the land"? Provide two examples of interests that run with the land.

10. I have been secretly dumping waste into your pond for 25

years. Provide at least one reason why I probably cannot claim that an easement has been created by prescription.

11. Explain the meaning of "adverse possession."

12. "A public easement is not really an easement." Is that statement correct? Explain your answer.

13. Describe a licence, and explain how it differs from an easement.

14. What is the difference between positive and negative covenants? Provide an example of each. In the context of restrictive covenants, why does the law draw that distinction?

15. Explain why the government may be able to grant a mineral lease with respect to oil that lies beneath your property.

16. What is a *profit à prendre*? If you have a *profit à prendre*, do you automatically own the things to which it applies?

17. Explain why a tenancy at sufferance is not really a tenancy at all, and why a tenancy at will may not really be a true lease either.

18. As a general rule, which party to a commercial lease has the obligation to repair the premises?

19. Describe two special types of remedies that may be available to a landlord under a commercial lease if the tenant fails to pay rent.

20. Explain five general differences between commercial leases and residential leases. Why have the legislatures felt the need to introduce those changes?

Cases and Problems

1. Five years ago, Romeo Enrique held the fee simple in a beautiful cottage, which he named Blackacre. As he had just turned 90, he began to worry about what would happen to his property after he was gone. He called his lawyer and arranged for his son-in-law, Jimmy Cobb, to have exclusive possession of the property as long as Louise, who was Jimmy's wife and whom Romeo had always regarded fondly, was alive. Romeo died the next year. Shortly before he passed away, he gave all of his assets, including any interest that he may still have in Blackacre, to his friend Evan Gilbert. Two years after Romeo's death, Jimmy sold his interest in Blackacre to Francesca Mucci. Francesca almost immediately began to clear all of the land around the cottage. While she realized that the property would be less valuable without the surrounding trees, she was annoyed by the wildlife that lived in the forest. Louise recently died. Who is entitled to Blackacre? Explain your answer. Discuss Francesca's rights and liabilities.

2. Joe Besser, Peter Bond, and Eric Childs bought a parcel of land as joint tenants with the intention of building a music studio on it within five years. After three years, however, Joe decided to put his money into a different venture and consequently sold his interest to Mick Shrimpton. Shortly after that sale was completed, the situation took a series of tragic turns. First, Joe was involved in a fatal traffic accident. Three weeks later, Peter died from electrocution. Two weeks after that, Eric was crushed to death beneath a bookshelf. And a mere three days later, Mick was killed in a gardening accident. Joe, Peter, Eric, and John all left valid wills. Joe's will left all of his property to his girlfriend, Celine; Peter's left all of his to Barbra; Eric's left all of his to Alanis; and Mick's left all of his to Whitney. Who now owns the land? Explain your answer.

3. Because of a number of problems that have arisen under the existing law, the provincial government intends to enact new legislation governing condominiums. Section 67(2) of that statute states: "Unless otherwise agreed, all common areas shall be shared among the individual unit

owners as joint tenants." Explain the difficulties that this provision would create. How could those difficulties be avoided?

4. For many years, Marina DelMare operated an outdoor adventure company from a cabin on a lake in northern Ontario. As a licensed pilot, she carried herself and her customers to the cabin in an aircraft that was capable of landing on the water. After a downturn in the economy, however, she was forced to close her business and sell her cabin. She found a willing buyer in Marc Ryan, a Canadian actor who had become a television star in Hollywood. Although he spent most of the year in California, Marc wanted to keep in touch with his roots. He became very disappointed, however, the first time that he tried to visit his new property. The cabin was accessible by two land routes. The first, which followed the public highways and then cut across part of the land that Marina had sold to him, was very long and inconvenient. Marc realized that if he was forced to rely upon it, he would seldom have the opportunity to use his cabin. The second route, which passed almost exclusively through land owned by Wendy Dais, was more direct and much quicker. Marc offered to purchase the road from Wendy, but she absolutely refused. His lawyer then informed her that Marc was entitled, by reason of necessity, to an easement over that road. Will that argument succeed? Provide two reasons for your answer.

5. Lester Tulk held the fee simple to a number of connected properties in Fredericton. Moxie Case, a wealthy land developer, offered to buy one of the properties, Elm Square, for $500 000. Although Elm Square had long been used as a park, Moxie explained that she wanted to clear the land and build an apartment complex. Lester was attracted by the price, but he did not approve of the purpose. Since he intended to retain the neighbouring properties for himself, at least for a decade, he much preferred the land to remain in its present condition. Therefore he made a counter-offer to Moxie under which he would sell

the land for $100 000, and she would covenant that she would not develop Elm Square for at least 25 years. Moxie accepted that offer, and the appropriate documents were carefully drafted to reflect the parties' agreement. Six months after the deal closed, however, Moxie resold Elm Square to François Cottenham, another local developer, for $400 000. Cottenham almost immediately began to clear the land in preparation for the construction of an apartment complex. Lester is outraged and has informed François that Elm Square must remain green for almost another quarter century. In response, François admits that he knew of the agreement between the original parties, but insists that he is not bound by a contract that he neither negotiated nor signed. What will happen to Elm Square? Explain your answer. Is that result fair?

6. Elias Gamel has the fee simple to a large area of land in northern Alberta. Six months ago, Choi Paper Products Inc persuaded him to enter into a contract. That agreement allowed Choi to harvest timber from Elias's land for a period of 50 years. In exchange, Choi promised to pay a fee based on the amount of timber that it removed on an annual basis, and it promised to undertake a reforestation project that would renew the source on a continuous basis. Choi intends to begin harvesting the wood within one year. The government recently announced a new tax incentive program that provides a tax credit to any individual or corporation "that owns timber that it has harvested or that it will harvest within a reasonable period." Choi has claimed a tax credit with respect to all of the trees on Elias' land. Is it entitled to do so? Explain your answer.

7. Ryan Furniture Ltd holds the fee simple in a large building that it uses for manufacturing, selling, and storing home furnishings. After a recent fire, Pol Lawn Care Inc was forced to temporarily relocate its business. It was able to quickly find a site for its manufacturing operations, but it still required storage space for its inventory. Because the owners of the two companies were old friends, Ryan and Pol signed a document that contained the following provisions.

> For as long as it requires the space, Pol is entitled to use the warehouse facilities in Ryan's building. Pol and Ryan will both be entitled to use the same storage space simultaneously. Each party, however, shall clearly label its goods. Pol will pay $1500 to Ryan for each month, or part of a month, that it stores its goods in Ryan's building.

Although that arrangement worked well initially, tensions have developed between the parties, largely due to the fact that renovations of Pol's own property have been considerably delayed. Therefore Ryan has ordered Pol to remove all of its goods within a reasonable time and no later than one week. Pol admits that storage space is available elsewhere, but only at a significantly higher price. It wants to remain in Ryan's building until its own premises are rebuilt. The parties' lawyers agree that, in light of other provisions in the document that have not been reproduced, Pol is entitled to remain on Ryan's premises only if a lease exists. Is that the case? Provide two explanations for your answer. If the parties did not create a lease, what interest, if any, did Pol receive?

8. Solomon Holdings Ltd entered into an agreement with Kostal Sporting Goods Supplies Inc. The agreement provided a formula for calculating monthly rent based on a combination of the market value of the premises and the net profit generated by Kostal's sale of sporting goods. The document also contained the following provision.

> Kostal shall have exclusive possession of the premises for a single five-year period commencing the first day of January in the next calendar year.

The agreement proceeded as planned. At the end of the five-year period, however, Kostal remained in the premises and continued to pay rent according to the formula established in the agreement. Solomon received such payments for nearly three years without objection. Recently, however, Kostal has discovered an alternative location at a lower rental price. On the first day of July, it provided Solomon with written notice that it intended to vacate the premises by the first of August. Solomon was generally agreeable to that proposal, but it insisted that Kostal was liable to pay rent for August, as well as July. Which party is correct? Explain your answer.

9. Takahana Sushi, a Japanese restaurant, rented its premises from Gunnar Schultz. The contract signed by the parties was very brief. For our purposes, these are the relevant provisions.

> 3. Schultz promises to provide Takahana with quiet possession.
>
> 5. Takahana shall pay an annual rent of $36 000, payable monthly in equal instalments.
>
> 7. This lease shall be for a single fixed term of 10 years.

Three months after taking possession of the premises, Takahana was informed by a public health inspector that the property was unfit for use as a restaurant because the plumbing in the toilets was defective. The cost of the necessary replacement was about $50 000. Takahana asked Schultz to make the necessary repairs. Schultz, however, refused because the lease did not require him to make repairs. He expressed some sympathy for Takahana's position, and indicated that he would not object if the tenant replaced the defective plumbing. He also insisted, however, that he was entitled to full rent for the remainder of the 10-year term. At that point, Takahana left the premises, relocated to a new building, and refused to continue paying rent to Schultz. Which party will prevail in this dispute? Explain your answer.

10. Yan Li owned and operated a large market. She rented space within that market to Manju Gupta under a weekly tenancy. That lease contained a covenant that restricted Manju to selling fruits and vegetables, and that expressly prohibited him from selling meats and cheeses. Despite being repeatedly told to adhere to the terms of the lease, Manju persisted in selling all sorts of foods. Yan received many complaints from her other tenants, a number of whom threatened to terminate their tenancies if the situation was not resolved. Therefore she exercised her legal right under her agreement with Manju, terminated his lease, and ordered him to remove his belongings from the market immediately. He initially refused to do so and carried on with his business for four more weeks. Finally, after the pressure from Yan and her other tenants became intol-

erable, Manju left the premises. He insists that the matter is now at an end. Yan, however, believes that she is entitled to the payment of money for the period that he stayed in the market following the termination of his original lease. Is she correct? Explain your answer. Describe the parties' relationship after Yan legally ordered Manju to leave the market.

11. Wilson Hum leased a commercial property to Frank Mosher for use as a pizzeria. The parties' agreement contained three important provisions.

   5. The tenant shall not during the term of the lease sell, assign, or sublet or part with possession of the said premises or any part thereof without the written consent of the landlord. Such consent shall not be unreasonably withheld.

   8. During the term of this lease, the tenant shall keep the premises in good repair, both interior and exterior. Damage by fire or other circumstances beyond the tenant's control are excepted.

   12. This lease shall be for a fixed term of five years. Annual rent of $30 000 shall be paid in equal monthly instalments.

Frank operated the pizzeria for two years, but he soon tired of the business. However, his friend Janine Gallant indicated that she would be willing to take control of the business for the three years remaining under the lease. Frank wrote to Wilson to seek consent for an assignment of the lease. At the same time, he provided documentation that established that Janine had good credit and was experienced in the food sales industry. Although Wilson simply ignored the request, Frank proceeded to assign his interest under the original lease to Janine. Unfortunately, for reasons that were completely unforeseeable at the time of the assignment, Janine's personal life fell into turmoil. As a result, she totally lost interest in the pizzeria. She failed to pay the rent and she allowed the property to fall into very poor condition. By the time that Wilson discovered that state of affairs, Janine had become destitute. She had no assets and was clearly not worth suing. Wilson therefore insists that Frank is responsible for paying the overdue rent and for the cost of repairing the premises. Do paragraphs 8 and 12 of the lease still apply to Frank? Explain your answer.

12. Igor Polska, an entrepreneur with varied interests, entered into two contracts with Ishtla Singh. The first was for the sale of goods. Ishtla promised to pay $5000 for a rare book. The second contract was for the rental of a property. Ishtla agreed to take possession for a one-year term beginning on the first day of July. The total rent was to be $36 000, paid in equal monthly instalments. Ishtla moved into the premises on the first day of July and paid $3000 in rent. Within two days, however, she informed Igor that she only intended to remain until the end of that month. She also told him that she had found another copy of the same book elsewhere at a lower price, and that she therefore was unwilling to pay the $5000 as promised. Igor nevertheless insists that he is entitled to the full value of both contracts, which he calculates to be $38 000 ($5000 for the book and $33 000 for the property). Ishtla believes that Igor's position is unreasonable. She relies on the fact that she has already introduced him to one person who is willing to pay $4000 for the book, and to another who is willing to occupy the property immediately under a monthly tenancy at a rent of $2000. Is Igor correct? Explain your answer. Do you require additional information to calculate the full value of Ishtla's liability?

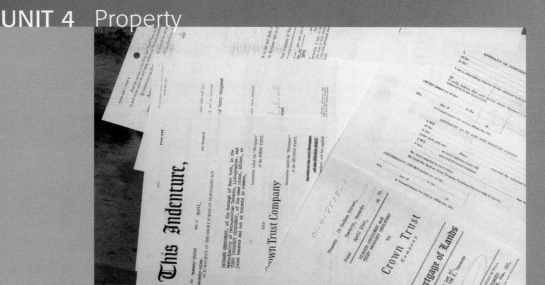

14 Real Property: Sales and Mortgages

CHAPTER OVERVIEW

OBJECTIVES

After completing this chapter, you should be able to:

1. Explain the basic differences between a registry system and a land titles system, and indicate which system operates in your jurisdiction.

2. Describe the concept of indefeasibility and its underlying principles.

3. Describe five types of unregistered interests that may be enforceable against the owner of a registered interest.

4. Explain the risk management issues that arise in the purchase of land.

5. Outline the purpose of an agreement of purchase and sale, and explain the role of the conditions that are frequently contained in that type of agreement.

6. Describe the remedies that may be available if an agreement of purchase and sale is breached.

7. Describe a mortgage, and identify the mortgagor and the mortgagee.

8. Outline the basic difference between a mortgage under a registry system and a mortgage under a land titles system, and identify three situations in which that difference has practical consequences.

9. Describe a subsequent mortgage, and explain the risk management issues that are associated with that type of arrangement.

10. Describe four types of remedies that may be available to a mortgagee if a mortgagor does not fulfill the terms of a mortgage.

In Chapter 13, we began our discussion of real property by describing a variety of interests and examining one important type of transaction: the lease. In this chapter, we discuss another important type of transaction: the sale. We also consider a form of financing that is often used to facilitate the purchase of land: the mortgage. First, however, it is necessary to briefly explain the registration systems that operate in Canada.

REGISTRATION SYSTEMS

A variety of interests may simultaneously exist in a single piece of land: a fee simple, a life estate, a lease, an easement, a restrictive covenant, and so on. We will discover even more possibilities in this chapter. As a matter of risk management, it is necessary to keep track of all of those interests. If you intend to purchase a particular property, you will want to know exactly what you are getting for your money. You certainly would not want to pay for a fee simple and then discover that you received only a life estate. Likewise, if you enjoy the benefit of a restrictive covenant, you would want to advertise that fact to a potential buyer of the servient tenement. Otherwise, the new owner might not be bound by the covenant. In either event, you will be able to rely upon one of two *registration systems*, depending upon where you live in Canada. A **registration system** documents the existence of interests in land.

Registry System

The four Atlantic provinces, as well as parts of Manitoba and Ontario, typically use *registry system*s (or *deeds registration*, as it is sometimes called).[1] A **registry system** provides an opportunity to inspect and evaluate documents that may affect real property. Suppose that you are interested in buying a cottage from me, but you are not sure that I actually own it. Therefore, before you go ahead with the purchase, you visit the registry office, search through all of the relevant records, and try to satisfy yourself that I am at the end of a good **chain of title**—that is, a series of transactions in which ownership was validly passed from one person to the next. Theoretically, it is possible to trace that chain all the way back to the time when the government held the land. Fortunately, as a result of legislation, it is only necessary to go back a much shorter period, for example, 40 years.

The task of *searching title* nevertheless is often difficult and hazardous. Consequently, it is usually best left to someone with expertise in the area, such as a lawyer specializing in real estate. The records may be unclear or misleading. Mistakes may be made, and errors may be overlooked for decades, only to be later discovered after many people have relied on the appearance of a good title. Continuing with our example, suppose that I thought that I had purchased the cottage 15 years ago from Alison. She in turn believed that she had inherited it from her uncle. In fact, her uncle's will actually left the property to her brother. Consequently, my chain of title is defective. Even though the records for the last 15 years seem to indicate that the property is mine, it really belongs to someone else (presumably Alison's brother). Furthermore, one of the defining features of the registry system is that the government's role is passive. It provides access to the documents, but it does not guarantee their accuracy. Therefore, even if you pay the price, you cannot get good title to the cottage

---

[1.] There is, however, a gradual shift toward land titles systems in a number of those jurisdictions.

from me. Because of that possibility, many insurance companies now offer *title insurance*, which provides a source of compensation if a transaction does not include everything promised.[2]

From a risk management perspective, the registry system leaves something to be desired. Although it does not happen often, a simple oversight during a title search may have disastrous consequences. You may end up paying a lot of money without actually getting any land in exchange. That is one reason for hiring a lawyer to assist in the purchase of land. It is the lawyer's job to ensure that the seller actually has a good chain of title. If the lawyer makes a mistake, you will not be able to get the land, but you will be able to sue the lawyer.

There is another point to note about risk management. If I did have a good chain of title, and if we did go through with the sale, you (or your lawyer) should return to the registry office as soon as possible to register the transfer documents. If that does not happen, you might actually lose the cottage. After selling the land to you, I might dishonestly sell it again to a third party named Tre. The general rule under a registry system is that competing claims are resolved by the *timing* of registration. If Tre did not have notice of your earlier transaction, and if he gave valuable consideration for his purchase, he gets the cottage if he registers before you. You can bring an action against me for damages, but you cannot get the property from Tre. In contrast, if you register your transfer first, you will provide Tre and the rest of the world with notice of your rights. Your claim to the land therefore cannot be defeated.

> competing claims under a registry system are generally resolved by the timing of registration

Land Titles System

To avoid many of the problems associated with the registry system, the three western-most provinces, the territories, and some parts of Manitoba and Ontario operate under a *land titles system* (or *Torrens system*, as it is sometimes called).[3] A **land titles system** does more than simply provide an opportunity to inspect and evaluate documents. It generates certificates of title that virtually guarantee the validity of the interests that are listed.

> a **land titles system** generates certificates of title that virtually guarantee the validity of the interests that are listed

The key to a land titles system is the doctrine of *indefeasibility*. **Indefeasibility** means that, with very few exceptions, the interests that are included in a certificate of title cannot be defeated. That doctrine is based on three principles. To illustrate this, we return to our earlier example.

> **indefeasibility** means that, with very few exceptions, the interests that are included in a certificate of title cannot be defeated

- *Mirror principle*: The **mirror principle** states that all of the interests listed in a certificate of title are generally valid. The certificate reflects reality. For example, when I purchased the land from Alison 15 years ago, the land titles office examined the transfer documents and issued a new certificate of title that named me as the owner. (It also would have listed any other type of interest that existed, such as an easement or a mortgage.) You are entitled to rely upon that certificate when buying the cottage from me. That is true even if my chain of title was defective because Alison never really inherited the property from her uncle.

> the **mirror principle** states that all of the interests listed in a certificate of title reflect valid interests

- *Curtain principle*: The **curtain principle** states that the only valid interests in a property are generally the ones that are listed in the certificate of title. Consequently, it is unnecessary for you to "lift the curtain" and look behind the certificate of title to determine whether anyone else has rights in the property. By the same token, even though Alison's brother

> the **curtain principle** states that the only valid interests in a property are the ones listed in the certificate of title

---

2. Insurance is considered in detail in Chapter 15.

3. Robert Torrens was a marine customs collector in South Australia, who developed the land titles system partially on the basis of the system that was used to register ships.

at one time was entitled to the cottage, his rights were lost when the land titles office issued a certificate of title naming me as the owner. The curtain fell on him.

- *Insurance principle*: The **insurance principle** states that a person who suffers a loss as a result of an error in the system is generally entitled to compensation. The land titles system includes an *assurance fund* that helps people like Alison's brother. Although he cannot get the cottage back, he is entitled to a payment of money.

the insurance principle states that a person who suffers a loss as a result of an error in the system is entitled to compensation

Unregistered Interests

Although the land titles system was designed to avoid uncertainty, a certificate of title is not entirely indefeasible. In some circumstances, an interest in land may be effective even if it is not registered. That is also true under a registry system. Consequently, when buying the cottage from me, you should conduct more than a single search at the land titles or land registry office. There are other places to look. Furthermore, unless you have expertise in this area, you should leave those tasks to your lawyer. Consider these common examples.

some unregistered interests in land may be enforceable

- *Short-term leases*: A short-term (say, three-year) lease may be enforceable against a purchaser even if it is not registered. For that reason, you should inspect the premises for any signs of tenants.

- *Prescription and adverse possession*: As we discussed in Chapter 13, it is sometimes possible for a person to acquire an interest in land as a result of a long period of use or occupation. That is true under registry systems and even under some land titles systems. Consider that fact when you inspect the premises.

- *Public easements*: As we saw in Chapter 13, a utility company or similar body may have the right to bury cables beneath a property or run wires overhead. Consequently, your lawyer should look for signs of activity on the land and perhaps contact the organizations in question.[4] If an easement does exist, its exact location should be determined. A house that sits directly on top of a sewer line may, for instance, be difficult to resell.

- *Unpaid taxes*: As a land owner, I am required to pay taxes on that property. If I fail to do so, the government may be entitled to seize and sell the land to raise the necessary money. Furthermore, its right to do so may continue to exist even after I have transferred the cottage to you. Before you buy, therefore, your lawyer should search the municipal and provincial records to ensure that there are no outstanding taxes.

- *Unpaid creditors*: Your lawyer should also search the records in the sheriff's office to determine whether there are any *writs of execution* (or *writs of seizure and sale*) against me. A **writ of execution** is a document that allows a court's judgment to be enforced. Suppose that someone successfully sued me in tort. If they filed the writ with the sheriff, that officer might then have the power to seize and sell any property registered in my name to pay the money that I owe.[5] And significantly, as long as the writ was filed while I was still the owner, the seizure and sale could

a writ of execution is a document that allows a court's judgment to be enforced

---

4. Private easements are generally enforceable only if they are registered.
5. The governing rules, which are quite complicated, vary between jurisdictions. In some instances, the power to seize and sell only arises when the writ is filed with the registry office.

take place even after I transferred the property to you. To keep the property, you would have to pay my debt.[6]

Is it fair that those interests can be enforced against you, even though they were not registered, and even though you were unaware of them when you bought the land from me? Consider Ethical Perspective 14.1.

ETHICAL PERSPECTIVE 14.1

Unregistered Interests in Land

Questions for Discussion

Suggest reasons why it might be fair to subject a purchaser to unregistered interests that are based on:

1. short-term leases
2. interests acquired by way of prescription or adverse possession

3. public easements
4. municipal taxes owed by the vendor
5. writs of execution filed against the vendor

In answering those questions, consider:

- the purchaser
- the person with the unregistered interest
- society as a whole

LAND SALES

Ownership of land can be passed between people in a variety of ways. We have already mentioned several possibilities, including expropriation, gifts, and adverse possession. From a business perspective, however, the most important possibility is *sale*. A **sale** occurs when ownership is transferred in exchange for consideration.

a sale occurs when ownership is transferred in exchange for consideration

Risk Management

The sale of land is a complicated matter, involving a large number of people performing a variety of tasks. That is true for both residential and commercial properties. The explanation lies in the need for risk management. A great deal can go wrong during a real estate transaction. In the last section, we saw that people other than the apparent owner may have interests in the land. There are many other dangers. Suppose you are interested in buying a factory from me. You should enlist the help of the following people.

- *Real estate agent*: Even if my property appeals to you, there may be others that better suit your needs. Given the time and expense involved in a real estate transaction, it is highly unlikely that you would want to relocate after only a few years in my factory. A real estate agent can search the market for alternatives and help you find the right property in the first place. An agent can also put you into contact with the other people you will need to safely purchase a property.

- *Lawyer*: It is important that you hire a lawyer. In addition to conducting the searches that we previously discussed, a lawyer will perform a large

---

[6.] You would then be allowed to sue me for the same amount, but I may not have it. If I did, I presumably would have paid the judgment myself.

number of other tasks, including: (i) communicating with the seller or the seller's lawyer, (ii) verifying which secondary pieces of property are included in the sale (such as machines in the factory), (iii) ensuring that local bylaws will allow you to use the land for your intended purpose, (iv) obtaining insurance coverage for the property, (v) checking mortgage arrangements (if any), and (vi) preparing, filing, and registering the formal documents that are needed for the transfer. It is also very common for the lawyer to secure the services of other professionals on this list.

■ *Appraiser*: It is often difficult to determine the correct price for a property, especially in the commercial context. Several factors can affect the value of land, including the condition of the buildings, the value of neighbouring properties, accessibility to public transport, the uses that are permitted under zoning regulations, and the municipality's plans for future development in the area. Consequently, before agreeing to a price, you should get an opinion from a professional appraiser.

■ *Surveyor*: During the course of negotiations, I will provide a *legal description* of my property, which includes its precise size and location. That description, however, may be inaccurate. For instance, it might overlook the fact that my building *encroaches* upon a neighbour's land by a few metres. A survey would reveal that fact. Since you would not be willing to pay full market value for a property that could lead you into a lawsuit, you would likely refuse to go ahead with our sale unless I either obtained the neighbour's consent to the encroachment or reduced the price.

■ *Inspector*: You are concerned about the physical condition of the premises, especially since the value of the property is affected by its state of repair. Furthermore, a dangerous structure could expose you to liability by causing injuries or deaths among your employees or guests. And even if no one is hurt, health and safety regulations might eventually require you to spend a lot of money fixing the defects. For those reasons, you should hire an inspector to check the premises for potential problems.

■ *Environmental auditor*: Depending upon the nature of my business, you might be concerned by the possibility that my factory has leaked toxic substances into the environment. Even if no one is killed or injured as a result, you may eventually be required, as the owner of the premises, to pay a substantial amount of money for a cleanup operation.[7] An environmental auditor could identify that possibility.

various professionals should be retained for risk management

One final, perhaps cynical, observation is appropriate. We opened this section by discussing the need for risk management. The individuals in the preceding list could minimize the risks by identifying potential problems at the outset. However, by hiring those people, you would also create a safety net for yourself. Suppose that you discover an underground pool of hazardous waste on the property shortly after our deal closed. If you sue me for the cost of the cleanup, I might honestly say that I simply do not have the money to pay damages. Therefore you will need another source of compensation. If you had hired an environmental auditing company, you might now be able to sue it for breach of contract or for the tort of negligence because it failed to detect the problem. As we discussed in Chapter 12, a professional can be held liable for doing a job carelessly. And furthermore, even if the environmental auditor does not have a lot of money, it very likely has liability insurance.[8]

[7.] Environmental regulations are discussed in Chapter 23.

[8.] When purchasing my factory, you should also have considered buying *property insurance* that would cover the cost of an environmental cleanup. Chapter 15 explains property insurance.

As we have seen, the purchase of land creates a number of risks. Concept Summary 14.1 provides a checklist of some of the dangers you should guard against. You should not undertake all of those tasks yourself, but arrange most through your lawyer.

Concept Summary 14.1

Risk Management and the Purchase of Land

Danger	Precaution
• subsequent purchaser acquiring interest in same property	• registration as soon as possible to provide notice or obtain certificate of title
• short-term leases	• inspection of property to discover tenants
• rights to use or occupation of land created through prescription or adverse possession	• inspection of property to discover signs of use or occupation
• public easements	• inspection of property to discover activity • inquiries to utility companies and similar organizations
• unpaid taxes creating a right of seizure and sale	• search of municipal records
• unsatisfied writs creating a right of seizure and sale	• search of sheriff's records
• payment of excessively high price	• valuation of property by professional appraiser
• misdescription of property	• description of land and buildings by professional surveyor
• defects in building and equipment	• inspection by engineer and similar professionals
• toxic or hazardous substances	• inspection of property by environmental auditor

Agreement of Purchase and Sale

Transactions involving commercial properties are often complicated by the fact that the parties are dealing with several matters at the same time. For instance, if you are buying my factory, you may also want to obtain the equipment in it.[9] You may even be interested in acquiring my business as a whole, including my customer lists and the name of my company. However, we will focus on the sale of the real property itself. That sale is created by an **agreement of purchase and sale**.

An agreement of purchase and sale is a contract and therefore must satisfy all of the usual contractual elements, including an intention to create legal relations, an offer and acceptance, and consideration. Furthermore, although most types of contracts can be created orally, a contract for the sale of an interest in land must be evidenced in writing.[10] And as always, there must be a mutual agreement between two parties with respect to all of the relevant terms. That does not mean, however, that the **vendor** (the person selling the property) and the **purchaser** (the person buying the property) must settle every point at the outset. It is very common for an agreement of purchase and sale to include *conditions*.

A **condition** (or a **condition precedent**) is a requirement that must be satisfied before the transaction can be completed.[11] It does not prevent the cre-

an agreement of purchase and sale creates a contract for the sale of land

the vendor is the person who sells the land

the purchaser is the person who buys the land

a condition or condition precedent is a requirement that must be satisfied before the transaction can be completed

---

[9] Chapter 15 explains that, when you buy land, you are generally entitled to the *fixtures*, which are things that are attached to the land.

[10] As Chapter 5 explained, the contract is valid if it is not evidenced in writing, but neither party can enforce it.

[11] As we saw in Chapter 6, there are different types of "conditions precedent."

ation of a contract, but it does suspend the parties' obligations to complete the deal. Several possibilities might arise in our earlier example.

- If my building was partially constructed on someone else's land, you might agree to buy the property from me, but only on the condition that I obtain my neighbour's permission for the encroachment.

- If a heap of toxic waste sits at the back of my lot, you might make our agreement conditional upon my ability to remove the hazard and obtain a clean report from an environmental auditor.

- If you intend to use the property differently than I did, you might make the sale conditional upon your ability to obtain zoning permission for the proposed activity.

- If you are unsure that you can afford to buy my land, you might make our agreement conditional upon your ability to obtain financing on reasonable terms.

If any condition is not met, then our sale will not be completed.[12] Nevertheless, one of us might still be held liable. Most conditions expressly or implicitly require at least one party to act in a certain way. For instance, I might be required to use my best efforts to obtain my neighbour's consent to the encroachment or to remove the toxic substances from the land. You might be required to use your best efforts to obtain zoning permission or to arrange financing. If a condition fails due to a lack of effort, the other party may be entitled to damages. Consider how you would respond in You Be the Judge 14.1.

YOU BE THE JUDGE 14.1

Agreement of Purchase and Sale and Conditions[13]

OK Detailing Ltd owns a large section of land. Dynamic Transport Ltd wants to buy part of it. The parties therefore entered into an agreement of purchase and sale. Dynamic promised to pay $250 000 and OK Detailing promised to transfer a specific portion of its property. There is, however, a problem. At the time of entering into that agreement, both parties knew that the sale could not proceed without permission under the *Planning Act* to subdivide the property into two lots. Unfortunately, their agreement does not expressly say that the sale is conditional on that fact. Nor does it expressly impose an obligation upon either party to obtain the planning approval.

Since the parties signed their agreement, the value of the land has increased from $250 000 to $400 000. OK Detailing realizes that it entered into a very bad bargain and is anxious to find some way out of it. Therefore it argues that the sale cannot be completed because the planning authority has not approved the necessary subdivision.

In response, Dynamic notes that OK Detailing has not even applied for permission to subdivide its property. Dynamic also argues that it would be unfair if the vendor could avoid the sale by simply refusing to seek planning approval.

The only relevant sections of the *Planning Act* state:

19(1) A person who proposes to carry out a division of land shall apply for approval of the proposed subdivision.
19(2) A subdivision means a division of a land by means of...transferring an interest in land to another person.

Questions for Discussion

1. Do the parties have a valid agreement?
2. If so, is the performance of that agreement subject to a condition?
3. If so, which party, if either, has an obligation to satisfy that condition?
4. What relief, if any, should be available if that obligation is not met?

---

12. In some circumstances, it is possible for the person who was intended to benefit from the condition to waive the need for satisfaction and to insist upon the completion of the sale: *Beauchamp v Beauchamp* (1973) 32 DLR (3d) 693 (Ont CA). Chapter 6 discusses waiver.

13. *Dynamic Transport Ltd v OK Detailing Ltd* (1978) 85 DLR (3d) 19 (SCC).

Closing

Once all conditions attached to the sale have been satisfied, the parties' transaction can be *closed*, or completed. It is common for *adjustments* to occur at that time. For instance, if the vendor has already paid the annual property tax, the price will be increased to reflect the fact that the purchaser will enjoy the benefit of that payment for the remainder of the year. The purchaser's lawyer will also conduct one last search at the various offices to ensure that competing interests have not been filed or registered against the land at the last minute. And at that point, the vendor's lawyer will provide the purchaser's lawyer with the formal document that is needed to convey ownership in the property. In jurisdictions under a registry system, a *deed* (or *deed of conveyance*) is used. In jurisdictions under a land titles system, a document called a *transfer* is used. The purchaser's lawyer will promptly register the deed or transfer to protect the client's rights. The lawyer will generally also help with the paperwork that is needed to obtain insurance coverage on the property, and to notify the municipality, the utility companies, and so on of the change in ownership.

Remedies

In most situations, an agreement of purchase and sale ends with a successful closing. The vendor receives full payment and the purchaser receives clear title. Occasionally, however, problems arise. The parties are entitled to rely upon the usual remedies for breach of contract that were discussed in Chapter 7. For instance, the plaintiff is normally entitled to recover the value of the property that it expected to obtain. Furthermore, at least historically, the courts would order *specific performance*. In other words, instead of being restricted to the monetary value of the property, the plaintiff could obtain the property itself by forcing the defendant to go through with the sale. That remedy was justified by the belief that every piece of land was unique, with the result that money could never truly provide an adequate substitute for actual performance.[14] Recently, however, the Supreme Court of Canada has expressed a different view. Case Brief 14.1 discusses its decision.

CASE BRIEF 14.1

Semelhago v Paramadevan (1996) 136 DLR (4th) 1 (SCC)

The plaintiff agreed to buy a house from the defendant for $205 000. As the closing date approached, however, the defendant said that he was not willing to go through with the sale. The plaintiff sued for breach of contract. By the time of trial, the property had increased in value to $325 000. The judge held that the purchaser was entitled to choose between: (i) an order for specific performance, and (ii) monetary damages that would place the plaintiff in the position that he would have enjoyed if the sale had been completed. The plaintiff chose the second option and therefore received about $120 000 from the defendant.

The defendant appealed all the way to the Supreme Court of Canada. Justice Sopinka agreed with the result reached at trial. In doing so, however, he rejected the

(continued)

[14.] Given that explanation, it seems strange that vendors can also demand specific performance. After all, a vendor is normally interested only in receiving the payment of money under a sale. Consequently, monetary damages should normally be an adequate remedy if the purchaser refuses to complete the sale. It might be different, however, if the vendor has a special or non-monetary reason for wanting to complete the sale: *Hoover v Mark Minor Homes Inc* (1998) 75 OTC 165 (Gen Div).

(continued)

traditional view that specific performance is almost *always* available for a contract dealing with the purchase of land.

While at one time the common law regarded every piece of real estate to be unique, with the progress of modern real estate development this is no longer the case. Residential, business and industrial properties are all mass produced much in the same way as other consumer products. If a deal

falls through for one property, another is frequently, though not always, readily available.

The Court therefore introduced a new rule that limits specific performance to situations in which the plaintiff has legitimate grounds for saying that monetary damages would provide an inadequate remedy.

On the facts before him, Justice Sopinka saw nothing special about the property in question. Nevertheless, since both parties had assumed that the property was unique, he did so as well.

We mention two more special remedies that may be available under a contract for the sale of land.

> **a purchaser's lien** allows the purchaser to have the land sold to satisfy the outstanding debt

- A *purchaser's lien* is generally created whenever the purchaser pays money to the vendor. For example, before the completion of a transaction, the vendor often requires payment of a deposit or part of the price. If the deal later falls through, the purchaser will want a refund. A **purchaser's lien** allows the purchaser to have the land sold to satisfy the outstanding debt. In practice, however, property is seldom sold under a lien. In most instances, the vendor simply repays the money. And in other cases, the purchaser may wait until the vendor voluntarily sells or mortgages the land to someone else, and then take part of the proceeds.

> **a vendor's lien** allows the vendor to have the property sold to satisfy the outstanding debt

- A *vendor's lien* is similar. Occasionally, a person may be willing to sell land on credit, without insisting upon full payment at the time of closing. In that situation, there is a danger that the purchaser will later refuse to pay the remaining amount even though it has already received ownership. The law therefore provides a **vendor's lien**, which allows the vendor to have the property sold to satisfy the outstanding debt.[15]

Note that a lien is a form of *security*.[16] That means that the lien holder may be entitled to priority over other types of claimants. Business Law in Action 14.1 illustrates this.

BUSINESS LAW IN ACTION 14.1

Vendor's Lien and Priority

Sukie Petroutsas sold a piece of land worth $90 000 to Anthony Sidhu. Anthony paid $30 000 at the time of closing and promised to pay the remaining $60 000 within two years. Unfortunately, shortly after obtaining ownership of the property, Anthony's business began to falter. He was unable to make any more payments to Sukie. And to make matters worse, he also incurred $120 000 in debts to other creditors. Anthony's only significant asset is the land that he bought from Sukie.

Questions for Discussion

1. Assume that Sukie has exercised her unpaid seller's lien and has had the property sold for $90 000. How much of that amount will she receive? How much will Anthony's other creditors receive?

2. What would likely happen if Sukie did not have the right to exercise an unpaid seller's lien? Assuming that Anthony sold the land to pay his debts, how much would Sukie receive? How much would the other creditors receive?

[15.] A lien should be registered as an interest in the property. If it is not, it can be defeated if a person who does not have notice of the vendor's claim buys the land from the purchaser.

[16.] Chapter 21 discusses security.

MORTGAGES

The purchase of land is often the largest single transaction that a person or a business will ever complete. Real property tends to be very expensive, especially if it is located in a commercially desirable area or if it contains a development, such as an apartment complex or a shopping mall. Consequently, the purchaser can seldom pay the full price from pre-existing resources. It is usually necessary to obtain a loan. A lender, however, will be reluctant to extend *credit* (that is, provide money in exchange for a promise of repayment) without some form of *security*. A bank, for instance, is unlikely to lend you the $500 000 that you need to buy a new factory unless you have something that the bank can take or sell if you do not repay your debt. The purchase of land is therefore usually financed through a *mortgage*. Broadly speaking, a **mortgage** is an interest in land that provides security for the repayment of a debt.[17] The person who borrows the money and gives an interest in land is the **mortgagor**. The person who lends the money and acquires an interest in land is the **mortgagee**. Take a moment to repeat those terms. They are often confused.

A mortgage can be used in several ways.

- The previous example presents a typical situation. The same property was involved in two transactions. First, you bought the factory from the vendor. Second, to pay for that purchase, you granted a mortgage over your newly acquired asset as security for a bank loan.[18]

- The two transactions can, however, be distinct. For instance, if you already own a factory, but wish to buy new equipment, you might borrow money for the purchase by allowing the lender to take a mortgage over the land. You would be using one asset (the factory) to acquire another (the equipment).

- Our examples to this point have involved three parties. You bought property from one person and borrowed money from another. But often, there are only two parties. For instance, in the first case, the vendor presumably received full payment when the sale closed. You paid with the money that you borrowed from the bank. Under a different arrangement, however, the vendor could have allowed you to take the factory on credit. And to secure your promise to pay the price in the future, the vendor itself could have taken a mortgage over the property that it just sold to you.

In any event, the basic operation of the mortgage itself remains the same. Figure 14.1 illustrates the process. (Some of the features of that diagram are discussed below.)

a **mortgage** is an interest in land that provides security for the repayment of a debt

the **mortgagor** is the person who borrows the money and provides the interest in land

the **mortgagee** is the person who lends the money and acquires the interest in land

mortgagor = borrower

mortgagee = lender

mortgages can occur in two-party or three-party situations

---

17. Although less common, a mortgage can also be created by using other types of property as security for a loan.

18. It is highly unlikely that the bank would give credit for the full value of the property. The reason is risk management. Suppose that the bank allowed you to borrow $500 000 on the basis that your new factory was worth that much when the mortgage was created. A downturn in the economy might have two effects: (i) it might prevent you from repaying the loan, and (ii) it might cause the value of the land to collapse. Consequently, at the end of the story, the bank might be left holding a property worth only $300 000, even though it had given you $500 000. It would suffer a loss of $200 000.

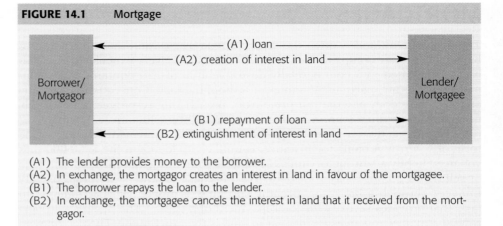

FIGURE 14.1   Mortgage

(A1) loan
(A2) creation of interest in land

Borrower/
Mortgagor

Lender/
Mortgagee

(B1) repayment of loan
(B2) extinguishment of interest in land

(A1) The lender provides money to the borrower.
(A2) In exchange, the mortgagor creates an interest in land in favour of the mortgagee.
(B1) The borrower repays the loan to the lender.
(B2) In exchange, the mortgagee cancels the interest in land that it received from the mortgagor.

Nature of Mortgages

Although we have provided a general definition of a mortgage, the specific rules are different in every jurisdiction. The most important differences depend upon whether the security is given under a land titles system or a registry system.

Registry System and Land Titles System

If the land in question is held under a land titles system, a mortgage creates a *charge* over the property. A **charge** occurs when the mortgagor agrees that the land will be available to the mortgagee if the debt is not repaid. As we will discuss, the mortgagee is required to remove that charge if the loan is repaid and if the other terms of the parties' agreement are satisfied.

However, if the land in question is held under a registry system, then a mortgage does not merely create a charge; it actually involves a *conveyance of title*. In exchange for the loan, the mortgagor transfers the property to the mortgagee, who then becomes the legal owner.[19] The mortgagor is, however, entitled to have the title reconveyed if the mortgage is fulfilled.

Subsequent Mortgages

Under the registry system, the mortgagee acquires the *legal title* to the property. But the mortgagor is not left without anything—it receives an *equitable interest* in the land. That interest arises because the borrower enjoys the *equity of redemption*. As Chapter 1 explained, there were traditionally two types of courts: courts of law and courts of equity. The courts of law initially adopted a very harsh approach to mortgages. If the mortgagor did not repay the loan within the required time, the mortgagee could keep the property for itself *and* it could sue for the late payment. Not surprisingly, the results of that rule were often grossly unfair. A mortgagor who missed the repayment schedule by even a single day could lose its land forever and still be liable for the debt. The courts of equity therefore created the **equity of redemption**, which allows the mortgagor to recover the property by repaying the loan even after the due date.[20]

a charge occurs when the mortgagor agrees that the land will be available to the mortgagee if the debt is not repaid

a mortgage under a registry system involves a transfer of ownership

the equity of redemption entitles the mortgagor to recover legal title to the land by repaying the loan

---

[19] In most cases, the mortgagor holds the fee simple to the property at the outset. However, it is also possible to mortgage other interests in land, such as a lease or even an easement: *Russell v Mifflin (SW) Ltd* (1991) 89 Nfld & PEIR 168 (Nfld SC TD).

[20] Although a mortgage under a land titles system does not involve the transfer of ownership to the lender, it is still common to use the term "equity of redemption" to describe the borrower's right to re-acquire clear title to the property upon fulfillment of the mortgage.

The two types of court are now combined, but the distinction between legal and equitable rights remains important.

The mortgagor therefore holds an interest in the land under either a land titles system (because it retains the legal title) or under a registry system (because it acquires an equitable interest). That is significant because it allows for the creation of subsequent mortgages. As the name suggests, a **subsequent mortgage** is one that takes effect after the initial mortgage. Suppose that you own a large piece of land, called Blackacre, that is worth $500 000. To acquire a new fleet of trucks, you borrow $300 000 from the Primus Bank and give a mortgage over Blackacre as security for that loan. At that point, the bank acquires either legal title or a charge, and you enjoy the equity of redemption. Your interest in the land, or your *equity*, is worth $200 000. That is a valuable property interest in itself. Consequently, you might be able to use it if you later want to buy a new computer system for $100 000. To secure a loan in that amount from the Nether Bank, you could grant a second mortgage over your interest in Blackacre.

As you might expect, subsequent mortgages raise a number of interesting risk management issues.

> a subsequent mortgage is one that takes effect after the initial mortgage

Vulnerability of Mortgagors

Although subsequent mortgages can help you to raise additional funds, they also carry an obvious danger. If you have two mortgages, you also have two outstanding loans. And if you fail to repay either one of them, you may lose your land.

Vulnerability of Subsequent Mortgagees

If a mortgagor does not repay a loan, the mortgagee may be entitled to *foreclose*, that is, permanently keep the land for itself. And in doing so, the mortgagee will extinguish not only the mortgagor's equity of redemption, but also the interest held by any subsequent mortgagee.[21] After all, if the mortgagor no longer has an interest in the property, there is nothing that the subsequent mortgagee can use as security. Consequently, in our previous example, Nether Bank is in a vulnerable position. If you fail to fulfill your first mortgage, Primus Bank could foreclose on Blackacre. And while Nether Bank could still sue you for repayment of its loan, it would probably have little chance of success. It no longer has any security, and since you were unable to repay Primus Bank, you presumably do not have much money. To avoid that result, Nether Bank would be required to prevent foreclosure by paying off your outstanding debt to Primus Bank. Not surprisingly, because of that possibility, Nether Bank would almost certainly charge a higher rate of interest than Primus Bank. A subsequent mortgagee will demand additional compensation for the additional risks that it faces.

In theory, it is possible to have any number of subsequent mortgages. However, very few lenders are willing to stand worse than second, since a subsequent mortgagee faces the danger of foreclosure by any of the earlier mortgagees.

> a subsequent mortgagee's security may be lost if an earlier mortgagee forecloses

Priority of Mortgages

Mortgages generally take priority in the order that they are registered, not necessarily in the order that they are created. Suppose that Primus Bank received all of the relevant documents from you on Monday, but did not take them to the land registry office until Friday. If Nether Bank received all of its documents from you on Tuesday and filed them promptly, it would take first priority as long as it did not have notice of your earlier transaction with Primus Bank. That could be important. Suppose that the economy collapsed, the value of Blackacre

> mortgages generally take priority in the order that they are registered

---

[21.] Subsequent mortgagees are also treated less favourably in other situations. For instance, if the property is sold rather than foreclosed, the first mortgagee will be paid off completely before a subsequent mortgagee can claim any part of the sale proceeds.

slumped to $250 000, and the land was sold to satisfy your debts. Nether Bank would be entitled to the full amount of its loan ($100 000) and Primus Bank would only receive half of its loan ($150 000 out of $300 000). The lesson is clear. As a matter of risk management, a mortgagee should register its interest as soon as it is created, because registration provides notice to the whole world.

Disposition of Interests

Since we have been discussing the people who may be involved in a mortgage, it is appropriate to briefly mention two more possibilities.

the mortgagee and the mortgagor may dispose of their interests

- *Disposition by mortgagee*: A mortgagee may wish to sell its rights to a third party. Although it is entitled to do so, the parties should act carefully. A mortgage is a *property interest* that is created by *contract*. The mortgagee can use a simple *assignment* to transfer its *contractual* rights (such as the right to demand repayment).[22] But the third party will not acquire the *security* unless it also receives the mortgagee's property interest—either title (under a registry system) or a charge (under a land titles system). Furthermore, as soon as the appropriate transfer takes place, the third party should promptly register its interest.[23] It should also notify the mortgagor of the assignment.[24] Figure 14.2 illustrates the basic process.

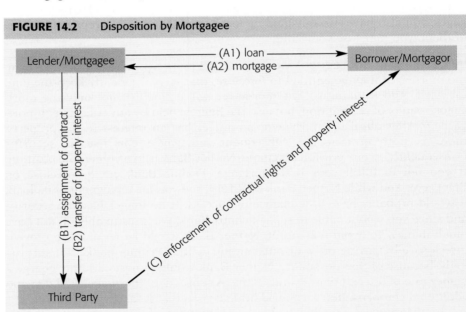

FIGURE 14.2   Disposition by Mortgagee

(A1) The lender loans money to the borrower.
(A2) The borrower creates a mortgage by giving the lender a proprietary interest in a piece of land. The borrower is the mortgagor and the lender is the mortgagee.
(B1) The lender/mortgagee assigns to a third party the contractual right to demand repayment of the loan from the borrower/mortgagor.
(B2) The lender/mortgagee transfers its proprietary interest to the third party.
(C) The third party enforces the contractual rights and the proprietary interest against the borrower/mortgagor.

[22.] Chapters 3 and 13 discuss assignments.

[23.] If the third party fails to register its interest, it can be defeated if another person later buys the mortgagee's interest and registers first.

[24.] The mortgagor is required to pay only once. If it pays the original mortgagee before receiving notice of the assignment, it is not required to make the same payment again to the third party assignee. (The third party can, however, sue the original mortgagee for its improper receipt of that payment.)

- *Disposition by mortgagor*: The distinction between the proprietary and contractual aspects of a mortgage is also important when a mortgagor sells its interest. Suppose that a third party wants to buy a piece of land that is already subject to a mortgage. The third party might pay for the property partially by providing cash and partially by promising to pay the balance of the vendor's loan.[25] Figure 14.3 illustrates the basic process. Note two more points about that arrangement. First, as long as the lender registered its mortgage, the land will still be subject to that security, even though it is in the third party's hands. Consequently, if the loan is not repaid, the land can still be used to satisfy the debt. Second, the general rule states that it is possible to assign contractual rights, but not contractual obligations. As a result, even though it no longer has an interest in the land, the original mortgagor (now the vendor) can be sued if the third party does not repay the loan as promised.

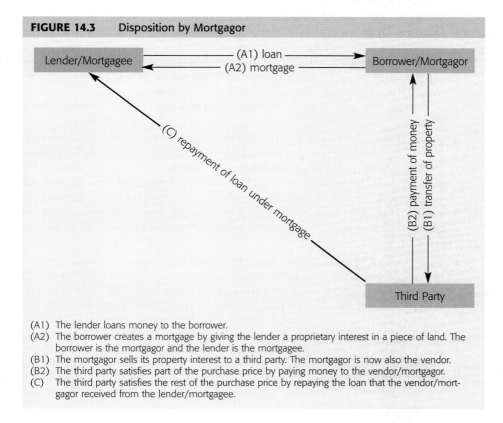

FIGURE 14.3   Disposition by Mortgagor

(A1)   The lender loans money to the borrower.
(A2)   The borrower creates a mortgage by giving the lender a proprietary interest in a piece of land. The borrower is the mortgagor and the lender is the mortgagee.
(B1)   The mortgagor sells its property interest to a third party. The mortgagor is now also the vendor.
(B2)   The third party satisfies part of the purchase price by paying money to the vendor/mortgagor.
(C)   The third party satisfies the rest of the purchase price by repaying the loan that the vendor/mortgagor received from the lender/mortgagee.

Terms of the Contract

Because a mortgage is created by contract, the parties are generally free to include any terms that are appropriate. Certain types of covenants (promises) are, however, standard. With respect to the mortgagee, the most important

---

[25.] Alternatively, the third party might arrange to discharge the existing mortgage by repaying the loan on the mortgagor's behalf. In that situation, the third party would probably finance its purchase by giving a new mortgage over the property as security for a bank loan. The choice between assuming an existing mortgage and creating a new one is usually based on whether the third party can get better terms than are contained in the existing mortgage.

concerns the duty to discharge the mortgage once the debt has been repaid. It will do so by either reconveying title to the mortgagor (under a registry system) or by registering a *cessation of charge* (under a land titles system). The mortgagor tends to have more obligations.

- *Repayment*: The borrower must repay the debt according to the parties' agreement. That will generally mean that payments must be made on certain days, in certain amounts, and with a certain amount of interest. Furthermore, it is very common for a mortgage to contain an **acceleration clause**, which requires the mortgagor to immediately repay the full amount of the loan if it misses a single payment. It is easy to see why a mortgagee would insist upon such a clause. Once the contract is breached, the mortgagee does not want to wait and see if it will be breached again. It wants to bring the matter to an end immediately.[26] An acceleration clause can be contrasted with a *prepayment privilege clause*. The mortgagor sometimes repays the loan earlier, or in larger instalments, than initially agreed. In most circumstances, the mortgagee will impose a financial penalty (or a *bonus*) on the mortgagor for doing so. After all, while the mortgagee wants the loan to be repaid, it also wants the interest to build up as much as possible. To avoid that problem, the mortgagor may insist upon a **prepayment privilege** that allows early or additional payments to be made without penalty.

- *Taxes*: If the mortgagee has registered its interest, its security is reasonably safe. However, even a registered interest can sometimes be defeated. For example, the government may be entitled to seize and sell a piece of land if the taxes on that property have not been paid. The mortgagor is therefore usually required to promise to pay the taxes. Indeed, to ensure that payment actually occurs, the mortgagee may insist upon receiving an appropriate amount of money so that it can pay the taxes itself.

- *Insurance*: The mortgagee's security is only as valuable as the property itself. For instance, a mortgage over an office complex that is worth $1 000 000 provides sufficient protection for a $600 000 loan. The situation will be much different, however, if the building burns to the ground and leaves the land with a market value of only $200 000. To protect itself against that danger, the mortgagee will require the mortgagor to purchase adequate insurance for the property.[27] Furthermore, the mortgagee will insist upon being named as a beneficiary of that insurance policy. Therefore, if the building is destroyed, the lender will effectively receive repayment of the loan from the insurance company.

- *Waste*: For similar reasons, mortgages usually contain a clause that prohibits the borrower from committing an act of waste. As we saw in Chapter 13, waste occurs when a property is changed in a way that significantly affects its value.

an acceleration clause requires the mortgagor to immediately repay the full amount of the loan if it misses a single payment

a prepayment privilege allows early or additional payments to be made without penalty

---

[26] An acceleration clause can create hardship. It might be unfair, for instance, to demand full payment from a mortgagor who simply missed a single payment due to illness. The courts therefore sometimes grant relief from acceleration if the borrower puts the loan back on track.

[27] Chapter 15 considers insurance policies in more detail.

Remedies for Default

A mortgage typically comes to an end when the borrower fulfills the terms of the parties' agreement, and the lender discharges its interest in the land. Difficulties do occasionally arise, however, especially during economic recessions or depressions. The most common source of problems is the mortgagor's failure to repay the loan. As we saw with respect to the equity of redemption, our legal system has struggled to find ways of fairly balancing the parties' interests in that situation. The mortgagor is often vulnerable and in need of protection. But at the same time, the mortgagee has a legitimate interest in recovering the debt that it is owed, by using its security if necessary. There is no obvious means of resolving that tension. Not surprisingly, the rules vary significantly between jurisdictions. Each province and territory has legislation that governs the remedies that are available in the event of default.[28] However, there are generally four possibilities:

- suing on the covenant
- possession of the property
- foreclosure
- sale

Suing on the Covenant

A mortgagee has both property rights and contractual rights. To enforce repayment of the loan, it is entitled to use the security interest that it holds in the mortgagor's land. But it is not required to do so. In most circumstances, it has the option of simply suing the mortgagor for the outstanding amount. There are, however, certain limitations on that right. Most significantly, legislation in Alberta, British Columbia, and Saskatchewan generally prevents an action from being brought against an individual or against a corporation that has not *waived* its statutory protection.

some jurisdictions limit a mortgagee's ability to sue on a covenant

Possession of the Property

Under a registry system, the mortgagee becomes the legal owner of the property. In theory, it is therefore entitled to possession at the outset. Almost invariably, however, the parties' agreement states that the mortgagor is allowed to occupy the premises unless it goes into *default* by breaching the contract. In theory, the situation is somewhat different under a land titles system because the mortgagee merely acquires a charge rather than ownership. It therefore has no natural right to possess the land. In practice, however, the situation is much the same. The parties' agreement generally states that the borrower's right to occupy the premises may be lost in the event of default.

the mortgagee may take possession of the property if the mortgagor defaults

The mortgagee's right to possession is far less attractive than it might seem.

- Most mortgagees are financial institutions that have little interest in occupying land. As a general rule, banks want money. They do not want the problems associated with the possession of real property.
- A mortgagee who takes possession acquires a number of responsibilities. It must keep the property in good repair and cannot commit acts of waste. It must also take reasonable steps to generate income from the

[28.] Given the large number of statutory provisions that are involved, citations are not provided.

property. And when it does generate income (such as rent), it is generally required to use that money to reduce the mortgagor's debt.[29]

■ The mere fact that the mortgagee took possession does not prevent the mortgagor from later exercising its equity of redemption (assuming that it is still available), repaying the amount that is due under the loan, and resuming possession of the property.

For those reasons, the mortgagee normally will not take possession of the property unless the mortgagor has either abandoned it or is acting in a manner that will decrease its value. Consider Business Decision 14.1.

BUSINESS DECISION 14.1

Mortgages and the Right of Possession

I bought a shipment of widgets from you on credit. Although the price was $100 000, you agreed to accept $25 000 in cash, plus a mortgage over my land to secure repayment of the remaining $75 000. The terms of our agreement required me to repay the debt in 25 monthly instalments. Although I made the first 10 payments without trouble, I missed the eleventh. I explained to you that my business had experienced difficulties due to the death of one of my key employees. I also asked if I could miss my payments for the next three months as well, while I put my business back in order.

Question for Discussion

1. Our agreement expressly allows you to take possession of my premises, which consists entirely of a factory and a warehouse. Will you do so? Is there any point in doing so? Explain the factors that will influence your decision.

Foreclosure

To understand the remedy of *foreclosure*, we must once again look at the history of mortgages. The mortgagee was traditionally entitled to keep the land that had been transferred into its name if the mortgagor was even a single day late with a payment. Because the effects of that rule were often unfair, the Court of Chancery created the equity of redemption, which allowed the mortgagor to recover the property by repaying the loan at a later date. In time, however, that led to complaints by mortgagees. They could never be sure that they were entitled to keep the land that they had acquired. A mortgagor was often allowed to redeem a property years after the loan had become due. The Court of Chancery therefore created a new rule that allowed mortgagees to apply for orders for foreclosure. **Foreclosure** (from the Latin words meaning "to close from outside") is a procedure for extinguishing the mortgagor's equity of redemption.

Once again, the remedy tends to be more attractive in theory than in practice.[30] Although the details vary between jurisdictions, the procedure tends to be quite drawn out. And surprisingly, it often lacks finality. After the mortgagee applies for foreclosure, the court initially grants an order *nisi* (Latin for "unless") as a way of informing the mortgagor and any subsequent mortgagees that the equity of redemption may be foreclosed unless the outstanding debt is

foreclosure is a procedure for extinguishing the mortgagor's equity of redemption

foreclosure tends to be less attractive in practice than in theory

---

[29.] The mortgagee is, however, entitled to deduct a reasonable amount for repairs and expenses.

[30.] The concept of foreclosure is best suited to a registry system, in which the mortgagee receives legal title at the outset. However, the same terminology, and essentially the same procedures, are used under a land titles system, in which the lender starts with only a charge.

repaid.[31] If that does not occur within the required period (usually six months), the court will grant a final order of foreclosure. But even at that point the mortgagee is not necessarily entitled to the property forever. As long as the lender still holds the land, the borrower can apply to the court to have the foreclosure set aside in exchange for repayment of the loan.

There are other reasons why foreclosure is often not a satisfactory remedy.

- Mortgagees tend to be lending institutions that are not particularly interested in owning land. They want money.

- Foreclosure often seems unfair from the perspective of the mortgagor and any subsequent mortgagees. The mortgagor will lose the property and the subsequent mortgagees will lose their security. Furthermore, the mortgagee may be overcompensated. Suppose that you borrow $60 000 from a bank by mortgaging a property that is worth $100 000. Some time later, you buy $20 000 worth of goods from a supplier. Because that purchase is made on credit, you are required to give a second mortgage over your land. Your business then experiences financial difficulties, and you are unable to repay either creditor. If the bank is able to foreclose, it will receive land worth $100 000, even though it was owed only $60 000 at the outset. By the same token, you will effectively pay $100 000 to discharge a debt of $60 000. And the person who holds the second mortgage will lose its security. For that reason, mortgagors and subsequent mortgagees can seek a court order that requires the mortgagee to proceed by way of *sale*, rather than foreclosure. The mortgagee also has the option of requesting sale.

Sale

The remedy of **judicial sale** occurs when the mortgaged property is sold under a judge's order. Although the rules vary from place to place, the process is carefully controlled. It is done under the authority of the court or another government official (the registrar of titles), who must approve the terms of the sale. In some jurisdictions, the court or the registrar of titles may set the minimum price for which the land can be sold.

the remedy of judicial sale occurs when the mortgaged property is sold under a judge's order

The sale proceeds are used to repay the loan that was granted by the first mortgagee.[32] If there is money left over, it is used to satisfy the claims of subsequent mortgagees. And if any money still remains at that point, it is paid to the mortgagor.[33] However, if the sale proceeds are insufficient to cover the debts, there is a *deficiency*, and the mortgagee may be entitled to sue the mortgagor for the shortfall.[34]

The use of sale varies significantly between jurisdictions. In Nova Scotia, the courts insist upon it, rather than foreclosure. Similarly, although foreclosure is available in Alberta, Saskatchewan, and the parts of Manitoba that are under the land titles system, the courts prefer a sale to be attempted first. It is only when no reasonable offer is made on the property that the mortgagee can

---

[31.] Foreclosure will extinguish both the mortgagor's equity of redemption and a subsequent mortgagee's security interest.

[32.] The mortgagee is also entitled to the payment of interest and compensation for the costs associated with enforcing its rights.

[33.] If the mortgagee forecloses and later sells the property to a third party, the mortgagor and the subsequent mortgagees are usually not entitled to a share of the sale proceeds, even if those proceeds exceed the amount that was owed under the first mortgage.

[34.] Some jurisdictions generally prohibit the mortgagee from suing the mortgagor on the covenant.

proceed to foreclosure. In the rest of the country, the lender generally has a greater choice between remedies.

As an alternative to seeking a court-ordered sale, the mortgagee can sometimes exercise a **power of sale** that is contained in the parties' agreement. Although quite common in some places (especially Ontario), that type of term is severely restricted in others (especially Alberta). In any event, the mortgagee is responsible for getting a reasonable price for the property. If it fails to do so, it can be held liable for the shortfall.

a power of sale is a contractual right that allows the mortgagee to sell the land in order to obtain payment

Combination of Remedies

various remedies may be used in combination

The preceding remedies can often be used in combination. For example, if the mortgagor has abandoned the property, the mortgagee may take possession of the land to prevent it from losing value, and then have it sold. As we have seen, some jurisdictions allow the mortgagee to sell the property and then sue the mortgagor on the covenant for any outstanding debt. And quite often, a financial institution will obtain a property by way of foreclosure and then sell it for its own benefit. Banks, as we have said, usually want "the money, not the mud."

Chapter Summary

A registration system documents interests in land. Two registration systems operate in different parts of the country. A registry system provides an opportunity to inspect and evaluate documents that may affect real property. It provides access to the documents, but it does not guarantee their accuracy. A land titles system does more than simply provide an opportunity to inspect and evaluate documents. It generates certificates of title that virtually guarantee the validity of the interests that are listed on those certificates. Although both systems are based on registration, some types of unregistered interests are enforceable.

The sale of land is a complicated matter, involving a large number of people performing a variety of tasks. As a matter of risk management, the purchaser should retain various professionals. A sale occurs through an agreement of purchase and sale that is created by the vendor and the purchaser. Such agreements often contain conditions that suspend the parties' obligations to complete the deal. A sale closes when the vendor provides the purchaser with the formal document needed to actually convey ownership in the property. As a matter of risk management, the

purchaser should register that document as soon as possible. If an agreement of purchase and sale is breached, the innocent party may be entitled to a variety of contractual remedies, including specific performance or a lien.

A mortgage is an interest in land that is created to provide security for the payment of a debt. The person who borrows the money and gives an interest in land is the mortgagor. The person who lends the money and acquires an interest in land is the mortgagee. Under a land titles system, a mortgage creates a charge over the property. Under a registry system, a mortgage involves a conveyance of title. In either event, the mortgagor enjoys an equity of redemption. The mortgagor can use the equity of redemption to create subsequent mortgages.

A mortgage involves both an interest in land and a contractual relationship between the parties. The contract imposes various obligations on the mortgagee and the mortgagor.

If the mortgagor defaults, the mortgagee may be entitled to a variety of remedies, including an action on the covenant, possession, foreclosure, and sale.

Review Questions

1. What is the major difference between a registry system and a land titles system? Why is it necessary to trace a good chain of title under the former, but not the latter?

2. "Title to land is always safer under a land titles system." Is that statement true? Explain your answer.

3. Explain the meaning of "indefeasibility," and describe the three principles upon which it is based.

4. List five types of unregistered interests that may be enforced against a person who purchases land. In each instance, briefly explain why enforcement is allowed without registration.

5. Identify six types of people who may be hired to minimize the risks associated with the purchase of land. Briefly explain the role of each.

6. "Unless a condition is satisfied, the parties do not really have an agreement of purchase and sale." Is that true? Explain your answer.

7. "The failure of a condition may prevent the parties from closing a sale, but it cannot expose either party to liability." Is that statement true? Explain your answer.

8. Why did the Supreme Court of Canada recently decide that specific performance should not always be available under an agreement for the purchase of land?

9. What is a purchaser's lien? What is a vendor's lien? Describe situations in which each type of remedy would be available.

10. What is a mortgage? Identify the two parties that are always involved in a mortgage.

11. Can a mortgage be used to finance the purchase of something other than the land that is being mortgaged? Illustrate your answer with an example.

12. The mortgagee receives an interest in land. Is that interest the same under both a registry system and a land titles system? Explain your answer.

13. "A mortgage involves a difficult tension between the rights of the mortgagor and the rights of the mortgagee." Discuss that statement in light of the history of the equity of redemption and the remedy of foreclosure.

14. What is a subsequent mortgage? How is a subsequent mortgage related to the equity of redemption?

15. Explain the vulnerability of a subsequent mortgagee in terms of risk management.

16. "Registration is irrelevant to priorities between competing mortgagees." Is that true? Illustrate your answer with an example.

17. What is an acceleration clause? What is a prepayment privilege? Which would you prefer to insert into a mortgage agreement if you were a mortgagor? What if you were a mortgagee?

18. Is the mortgagee always required to use its security interest to enforce the repayment of the loan that it gave to the mortgagor? Does your answer depend upon where you live in Canada?

19. Explain the effect of foreclosure. How does foreclosure relate to the equity of redemption? Does foreclosure always allow the mortgagee to permanently retain the land in question?

20. Describe a situation in which the mortgagor and a subsequent mortgagee would prefer the remedy of sale to the remedy of foreclosure by the first mortgagee.

Cases and Problems

1. Five years ago, Megarry Inc owned a large piece of land. It subdivided that property into ten equal parts and sold three of them, as a single unit, to Cheshire Ltd. (Each of the three parts was individually described.) The transfer documents were immediately registered. Although Cheshire had initially intended to construct a number of warehouses on its new property, it soon developed economic difficulties. Since it no longer has any use for the property, Cheshire recently sold it to the Burns Corp. Shortly after that sale closed, Burns began to survey the land with a view to building a shopping mall. When it did so, however, Megarry's lawyer sent a letter stating that her client still owned part of the property that Burns was in the process of developing. After some investigation, the parties agree that Cheshire accidentally registered itself as owner of four parcels, rather than three. That mistake was overlooked, both at the time of the original sale and at the time of the recent resale by Cheshire to Burns. Who owns the disputed fourth section of the property? Do you require additional information to answer that question?

2. Ivan Perez owned Harvard Place, which he operated as an apartment complex for many years. That property is located in a jurisdiction that is governed by a registry system. Two years ago, Ivan decided to switch his focus from the rental market to condominiums. To finance his new venture, he borrowed $2 000 000 from Elsa Kamaguchi and gave a mortgage over Harvard Place as security. Elsa promptly registered her interest. Several months later, Ivan notified his tenants of his intention to develop his property into a condominium complex. Most of the tenants gradually left the premises, and as they did, Ivan sold their units to individual purchasers. Some tenants, however, remained, including Nelson Wolodko. He arranged with Ivan to terminate his lease and to purchase his old apartment as a condominium unit. As a result of an oversight, however, Nelson did not register his interest.

A short time later, the economy went into decline, and Ivan found that he was unable to repay his loan. Elsa claims that she has at least two options. (1) She has informed Nelson that she may seek a court order for the sale of premises. He insists, however, that he is immune to a sale, either because he owns his unit or because he occupies it as a tenant under a lease. (2) Elsa has informed Ivan that she may sue him for repayment of the loan. He insists, however, that he is generally immune to such an action because he has sold most of the units to people like Nelson. He also insists that, as a general rule, a mortgagor cannot be sued on a covenant. Discuss Elsa's likelihood of success under each option.

3. Darren Munt is an unsophisticated man who has spent most of his adult life working as a custodian in an elementary school. Recently, he decided to use the money that he had inherited from his father to create a company that would sell books and videos over the Internet. Because he had no experience in that field, he visited Jenny Schmidt, the lawyer who had handled his father's estate. Jenny agreed to help Darren in exchange for a hefty fee. Several weeks later, she informed him that she had found a property with a building that would be suitable for a warehouse. They briefly toured the premises together. Darren was excited about the prospect, but expressed concern "about all of the little details." Jenny assured him that she had extensive experience in real estate matters and promised that, for a price, she would "do all of the legwork."

Jenny contacted the owner of the property. Two months later, the deal closed, and Darren acquired the fee simple to the premises. Shortly after he took possession, however, he became aware of a number of problems. (1) His neighbour complained that the warehouse, which had been built only three years earlier, was located partially on its land. (2) As a result of discussions with other people in the business, Darren realized that he had grossly overpaid for the property. (3) He discovered that the building's foundations were cracked and that its roof was in serious danger of collapse. (4) He was notified by government officials that a large pool of blood was buried only several metres underground on a part of the property that was adjacent to a river. The government explained that the land had previously been used as a slaughterhouse. Fearing that the water supply might become contaminated, the government has demanded a cleanup. (5) Several ex-employees of the slaughterhouse informed Darren that they had been injured on the job as a result of the previous owner's carelessness. They also informed him that they had successfully sued the former owner, and that they had filed writs of execution against the property two days before Darren's sale had closed. (6) And finally, Darren soon became aware that while he might be able to store merchandise in the warehouse, he could not process Internet orders from the same premises. Although he had not noticed them when he briefly visited the property with Jenny, and although they had not been registered against title, power lines had been installed directly overhead by a utility company. Those lines cause electrical interference with computer equipment.

Discuss Darren's situation from a risk management perspective. Is there any obvious solution to his various problems? Explain your answer.

4. Daniel Fossum entered into an agreement of purchase and sale with Visual Developments Inc. Fossum found the property unusually attractive for a number of reasons: (i) it was located on Whyte Avenue, in a historic part of Edmonton, where land seldom is offered for sale, (ii) it was situated across a narrow lane from another property that he already owned, (iii) it could accommodate an art gallery that he wanted to open, and (iv) it contained on-site parking and a rentable basement suite, both of which are rare in the area. Shortly before closing, however, Visual had a change of heart. It has offered to pay damages, but it refuses to complete the sale. Fossum has sued Visual for breach of contract, claiming that he is entitled to specific performance. In response, Visual argues that the Supreme Court of Canada no longer allows that remedy to be awarded in cases involving commercial property. Which party is correct? Can Fossum compel Visual to transfer the property to him? Explain your answer.

5. Irene Aust entered into an agreement of purchase and sale with George Chang. Under the terms of that contract, she paid a deposit of $25 000, which was to eventually count as partial payment of the total price of $150 000. Several weeks before closing, however, George was presented with a new business opportunity that would require him to keep the property. He therefore informed Irene that he was not willing to transfer ownership to her. Since she had not yet relied upon the contract in any substantial way, Irene agreed that she would not seek an order for specific performance. She also generously offered to waive any right to expectation damages that she might enjoy. She insisted, however, that the $25 000 deposit be returned to her. Although Irene's demand was entirely reasonable, George refused. He had already used that fund to establish his new business. In practical terms, he also believed that he could avoid repayment of the deposit, at least in the short term, because he simply did not have any other money. What should Irene do to enforce her claim?

6. As a result of a recent illness, Pierrette Dumont was forced to borrow money from her bank to meet a number of outstanding bills. When she initially negotiated the loan with the bank manager, she agreed to grant a mortgage over her home as security. However, before actually proceeding with that transaction, Pierrette discussed the matter with her brother, Gaston. She became alarmed when he suggested that the mortgage would require her to immediately transfer the ownership in her home to the bank. The house had been in their family for generations and had great spiritual significance for both of them. Pierrette agreed with Gaston that it would be catastrophic if they ever lost possession of it. Are their concerns well founded? What additional piece of information do you require before fully answering that question?

7. Dominion Widget Inc purchased an office complex from Premium Holdings Ltd for $1 000 000. Under the terms of that agreement, Dominion paid $400 000 immediately and gave a mortgage under which it promised to pay the remaining amount, with interest, in a lump sum five years after the date of closing. Although the time for payment has now arrived, Dominion has offered only $300 000 to Premium, along with a renewed promise to pay the outstanding amount within one year. Dominion has explained that its financial position is weaker than expected due to a trade dispute with the United States regarding government subsidies on the manufacture of widgets. However, it has also demonstrated that the situation will almost certainly be rectified within 12 months. Premium, however, insists

that it is entitled to obtain clear title to the property by fore-closing at once. There is, therefore, a tension between the parties' interests. Discuss that tension by tracing the historical development of the rules regarding foreclosure and redemption.

8. Panpac Holdings Inc owns Sino-Columbia Place, a piece of land in Vancouver. Although that property is worth $5 000 000, it is also subject to a number of security interests. (1) Panpac mortgaged Sino-Columbia when it borrowed $3 000 000 from the First National Bank five years ago. Since that time, $500 000 has been repaid. (2) Three years ago, Panpac once again mortgaged the property when it borrowed $1 000 000 from the Silver Financing Company. Under the terms of that agreement, Panpac is not required to make any payments for another six months. By that time, the size of the debt will have been increased by the accumulation of interest. (3) One year ago, Panpac bought $600 000 worth of goods on credit from Tertiary Supply Ltd. Tertiary secured payment for that transaction with a mortgage over Sino-Columbia. To date, Panpac has repaid $100 000. (4) Panpac recently came to you seeking a loan of $500 000. It explains that it has been offered a unique opportunity to invest in a fledgling software company in Victoria. You certainly have $500 000 to lend, and you would normally be inclined to comply with Panpac's request, especially since the company has offered to pay an unusually (though legally) high interest rate. What considerations will affect your decision regarding the proposed loan? Do you require any additional information before arriving at that decision? Explain your answer.

9. The Acme Food Company borrowed $500 000 from the Imperial Bank on the strength of a mortgage over Sunnydale, its farm. Acme quickly defaulted on the loan and has indicated that there is little likelihood that it will ever repay the debt. To make matters worse, Sunnydale has recently been the subject of public concern. Although nothing has yet been proven, there are widespread allegations that the site is contaminated by toxic waste. For the foreseeable future, the government has prohibited human consumption of anything grown on Sunnydale. It has, however, stated that the farm's produce can be used for animal feed. Nevertheless, Acme has abandoned the property. Not surprisingly, the value of the land has dropped from $750 000 to $350 000. What remedy (or remedies) should the bank pursue? Explain your answer.

10. The Newton Widget Company owned two properties, each of which contained a factory. After recognizing the need to modernize its operations, it requested a loan of $500 000 from the Bank of the Rockies. The bank agreed, but insisted on taking a mortgage over both properties as security. Even with the loan, Newton found it very difficult to afford the computerized equipment that it intended to purchase.

It therefore decided to cut back on other expenses. It accordingly stopped paying its property taxes and cancelled the insurance contract that previously provided compensation for any loss or damage that occurred to its land, buildings, or equipment. In an effort to streamline its production of widgets, it also leveled one of its factories, which was valuable but in need of repair and costly to maintain. It then consolidated all of its operations into the single factory. To this point, Newton has made mortgage payments as required under the parties' agreement. The bank nevertheless feels aggrieved. Why? Has Newton done anything wrong? Explain your answer.

11. Ahmad Vaughan borrowed $50 000 from Sarah Jamal. The parties' agreement required Ahmad to repay the loan in monthly instalments of $1000. As security, Sarah took a mortgage over Ahmad's nightclub, which was worth $200 000. Unfortunately, due to the unusual nature of his business dealings, Ahmad frequently experienced tremendous fluctuations in his monthly income. What would be the likely outcome if, three months into the agreement, Ahmad received a large amount of money and attempted to repay the entire outstanding balance immediately? What if, instead, Ahmad suffered an economic setback and was unable to pay three consecutive instalments? If Sarah did not want to use her security to enforce repayment, is there any way that she could nevertheless sue Ahmad for immediate repayment of the entire outstanding balance? Explain your answer.

12. Anna Hurst borrowed $100 000 from the Bank of New Brunswick. As security for that loan, she gave a mortgage over a property that was worth $150 000 at the time. The parties' agreement contained a schedule that required Anna to pay $5000 per month until the loan was completely repaid. Unfortunately, the local economy collapsed shortly after Anna paid the second instalment. That event had two consequences. First, it prevented Anna from making any more payments to the bank. Second, it caused the value of the mortgaged land to plummet from $150 000 to $90 000. Believing that she would never have the ability to redeem the loan, Anna co-operated fully when the bank brought an application for foreclosure. In time, the court granted a final order for foreclosure, and the lender acquired clear title. Several years later, after the local economy had substantially recovered due to an unexpected infusion of government resources, the bank sold the property to a third party for $130 000. Anna now claims that the bank has been overcompensated. She notes that, while there was only $90 000 owing under the loan when she defaulted, the bank has ultimately received a benefit of $130 000. The mortgagee, in her view, should not be able to retain its $40 000 windfall. Is she correct? Explain your answer.

15 Personal Property

CHAPTER OVERVIEW

OBJECTIVES

After completing this chapter, you should be able to:

1. Distinguish between real property and personal property, and between tangible and intangible property.
2. Describe four ways in which personal property rights can be acquired and four ways in which they can be brought to an end.
3. Define the term "bailment," and list the three elements of a bailment.
4. Explain the nature of a lien and a right of sale.
5. Explain five factors that a judge will consider in determining how a reasonable person would have acted in a bailment.
6. Describe the scope of liability for a common carrier, distinguish between the standard of reasonable care and the standard of insurer, and outline three sets of defences that may be available to a common carrier.
7. Describe the process of sub-bailment.
8. Distinguish between third-party insurance and first-party insurance by giving an example of each.
9. Explain the concept of indemnification, and explain how it is related to the ideas of an insurable interest, excessive insurance, and insufficient insurance.
10. Describe the process of subrogation.

Having looked at *real property* in the last two chapters, we can now turn to *personal property*. Although complications occasionally arise, the basic distinction is this: **real property** is immovable, and **personal property** is movable. You cannot carry a piece of land around with you, but you can take a cat or a car from one place to the next. Another distinction is that real property is usually permanent, whereas personal property tends to be transitory. Different owners will come and go, but a particular piece of land will always exist (unless, for instance, it falls into the ocean following an earthquake). In contrast, cats and cars come into the world through birth and manufacture, and eventually pass away through death and destruction. A third distinction is beginning to disappear. Historically, wealth was concentrated in real property. Position and power in society depended upon the ownership of land. Increasingly, however, wealth is held in other forms of property. The dot-com billionaires are proof of that.

real property is immovable

personal property is movable

The general concept of personal property can be broken down into several other categories. The most important distinction is between *tangible* and *intangible* property. **Tangible property** is a thing that can be touched. You can, for example, pick up your cat and sit in your car. Such things are sometimes called *goods* or *chattels*.[1] **Intangible property** is a thing that cannot be touched. For instance, while you can physically hold a cheque, your real concern, as we saw in Chapter 9, is with the rights that that piece of paper represents. You cannot put your hands around those rights. At most, you can require the debtor to fulfill an obligation.[2] As we will see in Chapter 16, much of our new economy consists of a special type of intangible property known as intellectual property, which includes copyrights, patents, and trademarks.

tangible property is a thing that can be touched

intangible property is a thing that cannot be touched

ACQUIRING PERSONAL PROPERTY RIGHTS

Personal property rights are usually acquired through the *intention* of one or more people. For instance, you probably bought this text. The bookseller intended to transfer ownership in exchange for a payment of money. The same sort of process occurs when you rent something, like a moving van. Your rights once again arise from a contractual arrangement. The only major difference between purchasing and renting is that you receive a smaller package of rights when you rent. You cannot keep the vehicle indefinitely. You must return it at the end of the agreed period.

personal property rights usually arise through intention

Property rights are not always acquired through contract. Sometimes, you can get something for nothing. Assuming that the other person intends to give, and that you intend to receive, you can become the owner of a gift once it is delivered to you. Furthermore, you can sometimes acquire property rights even if you act alone and do not enter into any sort of agreement with another person. The law says "finders keepers," but not "losers weepers." For instance, if you find a diamond ring and pick it up with the intention of taking control of it, you obtain rights that you can use against everyone *except* the true owner (if

rights can be acquired by gift or finding

[1.] The word "chattel" comes from the same source as the word "cattle." The root word first referred to movable wealth generally, and then to livestock specifically. The overlap is understandable. Domesticated animals were once a primary form of wealth.

[2.] For that reason, lawyers refer to intangible property as *choses in action*. A chose in action is a "chose" (the French word for "thing") that can only be enforced through legal action. A particular piece of tangible property is a *chose in possession*, because it is a thing that can be possessed.

there is such a person).[3] Consequently, if you took the ring in for an appraisal, you could sue the jewelry store in tort (as Chapter 10 explained) if it refused to return the item to you.[4] In the business world, however, a finder's rights may depend upon the circumstances. Although the law is rather unclear, it appears that an occupier is entitled to things that are found in the private, but not the public, parts of its premises.[5] Case Brief 15.1 discusses the leading decision.

CASE BRIEF 15.1

Parker v British Airways Board [1982] 2 WLR 503 (CA)

Alan Parker found a gold bracelet in the executive lounge at Heathrow Airport in London. He turned the bracelet over to the British Airways Board, which leased the airport, but made it clear that he wanted it back if the true owner did not come forward. The owner never appeared, and the board sold the jewellery for £850. Instead of paying that money to Parker, however, it kept it on the basis that it was entitled to anything found on its premises. Parker was understandably upset and sued.

The court ordered the board to pay the money to Parker. The judge agreed that an occupier is entitled to personal property *if* it is found in an area over which the occupier had a "manifest intention" to exercise control. That might be true, for instance, if Parker had discovered the bracelet under a desk in an office. On the facts, however, the item was discovered on the floor of a publicly accessible waiting area.

rights can be acquired through creation

Some rights can be acquired through an act of creation. An author enjoys copyright as a result of writing a new book. And for somewhat different reasons, the owner of a cow acquires rights to any calves that are born. As both of those examples illustrate, property rights sometimes arise when none previously existed.

LOSING PERSONAL PROPERTY RIGHTS

rights can be lost through contract, destruction, or abandonment

Personal property rights do not last forever. For example, you will lose all of your rights to this book if you sell it to someone else. And if you rent it to a classmate for a term, you will no longer enjoy the right to immediate possession (but you will gain a right to a payment). More dramatically, since you cannot own something that does not exist, your rights will be lost if this book is destroyed in a fire. And while we have already seen that your rights will continue to exist even if this book is *lost*, the situation will be different if you *abandon* the text with an intention of giving up control.

a fixture is a chattel that has been sufficiently affixed, or attached, to land

Rights can also disappear if your personal property becomes attached to, or mixed with, land or other chattels. Although there are several possibilities, we will focus on the most common situation, which involves *fixtures*.[6] A **fixture** is

---

[3.] There is no true owner if the goods were never previously owned, or if they were abandoned. Although a finder acquires substantial rights, it may also incur some obligations. A finder may be required to make a reasonable effort to locate the true owner and to preserve the goods.

[4.] *Armory v Delamirie* (1722) 93 ER 664 (KB).

[5.] There are other limitations. You cannot, for instance, acquire property rights in something that you discover while trespassing on another's land.

[6.] Similar rules apply when two chattels are joined together. For example, I may apply paint to your boat or tires to your car; my stallion may impregnate your mare and produce a foal; my grapes may become mixed with your grapes in a single barrel of wine; and my sheep may become mingled within your flock. Although the precise rules depend upon the situation, the courts will always try to strike a fair balance between the our competing interests. See B Ziff *Principles of Property Law* 3d ed (2000) at 111-8.

a chattel that has been sufficiently affixed, or attached, to land or to a building.[7] The important point is that once a chattel becomes a fixture, it belongs to the owner of the land. Suppose that you bought a dishwasher to use in your apartment. Although the decisions are frustratingly inconsistent, a court would be influenced by the following factors in deciding whether the machine became a fixture.

- *Degree of attachment*: A chattel is more likely to be considered a fixture if it is attached to a building rather then merely sitting under its own weight. Consequently, if you simply wheeled the machine into the corner of the kitchen, it would presumably remain yours. However, if you installed it within the kitchen counter with screws and plumbing, it might be a fixture and therefore belong to your landlord.

- *Purpose of attachment*: A court would be even more concerned with the objective intention served by placing the dishwasher in the apartment. The key issue is whether a reasonable person would believe that the dishwasher became part of the building. If it was installed to enhance the value of the apartment, then it is probably a fixture. However, if it was merely done to make better use of the dishwasher itself, then it is less likely to be a fixture.

- *Tenants' fixtures*: There are special rules that would apply because your apartment was rented. The courts are concerned that tenants might unfairly lose ownership over things that they add to their premises. Consequently, even if the dishwasher did become the landlord's fixture, you could turn it back into your chattel if you removed it, within a reasonable time after the end of the lease, and without doing irreparable damage to the apartment. The same rule applies to trade fixtures. For instance, you probably could remove shelves and signs that you installed in a warehouse that you rented for storage.[8]

BAILMENT

Many things can be done with personal property. We discussed a number of examples earlier in this text. For instance, contractual rights can be assigned, goods can be sold, and cheques can be negotiated. Another important type of arrangement, known as a **bailment**,[9] occurs when one person temporarily gives up possession of property with the expectation of getting it back. The person who delivers the property is the **bailor**. The person who receives it is the **bailee**. Examples of bailment are:

- renting a circular saw from a hardware store
- shipping furniture with a moving company
- delivering a machine to a shop for repairs
- placing equipment in a storage unit
- leasing a vehicle from a dealership
- borrowing a book from a library

a **bailment** occurs when one person temporarily gives up possession of property with the expectation of getting it back

the **bailor** is the person who delivers property

the **bailee** is the person who receives property

[7.] A building is usually a fixture itself because it is attached to land. An interesting issue sometimes arises with mobile homes.

[8.] Since the issue of fixtures is almost always addressed in a lease, the parties can generally create their own terms. The basic rules discussed in the text, however, are usually followed.

[9.] The word "bailment" comes from the French word *bailler*, which means "to deliver."

- sending a package by courier
- lending a lawnmower to a neighbour

Those illustrations cover a lot of ground. Some arise in a business context, others more informally. Some involve a payment of money, others do not. They are all considered bailments, however, because they all satisfy the same requirements:

- one person voluntarily delivers property to another
- for a particular purpose
- with the intention that the property will be returned or disposed of as directed

Although the second and third requirements are usually straightforward, the first occasionally causes problems. As a general rule, a bailment exists only if one person intends to deliver control and possession of property to another person.[10] Business Law in Action 15.1 provides an illustration.

BUSINESS LAW IN ACTION 15.1

Bailment and Parking Lots

You leave your car in the Convenience Plus parking lot while you attend a business meeting. After the meeting, you find that your vehicle has been vandalized and you are furious that Convenience Plus did very little to prevent the damage. You may be able to successfully sue Convenience Plus *if* that company received your car under a bailment.

In determining whether a bailment existed, a judge would consider the *degree of possession and control* that you delivered to Convenience Plus.

- If you simply put coins into a meter, or paid for the right to leave your car in a particular area, the law would probably recognize a *licence*, rather than a bailment. A licence is merely permission to act in a way that would normally be prohibited. In this case,

you would be allowed to leave your vehicle on Convenience Plus's land without committing the tort of trespass.

- If you not only paid for the right to leave your car on the lot, but also handed your keys over to an attendant, the law would probably recognize a bailment. Note the crucial difference between the two situations. In this case, you have given up *possession and control* of your car to Convenience Plus.

Questions for Discussion

1. Given that you would enjoy better rights under a bailment than under a licence, why would you ever enter into the second type of arrangement?
2. For which type of relationship would you expect to pay more?

Liability of Bailors

Most bailments occur without incident. The bailor delivers the property to the bailee, it is held for the intended purpose, and then returned in good condition. Exceptionally, however, difficulties arise on one side or the other. We consider the bailor's liability in this section and the bailee's in the next.

Consider a situation involving a lease. Suppose you are in the business of renting heavy machinery to construction firms. If you *sold* the same equipment,

---

[10.] That requirement is sometimes relaxed. For instance, a finder is often classified as a *quasi-bailee* (that is, *sort of like* a bailee) even though the person who lost the property did not voluntarily deliver possession and control of the goods. Likewise, if you leave your jacket in a store, the proprietors may be considered to be a type of bailee, at least if they pick it up with the intention of taking control of it.

your transaction would be caught by the *Sale of Goods Act*, and you might be required, among other things, to ensure that it was fit for its intended purpose. A lease, however, is not a sale. It is a bailment because you expect that the property will be returned to you at the end of the transaction. Nevertheless, the law requires you, as a bailor who is receiving consideration for the use of your property, to use reasonable care in providing appropriate machines.[11] Consequently, if a backhoe collapses and injures a worker, you might be held liable if you knew, or should have known, of the defect that caused the accident. You might also be required to provide a special warning regarding any unusual dangers, unless the bailee was already familiar with the type of equipment it was renting.

The other major basis of liability arises from a bailor's failure to pay a charge. Suppose that you deliver your car to a garage for repairs or leave your furniture in a storage unit. You are expected to pay for the benefit that you receive from the mechanic or from the warehouse. To ensure that you do so, the bailee is entitled to exercise a *lien* over your property.[12] A **lien** is the bailee's right to retain possession of the property until the bailor pays a debt. Note that the bailee is only entitled to *retain* your property. If you somehow honestly recover your goods, the lien usually disappears. If a lien is exercised, and if you do not respond to it in a timely manner, the bailee can also exercise a statutory *right of sale*. Although the exact requirements vary between jurisdictions, a **right of sale** allows a bailee to sell the bailor's property to obtain payment of the bailor's debt. If the sale proceeds are larger than the debt, the bailor is entitled to the extra money.[13]

> a **lien** is the bailee's right to retain possession of property until the bailor pays a debt

> a **right of sale** allows a bailee to sell the bailor's property to obtain payment of the bailor's debt

Liability of Bailees

A bailee's primary obligation is to return the property, in good condition, to the bailor at the end of the arrangement. A bailment, however, exposes the bailor to considerable risk. Suppose that you deliver your truck to me. The vehicle might become lost, damaged, or destroyed. Furthermore, those events may occur while I am in possession. Since you would have little way of knowing exactly what happened to your truck, you might find it difficult to satisfy the usual requirements of, say, the tort of negligence. The general rule in private law

---

[11.] The lease itself can impose additional obligations upon the bailor or reduce the obligations that are normally imposed by the law.

[12.] Every province and territory has legislation that provides such rights to people who warehouse or store goods: *Warehouseman's Lien Act*, RSA 1980, c W-3, s 3 (Alta); *Warehouse Lien Act*, RSBC 1996, c 480, s 2 (BC); *Warehousemen's Lien Act*, RSM 1987, c W-20, s 2 (Man); *Warehouseman's Lien Act*, RSNB 1973, c W-4, s 2 (NB); *Warehousers' Lien Act*, RSN 1990, c W-2, s 3 (Nfld); *Warehouse Keepers Lien Act*, RSNWT 1988, c W-2, s 2 (NWT); *Warehousemen's Lien Act*, RSNS 1989, c 499, s 3 (NS); *Warehouse Keepers Lien Act*, RSNWT 1988, c W-2, s 2 (Nun); *Repair and Storage Liens Act*, RSO 1990, c R.25, s 4(1) (Ont); *Warehousemen's Lien Act*, RSPEI 1988, c W-1, s 2 (PEI); *Warehousemen's Lien Act*, RSS 1978, c W-3, s 3 (Sask); *Warehouse Keepers Lien Act*, RSY 1986, c 176, s 2 (Yuk). Similar rights are given to people who repair or improve goods. However, the scope of mechanic's lien legislation varies between jurisdictions. See, for example, *Possessory Liens Act*, RSA 1980, c P-13, s 2 (Alta); *Repairers' Lien Act*, RSBC 1996, c 404, s 2(1) (BC); *Repair Shops Act*, RSM 1987, c R-90, s 1 (Man); *Liens on Goods and Chattels Act*, RSNB 1973, c L-6, s 2 (NB); *Mechanics' Lien Act*, RSN 1990, c M-3, s 6(1) (Nfld); *Garagekeepers' Lien Act*, RSNWT 1988, c G-1, s 2(1) (NWT); *Mechanics' Lien Act*, RSNS 1989, c 277, s 6(1) (NS); *Garagekeepers' Lien Act*, RSNWT 1988, c G-1, s 2(1)(Nun); *Repair and Storage Liens Act*, RSO 1990 c R.25, s 3(1) (Ont); *Mechanics' Lien Act*, RSPEI 1988 c M-4, s 2 (PEI); *Garage Keepers Act*, RSS 1978, c G-2, s 3(1)(Sask); *Garage Keepers Lien Act*, RSY 1986 c 77, s 2(1) (Yuk). A number of other statutes also confer rights on more specific types of people, such as threshers and woodsmen.

[13.] Note that statutory liens and rights of sale are generally limited to bailees who repair and store property. For instance, while common carriers have the ability to exercise a common law lien, they do not have a right of sale.

requires the plaintiff to prove that the defendant wrongfully caused a loss. But in our situation, I am the only one with access to all of the facts. The courts have therefore developed a special rule in this situation. If the bailor proves that goods were lost or damaged during a bailment, then the *burden of proof shifts* to the bailee. At that point, I would be required to prove that I was not to blame. If I could not do so, I would be held liable, even though you did not actually show that I was responsible for your loss. Although that rule provides a great benefit to the bailor, it is available only if the court is satisfied that the loss occurred during the bailment and that a shift in the burden of proof would not be unfair to the bailee. Consider the issue in You Be the Judge 15.1.

if the bailor proves that goods were lost or damaged during a bailment, then the burden of proof shifts to the bailee

YOU BE THE JUDGE 15.1

Shifting the Burden of Proof[14]

Wong Aviation Ltd rented a Cessna airplane to Douglas Taylor one morning in late October. The weather was cold, visibility was limited, and the air was turbulent. Taylor took off with the intention of flying the plane in a tight circle around the Toronto Island Airport. Unfortunately, he and the aircraft disappeared without a trace. Although there is no positive evidence whatsoever regarding the disappearance, the evidence indicates that, given the weather conditions, it would have been possible for Taylor to lose control of the plane even if he did not act negligently.

Wong Aviation has sued Taylor's estate for $250 000, the value of the Cessna. Wong admits that it cannot succeed in a simple claim in negligence because it has no basis for positively proving, on a balance of probabilities, that Taylor carelessly caused the loss. Therefore it has based its action on the contract of bailment that was created when Taylor rented the plane. In doing so, Wong believes that it can shift the burden of proof. More specifically, it argues that since it has established that property was lost during the bailment, to avoid liability, the defendant must prove that the loss was *not* caused by Taylor's lack of care. The defendant could not discharge that burden—no one has any idea what happened to Taylor and the aircraft.

Questions for Discussion

1. Under what conditions is the burden generally shifted in the context of a bailment?
2. Are those conditions satisfied in this case?
3. Would it be fair to shift the burden in any event?

Note that even if the burden of proof does shift, the bailee is not generally required to *guarantee* the safety of the bailor's property.[15] Liability will arise only from a failure to take reasonable care. But how much care must be used to avoid liability? Although the courts traditionally applied different standards of care to different types of bailments, they have moved toward a situation in which most bailees simply have to act as a reasonable person would act in similar circumstances.[16] Depending upon the circumstances, a reasonable person might exercise more or less caution and care. Several factors are especially important.[17]

the bailee must act as the reasonable person would act in similar circumstances

---

[14.] *Taylor Estate v Wong Aviation Ltd* (1969) 3 DLR (3d) 55 (SCC).

[15.] We will see an exception that applies to common carriers. Furthermore, the defence of reasonable care is not available in a case of *deviance*, where the bailee dealt with the bailor's property in an unauthorized way. For instance, if you left your furniture in my storage facilities while you were abroad for a year, I might, without your permission, let my brother use it for a few months. If so, I could be held liable even if I was not directly at fault for the fact that the goods were lost or damaged: *England v Heimbecker* (1977) 78 DLR (3d) 177 (Sask Dist Ct).

[16.] That is a general trend in the law. We saw a similar development for the tort of occupiers' liability in Chapter 11.

[17.] While it is important to know which factors affect the content of the standard of care, you should not become too caught up in the exercise. The distinctions between situations are even harder to apply than they are to describe. At the end of the day, a judge usually adopts a common sense approach to all of the facts.

- *Contract, custom, and statute*: If a bailment is contained within a contract, the parties are generally free to agree upon the level of care that the bailee must use. The court may also formulate the standard of care to reflect a practice that is customarily used in a certain type of business. Diamond merchants, for instance, use greater care than people who deal in bricks. Similarly, the standard may be affected by legislation.

- *Benefit of the bailment*: Greater care must be used if a bailment is entirely for the benefit of the bailee. That would be the case if I borrowed a truck from you, as a friend, because I was moving to a new apartment. In contrast, a lower level of care may be acceptable if a bailment is entirely for the benefit of the bailor. Perhaps I had possession of your vehicle simply because I allowed you, as a favour, to park it in my garage while you were on vacation.

- *Gratuity or reward*: A bailee's burden also depends upon whether it was *gratuitous* (free of charge) or for *reward* (for payment). If I was using your truck to move my furniture, I would have to exercise more care if I did not pay for that privilege. After all, I was getting something for nothing. However, if I rented the truck from you, a court might be more lenient, since the transaction benefitted you too.

- *Value and nature of the property*: A reasonable person's behaviour is influenced by the nature and value of the property. I would be expected to behave more cautiously if the truck that I borrowed from you was a fragile and priceless antique rather than a sturdy but well-used pick-up.

- *Bailee's expertise*: I might be expected to exercise greater care if I claimed to have special experience or training in handling the property. For instance, the standard would be higher if you stored your truck in my commercial parking complex rather than the garage attached to my house.

The expectation under the general standard of care can be quite demanding, especially if there is a gratuitous bailment entirely for the bailee's benefit. In exceptional circumstances, however, the bar is set even higher: the bailee is effectively treated as an *insurer*. In other words, the bailee can be held liable even if it was *not* careless. The bailor is entitled to compensation simply because its property has been lost or damaged. We will consider the most important example in the business context: *common carriers*.[18]

the bailee is sometimes treated as an insurer

Common Carriers

A **common carrier** is a company that offers to deliver any goods for any person in exchange for a standard price (assuming that it has available space). That definition can apply to companies that transport by trains, trucks, ships, or airplanes. Notice, however, that a company must do more than commonly carry goods for money. It must also offer its services without reserving the right to refuse to deliver some goods while taking others. Railways, for instance, are often common carriers. In contrast, a moving company is a *private carrier*, rather than a common carrier, if its owner frequently turns away work that

*a **common carrier** is a company that offers to deliver any goods for any person in exchange for a standard price*

---

18. A similar set of rules applies to innkeepers, who are people who offer food and lodging to the public without reserving a general right to turn away travellers: *Innkeepers Act*, RSA 1980, c I-4 (Alta); *Hotel Keepers Act*, RSBC 1996, c 206 (BC); *Hotel Keepers Act*, RSM 1987, c H-150 (Man); *Innkeepers Act*, RSNB 1973, c I-10 (NB); *Innkeepers Act*, RSN 1990, c I-7 (Nfld); *Hotel Keepers Act*, RSNWT 1988, c H-5 (NWT); *Tourist Accommodations Act*, SNS 1994-95, c 9 (NS); *Hotel Keepers Act*, RSNWT 1988, c H-5 (Nun); *Innkeepers Act*, RSO 1990, c I.7 (Ont); *Tourism Industry Act*, RSPEI 1988, c T-3.3 (PEI); *Hotel Keepers Act*, RSS 1978, c H-11 (Sask); *Hotel and Tourist Establishments Act*, RSY 1986, c 86 (Yuk).

involves particularly heavy lifting. So is an airline that reserves the right to refuse some sorts of goods.

A private carrier is liable only if it fails to exercise the level of care that is reasonably expected from someone in its line of work. A different rule applies to common carriers, for largely historical reasons. In ancient times, unscrupulous carriers often agreed to transport goods, but then delivered the property to highwaymen in exchange for a share of the loot. A *shipper* (a person who shipped the property) usually found it difficult to prove carelessness because it did not have easy access to the facts. The loss occurred while the goods were out of its possession. To remedy that problem, the courts held that a common carrier was generally liable for any loss or damage, even if it was not personally at fault. The shipper merely had to prove that: (i) the carrier was a common carrier, (ii) the property was given to the carrier in one condition, and (iii) the property either was not properly delivered to its destination or was delivered to its destination in worse condition.

That basic rule is still applied. Furthermore, a common carrier has very few defences.

- *War and act of God*: A carrier is not liable if goods are harmed as a result of war or an **act of God**, which is a natural catastrophe, such as an earthquake or flood. In either event, however, the carrier may be held responsible if it carelessly exposed the shipper's property to danger. A trucker, for example, might damage goods as a result of unreasonably driving under treacherous weather conditions.

> an act of God is a natural catastrophe

- *Inherent vice and shipper's fault*: The shipper's goods may have suffered damage as a result of an **inherent vice**, which is a defect in the goods themselves. For instance, cattle may die in transit because they were already diseased when they were brought on board. Similarly, the carrier is not responsible for loss or damage that is the shipper's fault. The person sending the property might, for example, improperly pack crystal bowls or fail to label their container as "fragile."

> an inherent vice is a defect in goods themselves

- *Exclusion clause*: By far the most important defence arises from the use of *exclusion clauses*. As we discussed in Chapters 5 and 7, an **exclusion clause** is a contractual term that protects one party from liability. Common carriers typically use standard form agreements that contain provisions along the following lines: "The carrier's liability is limited to $50 per package for any damage howsoever caused," or "The carrier shall only be liable for damage caused by negligence."[19] As usual, judges interpret such clauses narrowly and insist that they be sufficiently drawn to a shipper's attention before a contract is created. Furthermore, in the present context, exclusion clauses must be approved by the Canadian Transport Commission to ensure that customers are treated fairly. Within those limitations, however, exclusion clauses provide an important mechanism for risk management for both parties. The carrier is relieved of responsibility, and the person transporting the goods is alerted to the fact that it should purchase property insurance.

> an exclusion clause is a contractual term that protects one party from liability

Sub-Bailment

We need to briefly consider the concept of *sub-bailment*. As the name suggests, a **sub-bailment** occurs when property that is already held under a bailment is transferred into a further bailment. Suppose that you deliver property to me,

> a sub-bailment occurs when property that is already held under a bailment is transferred into a further bailment

---

[19.] In the second situation, since the burden of proving the defence is on the common carrier, it would have to prove that it had not been careless.

and that I then deliver it to someone else. You are called the *original bailor*. I am called the *bailee/bailor* (because I am the bailee under the original bailment, but the bailor under the sub-bailment). And the third party is called the *sub-bailee*. That sort of arrangement arises quite often in the business world. Three simple examples will illustrate the point.

- I own a general repair shop. You deliver a television to me with instructions to fix the picture tube. Because I do not have the proper equipment to deal with that problem, I deliver the television to another company, with instructions that is should be returned to me once the job is done.

- I own a trucking company. You deliver a load of kitchen fixtures to me for shipment from Vancouver to Charlottetown. When I arrive at the east coast of New Brunswick, I learn that the Confederation Bridge, which links Prince Edward Island to the mainland, is closed for repairs. I therefore deliver the goods to a local ferry company for the last leg of the journey across the water.

- You manufacture heavy machinery. I operate a local construction supply company. My stock includes several vehicles that I have leased from you, including a bulldozer. As part of my business, I sublease that bulldozer to a construction firm for use on a particular project.

Figure 15.1 illustrates the process of sub-bailment.

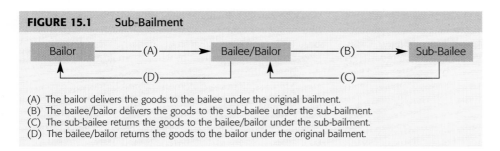

FIGURE 15.1   Sub-Bailment

(A) The bailor delivers the goods to the bailee under the original bailment.
(B) The bailee/bailor delivers the goods to the sub-bailee under the sub-bailment.
(C) The sub-bailee returns the goods to the bailee/bailor under the sub-bailment.
(D) The bailee/bailor returns the goods to the bailor under the original bailment.

A bailee is allowed to place the property into a sub-bailment only with the bailor's consent. A bailment contract may expressly state that the bailee is entitled to deliver the goods to a third party. However, the courts also often recognize implied consent from the circumstances. It is common for a court to assume that a person who delivers an automobile to a mechanic for repairs, or a package to a carrier for shipment, agrees to allow the bailee to transfer the property to a third party to complete the task if necessary. If a bailee places property into a sub-bailment without the bailor's permission, it can be held responsible for any resulting loss. It may even be held liable for the tort of conversion if its conduct seriously interferes with the bailor's ownership.

the bailor must consent to a sub-bailment

The most important issue concerning sub-bailment arises if property is lost or damaged while it is in the sub-bailee's possession. As a general rule, that party is expected to use reasonable care in dealing with the goods. There are two possible actions if it fails to do so.

- A claim may be brought by the bailee/bailor, even though that party did not own the property and merely enjoyed a right of possession under the original bailment. If that claim is successful, then the bailee/bailor normally receives the damages from the sub-bailee on behalf of the original bailor.

- The original bailor may also be entitled to sue the sub-bailee. That is true only if: (i) the original bailor expressly or implicitly agreed to the sub-bailment, and (ii) the sub-bailee knew, or ought to have known, that it received possession of goods that were already held under a bailment.[20]

The situation can become quite complicated if property is passed through a series of bailments and sub-bailments, especially if some of those arrangements involve exclusion clauses. Case Brief 15.2 provides a useful summary of the entire area.

CASE BRIEF 15.2

Punch v Savoy's Jewellers Ltd (1986) 26 DLR (4th) 546 (Ont CA)

Lenore Punch, who lived in Sault Ste Marie, received a ring from her aunt as a gift. It was a family heirloom that was worth more than $11 000. Because the ring was in need of repair, Ms Punch took it to a local shop, Savoy's Jewellers. Savoy realized that it could not perform the repairs itself and consequently sent the ring, by registered mail, to Harry Walker Jewellery in Toronto. In doing so, however, it purchased only $100 worth of insurance on the ring.

Harry Walker fixed the ring and was prepared to return it to Savoy. Due to a postal strike, however, it obtained permission from Savoy (but not from Ms Punch) to send the ring by CN Railway's courier service rather than by registered mail. A driver for CN collected the ring, and an employee for Harry Walker signed a shipping form that contained a provision that limited CN's liability for any loss to $100. Unfortunately, the ring disappeared. Although the exact cause of the loss was unknown, CN freely admitted that its driver may have stolen the property. (Oddly, CN never even bothered to discuss the matter with its employee.)

Ms Punch therefore relied on the bailment relationship and sued Savoy, Harry Walker, and CN. The Ontario Court of Appeal first held that she had implicitly consented to Savoy's sub-bailment to Harry Walker, and to Harry Walker's sub-sub-bailment to CN. Although Ms Punch had not discussed the matter with Savoy at the outset, she presumably knew that a sub-bailment was possible and she did not object. Furthermore, she admitted that if she had been asked, she would have consented. And finally, the evidence indicated that Savoy's use of a sub-bailment was common in the jewellery business.

Next, the court stated that since the ring disappeared while it was held on bailment, the burden of proof shifted from Ms Punch. Each defendant consequently could be held liable unless it established that its carelessness had *not* caused the loss. None of the defendants were able to do so. Indeed, the evidence pointed in the opposite direction. Savoy carelessly failed to purchase adequate insurance coverage for the ring. It should have been more cautious, especially since it agreed to allow Harry Walker to return the ring by way of a courier service with which it had no experience. Harry Walker was also careless. It should have explored the possibility of obtaining better insurance coverage. And CN was careless because it allowed the ring to disappear while in its possession, probably through theft by its own employee.

Finally, the court held that the exclusion clause contained in CN's shipping document might be effective against Harry Walker, but not against Savoy or Punch. The exclusion clause was contained in a contract. And as we saw in Chapter 3, contractual terms can generally only be enforced between contractual parties—in this case, CN and Harry Walker. An exception may be created if a bailor agrees to be bound by a term. On the facts of this case, however, neither Savoy (as the bailor/bailee) nor Ms Punch (as the original bailor) even knew about the exclusion clause.

The defendants were therefore all liable to Ms Punch. She was entitled to recover from any or all of them up to the full value of her ring. She could not recover complete compensation three times over. Between themselves, the defendants were equally liable. CN tried to limit its liability with regard to Harry Walker, but the Court of Appeal narrowly interpreted the exclusion clause and found that it was ineffective because it did not cover losses created through theft.

---

20. Even if the bailor did not initially consent to the sub-bailment, it can subsequently *ratify* that arrangement. In other words, it can later adopt the bailee/bailor's act of placing the property into a sub-bailment as having been performed on its behalf.

PERSONAL PROPERTY, RISK MANAGEMENT, AND INSURANCE

Personal property raises interesting risk management issues. In one sense, property rights are very strong. They usually exist until their owner intentionally disposes of them.

- If you lose your property, you can recover it from me even though, as a finder, I acquired rights against everyone else in the world.

- If a thief steals your goods and sells them to me, I may be liable for the tort of conversion even if I acted in the reasonable belief that the thief was the true owner.[21] As a general rule, people cannot give more than they actually have.[22] I could not buy from the thief something that still belonged to you.

In a number of other respects, however, personal property rights are quite fragile.

- Even if I found your goods, you cannot sue me unless you know that I have your property. However, personal property is easily moved from one place to another. And while there are registration systems for keeping track of some chattels (such as vehicles), it is often impossible to locate goods that have gone missing.

- Personal property may be damaged innocently or in a way that does not support a valuable cause of action. Your computer may be ruined by an electrical storm that causes a power surge, or it may be crushed by a common carrier under a shipping contract that contains an effective exclusion clause.

Those sorts of concerns create the need for risk management. Some strategies are proactive because they reduce the risk of loss in the first place. For instance, security systems can prevent thefts, and training programs can help employees avoid accidents. Perhaps the most important form of risk management, however, is *insurance*.

In Chapter 10, we discussed the need for *liability insurance*, which involves an insurance company's contractual promise to pay damages on behalf of a person who incurs liability. In exchange for that promise, the insured party pays a price, called a *premium*. Since an employer may be vicariously liable for an employee's torts, liability insurance is often a matter of survival. Few businesses have sufficient assets to pay for all of the damage that they may cause in the course of their operations. In this chapter, we look at another significant form of insurance: *property insurance*. **Property insurance** is a contract in which an insurance company, in exchange for a premium, promises to pay money if property is lost, damaged, or destroyed.[23] The basic difference between the two

property insurance is a contract in which an insurance company, in exchange for a premium, promises to pay money if property is lost, damaged, or destroyed

---

[21.] See Business Law in Action 10.2.

[22.] The rule of *nemo dat quod non habet* (or *nemo dat* for short) is subject to several exceptions. The most important occurs if value is given in exchange for money rather than goods. Suppose that a thief stole $5000 in cash from you. If I bought that money from the thief by selling a car to him, I can obtain ownership of the money. That exception is based on the need for cash to pass freely through the commercial world.

[23.] Although insurance is a type of contract, it is governed by special rules. Most significantly, while you generally are not required to volunteer information when you negotiate an agreement, the situation is different when you purchase insurance. Insurance is a contract of *utmost good faith*. You are therefore required to voluntarily disclose any facts that might affect the risks for which you are seeking coverage. If you fail to do so, your contract may be void.

types of insurance is reflected in the fact that the former is often called *third-party coverage*, whereas the latter is often called *first-party coverage*.

- *Third-party coverage*: Liability insurance provides third-party coverage because, in one sense, it is aimed at providing compensation to someone outside of the insurance contract.[24] The insurance company's obligation is triggered only if the insured party is accused of wrongfully inflicting a loss upon someone else.

- *First-party coverage*: Property insurance provides first-party coverage because it does not require the involvement of an outsider. The insurance company's obligation to pay is triggered by a loss to the insured party itself.

Figure 15.2 illustrates the difference between third-party and first-party insurance.

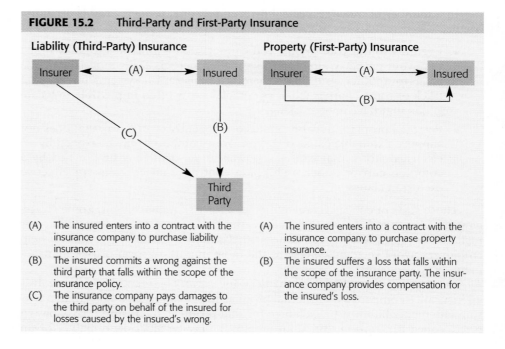

FIGURE 15.2   Third-Party and First-Party Insurance

Liability (Third-Party) Insurance

Property (First-Party) Insurance

(A) The insured enters into a contract with the insurance company to purchase liability insurance.
(B) The insured commits a wrong against the third party that falls within the scope of the insurance policy.
(C) The insurance company pays damages to the third party on behalf of the insured for losses caused by the insured's wrong.

(A) The insured enters into a contract with the insurance company to purchase property insurance.
(B) The insured suffers a loss that falls within the scope of the insurance party. The insurance company provides compensation for the insured's loss.

Although the rules are complex, we can briefly summarize the essential points that arise in connection with property insurance.

Scope of Coverage

First, as a matter of risk management, it is critical to understand the scope of coverage that is provided by an insurance policy. You only get what you pay

---

24. That statement is not entirely accurate. Liability insurance is actually intended to protect the insured party against the risk of being held liable to a third party. The important point, however, is that such coverage necessarily requires the involvement of a third party. Furthermore, a practical effect of liability insurance is that the third party is much more likely to receive compensation. The insurance company usually has enough money to pay damages even if the insured party does not.

for.[25] Most insurance contracts are based on standard form agreements (as discussed in Chapter 5) that cover common events, like fires, floods, storms, and thefts. That basic coverage, however, is subject to restrictions. Standard fire insurance, for instance, may not cover accidents that arise from the storage of explosives or from riots. As a general rule, you can obtain extra protection for those events, but you will have to pay higher premiums.

the scope of property insurance is limited

Indemnification

Second, property insurance is never profitable. At most, it provides **indemnification**, which is reimbursement for a loss that has occurred. And it seldom offers even that much relief.

indemnification is reimbursement for a loss that has occurred

- There are different ways of calculating the loss that occurs when property is lost, damaged, or destroyed. Suppose that a piece of equipment in your factory is badly damaged in a fire. Your policy may entitle you to replace it with a new machine. It is more likely, however, that your insurance company is merely obligated to pay the value that your equipment had the moment before it was destroyed. And if your equipment had been in use for some time before the accident, its *depreciated value* would probably be far less than the cost of a replacement.[26] Consequently, unless you can find a suitable second-hand substitute, the policy will not actually provide enough money to make your factory operational again.

- Property insurance policies usually include *deductibles*. A **deductible** occurs when the insurance company is not required to provide indemnification for the initial part of a loss. A common example involves cracked automobile windshields. The driver usually agrees to pay, for instance, the first $250 toward a repair. You can always ask for a policy that does not have a deductible and that provides full replacement cost. But again, you will pay accordingly.

a deductible occurs when the insurer is not required to provide indemnification for the initial part of a loss

As these paragraphs suggest, the choice of insurance coverage is often a very complicated and speculative matter. Business Decision 15.1 provides a dramatic example.

---

[25] And sometimes not even that much. In an effort to save money, insurance companies occasionally refuse to pay for losses that fall within the policies that they have sold. In doing so, they commit a breach of contract. To discourage that practice, a court may award punitive damages, as well as compensatory damages, against an insurance company: *Whiten v Pilot Insurance Co* (2002) 209 DLR (4th) 257 (SCC) ($1 000 000 in punitive damages).

[26] Insurance policies also often give the insurer the option of paying to repair, rather than replace, damaged property. An insurance company will choose the cheaper alternative.

BUSINESS DECISION 15.1

Insurance Coverage and the Price of Premiums

Piracy on the high seas continues to thrive. And while its traditional image may be romanticized, in reality it is a deadly serious business. Hundreds of ships are attacked every year and some estimates put the global cost at more than $23 billion.[27] In a common operation, pirates seize control of a vessel, possibly execute the crew, and off-load the cargo at a friendly port. They may then rename the ship, solicit new cargo from unsuspecting customers, and steal the second shipment. They can repeat this process many times over.

However, it is difficult to assess the actual risk of being attacked. Many instances of piracy are not reported because ship owners do not want their vessels and crews to be detained while port authorities conduct lengthy investigations. An idle ship can cost its owner $10 000 per day in lost income. Furthermore, while the risk of piracy is very real, the number of annual incidents is actually small when compared to the enormous amount of global shipping that occurs on a daily basis. Finally, the danger tends to be confined to certain areas, especially in the shipping lanes around southeast Asia.

Suppose that you own a medium-sized furniture manufacturing business. Unfortunately, because of some poor decisions in the past, your company's economic situation has become unstable. In an effort to increase sales, you decide to offer a new line of tables and chairs crafted from fine mahogany. For that purpose, you purchase $100 000 worth of the wood from a producer in a remote region of the Philippines. Your plans are upset, however, when you ask your insurance agent for coverage of your mahogany while it is shipped to Canada. Your agent explains that the geographical area in question has recently been hit by a wave of ruthless and highly efficient pirates. Consequently, while you expected to pay about $5000 for comprehensive coverage, you are told that you have a choice between: (i) paying $4000 for coverage that *does not* include protection from piracy, and (ii) $25 000 for coverage that *does* include such protection.

You are in a dilemma. You have already paid the producer for the mahogany. You realize, however, that if you pay $25 000 for insurance, you will have little chance of making a profit from your new venture. You also realize that if your shipment is pirated, and if you do not have insurance, you will be wiped out altogether.

Questions for Discussion

1. Will you purchase insurance coverage? What factors will influence your decision? Is your decision based entirely on an economic calculation, or is it also a reflection of your personality?
2. Can you suggest any other solutions to the problem?

Insurable Interest

an **insurable interest** exists if a person benefits from the existence of the property and would be worse off if it was damaged

You cannot obtain property insurance unless you have an *insurable interest*. That requirement is needed to avoid "moral hazards." Suppose that you could buy coverage over my car. You would have an incentive to destroy my vehicle later. Even though you would not actually suffer a loss (since the car belongs to me), you would be entitled to a payment under the insurance policy. The law therefore prevents you from obtaining insurance unless you have an *insurable interest*. An **insurable interest** exists if you benefit from the existence of the property and would be worse off if it was damaged. Consistent with the goal of indemnification, you can be protected only from a loss that you could actually suffer. However, you do not necessarily have to *own* the property in question. The Supreme Court of Canada has held, for instance, that you can have an insurable interest in a corporation's property if you own a substantial number of shares in that company. Any loss to the business would also be harmful to you.[28]

[27.] "Not since Captain Kidd has piracy been so rife" *National Post*, August 3, 2001.

[28.] *Kosmopoulos v Constitution Insurance Co* (1987) 34 DLR (4th) 208 (SCC).

Excessive and Insufficient Insurance

Since property insurance is limited to indemnification, it is important to avoid excessive insurance. There is nothing to be gained from purchasing the same coverage from two insurers. Suppose that you insured the full value of your building, say $500 000, against the risk of fire with both Insurance Company A and Insurance Company B. Even if your building was entirely destroyed by fire, you would be able to collect only $500 000, not $1 000 000. The premium that you paid to one of the companies therefore would be a waste of money. That extra payment would simply provide a benefit to the insurers. The doctrine of **contribution** states that if two parties are equally liable, they share the loss between themselves. Consequently, if you recovered $500 000 from Company A, it could demand $250 000 from Company B. In effect, the companies would enjoy a bargain at your expense. Each would be liable for only $250 000 even though it had charged you for $500 000 in coverage.

the doctrine of **contribution** states that if two parties are equally liable, they share the loss among themselves

Just as it is important to avoid *excessive* coverage, it is also important to avoid *insufficient* coverage. That proposition is especially important in one context. To encourage you to buy as much coverage as possible, insurance companies often put *co-insurance clauses* into their policies. A **co-insurance clause** states that, if you do not maintain a certain level of coverage, you may be held partially responsible if you suffer a loss of a *lesser* extent. We can demonstrate that difficult rule by using a simple example. Suppose that you buy only $6000 worth of insurance, even though your equipment is worth $10 000. The policy contains a co-insurance clause that requires coverage for at least 80 percent of the value of your machine.

a co-insurance clause states that if an insured party does not maintain a certain level coverage, it may be held partially responsible in the event of an accident

- If an accident occurs, and the damage to your machine is worth *at least* 80 percent of its value (say, $9000), you will be entitled to receive $6000, which is the full extent of the benefit that you bought.

- However, if an accident occurs and the damage to your machine is worth *less than* 80 percent of its value (say, $4000) then you will be a co-insurer to the extent that you did not buy enough coverage. Since you bought only 75 percent of the protection required under the co-insurance clause (that is, $6000 coverage rather than $8000 coverage), you can recover only 75 percent of your loss (that is, $3000 of the $4000 loss). Figure 15.3 shows the relevant calculation.

FIGURE 15.3   Co-Insurance

$$\frac{\text{amount of coverage purchased}}{\text{minimum coverage required under co-insurance clause}} \times \frac{\text{actual}}{\text{loss}} = \frac{\text{insurer's}}{\text{liability}}$$

$$\frac{\$6000}{\$10\,000 \times 80\% \,(= \$8000)} \times \$4000 = \$3000$$

Subrogation

There is one more point to make in connection with indemnification. So far, we have ignored the possibility that the property protected under a policy may be *wrongfully* damaged by a third party. Suppose that I destroy your factory by carelessly starting a fire. Generally speaking, the rights that you enjoy under your policy are not affected by the fact that I committed a tort against you. You will still receive compensation from your insurance company. But because your policy limits you to indemnification, you *cannot* also sue me in tort. If you did, you might recover twice for the same loss—once from me and once from the insurer. That is not to say, however, that I will not have to pay for my wrong. The terms of your policy will entitle your insurance company to *subrogation*. The doctrine of **subrogation** allows your insurance company to stand in your shoes and acquire the rights that you have against me. Consequently, after indemnifying you, your insurance company will, at its own cost, bring an action against me for negligently burning down your factory. Figure 15.4 illustrates the process of subrogation.

subrogation allows an insurance company to stand in the insured party's place and acquire any rights that it may have against a third party

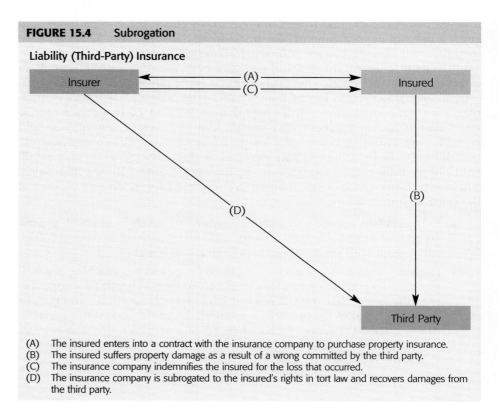

FIGURE 15.4   Subrogation

Liability (Third-Party) Insurance

(A)   The insured enters into a contract with the insurance company to purchase property insurance.
(B)   The insured suffers property damage as a result of a wrong committed by the third party.
(C)   The insurance company indemnifies the insured for the loss that occurred.
(D)   The insurance company is subrogated to the insured's rights in tort law and recovers damages from the third party.

Are the effects of the doctrine of subrogation fair? Consider Ethical Perspective 15.1.

ETHICAL PERSPECTIVE 15.1

Subrogation

Questions for Discussion

Answer these questions on the basis of the example in the paragraph on subrogation.

1. Would it be unfair if you were entitled to both claim indemnification from the insurer and sue me for damages in tort? If you could have obtained damages from me if you had not purchased a policy, then why did you pay the premium to the insurance company? Was the policy really a benefit to you? Explain your answer.

2. Assume that: (i) you paid $10 000 in premiums, (ii) you received $100 000 in indemnification, and (iii) your insurer recovered $100 000 in damages from me as a result of being subrogated to your rights in tort. Is it fair that the insurance company can retain the money that you paid in premiums even though it did not eventually suffer any loss in return? Explain your answer.

Other Forms of Business Insurance

Before leaving this topic, it is important to note that there are many types of insurance policies in addition to the ones that we have discussed. Some are especially important to the issue of risk management in the business world. In determining which are appropriate for a particular business, you should consult an insurance broker.

- Although property insurance may allow a business to replace or repair equipment and facilities that have been lost, damaged, or destroyed, there will usually be a delay before operations return to normal after an accident. And that delay may be very costly. Consequently, **business interruption insurance** is quite common. As the name suggests, it provides coverage for losses created by downtime. It can include, for instance, compensation for lost profits, wasted expenditures, and relocation expenses.

    business interruption insurance provides coverage for losses incurred as a result of downtime

- A similar issue arises as a result of computer saboteurs. The release of a single virus can easily cost the global economy billions of dollars as Web sites crash and hard drives are erased. Although the insurance industry is still coming to terms with that problem, it is certainly possible for a business to purchase **hacker insurance**. Because of the potential size of the losses, however, coverage tends to be expensive and therefore is often practical only for enterprises like eBay and Amazon that rely heavily upon the Internet.

    hacker insurance provides protection from the economic consequences of computer saboteurs

- A business may suffer a substantial economic loss if an important member of its organization dies or becomes incapacitated. Although that person inevitably will be missed, a company may find it easier to adjust to the loss if it has access to funds with which it can hire and train a replacement. **Key person insurance** provides such a fund.

    key person insurance provides protection against the loss of important members of a business

- Many businesses also help to arrange **life, health, and disability insurance** for employees and their families. Typically, the employer and the employee reach an agreement in which both contribute to the cost of the premium. The employer's portion is part of the employee's total remuneration package. Such arrangements are advantageous to employees because, while they could individually purchase insurance for themselves, the costs of group coverage are substantially lower.[29]

    life, health, and disability insurance provides protection for employees in the event of health problems

---

29. An injured employee may also be entitled to benefits under workers compensation schemes: Chapter 10 and Chapter 25.

a **fidelity bond** provides coverage when an employee steals money, equipment, or other assets from a business or one of its clients

a **surety bond** is used to assure a client that it will be financially protected if a job is not performed as promised

■ *Bonds* are used to provide comfort in some business contexts. A **fidelity bond** provides coverage when an employee steals money, equipment, or other assets from a business or one of its clients. First-party fidelity covers the company's own property. Third-party fidelity covers property belonging to a client. A **surety bond** is used to assure a client that it will be financially protected if a job is not performed as promised. For instance, you may be concerned about a construction company's ability to complete a new building on time. If so, you might insist upon a surety bond that would allow you to receive compensation from an insurance company if the project is delayed.

Chapter Summary

Broadly speaking, there are two types of property: real property and personal property. Personal property is either tangible or intangible. Personal property rights can be acquired in various ways: contract, gift, finding, and creation. They can also be lost in various ways: contract, destruction, abandonment, and fixture.

A bailment occurs when one person temporarily gives up possession of property with the expectation of getting it back. The person who delivers the property is the bailor, and the person who receives it is the bailee. Bailments arise in many circumstances, including leases for personal property.

A bailor may be liable for delivering goods that are not fit for the bailee's purpose. A bailor may also be liable to pay a price in exchange for the benefit of the bailment. If it fails to do so, the bailee may be entitled to exercise a lien and a right of sale.

A bailee's primary obligation is to return the property to the bailor in good condition. If the bailee fails to do so, the burden of proof may shift, and the bailee may be held liable unless it proves that it was not carelessly responsible for the loss or damage to the bailor's property. In rare circumstances, the standard of care is higher, and the bailee is treated as an insurer of the bailor's goods. That rule applies to common carriers.

A sub-bailment occurs when property that is already held under a bailment is transferred into a further bailment. In that situation, the sub-bailee may be held liable to either the bailee/bailor or the bailor if the property is lost or damaged.

Insurance is one of the most important forms of risk management in business. Liability insurance, which we examined in Chapter 12, is sometimes called third-party insurance because, in one sense, it is aimed at providing compensation to someone outside of the insurance contract. Property insurance, on the other hand, is sometimes called first-party insurance because it does not require the involvement of an outsider and because the insurance company's obligation to pay is triggered by a loss to the insured party itself.

Basic property insurance policies are usually limited in scope. Furthermore, insurance merely provides indemnification for a loss. There are different ways in which to calculate losses for the purpose of insurance. Insurance benefits are often subject to deductibles.

Insurance is available only to a person who has an insurable interest in property. An insurable interests exists if a person benefits from the property and would be worse off if it was damaged or lost.

Businesses should avoid obtaining excessive insurance and insufficient insurance. Excessive insurance often provides a benefit to the insurance companies as a result of the doctrine of contribution. Insufficient insurance often gives rise to the problem of co-insurance.

The process of subrogation allows an insurance company to stand in the insured party's place and acquire any rights that the insured may have against a third party.

Besides liability insurance and property insurance, a business may wish to purchase other types of insurance, including business interruption insurance; hacker insurance; key person insurance; life, health, and disability insurance; fidelity bonds; and surety bonds.

Review Questions

1. What is the difference between real property and personal property?

2. There are different ways of classifying personal property. Use examples to explain the difference between tangible and intangible property, and between choses in possession and choses in action.

3. List four ways in which personal property rights can be acquired.

4. "Finders keepers, losers weepers." Explain the extent to which the law adopts that phrase. Against whom does the finder of property have rights?

5. "You are always entitled to keep property that you find on someone else's premises." Explain the extent to which that statement is correct.

6. List four ways in which personal property rights can be lost.

7. What is a fixture? To whom does a fixture belong? Explain the factors that will influence a court's decision as to whether a chattel has become a fixture.

8. Define the term "bailment," and list the three elements of a bailment. Which party is the bailor, and which party is the bailee?

9. Using examples, describe situations in which leaving a car in a parking lot creates a bailment or a licence. In practical terms, what is the most important difference between a bailment and a licence?

10. "Since the bailor is simply delivering possession of goods to the bailee, the bailor never has an obligation with respect to the quality of the property." Is that statement true? Illustrate your answer with an example.

11. Explain when and how a bailee can use a lien or a right of sale to recover payment from a bailor.

12. Why does the law sometimes shift the burden of proof when the bailor complains that property has not been returned in a timely manner or in good condition? Briefly describe the situation in which the burden of proof will shift.

13. List and briefly explain five factors that will influence the judge's determination as to whether the bailee acted as a reasonable person would have acted in similar circumstances.

14. Define the phrase "common carrier." Is every business that transports goods for a price a common carrier? Explain your answer.

15. "A common carrier is an insurer of bailed goods." What does that statement mean? Will a common carrier always be held responsible if goods are lost or damaged while in its possession? List three types of defences that a common carrier can use against a bailor. In practical terms, which type of defence is the most significant? Explain your answer.

16. Explain the process of sub-bailment and identify the parties that are involved in that process. Is a bailee always entitled to place goods into a sub-bailment?

17. To whom can a sub-bailee be held liable for losing or damaging goods held on a sub-bailment? Outline the situations in which a sub-bailee can use the protection of an exclusion clause.

18. Use examples to explain the difference between third-party insurance and first-party insurance.

19. Define the term "indemnification." Explain how the concept of indemnification affects the ideas of: (i) an insurable interest, (ii) excessive insurance and insufficient insurance, and (iii) contribution and co-insurance.

20. Explain the process of subrogation.

Cases and Problems

1. As part of a special promotional campaign, the Blacksox Baseball Club printed tickets that contained a stub entitling the holder to a free deluxe meal at a local restaurant. Anna held season tickets to the Blacksox and followed the team closely throughout the summer as it struggled for a position in the playoffs. By the end of September, however, it was clear that the Blacksox would fall short, and Anna consequently began to lose interest. On the final night of the regular season, she therefore decided against attending the Blacksox game and went instead to a video rental shop that was owned and operated by Dmitri. While in the shop, she suffered a sneezing fit and asked Dmitri if she could use the washroom. Dmitri explained that his shop did not have a public restroom, but in the circumstances, allowed Anna to use the private facilities that are normally available only to staff members. While searching her purse for a handkerchief, Anna came across her ticket to the last Blacksox game. She crumpled it up, threw it on the floor, and continued to search for her handkerchief. By coincidence, Oscar also suffered a sneezing fit while in Dmitri's shop later that same evening, and he too was allowed to use the restroom. While there, he picked up the discarded ticket and was delighted to see that the stub for a free meal was still attached. When he mentioned his good luck

to Dmitri, however, the shop owner insisted that he was entitled to the meal. The pair then agreed to ask Anna who she thought should get the stub. Unfortunately, to complicate matters even further, she declared that she wanted the meal after all. Who should get the free meal? Explain your answer.

2. Iona Camponi purchased an acreage with a mortgage in favour of the Bank of Alberta. She also purchased a mobile home from Halcyon Houses. That sale was subject to terms that allowed Halcyon to reclaim possession of the home if payment was not made in a timely manner. Iona poured a concrete foundation on the land, placed the mobile home on top of it, and constructed a back deck that was attached to both the mobile unit and the concrete pad. She also hooked up utilities (water, power, and plumbing) to the unit. Iona settled in very nicely and quickly formed the opinion that she had found a permanent home. Within months, however, her financial situation took a turn for the worse, and she defaulted on both the land mortgage and the purchase of the mobile home. The Bank of Alberta consequently foreclosed on the mortgage and obtained ownership of the land. Some time later, Halcyon Houses attempted to remove the mobile home under the terms of its contract with Iona. The bank, however, insisted that the unit had become a fixture and that it consequently belonged to them as a result of their ownership of the acreage. Who owns the mobile home? Explain your answer.

3. Helen Cottee visited Franklins Hardware Store and purchased a number of items. Because of the size and weight of those items, a store clerk provided Helen with a shopping cart to allow her to more easily transport the goods from the store to her car. While she was pushing the cart across the parking lot, however, one of its wheels fell off. The cart collapsed on Helen and caused extensive injuries. Helen brought an action against Franklins seeking compensation for the accident. Will she succeed? Explain your answer.

4. Shortly before taking a three-year position as a nurse in Saudi Arabia, Noreen Rabby moved her furniture and personal belongings into a storage unit that she rented from Newtown Security Inc. The agreed price was $200 per month. For the next three years, Noreen purchased money orders on a monthly basis and sent them to the address that she had copied into her phone book before she left Canada. Unfortunately, Noreen had written that address incorrectly, so none of the cheques ever reached Newtown. Furthermore, for reasons that neither party can explain, her letters were never returned to her and the money orders have simply disappeared. And finally, Noreen had forgotten to give her address in Saudi Arabia to Newtown, so that the company had no way of contacting her in her absence. When Noreen returned from Saudi Arabia at the end of her job posting, she was surprised to learn that Newtown, acting under statutory authority, had sold her belongings to cover the rental payments that were never received. She is also very angry that the storage company insists on retaining all of that money, even though the proceeds from that sale exceeded her indebtedness by $2500. Newtown believes that it is entitled to the extra money on the grounds that it became the owner of the goods when Noreen failed to meet her obligations under the contract. Who is entitled to the $2500? Explain your answer.

5. Hitek Industries is one of very few companies in the world that manufactures a delicate and expensive piece of machinery known as a "widget phalanger." Widget phalangers are used for mapping and measuring underground oil deposits. One day last year, Perry Omoc, Hitek's owner, received a telephone call from Mathilde Waltsin, an old friend with whom he had studied engineering at university. She explained that she owned an oil exploration company and that she was interested in surveying a possible deposit in the Yukon. She indicated that she would require the use of a widget phalanger for that project, but then confessed that, due to a recent financial setback, she did not have enough money to buy, or even rent, that piece of equipment. She wondered if, for old times sake, Perry would be willing to simply lend her one of his spare units for 10 days while she surveyed the area in question. He initially refused, but her persistence eventually won him over, and he had a widget phalanger delivered to her the next day. Unfortunately, after using the machine for a week, she destroyed it by powering it on-site with a portable generator that emitted a power surge during an electrical storm.

Mathilde promptly told Perry of the accident and suggested that his lawyer contact her insurance company with a view to receiving compensation for the loss. After a brief round of preliminary negotiations, however, the insurance company refused to pay a benefit under Mathilde's liability coverage policy. It did so on the basis of *Schonky v Beano*, a decision of the Supreme Court of Canada. In many respects, the facts in *Schonky* were strikingly similar to events that occurred between Perry and Mathilde. Beano had temporary possession of a "litmus configurator" (a relatively sturdy and inexpensive machine that is also used in oil exploration) that was owned by Schonky. That machine was destroyed when an electrical storm caused a power surge to a portable generator that Beano was using on-site. The case report in *Schonky* further indicates, however, that Schonky had paid Beano to test the litmus configurator on a remote location. Beano was not itself actually searching for oil. Indeed, it did not have any special expertise in the oil industry. Nevertheless, it had been hired by Schonky to determine whether the equipment could properly function under various conditions. The relevant passage in the Supreme Court of Canada's decision states:

> As often is true, it is very difficult to determine whether or not the defendant acted as a reasonable person would have acted in similar circumstances. I believe that Beano's conduct in this case is very close to the line and I have wrestled a great deal with the issue of liability. Ultimately, however, I have come to the conclusion that Beano did not act carelessly. I recognize that it could have taken certain steps to prevent the accident that happened. It could, for instance, have incurred the expense of attaching a "surge inhibitor" to the generator, before connecting the generator to the litmus configurator. On the particular facts before me, however, I do not believe that a reasonable person would have done so. Schonky therefore is not entitled to compensation from Beano.

Does that decision *necessarily* mean that Mathilde (or her

insurer) is not liable to Hitek as a result of the bailment that arose between the parties? Explain your answer.

6. Occidental & Atlantic (OA) is a shipping company that offers to deliver goods for anyone anywhere in the world. Mediterranean Imports Ltd wished to have $500 000 worth of silk sent from a port in northeast Italy to Halifax. It entered into a contract with OA that included the following provisions.

37 The carrier shall use whichever route is the most appropriate in the circumstances.

73 The carrier's liability for loss or damage due to fire, storm, or act of God shall be limited to $500 per shipment.

127 Any disputes arising between the parties shall be resolved under the laws of Canada.

Shortly before the journey began, an armed conflict erupted in a region of the Balkans, which lie to the east of Italy. Although carriers regularly passed through the affected area when transporting goods from northeastern Italy to North America, most carriers chose to adopt alternative routes during the course of the conflict. The captain of OA's vessel, however, realized that any deviation from the standard course would be costly and therefore decided to proceed as usual. Unfortunately, the entire cargo of silk was lost when OA's ship was caught in a crossfire and sank. Mediterranean Imports did not purchase first-party insurance for its property and therefore is anxious to recover compensation from OA. Is it entitled to do so? Explain your answer.

7. Miles Sivad, a wealthy music producer, owned a large number of expensive paintings and *objets d'art*. As a favour, he agreed to loan several paintings to a business colleague, Gilmore Green. He also gave Gilmore permission to lend the same paintings to other people on a short-term basis. Several weeks later, Bess Porgy, who believed that Gilmore owned the paintings in question, asked him if she could borrow one to spruce up her home for a party that she had planned. Gilmore agreed and Bess hung *Sketches of Spain* in her living room. Although her party was generally a success, the painting was stolen by one of several uninvited and untrustworthy guests who had arrived at her place. Gilmore sued Bess for failing to use reasonable care to safeguard *Sketches of Spain* while it was in her possession. The trial judge agreed with the claim and ordered Bess to pay to Gilmore $250 000, which was the value of the painting. It was only after the trial that Miles learned what had happened. His anger over the theft was exceeded only by his anger over the fact that Gilmore refused to hand over the $250 000 that he had received as damages from Bess. Was Gilmore actually entitled to recover that money from Bess? If so, was he obligated to transfer it over to Miles? Explain your answer.

8. Brenna Corp wanted to ship $25 000 worth of office supplies from Kamloops to Moncton. For that purpose, it contacted Hanjin Transport Inc, a general moving company. Although Hanjin reserved a general right to refuse certain types of goods, it agreed to deliver Brenna's property as requested. The parties entered into a contract that contained the following provision: "The carrier is entitled to subcontract on any terms for the handling of the goods." Hanjin used its own truck to take the office supplies from British Columbia to Manitoba. Once it arrived in Winnipeg, however, it paid Pilgrim Container Ltd, a reputable shipper, to complete the journey to New Brunswick. Pilgrim was informed that the goods belonged to Brenna. The contract between Hanjin and Pilgrim therefore contained the following provision: "Pilgrim's liability to any party with an interest in the goods shall be limited to $500." Somewhere east of Thunder Bay, the driver of Pilgrim's truck fell asleep at the wheel and drove into a lake. Although he emerged unhurt, his entire cargo, including Brenna's office supplies, was totally ruined. Discuss Brenna's rights against Hanjin and Pilgrim.

9. Western Paper Inc's warehouse was located next to Thames Explosives Ltd's factory. As a result of a careless manufacturing process, a fire erupted in Thames' premises and soon spread next door. By the time the blaze was contained by the local fire department, $100 000 worth of Western's product had been destroyed. Western had purchased from Fortress Insurance first-party coverage that entitled it to compensation for losses attributable to fire. Thames had purchased from Sentinel Insurance third-party coverage that entitled it to complete protection from losses that it carelessly inflicted as a result of careless manufacturing processes. Explain how the insurance policies will apply in this case. Who will ultimately pay for the loss created by Thames and sustained by Western? Explain your answer.

10. Horst and Jurgen Romani grew up in Europe. As an adult, Horst immigrated to Vancouver. Jurgen remained behind and, while in France, developed an idea for a perfume company. He then began to purchase the necessary supplies and equipment. As his project neared fruition, he asked his brother to join him in the venture. Although Horst was initially skeptical, he was eventually persuaded and agreed to meet the expenses associated with transporting Jurgen and his materials from France to Canada. Horst also gave his brother $11 000 to purchase additional materials. Once they were reunited in British Columbia, the pair informally agreed that they would create a company named Roma France Ltd to manufacture and distribute perfume in this country. They did not, however, actually go through the process of incorporation. Furthermore, while all of the property was stored in Horst's basement, it still belonged to Jurgen. Horst nevertheless purchased a fire insurance policy for it. In fact, a fire did occur and destroyed all of the equipment and supplies that the brothers had intended to use in their business. The insurance company, however, has refused to honour the policy on the grounds that the property in question belonged to Jurgen, with the result that Horst did not have an insurable interest in it. Is the insurer's argument persuasive? Explain your answer.

11. Nocturna Mattress Ltd kept a large inventory of beds in its warehouse. As a matter of internal management, it tried to keep about $60 000 worth of stock on hand at all times. It purchased property insurance from Citadel Insurance. That policy contained a co-insurance clause that called for the insured to hold 80 percent coverage. Nocturna nevertheless chose to pay for only $30 000 worth of coverage. As a result of a cycle of heavy snowfall and warm weather, Nocturna's warehouse was flooded, and much of its inventory sustained irreparable water damage. It therefore

has made a claim under its policy with Citadel. How much will Nocturna receive if: (1) the total loss was valued at $50 000, (2) the total loss was valued at $40 000, (3) the total loss was valued at $30 000 and the policy also contained a $5000 deductible? Explain your answers.

12. Skynet Industries is one of several private corporations that manufacture components for the military. As such, it frequently is subject to various forms of protests from a number of interest groups. Although it employs almost 100 people, its chief engineer and CEO, Dyson Bennett, is the moving force behind the company. He is also primarily responsible for its most profitable branch: cyborg intelligence research. To protect its equipment and plant, Skynet purchased full coverage for any loss or damage that any of its property sustained from any cause. Given the unusually broad scope of that policy and the economic value of Skynet's assets, the annual premiums are very expensive.

As part of a controlled, in-house testing program, Skynet recently detonated a small incendiary device at its plant. Although the explosion proceeded as planned, the plant was substantially destroyed by a fire that followed. That fire should have been automatically extinguished by the company's state-of-the-art sprinkler system. It appears, however, that the system had been disabled by an unidentified protestor who had managed to break the security code for Skynet's main computer. Skynet consequently lost virtually all of its stock and equipment. Much more significantly, however, Dyson Bennett suffered severe burns while escaping from the building. Although he survived the incident, the medical evidence indicates that his injuries will prevent him from ever resuming his previous role with the company. And finally, while its financial position is strong enough to see the company through the disaster, Skynet has incurred substantial costs in temporarily relocating its operation to a new site while its own facilities are rebuilt. Among those costs is the loss of a large contract that it otherwise would have received from the Canadian military for the development of a new laser-directed missile-launching system.

On the basis of the information that has been provided, does Skynet have sufficient insurance to compensate it against all of its losses? If not, suggest alternative forms of insurance that it should have bought.

WWWeblinks

Interests in Land

Canadian Real Estate Law—Fee Simple Estates and Life Estates
www.duhaime.org/ca-re7.htm

This Web site offers a general introduction to real estate law in Canada, including a description of fee simple estates and life estates. It also provides links to summaries of Canadian real estate case law.

JURIST Canada—Property Law
jurist.law.utoronto.ca/cour_pgs.htm#Property

The JURIST Web site features links to course pages developed by Canadian law teachers. They include materials relevant to the study of property law.

Provincial and Territorial Mining-Related Acts and Regulations
www.nrcan.gc.ca/mms/provacts-e.htm

This Natural Resources Canada site provides links to mining-related information, acts, and regulations for each jurisdiction in Canada. The links offer information on how to obtain mineral rights.

Leases

Ontario *Commercial Tenancies Act*, RSO 1990, c L-7
192.75.156.68/DBLaws/Statutes/English/90107_e.htm

This Act sets out the rights and duties of the landlord and tenant in a commercial tenancy agreement, and describes the remedies available in the event of the breach.

Reference Guide to Landlord and Tenant Law in Alberta
www.acjnet.org/docs/landten/index.html

This guide to residential landlord and tenant law describes the rights and duties created under a tenancy agreement, as well as the offences and penalties set out in various pieces of legislation. It also has links to other landlord and tenant resources.

Registration Systems

British Columbia Real Estate Law
www.duhaime.org/cabcreal.htm

This Web site summarizes some of British Columbia's real estate laws and legislation, including a description of the land titles system under which the province operates.

Sales

ARVIC Search Services

www.arvic.com/library/Buychecklist.asp

This site includes a checklist of the items business people should consider when purchasing an existing business, including real estate, leases, insurance, and other legal issues.

Real Estate Institute of Canada

www.reic.ca/

REIC offers educational programs on a variety of commercial, legal, and ethical topics and issues related to real estate transactions; online articles; and links to other information resources.

Personal Property, Risk Management and Insurance

Insurance-Canada.ca

www.insurance-canada.ca/

This Web site provides consumers and insurance professionals with information on insurance-related topics, including general information about the importance of insurance as a risk management tool and specific information on types of insurance.

Insurance Bureau of Canada

www.ibc.ca/

The IBC identifies and monitors policy issues affecting the insurance industry. Its site provides numerous links to industry-related publications and resources.

Risk and Insurance Management Society Inc

www.rims.org

RIMS, a not-for-profit organization dedicated to advancing the practice of risk management, offers online articles and links to other risk management resources.

Export Development Canada

www.edc-see.ca/

The EDC is a department of the federal government that provides a wide range of risk management services, including insurance and financing, to Canadian exporters and their customers around the world.

COMMERCIAL LEASES: AN OVERLOOKED INVESTMENT

Every jurisdiction in Canada regulates residential tenancies through tenant-protection legislation. Canadian law has the incentive to become involved in that relationship because of the difference in bargaining power between residential tenants and their landlords. Commercial leases, on the other hand, do not benefit from the same legislative protection. It is generally considered acceptable to allow two businesses to freely negotiate the terms of their commercial agreement. In other words, all business people presumably have equal bargaining power. But that is not always the case for small business owners who feel pressured by their landlords.

Renting can sometimes cause problems that the small business person would not consider. For example, the business person might feel pressure from the landlord to give up the rented space or else pay more rent. By giving in to the landlord's demand and relocating, the business person risks losing their customer base. Another mistake a business person can make is relying on the goodwill of the landlord. Perhaps the business person has enjoyed a long-term relationship with the landlord and, on that basis, failed to put lease renewals in writing. In that situation, the landlord may be able to force the tenant out of the location. And what can a tenant do if the landlord leases space to a competitor in the same building? Unless their lease agreement contains a non-competition clause, the answer is "very little."

Business people can avoid these and other problems by practising risk management. One way of doing that is to negotiate your lease. Dale Willerton, a lease consultant, says that when it comes to commercial leases, "You don't get what you deserve. You get what you negotiate." Lease negotiation can produce two effects. First it may create incentives that you would not otherwise receive when signing a lease. For example, during periods when commercial space is readily available, you may be able to negotiate lower rents, moving costs, a period of free rent, interior refinishing, or other improvements. Willerton recommends that business people negotiate more than one location at a time. He explains that creating competition for your tenancy is the ideal way to ensure that you get the best deal. By playing one landlord's offer against another's, you can increase your bargaining power.

The second effect of lease negotiation is more important from a legal perspective. Negotiation can help business people avoid future business losses. Consider the ways that you can protect your business.

Writing Requirement To be enforceable, a lease has to be in writing in most Canadian jurisdictions. But as a general rule, *all* business agreements should be in writing. Writing helps prevent miscommunication between the parties. A written lease will outline the rights and duties of both the landlord and tenant. In the event of a dispute, the parties can refer to the terms of the lease.

Lease Length Selecting the best lease length is a crucial business decision. On the one hand, you may want a month-to-month lease because of the flexibility it affords. However, that type of lease does not provide much of security. On the other hand, you may prefer a long-term lease to recoup any investment you may have made in renovating the premises. The drawback in that type of lease is that you may be tied to a location that you no longer want. You also should be wary of demolition or construction clauses. That type of clause allows a landlord to give short-term notice if they decide to demolish the building or make substantial structural changes. The drawback in that situation is that you may have carefully planned and negotiated your long-term lease only to find out that you have to find new premises on short notice.

Business Space   Rent is often calculated by square footage. To prevent unnecessary losses, business people should ensure that the location is measured correctly. Over time, even a relatively small discrepancy can add up to a considerable overpayment.

Non-Competition (or Exclusivity) Clauses   Even if you have your landlord's word that they will not lease nearby space to a competitor, there is no guarantee that new owners will honour the same promise. For that reason, you should consider negotiating a non-competition clause to prevent the landlord from leasing to tenants with businesses similar to yours without your consent.

Option to Renew   One way to minimize the risk of a long-term lease is to sign a short-term lease with renewable options. A renewal clause allows you to renew your lease for an additional term after the lapse of the existing lease. But before renewing your lease, keep in mind that many aspects of your business may have changed since your original lease was signed. Your costs, labour, and real estate requirements may have changed. You should take all of those factors into account before you renew your lease. The timing of renewal negotiations is also very important. Some landlords may try to put themselves in a stronger bargaining position by leaving negotiations to the last minute, when it is too late for you to find another location. To avoid that problem, you should start renewal negotiations about a year in advance. If you include an option to renew in your lease, you should also negotiate a clause that sets out the amount of, or the formula for calculating, any rent increase.

QUESTIONS TO CONSIDER

1. List and discuss three clauses that you can include or exclude from your lease to avoid future business losses.
2. Does it seem fair that small business owners are treated in the same way as large corporations with respect to landlord-tenant matters? Give reasons for your answer.

Sources: Lease Consultants <www.theleasecoach.com>; Sean Silcoff, "Retail rainmaker: if you're a small retailer and you want to get a lot bigger, talk to Harley Oberfeld" (1998) vol 71(15) *Canadian Business* 28; Liz Katynski, "New digs: is a commercial agent an asset?" (1997) vol 19(8) *Manitoba Business Journal* 7; Michael Gelmon, "Practice management: getting the best deal from your landlord" (March 1997) *Strategy CMA* 11.

Video Resource: "Leasing Woes," *Venture* # 704, November 17, 1998.

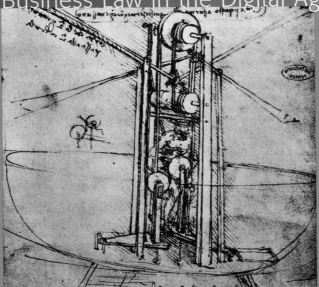

16 Knowledge-Based Businesses and Intellectual Property

CHAPTER OVERVIEW

OBJECTIVES

After completing this chapter, you should be able to:

1. Describe how information technologies have helped spawn a knowledge-based economy.
2. Demonstrate how the new economy is based on the commodification of information.
3. Distinguish between internal and external information-based assets.
4. Discuss how intellectual property laws are used to increase the value of information-based assets.
5. Determine whether a particular creation is protected under copyright legislation.
6. Outline the protection offered under trademark law, and determine whether an action for passing-off may succeed.
7. Discuss the patentability of inventions, and identify possible grounds of infringement.
8. Explain how intellectual property law protects industrial designs and integrated circuit topographies.
9. Discuss trade secrets as a means of protecting information-based assets.
10. Describe the nature of confidential information and the remedies available when confidentiality is breached.

Many believe that the power of high technology has ushered in a kind of industrial revolution, an economic shift that is transforming the way we do business. When they talk about the **new economy**, they are talking about a "world in which communications technology creates global competition—not just for running shoes and laptop computers, but also for bank loans and other services that cannot be packed into a crate and shipped. A world in which innovation is more important than mass production. A world in which investment buys new concepts or the means to create them, rather than new machines. A world in which rapid change is a constant. A world at least as different from what came before it as the industrial age was from its agricultural predecessor. A world so different its emergence can only be described as a revolution."[1]

in the new economy, investment buys new concepts or the means to create them rather than new machines

In the new economy, entrepreneurs recognize the power of information and knowledge. Knowledge-based work is qualitatively different from traditional forms of labour, such as working with bricks and mortar, plastics, or even silicon chips. To the extent that knowledge can be captured in digital form, it is much easier to manufacture and distribute than most of the stuff that you buy in department stores. At the same time, it is much harder to control.

in the new economy, entrepreneurs recognize the power of information and knowledge

In this chapter, we investigate the legal aspects of knowledge-based businesses. We begin with an examination of information as a commodity. We then investigate the central legal mechanisms by which such assets can be controlled and exploited for profit—the laws of intellectual property.

INFORMATION AS A COMMODITY

The *Gospel According to Matthew* speaks of the miracle of the loaves and the fishes. According to the gospel, the Christ's heavenly blessing allowed five loaves and a couple of fish to miraculously replenish itself, feeding more than 5000 people and leaving 12 baskets of food after everyone had their fill. At the time the miracle was recorded by Matthew, it would have been equally miraculous if Matthew had been able to reproduce 5000 copies of his written account. In fact, it took about 1400 years of technological development to achieve such a task. And even then, Johan Gutenberg was able to produce only 200 copies of the *New Testament* with the movable type printing press that he invented.

Miraculous Nature of Information

Gutenberg's 200 reproductions of the *New Testament* was itself a kind of miracle—although it is difficult to think of it that way today. Before his invention, the reproduction of 200 bibles would have taken considerable time, energy, labour, and natural resources. But it is not merely the tremendous increase in the speed at which the gospel could be reproduced that made the printing press miraculous. Nor was it the decreased transaction costs that were required for the reproductions. What is miraculous about the printing press is that it demonstrated the possibility that Matthew's gospel—and other information— might be *universally possessed*. The possibility of universal possession is what distinguishes information from tangible commodities. **Universal possession** is possible when a good is available to many people at the same time in a way that one person's enjoyment of it does not diminish another's.

universal possession is possible when a good is available to many people at the same time in a way that one person's enjoyment of it does not diminish another's

Sneakers, laptop computers, and other forms of tangible property are capable of *exclusive possession*. **Exclusive possession** characterizes an

exclusive possession characterizes an individual's exercise of power over a thing at their pleasure to the exclusion of all others

---

[1.] J Browning & S Reiss *Encyclopaedia of the New Economy* (2002) <hotwired.lycos.com/special/ene/>.

individual's ability to exercise power over a thing at their pleasure to the exclusion of all others. Exclusive possession is possible in the case of a tangible commodity, because tangible items occupy space and can therefore remain in the sole control of those who possess them. I can keep you from wearing my sneakers by tying them to my feet. I can stop you from using my laptop computer by locking it in my office. But I cannot easily prevent you from possessing knowledge of the miracle of the loaves and the fishes. Such information can be replicated by word of mouth. Innovations like Gutenberg's printing press, the photocopier, and digital technologies further enhance the possibility of the universal possession of information. Put another way, recent developments in information technology increase the difficulty of the exclusive possession of information and ideas.

Economics of Information

When the creator of an idea has the sole aim of spreading the gospel, the miraculous nature of information is a blessing. However, most creators of ideas have additional motives. As the saying goes, "Information wants to be free. It also wants to be expensive."[2] To continue with our example: many books and paintings have been produced on the miracle of the loaves and the fishes. Why would the creators of such works—whose livelihoods depend on the number of copies sold—spend years writing or painting, while passing up other financial opportunities, if they knew that anyone could easily reproduce their book or painting without their permission, without cost or sanction? There is far less incentive for creators of ideas to toil in their creation if those ideas, once developed, can be universally possessed with no compensation to them.

Bread and fish are commodities—they are bought and sold. My incentive to make bread or to catch fish depends largely on the *natural scarcity* of those items. **Natural scarcity** occurs when the supply of a natural resource is inadequate. Because natural resources are finite, the market value of those resources usually increases when supplies become inadequate. Consider what would happen if natural resources were not finite. Suppose I could buy loaves and fishes from you and then miraculously reproduce them in great numbers at no additional cost to me. That would allow me to affect your ability to sell loaves and fishes, since I could decide to give the newly created supply away for next to nothing to all of your potential customers. If natural resources were capable of universal possession in this way, there would be very little incentive for you to make the loaves or catch the fish. The phenomenon of natural scarcity is what allows bakers and fishers to make a living.

Our ability to reproduce, distribute, and universally possess information at virtually no cost means that its supply is not finite. Therefore, information is not as easily bought and sold as bread and fish. To create a market for information, an *artificial scarcity* must be introduced. **Artificial scarcity** makes the supply of an informational resource inadequate, by making the information incapable of universal possession. Knowledge-based businesses depend upon the creation of an artificial scarcity to increase the value of their information-based assets. This scarcity is brought about through the law of intellectual property.

Information-Based Assets

One aim of a business is to generate assets. A knowledge-based business generates information-based assets. Sometimes referred to as *invisible capital*, these

natural scarcity occurs when the supply of a natural resource is inadequate

artificial scarcity makes the supply of an informational resource inadequate

---

[2.] S Brand *The Media Lab: Inventing the Future at MIT* (1988).

assets are distinguished from bricks and mortar or other more traditional forms of business capital.[3] The invisible capital of a business is like the three parts of a cake.

- The bottom layer of the business is its *human capital*. **Human capital** is the special talents and expertise of those employed by the business. Bill Gates has said that the majority of Microsoft's assets walk out of the building at the end of the working day and, hopefully, return the next morning.

- The top layer is the *internal information-based assets* of a business. **Internal information-based assets** include the business plan and other business concepts, models, and information systems, as well as any inventions or content created by those involved in the business. It also includes its customer lists, data administration, and processing systems.

- The icing is the *external information-based assets* of the business. **External information-based assets** include the image and reputation of the business, its brand recognition, and the relationships it has developed with suppliers and customers.

Chapter 17 on electronic commerce considers other aspects of information-based assets. This chapter focuses on how businesses can protect such assets in a world where exclusive possession is no longer possible or desirable—the law of intellectual property.

> human capital is the special talents and expertise of those employed by the business

> internal information-based assets include business concepts, models, information systems, as well as any inventions or content created by the business

> external information-based assets include the image and reputation of the business

INTELLECTUAL PROPERTY

Intellectual property law aims to protect products of the mind. Although it does this to provide incentives to creators, intellectual property recognizes that creators cannot forever monopolize their ideas. To allow a monopoly of ideas would grind human progress to a halt. Consequently, **intellectual property law** is an intricate web of public and private interests. It is a set of rules that aims to balance the rights of a creator against the public interest. The tension between these interests is readily apparent when a court is asked to establish a new legal precedent. Consider the landmark decision in Case Brief 16.1.

> intellectual property law is a set of rules that aims to balance the rights of a creator against the public interest

CASE BRIEF 16.1

International News Service v The Associated Press (1918) 248 US 215 (US SC)

The Associated Press (AP) was a wire service. Its business was to supply news stories from overseas to American newspapers during World War I. Without permission, one of its competitors, International News Service (INS), retrieved some AP news bulletins and sold them to several of its customers in the United States, *and* presented those news items as though it had collected and reported them. AP sued INS, claiming that the news items belonged to them and that INS had published them illegitimately. INS argued that there can be no private rights in public affairs and insisted that no one can own the news.

The US Supreme Court was divided on the issue. Writing for the majority, Justice Pitney recognized that intellectual property law was not intended to confer upon an individual the exclusive right to control the flow of knowledge simply because that person happened to be the first to report the story. At the same time, Justice Pitney held that it is unjust to let a business competitor "reap where it had not sown,"

(continued)

[3.] L Downes "Invisible Capital" *The Industry Standard* (July, 10 2000) <www.thestandard.com/article/display/0,1151,16431-1,00.html>.

(continued)

especially when the result was to divert profit "from those who have earned it to those who have not." Consequently, he held that INS was not allowed to appropriate the story "until its commercial value as news... had passed away."

Writing in dissent from the majority, Justice Brandeis took a very different point of view. Justice Brandeis was not terribly moved by the fact that AP had made a substantial investment in collecting the wartime news. "The fact that a product of the mind costs its producer money and labor and has a sufficient value for which others are willing to pay, is not sufficient to ensure to it this legal attribute of property. The general rule of law is, that the noblest of human productions—knowledge, truths ascertained, conceptions, and ideas—become, after voluntary communication to others, free as the air to common use."

The tension between the public interest and private rights, the idea that information wants both to be free and expensive, is a recurring theme of intellectual property law.

Copyright

Copyright is the law of authorship. It rewards and protects an author's creative efforts by giving the author an exclusive right to publish or otherwise control the distribution of a work. Many people are under the mistaken impression that a copyright must be registered in order to be enforceable. In fact, copyright is automatic upon the creation of an original work in a fixed medium. To protect the creative process, the law prohibits others from copying an author's work for a specified period of time. Unless ownership of the copyright is somehow transferred to another person, only the author is permitted to produce or reproduce a work, and only the author can authorize others to do the same. In this context, an **author** is someone who produces an original work.

It is a common misconception that copyright protects ideas. As Case Brief 16.1 illustrates, copyright law does not protect ideas. What copyright does protect is the manner in which an idea is expressed.

*an **author** is the producer of an original work*

copyright protects the manner in which an idea is expressed

Forms of Expression That Are Protected

There are several ways in which an author can express an idea. The *Copyright Act* refers specifically to seven forms of expression that are protected.[4] Figure 16.1 provides examples of each.

FIGURE 16.1   Seven Forms of Expression Protected by Copyright

	Examples of Copyright Material
literary works	stories, textbooks, instruction manuals, compilations, translations, computer programs
dramatic works	films, videos, screenplays, choreography, scenic arrangements, recitals
musical works	compositions, melodies, harmonies, sheet music
artistic works	paintings, drawings, photos, sculptures, engravings, maps, charts

(continued)

[4.] *Copyright Act*, RSC 1985, c C-42 (Can).

FIGURE 16.1 *(continued)*

performances	—— acting, dancing, singing, drumming
sound recordings	—— records, cassettes, compact discs
communication signals	—— broadcast signals

Source: Industry Canada *A Guide to Copyrights* (2000) at 3.

Some forms of expression are not protected by copyright. Slogans, short phrases, titles, names, and factual information are not generally subject to copyright law. As we saw in Case Brief 16.1, news and other factual information are considered to be part of the public domain. Where a business report or magazine article contains factual information, it is the expression of the information that is subject to protection, not the facts themselves. Copyright does not apply to basic ideas. Figure 16.2 illustrates when copyright applies.

FIGURE 16.2 **When Does Copyright Apply?**

Copyright applies to:	Copyright does not apply to:
a song	—— the title for a song
a novel	—— the idea for a plot
a play	—— the method of staging a play
	Hamlet (a work in the public domain)
a magazine	—— the facts in the article
a computer program	—— the name of the program

Source: Industry Canada *A Guide to Copyrights* (2000) at 3–4.

Requirements for Copyright Protection

For a work to enjoy copyright protection in Canada, it must meet three requirements.

- The work must be *original*
- The work must be *fixed*
- The work must be *connected to Canada* (or to a World Trade Organization, Berne, Rome, or Universal Copyright Convention member state)

Originality Do not confuse the requirement of originality with the concept of novelty. The notion of an **original work** means that the work originated from the author and was not copied from any other source. After all, you cannot obtain a copyright for work that belongs to someone else. Note that the originality requirement has a low threshold. Although one must be able to prove that the work involved some intellectual effort, all that needs to be shown is that something has been done to create a potentially marketable commodity.[5] Business Law in Action 16.1 illustrates the meaning of originality.

an **original work** is work that is not copied from any other source

---

5. *Ladbroke (Football) Ltd v Williams Hill (Football) Ltd* [1964] 1 All ER 465 (HL); D Vaver *Intellectual Property* (1997) at 1.

BUSINESS LAW IN ACTION 16.1

The Low Threshold of Originality

Mark and Jenny had been scheming for some time about starting up a business that would capitalize on student laziness on campus. Sitting in the half-empty lecture theatres of their mega-class, they realized that there was a market for class lecture notes. Therefore, they ran an ad in the student newspaper calling for dean's honour roll students enrolled in mega-classes at the university to apply to be paid note-takers for their company, Campus Notes. Mark and Jenny met with a large group of applicants and explained that they would pay successful applicants a fixed fee in exchange for a copy of their class notes and permission to distribute them to Campus Notes customers. The note-takers were told that the best way to prepare the notes was not to transcribe the lecture word for word, but to organize the materials in a way that made sense, with many headings and subheadings and additional illustrations and examples.

Business boomed until the day that Campus Notes received a letter from several professors threatening to sue them for breach of copyright. In essence, the professors claimed that they held copyright in their lectures and that the lecture notes provided by the honour roll students were *not* original works.

Question for Discussion

1. Could Mark and Jenny claim that the lecture notes provided by their note-takers are original works?

---

copyright is usually restricted to the expression of a work in a fixed medium

Fixation   Although the Act does not expressly stipulate this, copyright is usually restricted to the expression of a work in a fixed medium. For example, a choreograph must have its scenic arrangement fixed in writing or otherwise. Likewise, a broadcast must be recorded on tape or some other medium while being transmitted. There is a similar requirement for computer programs. The aim of such requirements is to add certainty to the law. Ensuring that an author is capable of identifying the work and demonstrating that it persists in some medium will ultimately prevent spurious claims that spontaneous activity, including oral conversations, enjoy copyright protection. Case Brief 16.2 illustrates the meaning of fixation.

CASE BRIEF 16.2

Gould Estate v Stoddart Publishing Co (1996) 30 OR 520 (Gen Div)

In 1956, Glenn Gould was a young, up-and-coming concert pianist. That summer, while on vacation in the Bahamas, Gould invited a photojournalist named Jock Carroll to take pictures and conduct a series of informal interviews. While snapping some 400 pictures, Carroll also recorded a number of Gould's remarks both on paper and audio tape. The point of the interlude was to capture the spontaneity of Gould while he was on vacation. Nearly 40 years later, 13 years after Gould's death, Carroll published a book *Glenn Gould: Some Portraits of the Artist as a Young Man.* Gould's estate sued, claiming breach of copyright.

The court held that there was no copyright in the oral conversations between Gould and Carroll. In rendering its decision, the court cited *Canadian Admiral Corp v Rediffusion* as authority for the proposition that "for copyright to subsist in a work, it must be expressed in material form and having a more or less permanent endurance."[6] A person's oral conversations therefore are not generally recognized as literary creations and do not attract copyright protection. Rather, the person who takes notes or otherwise records the speech in a fixed medium is considered to be the author and thereby attains copyright in the expression.

[6.] *Canadian Admiral Corp v Rediffusion Inc* [1954] Ex CR 382.

Connection with Canada (or copyright convention member states)   A work is subject to Canadian copyright law only if it has some connection to Canada. All work created in Canada is protected. However, work created outside of Canada by a Canadian national or an ordinary resident of Canada is also protected. Thanks to a number of international treaties, copyright eligibility extends even further. Any author of an original work who is a citizen or a person ordinarily resident in a country that is subject to the Berne Copyright Convention, the Rome Convention, the Universal Copyright Convention, or the World Trade Organization is protected by Canadian copyright law regardless of where the work was created. This is an important point for managers in knowledge-based businesses, who must take care to minimize the risk of their employees copying foreign material under the mistaken impression that it is not subject to Canadian law.

Copyright Ownership

Our discussion of copyright has been only from the perspective of the author. Generally, the author of a work is the copyright owner. Recall that the copyright owner has the legal power to prevent others from copying the work. Some authors and artists are interested in exploiting such power for monetary gains, but others are not. Those who, for any reason, are not interested in monetary gains can use their legal power to prevent others from gaining access to their work. For example, the American author JD Salinger once used the law of copyright to thwart the publication of his private letters.[7] However, on several other occasions, Salinger did exploit the power of copyright law—he transferred aspects of the copyright he owned to a book publisher in exchange for *royalties*. **Royalties** are the monetary compensation given to an author in exchange for the use of their copyrighted materials. Royalties are usually expressed as a percentage of the publisher's receipts from the sales associated with the copyrighted material. Some publishers even offer an author an incentive by way of an *advance on royalties*. An **advance on royalties** is an interest-free amount that is paid to the author before the completion of a work and is later deducted from the sum of royalties.

Knowledge-based businesses can adopt many other ownership schemes. To understand the various business possibilities, you need to know the bundle of rights that the copyright owner can exploit. Figure 16.3 summarizes these rights.

royalties are monetary compensation given to an author in exchange for the use of their intellectual property

an **advance on royalties** is an interest-free incentive that is paid to the author before the completion of a work and is later deducted from the sum of royalties

---

FIGURE 16.3   The Bundle of Rights Held by the Copyright Owner

the right to *produce, reproduce, perform,* or *publish* a work

the right to *translate* a work

the right to *convert* a dramatic work into a novel, non-dramatic work, or sound recording

the right to *convert* a novel into a dramatic work through public performance or by sound recording

the right to *convert* a non-dramatic or artistic work into a dramatic work through public performance

(continued)

[7.] *Salinger v Random House Inc* 811 F2d 90 (2d Cir 1976).

FIGURE 16.3 *(continued)*

the right to *communicate* a work by telecommunication
the right to *reproduce*, *adapt*, or *present* a work by film or photograph
the right to *present* an artistic work at a public exhibition (works created after June 7, 1988)
the right to *create* a sound recording of a musical work
the right to *license* computer software
the right to *reproduce* any performance that has been fixed
the right to *fix* any performance that has not yet been fixed
the right to *reproduce*, *license*, or *publish* sound recordings
the right to *fix* or *reproduce* broadcast signals
the right to *authorize* another broadcaster to simultaneously retransmit the signal

Source: Industry Canada *A Guide to Copyrights* (2000) at 3–4.

Copyright can be unbundled into several discrete rights, many of which can be bought, sold, licensed, or given away. This gives those engaged in knowledge-based businesses a multitude of business opportunities. Business Decision 16.1 will help you explore these.

BUSINESS DECISION 16.1

Unbundling Copyright

Vladimir, a fairly well-known author, has just finished writing an excellent manuscript. Thinking that this will be his greatest work ever and fearing an impending writer's block, he has approached your knowledge-based business to see if you are interested in purchasing ownership of the copyright. You see great potential in the work.

Question for Discussion

1. What are some of the more effective ways in which your company might best profit from his written manuscript?

> copyright in a work created in the course of employment is usually owned by the employer

The author of a work is *generally* the copyright owner. However, an important exception occurs in the employment context. Generally, the copyright in a work created in the course of employment is owned by the employer. For example, copyright in a government brochure developed by a public servant belongs not to the brochure's creator but to the Crown. A similar result occurs if a particular work is commissioned, as long as it is clear that the person who commissions the work is paying for the copyright and not merely the physical object. Note that the rule does not generally cover independent contractors. Knowledge-based businesses that hire independent contractors to generate information-based assets should expressly provide that copyright is held by the business and not the contractor.

Duration of the Copyright

Intellectual property rights do not last forever. Unlike property in tangible objects—which continues to exist until such objects are given away, sold, used up, or ruined—the bundle of rights inherent in copyright *always* comes to an end. When it does, the work is said to belong to the *public domain*. **Public domain** is the realm of works that belong to the community at large and that can be used by anyone. For example, the works of Shakespeare are in the public domain; the song *Happy Birthday* is not.[8] When does a work enter the public domain? In Canada, the duration of copyright generally lasts for the life of the author and then for 50 years following the end of the calendar year in which the author dies.

public domain is the realm of works that belong to the community at large and that can be used by anyone

Moral Rights

In addition to the bundle of rights that compose copyright, the creation of an original work also gives rise to a separate package of *moral rights*, which are legally enforceable.[9] Moral rights are considered to be so important that they cannot be bought or sold—they are retained by the author even if ownership in a copyright is subsequently transferred to someone else. **Moral rights** include: (i) the right of attribution, (ii) the right of integrity over a work, and (iii) the right to be associated (or not associated) with a work.

moral rights include the right of attribution, the right of integrity over a work, and the right to be associated (or not associated) with a work

The right of attribution allows an author to ensure that their name is attached to the work. It also allows an author to remain anonymous or to work under a pseudonym. In either case, the attribution right prevents others, even if they own the copyright, from using the work and claiming it as their own.

The right of integrity provides an author with a further degree of control over the work after it is sold. It allows an author to prevent others from distorting, mutilating, or otherwise modifying the work where doing so would prejudice the author's honour or reputation. A famous Canadian artist exercised such a right by forcing a shopping mall to remove Christmas decorations from his sculptures.[10] Note that the right of integrity in a work is not always easy to enforce. Often what one party sees as the distortion or modification of a work is perceived as free speech by another. Although the distortion of a work is sometimes grounds for lawsuit, the courts will not always view the total destruction of a work as prejudicing the author's reputation. Consider the case in Ethical Perspectives 16.1 (p. 358).

The fact that an author retains moral rights in a work even after it is sold is offset by the fact that moral rights can be waived by the author. This is an important consideration for knowledge-based businesses that buy and sell copyrighted content. From a risk management perspective, a business should make a contractual condition requiring an author to waive their moral rights. This will provide the business with a greater ability to control the content that it has purchased with no strings attached.

knowledge-based businesses that buy and sell copyrighted content should require authors to waive their moral rights

Copyright Infringement

Since the copyright owner controls the work, any use of it without the owner's permission is a **copyright infringement**. If you publish, perform, or otherwise

copyright infringement includes any use of an original work without the owner's permission

---

[8.] L Shrieves "Restaurants wish customers a happy birthday" *Knight-Ridder Tribune* (March 6, 2001) <www.stater.kent.edu/kentertainment/food/article.asp?ID=9>.

[9.] The name derives from the French *droits moraux*, which is better understood as a "personal right."

[10.] *Snow v Eaton Centre Ltd* (1982) 70 CPR (2d) 105 (Ont HCJ).

ETHICAL PERSPECTIVE 16.1

Gnass v Cité d'Alma [1977] JQ No 2 (Que CA)[11]

The town of Alma was doing a spring cleaning. The cleanup crew decided to throw out a number of public sculptures that had deteriorated over the years due to neglect and vandalism. For some reason, the crew decided to dump the sculptures in a nearby river. When the artist, Gnass, heard what happened, he commenced a lawsuit against the city.

The court held that the relocation of the statues to the bottom of the river did not interfere with Gnass's moral rights and therefore dismissed his claim. According to the court, the reputation of the artist could not be said to suffer simply because his works were out of sight and out of mind.

Questions for Discussion

1. Did Cité d'Alma interfere with Gnass's right to integrity?
2. In your view, is it ever morally permissible to destroy art?
3. What relationship, if any, exists between an artist's moral rights and the ethics of preserving or destroying art?

---

copy my work without authorization, you are probably infringing my copyright. However, this is not always the case. Sometimes, an act done in private is not considered an infringement. Since copyright includes a right of public performance, the law permits you to engage in a private performance of my material without running afoul of the law. For example, you are legally permitted to sing *Happy Birthday* in your basement at your son's birthday party. The same would not be true if his birthday party is being broadcast on national television. Unless you pay a licensing fee to perform the song in public, you are infringing copyright.

> copyright protects not merely whole works but also substantial parts of a work

The law of copyright protects not merely whole works but also substantial parts of a work. The notion of a *substantial part* is as much a qualitative judgment as it is a quantitative one. The general principle is that copyright owners cannot protect every particle of a work, where the taking of that piece would not undermine the overall value of the work. For example, borrowing 60 lines of code in a software routine that consists of 14 000 lines was held not to infringe copyright.[12] On the other hand, taking just a few bars from the refrain of a pop song may be substantial. This has become a difficult issue given the recent interest in digital sampling coinciding with the commercial success of house, hip hop, and rap music.[13] Courts consider a number of factors, including: (i) whether the part taken is distinctive, (ii) whether the taking would significantly impair the incentive for similarly placed authors, (iii) whether the author's ability to exploit the copyright has been substantially affected, (iv) whether the taker is unjustly enriched at the author's expense, and (v) whether the two works compete in the same market.[14] Figure 16.4 outlines examples of copyright infringement.

[11.] Discussed in D Vaver "Authors' moral rights in Canada" (1983) 14 *Intl Rev of Industrial Property and Copyright Law* 329.

[12.] *Delrina Corp v Triolet Systems Inc* (1993) 47 CPR (3d) 1 (Ont Gen Div). This decision was not based merely on the actual percentage copied but also on the fact that "their extent was so slight, and their effect so small, as to render the taking perfectly immaterial."

[13.] *Grand Upright Music Ltd v Warner Bros Records* 780 FSupp 182 (DNY 1991); *Jarvis v A&M Records* 827 F Supp 282 (DNJ 1993).

[14.] D Vaver *Intellectual Property* (1997).

FIGURE 16.4   Examples of Copyright Infringement

Infringement	Not Infringement
reprinting an article without the copyright owner's permission	quoting a few lines of the article in a research paper (fair dealing)
playing records at a dance without the copyright owners' permission	playing records at home
giving a public performance of a modern play without permission	giving a public performance of a play by Shakespeare (no copyright exists—public domain)
photocopying articles for a class of students without permission	obtaining permission from the author and paying a fee to them (if requested) to use an article
taping your favourite band at a music concert without permission	borrowing a musical tape from a friend to copy onto a blank tape for private use (a royalty payment to the owner of the song rights has been paid when the blank tape is purchased)

Source: Industry Canada *A Guide to Copyrights* (2000) at 6.

Licensing Schemes

A number of licensing schemes have been developed to allow people to use copyrighted material without having to seek permission while, at the same time, providing compensation to the copyright owner for use of the material. For example, it is now permissible in Canada to make a copy of a musical recording for private use without seeking authorization (such as copying a recently purchased CD onto cassette to listen in your car). This is made possible by a blank audio recording media levy. Instead of trying to stop private copying, a compensation scheme transfers a percentage of revenue from the sale of blank recordable media back to the copyright owners through *copyright collectives*. **Copyright collectives** are organizations that administer certain rights granted by the copyright system on behalf of copyright owners, who are members of the collective. In the case of the audio recording media levy, the Canadian Private Copying Collective is responsible for collecting the levy. The monies collected are ultimately redistributed to performing artists, composers and lyricists, music publishers, and record companies through their own collectives, such as the Society of Composers, Authors and Music Publishers of Canada (SOCAN). Note that the same system does not currently apply to video recordings. Making a copy of a video without permission is therefore a copyright infringement.

copyright collectives are organizations that administer certain rights granted by the copyright system on behalf of copyright owners who are members of the collective

The Right to Use Another's Works

Intellectual property aims to balance the rights of a copyright owner against the public interest. Therefore, copyright law provides a number of broad exemptions. For example, music may be performed without permission or licence at an event held for an educational or charitable object, or any activity incidental to it.[15]

copyright law provides a number of broad exemptions

[15.] *CAPAC v Kiwanis Club of West Toronto* [1953] 2 SCR 111.

Likewise, what might otherwise amount to a copyright infringement is often excused where a person has good cause to deal with the material as a matter of public interest.

fair dealing involves the legitimate use of a work for private study, research, criticism, review, or news reporting

The most well-known exemption, and the one that is most important to knowledge-based businesses, is *fair dealing*. **Fair dealing** involves the legitimate use of a work for private study, research, criticism, review, or news reporting. For it to be considered fair, the person dealing with the work must provide proper attribution to the source and the author. Drawing a bright line between fair dealing and infringement is not always possible and is a matter that is ultimately determined by a court. Note that the concept of fair dealing in research and private study is often understood in the context of personal use. Here, one cannot copy for another's purpose. For example, I may copy fairly for my own private study, as may my students for their own private study. However, I cannot copy for my students, nor they for me. The same would hold true in a business context. Knowledge-based businesses often need to copy works for internal research. Risk managers should be careful about the means of disseminating such copyrighted materials within the company and to clients, even if those materials are being used exclusively for research.

Trademarks

trademarks protect external information-based assets, such as the image and reputation of the business

Copyright is meant to protect the internal information-based assets of a business. Trademarks, on the other hand, protect external information-based assets, such as the image and reputation of the business, its brand recognition, and the goodwill that it has developed.

Why Trademark Law Is Important to Knowledge-Based Businesses

the design, marketing, and protection of trademarks are often as important to a business as the products or services they represent

The success of a business frequently depends on how the public perceives its products or services. The fact that a business may offer the best product or the finest service is often irrelevant. If your competitor has a stronger market presence, and its products or services are more easily distinguished from the rest, your business could be in trouble. It is well known that consumers are inclined to choose products or services with familiar names or symbols, especially where those names and symbols are trusted as reliable. In fact, the design, marketing, and protection of trade names, trademarks, logos, and package designs are often as important to a business as the products or services they represent. As one intellectual property scholar put it, "Advertisers spend much money associating their marks with imagery designed to encourage impulse buying. Before seeing a Coke dispenser, one may not have been thirsty; but the product temporarily satisfies the craving—until one sees the mark again. Indeed, to consume Coke may really be to consume that mark rather than the drink. The mark serves to validate the consumer's position in society as a member of a privileged class: one who can afford the lifestyle the mark has come to symbolize."[16]

trademark law protects businesses that invest in brands and similar forms of corporate identity

a **trademark** is a word, symbol, or design that is used to distinguish one person's goods or services from another's in the marketplace

Trademark law is meant to protect businesses that invest in brands and similar forms of corporate identification. A **trademark** is a word, symbol, or design that is used to distinguish one person's goods or services from another's in the marketplace. Like other forms of intellectual property, trademarks can be sold, licensed, or otherwise exploited for profit. This is a fundamental premise of franchising and other business structures. In fact, obtaining a trademark is a prerequisite to franchising a business. But trademark law does not entitle the owner or licensee of the mark to exclusive use in the same way that copyright

---

[16.] D Vaver *Intellectual Property* (1997) at 176.

and patent do. For example, the law cannot stop me from using the word "Coke" in this sentence. What the law does prevent a business from doing is adopting a similar mark or name for its own purposes. If your business were to do so—even inadvertently—it could be liable.

Passing-Off

A business is not required to register its trademarks. By using its name or mark for a certain length of time, the business will be able to establish ownership at common law. However, businesses must be extremely careful not to use a name or mark that is already in use by another business. Representing your business, goods, or services as someone else's through a confusingly similar mark or name could give rise to the common law tort of **passing-off**. To succeed under this cause of action, the business claiming that its mark or name has been illegitimately used must prove three things: (i) that the business had established a name, mark, or logo coinciding with its reputation or goodwill, (ii) that the impostor represented itself in a manner that resulted in confusion between the two enterprises, and (iii) that the established business suffered or is likely to suffer harm. Is there passing-off in You Be the Judge 16.1?

passing-off occurs when one person represents its business, goods, or services as someone else's through a confusingly similar mark or name

YOU BE THE JUDGE 16.1

Trademark and Passing-Off[17]

After conducting thorough market research of its candy competitors, the maker of Smarties discovers a small candy maker merchandising a very similar product, which it called Smoothies. Although the smaller company uses noticeably superior chocolate (hence its choice of names), the candy-coated shells are identical in colour, though slightly smaller in size, and the packaging appears quite similar to the untrained eye. The maker of Smarties sues. The Smoothies people reply with the argument that the two names look and sound completely different and their dictionary meanings are entirely unrelated.

Questions for Discussion

1. Do you think that the general public might be confused between the two candies? Why?
2. Must the trade names look or sound alike to cause confusion in the marketplace? Provide examples to support your position.

Registering a Trademark

Knowledge-based businesses do not usually leave matters to the common law doctrine of passing-off. They usually register their names and marks. As with copyright registration, trademark registration is not absolute proof of ownership, but it does provide the registrant with certain advantages. In the case of a dispute, the fact that a trademark has been registered will shift the onus of proving ownership in the use of the mark to the challenger. Since businesses often engage in lengthy and expensive fights over the use of names and marks, a prudent risk manager will register all variations on the names and marks used to represent its goods and services in the marketplace. By registering the name or mark, your company is protected across Canada for 15 years (and can be renewed indefinitely). An unregistered mark is much narrower in terms of the scope of protection since the doctrine of passing-off extends only to the locality of the company's reputation.

trademark registration is not absolute proof of ownership, but it provides the registrant with certain advantages

Three basic categories of marks can be registered: *ordinary marks*, *certification marks*, and *distinguishing guises*.

17. *Rowntree Co v Paulin Chambers Co* [1968] SCR 134.

ordinary marks are words or symbols that distinguish the goods or services of your business

- **Ordinary marks** are words, symbols, or designs that distinguish the goods or services of your business. Sometimes, the words are names (for example, Tom's House of Pizza® in Figure 16.5) and other times slogans (for example, "Pizza Made to Perfection"™).

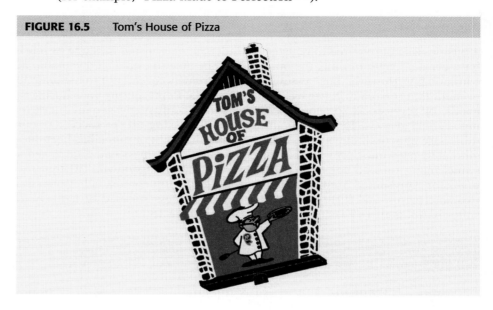

FIGURE 16.5   Tom's House of Pizza

certification marks identify goods or services that meet a standard set by a governing organization

distinguishing guises identify the unique shape of a product or its package

- **Certification marks** identify goods or services that meet a standard set by a governing organization (for example, "Recognized by the Canadian Dental Association").
- **Distinguishing guises** identify the unique shape of a product or its package.

Canada's *Trade-Mark Act* does not specifically require or prohibit the use of symbols such as ® (registered trademark) or ™ (unregistered trademark).[18] Still, businesses ought to use these symbols appropriately, especially if that use might find its way into another jurisdiction. A misleading use of the mark may not be prohibited in Canada (such as labelling ® on an unregistered mark), but it is prohibited in other jurisdictions, including the United States.

Trademark Infringement

A successful registration gives the owner a number of rights. Trademark law is meant to protect the owner against infringements of those rights.

a knock-off is an item for sale that looks very much like a product made by the trademark holder and is represented by an exactly similar mark but is usually of inferior quality

- The first and most obvious kind of infringement occurs when an exact imitation of the trademark is used without permission. A typical example is the *knock-off*. A **knock-off** is an item for sale that looks very much like a product made by the trademark holder and is represented by a similar mark. It is usually of inferior quality.
- A second kind of infringement occurs not through imitation, but when some other mark has the effect of confusing consumers. Often such infringements involve similar words, phrases, or symbols.

[18.] *Trade-Mark Act*, RSC 1985, c T-13 (Can).

- A third kind of infringement is known as *trademark dilution*. **Trademark dilution** occurs when a mark that is used in a non-confusing manner has the effect of sullying another trademark's image or somehow diminishing the value of its goodwill. According to the owner of the trademark for Perrier mineral water, this occurred when a Canadian company started selling a spoof known as Pierre Eh!. The court agreed.[19]

- A fourth kind of infringement sometimes occurs when a foreign party imports an authentically branded product (*not* a knock-off) into Canada as though it were the authorized Canadian distributor. Where the Canadian distributor holds a registered trademark for the product in Canada, the foreign party will usually have to seek permission to import the product even if it holds the trademark in other jurisdictions.

Trademark infringement gives rise to a number of legal remedies.

- Typically, the trademark holder will claim that the illegitimate use of the trademark injured its reputation, thus depreciating the value of its goodwill. When such a claim can be made out, the trademark holder is entitled to *damages*. This remedy will be applied in the same manner as it is in tort law.

- Sometimes the trademark holder does not suffer damages, but claims that the trademark infringer has been unjustly enriched through the illegitimate use of the mark. If a profit has been earned as a result of the infringement, the court may order an *accounting of profits*, requiring the infringer to transfer profits made through the use of the mark to the trademark holder.

- One of the more common and most important remedies sought by trademark holders is an *injunction*. When an injunction is appropriate, the court will make an order restraining the infringer from continuing to do business in a manner that involves the illegitimate use of the mark.

- Sometimes the infringing party is ordered to *deliver up* the infringing materials—turn over goods bearing the mark to the trademark holder or to otherwise dispose of them.

> trademark dilution occurs when a mark that is used in a non-confusing manner has the effect of sullying another trademark's image or somehow diminishing the value of its goodwill

> remedies available for trademark infringement include damages, accounting of profits, injunction, and delivering up

Patents

Many inventors believe that the chief value of a *patent* is that it gives them the time needed to develop and market their ideas. A **patent** grants a monopoly, allowing the inventor to exclude others from making, using, or selling the invention for a period of 20 years from the date of application.

Why the Patent System is Crucial to Knowledge-Based Businesses

From the inventor's perspective, patents provide an incentive for research and development. With patent protection, inventors can be confident that the time and money spent on creating new products will not be undermined by speedy copy-cat manufacturers trying to take advantage of inventions. It also allows inventors to profit by having the exclusive right to sell or license their inventions. In the knowledge-based economy, it also allows inventors to use their inventions as assets when trying to arrange corporate financing.

> patents grant a monopoly to inventors, allowing them to exclude others from making, using or selling their inventions for a period of 20 years from the date of application

> patents provide an incentive for research and development

[19.] *Source Perrier SA v Fira-Less Marketing Co* [1983] 2 FC 18 (TD).

the patent system plays a pivotal role in the way that information and knowledge are shared

The *patent system* is also crucial to business and to the broader public interest. Because a clear description of the invention must be filed in a public repository before a patent is granted, the patent system plays a pivotal role in the way that information and knowledge are shared. The Patent Office (and its Web site) is a critical resource not only for other inventors but also for businesses, researchers, academics, journalists, and others interested in keeping up with technological development. Given the breath-taking pace of innovation, knowledge-based businesses must regularly monitor the state of the art. Failing to do so may waste time and money. According to recent statistics, roughly 10 percent of all research and development in Canada results in duplicating patented technologies.[20] Businesses should therefore develop the habit of searching patent literature before developing new technologies.

Patentability

Not just any idea can be patented. Patent law protects inventions, which are defined in the *Patent Act* as an "art, process, machine, manufacture or composition of matter."[21] The Act also allows patents for new and useful "improvements" of existing inventions. In fact, 90 percent of patents granted in Canada are for such improvements.[22] Note that "useful" here does not mean that the invention must achieve some public benefit. It has always been thought that it is up to the market, not the Patent Office, to determine what inventions are useful.[23] Given that definition, a patentable invention may come in a number of forms, as Figure 16.6 shows.

FIGURE 16.6	Forms of Patentable Inventions
Form	Example
product	a knife
composition	chemicals that remove rust from knife blades
apparatus	a machine that makes knife handles
process	a method of assembling knives

Source: Industry Canada *A Guide to Patents* (2000) at 3.

a patent is the embodiment of an idea

Think of a patent as the *embodiment of an idea*. Just as one cannot copyright an idea but only its expression, one cannot patent a newly discovered natural law, scientific principle, or abstract theory. Other matters are unpatentable on the basis of public policy. For example, one cannot patent a medical treatment, although one can patent a drug used for the treatment of a disease. It is also said that computer programs and business methods are unpatentable, but recently, the courts have allowed them through indirect means.

[20.] Industry Canada *A Guide to Patents* (2000) at 15.

[21.] *Patent Act*, RSC 1985, c P-4; D Vaver *Intellectual Property* (1997) at 119.

[22.] Industry Canada *A Guide to Patents* (2000) at 3.

[23.] For example, patents continue to be granted for more lethal weapons. This approach was reinforced by Parliament in 1994 when it removed the requirement that inventions have *no illicit object in view*: *Patent Act*, RSC 1985 c P-4, s 27(3).

A patent is available only if it can be demonstrated that the proposed invention is:

- novel
- ingenious
- useful

Novelty

The **novelty** criterion does not mean that an inventor must prove that no one else has ever come up with the idea or built a similar product. It is enough to satisfy the *non-disclosure requirement*. One must be able to show that the invention had not previously been disclosed and become known, or otherwise made available, to the public. Understanding the novelty requirement as a public disclosure issue is very important to knowledge-based businesses. Even if your invention is novel in that it was the first of its kind in the world, if you allow your invention to become available to the public before your patent application, this could jeopardize its patentability.[24] Typical examples of such disclosures are: (i) delivering a presentation about the invention at a conference or trade show, (ii) displaying the invention in a public place, or (iii) showing the invention to someone without requiring confidentiality.

The novelty rule makes it crucial for business managers to institute safeguards against premature disclosure of products under development. Although some legal mechanisms exist to protect *trade secrets*, prudent managers prevent the risk of untimely disclosure through confidentiality clauses in employment contracts, and developing and distributing company policy on trade secrets.

It is also important for businesses to file a patent application as soon as the invention is complete. As a result of recent changes to the Act, if your business is working on a new invention, but a speedier competitor files it at the Patent Office before you do, your invention will not be seen as novel—even if you invented it first. This system has become known as a *first-to-file* (as opposed to a *first-to-invent*) system. Although a business must file a patent application before anyone else does, it must be careful to not file before the invention is complete. If the product is filed while still in the development stage, the application runs the risk of omitting key features, which may ultimately require a re-application. Besides the time lost in the process, an incomplete application creates the possibility that someone else will seek to patent a similar invention before your re-application is completed.

Ingenuity

The second requirement is that the invention or improvement must be *ingenious*. **Ingenuity** means that the item for which a patent is sought would not have been immediately obvious to people fluent in similar technologies. It must be capable of provoking a "Wow, why didn't I think of that!" reaction from other designers in the field. Note that the ingenuity requirement does not entail complexity. Simple ideas can be non-obvious. After all, someone invented the spoon straw. The spoon straw shown in Figure 16.7 (p. 366) illustrates the difference between ingenuity and complexity. At the same time, the simplicity of such an invention highlights the problem of hindsight. It is a feature of many great inventions that they appear obvious after their discovery. Inventors seeking patents must therefore think very carefully about how to present their work as a non-obvious improvement of the current state of the art.

Utility

The very definition of an invention implies that it serves some practical purpose. Product development merely for the sake of scientific curiosity is

novelty depends upon a non-disclosure requirement

prudent managers pre-empt the risk of untimely disclosure

the patent system is a first-to-file system

ingenuity means that the item for which a patent is sought would not have been obvious to people fluent in similar technologies

---

24. In Canada, there is a one-year grace period before filing during which a business can disclose: *Patent Act*, RSC 1985, c P-14 s 28(1).

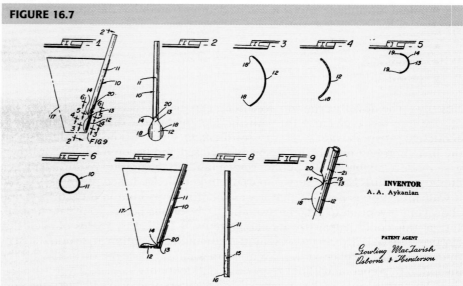

FIGURE 16.7

Patent CA 901307: Combination Drinking Straw and Spoon

Not all patents stem from complex ideas. Indeed many of the most ingenious inventions result from a relatively unsophisticated leap of logic that was non-obvious at the time of conception. The Spoon-Straw illustrates how two simple yet effective snips of plastic can result in significant utility. Once the market need was determined, the inventor quickly assembled the above drawing on the plane ride home from his meeting with the Coca-Cola corporation.

a product cannot be patented if it has no useful function

insufficient. If the product has no useful function or if it simply does not work, it cannot be patented. For example, if a manufacturing process has the effect of ruining the very items it is said to produce, it will be unpatentable.[25] The utility requirement does not preclude the patenting of a wasteful, unsafe, primitive, or commercially useless product.[26] As we have seen, it is up to the market and not the Patent Office to determine the value of the invention.

Exploiting a Patent

there are several ways of profiting from a patent

Once a patent is obtained, its owner must engage in a series of business decisions. What is the best means of profiting from this asset? There are usually several options.

- In some cases, the patent owner will choose to develop and market the product. By doing so, the owner retains full control over the invention. This choice allows the owner to select the image and branding of the product, its availability in the marketplace, pricing, profit margins, and so on. Retaining full control of the products also means assuming all of the risks. Even after years of research and development during the patenting process, it is possible to miscalculate what will happen in the market.

- If the owner of a patent is unable or unwilling to assume the risk, another option is licensing the patent, thereby permitting other businesses to bring the product to the market in exchange for royalties. Licensing schemes allow smaller businesses with information-based assets to cre-

---

[25.] *TRW Inc v Walbar of Canada Inc* (1991) 39 CPR (3d) 176 (FC CA).

[26.] D Vaver *Intellectual Property* (1997) at 138.

ate capital without large investments or expenditures. They can be granted in any jurisdiction where a patent is held.

■ The owner may choose to sell the patent outright. Although this usually requires assigning all rights as inventor, the owner receives in return a lump sum without incurring any risk in the marketplace. Sometimes it is difficult to know how to determine the value of the patent, especially when the product has not yet been to market. More recently, an inventory of information-based assets, including patentable product ideas, can be leveraged to raise capital for a growing company with few tangible assets.

Patent Infringement

A successful patent registration gives the registrant a number of rights, most notably, the exclusive right of "making, constructing and using the invention and selling it to others to be used."[27] Although these rights are generally given a wide range of application, there are limits. As we have seen, the patent system aims to balance private rights with the public interest. Even if you hold a patent, you cannot prevent me from building an exact replica of your machine for my own private research, as long as I am not exploiting your invention for profit. However, most companies in the business of improving existing inventions usually enter into mutually beneficial agreements with the original patent holder, rather than working secretly on them without the patent holder's knowledge and consent.

remedies exist for patent infringement

Similar to copyright and trademark, patent infringement gives rise to a number of legal remedies.

■ Typically, the patent holder will claim that the illegitimate use or sale results in damages. Again, this remedy will be applied in the same manner as it is in tort law.

■ Sometimes, the patent holder does not suffer damages directly but claims that the infringer has been unjustly enriched through the illegitimate use of the patented object or process. If there has been a profit as a result of the infringement, the court may order an accounting of profits, requiring the infringer to transfer profits made through the use of the patent to the patent holder.

■ Another common remedy is injunctive relief. When an injunction is successfully sought, the court will order the infringer to stop doing business in a way that interferes with the patent holder's rights.

The Right to Use Another's Patent

I have a right to use your patented invention for experimental purposes or other non-commercial uses. Like the fair dealings doctrine in copyright law, the lines are not always clear, and often the litigation process is required to balance private rights against the public interest. Similarly, although it is usually an infringement to make or construct a patented item, users have the right to repair and, in some cases, modify them. Although excessive modification might approach reconstruction, there is a public interest in permitting repairs if they conserve resources. There are other circumstances in which users have the right to use a patented product. For example, to obtain governmental approval, a patented product may be used when necessary for public health or safety reasons.[28]

---

27. *Patent Act*, RSC 1985, c P-14, s 42.

Industrial Designs and Integrated Circuit Topographies

Although the traditional forms of intellectual property are copyright, trademark, and patents, Canada protects two other distinct forms of intellectual property: *industrial designs* and *integrated circuit topographies*.

Industrial Designs

industrial design is the features of shape, configuration, pattern, or ornament applied to a finished article made by hand, tool, or machine

The success of a manufactured product often depends not only on its usefulness but also on its visual appeal. Because a distinctive product can be considered an intellectual asset, some manufacturers invest time and effort in the look of their product. An **industrial design** is the features of shape, configuration, pattern, or ornament applied to a finished article made by hand, tool, or machine. Because the *Industrial Design Act* seeks to protect only the visual appeal of an object, you will not be permitted to register designs that are purely functional in nature, or designs that have no fixed appearance or are not clearly visible, such as those hidden from view.[28] Nor can you register the use of particular materials or colours. Although the use of particular materials or colours will certainly enhance the visual appeal of an object, no one is entitled to a monopoly on these alone. In some cases, a unique pattern that is created through the arrangement of certain contrasting tones will qualify.

it is useful to mark all registered designs with the proprietor's name and a ⒟

Unlike copyright and trademark, an industrial design is protected only if it is registered. The Act protects registered original designs for up to 10 years by preventing others from making, importing for trade or business, renting, or selling the design. Once the 10-year term has expired, the design falls into the public domain, and anyone is free to make, rent, import, or sell it. It is useful to mark all registered designs with the proprietor's name and a ⒟. Doing so will entitle the registrant to seek monetary damage awards from anyone who infringes the design. A failure to mark the design will limit the remedy to an injunction, forbidding the offending party from continuing use of the design. Registrants must enforce their rights within three years of the alleged infringement.

knowledge-based businesses can commercially exploit industrial designs in several ways

As with other forms of intellectual property, knowledge-based businesses can commercially exploit industrial designs in several ways. Design rights can be assigned to others in exchange for cash, merchandise, or credit. They can also be licensed. The advantage of licensing the design is that ownership of the design is retained. As well, an entrepreneurial designer may license the design to a number of parties, for example, by geographic region to give the licensee exclusive rights to market the design within that region, or across Canada but for different periods of time.

Integrated Circuit Topographies

the *Integrated Circuit Topography Act* makes it illegal to copy registered topographies

With the growing importance of communications and information technologies, semiconductor integrated circuits (or *microchips*) have been given special protection. Microchips are constructed from a number of layers of semiconductors, metals, insulators, and other materials. In Canada, the *Integrated Circuit Topography Act* protects the three-dimensional configuration of these layers by making it illegal to copy registered topographies.[29] Such topographies, once registered, are protected even if they have not been physically embodied in a product. To be protected, a topography must qualify as original. This means that the topography must have been developed through the

---

[28.] *Industrial Design Act*, RSC 1985, c I-8 (Can).

[29.] *Integrated Circuit Topography Act*, SC 1990, c 37 (Can).

application of intellectual effort rather than the mere reproduction of an existing topography. Owners of registered topographies enjoy the right to exclude others from: (i) reproducing the topography or a substantial part of it, (ii) manufacturing a microchip that incorporates the topography, and (iii) importing, selling, leasing, or otherwise distributing a chip that embodies the topography.

However, a registered owner cannot prevent others from copying a registered topography for research and other non-commercial uses. In some cases, copying is allowed for *reverse engineering*. **Reverse engineering** is the process of disassembling and reassembling an integrated circuit to understand how it was built. Reverse engineering is allowed when its purpose is to design a new topography that meets the originality criterion set out in the Act. Allowing reverse engineering for this purpose is an attempt to balance intellectual property rights against the competing demands of the marketplace for the development of new products.

> reverse engineering is the process of disassembling and reassembling an integrated circuit to understand how it was built

A registered topography provides protection for 10 years within Canada. As with other forms of intellectual property, a prudent manager will ensure that all topographies embodied in products associated with its businesses are registered in every country where those products will be manufactured, sold, or otherwise marketed. Managers should also mark products containing registered topographies with the appropriate title. The failure to mark products containing a registered chip incurs the risk of allowing a successful defence. A person who infringes the rights of the owner is not liable if they had no knowledge of the registration of the topography.

TRADE SECRETS AND CONFIDENTIAL INFORMATION

Businesses should use intellectual property law to protect their information-based assets. However, they should also know that there are other ways of legally protecting business-related information.

The easiest, but most risky, means is a *trade secret*. One creates a **trade secret** simply by using legal means to keep the information-based asset a secret until it is sold. That often involves exacting promises of secrecy from employees and independent contractors in their employment contracts and contracts for services. Not surprisingly, one runs certain risks in doing this.

> a trade secret uses legal means to keep the information-based asset a secret until it is sold

- Even if you create such obligations contractually, it is possible for your employees and independent contractors (or anyone they might tell) to register your trade secret as though it were their own intellectual property. Despite your ability to prove that those information-based assets belong to you, you will still be forced to spend time and energy fighting to get back what was yours.

- Even if your employees and independent contractors are completely trustworthy, protecting information-based assets exclusively by way of trade secrets runs the risk that someone else might independently create the subject matter of the trade secret. If that happens, there is nothing to prevent that person from registering it as intellectual property or otherwise making it available to the public.

Although it is risky to use trade secrets as the *sole* means of protecting information-based assets, that does not mean that trade secrets lack utility. It is always a good idea to use contracts and other legal means of creating an air of secrecy around the research and development of new products.

breach of confidence occurs when a person who has been entrusted with confidential information uses that information improperly

Another way to protect business-related information is to ensure that it is *confidential information*. The advantage of being able to prove that someone has disclosed your confidential information is that you can sue for *breach of confidence*. A **breach of confidence** occurs when a person who has been entrusted with confidential information uses that information improperly. The plaintiff must prove: (i) that the information in question was of a confidential nature, (ii) that it was disclosed to the defendant in circumstances creating an obligation of confidence, and (iii) that its unauthorized use was detrimental.

The courts recognize that information may be confidential for a variety of reasons. Very often, however, it is difficult to decide whether knowledge acquired in the course of employment is confidential or merely common know-how. In situations of doubt, an employer should insert a detailed confidentiality provision into an employee's contract. In any event, to prove that information is confidential in nature, one must be able to demonstrate that the information was not generally known to a substantial number of people.

There is no specific test to determine whether information is known to a substantial number of people. A judge will assess all of the facts to determine whether information can still be considered confidential despite some degree of disclosure. In some cases, an idea, formula, or process may be confidential, even if parts of it are generally known to a substantial number of people, as long as it is original as a whole. With respect to the confidentiality requirement, it is most easily met by telling all recipients of the information that it is secret and must not be disclosed. However, it is usually sufficient if the information is disclosed under circumstances that imply secrecy; for instance, if you accidentally leave your diary on my office desk, or attach a notice at the top of a document clearly indicating that it is confidential. The final requirement entails proof that a disclosure of the information is detrimental to the interests of the person claiming confidentiality. Here, one need not prove a direct financial loss. It is sufficient to prove that the secret was disclosed against that person's wishes.[30] Concept Summary 16.1 reviews these requirements.

Concept Summary 16.1

Three Requirements of Confidential Information

The information must not be generally known to the public.
The information must have been imparted on a confidential basis.
Disclosure of the information is detrimental to the person claiming confidentiality.

Like the protections afforded by the law of intellectual property, the cause of action for breach of confidence supports a broad range of remedies, including injunctions, delivering-up, an account of profits, and compensatory damages.

[30.] *Cadbury Schweppes Inc v FBI Foods Ltd* (1999) 167 DLR (4th) 577 (SCC).

Chapter Summary

Information is distinguished from tangible commodities because it can be inexpensively reproduced, distributed, and universally possessed. Until recently, most businesses have focused on selling tangible commodities that are exclusively possessed by their customers. Traditionally, the value of tangible goods and services was determined in the market according to their natural scarcity. Information-based assets, however, require an artificial scarcity. This is achieved through intellectual property law.

Knowledge-based businesses use human capital to create internal information-based assets such as business plans, inventions, customer lists, data processing systems, and other tools that play an important role in the new economy. This invisible capital in turn generates the external information-based assets of a business—its brand recognition, goodwill, and reputation.

Intellectual property seeks to balance private rights and the public interest through an incentive system for creators and entrepreneurs, granting time-limited monopolies on various intellectual constructs, their expression, and their functionality. In addition to moral rights, authors are awarded a copyright in their works allowing them to prevent unauthorized copying and distribution. Exceptions are carved out for fair dealing and works that have fallen into the public domain. A copyright may be bought, sold, licensed, or given away. Moral rights may not be sold, but they may be indefinitely waived. To qualify for protection, a work must be original, in fixed form, and created in a copyright convention member state.

The law of trademarks is especially important to a business since its success often depends on how consumers perceive its particular products and services. Trademark owners are protected against competitors who try to confuse consumers through an illegitimate use of the mark, thereby diluting its value. Businesses are encouraged to register trademarks to increase the geographic range of their trademark. Unlike copyrights, registered trademarks do not automatically apply to countries that have intellectual property agreements with Canada.

The granting of a patent for an invention allows the inventor to exclude others from making, using, or selling the invention for a period of 20 years. Unlike trademarks, patents cannot be renewed. The patent system plays an important role in encouraging innovation, while ensuring the sharing of information and knowledge between businesses. Patent law protects original inventions and improvements to already existing inventions. Much like the fair dealing doctrine in copyright law, the public retains the right to use patents for experimental and non-commercial purposes.

Industrial design law protects the distinctive visual appeal of manufactured articles. Original designs are protected for up to 10 years by preventing others from making, importing for trade or business, renting, or selling the design. After 10 years, the design falls into the public domain. Like the patent system, the first party to file successfully will be the first to register, regardless of who came up with the design first. In the case of infringement, failure to register an industrial design limits its proprietor to an injunction rather than monetary damages.

Integrated circuit topographies may be registered for protection in Canada if they are original. Registered owners, however, cannot prevent others from copying the topography for research or for reverse engineering, a process of disassembling and reassembling an integrated circuit to understand how it was built. Unlike patents and industrial designs, the registration process does not require an examination for originality, and is much more expedient. Successful registration provides protection for 10 years within Canada.

Businesses further protect their information by using trade secrets and confidential information covenants. In determining the confidentiality of the information, courts will consider the degree to which the information had been disclosed to the public and the extent of the alleged infringer's duty of confidentiality.

Review Questions

1. Distinguish between "exclusive possession" and "universal possession," and give an example of each.

2. How does the scarcity of an asset affect its value? How can a prudent business manager increase the value of information-based assets?

3. Distinguish between internal and external information-based assets, and give an example of each.

4. Describe four ways a business can generate and capitalize on information-based assets?

5. What are the role and purpose of intellectual property law?

6. Does copyright law protect ideas? Explain.

7. What are the requirements for copyright protection? Expand on each requirement, and provide an example.

8. Who owns the copyright in a work created in the course of employment? How might a prudent business manager ensure that the employer is recognized as the copyright holder?

9. Explain the concept of "moral rights." How can a prudent

business manager ensure that these rights will not conflict with copyrights held by the business?

10. Must a copyright be registered to be enforceable? Why?

11. List three kinds of trademark, and give an example of each.

12. Describe three types of trademark infringement.

13. What is "passing-off"? How is it relevant to trademark law?

14. Outline the elements that must be proved to succeed under an action for passing-off.

15. What legal remedies are available for trademark holders in a judicial finding of trademark infringement by another party?

16. Why should a business manager thoroughly search patent literature before developing new technologies?

17. Can any idea be patented?

18. Outline three ways a patent owner can exploit the patent for financial gain. Briefly discuss the advantages and disadvantages of each option.

19. Explain the purpose of the protection afforded to industrial designs. Is registration required?

20. What are two means by which businesses can protect business-related information? Outline the elements needed to succeed in an action for breach of confidence.

Cases and Problems

1. The Toronto Metropolitan University has started a copyright infringement action against its arch nemesis, Toronto College, for allegedly copying lecture notes prepared by one of its professors. Toronto College has responded by arguing that although their manual is substantially similar, this is because it was compiled from common materials rather than because it was a direct copy of the Toronto Metropolitan University manual. What is the *Copyright Act*'s originality requirement for literary works? Does the subject matter of the manual preclude it from protection under copyright law? How could Toronto College have avoided this lawsuit?

2. The Beautiful Boy Modelling School hired Keith to prepare commercial artwork for their company materials. Upon completion of the work, Keith invoiced the modelling school for $1600 and was promptly paid. Later, when he realized that the modelling school was using the artwork more extensively than he was originally led to believe, Keith sued the school and its president, Dan, for copyright infringement. Dan, who was not only beautiful but was also a lawyer, argued that Keith's allegation of copyright infringement fails because his contract did not contain any limitations on the use of the work by the modelling school. Moreover, Dan argued that common business practices establish that in the case of work for hire, the commercial artist assigns all copyrights to the employer unless explicit restrictions are included as part of the terms of employment. What factors can the courts consider in determining whether Dan has infringed Keith's copyright? How could Dan, as a prudent business manager, have avoided this situation?

3. Miko Ltd and Karuzaro Inc are both distributors of colouring books designed for anatomy students at the college level. These companies were previously close collaborators. However, they are now at odds over the similarity of their recent publications, which contain very similar line drawings of the human form. Karuzaro has brought an action for infringement of copyright on the basis that Miko's drawings are substantially similar. Miko claims that

the drawings are quite dissimilar, and that any similarity is due to the forms that the parties developed together as part of their earlier collaborations. What factors might the courts consider in investigating Karuzaro's allegation? Support your position.

4. Tal sold his famous sculpture, *Angst of a Bicycle Tire*, to the owners of a new downtown shopping mall for a substantial price. The owners installed the sculpture in the foyer of the mall to the delight of both Tal and mall patrons. Years later, the mall owners allowed one of its tenants to use the sculpture to promote a bicycle tire sale. As part of the promotion, some of the sculpture's tires were adorned with the tenant's corporate logo as well as details of the sale. Tal, who was not consulted, was outraged. He sued, calling for the restoration of his sculpture to its original form. On what basis, if any, have the mall owners infringed Tal's intellectual property rights? How could the mall owners have avoided this situation altogether? Explain your reasoning.

5. Jai, always an enterprising young person, decided to start up a business after graduating. His first product was an abridged version of government reports with which he was well acquainted through his course work and independent study. After a tip from an anonymous caller, the government sought a court order prohibiting Jai from continuing to make such abridged reports available for sale on the basis of copyright infringement. In his defence, Jai says that although he copied large portions of the original report, his abridged report constitutes fair dealing. Discuss Jai's legal argument. As a prudent business manager, how could Jai have better protected his product against infringement claims?

6. Mangecakes International has decided to bring a passing-off action against competitor Liz Kalmanson Desserts Ltd. Mangecakes is seeking to prevent Liz from selling a cream-filled chocolate biscuit that is similar in size, shape, and ingredients to its celebrated Mangecake. Liz markets her biscuits under the name Choco Liz. Both versions of the biscuits are sold in clear plastic wrapping and display their

trademarked logos on the bottom of the packaging. Although Liz primarily sells her biscuits to caterers, they are also available for public purchase in several of the gourmet food shops that also sell Mangecakes. You are a senior manager at Mangecakes charged with stopping Liz before it is too late for the Mangecake empire. Outline the elements you must establish for a successful passing-off action and briefly make your case.

7. Greenberg Intelligent Agent Technologies, a recent start-up business, has just released its first product offering: a software bot capable of storing, indexing, and searching voice-mail messages. The bot is being marketed under the mark MAK2112. You have been retained to advise the company on intellectual property concerns associated with its products. Briefly explain the importance of trademark protection. Would the mark more likely qualify as an ordinary mark or as a certification mark? What are the advantages of trademark registration?

8. Backside Health Corp, the manufacturer and retailer of a very successful home-exercise device called Buns of Fury, is distressed by the emergence of a competitor marketing a strikingly similar product named Ferocious Buttocks. The Ferocious Buttocks machine is sold at a lower price due to the substandard materials used in its construction. Backside Health wants to sue the competitor on the basis of trademark infringement. How should they characterize the alleged infringement? What remedies may be available? Briefly outline each remedy and discuss which are preferred.

9. Depass Industries has contracted your intellectual property consulting firm for assistance in patenting their latest discovery. The company claims to have invented a way to prevent ice cream from leaking out of the bottom of waffle sugar cones, a problem that has plagued both the industry and consumers for years. The Depass process involves inserting a small amount of heated caramel syrup into each cone just before adding ice cream. The caramel must be heated to 48°C and added at 1 ml of syrup per 18 cm^2 of cone surface area. By doing so, the caramel collects at the bottom of the cone and hardens, forming an impermeable layer. The process, while seemingly unique, is subject to opposition as to its patentability. Does Depass's discovery seem to be a patentable form of invention? What requirements must the process meet to be patentable? Explain each. Briefly discuss how Depass might wish to exploit the patent, should it be awarded.

10. Bornfreund Brothers Inc, once a harmonious and profitable company, has recently dissolved into two separate companies, each run by one of the brothers. The former company was in the business of manufacturing token-dispensing machines for use in video arcades and amusement centres. The younger brother, Jordan, was granted the company's prized international patent for the dispensing method in the break-up and now wants to sue his older brother, Marcus, for patent infringement. Whereas the old method involved counting each token, Marcus has developed a new process in which the tokens are dispensed by weight. Marcus's invention has not yet been awarded a Canadian patent. Jordan wants to "put that bum out of business." What legal remedies would be available to Jordan if he is successful in making out his case against his older, wiser, and sneakier brother?

11. Kate Confectionery Corp has spent the last 15 years developing, marketing, and selling octagonal lollipops. Now that the company is about to go public, Kate is very concerned with registering all proprietary aspects of the business to increase its valuation. Her partner has advised her to pursue an industrial design registration for the unique shape of her lollipops. On what basis are the lollipops registerable? What are the advantages of registration? What is the length of protection granted if the registration application is approved? Is the protection renewable? How might Kate wish to exploit her design rights?

12. Louis Saint Chicken has sued its closest competitor, Bistro Poultry, for misappropriation of trade secrets, and a former employee, Nicolette Lemar, for breach of confidence with regard to its secret dipping sauce. Nicolette, who worked for Louis as a supervisor in its sauce laboratory for the last seven years, was recently recruited as the vice-president in charge of research and development at Bistro. Subsequently, Bistro began to produce and sell a garlic chicken wing sauce suspiciously similar to Louis's own world-famous dipping sauce. Louis alleges that, during the course of her employment, Nicolette was exposed to trade secrets with respect to its formula for its chicken wing sauce. There was no contractual clause barring Nicolette from disclosing the ingredients of the sauce, nor from undertaking future employment within the industry. What must Louis prove to succeed in its claim against Nicolette? How can Louis Saint Chicken better protect itself against the occurrence of a similar incident in the future?

17   Electronic Commerce

CHAPTER OVERVIEW

Electronic Commerce Legislation
Canada's *Uniform Electronic Commerce Act*
Provincial Electronic Commerce Legislation

Contracting Online
Contract Formation
Automated Electronic Commerce
Authentication
Information Security

Domain Names

Internet Access Provider and Online Service Provider Liability
Jurisdiction
Online Intermediaries

Online Consumer Protection

OBJECTIVES

After completing this chapter, you should be able to:

1. Outline the general strategies adopted in electronic commerce legislation to ensure business certainty in the online environment.
2. Define functional equivalence and its role in electronic commerce legislation.
3. State the considerations involved to ensure successful contract formation in electronic commerce.
4. Discuss the contractual issues specific to automated electronic commerce and the legislative method for correcting keystroke errors.
5. Explain the importance of authentication in online business transactions.
6. Describe how public key cryptography can be used to create electronic signatures.
7. Outline the business problems arising from the domain name system.
8. Discuss the jurisdictional implications of transacting in a global medium and how to minimize exposure to liability online.
9. Describe how an online business can shield itself from intermediary liability.
10. Explain how consumer protection principles can be used to promote the reputation of a business, generate goodwill, and build trusting relationships.

Knowledge-based businesses can distribute their products through various technological channels. Therefore, they are well positioned to participate in *electronic commerce*. **Electronic commerce** refers to technology-mediated business transactions. These take place across a network and usually involve the transportation of goods, services, or information—either physically or digitally—from one place to another. It is tempting to think of the Internet when one thinks of electronic commerce, but the definition is actually much broader. It also includes, for instance, a transaction that occurs between a customer and an automated bank machine.

Electronic commerce has a number of benefits. Once a system is in place, transactions become easy and affordable. Technology allows a business to reach more customers, in more places. It allows contracts to be performed more quickly. And it can reduce the expenses associated with marketing products and creating contracts. However, electronic commerce also has its costs. One such cost is uncertainty.[1]

One significant source of uncertainty is the law. The basic rules of commercial law were developed many years ago, when people usually dealt face to face. Not surprisingly, those rules are often poorly suited to transactions that are conducted over a network. As a matter of risk management, a business that is involved in electronic commerce must be aware of potential problems. This chapter therefore examines how the law has responded to technological changes in the business world. We begin with a survey of recent legislation that regulates electronic commerce. We then discuss how enforceable contracts can be created electronically and explore some specific issues that can arise from electronic commerce, including the use of domain names and the possibility of imposing liability in Internet-related services. We conclude with an outline of the fundamental principles guiding consumer protection in the sometimes dangerous online environment.

electronic commerce refers to technology-mediated transactions

ELECTRONIC COMMERCE LEGISLATION

A defining feature of electronic commerce is that it is global—it allows business to be done around the world. It is therefore desirable to have consistent laws from place to place. If every jurisdiction had a different set of rules, it would be impossible to achieve certainty in the electronic business world. As a result, the United Nations Commission on International Trade Law (UNCITRAL) encouraged countries to create uniform legislation based on a single model—a Model Law on Electronic Commerce.[2] That model law is not really a law. It does not create rights, powers, obligations, or immunities. It merely provides a *model* for the creation of a consistent set of laws. Ultimately, it is up to each government to decide how much of the model to adopt. Note that the model law is not intended to create entirely new types of legal relationships. Instead, its goal is to remove barriers that technology may impose upon the creation of traditional commercial relationships.

Canada's *Uniform Electronic Commerce Act*

Because our Constitution states that commerce is generally a provincial matter, electronic commerce legislation has been enacted on a province-by-province

---

[1.] The effects of uncertainty have been felt in the marketplace. That became evident at the outset of the new millennium, when many of the promises of the so-called *dot-com revolution* were disappointed.

[2.] The United Nations Model Law on Electronic Commerce: <www.uncitral.org/en-index.htm>.

basis. Still, the co-ordination of these rules was inspired on a national level. The strategy was similar to the international approach. A special working group of the Uniform Law Conference of Canada created its own model law—the *Uniform Electronic Commerce Act* (*UECA*).[3] Like UNCITRAL's model law, *UECA* has no legal force, but it has formed the basis for most electronic commerce laws in Canada. Some provinces have adopted all of it; others have adopted specific parts. Because of its significance, we will examine *UECA*'s most important provisions in detail. In particular, we will consider:[4]

- its *scope*
- the role of *consent*
- the notion of a *functional equivalent*
- the rules pertaining to *electronic contracts*
- the rules pertaining to *sending and receiving electronic documents*
- the treatment of *government documents*

Scope

UECA has a broad scope. Rather than listing all of the transactions to which it applies, it lists those to which it does *not* apply. For instance, it follows UNCITRAL's model law by specifically excluding wills and dealings in land. Those sorts of arrangement are still governed by the traditional rules. The list of exclusions differs, however, between jurisdictions. To manage risk, it is therefore important for a business involved with electronic commerce to know which exclusions apply in every jurisdiction in which it does business.

Consent

UECA does *not* require a business to use or accept electronic documents. It is meant only to facilitate electronic commerce for those people who *choose* to engage in it. It is important to realize, however, that your consent may be express or implied. The courts may decide that you consented to use *UECA* if you behave in a way that supports that inference.

Functional Equivalence

As we saw in Chapters 5 and 14, some types of contract traditionally were enforceable only if they were in writing. That is still true. *UECA*, however, recognizes that the writing requirement can sometimes be satisfied through *functional equivalence*. **Functional equivalence** identifies the essential purpose of a traditional rule and indicates how that purpose can be accomplished electronically.

For example, some statutes that regulate the enforcement of contractual terms require certain documents to be signed. That signature is intended to demonstrate the signer's willingness to be bound by the terms. However, that same purpose may be achieved through the click of a mouse. For instance, a dialogue box may appear on a computer screen that contains a box that says, "I accept these terms." Clicking on that box may be the functional equivalent of signing a document.[5]

functional equivalence identifies the essential purpose of a traditional rule and indicates how that purpose can be accomplished electronically

[3.] The *Uniform Electronic Commerce Act* (*UECA*): <www.ulcc.ca/en/us/index.cfm?sec=1 &sub=1u1>.

[4.] J Gregory "The *Uniform Electronic Commerce Act*," *Lex Electronica* 6(1) printemps 2000; <www.lec-electronica.org.articles/v6-1/gregory.htm>.

[5.] There are many other examples. The essential function of writing is memory, which can also be satisfied by electronic information, as long as it is accessible for future reference.

Electronic Contracts

UECA does more than permit functional equivalents. It even allows transactions to be achieved, without human intervention, by computer programs. For instance, contracts may be created by shopping bots (as we saw in Business Law in Action 2.2) and other automated electronic devices.

Sending and Receiving Electronic Documents

UECA also facilitates electronic commerce by removing uncertainty about *where* and *when* a message is sent or received.

UECA contains provisions to determine where and when a message is sent or received

A message is deemed to be sent from the sender's place of business and received at the recipient's place of business.[6] Suppose that your place of business is in Alberta, but that you send a message through your Internet server in Manitoba, while you are travelling in the Yukon. It can plausibly be said that your message was sent from any one of three places. *UECA* therefore eliminates the uncertainty and promotes commerce by consistently choosing one of those possibilities.

a message is deemed to be sent from the sender's place of business and received at the recipient's place of business

UECA also contains clear rules that determine *when* a message is *sent* or *received*. A message is deemed to be *sent* when it leaves the sender's control. Consequently, once you push a button and can no longer stop the message from being sent, that message is considered sent, even if it is never received. A message is deemed *received* when it reaches an information system in the control of the person to whom it is sent. That rule can be tough on recipients because they can be on the hook even if they never actually read the messages. However, a recipient can claim that a particular message was never received by proving, for instance, that it could not be downloaded from the server. The best way for a business to avoid disputes about the transmission of its messages is to either require acknowledgment or invoke a system of automated confirmation.

a message is deemed to be sent when it leaves the sender's control

a message is deemed received when it reaches an information system in the control of the person to whom it is sent

Note that *UECA*'s provisions do not change the common law rules regarding the communication of acceptance. As we saw in Chapter 2, contractual acceptance must be communicated to be effective. Furthermore, the time and the place of the acceptance depend upon the *medium of communication*. *UECA* has avoided the issue of instantaneous versus non-instantaneous communication, recognizing that the decision about whether to treat a particular electronic transmission as similar to a phone call or first-class mail depends upon the circumstances and must be determined on a case-by-case basis.

Note that the rules eliminating uncertainty about where and when a message is sent or received are merely default rules. In other words, parties can choose to adopt their own rules by mutual consent.

Government Documents

Governments electronically exchange an enormous amount of information with businesses and citizens and will do so even more as Canada's Government Online and similar provincial initiatives are fully implemented. *UECA* therefore contains a number of provisions regarding electronic documents that are sent to government.[7] For instance, some provisions protect governments from being swamped by electronic documents that arrive in various incompatible formats. A government can specify the formats that it is willing to accept.[8]

UECA contains provisions regulating electronic documents that are sent to government

---

[6.] The rules are more complicated if a company has several places of business or no place of business.

[7.] For the purposes of *UECA*, the term "government" does not include Crown corporations, but it may include municipalities, if the provincial or territorial legislature so decides.

[8.] Some jurisdictions, including Ontario, Nova Scotia, and the Yukon have adopted those provisions. Others, such as British Columbia and New Brunswick, have not.

Provincial Electronic Commerce Legislation

UECA is a model for provincial electronic commerce legislation.[9] Many provinces have adopted that model entirely or with minor variations.[10] Others have attempted to overcome the same problems by other means. Although it is impossible to provide a detailed comparison of each jurisdiction's approach, we can mention a few important differences.

The most substantial differences occur in New Brunswick and Quebec. For example, unlike most of its counterparts, the New Brunswick legislation does not regulate the process of offer and acceptance. And the Quebec legislation is much more extensive than its counterparts. For instance, it contains a number of detailed provisions regarding the consultation and transmission of documents that have legal implications for third parties, like online service providers. As a matter of risk management, the lesson is clear. While *UECA* has provided a model for electronic commerce statutes, there are occasionally substantial differences between jurisdictions. Businesses that are not confined to a single province or territory should consult the relevant legislation to avoid difficulties.

CONTRACTING ONLINE

Although *UECA* and the statutes that it inspired remove many sources of uncertainty about online commerce, a number of difficulties remain. In this section we will look at three issues:

- contract formation
- automated electronic commerce
- authentication and security

Contract Formation

The fact that commerce is conducted electronically creates certain problems for traditional rules governing the formation of contract. Some pertain to *shrink-wraps*, *click-wraps*, and *web-wraps*, while others pertain to the basic process of *offer and acceptance*.

Shrink-wraps, Click-wraps, and Web-wraps

A *shrink-wrap licence* occurs in the context of mass-marketed software. The software is placed in a package that is wrapped in clear cellophane. Underneath the cellophane is a card, which states the rules that are attached to the use of the software. That card also informs consumers that, by removing the

---

9. Bill 21, *Electronic Transactions Act*, 1st Sess 25th Parl, Alberta, 2001; *Electronic Transactions Act*, SBC 2001, c 10; *The Electronic Commerce and Information Act*, CCSM 2000, c E55, amending *The Manitoba Evidence Act*, RSM 1987, c E150 and amending *The Consumer Protection Act*, RSM 1987, C200; Bill 70, *Electronic Transactions Act*, 3d Sess, 54th Parl, New Brunswick, 2001; *Electronic Commerce Act*, SNS 2000, c 26 (NS); *Electronic Commerce Act*, SO 2000, c 17 (Ont); *Electronic Commerce Act*, SPEI 2001, c 31 (PEI); *Act to Establish a Legal Framework for Information Technology*, SQ 2001, c 32 (Que); *Electronic Information and Documents Act*, SS 2000, c E-722 (Sask); *Electronic Commerce Act*, SY 2000, c 10 (Yuk).

10. That is true of Alberta, British Columbia, Manitoba, Nova Scotia, Ontario, Prince Edward Island, Saskatchewan, and the Yukon.

cellophane, they are agreeing to abide by those rules—they can use the software, but they must honour the terms of the *licence* that has been created.[11]

The same basic process can be used for online commerce. A *click-wrap licence* is created when a person agrees to accept the terms of an online contract by clicking a mouse or touching an icon that says, "I accept." **A click-wrap licence** can be any licensing agreement triggered by the click of a mouse. A *web-wrap licence* is similar, but more specific. A **web-wrap licence** is triggered by some form of online interaction. For example, while viewing a document online, you try to download or install software, or order goods or services. A window pops up that (i) contains the terms of a contract, (ii) asks you to read those terms, and (iii) tells you to click on one box to accept those terms or on another to reject them. If you click on the first box, you may be bound by a contract. Canadian courts have said that, when properly constructed, such agreements are "afforded the same sanctity that must be given to any agreement in writing."[12] Case Brief 17.1 illustrates this.

a click-wrap licence can be any licensing agreement triggered by the click of a mouse

web-wrap licence is triggered by some form of online interaction

CASE BRIEF 17.1

Rudder v Microsoft (1999) 47 CCLT (2d) 168 (Ont SCJ)

Microsoft Network (MSN) provides online information services to members of its network. The plaintiffs were two Canadian law students who had entered into an online contract to receive MSN's services. They started a lawsuit in Ontario against MSN when they believed that they had been improperly charged for certain services.

MSN pointed to a provision in the online contract that it had created with the plaintiffs. That provision required any disputes to be resolved through the courts in the State of Washington. MSN therefore said that the case could not be heard in Canada. In response, the plaintiffs argued that they had not noticed the "forum selection clause" and argued that the clause should be treated as "fine print," since only a portion of the agreement was on screen at any given time.

The court held that the plaintiffs had agreed to obey the terms of the online contract when they clicked on the button that said, "I agree." The court then rejected the argument that any terms not wholly in view must be understood as fine print. Such a claim, it held, was no different from saying that only the terms and conditions that appear on the signature page of a printed document should apply. The court also said that ignorance of the relevant term was no excuse since MSN's agreement required potential members to view its terms on two occasions and signify acceptance on each occasion. In fact, the second display of the terms advised users that, "If you click 'I agree' without reading the membership agreement, you are still agreeing to be bound by all of the terms...without limitation."

The court in *Rudder v Microsoft* rejected the plaintiffs' argument partly because those arguments would "lead to chaos in the marketplace, render ineffectual electronic commerce and undermine the integrity of any agreement entered into through this medium." That decision recognizes the interests of businesses that engage in electronic commerce. However, the court also stressed the fact that click-wrap and web-wrap agreements are similar to traditional contracts in one important way—the terms of a contract are effective only if they are sufficiently brought to the parties' attention.[13] To manage risk, therefore, those terms should be as conspicuous as possible. If terms are hidden in a remote hyperlink or camouflaged in unusual fonts or footnotes, they may not be effective.

the terms of an online contract are effective only if they are reasonably brought to the parties' notice

---

[11.] A licence is simply permission to act in a way that would normally be prohibited. In this case, the licence allows the consumer to use the manufacturer's software.

[12.] *Rudder v Microsoft* (1999) 47 CCLT (2d) 168 at para 17 (Ont SCJ).

[13.] That was traditionally true in the "ticket cases," which were discussed in Chapter 4.

Offer and Acceptance

Online contracts also create challenges for the traditional rules regarding offer and acceptance. For instance, if a Web site proposes a contract, does it create an *offer* or merely an *invitation to treat*? As we saw in Chapter 2, if an offer is made to the world at large, it may be accepted by many people. If so, the offeror is required to fulfill many contracts, even if it really wanted to create only one. As a matter of risk management, you should design your Web site so that it extends only an invitation to treat. You should require each customer to place an order, that is, make offers, that you are free to accept or reject.

Electronic commerce also raises issues about the communication of acceptance. Chapter 2 explained how the traditional common law rule depends upon whether the communication is instantaneous (like a telephone call) or non-instantaneous (like a letter). Most jurisdictions in Canada have followed *UECA* by enacting legislation that deems when and where electronic communications are sent and received. However, most of those statutes do *not* specify whether particular forms of communication are instantaneous or non-instantaneous. Businesses should prepare for the possibility that an e-mail may be lost or delayed in cyberspace. The safest route is to use various means of communication. For example, if an e-mail message is important, it might be backed up by a fax, regular letter, or telephone call. While electronic commerce is generally intended to avoid that inconvenience, it is still sometimes better to have a back-up plan. The extra effort may save many years and much money in litigation. Admittedly, such safety mechanisms may become impossible as transactions become completely automated.

Web sites should generally provide invitations to treat rather than offers

electronic commerce raises issues about the communication of acceptance

Automated Electronic Commerce

As commercial transactions veer off traditional paths and swerve onto the information superhighway, the cornerstone of traditional contract theory, the notion of *consensus ad idem* (a "meeting of the minds") becomes more difficult to apply. As businesses move further into electronic environments, commercial transactions will no longer be created and performed exclusively by humans. Many transactions will be initiated and completed by computer software programs. These automated transactions will not easily fit within traditional notions of contract. In fact, the point of developing technologies that automate electronic commerce is to allow transactions to take place without any need for humans to review or even be aware of particular transactions. And significantly, unlike the technology that is currently used in things like vending machines and mechanical parking attendants, fully automated forms of electronic commerce will not simply act in predetermined ways by dispensing candy or parking stubs on demand. They will act intelligently and somewhat independently of their human creators. For example, when linked to a warehouse computer, they may detect a shortage of stock and order supplies without being instructed to do so by a human.

Most Canadian electronic commerce statutes allow contracts to be created by automated electronic devices.[14] However, while enforceable contracts can be created in that way, it may be dangerous to rely on such systems. Most of the statutes also say that transactions are unenforceable when purchasers make a *keystroke error* when dealing with an automated system. A **keystroke error** occurs when a person mistakenly hits a wrong button or key. For instance, you

a keystroke error occurs when a person mistakenly hits wrong buttons or keys

---

14. Section 21 of *UECA* states: "A contract may be formed by the interaction of an electronic agent and a natural person or by the interaction of electronic agents."

may order 1000 items instead of 100, or you may hit the "I agree" button instead of the "I decline" button. An automated system normally cannot recognize subsequent messages that you send in an attempt to correct a mistake. It will simply fill your order as originally received. The legislation may allow you to escape the consequences of your error in certain circumstances. Basically, you must prove that: (i) the automated system did not provide an opportunity to prevent or correct the error, (ii) you notified the other party of the error as soon as possible, (iii) you took reasonable steps to return any benefit that you received under the transaction, and (iv) you have not received any other material benefit from the transaction. An online business can avoid those sorts of situations by creating an automated mechanism to correct such errors. The simplest tactic is to require the purchaser to confirm the order by repeating the important steps (for instance, by retyping the number of items that it wants to receive).

Authentication

In our earlier discussion of functional equivalents, we saw that a signature can serve the important goal of demonstrating a person's willingness to be bound to a contract. But a signature can also provide an *authenticating function*. An **authenticating function** identifies the signatory and ties that person to the document. In many situations, contractual parties are not concerned about each other's identity. If you buy a bowl of matzo ball soup from my deli, I do not care who you are, and you do not care who I am. However, a party's identity is often important, especially in electronic commerce. Suppose that we create a contract online that requires you to pay $10 000 and that requires me to deliver an Internet server. Without some form of authentication, either you will have to pay and trust me to send the server, or I will have to send the server and trust you to pay. Although people often do business on the basis of trust, it is a dangerous practice, especially among strangers. Risk management therefore suggests the need for authentication. At least one of us has to be satisfied that the other can be trusted. *Electronic signatures* can be used for that purpose.

an authenticating function identifies the signatory and ties that person to the document

Electronic Signatures

An **electronic signature** is electronic information that people can use to identify themselves. The process in which a person uses an electronic signature usually involves two components:

an electronic signature is electronic information that people can use to identify themselves

- a trusted third party known as a *certification authority*
- technology known as *public key cryptography*

Although the process is complicated, we can briefly describe it.

Certification Authorities An electronic signature is reliable if it is used in conjunction with a *trusted third party*. A **trusted third party** is a person whom both contractual parties can trust. While I may not be willing to rely on information that I receive from you, I may be willing to rely on that same information if it has been verified by someone whom I know and trust. That trusted third party therefore uses a *digital certificate* to verify the identity of the person who provided the electronic signature. A **digital certificate** is an electronic document that authenticates the identity of a particular person. In many ways, it is like an electronic credit card—it is used to establish your credentials when doing business online. A trusted third party who provides that sort of certificate is known as a *certification authority*.

a trusted third party is a person whom both contractual parties can trust

a digital certificate is an electronic document that authenticates the identity of a particular person

public key infrastructure (PKI) is a set of policies and procedures that provides a high level of security and therefore allows businesses, consumers, governments, and courts to trust the information that they protect

cryptography is the science of encryption and decryption

encryption is the coding of plaintext into ciphertext to prevent access to the text by unauthorized people not privy to the code

ciphertext is the unreadable form of encrypted information

decryption is the process of converting ciphertext into its original form so that it can be understood

Internet users prefer *public key* cryptography

public key cryptography uses two keys-one is private; the other is public

PKI can be used to verify electronic signatures

Note that a certification authority need not be limited to verifying a person's identity for electronic signatures in online contracts. Digital certificates can also be used to certify a person's age, whether that person holds a licence to use certain online services, whether a person's level of security clearance authorizes access to an information system, and so on. These sorts of certification are now possible through the development of a special type of trusted third party system called a *public key infrastructure*. A **public key infrastructure (PKI)** is a set of policies and procedures that provides a high level of security and therefore allows businesses, consumers, governments, and courts to trust the information that they protect.[15]

PKI is based on *cryptography*. **Cryptography** is the science of encryption and decryption. Julius Caesar originally popularized it. Since he did not trust his messengers with the information that he sent to his governors and officers, he *encrypted* his messages. **Encryption** is the coding of plaintext into an unreadable form called **ciphertext** so that it cannot be understood by those who do not have the relevant code. Caesar used a simple system in which each character in his messages was replaced by a character three positions ahead of it in the Roman alphabet. Authorized recipients of his messages were provided with the code for *decrypting* them. **Decryption** is the process of converting ciphertext back into its original form so that it can be understood.

Caesar's system relied on the creation of a private code (nowadays referred to as a private key) that was intended to be shared only amongst confidants. That system had an obvious weakness. If the key ever fell into the wrong hands, the messages could be decrypted by unauthorized people. For that reason, Internet users prefer public key cryptography. In public key cryptography, *two* keys are created: one is private, the other is public. Although those two keys are distinct, they are created in a way that allows a message that was encrypted by your public key to be decrypted with your private key and vice versa. Because two keys are required—one to encrypt, the other to decrypt—no one has to share their private key with anyone else. The public key is made available online to the public at large. It allows anyone who possesses it to send encrypted information to you. The private key, however, is kept secret and remains solely in your custody. This system, when used in conjunction with a certification authority, ensures that no one else can read the encrypted messages that you send or receive.

A similar procedure can be used to create electronic signatures, although the key's functions are reversed. An electronic signature is the ciphertext that is created by an encrypted message. If you sign your message with your private signature key, I can decrypt that signature with your public signature key and compare it to the message. If they are identical, I can reasonably assume that the message was from you, since presumably you are the only one in possession of your private key. Thus, decrypting an electronic signature using a public key is one way to verify an electronic signature. Concept Summary 17.1 reviews the uses of PKI.

[15.] American Bar Association draft Public Key Infrastructure Assessment Guidelines: <www.abanet.org/scitech/ec/isc>.

Concept Summary 17.1

Uses of PKI in Electronic Commerce

to send and receive confidential messages
to create electronic signatures
to verify another's electronic signature
to validate digital certificates

FIGURE 17.1   Asymmetrical Cryptography or Encryption Is a Dual Key System

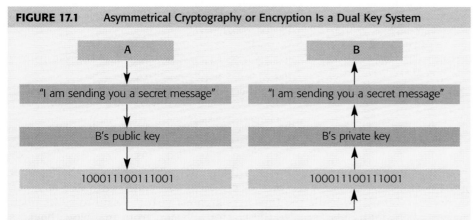

The sender, A, encrypts an e-mail "I am sending you a secret message" with B's public key. The message is transformed into a string of 1s and 0s. The recipient of A's message, B, uses her private key to decode the string of 100011100111001 as "I am sending you a secret message." Likewise, B could use A's public key to send an encrypted message to A.

Information Security

Although PKI systems are very useful, they have dramatic implications for privacy. As one author stated, "[t]he current approach to digital certificates and Public Key Infrastructures ignores the privacy rights of individuals, groups, and organizations. Digital certificates can be followed, traced, and linked instantaneously as they move around. Unless drastic measures are taken, individuals will soon be forced to communicate and transact in what could be the most pervasive electronic surveillance system ever built."[16] Ethical Perspective 17.1 discusses another side of the privacy question.

[16.] S Brand "Private credentials" <www.xs4all.nl/~brands/>.

ETHICAL PERSPECTIVE 17.1

Online Privacy[17]

To pump up advertising revenue, Dale and Bruce recently came up with an idea that would drastically increase traffic to their commercial Web site. They would cash in on the success of reality-based broadcasting by streaming live audio from cellular telephones onto the Internet. They used a scanner to intercept cellular telephone conversations. They then connected the scanner to the computer that was hosting their Web site. By streaming the scanner transmissions to their Web site, anyone anywhere in the world could listen in on people's private cell phone conversations.

Canada's *Personal Information Protection and Electronic Documents Act* (*PIPEDA*) adopts the following requirement:[18]

The knowledge and consent of the individual are required for the collection, use, or disclosure of personal information, except where inappropriate. [Exceptions exist where: (i) a crime is being investigated, (ii) for journalistic, artistic or literary purposes, or (iii) the information is publicly available].

Questions for Discussion

1. Would you say that Dale and Bruce have transgressed PIPEDA? Why?
2. How would you respond to an argument by Dale and Bruce that they are simply making more accessible information that is already available to the public?
3. What moral considerations should Dale and Bruce have taken into account before they decided to stream cellular phone conversations?

Since many corporations connect their internal networks to the Internet, most business people view the privacy concerns associated with **PKI** as a necessary evil. Similarly, while the Internet's greatest virtue is said to be its open-access, accessibility also creates the risk of invasion from malicious hackers, hacktivists, cyber-criminals, cyber-terrorists, and industrial spies. Online intruders can steal information-based assets; dilute corporate brands; cause critical infrastructure failures, service breaks and system failures; and scare away customers. Consider Case Brief 17.2.

CASE BRIEF 17.2

Mafiaboy[19]

In February 2000, a 15-year-old Montreal hacker known as Mafiaboy made headlines around the world when he brought several commercial networks—including those of Time Warner, ETrade Group Inc, and Dell Computer—to their knees. He used the power of more than 70 computers in 52 networks, most of them in universities, to flood the commercial Web sites and shut them down. Mafiaboy was arrested and charged almost a year later. He pleaded guilty to 55 counts of mischief. While RCMP and FBI officials originally estimated that Mafiaboy caused US$1.7 billion in damage,

the amount of money lost in the attacks was never fully established in court. The firms and institutions that he had targeted were unwilling to publicly disclose information that might reveal weak spots in their security.

Mafiaboy was sentenced in September 2001 to eight months in a youth detention centre and one year probation, and ordered to pay $250 to a charity. The judge said that, given the length and severity of the attacks, he could not accept Mafiaboy's argument that he just wanted to test the security of the corporations' Web sites. The Crown prosecutor felt that a clear message had to be sent to hackers that their activities could be tracked.

[17.] Privacy Commissioner of Canada "Web site broadcasts cell phone conversations" <www.privcom.gc.ca/cf-dc/cf-dc_010917_e.asp>.

[18.] *Personal Information Protection and Electronic Documents Act*, SC 2000, c 5.

[19.] "Crime—Mafiaboy" online QL (*National General News*, September 12, 2001); *National Post Online*, September 13, 2001 <www.mafiaboy.com>.

As the Mafiaboy case illustrates, PKI and other security measures are crucial to the success of Internet commerce. One expert has said that security is "what transforms the Internet from an academic curiosity into a serious business tool."[20] Security protects corporate assets from external threats. *Information security* can be used to protect your business against the threat of things like tampering, interception, worms, viruses, and logic bombs.[21] **Information security** is a combination of *communications security* and *computer security*. **Communications security** protects information while it is transmitted from one system to another. **Computer security** protects information within a computer system.

Hardware and software are not the only means of protection. A comprehensive information security system must include other forms of control, including strict workplace policies and personnel security. Businesses can also protect themselves by using the law as a deterrent, by informing those with access to information systems that they will be punished (perhaps by the loss of Internet privileges or even summary dismissal) if they engage in illegal activities like online gambling, possessing child pornography, sexual harassment, and fraud.

Businesses should also publicize that the *Criminal Code of Canada* contains a number of provisions designed to prevent security breaches.[22]

- Section 342.1 prohibits the *unauthorized use of a computer*, including theft of computer services, breaches of privacy, and trafficking in computer passwords.

- Section 430 (1.1) prohibits *computer mischief* that: (i) destroys or alters data, (ii) renders data meaningless, useless or ineffective, (iii) obstructs, interrupts or interferes with the lawful use of data, or (iv) obstructs, interrupts or interferes with any person in the lawful use of data or denies access to data to any person who is entitled to access thereto.

- Sections 183 and 184 prohibit the *interception of private communications*. The definition of "private communications" is quite broad, and includes any telecommunication made in Canada or intended to be received in Canada. Business managers charged with information security will be relieved to know that an exception exists where it is reasonable to expect that the communication may be intercepted, as in the employment context.

Businesses can use contract law to protect themselves against some security risks. As we saw in Chapter 16, they can adopt confidentiality agreements. Likewise, they should also create, publicize, and enforce against all company employees an Internet use policy. That policy should include provisions governing: (i) the use, disclosure, and return of confidential information, (ii) use of the Internet, and (iii) permission to monitor employee communications.

Businesses can also reduce some security risks by outsourcing to security providers, including certification authorities. By outsourcing, the security provider or its insurer assumes some of the risk of maintaining security.

information security is a combination of communications security and computer security

communications security protects information while it is transmitted from one system to another

computer security protects information within a computer system

businesses can protect themselves by using the law as a deterrent

[20] B Schneier "Managed security monitoring: Network security for the 21st century" <www.counterpane.com/msm.html>.

[21] Statement of Joel C Willemssen before the United States Senate. "Critical infrastructure protection" <www.gao.gov/new.items/d011132t.pdf>.

[22] *Criminal Code of Canada,* RSC 1985, c C-46 (Can).

DOMAIN NAMES

We have examined the core contractual aspects of electronic commerce. Now we will investigate other legal issues that can arise as a business migrates to the online terrain. Although a key benefit of electronic commerce is that geography becomes less important, the marketing slogan—location, location, location—is still relevant online. Perhaps the most important real estate in cyberspace is the *domain name*. A **domain name** locates an organization on the Internet. For example, by entering www.pearsoned.ca into an Internet browser or search engine, you will locate the Internet address for the company Pearson Education Canada, the publisher of this book.[23] Because of the enormous number of domains on the Internet, several organizations regulate their acquisition and use.[24]

a domain name locates an organization or other entity on the Internet

In the world of real estate, a person may buy a piece of land with a view to reselling it at a profit. The same sort of activity can happen on the Internet. A **cybersquatter** purchases a potentially valuable domain name with the intention of later selling it to the highest bidder. For example, some cybersquatters reserve domain names for common English words (like drugstore.com or furniture.com) to resell them to companies that are interested in dealing with the relevant products online. If no one claims a prior right to a particular domain name, the first person to register it becomes the owner and has the right to resell it. Problems arise, however, when a domain is not merely a common word but rather a name that someone else asserts some sort of proprietary interest in. Although the regulating authorities have received complaints about thousands of domain names, the disputes usually fall into three groups.

a cybersquatter purchases a potentially valuable domain name with the intention of later selling it to the highest bidder

- A person may innocently, or with some justification, register a domain name that is later disputed. For example, if your new-born nephew is named Ed Pearson, you might register the domain www.pearsoned.ca and post pictures of him at that address. You may receive a complaint from Pearson Education Canada, which holds a proprietary interest in that name.

- A person may register a domain name that resembles a trademark to which both parties claim a commercial right. For example, if you hold the US trademark Pearson International®, you may register www.pearsoninternational.ca. If so, you may receive a complaint from the Greater Toronto Airport Authority, which believes that, as operator of Pearson International Airport and holder of a similar registered Canadian mark, it has a stronger claim to that domain name.

- A person may register a domain name in which it has no commercial rights. For example, you might try to be the first to register www.pearsoned.ca, either to prevent Pearson Education Canada from using it or to offer it for sale to Pearson's competitors at a price far exceeding its cost.

Sometimes, cybersquatters feel that they are morally justified in taking a domain name. Consider the case in Business Law in Action 17.1.

---

[23] Like many other international companies, Pearson Education has registered several other domain names, such as <www.pearsoneducation.com>.

[24] For instance, dot-ca (as in <www.pearsoned.ca>) is administered by the Canadian Internet Registry Authority (CIRA) <www.cira.ca>.

BUSINESS LAW IN ACTION 17.1

Parody Web Sites[25]

Ken Harvey was a speculator in domain names who lived in Newfoundland. Upon registering walmartcanadasucks.com and a number of similar domains, Ken created and uploaded a Web page stating that, "This is a freedom of information site set up for dissatisfied Wal-Mart Canada customers." The site exhorted visitors to "Spill Your Guts" with a "horror story relating to your dealings with Wal-Mart Canada." Wal-Mart responded by filing a complaint to a dispute-resolution provider, indicating that the domains were registered in bad faith. According to Wal-Mart, Ken's free speech argument was merely a cybersquatter's convenient and transparent dodge. On that basis, Wal-Mart sought to have control of the domain name walmartcanadasucks.com.

The dispute resolution provider held that Ken's conduct, even if distasteful, should not result in an unwarranted expansion of the domain name dispute process. According to the arbitrator, the dispute resolution process is meant to protect against trademark infringement, not provide a general remedy for all misconduct involving domain names. Having held that the walmartcanadasucks.com domain name is not identical or confusingly similar to Wal-Mart's trademarked name, the arbitrator decided that Ken did not register the domain name in bad faith. In fact, the arbitrator ruled that Ken had "a legitimate interest in respect of the domain name, to use it as a foundation for criticism of the complainant." On this basis, the request to transfer the domain name to Wal-Mart was refused.

Questions for Discussion

1. Should consumers be allowed to say whatever they want about a business, even if what they say is harmful and results in a loss of profits?
2. If you were the Wal-Mart executive charged with handling the matter, how might you have avoided arbitration?

In some circumstances, the parties are entitled to litigate such matters. However, litigation requires a great deal of time and money to decide cases in the courts. Furthermore, because cybersquatting is a global activity, it is often difficult to decide *which* court should hear the matter. As a result, the bodies that regulate domain names have adopted procedures to resolve disputes primarily through arbitration.[26] As we discussed in Chapter 1, arbitration is a form of alternative dispute resolution (or ADR) that allows the parties to settle their argument without a court order. As a matter of risk management, the best strategy is to avoid difficulties altogether. While that is not always possible, businesses can take steps to minimize the potential for domain name disputes. For instance, a business manager who is responsible for a company's e-commerce development should register *bona fide* trademarks and business names as early as possible to avoid being held hostage by a cybersquatter. Note that even a registered trademark will not guarantee your business a proprietary interest in a particular domain name. Arbitrators have demonstrated a willingness to weigh the public interest in free speech and fair use against the rights of trademark holders.

domain name disputes are often resolved through arbitration

---

25. *Wal-Mart Stores Inc v walmartcanadasucks.com and Kenneth J Harvey*, WIPO Arbitration and Mediation Center, Case No D2000-1104 <arbiter.wipo.int/domains/decisions/html/2000/d2000-1104.html>.

26. Arbitration was discussed in Chapter 1. In some instances, a party can appeal the arbitrator's decision to a court. The rules for resolving a dispute regarding a dot-ca can be found at <www.cira.ca/en/cat_Dpr.html>.

INTERNET ACCESS PROVIDER AND ONLINE SERVICE PROVIDER LIABILITY

Problems cannot always be avoided, and disputes cannot always be settled through ADR. Litigation may be inevitable, especially if a business is engaged in global e-commerce. In that situation, it may not be enough to comply with local laws. Web site owners and operators must also consider the possibility of being dragged into court in some remote place. They must factor that possibility into the cost of doing business. And while it is expensive to ensure compliance in foreign legal systems, it is sometimes even more expensive to become embroiled in a far-away legal battle. Before considering compliance issues and the kinds of liability that might result from an electronic transaction, we need to first examine the question of *jurisdiction*.

Jurisdiction

jurisdiction refers to the ability of a court from a particular place to hear a case

Jurisdiction, in this context, refers to the ability of a court from a particular place to hear a case. Although the issue of jurisdiction can arise in any kind of case, it is particularly important for e-commerce disputes. Suppose that you have a company in British Columbia. That company has a registered trademark. You discover that a dot-com company in Saskatchewan that sells goods to people in Germany has improperly used your trademark on its Web site. That Web site is hosted by a server that is located in France. Where can you sue? British Columbia? Saskatchewan? France? Germany? At least three tests can be used to answer that question:

- a real and substantial connection test
- a passive versus active test
- an effects-based test

a real and substantial connection test asks whether the plaintiff's cause of action and the effects of the defendant's conduct are sufficiently linked to the place in which the plaintiff wants to sue

In Canada, the courts usually use a **real and substantial connection test**. They ask whether the plaintiff's cause of action and the effects of the defendant's conduct are sufficiently linked to the place in which the plaintiff wants to sue.[27] Unfortunately, the courts are not yet sure how to apply that test in an e-commerce case. Early cases in the US likened the Internet to a continuous advertisement.[28] On that basis, they said that information posted on a given Web site is directed to *every* place capable of accessing the site. Early decisions in Canada followed suit. For example, in *Alteen v Informix*, the defendant, an American manufacturer of information management hardware, allegedly issued untrue and misleading statements that led to an inflated stock price.[29] When Newfoundland shareholders tried to sue, Informix argued that the Newfoundland court had no jurisdiction. Informix argued that it had no real and substantial connection to Canada as it did not trade shares on a Canadian stock exchange, never made press releases in Canada, and had no direct contacts with the plaintiffs. Still, the court held that the mere availability of the misleading statements on the Internet was sufficient to assert jurisdiction. Note that the effect of this approach is to potentially make *every* business liable for *anything* that it posts online.

---

[27] *Tolofson v Jensen* (1994) 120 DLR (4th) 289 (SCC); *Morguard Investments Ltd v De Savoye* (1990) 76 DLR (4th) 256 (SCC).

[28] *Inset Systems Inc v Instruction Set Inc* 937 F Supp 161 (D Conn 1996).

[29] *Alteen v Informix Corp* (1998) 164 Nfld & PEIR 301 (Nfld SC TD).

Online business activity can take many forms, and the analogy between a Web site and a continuous advertisement is not always appropriate. Consequently, some courts now examine the online interaction to determine (i) the level of interactivity between the parties, and (ii) the commercial nature of the exchange of information that occurs on the Web site.[30] Under this **passive versus active test**, a court looks at the way in which each party does business online. Is it merely posting information, or does it require customers to interact through the exchange of information online? Does its site send e-mail to particular places? Does it encourage customers from foreign places to call by providing a local or toll-free number? The more interactive a Web site is in a particular country, the more likely that a court in that country has jurisdiction to hear a case. There is an important point for risk management. If a company does not want to be involved in litigation in a particular place, it should avoid interacting online with people in that place. Case Brief 17.3 illustrates how a company can avoid the assertion of jurisdiction in places where it has no business.

the passive versus active test requires a court to look at the way in which the parties do business online

CASE BRIEF 17.3

Desktop Technologies Inc v Colorworks Reproduction & Design (1999) WL 98572 (ED Pa)

Desktop Technologies was the owner of the US federally registered trademark "Color-works." It came to Desktop's attention that a Canadian company operating an identical kind of business not only used the same name as the mark (the Canadian company owned the Canadian trademark "ColorWorks"), it developed a Web site with the domain name www.colorworks.ca. That site contained several pages advertising ColorWorks services. The American company brought an action against the Canadian company in a Pennsylvania court.

The Canadian company had never done business or provided any of its services in Pennsylvania. It did business only in Canada. Though its Web site made available an online order form, it was purposely designed so that the form could not be filled out or sent via the Internet. To complete an order, the form had to be printed, filled out, and sent via fax or mail to Canada. Users were also provided with a telephone number in Canada as a point of contact.

After analyzing the commercial nature of the exchange of information that occurred on the Web site and the level of interactivity between the parties, the court held that every activity called for by the Web site was to take place in Canada. Consequently, the Web site functioned as little more than a passive form of advertising. Thus, the passive nature of the Web site was insufficient to permit the Pennsylvania court to exercise its jurisdiction over the defendant.

More recently, several courts have moved away from a test that examines the specific characteristics, or the *potential impact*, of a particular Web site. Instead, they have adopted a broader **effects-based approach** that focuses on the *actual impact* a Web site has in the place where jurisdiction is being sought. To the extent that the courts are tempted to look at *where* the harm is done rather than how it is done, it will be very difficult for businesses to insulate themselves from possible liability in remote jurisdictions.

One way a business can protect itself is to avoid *targeting a location*.[31] **Targeting a location** means specifically choosing to create relationships with people within that location. A business that targets individuals or corporations

an effects-based approach focuses on the actual impact that a Web site has in the place where jurisdiction is being sought

targeting a location means specifically choosing to create relationships with people within that location

---

[30.] *Zippo Manufacturing Co v Zippo Dot Com Inc* 952 F Supp 1119 (WD Pa 1997); *Braintech Inc v Kostiuk* (1999) 171 DLR (4th) 46 (Ont CA).

[31.] For an excellent legal and policy analysis of this approach, see M Geist "Is There a There There? Toward Greater Certainty for Internet Jurisdiction" (2001) Berkeley Tech LJ 1345.

within a particular place is more likely to have the courts there take its jurisdiction. There are a few things that a business can do to avoid targeting a jurisdiction.

- It can insert a jurisdictional clause into its standard form contract that requires any disputes arising from the agreement to be heard by the courts in a specified place. As we saw in our investigation of click-wrap and web-wrap contracts, such a clause will only be effective if adequate notice is given and if the other party is capable of assenting to it.

- A business can also use targeting technologies. Such technologies allow a company to manage the legal risks of e-commerce by restricting the geographical area in which it does business. You Be the Judge 17.1 illustrates this.

YOU BE THE JUDGE 17.1

UEJF et LICRA v Yahoo! Inc et Yahoo!France[32]

After viewing online auction sites that offered to sell thousands of Nazi objects (such as swastikas, daggers, uniforms and medals), two anti-racism groups based in Paris started an action against Yahoo! and Yahoo!France for "banalizing the Holocaust." Those groups demanded that Yahoo!France remove all hyperlinks to Yahoo!, which allowed Internet users to access racist material. Furthermore, these groups demanded that Yahoo!France explicitly warn its French users: (i) that Yahoo! contained racist content, and (ii) that they might break French law by browsing the US-based search engine that contained racist materials.

Yahoo!France argued that its site was customized to be free of Nazi-related content and that the main Yahoo! site targeted a US audience, which protects the sale of Nazi objects as free speech. The French court nevertheless agreed with the plaintiffs. The court commissioned an independent international panel to determine whether technological means were available that would allow Yahoo! to continue to auction Nazi memorabilia in countries where it is legal to do so without targeting France. The panel reported that such technologies, though imperfect, are available. Consequently, the French court asserted jurisdiction and ordered Yahoo! to technologically avoid targeting the offensive auctions at France.

Questions for Discussion

1. Do you agree with the decision of the French court? Why?
2. What are some possible global ramifications of this decision?
3. If your managerial duties included overseeing a Web site that hosts online discussion, what changes might you make to the availability of your site in foreign jurisdictions?

Online Intermediaries

Online activity creates unique difficulties for jurisdictional issues. But for the most part, the threat of liability is much the same as it has always been. The tort of deceit, for instance, is identical whether it is committed in person by a con artist or over the Internet by a dot-con artist. However, electronic commerce may generate new forms of liability for certain kinds of online businesses, because of the role that *online intermediaries* play in various online relationships. An **online intermediary** is a party that enables or facilitates an online transaction between others. Think about all the things that need to happen before you can sell me stuff that is advertised on your Web site. First, someone has to agree to host your Web site. Second, unless I am fortunate enough to own an Internet server, someone needs to provide me with access to the Internet. I also need an e-mail account. So do you. Someone is probably in the business of storing or managing most of that data. There are, then, many kinds of busi-

an **online intermediary** is a party that enables or facilitates an online transaction between others

---

[32.] Tribunal de Grande Instance de Paris (NRG 00/05308, 22 May 2000).

nesses that *intermediate* our transaction. They are all considered online intermediaries. In fact, you might even be one. If your business provides employees with access to the Internet or e-mail, then you are an online intermediary in any of their transactions. Here, we will focus on two different kinds of online intermediaries:

- Internet access providers
- online service providers

Internet Access Providers

An **Internet access provider** provides others with access to the Internet. Suppose you start a business that provides Internet access for a flat fee. What happens if one of your customers uses your service to defame someone, download obscene materials, or breach copyright? As an intermediary, can you be held accountable? Generally speaking, the law says "no." Internet access providers, like phone companies, are usually given special treatment, because they are in the business of supplying the pipeline, not monitoring its flow. That is not to say that an access provider is immune from all forms of liability. Suppose that you are an Internet access provider, and your standard contract absolutely guarantees customers uninterrupted service. One day, your service will go down. When it does, you will be liable for breach of contract. You could have avoided liability if you had anticipated service interruptions and provided for them in your standard contract. Or, suppose that you do not provide access for a fee, but for free to your employees. It is possible that they might do things online that attract liability to you as the access provider.[33]

an Internet access provider provides others with access to the Internet

Online Service Providers

Intermediary liability becomes much more difficult to determine in the context of *online service providers*. An **online service provider** offers goods or services, beyond mere Internet access, in exchange for something of value. Electronic commerce examples include e-mail suppliers, bulletin board operators, auction hosts, anonymous remailers, and commercial Web sites.

    An online service provider usually enters into a contract with its subscriber. As usual, it can be held liable to that person if it breaches their agreement. However, it can also manage that risk by inserting an exclusion clause into the contract. Significantly, however, that strategy cannot protect an online service provider from liability to a third party. Since that party is not part of any contract and is therefore not bound by any exclusion clause, it may sue the service provider *as an intermediary*. For example, when a customer uses Yahoo! or AOL Canada to distribute a defamatory statement, the victim of that tort may sue both the customer and the online service provider. The victim may also sue the service provider for failing to reveal the true identity of the customer if that statement was posted under a false name. It is important to recognize, however, that you do not have to be an Internet giant to expose your business to these kinds of lawsuits. Risk managers will want to shield their online businesses against liability for: (i) posting defamatory remarks, (ii) distributing materials subject to copyright, (iii) disclosing personal information, (iv) trademark infringement, (v) computer mischief, and (vi) possession or distribution of child pornography, to name a few.

an online service provider offers goods or services, beyond mere Internet access, in exchange for something of value

---

[33.] For example, an employee may download obscene materials in the workplace. By allowing the employee to create a hostile work environment, the employer may be held liable under human rights legislation, especially if the employer adopted a policy of monitoring employee conduct online but failed to enforce the policy.

The question of liability for online intermediaries is not perfectly settled. The confusion began with a pair of US decisions that reached opposite results on similar facts.[34] In each case, an online intermediary hosted discussion boards that allowed members to speak freely on various controversial topics. In both cases, a subscriber to the online service posted defamatory remarks about a high-ranking member of a competing business. In both cases, the competing business sued the author of the remark *and* the online service provider who hosted the discussion. In both cases, the online service provider was in the business of hosting so many different discussion forums that it delegated the responsibility for maintenance and oversight of the discussion board in question to a subcontractor.

In each case, the court asked whether the service provider was a mere *distributor*, or whether it was a *publisher*, of the defamatory message. The distinction is crucial. A **distributor** is liable only if it actually knows that an illegal message was posted but does nothing about it. A **publisher** of an illegal message is liable in any event. In the first case, the court said that the online intermediary was a mere distributor and therefore not liable. But in the second case, the court held that the online service provider was liable as a publisher since it had exercised editorial control over the contents of its bulletin boards. Those two decisions suggest that service providers who exercise no editorial control over their sites are immune from liability, while service providers who exercise even a low level of control may be held liable.

The implications of those two decisions are troubling. Suppose that your Web site allows people to post messages. One user posts illegal materials that infringe someone's trademark or, worse still, contain violent pornography. If you monitor the site, see the illegal materials, and remove them, your decision to exercise editorial control might actually mean that you could be held liable for failing to remove other illegal postings that you missed or decided to not remove. Because you invoked editorial control, the law might treat you as a publisher. As you can see, there is a problem with using the element of editorial control to determine an online service provider's liability. Such a rule discourages service providers from monitoring their sites and removing offensive material.

In the United States and the United Kingdom, that problem has been addressed by legislation that protects online services providers from liability in some circumstances.[35] Unfortunately, very few Canadian legislators have squarely addressed these issues.[36] One province that has is Quebec. According to section 27 of its *Act to Establish a Legal Framework for Information Technology*, service providers acting as intermediaries are not required to monitor the information communicated on their networks or in the documents stored on them, nor are they required to report communications or documents that may be used for illegal activities.[37] Even if a service provider chooses to monitor

---

[34.] *Cubby Inc v CompuServe Inc* 776 F Supp 135 (SDNY 1991); *Stratton Oakmont v Prodigy Services Co* WL 323710 (NY Sup Ct 1995).

[35.] In the US, the *Communications Decency Act,* 47 USC S 230(c) provides an extremely broad immunity: "No provider or user of an interactive computer service shall be treated as the publisher or speaker of any information provided by another information content provider." In the UK, a much more restricted immunity from liability is stipulated in section 1 of the *Defamation Act, 1996* (UK) 1996 c 31. Applying this provision to the online environment, a service provider who: (i) is not an author, editor, or publisher, (ii) takes reasonable care, and (iii) does not know, or have reason to believe, that what they did caused or contributed to the publication of a defamatory statement, will be protected from liability for defamation.

[36.] Industry Canada and Canadian Heritage *Consultation Paper on Digital Copyright Issues* (2001).

[37.] *Act to Establish a Legal Framework for Information Technology* SQ 2001, c 32.

Margin notes:

a distributor is liable only if it actually knows that an illegal message was posted but does nothing about it

a publisher of an illegal message is liable in any event

or report, its decision to do so will not automatically result in intermediary liability if illegal content is later found on its site. Section 36 of the Act states that service providers acting as intermediaries are not generally responsible for the illegal acts of service users. However, it also states that a service provider *may* incur liability if it *participates* in acts performed by service users.[38]

What about online service providers in other provinces? How can you shield your business from intermediary liability?

- You should have a clear contract with each user, possibly through a click-wrap agreement. Each user should be required to clearly consent to the *terms of service* that are contained in that contract. And those terms should allow you to claim *indemnification* from a user if you are ever held liable for something that they posted.[39]

- Those *terms of service* should clearly explain, with examples, which uses are acceptable and which are unacceptable.

- To avoid the risk of possible liability, you should, whenever possible, set up your business so that you can demonstrate that it merely acts as a conduit or pipeline for the materials that pass through the system.

- If you are sued, you should try to convince the court that while the legislation in Quebec, the US, and the UK are not binding in other places, they are based on policies that should be adopted.

ONLINE CONSUMER PROTECTION

Electronic commerce can expose a business to risks other than legal liability. Many of these risks arise from a lack of caution and a dangerous tendency to trust strangers. Since many online business interactions do not take place in a secure environment and therefore lack the authentication procedures, consumers and small businesses often fall prey to the *dot-cons*. A **dot-con** is a con artist who has gone high-tech, using the Internet to defraud consumers.

One scam involves *multi-level marketing*. **Multi-level marketing (MLM)** is a system of marketing that puts more emphasis on recruiting distributors than on selling products. The dot-con sends an unsolicited message to a number of people, telling them all that they can get rich by joining its salesforce and recruiting others to do the same. Just as it gets paid by the people under it, the dot-con promises that the recruiters will also get paid by the people under them. Unfortunately, the products at the heart of the sales pyramid are usually overpriced, shoddy, and perhaps downright dangerous. And for every MLM distributor who makes a decent living or even a decent supplemental income, there are many more who pay more for their supplies and promotional materials than they will ever earn in sales. Given the nature of online interaction, MLMs are becoming more prevalent in electronic commerce. So are hosts of other online scams including: (i) duplicitous auctions, (ii) hidden-term contracts, (iii) forged invoices, (iv) deceptive advertising, (v) fraudulent credit card charges, (vi) fictitious business opportunities, and (vii) miracle cures.[40]

a dot-con is a high-tech con artist who uses the Internet to defraud consumers

multi-level marketing (MLM) is a system of marketing that puts more emphasis on recruiting distributors than on selling products

---

[38.] For example, liability may be imposed if the service provider: (i) sends a document, (ii) selects or alters the information in a document, (iii) determines who transmits, receives, or has access to a document, or (iv) stores a document longer than is necessary for its transmission.

[39.] Indemnification would require the user to compensate you for any losses that you suffered (for example, by being successfully sued as an intermediary by a third party).

[40.] <www.ftc.gov/bcp/conline/edcams/dotcon/>.

Although business scams are as old as business itself, many con artists have begun to take advantage of high technology to peddle new and improved versions of traditional scams. We end this chapter with a brief look at consumer protection principles in the e-commerce environment. These principles are important to individuals as consumers; but they are also important to businesses. By adopting them, a business can enhance its reputation, strengthen consumer confidence, and ultimately increase sales.

Although some provinces have amended existing consumer protection legislation in light of electronic commerce, full-scale law reform has not yet occurred. Industry Canada promoted a set of guidelines in its *Principles of Consumer Protection in Electronic Commerce: A Canadian Framework*.[41] However, those guidelines are not laws; they are simply suggestions for ethical and effective business practices that are intended to supplement the laws that already protect consumers. We summarize those guidelines.

1. **Consumers should be provided with clear and sufficient information to make an informed choice about whether and how to make a purchase.**

   Online business should avoid jargon and use plain language whenever possible. They should clearly distinguish marketing and promotional material from the terms and conditions of sale. They should disclose the legal identity of their business, their business address, and any geographic limitations on where a product or service is for sale. They should fairly and accurately describe their goods. They should set out a complaints procedure and provide consumers with their own record of the transaction.

2. **Vendors should take reasonable steps to ensure that the consumer's agreement to contract is fully informed and intentional.**

   An online business should carefully set out the process of offer and acceptance. That process should require customers to confirm: (i) their interest in buying, (ii) the full price, terms and conditions, details of the order, and method of payment, and (iii) their agreement to purchase.

3. **Vendors and intermediaries should respect privacy.**

   An online business should set up its data collection and information systems with a view to respecting and protecting its customers' privacy.

4. **Vendors and intermediaries should take reasonable steps to ensure that transactions in which they are involved are secure.**

   An online business should use the technology and procedures discussed in this chapter to safeguard payment and personal information that is exchanged or stored as a result of a transaction.

5. **Consumers should have access to fair, timely, effective, and affordable means for resolving problems with any transaction.**

   An online business should have resources for handling consumer complaints efficiently and effectively. It should be aware that governments are working to clarify the rules governing online disputes, and to strengthen the enforceability of judgments, even in cross-border disputes.

[41.] Industry Canada *Principles of Consumer Protection in Electronic Commerce: A Canadian Framework* (1999). This document is itself based on the OECD Council *Recommendation of the OECD Council Concerning Guidelines for Consumer Protection in the Context of Electronic Commerce* (1999). It is excerpted from CSA Standard *Model Code for the Protection of Personal Information* (1999).

6. **Consumers should be protected from unreasonable liability for payments in transactions.**

An online business should not charge people for unauthorized transactions, as when a third party uses a person's credit information to purchase goods. If a person has already paid for an unauthorized transaction, the business should promptly provide a refund, even if the third party, who received the goods, cannot be found. Similarly, when a consumer mistakenly enters into a transaction, they should be allowed to cancel the agreement within a reasonable time. If a consumer disputes a sale because it did not receive adequate information about the relevant goods or services at the outset, the business should provide a refund, as long as the consumer returns the good or declines the service within a reasonable period of time.

7. **Vendors should not transmit commercial e-mail without the consent of consumers, or unless a vendor has an existing relationship with a consumer.**

Online businesses should avoid spamming, sending unsolicited e-mails to a large number of people. Not only is it bad netiquette, but spam exposes a business to the risk of being associated with products that are worthless, deceptive, and at least partly fraudulent. Many of the online scams that we discussed above are perpetrated through unsolicited mass e-mail. Why risk the reputation of your business when there are more sophisticated and successful means of advertising?

8. **Businesses should promote consumer awareness about the safe use of electronic commerce.**

A business's goodwill is enhanced when it demonstrates a commitment to consumer education and awareness initiatives. An online business should therefore provide consumers with advice on how to minimize the risks associated with electronic commerce, explaining to them how best to conduct transactions safely and securely. When possible, consumers should be given access to information that identifies disreputable electronic commerce practices.

Business Decision 17.1 lets you reflect on the value of these guidelines.

BUSINESS DECISION 17.1

Respecting Consumer Protection

At a meeting of senior managers of your nationwide retail business, a memo has been circulated asking you to support a corporate policy that would ignore the Industry Canada guidelines for consumer protection in the context of e-commerce. According to the memo, there are certain corporate advantages to ignoring the Industry Canada guidelines. The memo also indicates that the guidelines are merely suggestions and that there is no legal requirement to adhere to them.

Questions for Discussion

1. Will you support the proposed corporate policy?
2. What business reasons might there be to adopt the Industry Canada guidelines even if they do not have the force of law?

Chapter Summary

Electronic commerce refers to technology-mediated business transactions. Although e-commerce has facilitated the development of the knowledge-based economy, its success will ultimately depend on eliminating various legal uncertainties and impediments.

Electronic commerce legislation seeks to enable online transactions by removing commercial uncertainty and other impediments. The co-ordination of model laws at both the international and national level has facilitated the global implementation of uniform laws at the provincial level. Canada's model law, the *Uniform Electronic Commerce Act*, sets out a framework for inferring consent to participate in electronic transactions, the functional equivalents of paper-based requirements, the proper treatment of government documents, and a clarification of the rules of contract formation in the online setting (including the timing requirements for sending and receiving electronic documents). Although the adoption of electronic commerce in various Canadian jurisdictions differs in detail, many provinces and territories have maintained fidelity to much of the approach taken in *UECA*.

Online contracts, such as click-wrap and web-wrap agreements, have been recognized as enforceable provided the basic requirements of contract formation are adequately met. To ensure that an agreement is enforceable, managers charged with Web development should design online transactions with the requirements of electronic commerce legislation in mind. They should also ensure that the design of those transactions provides reasonable notice of the terms and conditions. Automated electronic commerce promises to dispense with the need for human supervision in the contract-formation process. Although most provincial legislation contemplates a method for rectifying keystroke errors, managers should incorporate safety mechanisms into their electronic contracts to protect their businesses against liability for computer-generated errors.

Public key infrastructure (PKI) promises to fortify the flimsy foundation of trust resulting from global online interaction. Information systems such as these can be used to authenticate transactions, ensure their integrity, and enhance online security. Technological measures are not, however, the sole means of ensuring information security. Business managers must also consider legal measures, including the adoption and enforcement of terms of service agreements and other strictly enforced corporate policies. A careful approach to information security will ultimately prove fundamental to the success of electronic commerce.

Although one key benefit of electronic commerce is that geography becomes less important, location is still relevant online. Domain names provide the virtual storefronts necessary for electronic commerce. Mimicking traditional real estate speculation, some individuals and companies are in the business of cybersquatting. Domain name registration authorities have developed uniform dispute resolution procedures to help resolve complaints brought by those claiming a proprietary interest in a particular domain name. For a fee, dispute resolution professionals will mediate and, if necessary, arbitrate disputes through various electronic media, thus decreasing the time and expense associated with traditional litigation.

The global reach of electronic commerce means that compliance with local laws is no longer sufficient insulation from legal risk. Web site owners and operators must consider the possibility that they may be dragged into a court battle in some remote jurisdiction. In resolving these disputes, Canadian courts consider whether there is a real and substantial connection between the cause of action, its effects, and the location in which the action has been commenced. Other considerations include the passivity or interactivity of the Web site and the actual effects of the alleged transgression in the location where jurisdiction has been sought. Targeting strategies, including the use of technological measures, will reduce the risk of being sued successfully in a foreign jurisdiction. The question of liability for online intermediaries is not perfectly settled. Early decisions have held that service providers who exercise no editorial control over their sites are immune from liability, whereas service providers who exercise even a low level of control might be held liable. Concerned that this approach provides a clear disincentive for service providers to read and remove illegal content from their Web sites, some jurisdictions have enacted legislation that provides a more balanced approach, extending further protection to online intermediaries under certain circumstances. The prospect of enhanced liability has led many Internet access and online service providers to insist on exclusion clauses in their terms of service. Prudent online intermediaries have also sought to implement practices to shield themselves from liability by demonstrating that they operate as mere conduits of electronic communication.

Full-scale law reform in the consumer protection area has not yet occurred. The most substantial development is a set of guidelines promoted by Industry Canada. Since these are not laws, any action taken by the Competition Bureau is merely educational in nature. Still, these guidelines offer insight to businesses and consumers about the shortcomings of conducting business online in a manner that does not ensure the development of trusting relationships with customers and clients.

Review Questions

1. In what sense is the law a source of uncertainty in the electronic commerce marketplace?

2. What are four potential benefits that electronic commerce offers to businesses willing to implement the use of information technologies?

3. What is the role and purpose of Canada's *Uniform Electronic Commerce Act*?

4. How is Canada's UECA enforced in each province and territory?

5. What are the relevant rules about sending and receiving electronic documents? As a risk manager, what steps can you take to avoid related disputes?

6. Given that electronic commerce legislation is provincially enacted, discuss several issues that a business manager should consider when engaged in interprovincial commerce.

7. Explain the difficulties associated with the formation of contracts online. What lesson can business managers learn from the case of *Rudder v Microsoft*?

8. How can information about products or services be designed to ensure that it is considered an invitation to treat? Why should a Web designer seek to do so?

9. Explain the complexities associated with automated electronic commerce. How can a business safeguard against the undesirable consequences of keystroke errors?

10. Explain how PKI is used for both security and authentication purposes. Why are the services of trusted third parties crucial to electronic commerce?

11. Summarize the process of cryptography. In what circumstances is public key cryptography preferable to private key cryptography? Explain.

12. How can businesses use the law as a deterrent to enhance information security? Provide two examples.

13. Distinguish between *communications* security and *computer* security, and provide an example of each.

14. What is cybersquatting? Is it ever legally permissible?

15. Describe three typical disputes arising from the domain name registration system, and provide an example of each. How can business managers avoid domain name disputes?

16. What factors should business managers consider when deciding whether to participate in electronic commerce on a global level? How can these risks be managed?

17. Name and discuss the variables that a court may consider in deciding if a specific online interaction falls under its jurisdiction.

18. Distinguish between online access providers and Internet service providers, and give an example of each. In which role is an online intermediary most likely to attract potential liability? Why?

19. As an online service provider in the province of Newfoundland, describe how you can shield yourself from possible liability as an online intermediary.

20. Describe how a business can incorporate consumer protection principles into its online contracting practices.

Cases and Problems

1. You are the general manager of a company that does business exclusively in Saskatchewan. With the aim of increasing efficiency and cutting costs, you are contemplating a change in corporate software that would enable filing all necessary government documents in electronic form. However, you are uncertain whether the provincial government will be obligated to accept documents in that form. Before paying a lawyer, you have decided to review the relevant legislation yourself to see if there is a clear answer. Using the legislation set out below, decide whether your company should switch to an electronic format. Can your provincial government force you to file solely by electronic means?

   The *Uniform Electronic Commerce Act* contains these clauses concerning the filing of electronic forms with the government:

6. (1) Nothing in this Act requires a person to use or accept information in electronic form, but a person's consent to do so may be inferred from the person's conduct.

   (2) Despite subsection (1), the consent of the Government to accept information in electronic form may not be inferred by its conduct but must be expressed by communication accessible to the public or to those likely to communicate with it for particular purposes.

9. A requirement under [enacting jurisdiction] law for a person to provide information to another person in a specified non-electronic form is satisfied by the provision of the information in an electronic document,

   (a) if the information is provided in the same or substantially the same form and the electronic document is accessible by the other person and capable of being retained by the other person so as to be usable for subsequent reference, and

(b) where the information is to be provided to the Government, if

(i) the Government or the part of Government to which the information is to be provided has consented to accept electronic documents in satisfaction of the requirement; and

(ii) the electronic document meets the information technology standards and acknowledgment rules, if any, established by the Government or part of Government, as the case may be.

Saskatchewan's *Electronic Information and Document Act* does not contain sections corresponding to 6(2) or 9(b) as do many of the other provinces. Instead it amends the following clause:

28. (1) A person may file a document or information in an electronic format with the appropriate department pursuant to a designated Act, but only if:

(a) the document or information is of a class that is prescribed in the regulations made pursuant to the designated Act as a document or information that may be filed electronically;

(b) the electronic format used is a format that is prescribed in the regulations made pursuant to the designated Act;

(c) the document or information is recorded on a system of electronic data storage that, in the option of the person responsible for the maintenance of the document or information to be filed, can be read by the computer or other equipment used in the information filing system; and

(d) the person filing the document or information is, or is a member of a class of persons that is, authorized to file the document or information in an electronic format by:

(i) a person who has the power to grant that authorization pursuant to the designated Act; or

(ii) if there is no person who has the power to grant that authorization pursuant to the designated Act, the member of the Executive Council to whom for the time being the administration of the designated Act is assigned.

2. As the president of a Web development company, you have been contacted by Alex Sadvari, the owner of the Naked Nature Art Studio. Alex wishes to revamp her Web site. Until now, the Web site functioned as a mere portfolio, inviting interested parties to contact her by telephone. Given her recent success and a seemingly never-ending demand for her drawings, she would like you to redesign her Web site so that it is capable of automated electronic commerce. As an astute business woman, Alex has expressed an interest in ensuring that the site's design will protect her against erroneous customer orders. Prepare a proposal outlining how your Web design will take into account the relevant legislative provisions to minimize potential liability.

3. You are the information manager of an electronic mailing service BadNews.ca. Your primary customers are collections agencies. BadNews.ca assists these agencies by locating debtors and delivering legal notices to them before the repossession of their assets. You were taking the position that simply sending an e-mail message would fulfill the written notice requirements set out in the provincial legislation that regulates the collection of debts. Recently, however, you discovered that the law requires such notices to not merely be sent but to actually be received. You have been asked to determine the effect that the *UECA* will have on your company's business practices. Prepare a brief memo explaining the rules governing the sending and receiving of electronic messages. Make sure that your memo provides some advice indicating the best way to avoid disputes with intended recipients.

4. Scroll Networks is a manufacturer of communications network hardware, including the XV11 routers used in wireless local areas networks (LANs). ICanSolve Logistics Inc installs corporate LANs, purchasing its supplies directly from Scroll. Periodically, Scroll sends ICanSolve and other customers an electronic price list. When supplies are low, and the price looks right, ICanSolve often purchases 25 to 50 units of the XV11 router through Scroll's online interface. During the course of Scroll's online ordering process, the customer receives a click-wrap prompt requiring them to agree to the terms and conditions of sale. Among other provisions, they are advised in boldface red letters that "prices are subject to change without notice at any time prior to shipment," and that "the seller is not liable for failure to deliver where materials are not reasonably available." Additionally, the terms and conditions state that "acceptance of the order is expressly conditioned on the buyer's assent to the seller's terms and conditions."

Upon obtaining inside information that XV11 router prices were scheduled to drastically increase the following day from $250 to $750 (due to a global shortage of integrated circuits), ICanSolve decided to place an order for 1000 XV11 routers. The following week, Scroll filled an order of 50 XV11 routers invoiced at $250 per unit. A letter accompanying the invoice stated that the enclosed portion of the order was priced at $250 as a gesture of goodwill but that the remaining 950 units would be priced at $750 per unit, due to the global shortage of integrated circuits. ICanSolve was offered 10 business days to cancel the balance of the order. ICanSolve accepted the initial delivery, but promptly contacted Scroll and demanded that the rest of the order be fulfilled at the advertised price. Scroll refused, arguing that its advertisements online and on paper indicated that the price was subject to change. What are the central legal issues in this case? How do you think that a court would resolve the dispute? If you were responsible for designing Scroll's online interface, what might you have done differently to avoid situations like this?

5. Unlike most of your friends in business, you are quite

familiar with encryption technologies and have been using them for a few years. Recently, you have done further research on the use of trusted third parties in electronic commerce. In so doing, it has come to your attention that it is possible for a hacker to forge a pair of encryption keys, using them to deceive you into thinking that you have authenticated the sender's identity when in fact you have not. Recognizing this possibility, you have decided to write a memo to the senior vice-president of your company explaining what a certification authority is and why your company should consider using one. Draft the memo.

6. Your company is drawing up an employee terms of service agreement. One paragraph states:

   The computer network and connected devices are the property of the employer. The employer retains ownership and associated rights of all files, documents, and communications received, created, or stored by employees. The computer system is to be used for business purposes only. The e-mail system must not be used to transmit, view, or store obscene, defamatory, discriminatory, pornographic, threatening, sexually explicit, harassing, or any other offensive material. The e-mail system must not be used to duplicate or transmit copyright-protected material without the appropriate permission. At no time should confidential or trade secrets be transmitted over the Internet. The employer reserves the right to monitor e-mail communication and Internet browsing, and to make use of keystroke technologies at any time without notice. The employer retains the right to disclose an employee's personal information, e-mail communication, and Internet browsing history upon request and without notice. Violation of this policy will result in employee discipline. By using the employer's communication facilities, the employee acknowledges and consents to the above terms and conditions of usage.

   Review this agreement. As a manager who is concerned about information security and intermediary liability, what is your opinion on its merits and shortcomings? What changes might be made to improve it?

7. Marcus is an employee of Scroll Networks. Alone at the office late one night with a pounding headache, deep concerns about meeting a deadline, and the knowledge that he was nowhere near finishing the assigned corporate memo, Marcus happened upon an idea. He decided that he would simulate a lightning strike on his company-issued laptop by stripping the Ethernet wire and inserting it into the 100 AC electrical wall outlet. Much to his surprise, he destroyed not only his laptop but also a cluster of workstations in the office. Although he stuck to his game plan, claiming that the office was struck by lightning, the hidden surveillance camera revealed otherwise. You are in charge of information security at Scroll Networks. What possible courses of action does the company have against Marcus? Assuming that you want to use the law as a means to educate employees at Scroll Networks and deter future information security breaches, which course of action will you choose, and why?

8. As the information manager of the XACTO Standard Weights and Measurements Corp, you have received an e-mail from a party identified as koko_k@pobox.com. The e-mail asks whether you are interested in purchasing the rights to the domain name www.xacto.ca. After entering the URL into your Web browser, you determine that the site is not currently in use. You then consult CIRA's Web site and ascertain that the domain name was registered to a party named Koko Kerasic of Edmonton, Alberta only one week ago. Somewhat curious, you decide to respond to the koko_k e-mail, inquiring about the price. A reply to your e-mail comes only moments later demanding $75 000. As the person charged with overseeing your firm's intellectual property enforcement, you are deeply concerned about securing that domain name.

   You seek preliminary advice from your lawyer, Erik, who asks whether your company owns the Canadian trademark for XACTO. Your answer is "yes." Erik then does a business search in Alberta to determine whether Koko has registered a business operating under the name XACTO. No such business name is registered. Upon further investigation, it turns out that Koko is an industrious 19-year-old high-school student who heard about cybersquatting in an ICQ chat room. Erik indicates that this matter must be resolved in accordance with the CIRA dispute resolution policy and quotes his fee for representing you in the matter. Given that your company is a financially-strapped start-up, you decide to handle the matter without representation. You point your Internet browser to www.cira.ca and review the CIRA *Domain Name Dispute Resolution Policy.* What position will you take when making XACTO's submissions to the CIRA dispute resolution provider? What argument can you expect from Koko or her parents? How is the matter likely to be resolved?

9. You are the owner of a small digital content provider based in Brandon, Manitoba. Your content is marketed under your Canadian registered trademark dFOX.® As well, you are the registered owner of the dFOX.com and dFOX.ca domain names. It has come to your attention that a US software company is advertising its newest voice-mailbot under the name dFOX on its Web site, codeworks.com. Code Works does not have a registered trademark for the dFOX product in the US or anywhere else. The Code Works site is targeted to Americans and explicitly warns that its voice-mailbot software may only work with US telecommunications hardware. The site has a US-only 1-888 number, but allows transactions to be completed online from anywhere in the world. The terms and conditions say that the warranty for the product is valid only for sales in the US. You decide to write a demand letter to Code Works, insisting that they cease using your trademark immediately. In the letter, you indicate that, for the past several weeks, customers confused by Code Work's use of your mark have flooded your Web server, causing e-mail transmission problems and irreparable damage to some of your corporate hardware. Code Works ignores your demand and continues to market dFOX voice-mailbots on its Web site. You decide to go to a Manitoba court to seek a remedy for trademark infringement and economic loss. Outline the jurisdictional issues and tests you will be facing. What will your argument be? What can you expect Code Works to argue? As a risk manager, how can you seek to avoid legal liabilities in foreign jurisdictions?

10. You have decided to go into business as an online intermediary. Among other things, you maintain an online discussion board dedicated to financial issues and publicly-

traded companies. At times—especially when stock prices drop—conversation on the discussion boards heats up, and people start to point fingers. Sometimes inflammatory and demeaning remarks are made. To maintain community standards and keep the peace online, you have on occasion directed your Web master to remove certain remarks that you believe to be defamatory. Sometimes, the decision to remove such remarks results from your own random monitoring of the discussions. Other times, the decision results from requests or demands made by discussion board participants.

Today, you received a statement of claim alleging that you are liable for defamatory statements posted on your discussion board. The claim, filed by a large corporation and its CEO, is seeking millions of dollars in damages. This is the first that you have heard of any disparaging remarks made about that company. Although you have a policy to remove postings when asked, neither the corporation nor its CEO made any such request, and no one on your staff had noticed the remarks. Needless to say you are very concerned. You immediately check the discussion group and, sure enough, six false, disparaging remarks had been posted. After checking various financial records, you see that the complaining company's stock prices plunged substantially the day after the remarks were made and have not since recovered. Is there any chance that the company might actually succeed against you? Explain why. How might a different approach to Web site management have reduced exposure to liability?

11. At a high-school reunion you run into an old classmate who has just returned from working in Malaysia. Upon hearing that you are now a renowned e-commerce entre-preneur, he corners you. After asking you several questions concerning online jurisdiction and consumer protection, he explains his latest business venture. It seems that he is marketing a cure for hair loss. According to him, he discovered the formula for a secret hair-regeneration tonic while working for a mining company deep in the heart of a rainforest. Apparently, the tonic can be manufactured from the ingredients found in the typical North American kitchen. He tries to recruit you to distribute his product online, promising you the recipe for the secret formula in exchange for a one-time payment along with a promise to buy a set quantity of promotional materials. To increase profits, you are also encouraged to recruit new distributors. Although your friend seems to be doing quite well for himself, as evidenced by the large diamond inlay in his gold tooth, you are suspicious. Could you be the target of a dot-con? Explain your reasoning.

12. The proliferation of electronic commerce has left consumer protection legislation slow to catch up. This has spurred Industry Canada to announce a policy that includes updated consumer protection principles tailored to the online environment. One of those principles is that, "Vendors should not transmit commercial e-mail without the consent of consumers, or unless a vendor has an existing relationship with a consumer." If followed, would this principle always provide more protection to consumers? As a Canadian corporation, is your business required to adopt this policy? What are the likely business consequences of adopting it and the other principles announced by Industry Canada? What are the likely business consequences of ignoring them? Develop an appropriate e-mail business practice policy statement for your company.

WWWeblinks

Information as a Commodity

Intellectual Capital—Industry Canada

strategis.ic.gc.ca/SSG/pi00004e.html

This Web site provides information on current developments and intellectual capital through links to journal articles, research papers, and interviews.

Cognos

www.cognos.com/products/datamining.html

This software company offers data mining products and solutions to companies interested in transforming otherwise senseless business transaction information into extremely valuable assets.

Intellectual Property

Intellectual Property Policy Directorate—Industry Canada

strategis.ic.gc.ca/SSG/ip00001e.html

This directorate is responsible for reviewing and modernizing federal intellectual property laws. Its Web site provides news, research papers, laws and regulations, treaties, and links related to intellectual property.

Canadian Intellectual Property Laws and Regulations—Industry Canada

strategis.ic.gc.ca/SSG/ip01077e.html

This site provides links to the Canadian acts regulating patents, copyright, trademarks, industrial design, and integrated circuit topography.

Canadian Intellectual Property Office (CIPO/OPIC)

strategis.ic.gc.ca/sc_mrksv/cipo/welcome/welcom-e.html

The CIPO was created to administer the intellectual property system in Canada and provide information on intellectual property. Its Web site links to the Web pages of each subsection of intellectual property law.

World Intellectual Property Organization (WIPO)

www.wipo.org/index.html

This Web site provides information on intellectual property, WIPO activities and services, and links to treaties, decisions, and publications.

International Intellectual Property Treaties

strategis.ic.gc.ca/SSG/ip01076e.html

This Industry Canada Web page provides basic information on the international intellectual property treaties which Canada has signed and links to their full text.

Intellectual Property Institute of Canada (IPIC)

www.ipic.ca

The IPIC is a professional organization concerned with patents, trademarks, copyright, and industrial design. It maintains a list of intellectual property agents and lawyers.

Copyright Board of Canada

www.cb-cda.gc.ca

This site provides information on public hearings, recent decisions of the board, links to copyright collectives, and general information on copyright.

CANCOPY

www.uniquename.com/cancopy/home.html

Canadian creators and publishers established this not-for-profit agency to license public access to copyright works. Its site provides access to information on copyright licensing, an interface for affiliates and licensees, and resources relating to copyright.

Society of Composers, Authors and Music Publishers of Canada (SOCAN)

www.socan.ca

SOCAN collects and administers tariffs for music copyrights. Its Web site provides information on events, news, and other resources for both music users and music creators and publishers.

Recording Industry Association of America (RIAA)

www.riaa.org

RIAA represents the joint interests of many American film and music studios. Its site provides information on industry news, copyright, freedom of speech, licensing and royalties, piracy, audio technologies, and the interaction of music and the Internet.

US Copyright Office

lcweb.loc.gov/copyright

This US government Web site provides a wealth of US copyright information, publications, legislation, announcements, and a searchable registration database.

Canadian Trade-marks Database

strategis.ic.gc.ca/cgi-bin/sc_consu/trade-marks/search_e.pl

This online trademarks database allows you to search by trademark, status, application number, and registration number.

Canadian Trade-marks Journal

napoleon.ic.gc.ca/cipo/tradejournal.nsf/$$ViewTemplate+for+TMJournal+English?OpenForm

This CIPO Web page archives the *Canadian Trade-marks Journal*, which operates under the authority of the *Trademark Act* and publishes applications for trademarks for public comment and opposition.

Canadian Patent Database

patents1.ic.gc.ca/intro-e.html

This online searchable database lets you search, retrieve, and inspect over 1 400 000 patent documents in Canada, and European and US patents via a link to the World Intellectual Property Organization (WIPO).

US Patent and Trademark Office (USPTO)

www.uspto.gov

This US Department of Commerce site allows users to search patents and trademarks, order copies, apply for patents, register trademarks, pay fees, and monitor file progress.

PATSCAN—Patent and Trademark Searching

www.library.ubc.ca/patscan/welcome.html

This site provides patent and trademark searches for both university and industry, intellectual property resources, and database access.

Bizarre Patents—PATSCAN

www.library.ubc.ca/patscan/bizarre_patents.html

This page features the "bizarre patent of the month" and access to the PATSCAN archive of wacky patents.

International Chindogu Society

info.pitt.edu/~ctnst3/chindogu.html

Strange yet brilliant tools and devices.

Electronic Commerce

Electronic Commerce

aix1.uottawa.ca/~geist/ecommerce.html

This page provides a useful topical index to articles, case law, conferences, legislation, and policy papers on electronic commerce in Canada.

Electronic Commerce

canada.justice.gc.ca/en/ps/ec

The Department of Justice site addresses proposed

statutes on electronic commerce and provides links to news releases, consultation papers and reports, and other resources.

Electronic Commerce Task Force

e-com.ic.gc.ca/english/strat/641.html

This Industry Canada site offers information for companies involved in electronic commerce on marketplace rules—legal and commercial frameworks, financial issues and taxation, and intellectual property protection.

Provincial Electronic Commerce Legislation and Regulation

www.innovationlaw.org/lawforum/pages/ecommerce_legislation.htm

This site not only provides links to provincial electronic commerce legislation and regulations, but also offers background documents and links to other Internet-related legislation.

Privacy Commissioner of Canada

www.privcom.gc.ca/legislation/index_e.asp

 This site provides links to Canadian privacy legislation, privacy guides, reference materials, and other privacy-related sites.

The Validity and Enforceability of Web-wrap Agreements

www.law.ualberta.ca/alri/ulc/current/ewebwrap.htm

This article examines the enforceability of online contracts with respect to traditional standard form contracts and fundamental contractual requirements.

UNCITRAL Model Law on Electronic Signatures

www.uncitral.org/english/workinggroups/wg_ec/wp-88e.pdf

This document contains a draft guide to the UNCITRAL Model Law on Electronic Signatures and provides insight into the principles of electronic signatures.

Canadian Internet Registration Authority

www.cira.ca

Operating as the authority for the registration of .ca domain names, this site also provides access to its official dispute resolution policy and rules.

Institute for International Capital Research Inc.

www.business.mcmaster.ca/mktg/nbontis/ic/

Used by both global organizations and governmental agencies, this institute offers consulting on knowledge management, intellectual capital, and organizational learning.

Intangible Assets Manager

www.sveiby.com.au/IntangAss/CompanyMonitor.html

This site offers a method for measuring intangible assets.

18 Basic Forms of Business Organizations

CHAPTER OVERVIEW

OBJECTIVES

After completing this chapter you should be able to:

1. Identify four basic forms of business organization.
2. Explain how a sole proprietorship is created and how it operates.
3. Identify the factors that determine when a partnership comes into existence.
4. Describe strategies for minimizing the risk of being a partner.
5. Identify the key elements of a partnership agreement.
6. Distinguish between general and limited partnerships.
7. Describe the process of incorporating and organizing a corporation.
8. Describe the implications of the separate legal existence of the corporation.
9. Explain the division of power among the shareholders, the directors, and the officers to manage and control the corporation.
10. Identify three basic characteristics of shares of a corporation.

Doing business has risks. A manufacturer, for example, faces the risk that no one will buy its products, or that its products will hurt someone. But who exactly bears those risks? The answer depends upon the type of organization that is carrying on the business. We will focus on four possibilities:

- sole proprietorship
- general partnership
- limited partnership
- corporation

In each type of organization, the law strikes a different balance between the interests of the people who have a stake in the operation of the business (identified in Figure 18.1). The law determines the extent to which entrepreneurs benefit when their businesses prosper and lose when they do not. By affecting the risk to entrepreneurs in this way, the law influences incentives for entrepreneurs to start and maintain businesses.

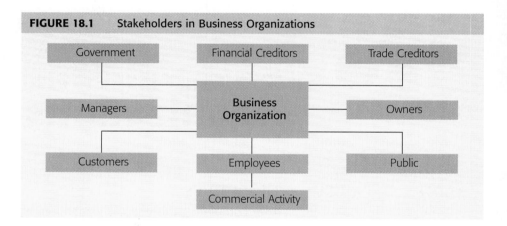

FIGURE 18.1   Stakeholders in Business Organizations

The law governing business organizations provides a structure for the *operation* of businesses, focusing on the relationship that owners and managers have with the business and with each other. It addresses such questions as these.

- What are the rights and obligations of the sole proprietor, the partner in a partnership, and the shareholder in a corporation to manage the business themselves and to monitor and control others who manage on their behalf?
- What remedies are available to owners when management acts in a manner contrary to the best interests of the business?

The law of business organizations also addresses the responsibilities that owners and managers have to other stakeholder groups—but only to a limited extent. For the most part, other types of laws govern those responsibilities.

- The rights and obligations of employees are governed by their employment contracts and by a range of regulatory laws, such as employment standards and occupational health and safety legislation, which are discussed in Chapters 25 and 26.
- The relationships between a business and its trade creditors (like suppliers of goods and services), financial creditors (like banks), and customers are dealt with under various types of law, including contract, tort,

property, commercial, and criminal law, which are discussed in other chapters.

■ Business organizations have a complex and multi-faceted relationship with the public. For instance, business decisions have a great impact on such areas as employment, the environment, and tax revenues. As a result, businesses are subject to various forms of direct regulation to protect the public interest, which we will examine in Chapter 23.

SOLE PROPRIETORSHIPS

The *sole proprietorship* is the simplest form of business organization. A **sole proprietorship** comes into existence when a person starts to carry on business on their own, without taking steps to adopt another form of organization, such as a corporation. If you agree to cut your neighbour's grass for money each week, you are carrying on business as a sole proprietor.

As a sole proprietor, you could enter into a contract to *employ* someone else to cut your neighbour's grass, but you remain the sole owner of the business and the only person responsible for it. Both legally and practically, there is no separation between the sole proprietorship business organization and the sole proprietor. As the sole proprietor, you cannot be an employee of the business because you cannot contract with yourself.

In this form of organization, the sole proprietor gets all of the benefits, and all of the burdens, of the business. This has several important implications in terms of the relationships between the business and its other stakeholders.

■ The sole proprietor is exclusively responsible for performing all contracts entered into in the course of the business, including sales contracts with customers, financial commitments, contracts with suppliers, and employment contracts.

■ The sole proprietor is exclusively responsible for all torts committed personally in connection with the business. That person is also vicariously liable for all torts committed by employees in the course of their employment. As we saw in Chapter 10, vicarious liability occurs when an employer is held liable for a tort that was committed by an employee.

■ For income tax purposes, the income or loss from the sole proprietorship is included with the income or loss from other sources in calculating the sole proprietor's personal tax liability.

The main advantage of a sole proprietorship is that it is simple and easy to set up. It is equally easy to dissolve: the sole proprietor simply stops carrying on the business. Just because you stop carrying on business, however, does not mean that you cease to be liable for the obligations that arose in connection with the business while it was being carried on.

The main disadvantage of a sole proprietorship is *unlimited personal liability*. **Unlimited personal liability** means that third parties may take all of the sole proprietor's personal assets—not just those of the business—to satisfy the business's obligations. As the scale of the business and the related liabilities increase, this exposure to personal liability becomes an increasingly important disincentive to using a sole proprietorship. Suppose that your grass-cutting business was wildly successful and you had entered into contracts to cut 1000 lawns each week and hired 100 students to do the work. As a sole proprietor, you would be personally responsible for all the work and to each employee. If one of your customers was not happy with the work and demanded a refund,

a **sole proprietorship** exists when a person carries on business without adopting any other form of business organization

the main advantage of a sole proprietorship is that it is simple and easy to set up

the main disadvantage of the sole proprietorship is unlimited personal liability

unlimited personal liability means that all of the sole proprietor's personal assets may be taken by third parties to satisfy the business's obligations or if an employee whom you fired sued you for wrongful dismissal, the liability would be yours alone. While you could try to manage the liability risk through contracts and insurance, incorporation is often a less expensive and more effective strategy.

there are limited ways to raise money for sole proprietorships

Another problem with sole proprietorships is raising money. Every business needs investment to grow. Since it is not possible to divide up ownership of the sole proprietorship, the only method of financing is for the sole proprietor to borrow money directly. An advantage of other forms of business is that they permit a wider range of financing possibilities. Consequently, sole proprietorships are used only for relatively small businesses.

Legal Requirements of the Sole Proprietorship

the name of a sole proprietorship may have to be registered

There are a few rules for carrying on a sole proprietorship. The name of a sole proprietorship must be registered if that name is something other than, or more than, the proprietor's personal name. Registration must be done in every province or territory in which the sole proprietorship carries on business.[1] For example, Amman Malik does not have to register if he carries on a grass-cutting business under his own name. But he does have to register if he uses the name "Malik's Gardening Services" or "Superior Gardening Services." Note that registration does not create any ownership interest in the business name. This interest is protected only under provincial passing-off laws and federal trademarks legislation, which are discussed in Chapter 16.

a business licence is government permission to operate a certain kind of business

A second rule, which applies to all forms of business organization including sole proprietorships, is that a *business licence* is required for some types of activities. A **business licence** is government permission to operate a certain kind of business. For example, most municipalities require the proprietors of taxi-driving businesses and restaurants to obtain a licence. Provincial governments have enacted licensing requirements for many types of businesses, including real estate agents, car dealers, and securities dealers. Anyone starting up a business should find out about the relevant licensing requirements.

GENERAL PARTNERSHIPS

a general partnership is a form of business organization that comes into existence when two or more persons carry on business together with a view to a profit

Where people pool their resources, knowledge, or skills, they may carry on business as a *general partnership* (or, more simply, a *partnership*). A **general partnership** is a form of business organization that comes into existence when two or more people carry on business together with a view to a profit. Partnership arises automatically by operation of law. Its creation does not require any formalities, although it may have to register the partnership name and obtain a business licence. For example, you and I agree to develop a business together: I agree to buy a lawnmower, and you agree to cut lawns with it. The profits are split between us. We have created a partnership.

Characteristics of General Partnerships

Like sole proprietors, partners carry on the business of the partnership themselves. Although the business can do some things in the name of the partnership, such as hold title to land or be sued, the partnership is not legally separate from the partners. That fact has several consequences.

[1.] This is the requirement in most provinces: for example, *Business Names Act*, RSO 1990, c B.17, s 2(2) (Ont).

- A partner cannot be employed by the partnership.
- All benefits of the partnership business accrue directly to the partners.
- All partners, even those who did not consent to a particular obligation, are personally liable for all of the obligations of the business, including torts committed by a partner or an employee of the partnership.

If a partnership is liable for an obligation, each partner is liable to the full extent of the obligation. *All* of a partner's *personal* assets—not just those that the partner committed to the business—may be seized to satisfy a partnership debt. This is contrary to the belief of many partners that only the partnership assets are exposed to risk.

The nature of a partnership means that its creditworthiness is partially based on the creditworthiness of the individual partners. For example, Eli and Taylor are partners in a restaurant business. The partnership has asked you to provide $200 000 worth of restaurant equipment on 90 days' credit. They need the equipment now, but will pay for it later. You should base your decision to enter into that contract on the assets that are held by the business *and* by Eli and Taylor personally. Suppose that you provide the equipment but are not paid on time. If the business's assets are worth only $100 000, you could get a judgment against the partnership and seize those assets *and* then seek to recover the remaining money from Taylor and Eli personally. You could collect $50 000 from each, or $100 000 from either. If you choose the second option and collect $100 000 from Eli, he can recover $50 000 from Taylor, unless they had some other arrangement.

To determine the liability of partners for income tax, the income (or loss) of the partnership is calculated by adding up all revenues of the partnership business and deducting all expenses. A share of the income (or loss) is allocated to each partner according to the partner's entitlement to share in the profits of the business. The partner's share of any business income must be included in their personal income, even if those profits were re-invested in the business and were not actually paid to the partner.

Partnership Property

Partnership property is all property acquired on behalf of the partnership or for the partnership business. If property is bought with partnership money, it is considered to have been bought on behalf of the partnership. Once property becomes partnership property, it must be held and used exclusively for the partnership and in accordance with the terms of the partnership agreement. Suppose that you bought a car for use in the partnership business. It would become partnership property. Even if you had paid for it out of your own pocket and were the registered owner, you could not convert it back to your personal use without the consent of the other partners.

Partnership Legislation and Partnership Agreements

The courts in England developed the law of partnerships and it was codified in the English *Partnerships Act* of 1890. All provinces, other than Quebec, have partnership legislation based on that English statute.[2] Because the acts are short and have never been substantially revised, they often do not provide a satisfactory set of rules for organizing a partnership. For that reason, partners often use a contract, called a **partnership agreement**, to supplement or modi-

all partners are personally liable for all of the obligations of the business

the creditworthiness of a partnership is partially based on the creditworthiness of the individual partners

partnership property is all property acquired on behalf of the partnership or for the partnership business

a partnership agreement is a contract between partners regarding the operation of the partnership

---

[2] For example, *Partnership Act*, RSBC 1996, c 348 (*BCPA*) (BC); *Partnership Act*, RSNS 1989, c 334 (*NSPA*) (NS); *Partnerships Act*, RSO 1990, c P.5 (*OPA*) (Ont).

fy the rules governing their relationship. Consequently, issues concerning the operation of a partnership are usually resolved on the basis of both the legislation and the partnership agreement.

Creating a Partnership

A partnership comes into being when two or more persons carry on business together with a view to profit.[3] Sometimes, it is unclear if that relationship actually exists. It is then necessary to consider a number of factors. The most important is the sharing of *profits*. The focus on profit sharing is directly related to the basic requirement that partners must *carry on business together*. Someone who is simply compensated out of revenues only has a stake in how much the business can sell. Furthermore, someone who is sharing profits must be concerned with the entire business operation, including the management of expenses. A partnership more likely exists if the parties both have a financial stake in the management of the business as a whole.

However, a partnership does not *necessarily* exist simply because the parties created a profit-sharing arrangement. They may do so *without* carrying on business together, such as in the following situations.

- Under the terms of a loan, the principal debt may be repaid out of the profits of the borrower's business. Alternatively, the lender's compensation may be an interest rate that varies with the borrower's profits.
- An employee's remuneration may vary with the employer's profits.
- A business may enter into an arrangement that requires it to pay a share of its profits to the spouse or child of a deceased partner.
- The purchaser of a business may agree to pay some of the business's profits to the seller as part of the purchase price.

Since profit sharing is not conclusive, it is often difficult to determine if a partnership exists.

- The idea of carrying on business together usually suggests the need for an enduring relationship, but even that factor may be inconclusive. There is probably no partnership if two competitors simply co-operate on an isolated transaction, as when a pair of software companies split the cost of a particular research project. The courts have held, however, that a partnership *may* arise even in relation to a single, time-limited activity.[4]
- A partnership is less likely to exist if the people involved are merely passive investors, for example, if they simply jointly own an apartment building and collect rent.[5] The situation may be different, however, if co-ownership of real estate is combined with active participation in its management and a sharing of profits.[6]

Margin notes:

profit sharing often indicates the existence of a partnership

a partnership does not necessarily exist simply because the parties created a profit-sharing arrangement

the existence of a partnership depends upon many factors

[3.] *BCPA* s 2; *NSPA* s 4; *OPA* s 2.

[4.] *Spire Freezers Ltd v The Queen* (2001) 196 DLR (4th) 210 (SCC).

[5.] *AE Lepage Ltd v Kamex Developments Ltd* (1977) 16 OR (2d) 193 (CA). In one case, the Supreme Court of Canada held that the receipt of rent under a number of equipment leases could constitute a business: *Hickman Motors Ltd v The Queen* (1997) 148 DLR (4th) 1 (SCC). Although this case did not address the issue of whether a partnership existed, it was cited in a more recent Supreme Court decision as authority for the proposition that the passive receipt of rents could be a business satisfying the requirements for the existence of a partnership: *Spire Freezers Ltd v The Queen* (2001) 196 DLR (4th) 210 (SCC).

[6.] *Volzkhe Construction v Westlock Foods Ltd* (1986) 70 AR 300 (CA).

In the final analysis, to determine if a partnership exists, a court will look at a number of factors:

- sharing profits
- sharing responsibility for losses, including guaranteeing partnership debts
- jointly owning property
- jointly controlling the business
- participating in management
- stating an intention to form a partnership in a contract
- filing certain government documents, such as registration under business names legislation as a partnership
- enjoying access to information regarding the business
- having signing authority for contracts and bank accounts
- holding oneself out as a partner
- being involved in the business full time
- using a firm name, perhaps in advertising
- hiring personnel
- establishing a separate address for the business

Every partnership needs money to set up business and to cover ongoing operating expenses, such as salaries and rent. Extra money may also be needed from time to time to buy new equipment or expand operations. Money can be raised from the partners or borrowed from a third party, such as a bank. The amount contributed by the partners is called the **capital**. The contribution of capital (in the form of money, property, or services) is indicative of a partnership, especially if the other parties also contribute capital to run the business.

capital refers to assets that the partners contribute to the business

You Be the Judge 18.1 and Business Law in Action 18.1 (p. 410) discuss the question of the existence of a partnership.

YOU BE THE JUDGE 18.1

Is There a Partnership?[7]

Groscki and Durocher were chartered accountants. Groscki ran a business giving tax advice and providing accounting services, which he operated out of premises that he owned. In 1989, he entered into an agreement with Durocher under which Durocher agreed to review financial statements and prepare tax returns for Groscki's clients for $20 an hour plus $913 a month. They agreed that Durocher would not be classified as an employee. That allowed Durocher to deduct certain expenses in connection with his work. Over time, Durocher assumed more responsibility for managing the business and supervising the staff. Groscki increasingly worked on other business ventures. In 1993, the name on the business letterhead and its sign was changed to say "Groscki and Durocher." Nevertheless, Durocher was never given signing authority for the business bank account and did not have access to the financial records of the business. In 1993, Durocher loaned $25 000 to Groscki for the business. In 1994, Durocher terminated his relationship with Groscki. Durocher argued that some of the firm's business belonged to him because he was a partner.

Questions for Discussion

1. What factors support the conclusion that the relationship between Groscki and Durocher was a partnership?
2. What factors suggest that it was not a partnership?
3. Which conclusion do you favour? Why?

---

7. *Groscki v Durocher* [1999] OJ No 2052 (QL) (SCJ), affirmed [2001] OJ No 39 (CA).

BUSINESS LAW IN ACTION 18.1

Partnership Tax Losses and the Creation of a Partnership[8]

Two recent Supreme Court of Canada cases clarified the requirement that investors must have a "view to a profit" for a partnership to come into existence.

A partnership was established to develop a luxury condominium project and operate a low-rent apartment complex. Through a complex series of transactions, Spire Freezers Ltd acquired a 50 percent interest in the partnership from Peninsula Cove Corporation, one of the original partners. In a subsequent transaction, the other original partner, BCE Developments Inc, sold its interest in the partnership to a number of other investors. It then bought the condominium development from the partnership for a price that created a $10 000 000 loss in the partnership.

Spire's main purpose in acquiring an interest in the partnership was to deduct its share of that loss against its other income and thereby reduce the income tax that it had to pay. Along with the other new investors, Spire continued to manage the apartment complex, which earned profits over a number of years, although not enough to offset the $10 000 000 loss. Revenue Canada refused to allow Spire to deduct the loss. It argued that Spire was not a partner because it was never carrying on a business "with a view to a profit."

The Supreme Court of Canada held that Spire *was* a partner and allowed the deduction. Even if Spire's main purpose was to deduct partnership losses, it also intended to carry on the business of the apartment complex. And even though the profits from that business were not sufficient to make up the $10 000 000 loss, that did not mean that the business was not being carried on with a view to a profit. The remaining business was not just "window dressing." Spire had an ownership interest in a substantial asset and performed significant management activity.

The Court reached the opposite conclusion in *Backman*. Again, a partner invested to take advantage of the deductibility of the partnership losses. In *Backman*, however, the remaining assets in the partnership were nominal and little management was required.

Question for Discussion

1. When should an investor who buys an interest in a partnership be allowed to deduct losses previously incurred by someone else in carrying on the partnership business?

Risk and Liability in General Partnerships

Business people need to know whether they are members of a partnership, primarily due to the risk of unlimited personal liability. An entrepreneur may be willing to accept that risk, either because it can be managed or because it is outweighed by the benefits of a partnership, such as the ability to deduct partnership losses for personal tax purposes. However, other people who are involved with a business, such as lenders, may want to avoid the risk of unlimited liability. For that sort of person, being found to be a partner may have unanticipated and disastrous financial consequences.

Managing the Risk of Becoming a Partner

As a matter of risk management, before joining a proposed relationship, you should examine it carefully to determine if you would indeed be entering into a partnership. If you have any concerns that you may get caught in a partnership, seek advice from a lawyer. In negotiating, you may insist on a contract with the other parties that expressly excludes a partnership.[9] You can also negotiate to

---

[8.] *Spire Freezers Ltd v The Queen* (2001) 196 DLR (4th) 210 (SCC); *Backman v The Queen* (2001) 196 DLR (4th) 193 (SCC).

[9.] Partnership status cannot be avoided, however, by a simple document to that effect: *Lansing Building Supply Ltd v Ierullo* (1990) 71 OR (2d) 173 (Dist Ct). There is no magic in words. A court will consider how the parties actually acted under their agreement.

structure the business organization to suggest that it is a not a partnership. If the matter is in doubt, you should insist upon sufficient compensation to reflect the risks that you are facing. And finally, as we will discuss, you can take steps to minimize the consequences if you actually are found to be a partner.

How Liabilities of the Partnership Arise

The provincial partnership statutes determine when a partnership incurs liabilities.[10] The basic principle is that each partner is an agent of the partnership. Therefore, each partner, when acting in the usual course of the partnership business, binds the partnership. That is the principle of **mutual agency**. An exception exists only if a partner did not have authority to act in a particular way (perhaps because of a restriction in the partnership agreement) *and* the outside party knew that that partner lacked authority.

mutual agency means that each partner, when acting in the usual course of partnership business, binds the partnership

The principle of mutual agency effectively places the risk of unauthorized behaviour on all of the partners. Partners are also liable for torts, such as negligence, that their fellow partners commit in the ordinary course of the partnership business. Given the unlimited personal liability of each partner, those liability risks are significant.

Managing Liability Risk If You Are a Partner

There are several legal and practical strategies for managing the risks associated with being a partner.

First, each partner owes a **fiduciary duty** to the others.[11] That duty requires each partner to act honestly and in good faith with a view to the best interests of the partnership. Partners must never put their personal interests ahead of those of the partnership. For instance, a partner cannot sell a piece of property to the partnership for an unfairly high price. A partner is also prohibited from competing with the partnership or using the name, property, or business reputation of the partnership to obtain a personal benefit. A partner who breaches the fiduciary duty must pay any resulting profits to the partnership.[12]

the **fiduciary duty** requires a partner to act in the best interests of the partnership

Second, the partnership agreement can be used to manage the risk of liability. Each partner can be expressly given limited authority and can be subject to formal control and monitoring mechanisms.[13] For instance, restrictions can be placed on who can write cheques or sign contracts. Note that these mechanisms do not prevent liability to a third party. When a partner fails to follow the rules and creates a liability, the firm will usually still be liable. These mechanisms are designed to reduce the risk that the liability will be created. When a liability is created in breach of the partnership agreement, the partnership

a partnership agreement can also be used to manage the risk of liability

---

[10] For example, *OPA* ss 6-19.

[11] Although there is no general expression of this duty in the *OPA*, it is well established that the fiduciary duty is a guiding principle of partnership law: *Hitchcock v Sykes* (1914) 23 DLR 518 (SCC). Section 22.1(1) of the *BCPA* expresses a general duty in the following terms: "a partner shall act with the utmost fairness and good faith towards the other members of the firm in the business of the firm."

[12] These obligations are specifically addressed in provincial partnership statutes: *BCPA* ss 32, 33; *NSPA* ss 32, 33; and *OPA* ss 29, 30.

[13] A partner may seek to minimize the risk associated with liability as a partner by holding the partnership interest in a corporation. A partner may also consider the scope for limiting liability of the partnership to those with whom the business has a contractual relationship by trying to negotiate protections in the contract. Alternatively, insurance may be a good mechanism for dealing with some risks. If some partners pay more than their share of a partnership debt, they can claim reimbursement from the other partners. That right, provided for in partnership statutes, is also a form of indemnification.

indemnification may be available between partners in connection with partnership liabilities

agreement may require the offending partner to compensate the others for the amounts that they are forced to pay to the third party. That is called a *right to indemnification*.

Third, partners can take practical steps to reduce the risk of partnership liability. Some partnerships involve only a small number of people who know each other very well. There is a natural relationship of trust and confidence. Furthermore, since each partner may be involved in the entire business on a daily basis, opportunities for informal monitoring exist. In that situation, there is relatively little likelihood of unauthorized activity. Those protections break down, however, as a partnership grows. The business becomes larger and more impersonal. In large law and accounting firms, for example, few partners are actively involved in all aspects of the business. Formal monitoring mechanisms therefore must be established under increasingly elaborate partnership agreements.

The lack of informal protections in large partnerships, coupled with an explosion in the number and size of professional liability claims, has encouraged professionals to lobby governments to change the law. That tactic recently worked in Ontario. Certain professional partnerships, such as lawyers and accountants, can now agree to become **limited liability partnerships**. Under that special form of general partnership, individual partners are not personally liable for the professional negligence of their partners if certain requirements are met.[14] Most large law and accounting firms have now become limited liability partnerships. All partners remain personally liable for obligations other than negligence, and the limited liability partnership is the same as a general partnership in all other respects.

in a **limited liability partnership**, individual partners are not personally liable for the professional negligence of their partners if certain requirements are met

Managing Liability Risk When You Are Not a Partner

You generally are *not* liable for partnership liabilities that arose before you joined, or after you left, the firm. However, you *may* be liable for a partnership obligation, if you **hold yourself out** as a partner or allow someone else to do so.[15] Suppose that you allow your name to be attached to a partnership even though you are not a partner. A bank lends money to the partnership because it knows that you are personally creditworthy. The bank can seek repayment from you if it relied on your *apparent* membership in the firm when deciding to make the loan.[16] You are also at risk if, for instance, you allow your name to appear on the partnership's letterhead, invoices, or business sign. Significantly, however, you cannot be held liable unless you actually *hold yourself out* as a partner or *know* that your name was being attached to the partnership and did nothing about it.[17]

holding out occurs when you represent yourself as a partner or allow someone else to do so

The issue of holding out often arises when a partner leaves a firm. In most cases, you want to avoid responsibility for any debts that arise *after* that time. There are two groups of clients that should concern you.

- Clients who dealt with the firm *prior* to your departure. These clients may honestly continue to rely on your creditworthiness when dealing with the firm. You will continue to be liable to them until they learn of your departure.
- Clients who deal with the firm for the first time after your departure, or

---

[14.] *Limited Liability Partnerships Act*, SO 1998, c 2. Ontario recently passed a law allowing small partnerships to incorporate for tax purposes. Full corporate limited liability is not granted under the statute: *Balanced Budgets for Brighter Futures Act, 2000*, SO 2000, c 42.

[15.] *BCPA* s 16; *NSPA* s 17; *OPA*s 15.

[16.] *Bet-Mur Investments Ltd v Spring* (1994) 20 OR (3d) 417 (Gen Div).

[17.] You cannot be held liable simply because you carelessly failed to realize that your name was attached to the firm: *Tower Cabinet Co v Ingram* [1949] 1 All ER 1033 (DC).

who never knew that you were a member of the firm. These clients cannot hold you liable unless you were held out to be a partner when they did business with the partnership.[18]

To manage those risks, you should ensure that clients who dealt with the firm before you left receive actual notice of your departure. You should also ensure that your name is deleted from the partnership registration. A notice published in a local paper may also be desirable, especially if the nature of the firm's business makes notice to each client impractical. And you should only allow the firm to continue using your name if the partnership agrees to indemnify you for any liabilities that you might incur as a result.

Internal Organization of the Partnership

Since partnerships involve more than one person, they need rules to settle basic issues, such as what each partner will do for the business, and how responsibility will be shared if something goes wrong. The partnership legislation in each jurisdiction provides a kind of standard form agreement that applies unless the partners agree to something else. These *default rules* give partners great flexibility to customize an internal structure to fit their particular needs.

default rules apply to partnerships unless the partners agree to some other arrangement

The default rules governing partners' relations are based on certain presumptions about the nature of the partnership. All partners are presumed to be *equal*, in terms of their financial interest *and* their rights to participate in management. In practice, however, that is hardly ever the case. Partners typically make unequal contributions of capital and services to the business, and their respective shares in the profits reflect those unequal contributions. Also, except in the smallest partnerships, partners generally delegate certain management functions to particular partners or committees. It is too cumbersome to have a firm run by many individuals.

the default rules are often inappropriate

In most cases, there is a significant difference between the statutory default rules and the parties' expectations. It is therefore important to know what the default rules are, if only so that they can be altered by the partnership agreement. These are the most important default rules.[19]

- Each partner shares equally both in the capital of the partnership and in any partnership profits. They must also contribute equally to any losses incurred.

- Each partner is entitled to be indemnified for payments that they make in the ordinary course of the partnership business or to preserve the business or its property.

- A partner generally is not entitled to interest on capital that they contributed. However, if a partner contributes more to the partnership than they agreed to, that partner is entitled to interest on the excess contribution.

- Each partner has a right to participate in the management of the partnership business.

- Decisions about ordinary matters connected with the partnership business may be decided by a majority of the partners.

- Each partner has equal access to the partnership books.

[18.] *BCPA* s 39; *NSPA* s 39; *OPA* s 36. In Ontario, publishing notice in the *Ontario Gazette* is sufficient to avoid liability to new clients of the firm.

[19.] This is the basic framework of default rules in *BCPA* ss 21-34, *NSPA* ss 22-34, and *OPA* ss 20-31. These rules vary slightly from one province to another.

- Unanimous consent is required for admission of a new partner, expulsion of a partner, or any change in the nature of the partnership business.
- Any person who takes an assignment of a partner's interest has no rights as a partner, except to receive the share of the partnership profits to which the assigning partner would otherwise be entitled.
- All property acquired by or for the firm must be used exclusively for the partnership.
- Any variation of the default rules requires unanimous consent.

We have now seen that a partnership agreement can be important to every phase of a partnership. Figure 18.2 summarizes some of the most important issues.

FIGURE 18.2	Key Issues to Address in a Partnership Agreement
Issue	**Content**
Name	What is the name of the partnership? Who will be entitled to use it if the partnership breaks up?
Membership of partnership	What criteria will be used for admission and expulsion? What process will be required to admit or expel a member?
Capitalization	What will be the capital contributions of the partners now and in the future?
Profits	How will the profits be shared between the partners? On what basis will they be paid?
Management	How will the partnership make decisions? What monitoring and control procedures will be put in place to guard against unauthorized liability and negligence? How will disputes be resolved?
Dissolution	What limits will be placed on the right of dissolution? Will death, insolvency, or resignation of a partner terminate the partnership for all partners? How will assets be distributed on dissolution?

Dissolution of Partnerships

dissolution is the termination of the partnership relationship

Dissolution is the termination of the partnership relationship. Partnerships can be dissolved easily. Any partner may terminate the partnership by giving notice to the others. Partnerships may also be dissolved if a partner dies or becomes insolvent.[20] If you set up a partnership for a specific purpose or for a limited time, such as to operate a painting business for one summer, it dissolves upon the achievement of that purpose or the expiry of that time.[21]

Partnership legislation provides a basic process to deal with the claims that arise upon dissolution.

- First, debts and liabilities to persons who are not partners are paid.
- Second, debts to partners (other than advances of capital) are paid.

[20.] *BCPA* ss 29, 36(1); *NSPA* ss 29, 36(1); *OPA* ss 26, 33.

[21.] *BCPA* s 30; *NSPA* s 30; *OPA* s 27.

- Third, invested capital is returned.
- Fourth, if anything is left, it is paid out to the partners according to their respective rights to the profits. The statutory scheme with respect to what the partners are entitled to on dissolution may be modified or fleshed out in an agreement.[22]

Business Decision 18.1 asks you to consider whether a partnership is an appropriate form of business organization in a specific situation.

BUSINESS DECISION 18.1

Creation of a Partnership

Melvin and Erin have known each other since childhood, and trust and respect each other. They have an idea for a new business—Ramps R Us. They have noticed that many businesses around Saint John (where they live) do not have adequate access for people in wheelchairs. They believe that they could make money by supplying low-cost ramps to businesses. Melvin has experience with metal fabrication, and Erin has worked for several years in retail marketing. Their plan is that Erin will get orders from local businesses, and that Melvin will construct and install the ramps. To get started, they need $100 000 for the metal-fabricating equipment, rent, and initial marketing expenses.

Melvin has a new car, owns his house, and has $50 000 in savings, which he is willing to contribute to the business. He is the sole supporter of two small children. He also currently operates as a sole proprietor under the name of Mel's

Metal. Mel's Metal has made a few wheelchair ramps in the past. Mel intends to continue working full time at Mel's Metal, at least initially. He will work in the new business at nights and on weekends.

Erin is single and has no dependants. She has no cash and no source of income at the moment. She also has substantial outstanding debts to various financial institutions.

Erin wants to be able to buy equipment and lease a shop for the proposed business. She also wants to do so without having to consult with Melvin. Even though Melvin trusts Erin and will be busy with his work at Mel's Metal, he does not want Erin to be able to bind the business without his consent.

Question for Discussion

1. What are the advantages and disadvantages of using a partnership to carry on this business?

LIMITED PARTNERSHIPS

All jurisdictions in Canada recognize limited partnerships. There are three essential distinctions between limited partnerships and general partnerships.

- First, in general partnerships, all partners have unlimited personal liability. But in **limited partnerships**, at least one of the partners, called a *general partner*, has unlimited liability, while at least one other, called a *limited partner*, has liability limited to the amount of their investment. Suppose that you had invested $5000 in a limited partnership as a limited partner. The partnership is being sued by an unpaid creditor. All of the partnership assets *and* the personal assets of the general partner can be used to satisfy that debt. Your liability, however, is limited to the amount of your investment—$5000.

- Second, limited partnerships come into existence only when a partnership declaration is filed with the appropriate government authority. A general partnership comes into existence as soon as the partners start carrying on business together with a view to a profit.

a **limited partnership** is a partnership in which the personal liability of at least one partner is limited to the amount of the partner's investment in the business

---

[22.] *BCPA* s 47; *NSPA* s 47; *OPA* s 44.

- Third, limited partners cannot participate in controlling the business or allow their name to be used in the firm name without losing their limited liability. A limited partner can, however, give management advice. In practice, it is often difficult to know when advice ends and control begins. For instance, in many limited partnerships, the general partner is a corporation. Someone may be both a limited partner in the partnership and a senior employee of the corporation. That person may manage the limited partnership, but in the capacity of an employee of the corporation. Since that limited partner is not in control of the business in a *personal* capacity, they may still have limited liability.[23]

Limited partnerships are usually attractive to passive investors who want to be treated as partners for tax purposes, but who want their liability limited.

CORPORATIONS

The corporation is the most common form of business organization. It is used for all types and sizes of businesses, from one-person operations to large multinationals. In this chapter, we will introduce the basic characteristics of the corporation and the process of incorporation. We will restrict our discussion to general business corporations and exclude publicly owned entities and specialized corporations, like banks and charities, that are governed under their own legislation. In Chapter 19, we will consider the legal rules for corporate governance.

Incorporation Process

Unlike sole proprietorships and general partnerships, corporations do not come into existence simply because one or more people start doing business. A corporation is created only when certain documents are filed with the appropriate government office under either the federal *Canada Business Corporations Act* (*CBCA*) or one of its provincial or territorial counterparts.[24] Once incorporated, the company is governed by the laws of the jurisdiction where incorporation occurred. The corporate laws in Alberta, Manitoba, Newfoundland, New Brunswick, Ontario, and Saskatchewan follow the federal model.[25] Though the structure of the corporate law rules in Prince Edward Island, Quebec, British Columbia, and Nova Scotia are somewhat different from the *CBCA*, the effect is similar in most respects.[26] Under the *CBCA* and the provincial acts that follow it, incorporation requires the filing of:

- articles of incorporation
- a name search report on the proposed name of the corporation
- the fee

---

[23] *Nordile Holdings Ltd v Breckenridge* (1992) 66 BCLR (2d) 183 (CA).

[24] *Canada Business Corporations Act*, RSC 1985, c C-44 (Can).

[25] *The Business Corporations Act*, SA 1981, c B-15 (Alta); *The Corporations Act*, RSM 1987, c C-225 (Man); *The Business Corporations Act*, SNB 1981, c B-9.1 (NB); *Corporations Act*, SN 1986, c 12 (Nfld); *Business Corporations Act*, RSO 1990, c B.16 (Ont); *The Business Corporations Act*, RSS 1978, c B-10 (Sask).

[26] *Company Act*, RSBC 1979, c 59 (*BCCA*) (BC); *Companies Act*, RSNS 1989, c 81, SNS 1990, c 15 (*NSCA*) (NS); *Companies Act*, RSPEI 1988, c C-14 (*PEICA*) (PEI); *Companies Act*, RSQ 1977, c C-38 (*QCA*) (Que).

The **articles of incorporation** set out the fundamental characteristics of the corporation—its name, the class and number of shares authorized to be issued, the number of directors, any restrictions on transferring shares, and any restrictions on the business that the corporation may conduct.[27] Once the required documents are properly filed along with the fee, the responsible official issues a certificate, which is then attached to the articles. That official document certifies that the corporation was incorporated on the date of the certificate.

The actual process of filing the requisite documents and receiving a certificate of incorporation is straightforward. Lawyers routinely incorporate businesses for their clients, as do other types of businesses at a lower price. Incorporation kits even permit do-it-yourself incorporations. However, since tax planning and other issues can arise in connection with incorporation, which is usually only the first step in organizing a business, it is sometimes wise to seek professional advice.

Upon incorporation, the company can start doing business. The business may be entirely new, or an existing business may be transferred to it. Several more steps are required, however, before the corporation is fully organized. First, the directors named in the incorporating documents must have a meeting and pass a resolution to issue shares to the shareholders. That is essential since, until the shares are issued, the only people who can act for the corporation are the directors named in the articles. Should anything happen to those directors, the corporation would be unable to act.

At the first meeting, the directors usually adopt arrangements for carrying on the formal legal business of the corporation. The directors decide, among other things:

- what notice must be given for meetings of directors and shareholders
- what constitutes a quorum
- who can sign contracts on behalf of the corporation
- what officers the corporation will have

Those arrangements are usually set out in a **bylaw**.[28] To take effect, a bylaw must be passed by the directors, but it only continues in effect if it is passed by the shareholders at their next meeting. Usually, a general organizational bylaw is passed by directors and approved by shareholders shortly after incorporation.

If a corporation has few shareholders, the final organizational step is usually the creation of a *shareholders' agreement*. A **shareholders' agreement** is a contract between shareholders that customizes their relationship. Corporate statutes set default rules for the rights and obligations of shareholders in a corporation. Shareholders' agreements, which are discussed in Chapter 19, allow shareholders to design rules that are better suited to their particular needs, including changing which matters require shareholder approval and the degree of shareholder support they need.

The corporation must maintain the articles of incorporation, bylaws, shareholders' resolutions, and any shareholders' agreement at its registered office, usually in a **minute book**. Shareholders and creditors must be given access to those documents. Articles, as well as any other documents (such as annual information filings) that are filed with a government agency, are maintained by the agency in a publicly accessible record.

> the articles of incorporation is the document that defines the corporation's basic characteristics

> a bylaw sets out the arrangements for carrying on the legal business of the corporation

> a shareholders' agreement is a contract between shareholders that customizes their relationship

> a minute book is a book in which corporate records are kept

---

[27.] The equivalent of articles under the *BCCA* and the *NSCA* is the memorandum of association; the equivalent under the *PEICA* is letters patent.

[28.] The equivalent of this bylaw under the *BCCA* and the *NSCA* is articles of association. Unlike bylaws, articles of association are mandatory and must be publicly filed.

A corporation does not have to register under provincial business names legislation unless it uses something other than its corporate name. However, it may require a business licence. If a corporation wants to conduct business outside of its home province or territory where it incorporated, it may need permission from the government of the jurisdiction where it wants to expand. Corporations incorporated under the *CBCA* have a right to carry on business throughout Canada.

Characteristics of Corporations

Separate Legal Existence

a corporation is a legal person distinct from its shareholders

Unlike a sole proprietorship or a partnership, a corporation has *separate legal existence*. The corporation *itself* carries on business, owns property, possesses rights, and incurs liabilities (including liability for crimes and torts). In most ways, a corporation has the same rights, powers, and privileges as a natural person. Shareholders have a bundle of rights in relation to the corporation through their ownership of shares. Shareholders do not, however, own the business that is carried on by the corporation, nor the property belonging to it. This contrasts with sole proprietors and partners, who carry on the business, own the property of the business, possess its rights, and are responsible for its liabilities directly.

Separate legal existence has three important implications.

- First, a shareholder can be an employee or a creditor of the corporation.[29] The shareholder and the corporation are, after all, two distinct entities—legally speaking.

- Second, for the same reason, the corporation is unaffected if a shareholder dies or withdraws from the business.

a **dividend** is a payment by the corporation to shareholders of cash or property which is authorized by the directors

- Third, the corporation is treated separately for income tax purposes. Income or losses that are generated through the business are attributed to the corporation and taxed at the corporate level. Shareholders are taxed only when they personally receive something from the corporation, such as a *dividend*. A **dividend** is a payment of cash or property by the corporation to shareholders, which is authorized by the directors. The payment of dividends is one way that shareholders receive a return on their investment in the corporation.

limited liability means that shareholders cannot lose more than they invest in the corporation in return for their shares

It is often said that shareholders have **limited liability** for the obligations of the corporation. Strictly speaking, however, shareholders have *no direct liability* for a corporation's obligations. To obtain shares, shareholders provide the corporation with money, property, or services. Shareholders are said to have limited liability because their maximum loss in connection with the business is limited to the value of what they transfer to the corporation in return for their shares. Creditors, employees, and other claimants against the corporation can demand to be paid out of the corporation's assets. But once the corporation's assets are exhausted, the creditors cannot claim against the shareholders personally. In the worst case, if all the assets of the corporation are taken by creditors, then the shareholder's shares may be worth nothing. They will have lost all their investment—but nothing more. Limiting the risk for shareholders in this way is intended to encourage entrepreneurship and shareholder investment.

Limited liability effectively shifts the risk of loss from the shareholders to the corporation's other stakeholders, such as creditors. Since creditors can

---

[29.] *Salomon v Salomon & Co* [1897] AC 22 (HL).

recover what is owed them only from the assets owned by the corporation, if the corporation has few assets they may refuse to lend money to the corporation unless a creditworthy shareholder provides a *personal guarantee* for the corporation's debt. If a shareholder gives such a guarantee and the corporation defaults, the shareholder is personally liable for the corporation's obligation.[30]

While the courts generally adhere to the concept of limited liability, they sometimes disregard the separate existence of the corporation in relation to a specific claim. In other words, they **pierce the corporate veil**.[31] For instance, a judge may permit a creditor of a corporation to claim directly against a controlling shareholder if the corporation has insufficient assets to satisfy the creditor's claim. Disregarding the corporation in this way does not destroy its separate existence for all purposes, but only for the *limited purpose* of granting relief to the creditor directly against the shareholder.

It is very difficult to predict when a court will pierce the corporate veil, although usually there must be some kind of serious impropriety or unfairness or both. When a business has been incorporated to do something (or facilitate the doing of something) that would be illegal or improper for the individual shareholders to do personally, the courts have disregarded the separate existence of the corporation. That occurs when a corporation was used to commit a fraud, as in Case Brief 18.1. Ethical Perspective 18.1 (p. 420) presents a case in which the arguments for piercing the corporate veil are not as clear.

> **piercing the corporate veil** occurs when a court refuses to give effect to the separate legal existence of the corporation and imposes personal liability on a shareholder

CASE BRIEF 18.1

Big Bend Hotel Ltd v Security Mutual Casualty Co (1979) 19 BCLR 102 (SC)

Kumar operated a hotel that was destroyed in a fire. Due to suspicious circumstances surrounding the fire, his fire insurance was cancelled. Kumar decided to acquire another hotel but knew that he would be turned down for fire insurance. He therefore incorporated Big Bend Hotel Ltd and had it acquire the hotel and apply for the insurance. The hotel burnt down. The insurance company refused to pay. The corporation sued for payment of the insurance proceeds.

The court denied the corporation's claim. It held that the insurance company would not have issued the policy to Kumar. Even though the corporation was a distinct legal person from Kumar, it was being used solely to disguise the real person behind the corporation. The insurance company should be able to disregard the separate personality of the corporation and treat the policy as if it had been applied for by Kumar directly. On that basis, the insurance company did not have to pay because Kumar had fraudulently failed to disclose the prior fire loss.

[30.] Chapter 19 discusses how shareholders may incur liability as directors and officers when they act in that capacity; Chapter 21 discusses guarantees.

[31.] *Littlewoods Mail Order Stores Ltd v Inland Revenue Commissioners* [1969] 3 All ER 855 (HL).

ETHICAL PERSPECTIVE 18.1

Limited Liability[32]

Carleton operated a taxi business using a number of separate corporations, each of which owned two cabs. Carleton owned all the shares of each corporation and managed the corporation's business. Each corporation maintained the minimum amount of third-party liability insurance coverage required by law—$10 000. Walkovszky was hit by a taxi cab owned by one of Carleton's corporations and suffered serious injuries. She sued the corporation that owned the car and was awarded compensatory damages in an amount that far exceeded $10 000. However, because the defendant corporation had no assets other than the cars, which were not worth much, she could not actually collect much more than the $10 000 that was available under the corporation's insurance policy.

Questions for Discussion

1. Is it appropriate for a person to carry on a taxi business though a corporation with assets that are insufficient to meet the reasonably foreseeable liabilities resulting from car accidents?

2. Should the court disregard the separate legal existence of the corporation and hold Carleton personally liable?

Separation of Ownership and Management

*a **board of directors** consists of the individuals whom shareholders elect to manage the corporation*

officers are the people to whom the board of directors delegates responsibility for managing the corporation

There is a legal distinction between managers of a corporation—the directors and officers—and the shareholders. By a majority vote, the shareholders elect a **board of directors** to manage the corporation. Those directors then delegate the responsibility for managing the corporation to the **officers** that they appoint. It is the directors who have the authority to monitor and supervise the officers' management of the corporation's business. Shareholders do not participate, as shareholders, in management. Unlike partners, they are not agents of the firm. In many corporations, especially small ones, however, these legally distinct roles are played by the same people: the shareholders are also the directors and officers. But in larger businesses, directors and officers are unlikely to hold all of the shares of a corporation, although they often do hold some. Large corporations, like Bell Canada Enterprises Inc, have thousands of shareholders, including the officers and directors.

shareholders must be concerned about management accountability

The separation of ownership and management creates a number of issues regarding internal relationships in the corporation, issues that are addressed by corporate law. Perhaps the most important relationship is the one between shareholders on the one hand, and officers and directors on the other. From the shareholders' point of view, the key issue is how shareholders can control management and ensure that management acts in their interests. That is addressed in Chapter 19.

Corporate Finance

Corporations are financed in two basic ways:

equity is what the shareholders have invested in the corporation in return for shares

- **equity**—the shareholders' investment in the corporation
- **debt**—loans that have been made to the corporation by shareholders, commercial lenders, or other creditors

debt consists of loans that have been made to the corporation

There is a basic difference between equity and debt. Debt is a claim for a *fixed amount*. Equity represents a claim on the *residual value* of the corporation after the claims of all creditors have been paid. The value of that residual claim

---

[32.] *Walkovszky v Carleton* 223 NE 2d 6 (NY CA 1966).

is a function of the value of the corporation's business. Valuing a business is complex and imprecise because it depends on numerous factors that change over time. The value of a business depends, in part, on the value of the tangible assets owned by the business, which may be difficult to assess. Increasingly, it also depends on intangible assets, which are even harder to value. How much is Microsoft's copyright in Windows worth? The value of a business is also affected by the corporation's plans for it. Most businesses are worth more as a **going concern**, that is, as an operating unit, than as a collection of assets that will be sold piecemeal. The expected future growth of a business is also a significant factor. Because businesses are hard to value, the residual claim that shares represent is also difficult to value. Shares are attractive because their value increases with the value of the business. Unlike debt, there is no limit on what they may be worth, nor, however, is there any guarantee that they will have any value at all.

the **going concern** value represents the value of a corporation as an operating unit

debt is a claim for a fixed amount

There is another critical difference between debt and equity. If a debt obligation is not repaid, there is a breach of contract. The creditor can sue for damages and even force the corporation into bankruptcy. But if an obligation to a shareholder, such as a dividend payment, is not met, the shareholder cannot put the corporation into bankruptcy. In fact, there may not be any remedy at all, as discussed in Chapter 19. Since shareholder rights are not as easily enforced as debt-holder rights, and because shares rank last in priority, shares are significantly riskier than debt.

shares represent a claim on the residual value of the corporation after the claims of all creditors have been paid

A corporation can have different **classes** of shares with different characteristics. Every corporation must have shares that cover three basic rights:

different **classes** of shares have different characteristics

- to vote for the election of directors
- to receive dividends declared by the directors
- to receive the property that remains after a corporation has been dissolved and all prior clams have been satisfied

Those basic rights do not have to be attached to any *single* class of shares—they can be spread out over several classes. All shareholders in a particular class must have the same rights. In practice, however, most corporations have one class of shares that includes all three basic rights called **common shares**. A corporation may also have *preferred shares*. Usually **preferred shares** are entitled to receive fixed dividends on a regular basis and a return of the amount invested. Their preference is to receive their dividends before any dividends may be paid on the common shares and, on dissolution, to receive their investment back before any payments are made to common shares. Preferred shares are therefore less risky than common shares. On the other hand, they usually have no voting rights and no claim to the residual value of the corporation after the amount invested has been repaid.

common shares carry all three basic rights

preferred shares are entitled to receive fixed dividends on a regular basis and a return of the amount invested before any payments are made to common shares

A wide range of names and characteristics can be given to shares. The specific bundle of rights that shareholders have is set out in the articles and is designed to create shares that will be attractive to prospective shareholders. The flexibility of equity financing is a significant advantage of the corporation.

Chapter Summary

The sole proprietorship is the simplest form of business organization. It comes into existence whenever a person begins carrying on a business. A sole proprietor has unlimited personal liability for the obligations of the business and is solely entitled to its benefits. Sole proprietorships (and other forms of business organization) may have to register under provincial business names legislation, and a business licence.

A partnership comes into existence when two or more people start to carry on business together with a view to a profit. Partnerships are governed by special statutes in each province that provide (i) default rules governing the relations of partners to each other and (ii) mandatory rules governing the relationship of the partnership to outsiders. Partners are personally responsible for the obligations of the business and are entitled to the benefits from it. Each partner is considered the agent of the partnership capable of creating partnership obligations within the course of its business.

The risks associated with unlimited personal liability and the ability of all partners to bind the partnership are addressed legally by the fiduciary duty owed by each partner to the partnership and by provisions in partnership agreements. In smaller partnerships, those legal protec-

tions are supplemented by informal monitoring of each partner by the other partners who work in the business. A limited partnership is a special form of partnership in which at least one partner's liability is limited to the amount it invested in the partnership.

A corporation is formed when certain documents are filed with the appropriate government authority. A corporation is legally separate from its shareholders and managers. The corporation alone is responsible for the obligations of the business that it carries on and is solely entitled to the benefits from the business. Shareholders have a financial interest in the corporation represented by their shares. They elect directors who have responsibility for managing the business and affairs of the corporation. Directors may delegate some of their management responsibility to officers.

A corporation can be financed in two ways. Equity is what the shareholders have invested in the corporation in return for shares. Debt consists of loans that have been made to the corporation. Shares represent a claim to the residual value of the corporation after all others with claims against the corporation are paid. Shares are a riskier investment than debt.

Review Questions

1. What is the main purpose of business organizations law?

2. What do you have to do to create a sole proprietorship?

3. Who is responsible for the obligations of a business that is carried on by a sole proprietor? What does this mean in practice for sole proprietors?

4. Can a person who is a sole proprietor also be an employee of the sole proprietorship? Explain your answer.

5. What are the major limitations of the sole proprietorship?

6. Is a partnership a separate legal entity? Are there some circumstances in which it is treated like a separate entity?

7. What are the criteria for the creation of a partnership?

8. Identify four situations in which sharing of profits does not result in the creation of a partnership.

9. If you were entering a business relationship and did not want to be a partner, what could you do?

10. What is mutual agency? What are the implications of mutual agency in terms of the risks that individual partners face?

11. If you are a partner, how do you protect yourself against the risk of other partners creating unauthorized obligations for the firm?

12. What is a limited liability partnership, and how is it different from a limited partnership?

13. How can you avoid being held liable for obligations that a partnership incurs after you have left that partnership?

14. What kinds of rules does provincial partnership legislation provide for the internal organization of partnerships? How are these rules addressed in a partnership agreement?

15. How is a corporation created? Why would you need a lawyer to advise you on creating a corporation?

16. What key documents define the characteristics of a corporation?

17. What does organizing a corporation involve?

18. "A corporation is a separate legal entity." What does that statement mean?

19. Does limited liability always protect a shareholder?

20. What are the differences between debt and equity from an investor's point of view? From the corporation's point of view?

Cases and Problems

1. Oren and Jenna carry on their business of buying and selling real estate as a partnership. Each is entitled to 50 percent of the profits from the business. Oren bought and sold a parcel of real estate without Jenna's permission or knowledge. Oren took all $100 000 of the profits from the sale himself. Is there a legal basis for Jenna to claim compensation from Oren? If so, how much is she entitled to receive?

2. Jordan and Sean are partners in a law firm. One of the firm's clients, Tran, became bankrupt recently. Just before his bankruptcy, Sean helped Tran to fraudulently sell his house to his wife for $1 to ensure that it would not be taken by his creditors. He did this at a meeting in the law firm's offices when he advised Tran how to transfer the house, prepared the necessary documents to give effect to the transaction, and then registered the transfer. Tran's creditors sued Sean and Jordan for fraud. Is Jordan liable for the fraudulent acts of his partner Sean?

3. You are the president of a large steel manufacturer, and all of your corporation's legal work is done by one of the largest law firms in the country, Osman & Co. Your company regularly relies on opinions from Osman & Co in making million-dollar business decisions. You have never worried about receiving bad advice from the firm because, if the firm was negligent and gave the wrong advice, the firm's insurance and the assets of all those rich partners would be available to satisfy any judgment in your favour. Today, you receive in the mail an announcement that Osman & Co is becoming a limited liability partnership. Would you have any concerns about this change and, if so, what might you do about it?

4. John and Rita are partners in a marketing firm. Under the terms of the partnership agreement, John and Rita each contributed $15 000 to the capital of the partnership and each is entitled to receive 50 percent of all profits of the business. Recently, the firm has been experiencing financial difficulty. John and Rita have therefore decided to dissolve the partnership. John and Rita are concerned that the partnership may not be able to pay off all of its debts and liabilities. The partnership owes $5000 to its landlord and has a bank loan of $10 000. As well, John has loaned $7000 to the partnership. They cannot decide which debts to pay off first, but believe that they are entitled to be paid first since they contributed the most to the partnership and have the most to lose. Can John and Rita pay themselves first? Assuming that the assets of the partnership are $30 000, how would they be distributed?

5. Bobby was one of several limited partners in a limited partnership called Typecast Limited Partnership, as well as the sole shareholder and president of a corporation named Live Life Magazine Inc, which was the general partner of Typecast. In his capacity as president of Live Life, he acted as the manager of the limited partnership. On behalf of the limited partnership, Bobby negotiated a contract with Gold Dust Graphics Ltd to supply printing services worth $50 000. Gold Dust paid the $50 000 to Typecast, but the limited partnership failed to perform the services. Gold Dust sued the limited partnership and got a judgment for $50 000, only to discover that neither Typecast nor the general partner, Live Life, has any assets. Can Gold Dust seek to recover its $50 000 from Bobby?

6. Sklar owns a computer software business that he has run as a sole proprietorship since 1995. Market conditions have been favourable to Sklar. His business has been a great success and is growing fast. Sklar has therefore decided to transfer the business of the sole proprietorship to a corporation in which he will be the only shareholder. As part of the consideration for the transfer of the business, the corporation has promised to pay him $50 000. Unfortunately, the corporation soon runs into serious difficulty despite Sklar's best efforts. On an application by its creditors, a court appointed Ernst & Young as a receiver to collect the assets of the corporation, pay off all debts, and transfer any remaining assets to the shareholder. Normally, each creditor would receive a share of the corporation's assets proportional to its respective claim. Ernst & Young says that the creditors other than Sklar should be paid before anything is paid to Sklar. They argue that the corporation is a sham and that Sklar is actually carrying on the business himself using the corporation as a disguise. In other words, Sklar's claim to the $50 000 is actually a claim against himself and, therefore, unenforceable. Do you agree with Ernst & Young?

7. For over five years, Rick was the CEO of JB Guitars Inc, a corporation operating a chain of retail guitar stores. He had gained tremendous practical experience and decided to start his own business selling guitars. However, he had entered into an agreement with JB Guitars when he first started working there, under which he promised that he would not carry on a competing business for two years after he ended his employment with JB Guitars. To avoid breaching that contract, Rick incorporated a corporation named Generation X Guitars Inc to carry on the business. He is the sole shareholder, director, and president. Rick's old employer claims that the new corporation is just a way of getting around the non-competition agreement and sued for a court order prohibiting Generation X Guitars from carrying a business competing with JB Guitars. Will JB Guitars be successful?

8. Tiffani and Armaan are sisters. Last year, they inherited $200 000 each from their grandfather's estate. Using all of both inheritances, they bought a small apartment building in downtown Vancouver. They entered into a co-ownership agreement which states that profits are to be paid to each co-owner in proportion to her 50 percent interest and that each is liable to contribute to any loss in the same proportion. Any sale or other dealing with the property by one co-owner requires the consent of the other. Tiffani and Armaan do not take part in the management of the apart-

ment building directly. They have hired a property management company to ensure that the apartments are rented and to collect the rents. Recently, Tiffani met someone willing to cut the grass and do the gardening around the building for a great price. She wants to enter into a contract for these services for a year. She believes that Armaan will not agree, so she is thinking about going ahead with the contract without advising her sister. If Tiffani does sign a contract, will it be binding on Armaan?

9. Seth and Marta have decided to start a travel agency business using a corporation. Seth will make only a small initial financial investment in the corporation, but will manage the business on a daily basis. Since the business will succeed or fail on his efforts, he wants to have his returns from the business depend entirely on how the business is doing. Marta works for the public service and is the sole support for her family of three. She recently sold her house and has $150 000, which she wants to invest in the business. Marta is not interested in working in the business and is content to have Seth manage it on his own. Her only concern is that she wants to receive a fixed annual return of 10 percent on her investment. What kind of shares would Seth and Marta each want?

10. Alice has been carrying on a sporting goods business in Ottawa as a sole proprietorship under the name A-Sport since 1996. By the spring of 2001, she was unable to cover the substantial costs associated with the business. By September 2001, she had sold many of her personal assets, including her house, to pay the businesses expenses. Alice is very worried that she will lose the business and not be able to support her daughter, since she is a single mother and has no other source of income.

In September 2001, Alice met Mario at a trade show in Montreal. Mario carries on a business similar to Alice's in Toronto, also as a sole proprietorship. The key to his success has been a combination of innovative inventory management techniques and the use of aggressive television advertising. Mario is married with three children.

Alice and Mario talk about the possibility of carrying on the A-Sport business in Ottawa together in some way. Mario is from Ottawa originally and wants to invest in Alice's business. Mario has $100 000 available for such a venture and has substantial assets, including three store premises and a warehouse in Toronto. They agree on the following.

- Alice will contribute all of her interest in the A-Sport business.
- Mario will contribute $100 000 in cash.
- Alice will manage the A-Sport stores on a day-to-day basis, while Mario will be responsible for marketing and inventory management. Mario will continue to spend most of his time in Toronto looking after his business there.
- All major decisions for the business will require the agreement of both Mario and Alice.

What issues should Alice and Mario address before going into business as a partnership?

11. Based on the facts in Problem 10, how would these issues be addressed differently if Alice and Mario were to set up a corporation to accomplish their business objectives.

12. Peter and Sarah were both accountants carrying on business as sole proprietors. They decided to enter into an arrangement that would reduce their expenses.

- They rented premises consisting of three offices and a reception area, out of which they would both practice. Each signed the lease as a tenant.
- They hired a secretary to work for both of them.
- They will each contribute equally to the office expenses.
- Apart from those shared expenses, all expenses are the responsibility of the person incurring them.
- All decisions regarding the management of the office (such as the secretary's rate of pay and the choice of long-distance provider) require the consent of both Peter and Sarah.
- Each will bill and be exclusively entitled to the fees received in return for their own work.

Is this a partnership? To be certain, what other information would you need?

19

Legal Rules for
Corporate Governance

OBJECTIVES

After completing this chapter you should be able to:

1. Describe the basic allocation of power and responsibility in the corporation among directors, officers, and shareholders.

2. Explain how the allocation of power contemplated in corporate law does not always operate in practice.

3. Determine what the fiduciary duty, the duty of care, and the oppression remedy require of management in specific situations.

4. Identify four common situations in which the personal interests of directors and officers may be in conflict with the best interests of the corporation.

5. Explain the legal standard of care that management must observe when making business judgments.

6. Describe one of the few corporate law rules that are designed to protect creditors.

7. Outline five legal strategies available to shareholders for ensuring that management is accountable to them.

8. Explain when a corporation will be liable for torts and crimes due to the actions of people working on its behalf.

9. Identify whether a corporation's employee has authority to enter into a contract on behalf of the corporation.

10. Identify the liability risks associated with being a director or officer and some strategies that can be used to avoid these risks.

The rules for how corporations are governed in Canada have a fundamental impact on how they are structured. Rules defining when someone can bind a corporation to a contract, for example, affect how corporations organize their contract approval process to ensure that contracts are not entered into unless they are authorized. Corporate governance rules also affect incentives for entrepreneurs to start and carry on their businesses, for investors to invest in businesses, and for managers to work for businesses. One key issue is how management is made accountable to investors. Without sufficient accountability, shareholders will not invest. However, accountability obligations must not be so great that they interfere with management's ability to do its job or discourage capable people from becoming managers.

In this chapter, we discuss the basic legal rules for corporate governance in Canada. We begin by laying out the distribution of power and responsibility among directors, officers, and shareholders as set out in the *Canada Business Corporations Act* (*CBCA*) and most other corporate statutes in Canada.[1] Next, we will look at the standards for management behaviour that are imposed by corporate statutes to ensure management accountability to shareholders. Those standards include the fiduciary duty and duty of care. We will also look at the procedures that shareholders can use to enforce those standards.

Management also has responsibilities to non-shareholder stakeholders, such as employees, creditors, and the public. In this chapter, we look at situations in which corporations become liable in contract, tort, and criminal law, and the implications that these liability rules have for corporate organization. Another important aspect of the governance scheme are the regulatory statutes designed to protect the public, many of which impose personal liability on corporate managers. Statutes that impose fines on directors for environmental damage caused by corporate activities are one example. Environmental and other forms of regulation are discussed in Chapter 23.

MANAGEMENT AND CONTROL OF THE CORPORATION

Power and responsibility in the corporation belong to different groups of people.

shareholders are the residual claimants to the assets of the corporation and elect the directors

- **Shareholders** are entitled to the assets of the corporation remaining after all the creditors are paid on its dissolution. Their only powers are to vote for the election of directors, to appoint the auditor, and to vote on proposals made to them. As shareholders, they do not participate in managing the ordinary business of the corporation.

directors are responsible for managing or supervising the management of the business of the corporation

- **Directors** are responsible for managing or supervising the management of the business of the corporation and its internal affairs, including issuing shares, declaring dividends, and calling shareholder meetings.

officers are appointed by the directors of a corporation and exercise management powers delegated to them by the directors

- **Officers** are appointed by directors and exercise substantial management powers delegated to them by the directors.

Figure 19.1 lays out the relationship between these three groups of people.

[1.] *Canada Business Corporations Act*, RSC 1985, c C-44 (*CBCA*) (Can); *The Business Corporations Act*, SA 1981, c B-15 (*ABCA*) (Alta); *The Corporations Act*, RSM 1987, c C-225 (*MBCA*) (Man); *The Business Corporations Act*, SNB 1981, c B-9.1 (*NBBCA*) (NB); *Corporations Act*, SN 1986, c 12 (*NCA*) (Nfld); *Business Corporations Act*, RSO 1990, c B.16 (*OBCA*) (Ont); *The Business Corporations Act*, RSS 1978, c B-10 (*SBCA*) (Sask). In subsequent notes, references will be made to illustrative provisions, rather than to all statutes.

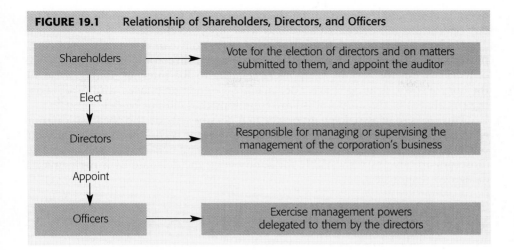

FIGURE 19.1   Relationship of Shareholders, Directors, and Officers

HOW DIRECTORS AND OFFICERS EXERCISE POWER

Directors

Under the *CBCA* and statutes modelled after it, the first directors of a corporation are those appointed at the time of incorporation in the articles. These directors hold office until the first meeting of shareholders, which must be held within 18 months of incorporation.[2] At that meeting and others at which an election is required, shareholders must, by simple majority vote, elect directors. Some corporate statutes impose Canadian residency requirements for some proportion of directors: under the *CBCA*, it is 25 percent for most corporations.[3]

Directors exercise their power collectively, primarily at meetings. However, a written resolution signed by all directors is as effective as a resolution passed at a meeting. As Chapter 18 explained, the corporation's articles or bylaws typically contain its rules for calling and conducting meetings, such as the necessary quorum and who is the chair. Corporate statutes provide some default rules if the corporation has not set its own.

Officers

Nothing in Canadian corporate legislation addresses what officers a corporation should have or what they are to do. Most corporations have officers called chief executive officer (CEO), president, and secretary. Other common officers are vice-president and treasurer. Directors can be officers, but they need not be.

Corporate statutes give directors the power to designate offices, like president and secretary, and to specify the duties of those offices. Usually this is done in a bylaw passed by directors and approved by shareholders just after incorporation. After setting up the offices, the directors appoint people to fill them. Although there are no fixed rules, a common corporate structure gives the CEO

---

[2] *CBCA* s 133; *OBCA* s 118.

[3] *CBCA* s 105(3), as amended by SC 2001, c 14, s 37. In some provinces, a majority of directors must be Canadian residents: for example, *OBCA* s 123.

overall responsibility for running the corporation's business, while the day-to-day operations are delegated to others who report to the CEO.

Under the *CBCA* and similar statutes, directors can delegate any of their powers to a managing director, to a committee of directors, or to one or more officers, except for certain key powers relating to the internal management of the corporation. Issuing shares, declaring dividends on shares, and repurchasing the shares of the corporation are functions that cannot be delegated.[4]

Directors may also delegate power to a person outside the corporation. For example, many corporations grant power to manage some specific area of their business to a management company that has special expertise in the area. The directors are always responsible for supervising the delegate as it performs its delegated responsibilities.

MANAGEMENT'S DUTIES TO THE CORPORATION

Fiduciary Duty

fiduciary duty is the duty of officers and directors to act honestly and in good faith in the best interests of the corporation

The **fiduciary duty** is the most important legal standard of behaviour for officers and directors. Section 122(1)(a) of the *CBCA* defines this duty.

> Each director and officer in exercising his powers and discharging his duties shall... act honestly and in good faith with a view to the best interests of the corporation....

what the fiduciary duty requires is elusive

Even though numerous cases have addressed the fiduciary duty, what it means in specific situations remains elusive. The duty to act honestly is straightforward: directors and officers cannot defraud the corporation, such as by stealing corporate assets. Beyond honesty, directors and officers must try to do what is best for the corporation and must not put their personal interests ahead of the interests of the corporation.

The fiduciary duty is owed to the corporation, not to the shareholders or to employees, customers, suppliers, creditors, the public, or any other corporate stakeholder. It is often difficult, however, to define what the interests of the corporation are. For example, is it in the corporation's best interests to pay high wages or to keep wages as low as possible? While high wages may lead to happy, productive workers, it may reduce cash flow available to pay off creditors. Does the obligation of management to act in the best interests of the corporation require it to try to accommodate the divergent interests of employees and creditors?

courts treat the interests of the corporation as defined by the interests of shareholders

The courts have avoided this problem by treating the interests of the corporation as defined by the interests of shareholders: whatever maximizes the value of shareholders' investment in the corporation's shares is in the best interests of the corporation. No corporation will maximize share value if it completely ignores the interests of its employees, customers, creditors, and other stakeholders, but management is not permitted to favour the interests of other stakeholders at the expense of share value.

Managers must be particularly concerned about their fiduciary duty when their personal interests and their duty to the corporation may conflict. We will discuss the most common situations in which such a conflict may arise.

[4.] *ABCA* s 110; *CBCA* s 115(3); *OBCA* s 127(3).

Transacting with the Corporation

A conflict of interest arises when a director or officer contracts with the corporation. Suppose that you have an opportunity to sell goods to a corporation of which you are a director. As the seller, you want to negotiate the highest possible price for your goods. However, the corporation's interest is precisely the opposite, as it wants to get the goods for the lowest possible price. If, as a director, you are responsible for negotiating the contract on behalf of the corporation, you have a serious conflict of interest. Your duty binds you to do whatever is in your power to get the lowest price for the corporation. At the same time, your personal interest is in selling for the highest price. Even if you are not directly involved in the negotiations on behalf of the corporation, as a director, you may be in a position to influence the corporation's decision making either directly, as a member of the board if the contract must be approved by the board, or indirectly, by virtue of your relationship with the corporation and its personnel. A conflict still exists and may result in a suboptimal transaction for the corporation.

a conflict of interest may arise when a director or officer contracts with the corporation

Historically, because of the inevitable conflict between duty and personal interest, a fiduciary was prohibited from participating personally in any transaction with the corporation. This creates a practical problem where the best price or even the only source of supply is a director or officer or a business related to a director or officer. This problem often arises in transactions between corporations with common ownership that do business with each other. Consider two corporations under common ownership where one supplies the raw materials that the other uses in its business.

The solution to this problem in the *CBCA* and most other Canadian statutes is to permit a transaction between the corporation and a director or officer (or a business related to them) if procedural *safeguards are observed*. The director or officer must give adequate notice of the interest and may not vote on the approval of the contract by the board of directors. As well, the contract must be fair and reasonable to the corporation. In practice, notice regarding the interest should be recorded in the minutes of the board meeting at which the contract is approved. Compliance with these requirements is the only way to avoid a fiduciary breach. If this scheme is not complied with, the corporation may refuse to complete the transaction.[5]

a director or officer can take steps to avoid breach of the fiduciary duty

Taking Corporate Opportunities

A conflict between personal interest and fiduciary duty arises when the fiduciary considers taking advantage of some project or opportunity in which the corporation has an interest. This situation often arises because a principal task of management is to choose the projects the corporation should invest in—acquiring an asset, establishing a business, or signing a contract. If fiduciaries were permitted to personally invest in projects, there is a risk that they would take for themselves valuable investment opportunities that they should have tried to obtain for the corporation. The fiduciary duty prohibits fiduciaries from allowing their personal interest to conflict with their duty to the corporation and taking an opportunity belonging to the corporation. If they do, any personal profit from the opportunity must be paid over to the corporation. This obligation is intended to eliminate any incentive for the fiduciary to take the opportunity in the first place.

a conflict of interest may arise when the fiduciary considers taking personal advantage of some project or opportunity in which the corporation has an interest

---

[5.] *CBCA* s 120; *OBCA* s 132.

When does the opportunity belong to the corporation, so that the fiduciary should be prohibited from taking it? Case Brief 19.1 illustrates how to deal with this question.

CASE BRIEF 19.1

Canadian Air Services Ltd v O'Malley (1974) 40 DLR (3d) 371 (SCC)

Canadian Air Services Ltd (Canaero) was in the business of mapping and geographic exploration. O'Malley, the president, was assigned to Guyana to obtain a contract for mapping the country. After working on this project for some time, he resigned from Canaero and incorporated his own business, Terra Surveys Ltd, to perform work similar to what he was doing for Canaero. The government of Guyana asked for bids to map the country and accepted Terra's bid over Canaero's. Canaero sued O'Malley, alleging that he had breached his fiduciary duty to Canaero by taking the benefit of an opportunity belonging to the corporation.

The Supreme Court of Canada held that O'Malley did breach his duty. The court cited several factors that showed that the opportunity to map Guyana belonged to Canaero.

■ *Specific nature of opportunity*: It was a specific

opportunity that the corporation had been actively pursuing, rather than one that was simply in the same area as the corporation's business.

■ *Maturity of opportunity*: It was also a mature opportunity in the sense that Canaero had done extensive work in preparing for it. It was substantially the same opportunity that Canaero had been working on through O'Malley, although the ultimate contract was different in some respects.

The court also decided that O'Malley's close relationship to the opportunity while at Canaero supported a conclusion that he should be prohibited from taking it. O'Malley learned all about the opportunity through his position, did the preparatory work relating to the opportunity, and negotiated for it on behalf of Canaero.

Whether a breach of fiduciary duty will be found in any case depends on several factors. In addition to the ones cited in *Canadian Air Services*, the courts have said that these factors indicate that the opportunity belonged to the corporation.

■ *Significance of opportunity*: The opportunity would have represented a major component of the corporation's business if acquired or was a unique opportunity rather than merely one of many considered by the corporation.

■ *Private opportunity*: The opportunity was not publicly advertised or otherwise widely known, but was one to which the fiduciary only had access by virtue of the fiduciary's position in the corporation.

■ *Rejection*: The opportunity had not been rejected by the corporation before the fiduciary acquired it.[6]

Competition by Directors and Officers

In general, it is not a breach of fiduciary duty to terminate one's relationship with a corporation and go into competition with it. Otherwise, the fiduciary duty might become an unreasonable restraint on a person's ability to earn a living. However, a fiduciary may not compete with the corporation while remain-

a fiduciary cannot compete with the corporation while remaining in a fiduciary relationship with the corporation

---

[6] *Peso Silver Mines Ltd v Cropper* (1965) 56 DLR (2d) 117 (BCCA), affd 58 DLR (2d) 1 (SCC). In this case, a rejection by the board of an opportunity was held to be sufficient to allow a board member to take the opportunity himself.

ing in a fiduciary relationship with it. And as Case Brief 19.1 showed, a fiduciary cannot quit to take an opportunity developed by the fiduciary while working for the corporation. Any competing fiduciary will be forced to pay over all profits from the competing business to the corporation.[7]

Hostile Takeover Bids

When a bidder makes a **takeover bid** by offering to purchase enough shares to gain control of a corporation, they are usually motivated by a belief that they can increase the value of the corporation by making some changes in management. Almost always, the changes include replacing existing directors and senior managers. The self-interest of directors and senior managers may lead them to try to defeat the takeover bid to preserve their jobs. Defensive measures often include issuing new shares to make the bid more expensive. If a bid is withdrawn as a result of such defensive measures, however, the shareholders may be worse off. Bidders typically offer shareholders a substantial premium over the current market price. Those who do not sell will benefit from the improvements made by the bidder to increase the value of their shares.

If no defensive measures were permitted, the only way management could prevent a takeover bid would be to manage the corporation so effectively that no bidder could improve share value by managing better. Following this argument, the courts should apply the fiduciary duty to prevent all defensive measures. The threat of takeover bids will be a strong incentive to good management. The problem with prohibiting management from defending against *all* bids is that some takeovers are not in the best interests of the corporation or its shareholders. For example, a bid may be at a price that the directors correctly believe is lower than the actual value of the corporation's shares. Unfortunately, reasonable opinions about the actual value of shares and thus the bid may differ substantially.

The courts have permitted some defensive actions taken by the directors, particularly those that have followed procedures to minimize the conflict of interest. These typically involve setting up a committee of directors to decide how to respond to the bid, which is independent of senior management, since they have the most to lose if the bid is successful. The courts have also endorsed measures designed to allow time to find a second bidder to compete with the first rather than simply to stop the bid. Defensive measures of this kind still permit shareholders to choose whether to sell and may increase the price offered to them.

a **takeover bid** is an offer to buy shares in a corporation, usually with a view to acquiring control of the corporation

Duty of Care

The second important standard of behaviour for management imposed by corporate law is the **duty of care**, which the *CBCA* defines in these terms:[8]

> Every director and officer of a corporation in exercising his powers and discharging his duties shall... exercise the care, diligence and skill that a reasonably prudent person would exercise in comparable circumstances.

The degree of care required by this standard depends upon the facts of each case. In all cases, however, directors must have at least a basic understanding

duty of care requires every director and officer to exercise the care, diligence, and skill that a reasonably prudent person would exercise in comparable circumstances

[7.] *Bendix Home Systems Ltd v Clayton* (1977) 33 CPR (2d) 230 (Ont HCJ).

[8.] Section 122(1)(b). Provincial statutes, other than those in Nova Scotia and Prince Edward Island, also impose a duty of care: for example, British Columbia's *Company Act*, RSBC 1979, c 59 (*BCCA*) s 142(1)(b) and *OBCA* s 134(1)(b).

of the business. A director who does not have this minimal level of understanding should acquire it or resign.[9]

In addition to a basic level of competence, the duty of care requires some
monitoring of the business. This does not require a detailed inspection of the
daily activities of the corporation; however, it does involve keeping informed
about the corporation's policies and its business, as well as regularly attending
board meetings.

The reference to a person "in comparable circumstances" means that the
duty has a subjective element. If you have significant knowledge or experience,
you have to meet a higher standard of care.[10] The standard of care also depends
upon a person's position. For example, all **public corporations**, which are large
corporations that have issued shares to members of the public, must have an
audit committee to review the financial statements and the financial reporting
process.[11] Directors who serve on this committee have more opportunity to
examine the financial affairs of the corporation than other directors. Therefore,
more is expected of them in terms of monitoring these affairs and warning
other directors about problems.

Being removed from some aspect of the corporation's business, however,
does not relieve directors of their duty. For example, in a small corporation with
few shareholders, one of the directors, a chartered accountant, may be responsible for dealing with the financial side of a corporation's business. However, all
the other directors are still required to comply with a standard of care in relation to financial matters. If one of these other directors learns that the corporation failed to properly withhold income tax from employee wage payments
and remit the tax to the Canada Customs and Revenue Agency, that director
must do everything reasonably possible to ensure that the corporation puts in
place procedures to prevent a recurrence. This might include requesting a
board meeting to discuss the problem, inquiring into the problem, designing a
solution, and monitoring to ensure that the solution is put into effect.[12]

The courts have been reluctant to find a breach of the duty of care when
this involves second-guessing management on issues of general business judgment, such as whether a particular deal was the best one for the corporation.
They have acknowledged their lack of business expertise. Courts often say that
they do not want to set the standard for the duty of care so high that it inhibits
business people from doing their jobs or discourages people from becoming
directors and officers at all. As a result, business decisions are presumed not to
be a breach of duty in the absence of fraud, illegality, or conflict of interest on
the part of the decision maker. The duty of care still requires that the process
for making the decision is reasonable in the circumstances. For example, managers must try to ensure that decisions are based on adequate information and
advice. The approach taken by courts to business decisions is sometimes
referred to as the **business judgment rule**.[13]

Especially in large corporations, officers and directors must rely on the
advice of experts, including accountants, lawyers, investment dealers, and engineers. Directors and officers are not liable for breach of their duty of care if they

public corporations have
issued their shares to the public

being removed from some
aspect of the corporation's business does not relieve directors
or officers of their duty

the **business judgment rule** is
a presumption that, in making
business decisions, directors
and officers are not in breach of
their duty in the absence of
fraud, illegality, or conflict of
interest

[9.] *Selangor United Rubber Estates Ltd v Craddock* [1968] 2 All ER 1073 (Ch).

[10.] *Re Standard Trustco Ltd* (1992) 6 BLR (2d) 241 (Ont SC).

[11.] In most cases, the shares of public corporations trade on a stock exchange, such as the Toronto
Stock Exchange.

[12.] *Fraser v MNR* [1987] DTC 250 (TCC).

[13.] *Schelensky v Wrigley* 237 NE 2d 776 (Ill App 1968). The business judgment rule has been
endorsed by Ontario courts: for example, *Pente Investments Management v Schneider Corp* (1998)
42 OR (3d) 177 (CA).

rely on financial statements or reports of lawyers, accountants, and other professionals.[14]

Protection for Creditors

Directors and officers have no duty to protect the interests of creditors of the corporation. For the most part, creditors are left to protect themselves by contract, as Chapter 21 discusses. There are, however, some corporate law provisions that benefit creditors. Corporate law tries to ensure that the corporation's money and assets are not distributed to shareholders, directors, officers, or employees, if that would threaten the corporation's ability to pay its creditors.

directors and officers have no duty to protect the interests of creditors of the corporation

Directors cannot authorize either the payment of a dividend to a shareholder or the corporation's purchase of a shareholder's shares if there are reasonable grounds for believing that (i) the corporation could not pay its liabilities to its creditors as they become due, or (ii) the realizable value of the remaining assets (after the payment) would be less that the total amount owed to creditors plus the total of all shareholder investments.[15] Directors are personally liable if they authorize such payments. Under some corporate statutes, the directors are also liable if they authorize the corporation to lend money or provide other financial assistance to directors, officers, shareholders, or employees of the corporation when either of these tests is not met.[16]

Even though the main purpose of these provisions is to protect the creditors, they are not enforceable directly by creditors. The directors' obligation not to authorize payments if the tests are not met, and to compensate the corporation if they do, is owed to the corporation. Only the corporation can enforce those obligations.

HOW SHAREHOLDERS EXERCISE POWER

For most purposes, shareholders must act collectively. This usually takes place at meetings during which shareholders have an opportunity to question and criticize management, as well as to discuss and vote on proposals made to them. Directors are responsible for calling meetings but, under most corporate statutes in Canada, a group of shareholders holding at least five percent of voting shares may require the directors to call a meeting.[17] Directors are obligated to call *annual meetings* at least every 15 months. At **annual meetings**: (i) directors are elected, (ii) the auditor is appointed for the coming year, and (iii) financial statements for the past year are discussed. Directors must ensure that shareholders receive advance notice of the meeting, along with information regarding these three items and any other business.

at **annual meetings,** shareholders elect directors, appoint an auditor, and review the annual financial statements

---

[14.] *BCCA* s 127; *CBCA* s 123(4); *OBCA* s 135(4). This defence is not available under the *NCA*.

[15.] *CBCA* ss 34, 35, 36, 42, 118; *OBCA* ss 30, 31, 32, 38, 130. To pass the second test, the realizable value of the corporation's assets must exceed the total of all liabilities plus the stated capital for all classes of shares. Stated capital is the net historical total of all money and other value contributed to the corporation in return for shares.

[16.] A recent amendment to the *CBCA* eliminates this restriction on the payment of financial assistance. The fiduciary duty would nevertheless prevent giving assistance when the corporation would be prejudiced. Directors are also liable to employees for up to six months' unpaid wages if the corporation is either bankrupt or in liquidation proceedings, or the corporation has been successfully sued for the debt and the judgment has been unpaid for six months: *ABCA* s 144; *CBCA* s 119; *OBCA* s 131.

[17.] *ABCA* s 131; *BCCA* s 147; *CBCA* s 143.

a proxy, or proxy holder, is a person designated by a shareholder to vote at the shareholders' meeting

a management circular is a document sent to the shareholders that contains management proposals and other information related to shareholder meetings

dissident shareholders disagree with management proposals and wish to solicit the votes of their fellow shareholders to defeat management

a dissidents' circular is a document sent to all shareholders by any shareholder who seeks the votes of other shareholders against management

Only a small percentage of shareholders of public corporations attend shareholders' meetings in person. Shareholders can participate without attending by appointing a *proxy*, who need not be a shareholder, to represent them at the meeting and vote their shares. The **proxy**, or **proxy holder**, has all the powers of the shareholder at the meeting, but must vote in accordance with any direction given by the shareholder.

For all public corporations, management must send the shareholders a form of proxy allowing them to appoint a proxy.[18] The form is sent along with a **management circular**, a document that contains information regarding the proxy, the business to be dealt with at the meeting, and certain other information. As the number of shareholders of a corporation increases, the information provided by the circular becomes an important way of enhancing shareholder participation.

Shareholders who disagree with management proposals may try to encourage their fellow shareholders to vote against them. Such **dissident shareholders** are entitled to obtain a list of shareholders and their addresses from the corporation and use it to contact other shareholders to influence their voting.[19] If the corporation is a public corporation, however, dissident shareholders must send out a **dissidents' circular** with information on the identity of the dissidents, their relationship to the corporation, and their interest in the proposal.[20] Dissidents' circulars are relatively rare in the Canadian marketplace. The costs of complying with the disclosure requirements are often too high.

At the meeting, voting is usually by a show of hands, but any shareholder may require that each vote be recorded on a ballot that is collected and counted. Approval is usually by an ordinary majority vote.[21]

Access to Information

All shareholders may have access to certain information to enhance their ability to monitor management and to exercise their rights as shareholders. A corporation must maintain these records and allow shareholders access to them:[22]

- articles
- bylaws
- minutes of meetings of shareholders
- a share register showing the owners of all shares

Shareholders as well as creditors may examine and copy these during business hours. They have no right to inspect minutes of directors' meetings.

The most important information shareholders receive are the annual financial statements of the corporation. For public corporations, these are usually contained in an annual report. Annual statements must be audited by an independent firm of accountants that determines whether the statements created by management were prepared in accordance with generally accepted accounting principles and fairly present the financial results of the corporation for the year. The auditor bases its opinion on an evaluation of the financial records of the corporation. Shareholders may unanimously agree to dispense with the audit

---

[18.] *ABCA* s 144; *CBCA* s 150; *OBCA* s 112. All corporations with more than 50 shareholders incorporated under the *CBCA* must meet this requirement.

[19.] *ABCA* s 21(3), (9); *CBCA* s 21(3), (9); *OBCA* ss 145, 146.

[20.] *OBCA* s 144, RRO 1990, Reg 62 ss 33-36. Under the *CBCA*, this obligation arises when there are more than 50 shareholders: s 150(b), SOR/79-316, ss 38-41.

[21.] *ABCA* ss 167, 176, 183, 204; *CBCA* ss 173, 183, 189, 211.

[22.] *ABCA* ss 20, 20.1, 21; *CBCA* ss 20(1), 21; *OBCA* ss 145, 146.

requirement. This is commonly done in small corporations where all the shareholders are closely involved in its business and do not consider the protection of an independent assessment of the corporation's financial statements to be worth the expense.

Shareholders' Agreements

If a corporation has few shareholders, they often customize their relationship, creating an arrangement that is different from that provided by the statute that governs the corporation. They may:

- change shareholder voting entitlements
- change shareholder approval requirements
- create rules for share transfers

Voting and Management

Shareholders may want to allocate decision-making power between themselves in a way that is different from the allocation that would result from the number of shares each holds. For example, Ellen, Ranjan, and Phillipe decide to set up a corporation to carry on a business of distributing computer software. Phillipe will contribute the $500 000 needed to set up the business and will be the sales manager. Ranjan, who recently completed his MBA but has little money, will be responsible for the financial side of the business. Ellen will contribute some software she has developed and will be in charge of supporting the software sold. Because of his large financial contribution, Phillipe will get 80 percent of the shares, while Ranjan and Ellen will get 10 percent each. If each share has one vote, Phillipe, as the holder of a majority of the shares, would have enough votes to determine who will be on the board. He does not have to include Ellen or Ranjan. But what if Phillipe, Ellen, and Ranjan consider themselves to be in a relationship in which each should have an equal say and each wants to be on the board?

They could address this in a shareholders' agreement. All three could agree that they will vote their shares to elect all three of them as directors. Ranjan, Ellen, and Phillipe may also agree that all shareholder decisions must be approved by shareholders unanimously.

The *CBCA* and statutes modelled on it permit all the shareholders of a corporation to agree to alter the allocation of power between directors and shareholders. Such **unanimous shareholders' agreements** may "restrict, in whole or in part, the powers of the directors to manage the business and affairs of the corporation." A shareholder who is a party to such an agreement has all the rights and powers, as well as the duties and liabilities, of a director to the extent of the restriction. The directors are relieved of their duties and liabilities to the same extent. This allows a small corporation to organize its structure to reflect the fact that it is the shareholders who are running the business by giving them management powers.[23]

a unanimous shareholders' agreement is an agreement of all shareholders to transfer some or all of the directors' powers to themselves

Share Transfer

In small corporations, share transfer is a problem. Typically, the business is tied up with the individuals who are the shareholders. To continue with our exam-

---

[23.] *ABCA* s 140; *CBCA* s 146(2); *OBCA* s 108. There are many unresolved issues with respect to how a corporation that is subject to a unanimous shareholder agreement will function. For example, would it still need to have directors if the shareholders have removed all of their powers?

ple: Ellen would probably have difficulty selling her shares if she leaves the business, because the business would have trouble operating without her expertise. Another problem with finding a buyer for an interest in a small corporation is that such interests are inherently hard to value. There is no market like the Toronto Stock Exchange to establish prices.

Share transfers are also difficult for non-financial reasons. Shareholders do not want other shareholders to be able to sell their shares to just anyone. They want some restrictions on share transfer so that they can control who becomes involved in the business as a shareholder. At the same time, all shareholders want minimal restrictions on their ability to sell their own shares, given the financial difficulties of selling them.

It is therefore common to set up some share transfer procedures in a shareholders' agreement and prohibit transfers except in accordance with these procedures. A common situation in which transfers are permitted is upon compliance with a **right of first refusal**. If Ellen wanted to sell her shares, a right of first refusal would require her to offer them first to the other shareholders at a price set by her. Ranjan and Phillipe would then have a limited time to purchase Ellen's shares, usually in proportion to their existing share interests, at that price. If they do not purchase her shares, Ellen may offer them for sale to someone else at the *same price* for a limited time. The requirement to sell at the same price that she offered the shares to the other shareholders discourages Ellen from setting an unreasonably high price for her shares in the first place.

In a corporation with just two shareholders, the shareholder agreement often contains a *shotgun buy-sell* provision. A **shotgun buy-sell** is a share transfer mechanism that forces one shareholder to buy out the other. If Marsha offers all of her shares to John at a price she specifies, John must then either (i) buy all of Marsha's shares, or (ii) sell all of his shares to her at the same price. Either way, one of them ends up with all the shares in the corporation. This drastic mechanism can by used to break a deadlock between shareholders.

> **right of first refusal** is the right for shareholders to be offered shares that a shareholder wants to sell first before they are offered to non-shareholders

> a **shotgun buy-sell** is a share transfer mechanism that forces one shareholder to buy out the other

SHAREHOLDER REMEDIES

Shareholders have remedies to ensure that management acts in their interests and to obtain relief when management fails to do so.[24]

Dissent and Appraisal Rights

When the shareholders approve by a two-thirds majority vote certain fundamental changes to the corporation, such as (i) specific major amendments to the articles, (ii) amalgamation with another corporation, or (iii) the sale, lease, or exchange of all, or substantially all, of the assets of a corporation, outside of the ordinary course of business, those who vote against the change are entitled to have their shares bought by the corporation for their fair value.[25] This **dissent and appraisal right** allows a change approved by most shareholders to go ahead, while permitting those who strongly disagree to exit the corporation. If many shareholders exercise their rights, however, implementing the change can become very expensive for the corporation. The corporation may even

> the **dissent and appraisal right** entitles shareholders who dissent from certain fundamental changes to have the corporation buy their shares

---

24. The directors are responsible for making the corporation pursue relief for injuries or losses it suffers. Nevertheless, shareholders may seek a court's permission to pursue relief on the corporation's behalf for breach of fiduciary duty or any other wrong done to the corporation. The action commenced by the shareholder is called a *representative*, or *derivative*, *action*.

25. *BCCA* s 231; *CBCA* s 190; *NBBCA* s 131; *NCA* ss 300-1.

decide not to go ahead with the change, even though it received the necessary shareholder approval, because of the expense.

Oppression

When actions by the directors or the corporation have oppressed or unfairly disregarded or prejudiced their interests, shareholders may claim relief under the **oppression remedy**.[26] The courts have broadly interpreted their authority to provide this relief. Relief is available when the *reasonable expectations* of shareholders about management behaviour have not been met. Relief can include anything the court decides is necessary to remedy the problem, including buying the oppressed shareholder's shares. These are examples of behaviour that the courts have found oppressive:[27]

- approval of a transaction lacking a valid corporate purpose that is prejudicial to a particular shareholder
- failure by the corporation and its controlling shareholder to ensure that a transaction between them was on terms that were comparable to the terms that would have been negotiated by parties who were not related to each other
- discrimination against shareholders in a way that benefits the majority shareholder to the exclusion or the detriment of minority shareholders
- lack of adequate and appropriate disclosure of information to minority shareholders
- planning to eliminate minority shareholders[28]

the **oppression remedy** allows a shareholder to claim compensation for a loss that was caused by an act or omission by the corporation or its directors, which oppresses the interests of the shareholder

Other Shareholder Remedies

Shareholders may seek other remedies, such as a court order that directs compliance with the governing statute or the rectification of corporate records that contain errors. On an application by a shareholder, a court may even direct that the assets of the corporation be sold, its creditors paid off, and any surplus distributed to the shareholders. This extreme remedy is called **liquidation and dissolution**, or **winding up**. It may be ordered when it is just and equitable to end the corporation's existence. For example, a court may order the winding up of a corporation with two shareholders who cannot agree on how the corporation should carry on business.[29]

under a **liquidation and dissolution**, or **winding up**, the corporation's assets are liquidated, its creditors paid off, the remaining money distributed to the shareholders, and the corporation brought to an end

CORPORATE GOVERNANCE IN PRACTICE

Corporations vary in size. At one extreme, a corporation may have only a single shareholder, who is also the sole director and officer. At the other, a large public corporation may have thousands of shareholders spread out around the world and more than 20 directors, some of whom work as managers in the

[26] For example, *BCCA* s 200; *CBCA* s 241; *NBBCA* s 166.

[27] *Arthur v Signum Communications Ltd* [1991] OJ No 86 (Gen Div) affd [1993] OJ No 1928 (Div Ct).

[28] Creditors and anyone else may seek permission to bring an oppression action and, in a number of cases, creditors have succeeded in obtaining permission: for example, *Prime Computer of Canada Ltd v Jeffrey* (1991) 6 OR (3d) 733 (Gen Div).

[29] Liquidation and dissolution may be ordered in other circumstances: *CBCA* ss 213, 214; *OBCA* s 207.

corporation. The operation of corporate governance rules vary significantly depending on where a corporation is on the continuum.

If one person is the sole shareholder, director, and officer, the allocation of rights and responsibilities contemplated in corporate statutes is a mere formality and generally irrelevant. Even if the sole shareholder elects other directors, it will be the shareholder who ultimately makes management decisions. If there are a few shareholders, usually they will also be the managers. The legal arrangements for management are likely to be set out in a shareholders' agreement and may be quite different from what the corporate statute provides.

As the number of shareholders increases, not all of them will be involved in management. In this situation, managers may be tempted to act in a way that benefits themselves at the expense of the corporation. If they pay themselves excessive salaries or other perquisites, they receive 100 percent of the benefit. While these kinds of actions may reduce the value of the corporation's shares, including those held by management, the loss experienced by management will be much less than the benefit to them. Furthermore, as the size of a corporation increases, it becomes more difficult for shareholders to detect and prevent managerial abuses. Managers therefore have even more incentive to misbehave.

In a large corporation, shareholders are at a disadvantage partly because they do not have enough information to understand and evaluate management's performance. Even if some are willing and able to gather sufficient information and analyze it, they may find it difficult and expensive to mobilize many other shareholders, who are spread around the country or the world. The relatively small financial stake of most individual shareholders will discourage them from incurring these costs. As a result, shareholders' legal rights to vote and pursue shareholder remedies may not be very useful.

Another problem with the legal corporate governance scheme is that it is designed to ensure only that the *board of directors* is accountable to shareholders. Little attention is paid to the accountability of *officers*, who run corporations in practice. In large public corporations, the board of directors tends to be dominated by the full-time professional managers of the corporation.

CORPORATE LIABILITY

The rules governing a corporation's liability for contracts, crimes, and torts determine how a corporation is legally affected by the behaviour of people acting on its behalf. Those rules influence how the corporation organizes itself to participate in the marketplace. The rules that determine when a corporation is liable in tort, for example, will determine how a corporation supervises its employees in their interaction with customers to minimize the risk of liability.

Liability in Contract

an **agent** is a person who is authorized to act on behalf of the corporation

A corporation only becomes liable to perform contracts as a result of actions by **agents**, who act on its behalf. Salespeople, purchasing clerks, directors, and officers may all be considered agents of the corporation for specific purposes. Agency will be discussed in detail in Chapter 20.

The rules on when a corporation is liable in contract balance the interests of the corporation with the interests of third parties seeking to enter into contracts with it.

- On the one hand, a corporation does not want to be bound by an agent who purports to act on its behalf but who, in fact, was not authorized to do so.

- On the other hand, a third party that enters into a contract with a corporation does not want to spend much time or money deciding whether the corporation has actually authorized that person. It wants to rely on commonly accepted indicators of authority, such as a letter of introduction from the corporation's president on the corporation's letterhead.

In large transactions, the parties will do a significant amount of investigation to satisfy themselves that the person executing a contract on behalf of a corporation has authority to do so. These investigations will be backed up by documentation, such as certified copies of board resolutions authorizing certain people to enter into the transaction and lawyer's opinions regarding authority. In most situations, however, the size of the transaction simply does not justify incurring the costs associated with that degree of certainty.

Authority of Agents

An agent can only bind a corporation if the corporation has given it one of these types of authority:

- **Actual authority**: The agent is authorized by the corporation to enter into the obligation in question.

- **Apparent (or ostensible) authority**: The corporation makes a representation that the agent has authority to bind the corporation to the obligation in question.

Actual authority may arise when powers are conferred on the agent by a resolution of the board of directors or another permitted delegation by the board, an officer, or an employee. When the authority is conferred on a position or office, such as president, a person properly appointed to that position or office has the authority that goes along with it.

It is often difficult for third parties to satisfy themselves that actual authority exists because they do not have access to the internal corporate records or other private documents that create the authority. They must therefore rely on apparent authority. A representation creating apparent authority may be express or implied from the conduct of the corporation. For instance, it may be enough if a corporation allows a person to act with certain authority. Putting someone in a particular position constitutes a representation that the person has the usual authority for that position. This kind of apparent authority is referred to as **usual authority**.[30] What is usual is determined by reference to the authority of agents in similar positions in similar corporations. Agents with such titles as vice-president, treasurer, and secretary, however, may have widely varying degrees of authority in different industries and even within industries. For a third party to rely on apparent authority, the representation creating it must be made by someone with authority to make the representation.

The final requirement that must be satisfied before a third party can rely on apparent authority is that the representation induced the third party to enter into the disputed contract with the corporation. As a practical matter, that is seldom hard to prove.[31]

actual authority is authority that is actually given to an agent by a corporation

apparent, or *ostensible*, *authority* is created by a representation on behalf of the corporation that an agent has authority to bind the corporation

usual authority allows a person appointed to a particular position to exercise the authority usually associated with that position

---

[30] *Freeman & Lockyer v Buckhurst Park Properties (Mangal) Ltd* [1964] 2 QB 480 (CA).

[31] Many Canadian corporate statutes contain provisions limiting the ability of corporations to rely on certain kinds of defects in their authority, such as a provision in their articles: for example, *CBCA* s 18; *OBCA* s 19.

Liability for Crimes

corporations create special
problems for criminal law

The consequences of imposing criminal liability on corporations are different from those of imposing criminal liability on individuals, because corporations have "no soul to damn; no body to kick."[32] Corporations will be concerned about the effect of a criminal conviction on their reputation, but the threat of a conviction may not deter them from misbehaving to the same extent. Also, criminal penalties are problematic when a corporation is the offender. Imprisonment of the corporation itself (as distinct from its officers and directors) is impossible. And if a fine is imposed on a corporation, its shareholders and all those with financial claims against the corporation, including employees, may suffer. Despite those distinctive characteristics of criminal punishment for corporations, they can be held criminally responsible. The practical issue is how to determine when a corporation has committed a crime.

There are three broad categories of offences, each with different rules about what is required for corporate liability.

an **absolute liability** offence
occurs upon the commission of
an act prohibited by law

- **Absolute liability** offences are committed whenever the accused engages in prohibited behaviour. Corporate liability arises when a person commits the prohibited act on behalf of the corporation. The acts of employees in the course of their employment will satisfy this test.[33]

a **strict liability** offence occurs
upon the commission of an act
prohibited by law unless the
accused acted reasonably in the
circumstances

- A **strict liability** offence occurs when a person, acting on behalf of the corporation, commits a prohibited act. Unlike an absolute liability offence, however, the *defence of due diligence* is available for a strict liability offence. That means that liability does not arise if the accused acted reasonably in the circumstances. A corporation can rely on that defence if the person with managerial responsibility for the relevant area of the corporation's affairs used due diligence. That person is described as the **directing mind and will** of the corporation. The care exercised by that person is considered to be the care exercised by the corporation itself.[34] As Chapter 23 explains, absolute and strict liability offences usually form part of a regulatory scheme, such as those protecting public health, safety, and the environment.

the **directing mind and will** is
the person who has responsibility to manage the business of
the corporation in the area in
which the offence occurred

a **mens rea** offence arises
upon the commission of an act
prohibited by law by a person
who had some degree of
knowledge or intention

- Most criminal offences, such as fraud, are committed only if the accused had some degree of knowledge or intention, referred to as **mens rea** (or "guilty mind"), when it performed a prohibited act. A corporation may be liable under this category of offence if the person who had the *mens rea* while committing the crime was also the directing mind and will of the corporation. In that case, the person who was the directing mind and will can be held *individually* responsible as well.

Any person who has governing executive control over an area of the corporation's business is considered to be the directing mind and will of the corporation in that area. A corporation may have many directing minds. Each person responsible for a discrete aspect of the corporation's business—whether that aspect is defined functionally, geographically, or otherwise—may incur criminal

---

[32.] Lord Thurlow, quoted by G Williams *Criminal Law: the General Part* 2d ed (1961) at 856.

[33.] Absolute liability offences punishable by imprisonment are likely to be found contrary to the protection against being deprived of life, liberty, and security of the person under s 7 of the *Charter of Rights and Freedoms*. Although corporations cannot be imprisoned, it has been held that they cannot be convicted under a law which would be unconstitutional if applied to individuals: *R v Big M Drug Mart* (1985) 18 DLR (4th) 321 (SCC).

[34.] *R v Sault Ste Marie* (1978) 85 DLR (3d) 161 (SCC).

liability for the corporation. It is not only the president or the board of directors who may do so. In *Waterloo Mercury Sales*, liability was imposed on a corporation operating a car dealership because the used car sales manager fraudulently had odometers on used cars turned back.[35] For the purposes of the criminal activity, the used-car sales manager was found to be the directing mind of the corporation. In essence, the test is whether the employee with *mens rea* was given—expressly, implicitly, or practically—the authority to *design and supervise* the performance of corporate policy. It is not enough, however, if that person had authority only to *carry out* policies that someone else in the corporation created.[36]

Note that the corporation will not necessarily escape liability merely because it had a policy *against* the behaviour that constituted the crime. In *Waterloo Mercury Sales*, the dealership had a policy against turning back odometers. The court still imposed liability. The lesson is clear. In some situations, the best that a corporation can do by way of risk management is to adopt clear policies *and* to hire responsible people who will carry them out.

Liability in Tort

A corporation may be liable in tort in two ways. It may be directly liable when a person who is the directing mind and will of the corporation itself has committed the tort. Or it may be vicariously liable for acts of employees in the course of their employment, as discussed in Chapter 10.

PERSONAL LIABILITIES OF DIRECTORS AND OFFICERS

Directors and officers are subject to a wide range of potential liabilities. Governments have imposed personal liability, including fines and imprisonment, as a way of encouraging corporations to better comply with laws relating to unpaid income taxes, payment of wages, environmental protection, and other regulatory schemes. Some of these laws are discussed in Chapter 23. As well, directors and officers are increasingly being held personally responsible for torts, such as the tort of inducing breach of contract discussed in Chapter 11.

Exposure to these liabilities creates a strong disincentive to becoming a director or officer of a corporation. To offset these risks, a corporation can reimburse directors and officers for any expenses that they *reasonably* incur in connection with the defence of any civil, criminal, or administrative proceeding that is connected to their position within the corporation. This reimbursement, called an **indemnity**, is mandatory if the directors or officers:

- were not found to have committed any fault
- complied with their fiduciary duty to act honestly and in good faith with a view to the best interests of the corporation
- had reasonable grounds for believing their conduct was lawful[37]

indemnity is compensation paid by a corporation to a director or officer for costs incurred in connection with performing their duties

---

[35] *R v Waterloo Mercury Sales Ltd* (1974) 49 DLR (3d) 131 (Alta Dist Ct).

[36] *Rhone (The) v Peter AB Widener (The)* (1993) 101 DLR (4th) 188 (SCC). In *R v Safety-Kleen Canada Inc* (1997) 145 DLR (4th) 276 (Ont CA), a truck driver was held not to be a directing mind of his employer corporation in connection with the employee's disposal of waste.

[37] *ABCA* s 124; *CBCA* s 124; *OBCA* s 143.

Even when a director or officer does not meet the first criterion, a corporation may still provide indemnification if the other two criteria are met. Indemnification may include amounts not directly relating to the defence, such as money paid to settle an action or satisfy a judgment. You Be the Judge 19.1 asks you to apply these rules regarding indemnification.

YOU BE THE JUDGE 19.1

Consolidated Enfield Corporation v Blair (1995) 128 DLR (4th) 73 (SCC)

Blair was the president and a director of Consolidated Enfield Corporation. At Enfield's annual meeting, a slate of nominees proposed by management, and including Blair, stood for election. Canadian Express Ltd, a major shareholder, nominated a candidate for director to replace Blair. Canadian Express had enough votes to ensure that its candidate would be elected. After the votes on the election of directors were cast, a lawyer advised Blair that he, as chair, had to make a ruling on the results of the vote, even though his own election was at stake and the votes cast by Canadian Express against Blair were invalid. He took the advice and ruled: (i) that the votes cast for the Canadian

Express nominee were invalid, and (ii) that the management slate was elected. In subsequent legal proceedings, a court ruled that the votes cast in favour of the Canadian Express nominee were valid, and so Blair had not been re-elected. Blair claimed indemnification from Enfield for his legal costs in connection with these proceedings.

Questions for Discussion

1. Should Blair be entitled to indemnification in these circumstances?
2. What arguments may be made for and against indemnification?

Indemnification commitments are only as good as the ability of the indemnifier to pay. If there is a risk that an indemnifying corporation may not have enough money to pay, a director or officer may seek a guarantee, perhaps from a shareholder, to provide greater security. It has become common for directors and officers to ask their corporations to pay for insurance against their personal liability. To make an insurance claim, directors and officers must have fulfilled their fiduciary duty.[38]

Ethical Perspective 19.1 asks you to think about when a corporation should pay an indemnity. Business Decision 19.1 (p. 443) requires you to consider what protection an indemnity provides and what other strategies you could use as a director to protect yourself. Figure 19.2 (p. 443) lays out sources of corporate liability and how to manage the risk.

ETHICAL PERSPECTIVE 19.1

Indemnification for Liabilities under Regulatory Statutes

Governments have tried to strengthen environmental and other regulatory schemes by

imposing liability on directors and officers. This has raised questions about when indemnification and insurance to cover these liabilities should be available. On the one hand, with the range and seriousness of potential liability increasing, indemnities and insurance become more important as a way

(continued)

[38.] In 2000, Nortel Networks Inc paid about $500 000 for $250 million in group liability insurance for directors and senior officers.

(continued)

of ensuring that competent people are willing to become officers and directors. On the other hand, the intended effect of imposing liability on directors and officers is to discourage businesses from acting illegally and, if directors and officers are insulated from this liability by indemnification and insurance, the effectiveness of the legislative scheme is reduced. In a recent case, several officers were convicted of the offence of failing to take all reasonable care to prevent the corporation from permitting the unlawful discharge of wastes. The judge ordered the officers to pay fines.[39]

Question for Discussion

1. Should the corporation indemnify the officers by paying their fines for them?

BUSINESS DECISION 19.1

Joining a Board of Directors

You run an environmental consulting business, and your major client is Medex Inc, which has carried on a business of collecting and disposing of medical waste in Ottawa and eastern Ontario since 1990. Jamal is the majority shareholder, CEO, and chair of the board of directors of Medex. He has asked you to join the board as its fifth member and to go on the environmental compliance committee, which the board intends to set up.[40]

Questions for Discussion

1. What concerns would you have about accepting this offer?
2. Can you limit your exposure by staying uninvolved except when the board calls upon you to provide advice in your particular area of expertise?
3. Are there any strategies that you could adopt to minimize these risks?

FIGURE 19.2   Corporate Liability and Risk Management

Sources of Personal Liability for Directors and Officers	Strategies Available to Manage Liability Risk
General standards of behaviour • fiduciary duty • duty of care • oppression remedy	Diligence • regularly attending board meetings • keeping informed and acting when put on notice • conducting risk assessment • establishing compliance policy and monitoring systems, including timely reporting and education • seeking advice • being sensitive to conflicts of interest
Examples of specific liability risks • environmental offences • failure to remit employee withholdings • authorizing dividends, share buy-backs or financial assistance to employees and other insiders when solvency and other financial tests not met • up to six months of unpaid employee wages • liability under many other statutes	Indemnification
	Insurance
	Resignation

---

[39] *R v Bata Industries* (1995) 127 DLR (4th) 438 (Ont CA).

[40] *Stuart v MNR* [1995] 2 CTC 2458 (TCC).

Chapter Summary

Under Canadian corporate statutes, directors are responsible for managing the business of the corporation. Officers are appointed by the directors and exercise powers delegated to them. Directors and officers are subject to a fiduciary duty to act honestly and in the best interests of the corporation. Fiduciaries may not: (i) be involved personally in transactions with the corporation unless certain safeguards in the corporate statute are observed, (ii) personally take opportunities belonging to the corporation, or (iii) compete with the corporation. Directors and officers also have a duty to exercise the care, diligence, and skill that a reasonably prudent person would exercise in comparable circumstances.

Shareholders are the residual claimants to the assets of the corporation, but their only power is to vote for the election of directors, on proposals made to them, and on the appointment of an auditor. Directors may not make payments to shareholders or others in a close relationship with the corporation if the corporation cannot meet financial tests designed to protect creditors. Corporate law requires that shareholders be given certain information to allow them to monitor management and exercise their rights as shareholders. Shareholders may enter agreements to exercise their powers differently from those provided in governing corporate law and to create rules to govern share transfers. When shareholder agreements are unanimous, they may transfer some or all of the directors' powers and responsibilities to the shareholders. Shareholders have several remedies to seek relief from the actions of the corporation and management, including the dissent and appraisal right and the oppression remedy. The legal scheme for corporate governance may be ineffective in public corporations because of the practical inability of shareholders to take advantage of the accountability mechanisms provided for and the failure of these mechanisms to impose direct accountability on officers.

Corporations are liable for contracts made by persons with actual or apparent authority to contract on their behalf. A corporation is liable for crimes and torts committed by a person who is the directing mind and will of the corporation. Directors and officers are subject to a wide number of statutory liabilities but, if they have discharged their fiduciary duty, they may be indemnified for liabilities incurred in connection with fulfilling their responsibilities.

Review Questions

1. Are directors always responsible for managing the business of a corporation and its internal affairs?

2. How does a corporation get its first directors? Its next directors?

3. Are there restrictions on the directors' ability to delegate management responsibility to officers or to people outside the corporation? Why would the directors give someone outside the corporation management responsibility for some of its business?

4. What is the fiduciary duty, and how is it "owed to the corporation"?

5. Is a director of a corporation allowed to be involved personally in a transaction with the corporation? If so, when?

6. How do you determine whether a fiduciary can pursue an opportunity?

7. What does the fiduciary duty require of directors of a corporation subject to a hostile takeover bid?

8. What are the basic elements of the duty of care that directors and officers have?

9. What is the significance of a person's position and personal characteristics in determining what the duty of care requires?

10. Explain how the duty of care applies to business judgments made by directors and officers.

11. How does corporate law try to facilitate shareholders' exercise of their rights?

12. Assume a corporation had two shareholders holding 10 percent and 90 percent of the corporation's common shares. Both shareholders wanted an equal say in any major decision about the corporation's business. Do these shareholders need a shareholders' agreement? If so, what would be its main provisions?

13. What is the "dissent and appraisal" remedy? What impact does it have on corporate governance?

14. Why is the oppression remedy more useful to shareholders than the derivative action?

15. Why do the legal mechanisms by which shareholders keep directors accountable to them not work very well in large corporations?

16. What must a person dealing with a corporation establish to enforce a contract with it?

17. Who is the "directing mind and will" of the corporation? What is the significance of this concept in relation to corporate liability for crimes? For torts?

18. How can corporations reduce the risk of being found liable for the criminal activities of their employees?

19. What limits are there on the ability of a corporation to indemnify its directors for costs incurred in defending an

action to which they were made a party only because they were directors? Are these appropriate?

20. How can directors and officers minimize their risk of liability for actions in the course of fulfilling their roles in the corporation?

Cases and Problems

1. Carl owns 51 percent of the shares of Probex Inc, a successful building supplies business. At the last shareholders' meeting, Carl elected Morris, Ellen, and himself as the directors of the company. Morris, Ellen, and Carl appointed Carl as the CEO and president of the company. The company has been successful for many years. However, business has been slow this year. Both Morris and Ellen believe that the current slowdown of the business is a direct result of Carl neglecting his duties of overseeing the day-to-day operations of the business due to his infatuation with his new dog, Roxy.

   By outvoting Carl at the next directors' meeting, Morris and Ellen replace Carl as CEO and president with Philip. Carl is furious and tells Morris and Ellen that since he owns 51 percent of the company, they had no right to replace him, especially since he elected them. Carl further advises them that, given his authority as the controlling shareholder, he is reclaiming his position as CEO and president of Probex Inc. Is Carl entitled to be the CEO and president of the corporation? What can he do to ensure that he is appointed to these offices?

2. Tim owns 60 percent and his sister Nancy owns 40 percent of the shares of Landco Shirts Ltd. Landco is incorporated under the *CBCA* and carries on a retail clothing sales business managed by Tim. Nancy is a doctor and is not involved in the daily affairs of the business. Nancy, Tim, and their father are the only directors of the corporation.

   Over the past two years, Tim has occasionally had Landco buy ski wear and other sports clothes from a corporation in which he holds 25 percent of the shares and of which he is a director. He has never disclosed his interest in these transactions to the other members of the board because (i) he thought it was none of their business, and (ii) he was careful to make sure that the prices paid by Landco were fair. Also, during the past two years, the business has been growing rapidly, and Tim has not spent the time necessary to prepare financial statements for the corporation and send them to Nancy. Can Nancy claim relief using the oppression remedy? Is there anything Tim can or should do to avoid liability?

3. Crook was employed as the scrap manager for Canada Labs Inc, a corporation incorporated under the *CBCA*. In that capacity, Crook regularly sold waste gold generated by the experimental work conducted by Canlab to Golden Corona Mines Inc for recycling. Corona also sold gold, although Canlab had never been one of its customers.

   Crook devised a scheme to make himself wealthy. One day, he sent a purchase order on a Canlab order form to Corona for $1 000 000 in gold. Because Corona had not

sold gold to Canlab in the past, it called Smith, the manager of purchasing for Canlab, to ask if the gold order from Crook was authorized. Smith, who was responsible for all purchases made by Canlab, said she would check into it. She called Crook, and he convinced her that the gold was needed for a particular set of experiments. Smith was too busy to inquire further and forgot to call Corona back. Corona called Smith several more times, but Smith did not call back. In frustration, after five days, Corona called Crook who, of course, confirmed that Corona should send the gold.

   Corona did send the gold to Canlab. It was received by Crook, who then skipped the country and took the gold with him. Corona sued Canlab for payment for the gold. On what basis could Canlab be liable to pay for the gold? Are any defences available to Canlab?

4. Sarah, a shareholder in Corporation X, wanted to sell her shares. She asked Peter, the chair of the board of directors, if he knew of anyone who wanted to buy shares of Corporation X. Peter said he would buy them for $10 per share. Peter did not tell Sarah that the corporation was having discussions with Tony, who was interested in buying all the shares of the corporation for $15. Should Peter have told Sarah about these discussions?

5. Xena, Yasmin, and Zenith (X, Y, and Z) are the original shareholders and directors of Aberdeen Management Consulting Ltd, incorporated under the *CBCA*. Each holds 10 shares. The corporation had been profitable, but it needed more capital to engage in new business projects. To raise capital, Aberdeen issued more shares. Raju, Sara, and Tristin (R, S, and T) agreed to purchase 20 shares each for $1000 per share.

   Upon reviewing the corporation's financial statements to be discussed at the next annual meeting, R, S, and T discovered that the corporation has a consulting contract with a company controlled by X, Y, and Z. The contract fees are much higher than the usual market rate for consulting services and have substantially reduced the profits of the business. R, S, and T decided that, at the next shareholders' meeting when the terms of X, Y, and Z expire, they would elect themselves as directors, terminate the contract, and put the business of the corporation on a much stronger financial footing. Upon hearing of this plan, X, Y, and Z issued themselves an additional 20 shares each. At the shareholders' meeting, much to R, S, and T's surprise, X, Y, and Z outvoted them, re-electing themselves as directors. R, S, and T are outraged and certain that something must be done to remedy this terrible situation.

   Is there anything R, S, and T can do?

6. Marilyn was the founder, majority shareholder, president, and a director of Escada Cosmetics Ltd. Since its incorporation in 1980 under the *OBCA*, the company has been successful due to Marilyn's hard work. However, after 20 years, she was ready to play a reduced role in the company. Marilyn believed that her daughter, Chloe, would make an excellent manager of the company. At Marilyn's suggestion and urging, the board appointed Chloe as director and president in July 2001.

   Things went well at first, but managing the business soon became too much for Chloe, who did not have any knowledge of or experience with the day-to-day operations. Consequently, Escada began to do poorly, and by the end of October 2001, its profits had disappeared. Despite its weak financial position, in November 2001, the board of directors of Escada paid a $1 000 000 dividend to Marilyn to help her buy a home in California.

   Full Moon Financial Group, a minority shareholder of Escada, is worried about its investment, which it made in August 2001 before the desperate financial condition of Escada was known. What options does Full Moon have for protecting its investment?

7. Florence Industries Ltd, based in Alberta, manufactures household cleaning products. Its president, Ebenezer, entered into negotiations with Second Class Disposal Services Inc for a service contract. Second Class promised Ebenezer that their disposal services, which were much less expensive than what other disposal businesses were offering, met all legal requirements. Ebenezer was satisfied by their assurances and signed the contract without further investigating Second Class or its track record.

   Three months into the contract, Ebenezer was accused of authorizing the disposal of industrial waste into the Bow River, contrary to the Alberta *Water Resources Act*. This statute provides that an accused who exercised reasonable care to prevent the corporation from disposing of the waste can avoid liability.

   Assuming that industrial waste was dumped into the Bow River on behalf of Florence Industries by Second Class, discuss whether the president *or* Florence Industries can be held criminally liable.

8. New Technology Co is a public company whose shares are widely held and listed on the Toronto Stock Exchange. In the last year, the corporation's business has struggled, and its share price has fallen from an all-time high of $150 to $15. Over the same period, its competitors have done well, and their shares have increased in value. This month, it was announced that the board of directors had decided that the president should be given a $10 000 000 bonus. Assume that you bought 1000 shares at the peak of the market for $150 000 and that your shares are now worth only $15 000. You are very angry that, while the shareholders are suffering, the president is getting this enormous bonus. What can you do?

9. FaxCo Inc is a distributor of fax machines. The corporation had ten shareholders, including Frances and her two sons, who together held 60 percent of the shares and were also the directors of the corporation. The sons ran the business. Frances had no experience in business and was not involved in any way. She paid no attention to what was going on, although she regularly attended board meetings. In 2001, the sons started taking large amounts of money out the business in the form of loans to themselves to finance their lifestyles.

   When the financial statements for the year were prepared, they showed that shareholder loans had ballooned from nil to $1 000 000 in a year, when revenues of the business had been only $2 000 000 over the same period. The board of directors approved the statements. Frances was at the meeting but did not look at the statements. Within two months, the corporation was not paying its debts, and one of its creditors obtained a court order appointing a receiver to take control of and run the business. The receiver discovered the loans to the sons. The sons, themselves, are now insolvent. Frances, however, has substantial personal assets. Is there any way that the receiver, acting on behalf of the corporation, can seek relief against Frances?

10. Aaron, Boris, and Corinne propose to set up a corporation to carry on a book-publishing business. The corporation would have only common shares—20 percent would be held by each of Aaron and Boris, and 60 percent by Corinne, based on their respective financial contributions. Aaron and Boris will run the business, while Corinne will be a passive investor with no involvement in the daily activities of the corporation. Nevertheless, Corinne wants a veto over certain things, including all expenditures over $10 000 and all decisions regarding the hiring and firing of employees. Aaron and Boris agree that Corinne should have such a veto. How should the corporation be structured to achieve the arrangement?

11. Simone is a director of Pace Computers Ltd, incorporated under the *Canada Business Corporations Act*. She is also the sole shareholder and director of Simtronics Supply Inc, which was incorporated under the *Canada Business Corporations Act* and which sells parts for personal computers. At a Pace board meeting, Simone suggests that Pace could get its parts inventory for less money from Simtronics than from its current supplier. Is there anything preventing Pace from entering into a supply contract with Simtronics? Should Simone take any steps to ensure that no legal problems arise?

12. Mona buys and sells commercial real estate. Recently, she joined the board of Tag Realty Inc, a real estate development business. At a party, a friend tells Mona about a property that will be coming onto the market soon for a good price. Can Mona buy the property herself, or is she obliged to try to obtain it for Tag? What factors would Mona have to take into account? Is there anything Mona can do if she wants to acquire the property herself and avoid any legal questions?

20 Agency and Other Methods of Carrying on Business

CHAPTER OVERVIEW

OBJECTIVES

After completing this chapter, you should be able to:

1. Identify four ways in which an agency relationship can be created.
2. Distinguish between the actual authority and apparent authority of agents to enter into contracts on behalf of their principals.
3. Identify three situations in which an agent's fiduciary duty to act in the best interests of a principal may limit the agent's business opportunities.
4. Describe one situation in which a principal will be bound by a contract entered into by an agent without any authority from the principal.
5. List five events that will terminate an agency relationship.
6. Explain the circumstances in which a principal may be liable for the torts of its agent.
7. Describe practical and legal strategies that a principal can use to manage the risk of its agent binding it to unauthorized obligations.
8. List four methods of carrying on business in which questions may arise as to whether a person is an agent.
9. Explain how franchises can reduce the business risk for franchisees.
10. Identify the risks for franchisees in entering into franchise agreements, and explain how the franchise laws in various jurisdictions address them.

an agent is a person who represents someone else for some specific purpose

a principal is a person whom an agent represents for some specific purpose

an agent may have authority to enter into legal obligations on the principal's behalf

an agent may simply represent the principal's interests

a franchise allows entrepreneurs to start their own business using the franchisor's established name and business concept

In business one person often represents another for a specific purpose. Stockbrokers are independent business people, but they represent you to execute your purchases and sales of shares. A manager employed by a car dealership represents the dealership when negotiating the terms under which the dealership will sell you a new car. In each case, the person acting on behalf of someone else is called an **agent**. The person being represented is called the **principal**.

Sometimes, the agent has authority to bind the principal to a contract. In the car dealership example, the manager has authority to agree to the terms on which the dealership will sell you the car. In this case, one concern of the dealership is whether the manager exceeds the authority the dealership has granted. If the dealership has not authorized the manager to give you a price reduction of more than 10 percent, it will not want to be bound to sell you the car if the manager does so. As the person negotiating the contract with the agent, you will want to be able to rely on the agent having authority to bind the dealership to give you the discount. The legal rules of agency govern the nature and scope of agents' authority in cases like this. As a result, these rules have a significant impact on the risks for principals and third parties when they deal through agents and define the risk management strategies available to each. The rules regarding an agent's authority to contract are one of the important subjects of this chapter.

Agents do not always have authority to enter into legal obligations on the principal's behalf. They may merely represent the principal's interests. If you are selling your house, for example, your real estate agent will not usually have the authority to commit you to selling for a particular price, but will be responsible for finding prospective purchasers and assisting with the sale process. Even in these situations, however, agents are subject to legal standards of behaviour that are designed to protect principals from the risks to which their agents may subject them. Principals have a much more limited set of obligations to their agents. In this chapter, we will discuss these basic standards of behaviour.

In some settings, these legal standards of behaviour for agents have been found to be insufficient to protect people dealing with agents. As a result, some agency relationships are governed by special statutes. For example, legislation addresses the risks that stockbrokers may not have sufficient assets to pay claims against them by their clients. This chapter provides a basic overview of some of these statutory regimes.

We will also look at *franchises*. A **franchise** is a common business method that allows entrepreneurs to start their own business using the franchisor's established name and business concept. That approach can substantially reduce the risks associated with a new business. It is less risky to set up a McDonald's franchise than it is to set up an independent fast-food restaurant specializing in hamburgers. An important trade-off for that risk reduction, however, is that franchisors insist on a high degree of control over the franchisee's operations to ensure the quality of the products and services. Franchisors also charge substantial fees for the right to operate the franchise. Like agency, franchising is a way for the franchisor to carry on its business through someone else. Legally, however, the franchisor and franchisee are separate businesses. No agency relationship is present.

Alberta and Ontario have enacted legislation to ensure that franchisors adequately disclose the risks and benefits of the franchise business and treat their franchisees fairly. We will discuss the characteristics of franchising and the legal rules governing the franchise relationship in the last section of this chapter.

BASIC RULES OF AGENCY

Creation

There are several ways to create an agency relationship. One of the most common is by express agreement. The principal and the agent enter into a contract that outlines the terms of the appointment of the agent, including the scope of the agent's authority and the agent's remuneration. In those provinces where the *Statute of Frauds* is still in force, the contract must be in writing if the relationship is to last longer than one year.[1] As well, the agreement must be in writing if the agent is going have the authority to sign cheques on behalf of the principal.[2] The listing agreement that you sign with a real estate agent is an example of an agency relationship that is created by express agreement.[3] What is commonly called a *commercial representation agreement* is also a kind of express agency. A **commercial representation agreement** occurs when a manufacturer of goods, such as sports wear, agrees to allow someone to enter into contracts with retail sporting goods stores on behalf of the manufacturer to sell its clothes. Figure 20.1 outlines the creation of agency.

many agency relationships are created through express agreements

a commercial representation agreement occurs when a manufacturer of goods agrees to allow someone to enter into contracts with customers to sell its goods

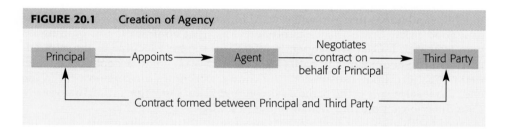

FIGURE 20.1   Creation of Agency

Many other business relationships may have the effect of making someone your agent, even if they are not referred to by that name. If you allow a lawyer to act on your behalf in closing a real estate transaction, the lawyer is acting as your agent.

An agency relationship can arise even though the parties never expressly agreed that the agent would have the authority to act on the principal's behalf.

- As we discussed in Chapter 18, in all partnerships, each partner is an agent of the partnership and can bind the partnership to obligations incurred in connection with carrying on the business of the partnership in the usual way.

- In Chapter 19, we discussed agency and corporations. Corporations can act only through human beings. Individuals acting on behalf of a corporation are acting as its agents.

- As we discussed in Chapter 19, the directors, officers, salespeople, purchasing clerks, and other employees may all be agents of the corporation for particular purposes. However, it is difficult to determine when someone acting on behalf of a corporation has authority to enter into a par-

---

[1.] Provincial writing requirements are discussed in Chapter 5.

[2.] *Bills of Exchange Act*, RSC 1985, c B-4 (Can).

[3.] In some provinces, listing agreements with real estate agents must be in writing: for example, *Real Estate Act*, SA 1995, c R-4.5, s 22 (Alta); *Real Estate Trading Act*, SNS 1996, c 28, s 26 (NS); *Real Estate and Business Brokers Act*, RSO 1990, c R.4, s 23 (Ont).

ticular obligation. That is the practical problem confronting a third party that wants to enter into a contract with a corporation. Does the person the third party is dealing with have authority to bind the corporation to the contract which it wants to enter into with the corporation?

- Sometimes, the agency relationship will arise outside a partnership or corporation without any express appointment of the agent. For example, when a principal represents or holds out someone as its agent in discussions with a third party, that person will have the authority suggested by the principal's actions to deal with the third party, despite never being properly appointed as an agent. Appointing someone to a particular position or allowing someone to act in a particular way may be sufficient to create an agency.

an agency relationship may arise even though the parties never expressly agreed that the agent would have the authority to act on the principal's behalf

Ratification

Even if an agency relationship never existed, in limited circumstances an agent can still enter into an agreement that ultimately binds a principal. Suppose that Gary, someone with no authority to act on your behalf, purports to enter into a contract to buy a fax machine for you from a third party, telling the third party that he is your agent. Perhaps Gary knows that you wanted to buy a fax machine and hopes that you will reward him if he negotiates for you to buy one at a good price. Since Gary has no authority, that contract is not binding on you. However, if Gary subsequently offers you the fax machine at the stipulated price, you could agree to **ratify** the contract—you could accept the contractual obligation. Upon ratification, the contract becomes binding on you. In the end, the legal result is the same as if you had given Gary the authority to negotiate the contract on your behalf in the first place.

a contract is ratified when someone accepts a contract that was negotiated on their behalf but without their authority

For ratification to be effective, it must meet these requirements.

- It must be clear. Ratification can, however, be either *express or implied* from behaviour. In the example above, your ratification of the contract would be implied if you took delivery of the fax machine and used it.[4]

- It must occur within a *reasonable time* after the creation of the contract. What is reasonable depends on the facts. If someone without your authority purported to act on your behalf to enter into a fire insurance contract on a building that you owned, you could not ratify it after the building burned down.[5]

- The principal must accept the *whole contract* or none of it. For example, if you had developed some software and someone purported to license the software to a third party on your behalf, you could not accept the royalties under the licence without also accepting the support and maintenance obligations in the contract.

- The principal must have been *identified* by the agent. An agent cannot make a contract, either on its own behalf or on behalf of some person the agent has not yet identified, and then try to find someone to ratify it.

- The principal must have had *capacity* to create the contract both at the time the agent created the contract and at the time of ratification.

What happens if an unauthorized contract is not ratified? Suppose that an

---

[4.] *Findlay v Butler* (1977) 19 NBR (2d) 473 (QB); *Canada Trust Co v Gordon* [1978] 5 WWR 268 (Sask QB).

[5.] *Portavon Cinema Co Ltd v Price and Century Insurance Co Ltd* [1939] 4 All ER 601 (KB).

agent purported to create a contract with a third party on a principal's behalf.[6] The agent did not actually have authority, and the principal never ratified the agreement. In that situation, the agent is not personally liable to the third party under the contract *unless* the third party and the agent intended the contract to be binding on the agent personally.

Pre-Incorporation Contracts Special ratification rules apply when a person purports to enter into a contract with a third party on behalf of a corporation that does not yet exist. Such a **pre-incorporation contract** might be created, for example, if there has not been time to set up the corporation before the agent started negotiating the contract with the third party.

Under most Canadian corporate statutes, a person that enters into a pre-incorporation contract with a third party is personally bound to perform the contract and is entitled to its benefits.[7] But if a corporation does come into existence and does adopt the contract, the agent steps out, and the corporation acquires those rights and liabilities. Those rules may, however, be varied.

- The third party and the agent can agree that the agent will not be bound by the agreement in any event.
- The third party can ask a court to impose liability on *both* the agent and the corporation, even if the corporation adopts the agreement. The third party would do so if the corporation was financially unable to perform the entire agreement.

Those rules allocate the risk that the corporation will not be created or adopt the contract. The third party bears that risk only if it agrees to release the agent from liability in either event. Otherwise, the agent bears the risk. This scheme reflects the fact that the agent is usually in the best position to ensure that the corporation is created and adopts the agreement with the third party.

When Is the Principal Liable?

Most disputes about agency relate to the scope of the agent's authority. Did the agent have authority to enter into the agreement that the third party is trying to enforce against the principal? As we saw in Chapter 19 in relation to corporate agents, an agent may have received **actual authority** from the principal to create the agreement in question. If an agent is appointed under the express terms of a contract, actual authority is usually spelled out in that contract. Actual authority can also arise in other ways. For instance, an employee can receive actual authority to act on an employer's behalf: (i) under the terms of the employment contract, (ii) through a resolution of a company's board of directors, or (iii) by virtue of holding a particular position, like a sales manager. Actual authority can also be granted less formally, such as through an oral delegation of authority. Whichever way the agent acquires actual authority, the principal is bound by any obligation that the agent creates within the scope of that authority. That is true whether or not the third party knows the exact scope of the agent's actual authority.[8]

an agent may be personally liable under an unauthorized and unratified contract

a pre-incorporation contract is a contract created by an agent on behalf of a corporation that does not yet exist

actual authority occurs when the principal actually authorizes the agent to act on its behalf

---

[6] If an agency relationship never arises, there may never really be an "agent" or "principal." These terms nevertheless are used for convenience.

[7] For example, *Business Corporations Act*, SA 1981, c B-15, s 14 (*ABCA*) (Alta); *Canada Business Corporations Act*, RSC 1985, c C-44, s 14 (*CBCA*) (Can); *The Business Corporations Act*, SNB 1981, c B-9.1, s 12 (*NBBCA*) (NB); *Business Corporations Act*, RSO 1990, c B.16, s 21 (*OBCA*) (Ont).

[8] *Freeman & Lockyer v Buckhurst Park Properties (Mangal) Ltd* [1964] 1 All ER 630 (CA).

Chapter 19 explained how a third party often does not know—and has no easy way of knowing—the extent of an agent's actual authority. That information is likely contained in a contract or other document to which the third party does not have access. The third party therefore may have to proceed on the basis of common indications of authority, such as a name tag that identifies a person as a "sales manager." The law helps in that situation by allowing the third party to rely on words or conduct by the principal that indicate that the agent has authority, even if that is not true. **Apparent authority** occurs when the principal creates the reasonable impression that the agent is authorized. The principal is liable to the third party under any contract that the agent created within the scope of that apparent authority.[9]

Apparent authority is not necessarily connected with actual authority. In practice, however, they often overlap. Suppose that you are the office manager of a business that is being conducted through a corporation. You want to buy a photocopier for that business. You may have actual authority to do so under the terms of your contract with the corporation. You may also have apparent authority because the corporation's president wrote a letter saying that you were authorized to buy the photocopier. Nevertheless, one form of authority may exist without the other. That would be true, for instance, if the president's letter was inaccurate because your employment contract said that only the vice-president was authorized to buy office equipment.

It is impossible to list every form of behaviour that can create apparent authority. Significantly, only the principal's conduct—not the agent's—is relevant. The court must be satisfied that the principal acted in a way that made the third party reasonably believe that the agent was authorized. The clearest example occurs when the principal actually says words to that effect to the third party. But less direct forms of communication may be enough.

Suppose that Jan is a wheat dealer. Tom gives her possession of 1000 tonnes of his wheat. Given the nature of both Jan's business and Tom's conduct, it might be reasonable for a third party to believe that Jan is authorized to sell the wheat.[10] Similarly, hiring a lawyer to defend a lawsuit may give that lawyer apparent authority to settle the claim on your behalf. If the lawyer does so, you may be bound by the settlement agreement, even if you never gave the lawyer actual authority to settle.[11] You could, however, then sue your lawyer for exceeding the scope of the authority that you did give.[12]

In each case, the court asks if it was reasonable for the third party to believe that the agent had authority. As our examples suggest, the answer to that question largely depends on two factors:

- the nature and content of the principal's communication to the third party
- the circumstances in which that communication occurs, including the kind of business that is involved

apparent authority occurs when the principal creates the reasonable impression that the agent is authorized

actual authority and apparent authority may overlap

apparent authority must be based on statements or conduct by the principal

---

[9] That form of authority is sometimes described as "ostensible authority," "agency by estoppel," or "agency by holding out." Estoppel is discussed in Chapter 3. Holding out in the context of partnerships is discussed in Chapter 18.

[10] *Pickering v Busk* (1812) 104 ER 758 (KB).

[11] *Sign-O-Lite v Bugeja* [1994] OJ No 1381 (Gen Div).

[12] As your agent, the lawyer has a duty to follow your instructions and has a fiduciary duty to you. Both of those duties would be breached if the lawyer agreed to the settlement without your consent.

A principal will be bound by the agent's apparent authority only if the third party relied on that appearance of authority. Consequently, the third party cannot enforce a contract if it knew, or should have known, the agent did not have authority.[13] Case Brief 20.1 illustrates how apparent authority can arise without any express representation by the principal.

the third party must reasonably rely on the appearance of authority

CASE BRIEF 20.1

Spiro v Lintern [1973] 3 All ER 319 (CA)

John owned a house. He directed his wife, Iris, to list the property with a real estate agent, but did not give her authority to sell the house. Iris entered into a contract to sell the house to Lintern. John was aware of what his wife had done but did nothing about it. He even permitted Lintern to come to the house with his architect to plan some repairs. At the time of the contract, Lintern had no idea that Iris was not the owner of the house. John refused to sell, arguing that Iris had no authority to sell his house. The court held that, by allowing Iris to act as she had, John had given her apparent authority to sell the house.

Special Rules for Corporations

Many corporations are complex organizations that use many types of agents with many types of authority. It is therefore difficult for a corporation's customers to determine whether the people they deal with are actually authorized to act on the corporation's behalf. Consequently, most corporate statutes prevent corporations from avoiding liability by relying on internal corporate restrictions. The risk of unauthorized conduct falls upon the corporation. The **indoor management rule** states that a corporation cannot rely on certain kinds of defects in the authority of an agent who purports to act on its behalf in entering into a contract with a third party, which may: (i) restrict the authority of any person to bind the corporation, or (ii) require some procedure to be followed before a contract can be created. More specifically, a corporation cannot rely on any provision in its articles or bylaws, or in any unanimous shareholder agreement, that creates a defect in the agent's authority. As well, a corporation cannot deny that a person held out by a corporation as an officer, director, or agent has not been duly appointed or does not have the authority that a person in that position usually has in the business of the corporation.[14]

the indoor management rule states that a corporation cannot rely on certain kinds of defects in the authority of an agent who purports to act on its behalf in entering into a contract with a third party

However, a third party cannot enforce a contract if it knew that there was a defect in the agent's authority, or if it should have known of that defect. Suppose that you are a director of a shoe company. The corporation's sales representative purports to sell you $1 000 000 worth of inventory. If you know that sales representatives cannot enter into contracts for more than $500 000 without the president's approval, the sale contract is unenforceable.

---

13. *Hazelwood v West Coast Securities Ltd* (1975) 49 DLR (3d) 46 (BC SC), affd (1976) 68 DLR (3d) 172 (CA).

14. For example, *CBCA* s 18; *NBBCA* s 15; *OBCA* s 18; *Corporations Act*, SN 1986, c 12, s 33 (Nfld).

FIGURE 20.2   When a Principal Is Bound by the Acts of an Agent

- Agent acts within the scope of actual authority given by the principal to the agent:
  - by express delegation to the agent
  - by appointing the agent to a position with that authority
  - implied from the circumstances

- Agent acts within scope of apparent authority created by principal's representation to a third party, which may consist of:
  - the principal's statement or conduct
  - the principal acquiescing to agent acting with that authority
  - the principal appointing the agent to a position that would usually have that authority

- Partner acts within the normal course of the partnership business.

- Agent enters into contract on behalf of an identified principal but without the principal's authority, and the principal subsequently ratifies the contract.

- Agent enters into a pre-incorporation contract, and the corporation adopts the contract after it comes into existence.

When Is the Agent Liable?

An agent is normally not liable because it is usually clear that it was contracting on behalf of an identified principal. However, the agent and the third party may agree otherwise. And even if the contract does not expressly provide for liability, a court may decide that the parties implicitly intended the agent to be personally liable. The agent can also be held personally liable if it presented itself to the third party as the principal.[15] That can happen if the agent fails to disclose that there was a principal. If the third party later discovers that the person it dealt with was only an agent, and if that agent had authority to act on behalf of the **undisclosed principal**, the third party can hold either the agent or the principal liable.[16] Therefore, to avoid the risk of personal liability, an agent should clearly explain its own role, and disclose the existence of a principal, to the third party.

Suppose that an agent purports to contract on behalf of a principal, but does not actually have authority to do so. The agent is not personally liable under that agreement unless it and the third party agreed otherwise. The agent nevertheless may be responsible for any losses that the third party suffers as a result of the transaction. An agent that knew it was not authorized to act on the principal's behalf may be liable for fraud or deceit.[17] And even if the agent did not act fraudulently, it may be liable to the third party for a *breach of warranty of authority*. A **breach of warranty of authority** occurs when an agent incorrectly indicates that it is authorized to act for a principal. That liability applies even if the agent honestly, but mistakenly, thought that it had the principal's authority.[18]

*an **undisclosed principal** exists when the agent did not disclose that it was acting on behalf of a principal*

*a **breach of warranty of authority** occurs when an agent indicates that it is authorized to act for a principal when it is not*

[15.] The agent will be liable only if there is clear evidence that the parties intended the agent to be liable: *Petro-Partners v Eastside Management 94 Inc* [1999] OJ No 2269 (CA).

[16.] The undisclosed principal can also enforce the contract against the third party.

[17.] *Keddie v Canada Life Assurance Co* [1999] 179 DLR (4th) 1 (BCCA). The tort of deceit was discussed in Chapter 11.

[18.] *Yonge v Toynbee* [1910] 1 KB 215 (CA).

The Agent's Duty to the Principal

When an agent is appointed by contract, its responsibilities may be set out in some detail. It must comply with those duties and follow any instructions given by the principal. The agent can be held responsible for failing to do so. In one case, a principal appointed an agent to insure a ship. The agent failed to do so, and the ship was lost. The agent was liable to the principal for the loss that the insurance would have covered.[19] Furthermore, an agent may have a duty that is not mentioned in the contract, but that arises from the context. For example, an agent that receives goods to sell may have the duty to insure them while they are in its possession.

In general, an agent's obligations cannot be delegated to anyone else—they are personal obligations. That rule recognizes that a principal often puts great trust in the judgment and skill of its agent. There are important practical exceptions to this general rule. For instance, if a law firm or a large business enterprise is appointed as an agent, responsibility necessarily is delegated to someone within that organization.

an agent's obligations generally cannot be delegated

Because an agency relationship exposes the principal to the risk of being held liable in unwanted ways, the common law also imposes two other types of duties on agents:

- a fiduciary duty
- a duty of care

Those duties reduce the principal's risk.

Fiduciary Duty

Like corporate directors and officers (discussed in Chapter 19), agents have a **fiduciary duty** to act in good faith and in the best interests of their principals.[20] While the precise content of that duty depends on the circumstances, one of its key requirements is that agents must avoid situations in which their personal interests conflict with the best interests of their principals. For instance, if you were appointed to negotiate a contract for the sale of your principal's land, you could not buy that property yourself. There would be an obvious conflict of interest. You would be acting for the principal as the seller *and* for yourself as the buyer.[21] You would be tempted to favour your own interests over the principal's.

a fiduciary duty requires an agent to act in good faith and for the best interests of the principal

A conflict of interest would also arise if, without your principal's knowledge, you arranged for the property to be sold to someone with whom you have a relationship.[22] Suppose that I had previously agreed to pay $5000 to you if you found a suitable piece of land for me. You then arranged for me to buy your principal's property for $200 000. You have breached your fiduciary duty. Your desire to obtain $5000 from me may have interfered with your obligation to find the best deal possible for your principal. You would have to pay the $5000 finder's fee over to your principal.[23] It would not matter that $200 000 was an entirely fair price for the sale of the land—the fiduciary duty may be breached even if the principal did not suffer any loss. That rule is based on the need to

the fiduciary duty may be breached even if the principal did not suffer any loss

---

[19.] *Turpin v Bilton* (1843) 134 ER 641 (CP).

[20.] *R v Kelly* (1992) 92 DLR (4th) 643 (SCC). We discussed the fiduciary duty that partners in a partnership owe each other in Chapter 18.

[21.] *Aaron Acceptance Corp v Adam* (1987) 37 DLR (4th) 133 (BC CA).

[22.] *Andrews v Ramsay* [1903] 2 KB 635.

[23.] *Raso v Dionigi* (1993) 100 DLR (4th) 459 (Ont CA).

ensure that agents never have any incentive to act in their own best interests at the expense of their principals. You would be entitled to keep the $5000 that you received from me only if you had explained the entire situation to your principal, who then allowed the sale to be completed.

The fiduciary duty involves several other obligations.

- An agent must disclose information that may be relevant to the principal's interests.[24] For example, if you are appointed to buy cars, you must reveal any bargains that you find.

- An agent cannot personally profit from the unauthorized use of information or opportunities that arose as a result of the agency relationship.

- An agent cannot compete with the principal. Consequently, if you are appointed to sell goods for your principal, you cannot also sell the same kind of goods for the principal's competitor.

a fiduciary duty may be displaced by the principal's instructions

An agent's fiduciary duty may, however, be displaced by the principal's instructions. If your principal specifically tells you to act in a certain way, you must do so, even if you think some other course of action would be in the principal's best interests.[25]

Duty of Care

the duty of care requires an agent to take reasonable care in the performance of the agency responsibilities

Every agent owes its principal a *duty of care*. The **duty of care** requires an agent to take reasonable care in the performance of the agency responsibilities. The precise content of that duty depends upon the circumstances and on what the agent agreed to do.[26] If that duty is breached, the agent generally must compensate the principal for any loss that it suffers. The principal may be denied recovery, however, if it knew that the agent was incompetent or unqualified.[27]

Case Brief 20.2 illustrates how an agent must understand the scope of its obligations, ensure that it is able to fulfill those obligations, and alert its principal to any deficiency in its skills.

CASE BRIEF 20.2

Fine's Flowers Ltd v General Accident Assurance Co of Canada (1977) 81 DLR (3d) 139 (Ont CA)

Fine's Flowers Ltd appointed an insurance agent to obtain "full coverage" for its garden business. The agent obtained insurance against a number of business risks—but not damage to plants caused by freezing as a result of a heating system failing. Unfortunately, that is exactly what happened. Fine's sued the agent for breach of contract and negligence.

The Court of Appeal held that the agent's undertaking to obtain "full coverage" created an obligation to ensure that Fine's was insured against all foreseeable and normal risks. The agent was liable for failing to fulfill its contractual duty to obtain adequate insurance and for breaching its duty of care to Fine's by failing to warn it about the gap in coverage.[28]

---

[24] *McCullough v Tenaglia* (1998) 40 BLR (2d) 222 (Ont Gen Div).

[25] *Bertram v Godfray* (1830) 12 ER 364 (PC); *Volkers v Midland Doherty Ltd* (1995) 17 DLR (4th) 343 (BC CA).

[26] *Tonks v Aetna Life Assurance Co of Canada* (1992) 98 DLR (4th) 582 (Ont Gen Div).

[27] *Hillcrest General Leasing Ltd v Guelph Investments Ltd* (1971) 13 DLR (3d) 517 (Ont Co Ct) (negligence in selecting sub-agent).

[28] Fine's could not recover compensation for the same loss twice. As discussed in Chapter 10, it was eventually required to elect between its concurrent actions.

The Principal's Duty to the Agent

Like an agent, a principal must fulfill any obligation that is set out in an agency contract. Furthermore, a principal generally must satisfy certain obligations that are imposed by law.

- Unless the parties agreed that the agent would work for free, the principal must pay reasonable remuneration for the agent's services.[29]
- A principal has an implied obligation to indemnify the agent for liabilities and expenses that are reasonably incurred in connection with the agency relationship. Suppose that you are asked to obtain insurance for your principal. You do so and pay the first premium on the principal's behalf. The principal must reimburse you for that expense. A principal is not, however, under any obligation if an agent acts illegally or in breach of the agency agreement.[30]

Termination

There are several ways to terminate an agency relationship.

- Either party can provide notice of termination.
- The relationship can end in accordance with the agency contract.
- If the agent is appointed for a specific project or a particular period, that project may be completed or the period may expire.
- Performance of the agency may become impossible.
- The principal may lose the capacity to contract as a result of death, insanity, or bankruptcy.[31]

an agency relationship can be terminated in several ways

That last ground can create practical difficulties if the agent is unaware that the principal has lost capacity. Since the principal cannot be liable for obligations that arise after the incapacity occurs, the third party may try to hold the agent personally responsible. In some circumstances, the agent may be liable for breach of warranty of authority.

Because an agency may be terminated by notice from either party, the relationship can be very fragile. For that reason, agency agreements often require a reasonable notice period before termination. Furthermore, if an agent is an employee, the law states that the agency-employment relationship can be terminated only for just cause, or with either notice or compensation in lieu of notice. Consequently, the precise nature of the parties' relationship may be significant with respect to which rules apply on termination. Agents may enjoy more rights as a result of also being employees.[32]

Risk Management Issues

Before concluding our general discussion of agency, it is appropriate to highlight the issue of risk management in regards to both contract and tort.

---

[29] *Banfield, McFarlane, Evan Real Estate Ltd v Hoffer* [1977] 4 WWR 465 (Man CA).

[30] *Duncan v Hill* (1873) LR 8 Ex 242, cited in GHL Fridman *Law of Agency* 7th ed (1997).

[31] Capacity to contract is discussed in Chapter 5. The agency relationship is also terminated if the agent dies or becomes insane.

[32] The question of when an agent should be considered an employee was considered in *Renmar Sales Agency Inc v 806897 Ontario Inc* [1999] OJ No 3956 (SCJ).

Contracts

A principal is liable for contracts created on its behalf by an agent with either actual or apparent authority. The principal must therefore be concerned about the risk of being bound to unwanted contracts. That risk is more easily managed with respect to *actual authority*. The principal can use an agency agreement to clearly state what the agent is and is not authorized to do. That document should be carefully drafted to ensure that it is broad enough to allow the agent to do a proper job, but not so broad as to permit the agent to create unintended liabilities.

Risks associated with *apparent authority* can also be managed, but not as easily. To avoid giving an agent apparent authority to enter into unwanted obligations, the principal must carefully monitor how it communicates, directly and indirectly, with third parties.[33] The principal must also realize that apparent authority may exist even after the actual agency relationship has come to an end. If a third party dealt with the agent before the agency relationship was terminated, it may continue doing so afterwards. And if that third party was unaware of the termination, it may be able to enforce any new agreements against the principal. To avoid that possibility, the principal should notify all of its customers whenever it terminates an agent's authority.[34]

Torts

If an agent commits a tort, the principal is vicariously liable to the victim if: (i) the agent was also an employee, and (ii) the tort was committed within the course of employment.[35] The basic rules for vicarious liability were discussed in Chapter 10. In Chapter 25, we will discuss the rules that determine when a person is, in law, an employee.

A principal may be liable even if an agent was not an employee. In general, if the agent is acting within the scope of its actual or apparent authority, the principal is liable for the agent's fraud or negligent misrepresentation.[36] Case Brief 20.3 illustrates this problem.

CASE BRIEF 20.3

Betker v Williams [1992] 2 WWR 534 (BC CA)

Williams was selling a vacant lot. His agent told the purchasers that the lot would be suitable for building a solar home. The purchaser bought the lot. In fact, the lot was too small to accommodate any kind of house because no sewer could be installed.

The agent was liable for the tort of negligent misstatement. The court held Williams liable as well, even though he had nothing to do with making the misrepresentation. Williams had to reimburse the purchaser for the difference between the contract price and the actual value of the property.[37]

---

[33] When the agent acts outside the actual authority given by the principal, but in circumstances in which the third party can rely on apparent authority, the principal is liable to the third party, but it can also sue the agent for breach of the agency agreement.

[34] This issue of managing the risk of liability after the departure of a partner is discussed in Chapter 18.

[35] If the principal is forced to pay compensation to the victim, it is generally entitled to recover that amount from the agent-employee.

[36] When an agent has made a misrepresentation, the third party may be able to rescind the contract, even when the principal did not authorize, or even forbade, the misrepresentation.

[37] The case also illustrates that an agent may have a duty of care to a third party.

As we have seen, a principal is exposed to substantial risks whenever it uses an agent. Often, the only strategy for avoiding such risks is to carefully select, train, supervise, and monitor agents. You Be the Judge 20.1 illustrates the importance of that strategy. Business Law in Action 20.1 suggests that another risk for principals is that an agency relationship may arise when the principal does not expect it. Ethical Perspective 20.1 (p. 460) addresses the appropriateness of using criminal penalties as a way of reducing the risk that agents will not fulfill their duties to their principals.

YOU BE THE JUDGE 20.1

Authority of Insurance Broker[38]

Horne carried on business as an insurance broker on behalf of several insurance companies, including Canada Life Assurance Company. Under his contract with Canada Life, he was authorized to solicit customers for life insurance and various other products, but he was not authorized to incur any liability for Canada Life without prior approval from the company.

In June 1990, Horne met Keddie, who was seeking to make an investment. He told her that he was a Canada Life broker operating under the name Royal Pacific Consulting. On Horne's advice, Keddie purchased a $375 000 Canada Life annuity contract. Horne subsequently gave Keddie a folder containing information about the annuity. The folder had a picture of the Canada Life building in Toronto on the front, and the name and address of Canada Life on the back.

In 1992, Keddie was interested in making another investment. Horne convinced her that she should purchase another Canada Life annuity. Keddie gave Horne a cheque for $300 000 payable to Royal Pacific Consulting. Horne invest-

ed $105 000 in an annuity offered by another financial institution and kept the remaining $195 000 for himself. Horne later gave Keddie a folder, similar to the first one, that contained information about the annuity inside. However, whereas the earlier policy simply referred to "Canada Life," the new policy statement referred to "Royal Pacific Group Representing the Canada Life/NN Financial Group."

There was no evidence as to how Horne got the folders. There was, however, evidence that he had been provided with a large quantity of material from Canada Life, including application forms and brochures. The only information that Keddie had about Horne's relationship to Canada Life was based on what he had told her.

When Horne eventually stopped making payments to her, Keddie successfully sued him for fraud. Unfortunately, Horne no longer had any assets and therefore could not satisfy that judgment. Keddie then sued Canada Life alleging that since Horne was Canada Life's agent, it was liable for Horne's fraud.

Question for Discussion

1. Should Keddie succeed against Canada Life?

BUSINESS LAW IN ACTION 20.1

When Is the Government Liable as Principal?

Private parties have recently tried to hold governments liable for the actions of other bodies, such as universities, by arguing that those bodies were agents acting within the apparent authority that they had been given by the government.[39] That strategy may be attrac-

tive because governments, unlike many private parties, have ample resources with which to pay compensation.

In *Springbank v Yukon Contractors*, the Yukon government wanted to build the Yukon Place Arts Centre in Whitehorse.[40] It appointed the Yukon Contractors' Association (YCA) to receive construction bids and to administer the bidding process. CRJ Springbank Electric and Construction Ltd

(continued)

[38.] *Keddie v Canada Life Assurance Co* [1999] BCJ No 2165 (CA).

[39.] *Dale v Manitoba* (1997) 147 DLR (4th) 605 (Man CA).

[40.] *CRJ Springbank Electric and Construction Ltd v Yukon Contractors Association* [1993] YJ No 216 (SC).

(continued)

submitted a bid. The YCA rules committee disqualified that bid on the basis that it was incomplete. In fact, the committee acted improperly in rejecting Springbank's bid, which would have been the lowest and therefore should have won the competition. By the time that was sorted out, however, the contract had already been awarded to someone else. Springbank sued the government for the loss of the contract. Springbank argued that the government had held the YCA out as its agent and therefore was responsible for the YCA's actions.

The Yukon Supreme Court rejected the claim because there was no reasonable basis for Springbank to think that YCA was an agent of the government. The court was influenced by the fact that the bidding rules never indicated that the YCA was acting as an agent. Nevertheless, the case sug-gests that it may be possible in other circumstances to impose liability on a government that delegates its responsi-bilities to a private party.

Questions for Discussion

1. Do you agree with the decision?
2. Would it be reasonable for Springbank to assume that in designating the YCA as a depository to receive bids to contract with the government, the government was appointing the YCA as an agent to act on its behalf?
3. More generally, should governments be subject to the same rules regarding a principal's liability for acts of its agents that apply to private parties? Are there reasons to hold governments to a higher standard?

ETHICAL PERSPECTIVE 20.1

Agent's Criminal Liability[41]

Over a two-year period, almost three dozen investors purchased shares in two companies on the advice of Hudec. The majority of the investors received no information about the companies and relied exclusively on Hudec's advice. Hudec continued to play a role in advising the investors from time to time as to the status of their investments. He later admitted that one company had given him $43 000 cash and the other 79 000 shares in return for directing his clients to them. He also later admitted that he did not tell any of the investors that he had received those benefits from the companies.

Hudec was found guilty under the *Criminal Code* for accepting commissions without his clients' knowledge and consent. He realized that he was an agent for his clients. And they were entitled to know that he was receiving benefits from the companies in question. If they had known that fact, they might have invested elsewhere.

Questions for Discussion

1. Is it appropriate for agents to be held criminally liable in these circumstances?
2. Should liability depend on whether the investors lost their investments?
3. Would civil liability to compensate for any investor losses be sufficient?

BUSINESS RELATIONSHIPS IN WHICH AGENCY ISSUES ARISE

Agency arises in a variety of business arrangements. We looked at partnerships in Chapter 18 and corporations in Chapter 19. In this section, we will consider several other situations that involve agency relationships:

■ joint ventures and strategic alliances
■ distributorships
■ agents governed by special statutes

[41.] *R v Hudec* [1992] OJ No 2992 (HCJ).

Joint Ventures and Strategic Alliances

A *joint venture* is not a distinct form of business organization, nor is it a relationship that has a precise legal meaning. A **joint venture** is simply any legal arrangement in which two or more parties combine their resources for a limited purpose, or a limited time, or both. For instance, a small exploration company may own the rights to mine gold from a certain area, but not have the financial resources needed to actually build the mine. It therefore could enter into a joint venture with a larger mining company that does have sufficient resources. That joint venture could operate through a corporation in which each party has one share, or through a partnership in which each party was a partner. Alternatively, the parties could regulate their relationship entirely through a contract.

Much of this description can apply to *strategic alliances*. A **strategic alliance** may be any arrangement in which two or more parties agree to co-operate for some purpose. That arrangement can be legal or informal. It can involve greater or lesser degrees of co-operation. A joint venture or partnership may be referred to as a strategic alliance. That term may also be used, for example, to describe an arrangement in which the parties (i) conduct a research project, (ii) jointly market products, or (iii) simply share information.

If a joint venture or strategic alliance is purely contractual, the participants are not automatically agents for each other.[42] They may, however, agree otherwise. In fact, joint venturers often agree that each will have authority to create obligations for both in connection with the joint venture business. When that is done, the precise scope of the agency relationship should be clearly stated in the joint venture agreement. Furthermore, even if there is no *actual* agency relationship, one party's actions may, in the circumstances, provide the other with apparent authority. And a third party may be entitled to rely on that appearance of authority.

> a **joint venture** is a legal arrangement in which two or more parties combine their resources for a limited purpose, or a limited time, or both

> a **strategic alliance** is any arrangement in which two or more parties agree to co-operate for some purpose

Distributorships

A **distributorship** exists when one business contractually agrees to sell another's product. In addition to selling the basic product, a distributor may also perform some of the responsibilities that would normally fall upon the supplier or manufacturer. The distributor may, for example, provide warranty service. In selecting a distributor, a supplier is primarily motivated by finding access to the greatest number of customers.

A distributorship does not normally involve an agency relationship. The parties can agree that the distributor acts on behalf of the supplier when it deals with customers. Usually, however, the distributor buys the products for itself and then resells them on its own behalf. In fact, most distributorship agreements expressly state that the distributor is *not* an agent and therefore has no authority to bind the supplier. Suppliers do not want to be exposed to the risk of unwanted obligations. For that reason, they also need to be concerned about the possibility of *apparent authority*. If a distributor is made to look like an agent, a customer may acquire rights against the supplier, regardless of what the distributorship agreement says.

> a **distributorship** exists when one business contractually agrees to sell another's product

> a distributorship does not normally involve an agency relationship

---

[42.] *Canadian Mortgage and Housing Corporation v Graham* is one case in which one contractual joint venturer was held responsible for the obligations of the other: (1973) 43 DLR (3d) 686 (NS SC TD).

Agents Governed by Special Statutes

Some kinds of agents are governed by special statutes that are intended to protect the people with whom they deal. For example, lawyers, real estate agents, insurance agents, stockbrokers, and travel agents are subject to regulations that complement the basic common law rules that we have discussed. In each case, a professional organization also governs the way that business is done.

For example, to work as a real estate agent, a person must be either licensed or employed by a licensed agent under provincial legislation.[43] Licensing bodies try to ensure that agents meet certain standards for competence, honesty, integrity, and financial responsibility. They enforce specific rules relating to trading (including prohibiting agents from supplying false information), handling clients' money, advertising, and disclosure when agents may have a personal interest in the transaction. For instance, real estate agents are required to tell the principal about any compensation they will receive from another party to the transaction. Typically, licensing bodies have the power to suspend or revoke licences when the required standards are not met.

Regulatory schemes often have a complaints process. Anyone concerned about the actions of a real estate agent can file a complaint with the licensing body, which has the power to inspect the agent's premises and records. If it discovers wrongdoing, it may subject the agent to disciplinary proceedings, which can lead to the suspension or revocation of the agent's licence, or even criminal charges.

Similar schemes apply to insurance agents and travel agents.[44] Stockbrokers are governed by a more comprehensive scheme of regulation, which includes standards for internal controls, insurance, and sufficient capital to ensure that brokerage firms are solvent.[45] The Canadian Investor Protection Fund covers customers' losses of securities and cash balances that result from the insolvency of a firm. It does not cover losses that result from changing market values, regardless of the cause of such losses.

FRANCHISING

A **franchise** is a purely contractual relationship under which the franchisor gives the franchisee the right to operate its "system" in return for a set of fees. The franchise agreement:

- includes a licence that allows the franchisee to use the franchisor's trademark[46]
- requires the franchisor to assist in the operation of the franchised business (by providing training, uniforms, and so on)
- requires the franchisee to maintain certain standards and follow certain rules

---

[43.] In Ontario, for example, licensing is under the *Real Estate and Business Brokers Act*, RSO 1990, c R.4. Since 1997, it has been administered by the Real Estate Council of Ontario, a non-profit body created by statute. Real estate agents in Alberta are regulated under the *Real Estate Act*, SA 1995, c R-4.5 and in Nova Scotia under the *Real Estate Trading Act*, SNS 1996, c 28.

[44.] For example, *Registered Insurance Brokers Act*, RSO 1990, c R.19 (Ont); *Travel Agents Act*, RSBC 1996, c 459 (BC); *Travel Industry Act*, RSO 1990, c T.19 (Ont).

[45.] For example, *Securities Act*, RSBC 1996, c 418 (BC); *Securities Act*, RSO 1990, c S.5 (Ont).

[46.] A licence gives permission to act in a way that would otherwise be prohibited.

- requires the franchisee to pay fees based, in part, on the volume of sales

While we often think of franchises in the fast-food context, they are common in many other areas, like retailing.

Advantages and Disadvantages for the Franchisee

Franchising has pros and cons from the franchisee's perspective. On the one hand, there are several advantages.

franchising has pros and cons for the franchisee

- Franchising reduces many of the risks that are associated with starting a business. The franchisor may provide an established reputation in the marketplace, a proven business concept, and assistance in the form of staff training, operational advice, and low supply costs.
- A franchisor may provide advice on the best location. It may even rent that location to the franchisee.
- Franchisor advertising benefits all franchisees.

On the other hand, there are important disadvantages.

- To ensure that every outlet operates under the same standards for quality and service, the franchisor imposes restrictions on the franchisee's ability to do business. Those restrictions are sometimes quite onerous.
- The franchisee may be left with little profit after paying the franchise fees.
- Franchising agreements tend to be very long and complex. Potential franchisees may find them difficult to understand.
- Potential franchisees may also find it difficult to obtain information about the actual operation of the business. That is especially true if the franchise business is new and unproven. Sometimes, the franchisor is the only source of information—and that party may not be entirely reliable.

Advantages and Disadvantages for the Franchisor

Franchising also has pros and cons for the franchisor. On the positive side, franchising provides a way of expanding operations without the need to either provide all of the investment capital or take all of the risks. On the negative side, the franchisor must share the profits with its franchisees. It also bears the risk that its reputation may be damaged by a shoddy franchisee.

franchising has pros and cons for the franchisor

A franchise could be set up as an agency relationship, whereby the franchisee could be allowed to conduct business on behalf of the franchisor. In practice, however, that arrangement is not used because an agency relationship would expose the franchisor to the risk of liability in connection with every franchised outlet. That is a risk that franchisors want to avoid.

franchises are not operated as agency relationships

Legal Rules Governing Franchise Relationships

A franchisor has certain advantages over a potential franchisee during negotiations. The franchisor knows its business better than the franchisee. The franchisor is also intimately familiar with the rights and obligations that are set out in the franchise agreement. Furthermore, some potential franchisees have little previous business experience. Together, those factors increase the risk that franchisees will make a bad bargain.

franchisors usually have negotiating advantages over franchisees franchises are often offered on a take-it-or-leave-it basis

Even if a franchisee identifies a potential problem with a proposed franchise agreement, the franchisor will probably be inflexible. A franchisor will usually strongly resist any attempt to modify its standard form agreement because it wants to ensure that all of its franchisees receive the same deal. Preferential treatment for one franchisee will encourage others to seek the same. For that reason, franchises are often offered on a take-it-or-leave-it basis.

The common law rules of contract that we discussed in Chapters 4 and 5 provide some protection for franchisees. For instance, if a franchisee is induced to enter into a franchising agreement on the basis of a franchisor's misrepresentation regarding an outlet's profitability, that contract may be set aside. That is also possible if an agreement is unconscionable. Following the usual rule, however, the franchisor does not have a general duty to disclose all information that might affect a franchisee's decision.

Because those common law protections are often inadequate, Alberta and Ontario have enacted legislation that imposes obligations on franchisors for the protection of current and prospective franchisees.[47] These are the key elements of the legislation.

- Franchisors have a minimum obligation to deal fairly with franchisees and prospective franchisees. Franchisors must act in good faith and in accordance with reasonable commercial standards.

- Franchisors must provide extensive disclosure to prospective franchisees regarding the risks associated with the franchise business.

- Any franchisee who signs a franchise agreement has a right to withdraw from the agreement within 60 days of signing, or within two years if the required disclosure documents were never provided.

- Franchisees have the right to damages for any misrepresentation in disclosure documents.

- Franchisees have the right to organize themselves to deal collectively with the franchisor.

Business Decision 20.1 asks you to decide on how best to structure a business relationship.

BUSINESS DECISION 20.1

Method of Carrying on Business

You are a new manufacturer of tennis rackets and you are looking for someone to help you sell your product in Alberta. Jordan has worked for several years as a distributor for in-line skates in Alberta and sells to many of the same retailers that you would like as customers.

You want to enter into some kind relationship with Jordan to help you sell to those retailers.

Questions for Discussion

1. What are the options for structuring your relationship with Jordan?

2. What are the advantages and disadvantages of each?

[47.] *Franchises Act*, SA 1995, c F-17.1 (Alta); *Arthur Wishart Act (Franchise Disclosure), 2000*, SO 2000, c 3. The Ontario statute is named after Arthur Wishart, who first proposed a public inquiry into the franchising industry.

Chapter Summary

Under an agency relationship, an agent represents a principal for some specific purpose. That purpose may include the creation of contracts. Agency relationships themselves are often created by a contract between the principal and the agent. They exist as a matter of law in partnerships. Agency can also be created by the principal holding out, or representing, a person as having the authority of an agent.

Even if a person is not an agent when an obligation is purportedly created on behalf of a principal, that obligation can become binding on the principal if the principal ratifies it. A special rule applies to pre-incorporation contracts. In most provinces, the agent is personally liable under contracts it enters into before the company is incorporated. Afterwards, the corporation can adopt the contract. If it does so, the contract becomes binding on the corporation, and the agent ceases to be personally responsible.

The principal is liable for a contract entered into by an agent on its behalf if it gave the agent either actual authority or apparent authority to do so. Most corporate statutes have special rules that prevent the corporation from relying on a failure to follow its own internal procedures to deny that an agent had authority. An agent is not normally personally liable for contracts entered into on behalf of a principal unless the agent and third party otherwise agreed. If an agent purports to enter into a contract on behalf of a principal and has no authority to do so, the agent may be liable to the third party for breach of warranty of authority.

An agent is required to fulfill any obligations created under the agency agreement. An agent also has a fiduciary duty to act in the principal's best interests, and a duty of care to act reasonably when performing the agency obligations. A principal must comply with the obligations specified in the agency agreement. In the absence of an express provision to the contrary, a principal must pay reasonable remuneration and indemnify the agent for any reasonable expenses.

An agency relationship can be terminated in several ways. If the agent is an employee, statutory and common law rules regarding notice must be observed.

An agency relationship can exist in the context of some methods for carrying on business, such as a contractual joint venture or a strategic alliance. Generally, distributorships and franchises are not agencies. Some agency businesses are subject to special regulatory schemes designed to protect the public and consumers.

Franchises are contractual relationships under which the franchisor gives the franchisee the right to operate its business system in return for fees. Franchises have advantages and disadvantages for both franchisors and franchisees. Alberta and Ontario have special statutes to protect franchisees.

Review Questions

1. Why would you appoint an agent to act on your behalf? What are the risks in using an agent?

2. Can a contract negotiated by an agent on behalf of an identified principal, but without the principal's knowledge or consent, be binding on the principal? Can it be binding on the agent?

3. The president of a corporation you are dealing with tells you that Alton has authority to sell you one of the corporation's cars. You find out that the president was mistaken because Alton's employment contract says that he does not have this authority. Can you go ahead with the contract relying on the president's statement to you?

4. If you were a third party negotiating a contract with an employee of a corporation, would you be concerned about the authority of that person to commit the corporation to the contract? Are there defects in authority that you would not have to worry about?

5. If you were a real estate agent acting for someone trying to sell a house, could you buy that house for yourself? How could you deal with that situation in a way that would allow you to buy the house and fulfill your duties as an agent?

6. If you appointed an agent to buy a car for you, what concerns would you have about the unauthorized actions of the agent, such as agreeing to a higher price than you were prepared to pay? How would you deal with those concerns?

7. Can you enter into a contract on behalf of a corporation that has not yet been incorporated? Who would be responsible for performing such a contract?

8. Explain the situations in which a principal can be held liable for torts committed by its agent? Is there anything that the principal can do to reduce those risks?

9. Are the parties to a contractual joint venture, strategic alliance, distributorship, or franchise agreement in an agency relationship?

10. You negotiated a contract with an agent, but later found out that the agent had no authority to contract on behalf of the principal. Assuming that the principal is not liable, do you have any recourse against the agent?

11. Jane appointed you to act as her agent to negotiate the purchase of some cattle. Before you signed the purchase contract, Jane died. What effect, if any, does her death have on your authority as agent?

12. You contracted with Lana to act as your agent in purchasing lumber. That contract does not say that she is entitled to be paid. Are you required to pay her? Are you required to pay her expenses for travelling to visit lumber producers to acquire lumber for you?

13. Allan has appointed you as an agent to sell his line of ski jackets to retailers. Another manufacturer asks you to carry its line of ski jackets as well. Can you agree to carry the other line?

14. At 9:00 a.m., you instruct your stockbroker to buy 1000 shares of Bolt Networks Inc as soon as possible at the current market price of $10. The stockbroker forgets to place your order until the next day when the price has gone up to $15. Do you have any claim against the agent?

15. Is there a difference between a strategic alliance and a joint venture?

16. You bought a piece of commercial real estate with the help of your agent. You now believe that the agent misled you regarding the zoning of that property. What could you do about it?

17. Why might you consider a franchise rather than starting a new business from scratch?

18. If you were negotiating with a franchisor in Manitoba, would you have any concerns about revenue estimates shown to you by the franchisor to encourage you to agree to become a franchisee? Would your concerns be different if you were in Ontario?

19. If you had appointed the operator of a marina as an agent to sell your boat for you, what would you have to do to terminate that agency relationship?

20. You have entered into a contract with Azam to supply your business with stationery. You have known Azam for a long time and trust him to be a reliable supplier. A few days later, Azam discloses that he was acting as an agent for a paper manufacturer that you have never heard of. Can you enforce the contract against the paper manufacturer or Azam?

Cases and Problems

1. Jensen entered into a contract to buy a mobile home from South Trail Mobile Ltd. The contract provided that all sales had to have the approval of the president of South Trail. When Jensen asked about this approval, Hiram, the salesman with whom Jensen was dealing, said that it had been approved as required. In fact, the president had not approved the contract. Can Jensen enforce the sale contract against South Trail?

2. Glen entered into a contract with Boris, an auctioneer, under which Boris agreed to sell some vacant land that Glen owned. The catalogue for the auction set out the conditions for sales at the auction and said that the auctioneer had no authority to make representations on behalf of anyone whose property was to be sold at the auction. Oded asked Boris whether the property was zoned for commercial development. Boris said it was, but he was mistaken. The zoning permitted only agricultural use. Oded bought the property at the auction, relying on what Boris had told him. However, when he discovered the truth about the zoning situation, he refused to pay. Can Glen enforce the contract against Oded?

3. Jennifer is an agent of MB Forest Products Inc. Under her agency contract, she buys raw logs from independent logging companies. While Jennifer is visiting some logging companies in the interior of British Columbia, MB goes bankrupt. Jennifer later signs a contract with ForCan Logging Ltd on behalf of MB for the purchase of 1000 logs. The contract is at a very favourable price for ForCan. Can they enforce the contract against MB? Do they have any rights against Jennifer?

4. Martina and Owen were interested in running a pizza business in Toronto, but have no business experience. They approach Mr Pizza, a franchisor that is advertising for new franchisees in the newspaper. The franchisor shows them some financial statements for a Mr Pizza location in Toronto, which suggest profits of over $1 000 000 a year. Mr Pizza tells Martina and Owen that the location can be theirs for $100 000. Martina and Owen are very interested. Mr Pizza asks them to sign a 75-page agreement. When they suggest getting some legal advice, Mr Pizza discourages them by saying, "Why share your future profits with lawyers?" Martina and Owen sign the agreement and begin carrying on the business. They work 15-hour days for six months and take home only $50 000. The basic business is profitable, but what they can take out of the business is limited by the fees they have to pay: advertising fees, royalties for use of the trade mark, fees for training employees, fees for their uniforms, and fees to have their premises inspected each month. Martina and Owen want out. Their agreement, however, provides for a two-year term. Is there anything that they can do? Would your answer be different if Martina and Owen's pizza restaurant was in Halifax?

5. Geomedia Inc helps retailers promote sales by arranging to distribute advertising flyers to consumers, usually in the form of newspaper inserts. Red Rose Inc sells arts and crafts supplies across Canada. In the past, it managed its own advertising by contracting with several newspapers, including the *Regina Post*, to distribute its flyers. Recently, Red Rose hired Geomedia to act as its agent to distribute flyers. It then faxed an announcement to the newspapers that said, "From this point forward, Geomedia will be managing all media distribution for Red Rose." The *Regina Post* interpreted that fax to mean that it would be contracting with Geomedia rather than Red Rose.

The *Regina Post* subsequently received several orders from Geomedia that involved advertisements for Red Rose. Those orders, printed on Geomedia letterhead, said: "Please bill Red Rose care of Geomedia." The *Post* published those ads, but has not been paid. To make matters worse, Red Rose has gone bankrupt. Is the *Post* entitled to receive payment from Geomedia?

6. Koh Corporation agreed to provide cleaning services for one year to Mid-Town Management Inc, which operated several large office buildings in Saskatoon. The contract price was much cheaper than for other cleaning services. In its dealings with Mid-Town, Koh always made clear that it was acting on behalf of a principal in contracting to provide the services, though it never identified who that principal was. In fact, Koh was acting on behalf of Down-Town Realty Inc, a competitor of Mid-Town's. After six months, Koh stopped providing the services. Is Koh liable to Mid-Town for breach of contract?

7. Orlof was interested in buying real estate from Danilova. He signed an agreement to purchase the property "on behalf of a corporation to be incorporated." Orlof then instructed his lawyers to prepare the necessary documents to complete the transaction. To close the transaction, a lawyer in the firm decided to use a corporation that had already been incorporated (a "shelf corporation") by another partner in the law firm. She drafted a transfer of the one issued share from the partner to Orlof, a shareholder's resolution appointing Orlof as the sole director, a director's resolution authorizing the transaction, a legal opinion, and some other documents in the name of the shelf corporation. She then sent that package to Danilova's lawyer for comments, together with a cover letter indicating that the shelf corporation would complete the purchase. When the date came to close the transaction, Orlof decided that the price was too high. He therefore refused to take a transfer of the share, to sign the resolutions, or to pay Danilova.

The law firm later transferred the partner's share in the shelf corporation to another client, who began to carry on a profitable business through the shelf corporation. Danilova sued the shelf corporation. She alleged that the agreement to buy her property was a pre-incorporation contract that had been adopted by the corporation based on the sending of the draft documents by Orlof's lawyers to Danilova's lawyers. Will Danilova succeed? What would you do if you were the client who was now carrying on business using the shelf corporation?

8. Sonia hired Klaus, a real estate agent, to sell her house. She told him that she would like to list the house for $350 000, but that she was willing to sell for as low as $300 000. Klaus's brother, Bjorn, was looking for a house. Klaus told him that Sonia would sell for $300 000. Klaus presented Sonia with an offer to purchase the house for $275 000. That offer was made in the name of Bjorn

Investments Ltd, a corporation that Bjorn controlled. Following some negotiations, Sonia sold the house to Bjorn Investments Ltd for $300 000. Sonia later learned that Bjorn Investments was controlled by Klaus's brother. Does she have any claim against Klaus? Does it make any difference if the actual market value was $300 000?

9. Porter entered into a contract with Hip Sports Inc under which Hip agreed to sell Porter's basketball shoes. Hip was authorized to enter into contracts to sell the shoes on Porter's behalf and Porter agreed to pay (i) a commission of 10 percent of the sale price of the shoes, and (ii) all of Hip's advertising expenses. Hip represented several other lines of products.

Hip planned to advertise Porter's shoes through a flyer campaign. The going rate for that service was $5000. However, Hip was able to negotiate a discount of $1000 because it did a high volume of business with the flyer producer. Hip saw no reason to pass that benefit on to Porter since it was granted on the basis of *all* of the business that Hip did with the flyer company—for Porter and for other customers. Hip therefore charged Porter the full $5000. Is Hip liable to give Porter the benefit of the discount?

10. Goran and Basil were partners in a partnership named GB Computer Leasing. GB carried on a business of leasing personal computers and related equipment from a retail store. It was an express term of the partnership agreement that neither Goran nor Basil would enter into contracts to buy personal computers without the consent of the other. Goran bought 20 computers from Ellen. Ellen agreed to defer payment for one month. Basil has discovered that transaction and refuses to approve it. Can Ellen enforce the contract against the partnership? Does she have any action against Goran?

11. Louise operated a flea market under a tent. She decided that she needed insurance to protect her in case snow caused the roof to collapse. Louise asked Barak, an insurance broker, to obtain insurance for her that would provide that protection. Barak agreed to do so and found a policy with Abda Insurance Co for the protection of property. He recommended it to Louise. Relying on that advice, Louise entered into a contract with Abda. Unfortunately, the policy had a rider that excluded liability for roofs collapsing under snow. After a heavy snowfall, Louise's roof did collapse. Abda refused to pay. Does Louise have any claim against Barak?

12. Able has acted as an agent for Solon Corp for several years. Solon was in the business of selling security services. Able's contract required him to seek customers for Solon's services. In the course of working with Solon, Able learned a great deal about the security business and the sophisticated software that Solon uses. Able wants to use this knowledge to start up his own security service business. Can he do so?

WWWeblinks

Business Organizations

Industry Canada—Corporations Directorate

strategis.ic.gc.ca/sc_mrksv/corpdir/engdoc/homepage.html

This Web site offers information on incorporation under the federal *Canada Business Corporations Act* (CBCA), including such important issues as how to choose a corporate name. It also allows you to conduct the entire CBCA incorporation process online.

Manitoba Companies Office

www.gov.mb.ca/cca/comp_off/index.html

This Web site is similar to other sites maintained by many provincial and territorial governments that offer information on the process of incorporation under provincial law. This site also enables searches for corporate, partnership, and sole proprietorship names in use in Manitoba.

Canada Legal.com

www.canadalegal.com/gosite.asp?s=4557

On this site is a detailed discussion on how to choose the right form of business organization, including both legal and business issues, such as selecting a corporate name and registering a sole proprietorship, partnership, or corporation.

Small Business Canada

sbinfocanada.about.com/library/weekly/aa052301a.htm

This site, specifically aimed at small business, provides information on how to choose which form of business organization to use. It has links to a variety of useful resources.

Royal Bank of Canada

www.royalbank.com/sme/index.html

This site provides information on issues associated with starting a business, including advice on financing, business plans, and risk management.

World Wide Legal Information

www.wwlia.org/ca-corp1.htm

This Web site provides information on companies, partnerships, and sole proprietorships, focusing on the law in British Columbia. It includes a comparison between BC company law and federal corporate law and links to the text of the BC *Companies Act*.

National Library of Canada

www.nlc-bnc.ca/caninfo/ep034.htm

This site provides links to sites containing all federal and provincial laws (except the laws of Prince Edward Island and Newfoundland). By visiting the sites for each jurisdiction, you can find their statutes on partnerships, limited partnerships, and corporations.

LawyersBC

www.lawyers-bc.com/partner/

British Columbia lawyers use their site to offer a guide to starting a business, including a comparison of the use of partnerships and corporations and a detailed discussion of issues relating to what clauses may be needed in partnership and shareholder agreements.

Nova Scotia Business.com

www.novascotiabusiness.com/nsbusiness/BusinessCase/setup.htm

This site provides information on how to choose which form of business organization to use, focusing on people seeking to do business in Nova Scotia. The site includes information on all aspects of doing business in NS.

Corporate Governance

Senate of Canada Task Force on Corporate Governance

www.parl.gc.ca/english/senate/com-e/corp-e.htm

This site provides a detailed overview of corporate governance rules and practices, including recommendations for improving corporate governance rules in the *Canada Business Corporations Act*.

Report of the Joint Committee on Corporate Governance by the Canadian Institute of Chartered Accountants and the Toronto Stock Exchange

www.icca.ca/cica/cicawebsite.nsf/public/JCCG

This report, issued in November 2001, assesses the state of governance in Canadian public companies in law and practice and makes recommendations for improving corporate governance practices. Besides addressing corporate law rules, it identifies problems associated with the organization of boards of directors and other management issues.

Osler Hoskin Harcourt

www.osler.com/index.asp?layid=117&csid=3029&csid1=0&csid2=0&menuid=294&miid=296

This law firm's Web site provides an excellent overview of legal corporate governance issues for business people in an online publication, "A guide to the responsibilities of directors in Canada," with information on directors' duties, statutory liabilities, and risk management.

PricewaterhouseCoopers

www.pwcglobal.com/ca/eng/ins-sol/spec-int/ipo-cgf.html

This accounting firm's Web site provides useful guidance

on organizing a corporation in anticipation of becoming a public corporation.

Franchising

Canadian Franchise Association

www.cfa.ca/

The CFA site contains a wealth of information for people interested in franchising, including the association's code of ethics and its disclosure rules, links to its magazine and publications, and an overview of the franchising legislation in Alberta and Ontario.

Canadian Franchise

www.canadianfranchise.com/

This site contains general information on franchising, including a glossary of franchising terms, tips on entering franchise relationships, and a searchable database of franchising opportunities.

Osler Hoskin Harcourt: Franchise Law Briefing

www.osler.com/index.asp?layid=73&csid=3039&menuid=304&miid=306

This law firm site provides information on current issues in franchising, such as Ontario legislation that protects franchisees and a detailed discussion of terms in franchise agreements.

FRANCHISE AGREEMENTS:
PROTECT YOUR INVESTMENT

A franchise is a purely contractual business relationship under which the franchisor gives the franchisee the right to participate in an existing business system in exchange for a set of fees. That arrangement offers a number of advantages to the franchisee, including the benefits of an established and successful business system, an increased chance of generating profits, access to widespread advertising campaigns, and continued management assistance. Many people choose franchises for the combined benefits of security and independence, but many end up disappointed.

One reason for that disappointment is that it takes the right kind of business person to operate a franchise. If you are the type of person who wants to control every aspect of your business, then a franchise probably is not for you. Some entrepreneurs may want to diversify and expand the existing business, but they soon find out that they are confined to the franchise agreement. One way to avoid that problem before it happens is to assess yourself and your business motivations. A franchisee profile can help identify whether you possess the attitudes and values necessary for the successful operation of a franchise.

Even if you determine that a franchise is the best form of business organization for you, there may be other disadvantages that you would not expect. Franchise owner Dale Hunt of Winnipeg learned that lesson the hard way. Hunt owned two successful locations of Robin's Donuts. In fact, his businesses were doing so well that he "thought [he'd] found the golden goose." That is, until Robin's Donuts went into expansion mode and opened three new stores around him within a year and a half. As you might expect, Hunt's customer base went down considerably, but he could not do anything about it because expansion by the franchisor was permitted in his franchise agreement.

Generally, the franchise agreement includes first refusal rights, which means that the franchisee has the right to purchase a new franchise in the same territory before it is offered to anyone else. In many cases, franchisees feel pressured into opening the new location to avoid losing a part of their market share. But when that happens, franchisees may stretch their resources dangerously thin.

Franchise agreements rarely give the franchisee protected territory, but there are mechanisms that can protect your franchise from the risk of expansion. A profit-sharing arrangement between the new franchisee and the original franchisee may work better for the original franchisee than buying the new location outright. Alternatively, the franchise agreement should specify a method for determining whether a new store has damaged the business of an existing location. Using that approach, the agreement specifies the level of impact that the original store can withstand. If the new store creates an impact that goes beyond that level, the franchisor compensates the original franchisee.

In addition to the problems of territory and expansion, there are other potential sources of conflict for the franchisee, including costs, fees, and the termination of the franchise agreement. Thankfully there are resources at your disposal to help you avoid the pitfalls. First, to ensure that you protect your investment, you should ask a franchise lawyer to review your agreement *before* you sign. It is also important for you to research the franchise carefully. The best way to gather information about the business is to speak to a number of franchise owners. That way you can learn first hand about the possible advantages and disadvantages of a particular chain. You can also get important information from the Canadian Franchise Association (CFA), which promotes ethical franchising and self-regulation through standardized disclosure documents, a code of ethics, and a screening process for members. Franchisees have some protection knowing that their franchisor is a member of the CFA.

Significantly, only two provinces have legislation governing the franchise industry. Franchising laws in Alberta and Ontario impose a duty of fair dealing on each party. In addition, the legislation contains extensive disclosure requirements that franchisors must follow. Interestingly, Alberta's *Franchises Act* has been blamed for the slow growth of franchising in that province. Ontario, on the other hand, is home to over half of the country's franchisors. Ontario's legislation is still very new. Consequently, it remains to be seen if the new laws will slow the growth of franchises in that province. It is also possible that other provinces will follow Ontario's lead.

QUESTIONS TO CONSIDER

1. If you were planning to invest in a franchise, what resources would you consult to manage your risks? Explain why.

2. Should the government regulate the franchise industry or should it be self-regulated? Give reasons for your answer.

3. Does it seem right that a franchisor can be held to different and higher standards in Alberta than in Nova Scotia? Do you think that other Canadian provinces should adopt franchise legislation? Why?

Sources: C Clark, "The new face of franchising," (1999-2000) vol 18(8) *Profit: The Magazine for Canadian Entrepreneurs* 36; "Inside franchising" (1996) vol 69(3) *Canadian Business* 49; <www.cbc.ca/business/programs/venture/onventure/071100.html>; Franchisee Profiling <www.franchise-profiles.com/franchize/cover.htm>; Canadian Franchise Association < www.cfa.ca>.

Video Resource: "Reading the Fine Print (Franchising)," *Venture* # 740, February 22, 2000

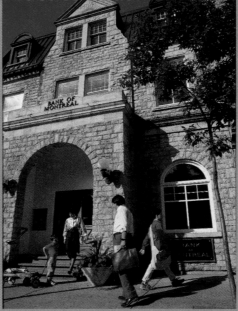

21 Secured Transactions

CHAPTER OVERVIEW

OBJECTIVES

After completing this chapter, you should be able to:

1. Explain why financial institutions and other creditors seek security for the performance of obligations owed to them.

2. Describe five types of transactions in which a creditor gets a right to seize the property if the debtor fails to perform its obligations to the creditor.

3. Explain how leases can be used to finance the acquisition of an asset.

4. Identify problems that secured creditors may encounter in trying to reduce the risk of a bad debt.

5. Describe the advantages of the current rules protecting security interests for creditors.

6. Explain how a supplier of goods can ensure that its claim for payment from the buyer will be most effectively secured.

7. List four steps used by secured creditors to enforce their rights against the personal property of debtors.

8. Describe the obligations of a creditor that seizes a debtor's property.

9. Outline the risks for a person acquiring personal property from someone who has previously given security interests in the property to a creditor, and explain how to manage them.

10. Explain four situations in which one person's guarantee of another's credit obligation becomes unenforceable.

We all rely on credit, at least some of the time. If you promise to pay later to get something now, you are a *debtor*, the person who owes the credit obligation. The other party is the *creditor*, the person who allows time to pass before requiring payment. The creditor has two main ways of reducing the risk of non-payment:

- security interests
- guarantees

A **security interest** allows a creditor to seize some of a debtor's personal property if a debt is not repaid. For instance, a bank may not be willing to lend you $10 000 unless you give it a security interest in your car. If you fail to repay the loan, the bank may be entitled to take your car. A security interest can be given over any type of *personal property*. Personal property, as discussed in Chapter 13 and Chapter 15, includes both *tangible* property (assets that can be touched) like cars, and *intangible* property (assets that cannot be touched) like corporate shares, life insurance policies, some kinds of licences, and intellectual property. In this chapter, we will discuss the creation, registration, and enforcement of security interests in personal property. We will not discuss security interests in *real property*, such as mortgages, which we examined in Chapter 14.

Even with a security interest, a bank may not be willing to lend you $10 000 unless you provide a *guarantee*. A **guarantee** is a contractual promise by a third party, called a *guarantor*, to satisfy the principal debtor's obligation if that debtor fails to do so. Suppose that you persuade a friend to act as the guarantor of your loan. If you fail to repay that loan, the bank can demand payment from your friend. In some situations, however, the law recognizes that the debtor and the creditor may act in a way that unfairly hurts the guarantor. For instance, if the debtor agrees to pay a higher rate of interest on the debt, the guarantor's potential liability is increased. If that occurs after the guarantee is signed and without the guarantor's consent, the law may release the guarantor from liability. Our discussion of guarantees will focus on the situations in which guarantors are relieved of their obligations.

> a security interest allows a creditor to seize a debtor's personal property if a debt is not repaid

> a guarantee is a contractual promise by a third party to satisfy the principal debtor's obligation if the debtor fails to do so

SECURITY INTERESTS AND PROVINCIAL PERSONAL PROPERTY SECURITY LAWS

To see how security interests work, we will look at a more complex example. Suppose that you want to borrow money to buy a new delivery truck for your business. A bank will base its decision to accept or reject your loan application largely on your ability to repay the loan. Unfortunately, after examining your income and expenses, the bank still has major concerns. What might encourage the bank to lend the money to you?

Perhaps your business has assets, including a computer system, some desks, and a photocopier. The bank would be more willing to give you credit if it received your permission to seize and sell those assets if you failed to repay the loan. In other words, you might offer to create a security interest by using your assets as *collateral*. **Collateral** is personal property that is subject to a security interest.

Provincial personal property security legislation (**PPS legislation**) comprises

> collateral is property that is subject to a security interest

secured creditors, or secured parties, are people who extend credit to a debtor and who receive a security interest from the debtor

PPS legislation makes it easier for a secured creditor to acquire an enforceable security interest

PPS legislation creates a system that allows a secured creditor to register its security interest

legal rules relating to security interests.[1] The main purpose of those laws is to make it easier for **secured creditors**, or **secured parties**, like the bank in our previous example, to acquire enforceable security interests. PPS legislation creates a system that allows a secured creditor to register its security interest. Registration generally gives that creditor priority over all unregistered interests in the same collateral and any interest in the collateral registered later. Once registered, the secured creditor's interest is listed in a publicly accessible database. Anyone thinking of extending credit to the same debtor can find out whether that person has already given a security interest over its assets.

HOW SECURITY INTERESTS ARE CREATED

Conditional Sales

In the commercial world, the buyer is often allowed to postpone paying at least part of the purchase price. As security for that debt, the seller may retain an interest, usually in the form of ownership, in the goods that are being sold. The buyer gets *possession* of the goods immediately, but it does not *own* them until it pays the full price. This arrangement is called a **conditional sales** contract.

a conditional sale occurs when the seller retains ownership of the goods to secure payment of the purchase price by the buyer

Conditional sales are very common in consumer transactions where a person buys furniture or other household items, but defers payment until some time in the future. They are also quite common if two businesses have an ongoing relationship for the purchase of goods. For instance, a manufacturer may retain a security interest in the equipment that it supplies to a distributor. And a franchisor may retain an interest in the supplies that it delivers to its franchisee. In each case, the security interest is taken to secure the payment of the purchase price. If the buyer defaults, the seller can take back the goods. Usually, the buyer is responsible for any damage to the goods. And sometimes, the buyer may be required to buy insurance to cover the goods while payment is pending. The seller may be named as the beneficiary under that insurance policy.

Special Cases

There are two kinds of transactions that are similar to conditional sales and are often used to create security interests:

- consignment
- lease

a consignment occurs when the owner of goods transfers possession, but not ownership, to someone else

the consignor is the owner

the consignee is the person who receives possession, but not ownership

A **consignment** occurs when the owner of goods transfers possession, but not ownership, to someone else. The owner is called the **consignor**. The person who receives possession, but not ownership, is called the **consignee**. There are many business reasons for creating a consignment.

---

[1] For example, *Personal Property Security Act*, RSA 1988, c P-4.05 (*APPSA*) (Alta); *Personal Property Security Act*, RSBC 1979, c 359 (*BCPPSA*) (BC); *Personal Property Security Act*, SM 1993, c 14 (*MPPSA*) (Man); *Personal Property Security Act*, SNB 1993, c P-7.1 (*NBPPSA*) (NB); *Personal Property Security Act*, SN 1995, c P-7.1 (*NPPSA*) (Nfld); *Personal Property Security Act*, SNS 1995-96, c 13 (*NSPPSA*) (NS); *Personal Property Security Act*, RSO 1990, c P.10 (*OPPSA*) (Ont); *Personal Property Security Act*, SPEI (1997), c 33 (*PEIPPSA*) (PEI); *Personal Property Security Act*, SS 1993, c P-6.2 (*SPPSA*) (Sask). Quebec's civil code also provides for security interests but its rules remain distinct. Our discussion is based on the rules in the other provinces.

- The consignee may be examining the goods for possible purchase.
- The consignee may have agreed to try to sell the goods on the consignor's behalf. This is what we usually mean when we say goods are held by someone "on consignment." A children's used-clothing store may take clothes on consignment from a parent, offer them for sale, and then pay the parent a percentage of the purchase price if the clothes are sold.

In a true consignment, the consignee is not bound to pay for the goods until it does something, such as selling them to a third party. However, the term "consignment" is also sometimes used to refer to a situation in which the "consignee" has already agreed to pay for the goods and the "consignor" holds onto ownership to secure full payment of the price. In effect, that situation involves a conditional sale, not a true consignment. Retention of ownership under the consignment is a form of security interest.[2]

A lease can also operate like a conditional sale and an alternative to a secured loan. Suppose that you want to buy an asset. You could try to borrow the amount of the purchase price under a conventional form of secured bank financing. Or you could use a *lease*. A **lease** occurs when the lessor retains ownership of an asset, but gives possession of it to the lessee for a period of time in return for the lessee's promise to make regular payments. When used for financing, the lessor's ownership of the leased assets is a security interest. Its purpose is to secure the lessee's obligation to make payment. The following example illustrates how a lease can have the same effect as a secured loan.

Suppose that you want to acquire a truck for $50 000. You have two options.

a **lease** occurs when the lessor retains ownership of an asset, but gives possession of it to the lessee for a period of time in return for the lessee's promise to make regular payments

- You could arrange to buy the truck from the seller. To finance that purchase, you could then borrow $50 000 from the bank by agreeing to repay that amount, plus interest, in 60 blended monthly instalments of $1000. As security for those monthly instalments, you could give the bank an interest in the truck. We call this arrangement the *bank financing model*.
- You could enter into an arrangement, which we will call a *lease financing model*, with a lessor, who would buy the truck that interests you. The lessor would then agree to lease that vehicle to you for 60 months in exchange for your promise to make monthly payments of $1000. The lessor would also give you an option to purchase the truck at the end of the 60 months for the price of $1.

Under the bank financing model, at the outset, you get ownership of the truck, which you use as collateral for the bank loan. The bank makes its decision to lend the money to you based on two factors: (i) its assessment of your ability to repay the loan, and (ii) its assessment of its own ability to acquire and sell the truck if you fail to make the payments.

Under the lease financing model, you do not get ownership of the truck at the outset. The lessor does. You merely get the right to possess the vehicle *and* the option to obtain ownership after making all of the payments. However, like the bank, the lessor makes its decision to enter into that arrangement based on two factors: (i) its assessment of your ability to make the lease payments, and (ii) its assessment of its own ability to acquire and sell the truck if you fail to make those payments.

[2.] *Re Stephanian's Carpets Ltd* held that if a consignee has an unrestricted right to return the goods under the consignment, the consignor does not have a security interest: (1980) 1 PPSAC 119 (Ont SC).

The two transactions also share these features.

- The same amount of credit is extended to you—$50 000 (the price of the truck).
- You are obligated to repay the price of the truck *plus* some interest. Consequently, while the truck only costs $50 000, you must make 60 monthly payments of $1000 each.
- You give up an interest in the vehicle to secure your payments.
- You will own the truck at the end of the arrangement. The only difference is that in the lease financing model, you must actually exercise your option to buy the vehicle for $1. Of course, it would be economically irrational for you *not* to exercise that option unless the truck was so badly damaged that it was worth less than $1.[3]

Granting a Security Interest in a Specific Asset or in All the Debtor's Assets

a **chattel mortgage** is a transaction in which a debtor gives a creditor title to some specific personal property to secure the performance of an obligation it owes to the creditor

The debtor often agrees under a lending transaction to provide the creditor with ownership, or some other form of security interest, in a specific piece of personal property. In our example of the bank financing model, you gave the bank an interest in your truck. From the creditor's perspective, that arrangement is attractive because it is easy to determine the value of the security, and it is relatively easy to enforce the security. The bank knew that the security was worth $50 000, and to enforce its rights, it simply had to seize the vehicle if you failed to repay the loan. When the debtor transfers title to the secured party, the transaction is sometimes called a **chattel mortgage**.

a **general security agreement** provides a creditor with a security interest in *all* of the debtor's assets

A creditor may not be satisfied with security over specific pieces of personal property. For example, if you are trying to buy a business, the bank may not lend you the purchase price unless you are willing to enter into a *general security agreement*. A **general security agreement** provides a creditor with a security interest in *all* of the debtor's assets. Since it is not in either party's interest to freeze operations, the debtor will be given permission to carry on business as usual, including selling inventory and replacing worn-out equipment. Nevertheless, the creditor's security interest covers all of the debtor's assets.

Assignment of Accounts Receivable

accounts receivable are the amounts that a business is entitled to collect from its customers

Most businesses sell at least some of their products on credit. For instance, customers may be given 30 or 60 days to pay for the goods or services they have received. The amounts that a business is entitled to collect from its customers are its **accounts receivable**. Those accounts usually represent a substantial asset, which can be used as security if the business wants to borrow money. The business can give the bank an **assignment of accounts receivable**, which would allow the bank to collect the debts (or "book debts") owing to the business if the loan is not repaid.

an **assignment of accounts receivable** allows a creditor to collect money owing to a debtor if the debtor does not fulfill its obligations

An assignment can cover both: (i) accounts that are receivable by the business at the time that the assignment is created, and (ii) accounts that become receivable by the business in the future. In either event, the creditor does not

---

[3.] In practice, option prices are usually more than $1. Even when the option price is substantial, however, a lease transaction may be functionally equivalent to a conditional sale or a bank-financed purchase if the price is at or less than the market value of the leased goods at the end of the lease term.

usually collect money that is owing to the debtor. In most cases, the debtor is allowed to collect its own accounts receivable and to carry on business as usual. The creditor steps in and demands payment from the debtor's customers only if the debtor fails to fulfill its obligations to the creditor.[4] Figure 21.1 illustrates the process of assigning accounts receivable as security.

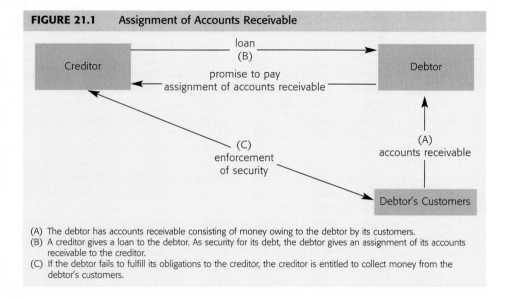

FIGURE 21.1   Assignment of Accounts Receivable

(A) The debtor has accounts receivable consisting of money owing to the debtor by its customers.
(B) A creditor gives a loan to the debtor. As security for its debt, the debtor gives an assignment of its accounts receivable to the creditor.
(C) If the debtor fails to fulfill its obligations to the creditor, the creditor is entitled to collect money from the debtor's customers.

After-Acquired Property

Banks and other financial institutions often take security over *all* of the debtor's assets, including assets that the debtor acquires *after* the security agreement becomes effective. Provincial PPS legislation specifically permits security interests in after-acquired property.

Before the PPS legislation was created, creditors often used a *floating charge* to take security in after-acquired property. A **floating charge** is a security interest that *hovers* above the debtor's assets until some event causes the charge to become *fixed* or *crystallized* on those assets. The contract that creates that interest usually states that the charge hovers over *all* of the debtor's property, both present and future. It also usually states that the charge descends and becomes fixed if the debtor misses a payment and is provided with notice of default by the creditor. Until then, the debtor can carry on business by buying and selling assets. However, once the relevant event occurs, the debtor can only sell its assets *subject to the creditor's charge*. That means that a purchaser of the debtor's assets does not own them outright—the creditor's interest continues to exist in them. Many of the cases on floating charges dealt with the difficult task of determining precisely when the charge became crystallized.

Floating charges are not often used any more. The PPS legislation allows a creditor to take a similar sort of security interest. A secured party's interest can attach to all of the debtor's current and after-acquired property as soon as the property is acquired by the debtor without any requirement for crystallization. And with some exceptions, that interest continues to exist even if the debtor disposes of its property to a third party. In practice, security agreements that deal with after-acquired property under the PPS legislation usually allow the debtor

Provincial PPS legislation specifically permits security interests in after-acquired property

a floating charge is a security interest that *hovers* above the debtor's assets until some event causes the charge to become *fixed* or *crystallized* on those assets

---

[4.] We discussed assignments of accounts receivable in Chapter 3.

to deal with its assets free of the secured party's interest to the extent necessary to carry on its business.[5]

Special Security Interests of Banks

In Canada, banks can be incorporated only under the federal *Bank Act*.[6] Section 427 of the Act allows banks to take a special kind of security in certain types of assets, which other creditors cannot take. Banks may take 427 interests *in addition* to other sorts of security, and often take more that one type of security for a single obligation.

Banks may take s 427 security interests only in the types of assets listed in the Act. These include the goods (usually inventory, but not always) of retailers, wholesalers, manufacturers, as well as mining and forest products. A bank may lend money to a farmer to buy seed and take an interest in the crops grown from the seed as security under the provision. Banks cannot take this special kind of interest in consumers' assets or the assets of most businesses providing services.

Under the Act, there is a special registration system for these interests. To protect the bank's interest against other creditors of the debtor, the bank must get the debtor to file a "notice of intention" to give security to the bank at the branch of the Bank of Canada closest to the debtor's place of business.

The main advantage of a s 427 security interest for banks is that a single registration applies to all the debtor's assets no matter which province or territory they are in, unlike registration under the PPS legislation in a province which is effective only in that province. Consequently, if the debtor has assets in several provinces, the secured party may have to register in each province to protect its interests in the assets in that province. Another advantage of s 427 interests is that they will prevail over most other forms of security interests in the same collateral.

Concept 21.1 reviews the common ways in which security interests are created.

Concept Summary 21.1

Common Ways Security Interests Are Created

Conditional sale	The seller of goods retains title, or some other form of security interest, to secure future payment of the purchase price by the buyer.
Granting a security interest in a specific asset or in all the debtor's assets	The debtor transfers title, or some other form of security interest, in some or all of its personal property to a creditor to secure performance of an obligation owed by the debtor. (If title to the asset is transferred, this form of security is called a chattel mortgage.)
Assignment of accounts receivable, or book debts	A person (the *assignor*) owed a debt (the *account receivable*) assigns it to someone else (such as a bank) to secure performance of an obligation owed by the assignor to the bank. That arrangement may include assignment of both present debts and debts arising in the future.
Security interest in after-acquired property	The debtor gives a secured party a security interest in all property acquired by the debtor *after* the date that the security agreement is created.
Special security interests created under the federal *Bank Act*	The debtor gives a bank a security interest in certain types of property described in the Act. A single registration protects this interest in the debtor's assets wherever they are in Canada.

[5.] *Re Credit Suisse Canada and 1133 Yonge Street Holdings Limited* (1998) 41 OR (3d) 632 (CA).

[6.] *Bank Act*, RSC 1985, c B-5 (Can).

PROVINCIAL PERSONAL PROPERTY SECURITY LEGISLATION

Each method we have discussed has the same function: to give the creditor an interest in the debtor's property to secure the debtor's performance of an obligation. Historically, each type was governed by special legislation or common law rules. They carried different remedies and enforcement procedures. And different types of security interests had to be registered at different places. That situation was inconvenient for at least these two reasons.

- Even within a single province, a potential creditor, who wanted to know whether a debtor had already given a security interest in a particular asset to another creditor, had to search separate registries for each type of registered interest.

- Since most of the relevant laws were provincial, a secured party had to search separately in every province where the debtor had assets that it offered as security.

> the traditional rules governing security interests were inconvenient

It is still necessary for secured parties to search in every province where the debtor has assets. And in some cases, it may be difficult to tell which provincial laws apply, such as when a truck that is collateral moves between provinces. Within each province, however, PPS legislation now integrates the sometimes conflicting common law and statutory rules for security interests. The details of the provincial systems differ; however, *most* security interests are now governed by a single legislative scheme. We will discuss exceptions.

The unified approach under the PPS legislation allows creditors to more easily and accurately assess and manage risks. It provides a simple and inexpensive system for secured parties to register their interests. That system can be searched to determine what security interests a debtor has granted, and it establishes a clear system for determining the **priority**, or ranking, of competing claims to the same collateral. Provincial legislation also provides a single system of default rights that apply to every type of security that is caught by the scheme. In all these ways, the PPS legislation provides greater certainty for creditors.

> PPS legislation allows creditors to more easily and accurately assess and manage risks

> priority is the secured creditor's right to enforce its claim against a piece of collateral before other secured creditors can do the same

Scope of Application

Most provincial legislation applies to all agreements between a debtor and a secured party that create a security interest in personal property.[7] A security interest is defined simply as an interest in personal property that secures the payment or performance of an obligation. This functional definition was intended to catch all kinds of security interests that arise by agreement, regardless of their form. It includes, for instance, conditional sales and assignments of accounts receivable.

Leases

One difficult, but important, issue is how to determine if a lease transaction creates a security interest. A lease of goods can be used as a substitute for a secured loan to finance the acquisition of the goods. Whether the lessor's title functions as a security interest depends upon the terms of the lease and circumstances of

---

[7.] For example, *BCPPSA* s 2(1); *NBPPSA* s 3(1); *OPPSA* s 2.

the transaction. Because leases can be structured in many ways, it is difficult to provide an accurate general rule. Some jurisdictions have tried to avoid the problem by saying that any lease that has a term of over one year is caught by the PPS legislation.[8] In Ontario, however, it is still necessary to analyze each transaction to see if the lease, in substance, creates a security interest.

leases may or may not be caught by PPS legislation

If a lease is subject to the provincial PPS legislation, the priority of the lessor's security interest is determined by the legislation. If a lease is not subject to the PPS legislation, the lessor's ownership of the leased assets typically gives it a claim ranking ahead of all other creditors of the lessee, including those who have registered under the legislation. This is always the lessor's preferred result.

Exceptions

The rules in provincial PPS legislation do not apply to all forms of interests in personal property.[9] Rights created by statute, rather than by agreement, are not subject to the personal property security schemes. These are the most important statutory rights.

- A landlord under a commercial lease usually enjoys the *right of distress*, or *distraint*, if the tenant has not paid rent (as discussed in Chapter 13). The **right of distress**, or **distraint**, allows a landlord to seize property that belongs to the tenant and is on the rented premises, sell it, and use the sale proceeds to pay the outstanding rent. That right generally cannot be used against non-commercial tenants.

*the **right of distress**, or **distraint**, allows a landlord to seize property that belongs to the tenant and is on the rented premises, sell it, and use the sale proceeds to pay the outstanding rent*

- *Deemed trusts* that are created under some statutes for the benefit of the government are exempt from the application of provincial PPS legislation. Under a **deemed trust**, some assets of a business are deemed as a matter of law to be held for the benefit of the government and cannot be used for the business. The most important deemed trust is the provision of the *Income Tax Act* that states that deductions from employee wages by employers are deemed to be held in trust for the government. As a result, the government beneficially owns the funds, which must be remitted to the Canada Customs and Revenue Agency.[10]

*under a **deemed trust**, some assets of a business are deemed as a matter of law to be held for the benefit of the government and cannot be used for the business*

- *Liens* for people who provide repair or storage services are usually excluded from the PPS legislation. A person who is in possession of personal property and either repairs or stores it can retain the property until the owner pays the price of the repairs or storage. For instance, a mechanic who fixes your car can keep the vehicle until you pay the repair bill. The mechanic's right against your car is like a security interest since it is used to reduce the risk that the bill will not be paid. It is different from a security interest, however, because it arises without you, as the debtor, consenting. That right, called a **lien**, usually exists only if the person providing the goods or services is in possession of the property. In some situations, however, a non-possessory lien may be available.[11]

*a **lien** allows a person who has not been paid to retain possession of goods that it has repaired or stored*

[8.] For example, *BCPPSA* s 3(b)(c); *NBPPSA* s 3(2); *NSPPSA* s 4(12).

[9.] Exceptions are provided for in *BCPPSA* s 4; *NBPPSA* s 4; *OPPSA* s 4.

[10.] *Income Tax Act*, RSC 1985 (5th Supp), c 1, s 227(4) and (4.1) (Can).

[11.] *Repair and Storage Liens Act*, RSO 1990, c R.25, Part II (Ont). Even though they are not generally subject to PPS legislation, the statutes in some provinces state that repair and storage liens prevail over interests that are subject to the legislation: for example, *OPPSA* s 31. As well, the Ontario *Repair and Storage Liens Act* sets out certain requirements for a lien and creates some exceptions to its priority: ss 7(3), 16(1)(c) and (d). Repairers and storers may register their liens under the Ontario PPS legislation.

Those exceptions mean that the specified creditors do not have to register under the PPS legislation, and, in most cases, they have priority over ordinary security interests that are subject to the legislation.

The rights of banks under s 427 of the *Bank Act* represent a sort of hybrid. In Ontario, the courts have determined a bank may register these under PPS legislation and take advantage of whatever rights it may provide in terms of priority over other creditors. Banks do not have to register, however. They may choose to register only under the special system set up under the *Bank Act* and enforce their rights under that statute.[12] In some other provinces PPS legislation provides that it does not apply to s 427 interests. Although no case has decided the issue, rights under the Act likely rank ahead of rights created under PPS legislation.

Protecting Security Interests under PPS Legislation

As we saw in Chapter 3, contracts usually can be enforced only against those who are parties to them. That rule generally applies to contracts that create security interests. Under provincial PPS legislation, however, a security agreement may be effective against third parties such as other secured parties if the security interest meets the requirements for *attachment* in the PPS legislation.

Attachment

Attachment occurs when three requirements are met:

- The debtor signs a written security agreement containing a description of the collateral, or the secured party gets possession of collateral.
- The secured party gives some value to the debtor.
- The debtor gets some rights in the collateral.[13]

attachment allows a security interest to be enforced against third parties

The debtor and the secured party may agree that attachment should be postponed, even if these requirements are met. This, however, is rare since secured parties have little to gain from agreeing to postpone the attachment of their interests.

Perfection

To fully protect the priority of its claims to a debtor's assets, a secured party must *perfect* its security interest. **Perfection** usually occurs when a security interest has attached, and the secured party has registered under the PPS legislation. It is also possible, though less common, for a secured party to perfect its security interest by taking possession of the collateral.[14]

To perfect by registration, the secured party must file a **financing statement** with the registrar responsible for administering the PPS legislation in that province, who notes the time and date of registration. That information is used to determine the priority of the secured party's interest in relation to any other security interest under the PPS legislation. A security interest perfected by registration has priority over all *subsequently* registered security interests, but not over *previously* registered security interests. Registration also ensures that the existence of a security interest is disclosed to people who search the

perfection usually occurs when a security interest has attached, and the secured party has registered under the PPS legislation

a **financing statement** is the document that is filed to register a security interest under PPS legislation

a security interest perfected by registration has priority over all subsequently registered security interests, but not over previously registered security interests

registration ensures that the existence of a security interest is disclosed to people who search the register

---

[12.] *Re Bank of Nova Scotia and International Harvester Credit Corp of Can Ltd* (1990) 73 DLR (4th) 385 (Ont CA); *Royal Bank of Canada v Sparrow Electric Corp* (1997) 143 DLR (4th) 385 (SCC).

[13.] For example, *BCPPSA* s 12; *OPPSA* s 11(2).

[14.] Under the *OPPSA*, perfection is possible through registration (s 23) or possession (s 22).

register, including other potential creditors. A secured creditor therefore has two incentives to register. Registration continues for a period chosen by the registering secured party. Registration fees increase with the duration of the registration.[15]

The financing statement identifies the debtor, the secured party, and the general nature of the security interest. Paper financing statements are scanned and stored in an electronic database. Financing statements can also be filed directly in electronic form. This *notice filing system* has several advantages over older systems that required the security documents themselves to be filed.

- It is easier to file, store, and search electronic records.
- The specific terms of the security agreement remain confidential, known only to the debtor and the secured party.
- A single financing statement can relate to more than one security interest given by a debtor to a secured party. For instance, a creditor who takes an interest in a debtor's inventory and accounts receivable in separate security agreements can perfect both interests by filing a single financing statement.
- A secured party can register before the security agreement is created.

Business Law in Action 21.1 illustrates the benefits of that last feature of the notice filing system.

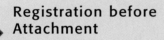

BUSINESS LAW IN ACTION 21.1

Registration before Attachment

Lenders generally file a financing statement to register their security interest *before* closing the financing transaction. This is a typical example.

Keeshon Construction Ltd and the Royal Bank discussed a loan from the bank to Keeshon of $1 000 000. The loan was to be secured on all of Keeshon's assets. They arranged that the loan and security agreements would be signed and the money advanced on September 19, 2002.

In anticipation of the loan, the bank registered a financing statement against Keeshon on September 15. Four days later, as anticipated, the parties signed the loan and security agreements, and the bank gave Keeshon a cheque for $1 000 000.

The bank's security interest attached in all of Keeshon's assets as soon as the security agreement was signed and value was given by the bank on September 19. Perfection occurred at the same time because the financing statement relating to the interest had already been filed. For perfection to occur, there must be attachment plus a registration, but the order in which the two requirements are met does not matter.

Question for Discussion

1. Why would the bank want to register its interest as soon as possible?

Priorities under PPS Legislation

A great advantage of PPS legislation is that it provides a system for determining who prevails when more than one secured party claims an interest in the same collateral. The relative priority of claims is often critically important. A debtor in default on its credit obligations probably does not have enough assets to pay off all its creditors.

The basic rule is that the first to register has the best claim. It does not matter whether a subsequently registered secured party knew about the other

---

[15.] In Ontario, a perpetual registration can be obtained for $500.

secured party's interest or that attachment occurred after registration.[16] In Business Law in Action 21.1, the relevant date for determining the bank's priority in any contest with another secured party is the date of its registration, September 15, 2002, even though perfection did not occur until September 19. If another secured creditor had obtained and perfected by registration a security interest in Keeshon's assets on September 18, it would still rank behind the bank.

An **unperfected security interest**, which is a security interest that has not been perfected, is subordinate to:

- any perfected interest
- other unperfected interests that attached earlier
- any lien created under any law
- any creditor who has both successfully obtained a judgment against the debtor and taken steps to enforce it by seizing the debtor's property.[17]

Unperfected interests are also ineffective against anyone who represents the debtor's creditors, such as a trustee in bankruptcy.[18] The secured creditors of a bankrupt debtor can enforce perfected security interests against the trustee, but *not* unperfected security interests. An unperfected security interest is treated as an unsecured debt. And a creditor with an unsecured debt is entitled only to share in whatever assets are left *after* the creditors with perfected security interests enforce their rights to the debtor's collateral. More precisely, each unsecured creditor will receive a share of the debtor's remaining assets equal to the proportion that the debt owed to that creditor represents of the debtor's total unsecured debt. For example, assume that a debtor's obligations exceed its assets by a 10:1 ratio. It owes $1 000 000, but it has assets worth only $100 000 and there are no creditors with perfected security interests. If you, as an unsecured creditor, are owed $50 000, you will receive only $5 000. If you were the only secured creditor with a perfected security interest, you would be entitled to seize $50 000 of the debtor's remaining assets, forcing the unsecured creditors to share the remaining $50 000. As a matter of risk management, you should have perfected your interest.

Purchase Money Security Interests

Banks and other financial institutions generally take security interests in *all* of the debtor's property, including that acquired after the loan is made and the security agreement created.[19] Such security interests in after-acquired property can be troublesome to a debtor who wants to acquire new assets on credit.

Suppose that a farm equipment distributor takes a bank loan. It uses all of its assets, both present and future, as collateral. The bank wisely files a financing statement to register its security interest under the PPS legislation. The distributor now wants to purchase more inventory from a manufacturer. And since it has little money, it wants to buy on credit. There may be a problem. The manufacturer may not agree to sell on credit unless it can take an effective form of security. However, all of the distributor's assets are *already* subject to the bank's

*an **unperfected security interest** is a security interest that has not been perfected*

unperfected interests are ineffective against anyone who represents the debtor's creditors

security interests in after-acquired property can be troublesome to a debtor who wants to acquire new assets on credit

---

[16.] *Robert Simpson Co v Shadlock* (1981) 119 DLR (3d) 417 (Ont HCJ). The rules are different where the secured party has perfected by taking possession of the collateral. In that case, the first to take possession or register prevails: *BCPPSA* s 30; *NBPPSA* s 30; *OPPSA* s 30.

[17.] For example, *OPPSA* s 20(1)(a); *SPPSA* s 20(1)(a)(b).

[18.] For example, *OPPSA* s 20(1)(b); *SPPSA* s 20(1)(d).

[19.] Security interests in after-acquired property are expressly permitted in s 12 of the *OPPSA*. After-acquired property clauses for the benefit of conditional sellers are not enforceable against consumers: *Consumer Protection Act*, RSO 1990, c C.31, s 22 (Ont); *BCPPSA* s 5.58(3).

perfected security interest. That means that the manufacturer's security interest would necessarily rank second at best. The first priority of the bank's security interest in after-acquired property may jeopardize the distributor's ability to carry on business.

Because this is a frequent problem, PPS legislation provides a special priority rule that applies in such circumstances. When a security interest in collateral is taken by a seller of personal property to secure payment of the purchase price, the seller's security interest can be given priority over all other security interests in the same collateral given by the debtor. This is called a **purchase money security interest (PMSI)**. A PMSI can also be acquired by a lender, such as a bank, if: (i) it lends money to the debtor to acquire an asset, (ii) the debtor actually uses that money to acquire that asset, and (iii) the debtor uses that asset as collateral for the loan.[20]

In either case, to obtain the super priority, the secured party must register its interest within 10 days of the debtor getting possession of the collateral. Suppose that you want to buy a car on credit, but you have already given your bank a security interest in all of your property, including after-acquired property. The car dealer could get a PMSI and rank ahead of the bank if it registered its financing statement to perfect its security interest within 10 days of your getting possession of the car.[21]

Special rules apply to PMSIs in **inventory**, those goods held for sale or lease by the debtor. They must be registered *before* the debtor gets possession of the collateral, and notice must be given to any secured party who previously filed a financing statement indicating an interest in inventory. Case Brief 21.1 illustrates these rules.

a purchase money security interest (PMSI) is a security interest in a particular asset given by a debtor to a secured party that either sells that asset to the debtor or finances the debtor's acquisition of that asset

inventory is goods held for sale or lease

CASE BRIEF 21.1

Clark Equipment of Canada Ltd v Bank of Montreal (1984) 4 PPSAC 38 (Man CA)

In 1977, the Bank of Montreal made a loan to Maneco Equipment Ltd. As security for the loan, the bank obtained a security interest in all property currently owned or acquired in the future by Maneco. It registered its interest in 1977 by filing a financing statement.

In 1978, Clark Equipment of Canada Ltd entered into an agreement to finance the acquisition of Clark equipment by Maneco, whose business was selling and leasing Clark equipment. On September 7, 1978, Clark gave notice to the bank that it would have a PMSI in the equipment that Maneco would acquire from Clark. Clark filed a financing statement in relation to this interest on September 20, 1978.

Subsequently, in 1979, 1980, and 1981, Maneco acquired three pieces of equipment from Clark, but did not pay for them.

In June 1981, Maneco defaulted on its loan, and the bank seized the equipment. Clark claimed that it had first claim to the equipment because it had a PMSI that ranked ahead of the bank's previously registered security interest.

The court held that the requirements for a PMSI had been met: (i) Clark's interest had been perfected by registration before Maneco got possession of the collateral, and (ii) Clark gave notice to the bank of its PMSI claim in Maneco's inventory. Clark was therefore entitled to recover the equipment.

---

20. **PMSIs** are defined in s 1 of the *OPPSA* and their super priority is provided for in s 33.

21. For example, *BCPPSA* s 33; *NBPPSA* s 33; *OPPSA* s 33.

Enforcement of Security Interests

In this section, we discuss the enforcement of security interests by secured parties, including the rules protecting the interests of debtors.

Default by the Debtor

A secured party can take possession of the collateral when the debtor has defaulted under the security agreement. A **default** occurs when

- the debtor fails to pay or to perform any other obligation secured under the security agreement, or
- an event occurs that is defined as a default in the security agreement

Security agreements often define default to include a failure to

- maintain the collateral in good working order
- maintain insurance on the collateral

A security agreement may give the debtor a period, such as 30 days, to remedy the default. The creditor cannot take steps toward enforcement until that period expires.

> **default** occurs if either the debtor fails to either pay or perform any other obligation secured under the security agreement, or an event occurs that is defined as a default in the security agreement

Taking Possession

The secured party's first step when a debtor defaults is to take possession of the collateral. Possession may not be taken by force.[22] If the debtor resists, the secured party must seek a court order for possession. If a secured party has taken possession of collateral, it has an obligation to take reasonable care of it.[23]

To take possession of the collateral, the secured party must give reasonable notice to the debtor.[24] What is reasonable varies from no notice at all to a few days. No notice would be appropriate if, for example, the debtor had no prospect of paying, and the collateral was at risk. Imagine that the collateral consisted of a truckload of ripe peaches. If collateral consists of accounts receivable, the secured party will simply give notice to the person obligated to make payment to the debtor that all future payments should be made directly to the secured party.[25]

> the secured party must give reasonable notice to the debtor to take possession of the collateral

Disposition of Collateral

Once the secured party has obtained possession of the collateral, it will probably want to sell it and apply the proceeds of the sale toward the outstanding debt. There are few legal rules regarding such sales. The secured party may advertise the sale to the public or enter into a private agreement with a buyer. The secured party may decide to lease the collateral to someone or do some-

---

22. *R v Doucette* (1960) 25 DLR (2d) 380 (Ont CA). Any method permitted by law may be used: *OPPSA* s 62(a). A conditional seller may not take possession of the property sold if the buyer is a consumer who has paid at least two-thirds of the purchase price: *Consumer Protection Act*, RSO 1990, c C.31, s 23 (Ont); *BCPPSA* s 5.58(3).

23. For example, *BCPPSA* s 17; *NBPPSA* s 17; *OPPSA* s 17.

24. *Ronald Elwyn Lister Ltd v Dunlop Canada Ltd* (1982) 135 DLR (3d) 1 (SCC). There are special notice requirements when a secured party intends to enforce its security interest against an insolvent debtor provided for in the *Bankruptcy and Insolvency Act*, RSC 1985, c B-3, amended SC 1992, c 27 (Can). See Chapter 22.

25. For example, *BCPPSA* s 61; *NBPPSA* s 61; *OPPSA* s 61.

the secured creditor must dispose of the collateral in a commercially reasonable manner

thing else.[26] Whatever it decides to do, the secured party must act in a manner that is commercially reasonable.[27]

What is commercially reasonable depends upon the circumstances. In general, the secured party must take reasonable care to ensure that it obtains the fair value of the collateral and does not act negligently. In some cases, the secured party will be obliged to either advertise the sale to ensure that a competitive bidding process takes place or obtain a professional valuation to ensure that the collateral is not sold for less than its worth.

The requirement for the secured party to act in a commercially reasonable manner provides important protection for the debtor. The secured party is interested only in recovering what it is owed, plus any expenses that it incurred as a result of enforcing its rights. Since the secured party cannot keep any excess money, it might be tempted to quickly sell the collateral for less than its worth. Consider the case in You Be the Judge 21.1.

YOU BE THE JUDGE 21.1

Commercial Reasonableness and the Disposition of Collateral[28]

Copp and Piccininni carried on a dental practice together through a management corporation. For that practice, the corporation leased equipment from Medi-dent Services Ltd under a number of long-term leases. Copp and Piccininni got into a fundamental disagreement about how to run the practice. Everything stopped, including the payments to Medi-dent. Eventually, Medi-dent seized the equipment. At that time, Medi-dent was owed $31 000 under the leases.

On April 18, 1990, Medi-dent gave a notice to the corporation, as well as to Piccininni and Copp, that it would sell the equipment at a public or private sale after May 14 if the full amount of the indebtedness was not paid before that

date. Piccininni contacted Medi-dent immediately after the seizure and offered to buy the equipment himself for $31 000. Medi-dent readily agreed since that was a simple and inexpensive way to get its money out. The sale was concluded on May 15.

Copp subsequently challenged the sale on the basis that it was not commercially reasonable. Copp argued that Medi-dent had not had a valuation done, nor had it tried to sell the equipment through a competitive bidding process. He also produced evidence that the equipment had a fair market value of at least $79 000.

Questions for Discussion

1. Did Medi-dent act in a commercially reasonable manner?
2. What should Medi-dent have done?

When a secured party sells the collateral, it can keep from the proceeds: (i) any reasonable expenses it incurred in connection with seizing and disposing the collateral, and (ii) the amount it is owed. Any amount left over must be paid to the debtor.[29] If the secured party does not recover all that it is owed, the debtor remains liable for any deficiency.

---

[26] For example, *OPPSA* s 63(2). If the secured party wants to sell the collateral, it must give at least 15 days notice of the sale to the debtor and others with an interest in the collateral: *OPPSA* s 63(4), (5), (6), (7).

[27] For example, *OPPSA* s 63(2); *SPPSA* s 59(2), (3).

[28] *Copp v Medi-dent Services Ltd* (1991) 3 OR (3d) 570 (Gen Div).

[29] If there are other secured parties, proceeds may have to be paid to them rather than the debtor, in accordance with the scheme in the provincial PPS legislation (for example, *OPPSA* s 64).

When a Secured Party Can Keep the Collateral

Sometimes, a secured party will decide to keep the collateral after it has taken possession. Suppose that the secured party runs a electrical contracting business. It sells some extra wiring it had on hand to another electrical contractor on credit and takes a security interest in the wiring to secure the payment of the purchase price. If the buyer defaulted and the seller took possession of the wiring, the seller might want to keep the wiring to use in its own business. Under **PPS** legislation, if the seller decides to keep the wiring, it gives up any claim it has against the buyer for payment of the price. Thus, the seller would have to be satisfied that the goods are worth at least the amount of the buyer's obligation before it decided to keep the collateral. Before the secured party can do so, however, it must give notice to the buyer and any other secured party with a security interest in the collateral. If either objects to the seller keeping the wiring, it has to be sold. Objections most commonly arise when the collateral is worth more than the debt owed to the secured party.[30]

a secured party can sometimes keep the collateral

When a Debtor Can Get the Collateral Back

The Ontario *PPSA* permits a debtor to **redeem collateral**—recover it back from a secured creditor who has seized it. However, the debtor is entitled to redeem the collateral only if it has: (i) fulfilled all the secured obligations, and (ii) paid all of the secured party's reasonable expenses.[31] A debtor does not have any right to cure a default and put the credit obligation back into good standing by making only its missed payments. Unless the secured party agrees, the debtor must pay the full amount of the obligation plus expenses before it can get the collateral back. Secured parties who rank behind the secured party in possession of the collateral can also redeem it.

In other provinces, the debtor can get the collateral back by making the missed payments plus paying the secured party's expenses.[32] This is called **reinstating the collateral**.

Concept Summary 21.2 reviews the rules for enforcing security interests.

redeeming collateral means recovering the collateral from a secured creditor, who has seized it, by fulfilling all obligations owed to the secured party and paying any expenses it has incurred

reinstating the collateral means the debtor gets the collateral back from a secured party that has seized it by making the missed payments plus paying the secured party's expenses

Concept Summary 21.2

Steps in Enforcing a Security Interest

1. Debtor defaults.

2. Secured party takes possession of collateral.

3. Secured party retains collateral in full satisfaction of the debtor's obligation, *or*
   Secured party disposes of collateral and applies proceeds to debtor's debt, *or*
   Debtor gets collateral back by redeeming it by paying all outstanding amounts owed to the secured party, *or*,
   in some provinces, reinstating it by paying amounts owing at the time of default plus the expenses of the secured party.

4. Debtor remains liable for any deficiency and any surplus is distributed in accordance with scheme of priority in the relevant PPS legislation.

---

[30] For example, *OPPSA* s 65(2)-(7).

[31] If collateral is consumer goods, the debtor has a right to reinstate the debt in Ontario: *OPPSA* s 66(2), (3).

[32] For example, *SPPSA* s 62, applied in *Bank of Nova Scotia v Sherstobitov* (1987) 64 Sask R 293 (QB); *MPPSA* s 62.

Security Interests When Collateral Is Transferred

a security interest in personal property may continue to exist even when the property is transferred by the debtor to a third party

One key protection for secured parties in PPS legislation is that a security interest in personal property may continue to exist even when the property is transferred by the debtor to someone else.[33] This means that the buyer of the property has to respect the secured party's interest, even if it knew nothing of it. If the debtor defaults, the property could be seized from the buyer. While the buyer will be able to sue the seller for what it paid plus any damages it suffers, that action may not be very useful. If the secured party has been driven to actually enforcing a security interest, the debtor presumably has little money.

Buyers will want to avoid this kind of risk. For each sale, a buyer could search the register maintained under PPS legislation to make sure that the seller had not granted a security interest in the goods. However, that tactic would be expensive and time consuming and would not disclose unregistered interests. If that were the only strategy for avoiding risk, it would discourage many commercial transactions. Consider the problem of having to do a search every time you bought something at a store. Because of that difficulty, the PPS legislation contains exceptions to the general rule that a secured creditor's security interest in collateral follows the collateral into the buyer's hands.[34] An exception arises if:

- the secured party has permitted the debtor to sell or otherwise deal with the collateral, or
- the debtor sells the goods in the ordinary course of the debtor's business

In either of those situations, the buyer receives the collateral free of any security interest given by the seller, even if the security interest is perfected and the buyer knows it. The only time that the buyer is not protected is when it knew that sale was a breach of the security agreement between the seller and a secured party. In practice, the buyer rarely knows anything about the security agreements the seller entered.

The first exception is hard to rely on, because a buyer seldom knows the content of a security agreement that exists between the seller-debtor and that party's creditor. Consequently, the key question from the buyer's perspective is whether the sale occurred in the ordinary course of the seller-debtor's business. A buyer who is in doubt on that question should search the register that is maintained under the PPS legislation. If the sale is *not* in the ordinary course of business, the security interest of the seller-debtor's creditor may follow the collateral into the buyer's hands.

an unperfected security interest is ineffective against a buyer that does not know about that interest

A buyer does not have to worry about unperfected security interests. PPS legislation provides that unperfected interests are not effective against the buyer if it has no knowledge of the interest.[35] This is another good reason for secured parties to register their interests.

[33.] For example, *OPPSA* s 25(1)(a); *SPPSA* s 28(1)(a). Provincial PPS legislation also requires that secured parties make a new filing, called a *financing change statement*, within a specified time after they find out about the transfer. That document, which names the buyer, is needed to maintain the perfection of the secured party's interest: *eg OPPSA* s 48.

[34.] For example, *OPPSA* ss 25(1)(a), 28; *SPPSA* ss 28(1)(a), 30.

[35.] For example, *OPPSA* s 20(1)(c); *SPPSA* s 20(1)(d).

GUARANTEES

A creditor can reduce the risk of non-payment by taking security. A creditor can also reduce that risk by receiving a *guarantee*, a contractual promise by a third party, called a *guarantor*, to satisfy the principal debtor's obligation if that debtor fails to do so. For example, if you were going to borrow money to buy a car, the bank might ask your parents to sign a guarantee of your obligation to make the loan payments. Your parents' guarantee would mean that if you failed to pay, the bank could demand payment from them.[36] A bank may also ask for a guarantee if the borrower is a corporation with few assets or is starting a new business. A guarantee from a shareholder with substantial personal assets may convince the bank to make the loan. The obligation under a guarantee is independent of the debtor's obligation, meaning that, after the debtor has defaulted, it is not necessary for the creditor to take steps against the debtor to enforce the debtor's obligation before making demand on the guarantor for performance. Figure 21.2 illustrates how a guarantee works.

a creditor can reduce the risk of non-payment by receiving a guarantee *of payment from someone other than the debtor*

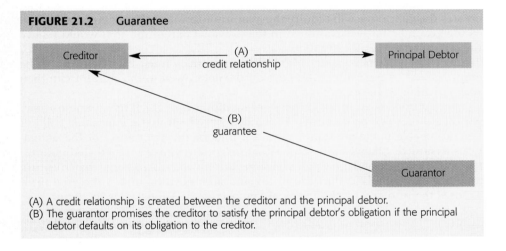

FIGURE 21.2   Guarantee

(A) A credit relationship is created between the creditor and the principal debtor.
(B) The guarantor promises the creditor to satisfy the principal debtor's obligation if the principal debtor defaults on its obligation to the creditor.

A guarantor is relieved of liability in several situations in which the creditor increases the guarantor's risk without the guarantor's consent.

a guarantor is relieved of liability in several situations in which the creditor increases the guarantor's risk without the guarantor's consent

- The contract between the creditor and principal debtor is modified without the consent of the guarantor in a way that is prejudicial to the guarantor.[37] This commonly occurs when the creditor and the debtor agree to increase the size of the loan or the rate of interest to be paid. Both increase the guarantor's exposure.

- The creditor breaches its contract with the principal debtor, and the guarantor's risk is affected. For example, the loan agreement stated that the debtor's failure to send the creditor annual financial statements was a default, but also that the creditor could take no action on the default for 30 days. If the creditor initiated enforcement proceedings when the statements were only one day late and refused to accept the statements on the following day in breach of its obligations, the guarantor would be

---

[36.] There are many business situations in which guarantees may be sought and given, but the rules in each case are as described in this section.

[37.] *Reid v Royal Trust Corp of Canada* (1985) 20 DLR (4th) 223 (PEI CA).

released. The creditor's action eliminated the debtor's right to cure the default.

- The creditor does something to hurt the value of collateral that the principal debtor gave as security. In this case, the guarantor's obligation is reduced to the extent that the creditor diminished the value of the collateral. Suppose that the security was a shipment of pork bellies. The bank took possession, but then let the goods sit for an unreasonable time. The pork became rancid and unsellable.[38]

- The creditor breaches the contract of guarantee. This might occur if the contract required the creditor to notify the guarantor before demanding payment, but the creditor failed to do so.

the guarantor can generally resist enforcement of the guarantee by using any defence that the principal debtor could use against the creditor

In general, the guarantor can resist enforcement of the guarantee by using any defence that the principal debtor could use against the creditor. Suppose that the creditor sold a television to your brother, and you signed a guarantee of your brother's obligation to pay the purchase price. If the television did not work, and your brother was entitled to refuse to pay the price, you could also refuse to make payment under the guarantee. Often, however, the contract that creates the guarantee will require the guarantor to waive those defences, as well as the grounds that we examined in the previous paragraph that would relieve the guarantor of responsibility.[39]

In every province except Manitoba, guarantees must be in writing to be enforceable.[40] A guarantor who pays off the debt owed to the creditor can then seek payment from the principal debtor.

A guarantee is often a significant obligation from which the guarantor may get little direct personal benefit. The courts have held that a guarantee will not be enforceable if the guarantor does not understand the nature of the obligations assumed. Likewise, in some situations, courts have insisted that guarantors receive independent legal advice regarding the obligations that they are assuming, especially if they are in a vulnerable position and if the guarantee exposes them to great risk.[41] Ethical Perspective 21.1 illustrates this issue.

ETHICAL PERSPECTIVE 21.1

Informed Consent of Guarantor

Aline carries on a trucking business and is negotiating a loan of $100 000 from her bank. The bank is concerned that Aline will not be able to make her payments and asks her for security. Aline says that she does not have any collateral. However, she also says that she lives with her grandmother, who has a portfolio of securities worth about $500 000. The bank suggests that

if Aline could get her grandmother to guarantee Aline's debt and give a security interest in the securities portfolio to secure her obligation under the guarantee, it would make the loan.

Aline comes back to the bank several days later with her grandmother. When the banker tries to explain what she is committing herself to, the grandmother says she does not want to be worried about the details, but just wants to help her granddaughter. The grandmother signs the guarantee and the security agreement, thereby giving the bank a security

(continued)

[38] *Bank of Montreal v Korico Enterprises Ltd* (2000) 190 DLR (4th) 706 (Ont CA).

[39] These sorts of waivers are interpreted strictly against the creditor: *Bank of Montreal v Korico Enterprises Ltd* (2000) 1990 DLR (4th) 706 (Ont CA).

[40] In Alberta, a guarantee must be acknowledged before a notary public to be enforceable: *Guarantees Acknowledgement Act*, RSA 2000, c G-11.

[41] *Bertolo v Bank of Montreal* (1986) 33 DLR (4th) 610 (Ont CA).

(continued)

interest in her securities portfolio. She does this without reading either document or hearing any explanation of either document.

Question for Discussion

1. Should the bank worry that the grandmother may not have fully appreciated the nature of the legal obligations to which she was committing herself? Assume that the grandmother's sole source of income is what she receives from her investments.

Business Decision 21.1 asks you to consider how you would apply your knowledge of securing transactions in a practical context.

BUSINESS DECISION 21.1

Setting up a Distributorship

Meena Inc is setting up a national chain of distributors for its tractors. Meena knows that most of its distributors will not have enough cash on hand to pay for the tractors when they are delivered. Therefore, it will not receive payment on any particular tractor

until it is actually sold by the distributor to a customer.

Question for Discussion

1. How should Meena Inc protect itself against the risk of non-payment in its distributorship agreements?

Chapter Summary

In credit transactions there is a risk that the creditor may not receive payment from the debtor. To reduce that risk, a creditor may take a security interest in the debtor's personal property. A security interest allows the creditor to seize and sell the collateral if the debtor does not fulfill its obligations.

Each province has personal property security (PPS) legislation, which creates rules for the creation, registration, priority, and enforcement of security interests in personal property. These rules make it more likely that secured creditors will be able to obtain and enforce their security interests in a cost-effective way. Security interests are created by agreement between the debtor and a creditor in five main ways: (i) conditional sales, including some leases and consignments, (ii) granting a security interest in a specific asset, (iii) assignment of accounts receivable, (iv) granting a security interest in after-acquired property, and (v) special security interests created under the *Bank Act*.

Provincial **PPS** legislation applies to every transaction that creates a security interest. Some exceptions exist, including statutory rights like landlords' distraint rights

and deemed trusts in favour of Canada Customs and Revenue Agency. Under **PPS** legislation, secured parties may perfect their interests in collateral if they have attached by registering a financing statement or taking possession of the collateral. PPS legislation creates a scheme of priorities. For registered security interests, priority is determined by the date of registration. An important exception to this rule is the super priority given to secured parties who supply goods to the debtor or directly finance their acquisition by the debtor. These purchase money security interests (PMSIs) have priority over all other security interests created by the debtor in the goods if certain requirements are met.

The steps followed in the enforcement of a security interest by a secured party are: (i) default by debtor, (ii) secured party takes possession of collateral, (iii) secured party retains collateral or disposes of it, or debtor redeems collateral, and (iv) after disposition, any surplus is distributed in accordance with scheme of priority in PPS legislation. The debtor remains liable for any deficiency. Security interests in collateral usually fall into the hands of anyone who buys the collateral from the debtor. To protect buyers, a security interest does not follow the collateral when: (i) the sale is in the ordinary course of business, (ii) the sale was permitted by the secured party, or (iii) the secured party's interest was unperfected, and the buyer was unaware of it.

Creditors can also reduce the risk of non-payment or non-performance by acquiring a guarantee from someone other than the principal debtor. Guarantors are released from liability in several circumstances when the secured party acts in a way that prejudices the guarantor's position without the guarantor's consent.

Review Questions

1. What is a security interest?
2. Why should a creditor perfect a security interest under provincial PPS legislation?
3. Identify two ways that a creditor can obtain a security interest in property that a debtor does not possess when the security agreement is created? Which is better from the creditor's point of view?
4. When is a consignment the same as a conditional sale?
5. When should a lease be treated as a transaction creating a security interest? When is it subject to provincial PPS legislation?
6. From a secured creditor's perspective, explain one advantage of taking a security interest in accounts receivable rather than other assets.
7. Why is the security that banks may take from debtors under section 427 of the Bank Act different from other types of security interests?
8. Why is PPS legislation an improvement over the previous legal regime for creditors?
9. What kinds of property can be used as security under provincial PPS legislation?
10. What types of interests are not subject to PPS legislation? What problems does this pose for secured parties?
11. What are the differences between security interests creat-

ed by contract and similar entitlements arising under statutes?
12. What advantage does a secured party obtain by perfecting its security interest? When should a secured party perfect?
13. What must happen before a secured party can seize collateral?
14. When does a creditor's obligation to act in a commercially reasonable manner arise, and what does it require?
15. If a manufacturer wanted to sell its product on credit to a dealer who had already given a security interest in all of its current and future property to a bank, could the manufacturer obtain a security interest in the product that it supplied that would rank ahead of the bank's?
16. If a secured party had perfected its security interest by filing a financing statement under the appropriate PPS legislation, can anyone else's interest have priority over it?
17. What rights does a debtor have once the secured party has taken possession of the collateral following a default?
18. If you were buying a boat from a friend, would you have any concerns about whether your friend had given a security interest in the boat? If so, what would you do about it?
19. When will a guarantor be relieved of its obligations?
20. When the debtor defaults on an obligation and a guarantor is required to pay, does the guarantor have any rights against the debtor?

Cases and Problems

1. Tornado Tyres Inc borrowed $1 000 000 from National Bank. As security for its loan, Tornado gave National a security interest in all personal property that it owned at the time that it entered into the security agreement or acquired later. National registered a financing statement relating to its interest on January 1, 2001. In June 2002, Tornado ran into financial difficulty and failed to remit to the Canada Customs and Revenue Agency $50 000 that it had withheld from employee wages for income tax. Tornado also stopped making its loan payments to National.

Acting under its security agreement, National seized all of Tornado's assets, including the $50 000 that was in its bank account at National. National has checked and there are no other security interests registered under the PPS legislation. Is there any reason that National should not apply the $50 000 against the liability of Tornado under the loan? Would it make any difference to your answer if National had never properly registered its interest under the PPS legislation?

2. RevCo Inc is the exclusive Ontario distributor of Automated

Teller Machines (ATMs) for E-Cash Ltd. In January 2000, RevCo entered into a general security agreement with A-Bank covering all the assets that it owned at the time or later acquired, including inventory, to secure a line of credit from the bank. A-Bank properly registered a financing statement that same month, indicating an interest in inventory and equipment. E-Cash supplied 10 ATMs to RevCo in 2002 and has not been paid. Before supplying the ATMs, E-Cash and RevCo had entered into an agreement that provided that the ATMs were only given to RevCo on consignment and that RevCo was not obliged to pay the wholesale price to E-Cash unless it sold the ATMs. E-Cash registered a financing statement against RevCo in January 2002, indicating a security interest in inventory.

RevCo has become insolvent. A-Bank is owed $200 000 under RevCo's line of credit, and a dispute has arisen with E-Cash as to who is entitled to the 10 ATMs supplied by E-Cash. Who is entitled to the ATMs, and why?

3. Cory leased a truck from Superior Leasing Inc for the snow-plowing business he carried on in Toronto. The lease allowed Cory to use the truck for three years with an option to purchase the truck at the end of the term for a fixed price of $7000. The option price was based on an estimate of the wholesale value of the truck at the end of the lease period. If Cory chose not to exercise the option, the truck would be sold at an auction and any surplus over the option price would be paid to Cory. If the truck sold for less than the option price, Cory would have to pay the difference. Superior did not file a financing statement in relation to its interest in the truck. Cory had also borrowed $40 000 from the Bank of Toronto and had given the bank a security interest in all his property. The bank properly registered a financing statement relating to this interest on January 1, 2000.

Who is entitled to the truck if Cory defaults on his payments to both the bank and Superior? Would it make any difference if this transaction and all the parties were in Manitoba?

4. Erin bought a new car from Davis Motors Inc for $20 000. Under the terms of the purchase, Erin paid $5000 down and agreed to pay the balance in regular monthly instalments. To secure her obligation, Erin gave Davis a security interest in the car. Erin defaulted on the payments when she had just $3000 left to pay. Acting under its security agreement, Davis repossessed the car. The manager of Davis liked Erin's car and offered to buy it from Davis for $7500. Davis agreed. When Davis received the money from the manager, it applied $3000 to the loan and paid the balance of $4500 to Erin. Erin is unhappy because she recently saw an identical car advertised for $10 000.

Is there any basis upon which Erin could complain about what Davis has done?

5. Samra had agreed to guarantee a loan of $50 000 that her brother, Amman, had received from the Bank of Vancouver. Amman had entered into an agreement with the bank giving it a security interest in all his personal property, which included several vehicles and some jewellery. After Amman had paid back $25 000, he approached the bank asking for permission to sell one of his rings to a friend for $5000. He convinced the bank that his remaining personal property would be more than enough to cover the amount of the debt still unpaid. The bank agreed. Amman and the bank signed an agreement releasing the bank's security interest in the ring, and Amman sold it.

Two year's later, Amman defaulted on his loan. Under the terms of the loan, the whole amount of the debt outstanding at the time of default, $5000, became due on default. The first thing that the bank did was to ask Samra to pay the full amount of the debt under her guarantee. Does Samra have to pay?

6. Goldie bought a new refrigerator from Cool Refrigerators Ltd, a retail appliance dealer, under a conditional sales agreement. In the contract, Goldie was given the right to possession of the refrigerator in return for promising to make six equal monthly payments of $150. Cool was to retain ownership of the refrigerator until the full price was paid. The contract also stated that if Goldie failed to make a payment, the total of all the outstanding payments became immediately due upon notice from Cool. Moreover, Cool was entitled to take possession of the refrigerator. Goldie has failed to make any payments since the initial instalment. What can Cool do? Describe all the steps that Cool would have to take to enforce its interest.

7. Orestes Clothing Corp intends to set up a clothing manufacturing business to make high-quality blouses. Orestes has no track record and few assets. However, its major shareholder and president worked for 20 years with another corporation that carried on essentially the same business. That person has substantial personal assets. Orestes needs a loan of $25 000 to pay for 50 sewing machines. The corporation already has a loan in the form of an operating line of credit from Montreal Bank, which is secured on all the present and future assets of the business. Orestes goes to Toronto Bank to ask for a loan to finance its acquisition of the sewing machines. Toronto Bank thinks that the basic business idea is sound and that Orestes will be able to earn sufficient revenues to make the loan payments. What can Toronto Bank do to protect itself against the risk of default?

8. Roma is going to buy a used tractor from a farmer. How can she protect herself from the risk that there are security interests in the tractor that would be enforceable against her?

9. Iaasic is interested in buying a computer from Electronic Gadgets Inc, but he does not have enough money to afford the purchase. His friend Ophelia agrees to lend him the money to buy the computer, but she is concerned that she may not get repaid. Iaasic is already in debt to his bank and has given a security interest in all of his assets, present and future, to the bank to secure his obligation to repay the loan. What can Ophelia do to protect her interests?

10. Giovanni bought a 1999 boat from West-End Marina under a conditional sales contract for $15 000. That contract provided that Giovanni would make regular monthly payments for five years. West-End retained ownership of the boat as security for Giovanni's obligations to make the payments. West-End assigned the boat and the conditional sales contract to Springliner Finance Corp. Giovanni was

unhappy with the boat from the beginning. It leaked and would not perform the way West-End had promised. After much discussion, West-End took the 1999 boat back and replaced it with a 2000 boat. Springliner was aware of the substitution and did not object to it, but no written amendment was ever made to the conditional sales contract, which continued to refer to the 1999 boat.

Within a few months, and after he had paid only $1000, Giovanni defaulted on his payments under the conditional sales agreement. When Springliner came to seize the boat, Giovanni said that Springliner has no claim to the 2000 boat since the conditional sales agreement refers only to the 1999 boat. What should Springliner do?

11. Eve is a loans officer at Commerce Bank. Arden Furniture Inc, one of her clients, carries on a retail furniture business in Winnipeg. Commerce has given Arden an operating line of credit, which is secured by a general security agreement on all the current and future assets of Arden. The bank's interest was registered under the Manitoba *Personal Property Security Act*. Arden comes to Eve to discuss a new cash register system that it wants to acquire on credit. The supplier has told Arden that it will sell to Arden only if it can get a security interest on the system that ranks ahead of Commerce. Should the bank agree to this? Is there anything else the bank should do upon learning about this proposed transaction?

12. Tomas wants to set up a wholesale appliance business. Knowing that most of his dealers will not be able to pay the full price for the appliances at the time of delivery, he is willing to finance the inventory of his dealers. He will secure the dealers' payment obligations by having each give him a security interest in all their present and future assets. One of the dealers has asked to have a clause included in the agreement that would permit the dealer to buy and sell its inventory and to replace worn-out assets. Should Tomas agree to including such a clause? What would be the effect if he did?

22 Dealing with Bankruptcy and Insolvency

CHAPTER OBJECTIVES

After completing this chapter, you should be able to:

1. Distinguish between bankruptcy and insolvency.
2. Explain how bankruptcy differs from creditor-debtor action.
3. Describe two ways in which bankruptcy in a consumer context differs from bankruptcy in a corporate context.
4. Identify four individuals involved in a bankruptcy and the roles they play.
5. Distinguish between an assignment, a petition, and a proposal.
6. Specify three categories of creditors, and describe the rights and responsibilities of each in bankruptcy.
7. Explain the principle of creditor equality.
8. Describe what exempt creditors are, and name two categories of exempt creditors.
9. Distinguish between settlements and preferences, and explain how each is treated in bankruptcy.
10. Describe three types of proposals, and explain the advantages of each.

This book has many examples in which a business is created or acquired. Generally speaking, those are the "good times," the times of planning, projection, and expansion, when things are well and operations are secure. It would be great to think that doing business is always this rewarding. Unfortunately, an unavoidable part of any venture—as we stress throughout this book—is risk. In this chapter we focus on the risk of business failure.

Business people work in the real world, where success is difficult. Cash is often in short supply. Liabilities may exceed assets. Even the future of operations can be in doubt. Statistics indicate that more than 80 percent of small businesses in Canada fail during the first five years of operation.[1] The liquidation of several well-established businesses during the past decade reminds us that big business is not immune from the threat of failure either. It is therefore prudent to know something about the law relating to business distress and failure.

Canadian law provides several methods for dealing with business failure. For the most part, they are borrowed from the common law of bankruptcy that was developed by English courts starting around 1500. They focus on people who are *bankrupt*. A person may be **bankrupt** when their debts exceed their liabilities, and they cannot meet their debts as they come due. A bankrupt party's assets are *liquidated*. **Liquidation** is the sale of assets so that they assume the "liquid" form of money and can be distributed to the bankrupt's creditors. Once that distribution occurs, no new claims can be launched against the bankrupt for pre-existing debts. Instead, the debtor is financially disabled for a time and is normally either *discharged* or wound up. **Discharge** is the release of a debtor from bankruptcy status. Another method of dealing with financial distress is for the debtor to make a *proposal* to creditors to re-establish its financial affairs. A **proposal** is a contract between a debtor and its creditors providing for a rearrangement of debts outside of formal bankruptcy. If the proposal is successful, the debtor continues to operate. If not, the debtor is placed in bankruptcy.

Bankruptcy law tries to reconcile financial failure with real business behaviour. Debtors work hard to prevent bankruptcy, as do creditors, who experience significant non-monetary costs in pursuing debtors. The aggravation and expense of collecting overdue debts may cause creditors to hesitate before strictly enforcing their rights to payment. Creditors may also hesitate for fear of suffering intangible losses during the bankruptcy process. Of particular importance are business synergies, client relationships, and accrued **goodwill**—a favourable and valuable public reputation. A creditor that acts too quickly and too harshly may be viewed unfavourably in the business community.

For all of those reasons, creditors are frequently patient when dealing with bad debts. They know that there are hidden costs to putting a debtor in bankruptcy. They also know that they frequently stand to gain more by adopting a flexible attitude. An important aspect of the legal regime regulating financial failure in Canada is therefore to encourage debtors and creditors to work out their differences co-operatively.

Canadian law is also shaped by a number of other considerations. Historically, one of the main purposes of bankruptcy was to reinforce the stigma of financial failure in order to encourage careful business behaviour. In England, for instance, it used to be common for bankrupts to spend time in prison. Some of these legal and social restrictions still exist in Canada, but the main focus of

most small businesses fail within five years

*a person may be **bankrupt** when their debts exceed their liabilities, and they cannot meet their debts as they come due*

liquidation is the sale of assets so that they assume the "liquid" form of money and can be distributed to the bankrupt's creditors

discharge is the release of a debtor from bankruptcy status

a proposal is a contract between a debtor and creditors providing for a rearrangement of debts outside of formal bankruptcy

goodwill is a business's favourable and valuable public reputation

the main focus of bankruptcy law today is rehabilitation

[1.] F Zaid *Canadian Franchise Guide* (1983) at 1-401.

the law today is rehabilitation.[2] If the bankrupt is a legal person (such as a corporation), they can seek extra time to rearrange their affairs and repay their debts. If the bankrupt is a natural person (that is, an individual), they can seek a prompt discharge and return to being a productive member of society. The forgiveness embodied in the law is a contemporary recognition of the fact that some risk taking is necessary for economic growth.

None of this should suggest that we approve of bankruptcy. There remain serious disabilities for those who are unfortunate enough to enter it, the most serious of which is that corporate and consumer bankrupts will usually find it difficult to re-establish their credit. But we do not suggest that bankruptcy is the end of a promising career, as it often was a century ago. We view bankruptcy law as necessary for achieving social purposes. Just as the risks of doing certain types of business have grown, so too have the potential downsides. With this has come a new appreciation of the need to see failure in context.

Bankruptcy laws also help to reduce uncertainty in the business world. They give creditors some idea of the risks that arise when they extend credit. They also provide debtors with several alternatives for rehabilitation. To parties on both sides of a credit transaction, they offer a preview of what will happen in the event of financial failure and, to that extent, they promote predictability in what is often a very difficult and emotional experience. Bankruptcy laws are therefore an essential tool in risk management.

REGULATION OF BANKRUPTCY

Canada's Constitution assigns the power to enact bankruptcy legislation to the federal government. The current federal act, the *Bankruptcy and Insolvency Act* (*BIA*), provides for officials to administer the bankruptcy process, various forms of proceeding in bankruptcy (assignments and petitions), non-bankruptcy alternatives (proposals), detailed regulations concerning the debtor's property, the administration of estates, the duties of a bankrupt, and miscellaneous matters.[3]

Broadly speaking, the Act aims:

- to provide for an equitable distribution of the bankrupt's assets to creditors in accordance with a generally recognized scheme
- to limit the possibility of discharging or eliminating certain debts, such as family support obligations and student loans, that are considered socially important
- to punish debtors for engaging in behaviour that undermines the principles of creditor equality and debtor rehabilitation, such as fraudulent pre-bankruptcy transfers and repeated financial failure
- to promote confidence and certainty in the credit system
- to provide for the rehabilitation of debtors
- to promote uniformity of laws in a field of importance to Canadian business

---

[2.] In many provinces, for example, an undischarged bankrupt cannot act as a chartered accountant or a corporate director: *eg Business Corporations Act*, RSO 1990, c B-16, s 118(1); *Canada Trustco Mortgage Co v Sugarman* (1999) 7 CBR (4th) 113 (Ont Gen Div).

[3.] *Bankruptcy and Insolvency Act*, RSC 1985, c B-3 (Can).

There are some important exceptions to the Act's coverage. It does not apply to banks, insurance companies, trust companies, and railways, key economic institutions that are dealt with under separate statutes. In addition, farmers and fishermen cannot be placed in bankruptcy. That reflects a policy decision based on the highly volatile nature of the economics of farming and fishing.

The Act is by far the most commonly looked-to statute concerning financial distress and failure in Canada, but it is not the only one. The federal *Companies' Creditors Arrangement Act* (*CCRA*) allows a debtor to seek a *stay*, or *bar*, of all claims pending the acceptance of a reorganization plan.[4] A **stay** is a court-ordered suspension of legal proceedings. And the federal *Winding-Up and Restructuring Act* applies to the liquidation of federally incorporated entities, banks, and insurance companies.[5] Later in this chapter, we will discuss how those statutes interact with the *BIA*.

> a stay is a court-ordered suspension of legal proceedings

A number of provincial statutes apply to debtor-creditor relations by virtue of provincial jurisdiction over property and civil rights. These may be invoked with certain advantages, but in case of conflict, the *BIA* prevails.[6] For instance, an early version of the Ontario *Employment Standards Act* purported to give priority to unpaid wages over all other claims. The applicable section of the Act was held to be inapplicable in the event of a bankruptcy because it directly conflicted with the *BIA*, which subordinates wage claims to the claims of secured creditors.[7] The priority that the federal bankruptcy law provides is sometimes an important bargaining tool for debtors who are seeking to manage their exposure to risk.

CORPORATE AND CONSUMER BANKRUPTCY

About 85 000 Canadians enter bankruptcy annually. Of these, about 88 percent are consumers and 12 percent are corporations. In 2000, total corporate liabilities amounted to $4.487 billion, or $446 314 per bankrupt, while total consumer liabilities were $4.09 billion, or $54 440 per bankrupt.[8]

The marked difference in the size and scope of bankrupts in each category suggests that there should be different rules for each type of bankruptcy proceeding. Two differences are especially important.

---

[4] *Companies' Creditors Arrangement Act*, RSC 1985, c C-36.

[5] *Winding-Up and Restructuring Act*, RSC 1985, c W-11.

[6] Federal jurisdiction over bankruptcy differs from provincial debtor-creditor legislation in at least three ways. First, bankruptcy law is federal law and is uniform across Canada. Most debtor-creditor statutes are provincial in scope and vary between jurisdictions. Second, provincial debtor-creditor legislation focuses on individual action by creditors. Bankruptcy is a form of court-supervised class action against the debtor. In bankruptcy, all claims are consolidated, prioritized, and satisfied. Third, the possibility for debtor relief and a "fresh start" are greater under bankruptcy than they are under debtor-creditor statutes, since the operation of a stay on further proceedings against the debtor are prohibited in bankruptcy. No such stay operates when an individual debtor-creditor action begins. Provincial statutes with application in financial recovery include provincial fraudulent conveyances, business corporations, and personal property security legislation.

[7] *Re Lewis Department Stores Ltd* (1972) 17 CBR (NS) 113 (Ont Reg).

[8] Office of the Superintendent of Bankruptcy Canada *Annual Statistical Report for the 2000 Calendar Year* (2000) at 4-5. There were also some 14 600 proposals filed in 2000 with liabilities of $2.1 billion.

- First, under federal law, corporations may make proposals with their creditors to settle their obligations. Creditors must vote upon these proposals, which require the approval of a majority in each class of creditors who represent at least two-thirds of the value of the assets in each class. Consumers can make a simplified form of proposal that only needs to be approved by a bare majority of creditors.

- Second, corporate debtors are rarely discharged from bankruptcy unless they pay all of their debts. However, first-time consumer debtors who demonstrate responsible behaviour are usually discharged within nine months.

Despite the differences, there are fewer explicit distinctions between corporate and consumer bankruptcies than might be expected.[9] This chapter focuses on corporate bankruptcy. Given the growing rate of consumer bankruptcies, however, they are an important source of the law, and we will refer to them from time to time.

BANKRUPTCY

Bankruptcy and Insolvency

English law concerning financial distress and failure originated in the courts of equity. As we saw in Chapter 1, equity was a separate system of rules that arose during the late Middle Ages, and was intended to soften the harsh results that were occasionally produced by the older, more rigid system of common law. The courts of equity had their own judges and procedures, and they devised their own solutions to deal with legal problems that the common law was incapable of handling effectively.

At common law, a debtor could be sued by creditors for non-payment. However, news of a single suit often triggered a legal stampede among creditors, who were all trying to get the same assets. Furthermore, once all the claims all came before a court, there was no systematic way of determining which claims were valid and which creditors should rank ahead of others.

The equity courts' response was to halt all claims against the debtor, pool that person's assets, and provide for their liquidation and disposition to the creditors. The net effect was a kind of "time out" for the bankrupt. Once the sale proceeds were distributed, no further claims could be brought against the bankrupt for debts previously incurred.

Equity's approach might appear unjust, particularly for creditors, who often received far less than the face value of their loans. However, equity's innovation also had several advantages.

- First, a single proceeding prevented the "race to the bank." All creditors were treated on the same basis by a single judge, who heard all of the evidence of the debtor's various debts.

- Second, because the debtor was exposed to only one set of legal proceedings, their assets were not depleted by the need to hire lawyers for a

---

[9.] The *BIA* s 66.11 defines a "consumer debtor" as an insolvent natural person whose total debts, excluding those secured by their principal residence, do not exceed $75 000.

variety of claims. Money that would have gone to the debtor's lawyers went to creditors instead.

■ Third, the bankrupt was given a fresh start. Although the stigma of bankruptcy was harsh, the bankrupt's rehabilitation could begin as soon as they were discharged.

Over time, some of those procedures changed, but on the whole they still apply in Canada. Similarly, the law and language of financial distress retain many of the features that originally developed in England. Two concepts that are particularly important to understand are *bankruptcy* and *insolvency*.

Almost every person is at some point unable to pay some financial obligation. Bankruptcy is a different matter. Canadian law formally defines **bankruptcy** as a situation in which someone is at least $1000 in debt and has committed an "act of bankruptcy." That act of bankruptcy usually involves failing to meet liabilities as they come due.[10] Simply meeting the definition is not sufficient, however. Before a person actually becomes bankrupt for legal purposes, the situation has to be serious, and a court must decide that bankruptcy has occurred.

Insolvency is an inability to meet financial obligations as they become due. That definition is close to the one for bankruptcy, but it is distinct. Many businesses operate in, or near, a state of insolvency for long periods of time, due to ordinary lags in payment and the general acceptability of assuming a certain level of debt in modern business.

The central distinction between bankruptcy and insolvency is one of degree: a bankrupt is less likely to be able to pay debts over a longer period than an insolvent. Under Canadian law, all bankrupts must be insolvent, but not all insolvents are bankrupt. Insolvency constitutes the threshold of bankruptcy. Most creditors are prepared to wait well beyond mere insolvency to begin bankruptcy proceedings due to desire to maintain business relationships, preserve assets, and avoid the expense of court action.

Petition and Assignment

Bankruptcy and insolvency involve different procedures. The power of the courts of equity was originally discretionary—it was exercised only when a judge thought it was necessary and appropriate.[11] Creditors therefore had to **petition**, or request, the court to place an individual or corporation into bankruptcy. The court could allow or dismiss the petition as it saw fit. If the court decided to allow the petition, it would usually issue a *receiving order* for the debtor's property. A **receiving order** is a command to the debtor to release all of its assets to the court or to a court-appointed agent, usually a trustee in bankruptcy. The law later developed to allow a person or a corporation to voluntarily **assign**, or place, itself in bankruptcy. In modern Canadian law, a person is bankrupt if they: (i) meet the requirements for bankruptcy, and (ii) have either been subject to a receiving order or voluntarily been assigned into bankruptcy. Figure 22.1 illustrates the methods of entering bankruptcy.

*in Canadian law **bankruptcy** is a situation in which someone is at least $1000 in debt and has committed an "act of bankruptcy"*

__insolvency__ is an inability to meet financial obligations as they become due

the central distinction between bankruptcy and insolvency is one of degree

*a **petition** is a request by creditors to a court to place an individual or corporation into bankruptcy*

*a **receiving order** is a command to the debtor to release all of its assets to the court or to a court-appointed agent, usually a trustee in bankruptcy*

*an **assignment** is a procedure by which a debtor voluntarily assigns itself into bankruptcy*

---

[10] Section 42 of the *BIA* sets out nine other possible "acts of bankruptcy," including the making of an assignment, a fraudulent conveyance or preference, a debtor's departure from Canada, the disposition of assets, a declaration of insolvency, a declaration of a moratorium on debt payments, and a bankrupt's default on a proposal.

[11] This is unlike the common law, where the law was applied mandatorily. During the nineteenth century, the common law and equity courts in England and Canada were combined. Today both forms of law are administered by the courts generally.

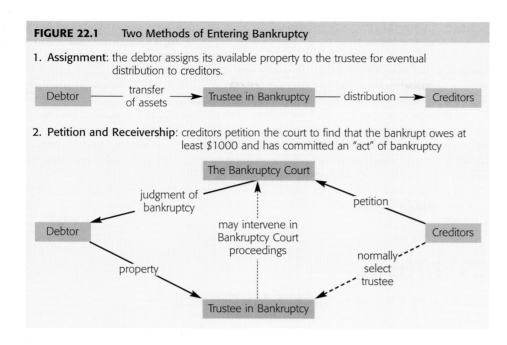

FIGURE 22.1   Two Methods of Entering Bankruptcy

1. **Assignment**: the debtor assigns its available property to the trustee for eventual distribution to creditors.

2. **Petition and Receivership**: creditors petition the court to find that the bankrupt owes at least $1000 and has committed an "act" of bankruptcy

We will examine the procedures for petitions and assignments later. Case Brief 22.1 deals with one aspect of bankruptcy procedure—commencement of proceedings in the debtor's locality.

CASE BRIEF 22.1

Re Malartic Hygrade Gold Mines Ltd (1966) 10 CBR (NS) 34 (Ont SC)

In Canada, bankruptcy proceedings must be started in the debtor's "locality." That requirement occasionally causes problems, because the debtor's locality may appear to be in several places. These include the places where the debtor is physically located, where the debtor carries on business, where the majority of their assets are situated, or where creditors reside. The *BIA* focuses on the place where the debtor carries on business, where they reside, or sometimes where the greater part of the bankrupt's property is located.

Malartic Hygrade Gold Mines Ltd carried on a substantial amount of business prospecting for gold in northern Quebec. It had creditors there and it was making plans to expand operations in that province. However, the head office of the company was in Ontario, the company was incorporated in Ontario, the company's books were located in Ontario, and the company's share register was in Ontario.

The court decided that in all of the circumstances, Ontario was the debtor's locality. Although some later cases have decided differently, that decision illustrates the importance of the *legal* presence of a debtor when other factors are conflicting or inconclusive.

Insolvency is a less-definite status than bankruptcy. It is also subject to several statutes related to creditor-debtor relations and fraudulent conveyances. Those statutes recognize that the payment of money is often a hotly disputed issue.

Proposals

Canadian law has recently encouraged greater co-operation between debtors and creditors by allowing for *proposals* as an alternative to assignment or

a **proposal** is a court-approved contract between a debtor and creditors that gives the debtor time to adjust its financial affairs while business operations continue

petition in bankruptcy. A **proposal** is a court-approved contract between a debtor and creditors that gives the debtor time to adjust its financial affairs while business operations continue. The great advantage of a proposal is that it keeps the debtor *out of formal bankruptcy*. That, in turn, usually permits the debtor to safeguard its credit-rating and to preserve its intangible assets, including its business relationships, reputation, and goodwill.

A proposal is voted upon by creditors. If successful, the proposal binds *all* creditors covered under the plan and allows the debtor to proceed with business. In exchange, the debtor often agrees to repayment at a higher rate of interest in future, to restructure its operations, to heighten scrutiny of its affairs, or some combination of these and other options.

Proposals can be made by any insolvent person, by a bankrupt, or by various bankruptcy officials. We will examine proposals in more detail later in this chapter.

CREDITORS

Creditors and the Market for Credit

Until now, this chapter has focused on debtors. After all, they are the ones upon whom the law of bankruptcy concentrates. For every debtor, however, there are also creditors. Business people should be aware that they will probably enjoy the status of both debtor *and* creditor at some point in the course of normal business operations. It is therefore useful to understand how the *BIA* regulates creditors.

Bankruptcy occurs because a debtor cannot pay its debts. By definition, therefore, bankruptcy protection involves *discounting*, or reducing, claims. For instance, if there is only a 50 percent chance that you will repay $2000 that you borrowed from me, my rights under that loan may be worth only $1000. That is something that professional creditors, like banks, know *before* they extend credit. For that reason, the interest rate on a bank loan reflects the bank's best guess as to: (i) whether a debtor will be able to repay a loan, and (ii) the amount that it will actually be able to recover if the debtor defaults under the loan.

a **secured creditor** is a creditor whose interest is directly linked to a particular asset

secured credit is the highest degree of protection available to a creditor

The *BIA* reflects and influences that situation. Under it, creditors may be secured, preferred, or unsecured. As we saw in Chapter 21, a **secured creditor** is a creditor whose interest is directly linked to a particular asset, such as a tractor or an assignment of the debtor's accounts receivable. The creditor is "secure" in the sense that there are definite assets that it can look to for payment. Secured credit represents the highest degree of protection and (at least initially) it is privileged under the *BIA* in being exempt from the stay that is placed on disposition of the debtor's assets.[12] This exemption means that the secured creditor can retrieve the secured asset for itself immediately. This is a critical advantage. Lower-ranked creditors can wait years for their *pro rata* shares to be paid, or they may not be paid at all. When there is a deficiency in the value of the asset, secured creditors enjoy the added protection of being able to claim for the balance of the debt owing as unsecured creditors.

a **preferred creditor** is a creditor that is preferred in relation to all other unsecured creditors, generally by operation of law

The *BIA* divides unsecured creditors into two categories. A **preferred creditor** is a creditor that is preferred in relation to all other unsecured creditors, generally by operation of law. For instance, those who are owed unpaid wages

---

[12.] *BIA* s 244(1) allows a secured creditor to enforce its security against a debtor ten days after giving notice of intent to enforce.

and taxes normally fall in this category, as do those bearing the administrative costs of carrying out the bankruptcy. These are "preferred" because society deems them to be important enough to enjoy priority over other unsecured creditors.

There is also the residual category of **unsecured creditors**. This is normally the largest class of creditor. Ordinary suppliers of goods and services, small lenders, and other creditors will be assembled and paid out of whatever is left over after the other priority claims are satisfied. Depending on the size of the bankrupt's estate, there is frequently little or nothing remaining. Creditors must take this risk into account when deciding to lend.

Concept Summary 22.1 reviews the three classes of creditors.

unsecured creditors are creditors that are neither secured nor preferred

unsecured credit has the least protection available to a creditor

Concept Summary 22.1

Classes of Creditors

Secured		Creditors whose interests are "secured" by some specific asset of the debtor, such as a piece of equipment, inventory, or accounts receivable. If the debtor defaults on the loan, the creditor is in a position to claim the asset and, depending on its value, claim for the balance of the debt owing as an unsecured creditor.
Unsecured	Preferred	Creditors who are "preferred" in relation to other general creditors by operation of law. For instance, creditors owed wages, taxes, rent, and support payments fall in this category, as do the administrative costs incurred in carrying out the bankruptcy.
	General	A residual class of creditor, paid after all other claims are satisfied.

Creditor Equality

One key point is the principle of creditor equality, which has two aspects.

- First, all unsecured creditors are caught by a stay on court proceedings against the debtor, once bankruptcy is formally determined. This means that they cannot bring independent actions against the bankrupt for their pre-existing debts. It also means that any proceedings that they previously began are stayed in favour of the bankruptcy action. The stay guarantees procedural equality among creditors.

- Second, all creditors in the same class recover on a *pro rata* basis. Suppose that the debtor has assets of $100 000, but owes $600 000 to creditor A and $400 000 to creditor B. A will get $60 000 and B will get $40 000. Sometimes, a creditor may try to "jump the queue" and receive a higher rate of recovery, either through a pre-bankruptcy transfer or other voidable *preference*. A **preference** is the payment to one creditor of a larger amount than they would be entitled to receive in a *pro rata* distribution. Improper transfers to a creditor can be cancelled or even punished by the bankruptcy court. For instance, the court may subordinate the guilty creditor to all other creditors and therefore lessen its chances of recovery.

bankruptcy generally involves the principle of creditor equality

a preference is the payment to one creditor of a larger amount than they would be entitled to receive in a *pro rata* distribution

Proof of Claim

To be officially recognized in the bankruptcy process, each creditor must prove its claim before a bankruptcy official. The claim process is designed to identify the pool of potential claimants, to eliminate ineligible claims, and to streamline

each creditor must prove its claim before a bankruptcy official to participate in the bankruptcy process

the bankruptcy process. Unsecured creditors must, by a certain date, submit a *proof of claim* setting out the amount at issue, how it arose, and whether the bankrupt has any counterclaim against the creditor.[13] Failure to do this usually voids a claim.

OFFICIALS

A number of officials play a role in the bankruptcy process. Since bankruptcy procedures arose in the courts of equity and remain to some extent distinct from ordinary court proceedings, it is important to know who these people are and what they do. Figure 22.2 provides an introduction.

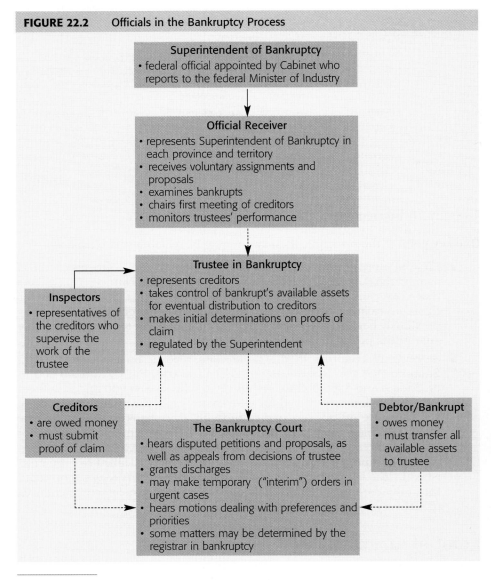

FIGURE 22.2   Officials in the Bankruptcy Process

Superintendent of Bankruptcy
- federal official appointed by Cabinet who reports to the federal Minister of Industry

Official Receiver
- represents Superintendent of Bankruptcy in each province and territory
- receives voluntary assignments and proposals
- examines bankrupts
- chairs first meeting of creditors
- monitors trustees' performance

Trustee in Bankruptcy
- represents creditors
- takes control of bankrupt's available assets for eventual distribution to creditors
- makes initial determinations on proofs of claim
- regulated by the Superintendent

Inspectors
- representatives of the creditors who supervise the work of the trustee

Creditors
- are owed money
- must submit proof of claim

Debtor/Bankrupt
- owes money
- must transfer all available assets to trustee

The Bankruptcy Court
- hears disputed petitions and proposals, as well as appeals from decisions of trustee
- grants discharges
- may make temporary ("interim") orders in urgent cases
- hears motions dealing with preferences and priorities
- some matters may be determined by the registrar in bankruptcy

---

[13] A counterclaim occurs when the debtor sues the creditor, usually to offset the amount owing under the original debt.

Superintendent of Bankruptcy and Official Receivers

The chief administrative official in bankruptcy in Canada is the Superintendent of Bankruptcy, a Cabinet appointee who reports to the Minister of Industry. The Superintendent has wide powers to inspect and investigate bankrupts' estates, to regulate and examine the work of trustees in bankruptcy, and to intervene in bankruptcy court proceedings across Canada.

The Superintendent is represented in each province and territory by an Official Receiver, whose office still "receives" a copy of receiving orders and other bankruptcy documents from the Bankruptcy Court. An Official Receiver's tasks include receiving voluntary assignments and proposals, examining bankrupts, chairing first meetings of creditors, and generally monitoring trustees' performance.

Trustee in Bankruptcy

Creditors in a bankruptcy are usually represented by a trustee, whom the debtor approaches to administer their assets after preliminary selection by the creditors. The trustee is professionally licensed by the Superintendent and assumes control of the debtor's assets once appointed by a court (in the case of a receiving order) or by the Official Receiver (in the case of an assignment). As we saw in Chapter 3, a trustee is someone who has possession of property for the benefit of someone else. In the bankruptcy context, a trustee becomes the beneficial owner of the bankrupt's property. The trustee takes possession of the bankrupt's assets, prepares essential documents in connection with the bankruptcy, reports on the bankrupt's affairs, adjudicates on creditors' proofs of claim, and then liquidates the assets and distributes the proceeds. The trustee is entitled to be paid for that work. Business Decision 22.1 examines some of the trustee's obligations in the context of a modern concern—environmental liability.

the trustee in bankruptcy takes control of the bankrupt person's assets

---

BUSINESS DECISION 22.1

Trustees and Environmental Liability[14]

Trustees assume responsibility for all property of the bankrupt, good or bad. Growing environmental awareness has highlighted the issue of environmental liability in bankruptcy. In particular, what happens if a trustee is saddled with property that is environmentally damaged? Is the trustee responsible for cleanups? Are creditors?

The answers to those questions used to be unclear. However, in 1997, the federal government passed legislation giving a trustee four options. When a court order requires a trustee to remedy any environmental condition, the trustee may: (i) comply with the order, (ii) abandon or dispose of the property to some other party, (iii) contest the order, or (iv) apply for a stay to determine the economic viability of complying with the order. If the property is abandoned and the government is required to undertake work to make the property compliant, the government's expenditure becomes a secured claim against the property.

Questions for Discussion

1. If the trustee decides to comply with the order, should there be any limits on what they are required to spend?

2. The relevant sections of the BIA now provide that the costs of environmental cleanups of a bankrupt's property conducted by the government prevail as a claim even over secured creditors. Who benefits from this shuffling of priorities? The general public? Creditors?

---

14. *BIA* s 14.06(2)-(8).

Bankruptcy Court

The law of bankruptcy was originally created in the courts of equity, which were separate from the courts of common law. Today, while most provinces continue to call a court a "bankruptcy court" when it hears a bankruptcy case, there is no separate system of courts for that purpose. Most bankruptcy courts are staffed by regular judges appointed for their competence in bankruptcy and commercial matters. The judges hear appeals from the registrar, disputed petitions and proposals, applications for discharge from bankruptcy, and certain motions dealing with preferences and priorities.

Registrar in Bankruptcy

The Registrar in Bankruptcy is like a deputy judge, with the power to hear unopposed petitions and proposals, grant discharges, make interim orders in cases of urgency, hear proofs of claim and appeals from decisions of a trustee, and deal with various administrative questions related to the trustee's administration of a bankrupt's estate.

Inspectors

Under the *BIA*, the creditors have the right to appoint a maximum of five inspectors to supervise the trustee in managing the bankrupt's estate. In practice, the inspectors are usually the representatives of the largest creditors, but they undertake their role as fiduciaries for all of the creditors.[15] Their decisions may be reviewed by the Bankruptcy Court if fraud or partiality is shown. Business Decision 22.2 illustrates their duty.

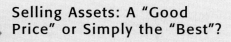

BUSINESS DECISION 22.2

Selling Assets: A "Good Price" or Simply the "Best"?

One of the trustee's duties under the *BIA* is to sell the assets of the bankrupt's estate to obtain proceeds to distribute to creditors. What, if any, obligations must the trustee satisfy in connection with the price that it seeks for those assets?

There are no easy answers. The trustee generally has a duty to maximize the sale proceeds. But the trustee must also defend the integrity of the bankruptcy process and therefore avoid improperly inflated prices. At the same time, individual circumstances such as a thin market, an unusual asset, or heavy carrying charges, may require the trustee to sell for less than the fair market value. Because those considerations may conflict, the courts often defer to the business decisions made by trustees and inspectors.[16]

Question for Discussion

1. How far should trustees have to go to demonstrate that they complied with the obligation to obtain the best price?

THE PROCESS OF BANKRUPTCY

A number of important tactical considerations arise *before* bankruptcy proceedings begin. They are largely informal and do not appear in the *BIA*, but they are critical to the task of risk management. Debtors must choose whether they

---

[15] The concept of fiduciary duties was discussed in Chapter 19. It is essentially a duty of utmost loyalty.

[16] *Re Hoque* (1996) 38 CBR (3d) 133 (NS CA); *Re Rassel* (1999) 177 DLR (4th) 396 (Alta CA).

want to leverage their existing assets to keep operations going or use the threat of assignment to play for time. For instance, a debtor may be so important in the community that financial institutions feel unable to "pull the plug," at least immediately. Likewise, creditors must decide whether to petition immediately or to keep the debtor afloat. Personal relationships and the hope of a turn-around may militate against quick creditor action. The outcome of strategic thinking usually dictates which procedure is used.

As we saw in an earlier section, bankruptcy has two basic requirements: (i) the debtor must owe at least $1000, and (ii) the debtor must have committed an act of bankruptcy—usually a failure to pay debts as they fall due. If those requirements are met, bankruptcy can be triggered in two ways:

- voluntary assignment
- involuntary petition

Assignment

Even before creditors have decided to take court action, the debtor may realize that its financial situation is dire. In such a case, assignment may be appropriate. Assignment is the most commonly used bankruptcy procedure in Canada. The debtor voluntarily assigns its property to a trustee for the benefit of its creditors. In doing so the assignee commits an "act of bankruptcy" under the *BIA*. If the debtor is a corporation, the directors must call a meeting so that the corporation can assign itself into bankruptcy.

In assignment, the debtor completes a preliminary statement of affairs that sets out a list of debts and creditors. After taking possession of the bankrupt's property, the trustee meets with the debtor to prepare a long-form statement of affairs and a notice of a first meeting of creditors. At that meeting, the trustee advises creditors how it intends to liquidate the assets and distribute the proceeds.

Individual debtors can apply for an automatic discharge from bankruptcy within nine months: (i) if there is no creditor opposition, and (ii) if the debtor attends mandatory counselling sessions. If the bankruptcy is the bankrupt's second, or if it is opposed, discharge can take a year or more. Corporate debtors are rarely discharged unless they have repaid all of their debts, which is uncommon.

Petition and Receivership

A petition for a receiving order is less attractive than an assignment. It is the creditors' attempt to force the debtor into bankruptcy. Not surprisingly, the debtor often resists that process. As a result, petitions are often contrary to the spirit of co-operation that should characterize the effort to resolve the debtor's financial difficulties.

A petition normally begins with clear evidence that the debtor is insolvent and can no longer pay their debts. Where one creditor is acting alone, it must prove that it is owed at least $1000 before it can start proceedings. Furthermore, it must prove that the debtor committed an act of bankruptcy within the past six months. As a result, a petitioning creditor often makes a fresh demand for payment to ensure that the evidence in support of the petition is timely. The creditor also needs evidence from other creditors that the debtor has ceased to meet their liabilities "generally," and therefore will *examine* other creditors for that purpose. Because that examination is informal, being outside or prior to a court action, there is no guarantee that the other creditors will co-operate.

Submitting a Petition

a class action is legal action taken by one or several people on behalf of a group that is too large to bring before the court

A petition can be submitted by one debtor acting individually or by several creditors acting together. In either event, once submitted, it becomes a *class action* in the name of all the creditors. A **class action** is legal action taken by one or several people on behalf of a group that is too large to bring before the court. The petition includes an *affidavit*, a voluntary written statement made under oath, that supports the statements made in the petition, as well as a notice that sets the date for hearing of the matter before the registrar or a bankruptcy judge.

An undisputed petition may be heard by the registrar who, after examining the documents, may grant the receiving order if they are satisfied that the requirements of the *BIA* have been met. Disputed petitions are heard by a bankruptcy judge. The main issues before the judge are usually whether the debtor has committed the alleged act of bankruptcy, and whether the debts claimed by petitioning creditors are valid.

After filing the petition, creditors should not contact the debtor's customers for any reason that is related to the debtor's financial condition. Contact can be seen to impair the business reputation of the debtor and may provide grounds for an action in interference by the trustee.[17]

Creditors should also realize that if they start proceedings too quickly, they may be held liable for any losses that the debtor suffers as a result, a situation that is examined in You Be the Judge 22.1.

YOU BE THE JUDGE 22.1

Demanding a "Demand" Loan—Can a Debt Be Called Too Soon?[18]

In today's economy it is common for financing to be fluid. Financial institutions often make "demand loans," which allow them to call the money back at almost any time. Can they actually exercise that right at any time, even if it forces the debtor into bankruptcy?

Joe Murano was a successful entrepreneur in the video store business. In 1989, he bought four video stores with the assistance of a loan from a bank. In March 1991, Murano was in the midst of expansion plans for the venture when the bank demanded immediate repayment of all the loans. In addition, the bank appointed a receiver, who took possession

of the stores two hours after the written demands were delivered. The bank also informed other bankers, lenders, business associates, and suppliers that it was appointing the receiver because of Murano's allegedly dishonest conduct. As a result, Murano lost other business opportunities.

Questions for Discussion

1. Does a "demand loan" imply that a bank may call a loan at virtually any time? What criteria could be used to evaluate such a demand?

2. How much damage should a creditor be responsible for? What if a creditor let other creditors know that the debtor is having trouble, resulting in the debtor suffering further losses, even though the information later turns out to be false? Should a creditor be liable for that behaviour as well?

The Receiving Order

If the petition is unopposed, the registrar reviews the petition and may grant it. Alternately, a judge will decide the petition in contested cases. The receiving order is in a standard form set out in the *BIA* and is often accompanied by a

[17] *Re Velvet Touch Furniture Stripping Ltd* (1980) 34 CBR (NS) 32 (Ont SC).
[18] *Murano v Bank of Montreal* (1995) 31 CBR (3d) 1 (Ont Gen Div).

notice directing the bankrupt, or their representative, to make themselves available to be examined by the trustee.

The receiving order allows the trustee to take control of almost all of the debtor's property. The trustee therefore must: (i) receive the keys, passwords, and operating instruments of the bankrupt, (ii) take possession of assets, (iii) and notify insurers, banks, sheriffs, and landlords about the change in management. The trustee must also tell the Official Receiver which of the bankrupt's officers will answer questions and perform the obligations that are imposed upon the bankrupt by the *BIA*. That officer is usually the person who oversaw the bankrupt party's day-to-day operations before bankruptcy occurred.

The Official Receiver examines or questions the bankrupt's officer about the causes of the bankruptcy, the whereabouts of creditors, and the status of debts. That information is written into a *statement of account*, which the trustee uses to plan and perform the liquidation of the bankrupt's assets.

Distribution of Assets

Once the trustee has taken possession of the bankrupt's property, several issues arise.

Undischarged Debt

Most of the bankrupt's debts are *released* once the bankrupt is discharged. That means that the debtor does not have to pay them. There is, however, a class of debts that are non-dischargeable. These survive bankruptcy in the form of obligations that, for policy reasons, the debtor should not be able to walk away from. Debts in this category include fines, spousal and child support orders, judgments against the debtor for assault and misrepresentation, and student loans made under federal or provincial statutes. Ethical Perspective 22.1 discusses the dischargeability of student loans.

most of the bankrupt's debts are *released* once the bankrupt is discharged

---

ETHICAL PERSPECTIVE 22.1

Discharging Student Loans in Bankruptcy—Think Again[19]

Like cars and computers, loans have become an increasingly common part of student life. Many students need loans to complete their studies. Many also want to know if they can discharge—get rid of—their student loans by going through bankruptcy.

Until October 1997, student loans were fully dischargeable. Soaring student bankruptcy rates, however, forced the federal government to rethink the law. In June 1998, the *BIA* was amended, making student loans *nondischargeable for 10 years* after full- or part-time studies cease. However, the *BIA* provides that a bankrupt can be discharged from such debt if the court is satisfied: (i) that the person acted in good faith, and (ii) that they will continue to experience financial difficulties that will likely prevent repayment.

The current state of the law reflects the fact that while bankruptcy is an opportunity to "clean the slate," it is rarely a cure-all. In many cases, student loans still remain payable. In addition, the bankruptcy normally has a serious effect on a person's credit rating, and it may be some time before they can apply for fresh credit without a guarantor.

Question for Discussion

1. Why should students not be able to discharge their student loans in bankruptcy?

---

19. *Re Minto* (1999) 14 CBR (4th) 235 (Sask QB).

Exempt Property

Generally speaking, all of the bankrupt's assets are available to the creditors. However, individual consumers who become bankrupt are entitled to certain *exemptions* that ensure they do not become destitute. Individuals are allowed to keep:

- tools of the trade up to $2000
- necessary clothing up to $1000
- household furniture and utensils up to $2000
- insurance proceeds
- statutory pension benefits
- damages for pain and suffering

Since both federal and provincial governments have the power to designate exempt property, entitlements vary slightly between jurisdictions.[20] In addition, bankrupts are entitled to keep wages that they earn during bankruptcy, but only to a maximum set by the Official Receiver.[21] Corporate bankrupts are not entitled to exempt property.

Exempt Creditors

Some creditors are partly or entirely exempt from the limits on recovery under the *BIA*. The most important of these are secured creditors, who are entitled to full repayment. The *BIA* allows secured creditors to deal with their security as if the bankruptcy never happened. And if they enforce their security, for example, by seizing a particular asset, they can claim as ordinary unsecured creditors for any *deficiency*.

Suppose that Nancy borrowed $250 000 from Mark and used a dump truck as collateral. Mark therefore had a security interest in that vehicle. Nancy defaulted on the loan and, indeed, went into bankruptcy. Three points are important.

- Mark can enforce his security in one of two ways. As we saw in Chapter 21, he may be entitled to simply seize and retain the dump truck. However, that option may create difficulties. For instance, he may insist that the vehicle is worth only $200 000, leaving a deficiency of $50 000. Nancy's trustee in bankruptcy, in contrast, may claim that the truck is worth $220 000, leaving a deficiency of only $30 000. If the parties cannot eventually agree, the court may order the truck to be sold.[22] Indeed, to avoid such complications, creditors often proceed directly to a sale of the collateral.[23]

- Whether or not the truck is sold, Mark is entitled to register a proof of claim as an ordinary unsecured creditor for the deficiency. While he is entitled to the full value of his security, he will not fully recover the deficiency. Nancy clearly has too many debts and too little money, and Mark

---

[20] *BIA* s 67(1)(b).

[21] The amount is calculated by a formula. In general, a family of four receiving a monthly income of $3000 would be required to contribute $50 to $75 monthly to the trustee for distribution to creditors. Those payments stop when the bankrupt is discharged: <strategis.ic.gc.ca/SSG/br01055e.html>.

[22] *BIA* ss 127-35.

[23] Mark might also proceed directly to sale simply because he does not have any need for a dump truck.

will have to share her inadequate assets with her other creditors. Generally, he will have taken this risk into account before extending the loan to her in the terms of the security agreement and the interest rate he charges on the debt.

- Mark cannot, in any event, recover *more than* the value of Nancy's debt to him. If, for instance, she owed $250 000, but the truck was sold for $275 000, he would have to pay the extra $25 000 to her trustee in bankruptcy.

In situations involving a *proposal*, landlords can also become exempt creditors. Insolvency often triggers the breach of a lease, and the landlord therefore becomes a significant creditor of the tenant. Under normal contractual rules, the landlord may be entitled to claim the value of the full rent until the end of the lease if no other tenant can be found. To assist in making proposals viable, the *BIA* modifies that rule by offering two options to an insolvent *commercial* tenant.

landlords can become exempt creditors when a proposal is made

- The first option allows the insolvent tenant to pay the landlord for its actual loss.

- The second option allows the insolvent tenant to pay the landlord the lesser of: (i) three years' rent, or (ii) 100 percent of the rent that would have been paid in the first year after the lease was prematurely terminated, plus 15 percent of the rent for the remainder of the term.

Those rules recognize that rental markets are often flexible and that landlords with insolvent tenants might try to "double-dip" when substitute tenants are otherwise available.[24]

Settlements and Preferences

The period leading up to bankruptcy can be hotly contested. Debtors and creditors may both be tempted to engage in questionable behaviour. Debtors may try to shift assets to related companies, friends, or relatives in the hope that these can somehow escape distribution. Such transfers are known as **settlements** if they are made for free or for nominal payment. Likewise debtors may attempt to **prefer**, or favour, some creditors over others by paying certain debts in advance of assignment or petition.

a settlement is the transfer of property that is made for free or for nominal consideration

Those kinds of leakage both impair the equality of creditors and decrease the assets available for distribution. Courts therefore developed rules for settlements and preferences that allowed creditors to void improper action by debtors and allowed trustees in bankruptcy to reclaim assets. Those historical doctrines are now contained in the *BIA*.

to prefer a creditor means to satisfy their claims in a larger amount than is permissible under bankruptcy law

- Any settlement made within a one-year period before bankruptcy is void.[25]

- A transfer made to a creditor 90 days before bankruptcy is void if the aim of the transfer was to prefer that creditor over others.[26]

- In the case of a non-arm's-length transaction between related parties, such as a husband and wife or affiliated companies, the avoidance period is one year.[27]

[24.] *BIA* s 65.2.

[25.] *BIA* s 91(1).

[26.] *BIA* s 95(1).

[27.] *BIA* s 96.

Director Liability

When a limited company goes bankrupt and does not have enough money to pay its creditors, its directors are usually not liable for the deficiency. However, a bankrupt company's directors may be liable if they have given personal guarantees for the company's debts or if a statute imposes liability upon them. For instance, the Ontario *Business Corporations Act* imposes liability on the directors of a corporation for:

- debts for services performed for the corporation in an amount equivalent to a maximum of six months' wages
- vacation pay of up to 12 months, as set out under the Ontario *Employment Standards Act*
- debts of the first two kinds accruing under any collective agreement with a union[28]

To cover such liability, most directors today maintain insurance.

PROPOSALS

a **proposal** is a court-approved contract between a debtor and creditors that gives the debtor time to adjust its financial affairs while business operations continue

A **proposal** is a court-approved contract between a debtor and creditors that gives the debtor time to adjust its financial affairs while business operations continue. The following are some of the most important kinds of proposals.

- A *composition* is an agreement between a debtor and its creditors whereby the creditors agree to accept, in satisfaction of their claims, less than the amount that is owing to them.
- An *extension of time* prolongs the time available for repayment. That may happen alone or together with a composition.
- A *scheme of arrangement* is a situation where the debtor's assets are vested in, or controlled by, a trustee for the benefit of creditors while the proposal is being performed.
- Under a *liquidation proposal*, the debtor agrees to sell assets and distribute the proceeds. The benefit of that procedure is that the debtor *itself* can assist in the recovery of receivables, such as payments from its *own* debtors. Under a normal bankruptcy, that job is performed by the trustee.
- A *share exchange* occurs when the debtor offers to exchange shares in a company for outstanding debt. That procedure is sometimes called a "debt-equity swap."

The first possibility may seem strange. Why would a creditor ever accept less than the full value of a debt? The answer is that the alternatives may be even less attractive. If a creditor enforces its rights to the letter, it will have to spend much time and expense in litigation. Even more important, that creditor will scare away customers—some good, some bad. You will probably be able to repay your loans. But in deciding which bank to borrow from, you will be influenced by reputation. If anything goes wrong, you would rather be dealing with Bank A, which has a reputation for fairness and flexibility, than Bank B, which has a reputation for squeezing debtors as hard as possible.

[28.] For the directors to be held liable under the statute, the employee must sue them while they are directors or within six months of their resignation. In the case of a debt, directors may be held liable for six months after the debt is incurred.

A proposal is, in some sense, an attempt to give the debtor another chance. Normally, the hope is that the debtor, by continuing to operate, will at least be able to pay off its immediate debts. The real benefit is time. By temporarily removing the pressure of repayment, the debtor may be able to return to profitability in future.

Form and Requirements

A proposal can be made by a bankrupt, an insolvent person, a liquidator or receiver, or a trustee in bankruptcy. Usually, the debtor drafts a plan that takes into account general business conditions and the wishes of its creditors.[29] The debtor has a strong incentive to be realistic, given that a proposal is less likely than either an assignment or a receiving order to impair its credit rating or attract the stigma of bankruptcy. Creditors may also be encouraged to participate since the proposal will be externally verified both: (i) by a trustee, who provides an independent opinion on a draft, and (ii) by creditors, many of whom will later vote on it.

The proposal itself is made to creditors who are categorized in classes according to their common interests. There may be, for example, a class of unsecured creditors with claims under $1000 and another with claims above that amount. The *BIA* is formally silent as to how classes are to be defined with respect to preferred and unsecured creditors. However, if the proposed classification is unfair, creditors will likely object, and the matter may be brought to court. Indeed, the debtor has the option of applying directly to the court for a determination of the appropriate classes.

The *BIA* does *not* require secured creditors to be dealt with under a proposal. The debtor may deal with them separately, as long as the debts owed to those creditors are *fully satisfied*. However, when secured creditors are included in a proposal, they must be placed in the same class if they are secured against the same assets. Again, it is possible for the debtor to apply to court for a determination as to the appropriate class or classes of secured creditor.

Besides dividing creditors into classes, proposals must meet other requirements. If secured creditors have given notice that they intend to enforce their securities, the proposal should provide that their claims are paid according to the terms of the security. In addition, the proposal must ensure that the ranking of creditors is respected. Thus, secured creditors must recover fully before preferred creditors, and preferred creditors must recover fully before general unsecured creditors.

Preparation and Voting

A debtor often does not file a proposal immediately. Rather, it files a notice of intent with the Official Registrar to provide a proposal and then consults with its creditors. Depending upon the outcome of those consultations, it may then file a formal proposal with the Official Registrar at a later date. It generally must do so within 30 days, but the Bankruptcy Court can extend that time by periods of 45 days. The court cannot, however, grant more than five months of extensions on the original 30-day period.

Once the proposal is submitted, it must be considered by a meeting of creditors within 21 days. The trustee then calls a meeting of creditors to consider

---

[29.] Before the court approves a proposal, it must be satisfied that the terms are reasonable. Therefore, the proposal should have a reasonable chance of success: *Re McNamara and McNamara* (1984) 53 CBR (NS) 240 (Ont SC).

and vote on the proposal. The court may, at any time before the first meeting of creditors, declare that the proposal has been refused by the creditors if it is satisfied that the debtor is not acting in good faith or that there is little real chance that the proposal will be accepted.[30]

For the proposal to be formally approved, it must receive the support of at least half the creditors in each class, who hold at least two-thirds of the face value of the debtor's assets in that class. Once the proposal is approved, it binds all creditors that are covered by its terms, including those who may have voted against it. A court must then approve the proposal within 15 days.

If the creditors do not vote in favour of the proposal, the debtor is automatically deemed to be bankrupt. The Official Receiver steps forward and conducts the first meeting of creditors. Alternately, it is possible for the trustee to use *voting letters* deposited by creditors and vote in favour of the proposal, or to call a second meeting to consider a revised or reformulated plan. **Voting letters** are letters that creditors use to vote on a proposal even though they did not attend the meeting.

voting letters are letters that creditors use to vote on a proposal even though they did not attend the meeting

OTHER STATUTES DEALING WITH FINANCIAL DISTRESS AND FAILURE

The *BIA* is not the only statute that deals with financial distress and failure. There are some provincial statutes that regulate general debtor-creditor relations, such as fraudulent conveyances, business corporations, and personal property security acts. Some may provide more favourable options for debtors or creditors than an assignment, receivership, or proposal under the *BIA*. In the relevant circumstances, they should be carefully considered.[31]

One important alternative is the *Companies' Creditors Arrangement Act* (*CCRA*), which applies to corporations that have issued *debentures* in series. **Debentures** are promissory notes or bonds backed by the general credit of a corporation. They are usually not secured by any specific property. An insolvent company that meets the requirements can apply to a court for protection while assembling a plan of reorganization—but only if its total outstanding debts exceed $5 000 000.

debentures are promissory notes or bonds backed by the general credit of a corporation

The benefit of applying under the *CCRA* is that action by *all* creditors, including secured creditors, is stayed. That is a significant advantage over the *BIA*, and most major companies in Canada have issued debentures in series or deeds of trust to take advantage of the option.

Unfortunately, the relationship between the *BIA* and the *CCRA* is somewhat unclear. It appears that an insolvent corporate debtor with debentures can take advantage of protection under either Act, or possibly both.

The *Winding-Up Act* (*WUA*) applies to the default of federally incorporated companies, banks, and insurance companies, as well as some insolvent provincial companies. Its application is mandatory for banks and insurance companies, but it is an alternative to *BIA* procedures for all other entities. The *WUA* differs substantially from the *BIA* in both substance and technique. Under the

---

[30.] *BIA* s 50(12).

[31.] For example, many provincial statutes allow a creditor to claim priority for both a debt *and* the costs associated with recovering that money through execution proceedings by the sheriff. Creditors in bankruptcy are governed by *BIA*-set priorities and normally recoup only a small percentage of their court costs: see *Royal Bank v R* (1981) 40 CBR (NS) 27 (Ont Div Ct).

WUA, for instance, proceedings may be commenced if the debtor is merely insolvent, whereas the *BIA* requires a bankruptcy. If proceedings have been commenced under the *BIA*, they preclude application of the *WUA*. Due to its limited application, the *WUA* has been rarely used in recent years.

BUSINESS LAW IN ACTION 22.1

International Bankruptcy[32]

As business becomes more global, the courts often have to address the situation in which a bankrupt person has assets in several countries. In such situations all of the problems that the *BIA* was intended to preclude—dispersed assets, multiple proceedings, and creditor inequality—reappear. No consolidation of claims takes place, and the scramble for assets occurs in different countries at the same time, with predictably mixed results.

There has been little progress toward an international agreement on bankruptcy co-operation. While some people would like to see a form of international bankruptcy in which a bankrupt's assets are pooled worldwide and distributed on an equal basis to all creditors, others assert that differing priorities in bankruptcy across countries reflect national policy preferences and that a uniform global system is improbable. Apart from an international bankruptcy convention between Nordic countries and repeated, but failed, attempts to con-clude a similar treaty in the European Union, truly international bankruptcy proceedings appear some way off.

Canada is not signatory to any international bankruptcy treaty. In 1997, the government amended the *BIA* to encourage Canadian courts to co-operate with their counterparts in foreign bankruptcy proceedings, and to allow foreign representatives to commence proceedings in Canada. The amendments also recognize that Canadian trustees and courts may look to foreign courts for help in Canadian bankruptcy actions.[33] The Canadian Bar Association has undertaken a study with its counterpart organizations in the United States and Mexico in an attempt to harmonize bankruptcy laws in the three NAFTA countries. That may lead to greater bankruptcy co-operation in North America.

Question for Discussion

1. Why would it be a good idea to have an "international" bankruptcy system? What problems would it avoid?

---

32. *Re Kaussen* (1988) 67 CBR (NS) 81 (Que CA).

33. Under Part XIII of the *BIA*, the Act recognizes foreign bankruptcy representatives and allows a foreign representative, such as a trustee, to stay or commence proceedings in Canada. Canadian courts are also empowered to issue orders facilitating foreign proposals and arrangements.

Chapter Summary

A key aspect of risk management is planning for the possibility of business failure. In Canada, bankruptcy law is designed to provide several means for resolving business failure and gives debtors and creditors options to choose from. In this respect, it is an important tool in risk management.

The main Canadian statute relating to bankruptcy and insolvency is the *Bankruptcy and Insolvency Act (BIA)*. It provides two principal procedures in bankruptcy: assignment or petition. An assignment is a voluntary act by the debtor placing itself in bankruptcy. A petition is a request by creditors to the court to place the debtor in bankruptcy. In both cases, the value of formal bankruptcy status is to provide a stay of action and a limit on recovery against the debtor. In exchange, creditors are paid in priority to the extent that the debtor's existing assets permit.

The *BIA* also provides for a third procedure outside bankruptcy in the form of a proposal. A proposal involves an understanding between the debtor and creditors in which the parties agree to compromise or rearrange debts. A proposal must be approved by at least half of the creditors in each class, comprising at least two-thirds of the value of the assets represented by that class. A proposal offers significant advantages to a debtor, given that a proposal is less likely than either assignment or a receiving order to impair its credit rating or stigmatize it as a bankrupt.

Each procedure has its own advantages. The ultimate choice of procedure is dictated by the appreciation of risk, including prospects for the debtor, the relationship between the parties, and general economic conditions. In some situations, common sense calls for an assignment, rather than the drawn-out struggle of a petition. In others, the debtor may be wiser to recognize financial reality and make a proposal or agree to a petition. Creditors should be careful about acting too quickly, as Canadian courts have found creditors liable for rash behaviour that destroys a debtor's business.

Canadian law relating to bankruptcy and insolvency attempts to strike a balance between the orderly repayment of debts, the rehabilitation of debtors, and economic growth. It is a realistic response to an unfortunate event.

Review Questions

1. What is meant by the terms "insolvency" and "bankruptcy"? How do they differ?

2. What is an act of bankruptcy? How is it related to insolvency?

3. What are the purposes of bankruptcy law? How does bankruptcy help the debtor? Creditors? Society?

4. How does bankruptcy differ from an individual debtor-creditor action? What problems in the common law did the development of bankruptcy overcome?

5. How does the law differ between commercial and consumer bankruptcies? Is the recent rise in the rate of consumer bankruptcy in Canada a good thing? Why?

6. Explain who is responsible for bankruptcy legislation in Canada, and why.

7. Distinguish between an assignment in bankruptcy and a petition. What are some of the advantages of an assignment? What is the priority between assignment and petition?

8. What are some of the advantages of a proposal? What majority is necessary for approval of a proposal? Who approves it?

9. Describe several important types of proposal? On what does the type or timing ultimately depend?

10. Against whom does the "stay" operate in bankruptcy? What does it stay?

11. Explain the distinction between a secured and an unsecured creditor. What is the relationship between categories of creditor and the market for credit?

12. What is a proof of claim? Why is it necessary, and who submits it? What happens if it is not submitted?

13. Describe the role of the trustee. Who does the trustee represent? Who regulates the trustee?

14. What is a discharge from bankruptcy? What debts are nondischargeable? Why?

15. What is "exempt property" under the *BIA*, and what is its purpose? Who is responsible for defining what property is permissibly exempt under the law?

16. Explain the concept of a reviewable transaction. How long a period may be reviewed? Is the interval of review a period pre-bankruptcy or post-bankruptcy?

17. Can student loans accrued as a result of a federal or provincial education loan program be discharged in bankruptcy? Why?

18. What are two aspects of the doctrine of creditor equality?

19. Who can take advantage of an arrangement under the *CCRA*? Explain why action under the *CCRA* is occasionally preferred to action under the *BIA*? How do the two statutes interact?

20. What problems present themselves when an entity with assets in Canada and abroad goes bankrupt? Why have efforts to provide for an international bankruptcy regime not progressed very far?

Cases and Problems

1. Elaine runs the Five Brothers restaurant in Niagara Falls. She has given the bank a general security interest on the property in exchange for a loan of $200 000. The restaurant is not successful and, due to a recent decline in tourism, has a fair market value of only $150 000. If Elaine decides to seek an assignment, what can the bank do to recoup its loan?

2. Bengt Norsson lives in Calgary. He works as a carpenter and drives into work at various sites everyday. Unfortunately, he does not really like his job and gambles on the side. Bengt lost thousands of dollars recently and is contemplating an assignment in bankruptcy. One of his principal concerns is whether an assignment would require him to give up his tools of the trade, without which he cannot work. Would he be able to keep them?

3. Ernie goes into bankruptcy, taking with him the dot-com online software company that he built from scratch. A trustee is appointed and starts running the business. He employs Ernie on a contingency basis to help an accountant prepare the business's income tax returns. Before discharge, Ernie also provides other services to ensure that the business continues to operate, with the happy result that it is sold for a higher amount than it would be otherwise. Ernie wants to know if he can claim wages from the trustee or if his efforts simply become part of the bankrupt's estate?

4. Belinda and Joe previously lived together. After a disagreement, Belinda and her daughter, Marianna, moved out 18 months ago. She had received an alimony order from a British Columbia court against Joe, who is required to pay $1200 a month to her for support. Joe sends cheques for seven months and then stops making payments. When Belinda calls, Joe tells her that he is "between a rock and a hard place." Can Belinda petition Joe into bankruptcy?

5. Tom Telleman sells piping and plumbing hardware from his home in Charlottetown. He sold 100 metres of piping worth $750 to a greenhouse in Summerside called Islandgrow. Once installed, the piping leaked badly and caused $28 000 worth of damage to Islandgrow's greenhouses. Islandgrow decides to sue Telleman for the return of the purchase price of the piping and damages. Telleman is known to have many creditors, including pipe suppliers, hardware manufacturers, and small lenders. Islandgrow's lawyer believes that Telleman has insufficient assets to pay any judgment against him. However, he has yet to take the case to court, and so the amount of recovery from any court case is unsettled. Could Islandgrow petition Telleman into bankruptcy?

6. Maria owes Karen $50 000. She has failed to repay that money for some time and has always been very secretive. As a result, Karen has difficulty locating Maria's creditors and begins to wonder if she alone can petition Maria into bankruptcy? After all, she remembers something about the need for evidence from multiple creditors to petition. Could Karen petition Maria into bankruptcy?

7. NorthStar is a pharmaceutical company in Montreal. It specializes in fertility drugs and HIV resistance products. Due to the heavy demand for its products, it seeks to expand production. To finance the expansion NorthStar takes out a loan from Bank X, which is secured against a building and new pieces of equipment it purchases with the loan. Shortly thereafter, however, NorthStar stumbles when competitors introduce a number of new drugs that eat into its most lucrative markets. As a result, the company is forced to assign itself in bankruptcy. Bank X then seeks to realize on its security. It claims the building and equipment and now wants to know whether it can operate them itself.

8. Tony has owned a hardware store on the west island of Montreal for the last 15 years. Business has been only so-so, and in an effort to generate publicity, he decides to give hardware kits worth $200 each to five local charities, which plan to use them as raffle prizes at various events in the coming year. A month later, Tony realizes that the business is no good and decides to make a voluntary assignment. Can the trustee seek a return of the hardware kits? What about a new colour television that Tony gave to his wife as a present for her birthday the year before?

9. Janetti Inc, a Montreal sweater manufacturer, concludes a security agreement with Bank X in which it gives the bank a general security over all of Janetti's accounts receivable. This is in exchange for a loan of $1 million. Janetti then files for bankruptcy, and the bank gives notice that it seeks to realize on its security. Bank X recovers only $300 000 from the accounts and wants to know if it can claim the balance of its loan in some way? What if, instead, it was able to recover $1.2 million?

10. Maria and Tony run a small restaurant in Charlottetown that serves specialties from their home region of Catania, Italy. They operate without the benefit of a corporate form because it is cheaper. They do everything they can, but the restaurant business is competitive in Charlottetown. In a few months they find themselves in the unenviable position of having to seek an assignment in bankruptcy for the very first time in their lives. The restaurant premises are taken from them, their meager bank deposits placed under the control of the trustee, and they are officially declared bankrupt. Maria and Tony come to you wondering what bankruptcy means for them and how long it will be before they can be discharged. What factors do you think a Bankruptcy Court would look at in deciding whether to grant a discharge?

11. Sunita used to run a convenience store in Burnaby but was petitioned into bankruptcy several months ago by her creditors. This was Sunita's second bankruptcy, and the period she is spending in bankruptcy is consequently lengthened. Never one to give up, she begins selling registered educational savings plans from home before discharge. Sunita borrows money from her brother and buys an expensive new computer to keep track of the transac-

tions. Subsequently, she is discharged, but the computer company comes after her, wanting payment. Sunita asserts that she has been discharged and owes nothing to anyone. Could the computer company commence action against her for the debt? Could the company have come after her *before* the discharge?

12. Joseph Inc, a retail fashion chain, contemplates making a proposal to its creditors. It is thinking about making the proposal to both secured and unsecured creditors in the form of an arrangement or debt-equity swap. Is it required to include secured creditors in its proposal?

WWWeblinks

Secured Transactions

Nova Scotia Personal Property Registry

www.gov.ns.ca/snsmr/property/ppsa.stm

This site is representative of the Web-based registers maintained by most provincial and territorial governments under their PPS legislation. Most permit secured parties to register their security interests online and search for registrations against a particular debtor, and provide general information about the PPS legislation in that province.

PPSA.Net

www.ppsa.net/body.htm

This Web site provides links to the text of all PPS legislation in each Canadian jurisdiction.

Uniform Law Conference

www.law.ualberta.ca/alri/ulc/priority/ecomlaw.htm#I.%20%20%20
COMMERCIAL%20LAW

This useful site discusses provincial PPS law in a broad commercial law context.

National Law Center for Inter-American Trade

www.natlaw.com/pubs/overview.htm

This site provides an excellent overview of the PPS system in Canada by a leading academic, Ron Cuming, who also comments on the effectiveness of the system.

Personal Property Security in Canada

www.duhaime.org/ca-ppsa.htm

This page provides a good general overview of PPS law in Canada, including Quebec. It provides a more detailed discussion of the rules in British Columbia.

Bankruptcy and Insolvency

Office of the Superintendent of Bankruptcy Canada

strategis.ic.gc.ca/sc_mrksv/bankrupt/engdoc/superint.html

This site contains a range of information, including an insolvency name search, statistics on bankruptcy, acts and regulations, a directory of trustees in bankruptcy, and credit counselling advice.

BankruptcyCanada.com

www.bankruptcycanada.com

This site is aimed at consumers who are contemplating assignment, the possibility of a petition, or a proposal to creditors under Canadian law. It features information on financial self-assessment, credit reporting, and finding a trustee.

Canadian Bankruptcy Law Centre

www.duhaime.org/bankr.htm

This site contains a list of Canadian bankruptcy and insolvency law articles on aspects of financial distress and failure, and links to other useful bankruptcy law sites.

Canada's Credit Doctor

www.thecreditdoctor.com/index.htm

This site is dedicated to helping people understand credit and how it affects their everyday lives, the work of credit-reporting agencies, and ways in which consumers can achieve and maintain a healthy credit rating.

Public Legal Education Association of Saskatchewan

www.plea.org/freepubs/freepubs.htm

This site has information about Canadian law and the law of Saskatchewan relating to debtor and creditor rights. It also has a useful section on farm financial difficulties.

Money*Problems*.ca

www.moneyproblems.ca

This private service is dedicated to helping Canadians avoid bankruptcy, repair their credit, get loans, and plan for the future. It provides information on credit-card debt, credit-counselling services, and tax problems.

Legal.com Bankruptcy Page

www.legal.com/bankruptcy

This site contains information on consumer bankruptcies in Canada and the US.

KPMG Personal Bankruptcy

www.personalbankruptcy.com

This site contains information on personal bankruptcy in Canada, including a question-and-answer section and a bankruptcy forum.

Financial Services Canada

www.financeca.about.com/cs/bankruptcy

This site gives suggestions and ideas on how to stay out of debt, both personally and in business, and contains articles on what to do to rebuild credit after bankruptcy.

23 Government Regulation of Business

CHAPTER OVERVIEW

OBJECTIVES

After completing this chapter, you should be able to:

1. Explain the importance to business regulation of the federal trade and commerce power and provincial power over property and civil rights.
2. Describe the relevance of the Canadian *Charter of Rights and Freedoms* for business in Canada.
3. Identify the jurisdiction and relevance of the Federal Court of Canada.
4. Describe why competition is important in the Canadian economy.
5. Explain the distinction between conspiracies, mergers, and abuse of dominant position under the *Competition Act*.
6. Define a restrictive business transaction, and give two examples.
7. Explain the difference between a reviewable matter and a criminal matter under the *Competition Act*.
8. Explain the role of the Agreement on Internal Trade.
9. Explain the legal framework for environmental regulation in Canada.
10. Identify one method for a person to commence action against anti-competitive conduct or environmental pollution in Canada.

Canada's federal and provincial governments are important regulators of business. They regulate when policy objectives or operating conditions make it necessary to do so. Their power is not, however, unlimited. In regulating business, they must respect the constitutional division of powers, basic considerations of fairness, and market requirements. Their success is vital to making Canada an attractive place to invest and work.

In this chapter, we examine government's regulation of business. Understanding how and what governments regulate is essential to properly managing business risks. Note that Canada's limited domestic market and harsh climate have traditionally made it necessary for governments to regulate business. These requirements have promoted a positive view of government, something very different from the view of government taken in the United States. While government is less of an active participant in the Canadian economy today than it was in the past, it remains a significant facilitator of business behaviour.

Note too that business can be done only through certain activities that are, strictly speaking, harmful if done in an unrestricted way. In other words, there must be *some* competitive conduct or *some* pollution permissible, or else business would grind to a halt. This trade-off dictates the adoption of a regulatory model of behaviour that allows certain activities to occur, and that adopts a more flexible approach to violations than is seen, for instance, in criminal law.

BUSINESS REGULATION

As we saw in Chapter 1, Canada's Constitution assigns responsibility over specific subjects of regulation, or "heads of power," to the federal and provincial governments. In the business context, for instance, the federal government is responsible for banking, currency and coinage, bankruptcy and insolvency, interprovincial transport, and trade and commerce. The provinces are responsible for property and civil rights, "local works and undertakings," and "all matters of a merely local or private nature in the province."

The original division of powers was created at the time of Confederation in 1867 and reflects the distribution thought appropriate then. It has since been amended to take into account new subjects that were not in existence at Canada's founding and to clarify the original partition in light of contemporary conditions.

The most important federal power related to business regulation is the express federal power over "trade and commerce." This power is exceptionally broad and potentially conflicts with the provincial power concerning "property and civil rights."[1] Most "trade and commerce" is carried out by contracts, which lie at the heart of "property and civil rights." It therefore has been necessary for courts to define the boundary between the federal and provincial powers.

the Canadian Constitution includes a division of powers between the federal and provincial governments

---

[1.] The Canadian term "trade and commerce" may seem broader than its American counterpart under the US Constitution, the Commerce Clause, which provides that the US federal government shall have the power "to regulate commerce with foreign nations, and among the several States, and with the Indian tribes." Professor Hogg notes that despite the broader Canadian language, however, the Canadian "trade and commerce" clause has been interpreted more narrowly than the Commerce Clause. As a result, the American Congress has more extensive powers than the Canadian Parliament over a wide range of business behaviour including competition law (antitrust), insurance, labour, marketing, securities, transportation, and communication: P Hogg *Constitutional Law of Canada* (1997) at 20-1.

The leading authority on the division of powers is *Citizens Insurance Co v Parsons*.[2] In that case, the court examined the validity of an Ontario law that required certain conditions to be included in all fire insurance contracts written in that province. The insurance company argued that the Ontario law was an intrusion into the federal government's domain of regulation. In rejecting that argument, the court held that the Ontario statute was a valid exercise of provincial power in relation to property and civil rights. The law did not infringe trade and commerce because that power did not encompass "the power to regulate by legislation the contracts of a particular business or trade, such as the business of fire insurance in a single province." Instead, the court said that the federal power extends to business activities of an inter-provincial nature, including the "general regulation of trade affecting the whole dominion."

Later cases upheld *Citizens Insurance*, and it is now generally accepted that provincial governments have the power to regulate business dealings of a purely local nature. Over time, however, the statements in *Citizens Insurance* about the extent of federal regulation over business activity have become important. In some cases, the federal power over trade and commerce has been held to support transactions that are completed *entirely* within a province, such as the local sale of domestically grown wheat or the marketing of farm products.[3] In other cases, it has not.[4] Nevertheless, the courts have clearly said that federal power can be exercised where there is a need for broad national standards, such as in trademarks or rules regulating competition.[5]

In comparison, provincial power over property and civil rights is local and specific. It involves the regulation of discrete business activities, including insurance, the professions and trades, labour relations, marketing, securities, property, debt adjustment, and consumer protection. Thus, provincial power has been held to validly regulate land ownership and the sale of goods. Given the frequency of such transactions, the provincial jurisdiction over property and civil rights is more often involved in daily business relations than federal jurisdiction and is an important consideration in assessing risk.[6]

Concurrency and Paramountcy

concurrency refers to the idea of shared powers between levels of government

In addition to subjects of exclusive federal and provincial jurisdiction, the drafters of Canada's Constitution recognized shared, or **concurrent**, powers in relation to such matters as labour, business organization, and the environment. Here, the exact division of jurisdiction was not clear and has only been partly resolved through subsequent negotiations and amendment of legislation.[7]

[2.] *Citizens Insurance Co v Parsons* (1881) 7 App Cas 96 (PC).

[3.] *R v Klassen* (1959) 20 DLR (2d) 406 (Man CA); *Re Agricultural Products Marketing Act*, (1978) 84 DLR (3d) 257 (SCC).

[4.] *Dominion Stores v The Queen* (1980) 106 DLR (3d) 581 (SCC); *Labatt Breweries v AG Canada* (1980) 52 CCC (2d) 433 (SCC).

[5.] *General Motors v City National Leasing* (1989) 58 DLR (4th) 255 (SCC).

[6.] P Hogg *Constitutional Law* (1997) at 21-4.

[7.] Three provisions expressly provide concurrent power. Section 92A(2) of the Constitution, added in 1982, gives provincial legislatures the power to make laws in relation to the export of natural resources. Section 94A, added in 1951 and amended in 1964, gives the federal government the power to regulate old-age pensions and other associated benefits. Section 95 gives concurrent power over agriculture and immigration to both levels of government. Concurrency can also arise from the way in which the courts interpret the Constitution. The judicial doctrine of "double aspect" provides that many powers fall under both heads of power. For instance, a law concerning drunk driving has a criminal (federal) and a highway safety (provincial) aspect. And the "pith and substance" doctrine states that where a power is exercised under one head of power, it is valid, even though it may incidentally regulate some matter within the other list. See P Hogg *Constitutional Law* (1997) at 40-1.

Concurrent jurisdiction remains a source of some tension and evolution in federal-provincial affairs.

The breadth of both federal and provincial power in relation to business raises the possibility of conflict. Where no other interpretation is possible, the courts must decide which government's legislation will prevail. In most instances, the doctrine of **paramountcy**, which is based on the Constitution's division of powers, determines which law is pre-eminent. However, the fact that many business activities have an overlapping federal and provincial aspect means that there is often a need for federal-provincial co-ordination. Examples include securities and highway regulation. Case Brief 23.1 illustrates this doctrine.

the doctrine of **paramountcy** determines which law is pre-eminent based on the Constitution's division of powers

---

CASE BRIEF 23.1

Bank of Montreal v Hall (1990) 65 DLR (4th) 361 (SCC)

The constitutional principle of paramountcy establishes which law prevails in the event of inconsistency between federal and provincial legislation. In *Bank of Montreal v Hall*, the issue was whether a procedure under the federal *Bank Act* for mortgage foreclosure overrode a provincial *Limitation of Civil Rights Act*. The Ontario statute required a creditor, as a prelude to any foreclosure proceeding, to notify the debtor that there was one last chance to repay the debt. The federal statute did not require such notice. The bank followed federal law, failed to serve the notice, and later found itself facing an argument that its foreclosure was invalid under provincial law.

The Supreme Court held that the bank was not required to comply with provincial law because the Ontario statute was inconsistent with federal legislation. In that situation, the conflict between federal and provincial law was direct. In other words, it would be impossible to comply with one set of laws without violating the other. The court observed that "there could be no clearer instance of a case where compliance with the federal statute necessarily entails defiance of its provincial counterpart."

THE CANADIAN *CHARTER OF RIGHTS AND FREEDOMS*

As we saw in Chapter 1, the *Charter of Rights and Freedoms* was added to Canada's Constitution in 1982 to protect fundamental democratic values. Those include the right to free speech, assembly, security of the person, and non-discrimination. Note that the *Charter* generally applies to both natural and legal persons—individuals and corporate entities—to different degrees.

- The *Charter* does not protect private property.[8] That deliberate choice of the drafters reflects Canada's social democratic tradition. It stands in sharp contrast to the US Constitution, whose Fifth Amendment provides that "no person shall be deprived of life, liberty, *or property*, without due process of law."

- As we saw in Chapter 1, some *Charter* provisions apply to "everyone" or "every individual." Those provisions are limited to natural persons (human beings) and are generally not considered to extend to legal persons (such as corporations). For instance, s 15(1) of the *Charter* prohibits discrimination against individuals on certain grounds. Because a corporation is not, strictly speaking, an "individual," and because it has no

---

[8.] *Home Orderly Services Ltd v Government of Manitoba* (1981) 32 DLR (4th) 755 (Man QB).

race, national or ethnic origin, nor any colour, religion, sex, age, mental or physical disability, it does not enjoy protection under s 15(1).[9]

- Some *Charter* provisions provide less protection to businesses than to individuals. For instance, advertising enjoys protection under s 2(b) as freedom of expression, but to a lesser extent than expression for a purely political, religious, or social purposes. Likewise, businesses enjoy protection under s 8 against unreasonable search and seizure. In practice, however, they may enjoy less privacy than natural persons because of the distinction that is drawn between searches in the criminal and quasi-criminal context.[10]

the Charter sometimes applies in favour of business

THE FEDERAL COURT SYSTEM

In Chapter 1, we discussed the Canadian court system. One court that we briefly considered was the Federal Court of Canada. In the context of government regulation of business, that particular court plays a major role.

The Federal Court cannot hear a case unless three requirements are met.

the Federal Court cannot hear a case unless certain requirements are met

- First, the Federal Court must have jurisdiction to hear the matter by virtue of the *Federal Court Act* or some other statute. The *Federal Court Act* refers to claims against the federal government, administrative remedies against federal agencies and tribunals, applications for judicial review, intellectual property, citizenship and immigration, maritime law, bills of exchange and promissory notes, and certain other matters. An example of a statute providing jurisdiction is the *Immigration Act*, which gives the Federal Court the exclusive competence to hear appeals of immigration rulings.

- Second, the Federal Court cannot hear a case unless it involves an issue that falls within the federal government's jurisdiction. For instance, a claim for damages arising out of a contract to build a marine terminal falls presumptively within the federal government's power to regulate shipping under the Constitution.

- Third, the resolution of a case must *also* be based on an existing body of federal law. Consequently, the Federal Court did *not* have jurisdiction in the previous example because the claim for damages was simply a contractual matter that fell under provincial government's power to regulate "property and civil rights."[11] The situation could have been different, however, if the dispute had concerned the operation of the terminal or

---

9. *Milk Board v Clearview Dairy Farm Inc* (1987) 33 DLR (4th) 158 (BC CA).

10. Corporations are more likely to be charged with regulatory offences than criminal offences. Criminal matters require proof "beyond a reasonable doubt." The standard of proof is somewhat lower in the administrative or regulatory context. For instance, the Supreme Court has held that searches and seizures conducted by the Canada Customs and Revenue Agency under the *Income Tax Act* to ensure the integrity of the tax system are permissible whether or not an inspector has reasonable grounds for believing that a particular taxpayer has breached the Act: *R v McKinlay Transport Ltd* (1990) 68 DLR (4th) 568 (SCC); *British Columbia (Securities Commission) v Branch* (1995) 123 DLR (4th) 462 (SCC).

11. *Quebec North Shore Paper Co v CP Ltd* (1977) 71 DLR (3d) 111 (SCC).

its employees' hours of work. Shipping and labour law are existing categories of federal law.[12]

The Federal Court has two divisions: Trial and Appellate. Federal Court judges sit in each province and territory. Appeals from Trial Division decisions may be taken to the Federal Court of Appeal. The Trial Division itself has jurisdiction to hear appeals from any "federal board, commission or other tribunal," except where appeal must be taken to the Federal Court of Appeal, as set out in s 28(1) of the *Federal Court Act*.[13]

COMPETITION

Competition is vital for the promotion of new ideas, products, and services. Competition itself has recently been stimulated by the progressive opening of Canada's borders to freer trade. That development has prompted both the federal and provincial governments to legislate to sustain and enhance competition in domestic markets.

Competition and the Common Law

The common law allows actions in *contract* against arrangements that unreasonably restrain trade, including some franchise arrangements, partnerships, shareholdings, and non-compete clauses. Restraints of trade are presumptively permissible, but the courts scrutinize them carefully to ensure that they do not unduly restrict competition. Chapter 5 discussed contractual covenants in restraint of trade. However, contractual actions are available only between contracting parties.

competition is sometimes governed by contract and tort law

As Chapter 11 explained, the common law also permits actions in *tort* for conspiracy and unlawful interference with trade. Those actions require an element of deliberate behaviour, either to conspire to restrain trade or opportunities or to interfere with the business of a third party. Both are hard to prove and are rarely successful.

A Law for Competition

In 1889, Canada became the first country to enact a competition law when it brought in anti-combines legislation. That law's emphasis was to prevent large-scale mergers among businesses that restrained trade. Later, as concern grew about the pervasive nature of anti-competitive conduct, the focus of legislative attention expanded to include monopolies, mergers, other anti-competitive practices, and consumer protection.

[12.] Consider *ITO-Int'l Terminal Operators Ltd v Miida Electronics Inc* (1986) 28 DLR (4th) 641 (SCC). The dispute concerned the validity of a contractual clause between Mitsui and Miida that limited Mitsui's liability for negligence and purported to cover Mitsui's agents as well. The question for the court was whether the issue of contractual limitations of liability had a sufficient maritime connection and therefore fell within the broad head of "navigation and shipping" under s 91(10) of the Constitution. The court held that it did. The Federal Court consequently had jurisdiction to hear the case.

[13.] The Federal Court of Appeal has jurisdiction to hear and determine applications for judicial review from 14 agencies, including the Canadian Radio-television and Telecommunications Commission, the Canadian International Trade Tribunal, and the Copyright Board of Canada.

the *Competition Act* is the main piece of federal legislation regulating competition

The main piece of federal legislation regulating competition today is the *Competition Act*.[14] Its aim is to restrict anti-competitive practices and stimulate competitive conduct. The Act contains key provisions relating to anti-competitive behaviour and such matters as misleading advertising, abusive marketing practices, and consumer protection.

Canadian competition law is similar to US anti-trust law, but it is also distinct. First, US law continues to be referred to as "anti-trust" law from its origins as a law against trusts, or industrial combinations. Canadian law, with few exceptions, has been updated to refer to "competition." That wider, less-negative term emphasizes the goal of *promoting* competition. Another difference is that Canadian law, with a few exceptions, generally cannot be used for private actions and remedies. In the US, in contrast, there are many statutes that allow private actions. Furthermore, the vigorous anti-trust attitude in the US is reflected in the fact that the plaintiff sometimes recovers treble damages, for three times the value of its actual loss.

Enforcement

The *Competition Act* is administered by the Commissioner of Competition, who oversees the operation of the Competition Bureau in Ottawa. The Commissioner is responsible for enforcement of the Act and three other standards-setting statutes.[15] Violations of the Act are categorized as civil, criminal, or dual matters.

reviewable matters involve civil claims under the *Competition Act*

- Civil matters under the Act are also known as **reviewable matters**, because they are investigated by the Commissioner. They may be referred to the Competition Tribunal, an administrative tribunal composed of judicial and lay members. The tribunal has the power to order that customs duties imposed on foreign goods be removed to stimulate competition, that a merger be dissolved, that entities contemplating merger be "held separate," or other remedies. Appeals from the tribunal's orders can be taken to the Federal Court of Appeal. Matters that are currently reviewable include refusals to deal, consignment selling, exclusive dealing, tied sales, market restriction, delivered pricing, foreign refusals to supply, and specialization agreements.

- The Commissioner refers criminal matters to the Attorney General for prosecution in court. Matters that are currently categorized as criminal include conspiracy, bid-rigging, price discrimination and predation, promotional allowances, and resale price maintenance.

- A small category of dual criminal-civil matters exists in the area of deceptive marketing practices, such as misleading advertising, deceptive telemarketing, and multi-level marketing. The Commissioner decides whether the behaviour was committed intentionally or recklessly. If so, it can be referred to the Attorney General for prosecution. If criminal prosecution is not pursued, the Commissioner retains the option of civilly reviewing the matter.

- Those enforcement mechanisms are reviewed in Concept Summary 23.1 and Figure 23.1.

[14.] *Competition Act*, RSC 1985, c C-34 (Can).

[15.] The bureau is also responsible for the *Consumer Packaging and Labelling Act*, the *Textile Labelling Act*, and the *Precious Metals Marketing Act*. All of those statutes deal with some aspect of consumer or industrial protection.

Concept Summary 23.1

Criminal Offences and Civil Reviewable Matters under the *Competition Act*

Nature of Offence/Matter	Activity Prescribed
Criminal offences	conspiracy, bid-rigging, price discrimination and predation, promotional allowances, resale price maintenance, deceptive notice of winning a prize
Dual matters	misleading advertising, deceptive telemarketing, multi-level marketing
Civil matters	refusals to deal, consignment selling, exclusive dealing, tied sales, market restriction, delivered pricing, foreign refusals to supply, specialization agreements

FIGURE 23.1   Enforcement Under the *Competition Act*

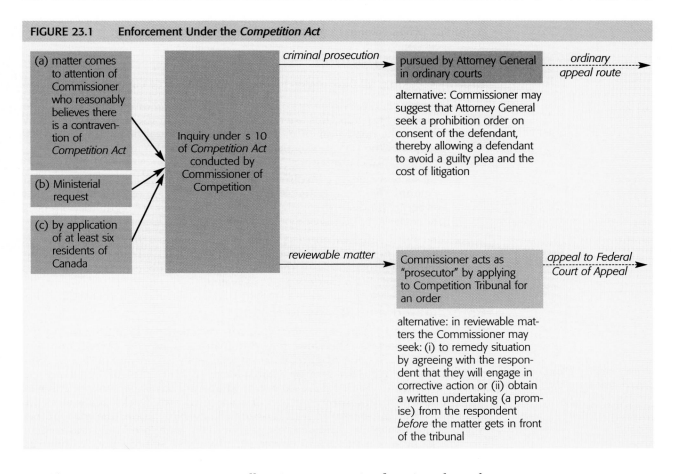

The Competition Bureau generally tries to serve its function through moral suasion and consent, and businesses normally comply after being asked to do so. The Commissioner enjoys broad discretion in enforcing the Act and may decide to resolve lesser matters by a written undertaking, or promise, with the defendant, or by recommending in a criminal matter that the Attorney General seek a consent order from the court. If the defendant does not co-operate or there is evidence of a continuing violation, the bureau may: (i) take coercive measures (such as a search or seizure), (ii) seek to review the matter before the tribunal, or (iii) refer the matter to the Attorney General for criminal prosecution.

Private Action under the Act

The ability to bring a private action against anti-competitive conduct under the Act is limited. Section 36 allows a civil action for damages if: (i) a person has suffered damage because of anti-competitive competition, and (ii) the accused's conduct is either being prosecuted as a criminal act *or* is in violation of a court or Competition Tribunal order. In addition, the *Competition Act* has been amended recently to provide for a private right of action in cases of refusals to deal, exclusive dealing, tied selling, and market restrictions, which are examined further below. In such cases the law requires that the complainant first obtain the tribunal's permission to take action by showing that it is directly and substantially affected by the behaviour complained of. If successful before the tribunal, the complainant is only allowed to obtain a cease-and-desist order against the defendant, *not* damages. It is, however, permitted to request reimbursement of its legal costs. Otherwise, the *Competition Act* does not currently allow a person to pursue private action in connection with a reviewable matter.

The *Competition Act*

Broadly speaking, matters under the Act fall within three categories.

- The first category consists of *co-ordinated conduct* or conduct relating to *pricing*. These activities are considered to be serious, either because they involve the behaviour of more than one individual or because they distort price, the very mechanism on which efficient markets depend. They are therefore criminalized.

- The second category involves *deceptive marketing practices*. These consist of claims *about* goods and services and, as such, are only indirectly about the actual products themselves. Consequently, they are regulatory offences under the Act and may be prosecuted either as criminal or civil matters.

- The third category consists of all other matters and generally involves issues of *supply*. These are considered to be lesser offences, because consumers will usually have the choice of a close substitute when supplies are limited. Such matters are reviewable.

Co-ordinated and Pricing Behaviour

Co-ordinated and pricing behaviour concerns conduct that is antithetical to the spirit of free markets. Therefore, it is criminalized under the *Competition Act*. Section 45 of the Act, for instance, makes it an offence to conspire to "lessen competition unduly." However, proving a **conspiracy**—a joint action of more than one party—is difficult. While the prosecutor must prove that the defendants' conduct was intentional, most conspirators are careful to cover their tracks. In addition, the statute has been interpreted to require specific knowledge among the conspirators that their agreement would lessen competition. That high threshold is rarely met.

a **conspiracy** is the joint action of more than one party

An example of a successful prosecution involved SGL Carbon, which was fined $12.5 million in 2000 for participating in an international conspiracy to fix prices and allocate markets for graphite electrodes, which are used in steelmaking. SGL and other members of the cartel agreed to restrict production capacity, fix prices, and allocate volumes of graphite electrodes sold worldwide. That scheme led to uniform pricing between SGL and its principal competitor in Canada. As a result, prices increased more than 90 percent between 1992 and 1997.[16]

---

16. The Act does not prohibit *conscious parallelism*, a common practice in highly competitive industries like gasoline or supermarket retailing. In those fields, prices tend to follow each other closely, sometimes moving within minutes. That kind of behaviour does not amount to a conspiracy if it is entirely voluntary and unforeseen. The bureau is also planning to modernize the conspiracy provisions to allow for strategic alliances. See *Annual Report of the Commissioner of Competition 2000-2001* (2001) at 36.

Bid-rigging is related to conspiracy.[17] It is another form of collusion. **Bid-rigging** occurs when a person either agrees to not submit a bid in response to a call for tenders or submits a bid that is based on a prior agreement. Bid-rigging is punishable by fine at the discretion of the court or imprisonment for up to five years.

In addition to conspiracy and bid-rigging, the Act prohibits three other pricing practices: price discrimination, predatory pricing, and price maintenance.[18]

- **Discriminatory pricing** occurs when a business systematically sells the same goods or services to competing customers at different prices without a valid reason or the like (eg, volume discount). For example, a seller might consistently provide more favourable credit terms to Buyer A than to Buyer B.

- **Predatory pricing** occurs when goods or services are sold below cost or at unreasonably low levels to drive a competitor out of business.

- **Price maintenance** involves an attempt to restrict the price at which a product is sold or resold. For example, it may be an offence for a wholesaler to impose mandatory pricing guidelines that require retailers to resell a product at a specific price. A wholesaler can, however, *suggest* an appropriate retail price.

Misleading Advertising and Other Representational Offences

The term **misleading advertising** refers to a representation about a product or business interest that intentionally or carelessly deceives the public. Since misleading advertising depends on the customer's perception, it involves an element of individual judgment and responsibility. It is therefore considered to be less serious than collusive or price-related behaviour. As a result, it forms part of a small category of dual-nature offences under the *Competition Act*, which can be either reviewed civilly or prosecuted criminally. It is not necessary to prove that any person was actually deceived or misled by the representation. However, in a prosecution, the court will look at both the literal meaning and the general impression of the words in question. A defence of *due diligence* exists to any such offence that is prosecuted criminally. **Due diligence** involves the exercise of reasonable care by an individual who is responsible for the performance of a duty.

Deceptive telemarketing may also be an offence. **Telemarketing** involves the sale of goods or services over the telephone. Legislation on point was introduced in 1999 in response to concern about misleading practices over the telephone, particularly those targeting senior citizens in the US. Section 52.1 of the Act requires telemarketers to promptly and fairly identify themselves, describe their product, state their prices, explain the purpose of their call, and so on. That section also prohibits misrepresentations, telephone contests and lotteries, and some pricing regimes. Section 53 of the Act has also been introduced recently to prohibit deceptive notices of winning a prize. Unlike other representational offences, which are dual in nature, deceptive notification is strictly a criminal offence.

Multi-level marketing plans may be an offence under the Act. A **multi-level marketing plan** occurs when participants in a scheme are promised benefits in exchange for persuading other people to join the scheme. A classic example involves a pyramid. You pay me for the right to participate in a sales scheme. In turn, you receive payments from the people whom you persuade to join the scheme. And they in turn receive payments from the people whom they enlist. And so on. The people at the bottom of the pyramid suffer the loss. The Act there-

bid-rigging occurs when a person either agrees to not submit a bid in response to a call for tenders or submits a bid that is based on a prior agreement

discriminatory pricing occurs when a business systematically sells the same goods or services to competing customers at different prices

predatory pricing occurs when goods or services are sold below cost or at unreasonably low levels to drive a competitor out of business

price maintenance involves an attempt to restrict the price at which a product is sold or resold

misleading advertising refers to representations about a product or business interest that intentionally or carelessly deceives the public

due diligence is the exercise of reasonable care by an individual responsible for the performance of a duty

telemarketing involves the sale of goods or services over the telephone

multi-level marketing plans occur when participants in a scheme are promised benefits in exchange for persuading other people to join the scheme

---

[17.] *Competition Act*, s 47.

[18.] Section 50. Few important convictions have been secured under that section. The Competition Bureau's Web site lists recent convictions: <strategis.ic.gc.ca/SSG/ct01709e.html>.

fore protects consumers from deceptive practices regarding the compensation to be received, bonuses, inventory requirements, and product return policies.

Distribution Practices

The Act prohibits certain distribution practices that restrict *supply*. For instance, in some circumstances, the Competition Tribunal can order a supplier to sell a product to a particular customer who is willing to meet the usual trade terms and who cannot otherwise obtain the product. Certain other distribution practices, such as *exclusive dealing*, *tied selling*, and *market restriction*, are reviewable.

- **Exclusive dealing** occurs when, as a condition of supply, a supplier requires a customer to deal only, or primarily in, products designated by the supplier. Such arrangements often arise in franchising.
- **Tied selling** occurs when the purchase of one product is tied to the purchase of another in some way. That can include the actual purchase of another product, more favourable terms for certain purchases, or prohibitions on the use of products supplied by third parties. An example might be the requirement to buy a certain brand of industrial lubricant when buying a piece of machinery.
- **Market restriction** occurs when a supplier restricts the people to whom the purchaser may resell a product. A violation may arise if a manufacturer prohibits retailers from selling its products beyond a given geographic region.

exclusive dealing occurs when, as a condition of supply, a supplier requires a customer to deal only, or primarily in, products designated by the supplier

tied selling occurs when the purchase of one product is tied to the purchase of another in some way

market restriction occurs when a supplier restricts the people to whom the purchaser may resell a product

Abuse of Dominant Position

abuse of dominant position occurs when competitive conduct results in an undue reduction of competition

A monopoly is most often considered as an *abuse of dominant position*. **Abuse of dominant position** occurs when competitive conduct results in an undue reduction of competition. Adoption of the broader concept reflects the fact that the prohibited behaviour often is not a "monopoly." There may be more than one entity that offers the same goods or services. Nevertheless, the government is concerned about entities that substantially control a particular type of business and that engage in behaviour which, if unchecked, will significantly lessen competition.

Section 78 of the Act lists several examples of abuse of dominant position. We look at three.

- The *cutting of profit margins* occurs when a supplier inhibits competition by directly selling goods in the market for a price that is lower than the one that it charges to retailers.
- The *use of loss leaders* involves temporarily introducing "fighting brands" into the market at below normal cost to discipline or eliminate a competitor.
- The *pre-emption of scarce facilities* involves withholding facilities or resources to impede competition.

A potential defence to these practices is whether the control comes about because of "superior competitive performance." Here, the tribunal must consider whether the defendant's record in the marketplace is simply a reflection of better business practices.

A recent case involving alleged abuse of dominance began in mid-1997 with an investigation of the marketing and selling practices of HJ Heinz, a well-known manufacturer of baby food. The bureau was concerned about Heinz's practice of: (i) making large, lump-sum payments to retailers that did not stock competitor brands, (ii) entering into multi-year contracts for exclusive supply with retailers, and (iii) providing discounts conditional on exclusive supply. In 2000, Heinz settled the matter with the Bureau by promising to stop those practices. Of more immediate concern to some consumers is the re-emergence of monopolistic practices in Canada's airline industry following the acquisition of Canadian Airlines International by Air Canada in 2000.[19] Ethical Perspective 23.1 illustrates the problem of exclusive dealership.

ETHICAL PERSPECTIVE 23.1

Single Source Contracts: Private Choice in Public Places[20]

There has recently been increasing concern about "single-source," or exclusive dealership, agreements in shopping malls and on school campuses across Canada. Brands buy the right to be marketed in certain public (or *quasi*-public) facilities in a way that makes true free choice difficult. For instance, on some university campuses, including McMaster and the University of Alberta, it is impossible to buy carbonated soft drinks that are not manufactured by Coca-Cola. The bookstore at McGill University is run by Chapters Inc.

Single-source marketing raises difficult issues. On the one hand, consumer groups are concerned about its impact on perceptions of choice and institutional freedom. On the other hand, marketers and facility managers argue that

exclusive dealership arrangements provide important market data and valuable revenue for cash-strapped public institutions. They do acknowledge, however, that targeting key groups—like students—pays off handsomely for many years. Captive audiences are more likely to remember brands and to select them even when they are presented with alternative products.

From a legal perspective, single-source contracts are presumptively valid long-term supply contracts for goods or services. However, they are not immune from attack and could be challenged under the *Competition Act*. But they usually avoid scrutiny because of the relatively small size of the market that is contained in a shopping mall, campus, or single workplace.

Question for Discussion

1. Are single-source contracts worthwhile? What alternatives could be proposed?

Mergers

A **merger** involves the combination of two or more business entities. There are three basic types.

> a **merger** involves the combination of two or more business organizations

- Entities that merge mainly to combine businesses that are complementary, such as a quarry and a cement manufacturer, engage in a *vertical merger*.
- Entities that merge mainly to combine businesses at the same stage of production, such as the acquisition of one car maker by another, engage in a *horizontal merger*.
- Entities that combine with other entities having little or no relevance to their existing business engage in a *diversification merger*.

Depending on the market, market dominance concerns are normally highest in a horizontal merger.

---

[19] Following the acquisition, the *Competition Act* was amended in July 2000 to provide the Commissioner of Competition and the Competition Tribunal with new powers to deal with potential abuses by Air Canada. Regulations now define new anti-competitive action in the airline industry, including the operation of routes at fares that do not cover avoidable costs, the use of low-cost second-brand carriers for such purposes, and the pre-emption of airport facilities or services.

[20] *McDonald's Restaurants of Canada Ltd v West Edmonton Mall Ltd* [1994] 10 WWR 662 (Alta QB).

Section 91 of the Act defines a merger as the acquisition of "a significant interest in the whole or a part of a business of a competitor, supplier, customer or other person." A reviewable offence occurs "where a merger is likely to lessen competition substantially in a trade, industry or profession." The Competition Tribunal is given the power to dissolve the merger, dispose of assets, or take other necessary action.

The Competition Bureau has been required to review an increasing number of mergers, mainly due to the effects of globalization, deregulation, and resulting concentration in certain markets. The bureau engages in pre-merger review of all transactions in Canada worth more than $35 million or where combined revenues of the entities involved exceed $400 million per year.[21] If entrepreneurs are uncertain about the anti-competitive effects of a proposed merger, they can seek an advance ruling from the bureau. You Be the Judge 23.1 reviews one merger case.

YOU BE THE JUDGE 23.1

Can Mergers Be Efficient?[22]

Much has been written in recent years about the validity of an "efficiency defence" to merger activity. All mergers are presumptively efficient. Otherwise managers would not engage in them. However, since 1996, the idea of efficiency has become more relevant with the inclusion of an efficiency defence in s 96 of the *Competition Act*.

The dominant idea behind an efficiency defence is that some markets are more perfect than previously thought and should be relied upon to self-correct for concentration. When a market is highly concentrated and prices for goods or services rise, theory suggests that other suppliers will enter those markets and bring prices back to an equilibrium. Critics contend, however, that there is ample evidence that markets for many products do not self-correct, particularly when there are significant barriers to entry. After all, when was the last time someone tried to start up a new aircraft or auto manufacturer?

One of the first opportunities for extended examination of the new efficiency defence came about in October 1998, when one of the two remaining propane suppliers in Canada, Superior Propane, tried to acquire its sole competitor, ICG Propane Inc. The acquisition was challenged by the bureau.

The issue before the tribunal was whether the "effects" of an anti-competitive merger considered under s 96 are limited to the loss of resources to the economy as a whole (the "dead-weight loss") or whether they include a wider range of the effects. The latter would include the wealth transfer from consumers to producers that occurs when the merged entity exercises its market power to increase prices, the elimination of smaller competitors, and the creation of a monopoly.

The tribunal found that the merger would prevent competition in Atlantic Canada and substantially lessen competition in many local markets. However, it concluded that since the merger was likely to result in efficiency gains of $29.2 million and would result in only $3 million of quantitative dead-weight loss and $3 million worth of qualitative dead-weight loss, the merger was saved by the efficiency defence.

(continued)

[21.] The thresholds are set out in ss 109-110 of the Act. In 2000–2001, the bureau performed 373 merger examinations. Of these, only five involved post-closing restructuring, one involved a consent order, and two involved situations where parties abandoned the merger at least partially because of the bureau's position. See *Annual Report of the Commissioner of Competition 2000-2001* (2001) at 25. The bureau guidelines concerning market share note that: "Mergers generally will not be challenged on the basis of concerns relating to the unilateral exercise of market power where the post-merger market share of the merged entity would be less than 35 percent. Similarly, mergers generally will not be challenged on the basis of concerns relating to the interdependent exercise of market power, where the share of the market accounted for by the largest four firms in the market post-merger would be less than 65 percent. Notwithstanding that market share of the largest four firms may exceed 65 percent, the Director generally will not challenge a merger on the basis of concerns relating to the interdependent exercise of market power where the merged entity's market share would be less than 10 percent. These thresholds merely serve to distinguish mergers that are unlikely to have anticompetitive consequences from mergers that require further analysis, of various qualitative assessment criteria." See Competition Bureau's *Merger Review Guidelines* at <strategis.ic.gc.ca/SSG/ct01026e.html>.

[22.] *Commissioner of Competition v Superior Propane* (2001) 199 DLR (4th) 130.

(continued)

The Federal Court of Appeal, on review of the case, disagreed. It preferred a wider definition of "effects." The majority said that "whatever standard is selected ... must be more reflective than the total surplus standard of the different objectives of the *Competition Act*. It should also be sufficiently flexible in its application to enable the tribunal fully to assess the particular fact situation before it."[23] The Federal Court of Appeal therefore overturned the tribunal's conclusion.

In September 2001, the Supreme Court of Canada decided that it would not hear a further appeal of the case, effectively leaving the tribunal to review its conclusion in light of the Federal Court of Appeal's decision.

Question for Discussion

1. How should "efficiency" be measured? What factors should be examined when one is determining efficiency in Canadian law?

BUSINESS DECISION 23.1

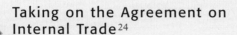

Taking on the Agreement on Internal Trade[24]

Until recently, trade between Canada's provinces was sometimes limited to protect key sectors from extra-provincial competition. For example, British Columbians could not buy beer from the Maritimes and Ontario construction workers could not work in Quebec. That aspect of domestic competition reflected the strongly local policies of another era, as well as the traditionally weak federal power over trade and commerce. As a result, Canada was a less-open economy than the US, where goods and services flow freely from state to state by virtue of the US Constitution's interstate Commerce Clause.

In an attempt to do away with restrictions on interprovincial trade, Canada's federal, provincial, and territorial governments signed the Agreement on Internal Trade (AIT) in 1995. The AIT promotes the free movement of goods, services, and people *within* Canada to make the country more competitive economically. It is based on six general principles that are designed to prevent governments from erecting new trade barriers and to reduce existing barriers: non-discrimination, the right of entry and exit, no obstacles to internal trade, legitimate objectives to government legislation, reconciliation of provincial standards, and transparency. Eleven specific business sectors are covered. Negotiations are continuing with respect to other sectors, and new subjects are being added over time.[25]

The AIT also features a formal dispute settlement mechanism to deal with grievances. It is administered by the AIT Secretariat in Winnipeg. The dispute settlement system can be invoked both by governments *and* private business, but it has been criticized recently because AIT rulings are *not* legally binding and cannot be enforced in court.

Implementation of several early decisions remains stalled. These include decisions condemning a ban by Prince Edward Island on milk from outside the province, a Quebec ban on the sale of coloured margarine, and a challenge by the Certified General Accountants Association of Canada (CGA) to force Ontario to allow CGA members to practise public accountancy there. The results have led some people to conclude that Canada's trade with other countries is freer than it is between provinces.

Questions for Discussion

1. If AIT decisions could be enforced in court, how could damages for loss of competitive opportunity be calculated?

2. What sectors of a province's economy should continue to be protected from goods and services originating in other provinces?

[23.] *Commissioner of Competition v Superior Propane Inc* (2001) 199 DLR (4th) 130 at 140.

[24.] See the AIT homepage at <www.intrasec.mb.ca>.

[25.] These are procurement, investment, labour mobility, consumer-related measures and standards, agricultural and food products, alcoholic beverages, natural resource processing, energy, communications, transportation, and environmental protection.

CONSUMER PROTECTION

The idea of a law of consumer protection is relatively new. In the past, most consumers knew their suppliers personally and could approach them directly about shortcomings, defects, and product safety. Actions arose in contract to resolve problems in quality and reasonable fitness, and in tort to cover cases of fraud.

Recently, federal and provincial governments have intervened to protect consumers through legislation in four key areas:

- misleading advertising
- product regulation
- regulation of business conduct
- disclosure of the true cost of credit

There is, however, little uniformity of coverage of these topics. The legislation has generally appeared in an unsystematic way.

Deceptive Marketing Practices

One important source of consumer protection legislation is the *Competition Act*. In addition to conspiracy and pricing arrangements, misleading advertising, and distribution practices, that statute also prohibits a broad range of anti-competitive behaviour that is targeted at consumers. Those practices fall under the heading of *deceptive marketing practices*. **Deceptive marketing practices** are representations that are made to promote a product or a business interest.

deceptive marketing practices are representations that are made to promote a product or a business interest

Many types of deceptive marketing practices are prohibited. For instance, goods cannot be offered for sale under a "bait and switch" or at a price for which they will not realistically be sold. Likewise, products cannot be promoted on the basis of misleading testimonials or product testing results. Those offences are all reviewable matters under s 74 of the Act, and the Competition Tribunal will consider the literal meaning of a representation as well as the general impression that it conveys. In the case of misleading advertising, however, the Commissioner has the option of applying to the tribunal for a remedy or referring claims for prosecution by the Attorney General.

Other Fair Practices Legislation

In addition to the *Competition Act*, a number of other federal statutes provide common standards for consumer products.

- The *Consumer Packaging and Labelling Act* requires the identification of products by their recognized name and amount of contents. Certain listed products, such as canned foods and milk, must be sold in standardized containers and bilingual labels must be provided.
- For clothing, the *Textile Labelling Act* establishes a set of requirements for garment labelling with generic identification of the origin of the garment and materials used. Most clothing now also conforms to recommended care labelling standards.
- For hazardous products, such as lead-based paints, glues, and industrial chemicals, the *Hazardous Products Act* creates two schedules for goods that are prohibited from production in Canada or that can only be produced and handled according to standards set out in regulations under the Act.

- The *Food and Drug Act* deals with many aspects of foods and drugs, including their processing, storing, and labelling. The Act's provisions deal with sanitary conditions maintained by producers; measures designed to prevent food, cosmetic, and pharmaceutical adulteration; requirements for the listing of ingredients; and dating for products with limited shelf life.

- The *Motor Vehicle Safety Act* applies to motor vehicles made or imported into Canada. Its provisions deal with safety features and procedures in case of vehicle recall.

Some provincial statutes also protect consumers. Terms that are implied by virtue of provincial *Sale of Goods* legislation, such as those relating to merchantability and fitness, were examined in Chapter 8. Such provisions are mandatory and cannot be eliminated by contract. In some instances, provincial legislation has extended liability by implying warranties or mandating coverage of foreseeable users of products and secondary purchasers.

The statutes that we have discussed all deal with goods. However, a growing section of our economy is now based on the provision of services. That makes regulation more difficult. In 2001, in response to a wave of complaints about bank branch closures and hidden costs in consumer credit, the federal government created the Financial Consumer Agency of Canada (FCAC) to protect and educate consumers of financial services.

ENVIRONMENTAL PROTECTION

Until recently, the environment was not seen to be a finite resource of popular concern. Now, there is growing apprehension about the quality of the environment and the government's ability to protect it.

Businesses are now subject to environmental protection legislation, which increase their legal risks. But at the same time, businesses are in the best position to design their operations in an environmentally sensitive manner. Companies that comply with the law and take a proactive approach to issues of environmental liability are bound to benefit from both public goodwill and reduced risk.

Common Law Approaches

Common law traditionally addressed environmental concerns through a variety of torts. We saw several possibilities in Chapters 11 and 12. Under the rule in *Rylands v Fletcher*, a person can be held strictly liable for a non-natural use of land if something escapes from its property and injures another person. The tort of nuisance occurs when the defendant unreasonably interferes with the plaintiff's use and enjoyment of its own land. The law of occupier's liability requires an occupier of premises to protect visitors from harm. The tort of negligence imposes liability upon a person who carelessly causes personal injury or property damage. The law of contract may also deal with environmental concerns. As we saw in Chapter 14, an agreement for the sale of land may require the vendor to ensure that the property does not contain any environmental hazards.

Common law actions for environmental damage can be maintained today, but they suffer from at least three drawbacks.

- First, they require court action and the related risk of protracted litigation.

common law protection of the
environment is deficient in
some ways

- Second, common law actions are normally property related. People who do not have property cannot complain about damage that is being done to society's collective property ("the commons," as it is sometimes called).
- Third, common law tort liability requires proof that is often hard to obtain, particularly given the transitory nature of many types of pollution. Without obvious causation, liability can be hard to prove.

These defects led to the introduction of comprehensive environmental legislation in Canada in the early 1970s.

Jurisdiction over the Environment

responsibility for the environment is split between levels of government

The original text of Canada's Constitution did not mention the environment. The provinces were given jurisdiction over local matters such as forests, minerals, and fresh water, whereas the federal government was given jurisdiction over matters of interprovincial concern, such as marine pollution. While that jurisdictional division continues, it is very difficult to apply neatly in practice. Consequently, a great deal of environmental management in Canada involves consultation, co-operation, and agreement between levels of government. Examples include constitutional amendments in 1982 to allow the provinces a greater say in natural resource management, and federal-provincial dialogue over Canada's commitments under international environmental agreements. Municipalities also have a substantial role to play in environmental protection through the passage of municipal bylaws on zoning, garbage disposal, and water use; however, we will not examine their role here.

Federal Legislation

CEPA entails the formulation of environmental quality objectives, guidelines, and codes of practice concerning the environment

The principal piece of federal legislation over environmental matters is the *Canadian Environmental Protection Act (CEPA)*.[26] *CEPA* entails the formulation of environmental quality objectives, guidelines, and codes of practice concerning the environment. The Act is concerned mainly with systemic threats to the environment, including nutrient-, marine- and fuel-based pollution, the release of toxic substances and animate products of biotechnology, and control over the movement of hazardous waste. It also sets out standards for the recycling, storage, and disposal of waste and other hazardous substances, and for conservation activities. The Act contains broad powers that allow the federal government to prosecute polluters and others who break environmental laws. Nevertheless, actions for environmental damage under *CEPA* can be brought only by the federal environment ministry. Civil suits are limited to actions for nuisance and possibly negligence when mandatory federal standards are not met.

Courts can require violators of federal law to cease polluting activities, to remedy failures to comply, or to pay for environmental cleanups. In addition, sanctions can be supplemented by fines and, when the conduct is particularly flagrant, by imprisonment. Corporate directors and officers can be held personally liable in this regard. *CEPA* is supplemented by other federal laws and detailed regulations that govern certain specific environmental activities. For instance, the *Transportation of Dangerous Goods Act* deals with safety in the movement of hazardous materials, the *Canada Shipping Act* sets emission standards for ocean-going vessels, and the *Fisheries Act* regulates marine pollution.[27]

---

[26] *Canadian Environmental Protection Act*, SC 1999, c 33 (Can).

[27] *Transportation of Dangerous Goods Act*, SC 1992, c 34 (Can); *Canada Shipping Act*, RSC 1985, c S-9 (Can); *Fisheries Act*, RSC 1985, c F-14 (Can).

Provincial Legislation

Provincial environmental protection legislation varies between jurisdictions, but all provinces have at least one general law concerning the subject. These are supplemented by laws related to specific activities such as the protection of water resources, environmental assessment, and pesticide use.[28] Several provinces and territories have also enacted environmental bills of rights to enshrine environmental protection as a fundamental value in society and emphasize the public's role in environmental protection.[29]

The coverage of most provincial laws is similar. In Ontario, for instance, the *Environmental Protection Act* covers motor and motor vehicle emissions, water, waste management, ozone depletion, and litter, packaging, and containers. Liability in each subject area arises on the basis of either *mens rea*, *strict*, or *absolute* liability offences.

- *Mens rea* offences require a culpable act *and* the intent of the wrongdoer. They are rarely prosecuted successfully under provincial environmental law because people rarely pollute deliberately.

- Strict liability offences are most common under environmental statutes. They are based on proof of a culpable act, but the defendant can prove that it took all reasonable care, or due diligence, as a defence.

- Absolute liability offences also require proof of a culpable act, but the defendant cannot avoid liability by proving due diligence. Such offences are rare.

Liability for environmental offences generally arises from one of four categories of activity. We use the Ontario *Environmental Protection Act* to illustrate.

- *Substantive offences* deal with actual pollution and improper waste disposal. Section 14 of the Act states that "no person shall discharge a contaminant or cause or permit the discharge of a contaminant into the natural environment that causes or is likely to cause an adverse effect."

- *Reporting offences* arise from the failure to notify the government that pollution has been released into the environment. If a business is convicted of polluting, its sentence may be reduced if it promptly reported the problem and co-operated in the investigation and cleanup.

- *Information offences* concern the failure to provide accurate and timely information to government inspectors and other officials. For instance, under s 184, it is an offence to hinder an inspector by concealing information or providing false particulars.

- *Regulatory offences* are committed through a failure to obey government orders, directives, certificates, and other mandatory requirements. Section 186, for instance, makes it a regulatory offence to exceed permissible discharge levels set out in a ministerial certificate of approval.

[28.] For example, the *Environmental Protection Act*, RSO 1990, c E-19, which is supplemented by the *Ontario Water Resources Act*, RSO 1990, c O-40, the *Environmental Assessment Act*, RSO 1990, c E-18, and the *Pesticides Act*, RSO 1990, c P-11. A number of other laws with environment-related application also exist.

[29.] For example, the *Yukon Environment Act*, SY 1991, c 5 and the Northwest Territories' *Environmental Rights Act*, RSNWT 1988, c 83. Other legislation containing limited aspects of an environmental bill of rights include the Quebec *Environmental Quality Act* (which has included, since 1972, a substantive right to environmental quality), LQ 2001, c Q-2, Alberta's *Environmental Protection and Enhancement Act*, RSA 2000, c E-12, and the *Environmental Act of Nova Scotia*, SNC 1994-95, c 1.

Corporate Exposure to Environmental Liability

Corporations are exposed to environmental liability in the course of day-to-day operations. It is important to understand how this liability arises, who is responsible, and what can be done to control the risk of liability.

Corporate exposure to environmental liability arises most often in one of three ways: (i) due to ownership of contaminants, (ii) as a result of the acts of a corporation's "directing mind," or (iii) through the acts of agents or employees.

Ownership Liability

Ownership liability arises from a corporation's legal relationship to contaminants. The extent of ownership liability has increased significantly under most provincial laws due to growing environmental awareness. Canadian governments have decided to cast the net of responsibility far and wide, with potentially onerous results.[30] In Ontario, for example, the current regime imposes a type of "no-fault" liability on owners. A business that owns a property is potentially liable for its condition and cleanup, even if: (i) the business acted in a careful and responsible manner, (ii) the pollution was created by a past owner or tenant, or (iii) the pollution migrated to the property from another site.[31]

The specific rules vary between provinces. Three general methods of limiting owner liability have, however, evolved.

- It is often possible for lenders, but not existing owners, to negotiate lender liability agreements with some provincial environment ministries. These agreements permit lenders to investigate land, secure the borrower's property, and take other measures without necessarily attracting liability.

- Officials may issue "comfort," or "no action," letters to help with the conveyance of property. While such documents may help with a given transaction, they lack uniformity.

- Some governments have begun to formally acknowledge records of site condition completed by private consultants that detail the state of a piece of property at a given time. These help to document the environmental conditions of a site, but do not guarantee immunity from action in future.

Given the ever-increasing nature of ownership liability, the best way to manage risk is to purchase environmental insurance. A number of environmental insurance products are on the market to protect against compliance cost overruns or against the possibility of future environmental liability.

Management Liability

Management liability refers to corporate responsibility for acts of the company's "directing mind." Under provincial law, anything that is done by someone

Canadian governments have decided to cast the net of ownership responsibility for environmental damage far and wide, with potentially onerous results

environmental insurance is an important form of risk management

---

[30] Canadian governments have not adopted American-style "Superfund" legislation to deal comprehensively with environmentally "hot" properties. Superfund laws were introduced by the US federal government in 1980 to impose liability for contaminated lands on responsible parties in the hope that this would help to clear the title and promote the redevelopment of environmentally questionable property. Under Superfund legislation, federal and state funds were established to pay for the cleanup of property, and statutory exemptions from liability were given to secured lenders and to parties meeting the definition of "innocent landowner."

[31] K van Rensburg "Brownfields Development—The Legal Liability Challenges" (2000) at <www.nrtee-trnee.ca/publications/WP_3_E.PDF>.

who is the directing mind of a company is automatically attributed to the corporation and may attract liability. If the individual commits an environmental offence, so does the corporation.

Identification of the corporation's "directing mind" depends on the situation and the way in which a corporation manages itself. The directing mind normally consists of those who manage the business, including officers, directors, and others with management capacity. Whether a corporation has exercised due diligence depends on whether the directing mind acted reasonably in the circumstances. The standard of behaviour required is a modified objective one. A director's behaviour is judged against the behaviour of a reasonable director, not against the behaviour of an ordinary person.

Liability for the Acts of Agents and Employees

A corporation can be held liable for environmental damage caused by its agents and employees in the course of their duties. Agents (described in Chapter 20) and employees (described in Chapter 25) are "the hands to do the work," rather than the corporation's directing mind.[32]

Due Diligence

Most environmental offences involve strict liability. While responsibility is based simply on a prohibited act, the defendant can avoid liability by proving that it acted carefully and with due diligence. In many provinces, however, due diligence is not only a defence; it is also a specific duty under law. Section 194 of the Ontario *Environmental Protection Act*, for instance, states that officers and directors of a company commit an offence if they do not act with due diligence.

> (1) Every director or officer of a corporation that engages in an activity that may result in the discharge of a contaminant into the natural environment... has a duty to take all reasonable care to prevent the corporation from causing or permitting such unlawful deposit, addition, emission or discharge.
> (2) Every person who ... fails to carry out that duty is guilty of an offence.

In one well-known case, criminal charges were brought against the president, a director, and a plant manager of Bata Shoes, a major Canadian shoe manufacturer.[33] Bata operated a plant that generated liquid waste. which was stored in drums and barrels on the plant site. Over time, many of the drums and barrels began to leak. The company was charged with allowing toxic waste to enter the environment. All three executives raised the defence of due diligence. Only the president invoked it successfully. He proved that he had taken all reasonable care by establishing a pattern of environmental responsibility. The court also found that he was entitled to rely on the experienced on-site director to bring problems to his attention. The director and plant manager could not use the due diligence defence and therefore were convicted. Evidence showed that the director knew of the situation, but failed to take remedial steps. Likewise, the court held that the plant manager's biweekly visual survey of the site was insufficient to meet the requirement of reasonable care.

When will a business need a due diligence program? The answer depends upon the identification of risk, which is a function of specific business conditions. For instance, chemical and pharmaceutical manufacturing usually

due diligence may be both a defence to a strict liability offence and a specific duty

---

[32.] *HL Bolton Engineering Co v TJ Graham & Sons Ltd* [1957] 1 QB 159 at 172.

[33.] *R v Bata Industries Ltd* (1992) 7 CELR (NS) 245 (Ont Prov Ct).

involve greater environmental risks than babysitting or book selling. However, expanded liability and aggressive attitudes toward enforcement in many jurisdictions means that there may well be more risk than imagined. It is therefore wise to have an outsider—preferably a professional environmental consultant—conduct an environmental audit of an enterprise. The exercise should identify infractions of environmental laws and the risks associated with past and present operations.

Environmental Remedies

The abstract nature of the environment raises the interesting issue of what remedies are available for environmental damage. After all, the environment is hard to "fix." Penalties for environmental offences have climbed in recent years, as public awareness and concern about the environment have grown. In Ontario, for instance, an individual can be fined up to $4 million dollars a day for the most serious offences.[34] Jail terms of up to five years can also be imposed. Fines for corporations are similarly onerous, with the upper range now being $6 million a day.

Although public attention tends to focus on the numeric value of penalties, *conduct remedies* are often just as severe. They can include long-term surveillance in the form of enhanced reporting requirements and regular inspections paid for by the defendant. Other remedies include orders for:

- seizure of vehicle plates and permits
- protection and restoration of the natural environment
- compensation for those harmed by the pollution
- confiscation of items seized from a defendant
- costs associated with the legal process

Sometimes, however, the courts struggle to find an appropriate response to environmental damage, as Case Brief 23.2 illustrates.

CASE BRIEF 23.2

R v Northwest Territories Power Corp [1990] NWTR 125 (SC)

The Northwest Territories Power Corporation was convicted of discharging waste harmful to fish. At trial, it was ordered to pay a $15 000 fine and to publish an apology to the people of the territory, which included the name and photograph of each corporate director. On appeal, the court held that the provisions of the *Fisheries Act*, under which the charges were brought, did not authorize a court to require the company to publish a forced apology. A court order requiring a public apology to be made when none has been offered is coercive and may violate fundamental rights to "life, liberty and security of the person" contained in s 7 of the Canadian *Charter of Rights and Freedoms*.

The court also held that it was improper to "pierce the corporate veil," to look beyond a legal entity to those who actually control it as we examined in Chapter 18, if the company—but not its directors—was convicted. It was, therefore, contrary to s 7 of the *Charter* to punish the directors for a corporate offence by requiring their names and photographs to be included in a public apology.

[34.] This includes offences resulting in adverse effects on the environment, breaches of a stop order, and infractions relating to hazardous waste or hauled liquid industrial waste.

Environmental Impact Assessments

The common law, criminal, and regulatory frameworks for environmental protection are generally retrospective—they focus on *past* injuries. Damage awards and criminal penalties may deter future wrongdoing, but that is not always true. In any event, the injury that pollution inflicts on the environment is often so serious that it pays to adopt a forward-looking approach.

The federal and provincial governments have introduced environmental impact assessments (EIA) to promote forward thinking. The typical EIA requires the preparation of a report by those interested in undertaking a project, followed by a process of review by government and the public. The final decision may lead to approval, approval with conditions, or rejection. Certain categories of a project can involve additional steps in the form of public hearings.

Given the potentially onerous nature of the EIA process, an important question arises for business people. What will an EIA entail? Federal EIA legislation requires reports for any project on federal lands, any project receiving federal government financing, and any project that requires federal permission or licensing before it can be undertaken.[35] In the case of some projects and classes of projects that are likely to have significant adverse environmental effects, such as steel plants, pulp mills, hydro-electric dams, as well as smaller undertakings that use specific chemicals or otherwise threaten the environment, a mediation or panel review must be conducted.[36]

International Environmental Protection: Climate Change and the Kyoto Protocol

There is a growing realization that many environmental problems are international in nature and are best solved through treaties that allow countries to take action together. Canada has signed several such agreements, including the Convention on International Trade in Endangered Species of Wild Fauna and Flora (CITES), the Montreal Protocol on Substances that Deplete the Ozone Layer, and the Basel Convention on the Control of Transboundary Movements of Hazardous Wastes and Their Disposal. The federal government has negotiated these agreements after consulting with the provinces. Once the agreements are created, they are implemented by the relevant level of government in accordance with the division of responsibilities under Canada's Constitution.

some environmental issues are addressed internationally through treaties

One recent international initiative is the Kyoto Protocol. That agreement, which was created in Kyoto, Japan in 1997, elaborates upon the earlier United Nations Framework Convention on Climate Change. The convention recognized that human activity risks altering the global climate, with potentially severe consequences for the world. The protocol sets legally binding targets and timetables for cutting developed-country emissions of six greenhouse gases. Canada's reduction target was set at six percent of the amount of gases that it emitted in 1990. That goal is to be achieved in the period of 2008-2012. That will require a 25 percent drop in emissions from "business as usual" projections. At a summit in Marrakech, Morocco in November 2001, countries nego-

---

[35.] *CEPA*, s 5.

[36.] *CEPA*, s 29. Detailed information on which types of undertaking require a comprehensive study, including reference to a mediator or panel review, can be found in the federal *Comprehensive Study List Regulations*, SOR/94-638.

tiating on climate change decided on the broad outlines of penalties for a country's non-compliance with emission targets.[37]

An innovative feature of the Kyoto Protocol is that it establishes three mechanisms for obtaining emission "credits." Eventually, individuals and countries that find it easier to reduce their emissions will be able to transfer or sell their permits to individuals and countries that find it more expensive to do so.[38] A federal emissions trading scheme is under discussion and promises to have a progressively greater impact on how business is conducted in Canada.

All of these achievements must be measured against the fact that the US, the world's largest emitter of greenhouse gases (responsible for 25 percent of annual global emissions), has refused to adhere the Kyoto Protocol because it is concerned that the protocol is overly generous to developing countries and will damage the US economy.

---

[37] Consequences include a declaration of non-compliance, submission of a compliance action plan to the delinquent country, deduction from the country's assigned amount future emissions of a number of tonnes equal to 1.3 times the amount, in tonnes, of excess emissions, and suspension of eligibility to use the CDM, JI, and IET mechanisms. Those mechanisms are discussed in the next note.

[38] The three mechanisms are the Clean Development Mechanism, Joint Implementation, and International Emissions Trading. The Clean Development Mechanism (CDM) is a way to earn credits by investing in emission reduction projects in developing countries. Joint Implementation (JI) is a way to earn credits by investing in emission reduction projects in developed countries that have taken on a Kyoto target. International Emissions Trading (IET) will permit developed countries that have taken on a Kyoto target to buy and sell credits among themselves.

Chapter Summary

Government regulation of business in Canada arises from two principal powers. Federal regulation is derived mainly from federal jurisdiction over trade and commerce. Provincial regulation is derived mainly from power over property and civil rights. The distinction is often drawn in practice between matters needing national co-ordination versus matters of purely local concern. Federal and provincial powers can also overlap, and the courts have developed techniques to determine which ones takes priority. In addition, there are several fields of co-ordinated jurisdiction, such as transportation, natural resources, and the environment.

A principal concern of government is to promote competition and protect consumers. For that reason, the *Competition Act* promotes choice by prohibiting a wide range of activities that decrease competition. That includes provisions against monopolies and conspiracies. It also requires the review of mergers, which recognizes that some mergers may result in worthwhile efficiencies, particularly if they enhance exports. At the same time, government has taken steps to promote competition through provisions against bid-rigging, price maintenance, price discrimination, and market restrictions.

Consumer protection legislation exists in several statutes. Legislation is necessary to supplement the traditionally weak power of consumers. The *Competition Act* contains provisions against misleading advertising, deceptive marketing, and telemarketing. Other laws attempt to protect consumers through the regulation of industrial or commercial activities like consumer packaging and labelling, food and drug safety, and the availability of basic services.

Environmental protection has also become an important issue today and is reflected in federal and provincial environmental protection statutes.

Review Questions

1. Under what federal and provincial powers is business regulated in Canada?

2. How is a conflict between federal and provincial law resolved in Canada?

3. Name two business-related subjects under federal jurisdiction and two under provincial jurisdiction.

4. Can the Canadian *Charter of Rights and Freedoms* be invoked by businesses? If so, how?

5. What role does the Federal Court system play in the regulation of Canadian business? When will the Federal Court have jurisdiction?

6. Explain why competition is important in the Canadian economy.

7. Identify the common law actions that can be brought for anti-competitive behaviour, and explain why a purely common law approach to anti-competitive behaviour is insufficient.

8. Name the official responsible for overall promotion of competition in Canada, and indicate what powers the Competition Bureau has to enforce competition.

9. What are four subjects of the Competition Bureau's competence? Describe a defining feature of each.

10. What is the status of private actions for anti-competitive behaviour under the *Competition Act*?

11. What is the distinction between a criminal matter and a reviewable matter under the *Competition Act*?

12. What are the elements of a conspiracy under the *Competition Act*? A merger? An abuse of dominant position?

13. What are "dual" offences under the *Competition Act*? What is due diligence?

14. Name three types of merger.

15. What are the quantitative and transaction-size thresholds for merger review? What percentage of market share by the merging entities will likely trigger review by the Competition Bureau?

16. Name two statutes concerned with consumer protection in Canada, and explain how they protect the public.

17. Why was it necessary for the federal government, the provinces, and the territories to conclude an Agreement on Internal Trade? What is one major advantage of the accord? One deficiency?

18. Which level of government is responsible for environmental protection in Canada?

19. What is a "nuisance" at common law?

20. Name three ways that a business can incur environmental liability.

Cases and Problems

1. Manitoba decides to legislate hours of work, pay, and unionization requirements. These are to apply "all employees in the province of Manitoba." Marina Papadopoulos is the president and CEO of Zeus.com, a small long-distance phone reseller whose main business is providing inexpensive long-distance service in the province. Several months after Zeus.com began operations and Marina hired several dozen people, one of her employees comes to her with a petition to unionize the company under provincial legislation. Marina contests the unionization petition in court because she claims that long-distance service providers are federally regulated. Will she be successful?

2. The federal government decides to enact national standards under the federal *Food and Drugs Act* for the composition of beer. According to federal standards, light beer has to contain no more than 2.5 percent alcohol. John Simpson Inc, a popular micro-brewery in Kingston, Ontario, violates this provision by retailing "John Simpson Lite" beer with an alcohol content of 4 percent. It decides to challenge the federal statute as outside government powers over trade and commerce. Note that most sectors of the food industry are highly concentrated, with large manufacturing suppliers advertising their products on national television and engaging in national distribution. It would be expensive and cumbersome for food manufacturers to have to comply with a variety of provincial regulations. Would the national beer standard survive attack?

3. The federal government decides to ban tobacco advertising and promotional events linked to the tobacco industry, such as sports events and entertainment sponsorships. The government claims that advertising increases tobacco consumption, particularly among young women. Could a cigarette manufacturer challenge the ban on the basis that it prohibits the exercise of a company's right to free speech?

4. Bigrow Inc imports saplings from the United States into Canada that, unknown to it, contain gypsy moth larvae. The gypsy moth is a pest that Canadian officials want to contain and eliminate. At a routine inspection of a shipment on Bigrow's premises, officials find larvae and order

Bigrow management to destroy the saplings. When they refuse to do so, a federal inspector, accompanied by provincial officers, enters Bigrow's premises and supervises the destruction of the saplings. Bigrow wonders if it can invoke the Canadian *Charter of Rights and Freedoms* to bring an action against the federal government. In particular, it wonders if it can claim a violation of s 8 of the *Charter*, which provides that "Everyone has the right to be secure against unreasonable search or seizure."

5. Josefina Makik and her sister, Aurora, lived in Saskatchewan. They noticed the bog-like conditions on some of their property and decided that they wanted to get into the business of growing and exporting wild rice, a delicacy grown only in Manitoba. They establish a corporation for this purpose. Years earlier, however, the federal government created the Wild Rice Marketing Agency to limit supply and support prices. The agency's statute requires that both a licence and quota be granted before a wild rice grower can legally export rice. Josefina decides to grow and export wild rice without either. The Wild Rice Marketing Agency commences an action against her corporation for damages for the illegal sales. Josefina wants to know if corporate activities are protected by the Canadian *Charter of Rights and Freedoms*, specifically the right to association under s 2(d) and mobility rights under s 6.

6. Several years ago, Betty established Care-at-Home Inc to provide nursing services to convalescents and seniors at home. Most of the revenues of Care-at-Home Inc came from government-provided healthcare coverage. However, the provincial government recently decided to assume responsibility for in-home care in a bid to control costs. That put Care-at-Home out of business. Betty sued the government claiming that her company's rights to "life, liberty and security of the person" under s 7 of the *Charter* were infringed. Is she likely to win?

7. Bluewater Inc, a pulp and paper manufacturer, agreed to purchase logs from various timber companies. Before agreeing to any prices, however, it met with other pulp and paper manufacturers and verified the timber needs of their mills, the quantities of wood produced by a given area in the last season, prospects for future production, and other factors. At those meetings, Bluewater and the other pulp and paper manufacturers discussed prices for the upcoming season on the basis that the amount of wood cut would be affected by the price offered. Bluewater insists that those discussions did not occur for any sinister reason, but merely to further the business interests of those involved in the pulp and paper industry. Have Bluewater and the other companies involved in the arrangement violated the *Competition Act*? If so, what provision?

8. For a number of decades, the six manufacturers of microscopes in Canada operated under an informal agreement that involved little or no competition on pricing, but high competition in performance and service. The manufacturers in the arrangement often re-designed their products and generally maintained the technology of their products at world-class levels. The government now wants to know if it could prosecute those manufacturers, either individu-

ally for abuse of their dominant positions or jointly for conspiracy.

9. Nancy and Bob Brown ran a successful locksmithing and security business in Perth, Ontario for 17 years. They were well known and highly respected in the community. The Browns were thinking of retiring and decided to sell their company to Vladimir Markovic, who had just moved to Perth. As a term of the sale, the Browns signed a non-compete agreement with their old business that prohibited them from operating a similar business similar within 100 kilometres of Perth for 10 years. Once out of the business, however, the Browns incorporated a business to act as a competitor to Markovic and their old company. Markovic brought an action to enforce the terms of the non-compete agreement. He wants to know if the non-compete clause can be enforced.

10. Jim Tate was store manager at Buyco on the outskirts of Edmonton. Buyco, a general retailer, always placed weekly advertisements in local newspapers. To move some high-tech toys sitting in a nearby warehouse, Tate decided to advertise a one-week fall sale. News of this sale went out in a flyer, not in the newspaper. As a result, there was a stampede into the store by customers when it opened on the first day of the sale. Later that day, the store had sold out. Many customers on subsequent days were disappointed. Tate offered them rain checks, but was later told by suppliers that they would not be able to get more product to Buyco until after the busy holiday season.

The Attorney General's office decided to prosecute Buyco and Tate under s 57(2) of the *Competition Act* for advertising high-tech toys at prices that they did not supply in reasonable quantities. What are the prospects of a successful conviction?

11. Storey's Landfill and Dump operated on the outskirts of Miramichi, New Brunswick. One side of the site was a river filled with fish; the other was an escarpment. The company had installed overflow pipes, ditches, a culvert system, and settling ponds to keep pollution from the landfill and dump from contaminating the water table underneath the property and the river. However, excessive rain caused a mudslide from the escarpment into the river. That contaminated the water and killed hundreds of fish. Storey's was charged with unlawfully permitting the release of a hazardous substance into the water. It wants to know what category of offence it will be prosecuted under and what defence it might raise.

12. Mr Zinger owned a farm near Bracebridge, Ontario, on which he raised tomato and cucumber crops. The Town of Bracebridge established a garbage dump near the farm, where large amounts of garbage were dumped each weekday. Other methods of disposing of the garbage, such as burial, were available, but the town chose to burn its garbage in the open air at the site, which caused offensive smells and smoke. The dump also attracted a large number of gulls, which attacked Zinger's tomato crop; the smoke also reduced his cucumber crop. Zinger wants to know what he can do about the situation.

24 Doing Business in a
Global Economy

CHAPTER OVERVIEW

OBJECTIVES

After completing this chapter, you should be able to:

1. Explain what domestic and international law are and how they differ.
2. Explain what public and private international law are and the roles they play in the global economy.
3. Identify three common risks in an international transaction, and explain how they can be overcome.
4. Explain why choice of law and choice of forum are necessary in international transactions.
5. Define arbitration, and discuss the advantages it offers to parties engaged in an international business transaction.
6. Describe the agreements that form part of a typical international sale of goods, and discuss what purpose each serves.
7. Identify what documentation is needed for an international sale of goods.
8. Describe the mechanics of an international sale of goods by letter of credit.
9. Describe the roles of the Department of Foreign Affairs and International Trade, the Canada Customs and Revenue Agency, and the Canadian International Trade Tribunal in international trade.
10. Explain what the "most favoured nation" and "national treatment" obligations are under international trade rules.

Until now, we have examined legal aspects of doing business *in Canada*. We have generally assumed that:

- the relevant events occur in Canada
- Canadian law applies
- a Canadian court will settle any disputes

While those assumptions simplify matters, sometimes they are not valid. In 2000, Canada exported $474 billion worth of goods and services, making it one of the 10 top trading countries in the world. Since Canadian business people are coming into greater contact with foreign partners and their legal systems every day, we need to consider the legal aspects of international transactions. The most distinctive features of an international transaction are that:

- some of the events occur outside of Canada
- Canadian law may not apply
- any disputes arising from the transaction may be settled by a foreign court

Note that additional risks arise when business is conducted across borders. As is generally true under a contract, the buyer must be concerned about receiving quality goods or services. The seller too must be concerned about receiving payment if it provides its product on credit. Those dangers are heightened in international sales. Minor misunderstandings can quickly escalate into major problems due to cultural and language barriers. Furthermore, while the buyer can bring a lawsuit in the seller's jurisdiction, or *vice versa*, international litigation involves a great deal of time, expense, and uncertainty.[1]

This chapter introduces the legal aspects of international business transactions. The first part focuses on private behaviour—the legal relationships created between business people in different countries. It explains the differences between domestic and international law, the problems that arise from their interaction, and the manner in which they operate together in an international sale. It also reviews ways to minimize the special risks that arise when a business transaction involves a foreign legal system.

> additional risks arise when a business enters into a transaction with a foreign partner

The second part of this chapter examines government regulation of international trade in Canada. Business people should be aware of the government departments and agencies that play a leading role in Canada's international trade relations. The chapter also surveys the concept of free trade, the role of the World Trade Organization (WTO), and Canada's involvement in that organization.

DOMESTIC AND INTERNATIONAL LAW

> domestic law is the law that applies within a particular geographical area

Most of this textbook is about *domestic law*. **Domestic law** is the law that applies within a particular geographical area, like Canada or the United States. Every country has its own domestic law. Some countries follow the common law tradition, with its emphasis on trials, judicial independence, and precedent. Others follow the civil law, which stresses written codes and inductive reasoning. Still others have been influenced by Hindu, Islamic, or Jewish law. And

---

[1.] The term "jurisdiction" has several meanings. In this context, it refers to a geographical area that is governed by a single set of rules and courts.

some are a blend of traditions. South Africa and Sri Lanka, for instance, have systems that are based on Roman law as later codified by the Dutch and more recently affected by indigenous influences.

International law is a distinct type of law that traditionally governed relations *between countries*. For that reason, it is often referred to as *public international law*. **Public international law** was classically concerned with international relations, the recognition of countries, nationality, and intergovernmental dispute settlement. The basic differences between domestic law and international law are illustrated in Figure 24.1. **Private international law** is a special kind of international law that is used to determine which courts and which laws apply in private disputes that contain elements from various jurisdictions.

public international law is concerned with international relations, the recognition of countries, nationality, and inter-governmental dispute settlement

private international law is used to determine which courts and which laws apply in private disputes that contain elements from various jurisdictions

FIGURE 24.1   Domestic and International Law: A Comparison

Domestic Law	International Law
• applies *within* a country	• applies to relations *between* countries or to establish which set of national laws will prevail in a given situation
• is based upon laws, regulations, and administrative practices	• is based upon treaties, the customary behaviour of countries in their international relations, and certain aspects of domestic law
• adjudicated upon by courts or arbitrators	• adjudicated upon by specialized international tribunals (International Court of Justice, WTO dispute settlement)

In most countries, domestic and international law are considered to be separate. This recognizes that national interests sometimes require governments to act abroad in ways that might be illegal at home. For example, by declaring war, Canada's government is permitted to use force against foreigners and foreign property. It probably could never act this way against Canadians or their property. That separation of public and international law has a by-product. Many countries, including Canada, hold the view that international law usually applies domestically *only* to the extent that it is adopted by the legislature. Thus, it is traditionally assumed that a given rule of international law applies in Canada only to the extent that Parliament or a provincial legislature has enacted it.

a given rule of international law applies in Canada only to the extent that Parliament or a provincial legislature has enacted it

What if domestic and international laws conflict? In Canada, domestic law normally prevails, although it is possible for the federal government to be held responsible for violations of international agreements that it has signed but failed to implement. Many scholars argue that there are certain fundamental obligations, like those set out in the Universal Declaration of Human Rights, that Canada could never justifiably violate.[2] Moreover, Canadian courts (like those in other countries) often interpret domestic law in a way that minimizes any conflicts with international law.

[2.] The Universal Declaration of Human Rights, approved by the United Nations General Assembly in 1948, seeks protection of human equality, liberty, and associated rights throughout the world. Although it has been superseded by other, more specific instruments, the Universal Declaration remains influential.

LEGAL RISK IN INTERNATIONAL BUSINESS TRANSACTIONS

there is no single international commercial code covering all private transactions

The issues that we discussed in the last section generally apply to international commercial matters. Although it has developed considerably in recent years, private international law remains incomplete in many respects. There is, for instance, no single international commercial code covering all private transactions. There are some international documents, such as the United Nations' Convention on Contracts for the International Sale of Goods (CISG), that provide neutral sets of rules that the parties may *choose* to adopt.[3] While Canada is a signatory to the CISG (along with more than 60 other countries), the UN convention is not mandatory. It applies only if the parties *choose* to adopt it. In practice, however, they seldom do, largely because the convention is still relatively new. Instead, parties to international transactions usually agree to use the rules that are provided by a specified domestic system of law.

there is no international court of general jurisdiction for commercial cases

Also, there is no international court of general jurisdiction for international commercial cases. The International Court of Justice in The Hague has jurisdiction only over disputes *between countries*. A few other international tribunals exist, such as WTO dispute settlement and the Court of Justice of the European Community, but these are often limited to hearing disputes between governments. As a result, there are three options for parties to an international transaction.

- When creating their contract, they may simply assume that their transaction will be performed without problems and hope for the best. As a matter of risk management, that is the worst possible strategy.

a forum is the courts of a particular jurisdiction or that jurisdiction itself

- It is much better for the parties to choose not only a system of law (as we saw in the last paragraph), but also a *forum*. A **forum** is the courts of a particular jurisdiction, or that jurisdiction itself. Consequently, if a dispute does arise, the parties know where they should turn for assistance.

arbitration is a process in which a neutral third person, called an *arbitrator*, imposes a decision on the parties

- Instead of (or in addition to) referring any disputes to a particular set of courts, the parties can agree to submit their disagreements to an *arbitrator*. As we saw in Chapter 1, **arbitration** is a process in which a neutral third person, called an *arbitrator*, imposes a decision on the parties. The arbitrator's decision can later be judicially enforced.

The parties can therefore adopt certain steps to reduce uncertainty and manage the risks that are uniquely associated with international transactions. Nevertheless, problems may still arise. We need to look at three issues in more detail:

- choice of law
- choice of forum and jurisdiction
- dispute settlement

Choice of Law

choice of law is the selection of the applicable set of rules

The starting point for a discussion about the treatment of international business transactions is the *choice of law*.[4] **Choice of law** is the selection of the applicable set of rules. The system selected is known as the **proper law of the contract**.

the proper law of the contract is the system of law that governs the contract

---

[3.] 1489 UNTS 3 (1980).

[4.] Special considerations apply in the context of international commerce transactions. Those rules for the choice of law and the choice of forum were discussed in Chapter 17.

The parties are generally free to choose any system of law. For instance, their contract may say, "This agreement shall be governed by the laws of Alberta."[5] The courts, both in Canada and abroad, try to honour the parties' choice, or at least take it into consideration. The parties' express choice of law is usually respected if it is in good faith, is legal, and does not violate any rule of public policy.[6]

If the parties fail to expressly state their choice of law, the issue becomes more complicated. Canadian courts often try to infer the parties' intentions by looking at the place where the contract was created, the form of the documents, the language used, and the currency of payment.[7] If that process fails to reveal a clear answer, the courts select the system of law with which the transaction has the *closest and most substantial connection*. While those two approaches are similar, the first focuses more on the parties' unstated intentions, while the second focuses more on the circumstances of the case.[8] Case Brief 24.1 illustrates the necessity of choosing the right law.

> the parties are generally free to choose any system of law

> the courts will select the system of law if the parties fail to do so

CASE BRIEF 24.1

Vita Foods Ltd v Unus Shipping Co [1939] AC 277 (PC)

Vita Foods, a New Jersey-based food importer, contracted to purchase several loads of Newfoundland herring. The herring were shipped from Newfoundland to New York. During the voyage, the ship carrying the fish ran aground on the Nova Scotia shore. The herring was damaged and, according to the case report, had to be "reconditioned" (that is, heat-treated).

Vita claimed damages from the carrier under Canadian law, claiming that the ship had run aground in Nova Scotia. The contractual bill of lading, however, said that the parties' agreement was governed by English law. There was, in addition, a third system of law in issue: that of Newfoundland, which was where the shipment had originated. At that time, Newfoundland was still an independent dominion within the British Empire. The carrier argued for the application of English law, which at that time would have relieved it of liability for negligence. Canadian law, on the other hand, imposed liability pursuant to the *Hague Rules on Maritime Liability*, which we will examine.

The court held that since the parties' choice of law was in good faith and legal and did not violate any rule of public policy, it should be respected. The choice of law expressed in the contractual bill of lading was English, and that choice prevailed. Vita was therefore unsuccessful.

---

5. Choice of jurisdiction and law clauses were discussed in the appendix to Chapter 4. When we discuss systems of law, we usually think in terms of countries. However, within a country like Canada, a different system of law exists in each province and territory, at least with respect to issues that the Constitution assigns to the provincial and territorial governments, rather than the federal government. We discussed the distinction between provincial (and territorial) matters and federal matters in Chapter 1.

6. *Vita Food Products v Unus Shipping Co* [1939] AC 277 (PC). The term "public policy" refers to a process of judicial reasoning that is based on what the court considers to be the current needs of the community. The express choice of law may also be overridden if contract is either concluded in bad faith or illegal. An example of both arose in *Golden Acres Ltd v Queensland Estate Pty Ltd* [1969] Qd R 378. The parties contracted for the purchase and sale of land in Australia under Hong Kong law. The court held the express choice of Hong Kong law was invalid because the parties had chosen that jurisdiction to be able to pay a broker's fee to the seller, a non-Australian, which would have been illegal under the relevant Australian law.

7. *Hamlyn & Co v Talisker Distillery* [1894] AC 202 (HL); *Sayers v International Drilling Co NV* [1971] 3 All ER 163 (CA).

8. *Imperial Life Assurance Co of Canada v Colmenares* (1967) 62 DLR (2d) 138 (SCC); *Amin Rasheed Shipping Corp v Kuwait Insurance Co* [1984] AC 50 (HL).

Choice of Law Not Necessarily Definitive

The parties' express choice of law does *not* necessarily determine all aspects of the transaction. There may be instances when, for instance, an important element of the transaction occurs in another jurisdiction. In such a case, and depending on the facts, the law of an entirely different system of law may be applied. Suppose that a seller in Vancouver agrees to send goods to a buyer in Australia. The parties also agree that their agreement is governed by British Columbia's law. Unfortunately, while being shipped, the goods are damaged in Honolulu.

the courts may decide to apply a different system of law than the one chosen by the parties in the contract

Despite the parties' choice of law, a court in Hawaii might decide that American law applies because Hawaii has the closest and most substantial connection with the actual incident that damaged the goods. For instance, it may be that the goods were damaged as the result of negligence by a stevedoring company at the wharf in Honolulu. The American court might say that that company had no reasonable expectation of being sued under Canadian law.

The lesson is both clear and unsettling. The parties' choice of law is never entirely conclusive. It is an important expression of their intention and is generally respected. However, it may be subject to variation, depending upon the circumstances. That possibility generates an important risk, because it can never be predicted and it upsets the parties' reasonable expectations. Furthermore, that risk is heightened because the laws of Canada's major trading partners, while often similar, are sometimes significantly different.[9]

Canadian business people should therefore prepare for the possibility that foreign law may apply to an international transaction by finding out about the business environment abroad and, when necessary, hiring an experienced lawyer.

Choice of Forum and Jurisdiction

The parties to an international transaction can select both the system of law and the forum for settling any disputes. Their choice of forum normally follows their choice of law. For instance, if they agree that the laws of Nova Scotia governs their agreement, they will likely also agree that the courts of Nova Scotia—or, more precisely, the courts in Halifax—will apply those laws.

Nevertheless, a court can always question whether it has authority to hear a case if the facts have a strong foreign connection. Suppose that all of the relevant events occurred and all of the witnesses and records are located outside of Nova Scotia. Furthermore, suppose that all of those significant elements consistently point to a particular foreign jurisdiction, such as England. A court in Nova Scotia might refuse to hear the matter.

forum non conveniens involves a court's discretion to decline authority over a case that should be heard elsewhere

Such a refusal is usually triggered by the doctrine of *forum non conveniens* (which literally means "inconvenient forum"). **Forum non conveniens** involves a court's discretion to decline authority over a case that should be heard elsewhere. Normally, the defendant argues that there is another jurisdiction or forum where it is more convenient and appropriate for the plaintiff to pursue its claim.[10] When presented with that argument, a court will look at such things as: (i) the place where the contract was created, (ii) the parties' choice of law, (iii) the place where the relevant events occurred, (iv) the place where the witnesses and the evidence is located, and (v) whether the plaintiff will suffer some disadvantage if the case is heard elsewhere.[11] If the court agrees with the defendant,

---

[9] In Canada, for instance, a worker dismissed without cause is usually entitled to a period of reasonable notice upon termination: Chapter 25. That is not normally the case in the US.

[10] The argument sometimes is made by someone other than the defendant.

[11] *Amchem Products Inc v British Columbia (Workers' Compensation Board)* (1993) 102 DLR (4th) 96 (SCC); *Guarantee Co of North America v Gordon Capital Corp* (1994) 18 OR (3d) 9 (Ont Gen Div).

it imposes a *stay*. A **stay** is a court-ordered suspension of legal proceedings. If that happens, the plaintiff can sue in another jurisdiction. Often, however, the prospect of hiring new lawyers and incurring more expenses will encourage the plaintiff to settle the dispute out of court, or even give up altogether.

a stay is a court-ordered suspension of legal proceedings

Dispute Settlement

Since there is no international court with general jurisdiction over private commercial disputes, the business world uses other mechanisms to resolve disagreements.

Courts

One alternative is for the parties to agree on a particular court, or forum, to hear their disputes. Some courts have a reputation for certain types of proceedings. For instance, the courts of London, England are known for their experience and expertise in international aviation and maritime litigation. Consequently, parties in those lines of business often agree in advance to send their disputes to London.[12]

Arbitration

Arbitration, a popular option, acts as a kind of "private court" through which the parties agree to settle their differences. A contractual arbitration clause will specify when arbitration will be used, how the arbitrator will be chosen, where the arbitration will take place, and what procedures will be followed.[13] For greater certainty, many arbitration clauses refer to established arbitration centres. Such centres facilitate hearings by providing a roster of potential arbitrators, a set of rules, and a list of fees. One well-known centre is the International Chamber of Commerce in Paris. Arbitration centres also exist in major Canadian cities.

The selection of the particular arbitrator is often contentious. A contractual arbitration clause usually allows the parties to agree on a person, if and when the need arises. They usually choose a senior lawyer or a law professor with a reputation for expertise and experience. However, because the parties may not be able to agree, the arbitration clause should also provide another procedure for selecting the arbitrator.[14] Whatever the selection process, the chosen arbitrator sets a date and place for the arbitration to occur. The hearing is usually conducted at a private facility, such as a hotel, where the parties bring their lawyers.

Arbitration is preferable to court proceedings for several reasons:

- First, arbitration offers a greater degree of neutrality than court proceedings. Parties are free to designate the place of arbitration, the language to be used, the applicable procedural rules, the nationality of the arbitrator, and the qualifications of their lawyers. In court proceedings, all of those matters are dictated by court rules.

[12.] *The Angelic Grace* [1995] 1 Lloyds Rep 87 (CA). Concern about arguments of *forum non conveniens* is diminished in these cases by the parties' deliberate selection of the London courts as the forum for their disputes, and by the courts' long tradition of accepting jurisdiction.

[13.] An example of an arbitration clause appears in the appendix to Chapter 4.

[14.] Many arbitration clauses provide that if the parties are unable to agree on an arbitrator, an independent appointing authority, such as the International Chamber of Commerce, will have the power to appoint that person.

■ Second, arbitration usually provides a less-expensive and faster way of resolving international business disputes. Arbitration clauses can be invoked quickly, hearing dates can be arranged on short notice, and final decisions can be rendered in a fraction of the time that it would take to bring most disputes to court. It is common, for instance, for cases in the Canadian court system to take several years to get to trial. Arbitration can occur in a matter of months. The cost of arbitral proceedings is therefore also reduced.

■ Third, because the parties have consented in advance, there is little a party can do to frustrate the proceedings by raising objections about the choice of law or *forum non conveniens*. Instead, the arbitrator normally has the power to determine all matters arising out of a dispute.[15]

an award is the written result containing an arbitrator's decision

■ Fourth, arbitral decisions, known as **awards**, are final and binding and can be judicially enforced. Because they are decided on the basis of neutral rules that are not associated with any one jurisdiction, arbitral awards enjoy greater international recognition than court judgments. The principal international treaty on the enforcement of foreign arbitral awards is in force and has been adopted by more than 130 countries, including Canada. There is no similar agreement for the enforcement of foreign judgments.[16] This, coupled with the speed of arbitral proceedings, offers a considerable advantage to parties seeking enforcement.

arbitration offers many advantages over court proceedings

■ Fifth, Canadian courts are increasingly willing to defer to the arbitration process.[17] Most arbitration clauses do *not* contemplate the possibility that the arbitrator's decision may be appealed or reviewed in a court. Furthermore, there are few grounds for challenging the validity of an arbitral award under federal or provincial law.[18] In Ontario, for instance, the *International Commercial Arbitration Act* says that an arbitral award can be set aside only if:

  ■ the contract that contained the arbitration clause was made by a party who lacked legal capacity,

  ■ there was no notice of the institution of arbitral proceedings,

  ■ the award deals with an issue that was not referred to arbitration,

  ■ there was some substantial procedural irregularity,

  ■ a court finds that the subject matter of the dispute was not capable of being resolved by arbitration, or

  ■ the award is contrary to public policy.[19]

That last point raises an important issue of risk management. Consider Business Decision 24.1.

---

[15] *Canada Packers Inc v Terra Nova Tankers Inc* (1993) 11 OR (3d) 382 (Gen Div); *Kaverit Steel and Crane Ltd v Kone Corp* (1992) 87 DLR (4th) 129 (Alta CA).

[16] See the New York Convention on the Recognition and Enforcement of Foreign Arbitral Awards, 7 June 1959, 330 UNTS 38. The draft Hague Convention on Jurisdiction and Foreign Judgments in Civil and Commercial Matters has been the subject of ongoing negotiations since the early 1990s but has yet to be been completed due to differences over the desirability of mandatory enforcement of foreign court decisions.

[17] *Gulf Canada Resources v Arochem* (1992) 66 BCLR (2d) 113 (CA); *Onex Corp v Ball Corp* (1994) 12 BLR (2d) 151 (Ont Gen Div).

[18] *International Commercial Arbitration Act*, SO 1993, c I.9, s 34 (Ont).

[19] Courts in other countries often follow a similarly restrictive approach: *Restatement (3d) of Foreign Relations Law* s 488 (United States of America).

Arbitration or Judicial Action?

Although arbitrators are usually appointed because of their experience and expertise in the relevant area, they are only human. They occasionally make mistakes. For instance, they may misunderstand the evidence or refuse to believe nervous, but honest, witnesses. Furthermore, they may deal with legal rules that are unclear and that equally support more than one interpretation.

If you take your claim to court, you know that you can generally appeal an unfavourable decision at least once.

There is greater opportunity to get a "correct" result. The decision of an arbitrator, however, may be final and binding.

Questions for Discussion

1. At the time of entering into an international business transaction, will you agree to the insertion of an arbitration clause?
2. What factors affect your decision? Are those factors purely economic? To what extent is your decision a reflection of your personality?

INTERNATIONAL SALE OF GOODS

We have looked at some of the basic legal distinctions of private international law. Now we will examine how they work in the context of a typical international sales transaction. We will focus on agreements involving the sale of goods, because that is the most common situation. Note, however, that services and intellectual property constitute a significant and growing component of global trade.[20]

Sale of Goods: Four Contracts in One

The typical international sale of goods involves at least four contracts.

- The first is *an agreement of purchase and sale* for the goods. A party in one country must agree to buy goods from a seller in another. Very often, that basic agreement will make provision for at least three other types of contracts. That gives rise to the idea of "four in one."

- Second, it is customary for the buyer to arrange financing through a bank in the form of a *letter of credit* opened in favour of the seller. The letter of credit is a promise by the buyer's bank to pay the seller upon the satisfaction of certain conditions, usually proof that the goods have been shipped. That arrangement is common in international sales, because few sellers have the luxury of waiting for payment until the goods arrive at the buyer's destination.

- Third, a contract of transportation is created to move the goods from the seller to the buyer. If the goods are being transported by marine cargo, the contract is normally referred to as a *bill of lading*.

- Fourth, a *contract of insurance* is created to ensure that there is some remedy if the goods are damaged in transit.

We will discuss each of the contracts in detail. Before doing that, we must stress that they are all interdependent—they all work together to spread risk. In

the typical international sale of goods involves at least four contracts

---

20. The WTO estimated in 2000 that world exports in commercial services were worth U.S. $1.3 trillion, and world exports of merchandise goods were worth $5.47 trillion. Growth in worldwide commercial service exports in the period 1990-1999 was 6 percent annually versus 6.67 percent for worldwide merchandise exports in the same period: *International Trade Statistics 2000* at 27, 40.

effect, they create a system of checks and balances that minimizes the danger that any one person will act improperly. For instance, the buyer and the seller may have never met. However, they each know their own banker. And while those two bankers may have never met, they probably know each other by reputation. Furthermore, each bank is probably wealthy enough to sue in foreign jurisdiction if anything goes wrong. The typical international sales transaction therefore places risk on the party best able to bear it.

Contract of Sale

Because we learned about contracts dealing with sales of goods within Canada in Chapter 8, our discussion about international contracts of sale can be brief. The agreement of purchase and sale generally must meet the usual requirements for an enforceable contract. For instance, there must be an offer and acceptance, and the parties must have intended to create legal relations. Depending upon the parties' choice of law, however, some of the normal requirement may not apply. The doctrine of consideration, for example, does not apply in many systems of law.

The sale contract typically contains a long list of terms. While their precise content depends upon the circumstances, they usually deal with: (i) the quantity and quality of the goods, (ii) the price, (iii) the method of payment, (iv) the shipping details, (v) the place of delivery to the buyer, and (vi) the point at which risk passes from one party to the other. Within the international context, the contractual terms also usually: (i) deal with the choice of law and the choice of forum, (ii) and specify the co-ordinate contracts of finance, transport, and insurance.

Contract of Finance

a **letter of credit** is a promise by the buyer's bank to pay the purchase price to the seller in exchange for certain documents

The contract of finance is normally contained in a *letter of credit*. A **letter of credit** is a promise by the buyer's bank to pay the purchase price to the seller in exchange for certain documents. The bank will not agree to that transaction unless it has the buyer's promise to pay for that credit. In some situations, the finance contract may be more specific. The parties to an international transaction may use an *irrevocable confirmed letter of credit*. Under an **irrevocable confirmed letter of credit**, both the buyer's bank *and* the seller's bank promise to pay the seller in exchange for certain documents. If the seller's bank actually pays, it seeks reimbursement from the buyer's bank, which in turn seeks reimbursement from the buyer. That sort of arrangement is very useful if the seller lacks confidence in both the buyer *and* the buyer's banker. The seller wants an assurance of payment from someone it trusts—its own banker.

under an **irrevocable confirmed letter of credit**, both the buyer's bank *and* the seller's bank promise to pay the seller in exchange for certain documents

Letters of credit are based on two principles.

the **autonomy principle** states that payment is based on the seller's ability to satisfy the terms of credit

- First, the **autonomy principle** states that payment is based on the seller's ability to satisfy the terms of credit (for instance, by handing over certain documents). Payment is *not* based on the condition of the goods that are provided under the parties' sales contract. The seller may be entitled to payment *even if* the goods are defective. Payment is therefore "autonomous" from the condition of the goods.

the **principle of strict compliance** states that the seller is entitled to payment only if it completely satisfies the terms of the credit arrangement

- Second, the **principle of strict compliance** states that the seller is entitled to payment only if it completely satisfies the terms of the credit arrangement. The seller cannot demand payment under a letter of credit merely because it provided goods that meet the requirements of the parties' sales contract.

Those principles make good business sense.

- Payment normally takes place while the goods are en route to their destination. It is therefore impossible for bankers to check the goods. The autonomy principle is based on the belief that the documents are a substitute for the goods themselves. A banker can, after all, verify a document even if it cannot examine the goods.

- The principle of strict compliance is also based on the need for certainty and efficiency in the business world. The parties and their bankers need a bright line rule. They do not want to be caught up in interpretation debates. Consequently, the seller is entitled to payment *only if* it provides documents that *perfectly conform* to the terms of the letter of credit.

An international set of rules known as the Uniform Customs and Practice for Documentary Credits (UCP) adopts the autonomy principle and the strict compliance principle. The UCP is both followed by banks as common practice and recognized by courts.

Supporting Documents

Although compliance with the letter of credit is usually a necessary condition for the seller's receipt of payment, it not normally sufficient. The bank typically requires the seller to produce a number of other documents, possibly including:

- a bill of lading
- an inspection certificate
- a certificate of origin
- a commercial invoice describing the goods
- an insurance certificate
- a draft (also known as a bill of exchange)

These supporting documents provide additional forms of risk management. A *bill of lading* provides the bank with evidence that the goods were actually shipped. Shipped goods are useless, however, if they are defective. Consequently, the parties may have agreed that the seller would not receive payment until it provided an *inspection certificate*. That document is completed by a neutral third party, who verifies the quality of the goods before they are shipped. A *commercial invoice*, which is completed by the seller, may also provide some evidence about the quantity and condition of the goods. In some situations, the parties may also agree upon the need for a *certificate of origin*. That document, which is normally completed by the producer of goods, verifies the product's country of origin. It can be used by customs officials in the importing country to assign tariff classification. An *insurance certificate* assures the buyer that if the goods are lost or damaged, compensation will be provided under an insurance policy.

The final document is the *draft*, or *bill of exchange*. A **draft,** or **bill of exchange**, is created when one person orders another person to pay a specific amount of money to a third person.[21] As Chapter 9 explained, this is a negotiable instrument, which the seller can transfer, or *negotiate*, to another person. Business Law in Action 24.1 highlights the most significant points.

a draft, or bill of exchange, is created when one person orders another person to pay a specific amount of money to a third person

---

[21] *Bills of Exchange Act*, RSC 1985, c B-4 (Can).

BUSINESS LAW IN ACTION 24.1

International Sales, Drafts, and Negotiation

Your company, which is located in Toronto, agrees to sell a shipment of widgets to a company in Mexico. Under the terms of that sales contract, the buyer creates a draft that orders his bank in Mexico City to pay the purchase price to you. You could present the draft to the buyer's bank in Mexico City to receive payment. However, after receiving the draft, you prefer to negotiate it to your own bank in Toronto. In exchange, your own bank pays you the value of the draft (minus any service charges). Your bank then seeks payment from the buyer's bank, which in turn receives payment from the buyer.

Questions for Discussion

1. What are the advantages to negotiating the draft to your own bank rather then seeking payment directly from the buyer's bank?
2. Do you want payment in Canadian dollars or Mexican pesos? From whom would it be easier to get such currency?
3. Who do you know and trust more: your bank in Toronto or the buyer's bank in Mexico City?
4. If you experience any problem in getting payment, would you rather sue your own bank in Toronto or the buyer or its bank in Mexico City?

It is possible that your bank will experience difficulties in receiving payment from the buyer's bank, but that seldom happens.[22] The international banking system operates quite well, largely because each bank values its own reputation. And if problems do arise, your bank is almost certainly large enough and sophisticated enough to take action against the buyer's bank in Mexico.

Contract of Transport

a bill of lading is a contract that is created between the seller and the carrier

It is necessary under an international transaction to deliver goods from one country to another. That task is usually performed under a *bill of lading*. A **bill of lading** is a contract that is created between the seller and the carrier.

Suppose that you agree to sell a shipment of widgets from your warehouse in Vancouver to a buyer in São Paulo, Brazil. To transport the goods, you enter into a contract with a shipping company that will act as the carrier. Under that contract, the carrier issues a bill of lading, which serves a number of functions. It provides a receipt for the goods that you handed over. It also contains the terms of the contract of carriage, including a description of the goods and instructions to the carrier to deliver them to a particular place within a particular time. Perhaps most interestingly, the bill of lading can also be used to transfer ownership in the goods. Several possibilities arise.

- You may ask the carrier to issue a *straight bill of lading*, which names the buyer (or the buyer's bank, if the buyer has used the goods as collateral for a bank loan for the price of the goods). Under that arrangement, the buyer normally becomes the owner of the goods as soon as they are shipped.

[22.] There are exceptions. The collapse of a single bank, or, more seriously, the insolvency of part of a country's banking system, as happened in Thailand, Indonesia, and Korea in 1997, can have profound implications. One infamous example involved the Bank of Credit and Commerce International, a Luxembourg-based financial conglomerate. BCCI was involved in questionable financial dealings around the world. It collapsed in July 1991 amid allegations of fraud following an investigation by the Bank of England. Its failure had a significant impact on the 1.4 million depositors that it had in 73 countries, including Canada.

- Or you may ask the carrier to issue an *order bill of lading*, which names a person who has ownership of the goods while they are in transit. For instance, if you have not yet received payment, you may not want to give up your title to the widgets. You therefore could name yourself under an order bill of lading. You could then take that bill and the other necessary documents to the buyer's bank to receive payment. In exchange for that money, you would *endorse* (that is, sign over) the bill to the buyer.[23]

- The buyer can also use the bill of lading to transfer ownership to a third party. Suppose that while the goods are still in transit, but after you have given up ownership, the buyer decides to resell the widgets to someone else. Even though the buyer does not yet have physical possession of the goods, they do have the bill of lading that represents their ownership. In exchange for a price, they may endorse that bill over to the sub-buyer. In that way, bills of lading are critically important to the flow of international commerce.

Other Transport Documents

In many countries, the term "bill of lading" is limited to contracts for marine cargo only. Contracts for goods carried by truck, rail, or air have different names. Those for trucking and rail transport are often referred to as "truck bills of lading" or "rail bills of lading," while those for air transport are "air way-bills."[24]

There has recently been an increase in *intermodal transport*. **Intermodal transport** involves the delivery of goods by several modes of transport. Pallets, containers, or trailers are transferred between trucks, trains, ships, or airplanes in the course of a single journey. Under the traditional system of transport documentation, intermodal transport would generate a blizzard of paperwork for every shipment. Each stage would involve its own bill of lading (or similar document). International business people therefore often use intermodal bills of lading. Such bills are issued by a combined transport operator, who assumes full responsibility for the shipment during all phases of the voyage for a fee.

intermodal transport involves the delivery of goods by several modes of transport

INCOTERMS

As we have seen many times, uncertainty is a critical concern for international sales. That problem can arise in a number of ways. It is relevant in this context because of the variety of terms that a contract may contain. We return to the example of your selling widgets, this time to a buyer in São Paulo, Brazil. Before you agree on a price, you must settle a number of other items.

- Does the buyer have to collect the goods from your warehouse? Or do you have to deliver them to a ship waiting in Vancouver, a wharf in Brazil, or the buyer's warehouse in São Paulo?

[23] In that sense, a bill of lading is similar to negotiable instruments, which we discussed in Chapter 9. Endorsement can be used to transfer not only the document, but also the rights underlying the document (in the case of a bill of lading, ownership of the goods). There are, however, important differences between a bill of lading and a true negotiable instrument (such as a bill of exchange). As we saw in Chapter 9, a person who receives a true negotiable instrument may take it "free of the equities." In other words, they may be immune to certain arguments and defences that could have been used against the person from whom they received the instrument. The same is not true of bills of lading: R Folsom *et al International Business Transactions* 4th ed (1995) at 199.

[24] Canada is not party to any international convention concerning unimodal or multimodal carriage of goods by rail or road. For regulations on bills of lading for carriage by air, see *Carriage by Air Act*, RSC 1985, c C-26, Art 11 (air waybill is presumptive evidence of the conclusion of a contract, receipt of cargo, and conditions of carriage).

- What happens if the goods are lost or damaged in transit? Who is responsible for obtaining insurance? Who must pay for that insurance? Who gets the benefit of that insurance?

Those questions must be answered. Furthermore, they should be answered as clearly as possible. For that reason, it is highly desirable to use *standardized terms*, terms that everyone knows and interprets in the same way. Ambiguity and inconsistency cause the business world to slow down.

INCOTERMS are internationally recognized terms and definitions relating to shipping and delivery

Because of the need for certainty, parties to international transactions usually rely on *INCOTERMS*. **INCOTERMS** are internationally recognized terms and definitions relating to shipping and delivery. They are not laws. Nevertheless, for the reasons that have been mentioned, they are usually incorporated into international sales agreements. For instance, your contract might say, "100 000 widgets will be $50 000 Canadian CIF INCOTERMS 1990 São Paulo." We will look at the precise meaning of that phrase in a moment. The important point is that you and the buyer have agreed that the abbreviation "CIF" ("cost, insurance, freight," which is a common shipping term) will be defined by INCOTERMS 1990.[25] There is no need for debate.

With respect to transportation, there are three basic types of INCOTERMS.[26] As Figure 24.2 shows, they impose progressively more obligations on the seller, who is required to: (i) make the goods available at its own warehouse, (ii) place the goods on board a ship, or (iii) deliver the goods to the buyer's location. As the seller's obligations increase, so does the price.

FIGURE 24.2   Transportation and Common INCOTERMS

EXW (ex works)
- The buyer under an EXW contract is required to collect the goods from the seller's place of business. The price therefore applies only to the goods themselves.
- The buyer is required to pay the costs associated with: (i) shipping the goods to its own place of business, and (ii) insuring the goods while they are in transit. The seller must, however, co-operate. For instance, it must provide any documents that the buyer requires.

FOB (freight on board)
- The seller under a FOB contract is required to place the goods on board a ship. It is therefore responsible for them until they have "passed the ship's rail." As a general rule, the buyer at that point both gets ownership of the goods and bears the risk of any loss or damage to the goods (as discussed in Chapter 8).
- The buyer is required to arrange the shipping and pay the costs associated with transportation once the goods are on board.
- Since the seller's responsibility ends once the goods have "passed the ship's rail," the buyer should also arrange and pay for insurance. After all, if the goods are lost or damaged in transit, the loss will fall upon the buyer. Since the buyer may not be familiar with the goods, the seller may agree to a FOB contract with additional services. In that situation, the seller *arranges* shipping and insurance on the buyer's behalf. The buyer is, however, still responsible for the associated costs.

(continued)

[25.] There have been several sets of INCOTERMS starting in 1936. For the sake of clarity, a contract should refer to the specific version, such as "INCOTERMS 1990." For added certainty, a separate provision in the contract should state that the entire agreement is subject to INCOTERMS 1990.

[26.] There are several variations on the basic options. For instance, instead of **FOB**, a contract may be **FAS**, in which case the seller's obligation ends when the goods are placed alongside a ship, rather than on board a ship.

FIGURE 24.2   (continued)

CIF (cost, insurance, freight)
- A CIF contract requires the seller to deliver the goods to the buyer's port.
- A CIF contract is similar to a FOB contract in that the risk of loss or damage usually passes to the buyer once the goods are placed on board the ship.
- A CIF contract, however, differs in two ways from a FOB contract.
- First, even though the risk of loss or damage passes to the buyer once the goods are placed on board, ownership in the goods generally remains with the seller until the price has been paid and the bill of lading has been endorsed to the buyer.
- Second, a CIF contract requires the seller to arrange and pay for shipping and insurance. Since the risk of loss passes to the buyer when the goods are placed on the ship, the insurance policy is arranged for the buyer's benefit.

Contract of Insurance

International trade gives rise to many risks. These can be classified into two categories: *operating risks* and *transport risks*. **Operating risks** arise from the use of goods or the operation of an investment in a foreign jurisdiction. We are more concerned with transport risks. **Transport risks** arise from the transportation of the goods to their final destination. Those risks include both *damage to the goods* that are being shipped and *damage that is caused by the goods* that are being shipped.

Ever since shipping became a global industry in the early twentieth century, there has been a debate about the liability of carriers for damage to goods. Ocean carriers successfully lobbied for a global system of limited liability known as the Hague Rules. These rules limited liability to a modest amount per package, and further gave carriers certain privileges, such as the right to jettison cargo if necessary to prevent a ship from sinking. Those rules were thought to be necessary to prevent the shipping industry from being driven out of business by liability. They also reflected the fact that carriers usually have little, if any opportunity, to inspect the goods that they carry. The Hague Rules were eventually accepted in most trading countries, including Canada, where they formed part of the *Carriage of Goods by Water Act*.[27]

Nevertheless, controversy persisted over limited liability. In 1968, a modification to the Hague Rules, known as the Hague-Visby Rules, was proposed. It slightly increased the liability limit per package and modified some of the defences available to carriers. Canada adopted the Hague-Visby Rules in 1993, and all goods shipped from Canadian ports are now subject to them. However, the US continues to apply the Hague Rules alone, as do many of Canada's other major trading partners.

From a risk management perspective, the lesson is clear. The parties to an international sales contract realize that they should not rely substantially upon their rights against the carrier if anything goes wrong. Instead, they should protect their interests through insurance, which we examined in Chapters 10 (third party, or liability, insurance) and 15 (first party, or property, insurance).

One important type of insurance against operating risk is available from the Export Development Corporation. The EDC is an extension of the federal government that sells insurance to cover the value of a shipment if a buyer fails to pay the price. The price for that insurance depends upon the risks associated with the country of destination. The EDC also provides financing assistance for foreign buyers of Canadian exports.

operating risks arise from the use of goods or the operation of an investment in a foreign jurisdiction

transport risks arise from the transportation of the goods to their final destination

---

[27.] *Carriage of Goods by Water Act*, SC 1993, c 21 (Can).

GOVERNMENT REGULATION OF INTERNATIONAL TRADE

We have examined the details of individual contracts for international sales. We can now look at how the area is regulated, both by the Canadian government and by international bodies.

In Canada, the main governmental department regulating international business is the Department of Foreign Affairs and International Trade (DFAIT). However, given the breadth and complexity of Canada's relations with the rest of the world, foreign affairs and international trade matters are actually co-ordinated between DFAIT and the departments of Finance, Revenue, Industry, Agriculture, Fisheries, Environment, Government Services, and Transport. Furthermore, a number of federal administrative tribunals and agencies are involved in implementing Canadian trade laws. Provincial governments also play a role in regulating international trade because they have exclusive juris-diction over a number of relevant areas. For instance, since the Constitution says that property and civil rights are a provincial matter, it is up to the provinces to implement some international agreements, such as the CISG, that relate to the sale of goods.

DFAIT's main trade responsibilities involve export promotion and export assistance. It also administers the *Export and Import Permits Act*, which governs trade sanctions on goods. That is done primarily through the Area Control List (ACL) and the Export Control List.[28] The ACL is a list of countries to which the Canadian government feels the need to control the flow of exports. As of early 2002, only Angola and Myanmar were listed on the ACL. The Export Control List is a list of goods for which the government believes it necessary to control exports. For example, Canada closely controls the export of military goods and technology to countries:

- that pose a threat to Canada and its allies
- that are involved in or under imminent threat of hostilities
- that are under United Nations sanctions, or
- whose governments have a persistent record of serious violations of the human rights of their citizens

The Department of National Revenue (DNR) also plays an important role in the administration and enforcement of trade policy through several key pieces of legislation. The DNR administers:

- the *Customs Act*, which provides the framework for customs adminis-tration
- the *Customs Tariff*, which sets out the specific tariffs charged on the entry of foreign goods into Canada
- the *Excise Tax Act*, which imposes the Goods and Services Tax and other revenue-generating taxes on imports[29]

Dumping and Subsidies

The DNR also investigates *dumping* and *subsidy* complaints. From a Canadian point of view, **dumping** occurs when foreign goods are sold in Canada for less

dumping occurs when foreign goods are sold in Canada for less than their fair value or total cost

---

[28.] *Export and Import Permits Act*, RSC 1985, c E-19 (Can).

[29.] *Customs Act*, RSC 1985, c 1 (2d Supp); *Customs Tariff*, RS 1997, c 36 (Can); *Excise Tax Act*, RSC 1985, c E-15 (Can).

than their fair market value or total cost. The foreign company's goal is to build up a stronghold in the Canadian market. **Subsidies** are financial incentives that foreign manufacturers receive from their own governments, that allow them to sell their goods in Canada at attractive prices. In either event, the Canadian government is legitimately concerned about the effect on Canadian businesses.[30] The government has developed ways of dealing with both dumping and subsidies.

If a substantial number of Canadian producers in a particular industry complain that they are being hurt by dumping, the DNR investigates and asks for a response from the foreign company. If dumping has occurred, the Canadian International Trade Tribunal (CITT) determines the extent to which the foreign company's activity has hurt the domestic industry. In appropriate circumstances, the government can then impose *anti-dumping duties*. An **anti-dumping duty** is a special charge that is placed on dumped goods as they are brought into Canada. The goal is to raise the price of those goods and thereby counteract the effect of dumping. Anti-dumping duties recently have been imposed on products as diverse as garlic from Vietnam and dishwashers from the US.

Anti-dumping measures are usually justified. However, the threat of such duties can also be used to improperly harass foreign producers. Consequently, anti-dumping legislation is now subject to the WTO Agreement. This sets specific thresholds that must be met before anti-dumping investigations or duties can be triggered. Unfortunately, those rules have not been entirely effective. Consequently, like many other countries, Canada is moving away from anti-dumping tactics. Instead, it is starting to use its own *Competition Act* (discussed in Chapter 23) to deal with sales that occur at less than fair market value.

While dumping is performed by a foreign company, a subsidy involves a foreign government. For instance, a foreign government may help a particular foreign company by paying for part of its research program. Since its research is being subsidized, that company has fewer costs and therefore can sell its products in Canada at prices that are lower than domestic producers can afford to offer. Subsidies are handled in much the same way as dumping. If a substantial number of Canadian producers complain, the DNR investigates and asks for a response from both the foreign company and the foreign government. If a subsidy is found to exist, the CITT determines its impact on Canadian producers. Depending upon the circumstances, the government may then take action. It may impose a *countervailing duty*, which operates in much the same way as an anti-dumping duty. Or it may impose a **quota**, which is a limit on the number of goods that can be imported into Canada.

Governments do many things that could be considered subsidies. For example, a government may build a road from a main highway to a remote factory, thereby sparing the company from the expense of doing so. The WTO Agreement, however, provides a narrow definition of "subsidy" and limits the situations in which one government can take action, based on an allegation that another government has subsidized a specific industry. Furthermore, subsidies are becoming less common for another reason. Since many governments are generally cutting funding, they are increasingly unwilling to subsidize their own industries. Today, subsidies are usually restricted to industries with great promise and to fields that traditionally have been of national interest, such as agriculture and military goods.

subsidies are financial incentives that foreign manufacturers receive from their own governments, that allow them to sell their goods in Canada at attractive prices

an anti-dumping duty is a special charge that is placed on dumped goods as they are brought into Canada

a quota is a limit on the number of goods that can be imported into Canada

---

[30] Canadian companies may also be accused of dumping goods in other countries or receiving improper subsidies from our own government.

Other Matters

Not only has the CITT partial responsibility for allegations of dumping and subsidies, it also serves a number of other functions. It can, for instance, be asked by the government to investigate a broad range of international trade matters and to provide advice based on its findings. As Ethical Perspective 24.1 demonstrates, the issues sometimes go beyond mere economics.

ETHICAL PERSPECTIVE 24.1

Talisman in Sudan?

In 1998, Talisman Energy, a Calgary-based oil producer, purchased a 25 percent stake in an oil-producing joint venture in Sudan, a poor country in northeast Africa. The joint venture was formed with other foreign partners to exploit oilfields in southern Sudan. A percentage of revenues from the project was to be paid to the Sudanese government.

The joint venture is very profitable and provides hundreds of jobs for unemployed Sudanese. However, there is some evidence that Talisman-built facilities, including an airstrip, warehouses, and a hospital, are being used by gov-

ernment forces in the course of military action against separatist rebels in the south. Talisman comes under pressure from shareholders in Canada and the US. Those shareholders claim that Talisman is indirectly promoting aggression against the southern population in violation of Sudanese and international law.

Questions for Discussion

1. What should a senior adviser to Talisman's management recommend in the circumstances?
2. What should be the role of Canadian companies that operate in zones of civil disturbance?

PUBLIC INTERNATIONAL LAW

Public international law traditionally governed relations between countries. More recently, it has begun to focus on economic matters. A number of international organizations are now concerned with cross-border trade.

GATT and World Free Trade

In 1947, 23 countries, including Canada, believed that open markets and free trade would result in greater efficiency and well-being for the global public. They created an international trade agreement, the General Agreement on Tariffs and Trade (GATT), which served several purposes.

a tariff is a tax that is imposed on goods that are imported from a foreign country

- GATT's main goal was to prohibit member countries from charging import *tariffs* beyond certain levels. A **tariff** is a tax that is imposed on goods that are imported from a foreign country.

- GATT required member states to apply their lowest, or most favourable, tariff rates to each other. That became known as the *most favoured nation* obligation.

- GATT members were required to treat foreign-produced goods from another member state in the same way as they treated domestic produced goods of the same type. That became known as the *national treatment* obligation.

The GATT restrictions promoted increased trade and provided an important stimulus to growth after the war.

Over the decades that followed, GATT members periodically negotiated lower tariff rates and developed rules in other trade-related fields, such as subsidies and dumping, customs valuation, pre-shipment inspection, licensing, and technical standards. Those rules recognized that trade can be hindered as easily by non-tariff tactics as by tariffs. GATT also created an informal mechanism for resolving trade disputes between member states. If a country violated the rules, GATT could allow the other countries that were hurt by the violation to close their markets to specified goods from the offending nation. That sort of retaliation was, however, rare. Most countries chose to settle their trade disputes between themselves.

World Trade Organization

GATT's mechanisms for dispute resolution were relatively informal. As global trade grew, both in size and in complexity, there was a need for a stronger, more integrated framework for international trade. GATT's members therefore decided to create a new treaty in 1994. GATT itself became part of the new World Trade Organization Agreement. The World Trade Organization (WTO) was created to administer that agreement. In early 2002, 142 countries and two customs territories (Hong Kong and Taiwan) were members.

The WTO Agreement adopts many of the GATT rules, such as the national treatment obligation. There are, however, important differences.

- First, GATT only covered trade in goods. The WTO Agreement covers trade in goods, services, and intellectual property. WTO coverage therefore accounts for intangible forms of wealth, a growing proportion of world trade.

- Second, the WTO Agreement retains GATT's tradition of decision making by consensus. In other words, decisions are adopted only if they enjoyed unanimous support from the members. That approach occasionally caused problems under GATT if one member state disagreed. The decision-making process under the WTO Agreement has greater flexibility, which has enhanced the impartiality and efficiency of the dispute settlement mechanisms.

- Third, the WTO Agreement introduces the possibility of appellate review. An appellate body has been established to hear appeals of panel decisions and to improve the consistency of dispute-settlement results.

- Fourth, the WTO Agreement consolidates most trade rules into a single package, bringing to an end the legal patchwork of agreements that emerged under GATT. Some inconsistencies remain, but the popular view seems to be that the WTO Agreement imposes more uniform requirements than existed in the past.

WTO Dispute Settlement

The WTO Agreement features an improved system of adjudication and implementation. If the WTO finds a violation of the rules, it instructs that offending country to implement changes. That country must respond within a specified time, either by appealing the decision or by complying with the rules. In most cases, the country changes or repeals its laws that were inconsistent with the WTO Agreement. If it fails to do this, the WTO may allow the injured country to close its markets to selected goods from the wrongdoer. You Be the Judge 24.1 discusses one aspect of WTO dispute settlement.

YOU BE THE JUDGE 24.1

Private Participation in WTO Disputes

WTO dispute settlement is a country-to-country affair. Governments decide when to bring complaints about other countries' laws. Countries found in violation also decide how to bring non-conforming laws into compliance with the WTO Agreement.

In some jurisdictions, like the United States and the European Community, private individuals can complain to their own government about an allegedly unfair foreign trade practice. If their government agrees and no solution can be reached with the offending country, the government may decide to bring action in the WTO. In Canada, however, there is no formal process for private complaints. Individuals and companies must lobby the federal government.

Questions for Discussion

1. Is private initiation of, or participation in, WTO disputes a good idea?

2. What problems might arise from private participation in WTO dispute settlement?

3. If private initiation or participation is allowed and that individual complainant's country wins, should that person be entitled to something from the wrongdoer?

North American Free Trade Agreement (NAFTA)

The North American Free Trade Agreement (NAFTA) entered into force between Canada, Mexico, and the United States in 1994. It was designed to act as a regional supplement to the WTO Agreement. The three NAFTA countries agreed to create a free trade area by eliminating substantially all tariffs on locally produced goods and services circulating between them. The tariffs are being removed in phases. The final phase is scheduled to be completed in 2008. NAFTA's central disciplines replicate those of the WTO in requiring most favoured nation and national treatment obligations. They also go beyond it, however, in protecting investment, providing liberalized access in selected service sectors, and removing specific restrictions on the cross-border transfer of professional persons. In addition, NAFTA features two side accords designed to ensure a high level of labour and environmental protection in North America.

Chapter Summary

Domestic law must be distinguished from international law. Public international law was classically concerned with international relations, the recognition of countries, nationality, and intergovernmental dispute settlement. Private international law is a special kind of international law that is used to determine which courts and which laws apply in private disputes that contain elements from various jurisdictions.

The rules governing international business transactions are still developing. Although some international documents provide neutral sets of rules, those documents are not mandatory. Furthermore, business people usually prefer to use the domestic laws of a specified country. They are generally free to choose any country; however, if they fail to do so, a court may select a system of law for them. There is also no international court of general jurisdiction for commercial cases. Business people therefore usually select a forum to resolve their disputes. In a case of *forum non conveniens*, however, a court in the chosen jurisdiction may refuse to hear the matter. The parties may also choose to settle their disputes through arbitration, which has both benefits and disadvantages.

An international sale of goods involves at least four contracts: (i) a sales contract, (ii) a financing contract, (iii) a transportation contract, and (iv) an insurance contract. The sales contract usually follows the rules that generally apply in connection with the sale of goods. The finance contract usually involves a letter of credit and a draft (or bill of exchange). It is used to facilitate payment to the seller. Payment usually depends upon the production of several documents as well. The transport contract usually consists of a bill of lading. Transportation is an important issue in international sales. For the sake of consistency and efficiency, the parties should use INCOTERMS. The insurance contract is particularly important because a number of international agreements have severely limited the liability of carriers.

Government plays an important role in international trade. It can, for instance, take action against foreign dumping and subsidies that hurt Canadian businesses. Canada is also a member of the WTO. The WTO provides mechanisms for the resolution of trade disputes between different countries.

Review Questions

1. What is domestic law? What is international law?

2. Name two categories of international law, and describe how they differ.

3. What is the United Nations' Convention on Contracts for the International Sale of Goods? Are Canadian businesses required to use it when they enter into international transactions?

4. Explain the meaning of the phrase "choice of law"? When will a court refuse to apply the parties' choice of law?

5. If the parties do not choose a system of law, how will a court decide which rules to apply?

6. Explain the meaning of the term "forum." Are the parties always entitled to choose their own forum?

7. Explain the doctrine of *forum non conveniens*. What is a "stay"?

8. List five advantages of arbitration. Explain why a party may not want to arbitrate a dispute and what other option exists in that situation.

9. Explain the meaning of the term "four-in-one" in the context of international sales.

10. Is it necessary for a Canadian business to provide consideration to create an enforceable agreement in an international transaction? Explain your answer.

11. What is a letter of credit? How is it used to finance an international transaction?

12. Explain the autonomy principle and the principle of strict compliance. How are they relevant to the issue of risk management?

13. Briefly explain six documents, in addition to a letter of credit, that a seller may be required to produce before receiving payment.

14. Explain how negotiation of a draft, or bill of exchange, may benefit a seller.

15. Describe a bill of lading, and explain how it works.

16. What is "intermodal transport"? What problem can it create with respect to transport documents? How can that problem be overcome?

17. What are INCOTERMS? Name three important INCOTERMS, and explain the obligations that each one imposes on a seller.

18. Briefly explain why it is difficult to successfully sue a carrier for goods that are lost or damaged in transit.

19. Outline the procedures that the Canadian government can use to deal with dumping or subsidies.

20. Explain how the WTO Agreement affects international trade.

Cases and Problems

1. Bobbi is in the business of making ice wine, a sweet dessert wine that Canada is becoming known for. Her brand has just been given marketing approval by the European Commission for all countries in the European Union. She decides that her first marketing push will be to Italy, a country where the market for dessert wine is growing. Bobbi is introduced to Sergio, an Italian wine broker in Milan, who offers to market her new product there. He faxes her an offer and asks her to fax it back after she has signed it. She does so. Several months later, after several trips to Italy, she learns that Sergio is no longer interested in marketing her ice wine and has started marketing the product of several of her competitors with good results. She sues in an Ontario court for development costs incurred in the venture and loss of profit. Sergio defends on the grounds that Ontario is *forum non conveniens* and that the proper place for such a dispute is an Italian court. What arguments can be made for and against her claim?

2. Diego, a recent arrival in Vancouver from Ecuador, is 18 years old. He wants to purchase a stereo for his apartment and goes to a local department store in Burnaby to do so. To Diego's surprise, the store offers him the stereo on credit, which Diego, being new to Canada, accepts. Several months later, the store comes after Diego demanding payment. Diego refuses on the grounds that the age of majority in Ecuador is 21. Would he be successful? What if he had remained in Ecuador and purchased the stereo after receiving a catalogue from a Canadian retailer? Who would be successful in that case? What if Diego had purchased the stereo while in Vancouver because of an offer made in a catalogue sent to him by an Ecuadorian retailer?

3. Ontario Bus Industries (OBI), an Ontario manufacturer of transport goods, bought a bus frame weighing several tonnes from a German seller. That frame was made in Hungary. The bill of lading was issued in Hamburg, Germany, and the bus was loaded onto a ship at Antwerp, Belgium, for transport to Toronto. The bill did not state whether the Hague or Hague-Visby Rules applied to the shipment. The bus was stored in the hold and damaged on the voyage to Canada. Under Belgian law, the Hague-Visby Rules apply to all shipments loaded in Belgium. They limit liability on a shipment or on a weight basis, whichever is higher. Under German law, the Hague Rules apply and limit the carrier's liability to £100 per shipment. The issue of which rules should apply comes before a Canadian court. How should it decide?

4. Edinger Inc is a Canadian computer consulting company doing business in North America and around the world. Its head office is in Kanata, Ontario. To serve its US clientele better, it establishes an American subsidiary in San Mateo, California. Edinger then hires a Canadian, Tim Winton, to run the US subsidiary. The contract was signed at Edinger's Kanata office, but no law is specified to govern the contract. Winton becomes a resident of California and is paid in US funds. Although Winton works primarily in the US, he makes frequent trips back to Canada and calls the Kanata office several times a day. After the market for consulting services collapses, Edinger lays Winton off in a cost-cutting move. Winton brings suit for wrongful dismissal in Ontario, claiming that he is owed notice pay and an amount for severance under Ontario law. The company's position is that Winton's contract was governed by California law, which does not recognize either notice or severance. What system of law governs Winton's contract?

5. Antony Gappah lends US dollars to his friend Peter Malunga in Zimbabwe. Both men agree that the loan will be repaid in US dollars, something that is illegal under Zimbabwean law. Both men subsequently emigrate to Canada, and Gappah demands repayment, asserting that both men are in Canada and that repayment of loans in US dollars is legal in Canada. Malunga disagrees. Who is correct?

6. Sidra Corp is a British Columbia-based manufacturer of microbrew equipment. It advertises itself on the Internet and through publicity at trade shows. Due to its promotional efforts, Sidra is approached by Good Times Inc, a Texas-based venture capital firm, about supplying microbrew equipment to a chain of 20 "relaxed dining" restaurants that Good Times is opening across Texas. A contract for purchase of the equipment is concluded. It contains this clause:

   "This Agreement will be governed by and interpreted in accordance with the laws of the Province of British Columbia, Canada and the parties can attorn to [that is, accept] the jurisdiction of the Courts of the Province of British Columbia, Canada."

   Sidra delivers the equipment as required in the contract. It also flies several technicians to Texas to help with installation. Nevertheless, in trials and after start-up, the brewery equipment purchased from Sidra malfunctions and leaks. Only after extensive repairs is Good Times' operation able to get off the ground. A month later, Good Times sues Sidra in a Texas court for the cost of the repairs and the delay. Sidra decides not to appear in the Texas court to defend. It is content to rely on the contract's jurisdiction and venue clause. Good Times wins a substantial judgment in Texas based on a Texas triple-damages statute and seeks to enforce it in British Columbia where Sidra has its bank account. Sidra contests on the grounds of the jurisdiction clause that Good Times had agreed to. What result will follow?

7. PierceAir, a small start-up in the airline business, entered into an agreement with Avia, an Ontario-based manufacturer of passenger planes, to buy several used Avia 111s. The contract of purchase and sale between the parties stated: "The parties may refer any disputes under this Agreement to arbitration, in accordance with the Ontario *Arbitration Act.*" After the sale, PierceAir discovered that several of the Avia 111s would not work. It therefore began an action against Avia in court alleging improper design, construction, and manufacture of the aircraft. Avia

immediately sought a stay of the court proceedings by pointing to the arbitration clause. PierceAir's position was that the wording of the clause (*"The parties* may refer...") required the joint agreement of both Avia *and* PierceAir before the arbitration clause could be invoked. Give reasons for and against PierceAir's position.

8. Elaine Gordimer operates three hamburger franchises in Mississauga, Ontario. The franchise agreement that she has with her franchisor, a major American company, requires that all disputes between her and the franchisor will be arbitrated in Connecticut. She agrees and commences operations. Some years later, Elaine's operations deteriorate due to business pressures. She fails to submit sales data. An inspector from the franchisor finds several deficiencies, including mouldy buns and fermenting condiments. The local board of health also cites her for maintaining too high a temperature in her refrigeration units, increasing the risk of food spoilage. For all of these reasons, the franchisor invokes the arbitration clause. Gordimer then brings a motion to stay the arbitration proceedings on the grounds that the arbitration clause is unconscionable and that Ontario was the more appropriate forum for arbitration. She therefore says that the arbitration clause is unenforceable in Ontario. Who will win?

9. Nazeem, a Mississauga, Ontario-based computer jobber, contracts to sell computer circuitry to a university in Portugal. The contract negotiated between the university specifies that the price is "INCOTERMS 1990 CIF Lisbon." Nazeem arranges shipping of the goods through Star Shipping Lines Co and delivers the circuitry to Star at the port of Montreal. The bill of lading that is issued when Star receives the goods on board is made expressly subject to Canadian law and to "the limits set out under the Hague-Visby Rules." The ship proceeds without mishap and arrives safely in the port of Lisbon. Unfortunately, Portuguese stevedores who unload the cargo accidentally drop the load containing the circuitry, destroying it. Does the university have a claim against Star or the stevedores for the mishap in Canadian law?

10. For several decades, Japan has maintained an 8 percent tax on shochu, a clear grain alcohol that is enjoyed in traditional ceremonies in Japan. Shochu is made by carefully distilling the alcohol from selected wheat. The resulting liquor is poured through fine charcoal filters to improve its purity and taste. Shochu is not manufactured outside Japan, although similar drinks are produced and consumed in nearby Korea and Taiwan. The Japanese government imposes a 10 percent tax on vodka, which is similar to shochu, but is made from potatoes and comes from abroad. There is some evidence that Japanese consumers are starting to turn to vodka as a substitute for shochu. However, recent research indicates that vodka appeals to a younger crowd and has none of shochu's traditional allure. Canada, the United States, and the European Union jointly decide to challenge the tax differential between shochu and vodka as a violation of Japan's national treatment obligation under the WTO Agreement. Would they be successful? What result might the complainants seek?

11. Loggers in British Columbia pay the provincial government there $1200 per hectare for the right to log on provincial property. This is far less than US loggers must pay their state governments for the right to log on state property, and allows the Canadians to undercut US lumber in both the US and other markets. US loggers complain that the Canadian lumber is subsidized. If the United States decides to place duties on Canadian lumber for this reason, would Canada be successful in challenging the US subsidy determination before the WTO?

12. In 1965, Canada signed the Auto Pact with the US. The pact was a bilateral agreement that allowed US automakers who had already established auto plants in Canada to bring cars into Canada duty-free. The more a company produced domestically, the more it was allowed to import. The pact applied only to US imports, but the Canadian government extended the same treatment to some European, Japanese, and Korean automakers on a case-by-case basis over the years, as they established Canadian manufacturing operations. Then in 1988, the Canadian government stopped doing so. Existing producers continued to be allowed to import duty-free, but the government denied treatment to other foreign automakers that contemplated establishing facilities in Canada. The European Union and Japan are deciding whether to launch a WTO challenge of the Auto Pact. Would they win?

WWWeblinks

Public Law Regulation

Canadian Centre for Policy Alternatives

www.policyalternatives.ca

This organization researches issues of social and economic justice designed to question current policies. Its Web site contains research reports, books, opinion pieces, fact sheets, and other publications, as well as a monthly digest of progressive research and opinion.

Library of Parliament Parliamentary Research Branch

www.parl.ga.ca/common/library_prb.asp?Language=E

The branch provides a consulting service for individual parliamentarians, responding to questions that require research and analysis on legal, economic, scientific, or social science matters. Its Web site contains a list of its recent research reports.

Competition

Industry Canada

www.ic.gc.ca/cmb/Welcomeic.nsf/ICPages/Mandate

This Web site describes the mandate and programming of Industry Canada, which is responsible for a range of economic regulation including consumer legislation, telecommunications, marketplace and trade regulation, and intellectual property.

Competition Bureau of Canada

strategis.ic.gc.ca//SSG/ct01250e.html

The Competition Bureau is responsible for administering and enforcing the *Competition Act* and other standard-setting statutes. The site contains information on its activities and ongoing work.

Consumer Protection

The Consumers' Association of Canada

www.consumer.ca

This association represents and articulates the interests of Canadian consumers to all levels of government. Its site contains a library of research on current issues of public policy, many of which deal with the government regulation of business.

Environment Protection

Environment Canada Environmental Law Enforcement

www.ec.gc.ca/enforce/homepage/english/index.htm

This site features information concerning all aspects of environmental law enforcement and links to related sites.

Legal Risk and International Business Transactions

International Chamber of Commerce

www.iccwbo.org

This Web site delivers information to help you on a variety of international transaction-related topics, including international commercial arbitration, INCOTERMS, and the UCP.

Government Regulation of International Trade

Canada Customs and Revenue Agency

www.ccra-adrc.gc.ca/customs

This Web site has details about what you need to know concerning Canadian import and export regulations, sources of small-business advice, anti-dumping and countervailing duty investigations, and services available at Canada's points of entry.

Department of Foreign Affairs and International Trade Canada

www.dfait-maeci.gc.ca

This site features information on trade policy, current political developments, international jobs, and internship opportunities.

NAFTA Secretariat

www.nafta-sec-alena.org

This Web site features general information on the history and provisions of NAFTA, as well as rules, decisions, and status reports arising from NAFTA activities.

NAFTA Claims

www.naftaclaims.com

This site contains hard-to-obtain decisions and information about NAFTA Chapter 11.

Public International Law

World Trade Organization

www.wto.org

This site contains detailed information about GATT, the WTO, and free trade in general, as well as database of all released GATT and WTO dispute settlement decisions.

WORLDTRADELAW.NET — The Online Source for World Trade Law

www.worldtradelaw.net

This site features a range of material on international trade law, including a number of decisions, links, and other trade law resources.

FAIR TRADE IN INTERNATIONAL BUSINESS

The rapid growth of international business activity has shaped a new awareness of international business behaviour, partly due to changing attitudes about corporate social responsibility. Broadly defined, corporate social responsibility is the relationship that a corporation has with all of its *stakeholders* (and not just its *shareholders*). According to the Canadian Department of Foreign Affairs and International Trade, corporate responsibility includes, among other things, human rights, respect for international labour standards, protection of the environment, prevention of bribery and corruption, and the impact of business activity on humanitarian concerns generally. Employees, governments, consumers, local communities, and anyone or anything within a corporation's sphere of influence are potential stakeholders to whom the corporation is responsible. Each of these stakeholders has responded to the corporate responsibility movement in different ways.

For its part, the Canadian government has introduced such legislation as the *Corruption of Foreign Public Officials Act*, and it actively participates in such interest groups as the Organization for Economic Co-operation and Development. Both of these initiatives are aimed at improving the standard of business conduct. The private sector also seeks to change corporate behaviour, but it takes a different approach. For their part, corporations can adopt voluntary codes of conduct. Codes of conduct establish a system of practices that influence, shape, or set benchmarks for behaviour in the marketplace. They encourage businesses to conduct themselves in ways that benefit both themselves and the community. Codes of conduct are *voluntary*, which means that the decision to adopt a code remains entirely within the corporation's control. However, public pressure may compel a corporation to adopt a recognized code. Public pressure may take the form of consumer protests, consumer boycotts, or shareholder divestment campaigns. In other words, the public changes the corporation's behaviour by threatening its bottom line. But even with this kind of stakeholder activity, the people of developing countries often are exploited. Consider the situation in the coffee industry and the potential impact of public pressure.

Coffee is the world's second most valuable commodity. Canadians drink 40 million cups of it per day, which generates huge profits for business people, and yet coffee growers receive only pennies a pound for their crop. Isabel and Pedro Velasquez grow a cash crop of coffee on their small mountainside property in Nicaragua. They receive the equivalent of $350 Canadian per year for the 600 pounds of coffee that their land produces. Put another way, the couple's annual income is less than what many individual Canadians spend on coffee each year. The price that the Velasquezes receive is not enough to live on, and they are forced to borrow to keep their farm in production. Pedro says, "I'd like to get a fair price for my coffee beans."

The gap between wealthy consumers and poor farmers has generated the fair trade coffee movement. The mechanics of fair trade are simple: coffee producers get a fair price for their crop; the middleman is eliminated; and consumers get premium coffee for a few cents more per cup. The benefits of fair trade are extensive: small-scale farmers are organized into co-operatives; they decide how to distribute their extra income on community, social, and environmental programs; and they avoid debt because fair trade buyers give them credit. Fair trade can radically improve the lives of farmers and their families and the communities in which they live.

Fair trade coffee buyers pay a higher price for the coffee produced on co-operatives. This assures the growers that they will receive both the cost of production and a living wage. But it also means that coffee retailers have to pay more to stock fair trade coffees in their stores. That was part of the reason why large specialty coffee chains were reluctant to sign on. That reasoning came as some surprise to Bob Thomson, the managing director of Fair TradeMark Canada, who argued that, "If a major chain were to carry one fairly traded coffee amongst their coffees they could significantly increase their sales.

They could increase their own profits in a higher priced product." In April 2000, the situation changed when major coffee retailer Starbucks announced that it had signed an agreement to sell fair-trade-certified coffee in its stores. That announcement came three days before an activist group was scheduled to protest in front of 30 Starbucks locations in the US. It is not clear whether Starbucks made its decision based on public pressure or profit projections or both. In any event, Starbucks patrons can now enjoy a cup of coffee knowing that their purchase has helped to make a better life for coffee producers and their families.

QUESTIONS TO CONSIDER

1. How does the government try to protect the interests of people of developing countries? What can the public do? What about businesses?

2. The advantages of fair trade to the individual coffee producer are clear. What are the advantages of fair trade from a business perspective?

Sources: "'Fair-trade' coffee makes inroads: Starbucks first champion" *Financial Post* (May 2, 2000) C7; "Premium blends: will coffee drinkers pay more to give growers their due?" (1996) vol 69(8) *Canadian Business* 16; <www.cbc.ca/consumers/market/files/food/coffee/>; International Code of Ethics for Canadian Business <www.cdp-hrc.uottawa.ca/globalization/busethics/codeint.html>; Merchants of Green Coffee <www.merchant.org/whoweare.html>.

Video Resource: "Coffee with a conscience," *Marketplace* #17, March 7, 2000.

25 Individual Employment

CHAPTER OVERVIEW

OBJECTIVES

After completing this chapter, you should be able to:

1. Develop business strategies to ensure that pre-employment practices comply with employment legislation.
2. Distinguish between employees and independent contractors.
3. Outline the circumstances in which a business is liable to third parties for the conduct of its employees.
4. Describe three ways in which a business can improve the supervision of its employees.
5. Identify five employer obligations imposed by employment standards legislation.
6. Discuss human rights in the workplace.
7. Explain the basic statutory measures designed to ensure safety in the workplace.
8. Distinguish between summary dismissal, wrongful dismissal, and constructive dismissal.
9. Define just cause for dismissal and the notice periods that must be provided when dismissing an employee without cause.
10. Distinguish between severance packages and settlement packages, and explain the effect of a signed release.

For Better or for Worse, one of the leading practical texts on Canadian employment law, likens employment to a close personal relationship.[1] Recognizing the level of personal investment that many people make in their work and the extent to which their jobs are central to their lives, the authors argue that the "relationship" analogy is appropriate. Like close personal relationships, the employment relationship can be understood as having a number of distinct phases:

- courting (recruiting employees)
- engagement (hiring employees)
- marriage (maintaining the employment relationship)
- separation (dealing with employment problems)
- divorce (employee dismissal)

In this chapter, we will consider these phases of the employment relationship under three separate heads. First, we will consider *pre-employment matters*, including recruiting, hiring, and the terms of employment. Then we will examine *employer obligations* and *worker protection* mechanisms imposed by statute and see how the employment relationship is maintained. Finally, we will investigate issues that arise when the employment relationship breaks down, including the *termination of employment* and *post-employment practices*, such as severance and settlement packages.

PRE-EMPLOYMENT MATTERS

Job Descriptions

a job description is a written list of the employment duties of a particular job

Before hiring for a position, an employer should define its requirements in a *job description*. A **job description** is a written list of the employment duties of a particular job. A well-drafted job description makes it easy for an employer to find the right person for the job. It also functions as a standard of measurement that can be used to discipline or, if necessary, dismiss an employee who is not living up to the employer's expectations. Although not technically a legal document, a job description that is poorly drafted is a liability. If the job description is too narrowly drafted, it can provide leeway for an employee to refuse certain tasks on the basis that they fall outside of their job. One way to manage this risk and achieve flexibility is to include a provision near the end of the job description that acknowledges that the job may include additional duties as assigned by the employer.

Advertising Positions

one possible risk in advertising is that an employer might post an ad that contravenes human rights legislation

After they have drafted a proper job description, many employers advertise the position. Advertising not only allows employers to select from a broad and diverse applicant pool, but also provides an appearance of impartiality during the hiring process. There are, however, also risks associated with advertising. For instance, an advertisement may violate human rights legislation. Consider the example in Business Law in Action 25.1.

[1.] RS Echlin & CM Thomlinson *For Better or for Worse: A Practical Guide to Canadian Employment Law* (1996).

BUSINESS LAW IN ACTION 25.1

Advertisements and Human Rights

Giuseppe's Pizza needs to hire someone to answer the phones and to take walk-in orders. Since Giuseppe regularly advertises in the local classified ads for delivery drivers, he decides to run his usual ad:

Giuseppe's is now hiring. Good wages, flexible hours and free pizza (while on the job). Call Giuseppe's today! Valid driver's licence required.

Although this ad may seem perfectly reasonable, it probably violates human rights legislation. Since the ad is for a phone attendant—not a driver—requiring a valid driver's

licence may discriminate against certain people who might otherwise apply for the job. For example, someone with a visual impairment might be perfectly well qualified for the job even though they may not be able to drive. By advertising a valid driver's licence as a requirement for the job, Giuseppe's has unintentionally discriminated against persons on the basis of physical disability.

Questions for Discussion

1. How could Giuseppe's Pizza have avoided that problem?
2. Would Giuseppe's Pizza lose anything if it re-wrote its advertisement to comply with human rights legislation?

Application Forms and Interviews

A successful advertisement will generate many job applications. To fill positions with appropriate people, employers need more information, often obtained through application forms and personal interviews. Many employers use an **employment application form**, which allows them to screen job candidates for the necessary qualifications. The more information they can obtain, the more likely they will find the best candidate. However, employers must be careful not to ask questions that are too invasive. Questions must relate to the applicant's ability to do the job. Unrelated questions may violate provincial human rights legislation. Figure 25.1 lists several kinds of information that may be sought in an application form or an interview, and suggests questions that should and should not be used.

an employment application form is a tool that allows employers to screen job candidates for the necessary qualifications

FIGURE 25.1   Employment Applications and Personal Interview Questions

Information Sought	Do not ask:	Do ask:
Name	What is your Christian name?	What is your surname?
Emergency contact	Who should be contacted in case of an emergency? What is your relationship with this person?	Who should be contacted in case of an emergency?
Eligibility for work	What is your nationality?	Are you legally entitled to work in Canada?
Education	What schools did you attend?	What is the highest level of education you have attained?
Ability	Describe any disabilities you may have.	Are you able to perform the following duties? If not, what is the nature of accommodation that you require?
Availability	What religious holidays do you celebrate?	Are you available for shift work? If not, what accommodations are necessary?

(continued)

	FIGURE 25.1 (continued)	
Languages	What is your mother tongue?	What languages do you speak?
Mobility	Are you married?	Are you able to transfer to another city?
Associations	Do you have any memberships in clubs or other organizations?	Do you have any memberships in clubs or other organizations that do not reveal your gender, race, religion, ancestry, or place of origin?

Source: Rearranged and reprinted with permission from RS Echlin & CM Thomlinson *For Better or for Worse: A Practical Guide to Canadian Employment Law* (1996) at 14-20.

Statements Made during Hiring

both employer and applicant must be careful not to misstate their positions

When the employer has selected an applicant, they usually negotiate the terms of employment. Following the general rule of contractual negotiations, both parties must be careful not to misstate their positions. As Chapter 4 explains, that could amount to a negligent misrepresentation, rendering any subsequent contractual agreement susceptible to rescission. For example, employers should avoid making over-the-top assurances about things like job title, job security, and promotions. Likewise, job applicants must not exaggerate their qualifications or pad their résumés. A misrepresentation by either party could allow the other to walk away from the employment contract with impunity. If a misstatement is negligent or fraudulent, it could even lead to a separate cause of action in tort or criminal law. Case Brief 25.1 illustrates the consequences of an employer's misstatement.

CASE BRIEF 25.1

Queen v Cognos Inc (1993) 99 DLR (4th) 626 (SCC)

Queen, an accountant, had a good job with decent pay, but was looking for something different. He saw an advertisement in a Calgary newspaper for a job with Cognos, a high-tech company. Queen applied for the job. During his interview, Queen was told that the position was a permanent one and that the successful applicant would play a lead role in developing a new accounting software program. The interviewer failed to mention that the entire project—including the budget for the lead position and the hiring of additional staff—was subject to further approval. Queen took the job. Soon after, Cognos decided to slash the funding allocated to the project. Consequently, no other staff were hired and, as a result, Queen's job became much less significant. He was dismissed 18 months later. He then sued Cognos for negligent misrepresentation, claiming that he never would have agreed to leave his former position if Cognos had not inflated the significance of the project and Queen's role in it.

The Supreme Court of Canada agreed with Queen. It held that employers have a duty during employment interviews to exercise reasonable care and diligence when making representations about the nature of an employment opportunity. According to the Court, it is not enough that the interviewers must be honest. They owe a further duty to make sure that their representations are accurate.

Nature of the Work Relationship

Our discussion has focussed on the employment relationship. However, not all work- or service-related contracts are contracts of employment. Nor are all workers considered to be employees.

Employees

An **employee** is a person who contractually agrees to work under the control and direction of an employer. Employees are legally protected in some ways that other workers are not. For example, an employee is entitled by both statute and common law to reasonable notice before being dismissed. The failure to give such notice entitles the employee to sue. The same is not true for workers who lack employee status.

an employee is a person who contractually agrees to work under the control and direction of an employer

Independent Contractors and Consultants

One kind of worker who lacks the status of employee is an *independent contractor*. An **independent contractor** contractually agrees to work but is *not* controlled by another person in how they accomplish a task. Independent contractors and consultants are not entitled to many of the rights that employees enjoy, such as:

an independent contractor is a person who contractually agrees to work but who is *not* controlled by another person in how they accomplish a task

- reasonable notice of termination
- statutory termination and severance pay
- overtime pay
- vacation pay
- statutory holiday pay

Being an independent contractor involves a trade-off. Employee benefits are sacrificed in exchange for independence. Independent contractors and consultants do not owe the same loyalty as employees. They therefore have more freedom in deciding when to work, how to work, where to work, for whom to work, and so on. As communications technologies continue to improve, employers are becoming more willing to relinquish control of those choices. This significantly reduces the costs generally associated with employee protection. For example, when a worker is classified as a consultant rather than an employee, the employer does not have to remit deductions for income tax, employment insurance, Canada Pension Plan, or workers' compensation. However, the fact that those deductions are not made does not necessarily mean that a worker is an independent contractor.

It is sometimes difficult to distinguish between employees and independent contractors or consultants. One test asks how much control is asserted by the party paying for the work. The **control test** is based on four significant factors: (i) the employer's authority to select individuals for employment, (ii) the employer's ability to decide the payment scheme, (iii) the employer's control and direction about the type, manner, and timing of the work, and (iv) the employer's right to discipline the worker.[2]

the control test may determine whether a worker is an employee or an independent contractor based on the degree of control exercised by the party paying for the work

Since highly skilled professional employees are not always subject to direct supervision, the degree of control is not always a determining factor. Therefore, courts have considered such other factors as: (i) who owns the equipment used to perform the job, (ii) whether the worker had the chance to profit, and (iii) who risks any loss. Courts have recently considered the overall role that the worker plays in the organization. The **organization test** attempts to determine whether the work is an integral part of the overall business.

the organization test attempts to determine whether a person's work is an integral part of the overall business

Given the variety of factors that judges take into account, it is difficult to ensure that a particular worker is an independent contractor rather than an

---

[2.] Echlin & Thomlinson *For Better or for Worse* (1996) at 43-4.

employee. Figure 25.2 gives a number of tips for companies that want to set up independent contractor relationships.

FIGURE 25.2	Ensuring an Independent Contractor Relationship

- Expressly state in the written contract that the party performing the services is not an employee and is not entitled to any of the statutory protections afforded to employees.
- Do not take any statutory deductions such as income tax, employment insurance, Canada Pension Plan, or workers' compensation.
- Do not provide vacation pay, statutory holiday pay, or overtime pay.
- Do not provide benefits such as health-care plans, stock options, or bonuses.
- Do not provide a company uniform, business cards, a company vehicle, company equipment such as a computer, voice-mail or e-mail, desk, or office space.
- Do not provide bookkeeping, invoicing, or secretarial services.
- Do not provide performance reviews or disciplinary measures. (This does not preclude a termination provision in the contract.)
- Expressly allow the worker to set their own work schedule.
- Expressly allow the worker to work for competitors or to generate income from other sources.
- Encourage the worker to set up a company, sole proprietorship, or a partnership with a GST number.

Source: Rearranged and reprinted with permission from RS Echlin & MJ MacKillop *Creative Solutions: Perspectives on Canadian Employment Law* (2000) at 17.

EMPLOYERS' OBLIGATIONS AND WORKER PROTECTION LEGISLATION

We now survey some of the more important obligations that employers owe to their employees and others:

- third-party liability
- supervision
- statutory protection

Third-Party Liability

A worker's status is important to the employer if that person causes damage to a third party. As we saw in Chapter 10, the injured third party can sue not only the individual worker, but also the company that commissioned the work. **Vicarious liability** occurs when an employer is held liable for an employee's tort. That doctrine is, however, subject to two important restrictions.

- The doctrine does *not* apply to independent contractors.[3]
- The doctrine applies to an employee's torts *if* the employee was acting in the course of employment.

vicarious liability occurs when an employer is held liable for an employee's tort

vicarious liability is limited to torts that an employee commits in the course of employment

---

[3.] A company may be held liable for failing to exercise reasonable care when hiring an independent contractor. In that case, the company's liability is not based directly on the independent contractor's wrong, but rather on its own wrongful act in hiring an inappropriate worker. Therefore, it is not vicarious.

Consequently, when a company is sued for vicarious liability, the court must decide: (i) if the worker was an employee and, if so, (ii) if the employee's tort was sufficiently connected to their employment. To determine the second requirement, a judge will look at several factors. The location of the incident, the time of day, and the fact that company equipment was involved are important, but they are not always conclusive.[4] The fundamental issue is whether the harmful act occurred while the employee was carrying out their assigned duties. You Be the Judge 25.1 focuses on that issue.

YOU BE THE JUDGE 25.1

Cole v California Entertainment Ltd [1989] BCJ No 2162 (BC CA)

Wayne Cole and some friends entered the Club California while wearing their matching red bomber jackets bearing the crest *Victoria Kick Boxing Club*. A doorman named Wolf explained the club's dress code and said they would have to take off their jackets if they wanted to enter. The group exchanged words with Wolf and other staff members. The club owner then instructed the bouncers to clear the entrance. When the altercation moved outside, the club owner went back into his office and closed the door. Cole and his friends left the club along with the four bouncers and walked to a nearby parking lot. Wolf challenged one of Cole's friends to a fight. A brawl broke out. Eventually, Wolf went after Cole who, being a lot smaller, backed away and said he did not want to fight. But Wolf kept coming. He grabbed Cole by the front of his jacket and hurled him through the plate glass window of a nearby store, pulled him out, and threw him against a car parked in front of the store. Wolf kept punching until two people finally pulled him off of Cole. Cole staggered across the street and collapsed. He was later taken to the hospital.

Questions for Discussion

1. Did the fight fall within the owner's instructions to clear the club's entrance?
2. Was Cole injured within the course of Wolf's employment?

Supervision

The risk of vicarious liability and other workplace hazards imposes certain responsibilities on employers to supervise their employees; however, even the most conscientious employer cannot stand guard around the clock. There are other ways in which employees can be controlled, including:

- employment policy manuals
- performance reviews
- promotion or probation

Employment Policy Manuals

The basis of a good employment relationship is communication. Each party must say how it expects the other to behave. Employers can express their expectations through *employment policy manuals*. Among other things, an **employment policy manual** explains the conduct that is expected of employees in the course of their employment. A carefully drafted policy manual not

an **employment policy manual** explains the conduct that is expected of employees in the course of their employment

---

4. Some provinces (such as British Columbia) have legislation that makes the registered owner of a motor vehicle vicariously liable for the accidents of any authorized driver of the vehicle, whether an employee or not: *Motor Vehicle Act*, RSBC (1996) c 318, s 86 (BC). In such case, the fact that a company vehicle was used is determinative.

only sets out the employer's expectations, but also details the manner in which its policies will be implemented, applied, and enforced. Ethical Perspective 25.1 illustrates the legal importance of a policy manual.

ETHICAL PERSPECTIVE 25.1

Smyth v Pillsbury Co 914 F Supp 92 (1996)

What began as a simple disagreement between Smyth and his work supervisor quickly turned into an online shouting match. Eventually, Smyth was dismissed from his employment for sending "inappropriate and unprofessional comments" over Pillsbury's internal e-mail system. Smyth then sued Pillsbury. He argued that the interception of his e-mails—many of which he had sent from his home computer—not only infringed his right to privacy but also was directly contrary to Pillsbury's employment policy manual. This manual assured its employees that "all e-mail communications would remain confidential and privileged" and that "e-mail communications could not be intercepted and used by [Pillsbury] against its employees as grounds for termination and reprimand."

In spite of the written policy, the court held that Pillsbury did not interfere with Smyth's right to privacy when it intercepted his e-mails and fired him on the basis of their content. According to the court, because Pillsbury owned the e-mail system and therefore did not invade any of Smyth's personal effects in the workplace, the interception of his communications was neither a substantial nor highly offensive invasion of his privacy. The court concluded that the company's interest in preventing "inappropriate and unprofessional comments, or even illegal activity over its e-mail system outweighs any privacy interest that Smyth might have had."

Questions for Discussion

1. Should the company be allowed to operate contrary to its written policy?
2. Can you suggest an alternative corporate e-mail policy?

Performance Reviews

a performance review is an evaluation of an employee that provides accurate and informative feedback about the quality of their work

One way to direct the behaviour of employees is to conduct regular *performance reviews*. A **performance review** is an evaluation of an employee that provides accurate and informative feedback about the quality of their work. Most performance reviews are conducted in person. However, employers should have a standard evaluation form to guide the process: (i) to ensure that employees are treated the same, and (ii) to provide a record in case the employment relationship breaks down. If an employer recorded a string of poor performance reviews in an employee's file, it is difficult for the employee to argue that they were wrongfully dismissed. Note that performance reviews do not merely serve a legal function. From a human resources perspective, a properly conducted performance review can be used to identify and correct workplace problems in their infancy, and thus prevent legal problems associated with a relationship breakdown.

Promotion and Progressive Discipline

a promotion usually entails new duties on the part of the employee, whether or not it includes a pay raise

a progressive discipline program involves a series of disciplinary steps

Employee behaviour can be directed through rewards and punishments. Employers should be able to recognize employees who consistently perform well and consider them for promotion to higher positions. This both rewards productivity and sets a behavioural benchmark for other employees. A **promotion** usually entails new duties on the part of the employee, whether or not it includes a pay raise.

When an employee has received a number of poor reviews or is otherwise misbehaving in the workplace, the employer should consider a *progressive discipline program*. A **progressive discipline program** involves a series of disciplinary steps that may progress from verbal or written warnings, through degrees of suspension, to dismissal.[5] It is useful to explain such a program in the employment policy manual. Suspension is a drastic measure and must be used only in reasonable circumstances, for example, if the employer legitimately suspects that the employee was involved in workplace fraud. When there is a plausible basis for commencing an investigation and the employer carries it out in good faith, courts have held that a brief period of suspension is a reasonable course of conduct.[6]

Statutory Protection

The employment relationship was once governed exclusively by the law of contract. Lately, legislators have been called upon to invoke statutory measures to protect workers. Much of the legislation falls under provincial jurisdiction and varies in detail between provinces.[7] Sophisticated employers usually hire human resource experts or employment law specialists to navigate the intricacies of these statutory measures. We will discuss these statutory regimes:

- employment standards
- human rights
- occupational health and safety
- workers' compensation

Employment Standards

Employment standards legislation requires an employer to meet minimum obligations, which apply only to employees but not to independent contractors, partners, or consultants. An employer cannot generally contract out of the legislation's minimum obligations. If an employment contract fails to meet those requirements, the employer must nevertheless compensate the employee. Furthermore, the legislation establishes *minimum* standards. If an employment contract actually provides the employee with greater protection, the employer cannot use the statute to reduce those rights. We briefly consider minimum standards in connection with:

employment standards legislation requires an employer to meet minimum obligations

- holidays
- wages
- work hours, overtime, and rest days
- leaves
- vacations

Holidays Every jurisdiction requires employers to pay employees for specific public holidays. This does not mean that employees cannot work on these days, nor does it prevent an employer from requesting its employees to work, as long as they are adequately compensated for it. Some provinces, such as British Columbia, Manitoba, and Prince Edward Island, entitle employees to public holidays only if they have worked 15 or more days in the month preceding the public holiday. Other provinces, such as Newfoundland, New Brunswick, and Ontario, allow certain kinds of employers, such as those in hospitals or the

---

[5.] Echlin & Thomlinson *For Better or for Worse* (1996) at 164-6.

[6.] *Pierce v Canada Trust Realtor* (1986) 11 CCEL 64 (Ont HCJ).

[7.] Federal legislation govern some employees, including those in federal government, transportation, shipping, radio, and banking.

hotel and restaurant industry, to require their employees to work on public holidays. Usually, these employees are entitled to additional compensation for working on those days. The most common public holidays are New Year's Day, Good Friday, Victoria Day, Canada Day, Labour Day, Thanksgiving Day, and Christmas Day.

Wages Every province has set a minimum wage. Minimum wage legislation ensures that an employee's pay increases in line with the cost of living. The minimum wage is determined on an hourly basis, but it also applies to employees who are compensated in other ways. In such cases, it is up to the employer to ensure that the statutory minimum is met. Some jurisdictions have set different minimums for different categories of employees. For example, Alberta sets a lower minimum for those under 18 years of age. Quebec and Ontario have lower minimums for people who usually receive tips. And the Northwest Territories sets a higher minimum for those not living along a highway. The typical minimum wage varies substantially between provinces and is influenced by such factors as the level of industry, the cost of living, and the political beliefs of the government in power.

Work Hours, Overtime, and Rest   Every jurisdiction regulates the number of hours that an employee can be asked to work. In most jurisdictions, this varies from 40 to 48. An employee can refuse to work more than that without fear of disciplinary action. Employees who choose to work more are entitled to overtime pay. In most provinces, the minimum rate of pay for overtime is 1.5 times the employee's regular wages. In a few provinces, the minimum rate is 1.5 times the minimum wage. A minimum daily rest period is also imposed in all jurisdictions, except Nova Scotia and the Yukon. In most provinces, employees are entitled to 30 minutes for every five-hour period worked.

Leaves   Many jurisdictions entitle employees to unpaid leaves of absence. For example, in British Columbia and Quebec, employees may take up to five days a year to meet the needs of their children. In some jurisdictions, bereavement leave is available for employees who grieve the loss of a loved one—sometimes it is paid, sometimes not. Employees are also entitled to take time to vote in elections. Every jurisdiction entitles women who have fulfilled a minimum service requirement to a leave of absence during pregnancy. Although most pregnancy leaves are unpaid, many employers continue to offer benefits, which may include part pay. Other employers offer no benefits, leaving the pregnant employee to claim employment insurance. Women who take pregnancy leaves are entitled to return to their job after the leave and do not lose seniority in their position. If it is impossible to reinstate the employee to her previous position, she must be provided with a comparable job with equivalent wages and benefits.

Vacations   Employees are entitled to paid vacation. In most jurisdictions, the length depends on years of service. Vacation allowance often begins to accrue from the first day of service, but employees often are required to work a full year before taking a paid vacation. The legislation usually provides a minimum of two weeks and sometimes allows employees to postpone vacations. Employees do not have a right to take vacations whenever they want—the employer may usually set the dates. As a practical matter, however, flexibility should be allowed, especially since most employees regard vacations as very important, as Business Decision 25.1 shows.

BUSINESS DECISION 25.1

Mandatory Vacation Dates

What started out for Sammy 15 years ago as a one-man, one-truck operation has turned into a very lucrative souvlaki empire. Sammy now owns 10 souvlaki trucks and one diner. Some say that Sammy is successful partly because he maintains certain traditional values. Among other things, he uses only the finest pita, he closes every Sunday to worship, and he shuts down his business for the month of August to take his entire family home to visit their European relatives. But things are not as simple as they once were. Sammy now has a payroll of 65 employees, many of whom have been complaining about not only having to take all of their holidays in the first two weeks of August, but also being forced to take two unpaid weeks for the remainder of the month.

Sammy traditionally closed for the entire month of August because his operation was small and he did not trust his business to anyone outside of his family. Recently, however, he hired an assistant manager who proves to be quite capable.

Questions for Discussion

1. Should Sammy continue to force his employees take their vacation in August?

2. What are the relevant business considerations in making this decision?

According to employment standards legislation, employers are usually required to keep accurate records as evidence that they have met the minimum statutory requirements. For example, employers must keep records of wages paid, hours worked, and vacations accrued. If a dispute arises and no accurate records have been kept, the employer risks having an employment standards referee defer to the recollection of the employee. If so, the employer may have to meet the statutory minimum for a second time if the employee's evidence is incorrect.

employers are required to keep accurate records as evidence that they have met the minimum statutory requirements

Human Rights

Both provincially and federally, special statutory provisions deal with human rights in the employment context. As we saw in connection with job advertising, such legislation is remedial in nature. Its main purpose is not to punish the employer, but to provide a remedy to the employee who has been discriminated against.

human rights legislation is remedial in nature

Discrimination, in this context, means treating someone differently on the basis of one of the grounds prohibited by human rights legislation, including race, ancestry, place of origin, colour, ethnic origin, sex, sexual orientation, disability, marital status, family status, and religion.[8]

discrimination is treating someone differently on the basis of a ground prohibited by human rights legislation

It is possible for an employer to discriminate either *directly* or *indirectly*. **Direct discrimination** occurs when an employer adopts a rule or practice that treats a person differently on the basis of one of the prohibited grounds. For example, if an employer refuses to hire a woman because she may decide to get pregnant, this would be direct discrimination. Such conduct is expressly prohibited under human rights legislation. Indirect discrimination is more subtle and is usually more difficult to spot. **Indirect discrimination** occurs when an employer treats a person differently on the basis of some characteristic other

direct discrimination occurs when an employer adopts a rule or practice that treats a person differently on the basis of one of the prohibited grounds

indirect discrimination occurs when an employer treats someone differently on the basis of some characteristic other than a prohibited ground, but in a way that adversely affects that person by virtue of a prohibited ground

---

[8]. *Human Rights Code*, RSBC 1996, c 210, s11 (BC). See also *Saskatchewan Human Rights Code* SS 1979, c S-24.1 s14 (Sask); *Human Rights, Citizenship and Multiculturalism Act*, RSA 1980, c H-11.7, s 8 (Alta); *Ontario Human Rights Code*, RSO 1990, c H19 s 23 (Ont); *Human Rights Act*, RSNB 1973, c H-11, s 3(4) (NB); *Fair Practices Act*, RSNWT 1988 (Supp), c11, s 3(3) (NWT).

than a prohibited ground, but in a way that adversely affects that person by virtue of a prohibited ground. For example, Giuseppe's Pizza refused to hire Aruna because she does not have a valid driver's licence. If Aruna does not have a licence because of some visual impairment, Giuseppe's Pizza is indirectly discriminating against her on the basis of a disability, which is a prohibited ground of discrimination.

An employer is not necessarily liable merely because it discriminated against an employee. Human rights legislation recognizes a number of defences. The nature of some jobs justifies discrimination that would normally be prohibited. The acronym for that sort of defence is **BFOR**, a *bona fide* occupational requirement.[9] To defend against a claim of discrimination, an employer must be able to demonstrate that the allegedly discriminatory requirement was imposed in good faith and with the sincere belief that it was imposed in the interests of adequate performance of the job.[10] For example, requiring a candidate for a firefighting job to meet some minimum requirement of physical ability is justified if the employer believes that such a requirement is truly necessary to carry out the job duties safely and economically. If the job involves climbing a ladder while carrying a heavy object, then the requirement would be justified. It would not if the position was a desk job.

Harassment is a form of discrimination in the workplace. **Harassment** involves any demeaning or offensive conduct connected to a prohibited ground of discrimination. As with other forms of discrimination, harassment can occur even if the conduct was not intended to be demeaning or offensive. A common form of workplace harassment is *sexual harassment*. In many jurisdictions, **sexual harassment** involves unwelcome or objectionable sexual advances, or any sexual comment, gesture, or conduct that the offender knew (or should have known) was unwelcome. In many jurisdictions, including Manitoba, New Brunswick, Prince Edward Island, and the federal jurisdiction, employers have an obligation to take reasonable steps to prevent sexual harassment. An employer that fails to do so it is vicariously liable for the acts of its employees.

The *duty to accommodate* is often used to remedy some forms of discrimination under human rights legislation. The **duty to accommodate** requires an employer to make adaptations to the workplace to meet the needs of an employee who would not otherwise be able to work there. These include wheelchair access, braille signage, and ergonomic workstations. Note that the scope of an employer's duty to accommodate is not absolute, but is limited to situations where it would not cause *undue hardship* to the employer. The application of the undue hardship standard largely depends on the particular circumstances. Relevant factors include: (i) the cost of the accommodation, (ii) the ease of its implementation, (iii) health and safety requirements, (iv) whether outside sources of funding are available to assist in making the accommodation, (v) whether the accommodation will disrupt a collective agreement, and (vi) whether the accommodation will affect the morale of other employees.[11]

It is generally up to the employees to express their need to be accommodated.[12] They also have a duty to take reasonable steps to assist their employers in making those accommodations.[13] The employee is not entitled to a per-

BFOR, or a *bona fide* occupational requirement, justifies discrimination that would normally be prohibited

harassment involves any demeaning or offensive conduct connected to a prohibited ground of discrimination

sexual harassment involves unwelcome or objectionable sexual advances, or any sexual comment, gesture, or conduct that the offender knew (or should have known) was unwelcome

the **duty to accommodate** requires an employer to make adaptations to the workplace to meet the needs of an employee who would not otherwise be able to work there

the duty to accommodate does not require a perfect solution

[9.] The wording in some provinces is "*bona fide* occupational qualification" (or BFOQ).

[10.] *Etobicoke (Borough) v Ontario (Human Rights Commission)* (1982) 132 DLR (3d) 14 at 19-20 (SCC).

[11.] Echlin & Thomlinson *For Better or for Worse* (1996) at 116.

[12.] *Emrick Plastics v Ontario (Human Rights Commission)* (1992) 90 DLR (4th) 476 (Ont Div Ct).

[13.] *Central Okanagan School District No 23 v Renaud* (1992) 95 DLR (4th) 577 (SCC).

fect solution—if the employer has made a reasonable adaptation to the workplace, it has discharged its duty to accommodate.

An employer is better able to protect itself from the risk of a human rights complaint if it knows the relevant laws. Therefore, the best strategy is to be proactive. Prudent business managers adopt company policies that comply with all of the requirements of human rights legislation. In addition, business managers should institute an informal complaints procedure and appoint a person in the workplace to investigate complaints in a neutral way. The creation of an informal complaints mechanism promotes better communication between workers and management, and encourages employees to solve workplace problems internally.

an employer can minimize exposure against human rights complaints

Occupational Health and Safety

Every employer must meet minimum standards for workplace health and safety. Health and safety legislation is aimed at preventing accidents, injuries, and industrial diseases by reducing the risk of dangerous conditions and poor safety practices. That is accomplished through educational and punitive measures. Many jurisdictions require the creation of workplace advisory groups composed of workers and managers. Employees have the right to refuse to work in unsafe conditions. If they do so, they must make a report to a supervisor. The employer is then required to investigate the problem. An employee who is not satisfied with the investigation may take up the matter with the workplace advisory group and, ultimately, with the responsible governmental agency. In exceptional circumstances, an unsafe workplace may be shut down.

health and safety legislation is aimed at preventing accidents, injuries, and industrial diseases

In most jurisdictions, a serious violation of occupational health and safety standards may be a crime. So is a violation of a health and safety inspector's order. Businesses are subject to fines, and individuals are subject to imprisonment. Companies and individuals may, however, use the defence of *due diligence*. **Due diligence** occurs when the accused took every reasonable precaution to avoid violating the safety standard.

due diligence occurs when the accused took every reasonable precaution to avoid violating the safety standard

Workers' Compensation

While occupational health and safety legislation is aimed at preventing workplace injuries, workers' compensation schemes (which we discussed in Chapter 10) were created to redress injuries that do occur by financially compensating injured workers. Many workplace injuries might be addressed through tort actions. However, there are at least two difficulties with formal litigation. First, it is very expensive. Second, it operates on an all-or-nothing basis. If the defendant wrongfully caused the injury, the plaintiff receives full compensation. Otherwise, the plaintiff does not receive any relief. Workers' compensation schemes use a much simpler and less expensive procedure. Furthermore, they provide some compensation even if a worker cannot prove that someone else was at fault. In exchange for those benefits, the legislation generally prevents a person from suing in tort for workplace injuries.[14]

workers' compensation schemes financially compensate injured workers

workers' compensation schemes generally preclude workers from suing their employers

Workers' compensation schemes are funded through compulsory contributions by employers. The amount that an employer must contribute depends on the industry in which it is involved—more dangerous industries naturally carry higher rates.

workers' compensation schemes are funded through compulsory employer contributions

---

[14.] Some provinces including British Columbia, Manitoba, New Brunswick, and Ontario, provide exceptions, such as when an employer negligently maintains defective machinery or when the injury was caused by another employee.

Workers' compensation schemes provide benefits in several circumstances.

- A partial disability allows the worker to continue performing in some capacity. Compensation for partial injuries is based on the difference between the worker's pre-accident earning capacity and post-accident earning capacity.

- A total incapacity prevents the worker from performing in any capacity. Workers who suffer a total, though temporary, disability are paid a set percentage of their pre-accident earning capacity for the duration of the disability.

- If a worker is killed in the course of employment, their dependants are entitled to compensation. For a spouse, some provinces provide periodic payments until the spouse remarries or reaches the age of 65. In other provinces, the spouse receives a lump sum payment equal to the amount that the worker would have received if they had been permanently injured rather than killed. The worker's children are also entitled to compensation until they reach the age of majority. In some provinces, dependent children are entitled to a further amount toward post-secondary education.

TERMINATION OF EMPLOYMENT

An employer's obligations do not last forever. They sometimes end abruptly—an employee may quit or be fired, or a company may cease to exist. Sometimes, a damaged relationship can be repaired. That task usually falls to a human resources expert. However, once it is clear that the relationship is irreparable, lawyers and risk managers may be needed.

We end this chapter by examining some issues that arise when the employment relationship breaks down. We will look at an employer's right to dismiss or fire employees who are in serious breach of their employment obligations, consider the rights of employees under the law of wrongful dismissal, examine the concept of constructive dismissal, and survey post-employment practices, such as severance packages and settlements.

Summary Dismissal

Employees sometimes misbehave on the job. If they do not perform their duties properly, they may be in breach of their employment contracts. The usual contractual rule applies. If the employee commits a serious breach, the employer is entitled to discharge the contract. In the language of employment law, the employer is entitled to a self-help remedy known as *summary dismissal*. **Summary dismissal** occurs when an employer dismisses the employee and thereby terminates the employment relationship without notice. That remedy is available only if the employer has *just cause*. **Just cause** means that the employer was justified in firing the employee without notice. It is limited to certain types of breach, including:

- absenteeism
- substance abuse
- incompetence and carelessness
- dishonesty and disobedience
- conflicts of interest
- criminal behaviour

summary dismissal occurs when an employer dismisses the employee and thereby terminates the employment relationship without notice

just cause means that the employer was justified in firing the employee without notice

Absenteeism

The employment contract requires the employee to regularly attend work during specified hours. If those hours are not expressly stated in the contract, the courts will imply a term that is in line with the employer's normal hours of business. Although the failure to report for work on a single occasion will not usually constitute grounds for dismissal, repeated *absenteeism* will.[15] **Absenteeism** is an unauthorized failure to report for work that is not the product of an illness. If the absenteeism hurts its business interests, the employer is justified in terminating the employee.

absenteeism is an unauthorized failure to report for work that is not the product of an illness

Under some circumstances, a repeated pattern of lateness will also constitute grounds for dismissal. After recognizing a pattern of lateness, the employer must clearly warn the employee that such lateness will not be tolerated. Similarly, if a worker leaves the job before a shift is over, and if that unauthorized departure causes harm or risk, the employer has grounds to dismiss the employee. However, an employer cannot dismiss an employee who had good reason to be absent, for instance, when the employee had already notified their employer that they were taking time off (after numerous consecutive days on the job) and had arranged for an alternate to work in their place.[16]

Before dismissing an employee on the basis of absenteeism or lateness, an employer should document a pattern of conduct as well as a series of warnings. The document should state that the employee did not have a legitimate reason for being absent or late.

Substance Abuse

Some employees have been known to come to work under the influence of alcohol or other drugs. This may be grounds for dismissal.

- First, courts consider whether the employee's job performance was impaired. The mere smell of alcohol on the breath of the employee is insufficient to warrant dismissal.

- Second, courts consider whether the employee's abuse of alcohol or other drugs threatened the safety of the workplace. It may be possible to dismiss a forklift operator who is drunk on the job, but perhaps not a secretary who is inebriated at an office party.

- Third, courts consider whether the employer's business reputation has been harmed by the employee's conduct.

- Fourth, courts consider whether the employer had a policy in place that prohibited such conduct and if it was known, or ought to have been known, by the employee.

Courts tend to be more lenient if it appears that the employer *condoned* the employees' conduct. **Condonation** occurs whenever an employer fails to reprimand an employee for their misconduct. If a business maintains an extremely permissive attitude in the workplace, its *apparent* condonation may deprive it of the authority to dismiss a drunken employee. To avoid that risk, a business should implement and enforce a clearly worded policy that defines acceptable and unacceptable conduct.

condonation occurs whenever an employer fails to reprimand the employee for their misconduct

Incompetence

Employers are often dissatisfied with worker performance. That alone does not mean that an employee has breached the employment obligations. One situa-

---

[15.] *Bowie v Motorola Canada Ltd* (1991) 44 CCEL 307 (Ont Gen Div).
[16.] *MacNeil v Ronscott Inc* (1988) 22 CCEL 89 (Ont HCJ).

incompetent employees lack basic skills or qualifications, or are otherwise unable to perform their assigned jobs

tion where poor performance does justify dismissal occurs when an employee is *incompetent*. **Incompetent** employees lack basic skills or qualifications, or are otherwise unable to perform their assigned jobs. To prove incompetence, the employer must do more than show that a job could have been done better; it must prove that the employee fell below the standard of basic competence.

A good risk manager will notify an employee that their work is substandard, and state that such shoddy performance will not be tolerated in the future. The employer should: (i) clearly identify the problems with the employee's work, (ii) establish a review process to assist the employee with improvement, and (iii) inform the employee that a continued substandard performance will result in termination.

Dishonesty and Disobedience

an employment relationship imposes a duty on the employee to be faithful and honest

An employment relationship imposes a duty on the employee to be faithful and honest. When dishonesty causes the employer to lose trust and confidence in the employment relationship, it is grounds for dismissal. In fact, the nature of some jobs requires an even higher standard of honesty. Employees who hold positions of trust, such as senior managers in financial institutions, are generally obligated to act in the best interests of the business. Although honesty is usually required only when the employee is acting in the course of their employment, courts have sometimes allowed an employer to dismiss an employee for dishonest conduct outside of the course of employment.[17]

employee fraud occurs when an employee intentionally deceives the employer in a way that is detrimental to its interests

Two kinds of dishonesty are *employee fraud* and *employee theft*. **Employee fraud** occurs when an employee intentionally deceives the employer in a way that is detrimental to its interests. The employee can be dismissed if the nature of the fraud is incompatible with a continuing employment relationship. **Employee theft** occurs when an employee steals from the employer. The law implies a term in every contract that prohibits employee theft. Since loyalty and honesty are at the core of the employment relationship, a single incident of theft may justify termination.

employee theft occurs when an employee steals from the employer

disobedience occurs when an employee repeatedly and deliberately defies a supervisor's clear instructions or refuses to perform without reasonable excuse

Disobedience is also a ground for dismissal. **Disobedience** typically occurs when an employee repeatedly and deliberately defies a supervisor's clear instructions or refuses to perform without reasonable excuse. The employment relationship is based on the idea that the employer controls or directs the work of its employees. A repeated failure to follow instructions not only results in unaccomplished tasks, it also undercuts the authority of the employer and generally lowers employee morale. Likewise, a repeated pattern of severe disrespect, or insulting behaviour directed at the employer or supervisors, may be grounds for dismissal.

Conflicts of Interest

a conflict of interest occurs when an employee acts in a way that conflicts with the employer's best interests

An employee is required to avoid a *conflict of interest*. A **conflict of interest** occurs when an employee acts in a way that conflicts with the employer's best interests. This may be: (i) carrying on a business that competes with the employer, (ii) accepting personal gifts or other advantages from a party who conducts business with the employer, (iii) having personal dealings with employer's clients, customers, or suppliers, or (iv) providing confidential information acquired during the course of employment to a competitor in exchange for some benefit. An employee may argue that the conduct in question did not *actually* hurt the employer. The lack of harm may be irrelevant,

---

[17.] *Marshall v Pacific Coast Savings Credit Union* (1992) 44 CCEL 261 (BC CA).

however, especially if the employer imposed a policy that prohibited the conduct in question.[18]

Criminal Behaviour

In addition to dishonest acts such as fraud or theft, other criminal conduct during the course of employment can lead to dismissal. Typical examples are physical assault and property offences. When an employee commits a crime on the job, they may be dismissed as soon as charges have been laid—even before there has been a conviction. The presumption of innocence applies in criminal law, but not in the workplace. However, as a matter of risk management, the employer should not dismiss an employee until a thorough investigation clearly finds that a crime has been committed. If it makes a false allegation, an employer may be liable for punitive damages.[19]

Concept Summary 25.1 reviews the grounds for summary dismissal.

Concept Summary 25.1

Grounds for Summary Dismissal

- absenteeism, lateness, and leaving work without permission
- substance abuse
- incompetence and carelessness
- dishonesty and disobedience
- conflicts of interest
- criminal behaviour

Wrongful Dismissal

Summary dismissal is an exception to the general rule. An employee may be summarily dismissed only in the sort of exceptional circumstances we have discussed. Normally, the common law and provincial employment standards legislation requires an employer to provide an employee with some reasonable period of notice before terminating the employment relationship. The notice period gives the employee an opportunity to avoid being without an income while looking for another job.

an employee normally must be given notice before being dismissed

It is not always possible to provide reasonable notice. If the employer fails to do so, the employee is usually entitled to money in lieu of notice. Sometimes, an employer will offer to pay that amount and ask the employee to leave immediately. Other times, the end is not so smooth. **Wrongful dismissal** occurs when an employee is dismissed without cause and without reasonable notice or money in lieu of notice. Although an employer generally cannot be forced to retain a particular employee, it may be held liable if it fires that person without reasonable notice. The employee may sue to recover not only money owed in lieu of notice, but also damages for the loss of commissions, bonuses, or benefits.

wrongful dismissal occurs when an employee is dismissed without cause and without reasonable notice or money in lieu of notice

The "reasonable notice period" depends upon the circumstances. Employment standards legislation always states a minimum notice period. Most jurisdictions require at least two weeks' notice for employees who have

employment standards legislation always states a minimum notice period

18. *Ennis v Canadian Imperial Bank of Commerce* (1989) 13 CCEL 25 (BC SC).
19. *Conrad v Household Financial Corp* (1992) 115 NSR (2d) 153 (SC TD), affd 45 CCEL 81 (SC AD).

been at a job for two years. Employees who have been at a job for ten or more years are often statutorily entitled to four to eight weeks' notice, depending on the jurisdiction. Note that these are the minimums, and courts often require much longer notice periods. Judges sometimes try to determine the length of the notice period that the parties themselves would have set if they had addressed the issue when they created their contract.[20] Usually, however, the courts look at such factors as: (i) the employee's age, (ii) the nature of the position held, (iii) the length of service, (iv) the salary level of the employee, and (v) the employee's likelihood of securing alternate employment. It is generally accepted, however, that the upper limit, even for the most senior executive, should not exceed 24 months.

Courts have recently begun to examine the behaviour of the employer around the time of dismissal. According to a majority of the Supreme Court of Canada, if an employee establishes that the employer engaged in *bad faith* conduct or unfair dealing in the course of dismissal, the resulting harm can be compensated by lengthening the usual notice period.[21] According to the Court, **bad faith** includes "untruthful, misleading or unduly insensitive conduct on the part of the employer." A bad faith dismissal resulting in such injuries as humiliation, embarrassment, and damage to one's sense of self-worth might give rise to a damage award greater than the amount owing to the employee in lieu of reasonable notice.

bad faith includes untruthful, misleading or unduly insensitive conduct on the part of the employer

where an employee establishes that the employer engaged in bad faith conduct or unfair dealing in the course of dismissal, the resulting harm can be compensated by a lengthened notice period

Constructive Dismissal

Employers sometimes try to avoid notice periods by making an employee's job so intolerable that they quit rather than wait to be dismissed. Such tactics may be stopped by the doctrine of *constructive dismissal*. **Constructive dismissal** occurs when an employer fundamentally changes the nature of a person's job. That doctrine does not prevent an employer from making minor alterations to an employee's tasks from time to time. In fact, in rapidly changing economic times, it is often necessary for employers to restructure operations and shuffle job duties, titles, locations, and compensation schemes. But employers who make fundamental changes without consulting the employee bear the risk of being sued. The three most common changes amounting to constructive dismissal are: (i) a reduction in salary or benefits, (ii) a change in job status or responsibility, or (iii) change in geographical location. If constructive dismissal can be proved, the employee is treated as though they were dismissed without notice and is therefore entitled to damages in lieu of notice. Business Law in Action 25.2 examines a question of constructive dismissal.

constructive dismissal occurs when an employer fundamentally changes the nature of a person's job

---

20. *Lazarowicz v Orenda Engines Ltd* (1960) 26 DLR (2d) 433 (Ont CA).

21. *Wallace v United Grain Growers Ltd* (1997) 152 DLR (4th) 1 at 33 (SCC). Iacobucci J justified the majority's extension of the notice period with this rationale:

> The point at which the employment relationship ruptures is the time when the employee is most vulnerable and hence most in need of protection. In recognition of this need, the law ought to encourage conduct that minimizes the damage and dislocation (both economic and personal) that result from dismissal. To ensure that employees receive adequate protection, employers ought to be held to an obligation of good faith and fair dealing in the manner of dismissal, breach of which will be compensated for by adding to the length of the notice period....

BUSINESS LAW IN ACTION 25.2

Pullen v John Preston Ltd (1985) 7 CCEL 91 (Ont HCJ)

Thomas Pullen worked for three years as Preston Ltd's marketing and sales manager in the Ottawa region. Because of a downturn in the economy, the company was restructured. As part of that development, Pullen was told that his salary would be reduced by 10 percent and that he would be stripped of some of his managerial duties. He promptly resigned his position and sued for constructive dismissal.

The court held that the change in Pullen's remuneration was significant, but not fundamental, given the harsh economic realities. Having considered all of the circumstances—

including the fact that all of the company's employees had to face a loss in salary and that Pullen was not deprived of all of his managerial duties—the court held that he was not constructively dismissed. The court approved the company's restructuring as a matter of last resort. Any less drastic action on the company's part would have led to the eventual loss of the company itself.

Question for Discussion

1. From a business perspective, how might Preston Ltd have avoided this lawsuit?

Severance Packages and Settlements

Fortunately, most employment relationships do not end with the employer having no regard for the employee's welfare. Conscientious and law-abiding employers usually offer *severance packages*. A **severance package** is a lump-sum payment that is meant to cover everything that is due to the employee at the time of termination. It is called a "severance" package because it includes *severance pay*. **Severance pay** is the amount that is owed to a terminated employee under employment standards legislation. A severance package may also include: (i) salary, commissions, or bonuses owing, (ii) benefits owing, (iii) contributions to Canada Pension Plan, (iv) contributions to registered retirement savings plans or private pension plans, (v) automobile allowance, (vi) vacation pay and sick leave, (vii) stock options, (viii) employee discounts and staff loans, (ix) interest owing, and (x) reference letters.

Sometimes an employer and employee negotiate the items to be included in the package so that it includes more than is required by legislation. This is sometimes called a *settlement package*. A **settlement package** is what the employer gives to the employee to bring an end to an employment dispute. As a matter of risk management, the employer should require the employee to sign a *release*. A **release** is the employee's written promise to refrain from suing the employer. Like other contracts, for the release to be effective, the employer must provide new consideration—something more than what the employee was already owed under the employment contract and the employment standards legislation. Case Brief 25.2 illustrates the importance of consideration.

a severance package is a lump sum payment meant to cover all items due to the employee at the time of termination

severance pay is the amount that is owed to a terminated employee under employment standards legislation

a settlement package is what the employer gives to the employee to bring an end to an employment dispute

a release is the employee's written promise to refrain from suing the employer

CASE BRIEF 25.2

Blackmore v Cablenet Ltd (1994) 8 CCEL (2d) 174 (Alta QB)

 After three years of dedicated service, a sales-man named Blackmore was dismissed without notice. To avoid a lawsuit, Cablenet offered Blackmore a settlement package that was less than the required severance. Blackmore knew that he could get more if he pursued the matter in court. However, Cablenet threatened that if he did not accept the package, it would refuse to give him his back-pay or a reference letter. Blackmore signed a release, but later sued.

The court held that the release was ineffective because Blackmore's promise not to sue Cablenet was gratuitous. Because Cablenet gave nothing of value to Blackmore in its so-called settlement package, there was no settlement. Ultimately, the court awarded Blackmore four months' pay in lieu of notice.

Chapter Summary

Before hiring an employee, an employer should draft a job description that accurately defines the duties attached to the position. Any advertisements should refer only to *bona fide* occupational requirements. When obtaining additional information from job applicants, employers must be careful to limit their questions to those relating to the applicant's ability to do the job. Both the employer and applicant should avoid misstatements during contract negotiations. The contract should be written.

Not all work- or service-related contracts are contracts of employment, nor are all workers employees. One way to test the nature of the work relationship is by determining how much control is asserted by the party paying for the work. Another test determines whether the work is an integral part of the overall business of the organization. The risk of vicarious liability and other workplace hazards impose responsibilities on employers to supervise their employees. Risk management requires employment policy manuals, performance reviews, and promotion or probation.

Statutory protection for workers includes: (i) employment standards—which is concerned with holidays, wages, work hours, overtime and rest periods, leaves, vacations, (ii) human rights—which is concerned with discrimination, harassment, and the duty to accommodate, (iii) occupational health and safety—which is concerned with the prevention of accidents, injuries, and industrial diseases through educational and punitive measures, and (iv) workers' compensation—which is concerned with redressing workplace injuries through an accident compensation scheme that is funded by compulsory contributions from employers. Due to the complexity of employment law, many employers hire trained human resource personnel or employment law specialists.

An employer's obligations may end abruptly.

Summary dismissal occurs when an employer dismisses an employee without providing notice—allowed when the employer can establish just cause. Just cause may exist if an employee is guilty of: (i) absenteeism, (ii) substance abuse, (iii) incompetence and carelessness, (iv) dishonesty and disobedience, (v) conflicts of interest, or (vi) criminal behaviour. The best way for a business to avoid being perceived as condoning employee misconduct is to implement and enforce a clearly worded policy that defines the limits of acceptable and unacceptable conduct.

The common law and provincial employment standards legislation generally require an employer to provide employees with some reasonable period of notice before terminating an employment relationship. Wrongful dismissal may arise if an employee is dismissed without cause and without reasonable notice or money in lieu of notice. The notice period will be further extended by a court in the case of bad faith dismissal. Constructive dismissal may arise if an employer fundamentally changes the nature of a person's job to force that person to quit.

A conscientious and law-abiding employer who wants to terminate an employment relationship usually puts together a severance package, which is a lump sum payment meant to cover everything that is due to the employee at the time of termination. That package will include severance pay, which is the amount that is owed to a terminated employee under employment standards legislation. Some employers provide their employees with additional items in their severance packages. If an employer wants to end the relationship amicably, it may offer the employee a settlement package, which generally includes more than the statutory minimums and is negotiated in return for the employee's willingness to sign a release, which effectively terminates the employment relationship and any potential disputes arising from it.

Review Questions

1. Why is it important to carefully draft a job description before advertising a position? Give an example that illustrates how a broadly drafted job description can be advantageous to both an employer and an employee.

2. Name an occupational requirement that might appear to be discriminatory. Give an example of how such a requirement might be justified as a *bona fide* occupational requirement.

3. What is the difference between an employee and an independent contractor? What are the benefits to an employer of hiring an independent contractor rather than an employee?

4. Compare the control and organizational tests for determining the nature of a work relationship.

5. Provide four examples of basic workplace issues that an employment policy manual should address.

6. What is the value of giving employees regular performance reviews?

7. When is the suspension of an employee a reasonable course of conduct?

8. Name several statutory regimes that have been created to protect employees. Give an example of each.

9. How many hours are in a standard work week? Under what circumstances is an employee entitled to a leave of absence?

10. Does an employee have the right to choose when to take a vacation?

11. Distinguish between direct discrimination and indirect discrimination.

12. Explain a situation in which being unmarried would be justified as a BFOR.

13. Can harassment be found to have occurred even if the conduct in question was not intended to be demeaning or offensive? Why?

14. Give two examples of how a risk manager can help to prevent violations of human rights legislation.

15. Which factors should be considered in deciding if, and to what extent, an employer has a duty to accommodate an employee's special needs due to disability?

16. Explain the aim of health and safety legislation. How can an employer defend itself against a violation of health and safety standards?

17. List six forms of employee misconduct that are considered to be just cause for a summary dismissal.

18. What factors should employers consider in determining a reasonable notice period for dismissing an employee? Is there a cause of action that exists for employees who feel that they have not been provided with reasonable notice of dismissal?

19. Define "constructive dismissal." What are the three most common kinds of changes that amount to constructive dismissal? What are the legal implications of proving constructive dismissal?

20. Distinguish between severance packages and settlement packages.

Cases and Problems

1. William Lee has been employed as a farmhand at Jean-Louis Mushroom Farms for four years. Following a decline in the value of mushrooms, Jean-Louis was forced to unilaterally alter the terms of William's pay. Jean-Louis also decided that it was necessary to abolish his custom of allowing employees to eat as many mushrooms as they desire while at work. He also reduced Jean-Louis's wages slightly to the current minimum wage. Despite the fact that it was only a minor reduction, William refuses to work for minimum wage and has brought an action for the balance of wages owing at his previous hourly rate. William is relying on his employment contract as well as past payment accounts, which prove his previous rate of pay. Discuss the factors that affect minimum pay rates. Is Jean-Louis justified in lowering William's wages if they continue to meet minimum wage requirements? Explain.

2. NumbersMagic Inc alleged that its bookkeeper, Chris Ginsberg, had stolen from it. The company made a claim against its insurer, Neverpay Insurance Ltd, to recover the loss. Neverpay refused the claim on the basis that the policy stated that:

In the event of loss and/or damages which can be attributed, even in part, to the acts of an employee, Neverpay Insurance will not be held responsible for compensating the company for said losses and/or damages.

The issue is whether Chris was a company employee at the time of the thefts. The evidence indicates that he performed basic bookkeeping services for the company, worked regular hours out of the NumbersMagic offices, and was subject to the direct supervision of a company manager. Chris was not a member of a recognized professional association, and his duties were those normally associated with a bookkeeper, not a professional accountant. Consequently, Chris was paid on an hourly basis—he did not set fees depending upon the nature of services he performed. He had no shares in the company, nor any incentive-based remuneration. No deductions were made from his cheques, nor did he receive holiday pay or any other company benefits. Apply both the control test and the organization test to determine whether Neverpay Insurance will likely have to make a payment under the policy. Support your position.

3. Erica performed deliveries for Speed of Sound Delivery Service. She used her own vehicle. She had the luxury of choosing when she wanted to work but, while on shift, she was subject to tight control by a Speed of Sound dispatcher. That meant that she could not deliver for anyone else during her shifts. Erica was paid by commission. No deductions were made on her cheques. After four years of uninterrupted work for Speed of Sound, Erica was dismissed without notice or cause. Erica brought an action for damages. Erica feels that her dedicated work for Speed of Sound Corporation entitled her to money in lieu of two months' notice, which is the amount recently received by another employee who was dismissed without notice. Do you think Erica will be successful in her claim? How much notice, if any, was Erica entitled to? Support your position.

4. WeBuildIt Construction Ltd hired Danele, an architect and construction manager, to build part of a tuna-canning plant. Danele was responsible for completing the project for a fixed sum. Her arrangement required her to employ workers and purchase materials, subject to the budgetary approval of WeBuildIt. The overall supervision of the workers remained under the direction of WeBuildIt's chief architect, Marty McPencil, who provided instruction to Danele and four other construction managers involved in the project. Following Marty's instructions, Danele designed and installed a giant metal tuna on the outside of the building. Ironically, on the opening day of the plant, the giant tuna fell and killed a fisherman who had just delivered his week's catch to the plant. The fisherman's wife is now seeking to recover damages from both Danele, who oversaw the installation of the giant tuna, and WeBuildIt Construction Ltd. Discuss the potential liability resulting from this situation.

5. Olga was a teller in the accounting department of the International Pirate Bank. She had been a loyal and dedicated employee for five years and had an unblemished work record, except for one letter warning her of disciplinary action, including possible dismissal, if her accuracy in balancing her cash each day did not improve. The letter required her to complete one full month of employment during which she was to make no mistakes. Olga managed to have a perfect record for that month. Unfortunately, during the next month, her cash did not balance. Olga was dismissed on the basis that she had consistently failed to meet the performance standard expected of a teller. Olga complained to her employer that she had been given only one written warning in over five years of employment, and, even in that case, she had fulfilled the employer's condition by balancing correctly for the one-month probation period. She also complained that the bank had failed to apply a mechanism of progressive discipline. As one of the Pirate Bank's risk managers, you have been called upon to resolve Olga's complaint and thereby decide her future. Did the bank have just cause for Olga's dismissal? Develop a policy to ensure that such complaints do not recur.

6. Following the conclusion of his contract, Puneet is seeking to recover overtime pay for time worked in excess of a 48-hour week. The facts are as follows. His contract is silent as to the number of hours to be worked in consideration for stated remuneration. His tendered record of the exact number of hours worked, although detailed, is uncorroborated. He has already been paid well in excess of the minimum hourly rate for all recorded hours worked. He is not a farmer or an emergency worker of any kind. Puneet has approached you to represent him in this matter. What legal issues does this scenario raise? What type of employment legislation is relevant to the resolution of this dispute? Does Puneet have a legal basis upon which to make this claim?

7. The Bank of Acadia adopted a policy that requires employees to provide urine samples for drug testing. That policy applies to all employees, although it is mandatory only for some, including new employees. The stated purpose of the policy is "to maintain a safe, healthy, and productive workplace for the employees; to safeguard customers, bank and employee funds; and to protect the bank's reputation." An employee who tests positive is required to attend treatment and rehabilitation counselling, which the bank pays for. If rehabilitation is unsuccessful, refused, or abandoned, the employee may be terminated from their employment. Concerned about the effect of such a policy on civil liberties, an activist group has filed a complaint with the Canadian Human Rights Commission, claiming that the bank is engaged in a practice of indirect discrimination. According to the group, the bank's policy has the effect of depriving certain people dependent on drug use of their jobs. Do you think that the bank's policy constitutes direct or indirect discrimination? Are there *bona fide* occupational grounds for doing so? Explain your answer.

8. Sylvan was employed as the garage manager for Tough Lucy's Trucking Ltd for seven years. During that time, he reported directly to the owner, Lucy LaRue. Sylvan proved to be an exemplary manager. He was known for his charm and got along well with other employees. However, according to several witnesses, Lucy seemed to think that Sylvan was not getting along with one employee in particular, namely Lucy's 24-year-old nephew she had hired to be the garage bookkeeper. Upon arriving to work one snowy January day, Sylvan was informed by Lucy that due to financial difficulties, Lucy would take over as garage manager and Sylvan would be reassigned to drive a company manure truck. There is no evidence that the garage was anything but profitable. The change in Sylvan's position involved a considerable change in responsibility as well as a lower salary, longer working hours, and substantially smellier working conditions. Sylvan was flabbergasted and appealed to Lucy on the basis of their long and pleasant working relationship. Lucy told him he could take it or leave it. Sylvan refused, resigned, and commenced a lawsuit. What is Sylvan's cause of action? What will he have to prove to win? Do you think that he will succeed? How

might Lucy have otherwise achieved her purpose without risking a lawsuit?

9. Shortly after his high-school graduation, Sweyn agreed to help his older sister, Svetlana, and her husband construct their home. The first day, Sweyn wore tennis shoes instead of proper boots. Although the issue was raised by another person who was on the construction crew, nothing was done about it. Since Sweyn had been driven to the construction site by Svetlana, he had no way to acquire adequate footwear, and his sister did not offer to drive him home. In fact, she and the rest of the crew seemed eager to commence work immediately. After walking through wet cement for several hours, Sweyn's feet began to turn yellow. Everyone knew this, but no one told him to stop working. Svetlana's husband said that he could continue working and would be fine as long as he washed his feet off, which he did. However, Sweyn suffered severe burns to his feet. He was on crutches for several weeks and has had trouble walking ever since. Sweyn has sued Svetlana. He contends that, during the construction project, he was effectively her employee, and therefore she had breached her duty of care as an employer when she brought Sweyn onto the work site without providing him with proper work boots. Do you think that the minimal standards set out by occupational health and safety legislation apply in this case? Explain your position. What kind of evidence would Svetlana need to prove to invoke a defence of due diligence?

10. Lucia, the district sales manager of the Sharky's Credit Union, extended credit to a customer contrary to company policy. Mike, Sharky's CEO, responded by personally reprimanding Lucia and suspending her scheduled pay increase. Slightly poorer but still unable to control her corporate generosity, Lucia subsequently extended substantial additional credit to the same customer. Mike discovered this during his weekly review of the company's accounts and immediately dismissed Lucia without notice. According to Mike, Lucia had attempted to withhold reports from the company that would have revealed the extension of credit to this and other customers. Were Lucia's breaches of company policy just cause for her summary dismissal? Is it necessary for Mike to prove fraud to justify the dismissal?

11. Dick Vernon, a school superintendent, was convicted of a criminal offence for defrauding the province of $194 when he failed to report his son's summer work program on a financial statement. In the criminal proceedings against him, Dick was fined $400 and sentenced to probation. Although the crime was completely unrelated to Dick's own employment, he was dismissed as soon as the conviction was registered against him. In its dismissal notice, the board of education cited the fact that his failure to disclose was premeditated and dishonest. Do you agree that Dick's offence constitutes just cause for his dismissal as school superintendent? Support your opinion.

12. Jamal was dismissed from his position as chief scientist at fledgling.com. To minimize exposure to liability and so improve chances of obtaining venture capital financing, Raquel, the chief operating officer of fledging.com, asked Jamal to sign a written release absolving the company of any claims against it. He asked whether he could take it away to have someone look at it, but Raquel said that it would be more convenient for everyone if he just signed it right away. Jamal decided to sign. After signing the release, Jamal received a cheque that covered two weeks' severance pay and a contribution to his relocation expenses.

Now, several months later, he has brought a wrongful dismissal action against fledgling.com. Jamal claims that the release was presented to him as an ultimatum—either he sign it or fledgling.com would refuse to pay his severance. Raquel claims that she did not exert any actual pressure on Jamal and that signing the release was simply a procedural formality associated with the severance process. Is the release enforceable? What would a better business manager have done differently to ensure that the release would be enforceable? How would the inclusion of relocation expenses, if not included in Jamal's terms of employment, help to render the release enforceable?

26 Organized Labour

OBJECTIVES

After completing this chapter, you should be able to:

1. Distinguish between individual employment and organized labour.
2. Understand the nature and function of collective bargaining.
3. Explain the collective bargaining process and the manner in which bargaining rights are acquired.
4. Describe provisions typically contained in a collective agreement.
5. Discuss the nature and function of grievance arbitration.
6. Identify three typical employee grievances in the context of organized labour.
7. Describe several remedies typically awarded by labour arbitrators.
8. Distinguish between the jurisdiction of labour arbitrators and courts.
9. Summarize four aspects of industrial conflict, and identify the relationships between them.
10. Discuss the role played by labour relations boards in the resolution of industrial conflict.

Not all work relationships are *individual* relationships between workers and their employers. In fact, much of the Canadian labour force is organized and governed *collectively*. Therefore, we distinguish *employment law* from *labour law*. As we saw in Chapter 25, employment law is the system of rules that governs the relationship between individuals and their employers. **Labour law** is the system of rules that governs collective relations between management, trade unions, their members, and the institutions involved in such relations.[1] It is the collective nature of organized labour that distinguishes it from other kinds of employment.

> **labour law** the system of rules that governs collective relations between management, trade unions, their members, and the institutions in such relations

In this chapter, we will investigate the features of organized labour that distinguish it from individual employment and consider their impact on the legal aspects of doing business. We will then consider collective bargaining and examine the trade union, the instrument through which collective bargaining is achieved. We will discuss the aim of bargaining through unions—the establishment and maintenance of a collective agreement. We will look at the system of grievance arbitration that is used in connection with disputes under a collective agreement, and conclude with a survey of the legal treatment of such industrial conflicts as strikes, picketing, lockouts, and boycotts.

COLLECTIVE BARGAINING

Nature and Function of Collective Bargaining

Slavery is a dramatic example of what can happen when individual workers are powerless. Even in less-extreme circumstances, individual workers may have little influence over their employers. By banding together, however, workers can exert considerable force. In fact, they may exert too much force. While collective power can be used to escape intolerable working conditions, it can also be used to illegitimately intimidate and coerce employers. Consider the plight of a ship's captain when its crew members engage in a mutiny. For that reason, organized labour was once a crime in Canada. Eventually, the right to organize gained legal recognition in the United States and then in Canada. But even then, there were roadblocks. Workers who tried to organize unions were initially confronted with economic reprisals from their employers. Today, trade unions are recognized as a legitimate way of empowering individual workers and enforcing their collective rights.

Labour law aims to find the appropriate balance between slavery and mutiny by imposing a system of rules around *collective bargaining*. **Collective bargaining** is the process whereby an employer and a *trade union* seek to negotiate a *collective agreement*. A **trade union** is an organization of employees formed to regulate the relations between the employer and the collective of employees. A **collective agreement** is a document containing the terms of employment, as well as the rights and duties of the employer, the trade union, and the employees. In most jurisdictions, the collective agreement of any organized group of workers can be enforced only through an arbitration procedure that has been started by either the employer or the union.

> **collective bargaining** is the process whereby an employer and a trade union seek to negotiate a collective agreement

> a **trade union** is an organization of employees formed to regulate the relations between the employer and the collective of employees

> a **collective agreement** is a document containing the terms of employment, as well as the rights and duties of the employer, the trade union, and the employees

Collective bargaining rights are based on legislation. Industries regulated by the federal jurisdiction are governed by the *Canada Labour Code*.[2] Other industries are regulated by similar provincial legislation, each of which estab-

---

[1.] HW Arthurs *et al*, *Labour Law and Industrial Relations in Canada* 4th ed (1993) at 32.

[2.] *Canada Labour Code*, RSC 1985, c L-2 (Can).

lishes a statutory tribunal usually known as a *labour relations board*. A **labour relations board** administers labour relations legislation within a jurisdiction.

Not every worker is entitled to the benefits and protections of collective bargaining. Each jurisdiction defines which employees are eligible to bargain collectively. Most jurisdictions use the term "employee" in the context of organized labour almost the same as in the context of individual employment. However, there are differences in its meaning. For example, a corporate manager is usually an employee in the context of employment law, but not in the context of collective bargaining. In other words, managers can not take part in collective bargaining on their own behalf. In collective bargaining, the role of management is to bargain on behalf of the employer. Only eligible employees can be represented by trade unions.

There is no definitive test to determine who is a manager and who is an employee, but items typically considered are: (i) the nature of the organization, (ii) the person's position in the organizational structure, (iii) the extent of the person's authority over other workers, and (iv) the proportion of that person's work that is non-managerial.[3] Managers are not the only workers who are ineligible to bargain collectively. Other workers excluded from the collective bargaining process may include such public employees as firefighters and police, as well as such professional employees as doctors, dentists, and lawyers.

Acquisition of Bargaining Rights

Just as some employees are ineligible to bargain collectively, some employee organizations are not qualified to take part in the collective bargaining process. Those that do not meet the qualifications do not have the right to bargain collectively, for example, many employee associations that organize primarily for social or recreational purposes. In addition to being qualified, the organization must be recognized by the jurisdiction's labour relations board as an *appropriate bargaining unit*. An **appropriate bargaining unit** is a group of workers recognized by the labour relations board as having a common interest in the outcome of negotiations. It is important to distinguish the bargaining unit—the constituency of workers—from its *bargaining agent*. The **bargaining agent** is the trade union that is legally recognized as representing the interests of the bargaining unit.

A trade union can become recognized as a bargaining agent for a particular bargaining unit through *voluntary recognition* by the employer. **Voluntary recognition** occurs when the employer agrees to recognize a trade union as the bargaining agent for its employees. Given the simplicity of its procedure, voluntary recognitions occur more frequently in industries where job duration is of a temporary nature, such as the construction industry. The downside of voluntary recognition is that such arrangements are often challenged by employees who do not want to be represented by the employer's chosen bargaining agent.

The more common method of acquiring bargaining rights is through a *membership drive*. The aim of a **membership drive** is to persuade a majority of employees in an appropriate bargaining unit to become union members. In most provinces, a union that secures the required number of members automatically becomes a **certified bargaining agent** and thereby acquires exclusive bargaining rights on behalf of the bargaining unit. In Alberta and Nova Scotia,

---

a **labour relations board** administers labour relations legislation within a jurisdiction

not every worker is entitled to the benefits and protections provided by collective bargaining

besides managers, some jurisdictions exclude firefighters, police, and some professionals from the collective bargaining process

an **appropriate bargaining unit** is a group of workers recognized by the labour relations board as having a common interest in the outcome of negotiations

a **bargaining agent** is a trade union that is legally recognized as representing the interests of a bargaining unit

voluntary recognition occurs when the employer agrees to recognize a trade union as the bargaining agent for its employees

a **membership drive** aims to persuade a majority of employees in an appropriate bargaining unit to become union members

a **certified bargaining agent** acquires exclusive bargaining rights on behalf of the bargaining unit

---

3. HW Arthurs *et al*, *Labour Law and Industrial Relations in Canada* 4th ed (1993) at 214.

however, the employees must vote for a union to be certified, regardless of the success of a membership drive. In other jurisdictions, a vote is necessary if the membership drive fails to recruit a majority of employees. And in some jurisdictions, employees who do not want to be represented by a particular union may, under some circumstances, complain to the labour relations board.

Collective Bargaining Process

Once a union has acquired the bargaining rights for an appropriate bargaining unit, it must negotiate with the employer to reach a collective agreement that protects the collective interests of the employees. Most collective agreements not only set out the terms of employment for the members of the bargaining unit, they also contemplate the nature of the interaction between the employer and the union. Therefore, a union must be careful during negotiations. A business that does not want its employees to organize, or that does not want to deal with the employees' chosen bargaining agent, may try to delay the creation of a collective agreement. That tactic sometimes threatens the very survival of the union as the bargaining agent.

Once a bargaining unit has selected and certified its bargaining agent, that union has the exclusive right to bargain on behalf of its members. Even if a collective agreement has not yet been created, other unions can not attempt to bargain on behalf of the employees in that bargaining unit, even if some of those employees would prefer being represented by another bargaining agent. Likewise, individual employees are prohibited from bargaining for themselves with their employer.[4] The exclusive right to bargain also includes the right for a certified union to bargain for its own financial security.

During negotiations, the employer and the union often reach an impasse. To avoid strikes, lockouts, or other forms of industrial conflict, most jurisdictions have imposed an array of dispute resolution procedures. One procedure is conciliation. Usually, an appointed conciliation officer talks with each party separately in a series of confidential discussions. The conciliation officer then makes a series of recommendations to persuade the parties to resume negotiations and to avoid the expense and conflict associated with strikes and lockouts.

One controversial obligation in the collective bargaining process is the *duty to bargain in good faith*. The **duty to bargain in good faith** imposes an obligation on both parties to make every reasonable effort to successfully negotiate a collective agreement. An employer or a union that intentionally tries to thwart the negotiation process violates that duty. Some business managers believe that either party should be entitled to negotiate as forcefully as it wants, and that the point of collective bargaining is to match the economic strength of the collective against that of the employer. Recall that the aim of labour law is to strike a balance between slavery and mutiny. The duty to bargain in good faith is a reminder that the entire process will break down if both parties feel free to engage in tactics that are inherently destructive of the employer-employee relationship. The duty therefore has been interpreted by most labour relations boards as an obligation about the manner in which negotiations are conducted, not about the actual content of particular proposals. The duty to bargain in good faith includes: (i) the duty to meet with the other party, (ii) the duty to engage in full and informed discussion, (iii) the duty to supply information, (iv) the duty to complete negotiations.[5] Case Brief 26.1 illustrates a violation of this duty.

a union has the exclusive right to bargain on behalf of its members once it has been selected and certified as the bargaining agent

the duty to bargain in good faith imposes an obligation on both parties to make every reasonable effort to successfully negotiate a collective agreement

[4] *Syndicat catholique des employés des magasins de Québec Inc v Cie Paquet Ltée* (1959) 18 DLR (2d) 346 (SCC).

[5] HW Arthurs *et al, Labour Law and Industrial Relations in Canada* 4th ed (1993) at 259-63.

CASE BRIEF 26.1

Governing Counsel of the University of Toronto v Royal Conservatory of Music Faculty Association
[1985] 11 CLRBR (NS) 219

The University of Toronto was negotiating its first collective agreement with the union representing the Royal Conservatory. The university wanted to streamline its administration. It announced its desire to sever the conservatory from the university entirely so that it could be dealt with as a separate, independent corporate entity. The Royal Conservatory's faculty association did not believe that such a move would be in its best interests. It asked the university management team for further negotiations. The university responded by saying that the request was an intrusion on its management rights, insisted that severance was non-negotiable, and refused to discuss the matter further. The union then filed a complaint with the labour relations board, claiming that the university had failed to bargain in good faith.

The labour relations board held that the university's outright refusal to discuss the issue of separation constituted a violation of its duty to bargain in good faith. Although the board made it clear that the university was not duty-bound to agree to the union's proposal, it did have a duty to hear and consider the union's proposal. The university's unwillingness to entertain the union's proposal, let alone respond to the union with an explanation of why it was opposed to the proposal, was in breach of the duty to engage in full and informed discussion. It was therefore a breach of its duty to act in good faith.

COLLECTIVE AGREEMENTS

There are three essential requirements for any collective agreement.

- First, it must be in writing.
- Second, it must be entered into by the employer and a trade union with a signature indicating the assent of each party.
- Third, it must contain provisions respecting the terms and conditions of employment.[6]

Although it is tempting to think of the collective agreement as a multi-party contract, there are several important differences between collective agreements and contracts. Collective agreements are enforceable not by common law but by labour legislation. Furthermore, labour legislation in most jurisdictions dictates the inclusion of particular statutory provisions that make the character of a collective agreement quite different from a common law contract. Some authors have suggested that the collective agreement is a kind of labour relations "constitution."[7] These are some of the standard provisions.

Strike and Lockout Provisions

To promote industrial stability, most jurisdictions in Canada, unlike other countries, require collective agreements to prohibit strikes and lockouts while the collective agreement is binding. Consequently, some labour practices that would otherwise be legitimate are actually unlawful. Consider Business Law in Action 26.1.

---

[6] G Adams *Canadian Labour Law* (1985) at 671.

[7] HW Arthurs *et al, Labour Law and Industrial Relations in Canada* 4th ed (1993) at 676.

BUSINESS LAW IN ACTION 26.1

The Lockout Provision[8]

To cut costs and increase plant efficiency, Kerasic and Sons Meat Packing Ltd attempted to shorten their work week by one day to create a four-day work week. The International Brotherhood of Meat Packers filed a grievance on behalf of its employees, claiming that the attempt to alter the traditional work week was unlawful.

The labour relations board concluded that such an alteration was in breach of the mandatory provision in the collec-

tive agreement, which prohibited strikes or lockouts during a binding collective agreement. According to the board, the effect of changing to a four-day work week was to prevent workers from working on the fifth day, which is, in essence, an attempt to lock out workers on that day.

Questions for Discussion

1. Do you agree with the labour relations board?
2. How might management have achieved its desired result without causing a grievance?

Grievance Provisions

Since strikes and lockouts are prohibited during a collective agreement, most jurisdictions in Canada set out other mechanisms for resolving disputes about the interpretation, application, administration, or alleged violation of a collective agreement. The most common mechanism is the process of *grievance arbitration*. As we saw in Chapter 1, arbitration is a process in which a neutral third person, an arbitrator, imposes a decision on the parties. Some collective agreements have a very detailed grievance provision that sets out the entire procedure step-by-step. Others are completely silent on the issue. Labour relations boards sometimes amend arbitration provisions that are inadequate and, in some cases, impose a statutory "model arbitration" clause. Therefore, business managers who employ organized labour should include in their collective agreement a procedure they like, for example, a provision that requires arbitration decisions to be released within a specified period of time. Otherwise, a process will be put into place to expedite the matter.

business managers should include in their collective agreement a grievance arbitration procedure that they like

Union Security Clauses

Every jurisdiction permits the inclusion of a *union security clause*. A **union security clause** states how a union will be paid—whether by its membership or otherwise. Usually a union is remunerated through the payment of union dues. Unions typically adopt one of these three structures.

a union security clause states how a union will be paid

- First, the union might decide to operate as a *closed shop*. A **closed shop** is a requirement that management will not hire anyone who is not already a member of that union.

a closed shop requires that management hire only people who are already union members

- A second approach is a *union shop*. A **union shop** requires a person to become a union member before starting their employment.

a union shop requires a person to become a union member before starting their employment

- A third approach is the *Rand formula*, or *dues shop*. A **dues shop** requires a person who is hired to pay union dues, but does not require that person to join the union.

a dues shop requires a person who is hired to pay union dues, but does not require that person to join the union

In some jurisdictions, an employer is required to include a union security clause in a collective agreement if the union requests it. To ignore such a

8. *CE Lummus Canada Ltd* [1983] OLRB Rep Sept 1504.

request is considered to be a breach of the duty to bargain in good faith and is grounds for complaint to the labour relations board. Concept Summary 26.1 reviews these three approaches.

Concept Summary 26.1

Union Security: The Means by Which a Union Will Be Remunerated

Closed shop	Employers cannot hire a person unless they are already a union member in good standing.
Union shop	Employers cannot hire a person unless they undertake to become a union member in good standing when starting employment.
Dues shop	Employers cannot hire a person unless they promise to pay union dues (though actual union membership is optional).

GRIEVANCE ARBITRATION

Arbitration Process

grievance arbitration is an external method of resolving labour disputes that cannot be resolved by the parties alone

Most collective agreements contain an *internal* procedure for dealing with employee grievances. In addition, labour law provides an *external* method of resolving such disputes—*grievance arbitration*. **Grievance arbitration** is an external method of resolving labour disputes that cannot be resolved by the parties alone. It is the final stage in the process of resolving an industrial dispute. Usually the process begins with the union notifying the employer of the dispute and their attempt to resolve it internally. If a settlement cannot be reached between the employee and management, the parties will engage in arbitration. In some cases, the process can be overseen by a sole arbitrator; in others, it may involve an arbitration panel.

it is important to distinguish disputes before an arbitration panel and those before a labour relations board

It is important to distinguish between: (i) disputes brought before an arbitration panel, and (ii) disputes brought before the labour relations board. The labour relations panel usually hears disputes about the violation of labour relations legislation. The arbitration panel or sole arbitrator hears and resolves disputes about the collective agreement. The role of arbitration therefore is to resolve a dispute between employee and management under an existing collective agreement. Although some arbitrations are open to the public, arbitrators have a discretion to exclude the public, including the press, from the proceedings.[9]

The parties to a collective agreement are jointly responsible for appointing an arbitrator. If the matter can be resolved by a sole arbitrator, the parties must agree to that person's selection. If a panel of arbitrators is required, each party selects its own arbitrator to sit as a member on the panel, and then jointly selects a third member to chair the panel. The cost of the proceedings, including the expense of the arbitrators, is generally shared equally by both parties. Management and unions must therefore be careful to budget for these expenses.

management and unions must budget for grievance arbitration expenses

There are similarities and differences between decisions made by a labour arbitrator and decisions made by a judge. Like judges, arbitrators must find certain facts on the basis of evidence and argument. Unlike judges, arbitrators are permitted to consider parole evidence.[10] Once the facts are established,

9. *Toronto Star* (1977) 14 LAC (2d) 155.

10. The application of several other traditional rules of evidence strictly adhered to in courtrooms is relaxed in arbitration.

arbitrators apply them to the collective agreement. If the collective agreement is insufficient to resolve the dispute, arbitrators look to outside sources, including: (i) the traditional rules of interpretation, (ii) the labour legislation itself, and (iii) *arbitral jurisprudence*. **Arbitral jurisprudence** is the body of existing arbitration decisions. Although arbitrators do not strictly adhere to the doctrine of precedent—following decisions from earlier cases—previous arbitral decisions often play an important role in the decision making. Usually, an arbitrator follows a previous decision that is relevant unless they think it is wrong. Finally, an arbitrator will apply many of the principles of equity.

To determine whether the grievance is a proper subject for arbitration, some arbitrators allow the parties to make preliminary submissions before the formal hearing begins. An employer can make several arguments to try to end the grievance before the matter is formally heard, including: (i) the grievor is not a person covered under the collective agreement, (ii) the issue falls outside the scope of the collective agreement, and (iii) the submission of the grievance fell outside of the required time limits.[11]

arbitral jurisprudence is the body of existing arbitration decisions

Typical Grievances

Business people who will be operating in an organized labour environment need to know about the most typical grievances. We briefly consider three basic grounds of complaint:

- discipline and discharge
- seniority
- compensation

Discipline

Like individual employment contracts, collective agreements often say how employee misconduct will be treated. In many respects, the basis for discipline is similar to that in individual employment. One main difference is that disciplinary procedures are generally spelled out in the collective agreement. Disciplinary measures usually include suspensions, formal warnings, and sometimes demotion. Extreme misconduct leads to discharge. Another difference is that many collective agreements provide that the employer is allowed to discipline or discharge an employee only if there is just cause. Where such a provision exists, an arbitrator will interfere with the employer's handling of a disciplinary matter only if the arbitrator believes that cause was lacking. Where a collective agreement does not contain such a provision, arbitrators will not usually interfere with an employer's decision to take action. For more leeway, business managers should therefore try to avoid a just cause provision.

It is sometimes difficult to tell if an employer's particular conduct is of a disciplinary nature. *Demotion* is a typical example. **Demotion** occurs when an employer transfers an employee to a lower-rated job. Often employers demote employees due to their misconduct. In this context, demotion is a form of discipline and is subject to review if the collective agreement contains a just cause provision. What if an employee is demoted due to their incompetence? This is generally seen as a non-disciplinary demotion and is not subject to review by an arbitrator. Sometimes the line between disciplinary and non-disciplinary demotion is difficult to draw, as You Be the Judge 26.1 demonstrates.

demotion occurs when an employer transfers an employee to a lower-rated job

---

11. HW Arthurs *et al*, *Labour Law and Industrial Relations in Canada* 4th ed (1993) at 332.

YOU BE THE JUDGE 26.1

Demotion[12]

Hilda had worked for a unionized bakery as a cashier for six months. Although she received some training from the bakery manager in handling cash, she made many errors on the deposit slips. Something seemed suspicious. Rather than warning Hilda about the possible consequences of continued errors, the bakery's management decided to see if she continued to mishandle cash. She did. Instead of making a fuss about it, the bakery's management simply demoted her to a packaging clerk. The bakery claimed that the demotion was non-disciplinary in nature and was purely a response to her

inability to competently perform the job of cashier. Hilda felt that her demotion was disciplinary since the bakery's management had obviously formed the wrong impression about her and was suspicious that she was trying to steal cash. Consequently, Hilda decided to grieve the bakery's decision.

Questions for Discussion

1. If you were asked to arbitrate this dispute, how would you characterize the demotion?
2. What additional facts might you wish to know before deciding?

Seniority

seniority grants preferences to certain employees based on their accumulated length of service

non-competitive clauses require seniority to be the determining factor, as long as the more senior person is competent

competitive clauses require seniority to be the determining factor only when the skill and ability of the competing employees are relatively equal

bumping occurs when a senior employee who is about to be laid off is allowed to invoke their seniority and *bump* a more junior employee from a junior position

A complaint that often arises in grievance arbitration is that an employer has acted without proper regard to an employee's *seniority*. The concept of seniority is central to virtually every collective agreement.[13] **Seniority** grants preferences to certain employees based on their accumulated length of service. Not only does seniority define who is eligible for certain monetary benefits, it also provides a way of determining which employee is entitled to job promotion and which employee is subject to a transfer or lay-off. Seniority provisions in collective agreements are usually one of two types: (i) *non-competitive clauses* and, (ii) *competitive clauses*.[14] **Non-competitive clauses** require seniority to be the determining factor, as long as the more senior person is competent. **Competitive clauses** require seniority to be the determining factor only when the skill and ability of the competing employees are relatively equal.

Many collective agreements contemplate *bumping*. **Bumping** occurs when a senior employee who is about to be laid off is allowed to invoke their seniority and *bump* a more junior employee from a junior position. In many instances, this sets off a chain reaction. The junior person who was just bumped asserts their seniority against a still more junior person, and so on. Most collective agreements either explicitly or implicitly provide that an employee who has elected to bump into a lower position does not forfeit the right to return to their previous job if it is eventually recalled. Collective agreements that include bumping rights usually carry a minimum requirement that the senior person is capable of doing the junior person's job. However, as Case Brief 26.2 illustrates, if the junior position requires a specialized skill, the senior employee is usually entitled to the necessary training to learn that skill.

---

12. *SP Bakery Co and Teamsters Local 464* [1997] BCDLA 500.15.40.45-06 A-139/97.

13. DJM Brown & D Beatty, *Canadian Labour Arbitration* 3d ed (2000) 6:000.

14. HW Arthurs *et al*, *Labour Law and Industrial Relations in Canada* 4th ed (1993) at 343.

CASE BRIEF 26.2

Re Saskatchewan Health Care Assn and Saskatchewan Union of Nurses [1994] 45 LAC (4th) 33

Nancy Hamm was a registered nurse who had been employed at St Paul's Hospital for 23 years. Although she had worked in a variety of positions during her tenure at the hospital, for the past few years, she had been employed in a general duty nurse classification on the general surgery unit. During those years, she had received performance appraisals of "very good" to "excellent or outstanding."

In 1993, the hospital entered a period of fiscal restraint. It notified Nancy that it would be reducing staff and that her position would be eliminated within three months. Nancy chose to exercise her right to displace a less senior employee under the terms of the collective agreement. She elected to move into a lower position in the post-anaesthetic care unit, a specialty unit that required a significant degree of skill and knowledge to care for its patients. According to the collective agreement, "A laid off or displaced Nurse may only dis-

place a Nurse in an equal or lower paid classification, with less seniority, *subject to the Nurse having ability, performance and qualifications for the position.*" Referring to this provision of the collective agreement, the hospital argued that Nancy could not bump into that position since she had not been trained to perform all of the duties required in post-anaesthetic care. Although Nancy had excellent general nursing skills, she lacked the specialized training required to perform some of the work in the unit.

The panel of arbitrators disagreed. Since Nancy had excellent general ability and all of the appropriate qualifications, they said the hospital was obligated to provide her with an opportunity to be certified in the necessary skills. According to the panel, the hospital could refuse to allow Nancy to bump into the position only if she had been given the proper training but still demonstrated an inability to perform the work.

Business managers involved in negotiating a collective agreement should realize that employees may want to use the bumping procedure in reverse. **Bumping up** is an application of seniority rights in the context of promotion. Prudent business managers will not want a system of promotion that is based solely on seniority. To avoid that risk, management should negotiate an exclusive right to make appointments in a manner that applies seniority rights differently in promotions than in lay-offs.[15]

> **bumping up** is an application of seniority rights in the context of promotion

Compensation

Compensation is a ground of complaint that often leads to grievance arbitration. Like the individual employment scenario, typical complaints involve: (i) equal pay for equal work, (ii) unilateral change in wages, (iii) overtime pay, and (iv) entitlement to benefits. One issue that arises more often in the context of organized labour is *retroactive pay*. **Retroactive pay** is money that is owed by the employer to the employee as a result of a collective agreement that is deemed to come into effect some time before the date of its creation. The law generally presumes that wage increases apply retroactively. Although most employers are willing to comply with collective agreements for retroactive wages in the form of back-pay, disputes often arise about whether employees are also entitled to other benefits as of that date. Traditionally, arbitrators have drawn a distinction between monetary and non-monetary provisions.[16] Therefore, they usually require clear language that expressly includes benefits before awarding them retroactively.[17]

> **retroactive pay** is money that is owed by the employer to the employee as a result of a collective agreement that is deemed to come into effect some time before the date of its creation

> there is a general presumption that wage increases—but not other benefits—apply retroactively

---

[15.] Brown & Beatty *Canadian Labour Arbitration* 3d ed (2000) at 6:2340.

[16.] *Onesimus Community Resources* (1994) 39 LAC (4th) 289 (Thorne); *Sturgeon General Hospital* (1974) 6 LAC (2d) 360 (Taylor).

[17.] *Toronto Hospital* (1995) 49 LAC (4th) 1 (Thorne); *York Regional Board of Education* (1990) 11 LAC (4th) 345 (Marszewski).

A business sometimes has to decide whether to offer back-pay to people who were employees at the time the collective agreement retroactively became effective, but ceased to be employees before the agreement was signed. Consider Business Decision 26.1.

BUSINESS DECISION 26.1

Retroactive Pay to Former Employees

Avi worked as a professor at Western University for three years. In his third year, another university recruited him, offering him a position starting on July 1 of that year. He accepted the position and gave proper written notice to Western University. During the same year, Western's faculty association had unionized and was in the process of negotiating a collective agreement with the university's management team. One subject of negotiation was retroactive pay for professors who had been employed at the university for a certain period of time and who were members in good standing in the faculty association. Avi met both of these requirements. However, the university was considering certain cost-cutting measures and took the position that it did not want to offer back-pay to professors who were voluntarily leaving as of July 1 to seek out greener pastures. The faculty association's representatives argued throughout negotiations that back-pay is meant to compensate employees for work done in the past and has nothing to do with what people decide to do in the future. However, those representatives also knew that the university management team might consider that issue to be a deal breaker.

Questions for Discussion

1. If you were asked to represent the university management's bargaining team, would you want to cut out employees like Avi who had voluntarily chosen to leave? Why?

2. If you were asked to represent the faculty association's bargaining team, would you allow the university to cut out employees like Avi who had voluntarily chosen to leave? Why?

3. Would your decision be any different if the reason Avi was cut out of the retroactive pay deal was because the university decided on June 30 that Avi should be laid off? Why?

Arbitration Awards

An arbitrator's authority to award remedies is limited by both the labour legislation and the terms of the collective agreement. Consequently, if the parties want to allow arbitrators broad power in resolving grievances, they must consider this in negotiating the collective agreement. One remedy generally available to arbitrators is an award of damages. The approach to damages in arbitral jurisprudence is similar to common law breaches of contract. The aim is to put the party who has suffered a breach of the collective agreement in the position that they would have been in had the breach not occurred. Other traditional contract principles come into play, including the duty to mitigate damages. However, some contractual remedies available to judges are not generally available to arbitrators. One such common law remedy is *rectification*. **Rectification** is the process by which a contract is rewritten to better reflect the actual agreement contemplated by the parties. According to the Supreme Court of Canada, arbitrators do not have the inherent power to rectify a collective agreement unless that agreement expressly gives them the power to do so.[18]

Arbitrators do have the power to grant a declaration of a party's rights by way of a *compliance order*. A **compliance order** usually requires a specific obligation in the collective agreement to be fulfilled or a particular course of conduct to be brought to an end. In deciding whether to make such an order, arbi-

rectification the process by which a contract is rewritten to better reflect the actual agreement contemplated by the parties

arbitrators do not have the inherent power to rectify a collective agreement unless that agreement expressly gives them the power to do so

a compliance order requires a specific obligation in the collective agreement to be fulfilled or a particular course of conduct to be brought to an end

---

18. *Port Arthur Shipbuilding Co v Arthurs* (1968) 70 DLR (2d) 283 (SCC).

trators often consider: (i) the difficulty of enforcing the order, (ii) the likelihood of future violations, (iii) whether the collective agreement is still in effect, and (iv) whether the balance of convenience justifies the order.[19]

Arbitrators also have the power to reinstate employees who were discharged without cause. And unless the jurisdiction's labour legislation or the collective agreement provides otherwise, arbitrators generally have the power to substitute a lesser penalty in the case of a suspension or discharge.[20]

arbitrators have the power to reinstate employees who were discharged without cause

Enforcement of Arbitration Awards

Although arbitrators have the power to order awards, they do no have the power to enforce them. Labour legislation in each jurisdiction provides that arbitration orders are to be filed with the courts and enforced in the same way as any other judicial order. Consequently, a party that fails to abide by an arbitration order could ultimately find itself in contempt of court and therefore be subject to state coercion.

INDUSTRIAL CONFLICT

Disputes under a collective agreement are usually resolved through grievance arbitration. However, when the parties reach an impasse before establishing a collective agreement or after it is no longer in effect, one party may decide to use economic pressure to persuade the other to make the appropriate concessions. The most common practice used by employees is a *strike*, while employers often respond by *locking out* their employees. Strikes and lockouts sometimes lead to secondary activities, such as *picketing* and *boycotts*. We finish this chapter by briefly considering strikes, lockouts, picketing, and boycotts, and their legal effect on businesses that employ organized labour. We will discuss both lawful and unlawful industrial action.

Strikes

The term *"strike"* does not enjoy a uniform definition across Canadian. Most statutory definitions of a **strike** require that there be: (i) a cessation of work, (ii) resulting from a concerted activity, (iii) that has a common purpose, (iv) designed to limit or restrict output. Some jurisdictions such as Alberta, Manitoba, and Nova Scotia require a fifth element: (v) the common purpose is to compel the employer to accept certain terms and conditions of employment.

a strike is a cessation of work, resulting from a concerted activity, that has a common purpose to limit or restrict output

Although employees who go on strike usually do so in a clear way, less obvious activities may also constitute a strike. Consider Case Brief 26.3.

---

[19] Brown & Beatty *Canadian Labour Arbitration* 3d ed (2000) at 2:1450.

[20] *Heusis v New Brunswick Electric Power Commission* (1979) 98 DLR (3d) 622 (SCC).

CASE BRIEF 26.3

Re British Columbia Terminal Elevator Operators' Assn and Grain Workers' Union Local 333
(1994) 23 CLRBR (2d) 286 (Can LRB)

Due to a decline in shipping demand, the management of the Saskatchewan Wheat Pool decided that it had to temporarily stop operating its night shift. This resulted in a lay-off of 10 employees. In response to the lay-offs, other members of the Grain Workers' Union Local 333 were instructed to refuse to work overtime. According to the union, the refusal to work overtime was justified under the collective agreement, which expressly stated that overtime shifts were voluntary. Management, on the other hand, argued that the refusal to work overtime was a concerted effort to stop working with the aim of limiting the Wheat Pool's output.

In determining whether the refusal to work overtime constituted an unlawful strike, the labour relations board held that a continued concerted refusal to work overtime would ultimately result in the employer's failure to fulfill its loading commitments. It therefore held that the refusal to work overtime was an unlawful form of strike. It ordered union members to cease and desist in their overtime refusal policy.

Although striking is a fundamental practice in the labour movement, neither the common law nor the Canadian *Charter of Rights and Freedoms* expressly identifies a general right to strike. If there is a right to strike, it is limited to those circumstances in which striking is not otherwise prohibited under the governing labour legislation. Typically, a strike is unlawful if it occurs while a collective agreement is in force or during a statutory freeze period or if it takes place before exhausting certain bargaining procedures. Since most jurisdictions state that workers enjoy the right to participate in lawful trade union activities, there is no need for workers to seek permission to participate in a strike, as long as the strike is lawful.[21]

- A strike is generally lawful if it is designed to gain economic objectives and if it starts after the statute's compulsory conciliation procedures have been exhausted.
- Strikes are unlawful when they are designed to gain sympathy and bring pressure on a secondary employer, or when their actual purpose is political protest.[22]

union members generally must vote before striking

Most jurisdictions require union members to vote before striking. Usually, a strike is permitted only if a majority of those who voted were in favour of striking, thus avoiding strikes unless the general membership believes that such action is necessary to resolve a dispute. Governmental supervision of the strike vote is not required in most jurisdictions. It is usually necessary for the union to give notice of the vote to the employer and, in some cases, to the ministry of labour. Typical notice periods do not exceed 72 hours.

Although workers sometimes are free to strike, they may not have any guarantee that they will be able to return to their jobs afterwards.

- Some strikes put employers out of business permanently. When that occurs, there are no such jobs to return to.
- In other instances, some types of employees may lose their positions because their union could not negotiate a position for them under the new collective agreement.

[21.] *CPR v Zambri* (1962) 34 DLR (2d) 654 (SCC).

[22.] HW Arthurs *et al, Labour Law and Industrial Relations in Canada* 4th ed (1993) at 276.

- Even if a business can withstand the financial hardship of a strike, employees sometimes cannot. Although some unions can provide strike pay to their members, some employees cannot afford to live on that lower amount and are therefore forced to look for other jobs.
- Alternatively, rather than looking for a new job, some workers are willing to abandon the strike and return to their job.

In most jurisdictions, if an employee's position remains intact after a strike has ended, that employee has the right to be reinstated. But the right to reinstatement is not absolute. Employers have grounds to discharge an employee during a strike if the worker engaged in serious misconduct, such as sabotage against plant property or violence on a picket line.

workers may not have any guarantee that they will be able to return to their jobs after a strike

an employer cannot discharge an employee simply because that person took part in a lawful strike

Lockouts

The flipside of an employee strike is an employer *lockout*. A **lockout** occurs when an employer closes the workplace, or refuses to continue to employ its workers, with the intention of compelling them to agree to certain conditions of employment. Note that there is a subjective element to this definition. For the business closure to be classified as a lockout, the employer must have intended to use it to compel its employees to agree to its terms. In some instances of industrial conflict, it is hard to tell what the employer's intentions are in shutting down operations. Industrial conflict often coincides with economic hardship on the business. The employer is free to make sound business decisions to suspend or cease operations altogether, and such decisions must be distinguished from closures designed to force concessions from a union. Consequently, if a business can show that its decision to shut down was irrevocable, it is better able to argue that it did not shut down with the intention of forcing an agreement.[23]

a lockout occurs when an employer closes the workplace, or refuses to continue to employ its workers, with the intention of compelling them to agree to certain conditions of employment

As is true of strikes, some lockouts are lawful, while others are not. The strategy of compelling workers to accept the employer's terms is completely legitimate if it is carried out within the statutory requirements that governs strikes. If the lockout follows the exhaustion of negotiation and conciliation procedures prescribed by statute and does not involve any other unlawful activity, a business's management team can choose to shut down operations to achieve its bargaining position.

Picketing

Picketing is one of the most well-known features of labour disputes. Picketing is used as a response to a variety of situations including strikes, lockouts, and boycotts. **Picketing** involves:

- the presence of one or more people
- the communication of information
- the intention to secure a sympathetic response from some third party[24]

picketing involves the presence of one or more persons, the communication of information, and the intention to secure a sympathetic response from some third party

Well-meaning picketers try to distribute information in a peaceful way to convince customers, other companies, the employees of other companies, and

---

[23.] *Doral Construction Ltd* [1980] OLRB Rep Mar 310; *Westinghouse Canada Ltd* [1980] OLRB Rep Apr 577.

[24.] AWR Carrothers "Recent developments in the tort law of picketing" (1957) 35 Can Bar Rev 1005.

even potential replacement workers, to support their strike. Although picketing is often meant to be a peaceful communicative process, there are times when the discussion between picketers and those nearby gets emotionally charged and sometimes even violent. Picketing can therefore be seen in two very different ways.

- It is an important form of social expression, when conducted peacefully.
- It is a coercive activity that interferes not only with commercial activity and industrial peace, but sometimes with traditional property rights.

Picketers often ask others not to cross picket lines. If successful, that tactic interferes with the employer's ability to carry on business in spite of the strike. Given the solidarity between many industrial workers, some collective agreements even contain provisions that allow workers to respect the picket lines of co-workers from different bargaining units. The potential effect of such a clause in a collective agreement is significant. After all, if enough people refuse to cross a picket line, the entire enterprise could be forced to shut down. Some shrewd business managers react by treating the actions of co-workers who refuse to cross a picket line as a *"concerted effort designed to limit business output."* In other words, they claim that workers who refuse to cross the picket lines are themselves engaging in an unlawful strike. That argument often succeeds.[25] Consequently, although an industrial employer cannot always force the end of a lawful strike, it can often require those not on strike to report to work even if their collective agreement contains a provision to the contrary.

Picketing is generally governed by the courts, because most issues that arise in a picketing dispute are based in either criminal or tort law. For example, under s 423 of the *Criminal Code*, it is a crime to surround or watch a workplace for the purpose of compelling a person to do, or refrain from doing, something lawful.[26] Similarly, picketing may violate the law of tort. Since picketing is a form of communication, picketers must be careful with the message they are disseminating—false statements about an employer may be defamatory. When picketing behaviour leads to physical injury, picketers may be sued for either battery or negligence. Sometimes, when picketing interferes with another's property rights, picketers can be sued for the torts of nuisance or trespass. For this reason, many picketers are careful to picket on public property, where an employer has little recourse unless the picketers are actually blocking a public passage way.

secondary picketing indirectly exerts pressure on a business by threatening or imposing sanctions against some third party

Picketers expose themselves to additional liability when they engage in the practice of *secondary picketing*. **Secondary picketing** exerts pressure on a business indirectly by threatening or imposing sanctions against some third party. When picketers exert secondary pressure, they exceed the primary purpose of picketing, namely the peaceful dissemination of information about the strike. Picketing of this sort is prohibited by statute in some provinces.[27] As well, it

---

[25.] *Re Otis Elevator and Elevator Constructors* (1973) 36 DLR (3d) 402 (NS CA); *Ducard Mechanical Contractors*, [1971] OLRB Rep Feb 86.

[26.] *Criminal Code*, RSC 1985, c C-46 (Can).

[27.] In *RWDSU Local 558 v Pepsi-Cola Canada Beverages (West) Ltd* (2002) 208 DLR (4th) 385, the Supreme Court of Canada affirmed that (unless prohibited by statute) secondary picketing is generally lawful, as long as it does not involve tortious or criminal conduct. Asked to determine whether picketing the homes of Pepsi-Cola's management was unlawful, the Court applied the "wrongful action" approach, focusing on the character and effects of the activity rather than merely its location. The Court held that the conduct of union members amounted to disorderly conduct accompanied by threats of harm in an effort to make members of Pepsi's management refrain from doing what they had every right to do. Given its tortious nature, the conduct of the union members was held to be unlawful.

sometimes gives rise to a cause of action in tort for *inducing breach of contract*. When picketers intentionally induce a breach of contract, they wrongfully interfere with the economic relations between the employer and third party. If they find that the aim of secondary picketing is not merely to disseminate information but to induce a breach of contract, the courts may issue an order that brings the picketing to an end. Third-party businesses caught in the crossfire of an industrial conflict must often protect their own business interests, as Ethical Perspective 26.1 illustrates.

ETHICAL PERSPECTIVE 26.1

Brett Pontiac Buick GMC Ltd v NABET Local 920 (1990) 94 NSR (2d) (SC AD)

During an industrial conflict, a radio station owned by CHUM FM locked out its employees, who were members of the National Association of Broadcast Employees and Technicians, Local 920. In response, the union members decided to picket in front of the business premises of one of CHUM's more important advertising clients, Brett Pontiac Buick. One day during the lockout, 15 picketers showed up at the dealership with union placards and positioned themselves in front of the driveway that provided customers with access to the premises. They began distributing pamphlets that referred to the dispute between the employer and the union, and concluded in bold print: "DON'T BUY FROM BRETT PONTIAC."

The owner of the dealership also received a letter that stated, "I have been advised that your Company continues to advertise on C-100 FM radio despite requests by illegally locked-out employees that you refrain from doing so. It is my intention to call upon the 2500 inside and outside postal workers in this area to boycott all companies who continue to support the Toronto-based CHUM radio in this illegal lockout, through their advertising. If I do not hear from you within the next 7 days your Company will be included on the boycott list. I trust that you will decide to withdraw all ads until this labour dispute is settled."

The owner of Brett Pontiac did not take kindly to this letter, nor to several other attempts by the picketers to interfere with its business. Brett Pontiac applied for an injunction against the union to prevent it from interfering with its business operations.

Questions for Consideration

1. Have the union members exceeded the morally permissible bounds of free expression?

2. Can you think of a more ethical, though equally effective, strategy for the union members to achieve their goals?

Boycotts

As the *Brett Pontiac* case illustrates, boycotts are often created by way of secondary picketing. A **boycott** occurs when people refuse to interact with a business, or to handle goods that are associated with that business, as support for a collective bargaining position. Although a boycott may involve picketing, it need not. Some boycotts are carried out through advertising or telephone campaigns. Regardless of the manner of the campaign, boycotts are economically dangerous. By definition, boycotts interfere with the interests of parties who are not directly involved in the industrial conflict. In some instances, businesses are forced to suffer financially even though they have absolutely nothing to do with the labour dispute. Not only are innocent third-party businesses affected by a boycott, such campaigns also cause harm to the employer—often even greater harm than would be caused by direct picketing.

The economic effect of strikes, lockouts, picketing, and boycotts has led to a response by both federal and provincial governments to temporarily revoke the right of some public sector groups to strike. In some instances, this has even led to wage control.[28] A number of jurisdictions have recently felt the need to

a **boycott** occurs when people refuse to interact with a business, or to handle goods that are associated with that business, as support for a collective bargaining position

---

[28.] AWR Carrothers *et al Collective Bargaining in Canada* (1986) at 108-25.

invoke back-to-work legislation that forces workers to return to their jobs while their labour disputes are settled through compulsory arbitration. These rather drastic measures demonstrate governments' desire to keep the economy productive. Occasionally, when a large enough sector of organized labour is involved in an industrial dispute, there is a clash of wills. On such occasions, the matter is no longer merely a legal dispute between a business and its employees, but a political battle involving the public interest.

Chapter Summary

Not all work relations are individual relationships. A substantial portion of Canadian industry is organized and governed collectively under labour legislation. Labour law is the system of rules that govern collective relations between management, trade unions, their members, and the institutions in such relations. The collective nature of organized labour distinguishes it from other kinds of work.

Labour law aims to find an appropriate balance between employer and employee objectives by imposing a system of rules on collective bargaining. Collective bargaining is the process by which an employer and a trade union seek to negotiate a collective agreement. A collective agreement is a document containing the terms of employment and the rights and duties of the employer, the trade union, and the employees. Not every worker is entitled to the benefits and protections of collective bargaining. Each jurisdiction defines those employees who are eligible to bargain as a collective and those who are not.

In addition to being eligible, employees who wish to bargain collectively must be recognized by the jurisdiction's labour relations board as an appropriate bargaining unit. Once recognized as such, the bargaining unit must choose a trade union to act as its bargaining agent. As soon as its bargaining agent has been selected and certified, that union has the exclusive right to bargain on behalf of its members. As its bargaining agent, the trade union must try to represent the interests of all of the employees in the bargaining unit. One of the more controversial obligations in the collective bargaining process is the duty to bargain in good faith. This duty imposes an obligation on both parties to make every reasonable effort to successfully negotiate a collective agreement.

Most businesses that employ organized labour put into place an internal procedure to deal with employee grievances. In addition to the internal grievance procedure that is usually stipulated in most collective agreements, labour law provides an external method of resolving such disputes through a process known as grievance arbitration. Grievance arbitration is the final stage in the attempt to resolve an industrial dispute under an ongoing collective agreement. Typical grievances issues are discipline and discharge, seniority, and compensation. Disciplinary measures include suspensions, formal warnings, and demotion. The concept of seniority is central to almost every collective agreement. Not only does seniority define who is eligible for certain monetary benefits, it also provides a way for determining which employee is entitled to job promotion and which employee is subject to a transfer or lay-off. Typical complaints about compensation concern equal pay for equal work, a unilateral change in wages, overtime pay, entitlement to benefits, and retroactive pay.

The authority of an arbitrator to award remedies is limited in scope both by the labour legislation and by the terms of the collective agreement. Arbitrators usually have the power to award damages, issue compliance orders, and reinstate employees to their previous positions. Although arbitrators have the power to order such awards, they do not have the power to enforce them. The enforcement of arbitration awards is carried out by a court of competent jurisdiction.

When industrial disputes arise before or during the negotiation of a collective agreement, one party may decide to use economic pressure to convince the other party to make the appropriate concessions. The most common practice used by employees is a strike. Employers often respond in such situations by locking out their employees. Strikes and lockouts sometimes lead to secondary activities, such as picketing and boycotts. A strike or lockout is generally lawful if it is designed to gain economic objectives and if it is timely. Although workers are permitted to strike in certain circumstances, they do not always enjoy a guarantee that they will be able to return to their previous jobs afterwards. Under some conditions, an employer is permitted to shut down operations to convince employees to accept its bargaining position. In extreme cases, an industrial conflict may force a business to shut down operations permanently. Picketing is a mechanism used in response to a variety of situations including strikes, lockouts, and boycotts. Secondary picketing exerts pressure on a business indirectly by threatening or imposing sanctions against some third party. Boycotts interfere with the interests of parties who are not directly involved in the industrial conflict. Businesses that are the victim of secondary picketing and boycotts often have recourse in the courts.

Review Questions

1. Distinguish labour law from employment law. On what basis can organized labour be differentiated from other kinds of work?

2. Do all employees have collective bargaining rights? Does it matter what industry they are employed in? How are collective bargaining rights acquired?

3. Describe the test that is used to determine whether a person is a manager or an employee.

4. How does a trade union become recognized as the bargaining agent for a particular bargaining unit?

5. What is the first step when a union and management reach an impasse while negotiating a collective agreement?

6. What are the different elements of the duty to bargain in good faith? Why does labour law impose such a duty?

7. List the three essential requirements of an enforceable collective agreement. Are there other provisions that one of the parties can insist in including?

8. How does Canadian legislation differ from that in other countries in its treatment of strikes and lockouts?

9. Name and describe examples of three structures that a union might adopt in a workplace.

10. Failing an internal resolution, what can the two parties do to resolve an employee grievance? Outline the steps typically involved in this process.

11. Define "arbitral jurisprudence." How much deference must a labour arbitrator show to previous arbitration decisions?

12. Give three examples of disciplinary measures that an employer may take in the context of organized labour.

13. Describe the industrial practice known as "bumping." Distinguish between "bumping-up" and "bumping-down."

14. Provide examples of typical compensation complaints. How can managers prevent disputes over retroactive pay or benefits?

15. Do labour arbitrators and labour relations boards generally have remedial powers similar to those of judges? Be specific. Is it possible to expand or limit the authority of labour arbitrators? What about labour relations boards?

16. What factors should a panel of arbitrators consider when exercising its power to issue a "compliance order"?

17. List the four requirements common to most statutory definitions of a strike. What is a fifth requirement in some jurisdictions?

18. What is the defining feature of a lawful employer lockout? How can this factor sometimes be difficult to isolate?

19. Outline the three elements that together define lawful picketing. In what venue is the resolution of picketing disputes generally achieved?

20. Define "secondary picketing" and "boycotts." Under what circumstances are these practices legal?

Cases and Problems

1. Local 54 has retained James Love to represent it in a grievance against Dilated Peoples Optical Inc. The union is grieving the employer's decision to exclude from the bargaining unit the position of dilation officer—which the employer decided to move from Edmonton to San Francisco. Dilated Peoples argued that dilation officers are excluded from the bargaining unit based on the collective agreement, which specifies that only staff "employed in the offices located in Edmonton" are to be included in the bargaining unit. Local 54 responded with the argument that the words used in the collective agreement were meant to be descriptive, rather than limiting. Which interpretation do you think should prevail? Explain your reasoning.

2. Scrappy Aluminum Inc has asked the labour relations board to direct its employee union, Local 233, to sign a collective agreement. The terms of that agreement, set out in a memorandum of settlement, received the support of an overwhelming majority of union members in a recent vote. While Scrappy alleges that the agreement is all but signed, Local 233 holds a different view. It claims that the agreement has not yet been completed, in part due to a lack of understanding between the parties about a proposed employee dental plan. It seems that the majority of Local 233 members need orthodontic work, which is not explicitly included under "dental benefits." Therefore, despite the results of its recent member vote, Local 233 would like to see a further clarification of this issue before signing the collective agreement. Consequently, Local 233 insists that the collective agreement has not yet been reached. You have been called upon to decide the validity of Scrappy's request. In your opinion, did the parties achieve a collective agreement? Was Local 233's refusal to sign the collective agreement a violation of its duty to bargain in good faith? Support your position.

3. Employees at Rasta Pasta Ltd, represented by Local 111, have continued to work following the expiry of their collective agreement. Management at Rasta Pasta quickly

drafted a short-term agreement to act as a bridge between the initial collective agreement and a future collective agreement to be negotiated by both parties. Both parties signed the short-term agreement. Although the issue was not specifically contemplated by either party in the agreement, Local 111 has recently tried to compel Rasta Pasta to continue certain payroll deductions in a manner set out in the initial collective agreement. Rasta Pasta's accountant has been consulted and has indicated that there are negative tax implications associated with continuing such deductions. As a member of Rasta Pasta's risk management team, you have been asked to determine how best to deal with this situation, given that the specific clause in question was not contemplated by either party when the short-term agreement was signed. Use your good judgement and sound risk management principles to generate a response that will satisfy Local 111. How might this problem have been prevented?

4. Local 393, a trade union representing employees of an Internet start-up company, is upset by a recent business decision made by the start-up. The plan is to transform many of the employees currently working in head office into teleworkers—requiring them to perform their jobs from home via the Internet. The employees are concerned because the collective agreement provides certain corporate benefits only to those employees who are "working at corporate headquarters." In adopting this cost-saving measure, the chief operating officer (COO) of the Internet start-up has relied on a labour relations board decision that defined "headquarters" as the main office, or centre of control, in any organization. The COO of the start-up agrees with the board that the main office is rightly considered the headquarters. The employees, however, argue that the Internet has decentralized the corporate structure in a way that makes the designation of headquarters meaningless; therefore, they are entitled to the benefits provided for in the collective agreement whether they are located in the corporate office tower or are connected to it through the Internet. Is the board bound to follow its previous decision? Create an argument on behalf of the employees indicating why it should not be bound to follow the previous decision. Explain your reasoning.

5. After nearly 17 years of dedicated employment and a perfect record, Sheila was dismissed from her restaurant job at Le Café for allegedly stealing candy from a vending machine in the foyer with her co-workers, Felix and Malcolm. Le Café had a policy that allowed for immediate discharge in the case of theft in the workplace. In fear of losing her job, Sheila initially maintained that she had put money into the machine and had simply tried to extract candy when it malfunctioned and failed to deliver chocolate-covered espresso beans. Later, Felix, who was guilt-ridden and honest to a fault, admitted that Sheila had accidentally discovered how to get candy out of the machine without paying and was demonstrating this to him and Malcolm. Although willing to admit that disciplinary measures were in order, Sheila grieved the decision to discharge as excessive and sought reinstatement. You are a manager at Le Café. Will you advise Le Café to enforce its policy by disputing the grievance or to settle the grievance and amend the policy? Why?

6. Mike Ladd was hired as a permanent express clerk for Dubb Express. After two years in that position, he was given the opportunity to move temporarily into the higher position of a "grade 2 dispatcher." After two years, he was given the position on a permanent basis. Two years later, Dubb Express merged with the Antipop Consortium, and Mike's grade 2 dispatcher position was temporarily eliminated. Rather than being laid off, Mike wanted to bump into a grade 1 dispatcher position. Upon making this request, Mike was told that, although he was at least two years more senior than either of the two grade 1 dispatchers, he was less qualified for that position than either of the people who occupied it. The job classification scheme in Dubb Express's collective agreement is determined by the employee's level of qualification, which is based solely on the employee's daily performance as a dispatcher. Qualification is measured as a ratio of the number of drivers that the employee is capable of supervising on a shift divided by the number of dispatching errors made during that shift. The collective agreement in place specifically gives Dubb Express the right to decide bumping requests on the basis of qualification. However, the collective agreement also contains a clause that recognizes various seniority rights, including "the right of a senior person to bump a more junior person." As a business manager at Dubb Express, you are asked to decide whether Mike should be allowed to bump one of the less senior dispatchers. Support your position. Does the concept of seniority include bumping-down when laid off?

7. Local 861 has brought a grievance against ESPO Broadcasting on behalf of one of its former employees, Addey Farberino. The grievance alleges that employees who had resigned during the term of the first collective agreement, but before ratification of a retroactive wage increase, were entitled to the wage increase recently issued by ESPO. The union alleges that it had proposed specific entitlement of retroactive pay to anyone who had been an employee under the first collective agreement, but that the proposal had somehow been dropped during the course of negotiations. The union claims that it had allowed the specific proposal to be dropped because it had relied upon a general presumption of retroactivity for wages and benefits. Nothing in the collective agreement explicitly contemplates this presumption. What position should management at ESPO take?

8. Khalil was transferred to a remote workplace contrary to the collective agreement between his union and his employer, Self Scientific Inc. Khalil filed a grievance. Although Self Scientific is prepared to reimburse Khalil for automobile and parking expenses, it argues that an arbitrator does not have the authority to provide any further remedies, and therefore is not in a position to order payment of salary in lieu of travel time. Does Self Scientific's argument have any merit? Is the arbitrator limited to remedies set out in the terms of a collective agreement?

9. Peter & Harvey Furs and Local 275 had previously entered into a collective agreement that explicitly prohibited strikes and lockouts before the end of the calendar year. However, on July 30, the union applied to the labour relations board to request a strike vote, referring to the labour legislation that stated: "Employers are prohibited from

imposing conditions in contracts of employment which would restrain employees from exercising rights under this Act."

Peter & Harvey has countered by seeking an order to prevent the strike vote by its employees. To support its position, it made reference to another section of the relevant legislation which provides that: "This section does not affect agreements between employer and union."

Prepare an argument for the resolution of these two apparently contradictory provisions, first arguing on behalf of the employer and then on behalf of the union. Explain your reasoning in each case.

10. Randall's Motorcycle Shop employed the 208 members of LOCO 666. Until recently, every union member was employed on a full-time basis. Unfortunately, due to financial difficulties, Randall determined that he would have to unilaterally change the status of some employees to part time to remain in business. In announcing his intention to the union, Randall stated that those employees with seniority would be given the opportunity to bump junior persons into the part-time positions. When they heard about these arrangements, several unruly junior employees refused to accept part-time status and threatened Randall with physical harm if he refused to reinstate everyone to a full-time position. Many of them also left work in the middle of their shift. Randall wants a declaration that those employees who left in mid-shift engaged in an illegal strike. In turn, the union is seeking a declaration that Randall had imposed an illegal lockout. Your business consulting firm has been called upon to mediate this dispute in an attempt to find a resolution without having to take matters before the labour relations board. You have wisely chosen to meet with each of the parties separately before making any recommendations. What will you say to each party? How will you try to reach some sort of consensus?

11. Ugly Ducklings Inc lawfully locked out its unionized employees from Local 747 after the union members refused to adopt its new corporate mission statement: "To be uglier than any other company, period." Outraged by its corporate mandate—which included a policy requiring employees from local 747 to get bad haircuts—the union leaders called a meeting to discuss an appropriate strategy to be adopted. The union leaders found themselves in a dilemma. Although their impulse was to picket, they also knew that the whole point of Ugly Ducklings' corporate mission was to attract media attention. Consequently, the decision by Local 747 to picket the corporate offices of Ugly Ducklings Inc would simply help the company achieve its aim of being in the limelight at the expense of the reputation of the employees of Local 747. Caught in this quandary, Local 747 felt a need to find a different way to get its message out. Your business consulting firm has been retained by Local 747 to find a lawful solution. What course of action will you suggest?

12. Despite the recent announcement that Leiser Soda Co had achieved record-breaking profits during the first quarter of the year, it refused to give its assembly-line workers a raise. In retaliation for this, the leader of Local 187 came up with what she thought was a brilliant plan. Although a general strike at the time would have been unlawful, she decided that she alone would walk out from her job and would picket the workplace with other employees who were not currently on shift. They agreed that all of the other workers would continue to work but that each would take a turn picketing while off-duty. Concerned about the potential disruption in the workplace and unwanted negative publicity, CEO David Leiser has instructed you and two other members of the management team to determine the appropriate response. In your opinion, will the actions of Local 187 be classified as a strike? A boycott? Both? Neither? Assume that the collective agreement makes no mention of strikes or boycotts. Is the union's activity unlawful? Explain your reasoning.

WWWeblinks

Pre-Employment Matters

Application Forms and Interview Guide

www.gov.sk.ca/shrc/appforms.htm

This site offers employers a guide to application forms and interviews, complying with the Saskatchewan Human Rights Code.

University of Lethbridge—Human Resources

home.uleth.ca/pab/policies/contractvsemployee.html

This page offers guidelines for differentiating between employment and contracted services.

Employer's Obligations and Worker Protection Legislation

Nova Scotia Department of Environment and Labour—Labour Standards

www.gov.ns.ca/enla/labstand/lstcode/

This Web site offers information related to the minimum employment standards and the complaint process under the Nova Scotia Labour Standards Code.

OHRC—Employment and Human Rights

www.ohrc.on.ca/english/publications/hr-at-work.shtml

This Ontario Human Rights Commission site provides

information on human rights in the workplace, with links to the complaint process and related documents.

Workplace Equity

info.load-otea.hrdc-drhc.gc.ca/workplace_equity/home.htm

This Web site provides general information on employment equity and equal pay, legislation, guides for employers, descriptions of particular programs, and contacts.

Termination of Employment and Post-Employment Practices

Substance Abuse in the Workplace

www.ucalgary.ca/UofC/faculties/MGMT/inrm/industry/abuse/abuse.html

This site provides information on designing workplace drug policies, educating employees, drug testing, and employee assistance programs, as well as offering links to other resources.

Constructive Dismissal

www.smithlyons.ca/practiceareas/Labour/Publications/Labour_99_10_1.htm

This site outlines the law of constructive dismissal in Canada and advises both employers and employees on how to avoid negative consequences of such a claim.

Collective Bargaining

Office of Collective Bargaining Information

www.gov.on.ca/LAB/lms/ocbie.htm

This office collects, analyzes, and distributes information on Ontario's collective bargaining relationships. Its site includes comprehensive information for small, medium, and large workplaces.

Collective Bargaining—Alberta Labour Relations

www.gov.ab.ca/alrb/guide/4guidechap.htm

This page provides a guide to collective bargaining in accordance with applicable legislation. Topics include bargaining, strikes, lockouts, picketing, and dispute resolution measures.

Collective Agreements

Collective Agreements and Rates of Pay

www.tbs-sct.gc.ca/pubs_pol/hrpubs/hr_941_e.html

This Treasury Board of Canada Secretariat site provides links to publications and policies governing the collective agreements and rates of pay for many group-specific agreements, and contains the adjustment appendix to PSAC collective agreements.

CIRB—Unlawful Strikes and Lockouts

www.cirb-ccri.gc.ca/publications/info/7_e.html

This information circular prepared by the Canada Industrial Relations Board provides information to employees, trade unions, and employers on unlawful strikes and lockouts to help them understand the board's processes.

Grievance Arbitration

Model Clause on Grievance Arbitration

www.caut.ca/english/member/bargaining/mc_grievarb.asp

The CAUT-ACCPU provide a model clause dealing with arbitration in the collective bargaining process.

Collective Agreement Arbitration Bureau

www.labour.gov.bc.ca/caab

This bureau, which provides personnel to resolve grievances between employers and trade unions during the term of a collective agreement, offers information on its site.

Industrial Conflict

LRB—Strikes, Lockouts, and Picketing

www.lrb.bc.ca/bulletins/part5.htm

This bulletin from British Columbia's labour relations board provides information on strikes, lockouts, and picketing under the *Labour Relations Code*.

Canada Labour Code, **Part I, RS 1985, c L-2**

info.load-otea.hrdc-drhc.gc.ca/federal_legislation/part1/legislation/l1toc.htm

Division VI of the *Canada Labour Code* sets out regulations and punishments with regard to workplace strikes and lockouts.

MANAGING RISK DURING THE RECRUITMENT PROCESS

Many business people see the recruitment process as a means to an end, but there is much more to it than that. The interviewing and hiring process can be one of the most effective risk-management tools at your disposal. Failure to be proactive during this process can lead to losses you never thought possible. Correcting a hiring mistake can cost a considerable amount of time and money. At minimum, your losses could amount to the time spent preparing the job description, the cost of placing the ad, and the time spent reviewing applications and interviewing and training the successful candidate. But you can incur even greater business losses if your hiring mistake turns into a full-blown legal dispute. The lawsuit you might face could range from a wrongful dismissal claim to being held vicariously liable for the damages caused by your employee. For risk management, it is better to spend the time and effort during the interviewing and hiring phase than it is to risk damage to your business and deal with the associated personal and financial losses.

Some business people have learned that lesson the hard way. Restaurant owner Karen Hall lost thousands of dollars after hiring a chef without checking her references or investigating her background. Some of those losses were pure business losses. For instance, the new chef ordered a monthly total of over $40 000 of supplies, but the restaurant typically used less than half that amount per month. The food spoiled, and Hall was unable to recoup the loss. When Hall fired her new chef, she found herself faced with a wrongful dismissal claim. The rest of Hall's losses resulted from legal fees. From a risk management perspective, there are a number of things that business people can do during recruitment to prevent those kinds of losses.

The Job Description

An effective job description has several valuable benefits. First, it establishes the minimum requirements necessary to perform the job, thus serving as the foundation for determining whether a particular candidate has the necessary skills. At this, and every stage of the recruitment process, employers must take care not to violate a candidate's human rights. They can follow provincial human rights guidelines to avoid making this type of mistake. Second, the job description serves an important time-saving function by reducing the number of applications and résumés that need to be reviewed. Presumably, only serious candidates who possess the specified qualifications, or who come close, will bother applying for the position. Third, the job description can help the business organize its operations more efficiently. For instance, complete descriptions of each job can help the company see how each position works within its overall structure.

The Job Interview

Employers should schedule more than one interview with the potential employee. It is important that different interviewers be present at each interview for several reasons. First, it shows the job applicant that you value the business, its employees, and its clients. Therefore, you are willing to take the time that is necessary to fill the position with the most qualified candidate. Using several interviewers also exposes the potential employee to different personalities and can reveal how well the applicant will interact with them. It also allows the business to use the collective experience of its members to make a well-informed decision. Finally, the successful candidate will feel a sense of accomplishment and have a greater attachment to the business and its members if they have successfully made it through a series of interviews.

References

Trust is an important feature of any employment relationship. Both the employer and the employee must feel that they can rely on each other. It is difficult, however, to gather information about a person's trustworthiness during the job interview. One effective way to gain that kind of knowledge is to check the candidate's references. Somewhat surprisingly, small business owners rarely check references, possibly due to the necessary time commitment. However, that investment at the beginning of the employment relationship can help to prevent expensive losses in the future. Note that referees do not know everything about an applicant's background. Therefore, business people should also conduct an independent, thorough investigation of each candidate—verifying information on application forms, résumés, letters, and any other documents provided by the applicant.

Orientation

Orientation is too often overlooked in the recruitment process. A properly conducted orientation has immediate and long-term benefits that can help prevent future losses. First, it allows the new employee to become a more productive member of the organization early on in their employment. Second, properly informing an employee of the norms and practices of the workplace can help prevent tension and conflict later on. Third, if the new employee has an opportunity to meet and interact with many of their co-workers early on in the employment relationship, it will make it easier for them to work together in the future. Finally, a thorough orientation will once again show the employee that you value the business, its employees, and its clients.

QUESTIONS TO CONSIDER

1. List three things that you can do during the recruitment process to protect your business from employee-related business losses. Explain how those practices can help to reduce losses.

2. Even though you carefully checked your new employee's references, you have been sued for negligence as a result of the damages caused by your employee. Is there anything you can do to avoid those losses?

Sources: H Levitt "A bad hire could cost you dearly: To minimize the risk of harm, be diligent when recruiting" *Financial Post* (October 18, 1999) C15; L Bernardi, "Best practices in employment law" (2000) vol 25(1) *Canadian Manager* 18; "Minimizing hiring risks: Hiring the wrong person can cost you plenty" (1989) vol 6(1) *Human Resource* 6.

Video Resource: "Perils of hiring" *Venture* #700, October 20, 1998.

Index

Note: Key terms and their page references are in bold.